Digital Resources to Enhance Performance

YOUSEEU
Record. Share. Interact. Learn.

A robust online platform that enables instructors to facilitate individual and group assignments such as speeches, presentations, and oral exams. This video-centric program offers:

- Speech recording
- Access to more than 80 speech video clips paired with assessment
- Group work features such as video conference, document collaboration, and more!
- Mock interview practice

Package your book with YouSeeU:
ISBN: 978-1-5063-7990-6

SpeechPlanner Sp

This interactive, web-based tool guides students through the process of planning, preparing, and rehearsing speeches, one step at a time.

- Create full sentence or keyword outlines
- Includes videos of sample speeches
- Unique practice timer

Package your book with SpeechPlanner:
ISBN: 978-1-5063-8459-7

YouSeeU + SpeechPlanner = A complete speech training routine

PACKAGE your book with *both YouSeeU and SpeechPlanner* ISBN 978-1-5063-8457-3

For additional information and the most current list of speech resources available for use with *The Public Speaking Playbook, Second Edition*, please contact your SAGE representative or visit www.sagepub.com

Our Content Tailored to Your Learning Management System

SAGE coursepacks

SAGE coursepacks makes it easy to:

- Import our quality instructor and student resource content into your school's learning management system (LMS)
- Customize course content to meet your students' needs
- Access resources without special access codes

Your Play-by-Play Guide to Better Presentations

The Public Speaking Playbook, Second Edition, was developed to coach students on preparing, practicing, and presenting speeches for diverse audiences. This theme is woven throughout the text, repeatedly demonstrating for students that preparation and practice will take the fear out of public speaking.

PREPARE, PRACTICE, AND PRESENT SPEECHES

- **New speech examples** throughout provide students with a deeper understanding of effective speech construction through review and critique.
- Includes expanded and updated coverage of **presenting online**!
- New **sample student speech videos** show students effective models for presenting and structuring their speeches.
- More than 80 speech clips, available in YouSeeU, highlight best practices and common student errors.
- Infused with relevant coverage of **real-world public speaking** issues from speaking ethically, to researching effectively, to presenting online

"The text does a great job of providing clear discussion and examples to assist novice speakers. It is written in a clear and concise manner with extensive illustrations and examples."
—Erica Cooper, *Roanoke College*

"A useful textbook for speech that covers several topics you don't normally find covered in detail, like language usage, and also has great exercises for in-class activities."
—Dr. Christy Mesaros-Winckles, *Adrian College*

- **Special occasion speeches are covered extensively** in Chapter 22, introducing students to eight types of ceremonial speaking, including the speech of introduction, the eulogy, and the after-dinner speech, along with a sample speech illustrating every occasion.

- **Game Plans** help highlight areas where students excel or need improvement and set the tone for building skills and confidence through routine practice.

"The theme of Gamble and Gamble's book makes the content feel more accessible from the start and makes for a book that is trying to move students from practice to 'the real game' that they will encounter after graduation."
—John Jarvis, *Bay Path College*

"I love the idea of coaching. Practice is what students need, and the authors give students plenty of activities to do that."
—Kathleen M. Golden, *Edinboro University of Pennsylvania*

"Excellent examples, easy to use, and appropriate for beginning and more advanced students."
—Amy Lenoce, *Naugatuck Valley Community College*

"I am so glad the topic of storytelling was included. Stories are so vital for speakers and for the success of our students in the workplace—stories are how we sell ourselves and how we learn and teach the organizational culture."
—Debbi Vavra, *Blinn College*

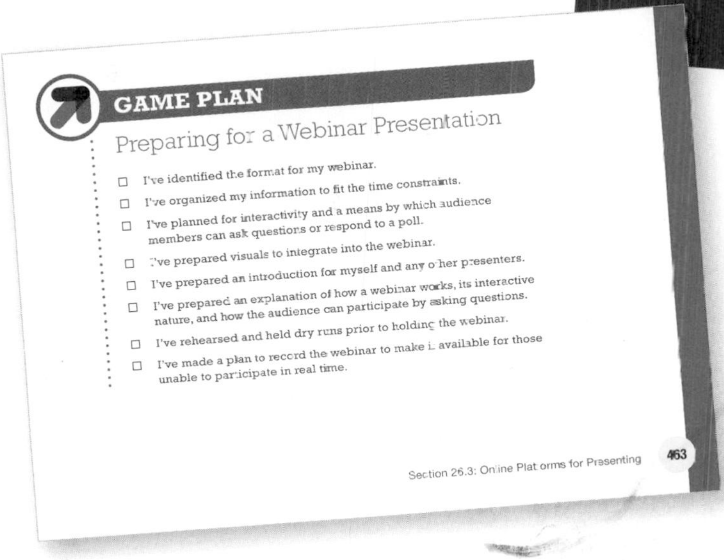
GAME PLAN

Preparing for a Webinar Presentation

- ☐ I've identified the format for my webinar.
- ☐ I've organized my information to fit the time constraints.
- ☐ I've planned for interactivity and a means by which audience members can ask questions or respond to a poll.
- ☐ I've prepared visuals to integrate into the webinar.
- ☐ I've prepared an introduction for myself and any other presenters.
- ☐ I've prepared an explanation of how a webinar works, its interactive nature, and how the audience can participate by asking questions.
- ☐ I've rehearsed and held dry runs prior to holding the webinar.
- ☐ I've made a plan to record the webinar to make it available for those unable to participate in real time.

Section 26.3: Online Platforms for Presenting 463

- **End-of-Chapter Exercises** provide next steps that take students from speech tips, to analyzing speech situations, to approaching the speaker's stand.

SECOND
EDITION

THE PUBLIC SPEAKING PLAYBOOK

We dedicate this book to our parents, Martha and Marcel Kwal and Nan and Wesley Gamble, and our children Lindsay and her husband Dan, and Matthew and his love Tong, who through the years have taught us so much about persistence, passion, and what really matters in life.

SAGE was founded in 1965 by Sara Miller McCune to support the dissemination of usable knowledge by publishing innovative and high-quality research and teaching content. Today, we publish over 900 journals, including those of more than 400 learned societies, more than 800 new books per year, and a growing range of library products including archives, data, case studies, reports, and video. SAGE remains majority-owned by our founder, and after Sara's lifetime will become owned by a charitable trust that secures our continued independence.

Los Angeles | London | New Delhi | Singapore | Washington DC | Melbourne

SECOND EDITION

THE PUBLIC SPEAKING PLAYBOOK

TERI KWAL GAMBLE

MICHAEL W. GAMBLE

SAGE

Los Angeles | London | New Delhi
Singapore | Washington DC | Melbourne

SAGE

FOR INFORMATION:

SAGE Publications, Inc.
2455 Teller Road
Thousand Oaks, California 91320
E-mail: order@sagepub.com

SAGE Publications Ltd.
1 Oliver's Yard
55 City Road
London, EC1Y 1SP
United Kingdom

SAGE Publications India Pvt. Ltd.
B 1/I 1 Mohan Cooperative Industrial Area
Mathura Road, New Delhi 110 044
India

SAGE Publications Asia-Pacific Pte. Ltd.
3 Church Street
#10-04 Samsung Hub
Singapore 049483

Acquisitions Editor: Karen Omer
Development Editor: Anna Villarruel
eLearning Editor: Gabrielle Piccininni
Editorial Assistant: Sarah Dillard
Production Editor: Jane Haenel
Copy Editor: Taryn Bigelow
Typesetter: C&M Digitals (P) Ltd.
Proofreader: Jeff Bryant
Indexer: Nancy Fulton
Designer: Scott Van Atta
Marketing Manager: Amy Lammers

Printed in Canada

Library of Congress Cataloging-in-Publication Data

Names: Gamble, Teri Kwal, author. | Gamble, Michael, 1943– author.

Title: The public speaking playbook / Teri Kwal Gamble, Michael W. Gamble.

Description: Thousand Oaks, CA : SAGE, [2017] | Includes bibliographical references and index.

Identifiers: LCCN 2016032688 | ISBN 9781506351643 (spiral : alk. paper)

Subjects: LCSH: Public speaking. | Oral communication.

Classification: LCC PN4129.15 .G36 2017 | DDC 808.5/1—dc23 LC record available at https://lccn.loc.gov/2016032688

This book is printed on acid-free paper.

17 18 19 20 21 10 9 8 7 6 5 4 3 2

Brief Contents

Detailed Contents

© iStockphoto.com/IzabelaHabur

© iStockphoto.com/SteveDebenport

© iStockphoto.com/2008GettyImages

Hero Images/Getty Images

© iStockphoto.com/Rawpixel Ltd

BananaStock/BananaStock/Thinkstock

© iStockphoto.com/poba

© iStockphoto.com/champja

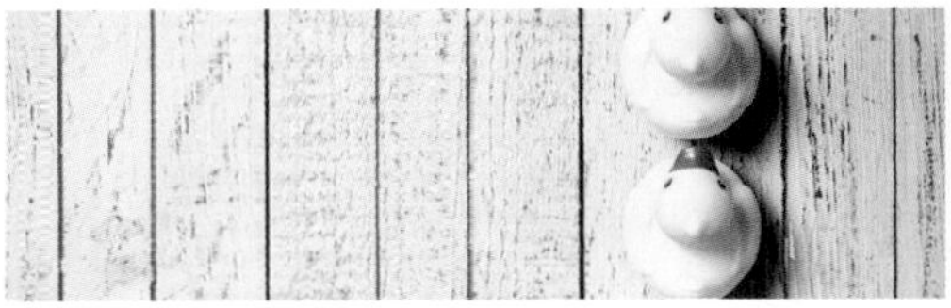

© iStockphoto.com/ThomasVogel

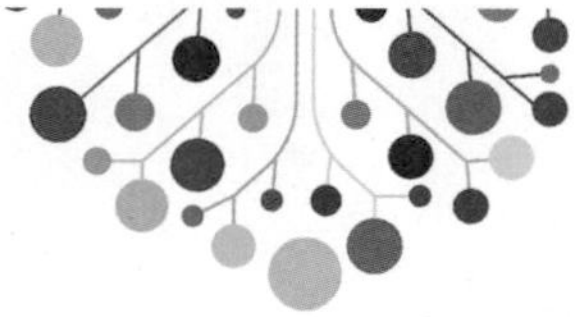
© iStockphoto.com/EnisAksoy

© iStockphoto.com/egon69

Duncan Smith/Photodisc/Thinkstock

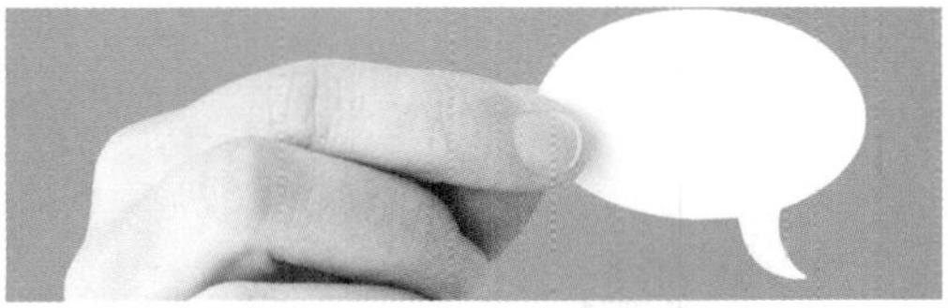

© iStockphoto.com/mrPliskin

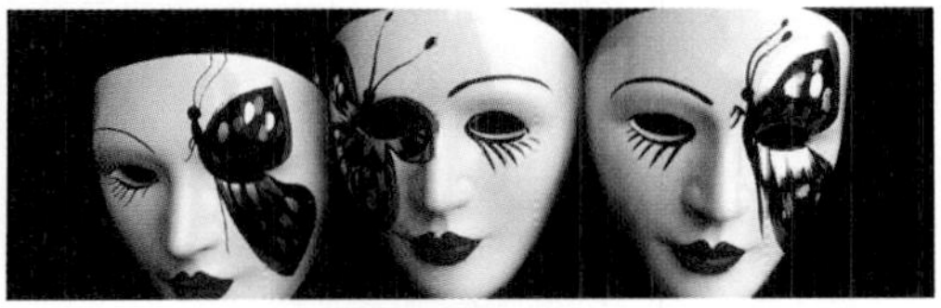

© iStockphoto.com/Christian J. Stewart

© iStockphoto.com/[joshblake]

© iStockphoto.com/ Groomes Photography

© iStockphoto.com/ GlobalStock

© iStockphoto.com/Geber86

AP Photo/Susan Walsh

Siri Stafford/ Photodisc/Thinkstock

© iStockphoto.com/skynesherc

© iStockphoto.com/track5

© iStockphoto.com/vm

Preface

How exciting it is for us to have completed the second edition of *The Public Speaking Playbook*. We hope you find it even more engaging and useful than this text's first edition. Our goal in writing the second edition remained faithful to our goal for the first edition—to create a resource that coaches students on how to prepare, practice, and present speeches for diverse audiences of varying sizes who gather in an array of forums—from classrooms to community centers, from organizational to public venues, from face-to-face settings to online.

Playbooks, of course, serve multiple audiences—athletes, actors, musicians, dancers, politicians, community organizers, leaders, and speakers—who rely on them to learn their craft, hone their skills, and accomplish their goals. All work under pressure, achieve individually or as part of a team or ensemble, and regularly plan and practice and evaluate in order to grow and improve performance outcomes. We weave the analogy throughout the pages of this text, repeatedly demonstrating for students how practicing and executing the right plays takes the fear out of public speaking and frees them to share their interests and knowledge, passions and concerns with others.

While the contents of the second edition have been streamlined, the *Playbook* retains its interactive focus, coaching students in building skills and training them actively in public speaking fundamentals. Every section of the *Playbook* includes brief learning modules that let students get to the "how-to" quickly, giving them the essentials they need to work both independently and collaboratively in preparing, rehearsing, and presenting a speech. The *Playbook* is spiral bound and tabbed for easy reference. Its eight main tabbed parts are divided into a series of sections or "plays" that facilitate students working play-by-play to deliver winning presentations at higher and higher levels. Embedded in every section are objectives, self-evaluation opportunities, coaching tips, and exercises to build skills and reinforce key competencies.

Also woven through the *Playbook,* and central to our goals, is a concern for diversity, ethics, and civic engagement, which we so hope students come to share. Bigotry, personal attacks, and divisiveness have no positive role to play in public speaking. Taking this to heart, this new edition of *The Public Speaking Playbook* now gives students the tools they need to build bridges of understanding between themselves and the audiences they address.

We hope you find *The Public Speaking Playbook* a resource not only worth using, but also worth keeping. Consider it a resource that you can consult throughout your life, honing your skills to reach the top of your game.

New in the Second Edition

The *Second Edition* of *The Public Speaking Playbook* incorporates many changes informed by feedback from instructors and students.

- **Streamlined for clarity and focus.** We have carefully edited each chapter to highlight the most important content and skills, allowing students to get to the information they need quickly and efficiently. We retained our focus on all of the key components to effective speechmaking, while reducing the overall length of the book by nearly 100 pages.
- **Updated for currency and relevance.** We have updated examples extensively throughout the text to provide students with more contemporary and relatable models for effective speeches.
- **New annotated speeches for deeper analysis.** We have provided four new annotated speech examples to promote deeper understanding of effective speech construction through review and critique. The new examples include a new sample commencement address, President Barack Obama's eulogy of Muhammad Ali, and two new persuasive speech samples from students on social media and football-related brain injuries.
- **Expanded and updated coverage of presentation aids.** Chapter 17 has been heavily revised and updated to include the most recent scholarship on presentation aids, covering everything from pie charts to Prezi. Additional coverage includes a new table outlining the pros and cons to using common presentation software to help students select the right tools for their presentations.
- **More than 80 new speech video clips.** Available through **YouSeeU for The Public Speaking Playbook** (more details under "Digital Resources" section below), the new edition provides dozens of new videos of *real students* delivering *real speeches* tied directly to each chapter's learning objectives. Many videos showcase both "needs improvement" and exemplary speech excerpts to help students grow their skills. Over 15 full speeches are available for students to review for guidance.

DIGITAL RESOURCES

SAGE edge™

edge.sagepub.com/gamblepsp2e

We know that high-quality resources are essential to effectively teach public speaking. Our goal has been to create resources that not only support but enhance the book's coaching theme. SAGE edge offers a robust online environment featuring an impressive array of tools and resources for review, study, and further exploration, keeping both instructors and students on the cutting edge of teaching and learning. SAGE edge content is open access and available on demand. Learning and teaching has never been easier! We gratefully acknowledge Sorin Nastasia, Kristyn Hunt Cathey, Gillie Haynes, and Suzanne Atkin, for developing the digital resources on this site.

SAGE COURSEPACKS FOR INSTRUCTORS makes it easy to import our quality content into your school's LMS. Intuitive and simple to use, it allows you to

Say NO to . . .

- required access codes
- learning a new system

Say YES to . . .

- using only the content you want and need
- high-quality assessment and multimedia exercises

For use in: Blackboard, Canvas, Brightspace by Desire2Learn (D2L), and Moodle

Don't use an LMS platform? No problem, you can still access many of the online resources for your text via SAGE edge at edge.sagepub.com/gamblepsp2e.

SAGE coursepacks includes:

- Our content delivered directly into your LMS.
- **Intuitive, simple format** that makes it easy to integrate the material into your course with minimal effort.
- Pedagogically robust **assessment tools** that foster review, practice, and critical thinking and that offer a more complete way to measure student engagement, including:
  - Diagnostic chapter **pre tests and post tests** that identify opportunities for improvement, track student progress, and ensure mastery of key learning objectives.
  - **Test banks** built on Bloom's taxonomy that provide a diverse range of test items with ExamView test generation.
  - **Activity and quiz options** that allow you to choose only the assignments and tests you want.
  - **Instructions** on how to use and integrate the comprehensive assessments and resources provided.
- **Chapter-specific discussion questions** help launch engaging classroom interaction while reinforcing important content.
- **Video and multimedia resources** that bring concepts to life make learning easier.
- Editable, chapter-specific **PowerPoint® slides** that offer flexibility when creating multimedia lectures so you don't have to start from scratch but can customize to your exact needs.
- **Sample course syllabi** with suggested models for structuring your course that give you options to customize your course in a way that is perfect for you.
- **Lecture notes** that summarize key concepts on a chapter-by-chapter basis to help you with preparation for lectures and class discussions
- **Integrated links to the FREE interactive eBook** that make it easy for your students to maximize their study time with this "anywhere, anytime" mobile-friendly version of the text. It also offers access to more digital tools and resources, including SAGE Premium Video.
- Comprehensive list of suggested **student speech assignments** for each chapter with relevant web resources to jump-start research.
- **Best practice guide** to aid instructors in teaching public speaking courses (both on-site and online), with tips on integrating online resources and media in lectures.
- All tables and figures from the textbook.

SAGE edge FOR STUDENTS enhances learning in an easy-to-use environment that offers:

- Mobile-friendly **eFlashcards** to strengthen understanding of key terms and concepts.
- Mobile-friendly practice **quizzes** that allow for independent assessment by students of their mastery of course material.

- A customized online **action plan** that includes tips and feedback on progress through the course and materials, allowing students to individualize their learning experience.
- Chapter-specific **learning objectives** that reinforce the most important material.
- Chapter-by-chapter **study questions** to help students prepare for quizzes and tests.
- Carefully selected chapter-by-chapter **video and multimedia content** which enhance classroom-based explorations of key topics.

YouSeeU for *The Public Speaking Playbook*

SAGE Video Assignments powered by YouSeeU for *The Public Speaking Playbook, Second Edition,* offers a better way to develop and enhance your students' public speaking skills through engaging, easy-to-use, video recording and assessment tools. Directly tied to the chapter learning objectives in the text and accessible within your school's LMS, YouSeeU makes it possible for students to apply what they learn by video recording speech assignments within the YouSeeU platform, specifically customized for ***The Public Speaking Playbook, Second Edition.*** Instructors and peers can access the recordings to provide targeted, frame-by-frame feedback, allowing for more robust advice and more effective learning—all adapted to meet the unique needs of each student. Students also gain exclusive access to **more than 80 sample speech video clips** within the YouSeeU platform, paired with assessment questions specifically tailored to reinforce chapter content and learning objectives. Add YouSeeU to your course and build your students' confidence as you prepare them for real-life success beyond the classroom!

We've made it easy for students to get **SAGE Video Assignments powered by YouSeeU for *The Public Speaking Playbook, Second Edition,*** all in one convenient package at a student-friendly price when bundled with the second edition of the text. *Contact your SAGE representative* today to request a demo and see how **YouSeeU** offers a better way to teach and learn communication skills.

Acknowledgments

What fun it is to work with the professionals on the SAGE team. We again thank Brenda Carter for her support; associate director of SAGE Publications Matthew Byrnie for his belief in and firm commitment to the *Playbook*'s success; Karen Omer for adding her creativity and insight to this project and stepping in as our editor without missing a beat; Sarah Calabi, our developmental editor, understanding our goals and guiding us so skillfully in revising and improving the text; associate developmental editor Anna Villarruel for her careful reading and follow-up; editorial assistant Sarah Dillard for stepping in whenever needed; and copy editor Taryn Bigelow for asking us all the right questions and working painstakingly to maintain the book's accurateness and readability. We also offer a special thank you to production editor Jane Haenel for gently keeping us all on track, marketing manager Amy Lammers for seeing the promise in possibilities, and Scott Van Atta, the book's designer, for the fresh look and visual appeal of this edition.

It is to the book's reviewers that we owe our most heartfelt thank you. The individuals listed here gave so generously of their time and talents, contributing ideas and recommendations that were invaluable in helping us produce a book of which we are so proud:

Second Edition Reviewers and Focus Group Participants

Traci E. Alexander, Harrisburg Area Community College; **Nicole Allaire,** Iowa State University and Des Moines Community College; **Suzanne J. Atkin**, Portland State University; **Diane M. Badzinski**, Colorado Christian University; **Susan L. Cain**, Southwestern University; **Kristyn Hunt Cathey**, Lamar University; **Laura H. Crosswell**, University of Nevada, Reno; **Becky DeGreef**, Kansas State University Polytechnic Campus; **Jeff Drury,** Wabash College; **Jennifer S. Hallett**, Young Harris College; **Benjamin M. Han**, Concordia University; **Paul T. M. Hemenway**, Lamar University; **Kim Higgs**, University of North Dakota; **Christina M. Knopf**, SUNY Potsdam; **Satish Kolluri**, Pace University, New York City; **Douglas J. Marshall**, Southern University at New Orleans; **Richard Maxson,** Drury University; **Christy Mesaros-Winckles**, Adrian College; **Elizabeth A. Nelson**, North Carolina State University; **Anthony Ongyod**, MiraCosta College; **Emily Berg Paup**, College of St. Benedict and St. John's University; **Sandy Pensoneau-Conway,** Southern Illinois University–Carbondale; **Leola M Powers**, MiraCosta College; **George B. Ray**, Cleveland State University; **Rheanna Rutledge**, NOVA Southeastern University; **Chris Smejkal,** St. Louis Community College; **Brigit K. Talkington**, Midland University; **Ty Williams**, St. Philip's College

First Edition Reviewers

Sandra Wheeler Abeyta, Cosumnes River Community College; **John E. Anglin**, East Central College; **Derek Arnold**, Villanova University; **Robert L. Arnold**, Richland College; **Diane M. Badzinski**, Colorado Christian University; **Kay B. Barefoot**, College of The Albemarle-Dare; **Cameron Basquiat**, College of Southern Nevada; **Valerie C. Bello**, Genesee Community College; **Mary D. Best**, Christopher Newport University; **Annette Bever**, Vernon College; **Kenneth W. Bohl**, Westmoreland County Community College; **Jennifer Emerling Bone**, Colorado State University; **Michael T. Braun,** Milliken College; **Deborah Cunningham Breede**, Coastal Carolina University; **Anna Maria Ruffino Broussard**, Nicholls State University; **Barbara Ruth Burke**, University of Minnesota, Morris; **Megan Burnett**, Alice Lloyd College; **Rebecca Carlton**, Indiana University Southeast; **Gregory S. Carr**, Harris-Stowe University; **Rod Carveth,** Charter Oak State College; **M. Chislom Jr.**, University of Wisconsin-Platteville; **Scott Christen**, Tennessee Technological University; **Jeanne Marie Christie**, Western Connecticut State University; **James D. Cianciola**, Truman State University; **Marcia J. Clinkscales**, Howard University; **Erica F. Cooper**, Roanoke College; **Jennifer Dahlen**, Northland Community and Technical College; **Thomas Damp**, Central New Mexico Community College; **Lissa D'Aquanni**, University at Albany; **Dale Davis**, University of Texas at San Antonio; **John R. Deitrick,** Becker College; **Norman F. Earls Jr.**, Valdosta State University; **Belle A. Edson,** Arizona State University; **Karen L. Eichler**, Niagara University; **Dana Emerson,** Linn Benton Community College; **Jerry M. Engel**, State University of New York, College at Geneseo; **Mary M. Ertel**, Erie Community College; **Rebecca J. Franko**, California State Polytechnic University, Pomona; **Kathleen M. Golden**, Edinboro University of Pennsylvania; **Ronald P. Grapsy, Jr.**, Kutztown University; **Stacy Gresell,** Lone Star College–CyFair; **Neva K. Gronert**, Arapahoe Community College; **Howard Grower**, The University of Tennessee; **Donna L. Halper**, Lesley University; **Edward Hatch**, Thomas College; **Gillie Haynes,** American University; **Keith Hearit**, Western Michigan University; **Ronald W. Hochstatter**, Northland Community and Technical College; **Tracey Quigley Holden**, University of Delaware; **Lisa Holderman**, Arcadia University; **Tracey Holley**, Tarleton State University; **Samuel Holton**, Southeastern Technical College; **Jason Wayne Hough**, Hartnell College; **Mary E. Hurley**, St. Louis Community College at Forest Park; **Jacqueline A. Irwin**, California State University, Sacramento; **Kathleen Jacquette**, Farmingdale State College; **John Jarvis**, Bay Path College; **Rebecca Kamm**, Northeast Iowa Community College; **Pamela A. Kaylor**, Ohio University Lancaster; **Chris Kennedy**, Western Wyoming Community College; **Dave Kosloski**, Clark College; **Reeze LaLonde Hanson**, Haskell Indian Nations University; **Kimberly A. Laux**, University of Michigan–Flint; **Amy K. Lenoce**, Naugatuck Valley Community College; **Tammy Swenson Lepper**, Winona State University; **Linda Levitt**, Stephen F. Austin State University; **Sandra Lieberg**, Lake Michigan College; **Andrew Lovato**, Santa Fe Community College; **Tobi Mackler**, Montgomery County Community College; **Matthew Thomas Malloy**, Caldwell Community College and Technical Institute; **Jeanette Martin**, United Tribes Technical College; **Chandra K. Massner,** University of Pikeville; **Janet Rice McCoy,** Morehead State University; **Susi McFarland**, Modesto Junior College and San Joaquin Delta College; **Shellie Michael**, Volunteer State Community College; **Nicki L. Michalski,** Lamar University; **Thomas P. Morra**, The Catholic University of America; **Laura D. Morrison**, College of The Albemarle; **Katie Kavanagh O'Neill**, University of Pittsburgh; **Lynne Orr**, William Paterson University; **Lisa Pavia-Higel**,

East Central College; **John H. Prellwitz**, University of Pittsburgh at Greensburg; **Brandi Quesenberry**, Virginia Tech University; **Rasha I. Ramzy**, Georgia State University; **Ramesh N. Rao**, Longwood University; **Renton Rathbun**, Owens Community College; **Christina L. Reynolds**, Otterbein University; **Emily Richardson,** University of Pikeville; **Jeanette Ruiz,** University of California, Davis; **Ann B. Russell**, Bladen Community College; **Stephanie Shimotsu- Dariol**, Western Governors University; **John Spinda**, Murray State University; **Roberta G. Steinberg**, Mount Ida College; **Lesa A. Stern**, Westmont College; **Karen Stewart,** Arizona State University; **Chelsea A. H. Stow**, Front Range Community College; **William Swanger**, Susquehanna University; **Brigit K. Talkington,** Midland University; **Belinda Collings Thomson**, Brescia University; **Debbi Vavra**, Blinn College; **Mark "Dog" Wallace**, Thomas College; **R. Lester Walsh**, Valley City State University; **Kathleen Watters**, University of Dayton; **Susan M. Wieczorek**, University of Pittsburgh at Johnstown; **Jonna Reule Ziniel**, Valley City State University

We also want to thank the following students and faculty for providing us with a treasure chest of speeches that added to the richness of this text's contents: Austin J. Beattie, Eric Mishne, and Tanika L. Smith.

About the Authors

Teri Kwal Gamble, a full professor of communication at the College of New Rochelle in New Rochelle, NY (PhD, New York University; MA and BA, Lehman College, CUNY), and **Michael W. Gamble**, a full professor of communication at the New York Institute of Technology in New York City (PhD, New York University; BA and MFA, University of Oklahoma), are partners in life and work. Professional writers of education and training materials, the Gambles are the coauthors of numerous textbooks and trade books. Their most recent publication is *Nonverbal Messages Tell More: A Practical Guide to Nonverbal Communication* (2017). Teri and Mike also are the coauthors of the best-selling text *Communication Works* (11th ed., 2013). Among other books the Gambles have written together are *Interpersonal Communication: Creating Connections Together* (2013), *Leading With Communication* (2013), and *The Gender Communication Connection* (2nd ed., 2014).

Previously, Michael served as an officer and taught Leadership Skills for the U.S. Army Infantry School during the Vietnam War. The Gambles also are the founders of Interact Training Systems, a consulting firm that conducts seminars, workshops, and short courses for business and professional organizations. Teri and Mike also produce training and marketing materials for sales organizations and are the coauthors of the trade book, *Sales Scripts That Sell.*

PART ONE

Get Ready to Speak

© iStockphoto.com/IzabelaHabur

1

Public Speaking and You: Building Confidence

UPON COMPLETING THIS CHAPTER'S TRAINING, YOU WILL BE ABLE TO

1. Demonstrate how developing public speaking skills can help you realize personal, professional, and societal goals
2. List and explain the essential elements of communication
3. Assess your confidence as a speaker
4. Identify the sources of public speaking anxiety
5. Use systematic desensitization, power posing, cognitive restructuring, centering, and skills training to alleviate symptoms of speech apprehension and build confidence

Contents

A playbook is a game plan—a plan of action designed to help you become a peak performer.[1] We wrote this playbook because we believe every public speaking student needs a game plan to succeed. Why? Because effective speakers prepare, practice, and present speeches that others judge to be of high quality. To rise to this level, effective speakers first master and then apply skills. And just like elite athletes and others who appear in public, they perform under pressure, either individually or as members of a team. They also practice consistently so that every one of their presentations is as good as or better than their last. With practice, you can join their ranks.

We place a high value on public speaking ability because it is such a vital means of **communication**. The ability to speak in public is a powerful skill to be honed. Audiences have been drawn to the words of Tony Robbins, Oprah Winfrey, Bill Clinton, Suze Orman, and the late Steve Jobs beause each has been able to inspire, reassure, convince, or simply reach out to audiences. Being able to speak in public without injecting vitriol, is similarly powerful. What will you do? You can be the smartest person in the room, but if deficient speaking skills keep others from understanding your ideas, being smart isn't enough. A class in public speaking gives you and your peers the opportunity to work together on improving your public speaking skills.

COACHING TIP

"Tell me and I forget. Teach me and I remember. Involve me and I learn."

—Benjamin Franklin

Merely reading and talking about public speaking won't make you a better speaker. Only involving yourself in the process and doing it will help you improve. The more you speak in public, the easier it will become, and the more you will improve. Doing it builds confidence.

section
1.1

Identify Speechmaking's Benefits

1.1a Benefits for Your Personal Life

1.1b Benefits for Your Career

1.1c Benefits for Society

Becoming a skilled public speaker has benefits for the individual, both personal and professional, and for society as a whole.

1.1a Benefits for Your Personal Life

Speaking in public precipitates self-discovery and builds confidence and can even trigger self-discovery as well as creative self-expression. For instance, as a result of researching a topic of interest, such as the problems faced by soldiers returning from a war zone, you might discover that you have the desire to engage in service learning by volunteering at a veteran's facility.

As a public speaker you are expected to reflect on your interests, to explore where you stand on controversial issues, and to consider the needs and concerns of others. You would need to consider your position and how to best make your argument so that even those who disagreed with your stance initially would listen to and understand it.

Becoming a more confident speaker will also make you a more confident student. By developing the ability to speak in public, you develop your ability to speak up in class—any class.

At the same time, as you build speaking confidence, you might find yourself wanting to become more civically engaged, speaking up and sharing ideas beyond the classroom as well.

While mastering the material in a major field is necessary, whether your major is business, computer programming, nursing, or any other subject, unless you also can present information clearly and effectively, no matter how intelligent you are, others may question your credibility and knowledge. By mastering the ability to communicate your ideas in public, you harness the power of speech. By being better able to control yourself and your ideas, you enhance your ability to control your environment.

1.1b Benefits for Your Career

Success in public speaking helps you grow professionally. Your ability to attain professional success is related to your ability to communicate effectively what you think, know, and can do. This is especially helpful in a job interview, since prospective employers favor candidates who have public speaking abilities.[2]

How far you advance in your career may well depend on how capable you are in addressing, impressing, and influencing others and in communicating your ideas clearly and effectively.[3] The executives and entrepreneurs of tomorrow need to be skilled public speakers—masters of the art of speaking before groups of all sizes, including the news media and online audiences.

1.1c Benefits for Society

Developing public speaking skills gives you a voice in influencing the direction of your college, community, and society as a whole. It gives you opportunities to let others know the issues you care about and want them to care about, too. By speaking up, and listening to others who speak up, you exercise effective citizenship. Freedom of speech has always been viewed as an essential ingredient in a democracy. What does freedom of speech mean? It means

1. You can speak freely without fear of being punished for expressing your ideas.
2. You can expose yourself freely to all sides of a controversial issue.
3. You can debate freely all disputable questions of fact, value, or policy.
4. You can make decisions freely based on your evaluation of the choices confronting you.

Our political system depends on a commitment by citizens to speak openly and honestly and to listen freely and carefully to all sides of an issue. It depends on our ability to think critically about what we listen to, so that we are able to accept or reject the speaker's goal. In so doing, we can make informed decisions about our future. Democracy depends on our willingness to understand and respond to expressions of opinion, belief, and value that are different from our own.

© iStockphoto.com/KIVILCIM PINAR

Rally around ideas. How can a speech influence your political attitudes and choices?

section 1.2

Understand the Context of Public Speaking

1.2a Picture the Parts Working Together

1.2b Consider Audience Expectations

Skilled public speakers have unique powers to influence. But like other forms of communication, public speaking is a circle of give-and-take between presenter and audience. The better you understand how communication works, the better your ability to make it work for you. The following elements are an integral part of the process:

- The source
- The receiver
- The message
- The channel
- Noise
- Feedback
- Situational and cultural contexts

One way to study the interactions of these elements is with a model of the communication process in action (see Figure 1.1).

Look closely at the variables depicted in Figure 1.1 to identify how they relate to each other dynamically during public speaking. Both the speaker, or **source**, and the listener, or **receiver**, participate in communication. Each party simultaneously and continually performs both sending functions (giving out messages) and receiving functions (taking in messages). Neither sending nor receiving is the exclusive job of any person.

Between the source and receiver, **messages**—both verbal and nonverbal—are sent and received. The words and visuals we use to express our ideas and feelings, the sounds of our voices, and our body language (or nonverbal communication) make up the content of our communication and convey information. Everything we do as senders and receivers has potential message value for those observing us. If a speaker's voice quivers or a receiver checks his or her watch, it conveys a message.

FIGURE 1.1
The Communication Process in Action

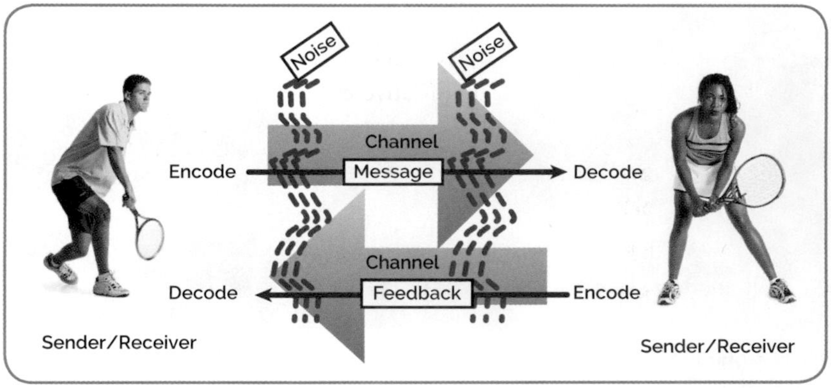

Channels are pathways or media through which messages are carried. The auditory channel carries our spoken words; the visual channel carries our gestures, facial expressions, and postural cues; and the vocal channel carries cues such as rate, quality, volume, and pitch of speech. Communication is usually a multichannel event.

Noise is anything that interferes with our ability to send or receive a message. Noise need not be sound. Physical discomfort, a psychological state, intellectual ability, or the environment also can create noise. As the model in Figure 1.1 shows, noise can enter the communication event at any point; it can come from the context, the channel, the message, or the persons themselves. Different languages, translators, generational terms, jargon, and technical terms play a role in the day-to-day noise of communication in our diverse world.

The **situational/cultural context** is the setting or environment for communication. Because every message occurs in a situation with cultural and social meanings, conditions of place and time influence both behavior and the outcome of the communication event. The after-dinner speaker addressing a large number of people who have just eaten and are full will need to give a different kind of speech than the person whose task is to address the members of a union protesting a layoff.

Feedback is information we receive in response to a message we have sent. Feedback tells us how we are doing. Positive feedback, like applause, serves a reinforcing function and causes us to continue behaving as we are, whereas negative feedback, such as silent stares, serves a corrective function and leads us to eliminate any ineffective behaviors. Internal feedback is that which you give yourself (you laugh at a joke you tell); external feedback comes from others who are party to the communicative event (receivers laugh at your joke, too).

It's all about the audience. Your goal as a public speaker is to anticipate and interpret listener feedback and adjust your message accordingly.

1.2a Picture the Parts Working Together

All parts of the communicative model continuously interact with and affect each other—they are interconnected and interdependent. When something happens to one variable, all the other variables in the process are affected. Communication is also cumulative; the communicative experiences we have add up and have the potential to alter our perceptions and behaviors. The **effects of communication** cannot be erased; they become part of the total field of experience we bring to the next communication event. Ultimately, our **field of experience**—the sum of all our experiences—influences our attitudes toward the speech event and our receivers, affecting both our desire to communicate and the way we do it.

Your success as a source ultimately depends on your ability to

- Establish common ground with your receivers
- Encode or formulate a message effectively
- Adapt to cultural and situational differences
- Alleviate the effects of noise
- Understand and respond to the reactions of those with whom you are interacting

Your effectiveness depends not only on what you intend to communicate, but also on the meanings your receivers give to your message. A self-centered communicator is insensitive to the needs of receivers, which limits his or her effectiveness. Keep your eyes on your communication goal, instead of focusing solely on yourself.

Know your parts. As you put your presentation together, keep your eyes on your goal to create a more dynamic and influential speech.

1.2b Consider Audience Expectations

Although being able to (1) organize ideas logically, (2) encode or express ideas clearly, and (3) analyze and adapt to receivers readily are skills every communicator needs, they are particularly important for public speakers.

Receivers usually have higher expectations for public speakers than for other communicators. For example, we expect public speakers to use more formal standards of grammar and usage, pay more attention to their presentation style and appearance, fit what they say into a specific time limit, and anticipate and then respond to questions their receivers will ask.

So, when speaking in public you will need to polish, formalize, and build on your basic conversational skills to reach your goal.

© iStockphoto.com/PeopleImages

Consider your audience's goals. How does your speech connect to their interests, needs, and knowledge?

COACHING TIP

"We live in an era where the best way to make a dent on the world may no longer be to write a letter to the editor or publish a book. It may be simply to stand up and say something . . . because both the words and the passion with which they are delivered can now spread across the world at warp speed."

—Chris Anderson, *TED TALKS: The Official TED Guide to Public Speaking*

Picture the model in Figure 1.1. Communication and understanding are key. Focus on your audience. Make it easy for those in it to understand you. You just might significantly affect their lives.

section

1.3

Build Confidence

1.3a Understand Public Speaking Anxiety

1.3b Address the Physical Effects of Speech Anxiety

1.3c Address the Mental Effects of Speech Anxiety

1.3d Use Skills Training

1.3e Anxiety Can Be Transformative

You are in good company if the thought of speaking in public causes you some concern. Speakers are not alone in experiencing fear or feeling stressed at the thought of performing in public. Athletes, dancers, actors, and musicians also have to handle their fear and emotional stress, which, if not channeled effectively, can interfere with their ability to perform.[4] When they control their fear, however, the stress becomes useful, helping them gain a competitive edge, boosting their energy, and readying them to deliver a peak performance. How does this happen? Quite simply, athletes and others who perform in public focus, face their fears, and train to handle pressure. And they do this gradually over time, not once, but regularly.[5] You can, too. Start by confronting your feelings about giving a speech.

Self-Assessment: How Confident Are You About Public Speaking?

In the space before each of the following statements, enter the number in the rating scale that best represents your feelings about each statement:

Not at all concerned   1   2   3   4   5   Extremely concerned

1. ____ I will forget what I plan to say.
2. ____ My thoughts will confuse listeners.
3. ____ My words will offend listeners.
4. ____ Audience members will laugh at me when I don't mean to be funny.
5. ____ I'm going to embarrass myself.
6. ____ My ideas will have no impact.
7. ____ I will look foolish in front of my audience because I won't be able to look them in the eye and I won't know what to do with my hands.
8. ____ My voice and body will shake uncontrollably.
9. ____ I will bore my audience.
10. ____ Audience members will stare at me unresponsively.

TOTAL ___

To determine your score, add the numbers you selected:

41–50	You have speech anxiety.
31–40	You are very apprehensive.
21–30	You are concerned to a normal extent.
10–20	You are very confident.

Although this self-survey is by no means a scientific indicator of your oral communication confidence, it can help you face your concerns. This is your first step in gaining control of your excess energy and using it to elicit a strong public speaking performance.

1.3a Understand Public Speaking Anxiety

Public speaking anxiety, also known as PSA, is a variant of communication anxiety that affects some 40 to 80 percent of all speakers.[6] PSA has two dimensions, process anxiety and performance anxiety.

- **Process anxiety** is fear of preparing a speech. For example, when you experience process anxiety, you doubt your ability to select a topic, research it, and organize your ideas.
- **Performance anxiety** is fear of presenting a speech. It finds you stressful about delivering the speech, fearful that you'll tremble, forget what you want to say, do something embarrassing, be unable to complete the speech, not make sense to receivers, or simply be assessed as a poor speaker.[7]

Why are some of us afraid to speak before a group? What makes us fear public speaking more than we fear snakes, heights, bee stings, or death?[8]

Fear of Failure

We all fear failure.[9] If you choose not to take risks because you visualize yourself failing rather than succeeding, if you disagree with what you hear or read but choose to keep your thoughts to yourself, then you are probably letting your feelings of inferiority limit you.

Fear of the Unknown

Some fear what they do not know or have not had successful experience with. The unknown leaves much to the imagination—and far too frequently, we irrationally choose to imagine the worst thing that could happen when making a speech.

Fear of Evaluation

Some speechmakers also fear that others will judge their ideas, how they sound or look, or what they represent. When faced with such an option, we prefer not to be judged.

Fear of Being the Center of Attention

We may also fear being conspicuous or singled out. Audience members usually focus directly on a speaker. Some speakers interpret receivers' gazes as scrutinizing and hostile rather than as revealing a genuine interest in them.

Fear of Difference

Ethnocentricity—the belief that one's own group or culture is better than others—makes some speakers think they share nothing in common with the members of their audience. Feelings of difference make it harder to find common ground, which in turn increases the anxiety about making a speech.

Fear Imposed by Culture

Culture can influence attitudes toward speaking in public. For example, according to research, Puerto Ricans, Filipinos, Israelis, and other Middle Eastern peoples are typically less apprehensive about public speaking than Americans.[10] In these cultures, children are rewarded for merely trying, making judgment and communication anxiety a less intrusive force.[11]

Ryan McVay/Digital Vision/Thinkstock

Conquering fear. Like an athlete visualizing a dive, visualize yourself giving a successful speech days, hours, and minutes beforehand to help combat public speaking anxiety.

Talking about practice. Practicing the proper posture and keeping an open power stance can physically promote confidence for your speech.

1.3b Address the Physical Effects of Speech Anxiety

When we experience the physical effects of anxiety, adrenalin is released into our systems and our respiration rate and heart rate increase. When our anxiety levels get too high, we need to manage the physical effects of speech fright. For example, if we're runners, we could go for a run. If not, we could take a moment to stretch our limbs.

Another technique is systematic desensitization, a way to reduce the physical responses of apprehension.[12] The principle behind systematic desensitization is that after being tensed, a muscle relaxes. Try these methods:

Tense/Relax

Tense your neck and shoulders. Count to 10. Relax. Continue by tensing and relaxing other parts of your body including your hands, arms, legs, and feet. As you continue this process, you will find yourself growing calmer.

Strike a Powerful Pose

How we stand can affect our speaking success. Merely practicing a "power pose" in private before presenting a speech lowers speaker stress levels, thereby reducing outward signs of stress and enhancing confidence:[13]

- Stand tall.
- Stand tall and lean slightly forward.
- Stand tall and open your limbs expansively.
- Leaning slightly forward, stake out a broad surface with your hands.

Leaning slightly forward engages an audience. Opening the limbs expresses power. Staking out a broad surface conveys a sense of control. In contrast to power poses, low-power cues increase stress and decrease confidence. Adopting a close-bodied posture conveys powerlessness, touching your neck or face is a symptom of anxiety, and folding your arms comes off as defensive. Use power poses that convey authority instead. Doing so will boost confidence at the same time.

1.3c Address the Mental Effects of Speech Anxiety

Far too often, our **self-talk**—our internal communication—fans the flames of our fears instead of extinguishing them.[14] We create a self-fulfilling prophecy, meaning that we form an expectation and adjust our behavior to match. As a result, the expectation we created becomes true. This can cause unnecessary problems if our thoughts are negative.

The goal is to use **thought stopping** to make self-talk work in your favor. Every time you find yourself thinking an upsetting or anxiety-producing thought, every time you visualize yourself experiencing failure instead of success, say to yourself, "Stop!" and tell yourself, "Calm." Thought stopping is an example of **cognitive restructuring**, a technique that focuses attention on our thoughts rather than on our bodily reactions. Cognitive restructuring works by altering the beliefs people have about themselves and their abilities.

A second technique is **centering**.[15] When centering, we direct our thoughts internally. Key in this procedure is the **centering breath**, designed to help us focus on the task mentally. Try it. Take a deep breath. Follow it with a strong exhalation and muscle relaxation. This done, you'll be better able to narrow your focus on the external task.

Using thought stopping and centering together allows you to gain control by diverting attention from thoughts that threaten your success to positive ones.

© iStockphoto.com/AntonioGuillem

Deep thoughts. Taking deep breaths and relaxing your muscles can help mitigate the effects that negative thoughts have on your speeches.

COACHING TIP

"There are two types of speakers—those that are nervous and those that are liars."
—Mark Twain

Nerves are not your enemy. Face them, control them, and you transform normal anxiety into a positive. Harnessing the excess energy that accompanies any apprehension you feel energizes you and enhances your development as a speaker.

1.3d Use Skills Training

We can combat both the physical and the mental effects of speech anxiety by making an effort to

- Speak on a topic about which we truly care
- Prepare thoroughly for the speechmaking event
- Keep in mind that our listeners are unlikely to perceive our signs of anxiety

Because you are just beginning your training to become a better speaker, it is reasonable to expect you may still feel anxious about speaking in public. As you increase your skill level by learning how to prepare and deliver speeches, you become consciously competent and aware of your competence. The idea of public speaking becomes less threatening.[16] By making your anxiety work for you, by converting it into positive energy, you learn to fear anxiety less, and you learn to like public speaking more.

GAME PLAN

Conquering Speech Anxiety

- ☐ I have assessed my own feelings and fears about giving a speech.
- ☐ I have chosen a topic that I know and about which I feel passionate.
- ☐ Last night, I practiced a powerful pose—I stood tall, I leaned forward, and opened my arms to the audience, staking out a broad surface with my hands.
- ☐ The morning before my speech, I went for a walk, a run, or a swim.
- ☐ Just before my speech, I took a moment to center my breathing and thoughts.
- ☐ I am ready to deliver my speech.

1.3e Anxiety Can Be Transformative

Contrary to what you may think, as a speaker you neither can nor should rid yourself of all speech anxiety. Rather, using your anxiety to perform more effectively is better than experiencing none at all.

In the book *Face of Emotion,* author Eric Finzi suggests that "putting on a happy face" not only erases a frown, it actually can lift your mood.[17] Nonverbal communication expert Paul Ekman agrees, acknowledging the possibility that facial expressions can affect our moods.[18] It follows then that changing any negative thoughts you have about giving a speech to positive ones can similarly influence your performance. With that in mind, follow these suggestions:

Prepare Thoroughly and Rehearse

Preparation helps instill confidence. It includes everything you do between thinking up a topic and speech delivery. Prepared speakers are competent speakers.

Visualize a Positive Experience

Instead of focusing on your negative thoughts and fears, focus on the potential positives of your performance. Visualize yourself being successful from start to finish.

Remind Yourself That Receivers Usually Cannot See or Hear Your Fear

Although you may feel the flutters that speech anxiety causes, the audience generally cannot detect these in your performance. In fact, observers usually underestimate the amount of anxiety they believe a speaker is experiencing.[19]

Choose a Topic You Are Knowledgeable About and Are Comfortable With

One of the best means of controlling your fear and laying the groundwork for a successful speech is to choose a topic that is important to you, that you know something about, and about which you want to find out even more. Highly anxious speakers rarely do this. As a result, they spend far too much preparation time trying to interest themselves in or master a subject, and far too little time rehearsing the presentation itself.[20]

Focus on Your Audience, Not on Yourself

Highly anxious speakers tend to be self-obsessed, but more effective speakers focus their attention on their listeners. When you avoid focusing on your anxiety and concentrate on your audience instead, you shine the communication spotlight on those you are speaking to and you minimize your anxiety.

COACHING TIP

"Think you can or think you can't; either way you will be right."

—Henry Ford

It is important to believe in yourself. You can become a skilled, confident, and proficient public speaker. Do you believe in you?

Exercises

GET A STRONG START

Becoming proficient at public speaking, like any other skill, is accomplished with practice. With introspection comes insight; with practice comes mastery. Take advantage of every opportunity to build your speaking skills.

1. Deliver a Tip on How to Enhance Confidence

For practice, customize a topic related to speech apprehension, such as "Taking the Fear Out of Public Speaking," "The Uses of Hypnosis," or "How to De-stress." Once you select a topic, research it, and explain the guidelines given to reduce apprehension.

2. TED on Power Poses

Watch the TED Talk about power poses available at **http://www.ted.com/talks/amy_cuddy_your_body_language_shapes_who_you_are.html**. In this presentation, Amy Cuddy reveals the extent to which body language shapes assessments of a person. Based on what you learn, identify what you can do to help others judge you to be a "powerful" presenter.

3. Analyze This: The Opening Monologue

View the opening monologue of an afternoon or late-night TV show such as *Saturday Night Live*, *The Tonight Show With Jimmy Fallon*, or *The Ellen DeGeneres Show*. Assess the host's confidence delivering the opening monologue. What was the host's topic? Did it appeal to the audience? Why? Did the host come across as knowledgeable? Why? Did she or he come across as confident? Why? What signs of anxiety, if any, did you see the host exhibit? Was the host's focus on the audience or on him- or herself? How do you know? What three adjectives would you use to describe the host's performance? What aspects of your analysis can you apply to your performance as a speaker?

4. Approach the Speaker's Stand

Choose one of the following assignments and share your thoughts with your peers in a two- to three-minute presentation. Structure your presentation so it has a clear introduction, definite body, and strong conclusion.

- **a.** Interview another member of the class to identify a number of interesting facts about that person. Be as creative as possible in organizing and sharing what you discovered about your partner and what it has taught you.
- **b.** Describe a significant personal experience that challenged your sense of ethics.
- **c.** Based on a review of recent news stories, share a concern you have regarding the ability of members of society to respect one another and get along.
- **d.** Bring to class a picture, object, or brief literary or nonfiction selection that helps you express your feelings about a subject of importance to you. Share the selection with the class, discuss why you selected it, and explain how it helps you better understand yourself, others, or your relation to the subject.

RECAP AND REVIEW

1. **Demonstrate how developing public speaking skills can help you realize personal, professional, and societal goals.** Public speaking precipitates self-discovery and the art of creative self-expression. It enhances self-confidence and the ability to influence or control one's environment. In addition, prospective employers favor persons with public speaking abilities. And society benefits from people who are able to function as responsible citizens and participate in the exchange of ideas.
2. **List and explain the essential elements of communication.** The following elements are integral to communicating: the source formulates and delivers a message; the receiver interprets the source's message; the message is the content of the speech; the channel is the pathway that carries the message; noise is anything that interferes with the sending or receiving of a message; the cultural context is the environment in which communication occurs; feedback is information received in response to a sent message; effect is the outcome or exchange of influences occurring during communication; and the field of experience is the sum of all the experiences that a person carries with him or her when communicating.
3. **Assess your confidence as a speaker.** Public speaking anxiety is composed of process anxiety (the fear of preparing a speech) and performance anxiety (the fear of presenting a speech). It is important to acknowledge and face whatever fear you have so that you are able to harness the excess energy that accompanies it.
4. **Identify the sources of speechmaking anxiety.** Among the common sources of speechmaking anxiety are fear of failure, fear of the unknown, fear of evaluation, fear of being the center of attention, fear of difference, and fear imposed by culture.
5. **Use systematic desensitization, power posing, cognitive restructuring, centering, and skills training to alleviate the symptoms of speech apprehension.** A variety of strategies can help you address both the physical and mental effects of speech anxiety. Practice tensing and relaxing your muscles, strike a powerful pose, focus on changing your own negative thoughts, and take comfort in honing your own competence by practicing and delivering speeches.

KEY TERMS

Centering 13
Centering breath 13
Channel 7
Cognitive restructuring 13
Communication 3
Effects of communication 8
Ethnocentricity 11
Feedback 7
Field of experience 8
Message 6
Noise 7
Performance anxiety 11
Process anxiety 11
Public speaking anxiety 11
Receiver 6
Self-talk 13
Situational/cultural context 7
Source 6
Thought stopping 13

2

© iStockphoto.com/SteveDebenport

Give Your First Speech

UPON COMPLETING THIS CHAPTER'S TRAINING, YOU WILL BE ABLE TO

1. Understand the basic moves used in speechmaking
2. Approach public speaking systematically
3. Deliver a brief first speech
4. Score your first speech performance to establish a baseline on which to build your skills

Imagine yourself standing smack in the middle of a sports field. "What am I doing here?" you ask yourself. You don't play sports. You are unprepared to participate in the game that's about to start. Because of your lack of familiarity with the sport, lack of training, and lack of equipment, you have absolutely no idea what to do as more skilled players take the field, milling about, looking at you. You feel like an idiot.

Now let's change the setting. You are seated in your public speaking class. And your instructor has just told you that you're going to have to come to the front of the room and give a speech. But public speaking is something you've had no formal training in and little, if any, experience with. You feel unknowledgeable, unprepared, and unconditioned. "What?" you ask, stunned. "The course has just begun and you already want me to give a speech. How am I supposed to do that?"

Though few, if any, coaches would expect you to have mastered a game by your first practice, they would expect you to be familiar with how it is played—and to have a sense of the kinds of rules and moves you will be expected to learn. So let's begin by previewing the four primary plays involved in giving a speech for the first time.

Every play is made up of one or more key steps—each necessary for the play's success. The four key plays to delivering your first speech are (1) topic selection; (2) speech development, support, and organization; (3) practice and delivery; and (4) post-presentation analysis.

Contents

COACHING TIP

Believe everything you say.

When you share your message, you share yourself. Having a personal connection affects the delivery of your speech and your relationship with your audience. Belief in the significance and relevance of your words is contagious.

section

2.1

Select Your Topic

This move is made up of three basic steps. First, analyze your interests and use this information to select a general subject area. Second, compare this general subject area to your audience and the occasion. Third, vet the topic, selecting your goal and narrowing your subject.

2.1a Analyze Yourself

Learning what motivates you and makes you tick will help you become a better speaker.[1] In fact, conducting a **self-analysis** is a prerequisite. Although at times you may be handed a specific topic assignment, most often the choice of topic will be yours. Even if given a topic, we recommend that you still conduct a self-analysis to uncover aspects of yourself that may be particularly interesting or appealing to others.

Conduct a Life Overview

Whatever your age, divide your life into thirds—early life, midlife, more recent life. Compose a sentence to summarize your life during each stage, for example, "During high school, I lived in Norman, Oklahoma, where my dad worked for an oil company, and I went to Sooner football games." Under each summary statement list your main interests and concerns during that life period. Examine your list. Which topics still interest or concern you?

Focus on This Moment in Time

Fold a sheet of paper in half. On the left side, list sensory experiences—whatever you are able to see, hear, taste, smell, or touch right now. On the right side, list topics suggested by each sensory experience. For example, if you wrote "balloon" on the left side, you might enter "party planning" on the right side.

Be Newsy

Peruse a newspaper, newsmagazine, or online news aggregator to find potential topics. Read a story and list topics suggested by it. For example, the February 19, 2016, *New York Times* featured an article titled "The Résumé and References Check Out. How About Social Media?" Imagine the possible speech topics the article suggests: how to prepare a résumé, how to use social media responsibly, interviewing skills, and so on.

Use Technology

Explore websites such as About.com, eHow.com, or YouTube, searching for sample presentations. Additionally, the speech topic resources at edge.sagepub.com/gamblepsp2e can prove helpful.

▶ See **Chapter 6** for more information on selecting a topic.

2.1b Consider Your Audience and the Occasion

Once you've conducted your self-analysis, you turn your attention to your audience, conducting an audience analysis. Why? Because if you consider only your interests and don't take the needs and interests of your audience into account, audience members are more likely to experience boredom and become easily distracted. If this happens, you lose the attention of receivers, which prevents your message from getting through.

Pay attention to your audience, and they will pay attention to you. This means you will want to consider how familiar audience members are with your selected topic area, what their attitudes toward it are, and what they would like to know about it. Take into account some of the demographic characteristics of the audience, such as their genders and ages, the cultures represented, their socioeconomic backgrounds. Think about how factors like these could influence how they feel about your topic and, consequently, how you should frame it. For example, if you decide to speak about student services for on-campus residents, but your class is made up primarily of students who commute to campus, a substantial number of students could find your talk irrelevant.

Take the time needed to get to know your receivers. Talk to them, asking about their interests and concerns. For this first assignment, chatting with three to five students should be sufficient. Ask them what they already know about your topic, whether it appeals to them, and what else they'd be interested in finding out about it. Their answers will help you narrow your subject and relate it more directly to them.

▶ **Chapter 5** will help you analyze your audience and adapt your presentation to them.

© iStockphoto.com/RawPixelLtd

Getting to know you. Speak more directly to your audience by knowing their demographic characteristics and relationship to your speech topic.

2.1c Criteria for Choosing Your Topic

There are a number of other criteria aside from your interests to consider when selecting a topic for your initial speech.

1. Avoid overused topics, unless you will be taking an unusual slant or offering a fresh perspective. Thus, rather than speaking on the legalization of marijuana, speak on how it helps deter the ill-effects of chemotherapy.
2. Select an appropriate topic—not one that will be alienating or that you or your receivers have no interest in learning more about. Make the effort to meet their needs and expectations.
3. Limit the scope of your topic so that it fits the time allotted for your speech. For example, speaking on The Story of My Life or The History of the Computer could be too broad, making it impossible for you to cover the topic in the time available.
4. Make sure you have access to the material you will need to prepare the speech.

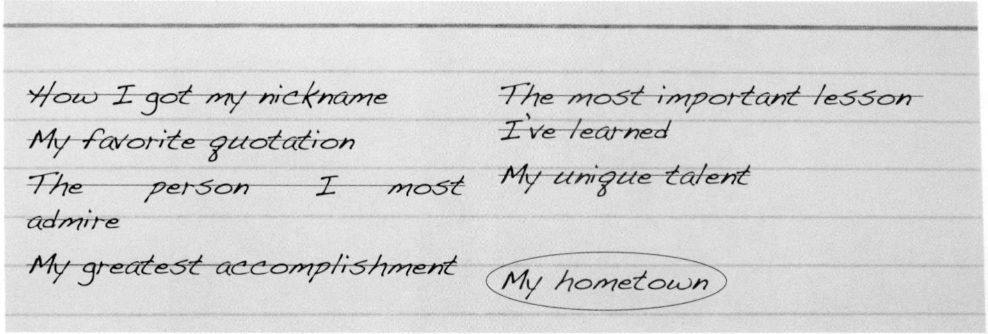

Choices matter. What topics would be engaging, fresh, and easily understood by your audience?

It is of paramount importance that your selected topic interests your audience. Among the topics students have used for a first speech are

- My Favorite Ancestor
- What I Learned Studying Abroad
- My Greatest Fear
- A Difficult Choice I Had to Make
- Why You Need a Mentor
- How Discrimination Affects Me
- How to Avoid Boredom
- The Dangers of Texting and Driving
- How to Get the Most Out of College

Which of these, if any, interests you? What topics would you like to hear about?

▶ **Chapters 5** and **6** will give you more strategies for selecting a topic that is appropriate for your audience.

© iStockphoto.com/IvelinRadkov

Don't procrastinate. Choosing a topic isn't necessarily easy, so start weeks in advance to have ample time to prepare.

section

2.2

Develop, Support, and Organize Your Speech

Once you have chosen a topic, decide what you want to share about it with receivers. This becomes your speech's goal. For example, is your goal to inform, persuade, or mark a special occasion? Once you answer this question, you are ready to formulate your speech's purpose.

2.2a State Your Speech's Purpose

Your speech should have a specific purpose—a single sentence specifying your goal. For example, if your goal was to inform receivers about self-driving cars, your specific purpose might be "to inform my audience about three ways self-driving cars will impact society." You then use the specific purpose to develop your central idea or thesis.

▶ **Chapter 6** will show you how to develop the general and specific purpose of your speech.

2.2b Compose a Thesis Statement

A **thesis statement** expresses the central idea of your speech in just one sentence. Here are three examples of thesis statements:

> Self-driving cars will change the way we live and get around in three ways: (1) by reducing accidents, (2) by permitting overnight travel, and (3) by fundamentally changing the taxicab and ride-sharing industries.
>
> Excessive personal debt is burdensome, inhibits a person's quality of life, and also results in financial instability.
>
> Fears of an epidemic of birth defects due to the Zika virus and questions about how to respond are prevalent in society.

The thesis statement, along with the specific purpose, acts as a road map for building your speech. Your next move is to develop the main points that flesh out the thesis.

▶ **Chapter 6** will show you how to create an effective thesis statement.

2.2c Identify Your Speech's Main Points

If your specific purpose and thesis are clearly formulated, it will be easy for you to identify your speech's main points—the major ideas your speech will relay to receivers. Most of your speeches will contain two or three main points, with each main point supporting your expressed thesis. For example, let's look at the last thesis statement identified in the previous section. Its two main points might read:

I. There is fear of a surge in birth defects due to the Zika virus.

II. There are questions about how to protect the population and prevent birth defects in the event that Zika becomes widespread.

We see the speaker plans to first confront the fears about Zika and then discuss questions about how to control and treat the disease if it develops into a pandemic. Once you formulate the main points, your next move is to locate and select supporting materials.

▶ **Chapter 10** will help you to establish your main points.

2.2d Research and Select Materials to Support Main Points

At this point, your focus is on conducting research and gathering supporting materials for your speech. To develop your speech, for example, you will use personal experiences, examples and illustrations, definitions, expert testimony, statistics, and analogies. The better your research and selection of support, the more credible receivers will find your speech.

▶ **Chapters 7** and **8** will show you how to find relevant research and use it in your speech.

Michael Blann/Digital Vision/Thinkstock

Support your points. Research adds credibility to your speech.

2.2e Outline Your Speech Indicating Transitions and Signposts

Every speech can be divided into three major parts: the introduction, the body, and the conclusion. Develop the **body of the speech**, the part that elaborates on the main points, first. When it is done, you then bring it together with an **introduction** and a **conclusion**. In the introduction, orient the audience to your topic, pique their attention and interest, state your thesis, and preview your main points. In the conclusion, restate your thesis in a memorable way, remind receivers of how your main points supported it, and motivate them—leaving them thinking and/or ready to act.

An **outline** provides the skeleton upon which you hang your main ideas and support. Two principles guide its creation: **coordination** (the main points should be relatively equal in importance) and **subordination** (the support underlying your main points). The outline of your speech's body will look something like this:

INTRODUCTION

BODY

I. Main Point I
   A. First level of subordination
      1. Second level of subordination
      2. Second level of subordination
II. Main Point 2
   A. First level of subordination
      1. Second level of subordination
      2. Second level of subordination
III. Main Point 3
   A. First level of subordination
      1. Second level of subordination
      2. Second level of subordination

CONCLUSION

When outlining your speech, you'll want to keep each of the speech's main sections in mind—paying careful attention to the introduction, body, and conclusion. The first component in your introduction should be an attention getter, followed by your thesis statement, then a statement of what's in it for the audience (why they should care), a credibility enhancer for yourself (why they should listen to you), and a preview of your main points. Similarly, the outline of your conclusion should contain a summary of your main points and your "home run"—a move that clinches audience support for and belief in your message.

▶ **Chapters 9** and **10** will demonstrate how to organize and outline your speech.

Once the outline is complete, you'll want to create transitions that connect the parts. You can use signposts, such as "first," "next," and "finally," to let receivers know where you are in your speech, and brief statements, such as "most important," to help focus the audience's attention.

2.2f Consider Presentation Aids

Once your outline is done, consider whether visual or audio aids such as physical objects, drawings, charts, graphs, photographs, or sound recordings will enhance the understanding and interest of receivers. Be sure to indicate in the outline when you will use such aids, if you choose to do so.

▶ **Chapter 17** will offer you tips on using presentation aids effectively.

Consider presentation aids. When used effectively, visual aids can reinforce your main points.

section

2.3

2.3a Rehearse and Revise as Needed

2.3b Anticipate Questions From the Audience

2.3c Take the Podium, Harness Nervous Energy, and Present the Speech

Practice Delivery

How well you do in your first speech depends in part on how effectively you have prepared, practiced, and overcome any anxiety. Instead of reading a speech word for word or, worse, choosing to wing it, practice speaking in front of a mirror or friends. Make it a habit to plan and prepare the structure of your speech and all content including supporting materials and visuals. Then rehearse extensively so that on the day you present your speech, you are comfortable using your notes to remind yourself of its content.

2.3a Rehearse and Revise as Needed

You will want to become so familiar with the contents of your speech that you can deliver it seemingly effortlessly. Focus on the word *seemingly* for a moment. Preparing and presenting a speech require real effort on your part. But if you work diligently and conscientiously, your audience will see only the end results—to them it will seem as if you are a natural.

When it comes to vocal cues, for example, you'll want to regulate your volume, rate, pitch, and vocal variety, being especially careful not to speak in a monotone, and being certain to use correct pronunciation and clear articulation so you convey ideas accurately and clearly. Beyond words, you'll also want to use appropriate facial expressions, sustain the right amount of eye contact, and use gestures and movement in support of your message.

Practice delivering the speech at least four to six times, initially to a mirror, and then to a small audience of family and friends. Stand when you practice. Always say your speech aloud. Use a timer. Revise your words or presentation as needed. Replicate the same conditions you will have when delivering it for real. Practice from the speech's beginning to its end without stopping. You might even record a rehearsal to assess how you're doing.

▶ See **Chapters 14, 15,** and **16** for more help with the delivery of your speech.

2.3b Anticipate Questions From the Audience

When you've finished speaking, audience members may have questions to ask you. When prepping for your presentation, think about what you would ask if you were a member of the audience. Also solicit questions from the rehearsal audiences made up of family and friends.

▶ **Chapter 27** will prepare you for questions that the audience may ask about your speech.

2.3c Take the Podium, Harness Nervous Energy, and Present the Speech

You've prepared. You have rehearsed and revised, and now it's time to have fun! Harness any nervous energy and remember to use the confidence building techniques you learned in Chapter 1. Visualize yourself succeeding!

▶ See **Chapter 1** for tips on managing speech anxiety and building your confidence before you speak.

Fuse/Thinkstock

Effortlessly. Practice a lot so your speech flows naturally—you'll have more confidence and more credibility with the audience.

COACHING TIP

See yourself enjoying your speech.

Enjoy delivering your speech, and the audience will enjoy it too! Enjoyment is an attractor. It is also inclusive.

section

2.4 Conduct a Post-Presentation Analysis

2.4a Assess Your Performance

Like an athlete or any performer, you'll want to review and critique your own performance, comparing and contrasting your expectations with your actual experience. Try to learn as much as possible from the first speech so you can apply these lessons to your next one. Complete a self-assessment scorecard or checklist that you can compare to the one your professor and/or peers offer.

- **Chapter 4** will help you listen effectively in order to analyze your fellow students' speeches and assess your own presentation.

© iStockphoto.com/filo

Self-review. What are some goals and areas about your performance that you can highlight prior to your speech for review after?

COACHING TIP

A scorecard is a speaker's friend.

How are you doing? Use a scorecard to track your progress. Needing to improve isn't a negative. It's a step on the road to mastery. It's time to measure up!

2.4a Assess Your Performance

Use the accompanying preliminary scorecard to assess your performance. Score yourself on each item using a scale of 1 to 5, with 1 meaning least effective and 5 meaning extremely effective.

POST-PRESENTATION SCORECARD

Introduction: How Well Did I Do?

- Capturing attention _____
- Conveying my thesis _____
- Previewing my main points _____
- Relating the topic to my audience _____

Body: How Well Did I Do?

- Communicating each main point _____
- Transitioning between main points _____
- Integrating support for each main point _____

Conclusion: How Well Did I Do?

- Restating the thesis _____
- Summarizing my main points _____
- Motivating receivers to think and/or act _____

Delivery: How Well Did I Do?

- Using vocal cues to create interest and convey meaning _____
- Using eye contact to connect with receivers _____
- Using gestures and movement that were natural and effective _____

Overall, I would give myself ________ points out of 5.

I believe my strong points were ____

____

____.

I believe I need to improve when it comes to ___________________________

____

____

____.

Based on this scorecard, I set the following goals for my next speech: _____

____

____

____

Exercises

FIRST SPEECH

Use these chapter exercises to apply your understanding of this chapter's content. When you commit to a practice regimen, you commit to building your public presentation skills.

1. First Speech Primer

Prepare a list of "do and don't" suggestions for preparing a first speech. Include the speaker's role in selecting a topic, formulating a goal, researching, thinking about his or her relationship to the audience, organizing ideas, preparing to present, and assessing the extent to which the speaker and the speech succeeded.

2. Cue the Critiquer

Offer advice to a student whose task it is to critique the first speech. What should he or she look for? How should he or she offer feedback?

3. Analyze This: A First Speech

Let's look at one student's first speech. (Comments or annotations on the speech are presented as side notes, or SN.) The topic was "My Hometown." As you read the speech, imagine it being delivered. Here are some questions for you to consider when evaluating it:

1. How do you think students in your class would respond to the speech? Would they, for example, find the topic as relevant and appealing as the speaker? Why or why not?
2. Is the speech organized effectively? What do you believe is its purpose? Can you identify the thesis? Does the speech have an introduction that captures your attention, a clear body, and a sound conclusion? Are there transitions to link ideas? Is there sufficient support for each of the speaker's points?
3. What changes, if any, would you suggest making to improve the speech? For example, would you add presentation aids?
4. What questions would you like to ask the speaker?

4. Approach the Speaker Stand: My First Speech

Use what you have learned about topic selection; speech development, support, and organization; presentation, practice, and delivery; and harnessing positive energy to prepare and give a brief speech on your hometown or another topic selected by your instructor. After delivering the speech, offer a self-assessment of your performance.

MY HOMETOWN

Good afternoon. I have learned a lot from all of you about your hometowns in the United States by listening to your speeches over the last few weeks. You've shared fascinating details that have helped me form mental pictures of many places I have never seen. Now I would like to take you to my hometown, the city of Shanghai, China.

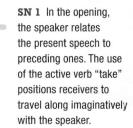

SN 1 In the opening, the speaker relates the present speech to preceding ones. The use of the active verb "take" positions receivers to travel along imaginatively with the speaker.

Have you ever been to New York City?

SN 2 The speaker's use of a question is involving. The speaker builds rapport by comparing what receivers know about New York City with his own city of Shanghai.

Did you know that Shanghai has almost twice as many skyscrapers as New York City, and will soon have 1,000 more? It is one of the biggest and most modern cities in China, and 18 million people live there. Shanghai already has many elevated highways and a subway, and the government is building a new ship terminal. The city even has a high-speed train line, the fastest in the world, that brings visitors from Shanghai's international airport into the city. And there are thousands of cars, many of them taxi cabs in bright gold, red, and blue.

There are big changes taking place in Shanghai today, and they are happening very fast, but first I want to tell you about the city the way I remember it. Try to picture it with me.

SN 3 The speaker demonstrates a deep emotional connection to the topic. The sense of change is in the air.

Over the past hundred years, many Chinese people were able to improve their lives by moving into "the city about the sea"—that's what the name Shanghai means, the city about the sea. Leaving the undeveloped countryside behind, they came to the city to work and live, and they made their homes in small apartment buildings near the Huangpu riverfront, or at the northern and southern edges of the city. My parents came to the city when they were young, leaving their families behind in the countryside. They worked hard, riding bicycles to their jobs and saving as much as they could. For a long time, they didn't have very much.

SN 4 The speaker's use of narrative draws receivers into the body of the presentation.

I grew up in our two-room apartment on the third floor and knew everyone in our neighborhood. Everyone knew everyone, in fact! We lived on the western riverbank, near the famous Shanghai Bund, which is a thoroughfare about a mile long of historic old buildings in the Western style. Our own neighborhood was also old, but crowded and full of busy apartment buildings. Our building was separated from the others by narrow lanes filled with bicycles and motorbikes, and there was laundry hanging everywhere to dry. I could often hear our neighbors laughing, arguing, or playing the radio, and the smell of food cooking was always in the air.

SN 5 The speaker's use of description and sensory images resonate.

continued

continued

I walked or rode my bicycle to school, and my route took me past the open-air markets and street vendors selling all kinds of food. Sometimes it was hard not to stop and buy something, or to linger by the park where there was always a little crowd of people performing their morning tai chi exercises, but I would never want to shame my parents by being late for school.

Sometimes when we had a school holiday, my friends and I would go to Nanjing Donglu. That is the big shopping area in the middle of Shanghai, where there are all kinds of stores. There are places to buy food of all kinds, like duck, sausages, fish, oysters and shrimp, and of course tea, and you can also find tools, hardware, art, clothes, and even pets. My friends at home have told me that, because one part of it is now closed to cars, Nanjing Donglu has even more tourists than ever before. These are mostly Chinese tourists, from other parts of the country, who enjoy coming to Shanghai to see the sights.

SN 6 The speaker changes tone to make clear the downside of modernization.

There were still cars allowed in Nanjing Donglu when I was growing up in Shanghai, but as I said there are many changes happening there. One of the biggest is the change in old neighborhoods like mine, which are being torn down to make way for the new skyscrapers I told you about, and other developments like new ports, factories, shipyards, and parks and pavilions. The World Expo took place in Shanghai some years back, and the government was very anxious and worked really hard to make the city as modern and as developed as possible, and it did this very quickly at great cost. There are many people who worked to preserve as much of old, historic Shanghai as they could, but hundreds of people lost their homes in the old town and moved away into the suburbs.

SN 7 In the conclusion, the speaker prompts continued interest by leaving the audience wondering what will happen when the speaker returns to Shanghai.

Next time I return to the city, my neighborhood near the Bund will be the first place I visit. I want to see whether my old home and my neighbors are still there.[2]

RECAP AND REVIEW

1. **Understand the basic plays used in speechmaking.** There are four basic plays in speechmaking: (1) topic selection; (2) speech development, support, and organization; (3) practice and delivery; and (4) post-presentation analysis.
2. **Approach public speaking systematically.** By working your way through all the sections step-by-step, you approach speechmaking systematically.
3. **Deliver a brief first speech.** Only by preparing and delivering a speech can you tell how well you understand and how effectively you are able to execute the plays involved.
4. **Score your first speech performance to establish a baseline on which to build your skills.** Like athletes, actors, and musicians, speakers review and critique their own performances, attempting to learn as much as possible from each experience so they can apply the lessons to future events.

KEY TERMS

Body of the speech 26
Conclusion 26
Coordination 26
Introduction 26
Outline 26
Self-analysis 20
Subordination 26
Thesis statement 24

SAGE edge™

Sharpen your skills with SAGE edge at edge.sagepub.com/gamblepsp2e.

SAGE edge for students provides a personalized approach to help you accomplish your coursework goals in an easy-to-use learning environment.

© iStockphoto.com/2008GettyImages

3

Ethics and Public Speaking in a Global World

UPON COMPLETING THIS CHAPTER'S TRAINING, YOU WILL BE ABLE TO

1. Explain how cultural understanding affects speakers and audiences
2. Define and discuss the importance of ethics, identifying where you draw the line when faced with specific ethical dilemmas
3. Define plagiarism, explaining why it is an ethical issue
4. Define critical thinking, explaining its significance for speakers and audiences
5. Describe the relationship among ethics, critical thinking, and multiculturalism/cultural understanding

Contents

When traveling in Australia, President George H. W. Bush unintentionally ended up insulting those Australians who came to see him when he raised his hand and gave the V sign. The gesture in America means "Victory." However, when two fingers are raised and the palm faces inward as President Bush's did in Australia, to the Australians this is the equivalent of raising the middle finger in the United States. What do cultural diversity, ethics, and critical thinking have to do with public speaking? Winning public speakers practice certain skills to reach diverse groups of receivers and to make each speaking engagement meaningful and respectful. Speakers who take cultural differences into account develop messages with broad appeal. But it doesn't stop there. **Ethics** matter too. Just as we expect athletes to play by certain rules, and game referees to make fair calls, we expect speakers to make sound ethical choices—to present their ideas, arguments, and information in a fair and balanced way. If a speaker is being unfair, we the audience then need to rely on our critical thinking skills to keep from being unknowingly manipulated. In this chapter, our goal is to help you become a culturally aware, ethical, and sound thinker—equipped with assets you can use not only on your campus, but also well beyond it, including at work and in your community.

COACHING TIP

"We all should know that diversity makes for a rich tapestry, and we must understand that all the threads of the tapestry are equal in value no matter what their color."

—Maya Angelou

Make diversity your friend. Every audience member merits respect. Diversity is not divisive. Its recognition is inclusive. Use diversity to build a new sense of community.

section

3.1

Respect Different Cultures

3.1a Attune Yourself to Difference

3.1b Assess Your Understanding of Cultural Diversity

3.1c Reflect Cultural Values

3.1d Understand Cultural Identity

3.1e Consider Preferred Learning Styles

3.1f Understand Difference to Build Bridges and Confidence

Public speakers can prepare themselves for situations that require them to speak before diverse audiences.[1] **Cultural diversity** is the recognition and valuing of difference. It encompasses such factors as age, gender, race, ethnicity, ability, religion, education, marital status, sexual orientation, and income.

Speeches, and our responses to them, demonstrate our understanding of difference and our tolerance for dissent. Beyond mutual respect, however, lies our own self-interest. When we demonstrate respect for cultural diversity, we reduce the chances of alienating members of the audience and increase the chances of eliciting the audience response we seek. By recognizing, for instance, that receivers from different cultures may be offended by different things, and that speakers from other cultures may display more or less expressiveness than their receivers, we become more culturally attuned and less culturally tone-deaf (see Table 3.1).

TABLE 3.1 FOCUS ON CULTURAL DIVERSITY

A SPEAKER WHO RESPECTS DIVERSITY	A SPEAKER WHO NEGLECTS DIVERSITY
Develops a complex view of issues	Develops a simplistic view of issues
Does not stereotype, avoiding its consequences	Frequently stereotypes, having to face the consequences
Sees things from others' viewpoints—empathizing with them	Sees things only from his or her perspective; assumes others share his or her values
Is comfortable speaking before a culturally diverse audience	Becomes anxious when speaking before a culturally diverse audience
Does not alienate receivers by trying to impose his or her views on them	Tries to impose his or her views on others, risking open hostility from receivers

3.1a Attune Yourself to Difference

Why should attuning yourself to cultural differences be part of your public speaking training? According to U.S. Census Bureau statistics, the United States is composed of five large ethnic groups who identify themselves as White (207.7 million), Hispanic (38.8 million), African American (36.6 million), Asian American (12.7 million), and Native American (3.5 million).[2] Given such statistics, there is a good chance you will find yourself speaking before audiences whose cultural backgrounds and perspectives differ from your own.

Your success depends on your ability to face up to cultural diversity and speak and listen across cultures.

3.1b Assess Your Understanding of Cultural Diversity

When speaking before audiences small or large, if we want to share ideas successfully, we need to take cultural differences into account.

Self-Assessment: Are You Prepared to Speak Before and Listen to People of Diverse Cultures?

To assess your personal preparedness to speak and listen to people of different cultures, respond to each of the following statements by labeling it as either true or false. Answer honestly.

1. I am equally comfortable speaking before people who are like me and speaking before people who are different from me. _______
2. I consider the concerns of all groups in society equally. _______
3. I am aware of how people from other cultures perceive me, including how they receive my words and actions. _______
4. I am equally comfortable listening to people from other cultures and listening to people from my own culture. _______
5. I believe in respecting the communication rules and preferences of people from other cultures, just as I would want people from other cultures to respect the communication rules and preferences of my culture. _______
6. I support the right of people from other cultures to disagree with my values and beliefs. _______
7. I understand that people from other cultures may choose not to participate in a dialogue or debate because of their culture's rules. _______
8. I recognize that some cultures are more expressive than others. _______
9. A culture provides its members with a continuum of appropriate and inappropriate communication behaviors. _______
10. I do not believe that my culture is superior to all other cultures. _______

Interpreting Your Response

The more statements you answered with "true," the better equipped you are to enrich the public speaking arena by welcoming people from diverse cultures into it.

3.1c Reflect Cultural Values

Culture is the system of knowledge, beliefs, values, attitudes, behaviors, and artifacts (objects made or used by humans) that we learn, accept, and use in daily life. Typically, cultural norms and assumptions are passed from the senior to the newer members of a group. Adept speakers use these cues to adapt to different audiences.

Co-Cultures

Within a culture as a whole are co-cultures. **Co-cultures** are composed of members of the same general culture who differ in some ethnic or sociological way from the parent culture. In American society, for example, African Americans, Hispanic Americans, Japanese Americans, Arab Americans, the disabled, LGBTQ, and the elderly are just some of the co-cultures belonging to the same general culture[3] (see Figure 3.1).

People belonging to a **marginalized group**—a group whose members feel like outsiders—may passively, assertively, or aggressively/confrontationally seek to reach their goals relative to the dominant culture.

- Co-culture members who practice a *passive approach* usually avoid the limelight or the lectern, accepting their position in the cultural hierarchy. They embrace the cultural beliefs and practices of the dominant culture. Recent immigrants to the United States who desire to attain citizenship may choose this path, hoping to blend in.
- Co-culture members who employ an *assertive approach* want members of the dominant group to accommodate their diversity. At the same time, they are receptive to rethinking their ideas, giving up or modifying some, but holding strong with regard to others. For example, many Muslim Americans spoke openly of their support for the War on Terror, while also expressing their desire to live according to their religious values and beliefs, which were falsely conflated with those of the terrorists behind the attacks of September 11, 2001.
- Co-culture members who take an *aggressive/confrontational approach* more intensely defend their beliefs and traditions, leading to their being perceived by members of the dominant culture as "hurtfully expressive" or "self-promoting." They make it difficult for members of the dominant culture to ignore their presence or pretend they do not exist.[4] Co-culture members adopt this strategy in an effort to demarginalize themselves and actively participate in the world of the dominant culture. In their early years, the members of ACT UP, a gay rights organization, employed such an approach.

FIGURE 3.1

A Culture and Its Co-Cultures

The term *co-culture* is preferred over *sub-culture* because the prefix *sub* denotes inferior status. A co-culture is a culture within a culture.

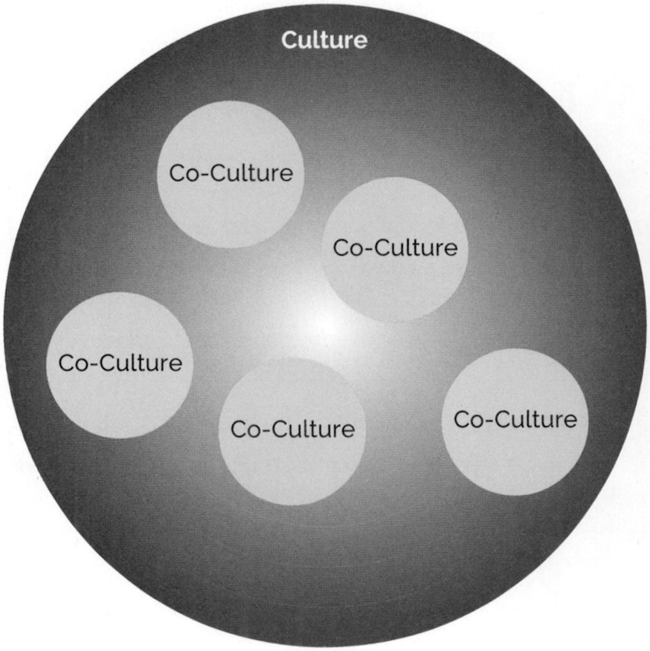

Within the context of cultural diversity, how would you identify yourself? Consider your own classroom or workplace. When you look around, do you recognize groups that constitute co-cultures? When taking a podium, remember to avoid speaking solely to one group. Public speaking is about communicating to as many listeners as possible.

Different Communication Styles

We need to recognize both how the culture we belong to affects our communication and how other peoples' cultures affect theirs.

Individualistic cultures tend to use **low-context communication**, while **high-context communication** is predominant in collectivistic cultures. As members of an individualistic culture, North Americans tend to speak in a low-context way, addressing an issue head-on, while persons from Asian countries usually avoid confrontation, relying on a high-context communication style that allows others to save face.[5] Thus, a North American speaker may directly contradict what another person has said, while an Asian speaker's comments are likely to be more indirect and subtle, even vague.

In some cultures, dissent and disagreement with friends and relatives is considered normal—it is possible to separate a speaker from her words—while in other cultures, speakers and their words are perceived as one. In the latter case, when you dispute someone's words, you also cast aspersions on his or her character. As a result, rarely will one Saudi Arabian publicly criticize or chastise another because doing so would label that speaker as disloyal and disrespectful.[6] It is important that speakers and audience members not interpret each other's behavior based on their own frames of reference or cultural norms, but work to understand the cultural dynamics of persons from their own as well as other cultures.

COACHING TIP

"What we have to do . . . is to find a way to celebrate our diversity and debate our differences without fracturing our communities."[7]

—Hillary Clinton

Creating community out of diversity depends on keeping the "isms" at bay. Because they exclude rather than include, ethnocentrism, racism, sexism, and ageism have no place in your speaker's toolbox.

3.1d Understand Cultural Identity

We also need insight into **cultural identity**, the internalization of culturally appropriate beliefs, values, and roles acquired through interacting with members of our cultural group. Cultural identity also is a product of our group memberships. We all belong to a number of different groups and form identities based on these group memberships, with cultural notions influencing what it means to be a group member.

- ***Gender*** affects the way males and females present themselves, socialize, work, perceive their futures, and communicate. Men tend to adopt a problem-solving orientation and prefer to use a linear approach to storytelling and presentations, while women typically offer more details and fill in tangential information.[7]
- ***Age*** influences our beliefs about how persons our age should look and behave. An older person may be perceived as wiser. Age can also influence judgments of credibility and precipitate disagreements about values and priorities. For this reason, persons belonging to different age groups are likely to perceive issues such as Social Security reform, transgender rights, and the value of rap music differently.
- ***Racial and ethnic identities,*** in addition to being based on physical characteristics, are also socially constructed. Some racial and ethnic groups share experiences of oppression; their attitudes and behaviors may reflect their struggles. Thus, race influences attitudes toward controversial issues such as affirmative action, welfare reform, and interracial marriage and adoption.
- ***Religious identity*** is at the root of countless contemporary conflicts occurring in the Middle East, Northern Ireland, India and Pakistan, and Bosnia-Herzegovina, and it sometimes influences receiver and speaker responses to issues and world events. In the United States, for example, evangelical Christians may have a different view of the relationship between church and state than do members of other Christian groups.
- ***Socioeconomic identity*** frames our responses to issues, influencing our attitudes and experiences as well as the way we communicate. The widening gap between the ultra-wealthy and the middle and lower classes in this country contributes to different attitudes on a host of issues, including tax cuts.
- ***National identity*** refers to our legal status or citizenship. People whose ancestors immigrated to the United States generations ago may still be perceived as foreigners by some Americans.

A speaker should be aware that the culture, economic and social class, and gender of receivers might influence the way audience members will process the examples the speaker employs. For example, based on their personal experience, audiences of mostly women, mostly men, or mixed gender likely would react differently to the examples used in this excerpt from a speech on "Why Girls Matter" by Anna Maria Chavez, CEO of Girl Scouts of the United States of America:

> Our alumnae have made huge impacts on all sectors of our communities. In the world of entertainment, for example, Taylor Swift is a Girl Scout. In the world of athletics, so is tennis star Venus Williams. Media great Robin Roberts is a Girl Scout alumna. Virtually every female astronaut who has flown into space was a Girl Scout. And one successful businesswoman who was a Girl Scout is Ginny Rometty, CEO of IBM. . . . All the former female U.S. secretaries of state were Girl Scouts: Madeline Albright, Condoleezza Rice, and Hillary Clinton. Fifteen of the 20 women in the U.S. Senate are Girl Scout alumnae. So are more than half of the 88 women in the House of Representatives. And of the five women who currently serve as governors across our nation, four were Girl Scouts.
>
> Embracing the values of tolerance and civility is not a hindrance to success, it is clear, but an asset because it instills the values of character, confidence and courage. That is more than a matter of opinion. According to a recent survey, nearly two-thirds of Girl Scouts view themselves as leaders, compared with 44 percent of other girls, and 52 percent of boys.[8]

Speakers also need to be aware of how different cultures process humor. When integrating humorous stories, keep in mind that humor does not always translate. For example, topics such as sex and dating could be unwelcome to Muslims, and "your mama" jokes could be unwelcome to Zambians, because Zambian parents are revered like gods.[9]

By considering ethnic and cultural identity, respecting diversity, and developing our understanding of people who are unlike us, we improve our ability to use public speaking to create community.

3.1e Consider Preferred Learning Styles

Speakers need to be sensitive to how receivers prefer to learn and process information. Some of us are aural learners, others are visual learners, and some of us need to be approached at an abstract level. If a speaker offers a variety of support that appeals to more than one learning style, that speaker will succeed in reaching the audience.

Stockbyte/Thinkstock

We are unique. Take into account that diversity means audience members may learn differently.

3.1f Understand Difference to Build Bridges and Confidence

Acknowledging that all cultures do not share the same communication rules benefits us both as citizens and as public speakers. The more we know about those from other cultures, the more confident we become speaking or listening to others. Use these two tips as guides:

Avoid Formulating Expectations Based Solely on Your Own Culture

When those you speak to have diverse communication preferences, acknowledge them and accept their validity. By not isolating yourself within your own group or culture, you become a more effective speaker.

Make a Commitment to Develop Speechmaking and Listening Skills Appropriate to Life in the Age of Multiculturalism and Globalization

By talking openly about controversial topics, listening to different viewpoints, and understanding how policies may inequitably affect people belonging to different cultural groups, you take a giant step toward understanding why diversity matters.

Although culture is a tie that binds, the global world grows smaller and smaller each day through technological advancement and ease of travel. Respecting difference, speaking and listening responsibly, and ethics go hand in hand. With this in mind, make it a priority to

- Be a respectful and patient listener
- Engage and ask questions—rephrase if confusion persists
- Have empathy and imagine yourself in another's shoes

Speak Ethically

section
3.2

3.2a What Audiences Expect of Speakers

3.2b What Speakers Expect of Audiences

Ethics express society's notions about the rightness or wrongness of an act, the distinctions between virtue and vice, and where to draw the line between what we should and should not do.[10] For example, what ethical code do we expect college athletes to follow? We expect them to follow the rules and avoid performance-enhancing drugs. To play fair, not cheat. Is it any different in public speaking? The kinds of cheating that speakers and audience members engage in involve breaches in trust similar to those committed by athletes and other performers. Would you cheat to impress an audience? Or would you sacrifice your goals if they turned out not to contribute to the overall well-being of others?

Here are some more ethical quandaries to resolve:

- Is it an ethical breach to speak on a subject about which you personally don't care?
- Is it ethical to use a fabricated story to increase personal persuasiveness but not tell the audience the story is made up?
- Is it right to convince others to believe what you do not yourself believe?
- Is it ethical to refuse to listen to a speaker you find offensive?

When facing ethical dilemmas or potentially compromising situations, our personal code of conduct guides us in making ethical choices.[11] Ethical speakers treat receivers as they would want a speaker to treat them; they do not intentionally deceive listeners just to attain their objectives. You should reveal everything your listeners need to know to be able to assess both you and your message, and not cover up, lie, distort, or exaggerate to win their approval and support. A functioning society depends on our behaving ethically.

Play fair. As in sports, being honest and ethical in public speaking is essential for success.

Ethical communication is honest and accurate, and reflective not only of your best interests, but also the best interests of others. **Ethical speechmaking** has its basis in trust in and respect for the speaker and receivers. It involves the responsible handling of information as well as an awareness of and concern for speechmaking's outcomes or consequences.

3.2a What Audiences Expect of Speakers

When receivers judge a speaker to be of good character, they are more likely to trust the speaker's motives, concluding that the speaker will neither take nor suggest they take any action that would bring them harm.

When receivers discover that speakers have been less than candid, they lose faith in the speaker's trustworthiness, integrity, credibility, and sincerity. Once receivers doubt a speaker, his or her words soon lose their impact, and trust, once lost, is extremely difficult to restore.

To be perceived as ethical in the eyes of audience members, adhere to the following tips:

Share Only What You Know to Be True

Receivers expect you to be honest. They have a right to believe that you will not

- Misrepresent your purpose for speaking
- Distort information to make it appear more useful
- Deceive them regarding the credentials of a source

Avoid committing an **overt lie** (deliberately saying something that you know to be false) or committing a **covert lie** (knowingly allowing others to believe something that isn't true). Whenever you hope to convey a false impression or convince another to believe something that you yourself do not believe, you are lying.[12] Such deceptive behavior is a violation of the unspoken bond between speaker and receivers.

Respect the Audience

Your audience doesn't want you to exploit their wants and needs, manipulate their emotions, or trick them into believing a fabrication to fuel your own desire for power or profit. Instead, they expect you to be honest and open—to engage them in dialogue and critical inquiry.

COACHING TIP

"If you say it enough, even if it ain't true, folks will get to believing it."

—Will Rogers

Repeating what you want others to believe doesn't make what you are saying any more true! Personal biases can affect the impact messages have. Step back and examine yours. Then add logic and reason to the mix.

Audience members have the right to be treated as your equals: Consider their opinions, try to understand their perspective on issues, respect their right to hold opinions that differ from yours, and acknowledge that you do not know it all.

Prepare Fully

Receivers expect you to be thoroughly informed and knowledgeable about your topic. They should be confident that you will present them with correct information, more than one side of an issue, and not knowingly mislead them by shaping, slicing, and selectively using data. You need to explore all sides of an issue (not just the one[s] you favor), and "tell it like it is" (not like you want your receivers to think it is).

Put the Audience First

Audience members have a right to expect that you will attempt to understand and empathize with them and the situations they face. A person who speaks on the importance of tax cuts for the rich without exploring the impact of such a policy on working families fails in his or her duty. Receivers also have a right to know that you will not ask them to commit an illegal act or do anything that is destructive of their welfare. For this reason, it would not be ethical to speak on a topic like the virtues of underage drinking or getting out of speeding tickets.

Be Easy to Understand

Audience members have a right to expect that you will talk at their level of understanding, rather than below or above it.

The audience should come away feeling they have sufficient grasp of your content to make an informed decision. If you use language unfamiliar to receivers, they will fail to grasp your message. And if you talk down to receivers, failing to recognize the knowledge base they have, they will feel insulted or belittled.

Don't Turn Words Into Weapons

Although your words may not literally wound others, they can do psychological damage. Willfully making false statements about another, engaging in name-calling or other personal attacks, or using inflammatory language to incite panic is unethical. Speak civilly.

Don't Spin

The audience has a right to expect that you will not manipulate their reactions by providing half-truths or failing to share information that proves you wrong. A speaker who knowingly suppresses information that contradicts his or her position destroys whatever bond of trust existed between speaker and audience.

Number one. Putting the audience's needs first will help you deliver a speech that is ethical and has greater impact.

Respect Difference

Audience members may have different ideas about what constitutes an interesting topic, proper language, appropriate structure, or effective delivery. In order to meet their expectations, speakers need to look at the contents of a speech through the eyes of the members of different cultures rather than assume that all audience members see things the same way. By acknowledging the differences among receivers, speakers can accomplish their goals. For example, members of some cultural groups—Africans, for example—expect to participate overtly in a speech event, even to the point of helping to co-create it, while members of other cultural groups consider such participation to be disrespectful of the speaker.[13] Similarly, Americans may judge a presentation that is blunt and opinionated acceptable and even preferable, while Asian audience members may judge it to be rude or insensitive.[14] Whatever their cultural backgrounds, receivers have a right to their attitudes and beliefs. They have a right to expect that you will acknowledge and respect their right to disagree with you.

TABLE 3.2 FOCUS ON ETHICS

AN ETHICAL SPEAKER	AN UNETHICAL SPEAKER
Is intent on enhancing the well-being of receivers	Is intent on achieving his or her goal, whatever the cost
Treats audience members as she or he would like to be treated by a speaker	Treats audience members strictly in terms of her or his needs, ignoring their needs
Reveals everything receivers need to know to assess both speaker and message fairly	Conceals, lies, distorts, or exaggerates information to win the approval and support of receivers
Relies on valid evidence	Juices evidence, deliberately overwhelming receivers with appeals to emotion
Informs receivers whom, if anyone, she or he represents	Conceals from receivers the person or interest groups she or he represents
Documents all sources	Plagiarizes others' ideas, exhibiting a reckless disregard for the sources of ideas or information

Hold Yourself Accountable

Listeners expect you to be morally accountable for your speech's content and to distinguish your personal opinions from factual information. You are not merely a messenger; you bear responsibility for the message.

Receivers also have a right to believe that, when uncredited, the words are yours. If you present the ideas and words of others as if they were your own, then you are committing **plagiarism**. The word itself is derived from the Latin word *plagiarius,* meaning "kidnapper." Thus, when you plagiarize, you kidnap or steal the ideas and words of another and claim them as your own.

Here are three simple steps to follow to avoid passing off someone else's ideas or words as your own:

1. Attribute the source of every piece of evidence you cite. Never borrow the words or thoughts of someone else without acknowledging that you have done so.
2. Indicate whether you are quoting or paraphrasing a statement.
3. Use and credit a variety of sources.

When students fail to adhere to these guidelines, they expose themselves to serious personal consequences, such as academic probation or expulsion.

Credit where credit's due. Citing sources for all your research and anything you borrow is an essential task of ethical behavior.

3.2b What Speakers Expect of Audiences

Civility, the act of showing regard for others, should be the watchword of receivers. Even if receivers disagree with a speaker, they should not heckle or shout down the speaker. Instead of cutting off speech, receivers need to hear the speaker out, work to understand the speaker's ideas, and, in time, respond with speech of their own.

Give All Ideas a Fair Hearing

Do not prejudge speakers. Evaluate what they have to say, see it from their perspective, and honestly assess their speech's content based on what they share, and not on any preconceptions you may have.

To act ethically, listen to the whole speech and process the speaker's words before deciding whether to accept or reject the speaker's ideas. Do not jump to conclusions and blindly accept or reject the speaker's ideas on the basis of the speaker's reputation, appearance, opening statements, or manner of delivery. Be a patient receiver.

Be Courteous, Attentive, and React Honestly

Speakers have a right to expect that you will listen and respond honestly and critically, not merely politely or blindly, to a presentation. To do this, you need to focus fully on the ideas being presented. Although you need not agree with everything a speaker says, you do need to provide speakers with accurate and thoughtful feedback that indicates what you have understood and how you feel about the message.

When questions are permitted after a speech, effective questioners first paraphrase the speaker's remarks to be sure they accurately understand the speaker's intentions, and then go on to ask a question or offer an opinion.

Speakers have a right to expect that you will listen to them regardless of any differences in age, culture, religion, nationality, class, sex, or educational background. An ethical listener recognizes that not all speakers share their perspective. But above all else, the behavior of ethical listeners does nothing to undermine a speaker's right to be heard.

COACHING TIP

"Of all feats of skill, the most difficult is that of being honest."

—Comtesse Diane-Marie de Beausacq

"Tell the truth, the whole truth, and nothing but the truth." If others don't view you as trustworthy, your words won't matter. Truth telling is not necessarily easy. In fact, telling others the truth is often more difficult than lying. But audiences deserve the truth. Telling them lies undermines their best interests. Make truth telling part of your personal code.

Think Critically

section
3.3

3.3a Set Goals

3.3b Analyze Consequences

3.3c Assess Outcomes and Their Effects

Critical thinking—the ability to explore an issue or situation, integrate all the available information about it, arrive at a conclusion, and validate a position—plays a key role in public speaking.[15] Both speakers and their audiences need to be critical thinkers, arriving at a judgment only after an honest evaluation of alternatives based on available evidence and arguments. Critical thinkers are honest inquirers who do not accept information without weighing its value.[16]

It is up to you as both public speaker and listener to take an active role in the speechmaking and speech evaluation process so that you practice critical thinking rather than subvert its use. When a speaker makes an emotional appeal for your support, be diligent in determining whether information exists that justifies responding as the speaker suggests. Examine the evidence on which conclusions are based to ensure they are valid and sound, to spot weaknesses in arguments, and to judge the credibility of statements.

It is important, however, to think creatively. Play with existing ideas so they yield new and fresh insights. Work to see the interconnectedness among ideas. It is also up to you to avoid presenting or accepting stale or faulty arguments. Look for differences or inconsistencies in various parts of a message. Ask questions about unsupported content. Decide whether conclusions are convincing or unconvincing and whether an argument makes sense. Base your opinion about the message on the evidence.

Critically thinking speakers expand receiver knowledge, introducing them to new ideas and challenging them to reexamine their beliefs, values, and behaviors. Similarly, the listener who is a critical thinker does not judge a speaker or the speaker's remarks prematurely, is willing to challenge him- or herself to reexamine ideas and beliefs, and refuses to use shoddy thinking habits to substantiate invalid conclusions. Speakers and listeners must hold each other accountable for both truth and accuracy. To accomplish this, follow the guidelines outlined on the next page.

© iStockphoto.com/Siphotography

The thinker. As a speaker, try to see ideas from fresh perspectives, and as an audience member, don't take all pieces of information at face value.

TABLE 3.3 FOCUS ON CRITICAL THINKING

A SPEAKER WHO THINKS CRITICALLY	A SPEAKER WHO THINKS UNCRITICALLY
Recognizes the limitations of his or her knowledge	Thinks he or she knows everything
Is open-minded, taking time to reflect	Is closed-minded and impulsive, jumping to unwarranted conclusions
Pays attention to those with whom he or she agrees and disagrees	Pays attention only to those he or she agrees with
Looks for good reasons to accept or reject others' opinions	Disregards opinions others offer, even if valid
Insists on getting the best information	Picks and chooses information to suit his or her purpose
Explores what is stated and unstated, investigating all assumptions	Focuses only on what is stated, ignoring unstated assumptions
Reflects on how well conclusions fit premises and vice versa	Disregards a lack of connection between evidence and conclusions

3.3a Set Goals

Prior to attending a speech, consider the speaker's and/or the listener's motivations for being there. Think about the degree to which the speaker is speaking to serve his own interests or the interests of others. Reflect on the degree to which your mind is open to receive the speaker's ideas.

3.3b Analyze Consequences

After a speech, speaker and receivers evaluate one another's behavior, their own behavior, and the likely consequences of their behavior.

For every speech event, seek to determine

- If honesty prevailed
- If language was used ethically
- If convictions were clearly expressed
- If logical evidence was used
- If emotional appeals added interest, but did not conceal the truth, and
- If selfish interests were disclosed

3.3c Assess Outcomes and Their Effects

Was the speech a success or a failure and why do you think so? Think in terms of how effective the speechmaker was rather than whether he or she was *entirely* effective or ineffective.

For example, seek to

1. Identify what the speaker did to demonstrate respect for difference.
2. Explain what the speaker did to earn your trust.
3. Assess the effectiveness of both the words and support the speaker used. What sources did the speaker use? Were they credible?
4. Recognize the kinds of information the speaker used to support claims. Were they unbiased? Were perspectives other than those held by the speaker addressed?
5. Identify which of the speaker's ideas you accept, which you question, and which you disagree with.
6. Determine the extent to which the speech changed you.
7. Evaluate the extent to which the speech enhanced consideration of an important topic.
8. Identify any questions you would like to ask the speaker, and any information you need the speaker to clarify.

Personal record? Which goals did you achieve, fall short of, or easily surpass?

GAME PLAN

Sensitivity, Ethics, and Critical Thinking

- ☐ I have reviewed my speech for derogatory words or statements that might alienate members of the audience.
- ☐ The main ideas of my speech are supported by truthful evidence.
- ☐ All evidence, ideas, quotes, and statistics from other sources are properly cited with full credits.
- ☐ In writing my speech, I accounted for differences of opinion.
- ☐ I have reviewed my speech for instances of "spin."
- ☐ I stand behind the words and ideas in my speech—I am accountable for my presentation.

Exercises

CULTURAL DIVERSITY, CRITICAL THINKING, AND ETHICS

Participating in the following exercises will broaden your understanding of what it means to value cultural diversity, think critically, and live up to high ethical standards.

1. The Danger of Overgeneralizing

Sometimes, when faced with people and situations we don't know, we resort to stereotyping—a thinking shortcut that organizes our perceptions into oversimplified categories. Stereotypes exist for short people, blondes, Asians, Black people, Millennials, and older adults, just to name a few. Though many of us have been the target of others seeking to stereotype us, we likely have done the same. List assumptions you have made about others, what you did to pigeonhole and classify them, and why you now believe the assumptions you made are true or flawed.

Facing up to your assumptions about others should help prepare you to speak before them. Whenever you speak, it is important to treat the members of your audience respectfully and as individuals rather than as members of a category. Doing so demonstrates not only cultural awareness, but also sound critical thinking and ethical judgment skills.

2. How We Learn Matters

If you were delivering a speech to college students on "The Effects of Grade Inflation," what kinds of materials would you use to ensure your speech appealed to each style of learner? To facilitate this task, imagine yourself as each type of learner as you consider possible materials.

Similarly, ask yourself how persons from cultures other than your own would respond to the kinds of material you selected. To what extent, if any, do you imagine their responses would differ from your own?

By stepping outside of who you are and considering your speech from the perspective of others who differ from you, you gain fresh insights.

3. Analyze This Speech: Thinking Critically About Diversity

Holger Kluge was president of the Canadian Imperial Bank of Commerce. He delivered the following remarks during a speech made to the Diversity Network Calgary, Alberta, Canada. As you read his words, consider these questions:

- What assumptions did the branch manager make?
- What did Holger Kluge learn about diversity? What have you learned?
- What ethical issues are exposed in this excerpt?
- How might critical thinking skills have avoided the problem altogether?

I'd like to begin my remarks with a story. A number of years ago we hired an employee as a teller in one of our branches. A few weeks after this individual began work, he was called into the branch manager's office for a discussion.

The manager was a good boss and a good mentor, and he wanted to tell the employee the facts of life about working for the bank.

He told him not to expect to rise too far in the organization.

When the young man asked why, the manager replied:

"You've got an accent. You weren't born in Canada. And you're not Anglo Saxon. Basically, you've got the wrong name and the wrong background for advancement."

He went on to say that the best the employee could hope for was to someday become a branch manager.

I was that employee.

The irony is, that at the time I was considered an example of the bank's progressive hiring practices.

Somehow, the significance of this honor eluded me. In the space of a few moments, I had been banished to a wilderness of diminished expectations all because of my name, the way I spoke, and my country of origin.

That's one experience that shaped my views on diversity, knowing what it's like to be on the outside, having to overcome obstacles which others don't, simply because you're different.[17]

SN 1 Kluge uses a story to involve the audience.

SN 2 Kluge uses the manager's words verbatim before paraphrasing the remainder of the manager's comments.

SN 3 Identifies himself as the subject, surprising the audience.

SN 4 Explains why he is sensitive to diversity, providing receivers with an important lesson.

4. Approach the Speaker's Stand

Speakers need to educate receivers, not merely tell them what they want to hear or serve their personal self-interests, but politicians, public relations practitioners, advertisers, talk show hosts, and other public figures often seem to violate this advice. Indeed, the use of deception by those in the public arena is not new. Keeping this in mind, choose one of the following three- to four-minute speaking assignments or one of your instructor's choosing

A. Identify a public figure who you believe deliberately deceived the public. Describe the alleged deception for the audience, and offer your opinion of the public figure's behavior, specifying how you believe she or he ought to have behaved.

B. Describe an ethical choice that you had to make, how you decided what to do, and why you believe your decision was right.

C. Prepare an ethical analysis of a recent speech, commercial, tabloid news report, or infomercial.

RECAP AND REVIEW

1. **Explain how cultural understanding affects speakers and audiences.** It is likely you will speak before audiences whose cultural backgrounds and values differ from your own. By respecting and adapting to difference, speakers and audiences bridge their diversity.
2. **Define and discuss the importance of ethics, identifying where you draw the line when faced with specific ethical dilemmas.** Ethics reflect a society's feelings about right and wrong. Questions of ethics arise whenever speakers and audiences interact. Receivers expect speakers to share only what they know to be true, to be fully prepared to present a speech, to consider what is in the best interests of receivers, to make it easy for others to understand them, to refrain from using words inappropriately, to refrain from putting either a positive or a negative spin on information just to win a point, to respect cultural diversity, and to be accountable for the message. Speakers expect receivers to give them a fair hearing, and to be courteous, attentive, and honest about their responses.
3. **Define plagiarism, explaining why it is an ethical issue.** Plagiarism includes both misrepresentation and lying. A plagiarist steals the ideas and words of another and claims them as his or her own.
4. **Define critical thinking, explaining its significance for speakers and audiences.** Critical thinking is the ability to explore an issue or situation by integrating all available information, arriving at a conclusion, and being able to validate the position taken. Both speakers and receivers need to arrive at judgments only after honestly evaluating alternatives rather than on the basis of faulty assumptions.
5. **Describe the relationship among ethics, critical thinking, and multiculturalism/ cultural understanding.** Critical thinking and respect for multiculturalism are integral in ethical speechmaking. By broadening the lens through which we process people and experience, and working to ensure that emotion does not overcome rationality, we demonstrate our ethical commitment to and respect for the speechmaking process.

KEY TERMS

Co-culture 40
Covert lie 46
Critical thinking 51
Cultural diversity 38
Cultural identity 42
Culture 40
Ethical communication 45
Ethical speechmaking 45
Ethics 37
High-context communication 41
Low-context communication 41
Marginalized group 40
Overt lie 46
Plagiarism 49

SAGE edge™

Sharpen your skills with SAGE edge at edge.sagepub.com/gamblepsp2e.

SAGE edge for students provides a personalized approach to help you accomplish your coursework goals in an easy-to-use learning environment.

Look and Listen

Hero Images/Getty Images

4

Listening Critically

UPON COMPLETING THIS CHAPTER'S TRAINING, YOU WILL BE ABLE TO

1. Define listening
2. Explain listening's role in a free society
3. Identify benefits of effective listening
4. Explain four types of listening
5. Describe cultural diversity's impact on listening
6. Be an effective audience member, demonstrating critical thinking and listening skills

Contents

In order to assess the quality, appropriateness, and value of spoken words, we need to possess two key skills: (1) the ability to listen and (2) the ability to think critically. Both skills have their basis in making valid judgments about the speaker's claims and conclusions and evaluating the speaker's information and arguments. In fact, research reveals that listening and the ability to influence others are positively related.[1] We tend to accept the words of those who listen to us.

When we put critical listening and thinking to work, we distinguish facts from inferences, valid from invalid evidence, and logical from flawed reasoning. We resist taking the easy way out, by questioning flimsy or unsupported claims and arguments. We refuse to accept a speaker's words at face value. Rather, we work actively to get the most out of a speech by setting listening goals to support our listening efforts.[2]

What do we listen for? We listen for facts, examples, testimony, and statistics that support the speaker's position. We assess whether or not the evidence the speaker offers is accurate or faulty, provided by a credible or biased source, and if it strengthens or weakens the speaker's position. We make a concerted effort to resist false assumptions, overgeneralizations, and other reasoning errors.

COACHING TIP

"Tell me to what you pay attention and I will tell you who you are."

—José Ortega y Gasset

If you are like most people, you pay attention to what interests you. It is equally important, however, to pay attention to what might not interest you but could be beneficial to you.

section

4.1

The Six Stages of Listening

4.1a Stage 1: Hearing

4.1b Stage 2: Understanding

4.1c Stage 3: Remembering

4.1d Stage 4: Interpreting

4.1e Stage 5: Evaluating

4.1f Stage 6: Responding

Hearing and listening are very different processes. **Hearing** is an involuntary physiological process, while **listening** is a voluntary mental process. In other words, just as we do not need to think to breathe, so we do not need to think to hear. But listening is a system of interrelated components, inclusive of both mental processes and observable behaviors, and occurring in six stages: hearing, understanding, remembering, interpreting, evaluating, and responding (see Figure 4.1).[3]

4.1a Stage 1: Hearing

During the hearing stage we receive aural stimuli—or sounds. We may choose to ignore some stimuli, like advertisements, while we choose to focus on others, such as instructions for an assignment in class.

We all attend to some sounds but block out others. **Attending** involves our willingness to focus on and organize particular stimuli. Unless our attention is held, however, we soon refocus on something else. Speakers quickly learn that it is not enough to capture the attention of listeners; they also have to work to retain it. To do this, speakers may

- Focus on subjects of particular interest to receivers
- Use words and images that evoke pictures in the minds of receivers
- Incorporate activity and movement into presentations, or
- Tell stories that create suspense, describe conflict, or evoke humor

FIGURE 4.1
Listening Stages

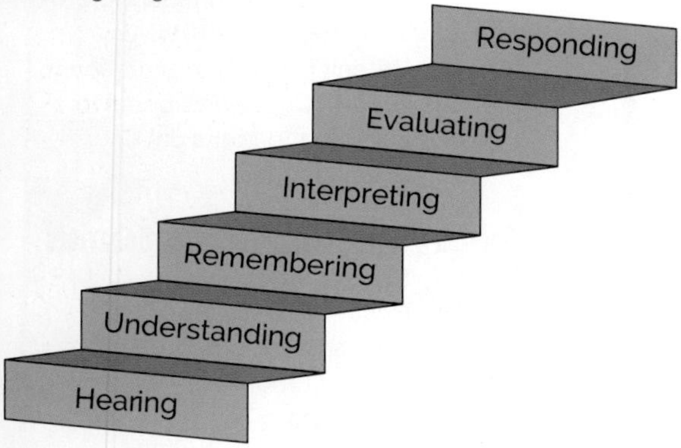

4.1b Stage 2: Understanding

During the **understanding** stage, we focus on meaning, using our own reservoir of information to decode a message. Refrain from judging the message until you are certain you comprehend it and can summarize the key ideas and evidence.

4.1c Stage 3: Remembering

During **remembering**, we mentally save what we've gained from the speaker's message for further use. Here again, we make choices as we decide what is worth remembering and what we can discard. A good speaker builds redundancy into his or her message to increase the audience's chances of remembering it. Sometimes we may also take notes, or, if permitted, record the speaker's remarks. If you anticipate a speech will be particularly important, ask the instructor or speaker if you can make an audio or video recording of the presentation to be sure you are able to retrieve it for future reference.

4.1d Stage 4: Interpreting

During the **interpreting** stage, we seek to understand the message from the speaker's perspective. Doing this keeps us from imposing our meaning onto the speaker's ideas. To interpret a speaker's message accurately we may

- Relate what the speaker says to what we already know
- Compile questions to ask to clarify things, or
- Paraphrase the speaker's thoughts in our own words

By adopting these behaviors, we ensure our listening is focused as well as purposeful.

© iStockphoto.com/ SteveDebenport

Instant replay. You can get feedback during the speech based on audience response and afterward by talking with others.

4.1e Stage 5: Evaluating

In the **evaluating** stage, we use critical thinking skills to weigh the worth of the speaker's message, evaluating what we have heard and understood. We decide whether we accept the speaker's point of view, whether the message has relevance for us, and whether we find it to be valid and well-intentioned, based on what we know. Whether we find the speaker's position valid or well-intentioned should depend on the kind of evidence and reasoning a speaker offers and our understanding of the issues involved.

4.1f Stage 6: Responding

During the **responding** stage, we react and provide feedback. We communicate our thoughts and feelings about the message we've received. Both during and after a speech, we let the speaker know whether we thought the message was successful or flawed.

The last time you applauded a speaker or failed to laugh at a joke or told your friend how much you appreciated the toast he made at your party, you were responding and providing feedback.

section 4.2

Listening and Cultural Differences

Each of the six stages of listening is influenced by affectors—emotional and intellectual biases—that can prevent us from processing a speaker's message in an impartial way. For each of us, culture, lifestyle, attitudes, and values influence and help determine

- What we attend to
- What we comprehend
- How we evaluate communication, and ultimately,
- What we retain

Culture affects willingness to listen. For example, **ethnocentrism**, the tendency to assess the values, beliefs, and behaviors of our own culture as superior to those of other cultures, can impede our ability to be receptive to the words of a speaker from a culture other than our own. Effective listeners need to recognize and adapt to potential biases brought on by ethnocentrism. They also need to pay attention to the other ways culture may intervene.

© iStockphoto.com/peshkov

We all wear glasses. Culture, lifestyle, and other biases shape the lenses through which you view the world, so be aware of how they impact your perception.

Because culture affects speaking style, it also can impede listeners from fairly processing a speaker's words. For instance, whereas some cultures advocate for succinctness and directness, others practice elaboration and exaggeration. The Arab proverb "A man's tongue is his sword" gives us insight into the Arab perception that words can be a punishing weapon. The speech of members of Arab cultures, for example, often contains forceful assertions and significant repetition, causing many who do not understand their culture well enough to conclude that they are being aggressive or threatening.[4]

Attuning ourselves to differences between cultures can help diminish the impact of the prejudices, biases, and misconceptions we have developed over the years.[5]

The Benefits of Critical Listening

section 4.3

Effective audience members listen to gain knowledge, think critically about the message's meaning, and evaluate a message's validity and worth. They distinguish between main and minor points, differentiate facts from opinions, assess evidence, and identify errors or weaknesses in reasoning. They do much more than simply "hear" the speech and their efforts are rewarded with a host of benefits.

4.3a Reduced Stress

As information is communicated, complex data are simplified, objectives are clarified, and the stress levels of listeners drop. The stress level of speakers also goes down as they are provided a forum to speak their minds, fulfilling their communicative needs.

4.3b More Learning

Listeners learn more about the speaker and the subject. Speakers learn more about what audience members respond to, and how they react to the speaker's ideas. As a college student, you spend approximately 60 percent of each class day listening.[6] Becoming a better receiver will increase both your personal confidence and your grades. Because you understand what has been said, you gain confidence in your ability to participate and express your opinions.

4.3c Improved Speaker–Audience Relationship

We all need someone to respond to us. We appreciate those who listen to us much more than those who ignore us. We also tend to tune in to those people who listen to us. Listening can create bonds between people from diverse backgrounds.

4.3d Improved Decision Making

Exposure to a wide range of information, attitudes, and beliefs provides you with a bigger picture and the kind of input you need to develop better judgment.

4.3e Improved Speaking

When speakers perceive themselves to have the rapt attention of their listeners and when they perceive their listeners to be open, alert, and active, then they are more comfortable in the speaking role and able to do an even better job of communicating their ideas.

4.3f A Better Society

People who listen critically to the messages of others and do not just accept what is presented to them can spot faulty reasoning, invalid arguments, and gross appeals to prejudice.

section 4.4

The Four Types of Listening

Listening theorists identify four different types of listening.

4.4a Type 1: Appreciative: Listening for Pleasure

You recently may have attended a live concert, taken in a movie or play, or spent an evening at the local comedy club. Why? You probably wanted to have a good time. Often we listen simply because doing so enables us to unwind, relax, or escape. The appreciative listener's purpose is to enjoy the power and impact of words that are well chosen.

4.4b Type 2: Empathic: Listening to Provide Emotional Support

Empathic listening serves a therapeutic function. It helps speakers come to terms with problems and develop clearer perspectives on the situations they face, and aids them in restoring emotional balance to their lives. Used most in interpersonal relationships, empathic listening also occurs during public presentations, such as when a speaker who lived through genocide describes his or her experiences for us.

4.4c Type 3: Comprehensive: Listening to Get Information

When you are lost and ask another person for directions, when you attend a presentation and seek to comprehend the speaker's message, when you sit in class and listen to a lecture, you are listening with the objective of gaining knowledge. Similarly, when we listen to news reports or to a physician delivering a diagnosis, we are listening comprehensively. Being able to listen comprehensively requires us to be able to recall facts, distinguish main and supporting points, and summarize what we have learned.

4.4d Type 4: Critical/Deliberative: Listening to Make an Evaluation

Frequently, in addition to working to understand the content of a message, we must also make judgments about its worth and validity, and ultimately whether we accept or reject it. Critical or deliberative listening goes a step beyond comprehensive listening, requiring us to separate fact and opinion, point out weaknesses in reasoning, and assess whether evidence is sound.

Improving Listening Behaviors

section
4.5

Consider the very best listeners you know. What words would you use to describe their behavior? Most people choose words like *concerned*, *open-minded*, *intelligent*, *attentive*, *interested*, and *respectful*. Now do the same for the worst listeners you know. Probably among the words you've chosen to describe them are *inattentive*, *closed minded*, *bored*, *impatient*, *nonresponsive*, and *rude*. Which list of words would you prefer to have others apply to you? Which would you prefer to use when describing the members of your listening audience?

Far too often, problem behaviors interfere with listening. To become more effective at both speaking and listening, you need to recognize those internal and external factors that contribute to deficient listening—or nonlistening—and then act to eliminate them. The kinds of listening problems that violate the mutual trust that should exist between speakers and listeners are identified in Table 4.1. Which, if any, of them have you been guilty of?

TABLE 4.1 PROBLEM LISTENING BEHAVIORS

BEHAVIOR	CONSEQUENCES
Tuning out	Loss of focus decreases understanding
Faking attention	Pseudolistening is deceptive
Prejudging	Prematurely evaluating can contribute to missing most of a message
Becoming overly emotional	The message's meaning can be distorted
Being lazy	Avoiding difficult material and taking the easy way out decrease comprehension
Being egocentric	Placing the focus on the self, not the speaker, makes it more difficult to understand others, positions and points of view
Being easily distracted	Oversensitivity to setting or context, personal appearance or delivery, decreases understanding, as does multitasking
Wasting time	Failure to use the thought-speech differential to advantage increases daydreaming

4.5a Stay Tuned In

Poor listeners do not pay the speaker sufficient respect or attention. It seems as if their ears and minds are "out to lunch." Words bounce off them. Nothing penetrates. We have all committed an unlistening act, preferring to pursue our private thoughts, reminisce, worry about a personal problem, or make silent plans for an event rather than concentrate on a speaker. To guard against tuning out, expend energy from the outset of a speech to its conclusion. Adopt an attentive posture, keep your eyes focused on the speaker, and work to remain alert. By looking at the speaker, you help your mind follow the lead set by your body.

4.5b React Honestly

Nonlisteners pretend they are listening. They look at the speaker, smile or frown appropriately, nod their heads approvingly or disapprovingly, and even utter remarks like "ah" or "uh-huh." All the external cues tell the speaker they are listening. But nonlisteners only pretend to listen.

Stop faking attention during a speech; instead, take notes. Note taking prevents you from becoming distracted and helps you listen for main ideas, transitions, and supporting materials. It also increases the probability that you will retain the speech's content.

4.5c Give a Fair Hearing

Before even giving the speaker a fair hearing, nonlisteners decide that the speaker looks uninteresting, sounds boring, or does not merit their attention because she or he does not represent their views. Such prejudgments contribute to their missing the real value in the speaker's remarks.

For example, a staunch Democrat more than likely registered full support for the 2016 documentary film *Where Do We Invade Next?* A staunch Republican would have been more likely to argue that the film's creator, Michael Moore, was a biased, inaccurate storyteller, and that his examples were flawed. Were those who supported and opposed the film reacting to the same stimulus? Yes, but prejudgments by both may have limited their ability to critically listen to the film's message.

To avoid prejudging speakers on the basis of their reputation, appearance, or manner, allow them to complete their presentations before you even begin to evaluate their effectiveness. Keep an open mind and hear the speaker out.

Bye bipartisanship. The major political divide in the United States means that it's less likely that party members will give fair hearings to those outside the party.

4.5d Control Emotional Reactions

Sometimes nonlisteners let their disagreement with the speaker's position get in the way of listening. They avoid anything with which they do not agree, that they believe has little relevance to their lives, or that they feel will be too difficult for them to comprehend. Personally threatened by a speaker's position, they do not really listen to it.

Nonlisteners also allow particular words spoken by a speaker to interfere with their ability to listen. These words, referred to by listening pioneer Ralph Nichols as "red-flag words," trigger an emotional deafness among nonlisteners, causing listening efficiency to drop to zero. Among them are words like *taxes, Nazi, Ebola, Zika,* and *welfare.* Are you aware of any specific words or phrases that cause you to erupt emotionally, thereby disrupting your ability to process a speaker's remarks accurately?[7]

To avoid reacting too emotionally and jumping to conclusions, don't mentally argue with a speaker during a presentation. If you listen first to what the speaker has to say, rather than assuming you know what's coming next, and if you refrain from focusing on something the speaker does or says that sets you off, then you will be better able to fairly evaluate the speaker's presentation.

4.5e Challenge Yourself

Nonlisteners often avoid material that is challenging. Believing they won't comprehend it anyway, they pass up the chance to exercise their minds.

Would you willingly attend a speech on thermonuclear engineering, molecular biology, or the privatization of industry, or would you tune out because you would have to work too hard? Oliver Wendell Holmes once noted, "The mind, once expanded to the dimension of larger ideas, never returns to its original size." Nonlisteners, however, refuse to stretch their minds; they won't work at listening.

Because listening is not easy, you need to commit to making the effort to do it. In other words, prepare yourself to listen by mentally clearing your mind of extraneous thoughts, reading up on the speaker's subject prior to the presentation, or researching the speaker.

COACHING TIP

"Nothing new can enter the mind through an open mouth."

—Unisys Corporation

We learn by listening. Audience members learn from listening to speeches, and speakers learn from listening to audience members. How you listen facilitates or debilitates the speaker's performance and/or the audience's response to and evaluation of your speech. What kinds of questions should listeners ask themselves when preparing to listen to a speaker? What kinds of questions should speakers ask themselves about how to encourage a receptive audience?

4.5f Focus on the Value in the Speech

Nonlisteners tend to be egocentric; they view themselves as the center of the universe, and they dismiss speeches that might be relevant to society but not to them personally. Seeking only self-satisfaction, nonlisteners are so wrapped up in themselves that they fail to realize the interconnectedness of all human beings.

Instead of focusing on yourself, focus on the value to be found in every speech.

4.5g Control the Physical Environment

Think of the story of Goldilocks and the three bears, in which the porridge was too cold or too hot and the beds too soft or too hard. If we let them, physical factors can function as distractions. Nonlisteners let themselves be distracted by the temperature, the arrangement of seats, or the acoustics of the rooms. They find themselves obsessed with a speaker's accent, mannerisms, or appearance. Once they succumb to such distractions, they are unlikely to listen to what the speaker is saying because they have neglected to focus on the message.

Even if the environment for the presentation is less than optimal, it is up to you to do whatever you can to maintain your focus. It is also up to you to resist multitasking while listening, which similarly distracts your focus.[8] Put away other books and papers and turn off your phone.

Daydreamer. While not always easy, focusing on the value in every speech is an excellent skill to develop.

4.5h Use Time Wisely

The average person speaks at a rate of 150 to 175 words per minute. The average listener, however, comprehends at about 400 to 500 words per minute. The difference between the two is referred to as the **speech-thought differential**. Nonlisteners waste this extra time by daydreaming instead of focusing on, summarizing, and asking themselves questions about the substance of a speaker's remarks.

Make good use of your "spare" mental lag time. Interact with the speech's content by producing your own examples, or relating what the speaker is saying to your own experiences.

No free time. How can you use the speech-thought differential to your advantage in a speech?

GAME PLAN

Preparing to Listen

- ☐ I have turned off my phone and put away other books and papers.
- ☐ I have a sheet of paper to take notes.
- ☐ I am ready to listen with an open mind.
- ☐ I am prepared to learn something new.
- ☐ I am prepared to critically evaluate the speaker's message.

Exercises

LISTENING CRITICALLY

Active listening is hard work. When you listen actively, your body temperature rises, your palms become moist, and your adrenalin flow increases. Your body prepares itself to focus. Let's look at what you can do to improve your skills as listener and thinker.

1. Analyze Your Listening Skills

Assess the current state of your listening behavior by responding "Yes" or "No" to each of the following questions:

	YES	NO
1. Do you ever find yourself thinking that you know better than a speaker and tuning out?	☐	☐
2. Do you ever daydream when you should be listening to a speaker?	☐	☐
3. Do you ever jump ahead of a speaker?	☐	☐
4. Do you ever fake paying attention to a speaker?	☐	☐
5. Do you ever try to avoid listening to difficult material?	☐	☐
6. Do you ever stop listening to a speech because the topic doesn't interest you?	☐	☐
7. Do you ever try to process every word a speaker says?	☐	☐
8. Do you ever let the speaker's delivery or mannerisms interfere with your reception of his or her remarks?	☐	☐
9. Do you ever let the environment or personal factors distract you from paying attention to the speaker?	☐	☐
10. Are there some topics you refuse to listen to?	☐	☐

Every "Yes" is a listening behavior that merits additional work on your part.
As you focus on how well you listen, keep the following seven points in mind:

Point 1. Listening is a conscious process. It requires your full attention. You can't half-listen; the half you miss could be critical.

Point 2. Evaluation should follow, not precede, reception. Effective listeners withhold evaluation until they are certain they have understood the entire message. Never allow what the speaker says or how he or she says it to close your mind.

Point 3. Every speech presents you with the opportunity to learn something new. Use—don't abuse—that opportunity. At times, you might need to overlook a speaker's monotone or lack of eye contact. Instead try to concentrate on the message.

Point 4. Both negative and positive prejudices toward a speaker or a topic can cause you to judge quickly. Either you will be too busy arguing against the speaker or too quickly impressed by what he or she is saying to listen accurately to the message.

Point 5. Effective listeners focus their listening efforts; rather than working to absorb every isolated fact, they concentrate on identifying the main points and the evidence used to support them.

Point 6. Your job is to look for relationships among a speaker's ideas, not to jot down or retain every word the speaker says.[9] Learning to take notes effectively will help you listen effectively, and vice versa.

Point 7. If you seek opportunities to practice skillful listening, you will become a more skillful listener. Work to increase your attention span, and you'll find quite a lot worthy of attending to. By challenging yourself to listen to difficult material, you will also prepare yourself to meet the speaker's challenge.

2. Take Notes

Active listening requires you to take an active role in setting listening goals and listening for main ideas and supporting information. The following suggestions will help you improve both your notetaking, whether initially live or electronic, and your listening abilities.

A. Divide a piece of paper in half. At the top of the left column write "Facts and Evidence." At the top of the right column write "My Questions and Reactions."

B. Jot down key words, but not a verbatim transcript of the speaker's ideas. You are attempting to summarize and then evaluate the speaker's message, not reproduce it.

C. Use your extra thinking time to analyze whether the speaker answers the questions you noted in the right column, and determine whether your responses to the message are favorable, unfavorable, or mixed.

D. Finally, decide on the extent to which you agree with the ideas and point of view expressed by the speaker, and evaluate the speaker's presentation.

3. Respond With Constructive Criticism

By using "I messages" you directly attribute what you found right and wrong to yourself and not someone else. After noting a negative in the speech or weak behavior in the speaker, be sure to suggest how it might be improved. Try "I couldn't determine the support for your second main point. It would have been helpful to me if you had offered examples and statistics to reinforce your position," instead of, "You failed to provide evidence for the second main point of the speech."

Following this advice, respond with constructive criticism to the following speaker weaknesses:

1. The introduction failed to arouse your interest.
2. A lack of transitions made the speech hard for you to follow.
3. You couldn't tell the speech was ending.

4. Approach the Speaker's Stand

Find a partner and pick a topic in the following list or another of your choosing. Each of you will represent an opposing side of the argument. Discuss the following as you craft your speeches:

- What core messages do both of you want to convey?
- What buzzwords might turn others off from listening about the topic?
- How might you craft a message to ensure listeners give you a fair hearing?
- Do certain facets of the argument elicit particularly emotional responses?

	AGREE	DISAGREE
1. Flag burning should be banned in the United States.	☐	☐
2. Capital punishment should be abolished.	☐	☐
3. Condoms should be distributed in all public schools.	☐	☐
4. Americans should buy only American products.	☐	☐
5. Handguns and assault weapons should be banned in the United States.	☐	☐
6. All Americans should pay the same income tax rate.	☐	☐
7. College should be free for all Americans.	☐	☐
8. Colleges should consider race when making admissions decisions.	☐	☐
9. Online gambling should be legal in the United States.	☐	☐
10. Prayer should be permitted in public schools.	☐	☐

RECAP AND REVIEW

1. **Define listening.** Listening is a voluntary psychological process composed of the following stages: sensing, attending, understanding and interpreting, evaluating, responding, and remembering.
2. **Explain listening's role in a free society.** Critical listening and critical thinking skills are necessary to distinguish facts from inferences, valid from invalid evidence, and logical from flawed reasoning. Both skills enable people to make informed choices and help preserve democracy.
3. **Identify benefits of effective listening.** Effective listeners experience less stress, learn more, develop better relationships, make better decisions, and are able to contribute more to society.
4. **Explain four types of listening.** There are four different types of listening. They are (1) appreciative: listening for pleasure; (2) empathic: listening to provide emotional support; (3) comprehensive: listening to derive information; and (4) critical: listening to make an evaluation.
5. **Describe cultural diversity's impact on listening.** Both our culture and our values affect our listening ability. In order to become better listeners, we need to work to eliminate the prejudices, biases, and misconceptions we have erected. Members of different cultures exhibit different listening styles. Those who do not understand a culture may misinterpret the communication of the culture's members.
6. **Be an effective listener, demonstrating critical thinking and listening skills.** The average person listens at only 25 percent efficiency, losing 75 percent of what he or she hears. By taking the time to understand the listening process and practicing effective listening habits, this deficiency can be alleviated.

KEY TERMS

© iStockphoto.com/Rawpixel Ltd

5

Analyzing and Adapting to the Audience

UPON COMPLETING THIS CHAPTER'S TRAINING, YOU WILL BE ABLE TO

1. Analyze your audience using formal and informal tools
2. Use the makeup of the audience as a guide
3. Plan your speech to reflect audience demographics
4. Plan your speech to reflect audience psychographics
5. Plan your speech to reflect the nature of the situation

Speeches are meant to be delivered to and for an audience. Successful speakers do not speak to inform, convince, motivate, or entertain themselves. Rather, the audience is central and serves as the speaker's compass.

Your success depends on reaching the audience—building your relationship and sharing your message. That's why you need to learn about **audience analysis**, the process of gathering and interpreting information about receivers, so you can adapt your message to meet and reflect their needs and interests.

COACHING TIP

"When I get ready to talk to people, I spend two thirds of the time thinking about what they want to hear and one third thinking about what I want to say."

—Abraham Lincoln

Actors are a lot like speakers. Actors who are in tune with audience members reach them on a level that those who perform only to hear themselves speak cannot hope to attain. If you consider only your words without considering the needs and wants of audience members, you risk having the words that are so important to you fall on deaf ears. To accomplish your goals, take time to customize your speeches for the people you are trying to reach—whether your purpose is to inform, persuade, or entertain them.

Contents

section
5.1

Reach Out to Your Audience

5.1a Consider the Audience's Makeup

5.1b Be Audience Centered

Imagine your potential audiences in the near future. You might speak to a student group; the members of a temple, church, or mosque; a teachers' organization; coworkers; a sales force; a community group; or a fraternity, sorority, or alumni group. Would you know each of these audiences equally well? Would you speak to each group about a topic in the same way? Probably not. Your knowledge of each audience would influence your approach.

To decide how best to reach, influence, motivate, or entertain an audience, you need to figure out its members. This is not a new notion. More than two millennia ago, in his *Rhetoric,* Aristotle noted, "Of the three elements in speechmaking—speaker, subject, and person addressed—it is the last one, the listener, that determines the speech's end and object."[1]

5.1a Consider the Audience's Makeup

Adapt your speech to reflect your audience's makeup. Not only do audiences differ, individual members also differ. Not all African Americans, 20-year-old women, or college students, for example, think alike. You will be well served to discover just how much you and the receivers have in common.[2]

5.1b Be Audience Centered

If you center attention on audience members, they will make you the center of their attention. When your words resonate, audiences are more likely to respond as you hope. Although you can't, of course, expect to interact individually with each audience member, the more you find out, the more adept you become at adapting your presentation.

Effective speakers select topics based on both their expertise and their knowledge of what audience members need or want to listen to. The audience-centered speaker is not self-centered, but is motivated by an understanding of receivers.

Journalist and political consultant Peggy Noonan served as a speechwriter for presidents Ronald Reagan and George H. W. Bush. In her book *What I Saw at the Revolution,* Noonan advises speechmakers to find inspiration from unlikely public venues—one place being a shopping mall—that are filled with people from all walks of life, like the audiences whom speakers seek to reach. She counsels, "Show [your audience] respect and be honest and logical in your approach and they will understand every word you say and hear—and know—that you thought of them."[3]

Answer Preliminary Questions

section
5.2

Audience members pay closest attention to messages they perceive to be meaningful, filtering out the information they deem less important. To penetrate the invisible shield individuals use to protect themselves from information irrelevance, relate your ideas to their values, beliefs, needs, and wants.

Answering the following questions can guide you in designing a speech that your audience will tune in to:

- To whom am I speaking?
- How do they feel about my topic?
- What would they like me to share with them?
- What kind of presentation do they expect me to deliver?
- What do I hope to accomplish?
- How important is my presentation to them?
- What do they know, want to know, and need to know about my subject?
- How do they feel about me?
- What problems or goals do the members of the audience have?
- What should I do to gain and maintain their interest and attention?

Drawing on her knowledge of what new college graduates expect to hear from her, in an address to the graduating class of Tulane University, comedian Ellen DeGeneres told them, "Follow your passion. Stay true to yourself. Never follow someone else's path unless you're in the woods and you're lost and you see a path. Then by all means, you follow that."[4] Because she knew her audience well, she drew a big laugh.

AP Photo/Bill Haber

Finding Ellen. Commencement speakers often try to relate their life experiences and values with those of the graduating class.

section
5.3 Compose a Demographic Snapshot

Developing an understanding of an audience starts with drawing its demographic profile. A **demographic profile** is a composite of characteristics including age; gender; educational level; racial, ethnic, or cultural ties; group affiliations; and socioeconomic background.

For example, imagine that you are asked to speak to two different audiences on the value of taking socioeconomic diversity into consideration in college admissions. Your first audience is composed primarily of middle-aged, well-educated, wealthy people employed in professional or executive jobs. Your second audience is composed primarily of middle-aged, high school–educated Americans who live in the inner city, work in service or trade jobs, and occupy the lower or lower-middle rungs on the socioeconomic ladder. Which group do you believe would be more sympathetic to your position? Why? Would a successful speaker give the same speech to both groups? Without sacrificing your own stand on the issue, how could you adapt your message to these and other groups?

A **homogeneous audience**—one whose members are similar in age, have similar characteristics, attitudes, values, and knowledge—is rare. More often than not, you will speak before a **heterogeneous audience**—one composed of persons of diverse ages with different characteristics, attitudes, values, and knowledge. When this is the situation, be sure you include all groups, paying attention to the kinds of demographic data you can use to help enhance communication with them.

5.3a Consider Age

How old are the members of your audience? One of your key goals is to diminish the age difference between you and those you hope to reach. To accomplish this, you need to be sensitive to the references you employ and the language you use. Ask yourself questions like the following:

- Will they give the same meanings to the words I use?
- Will they be able to identify with my examples and illustrations?
- Are they old or young enough to be familiar with persons and events I refer to?

Speakers would be wise to understand how generational differences influence receivers. According to Lynne Lancaster and David Stillman's *When Generations Collide*, age is a key determiner of audience attitudes.[5] They note, for example, that those born before 1945 are more apt to lean toward the conservative end of the spectrum, respecting both authority and symbols such as "the flag," and are less likely to be easily persuaded. Their guide word is *loyal*. Baby Boomers, born between 1946 and 1964, tend to be belongers, competitive, more cynical, and less likely to bow to authority. Their guide word is *optimism*. Generation X members, born between the mid-1960s and 1980, are more apt to have grown up in blended or single-parent households and tend to be more independent and media savvy. Their watchword is *skeptical*. Finally, Millennials, born between 1981 and 2000, have grown up with technology, and are both friendship and safety focused.[6] Their watchword is *reality*. Speakers can use the events and trends that serve as generational markers to guide them in appealing to different audience segments.

Cultural diversity. How can you make yourself more cognizant of the diverse experiences your audiences bring to your speeches?

Of course, age is more relevant to the development of some topics than others. For example, the age of listeners is crucial if you are speaking about life after retirement, but it would be less important if your topic were taking care of planet Earth.

5.3b Consider Gender

Another key variable to consider when analyzing your audience is the ratio of males to females. According to sociolinguist Deborah Tannen, whereas "women speak and hear a language of connection and intimacy . . . men speak and hear a language of status and independence."[7] Whether you are a male or a female speaker addressing a predominantly male, female, or mixed-sex audience, this finding should affect the amount of time you spend building rapport with your listeners and could alter the approach you select to deliver your information and ideas to them. For example, if you were speaking about national security to an audience of mostly men you might focus on the importance of strengthening defenses and the necessity for surveillance. On the other hand, were you speaking on the same topic to an audience composed of mostly mothers of school-aged children, you might focus instead on what needs to be done to ensure that children learn in environments that are safe and secure.

5.3c Respect Sexual Orientation

Although sexual orientation is often an invisible variable, it is important to recognize that not everyone in your audience will be the same orientation as you. Just as using racially insensitive remarks or demeaning the race or ethnicity of receivers is inappropriate, so is speaking disparagingly of, or displaying a bias against, someone's sexual orientation. By making the effort to include supporting materials that feature the LGBTQ community and heterosexuals, you ensure that you include all types of receivers. For example, if you were to speak about adoption, you may include in your speech information about local and state resources for both heterosexual couples and same-sex or transgender couples who seek to adopt.

5.3d Gauge Knowledge Level

Knowing the average level of education of receivers will help you make choices regarding vocabulary, language style, and supporting materials. Your goal is to adapt your words to your listeners' knowledge. If you miss your mark and speak above their knowledge level, they will not understand you; if you speak below their knowledge level, you will insult and bore them.

When speaking before a more knowledgeable audience, you will want to deliver a **two-sided presentation**, that is, a presentation that considers alternative perspectives, rather than the more simplistic **one-sided presentation**.[8] For example, if you were speaking on the trade policies of the United States to a well-informed audience, you would want to show receivers how familiar you were with the variety of viewpoints on this issue and explain why, after reviewing existing trade stances, you chose the position you now want them to adopt. Because individuals who are knowledgeable are used to processing complex communication and distinguishing among a variety of options, they will be more accepting of your ideas if you present them with strong evidence to back them up and include arguments that are logically sound.[9]

What's their expertise? Speaking on a new type of medicine would lead to two very different speeches for an audience of doctors and an audience of non-doctors.

5.3e Understand Racial, Ethnic, Religious, and Cultural Ties

As you prepare your speech, keep in the front of your mind any potential misunderstandings that racial, ethnic, religious, and cultural differences could foster. For example, a predominantly Catholic or Orthodox Jewish audience is likely to support the abolition of abortion. If you have an audience of diverse listeners, it is helpful to acknowledge that some of your listeners may disagree with your stance or point. However, it is also up to you to find ways to encourage them to consider different ideas.

5.3f Identify Affiliations

Memberships in occupational, political, civic, and social groups also provide speakers with a pretty accurate prediction of the way audience members will react to a topic. Group affiliations serve as a bond. Workers who belong to the same union, citizens who support a political candidate, or parents who are active in the PTA (Parent Teacher Association) probably share a number of key interests, attitudes, and values with others in the group.

Whenever you function as a speaker, you need to consider how the various affiliations of audience members could influence both your topic and your approach. Remember, your goal is to identify clues regarding how listeners will respond to your presentation.

5.3g Consider Socioeconomic Background

People from different socioeconomic backgrounds naturally look at situations, events, and issues from very different perspectives. A wealthy audience might not appreciate what it means to grow up in poverty. It is up to you to increase audience understanding of, and identification with, your subject.

Writing about this issue some years ago, journalist Anthony Lewis noted, "Upper-income Americans generally, whether in public or private employment, live not just a better life but one quite removed from that of ordinary families. They hardly experience the problems that weigh so heavily today on American society." How can you as a speaker close the perceptual gap created by this disparity?

First, you need to develop insight into how income affects life experiences. For example, a more privileged audience member listening to a speech against the Affordable Care Act might think $400 a month for health insurance for a family of four is quite reasonable, without considering the family's other expenses—rent, food, utilities, transportation—on an overall income of only $4,000 a month. Second, you need to locate examples and appeals that relate your topic to the varied experiences of your audience and make direct references to them during your speech.

Although each member of your audience is a unique individual, he or she is also a composite of a set of demographic factors. Rather than functioning as a means for stereotyping receivers, demographic variables should guide you in knowing your audience.

section

5.4 Compose a Psychographic Snapshot

5.4a Understand Values, Beliefs, and Attitudes

5.4b Understand How the Audience Perceives Your Topic

5.4c Understand How the Audience Perceives You

Learning about your audience members' **psychographics**—how they see themselves; their attitudes toward various issues; their motives for being there; and how they feel about your topic, you, and the occasion or event—provides additional clues to their likely reactions. To draw this kind of audience picture, you need to understand the beliefs and values that underlie audience members' attitudes.

5.4a Understand Values, Beliefs, and Attitudes

Values are the principles important to us; they guide what we judge to be good or bad, ethical or unethical, worthwhile or worthless. They represent our conception of morality and are the standards against which we measure right and wrong. Knowing that respect for elders is among the core values shared by Chinese people; machismo and saving face are important to Mexicans; devoutness and hospitality are valued by Iraqis; and family, responsibility to future generations, and a healthy environment are valued by many in the United States, how might you adapt a speech on the National Security Agency's wiretapping program to appeal to members of each group?[10]

Beliefs are what we hold to be true and false. They are also the building blocks that help to explain our attitudes. For example, those who believe that individuals will make better decisions with their money than the government often favor lower taxes. Because our belief systems are composites of everything we hold to be true and untrue, they influence the way we process messages. Some beliefs are more important to us than others. The more important our beliefs, the harder we work to keep them alive and the less willing we are to alter them.

Our values and beliefs feed into our **attitudes**, the favorable or unfavorable predispositions that we carry with us everywhere we go. The attitudes we hold help direct our responses to everything, including a speech. Attitudes are evaluative in nature and are measured on a continuum that ranges from favorable to unfavorable. For example, some hold favorable attitudes toward school voucher programs; others do not. Our attitudes reflect our likes and dislikes and are shaped by myriad influences, including family, education, culture, and the media.

5.4b Understand How the Audience Perceives Your Topic

Before class starts or right after it finishes are good times to make small talk with your peers in an effort to discover what they think about certain topics. Even just listening to what's on their minds as they chat with others can provide you with clues to their mind-set. Knowing your audience's attitudes toward your topic can help you determine how to handle your material. If you can gauge your audience's predisposition to respond favorably or unfavorably, you can adapt your approach so that you address their beliefs and reflect their values and more readily identify the kind of information you need to add, or the misconceptions you need to correct. And if you can demonstrate for them how your message supports the values they already hold dear, you are much more likely to succeed.

5.4c Understand How the Audience Perceives You

No matter how audience members feel about your topic, if they believe you to be a credible source, they are much more apt to listen to what you have to say.

What if you know audience members don't look favorably on you? Ask yourself whether they lack information, have received misinformation, or have a legitimate reason for holding the judgment. Then identify what you can do to influence them to view you more favorably. For example, if they don't believe you are an authority on your subject, you can work into your presentation experiences you've had that qualify you to speak on the topic. One student who asked his audience to accept that the U.S. government should significantly increase social services to the homeless made his message stronger by relating his own experiences as a homeless person some years earlier.

Know your audience. What's your audience's perception of you, and how will that impact your credibility and their listening?

What your audience thinks of you could change the way they respond to your message. Your credentials and your reputation accompany you to the podium.

section

5.5

Consider the Speaking Situation

An important component of your audience analysis is considering the reason for their attendance, as well as the occasion, location, and time at which your speech will take place.

5.5a Analyze the Occasion

Is your audience attending the speech voluntarily or are they required to attend? If you know in advance why people are present for your speech, you can adjust your remarks accordingly.

When thinking about the occasion, you also need to consider the kind of speech audience members are expecting you to deliver. If you are speaking to commemorate someone who has passed away, they expect you to deliver a eulogy. If you are speaking at a rally to encourage fund-raisers, listeners might well anticipate a motivational speech.

Whenever possible, it is wise for you to fulfill audience expectations. Be sure you can answer these questions:

- What is the nature of the group you are to address?
- What is your reason for speaking?
- What is the length of time allotted for your presentation?

Environmental variables like place, time, and audience size similarly affect the audience, influencing their reaction to you and your presentation. Consider how these factors could affect your style, language, and manner of delivery, and take steps to ensure that "little things" like the room being too small or the presentation running overtime don't stand in the way of communication.

5.5b Consider the Location

Consider some of the ways that the physical setting could affect the receptivity of listeners by answering these questions:

- Why do we find it difficult to concentrate when we're too hot or too cold?
- Why do we find it tough to focus on or pay attention to a speaker when a room is poorly lit or noisy?
- Why might an environment that is unattractive, or too attractive, adversely affect audience response?

Adapt your presentation to reduce listener discomfort and promote understanding and acceptance. That could mean talking louder or more softly, turning a thermostat down or up, bringing extra lights, or working extra hard to attract and maintain audience interest.

5.5c Consider the Time

If you are giving a speech early in the morning, right after lunch, later in the evening, or late in the week, you probably will have to wake up members of your audience by doing something unusual or by including some intriguing or startling example or illustration that compels their attention. You might, for example, ask a question or relate an experience that reveals your understanding of the situation.

Also consider the length of time you are given to speak. If you go over the time allotted, don't expect audience members to necessarily listen. If you speak for much less time than expected, don't expect that audience members will necessarily be pleased. Instead, find out the amount of time you are given, and work to fill that time with as stimulating and as informative a presentation as you possibly can.

Another consideration is the number of speakers sharing the program with you. Will you speak first, last, or somewhere in-between? Will you be flexible enough to tie your remarks to the remarks of those who precede you? Will you be sensitive to the lethargy that could affect your audience after a long evening of virtually uninterrupted listening? Former CEO of Fox News and communications consultant Roger Ailes observes that speakers need to be aware that during their speech the minds of audience members might wander off to thoughts of baby-sitters or other personal concerns. It is up to the speaker to draw them back in, even shortening the speech to maintain their interest. As he put it, "If the time is short, don't talk *faster*. Talk *less*. Edit your text."[11]

Speakers need to empathize with what the audience is feeling and decide how best to communicate that empathy. Accurate perception can prevent audience rejection.

5.5d Gauge Audience Size

How many people will be in your audience: ten, fifty, a hundred, a thousand, tens of thousands, or millions?

Audience size and formality are directly related. As audience size increases, speaker formality increases. Audience size also directly influences the amount of interaction you are able to have with members of your audience, the kinds of visual aids you use, and whether you will use an amplification system and a podium. Adept speakers are ready to vary their manner and means of presentation to meet the requirements of different audience sizes. In fact, audience size is one of those variables that help make every speech situation different. When you are sensitive to it, you increase your chances for success.

section
5.6 Get Information About Your Audience

By now you should understand the kinds of information it would benefit you to have about your audience. How can you collect it? What do you ask, where do you go, and what kinds of tools can you use to gain insight into the audience?

5.6a Ask Your Contacts

A sensible starting point is the person who invites you to speak. Ask that individual about the group he or she represents. Questions such as the following will yield valuable information:

- Why does the group exist?
- What goals does the group hope to fulfill?
- What is the nature of the occasion at which I will speak?
- How many people do you anticipate will be in attendance?
- Can you share any insights about the composition of the audience?
- What expectations do you believe audience members will bring with them to the presentation?
- Are you aware of any attitudes held by audience members on the whole that could positively or negatively affect how they receive my presentation?
- How much time will be allotted for the presentation?
- Will any other speakers be sharing the program with me?
- At what point in the program will I speak?
- What will the physical setting be like?
- Will I be introduced?

Of course, your sponsor is not the only person you might query. If you know anyone who has spoken to the group before, or if you know members of the group, you might also ask them similar questions.

Observe and report. Make observations of your audience members beforehand to make educated guesses about their characteristics.

5.6b Use Personal Knowledge and Observations

If you'll be speaking before a group that you belong to, such as a class, club, or civic organization, you can make decisions regarding your presentation based, at least in part, on prior conversations you have had with audience members, your perceptions of their opinions of you, and insights you have gained from hearing many of them voice personal opinions. Don't be afraid to watch people in action prior to the speech and to make educated guesses regarding ages, education and income levels, and cultural backgrounds.

5.6c Research Audience Attitudes

The library and the Internet hold clues to the attitudes of audience members. By researching what local, regional, and national opinion polls reveal about the attitudes of various groups on a variety of social and political issues, you might be able to make a number of assumptions regarding the attitudes of those before whom you will speak.

To increase specificity and add to the knowledge you are gathering about the group you will address, you can also use a questionnaire.

The Questionnaire

Your instructor may allow you to distribute questionnaires in class. A well-thought-out questionnaire helps you estimate the amount of knowledge your listeners already possess about your subject and their attitudes toward it. Questionnaires generally contain three different kinds of questions: closed-ended questions, scaled questions, and open-ended questions.

Closed-ended questions are highly structured, requiring only that the respondent indicate which of the provided responses most accurately reflects his or her opinion and so generate clear, unambiguous answers. The following are examples of closed-ended questions:

Do you think drones should be banned in the United States?

☐ Yes ☐ No ☐ Undecided

Should condoms be distributed in public schools?

☐ Yes ☐ No ☐ Undecided

In contrast, **scaled questions** make it possible for a respondent to indicate his or her view along a continuum or scale that ranges by degree from polar extremes such as *strongly agree* to *strongly disagree, extremely important* to *extremely unimportant,* and *extremely committed* to *extremely uncommitted,* thereby allowing the respondent to indicate the strength of his or her feeling.

The following are scaled questions:

How important is it for Congress to raise the minimum wage?

__ Extremely Important __ Important __ Neutral __ Unimportant __ Extremely Unimportant

To what extent do you agree or disagree with the following statement? "Colleges should consider race when making admissions decisions."

__ Strongly Agree __ Agree __ Neutral __ Disagree __ Strongly Disagree

Open-ended questions invite participants to answer in their own words and so produce more detailed and personal responses; however, they are also harder to interpret and may not provide the desired information. For example,

- How do you feel about schools that require students to wear uniforms?
- *Respond to this statement:* "A politician's private life is not the public's business."

Because each kind of question can aid you in drawing a profile of your audience, use a mix in any questionnaire you design. (See the sample questionnaire in Figure 5.1.)

FIGURE 5.1

Sample Questionnaire on Abortion

1. Age:
2. Sex: ☐ Male ☐ Female
3. Race: ☐ White ☐ African American ☐ Hispanic ☐ Asian ☐ Native American ☐ Other
4. Religion: ☐ Catholic ☐ Protestant ☐ Jewish ☐ Buddhist ☐ Atheist ☐ Muslim ☐ Other
5. Highest Educational Level Attained: ☐ High School ☐ College ☐ Graduate School
6. Occupation:
7. Organizational Memberships:
8. Income: ☐ Under $25,000 ☐ $25,000–$49,999 ☐ $50,000–$74,999 ☐ $75,000–$99,999 ☐ $100,000–$149,999 ☐ More than $150,000
9. Marital Status: ☐ Married ☐ Single ☐ Widowed ☐ Divorced ☐ Separated
10. Political Affiliation: ☐ Democrat ☐ Republican ☐ Independent
11. Have you or your significant other ever had an abortion? ☐ Yes ☐ No
12. Do you know anyone who has had an abortion? ☐ Yes ☐ No
13. How many persons would you estimate have abortions in the United States every week?
    ☐ 100 ☐ 500 ☐ 1,000 ☐ 10,000 ☐ More than 10,000
14. Which answer best reflects your opinion of the following statement: "Abortion should be prohibited"?
    ☐ Strongly Agree ☐ Agree ☐ Neutral ☐ Disagree ☐ Strongly Disagree
15. Explain your response to question 14:

Developing a comprehensive understanding of your audience will have profound effects on your speechmaking. Your challenge as a speaker is to find ways to make your message inclusive of the different ages, religions, educational levels, sexual preferences, races, cultures, group memberships, and psychographic profiles represented among the receivers. As you prepare and plan your speech, keep in mind everything you have learned about your audience, as well as the specifics of the speaking situation. You need to

- Phrase your topic in such a way that audience members will not be turned off by it or tune it out.
- Resist the urge to concentrate exclusively on what you want to say; spend more time understanding what the audience wants to hear.
- Convince audience members early in your presentation that what you are communicating will solve a problem they have, help them reach their goals, or otherwise enrich their lives.
- Use your creative powers to encourage your listeners to care about your subject.
- Build on whatever common ground exists between you and your audience; make a personal connection with them.
- Always refer first to areas of agreement before speaking about areas of disagreement.
- Demonstrate that you respect your listeners; if they sense that you think you're superior to them, chances are they won't listen to you. If you communicate to them in words they don't comprehend, your speech won't matter even if they listen to it.
- Hear and see yourself and the speaking environment through the ears and eyes of the members of your audience. Put yourself in their place and they will more readily give you their attention.

GAME PLAN

Analyze Your Audience

- ☐ I have considered the demographic factors of my audience and strategized the best approach for my speech.
- ☐ I have a good understanding of my audience's values, beliefs, and attitudes toward my topic.
- ☐ I understand the purpose of my speech, and I know what my audience expects of me.
- ☐ I have queried my contact about the physical setting and order of speeches, and I've adjusted my speech to suit the occasion.

Exercises

AUDIENCE ANALYSIS

Participating in the following activities will enhance your audience adaptation abilities.

1. What Do You Know?

Use what you know about demographics and psychographics to analyze the members of this class and another class. Explain how you will apply the information in your next speech or presentation in each class.

2. Adapt This

Imagine that you were asked to deliver a speech on the contributions of the women's movement twice—once to an audience composed of primarily feminist receivers, and then to an audience composed of predominately antifeminist receivers. Describe how you might prepare your address to appeal to members of these diametrically opposed audiences without sacrificing your personal principles.

3. Analyze the Audience: Do Audience Members Want to Be Present?

Some audiences attend speeches voluntarily, while others have to be present, which affects how you go about presenting your message. Explain what you will do to try and win over audience members who don't want to be there. What will you do to make your speech relevant and interesting to them?

4. Approach the Speaker's Stand

Develop a survey to analyze an audience on an issue of your choice; your survey should contain closed-ended, scaled, and open-ended questions. Once you are sure your survey's questions are clear and unambiguous, have class members complete it. Then explain how you would take that information and your personal knowledge about your audience into account when planning a presentation.

Specifically, in a two- to three-page paper explain how conducting such an analysis helps in addressing both the needs and interests of receivers, and describe how you could use the insights you gained from surveying receivers to guide you in

- Formulating your objective
- Creating an introduction and a conclusion
- Organizing your main points
- Wording a speech

Once this is done, develop a presentation that puts your plan into action.

Finally, after delivering your presentation, ask your classmates to rate your speech on a five-point scale indicating

- How relevant it was to them, and
- How interesting it was to them

If the outcome is not what you anticipated, discuss steps you might have taken to increase receptivity and interest.

RECAP AND REVIEW

1. **Analyze your audience using formal and informal tools.** In addition to drawing three key audience analysis profiles—a demographic profile, a psychographic profile, and an environmental situational profile—speakers need to query contacts, use their personal knowledge and observations, and when possible also research the attitudes of their audience using a questionnaire.
2. **Use the makeup of the audience as a guide.** Speakers need to adapt their speeches to account for the makeup of the audiences they address. In addition to acknowledging differences, speakers also need to discover how much they and their audience members have in common.
3. **Plan your speech to reflect audience demographics.** By developing an understanding of audience characteristics including the age, gender, educational level, racial, ethnic, or cultural ties, group affiliations, and socioeconomic status of audience members, public speakers are better able to customize and adapt their messages to reflect the specific needs and interests of receivers.
4. **Plan your speech to reflect audience psychographics.** By learning about audience member psychographics—what's going on in the minds of receivers, and their attitudes, beliefs, and values—speakers are better able to fine-tune their speeches and develop presentations that speak to the lifestyle choices and preferences of receivers.
5. **Plan your speech to reflect the nature of the situation.** By conducting environmental or situational profiles, speakers develop a fuller understanding of how the "where and when" of presentations affects speech content, delivery, and audience reaction.

KEY TERMS

Attitude 82
Audience analysis 75
Belief 82
Closed-ended questions 87
Demographic profile 78
Heterogeneous audience 78
Homogeneous audience 78
One-sided presentation 80
Open-ended questions 88
Psychographics 82
Scaled questions 87
Two-sided presentation 80
Values 82

SAGE edge™

Sharpen your skills with SAGE edge at edge.sagepub.com/gamblepsp2e.

SAGE edge for students provides a personalized approach to help you accomplish your coursework goals in an easy-to-use learning environment.

Topic and Research

BananaStock/BananaStock/Thinkstock

6

Select a Topic and Purpose

UPON COMPLETING THIS CHAPTER'S TRAINING, YOU WILL BE ABLE TO

1. Choose a topic appropriate for you, your audience, and the occasion
2. Develop an effective general purpose statement
3. Develop an effective specific purpose statement
4. Formulate a behavioral objective for audience members
5. Create an effective thesis
6. Evaluate the effectiveness of your general and specific purpose statements as well as your thesis

So you're going to give a speech. You must therefore confront a dilemma all speakers face: what to speak about. Choose the right topic—one that is appropriate for you, your audience, and the occasion—and you enhance your chances of delivering a "total quality speech." Choose the wrong topic—one that you and your audience do not care about, or that is inappropriate to the speaking situation—and you'll probably find yourself unable to maintain your own interest, let alone the audience's.

There are infinite topics to choose from.[1] Let's explore the plays involved in selecting one that will fulfill your general and specific purposes for speaking. Mastering these pages of the *Playbook* requires you to approach your speech both systematically and creatively—that is, it asks that you work within a format but think creatively every step of the way. Once you combine a reliable system with a spirit of innovation, no speaking hurdle will be insurmountable. Becoming an elite speaker is closer than you imagine.

Contents

section
6.1

Formulate a Topic

In professional and civic situations, topic choice is likely to be predetermined or significantly limited. However, this typically is not the case in public or professional speaking classes where the choice of topic is often left up to you. If you know what to talk about with your friends, you already hold the key to discovering a good topic for a class speech. Choose a topic that you are familiar with or would like to know more about, one that reflects your personal concerns or convictions, and one you believe will interest listeners and allow them to gain knowledge and insight. To reach this point, you will first need to undertake some self-analysis.

6.1a Learn Brainstorming Techniques

6.1b Use Other Topic Selection Techniques

6.1a Learn Brainstorming Techniques

The first step in topic selection is to compile a list of possible subjects that interest you and appeal to your audience. **Brainstorming** is a process of free association in which your goal is to generate as many ideas as possible without fear of critique. Give each of the following idea-generation techniques a try:

- **Brainstorm.** Get every possible idea down on paper.[2] Don't rule out any topic until you have had a chance to evaluate it.
- **Piggyback ideas.** Mix and match ideas you've generated to form interesting combinations. You might combine interests in the environment and in transportation for a speech on why people should drive environmentally friendly cars.
- **Don't censor.** Go idea-wild. You'll have ample opportunity to tame an idea once you evaluate it for usefulness and appropriateness to the speaking situation. During a brainstorming session, one student suggested a wild idea—implanting human stem cells in animal brains to produce animals that think like humans—only to discover that such research was actually being considered in scientific circles.

Brainstorm. It's best to write down anything that comes to mind and refine and discard topics that don't work later.

Technique 1: Brainstorm to Develop a Personal Inventory of Interesting Subjects

Think about subjects you either have some knowledge of or would like to learn more about. They may relate to something you have experienced personally, like a hobby, or something you would like to explore, like tornadoes.

Another possibility is to take an "on looking" walk with your phone or other recording device as your companion. As you walk, notice potential topics hidden in plain sight. Record examples that come to mind from architecture, street signs, passersby, dog walkers, and anything else you see.[3]

A variation of the same exercise is to focus on *the here and now* for a source of potential topics. On the left side of a sheet of paper list everything you are able to see, hear, taste, smell, or touch from your present location. Once you have identified 10 to 15 items, note on the right side of your paper topics that might naturally evolve from each observation or experience (see Table 6.1). Do not censor your ideas; write down everything that comes to mind. A general subject area may surface that you can then develop into a more specific speech topic.

TABLE 6.1 TOPIC INVENTORY

THE HERE AND NOW	POSSIBLE TOPICS
A passing airplane	Mass Transportation, Flight Safety, The History of Flight, How Airplanes Fly, The Future of Air Transport
The hum of the air conditioner	How Coolants Affect the Environment, The Invention of the Air Conditioner, How People Kept Cool Before Air Conditioning, The Energy Impact of Air Conditioning, Alternative Energy Sources
A television	Media Censorship, The History of the Sitcom, How Televisions Work, The Impact of *The Today Show,* The Changing TV Industry
A stuffed bear	Toy Manufacturing, Consumer Safety Regulations, The History of the Teddy Bear, Child Development
A dog	The Life of a Seeing Eye Dog, Dogs as Caregivers, The Importance of Supporting the ASPCA, The Domestication of Dogs
A lamp	The Development of the Light Bulb, Light Pollution, Life in America Before Electrification, How Light Bulbs Work

Technique 2: Brainstorm Using Categories as a Stimulus

Divide a sheet of paper into six columns. At the top of each column list one of the following words: *people, processes, phenomena, possessions, products,* and *programs.*[4] Then devote the next 30 minutes (5 minutes per category) to writing down every word you associate with each category, in turn (see Table 6.2). Review your lists of responses and see which, if any, of the general subject areas you might develop into a specific topic.

TABLE 6.2 BRAINSTORMING USING CATEGORIES

PEOPLE	PROCESSES	PHENOMENA	POSSESSIONS	PRODUCTS	PROGRAMS
the mayor	recycling	meteor shower	sunglasses	chocolate	literacy
Michelle Obama	digestion	earthquake	gold necklace	smart watch	orientation
Mom	rusting	sinkhole	treasury note	lawnmower	Peace Corps
novelist	baking a cake	tornado	jade statue	handbag	Medicaid
Albert Einstein	making origami	lightning	car	stereo	Boy/Girl Scouts

© iStockphoto.com/solidcolours

Get Creative. You never know which ideas will spark your interest!

Technique 3: Brainstorm Using the A-B-C Approach

The A-B-C approach uses the alphabet to help find a potential topic. This technique is particularly useful in helping prevent "idea paralysis." We provide you with one potential topic idea for each alphabet letter; generate at least one more on your own.

	Topic 1	Topic 2
A	Autoimmune diseases	________
B	Black holes	________
C	Coffee	________
D	Date rape	________
E	Echolocation	________
F	Fly fishing	________
G	Gun control	________
H	Hair loss	________
I	Influenza	________
J	Justice system	________
K	Kentucky Derby	________
L	Liberia	________
M	Missionaries	________
N	Nobel prizes	________
O	Organ donation	________
P	Paper	________
Q	Quantum physics	________
R	Radiation	________
S	Social networking	________
T	Ticklishness	________
U	UFOs	________
V	Volcanoes	________
W	Wilderness	________
X	Xenophobia	________
Y	Yeti	________
Z	Zoos	________

6.1b Use Other Topic Selection Techniques

These idea-generation exercises will help you develop areas of interest into a topic for presentation.

Technique 4: Scan the Media

Newspapers, magazines, books, advertisements, films, broadcast news, sitcoms, or the Internet might just provide the spark that lights our fire on a particular subject. Browsing through sources like these, as well as listening to or watching specialized programs, could result in a list of possible topics like the following:

Copyright Protection and Music Downloaded From the Internet

Right to Privacy

The Death Penalty

Fertility Clinics

The Electoral College

Manned Mission to Mars

Diversity and the Corporation

Depression and Holidays

Volunteerism

Trans Rights

Immigration

Virtual Reality

Women as Global Leaders

Robotic Surgery

Sustainable Fishing

Sexual Harassment

Cuba–U.S. Relations

Prison Privatization

Airline Safety

Job Hunting

24/7 news. The Internet and the world are at your fingertips, so just browsing your phone can spark an idea.

Technique 5: What's Taboo to Whom?

Consult resources such as David Livermore's *Leading With Cultural Intelligence,* or conduct an online search of "cultural mistakes" or "cultural taboos" around the world to identify speech topics that specific groups of people might find offensive or inappropriate for public discussion.[5] For example, in many Arab, Asian, and African cultures, talking about sex to audiences made up of both men and women is likely to be judged offensive.[6] Of course, some U.S. audiences might find it offensive as well. That said, not every potentially sensitive topic is taboo or off-limits. We need to remain open and process ideas we find disagreeable fairly.

On a smaller scale, be careful not to assume that because you are interested in a topic, others in your class will automatically be interested in that topic as well.

Technique 6: Draw a Mind Map

A mind map is a visual means of showing relationships among brainstormed ideas (see Figure 6.1). To create a mind map, begin by writing a word or phrase smack in the middle of a blank piece of paper. Then, as ideas about the center word come to mind, surround it with related words and images using arrows to indicate linkages between ideas, and colors to make your different ideas stand out.[7] As your ideas get clearer, feel free to redraw the map.

FIGURE 6.1

Mind Mapping

It's key in visualizing possibilities and idea relationships.

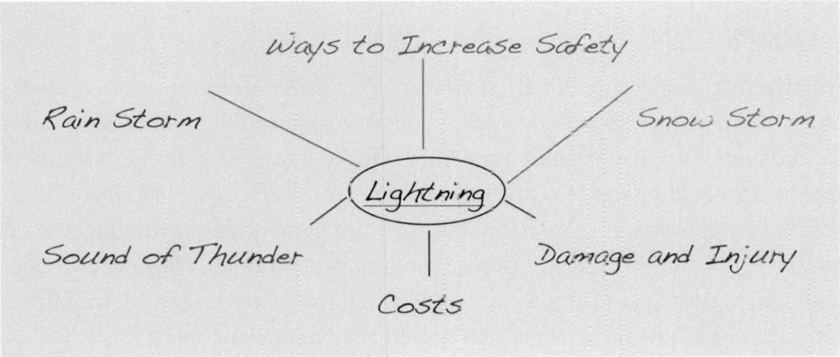

After completing these exercises and compiling an extensive list of possible topics, you are ready to assess each topic's viability. As you review the possibilities, remember that you should be passionate about the topic you ultimately select. Your topic should be adaptable to the diverse interests and concerns of receivers, have significance for you and them, and allow you to add to or acquire information.

section
6.2

Formulate General and Specific Purposes

6.2a Formulate the General Purpose

6.2b Formulate the Specific Purpose

6.2c Consider the Audience's Perspective

Once you have picked a general topic, select a general purpose that reflects your assignment, facilitates the attainment of your primary objective, or both. Answer the question: "What purpose do I want to fulfill by speaking on this topic?"

6.2a Formulate the General Purpose

The **general purpose** is the overall effect you hope to have on your audience. Virtually all speeches fulfill one of three general rhetorical purposes: to inform, to persuade, or to entertain.

Speaking to Inform

An informative speech is designed to teach. Thus an informative speaker resembles a teacher whose primary goal is to communicate and share knowledge with an audience—to give listeners new information. Speakers deliver informative speeches when they want to explain a process, procedure, organization, or function; when they describe a person, place, or thing; or when they define a word or concept. Most informative speeches are not controversial. They occur in virtually all classes you take and are equally common in work and community settings. The following are examples of informative speech topics:

- The Effects of Caffeine on the Body
- How Photosynthesis Works
- How to Save Money
- How to Dress for a Job Interview
- The Effects of Lead Poisoning
- How to Count Cards

Speaking to Persuade

The speech to persuade is designed primarily to change the thoughts and/or the behaviors of receivers. The persuasive speaker hopes to alter not only what the audience members know, but also how they feel and/or act.

Persuasive speech topics are more controversial than informative speech topics because others may oppose what the speaker advocates. Thus, while a speaker may deliver a speech supporting abortion rights, a number of audience members may hold very different opinions about the subject. The following are examples of persuasive topics:

- Televised Ads for Electronic Cigarettes
- The Right to Health Care
- The Tax Burden on the Middle Class
- The Dangers of Factory Farming
- Alcohol Consumption During Pregnancy
- The U.S. Space Program
- Opt-Out Organ Donation

Speaking to Entertain

The speech to entertain is designed to amuse an audience. If, as a result of the speaker's efforts, audience members smile, laugh, and generally feel good or have a good time, the speech is a success.

You might be called on to deliver a speech to entertain when serving as an after-breakfast, luncheon, or dinner speaker, or when delivering a comic monologue at a comedy club, for example. Humor is usually an essential ingredient in the speech to entertain; skill in using it is necessary. The following are examples of topics of speeches to entertain:

- How to Fail a Course
- Least Effective College Essays
- The Part of the City I Wouldn't Show a Tourist
- How to Lie
- Text Messaging Mistakes
- Handshakes I Have Experienced
- The Best Ways to Waste Time

After you have chosen a general purpose, the next step is to fill in the details.

6.2b Formulate the Specific Purpose

The **specific purpose** of a speech is your statement of the speech's main objective. It identifies what you want your speech to accomplish or what you hope to do with your speech.

The specific purpose statement of an informative speech often contains such words as *show, explain, report, instruct, describe,* and (not surprisingly) *inform.* The following are examples of specific purpose statements for various kinds of informative speeches:

- To *describe* for audience members how decreases in state funding to colleges will affect them
- To *inform* my audience about the effects of sickle cell anemia
- To *explain* to my audience the signs of a stroke
- To *report* on efforts to raise college graduation rates
- To *instruct* class members on how to interview for a job

Words like *persuade, motivate, convince,* and *act* are characteristic of specific purposes for persuasive speeches, as in the following examples:

- To *motivate* listeners to buy organic food
- To *persuade* listeners to register as organ donors
- To *convince* audience members to maintain a financial "rainy day" fund

COACHING TIP

"Communication is 'purpose driven.'"

—Larry A. Samovar and Edwin R. McDaniel

The purpose of a speech is the driver of the speech. Make that purpose crystal clear. There should be no doubt in the audience's mind regarding what you hope to accomplish.

What do you notice about each of the preceding specific purposes? Though formulated for very different topics, they share at least five characteristics.

1. The specific purpose is stated as an infinitive phrase, that is, *to explain* or *to convince.*
2. The specific purpose is for your personal use and is written from your perspective; it identifies your concrete goal and can guide your research and the direction of your speech.
3. The specific purpose focuses on a single, distinct idea.
4. The specific purpose relates your topic to your audience by specifying what you want the audience to know, think, or do as a result of your speech.
5. The specific purpose is clear and concise, not muddled or unfocused.

While a good specific purpose is ambitious rather than trivial, it does not overreach. If you're unable to develop a speech that reflects your specific purpose in the time available, then you need to narrow your specific purpose even more.

The sharper your specific purpose, the easier you will find it to develop your speech. So while formulating your specific purpose, complete this checklist:

Jupiterimages/Creatas/Thinkstock

Activate your audience. What do you want people to *do* after hearing your speech?

- ☐ Does my specific purpose reflect the assignment or speech situation?
- ☐ Will I be able to obtain my specific goal in the speaking time allotted me?
- ☐ Will I be able to prepare a speech that fulfills my specific purpose in a manner my listeners will be able to understand and respond to?
- ☐ Will my audience assess my goal to be relevant to their needs and reflective of their interests?
- ☐ Will my audience judge my purpose to be significant and worthy of their attention?

Be sure you answer each of these questions with a "yes" and with a reason before you proceed.

6.2c Consider the Audience's Perspective

In addition to formulating a specific purpose written from your own perspective, it is also helpful to assess the speech from the audience's perspective. You might find it useful to compose a desired **behavioral objective.** Complete the sentence "After experiencing my speech, audience members will . . . " to describe the response you expect from audience members.

Sample Behavioral Objectives for Informative Speeches

After experiencing my speech, audience members will be able to

- List three symptoms of West Nile virus
- Name four effects of global warming
- Explain how U.S. trade policy will affect them

Sample Behavioral Objectives for Persuasive Speeches

After experiencing my speech, audience members will

- Contribute money to support art museums
- Register to vote
- Sign a petition advocating that the U.S. government regulate carbon emissions

Writing a behavioral objective will help you focus the content of your speech on those aspects that audience members will find most interesting or appropriate. By identifying what audience members should know, think, or do after listening to your speech, you position the audience and its behavior in the forefront of your mind.

The next task facing you is to formulate a central idea or thesis.

GAME PLAN

Choosing a Topic

- ☐ Am I genuinely interested in my topic?
- ☐ Am I willing to research the topic to enhance my knowledge of it?
- ☐ Will an exploration of this topic benefit my listeners?
- ☐ Is my topic suitable for this particular situation?
- ☐ Will my listeners find a discussion of my topic worthwhile, important, and interesting?
- ☐ Have I narrowed my topic sufficiently to fit the speaking time allotted me?
- ☐ Have I identified a general speech purpose appropriate to the assignment or speaking situation?
- ☐ Have I formulated a clear specific purpose?
- ☐ Have I composed a behavioral objective that identifies the specific response I desire from audience members?
- ☐ Have I phrased my thesis/central idea so that it helps me control the development of my speech?
- ☐ By making careful choices, you focus your content and communicate more clearly, concisely, and confidently. Narrowing your focus will better enable you to get your message across.

section
6.3

Formulate the Thesis Statement

6.3a Thesis Statements for Informative Speeches

6.3b Thesis Statements for Persuasive Speeches

6.3c Evaluating the Thesis Statement

Speakers are often encouraged to develop theses for their speeches, just as writers do for papers. A **thesis** is a declarative sentence that divides a topic into its major components and summarizes the main points of your speech.

6.3a Thesis Statements for Informative Speeches

When your speech is an informative one and not intended to be primarily persuasive, the thesis statement (which some practitioners prefer to call the **central idea**) is phrased in a relatively objective and neutral manner. Its focus is on what you want audience members to understand or learn—for example, "Nuclear power plants have three major parts: the reactor core, vessel, and control rods."

6.3b Thesis Statements for Persuasive Speeches

When your speech is persuasive, the thesis is sometimes called a **claim**. It expresses an arguable opinion or point of view; for example, a thesis for a persuasive speech against the use of nuclear energy plants might be "Nuclear power plants should be decommissioned."

Whether the speech is informative or persuasive, the thesis statement is your speech "in a nutshell." It is a statement of the key concept of your speech that all the facts, quotations, and ideas in the speech are designed to support.

COACHING TIP

"Education is the most powerful weapon which you can use to change the world."
—Nelson Mandela

A speaker is an educator. Formulating an effective thesis provides receivers with an understanding of the speech's major components, paving the road to learning.

6.3c Evaluating the Thesis Statement

An effective thesis statement fulfills five criteria. Use this checklist of criteria to evaluate yours:

- ☐ It is a single sentence that conveys the essence of the speech.
- ☐ It focuses the attention of audience members on what they should know, do, or feel after experiencing the speech.
- ☐ It forecasts the development or organization of the speech.
- ☐ It is phrased diplomatically, avoiding figurative language that is apt to inflame.
- ☐ It supports the specific purpose.

When listeners are asked what your speech was about, they should be able to respond by offering your thesis. Even if they remember nothing else, it is the thesis you hope they retain. To show how this works, let us examine one of the examples we used earlier and develop it into a usable thesis.

Specific purpose: To explain to my audience the signs of a stroke

Thesis: Face drooping, arm weakness, and difficulty speaking are signs of a stroke and require immediate medical attention.

From this thesis, we can say that the speaker will explore three main points in his or her speech, each point corresponding to one of the three symptoms of a stroke.

Unlike the specific purpose, the thesis is usually delivered directly to the audience. Thus, a well-phrased thesis not only helps you divide your presentation into its major components, it helps your listeners follow the speech's progression. The following are examples of effectively phrased theses:

Thesis: Universal health care would improve the lives of Americans and bolster the economy.

Thesis: Practicing yoga will enhance your personal and professional life in four key ways.

Phrasing your thesis brings you a step closer to developing the structure of the speech itself.

Exercises

TOPIC AND PURPOSE

Participating in the following activities will let you apply what you know, putting your skills into action.

1. Top Ten Topics

Create a list of ten topics you believe worthy of both your and an audience's time. For each topic on your list, develop a thesis, and explain what makes the topic meaningful and worthwhile.

2. Purposeful Purposes

Using the ten topics in Exercise 1, demonstrate how each topic can be adapted to reflect the general purpose of an informative speech as well as the general purpose of a persuasive speech.

3. Analyze This: Is It Clear?

Read the following speech on disenfranchisement given by Dan Shuey, a student at Muskingum College.[8] Focus on how well the speaker clarified the following for receivers: (1) the general purpose, (2) the specific purpose, (3) behavioral objectives, and (4) the thesis of the speech. Phrase each of the preceding speech components in your own words. Then, using the criteria discussed in the text for each component, assess the extent to which each component fulfills its function.

SN 1 The speaker begins by supplying receivers with historical context. By ending this section with a startling thought, the speaker draws receivers into the speech.

In writing the Declaration of Independence, Thomas Jefferson openly plagiarized his hero John Locke when he categorized life, liberty, and the pursuit of happiness as inalienable rights. Eighty years later, the nation followed through on Jefferson's words by passing the 13th through 15th Amendments. These additions to the Constitution guaranteed full civil rights to all citizens, or at least male ones, regardless of ethnicity or condition of former servitude. Not surprisingly, several parts of the U.S. weren't keen on these laws, and for over one hundred years, communities faced opposition to the 15th Amendment—the right to vote—in the form of poll taxes, literacy tests, and other Jim Crow laws designed to keep blacks from the ballot box. Luckily, Congress has taken action and today has ensured all adult Americans are unconditionally guaranteed the right to vote. Or so we thought . . .

According to the *San Francisco Chronicle* . . . 4.65 million Americans are stripped of their "inalienable" right because of laws depriving current and former prisoners of the vote. These 4.65 million tax-paying, full American citizens—1.4 million of whom are African American, are disenfranchised as a result of laws, which, you'll soon learn, have an explicitly racist past. Today, we'll examine the problems that arise from laws that restrict a full 13 percent of all African American males from voting, how these laws came to be and why they're still in effect in many states, and what you and I can do to ensure that our elections are open to all adults—regardless of past convictions.

SN 2 The speaker uses statistics to demonstrate the magnitude of the disenfranchisement problem.

SN 3 The speaker previews the main points of his speech.

If you need a more direct reason to consider my proposition, consider this: in Florida alone, 750,000 citizens are deprived of the right to vote. That's over one thousand times the state's declared margin for President George W. Bush in the 2000 election.

Forty-eight states don't permit incarcerated felons to vote, 33 restrict voting for a time period after release, and seven permanently disenfranchise those convicted of a felony. The problems that arise from these laws affect us first, because the laws simply aren't just on a moral basis, and second, because they have a significant influence on our elections. According to the *New York Times*, the bulk of states that disenfranchise black voters are former members of the Confederacy, including Florida, Alabama, Mississippi, Tennessee, and Virginia. It's estimated that in Alabama, Mississippi, and Florida, 25 percent or more of all black men are permanently barred from voting because of past felony convictions. Nationwide, one of every eight black men is forbidden from voting by law. . . .

SN 4 The speaker introduces the first main point and uses a variety of support to build credibility for his position on disenfranchisement.

continued

continued

According to the . . . *San Francisco Chronicle*, in Florida alone, one of every three black men is disenfranchised. The article goes on to explain that if even a small number of these disenfranchised voters voted, and then voted 60 percent to 40 percent in favor of Al Gore . . . we should have a different President of the United States. And the . . . *New Orleans Times-Picayune* states that minorities as a whole actually turn out to vote at a higher percentage than whites. Furthermore, it's been calculated that four Senate seats won by Republicans . . . would have been won by Democrats if former convicts had not been disenfranchised. These four seats would have given the Democrats a majority in the Senate . . . possibly changing the face of U.S. policy entirely. . . .

SN 5 The speaker once again uses statistical support to reinforce the problematic nature of the situation.

The history of felon disenfranchisement laws is a frightening one to confront. Our nation does not have a strong history of civil rights and clearly there's a long way to go. Most felon disenfranchisement laws were enacted in the post–Civil War period with the unveiled motive of discriminating against the newly freed slaves. According to . . . the *San Diego Tribune* and verified in the 1977 Richard Kluger book, *Simple Justice*, a delegate to the Virginia convention in 1906, which helped establish disenfranchisement laws, said, and this is a direct quote, "This plan will eliminate the darkey as a political factor in this state in less than five years." Meanwhile, in Alabama, lawmakers inserted a provision into the state constitution banning those convicted of "moral turpitude" from ever voting. In the South, that was defined as a black man who directly spoke to white women. The Alabama legislature declared that its goal was to establish and preserve white supremacy. Sadly, the plan to push blacks out of the polling place worked. *The Union-Tribune* found that by 1903, disenfranchisement laws in Alabama had excluded nearly 10 times as many blacks as whites from voting.

SN 6 The next main point of the speech finds the speaker using an array of supporting materials, including testimony and statistics to review the history of disenfranchisement.

So why haven't these clearly racist laws been repealed? Blame politicians wary of being considered soft on crime. According to the . . . *New York Times*, in Alabama, the state legislature passed a law which would have ended the disenfranchisement of ex-felons in their state because it was a racially discriminating law. However, Governor Bob Riley vetoed the bill, calling it "unnecessary." The previously cited *San Francisco Chronicle* article explains that Republicans have little to gain from giving felons the vote and Democrats are fearful of being associated with them. . . .

SN 7 The speaker asks and answers a rhetorical question.

The solutions to the problems caused by felon disenfranchisement lie not in changing American attitudes. . . . Already 80 percent of American citizens support restoring voting rights to convicts after they've carried out their sentence. So it's time for those of us who do support it to make our voices heard in Washington. A policy is already on the table—we just need to tell Congress we want it passed. . . . However, this bill was not even let out of subcommittee. It was reintroduced . . . and once again was struck down in subcommittee before being heard before the entire House.

SN 8 The speaker introduces his solution to the problem raised in the speech using specific examples to underscore why action is necessary.

The full House needs to hear this bill. Most U.S. states have a House member on the committee for the Judiciary. Assignments can be viewed at www.house.gov. As the Reverend Jesse Jackson said . . . "It is time for people of conscience to come together to remove this modern version of Jim Crow discrimination." Furthermore, we can get involved in a national campaign to change these laws in our own states and make some money by joining the Sentencing Project. This registered nonprofit organization offers monetary stipends to students willing to research felon disenfranchisement laws. . . .

SN 9 The speaker explains what receivers can do to become involved in solving the problem.

Today, we looked at the inherent problems in a democratic system that disenfranchises felons. We analyzed the reasons these racially unequal laws exist, and we realized ways that each of us can act in order to allow all American citizens that right to vote. We are guaranteed life, liberty, and the pursuit of happiness. It's time we extend this guarantee to every American.

SN 10 The speaker summarizes the speech. By referring to the introduction in the concluding lines, the speaker achieves closure.

4. Approach the Speaker's Stand

Understanding and sharing the steps you take when moving from a general topic to a specific purpose to behavioral objectives and finally to a thesis can help others. In a presentation not to exceed two minutes, provide an example for your peers that illustrates your progression of thought as you move from a broad subject to a much more specific and focused thesis or central idea.

RECAP AND REVIEW

1. **Choose a topic appropriate for you, your audience, and the occasion.** A good topic is one that is appropriate for the speaker, the audience, and the occasion. Speakers use a variety of idea-generation exercises to help examine their personal behaviors and interests, they scan the media, and they survey reference books and indexes.
2. **Develop an effective general purpose statement.** The general purpose statement describes the overall effect a speaker hopes to have on an audience.
3. **Develop an effective specific purpose statement.** The specific purpose statement is the speaker's personal statement of the speech's main objective. It describes what the speaker wants the audience to know, think, or do as a result of the speech.
4. **Formulate a behavioral objective for audience members.** A behavioral objective is a specific outcome, an observable, measurable audience response that begins with seven words—"After experiencing my speech, audience members will"—and then describes the response the speaker expects from audience members.
5. **Create an effective thesis.** A thesis divides a speech into its major components and makes a clear point about the topic. A declarative sentence, it summarizes the speech's main points.
6. **Evaluate the effectiveness of your general and specific purpose statements as well as your thesis.** Speakers must answer "yes" to ten key questions to determine whether they can move forward with the speech; otherwise, they have more thinking and refining ahead of them.

KEY TERMS

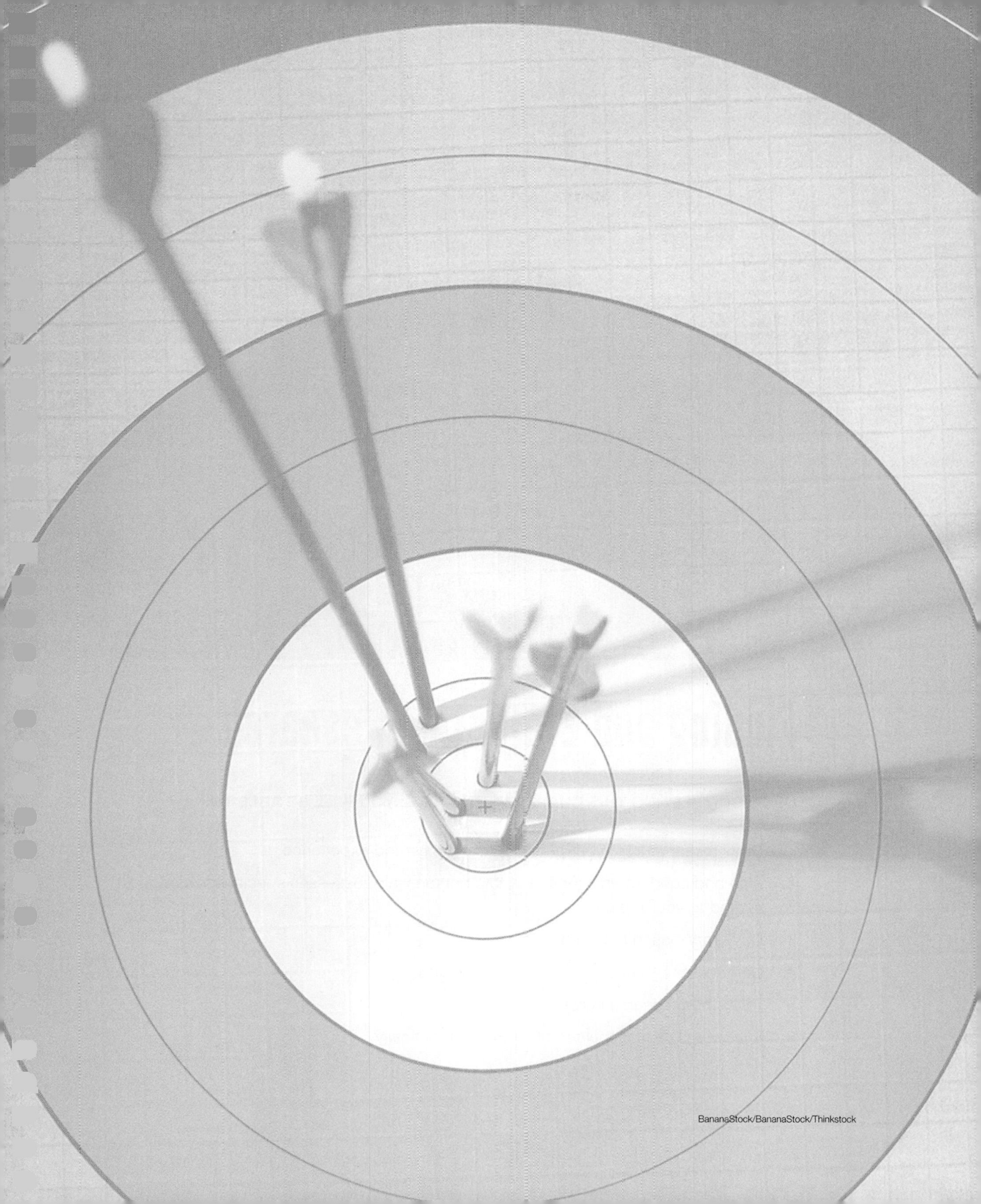

BananaStock/BananaStock/Thinkstock

© iStockphoto.com/poba

7

Finding and Evaluating Research

UPON COMPLETING THIS CHAPTER'S TRAINING, YOU WILL BE ABLE TO

1. Draw research from your personal knowledge and experience
2. Plan and conduct an interview with a person who possesses special knowledge related to your topic
3. Do library-based research
4. Demonstrate the value of researching online
5. Take good research notes
6. Evaluate potential sources of information critically

What distinguishes an effective from an ineffective speech? An effective speech integrates an array of relevant research in support of the speechmaker's thesis. Good speakers discover, evaluate, and cite research to document their speech's content and build credibility. Research adds substance, believability, and impact.

Consider the self-talk you engage in when listening to a speech. If you are a conscientious receiver, you listen critically and look for concrete support for the speech's thesis.

Now, how do you gather research? If you want to try a new restaurant, you might ask your friends for recommendations, peruse a restaurant guide such as *Zagat* or Yelp, or review various restaurant home pages on the Internet.

What does this have to do with public speaking? The research we do when preparing to speak in public is very much like the personal research we conduct daily. However, because a speech is shared with others in a more formal setting, we use more formal approaches when gathering materials for it. Researching a speech is a kind of investigation, and it is your job to take nothing for granted in investigating your topic.

Contents

COACHING TIP

"Every fact depends for its value on how much we already know."

—Ralph Waldo Emerson

Your speech is only as strong as the research and personal experiences upon which it is based. If you want audience members to accept what you say, then you have to impress them with how much you know.

section

7.1

Use Primary Research

Public speaking students frequently overlook **primary research**. Primary research is original research involving the collecting of firsthand data, including using your knowledge and experiences, conducting surveys, and interviewing credible sources.

7.1a Use Personal Knowledge and Experience

By the time you enroll in this class, you probably have some job experience to your credit, and you have certainly been in school studying a wide variety of subjects for many years. In your lifetime, you have probably read a vast number of newspaper and magazine articles, watched countless hours of television, written papers, and talked with an array of individuals—many who are more knowledgeable than you. Just going about the business of living provides you with many experiences from which to draw raw material for a speech. Yet many college students often discount the value of their own lives when they begin to research a topic.

Once we write down our experiences, they serve as a form of personal research and enhance our credibility. This is not to suggest that you can't speak about a topic unless you have lived it. By researching the subject, you can talk about poverty without actually having been impoverished. However, if you have experience with a topic that is important to you, that experience—when supplemented with additional outside research—will greatly increase your credibility with your audience. Thus, you can capitalize on your own experience to provide effective explanations, examples, or definitions.

For instance, one student, a survivor of Hodgkin disease, explained to his class how he coped with the impact of the illness. He described first discovering that he had Hodgkin's, its symptoms, his treatment, and survival rates. He buttressed his message by revealing his personal fears in depth. The speaker's simple words conveyed his message more meaningfully and eloquently than if he had quoted another source. Even if your experiences are not as dramatic or as emotionally powerful as surviving cancer, you can still use them to your advantage. Think over your life and consider how you could integrate one or more experiences into a speech to add a sense of freshness and authenticity to your message.

7.1b Interview Others Who Have Specialized Knowledge

Although personal experience is often a starting point for speech research, rarely will it be sufficient, if only because few—if any—student speakers have enough material from their own lives on which to base an entire speech. Thus, you must consult other sources, too.

Interviewing those with special knowledge is a key means of acquiring both information about and insight into a topic. One possibility is to talk to individuals who others will find credible because they possess special knowledge or are experts on the subject. For example, if your goal is to speak about the dangers of nuclear power plants, a call or email to a nuclear physicist at the Nuclear Regulatory Agency in Washington, D.C., could bring you up to date on the issues you plan to discuss in your speech.

Conducting interviews with specialists will not eliminate your need to conduct other research, such as examining newspaper and magazine articles or reading relevant books on the subject. But questioning experts can help you structure your research and provide you with ideas and information to bring your speech alive. However, you must begin by doing some preliminary research that will enable you to formulate the particular questions for which you need an expert's answers.

Prepare for the Interview

The first task is to determine why you are interviewing someone. What qualifies the individual as an expert? For example, one student decided to talk about controversial road construction near his campus that would likely disrupt access to the college and its nearby business district. He began his research by reading news reports on the topic and discovered one particular shopkeeper had surfaced as the voice of opposition to the project and was often quoted in local articles. A phone call produced specific insights about the building project that the student was able to use in his speech. Because he wanted to be sure to inform his audience about multiple perspectives, the student also interviewed a government official as well as an engineer familiar with the project, and incorporated the results of those interviews into his speech.

To set up an interview, all you need to do is pick up the phone and ask permission. You might use the following template:

> Hello, (Mr., Ms., Dr., Professor) ____________________. My name is ________________, from ____________________ College/University. I am researching a presentation for my public speaking class on the subject of ______________. I understand that you are well versed in this field and I wondered whether it would be possible for us to talk about it now or in the near future.

If you fail to reach the person you want to interview by phone and time allows, you could send a letter or email to the desired source. You might begin such a letter like this:

Dear (Mr., Ms., Dr., Professor) ________________:

I am a student at ________________ and am currently working on a speech on the topic of ________________. It is my understanding that you are an expert in this field, and I was wondering whether it would be possible for us to get together either in person or over the phone to discuss it.

I would only need a few minutes of your time to answer some basic questions about ________________. My peers would really enjoy hearing your views.

Please contact me at ________________, so we can work out the details of such a meeting. Thank you for your help. I look forward to meeting you.

Sincerely,

____

Before you make a phone call or conduct an interview, be certain that you have a series of questions to ask your interviewee that display a sense of purpose, direction, and familiarity with the subject. Here are sample questions you might use if you were interviewing a source from the American Polygraph Association about the use of lie detectors.

Preliminary Questions for the American Polygraph Association Representative

1. What is the scientific basis of the polygraph?
2. How do people train to administer lie detector tests?
3. How and when was the test developed?
4. How many tests are administered each year?
5. What are polygraph tests used for?
6. Is it possible to cheat on a polygraph test? How?
7. How does an administrator prepare to give a polygraph test?
8. How should a person prepare to take a polygraph test?
9. What ethical guidelines do polygraph administrators follow?
10. Why did you decide to become a polygraph administrator?

Whenever you conduct an interview, preserve its results. Take detailed notes or, if the interviewee grants you permission, record your conversation. You might use the following template for documenting that you have the interviewee's permission to record the interview:

This is ________________, and today's date is ________________. I am with ________________, who has consented to this interview being recorded. Is that correct ________________ [insert interviewee's name]?

If the interviewee answers "Yes," then you can proceed with the interview, safe in the knowledge that not only your interview, but also the permission to record will be captured on tape.

Let's say you plan to speak on an issue that especially concerns you—perhaps terrorism. Though some people are unlikely to consent to an interview, for the purposes of this exercise, assume that you can reach any public figure. Identify the desired interviewee and his or position, and explain why you consider him or her an expert on your chosen issue. Then compile a list of at least ten specific questions you would like to ask the expert either in person, via email, or by phone.

Conduct the Interview

You now have an interviewee lined up and have prepared your questions. How do you proceed?

First, arrive on time. It is better to find yourself waiting for the interviewee and using the extra time to strategize than it is to make the interviewee wait for you.

Second, explain your reasons for the interview right away. *You* know why it was important to interview the subject, but your interviewee may not be sure why you're there. If you need to set up a recorder, you can use that time to establish some common ground with the interviewee and give him or her a few extra seconds to focus on your topic.

Once you begin, the person you are interviewing may take your discussion into other areas. If the tangents are adding material to the interview that is relevant to your objectives, by all means let the interviewee pursue the area. If the detour is irrelevant, gently guide the interviewee back by returning to your prepared list of questions.

During the interview, ask questions designed to elicit needed information. Don't waste time asking questions you can get answered elsewhere. Ask open questions that require more than one-word answers. Follow up with **probing questions** that seek more information, such as "Why did you make that decision?"

Stockbyte/Stockbyte/Thinkstock

Investigative journalism. Interviewing someone knowledgeable on your topic is a great way to conduct research.

Also remember to give the interviewee feedback. For example, you may want to say, "So, what you are saying is . . . " or "What I hear you telling me is . . . ." Asking mirroring questions—such as "You said attitude is more important than aptitude?"—encourages discussion while also verifying the interviewee's meaning. An even more effective approach is to combine a mirroring response with a probing question: "So you are suggesting that emotional intelligence is as important as IQ. Are you implying that schools should be teaching this as well?"

Techniques like these help ensure that you have accurately processed and understood the information that the interviewee is giving you, and also show the interviewee that you really care about what he or she is sharing.

Conduct a Post-Interview Review

You should review your notes or recording immediately after the interview to clarify what you've written and so that you do not misquote your expert. Concentrate on isolating the main points from the conversation. Be alert for specific examples and information that you can incorporate into your presentation.

Compile a list of key ideas covered during the interview. Having such a list will make it easier to determine which pieces of information are relevant to your speech and which can be discarded. Transcribe or rewrite your notes, focusing on the most relevant material. You may want to write each piece of information on an individual index card so it will be easier to organize your presentation. For example, you might record information resulting from an interview about damage caused by a recent hurricane as shown in Figure 7.1.

FIGURE 7.1

Note Card Derived From an Interview

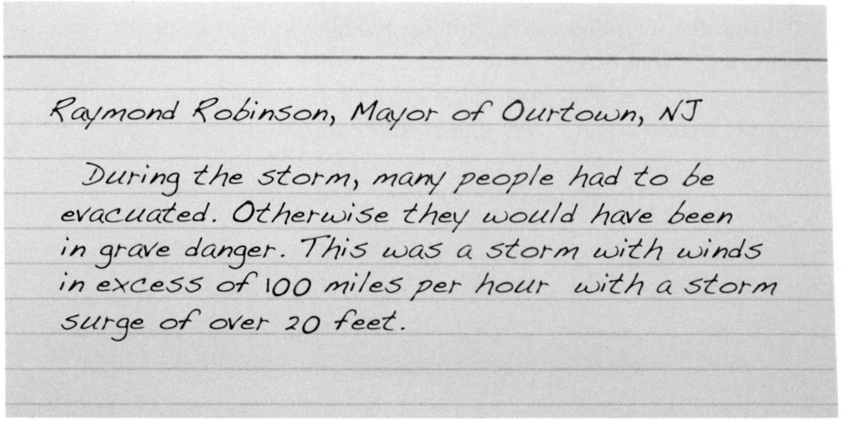
Raymond Robinson, Mayor of Ourtown, NJ
During the storm, many people had to be evacuated. Otherwise they would have been in grave danger. This was a storm with winds in excess of 100 miles per hour with a storm surge of over 20 feet.

Gather Secondary Research

section
7.2

Secondary research includes published statistics, texts and articles by experts, and media and personal documents. As a repository for a wide variety of such research materials, the library is your ally. If you are familiar with your college's library this section will simply be a quick review. If your library is still a mystery (perhaps because you do your research online), this is your opportunity to get to know it better. Even with the ease of researching online, the library has resources such as librarians, reference works, and the catalog that you may want to consult.

7.2a Library Resources

The library is a prime source for research materials. You can visit it in person (which we advise) and access it from afar. You'll want to consult its research librarians, catalog, reference works, and databases.

The Catalog

Using the library's online catalog, you can find resources even if you do not know a specific author or title. All you need to do is enter two or three key words into the computer, and it will search the library's collection for you to find relevant material. A librarian can guide you in searching your school's catalog most effectively.

COACHING TIP

"We live for self-expression and the opportunity to share what we believe is important."

—Garr Reynolds

You have a speech in you. You think it's important and want receivers to think so too. For this to happen, you need to give the audience good information. Choose wisely! If your audience remembers only one piece of research, what do you want that to be?

Reference Collections and Other Resources

The catalog is only one stop along your investigatory road. Visit the reference section of the library, where you will find encyclopedias, yearbooks, dictionaries, biographical aids, atlases, and an array of indexes.

- The *Statistical Abstract of the United States* is a U.S. Census Bureau–produced reference that includes an incredible array of facts about U.S. birth rates, death rates, family income, employment data, and hundreds of other topics.
- *The World Almanac and Book of Facts* lists award recipients, sports record holders, natural resources in various countries, and much more.
- *Facts on File* collects news articles on major topics like science, sports, medicine, crime, economics, and the arts in weekly issues bound in a yearbook every 12 months.
- Monthly magazine *Current Biography* provides complete articles about newsworthy people from around the world.
- *Who's Who* references, including *Who's Who in America* and a number of volumes for specific fields, including business, science, math, and engineering, are valuable biographical resources.
- The *Biography Index* collects biographical information from magazines and newspapers.
- Subject-specific dictionaries—*Black's Law Dictionary,* for example—can help you define technical terms or jargon.
- The *Oxford English Dictionary* provides detailed history of a specific word.
- *Bartlett's Familiar Quotations* contains more than 20,000 quotations.
- *Merriam-Webster's Geographical Dictionary* is a gazetteer that gives facts about nearly 50,000 locations around the world.
- *The Readers' Guide to Periodical Literature* is a general index of periodicals (also available online at http://www.ebscohost.com/academic/readers-guide-to-periodical-literature). Articles that appeared in more than 450 major magazines are cited by author, title, and subject. Each listing gives you all the information you need to locate a particular issue.
- Major U.S. newspapers are indexed, with back issues available on microfilm and online. (Most local newspapers in the United States are not indexed. If you see an article in a local paper that would be appropriate for your speech, clip it out and save it.)

AP Photo/Phil Sears

Ask an expert. Focus your interview questions on gaining new insights into your speech topic.

7.2b Online Sources

We have already seen that a variety of sources are available for you to research online. For example, most college libraries pay to subscribe to the *Encyclopedia of Associations* through GALENet, LexisNexis, or another online directory resource. All the major associations listed within it—the National Rifle Association, the American Civil Liberties Union, the Children's Defense Fund, and many more—have their own websites that are full of helpful information.

Other online resources include

- The *Catalog of U.S. Government Publications* searches current and historical federal publications (http://catalog.gpo.gov/).
- The *Consumer Information Catalog* lists free and low-cost publications available from various federal agencies on a wide range of topics (http://www.pueblo.gsa.gov/).
- The site http://fedstats.sites.usa.gov pulls together statistical information from 14 federal agencies.
- *The World Factbook,* published by the CIA (Central Intelligence Agency), contains maps and detailed information on every country, dependency, and geographic entity in the world (https://www.cia.gov/library/publications/the-world-factbook/).
- *Infotrac* covers general publications and government documents (see Figure 7.2).
- Business Index ASAP provides bibliographic references, abstracts, and full articles from more than 800 business, management, and trade organizations.
- Various search engines, such as Google, also function as online databases (see Figure 7.3).

A variety of sophisticated databases containing journal articles written by scholars on virtually any subject are available for you to consult via computer.

- ERIC (http://www.eric.ed.gov/)
- ASI (https://library.truman.edu/microforms/american_statistics_index.asp)
- Academic Search Premier (www.ebscohost.com)
- LexisNexis (www.lexisnexis.com/)
- Infotrac (www.infotrac.net)
- JSTOR (www.jstor.org)
- GoogleScholar (scholar.google.com)

When consulting some academic databases, you may want to seek help from a research librarian. Because some of these resources require the payment of a fee, if your library does not subscribe, be certain of the specific information you need before using them.

In many ways the Internet now functions as a well-equipped international library of information resources. Among the most effective search engines are Google (www.google.com), Bing (www.bing.com), and Yahoo! (www.yahoo.com). Video search engines also are becoming commonplace. Search online for relevant videos on YouTube, Google, Blinkx, and Bing Videos.

FIGURE 7.2
Infotrac

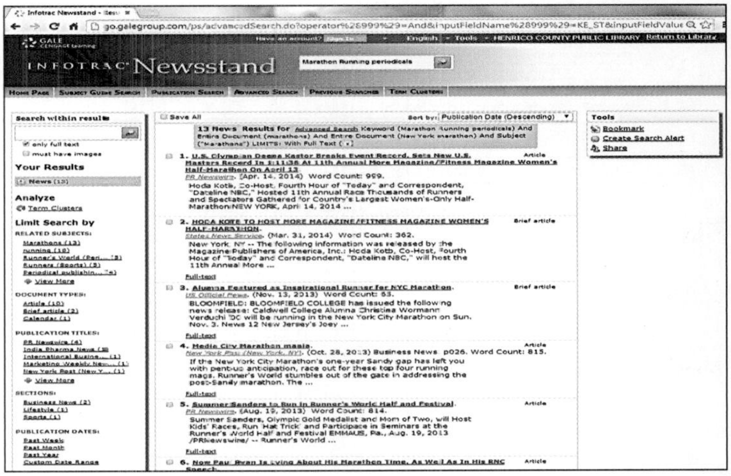

7.2c Websites

Websites can provide relevant information for a speech. Again, be sure to evaluate each site's objectivity together with the credentials of its author(s) and its sponsor(s). Websites maintained by faculty, think tank members, or nonprofit and governmental organizations tend to be more valid sources of information than many commercial websites designed for promotional purposes. Some websites present one-sided perspectives, rather than multisided consideration of issues, so you'll need to balance the information provided.

7.2d Blogs

When blogs engage qualified academics or other professionals in conversation, they can be enlightening. There is a difference, however, between such postings and those offered by random members of the public, who may not be as well informed about the subject. Therefore, unless you can determine the expertise of the blogger and responders, it is better to view them skeptically. Another reason to be wary is that blogs often represent the point of view of the blogger and may be biased. So pay careful attention to the evidence put forth and make an effort to assess its accuracy.

FIGURE 7.3
Google Search Results

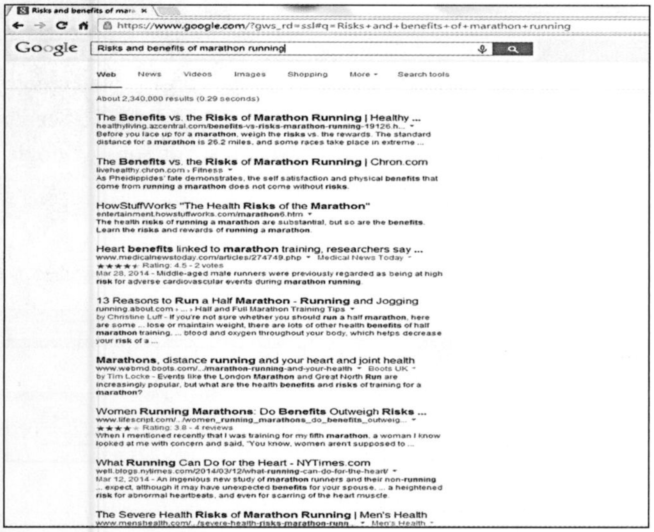

7.2e Wikis

A **wiki** is a website whose content is composed and edited by members of the public. Useful in introducing a subject and potential sources, wikis' use should be limited because anyone can post and edit material, the expertise of the person posting is not necessarily considered, and thus the information provided is sometimes inaccurate or outdated.

Thus, other than as a starting point, do not rely on wikis such as Wikipedia for information. In fact, citing Wikipedia as a source may damage your credibility. It is important to take the time to locate more reliable source material.

Think Critically About Research

section 7.3

When assessing the credibility of information, determine whether the sources you consulted are qualified and unbiased. Specifying the names, positions, and affiliations of your sources enhances credibility. Referring to a source generally, such as "Researchers have found . . . ," tends to detract from credibility.[2] Verifying and thinking critically about the quality of the information, whether you find it in traditional print research sources or online, is a serious responsibility.

7.3a Assess Traditional Research Sources

Sources that have an economic self-interest in the subject are less credible than sources that have nothing to gain. For example, a little over a decade ago, a study in the American Heart Association journal *Circulation* precipitated a call for the lowering of cholesterol limits. The government panel issuing the new recommendations failed to disclose its members' links to pharmaceutical companies, many of which manufactured cholesterol-lowering drugs. This omission called the impartiality of the research and the validity of the conclusion into question.[3]

7.3b Evaluate Online Sources

Although the information contained in traditional research sources, including books, magazines, and journal articles, is typically reviewed and checked by several people before being published, virtually anyone can post information on a website or through social media. As you decide what to include in your speech from your Web search, ask yourself the following questions about information you find on websites and on social media:

- ☐ Who is the site's sponsor? Was it found through a search engine or a library database? (Generally, library databases direct you to more reliable and higher-quality information.)
- ☐ To what sites, if any, is the site linked?
- ☐ What is the connection between the site and the links? Are the links from reputable sites?
- ☐ What clues does the Internet address of the site provide? Is it, for example, an advocacy organization (.org), a business (.com), the government (.gov), a network or Internet service provider (.net), an educational institution (.edu), or someone's personal site? The origination of the site offers clues to its mission or function.
- ☐ Who wrote the material that appears on the site?
- ☐ Is the author a qualified and reliable source?
- ☐ How recent is the webpage?
- ☐ How often is information on it updated?
- ☐ Why is the site on the Web?
- ☐ Is its primary purpose to provide information or to sell a product or idea?

© iStockphoto.com/diego cervo

Assess reliability. Even sources you find traditionally, such as in a library, should be checked for their objectiveness and credibility.

By attempting to determine whether the source or site sponsor has any apparent or hidden bias, whether claims made are justifiable, and whether postings are specific or general and up-to-date, you demonstrate your commitment not to trust information simply because it is published on the Internet. Always seek confirming sources for what you discover.

GAME PLAN

Reviewing Your Research

- ☐ I have explored and included information from a variety of sources, including my own personal experience, library resources, as well as online resources such as websites.
- ☐ I have kept a clear record of research notes with roughly enough sources to fit the "rule of one to three."
- ☐ I have reviewed my sources with a critical eye to make sure they are independent and reliable.
- ☐ I have incorporated my sources into my speech to acknowledge the words and work of others.
- ☐ I have compiled a list of works cited as well as a list of works consulted to show that I did not misuse or plagiarize the work of others.

Keep a Research Record

section
7.4

7.4a Take Good Notes

7.4b Cite Source Materials Carefully

As you work your way through your research materials, you'll find yourself adjusting and editing the information that you actually plan to present to your audience. Keep your mind open: New and exciting roads for inquiry will surface only if you are willing to explore them. If your explorations are to be meaningful, you will need to record the information you hope to use.

7.4a Take Good Notes

Many researchers use a notebook to keep track of information, allocating a new page for every source they use; this makes it easier for you to organize and document your work when it is time to construct your speech. Others use 4-by-6-inch index cards, which allow you literally to shuffle the cards into the order in which you will use the information in your presentation. Try this approach:

- Use a unique card for each article you reference.
- Record the title, author, and subject on the top of each card.
- Record one piece of information per card.

For examples of what note cards look like, see Figure 7.4. Notice how each card contains either a direct quotation from the material or paraphrased information. Using a computer to take notes allows you to move information around wherever you need it or want to use it in the speech itself. You will want to treat each page of your document as you would a note card.

Write it down. Take careful notes as you conduct your research.

FIGURE 7.4
Sample Bibliography Cards

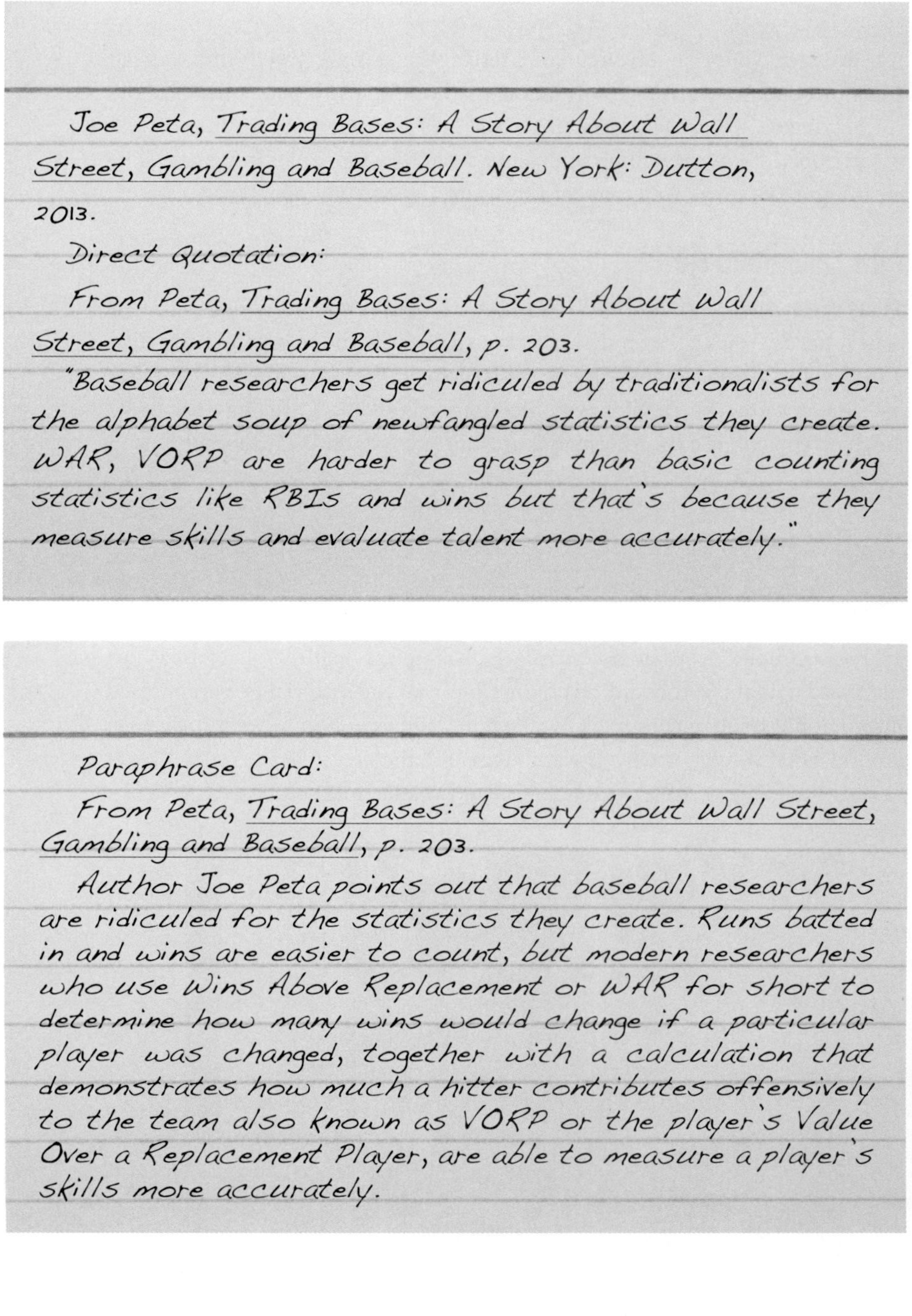

Joe Peta, Trading Bases: A Story About Wall Street, Gambling and Baseball. New York: Dutton, 2013.

Direct Quotation:

From Peta, Trading Bases: A Story About Wall Street, Gambling and Baseball, p. 203.

"Baseball researchers get ridiculed by traditionalists for the alphabet soup of newfangled statistics they create. WAR, VORP are harder to grasp than basic counting statistics like RBIs and wins but that's because they measure skills and evaluate talent more accurately."

Paraphrase Card:

From Peta, Trading Bases: A Story About Wall Street, Gambling and Baseball, p. 203.

Author Joe Peta points out that baseball researchers are ridiculed for the statistics they create. Runs batted in and wins are easier to count, but modern researchers who use Wins Above Replacement or WAR for short to determine how many wins would change if a particular player was changed, together with a calculation that demonstrates how much a hitter contributes offensively to the team also known as VORP or the player's Value Over a Replacement Player, are able to measure a player's skills more accurately.

7.4b Cite Source Materials Carefully

As you take notes, be sure to give each source correct attribution to avoid plagiarism. Giving sources the credit due them not only protects you but also increases your credibility. Let your research show. Do not ever cover it up or try to claim someone else's ideas as your own.

Audiences do not expect you to have developed all the ideas contained in your speech. During the presentation, you will need to provide oral citations that reveal the sources of your information to the audience. Such citations are not difficult to include as long as you have done your research and recorded your information carefully. What do you say in an oral citation? Here are some samples.

If you are citing a speech or article, you might say,

> *"Back in a January 2016 speech on the future of the United States, president Barack Obama, told a joint session of Congress . . . "*

If you are using a direct quotation, state the name of the author and the source:

> *"In his 2006 paper, 'The Importance of Accurate, Reliable and Timely Data,' Australian economist Saul Eslake writes . . . "*

If you are paraphrasing a book or article, you might tell your audience,

> *"Howard Gardner, author of the best-seller* Changing Minds, *feels that most of us change our minds gradually. The notion that mind change happens suddenly is wrong."*

Use a specificity progression in your oral citation of a source. The first time you cite a particular source, you want to be fairly specific. For example, in a speech on veteran suicides, one speaker told his audience, "As Melanie Haiken notes in her article for the February 2013 issue of *Forbes* magazine, 22 veterans are committing suicide every day." The student's second reference to the Haiken article was briefer, with him saying, "In her article for *Forbes,* Haiken also reveals that the number of veterans committing suicide has actually dropped from 1999 statistics." The speaker's third reference to Haiken's article contains even less source specificity, with the speaker stating, "Haiken points out that the VA Call Center has effected some 25,000 rescues since the inception of the veteran suicide intervention program."

As you build your speech, you bring experts onto your team in order to gain credibility and give your message the maximum impact. A Works Cited page lists the sources you mentioned during your speech. A list of all the sources you referenced when conducting your research is known as a Works Consulted page. Your instructor will probably ask you to turn in your Works Consulted when you submit the formal outline of your speech. When preparing either one, be sure to a use a consistent referencing style. The MLA (Modern Language Association) or APA (American Psychological Association) formats are the most popular.[4] (See Figures 7.5 through 7.8 for information on using these formats.) When using either format, arrange the list alphabetically—either by the last name of the author, by the title if no author is mentioned, or by the last name of the person interviewed. For examples, see the Works Consulted sections of the sample speech outlines included in the chapters on informative (Chapter 18) and persuasive speaking (Chapter 19).

FIGURE 7.5
What to Include When Citing a Work

Name of author(s) or editor(s)
Title of the source
Title of specific article
Publisher or website sponsor
Date of publication
Date of retrieval of electronic source(s)
Web address (URL)
The issue or volume of the journal
The name of the database used
Page numbers

FIGURE 7.6
Quick Guide to Citations

QUICK GUIDE	APA	MLA
Book	Last name, A. A., & Last name, B. B. (date). *Title of book*. City: Publisher.	Last name, First name and First name Last name. *Title of Book*. City: Publisher, date.
Journal	Last name, A. A. (date). "Title of article." *Journal Name, volume,* page numbers.	Last name, First name. "Title of Article." *Journal Name*, volume (date): page numbers.
Magazine	Last name, A. A. (date). "Title of Article." *Magazine name, volume,* page numbers.	Last name, First name. "Title of Article." *Magazine name*, date: page numbers.
Newspaper	Last name, A. A. (date). "Title of Article." *Newspaper name*, page numbers.	Last name, First name. "Title of Article." *Newspaper name*, date: page numbers.
Internet	Organization. (date). Title. Retrieved from <address>. Date.	Document Title Site. Date. Organization Publishing site. Retrieval date. <address>
Email	Email is not included in APA.	Last name, First name. Personal email. Date.
Interview	Interviews are not included in APA.	Last name, First name. Personal telephone interview. Date.

Aim for Source Variety

How many sources do you really need? Of course, the topic and the available material will be a major part of that answer. However, if you are looking for a guideline, keep the *rule of one to three* in mind. This says that you should aim for three sources ("the rule of three") for every minute of the presentation. So if you need to prepare a 5-minute speech, you would start with a goal of 15 sources. As you work, however, you will quickly find that many of these sources are not appropriate to the presentation, and you can then refine the materials to the "rule of one." That is, you should aim to refer to at least one source for every minute of your presentation.

FIGURE 7.7
Guide for APA Style Citations

Book—One Author

Family name, Initial. Initial. (date). *Title of book*. City: Publisher.

King, S. E. (2013). *Doctor sleep*. New York: Scribner.

Book—Two Authors

Family name, Initial. Initial., & Family name, Initial Initial. (date). Title. City: Publisher.

Jason, F., & Hanson, D. H. (2013). *Remote: Office not required*. New York: Crown Publishers.

Journal Article

Family name, Initial. Initial. (date). Title. *Journal Title volume number*, page numbers.

Alibali, M. W., Phillips, K. O., & Fischer, A. D. (2009). Learning new problem-solving strategies leads to changes in problem representation. *Cognitive Development*, *24*, 89–101.

Magazine

Family name, Initial. Initial. (year, month, week or day). Title of article. *Magazine Name*, page numbers.

Seabrook, J. (2013, October 14). The doctor is in: A technique for producing number one songs. *The New Yorker*, 44–56.

Newspaper

Family name, Initial. Initial. (year, month, day). Title of article. *Newspaper Name,* page numbers.

Berkman, S. (2013, October 19). Bronx renaissance. *The New York Times*, p. D1.

Internet

Organization publishing website. (date). Document title. Retrieved date, from address.

National Football League. (2013). *Football 101: Offense*. Retrieved October 1, 2013, from http://www.nfl.com/news/story/0ap.

Email

Email messages are categorized as personal information in the APA and are not included in a reference list. You can refer to them in your speech.

Interview

The interview is categorized as personal information in the APA system and is not included in a reference list. You can refer to interviews during your speech.

Don't become too hung up on these rules. They are merely guidelines. If you've selected 80 sources for your 5-minute presentation, you probably have far more information than you could use. If, however, you could find only one source of information for your speech, the rule of one to three tells you that you have far too little material, and that you may need to consider broadening your topic. For example, if you want to talk about homelessness in your hometown and you find only one newspaper article, you need to widen the scope of your work, perhaps to include the surrounding country or even your state.

FIGURE 7.8
Guide for MLA Style Citations

Book—One Author

Family name, First name. *Title of the Book*. City: Publisher, date.

Hosseini, Khaled. *The Kite Runner.* New York: Penguin Books, 2004.

Book—Two Authors

Family name, First name and First name, Last name. *Title of the Book*. City: Publisher, date.

Mahzarin, R. Banaji and Anthony G. Greenwald. *Blindspot: Hidden Biases of Good People*. New York: Random House, 2013.

Journal

Last name, First name. "Title of Article." *Journal Name*, date: page numbers.

Olson, Kathryn. "An Epidectic Dimension of Symbolic Violence in Disney's *Beauty and the Beast*." *Quarterly Journal of Speech*, November, 2013: 448–480.

Magazine

Last name, First name. "Title of Article." *Magazine Name.* Date: page numbers.

Wallace-Wells, Benjamin. "The Truly Paranoid Style in American Politics." *New York Magazine.* 25 November 2013: 31–43. Print.

Newspaper

Family name, First name. "Title of Article." *Newspaper Name*, date: page number. Print.

Eisenberg, Ann. "When Algorithms Grow Accustomed to your Face." *The New York Times*. 1 December 2013: B3. Print.

Internet

Organization website. (date). *Article Title*. Retrieved date, from Web address.

International Association of Skateboard Companies. (2013). *Just One Board*. Retrieved December 1, 2013 from http://thelasc.org.

Email

Family name, First name. "Subject Line." Email to Family name. Date.

Robinson, James. "My Attempts at Rope Climbing." Email to Johnson, Judy. 3 August 2013.

Interview

Family name, First name. Personal telephone interview. Date.

Guiliano, Edward. Telephone interview. 10 April 2012.

Exercises

RESEARCH

Becoming an adept researcher is a serious responsibility. Let's look at other research-based activities to get you in quality researcher shape.

1. Use a Checklist

Select a topic of interest to you. Go to the library and online and locate as much information as possible on your topic. Classify the material you find using categories such as scholarly, professional, or popular. Also decide whom you might interview on the subject and the extent to which you personally can contribute.

Use the following checklist to guide your search:

- ☐ The library's catalog
- ☐ Periodical indexes
- ☐ Newspaper indexes
- ☐ Research room
  - ○ General encyclopedias
  - ○ Specialized encyclopedias
  - ○ Yearbooks
  - ○ Biographical references
  - ○ Dictionaries
  - ○ Quotation books
  - ○ Atlases and gazetteers
- ☐ Computerized sources and databases
  - ○ Email and Listservs
  - ○ Websites
  - ○ Blogs
- ☐ Potential interviewees identified
- ☐ Any other research

2. Analyze Research Cited

In the following speech on dry cleaning, student Suzi Kim draws on personal experience, interviews, webpages, and published articles on the use of the chemical *perc* in dry cleaning. After reading the accompanying excerpt from her speech, and considering the sidenotes that accompany it, answer these questions:

1. Do you think the speaker interviewed the best people? Why or why not?
2. How many different sources and forms of support did the speaker use? Were they equally effective? Explain.
3. How do you feel about the speaker's use of webpages as sources? How else might she have used the Internet?
4. What additional kinds of research materials, if any, might the speaker have benefited from using?
5. Did any speechmaking errors impede the speaker's effectiveness? If yes, identify and explain them.
6. Based on this excerpted speech, to what degree do you believe the speaker realized her speaking goal?

DRY CLEANING

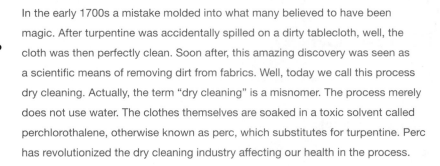

SN 1 The speaker uses the introduction to introduce the topic, exposing misconceptions about its nature. The speaker's interjection of the word "well" could become a distraction if continued throughout the speech.

In the early 1700s a mistake molded into what many believed to have been magic. After turpentine was accidentally spilled on a dirty tablecloth, well, the cloth was then perfectly clean. Soon after, this amazing discovery was seen as a scientific means of removing dirt from fabrics. Well, today we call this process dry cleaning. Actually, the term "dry cleaning" is a misnomer. The process merely does not use water. The clothes themselves are soaked in a toxic solvent called perchlorothalene, otherwise known as perc, which substitutes for turpentine. Perc has revolutionized the dry cleaning industry affecting our health in the process.

SN 2 The speaker clearly defines the subject of her speech, perc, using a local newspaper as a source.

According to the Galveston/Houston Association for Smog Prevention home page, last updated on January 28th, perc is a chemical that is listed under the Clean Air Act as a hazardous waste. Yet today more than 80 percent of U.S. dry cleaners rely on this toxic solvent. In the past, clothes made of such fine fabrics were worn until they became so filthy they needed to be thrown away. Well, clothes continue to be a luxury, and in a world that demands such fine fabrics to fulfill so many needs, we can no longer afford to throw away our lives or our health with perc.

SN 3 The speaker previews the speech's content.

Therefore, to best combat the threat of perc we must first understand the negative ramifications of dry cleaning that affect our health, then reveal some of the ineffective measures of governmental and industrial control of this toxic process, and finally learn some of the realistic measures we can adopt to keep our clothes clean and maintain our health.

SN 4 The speaker uses statistical evidence, identifying their source, as she builds a case against perc's use.

Dry cleaning has turned itself into an art and a science. We incorporate the cleaning into high, fast style. However, the history of dry cleaning . . . well, it's really quite humble. The process has gone from petroleum solvents that burst into flame into what many have believed to be a safe solvent—perc. So finally the *World and I* on November 5th reveals that up to 40 to 50 percent of the five hundred million pounds of perc produced annually is by dry cleaners.

SN 5 The speaker cites a series of sources including a website, research studies, and a personal example to underscore perc's dangers.

The main route for human exposure is via inhalation, but this chemical is also passed through skin and mouth contact. It is extremely soluble in blood. According to the Information Ventures home page, last updated on March 3rd . . . this chemical is also spread through blood, water, and other toxic solvents. In a study done at the University of California of individuals who frequented dry cleaning establishments at least three times a month, there were found decreased fertility and misshapen sperm in men, and pregnant women experienced nearly five times the rate of spontaneous abortions. In other studies, individuals were found to have a high incidence of pelvic cancer. And children who were exposed to perc solvent through water had an unusually high incidence of leukemia. New York City apartment owner Sue Kassier is living proof of these studies.

After experiencing a toxic odor coming from her bedroom vent, Kassier was later diagnosed with upper respiratory problems and retinal nerve destruction. These enhanced perc levels are due largely to the emissions from the clothing of dry cleaning workers. And according to the November issue of the *Archives of Environmental Health*, the exhalations from the lungs of dry cleaning workers are actually toxic. Perc is not particular in choosing its victims attacking individuals who live in neighborhoods near dry cleaning establishments.

3. Do You Know What They Know?

As Ralph Waldo Emerson said, "Every fact depends for its value on how much we already know." Conduct research to figure out what your audience already knows about the health dangers of a sedentary lifestyle or another topic of your choosing.

4. Approach the Speaker's Stand

Your instructor has asked for examples of the primary and secondary research you plan to incorporate into your next speech. In preparation for this, develop a list of sources you intend to consult. Then, prepare note cards showing proper citation for the following: a direct quotation and a paraphrase of a quotation from one primary and two secondary research sources, one of which is a Web source.

RECAP AND REVIEW

1. **Draw research from your personal knowledge and experience.** By using personal experience, a speaker enhances his or her credibility and adds believability to his or her presentation.
2. **Plan and conduct an interview with a person who possesses special knowledge related to your topic.** By conducting interviews with authorities on a subject, the speaker comes into direct contact with recognized experts and invests the presentation with even greater validity and relevance.
3. **Do library-based research.** Library and computer-assisted research enable the speaker to discover and integrate the latest in credible, authoritative information into the speech.
4. **Demonstrate the value of researching online.** The Internet has a wealth of resources you can consult to find material for your speech including databases of scholarly journals, professional websites, news and magazine indices, and image and video repositories. As with all research, evaluating the trustworthiness of sources is essential.
5. **Take good research notes.** Note cards featuring facts, quotes, and complete source information facilitate the organization and documentation of materials you integrate into your speech.
6. **Evaluate potential sources of information critically.** Evaluating the credibility, authoritativeness, currency, and relevance of the sources and information you intend to use is integral to an effective presentation.

KEY TERMS

Primary research 116

Probing question 119

Secondary research 121

Wiki 124

© iStockphoto.com/champja

8 Integrating Support

UPON COMPLETING THIS CHAPTER'S TRAINING, YOU WILL BE ABLE TO

1. Use and assess the effectiveness of examples
2. Use and assess the effectiveness of explanations and descriptions
3. Use and assess the effectiveness of facts and definitions
4. Use and assess the effectiveness of analogies
5. Use and assess the effectiveness of statistics
6. Use and assess the effectiveness of testimony
7. Properly cite support in a speech

Like a presidential candidate who studies a range of subjects before being interviewed by a reporter such as Charlie Rose or George Stephanopoulos, a speechmaker loads up on support before speaking. Consider how the interview with the candidate is covered. A team of researchers supports the interviewer. Information about the candidate's past wins and losses, strengths and weaknesses, and personal dramas are available for the interviewer to consult and refer to during the interview. Video profiles detailing the struggles and successes of the candidate have been recorded and are cued up. Were it not for such support, the interview itself might be dry and viewers might tune out. The same holds true for your speech and its audience.

A speech should be infused with support that amplifies, clarifies, and vivifies its ideas. To avoid having your speech fall flat, it is essential that you search diligently for supporting materials to elaborate on, prove, or enliven your points. And you must use the right type of support for the situation (see Table 8.1).

TABLE 8.1 SUPPORT

TYPE OF SUPPORT	PRIMARY USE(S)
Examples	To support specific points; to engage the audience
Explanations and descriptions	To clarify; to evoke a sensory response
Definitions	To explain words and concepts
Analogies	To promote understanding via comparisons and contrasts
Statistics	To strengthen claims and reinforce facts
Testimony	To increase believability and credibility

Contents

section
8.1

Use Examples

The right kind of examples can breathe life into a dull or uninteresting speech. Listeners are more likely to believe speakers who include and cite factual information, and they are more likely to engage in a story. As Nancy Duarte, the author of *Resonate,* notes, "Personal stories are the emotional glue that connects your audience to your message."[1]

8.1a Short Examples

You can use short examples to support a specific point. Although most of these examples are typically no longer than a sentence or two, when used in a series they gain power. In a speech on the pay gap between men and women, one student used the following series of brief examples to document disparities in pay by sex:

> Typically women earn less than men throughout their lives. According to a 2016 analysis compiled by *Time* magazine, on average, women earn 15% less than men do between ages 22 to 25. They earn 38% less than men between ages 51 and 64. The fact is that men out-earn women in hundreds of occupations from medicine to law, from athletic coaching to umpiring, from administrative assistants to bartenders.

Each example the student used demonstrated that there were virtually no careers in which women earned more than their male colleagues.

COACHING TIP

"Personal example carries more weight than preaching."

—Chinese proverb

Don't go it alone when speaking in public. You have a support team to take to the podium with you. Use examples, definitions, analogies, statistics, and testimony appropriately and creatively, and you will increase the likelihood that your audience engages with and responds favorably to your ideas.

8.1b Narrative Examples

Extended examples are also known as illustrations, **narratives**, or anecdotes. More detailed and vivid than brief examples, extended examples are built very much like a story: They open, reveal a complication, contain a climax, and describe a resolution. Though narrative examples are longer, and thus consume more time, when well planned and placed they are also more emotionally compelling and add a real sense of drama to the speech.

In a speech at the 2004 Democratic National Convention, then–U.S. Senate candidate Barack Obama used a personal illustration to demonstrate that his life story was typical of the American dream:

> My father was a foreign student, born and raised in a small village in Kenya. He grew up herding goats, went to school in a tin-roof shack. His father—my grandfather—was a cook, a domestic servant to the British. But my grandfather had larger dreams for his son. Through hard work and perseverance my father got a scholarship to study in a magical place, America, that stood as a beacon of freedom and opportunity to so many who had come before. . . .
>
> My parents shared not only an improbable love; they shared an abiding faith in the possibilities of this nation. They would give me an African name, Barack, or "blessed," believing that in a tolerant America your name is no barrier to success.
>
> They imagined me going to the best schools in the land, even though they weren't rich because in a generous America you don't have to be rich to achieve your potential. . . .
>
> I stand here knowing that my story is part of the larger American story, that I owe a debt to all of those who came before me, and that, in no other country on Earth, is my story even possible.[2]

By touching audience members in a way a generalization never could, an illustration helps the speaker pull listeners into the speech and focuses their attention on the issue at hand.

8.1c Hypothetical Examples

The examples cited in the preceding sections were factual. Sometimes, however, you will find it useful to refer to examples that describe imaginary situations. When you integrate brief or extended examples that have not actually occurred into your speeches, you are using **hypothetical examples**. Speakers are ethically bound to let audiences know whenever they use one.

In order for hypothetical examples to fulfill their purpose, audiences must accept that the fictional scenarios you create could really happen. The function of hypothetical examples is not to trick your listeners into believing something that is not true. Rather, you use hypothetical examples when you are unable to find a factual example that suits your purpose, you want to exaggerate your point, or you want to encourage your audience members to imagine facing a particular scenario. Sometimes, rather than being totally contrived, the hypothetical situations you cite will be a synthesis of actual situations, people, or events. But be careful. If you use a hypothetical example that is too far-fetched, audience members won't judge it credible.

Ron Reagan, the son of the former president of the United States Ronald Reagan, used the following hypothetical example in an effort to convince receivers to support stem cell research:

> Let's say that 10 or so years from now you are diagnosed with Parkinson's disease. There is currently no cure, and drug therapy, with its attendant side effects, can only temporarily relieve the symptoms.
>
> Now, imagine going to a doctor who, instead of prescribing drugs, takes a few skin cells from your arm. The nucleus of one of your cells is placed into a donor egg whose own nucleus has been removed. A hit of chemical or electrical stimulation will encourage your cell's nucleus to begin dividing, creating new cells which will then be placed into a tissue culture. Those cells will generate embryonic stem cells containing only your DNA, thereby eliminating the risk of tissue rejection. These stem cells are then driven to become the very neural cells that are defective in Parkinson's patients. And finally, those cells—with your DNA—are injected into your brain where they will replace the faulty cells whose failure to produce adequate dopamine led to the Parkinson's disease in the first place.
>
> In other words, you're cured.[3]

Hypothetical examples are especially useful when someone's privacy is at stake. Persons whose work involves confidentiality—physicians, lawyers, ministers, and therapists—often choose to use hypothetical, rather than real, examples when discussing cases. Still, when faced with the option of whether to use a real or hypothetical example, consider whether your receivers will be influenced more by something that did take place or by something that might take place.

8.1d Assess the Power of Your Examples

Whether you use real or hypothetical, brief or extended examples, what matters most is that they reinforce, clarify, and personalize your ideas, as well as relate directly to your listeners. If you think of yourself as a storyteller, and each example as a key part of your story, then you'll be better able to use your words, your voice, and your body to paint mental pictures that engage, touch, and bring your listeners into the center of your story's plot. To do this successfully, you need to search for and/or create examples that your listeners can get excited about and identify with. Use the following checklist to gauge the power of each example.

- ☐ Is the example universal?
- ☐ Does the example involve people?
- ☐ Does the example make an abstract idea more concrete?
- ☐ Does the example clarify your message?
- ☐ Is the example directly relevant to your message?
- ☐ Is the example vivid—that is, is it filled with detail?
- ☐ Can you relate the example to your audience without relying excessively on your notes?
- ☐ Can you use speaking rate and volume to increase the impact of the example?
- ☐ Will your listeners readily identify with the example?
- ☐ Will your listeners accept the example as credible?

As the checklist suggests, it is important that any examples you use are suitable for your audience, topic, and occasion.

COACHING TIP

"The human species thinks in metaphors and learns through stories."

—Mary Catherine Bateson

Get the audience involved. Don't leave them confused or standing on the sidelines. Share analogies and stories. Dig deep. Personal narratives add drama, infusing your speech with emotion. Keep it real. Make your audience feel.

section

8.2

Use Explanations and Descriptions

Explanations and descriptions are important tools in public speech. We use explanations to clarify what we have said, and we use descriptions to help our audience imagine they can see, hear, smell, touch, taste, or feel what we do. Both types of support help to engage our listeners in our topic.

8.2a Explanations

One speaker who anticipated a lack of subject familiarity on the part of her audience used an **explanation** to clarify the nature of Tourette syndrome.

> Put your hands in your lap. Now keep them there and don't scratch that itch on your head. Don't scratch it. It itches so badly, but keep your hands in your lap. That's what it feels like to have Tourette syndrome and to try to control it. Tourette's is a medical condition characterized by involuntary movements or sounds known as tics. People like me who have Tourette's are unable to control our actions.[4]

Because the speaker believed that most people lacked knowledge on her subject, her explanation was designed not to overexplain, but to facilitate their understanding.

8.2b Descriptions

While speakers use explanations to clarify the unfamiliar for their receivers, they use **descriptions** to produce fresh and striking word pictures designed to provoke sensory reactions. Novelist, essayist, and screenwriter Joan Didion relied heavily on description in a speech entitled "Why I Write."

> I was in this [Panamanian] airport only once, on a plane to Bogota that stopped for an hour to refuel, but the way it looked that morning remained superimposed on everything I saw until the day I finished *A Book of Common Prayer*. I lived in that airport for several years. I can still feel the hot air when I step off the plane, can see the heat already rising off the tarmac at 6 A.M. I can feel my skirt damp and wrinkled on my legs. I can feel the asphalt stick to my sandals. I remember the big tail of a Pan American plane floating motionless down at the end of the tarmac.[5]

Notice how the speaker's descriptions transport you to the airport, helping you feel and see what she experienced.

8.2c Assess the Power of Your Explanations and Descriptions

Consider how your audience will respond to each explanation or description. Use the following checklist to gauge the power of each explanation and/or description you use.

- ☐ Am I using the explanation to deliver information the audience clearly does not know?
- ☐ Have I avoided overexplaining or underexplaining?
- ☐ Is the description rich in specific detail?
- ☐ As a result of the description, will the subject of my description come more alive for listeners?
- ☐ Have I been appropriately selective in choosing what I explain and/or describe?

Ryan McVay/Digital Vision/Thinkstock

Move your audience. Vivid descriptions should elicit reactions from your audience.

section

8.3

Use Definitions

Definitions help bridge cultural divides, enhance audience understanding, and facilitate audience acceptance of a speaker's ideas. Definitions are especially useful when your audience members are unfamiliar with the way you are using key terms, or when they might have associations for words or concepts that differ from your own.

8.3a Which Words Should You Define?

When speaking, you need to define words that are technical in nature, that have specialized meanings, that are rarely used, that you are using in unique or unusual ways, or that have two or more meanings. If the context fails to make the meaning of the word immediately apparent to your listeners, then it is up to you to define it. For example, in a speech on the importance of teaching the sciences, William Durden, the president of Dickinson College, defined *interdisciplinarity* as an appreciation for collaboration and the breaking down of disciplinary silos in order to encourage problem posing and solving from multiple vantage points.[6]

© iStockphoto.com/Aslan Alphan

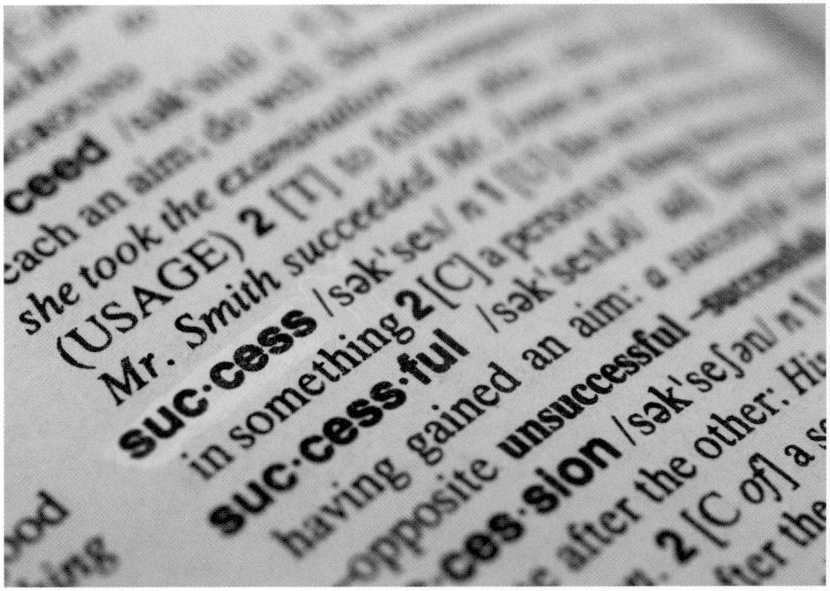

Get defined. If a definition cannot be grasped from the speech's context, you should define it.

8.3b How Do You Define a Word?

When you take your definition from a dictionary, you invest the meaning you cite with a degree of authority and credibility. At the same time, using an original definition could help audience members share your personal meaning for a word and could help make the speaker–audience connection more intense. Of course, using definitions supplied by experts also could help precipitate audience understanding and acceptance.

In a speech debunking the idea that the purpose of college was to train students for a job, one speaker used a definition from dictionary.com to explain why this is impossible:

> To train is to develop or form the habits, thoughts, or behavior by discipline and instruction, such as—to train an unruly boy; to make proficient by instruction and practice, as in some art, profession, or work: to train soldiers; to make fit by proper exercise, diet, practice, as for an athletic performance; to discipline and instruct (an animal), as in the performance of tasks or tricks; to treat or manipulate so as to bring into some desired form, position, direction: to train one's hair to stay down.
>
> We can't be in the business of "training" you for specific jobs because those jobs won't even exist in the future.[7]

In this way, the speaker made it clear that change is a constant and as a result the educating that colleges accomplish cannot be job specific.

8.3c Assess the Power of Your Definitions

Definitions are intended to increase listener understanding or acceptance of your ideas. By helping you explain the nature of a term or situation to your audience members, a definition may help you inform and persuade them. You can use the following checklist to gauge the power of each definition you employ.

- ☐ Does my definition contribute to the overall goal and purpose of my speech?
- ☐ Is my definition easily understood?
- ☐ Am I consistent in the way I define or explain a term or problem?
- ☐ Will audience members readily accept my definition?

section
8.4

Use Analogies

- 8.4a Literal Analogies
- 8.4b Figurative Analogies
- 8.4c Assess the Power of Your Analogies

Sometimes the most effective kind of support available to a speaker is an analogy. Like the definition, the analogy functions to increase understanding, but unlike the definition, it does so through comparison and contrast. There are two main types of analogies: *literal* and *figurative.*

8.4a Literal Analogies

A **literal analogy** compares two things from similar classes, for example, two viruses, two novels, or two crises. When delivering a speech on why we love horror movies, a student used a literal analogy, noting "If you loved the film *Saw,* you'll also love *The Grudge.* Both films are cut from the same cloth." Another student used a literal analogy to compare the Dodge Intrepid to a NASCAR vehicle, noting that when accelerating in her Intrepid she felt like she was beginning a NASCAR race. She then went on to describe the engine characteristics of NASCAR race cars that share much in common with the engine in the Intrepid.

As long as the things being compared are close enough to one another, the speaker will benefit from using a literal analogy. Because literal analogies tend to come off as more logical than emotional, the audience is likely to accept them as true.

8.4b Figurative Analogies

A **figurative analogy** compares two things that at first appear to have little in common with each other—a war and a dragon, or mad cow disease and an alien. A student giving a speech on horror movies made use of a figurative analogy in his speech, noting "A horror move is like a fairy tale on steroids."

Former secretary of state Hillary Clinton used a figurative analogy in her farewell speech to the State Department. Referring to the modern architect known for his multifaceted building designs, she said,

> We need a new architecture for a new world—more Frank Gehry than formal Greek. Now some of his work at first might appear haphazard, but in fact, it's highly intentional and sophisticated. Where once a few strong columns could hold up the weight of the world, today we need a dynamic mix of materials and structures.[8]

Speakers use figurative analogies to awaken the collective imagination of the audience—to prod them into accepting that two things that appear to have little, if anything, in common, actually share one or more vital similarities.

Your primary purpose in using an analogy is to explain the unfamiliar by relating it to something the audience is more familiar with. The essential similarities inherent in your analogies should be readily apparent. If you strain to create them, audience members may conclude that your analogies are far-fetched, inappropriate, unbelievable, or unpersuasive.

Now, try this. Create a literal and figurative analogy for each of the following: a course in public speaking, your job, and your love life.

8.4c Assess the Power of Your Analogies

Analogies enhance audience understanding and acceptance of a message by making the unfamiliar familiar or prompting audience members to use their imagination to consider the point being made. You can use the following checklist to gauge the power of the analogies you use:

- ☐ Does the analogy have a clear purpose within the context of the speech?
- ☐ Is the analogy easily understood?
- ☐ Is the analogy easily visualized?
- ☐ Is the analogy original?
- ☐ Is the analogy apt and colorful?

Drive audience understanding. Use analogies to compare and contrast.

section

8.5

Use Statistics

8.5a Understand What Statistics Mean

8.5b Put Statistics to Use

8.5c Use Statistics Ethically

8.5d Present Statistics Visually

8.5e Assess Your Use of Statistics

There is something comforting in the fact that we can express what we know with numbers. We use **statistics** to clarify and strengthen our ideas and claims, and to express the seriousness of a situation and/or the magnitude of a problem.[9]

8.5a Understand What Statistics Mean

You need to be able to distinguish among common statistical measures. Figure 8.1 explains the concepts of range, mean, median, mode, and percentage. Understanding these statistical measures strengthens your ability to highlight their importance and significance for receivers.

8.5b Put Statistics to Use

Speaking on the prevalence of guns, a speaker reported that being murdered with a gun was the number one cause of death for African American men ages 15 to 34. Then to drive home the seriousness of the situation, she added that since 1979, 44,038 black children were killed by guns—13 times more than all the black people killed by lynching from 1882 to 1968.[10]

Notice how the second set of statistics cited help to establish the problem's magnitude by adding context.

FIGURE 8.1
Making Sense of Numbers

Given the monthly salaries listed on the left, we can determine the following:

$12,000	This salary is **21.09%** of all salaries combined: 12,000 / 56,900 = .2108963.
$10,000	
$8,400	
$7,000	
$5,000	This is the **median salary**: 50% of salaries fall above and below it.
$4,000	
$4,000	This is **the mode**: the number that occurs most frequently in the number group.
$4,000	
$2,500	

The mean salary is the total of all salaries divided by the number of salaries: $56,900 / 9 salaries = $6,322.22.

The range is 9,500; the difference between 12,000 and 2,500.

8.5c Use Statistics Ethically

It's easy for unethical speakers to use numbers to fool the public. Factual information offered by biased sources may contain distortions or omissions.[11]

- Examine the following two groups of numbers.

GROUP 1	GROUP 2
12,000	16,000
10,000	15,000
8,400	9,500
7,000	8,400
5,000	5,000
4,000	4,200
4,000	4,000
4,000	3,000
2,500	3,000

- Determine the range, mean, median, and mode for each group and a percentage measure for the first number in each group. Check your answers by comparing them with these:
    - The range is 9,500 for Group 1 and 13,000 for Group 2.
    - The mean for Group 1 is 6,322. The mean for Group 2 is 7,567.
    - The median is the same for both groups; it is 5,000.
    - The mode is 4,000 for Group 1, and 3,000 for Group 2.
    - The number in the top row is 21 percent of the Group 1 total and 23 percent of Group 2.

Imagine that these figures were the monthly commissions earned by sales executives with the Triple X Corporation (Group 1) and the Triple Y Corporation (Group 2). Now imagine a sales professional has been offered a job by both companies. How might the recruiters at Triple X and Triple Y use these figures to convince the applicant to take the job?

How would you feel if the recruiter for Triple X cited the median salary ($5,000) to show that the "average" earnings of sales representatives in both corporations were identical while the recruiter for Triple Y cited the mean salary of her sales representatives ($7,567) and the mean salary at Triple X ($6,322) to demonstrate that Triple Y employees earned on the "average" $1,200 more a month?

Although both recruiters would technically be telling the truth, unless the sales representative considering the job offer understood how each recruiter was selecting statistics, he or she could be misled.

Because the results obtained depend on the measure used, it is important that you fully explain your statistics to your audience. It is equally important that you not engage in numerical exaggeration.

8.5d Present Statistics Visually

A visual aid can save time and make it easier for the audience to understand the significance of the statistical evidence you cite. Suppose, for example, you chose to speak on the relationship between vitamin D and breast cancer. In the course of your presentation you might well include a number of these findings: the breast cancer death rate was lowest in the sunny South and West and highest in the Northeast; breast cancer rates were more than 1.5 times as high in New York and Boston as in Phoenix or Honolulu; and breast cancer is more prevalent in communities with the most light-blocking air pollution and less prevalent where more solar radiation is received by residents.[12] These are interesting findings, but they probably would be even more effective if shown on a simple graphic, like Figure 8.2.

It is your responsibility to ensure that the statistics you use represent what you claim to be measuring, that you obtain them from a reliable source, that you use them correctly, and that you interpret them accurately. If you follow these precepts, then your statistical support will help you make your speech both more understandable and more memorable.

FIGURE 8.2

Age-Adjusted Breast Cancer Mortality Rates, by County Area, and Contours of Annual Mean Daily Solar Irradiance in Langleys (calories/cm2), United States, 1970–1994

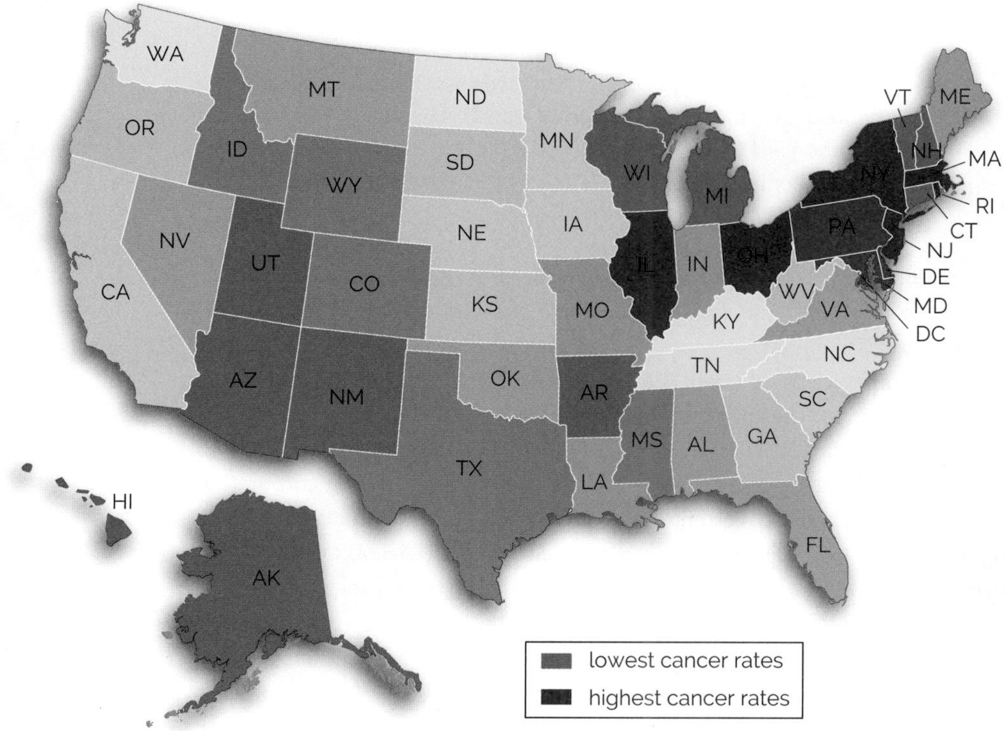

Sources: Developed through use of National Cancer Institute and National Oceanic and Atmospheric Administration data (available at www.cancer.gov and http://www.noaa.gov).

8.5e Assess Your Use of Statistics

The impact of examples is strengthened when they are followed by statistics that demonstrate their representativeness. But before you integrate any statistics into your speech, you need to use your critical thinking skills to evaluate their usefulness. Use the following checklist to gauge the effectiveness of your statistics.

- ☐ Are the statistics representative of what I claim they measure?
- ☐ Am I being totally honest in my use of these statistics?
- ☐ Have I obtained my statistics from a reliable source that has no vested interest in the figures?
- ☐ Have I interpreted the statistics correctly?
- ☐ Have I used statistics sparingly?
- ☐ Have I explained my statistics creatively?
- ☐ Have I rounded off my statistics to facilitate understanding?
- ☐ Have I used a visual aid to increase the memorability of my statistics?
- ☐ Have I provided context for the statistics?
- ☐ Have I used statistics to clarify and enlighten rather than confound and confuse?
- ☐ Are the statistics I used complete and current?

GAME PLAN

Choosing Speech Support

- ☐ I have chosen support that will help me communicate my ideas more clearly and creatively.
- ☐ I have found examples that are useful and representative of my topic.
- ☐ I have used statistics that are relevant, reliable, and solid.
- ☐ I have incorporated testimonials from qualified and unbiased sources.
- ☐ My audience will find each piece of support relevant and appropriate.
- ☐ Each piece of support I have used increases the memorability of my speech.
- ☐ I am offering receivers a sufficient variety of supporting materials.

section
8.6

Use Testimony

When speakers use the opinions of others to reinforce claims they are making, they are using **testimony**. Though, of course, your own opinions do count, you will find that audiences, in general, are more influenced when you supplement your personal opinions with an expert opinion.

8.6a Expert Testimony

Expert testimony is provided by sources recognized as authorities on your topic; when you cite an expert and establish his or her reputation, you enhance your credibility and that of your speech as well. One student used expert testimony to try to convince her receivers that campus fraternities should be abolished:

> John Foubert is the founder of *One in Four,* a private nonprofit rape prevention center with 15 chapters on college campuses. He is also the author of *The Men's and Women's Programs: Ending Rape Through Peer Education,* as well as a researcher on the subject. In a 2013 report about "rape-bait," for CNN, Foubert reported the following: "Guys who joined a fraternity committed three times as many sexual assaults as those who didn't join. It is reasonable to believe that fraternities turn men into guys more likely to rape." Foubert believes that what should worry us is the culture of male peer support in fraternities that permits bad attitudes to escalate, inciting violence against women.[13]

Because the student's topic was controversial, and the audience may have been hesitant to accept her stance, relying on an expert on the subject makes sense. Speakers integrate expert testimony into their speeches by using a source's direct quotations or by paraphrasing the source's words. Notice how in the preceding example the student used both when speaking of Foubert's findings.

Supporting materials are evaluated twice: initially by the speaker, and subsequently by receivers. Speakers and receivers who are well trained to think critically are able to spot the strengths and the weaknesses in the messages they deliver to others and that others deliver to them. Critical thinkers assess the credibility of the speaker's statements and the validity of the evidence supplied by the speaker.

8.6b Peer or Lay Testimony

In contrast to expert testimony, **peer** or **lay testimony** comes from people who are not necessarily recognized authorities, but "ordinary people" who have firsthand experience with the subject. Peer or lay testimony provides audience members with greater personal insight; such a speaker shares the feelings, the reactions, and the knowledge of individuals who have "been there."

In a speech called “Homeless Children: A National Crisis,” the speaker used the testimony of Sherry, a homeless girl who had a written a poem about her experiences. By asking the audience to listen to Sherry’s own words, the speaker was able to convey the girl’s innermost feelings to the audience.

I Want to Live in a House

I saw them at their house today.
They had new coats and mittens.
I don’t have a house like that,
I don’t have a coat or mittens.
Things will change; Mommy said they will
As she buttoned my cotton blouse.
I sure hope it’s true, you know,
’Cause I really want to live in a house![14]

What determines whether you paraphrase an opinion or quote it directly? You should paraphrase testimony—that is, restate it in your own words—if doing so would increase audience members’ understanding of or response to it. If the quotation is not too long or too difficult for audience members to comprehend and if you believe it has sufficient force and clarity the way it is, a direct quotation is generally preferred.

8.6c Assess the Power of Your Testimony

Testimony works because it lets you borrow someone else’s credibility. In effect, testimony enables you to associate your ideas with the knowledge, experience, qualifications, and reputation of another. It will do you no good to associate yourself with someone who is not an authority on your topic, is not highly regarded by others, or does not have firsthand experience with your subject. Use the following checklist to gauge the effectiveness of the testimony you cite.

- ☐ Have I clearly identified the source of the testimony?
- ☐ Is the source I cite recognizable, objective, and credible?
- ☐ Is the testimony I am using absolutely relevant to my presentation?
- ☐ Have I quoted or paraphrased the source accurately and used his or her words in proper context?
- ☐ Have I used verbatim quotations whenever possible?
- ☐ Have I used lay or peer testimony to enhance the audience’s ability to identify with my topic?
- ☐ Did I use the most up-to-date testimony available?
- ☐ Have I stressed the source’s qualifications so audience members will not have to strain to find his or her statement credible?

section

8.7 Citing Sources in Your Speech

It's one thing to find support, another to integrate it into your speech, and a third to cite it correctly when giving your speech and in your bibliography. Keep in mind that your audience members will have access only to the sources you identify orally; typically listeners do not see the bibliography you may have to submit to your instructor. Thus, to enhance your credibility, you need to tell audience members where you got your information and what makes its credible. This requires citing your sources, that is, sharing with receivers the name and author of a book, article, newspaper, or Web document; explaining what makes the author a qualified source; and revealing the date the material was published or posted. The goal is to seamlessly integrate such citations into your speech (see Table 8.2).

The following excerpt from a speech fulfills requirements for oral citation:

> **Oral Citation:** The website of the United Network for Organ Sharing, unos.org, reports as of this morning, 120,925 Americans are waiting for healthy organs, but only about 15 percent of these people can expect to receive the organs they need.
>
> **Bibliographic Citation:** "Transplant Trends." United Network for Organ Sharing. http://www.unos.org/ (accessed December 8, 2013).

The speaker gave the name of the organization and its Web address, adding the needed credibility to the statistics she was offering. Notice how in her remarks she also established the information's timeliness.

In another speech given before the National Association of Broadcasters, its president, Gordon Smith, included a reference to a source, saying,

> **Oral Citation:** A recent Wall Street Journal article had the headline: "Don't Look Now: A Car That Tweets."[15]
>
> **Bibliographic Citation:** Ramsey, Mike. "Don't Look Now: A Car That Tweets." *New York Times,* February 10, 2012. http://www.wsj.com/articles/SB10001424052970203824904577213041944082370.

Although his audience might have been better served if he had given the date of the article and its author when citing it, it isn't always necessary for you to include the exact date in your presentation, but it should appear in your bibliography as a complete citation. Written citations contain more detail.

Use the following checklist for citing oral sources:

- ☐ Did I share the name of the author or origin of the source?
- ☐ Did I include the title or description of the source?
- ☐ Did I set the source in context by providing a date?
- ☐ Did I establish any relevant credentials or affiliations of the source?
- ☐ Did I establish the source's credibility?
- ☐ Did I cite the source without interrupting the flow of my presentation?
- ☐ Could an audience member locate the source I cited if they wanted to?

TABLE 8.2 ORAL CITATIONS

SOURCE CITED	INFORMATION TO SHARE
Book	The book's title, author, some information on the author's qualifications, and the publication date
Journal or magazine article	The name of the journal or magazine, the article title, the author's qualifications, the publication date
Newspaper	The name of the newspaper, the article title, the author of the article and his or her qualifications, the date the article appeared
Government document	Agency name or branch of government that produced the document, publication name, and date
Brochure/pamphlet	Title, publisher, date of publication
Weblog	Blog site, name of blogger, qualifications, date of posting
Interview conducted by you	Cite yourself as the interviewer, identify the person interviewed, and the date and place of the interview

Exercises

SUPPORT

You can apply what you have learned by participating in the following activities:

1. Finding Facts, Statistics, and Examples

Locate an interesting fact, statistic, and example to use in a speech on one of the following subjects. Explain the value of each and properly identify its source:

- Recycling
- Benefits and Risks of Vaccinations
- Introverts

2. Reliable Sources

Identify a reliable source whose testimony you could cite in a speech on each of the topics listed in the preceding exercise.

3. Assess the Speech: Identifying Support

Read or view a speech given by the current president of the United States. The president's inaugural or State of the Union addresses should be readily available online. Identify the kinds of support the president used to support the goals of the speech.

4. Approach the Speaker's Stand

Using the right support and citing sources appropriately takes practice:

1. Select a topic that concerns or interests you.
2. Formulate a statement related to the topic that you are prepared to support. Your statement should begin "I think that . . ." or "I believe that . . ."
3. Locate two types of support from two different research sources that you can use to make your point.
4. Develop a 60-second presentation.

Once you select your issue, ask yourself these questions:

- Have I selected an issue that I can support?
- What types of support should I use?
- Does each potential piece of support back up my claim?
- How can I use other forms of support to further enhance the impact of my remarks?

RECAP AND REVIEW

1. **Use and assess the effectiveness of examples.** When examples are useful and representative they help you develop ideas. Although short examples support specific points, lengthier narrative examples deeply influence receivers. Hypothetical examples encourage audience members to imagine what it would be like to face the situation described.
2. **Use and assess the effectiveness of explanations and descriptions.** Explanations help clarify content. Descriptions rely on sensory appeals to engage receivers.
3. **Use and assess the effectiveness of facts and definitions.** Facts are the verifiable information in your speech. Definitions are needed when audience members are unfamiliar with terms used or might have different associations for them.
4. **Use and assess the effectiveness of analogies.** Analogies rely on comparison to enhance understanding. When used appropriately, they help make the unfamiliar more familiar.
5. **Use and assess the effectiveness of statistics.** If fully explained, statistics clarify and strengthen ideas and claims.
6. **Use and assess the effectiveness of testimony.** Use both expert and lay opinion to borrow credibility and supplement your use of personal opinion.
7. **Properly cite support in a speech.** Orally identify sources in your speech and provide complete information in your bibliography. Doing this correctly enhances both your and the source's credibility.

KEY TERMS

PART FOUR

Organize and Outline

© iStockphoto.com/ThomasVogel

9

Organizing Your Speech

UPON COMPLETING THIS CHAPTER'S TRAINING, YOU WILL BE ABLE TO

1. Explain why organization matters
2. Explain the principle of redundancy and why it is useful in a speech
3. Identify linear organization and list some examples of this format
4. Identify configural organization and list examples of this format
5. Discuss how culture influences organizational preference

Contents

Organization empowers a speech. In fact, organization and content are equal partners in speech development. If a speech is poorly organized, even if the information you present is first rate, audience comprehension suffers.[1]

Can you, for example, imagine trying to follow a ballet troupe, a theatrical ensemble, or a sports team if the performers or players involved had no idea where they were supposed to be positioned or what they were supposed to do? The dancers would bump into one another. The actors would stumble about the stage. The athletes would be in disarray. What is more, there would be no pattern for those watching to follow, so they wouldn't know where to look to make sense of the performance or game they were attending. The ability to organize a game's plays is critical for most sporting events. The same principle holds true for public speakers and audiences. The ability to organize ideas into one or more effective patterns is critical for effective speechmaking.[2]

Unless audience members are able to follow and understand your speech, they might as well not listen to it. Research supports what we know intuitively—we learn more from a speech that is well organized.[3] For this reason alone, it is important to learn to craft a speech that doesn't ramble, but instead is coherent and balanced.

In addition, developing an understanding of organizational patterns has advantages, making it easier for you—both as a speaker and a listener—to give and follow lectures, process information, weigh persuasive appeals, and function as a critical, effective communicator.

COACHING TIP

"Organize, don't agonize."

—Nancy Pelosi

Never let your ideas wander about aimlessly. Give them order. Strategize when selecting an organizational pattern. Choose the organizational strategy that will work best for your speech's purpose, content, and audience. Select wisely, and your main and supporting points will flow, virtually effortlessly, from the strategy.

section

9.1 Understand Speech Organization

Creating a speech has been compared to writing an essay. Yet, in some ways creating a speech and an essay are very different experiences (see Table 9.1). Whereas audience members usually listen to a speaker deliver a speech only once, readers are able to revisit written passages in their search for meaning. In order to facilitate comprehension of a spoken message, speakers normally use shorter sentences than do writers, and they also repeat the main ideas of their work more frequently than writers. Writers may use clearly visible headings and subheadings. When presenting, however, we must find ways to let the organization of our speech reveal itself naturally to the members of our audience.

Just like an essay, a speech benefits from having a clear beginning, middle, and end. In writing a speech, think of the often-repeated adage: "Tell them what you are going to tell them. Tell them. Tell them what you told them." We begin by introducing the topic, offering a preview of what's to come. This done, we go on to discuss the topic, developing it fully. Then we wrap up with a concluding statement that summarizes the main points and ties the presentation together. This formula acknowledges the principle of *redundancy*—the use of repetition to reduce the uncertainty of receivers—and is especially important because not every audience member is adept at listening skillfully. By building a certain amount of repetition into a speech, a speaker improves receiver comprehension.

TABLE 9.1 THE SPEECH VERSUS THE ESSAY

SPEECH	ESSAY
Is heard once	May be read many times
Contains short sentences	Contains complex sentences
Contains repetition	Contains less repetition
Organization revealed naturally	Organization revealed by heads and subheads

Use Linear Organizational Formats

section
9.2

Traditional organizational formats use a linear logic that is representative of the way many North American speakers organize their thoughts. A speech has a **linear format** if its main points develop and relate directly to the thesis or topic sentence that comes early in the presentation. When exhibiting linear logic, a speaker develops ideas step-by-step, relying on facts and data to support each main point. Then the speaker links each main point to other main ideas via a series of bridges or transitions.

Members of low-context cultures, such as the United States, often use a linear format. They characteristically relay information explicitly. Why? Because they expect receivers will have difficulty understanding what is not said overtly. Rather than rely primarily on emotional appeals and stories to make their points, they offer relevant supporting facts—that is, hard evidence and proof in defense of positions taken.

We will look at five traditional or linear approaches to ordering material: (1) chronological order; (2) spatial order; (3) cause-and-effect order; (4) problem–solution order; and (5) topical order (see Table 9.2).

TABLE 9.2 LINEAR FORMATS

FORMAT	PURPOSE	ESPECIALLY USEFUL IN
Chronological	To explain to audience members the order in which events happened; to describe a series of sequential developments	Informative speaking
Spatial	To describe the physical arrangement of objects in space	Informative speaking
Cause and Effect	To categorize a topic and relevant materials into those related to the causes and consequences of a problem	Informative and persuasive speaking
Problem–Solution	To identify a significant problem that needs a resolution and then a solution to alleviate the problem; to demonstrate a problem's nature and significance, then solution(s)	Persuasive speaking
Topical	To highlight the natural divisions of a topic; to identify the natural clusters or subtopics of a speech	Informative, persuasive, and special-occasion speaking

9.2a Time Order: It's Chronological

When you use time or **chronological order** to organize the body of your speech, you explain to your audience members the order in which events happened. For example, you may deal with your topic by taking an historical approach.

Purpose: To inform the audience about the evolution of marijuana laws

Thesis: Laws about marijuana have changed dramatically since the early 1900s.

I. Marijuana was a common ingredient in 19th-century medicines.

II. The government began to regulate marijuana starting around 1910.

III. In 1996, California legalized medical marijuana.

IV. In 2012, Colorado became the first state to legalize recreational marijuana use.

Chronological organization can move from the past forward to the present.

A time pattern can also be used in a subsection of a speech where the overarching organization is of another style. For example, a speaker delivering a speech on the problem of institutionalizing the mentally ill might first chronologically explain how mental institutions developed in this country. Such an organizational tactic would offer receivers a context against which to process those points the speaker will explore during the remainder of the presentation.

Time warp. A time pattern can be either earliest to latest or vice versa in order to convey a point.

Especially useful in informative speaking, a chronological structure helps when you organize your main points from earliest to latest or vice versa in order to illustrate a particular progression of thought, as in the following examples.

Purpose: To inform the audience about the development of the Internet

Thesis: The Internet has changed dramatically since its invention.

I. More than 3 billion people have access to the Internet today.

II. The World Wide Web was invented in 1989 and made the Internet accessible to nonexperts.

III. The first computer networks were developed in the late 1960s and early 1970s.

Some chronological organizations move from the present backward to the past.

Purpose: To inform the audience about the three stages of labor and childbirth

Thesis: There are three stages of labor.

I. The first stage of labor has two phases.
   A. Early labor is the first phase, which begins with very mild contractions.
   B. Active labor is the second phase, when contractions become more intense.

II. Stage two is birth.

III. Stage three is the delivery of the placenta.

Chronological organization can be used to describe the sequence of any event.

9.2b Spatial Order: It's Directional

If you can observe your subject in space, it may be a candidate for **spatial order**. For example, we can discuss the planets in order of their proximity to the sun or describe the street plan of Washington, D.C. In spatial order, main points proceed from top to bottom, left to right, front to back, north to south, and so forth—or vice versa. Here is an example of how a speaker used a spatial pattern in talking about the White House.

Purpose: To inform the audience about the layout of the White House

Central idea: The White House includes 67,000 square feet of offices, reception and meeting rooms, and living space in three distinct areas

In this example, main points move from east to west.

I. The East Wing houses the offices of the First Lady and the social secretary.

II. The Residence is the site of public events like state dinners and receptions and is the home of the first family.

III. The West Wing contains the Oval Office and the offices of other key executive staff.

Like chronological order, spatial order is used most frequently in informative speeches.

9.2c Cause-and-Effect Order: It's Relational

Cause-and-effect order requires you to categorize your materials into those related to the causes of a problem and those related to its effects. You then decide which aspect to explore first.

Cause-and-effect order and effect-and-cause order are quite versatile. They are used in both informative and persuasive speeches. Here's an example from a speech about drunk driving:

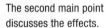

The first main point focuses on causes.

The second main point discusses the effects.

I. In 2013, more than 28 million people admitted to having driven drunk.

II. In 2014, nearly 10,000 people were killed by drunk drivers.

© iStockphoto.com/imaginima

Context. With a cause-and-effect argument, you can establish why something happens so you can talk about changing it.

9.2d Problem–Solution Order: It's Workable

Speakers seeking to influence often select a **problem–solution order** whereby the speaker first reveals a significant problem that needs a resolution and then offers a solution to alleviate the problem. Notice in the following example how the emphasis is on how the problem can best be resolved.

Purpose: To convince my audience that national health insurance can help solve our health care problems

Thesis: National health insurance will solve many of the problems caused by rising health care costs.

I. Rising health care costs have resulted in an uninsured class of people. ← The problem

II. Implementing national health insurance will solve this problem. ← The solution

When using a problem–solution format, a speaker may discuss the advantages of the solution as well. When this occurs, the speaker's organization includes a third main point: the advantages of adopting the solution. The next example also presents a pragmatic solution to a problem.

Purpose: To convince my audience that we need to revise the reporting of poverty statistics

Thesis: We should act now to solve the problem caused by the way poverty statistics are currently reported.

I. The poverty level is currently understated in order to keep people off welfare rolls. ← The problem
   A. The income level defined as poverty for families of four is absurdly low.
   B. Poverty thresholds for single-parent families are even more outrageous.

II. Minimally acceptable income levels must be raised. ← The solution
   A. Government levels of aid must be raised for families.
   B. Additional help must be given for single parents.

III. These increases will solve some of the problems of the poor. ← The advantages of adopting the solution
   A. They will make life easier for families.
   B. Additional aid to single parents will help them help themselves and their children.

Problem–solution order is most frequently employed in persuasive presentations.

9.2e Topical Order: It's Part of the Whole

When your speech does not fit into any of the patterns just described, you may arrange your material into a series of appropriate topics. This is **topical order**. For example, you use a topical order to speak about the pros and cons of a particular issue.

Purpose: To inform audience members of the advantages and disadvantages of a vegetarian diet

Central idea: Eliminating meat from your diet presents both advantages and disadvantages.

A topical organization clusters ideas into a series of appropriate topics.

I. There are two advantages of a vegetarian diet.
   A. It does not support inhumane factory farming or require the death of any animal.
   B. A vegetarian diet is linked to better overall health.

II. There are two disadvantages to a vegetarian diet.
   A. Some people are unable to get the nutrients they need without eating meat.
   B. It can be difficult to eat out at restaurants or at friends' homes and maintain the diet.

Other examples of topical order also may include categorical arrangements that look at the social, political, and economic factors that contribute to a problem, the perceptions of upper-class, middle-class, and lower-class people on an issue, or any other divisional structure that breaks the material into units. When employing topical order, you may find that you can intermingle time, spatial, cause-and-effect, or problem–solution order within the topical order. In addition, although the subdivisions of a topical-ordered speech typically correspond to different aspects of the topic, subdivisions may also serve as a *mnemonic* (a device that is used to trigger memory). For example, in a speech on speechwriting, one speaker used the word *BRIEF* as follows to organize the body of the presentation:

Brainstorm ideas

Research ideas

Interpret ideas

Energize ideas

Finalize ideas

Because it lends itself to almost any subject, topical organization is a very popular organizational format.

Use Configural Formats

section
9.3

According to most intercultural communication theorists, English is primarily a "speaker-responsible" language, but other languages, including Japanese, Chinese, and Arabic, are more "listener responsible." Native users of speaker-responsible languages typically believe it is up to the speaker to be explicit about what he or she wants the listener to know. In contrast, native speakers of listener-responsible languages typically believe that speakers need indicate only indirectly what they are speaking about. They believe it is up to the listener, and not the speaker, to construct the speech's meaning.[4]

Speech strategies organized by linear logic present support and evidence in a very direct, speaker-responsible way. In contrast, **configural formats** are less explicit in offering hard evidence in defense of a position.

Instead of previewing and discussing main points one a time, configural thinkers approach their subject from a variety of perspectives, using examples and stories to carry the crux of their message. Because configural speakers believe the explicit stating of a message is unnecessary, those who use this style expect receivers to understand more of the subtleties in their presentation. Instead of directly stating the conclusion, the speakers lead receivers to their goal indirectly and by implication.

Think it out. What types of speeches would work best with configural formats, and what types should follow more traditional formats?

Communication scholars identify three main systems of configural organization.

1. First is the **deferred-thesis pattern**, in which the main points of a speech gradually build up to the speaker's thesis, which the speaker does not reveal until the speech is nearly over.
2. Second is the **web pattern**, in which threads of thought refer back to the speaker's central purpose; although to Western ears the speaker may seem to be off topic at points, to receivers in other cultures the tangents the speaker explores are connected to the speaker's topic and make it more meaningful.
3. Third is the **narrative pattern**, in which the speaker tells a story or series of stories without stating a thesis or developing it with main points. When using this pattern, the speaker may only "discover" the main point via a series of illustrations and parables.[5]

Speakers who use configural patterns devise a series of "stepping stones" that circle their topic; they do not hit it head on.

The following speech outline is organized configurally. Because the speaker does not explicitly state the speech's main points, the audience will need to participate actively in interpreting what the speaker only implies.

Purpose: To persuade my audience that biological weapons research is a problem

In a configural organization, the speaker implies, rather than explicitly states, the main points.

I. A hypothetical worker, Alan, who works in a lab funded by the defense department, inadvertently infects himself with the biological weapon he is studying.

II. Alan suffers the kind of death that our enemies would suffer were biological weapons used during episodes of warfare.

III. Alan's family suffers with him.

IV. Today, members of Alan's family address Congress, asking, "How can America be involved in something like this?"

According to Richard Nisbett, there is a *geography of thought* when it comes to both the development of a worldview and the frameworks of thinking that support it.[6] In the West, speakers summarize and offer a conclusion. In the East, speakers tend to cycle back into the same topic from different directions.[7] The following example—offered by a professor—addresses the difference in approach:

> I was surprised when one of my students who had been a teacher in China before coming here told me that she didn't understand the requirements of essay structure. I told her to write a thesis statement and then prove its three points in the following paragraphs. She told me if she wrote this way in China she would be considered stupid. "In China," she said, "essays were written in a more circular fashion moving associated ideas closer and closer to the center."[8]

While we need to be cautious about overgeneralizing—especially because people from one culture who spend time in another culture tend to adjust their thinking styles—when speaking to an audience composed of people from diverse cultures, speakers may consider adjusting their organizational preferences.

Keep this in mind when in the next chapter we turn our attention to outlining.

GAME PLAN

Organizing Your Speech

- ☐ I have reviewed all of my options for organization, and I understand their similarities and differences.
- ☐ I have chosen an organizational format that best suits my topic and goal.
- ☐ I have taken culture into account and used the organizational format that best conveys my message while adhering to speaker-responsible and/or listener-responsible strategies.
- ☐ I have considered my audience and plan to present my topic in a way that is accessible to them.

Exercises

ORGANIZATION

Use the following chapter exercises to think strategically about speech organization.

1. Organization Matters

Create a PowerPoint storyboard of a recent event or sports game at your college. Be sure to take photos of the performers or players warming up, key moments, the crowd reacting, and the performers walking off the stage or field at the end. Post the photos in random order. Ask a student who has not yet taken a course in public speaking to tell you a story about the event or game based on your PowerPoint presentation. Next, rearrange the photos in the correct sequence. Have the student describe how his or her understanding of how the event changed when the sequence of events was properly ordered.

2. Pick a Pattern

A. Take a speech topic such as "the search for alien life." How could you develop a speech on the subject using chronological, spatial, cause-and-effect, problem–solution, topical order, or any linear format of your choice?

B. Using the same topic, how could you develop a speech on the subject using a configural pattern?

3. Analyze the Speech: Contemplate Cultural Perspectives

According to cultural anthropologist Edward T. Hall, culture guides attention, helping us decide those stimuli to which we will pay attention and those we will ignore.

With this in mind, what steps should a speaker take to ensure that audience members who prefer an organizational pattern other than the one the speaker has chosen pay attention to the right things in the presentation? For example, let's say a speaker from a low-context culture such as the United States were asked to give a speech on how globalization affects the U.S. middle class to an audience composed of economists from Saudi Arabia or Mexico. How might the speaker adapt the speech's organizational format to appeal to members of a high-context culture? In your opinion, does changing the organizational structure also change the speech's content, so that a speaker who makes such adaptations is no longer being true to his or her beliefs? Explain your position.

4. Approach the Speaker's Stand

Select a topic such as organ donation, global warming, U.S. refugee policies, the death penalty, or the European Union. Research your choice, identifying main points for the topic that would be appropriate if you were to use a chronological, spatial, cause-and-effect, problem–solution, topical, or alternative organizational pattern. Consider how each of these organizational formats affects the speech. Then, identify the organizational pattern you believe works best and why.

RECAP AND REVIEW

1. **Explain why organization matters.** When ideas are unorganized, they are disorienting to receivers, making it difficult for them to make sense of your speech.
2. **Explain the principle of redundancy and why it is useful in a speech.** A speech is listened to—usually once. By summarizing main points we reduce the uncertainty of receivers and increase their comprehension.
3. **Identify linear organization and list some examples of this format.** Linear formats are more commonly used in the West to convey information in a direct and straightforward manner. Key linear formats include (1) chronological, (2) spatial, (3) cause and effect, (4) problem–solution, and (5) topical.
4. **Identify configural organization and list examples of this format.** Configural formats are nonlinear and built using subtleties, intuitive thinking, and informal logic that cycles back to the same topic from different directions. Key configural formats include (1) the deferred-thesis pattern, (2) the web pattern, and (3) the narrative pattern.
5. **Discuss how culture influences organizational preference.** Culture attunes us to different ways of thinking and processing information. We adhere to the "geography of thought" in both the development of a worldview and the frameworks of thinking that support it.

KEY TERMS

Cause-and-effect order 168
Chronological order 166
Configural formats 171
Deferred-thesis pattern 172
Linear formats 165
Narrative pattern 172
Problem–solution order 169
Spatial order 167
Topical order 170
Web pattern 172

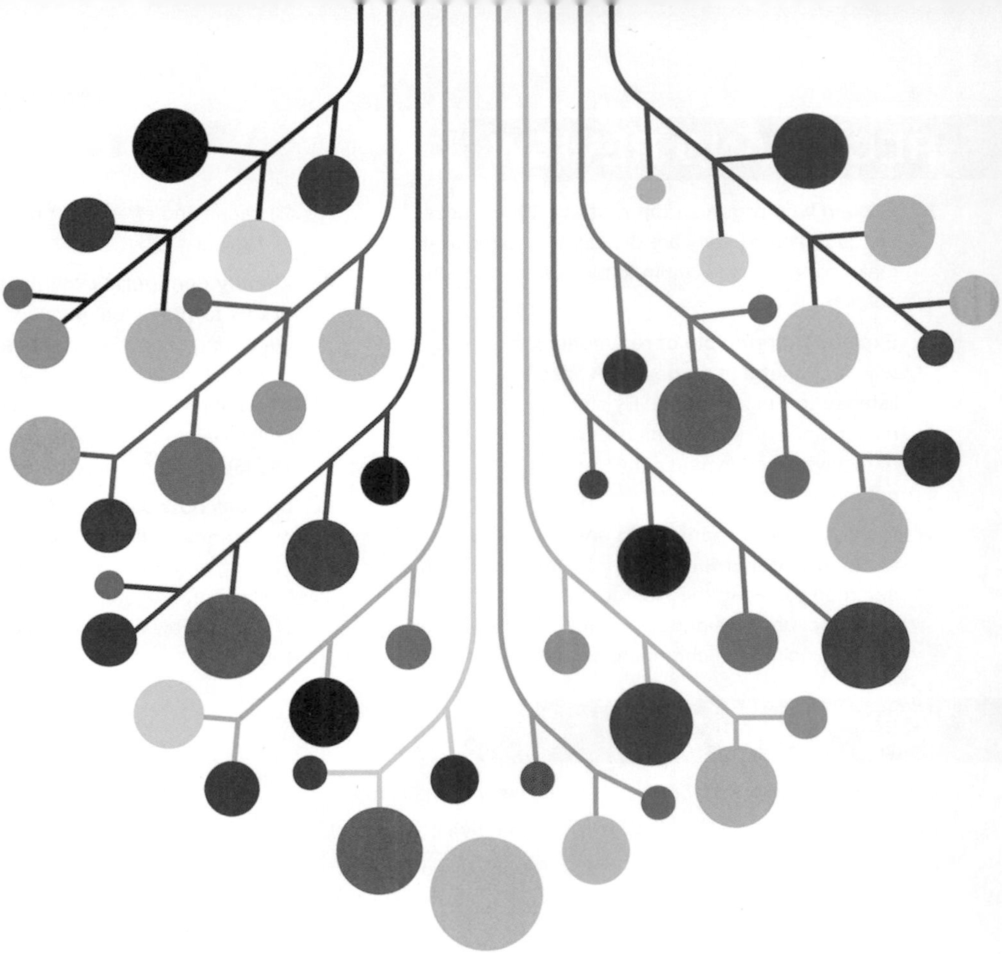

© iStockphoto.com/EnisAksoy

10

Outlining Your Speech

UPON COMPLETING THIS CHAPTER'S TRAINING, YOU WILL BE ABLE TO

1. Identify the parts of an outline
2. Develop a full sentence outline, adhering to appropriate form and structure
3. Prepare an extemporaneous outline or speaker's notes from a formal outline

Once you select the organizational pattern that best supports the subject matter of your speech, you are ready to develop your outline. An outline helps organize and clarify your ideas. It guides you in deciding what material is important and what is not by forcing you to assess the relationships among ideas. When relationships are clear, the audience is better able to process and think critically about your points.

An outline also functions as a road map for your presentation. It helps you visualize how the parts of your speech fit together. An outline ensures that each part of your speech has unity and coherence, and that your main points and subpoints are well developed and supported. Use it to assess if your speech holds together before delivering it to an audience.[1] By using an outline you can

1. Confirm clarity of both the purpose statement and thesis
2. Critique construction of both main and subpoints
3. Identify placement of transitions or idea connectors

In other words, the outline helps to control the development of your material and the flow of your speech.

Contents

COACHING TIP

"The benefit of this kind of outlining is that you discover a story's flaws before you invest a lot of time writing the first draft. . . ."

—George Stephen

Outlining works. Begin the outline as soon as you start preparing your speech. Use it to double-check the underlying logic of your ideas. Fix any flaws you discover. The outline is your visual depiction of your speech. It will show you if the parts fit together well. If something doesn't belong, take it out. If something is missing, add it. Put the effort in up front and your audience will thank you by following your road map, and maintaining their focus and direction.

section 10.1

Create an Outline That Works for You

10.1a Establish Your Main Points

10.1b Support Main Points With Subordinate Points

10.1c Use Coordinate Points

10.1d Exhibit Parallelism

10.1e Label All Parts

As soon as you start working on your presentation, you should begin putting your ideas into outline form. In many ways, the outline resembles a building constructed using a modular design. Instead of working with building blocks, however, you work with idea blocks and structure the outline in stages.

- During the first stage, create a preliminary *working outline* composed of a few words to identify the key points of your speech. You can also create a mind or concept map to visualize the relationship between ideas (see Figure 10.1, from a speech about bees).

FIGURE 10.1
Mind/Concept Map

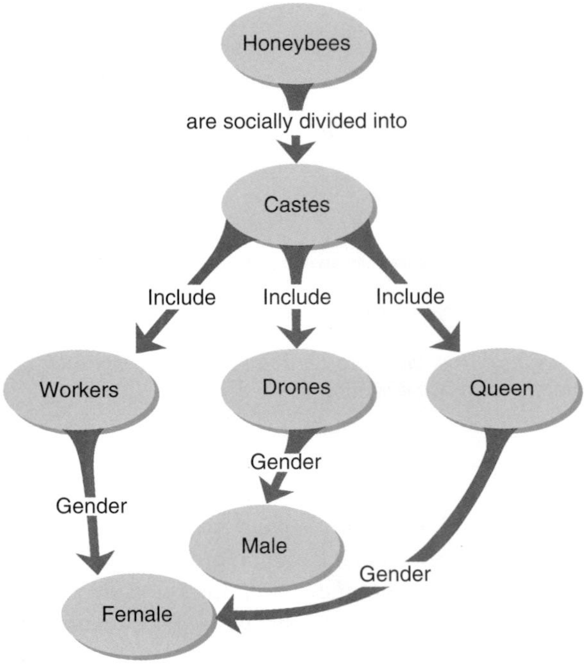

- The *full-sentence outline* is more detailed. Develop this version only after you have researched and fully fleshed out the ideas contained in the working outline.
- Finally, transform your full sentence outline into an extemporaneous outline, or speaker's notes. This becomes the outline you use to guide your delivery of the speech (see Table 10.1).

Let's imagine that you have devised the following preliminary working outline for a speech about affirmative action:

I. Definition

II. Purposes

III. Outcomes

IV. Why under attack

TABLE 10.1 THREE STAGES OF OUTLINE DEVELOPMENT

STAGE	OUTLINE TYPE	DESCRIPTION
One	Preliminary working outline	Words or phrases identifying a speech's points
Two	Full sentence	Elaborates main and subpoints
Three	Extemporaneous	Speaker's notes, used when delivering a speech

Your next task is to conduct your research and flesh out the full-sentence outline. The outline should fulfill the following criteria:

1. It identifies the specific purpose and thesis statement or central idea.
2. It exhibits coordination and consistency.
3. It presents a visualization of the speech, distinguishing between your main points, your speech's subtopics that directly support your thesis, and your subordinate points—those ideas that function as support or amplification for your main ideas or subtopics.
4. It reveals a division of the whole.
5. It exhibits parallelism.
6. It labels as well as indicates transitions between your introduction, the main points of the body, and the conclusion.
7. It identifies the works you consulted.

Though we later discuss and provide examples of these criteria in action, a few merit special attention.

10.1a Establish Your Main Points

The basic structure of an outline begins with its **main points.** Like a skeleton that gives our body shape and purpose, these ideas serve as the framework of the outline that makes a successful speech.

You want your receivers to retain the main ideas of your speech; otherwise, there would be little reason to have an audience listen to you. For example, if you were speaking on the Zika virus, you might structure your outline as one student did with two main ideas.

Purpose: To inform audience members about the fears and questions concerning the Zika virus

I. Fears about Zika are prevalent in society today.

II. Questions about efforts to protect against a Zika pandemic remain unanswered.

© iStockphoto.com/stock_colors

Map it out. Not every speech has to follow one format, but no matter how you deliver it, you should always plan and outline it first.

The ordering of points should flow logically so receivers can follow the presentation easily. In the above example, the speaker chose first to confront existing fears about Zika and then to discuss the questions revolving around the disease's control and potential treatment should it develop into a pandemic. It would have made less sense for the speaker to start with how researchers plan to combat the disease and end with existing fears. However, sometimes the main points of a presentation can be attacked in any order. For example, suppose you were presenting a speech on popular hobbies. Your speech might focus on

I. Hobbies conducted with a group

II. Hobbies conducted alone

No particular reason exists to put main point I before II or vice versa. The order depends only on how you choose to approach the subject.

10.1b Support Main Points With Subordinate Points

Subordinate points, or subpoints, are the foundation on which larger ideas are constructed. Begin the organizational process by arranging your materials into clusters of main and subordinate ideas. As you proceed, identify which evidence supports which ideas, and keep in mind all the kinds of support identified in Chapter 8.

When you take the time to prepare an easy-to-follow structure for your speech, your main points alert receivers to listen for supporting information. Because they are not struggling to give order to a disordered array of information, they are able to focus instead on the thesis of your speech and the support you offer to build your presentation. Since your ideas are carefully laid out, you can focus on establishing a good relationship with audience members, instead of concentrating on what to say next.

The outline you develop will indicate the relative importance of each item included in it. The main points (indicated with Roman numerals I, II, III, and so on) are the most important items you want your audience to remember. Your subpoints (capital letters A, B, C, and so on) are supportive of but less important than the main points. Likewise, sub-subpoints (Arabic numerals 1, 2, 3, and so on) are supportive of but less important than subpoints. Remember to line up the entries in your outline correctly. Locate the main ideas closest to the left margin. The subpoints should begin directly underneath the first letter of each main point. Generally, at least two subpoints must support every main point.

© iStockphoto.com/AnatoliStyf

Rock solid. Even with strong main points, a speech will fall apart without meaningful subpoints and sub-subpoints to support it.

Items that support the subpoints begin directly underneath the first letter of each subpoint. If needed, indicate the supporting materials for the sub-subpoints with lowercase letters (a, b, c, and so on). In this way, the full sentence outline functions as a visual representation of the supportive underpinnings for ideas. In general, there should be at least a 3-to-1 ratio between the total words in your speech and the number of words in your outline.

A full sentence outline using symbols and indentations for a speech on the avian flu might look like the following:

SN 1 Make your main points the most prominent part of the outline by using Roman numerals and aligning them with the left margin of your page.

SN 2 Use capital letters for subpoints and indent them evenly below the first word of each main idea they support.

SN 3 Use Arabic numerals for sub-subpoints and indent them evenly below the subpoints they support.

SN 4 All main points should be of equal importance.

SN 5 Include at least two subpoints for each main point.

Full Sentence Outline

Specific purpose: To inform audience members about the fears and questions concerning the H5N1 avian flu (bird flu)

Central idea: Acknowledging the fears concerning avian flu and understanding the questions regarding protection can help us meet the challenges the disease presents.

I. There is widespread fear concerning the H5N1 avian flu.
   A. Many people fear that H5N1 avian flu is the next pandemic.
      1. There is concern that cases of human infection of H5N1 avian flu have been reported in a number of countries, including China, Cambodia, Turkey, and Iraq, among people who handled infected birds.
      2. There is concern that the H5N1 avian flu virus will mutate spontaneously, giving it greater ability to jump from human to human.
      3. There is concern that travel, especially by air, will accelerate transmission of the disease around the world.
   B. Currently, chances of contracting H5N1 avian flu are small for people who do not have close contact with birds.
      1. Not a single bird in the United States has been found to suffer from avian influenza.
      2. Casual contact with birds will not spread flu because of the species barrier.

II. Many questions remain regarding future efforts to protect against a pandemic strain of avian flu.
   A. Developing a vaccine to attack a pandemic avian flu virus is problematic.
      1. Whether Tamiflu and Relenza will be effective against the pandemic version of the avian flu virus is unclear.
      2. Because scientists do not know what the pandemic flu virus will look like, a vaccine cannot yet be made.
      3. Scientists hope that the H5N1 vaccines now in trials will provide at least some protection in a pandemic.
   B. Developing international cooperation is critical.
      1. We need to increase awareness of the threat.
      2. We need to improve surveillance and diagnosis of the disease in birds.
   C. Developing a biosecurity system is key.
      1. The president signed an executive order adding pandemic influenza to the list of quarantinable diseases.
      2. The N95 mask provides aerosolization protection from the droplets that spread the virus.
      3. Discouraging personal stockpiling, the government is calling for the maintenance of national and regional supplies of vaccine.

10.1c Use Coordinate Points

The best outlines should consist of **coordinate points**. This simply means that all the main points you discuss should be of equal weight or substance. For example, if you were to speak about Mexican customs, you might organize them topically according to social, business, and religious customs as follows:

- **I.** Understanding the social customs of Mexico can improve Mexican–American relations.
- **II.** Understanding the business customs of Mexico can improve Mexican–American relations.
- **III.** Understanding the religious customs of Mexico can improve Mexican–American relations.

The outline reveals that the speaker plans to spend about the same amount of time discussing the three divisions of Mexican customs. What if the speaker were unable to find much material on religious customs? One solution would be to limit the speech to business and social customs. If there were some religious customs that were essentially social in nature, those elements might be subordinated under the social category.

I. Here is where you put your first main point.
   - A. Your first subpoint includes evidence that supports the main point.
     - 1. The first sub-subpoint gives additional information about subpoint A.
     - 2. The second sub-subpoint gives additional information about subpoint A.
   - B. Your second subpoint includes evidence that supports the main point.
     - 1. The first sub-subpoint gives additional information about subpoint B.
     - 2. The second sub-subpoint gives additional information about subpoint B.

10.1d Exhibit Parallelism

A good outline must be devised in such a way that the concepts in it exhibit **parallelism**, that is, words, phrases, or sentences parallel each other or balance with one another, often mirroring each other. This approach also helps the audience to process and retain your speech's points.

Note that every entry is subdivided into two or more points. The entries all rely on the same grammatical pattern and are complete simple sentences. This technique also lets you think through your ideas without writing a complete manuscript.

10.1e Label All Parts

Effective outlines clearly label all parts, which eventually will include the body, which we have focused on in this chapter, together with the introduction, the conclusion, transitional tools (see the next section), and the works cited list. By handling each of the parts of your speech separately, and labeling them clearly, you take the steps necessary to ensure that you

1. Develop an adequate body of material to share
2. Prepare an effective introduction and conclusion
3. Anticipate how you will get from section to section and point to point
4. Highlight the sources (books, magazines, newspapers, government documents, television programs, interviews, and Internet sites) you consulted during the speech preparation process

You thereby improve the chances that you will realize your essential speechmaking objectives.

section 10.2

Make Your Speech Seamless

Audience members who rely on linear logic will expect you to transmit your ideas with clarity and fluidity. They will count on you using transitional tools—transitions, internal previews, and internal summaries—as you move from one idea to the next to create a sense of coherence and unity.

10.2a Use Transitions

Moving from one main point to the next is very much like getting from one side of a river to the other. In the world, a bridge serves that purpose very nicely. In public speaking, **transitions** work as bridges from idea to idea. A transition also serves as the glue that binds your ideas into a completed presentation rather than an array of unrelated concepts.

As you work with transitions, remember that they fall into one of the four Cs:

- **Chronological transitions** help the listener understand the time relationship between the first main point and the one that follows. Words and phrases such as *before, after, later, at the same time, while,* and *finally* show what is happening in time order.
- **Contrasting transitions** include terms such as *but, on the one hand/on the other hand, in contrast,* and *in spite of.* These words show how the idea that follows differs from the ones that precede it.
- **Causal transitions** are words like *because, therefore,* and *consequently;* they help show the cause-and-effect relationships between the ideas.
- **Complementary transitions** help the speaker add one idea to the next. *Also, next, in addition to,* and *likewise* are examples.

See Table 10.2 for some examples of transitions in action.

You also may use more than words to bridge ideas. Visuals, for example, can help you transition, as can physical movement. Walking from one side of the podium to the other as you move to the next main point can serve to show your audience that you are literally changing direction from one idea to the next in your presentation.

TABLE 10.2 TRANSITIONS

TYPE	EXAMPLES
CHRONOLOGICAL	After we completed the first phase of the project . . . At the same time that we were exploring cultural values . . .
CONTRASTING	Although the money was available to build the senior center . . . On the contrary, we should also consider . . .
CAUSAL	As a result of the ways the members of different cultures define what is "real," "good," and "correct," their interpretations of . . . Because the maintenance needed on the bridge was ignored . . .
COMPLEMENTARY	Likewise, our experiment was designed to demonstrate that . . . It is just as important to examine the ways in which animals . . .

10.2b Use Internal Previews

An **internal preview** also helps hold your speech together, but is generally longer than a simple transition. It prepares audience members for the information that will follow. Let's examine how previews can work for you

In a presentation on genetic engineering, a speaker told her audience the following:

> We will next consider a technique that allows biologists to transfer a gene from one species to another. It is called recombinant DNA technology.

More than just a transition, this speaker's statement gives the listener a specific indication of what to look for as the speech progresses.

© iStockphoto.com/andresr

Pass the baton. The audience should know when you're transitioning to a new point no matter how you accomplish it.

10.2c Use Internal Summaries

The internal preview precedes the information you are discussing; the **internal summary** follows it. Summaries help speakers clarify or emphasize what they have said. For example, here the speaker provides a mini-conclusion by noting what she just covered before introducing her next point:

> It should now be clear why violent video games can desensitize young people and make them meaner. We next need to turn our attention to what we can do about it.

In this case, the internal summary is combined with an internal preview, creating a bridge to the next section of the speech.

10.2d Use Signposts

Speakers use **signposts** to make receivers aware that they are about to explain something, share an important idea, or let the audience know where they are in the progression of a speech. Signposts are indicated by an array of signaling cues such as

- Numbers ("first," "second," and "third")
- Phrases designed to focus receiver attention ("You'll especially want to keep this in mind" or "Above all else, remember this")
- Phrases that indicate an explanation is forthcoming ("For example" or "To illustrate what I mean")
- Rhetorical questions ("What steps can we take to make things better?" or "Why is this important?")

In addition to facilitating the speaker's movement from idea to idea, signposts serve as a guide for receivers, focusing the spotlight on what the speaker believes is most important. When giving a speech on the challenges posed by violence in schools, a speaker used the following signposts to mark or signal each of the main points in her speech:

I. The first challenge I'll discuss is the one students face.

II. The second challenge I'll discuss is the one teachers face.

III. The last challenge I'll discuss is the one communities face.

Signposts also signal the end of a speech. When a speaker says something like "Finally," or "To sum up," the speaker is signaling the receiver that the speech is about to end. So in addition to moving a speech forward, signposts also draw it to a close.

© iStockphoto.com/_ba_

Read the signs. Help your audience out by signaling important information and guiding them through the speech.

Now it's time to put all of the elements together. The following is an example of one student's outline. As you read it, note the student's use of attention-getting material at the outset, how the introduction provides a preview of the speech, which ideas the student chose to emphasize, the relationship of main points to the central idea, how subordinate ideas are used to support the main ideas, how transitional tools link ideas, and how the conclusion reinforces the speech's purpose and make it memorable.

SAMPLE OUTLINE

Title: Abandonment of the Elderly

Specific purpose: To explain the growing abandonment problem that thousands of our elderly are left to experience

Central idea: Increased family stresses and a lack of government assistance are causing families in the United States and abroad to abandon their older relatives.

Introduction

I. Nearly a half-century ago the late playwright Edward Albee wrote *The Sandbox,* a drama telling the story of a family who bring their grandmother to a playground and dump her in a sandbox.

II. Back then Albee's play was labeled as absurd.

III. Now that this is happening in many countries, it is all too real.

IV. Today, I would like to talk to you about the growing problem of granny-dumping that the elderly face.

SN 1 See Chapter 11 to learn how to introduce your speech.

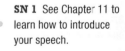

continued

SN 2 Signposts signal the progress of the speech.

SN 3 Transitions bridge one idea to the next.

continued

(Transition: Let's begin by examining the story of one elderly person.)

I. Thousands of families in the U.S. are abandoning aging parents.
   A. John Kingery, 82, was abandoned outside a men's room in Post Falls, Idaho.
      1. His clothes were stripped of their labels.
      2. An Alzheimer's sufferer, Kingery was not able to remember his name.
   B. Thousands of elderly Americans face similar abandonment situations, often being left in hospitals.
      1. The American College of Emergency Physicians estimates that 70,000 people are abandoned each year in hospital emergency rooms.
      2. Most of the families who abandon relatives do so because they cannot pay for the necessary care.

(Transition: This is not only an American problem. In South Korea, China, and India the elderly face a similarly uncertain future.)

II. In South Korea, the breaching of the Confucian social contract has left many elderly people to fend for themselves.
   A. Denied welfare, thousands of South Koreans age 65 and over commit suicide.
      1. One 78-year-old widow staged her death as a final act of public protest against a society she said had abandoned her by drinking pesticide in front of her city hall.
      2. South Koreans are denied welfare because their children are capable of supporting them.
   B. Thousands of older Chinese face equally horrific fates.
      1. Chinese parents invest heavily in their children's education thinking the children will repay the debt to them later in life.
      2. The children do not live up to their responsibilities.
      3. Elderly parents find themselves with no financial reserves.
   C. The elderly in India are also abandoned.
      1. Every year, thousands of grown Indian children abandon their parents.
      2. With society no longer parent-oriented, the elderly in India are left to fend for themselves.

(Transition: Why are family members and governments not living up to their responsibilities?)

III. Responsibilities are overwhelming those here and abroad who in the past would have cared for elderly relatives.
   A. The social fabric of societies is fraying.
   B. Governments have not responded to the erosion of the family structure.
   C. Caregivers suffer physical and mental stress.
      1. Exhausted caregivers become susceptible to high blood pressure and strokes.
      2. Caregivers suffer from depression.
      3. Caregivers experience guilt.

(Transition: So much for the reality of granny-dumping what about the future?)

IV. There are a number of ways to ensure granny-dumping ends.
   A. Families can do more.
      1. They can avoid placing all of the responsibilities on one person.
      2. Relatives can help out with the never-ending stack of paperwork required by government agencies.
   B. Governments can do more.
      1. Programs need to be added so that elderly parents can be cared for outside the home at least part of the time.
         a. This would provide variety for the elderly parents.
         b. Such programs would also give a much-needed rest to the family so they could avoid burnout.
      2. Suicide prevention centers need to be established.
         a. The government needs to protect its people.
         b. The elderly need to feel there is hope.
      3. A holistic approach to elder care needs to be adopted.

Conclusion

I. Though Albee's *The Sandbox* was labeled as an example of absurdism some fifty years ago, granny-dumping has become an all too real and all too tragic way of life for tens of thousands of people around the world.

II. It is time to treat our aging and elderly relatives with the respect and dignity they deserve.

SN 3 See Chapter 12 for guidance on concluding your speech.

Bibliography

"Abuse Underreported in Many States." *USA Today Magazine,* April 2004, 3.

Albee, Edward. *The Sandbox.* New York: New American Library, 1961.

Boaz, Rachel. "Why Do Some Caregivers of Frail Elderly Quit?" *Healthcare Financing Review,* 30 (Winter 1991): 41–47.

Bradsher, Keith. "In China, Families Bet It All on College for Their Children." *New York Times,* February 16, 2013. http://www.nytimes.com/2013/02/17/business/in-china-families-bet -it-all-on-a-child-in-college.html (accessed May 28, 2014).

Butler, Robert. "Health Care for All: A Crisis and Cost Access." *Geriatrics,* 47 (September 1992): 34–48.

"Elder Abuse: A Hidden Tragedy." *Biotech Week,* October 20, 2004, 195.

"Granny Dumping by the Thousands." *New York Times,* March 29, 1992. http://www.nytimes .com/1997/03/09/oinion/grannydumping-byt-the-thousands.html (accessed May 27, 2014).

Krugman, Paul. "Does Getting Old Cost Society Too Much?" *New York Times Magazine,* March 9, 1997, 58–60.

Ley, Rebecca. "Why DO So Many Children Abandon Parents in Their Darkest Hour?" *Daily Mail,* May 28, 2014. http://www.dailymail.co.uk/femail/article-2642006/Why-DO-children-abandon-parents-darkest-hour-Im-stunned-Ian-Botham-didnt-visit-dementia-stricken-father.html (accessed May 29, 2014).

Lin, Judy. "Honor or Abandon: Societies' Treatment of Elderly Intrigues Scholar." *UCLA Today,* January 7, 2010. http://www.today.ucla.edu/portal/ut/jared-diamond -on-aging-150571.aspx (accessed May 27, 2014).

Sang-Hun, Choe. "As Families Change, Korea's Elderly Are Turning to Suicide." *New York Times,* February 17, 2013. http://www.nytimes.com/2013/02/17/world/asia/in-korea-changes-in -society-and-family-dynamics-drive-rise-in-elderly-s (accessed May 28, 2014).

section

10.3 Practice Speaking With Your Outline

10.3a Prepare an Extemporaneous Outline

Once you have researched your topic, identified your supporting materials, and outlined your presentation, it's time to become your own audience and explore the sound and feel of your speech. Three essential ingredients in your first tryout are (1) your speech notes, (2) a clock or wristwatch, and (3) an audio or video recorder so that you can review the exact words you used to express your ideas. Before starting, check the time and turn on the recorder. Then begin speaking. In effect, what you are doing is preparing an oral rough draft of your presentation.

Look for the following elements:

1. Does your presentation consume too much or too little time?
2. Are any ideas not expressed as clearly as you would like?
3. Have you expressed the same thoughts again and again?
4. Is the structure confusing because of missing or inappropriate transitions?
5. Did you remember to include an effective attention getter?
6. Is the information in the body of your presentation too detailed or technical for receivers?
7. Does your conclusion satisfy the psychological requirements you established for it?

If you find that your main attention getter is not as effective as it could be, improve it. If the supporting material under, say, the second main point is confusing, rewrite it. Refine your speech until it is as close as possible to what you want to present. Once you reach that point, you are ready to prepare to give your speech extemporaneously.

GAME PLAN

Creating a Successful Outline

- ☐ I have a good idea of both my purpose for speaking and my topic.
- ☐ To help me brainstorm and organize my ideas, I drew a concept map and/or converted my thoughts into a written working outline.
- ☐ I developed my working outline into a full sentence outline and added subordinate points to support the main ideas.
- ☐ I have included at least two main ideas that I have supported with at least two subordinate points.

- ☐ I have added transitions so my speech flows seamlessly from one idea to the next.
- ☐ I added an introduction and conclusion that preview and review my speech's main ideas.
- ☐ I have revised my outline into speaker's notes that I used to practice my speech out loud.

10.3a Prepare an Extemporaneous Outline

When you deliver an extemporaneous speech, instead of speaking from a script, you typically refer to a set of brief notes, called an **extemporaneous outline** or speaker's notes. This outline reminds you of the key parts of your speech and the support you will use to develop each point. The time to prepare your extemporaneous outline is after you have practiced delivering the speech a few times using a more detailed outline. Only when you are comfortable and familiar with your speech are you ready to rely exclusively on the extemporaneous outline.

Your primary goal when preparing speaker's notes is to keep them as brief as possible so you won't be tempted to read them aloud instead of maintaining eye contact with the members of your audience. It is okay, however, to include a number of delivery cues in the margins of note cards, such as "emphasize" or "hold up the visual aid," much as an actor marks up a script, to help facilitate speaking smoothness.

When creating your speaker's notes, print or type in large block letters and use just a key word or two in place of the complete sentences in your outline to remind you of your main points and subpoints.

FIGURE 10.2
Sample Speaker's Notes

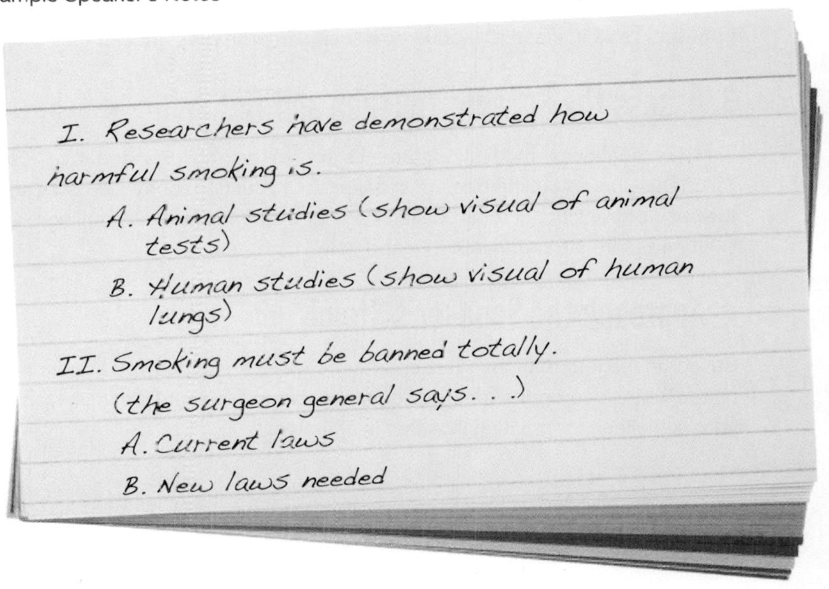

I. Researchers have demonstrated how harmful smoking is.
A. Animal studies (show visual of animal tests)
B. Human studies (show visual of human lungs)
II. Smoking must be banned totally.
(the surgeon general says. . .)
A. Current laws
B. New laws needed

© iStockphoto.com/wdstock

Exercises

OUTLINING

Use the following activities to help you refine your outlining skills.

1. Develop an Outline of a Speech

In addition to helping you prepare your own presentation, a speech outline also helps you prepare to analyze others' presentations. If, as you listen to a speaker's ideas, you can also picture the structure of his or her ideas, you will be better able both to recall the main points of the speech and to determine whether the support the speaker supplies is adequate. After you develop a clear image of the visual framework of a speech, you are also better equipped to critique the speech and ask the speaker relevant questions.

For practice, read a speech of your choice or one assigned by your instructor. Working alone or in a group, develop a sentence outline of the main points of the speech's body. Once your outline is complete, answer these questions:

- Is the body of the speech well organized?
- Does the speech exhibit structural integrity?
- How does making an outline of the speech help you answer the two preceding questions?

2. Take the Transitional Challenge

In your next class, keep track of the transitions, internal previews, and summaries and signposts that your professor uses in class. Describe how their use promotes understanding and learning.

3. Assess the Speech: YouTube and TED

View two speeches: the first, a student's speech on YouTube; and the second, a professional speaker's "TED Talk." Develop an outline of each speaker's introduction, body, and conclusion, comparing and contrasting their use of transitional tools. Based on your examination of the outlines, which speech do you believe exhibited more structural integrity and why?

4. Approach the Speaker's Stand

Based on the information in this chapter as well as research you conduct independently, prepare a podcast or YouTube video on the tenets of outlining, being certain to discuss each of the outline's parts along with your guidelines for creating one that is effective.

RECAP AND REVIEW

1. **Identify the parts of an outline.** An outline is a speech road map. It contains the following parts: the specific purpose, the thesis, the main ideas, the introduction, the body (composed of key main and supporting points), transitions, and the conclusion.
2. **Develop a full-sentence outline, adhering to appropriate form and structure.** Developing an outline helps the speaker organize his or her thoughts into a meaningful framework. An effective outline exhibits (1) coordination and consistency, (2) subordination, (3) a division of the whole, and (4) parallel structure.
3. **Prepare an extemporaneous outline or speaker's notes from a formal outline.** Once an outline is completed, the speaker then develops a shortened version of the outline containing key words to use during the presentation.

KEY TERMS

SAGE edge™

Sharpen your skills with SAGE edge at edge.sagepub.com/gamblepsp2e.

SAGE edge for students provides a personalized approach to help you accomplish your coursework goals in an easy-to-use learning environment.

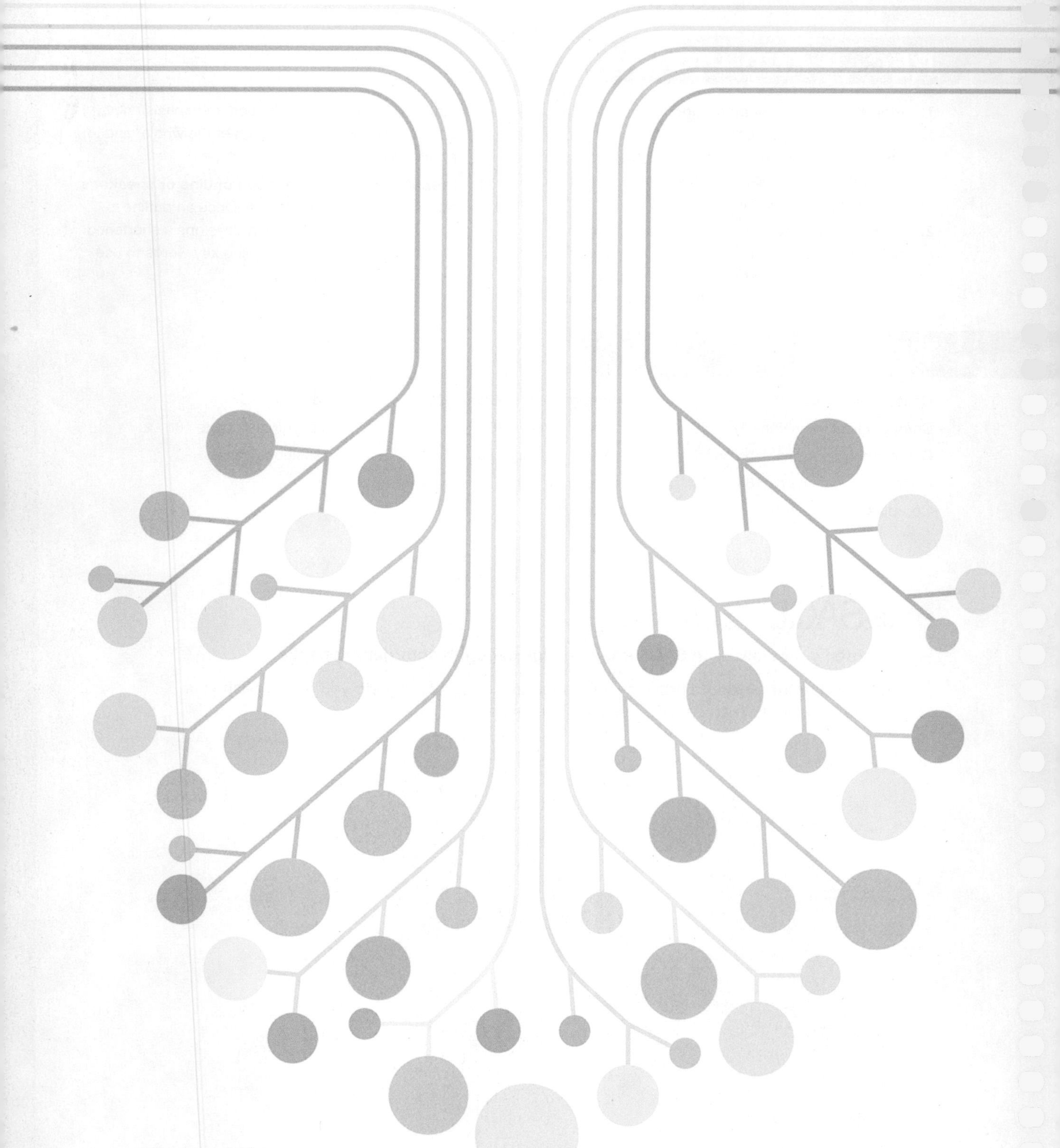

PART FIVE

Present Your Speech

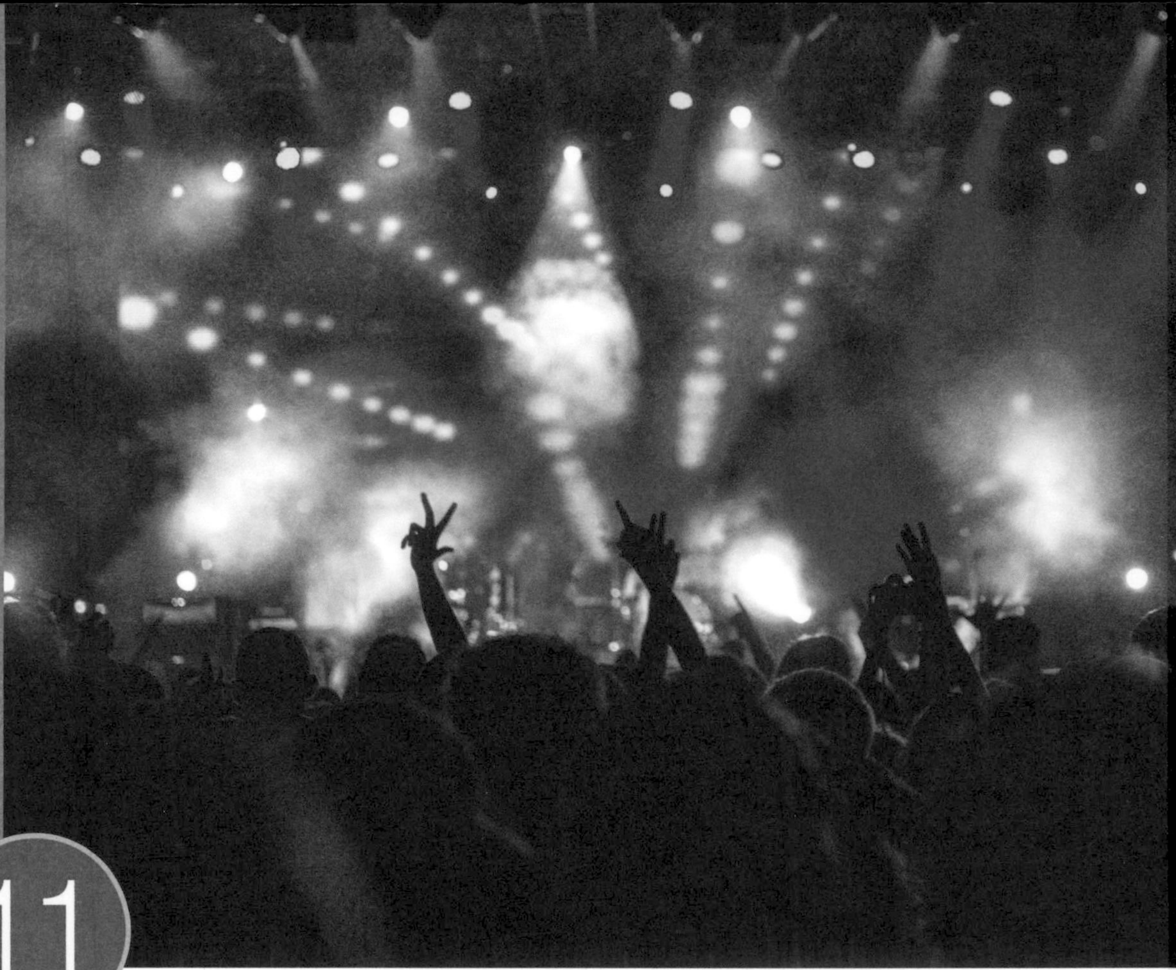

© iStockphoto.com/egon69

11

Introducing Your Speech

UPON COMPLETING THIS CHAPTER'S TRAINING, YOU WILL BE ABLE TO

1. Explain how an introduction affects a speech
2. Describe the purposes served by introductions
3. Identify at least five ways to introduce a speech
4. Use the introduction to capture attention, build credibility, and preview the speech's main ideas
5. Avoid introduction pitfalls

Think about the opening song at a rock concert and its effect on fans. The introduction of your speech works the same way. During the first few moments of a presentation, audience members form their initial impression of both the speaker and the speech. How you begin affects the motivation to listen.

There is wide agreement that opening strong is vital to speechmaking success. According to speech coach Stephen C. Rafe, author of *How to Be Prepared to Speak on Your Feet,* "You have to develop the best possible opening—one that will catch your audience's attention from the first words you speak."[1]

If you succeed in convincing the audience that what you have to share merits their attention, their faces will register appreciation and concentration, their bodies will display interest and concern, and they will sit still and listen to you.

Though it is often the last part of a speech to be written, and usually takes only about 10 percent of total speaking time, an effective introduction captures attention and interest, builds your credibility and goodwill, and orients receivers to the organizational pattern your speech will follow. The better you are at accomplishing these objectives, the more likely it is that your audience will listen.

Contents

section **11.1**

Get Your Audience's Attention

Audience members quickly form impressions of you. Unless your speech attracts attention and builds interest from the outset, you may fail to communicate your point simply because the audience isn't listening. Let's look at several effective attention-getting techniques:

- Startle or shock the audience
- Directly involve the audience
- Arouse curiosity and build suspense
- Use an interesting quote from a relevant source
- Use humor
- Use a story to arouse emotion

11.1a Startle or Shock the Audience

The goal of an introduction is to compel attention. The speaker's initial words make such an impact that it becomes virtually impossible for the thoughts of audience members to stray. Consider the opening of this speech, titled "The Story of the Lost Corpse":

> I've spent my career as a hospital administrator talking about the need for values, but it's not always easy to walk the walk, especially when a crisis erupts and the most expedient response is often the unethical one—I learned that the day we lost a corpse. We had two bodies in the morgue of a hospital I previously led; one was going to be taken to a mortuary for a traditional funeral and the other was going to a university as a donation to science. As it turned out, the wrong body went to the university. . . . My risk manager gave me the news. I asked him what he thought we should do, and he promptly responded, "No harm, no foul. No one knows, so let's leave it that way." . . .
>
> That didn't seem the appropriate response, and it was contrary to the values of the hospital. I told him, "If it was your loved one, you wouldn't have wanted the body to be taking a ride across the state to the university." . . . I decided to inform the family.[2]

Storytime. Opening with a story, whether it's a personal anecdote, about someone's life, or a fictional plot, can grab your audience's attention.

Startling or shocking statements are effective and easy to use. However, you need to weigh carefully how much shock effect is consistent with an honest treatment of the topic. With that in mind, evaluate your attention getter:

- Will audience members perceive it as relevant to the topic?
- Will they follow it without difficulty?
- Will it ignite their interest?

Using an introduction only because of its shock value but failing to connect it to your remarks can lead audience members to become confused or irritated rather than interested. Startling statements must be both true and supportable.

11.1b Involve the Audience

When audience members believe your topic directly affects them, or is something for which they share personal responsibility, they will pay closer attention.[3] Notice how in the very first sentence of a speech on the Prozac family of drugs, the speaker immediately draws you in:

> Congratulations! You have all been invited to play "Choose Your Own Personality," and take a spin at the Prozac wheel. What do you win? A legitimate cure to chronic depression? A chance at one of a dozen annoying and dangerous side effects? Or a whole new personality![4]

11.1c Arouse Curiosity and Build Suspense

Rhetorical questions—questions requiring no overt answer or response—are curiosity arousers and suspense builders. As your listeners mull over how to respond to your question(s), their participation is ensured.

In a speech on the five stages of sleep, one student asked the audience:

> Have you ever bragged that you don't need sleep? Well according to the American Academy of Sleep Medicine people who sleep less than seven hours nightly have a 26 percent greater death rate than those who sleep seven to eight hours a night.[5]

Imagine being in that audience. How would you respond if asked that same question? You'd probably start thinking about how much you sleep, and thus one objective of the introduction would be realized. You would then begin to wonder "How?" and "Why?" The speaker can pave a path for you to travel with him or her with a single question.

HeroImages/Getty Images

Keep them guessing. Building suspense and relying on the natural curiosity of audience members are effective attention getters.

11.1d Quote a Relevant Source

Sometimes a quotation is the most effective technique you can use both to impress your audience and to capture their attention. The words of a well-known figure, a passage from a work of literature, or a familiar phrase may help you communicate information in a more persuasive or comprehensible manner than your words alone could otherwise accomplish.

Delivering a speech at the Israeli Embassy in Washington D.C., president Barack Obama enhanced his credibility by quoting from the Talmud:

> The Talmud teaches that if a person destroys one life, it is as if they've destroyed an entire world, and if a person saves one life, it is as if they've saved an entire world.[6]

The words of ordinary people can also be used when appropriate to arouse greater interest. So can nearly any other quotable source. Speaking about past racial and economic injustices, one student began her speech with these words:

> Have you ever wondered how your world differs from the world your grandparents grew up in? When I was in high school, I asked my great-grandma what it was like growing up when she was young. Her words stung: "When I was your age, the high school was all white. No blacks were allowed to attend it. I played sports on an all white team because no blacks were allowed to play on our teams. I rode in the front of the bus. They could not. They also couldn't drink out of the fountain I drank from. And they couldn't sit next to me in the luncheonette. I never even met a black person until I left our town and went off to college." My grandmother's world lacked diversity. It was colorless rather than color-full.

11.1e Use Humor

When used wisely, appropriately, and with discretion, humor encourages audience attention and portrays the speaker as a likeable, friendly person.[7] In many ways humor acts as a bridge to goodwill.

Humor works best when it is directly related to the content of a speech and not merely "stuck on" for effect or as an afterthought. Addressing Dartmouth's graduating class, Conan O'Brien began with these words:

> Before I begin, I must point out that behind me sits a highly admired president of the United States and decorated war hero while I, a cable television talk show host, have been chosen to stand here and impart wisdom. I pray I never witness a more damning example of what is wrong with America today.[8]

If you think audience members might find the humor you are considering using offensive, don't use it. While humor that pokes fun at the speaker him- or herself or the human condition usually is effective, at no time are racist, sexist, ethnic, and off-color jokes or stories appropriate.

11.1f Arouse Emotion

When integrated effectively into introductions, stories also capture listener attention and hold listener interest. We all enjoy a good story, and if that story is filled with the drama of human interest and is amusing or suspenseful, we enjoy it even more. Of course, the story you use should not only involve the audience, it should also be clearly relevant to the issues you discuss in your speech.

A student used the following story in the introduction of her speech on fraternities to depict a problem in a way her audience would understand.

> Chuck was a sophomore at Alfred University in New York. He was a typical student with goals and dreams, just like yours and mine. He was a student who wanted to be accepted by his peers so badly that he'd do almost anything for his newly found "brothers," including allowing himself to be locked in a car trunk in the middle of winter, and consuming a bottle of wine, a quart of Jack Daniels, and a six pack. This pledge's dreams went the way of alcohol poisoning and overexposure.[9]

In addition, if the story involves you or someone you know personally it can also help establish your experience with the topic. Michael Eisner, former CEO and chairman of the Walt Disney Company, used this story to introduce his speech on what it takes to manage a creative organization:

> Humbling is something at Disney we encourage. It reminds me of an experience one of our young American Disney executives had when he was opening a new office for us in London and wanted to impress his new British secretary. As she entered his office, he was speaking on the telephone and said, "Why, of course, your majesty, think nothing of it. You can call me any time. See you soon. Regards to Prince Philip."
>
> Then he hung up and said, "Oh, hello, Miss Brown. Did you want to see me?"
>
> "I just wanted to tell you, sir," says the secretary, "that the men are here to hook up your telephone."[10]

In addition to capturing the attention of receivers, stories add color to a speech and also help the speaker make the ideas in the speech less abstract and more concrete.

section

11.2 Build Your Credibility

11.2a See Yourself Through Their Eyes

11.2b Demonstrate Your Credibility

11.2c Establish Topic Credibility and Relevance

11.2d Connect Credibility and Culture

Aside from capturing your audience's attention and engaging them in your ideas, your introduction also should build your credibility. Part of your job is to convince receivers that you are a knowledgeable and believable source.

11.2a See Yourself Through Their Eyes

Credibility is based on a receiver's judgment of a source's expertise on a particular topic. Once a speaker convinces you that he or she is qualified, sincere, and someone with whom you can identify, you will likely perceive that person as trustworthy and believable. Whether the speaker actually possesses those qualities is not the issue; in your eyes, the speaker is someone whom you believe is competent to offer you advice, has your best interests at heart, and is a person of goodwill.

You may, of course, respect the speaker's competence when it comes to some subject areas but not others. You may, for example, be ready to listen to the advice the television personality Dr. Phil offers on psychological matters but discount his beliefs regarding financial issues. Thus, you need to help your receivers understand why you are qualified to speak on your chosen topic. You might show them that you know what you are talking about by sharing experiences, interests, and research findings related to your topic.

Your audience members' initial impressions of you will be based on how you look, what you say, and how you communicate during your opening remarks. Speakers who are well dressed, passionate about the importance of their topics, speak clearly, use inclusive language, make eye contact, and stand with an open body position are seen as more credible than speakers who lack these qualities. If at the end of your introduction audience members believe you are qualified to speak on your chosen topic, if they identify with you and respond to you because they like and trust you, then in their eyes you will be a credible source.

In the mirror. Be aware of how you will come across to others in the introduction of your speech.

11.2b Demonstrate Your Credibility

To hone your own level of credibility, answer these five questions as you draft your speech.

1. Why should audience members listen to *me?*
2. What have I done or experienced that qualifies me to speak on the topic?
3. How personally committed am I to the ideas I am about to share with my audience?
4. What steps can I take to communicate my concerns and enthusiasm to the audience?
5. How can I use my appearance, attitude, and delivery to help establish my goodwill and make my case?

If you are mindful of the ways listeners perceive you, then you will find that you can use attitude, demeanor, and content to build your credibility in their eyes.

Notice how student Ann Marie Ursini uses her abilities as well as research to build credibility with receivers in a speech on the need for Americans to speak a foreign language. As you read this excerpt, consider how effectively she communicates her thesis to receivers:

> America is facing a crisis of ignorance. *Es muy probable que ustedes no estan entendiendo lo que yo digo ahora.* If you are like the majority of Americans, you have no idea what I just said. Which is essentially what I said, only I said it in Spanish and therein lies the problem. Since you are all "speechies" of one sort or another, I certainly do not need to impress upon you the importance of communication. However, most Americans are currently depriving themselves of a tremendous tool that could open up whole new worlds—the ability to communicate in a foreign language.[11]

Your ability to show your audience members your concern for them will encourage them to listen to you. Both the sincerity of your voice and the commitment portrayed by your facial expressions, eye contact, and gestures can enhance your audience's opinion of you and do much to cement the feeling of goodwill that is so integral to their assessments of your credibility. When your listeners understand how you personally relate to the subject, they are better able to relate to it and to you.

Believable. How can you effectively use your tone, demeanor, eye contact, and stance to convey passion and genuineness in your speech?

11.2c Establish Topic Credibility and Relevance

The audience needs to understand how your topic affects them. They need to be provided with a credible reason to listen—an answer to the question: What's in it for me?

Would these words from a student speech about the cost of a college degree have relevance for you? Do you find them credible?

> Here we are at college. Many of us have taken loans to finance our educations. The average debt of a student in a liberal arts college is over $20,000, which works out to a loan payment of about $248 a month. That's a lot when you consider that graduates of liberal arts colleges will only earn about $40,000 a year according to PayScale.com. How much will you owe when you complete your education?

Since many students take out loans that will take years to repay, the speaker enhanced her credibility by establishing a problem she and her audience shared in common.

11.2d Connect Credibility and Culture

In some cultures, speakers are emotional and passionate, while in others they are restrained and unexpressive. If you are of the same sex, ethnic background, and age as the majority of your audience members, you have an obvious advantage. But most speakers cannot count on having such a uniform audience. Again, it is up to you to think critically and plan your opening not only to excite and motivate listeners but also to establish common ground with them.

Former president Bill Clinton accomplished this in a speech given to African American leaders on the site in Memphis where the Reverend Martin Luther King Jr. delivered what turned out to be the last speech of his life. The president began his remarks with phrases that reflected the words King had used nearly three decades earlier. Clinton adopted King's tone, words, and style in an effort to establish his own credibility and win over his audience.[12]

Clinton began his address:

> I am glad to be here. You have touched my heart. You have brought tears to my eyes and joy to my spirit.[13]

He then continued by referring to the Bible:

> The proverb says, "A happy heart doeth good like medicine, but a broken spirit dryeth the bone."[14]

By emulating King, Clinton sounded a lot like a preacher. He also established himself as a concerned member of the community, one who shared the same interests as his receivers, and whom they now viewed as more credible. By identifying and sharing the concerns of your receivers, you can enhance your cultural credibility as well.

section 11.3

Preview the Big Ideas

In addition to attracting attention and building your credibility, a good introduction sets the scene for your presentation, preparing audience members for what is to come. If you focus on your goal, your listeners' eyes, ears, and hearts will follow. A preview

1. Lets the audience know your speech's subject and purpose
2. Identifies the main ideas that will constitute the body of your speech

From the very beginning, your audience should have a pretty clear understanding of your intended topic (unless you are using a configural format; see Chapter 9). If your introduction fails to introduce the subject of your speech, the audience's attention will remain unfocused. Your introduction should clarify, and not confuse receivers.

Notice how one student used this brief, but effective, introduction to prepare the audience for the body of the speech:

> Gossip has a bad reputation. It hasn't always had, and it doesn't always deserve it. Allow me to give you the real scoop. . . . First, I will give you a brief overview of the history of gossip. Then, I'll explain how it fulfills psychological needs, how it functions anthropologically, and finally, how gossip is real news.[15]

Coming attractions. Your introduction should set the scene of your argument to pique the interest of your audience.

section

11.4 Avoid These Common Introductory Bloopers

To ensure all goes smoothly and avoid committing an introductory foul, follow these guidelines:

- ***Don't forget to prepare.*** Lack of preparation is not something audience members readily forgive. Lack of preparation demonstrates a lack of commitment on your part. Simply be prepared.
- ***Don't pretend to be what you are not.*** Audience members want to know you; they want to know what you think, what you feel, and why. If you pretend to know something when you don't, or pretend to feel something when you don't care, then in time—usually sooner rather than later—you will be exposed as a fraud.
- ***Don't rely on gimmicks.*** Treat the audience fairly. If you trick them into paying attention, in the end, they won't. If an introduction doesn't suit your topic, don't use it.

COACHING TIP

"You have only one chance to make a good first impression."

—Anonymous

Attention! The first words you speak to an audience should both command attention and establish a connection. Involve the audience. Build your esteem in their eyes. Add momentum to your speech. By crafting a winning attention getter, you give your speech a running start.

- ***Don't be long-winded.*** Under ordinary circumstances your introduction should use about 10 percent of your speech. If you persist in introducing your ideas, you'll find that by the time you get to the body of your speech, your audience will be short on patience and endurance.
- ***Don't create the introduction first.*** It's a lot easier to make a good decision about how to begin your speech after you have prepared the body of your presentation.

Remember, although a good introduction is no guarantee that your speech will be successful, if you don't invest time and effort in preparing it, you are almost certain to build an impenetrable wall between you and your listeners.

GAME PLAN

Creating a Captivating Introduction

- ☐ Based on my topic and personality, I am using curiosity and suspense/humor/emotion/a relevant quotation to capture the attention of my audience members.
- ☐ I've considered our shared experiences and built upon our common ground to develop an introduction that establishes a positive relationship with my audience.
- ☐ I've made sure that my introduction includes the necessary information to orient receivers to the thesis of my speech by previewing its main ideas.
- ☐ I have established my own credibility and relevance to the topic to satisfy audience members' skepticism.

Exercises

THE INTRODUCTION

Creating an effective introduction takes practice and skill. To hone your ability, use these training camp drills to get your introduction in shape.

1. Captivate Me

First prepare hypothetical startling statements you could use to introduce a speech on one of the following topics:

- Gun Safety
- Transgender Rights
- Preparing for Final Exams
- Hazards of Bicycle Riding

Then create an introduction that is designed to arouse the audience's curiosity or emotion about one of these topics:

- Affirmative Action
- Vaccinations
- Gluten
- Doctors Without Borders

2. Learn From TV

Spend time carefully watching television advertisements. Describe examples of ads that use startling or shocking openers, rhetorical examples, humor, or emotion to capture audience attention and encourage involvement. Then find examples of openers that are used by local or national news programs to do the same.

3. Analyze This Introduction

Select a recent speech from *Vital Speeches of the Day* or TED Talks. Evaluate the extent to which the speaker used the introduction to capture attention, build credibility, and preview the content of the speech.

4. Approach the Speaker's Stand

Develop three possible introductions for a speech on any one of the following subjects, or a subject of your choice:

Ageism	Depression	Free Speech
NSA Spying	Bullying	Eleanor Roosevelt
Comets	Political Correctness	Space Travel

Present your introductions to the class. Then ask your classmates to tell you whether they found them effective and which they found most effective.

In a one- to two-page paper explain the techniques you relied on in each introduction to attract audience attention, build your own credibility, and forecast what is to follow.

RECAP AND REVIEW

1. **Explain how an introduction affects a speech.** The way a speaker introduces a presentation influences the interest level of receivers and affects receivers' initial perception of the speaker.
2. **Describe the purposes served by introductions.** Effective introductions serve these key functions: (1) they capture attention, (2) they build credibility, and (3) they orient receivers to the organizational development and tone of the speech.
3. **Identify at least five ways to introduce a speech.** To fulfill the functions of an introduction speakers rely on a number of techniques: they startle or shock receivers, directly involve receivers, arouse curiosity or build suspense, make their listeners smile or laugh with them, or move them with stories.
4. **Use the introduction to capture attention, build credibility, and preview the speech's main ideas.** Speakers seize attention by surprising the audience, involving them, relating an interesting quote, using humor, and appealing to emotion. In order to build credibility, the speaker first must understand how receivers perceive them and then help the audience view them as qualified. To accomplish this, they relate personal experiences, identify credentials, use reputable sources, establish topic relevance, and build common ground. Effective introductions also communicate the subject of a speech and its purpose, as well as preview what's to come.
5. **Avoid introduction pitfalls.** During introductions speakers should not apologize for lack of preparation, pretend to be what they are not, rely on irrelevant gimmicks, or be long winded. The introduction should also not be created before the speech's body.

KEY TERMS

Rhetorical questions 199

SAGE edge™

Sharpen your skills with SAGE edge at edge.sagepub.com/gamblepsp2e.

SAGE edge for students provides a personalized approach to help you accomplish your coursework goals in an easy-to-use learning environment.

Duncan Smith/Photodisc/Thinkstock

12 Concluding Your Speech

UPON COMPLETING THIS CHAPTER'S TRAINING, YOU WILL BE ABLE TO

1. Describe the purposes conclusions serve
2. Identify at least five ways to conclude a speech
3. Avoid conclusion pitfalls
4. Develop conclusions that achieve multiple goals

Contents

Picture this. You're at a soccer game. The game is almost over. The score is tied. All the fans are on edge. The star striker, taken down in the box just as she was about to shoot, is given a free kick. She lines up, fakes to the right, then drives the ball past the goalie into the net! A thrilling finish means everyone will remember the game's outcome. That's the kind of reaction you want to create in the audience as you deliver your speech's conclusion.

During a presentation's final few moments, the audience listens and observes as the speaker does his or her best to drive home the message of the speech while leaving the audience with a favorable impression. An appropriate ending can make or break the entire speech. It should compel the audience to continue thinking about your speech—even after you have stopped speaking.

COACHING TIP

"You've got to be very careful if you don't know where you are going, because you might not get there."

—Yogi Berra

End your speech with flair. The conclusion is a significant moment in your speech's life. It is when you "get there." Take advantage of your last few moments speaking to remind the audience why your ideas are important and why they should care. You have one final chance to be sure you reach your goal and connect with the audience. Make it memorable!

section

12.1

End Strong

12.1a Keep It Short

12.1b Forecast the Finish Line

12.1c Restate the Central Idea or Thesis

12.1d Motivate the Audience (Again)

12.1e Achieve Closure

Sharon Bower, speech consultant and author of *Painless Public Speaking*, explains, "Listeners forget long, colorless, and complicated endings. . . . A final statement should be short and sweet: short to listen to and sweet to remember."[1] And speech coach Stephen C. Rafe, author of *How to Be Prepared to Speak on Your Feet*, advises that you "look over your material and ask yourself, 'What is the most important or logical way to end this communication?' Pick the kind of ending that works best for your audience, your situation, your topic, and your intentions."[2]

A well-designed conclusion fulfills these functions:

1. It lets the audience know a presentation is drawing to a close.
2. It summarizes key ideas the speaker shared.
3. It "wows" receivers, reenergizing them and reminding them of the response the speaker seeks.
4. It provides the speech with a sense of closure.

The final minutes you and your audience are together constitute your last opportunity to position your ideas firmly in their minds. It takes great skill to end a game in a way that brings fans to their feet. The same is true for a speech. Although you might be tempted to take the easy way out and bring your speech to a close with a "That's all folks" or "And so it goes," doing so could destroy an otherwise fine presentation. Instead, put audience members in a mood conducive to achieving your goals by ending your speech in as memorable a way as you began it. If you do this, you'll add additional "wow" power to your words and achieve closure, much like early colonial patriot Patrick Henry did when he delivered these closing lines to his speech: "I know not what course others may take, but as for me, give me liberty or give me death." His ending is part of our national heritage and an example of how a great ending to a speech is constructed.[3] Although the conclusions you create may not become part of our national heritage, you can design conclusions that rouse your audience.

12.1a Keep It Short

A conclusion should not be lengthy. The average conclusion makes up about 5 percent of a speech. However, just as with your introduction, the materials you use in your speech's conclusion must be relevant to your topic, appropriate to the audience and occasion, interesting, and involving. They also need to provide audience members with a sense of completion. The conclusion is your last chance to put the spotlight exactly where you want it to shine.

At the close of one student's speech on the importance of regular exercise, for example, in about 60 seconds he reminded the audience of the results of the physical activity survey he provided when he began the speech, reviewed the health risks that regular exercise reduces, and then ended with these words: "The bottom line is that while many people fail to appreciate that exercising, even a little, is the quick fix to improving our health and quality of life, we thankfully are no longer among them. We get it. And we'll do it."[4]

12.1b Forecast the Finish Line

A conclusion should not take the audience by surprise. Instead, cue the audience that you are about to stop speaking. You might pause, decrease or increase your speaking rate, build momentum, alter your voice tone, or cue them with a transitional phrase. For example, you might say, "In conclusion," "To review," or "Let me end by noting . . . " Such techniques help your audience adjust to the fact that you are approaching the speech's end.

Here is how Talbot D'Alemberte, one-time president of the American Bar Association, signaled the end of a speech on civil justice reform:

Comstock/Stockbyte/Thinkstock

Finish strong. A well-crafted conclusion should be memorable and reinforce the goals of your speech.

> In closing, I want to pay special tribute to lawyers like you who have devoted so much time and energy to our profession. The bar binds us together as a profession uniquely responsible for ensuring justice in our society. Our involvement reminds us that the law is a calling and not simply an occupation or a business.[5]

12.1c Restate the Central Idea or Thesis

New ideas have no place in the conclusion to a speech. Instead, use the conclusion to reinforce the main points you want audience members to remember. Think of it this way: You are putting your presentation on "rewind" for a moment. In order to accomplish this, you can

- ☐ Recap your central idea or thesis and your main points one last time so your audience enjoys an instant replay of your position and your rationale.
- ☐ Use a quotation that summarizes or highlights your point of view.
- ☐ Make a dramatic statement that drives home why audience members should be motivated and committed to respond as you desire.
- ☐ Take the audience full circle by referring to your introduction.

John F. McDonnell, chairman and CEO of McDonnell Douglas, used the conclusion of a talk entitled "PaxPacifica" to reemphasize his speech's thesis and main points:

> In closing, I want to restate the point I made at the outset. There are good and compelling reasons why the U.S. should encourage the export of U.S.-made weapons to friendly nations around the globe. This would serve U.S. strategic interests and it would help shape up the U.S. defense industrial base at a time of declining defense spending. When it is allowed to compete, the U.S. defense industry is not only competitive, but is almost always the first choice of the most knowledgeable customers around the world.[6]

12.1d Motivate the Audience (Again)

Just as an effective introduction motivates audience members to listen to a speech, an effective conclusion motivates receivers to respond appropriately. Your conclusion is no place for you to let up on effort or energy. It certainly is no place for you to let down your audience. Instead, take the time you need to create a striking ending that supports and sustains your speech's theme.

Many of the same kinds of materials you used to develop your introduction can help you set a proper concluding mood. Reminding receivers of a startling fact, using a quotation, integrating humor, asking a rhetorical question, or using an effective story can pump up a conclusion.

For example, one speaker used a humorous quotation to set the mood for continued contemplation and action by audience members. In a speech entitled "Rediscovering a Lost Resource: Rethinking Retirement," the speaker closed with this anecdote:

© iStockphoto.com/blackred

Don't let up. Maintain your energy at the conclusion of your speech to motivate and inspire your audience.

> Listen to Warren Buffet, who has built an investment empire. When asked a few years ago about leaving a woman in charge of one of his companies after celebrating her 94th birthday, he replied, "She is clearly gathering speed and may well reach her full potential in another five or ten years. Therefore, I've persuaded the board to scrap our mandatory-retirement-at-100 policy. My God, good managers are so scarce I can't afford the luxury of letting them go just because they've added a year to their age."[7]

12.1e Achieve Closure

An effective means of giving a speech balance is to refer in the conclusion to ideas explored in the introduction, achieving **closure**. You might reuse a theme you introduced at the beginning of your speech, ask or answer the rhetorical question you used at its outset, refer to an opening story, or restate an initial quotation. Integrating any one of these strategies helps to provide audience members with a desired sense of logical and emotional closure. Because such strategies help your speech sound finished, audience members are not left wondering whether your speech is actually over. Leave your audience hanging and you leave your ideas hanging. If your conclusion convinces audience members that you have delivered what you promised in your introduction, they are more likely to accept your thesis and take the action you advocate.

After opening her speech celebrating the legacy of Martin Luther King Jr. with references to a letter about racial injustice that King had written from a Birmingham jail back in 1963, the speaker ended her speech by coming full circle:

> We have a chance to glimpse what Dr. King described in his closing words of the Letter from the Birmingham Jail . . . "the radiant stars of love and brotherhood will shine over our great nation with all of their scintillating beauty."
>
> And all God's people said . . . Amen.[8]

By referring back to ideas explored earlier in their speeches, speakers help audience members acknowledge the wholeness and completeness of their presentations.

Avoid These Common Concluding Pitfalls

section
12.2

An effective conclusion leaves the audience fulfilled and in the mood to think about or do what you recommend. Your closing comments are your last chance to make a good impression and fulfill the purpose of your speech. Because it comes last, the conclusion is the part of the speech your audience will remember most clearly. Make sure to leave a positive final impression by avoiding these pitfalls:

- ***Don't end abruptly.*** A conclusion needs to be built carefully, or the ideas you've worked so hard to develop will topple like a house of cards. Let your audience know you are wrapping up so they aren't caught by surprise.
- ***Don't be long-winded.*** When you end a speech, you cross the finish line. Hang around that finish line too long without crossing it, and your audience could lose interest in you and your ideas at a very critical juncture. Build your conclusion, but keep it tight.
- ***Don't introduce new ideas.*** Though it's appropriate to restate in a fresh way the ideas you've covered in your speech, it's not appropriate to introduce new ideas in the conclusion. The conclusion is your last opportunity to drive home important points, not the time to start making new ones.
- ***Don't end with a thud.*** Devise a conclusion that will stick in the minds of your listeners, not one that may have little, if any, impact on what they retain. If you create an ending that has real emotional appeal, you will inspire rather than let down your audience. Your ending should be striking, not count as a strike against you.

GAME PLAN

Writing a Compelling Conclusion

- ☐ I know how much time is allotted for my speech, and I've made sure that the conclusion is no more than 5 percent of the total time.
- ☐ I have included transition words such as "in closing" to forecast the speech's end for my audience.
- ☐ After I transition into my conclusion, I don't introduce new ideas but rather focus on recapping my thesis and key ideas.
- ☐ I've used one of the techniques discussed in this chapter to elicit an appropriate reaction from audience members so my words will linger in their minds.

Exercises

THE CONCLUSION

Learning to create a memorable conclusion will help you keep your speeches from simply petering out.

1. Reinforce Common Ground

A speaker can use a conclusion as a communication bridge. By reaffirming the concerns and interests a speaker and audience share in common, the speaker reinforces their **common ground** and increases the likelihood that the audience will respond as the speaker desires. For example, Coca-Cola created a global marketing campaign that focused on the unifying themes of joy, laughter, sports, and music. By "selling" these universal themes, company executives contended they could "achieve more by doing one promotion globally."[9]

A public speaker is able to accomplish much the same thing—that is, a speech can be written so that it is understood and responded to similarly by audiences in different parts of the world. You are asked to create a speech on Self-Driving Cars that would speak to audiences in New York City, Shanghai, Moscow, and Rome. What themes would you employ to make the speech appealing across borders?

2. Analyze This Conclusion

Lauren had outlined the body of a presentation on the dangers of drinking and driving. She chose the topic because her brother had been hit and killed by a drunk driver and she conducted extensive primary and secondary research in preparation for her speech. Now nearing the end of her preparation, Lauren began crafting her speech's conclusion. She had agonized over the introduction, but ultimately chose to discuss the death of her brother in the introduction, telling the sad story as if it had happened to someone else. Lauren had an idea. "Maybe, what I should do," she thought, "is reveal in the conclusion that the person killed was not a stranger, but my own brother."

- Respond to Lauren's idea. Does it fulfill the guidelines discussed in this chapter?
- What other options would you recommend she consider?
- Locate a speech on drinking and driving on YouTube. Analyze its conclusion according to the following criteria: Did the speaker signal that the speech was coming to an end? Summarize the speech's key points? Restate the speech's central idea or thesis? Achieve closure? Did the speaker's conclusion invite the audience to respond? Did the conclusion add to the speech's memorability?

3. Approach the Speaker's Stand

Review the introductions you created in Chapter 11's Approach the Speaker's Stand. Develop a conclusion to join each of the introductions you created, or develop three conclusions on different topics identified here or other topics you find interesting.

Ageism	Depression	Free Speech
NSA Spying	Bullying	Eleanor Roosevelt
Comets	Political Correctness	Space Travel

Present your conclusions to the class. Then ask your classmates to tell you whether they found them effective.

In a one- to two-page paper, explain the techniques you relied on to signal the conclusion, reemphasize your theme and main points, and motivate listeners to respond as you desire. Explain which introduction and conclusion you believe audience members would find most effective and why.

RECAP AND REVIEW

1. **Describe the purposes conclusions serve.** Effective conclusions serve four key functions: (1) forecast the end of a speech, (2) reemphasize the central idea of a speech, (3) motivate receivers to respond as a speaker desires, and (4) provide a speech with a sense of closure.
2. **Identify at least five ways to conclude a speech.** To achieve the functions of conclusions, speakers should keep their closing words short, use cues to help receivers adjust to the fact that a speech is ending, review key points covered, use a dramatic statement or quotation to reinforce a speech's central idea(s), and take the audience full circle by referring to the speech's introduction, thereby creating a sense of closure.
3. **Avoid conclusion pitfalls.** When concluding, speakers should not end too abruptly, be long-winded, introduce new ideas, or end with a thud.
4. **Develop conclusions that achieve multiple goals.** Develop conclusions that forecast a speech's end, summarize a speech's main points, elicit a desired response from receivers, compel them to continue thinking about your message, and provide closure.

KEY TERMS

Closure 216

Common ground 218

SAGE edge™

Sharpen your skills with SAGE edge at edge.sagepub.com/gamblepsp2e.

SAGE edge for students provides a personalized approach to help you accomplish your coursework goals in an easy-to-use learning environment.

PART FIVE: Present Your Speech

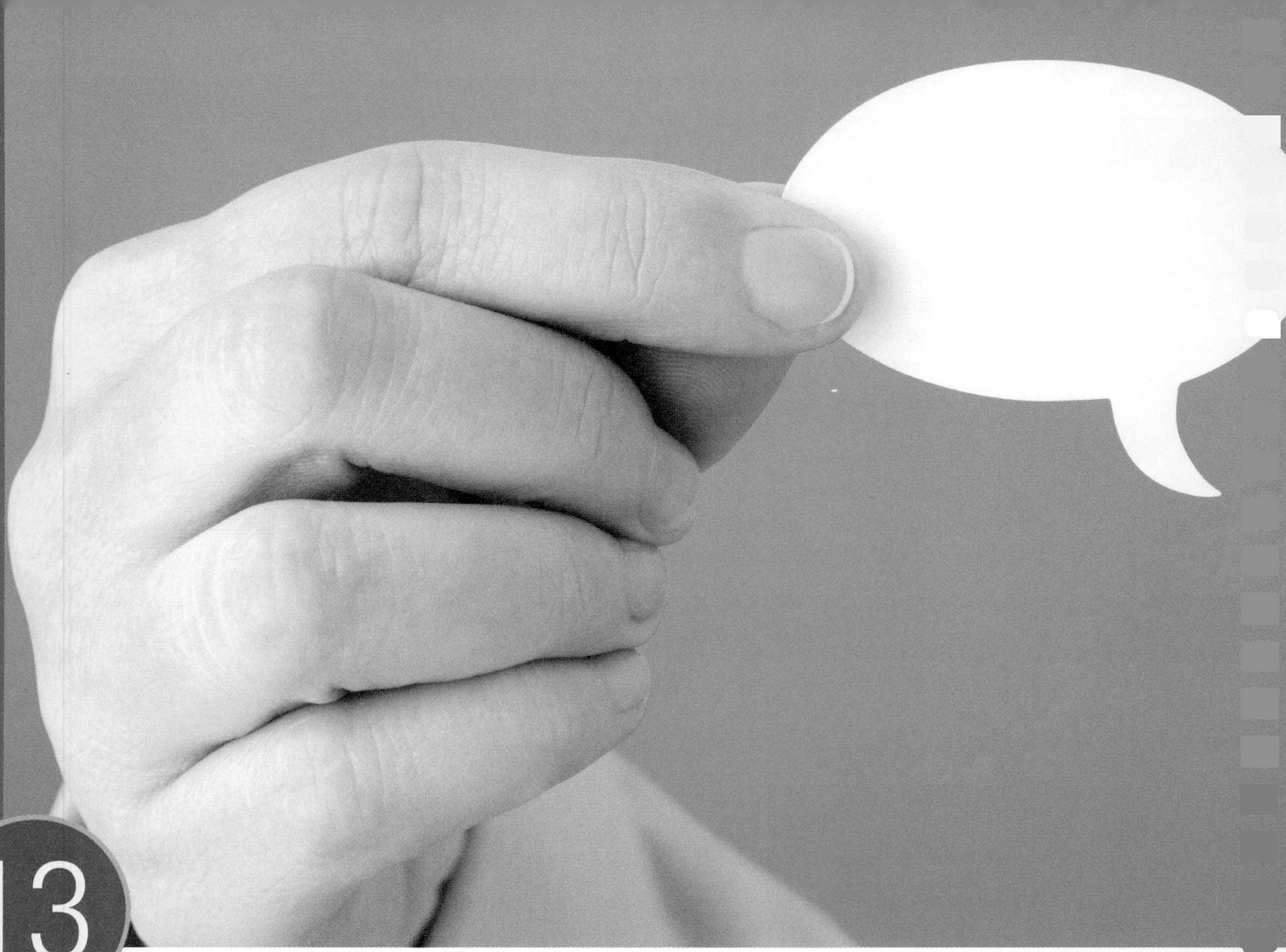

© iStockphoto.com/mrPliskin

13

Wording the Speech

UPON COMPLETING THIS CHAPTER'S TRAINING, YOU WILL BE ABLE TO

1. Explain how words work
2. Use words that connect with receivers
3. Use words that demonstrate your consideration of the audience
4. Make strategic word choices
5. Adopt an oral style

In hockey, when a player commits a dangerous foul, the referee orders the player into the penalty box. As long as that player is off the ice, the team remains a player short. When this happens, the opposing team has the advantage—and with the advantage comes the opportunity to make a power play. In public speaking, the player who has a way with words has the advantage. Speakers whose words are ineffective put themselves in a figurative penalty box. Thus, using words well is key in scoring a speechmaking power play. In large part, the message you communicate to the audience and the meaning receivers extract depend on your word choices.

Your words can cause ideas to live in the minds of your receivers long after you finish speaking. But only if you select words that have audience appeal—words that succeed in moving others emotionally and intellectually—are you likely to establish the audience connection you seek. Choose the wrong words—words that lack vividness, are difficult to understand, or fail to capture the imagination—and you might well contribute to the audience's boredom or confusion. Communicating simply, accurately, and effectively increases your chances of delivering a memorable speech.

In this chapter we explore your role as a creator of word power plays. We'll look at how language works and how the word choices you make spell the difference between speechmaking success and failure.

Contents

COACHING TIP

"Words. . . . They're innocent, neutral, precise, standing for this, describing that, meaning the other, so if you look after them you can build bridges across incomprehension and chaos."

—Tom Stoppard

Words help you connect. Select the right ones and they convey your ideas with clarity and power. Remember to keep your words simple. Speech is for the ear, not the eye. Speak in short units. Eliminate jargon. Keep it personal.

section

13.1 Understand How Words Work

Language is a unified system of symbols that permits us to share meaning.[1] A *symbol* stands for, or represents, something else. Words, as symbols, represent things or ideas. For example, the word *homeless* is not the thing "homeless." Because words can convey different meanings to different listeners, good speakers must understand the relationship that exists among words, thoughts, and human behavior.

The **Triangle of Meaning**, devised by communication theorists C. K. Ogden and I. A. Richards, provides a model of the tenuous relationships among words, thoughts, and things (see Figure 13.1). The dotted line connecting a word and a thing indicates that there is no direct connection between the two. The only connection between the word *coat*, for example, and a physical coat is in people's thoughts. It is feasible that a number of us could look at the same object, think entirely different thoughts about it, and thus give it entirely different meanings based on our experiences. One person might hear the word and think of a winter jacket, another a suit coat, and a third a coat of paint.

It is dangerous to assume everyone understands what you mean. Once communication is the goal, we can no longer consider only one meaning for a word. We must also focus on what our words mean to those with whom we are communicating.

FIGURE 13.1
The Triangle of Meaning

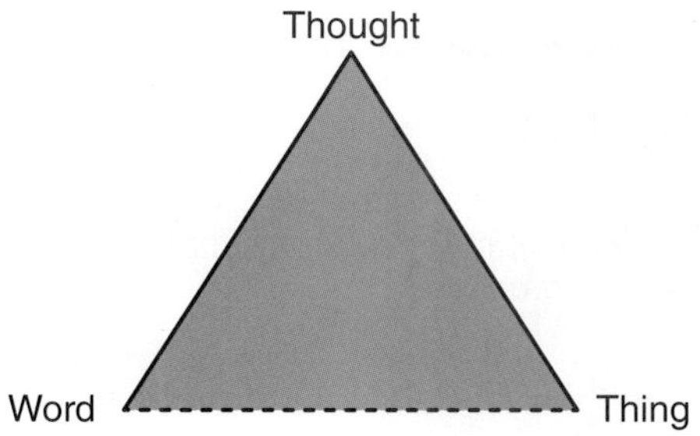

Use Words to Connect

section
13.2

For language to work, there must be a common understanding about what the words we are using mean to others. Only then can we share meaning and experience.

Different words that describe the same event can evoke very different responses. For example, how do you react to each of the following words or phrases? What kinds of thoughts does each generate? What image(s) do you visualize for each?

war   defensive response   massacre

Though the event being described could be the same, the words used to describe it express our perception. If we use the word "massacre," we suggest disapproval, while a "defensive response" might be a justified reaction to an attack. And this influences how our audience responds as well. Our words can help listeners perceive our ideas as we want, influencing their attitudes, values, and actions. Used well, words can cause an audience to feel intensely, overcoming their apathy.

© iStockphoto.com/kaantanman

Words matter. Words should not be easily thrown away, so be precise and considerate in your word choices.

COACHING TIP

"Words can wring tears from the hardest hearts."

—Patrick Rothfuss

Your words can help you win the hearts of your audience. Reason reaches receivers on a logical level. Figurative language rich in sensory appeals reaches them on an emotional level. So choose your words with care. Make the audience feel and you make your message real!

section

13.3

Consider Your Audience

13.3a Overcome Communication Obstacles

13.3b Consider Time and Place

13.3c Observe Reasoning and Thinking Preferences

13.3d Use Plain, Unbiased Language

Meaning exists not in words, but in the minds of people using the words. Your goal in communicating with your audience is to create meaning overlap. Only if the audience gives similar meanings to your words will they be able to make sense of your message and respond as you desire. Accordingly, one of your prime objectives is to translate your ideas into language your listeners will understand and respond to. This requires you to be culturally sensitive.

13.3a Overcome Communication Obstacles

Words have both denotative and connotative meanings. The **denotative meaning** is the word's dictionary definition, precise and objective. Audience members are not dictionaries; when you use a word they should not have to consult a dictionary to find meaning number four for that word. What audience members do carry with them in their heads is the connotative meaning of words. **Connotative meaning** is variable and subjective. It includes all the feelings and personal associations that a word stimulates. For example, the feelings and personal associations people have for words and phrases such as *home, immigrant, gun control,* or *childhood* differ depending on whether the experiences they associate with each word are good or bad.

If you fail to consider the possible connotative meanings a word could evoke among audience members, you increase your chances of being misunderstood. Search for words that seem likely to elicit the meanings and responses you desire from as many audience members as possible. Focus on the audience instead of simply speaking the first words that pop into your mind. Take time to identify the best way and the best words to use to evoke a desired reaction.[2]

13.3b Consider Time and Place

Every generation evolves new meanings for old words. It's as if we recycle language. This fact becomes important when you are speaking to audiences composed primarily of persons not your own age. Consider, for example, how an audience of your peers, an audience of people in their seventies, and an audience of elementary school-aged children might interpret any of the following words: *radical, net, surf, rap, bitcoin, red, straight, chill, hook-up, bad, sick, cell, awesome.* Because time can affect a word's meaning, speakers must be aware of the meaning any given audience member could attach to a word.

The meanings of words change not only through time. Words also change meaning from one section of the country to another. Pop, soda, and Coke are all the same drink, depending on where you live. Public speakers need to be sensitive to how regional differences affect word meanings or they could find themselves facing a widening communication gap.

© iStockphoto.com/microgen

Words are worlds. Be considerate of your audience, know what words have value to them, and be thoughtful in how you employ them.

13.3c Observe Reasoning and Thinking Preferences

Our words provide clues to our worldviews, interests and concerns, and what we believe to be important. They also reveal how we think.[3]

People in Western cultures tend to rely on both inductive and deductive reasoning to make points and to understand those made by others. Inductive reasoning relies on observation and specific instances or examples to build a case or argument. Deductive reasoning takes a known idea or general principle and applies it to a situation.

People from non-Western cultures, however, may prefer to rely on other ways of presenting their messages in lieu of making objective observations. Rather than limiting themselves to inductive and deductive reasoning when speaking before others, for instance, people in the Arab world sometimes express their emotions and religious faith.[4] Westerners who aren't attuned to Arabs' preferences may therefore have difficulty locating the main ideas in speeches given by Arabs, and vice versa.[5] Arab speakers, for example, sometimes change course mid-speech. To Westerners, it may seem as if they have gone off on a tangent as they personalize and emote. As a result, Western audiences often find themselves working harder to identify an Arab speaker's purpose than they do when listening to a speaker of their own background. Arab speeches also may contain exaggerations and repetitions. Additionally, Western receivers often interpret the stress patterns of the Arabic language incorrectly, perceiving them as aggressive or disinterested when that likely was not the intent of the speaker.[6]

Asians also differ from Westerners in their language use and preferences. Whereas North Americans tend to exhibit a frank, direct speechmaking style that is sometimes confrontational, Asians tend to place a high value on politeness and are more likely to use hints and euphemisms to convey their meaning.[7] They typically neither preview nor identify their speech's purpose or main points for receivers. Instead, both are suggested through stories and personal testimonies.[8]

Brand X Pictures/LauriPatterson

Hero, hoagie, sub, or wedge? Consider whether the language of your presentation is attuned to regional differences.

Clearly, there is more than one way to express ideas verbally. In our diverse world, it is counterproductive to consider the expression preferences favored by the members of one culture superior to another's. We run into problems when we allow feelings of ethnocentrism to interfere with our ability and willingness to process others' thoughts as accurately as possible and without bias. Our goal should be to shrink the language divide, not widen it.

13.3d Use Plain, Unbiased Language

It is important to respect all members of the audience, acknowledging their cultural beliefs, norms, or preferences, and taking their perspectives into account when selecting your words.

- ☐ Eliminate idioms and jargon that persons unfamiliar with your topic would find confusing or frustrating.
- ☐ Speak in short units that facilitate the processing of your words, while making certain that you do not "dumb down" your content or talk down to the members of your audience.
- ☐ Avoid using overly technical language as well as overblown language that overwhelms rather than interests listeners.

For example, generally the words *gay* and *lesbian* are preferred to refer to men and women, respectively, who have an affectional preference for persons of their same sex. The word *woman* is preferred to *girl* or *gal* when referring to a female adult. The phrase *physically challenged* is preferred to *disabled.* The word *Hispanic* is appropriate when referring to persons who identify themselves as belonging to a Spanish-speaking culture, while *Latina* or *Latino* is the preferred term when speaking of someone who is from a Latin American country. Most African Americans prefer the term *African American* to *black* or *Afro-American.*[9] When referring to American Indians, *Native American* is the preferred term, not *Indian*, which is best reserved for referencing persons from India. The correct means of identifying persons from Asia is *Asian,* not *Oriental,* which is suggestive of a European bias.

Be respectful. Word choice is always important in avoiding showing disrespect or prejudice toward any one culture, gender, religion, sexual orientation, and so on.

section

13.4

Be Strategic

Only if your audience shares your meaning will they truly perceive your message accurately. To achieve this, you need to make strategic word choices—choices that favor the simple over the complex, the concrete over the abstract, the appropriate over the inappropriate, and the vivid over the vague. Let us explore each of these language options in turn.

13.4a Keep It Simple

Whenever you have the choice, select the simplest, most familiar word available to you. Never use a technical word like *cephalalgia* when a simpler one like *headache* will do—the latter is usually clearer to your listeners (see Table 13.1).

Far too often, speakers who spout unfamiliar words and **jargon and technospeak** (specialized language) to uninitiated audiences succeed only in communicating their stuffiness and pretentiousness. No real sharing of meaning can occur between such a speaker and his or her audience because the audience has no idea what the speaker is talking about.

The following story illustrates how poorly chosen language can obscure meaning:

> A plumber who had only a limited command of English knew that hydrochloric acid opened clogged drainpipes quickly and effectively. What he didn't know, however, was whether it was the right thing to use. So the plumber decided to check with the National Bureau of Standards in Washington, D.C. Seeking confirmation that hydrochloric acid was safe to use in pipes, he wrote the bureau a letter. After processing his letter, a scientist at the bureau wrote back this response: "The efficacy of hydrochloric acid is indisputable, but the corrosive residue is incompatible with metallic surfaces."
>
> The plumber interpreted the scientist's response as a confirmation and wrote a second letter to the bureau thanking the scientist for the quick reply and for giving him the go-ahead to use hydrochloric acid.
>
> The plumber's thank you really bothered the scientist who showed it to a superior. His superior decided to write the plumber a second letter. This letter read, "We cannot assume responsibility for the production of toxic and noxious residue which hydrochloric acid can produce; we suggest that you use an alternative procedure."
>
> Though this response left the plumber a bit baffled, he hurriedly sent the bureau a third letter telling them that he was pleased they agreed with him. "The acid was working just fine."
>
> When this letter arrived, the scientist's superior sent it to the head administrator at the bureau. The head administrator ended the confusion by writing a short, simple note to the plumber: "Don't use hydrochloric acid. It eats the hell out of pipes."

The more difficult your language, the more likely your audience—particularly if unspecialized—will have difficulty understanding it. For this reason, before using the jargon of a field always check whether audience members share the specialized vocabulary.

TABLE 13.1 USING SIMPLE LANGUAGE

INSTEAD OF	USE
endeavor	try
commence	begin
altercation	fight
vista	view
eschew	avoid
ediface	building
remunerate	pay
precipitation	rain

13.4b Keep It Concrete

Using concrete rather than abstract language helps your audience members picture what you want them to. It leaves no doubt about your meaning and it will help prevent possible misinterpretation of your message.

Remember, the more abstract the word, the more meanings people will have for it. To reduce ambiguity, be concrete (see Table 13.2).

TABLE 13.2 USING CONCRETE LANGUAGE

INSTEAD OF	USE
expensive car	Mercedes-Benz
help the manufacturer	help the U.S. car manufacturer
livestock	cattle
dog	Bichon Frisé
sound business principles	employee participation
a bundle	$1,000,000
be fair	use the same standard for all
help the homeless	volunteer at a soup kitchen
physical activity	aerobics

Concrete words evoke more precise meanings. If you make a conscious effort to be more specific and less general, the speeches you deliver will become clearer, more interesting, and easier to remember.

Indirect expressions, called **euphemisms**, make it easier for speakers to handle unpleasant subjects, but often they also make it harder for audiences to develop a clear and accurate perception of what the speaker is saying. Notice how your reactions are changed by the words used in the trios in Table 13.3.

TABLE 13.3 WORD CHOICE AND AUDIENCE PERCEPTION

put to sleep	euthanized	killed
loved one	dead body	corpse
slumber chamber	coffin	casket
break wind	pass gas	fart
expecting	in the family way	pregnant
let go	laid off	fired
sanitation worker	garbage collector	garbage man

© iStockphoto.com/Ben Harding

Pre-owned or used car? Choose your words carefully.

The words in the first column are the most polite. Receivers generally find them less harsh and more pleasing, but do they convey the clearest meaning? How do the pictures they create in your mind differ from the pictures created by the words listed in the second and third columns?

A speaker's word choices play a role in our reaction to his or her speech. For example, the words *janitor* and *sanitary engineer* both mean *custodian*. Yet, the terms have very different connotations. We frequently react to the words the speaker uses instead of what the words actually refer to. Receivers need to work hard to prevent a speaker's words from blinding them to what those words represent.

13.4c Keep It Appropriate

Phrase your speech using words that you understand and are comfortable saying, and that your audience will understand, accept, and respond to positively. Obscene, racist, ageist, or sexist remarks are usually judged offensive by audiences, reducing your credibility. Thus, common sense must prevail. Although we may use certain terms when conversing with our close friends, such expressions may be inappropriate in a speech. For example, back in 1984, one-time presidential hopeful billionaire Ross Perot made a mistake when he delivered an address before the NAACP (National Association for the Advancement of Colored People) convention in Nashville and referred to African Americans as "you people."

Confront the Issue of Political Correctness

For some, **political correctness** means using words that convey respect for and sensitivity to the needs and interests of different groups. Thus, when we find ourselves speaking about various issues to audiences composed of persons who are culturally different from us, we may also find ourselves adapting our language so that it demonstrates our sensitivity to their perspectives and interests. For others, however, political correctness means that we feel compelled by societal pressures *not* to use some words for fear that doing so would cause members of our audience to perceive us as either racist or sexist. For example, some years back, when David Howard, a Caucasian aide to then mayor of Washington, D.C., Anthony Williams, used the word *niggardly* in reference to the budget, a controversy erupted. Howard was compelled to resign even though the word he used was in reality unrelated to the "N" word. (Using the "N" word in place of the actual word is also a form of political correctness.) Some might opt to do whatever is necessary to avoid offending anyone. Still others view political correctness as a very real danger to free speech. Which of these viewpoints comes closest to representing your own?

Avoid Sexist, Racist, and Ageist Language

We can show our respect with words, but we can also use words to signal our lack of respect or contempt.

Sexist language suggests that the two sexes are unequal and that one gender has more status and value and is more capable than the other. For example, in past decades, masculine words were used to include both males and females. But the use of *he* for he or she or *mankind* for the human race in written and spoken discourse excluded women by ignoring them.

A sexist language practice called **spotlighting** was also used to reinforce the notion that men, and not women, set the standard. Though a person was rarely described as a *male physician*, *male lawyer*, or *male physicist*, terms such as *woman doctor* and *female mathematician* were widely used. Today, however, spotlighting is rarer and we are somewhat more apt to substitute gender-inclusive terms such as *chairperson* and *spokesperson*, and to use language that equalizes rather than highlights the treatment of gender.

Racist language expresses bigoted views about a person or persons from another group, based on a person's ideas of that race. Racist language dehumanizes the members of the group being attacked. It is the deliberate, purposeful, and hurtful use of words intended to oppress someone of a different color.[10]

Ageist language discriminates on the basis of age. U.S. culture tends to disparage the elderly and exalt the youthful. Negative stereotypes such as "She's an old hag," "She's set in her ways," or "He's losing his mind" abound. Ageism is often based on a distaste for and fear of growing older.[11] We need to decategorize individuals and change our expectations to improve our communication effectiveness with persons of all ages.[12]

13.4d Keep It Distinctive and Vivid

A distinctive speech grabs your attention and stays in your memory.

To be a vivid speaker, you need to be a vivid thinker. You need to see a vivid mental picture in your mind's eye before passing it on. You must hear the cadence of your words and sense the rhythm of your speech's movement before expecting others to do so. To achieve vividness,

- ☐ Give yourself the freedom to think imaginatively.
- ☐ Make a conscious effort to use figures of speech and selected sound patterns that add force to your thoughts.

Using **figurative language** helps your audience picture your meaning, while the sound and rhythm of certain words help them sense your intensity. For example, were you to deliver a speech on competitive racers Usain Bolt or Paula Radcliffe, saying that either ran like the wind would be more descriptive than saying he or she ran fast. Both figurative language and vivid speech will help you gain and sustain the attention of your audience.

Imagery is your partner in keeping your message vivid. Part of your task is to use words to create vivid mental pictures designed to influence how audience members see things, process your message, and share more fully in the speechmaking experience. Colorful and concrete words that appeal to the senses help awaken the imaginations of receivers, shortening the distance to your goal. Notice how Jesse Jackson used the image of a quilt to share his vision of America:

> America's not a blanket woven from one thread, one color, one cloth. When I was a child growing up in Greenville, South Carolina, and grandmother could not afford a blanket, she didn't complain and we did not freeze. Instead, she took pieces of old cloth—patches, wool, silk, gabardine, croakersack on the patches—barely good enough to wipe off your shoes with. But they didn't stay that way very long. With sturdy hands and a strong cord, she sewed them together into a quilt, a thing of beauty and power and culture.[13]

Jackson then went on to describe for receivers why the people of this country—its farmers, laborers, women, and mothers—needed to work together and pool their resources (their patches) to piece together such a quilt, one that would provide the people of this nation with health care, housing, jobs, and hope.

Use Figures of Speech

Using figures of speech makes ideas vivid. Words that suggest striking mental images add freshness and vitality to a speech.

Among the most commonly used figures of speech are similes and metaphors.[14] A **simile** is an indirect comparison of dissimilar things, usually with the words *like* or *as*.

Chief Seattle, a Native American leader, used effective similes to make his point:

> The white people are many. They are like the grass that covers vast prairies. My people are few. They resemble the scattering trees of a storm-swept plain.[15]

In contrast to a simile that builds an indirect comparison, a **metaphor** builds a direct identification by omitting the words *like* or *as*. In a metaphor, two things not usually considered alike are compared directly, and their relationship is implied. Professional speaker and writer Wayne Dyer used a metaphor when he wrote,

> Your body is nothing more than the garage where you temporarily park your soul.[16]

In this example, the metaphor used helped give concreteness to a more abstract concept. Metaphors enhance the audience's ability to visualize the speaker's message.

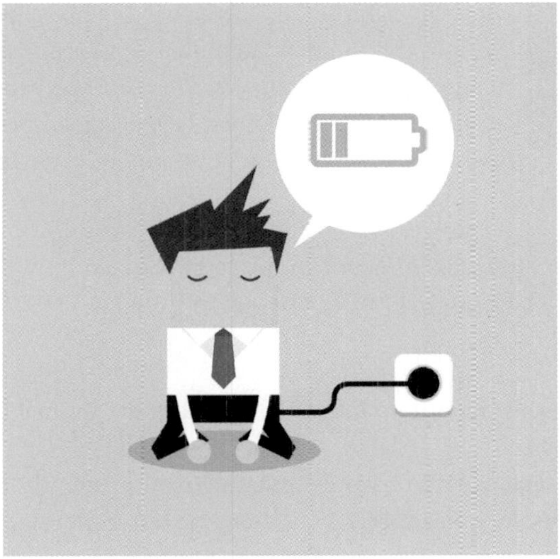

© iStockphoto.com/Nueng

Recharge your batteries. A figure of speech can help an idea stick in your audience's heads.

Use Sound and Rhythm

Sound and rhythmic patterns can also help improve a speech. Consider using parallelism, alliteration, and antithesis.

Parallelism makes your speech vivid through the repetition of words, phrases, or sentences. In his "I Have a Dream" speech, Martin Luther King Jr. buttressed the forcefulness of his message by adding parallelism and figures of speech to it:

> One hundred years later, we must face the tragic fact that the Negro is still not free. One hundred years later, the life of the Negro is still sadly crippled by the manacles of segregation and the chains of discrimination. One hundred years later, the Negro lives in a lonely island of poverty in the midst of a vast ocean of material prosperity. One hundred years later, the Negro is still languishing in the corners of American society and finds himself in exile in his own land.[17]

© iStockphoto.com/Atypeek

Read "The Raven." Edgar Allen Poe's famous poem includes alliteration abundantly.

Each time King used the phrase "one hundred years later" and evoked an image of the plight faced by African Americans a century after the abolishment of slavery, he was using parallelism.

Alliteration is the repetition of initial consonant sounds in nearby words. In a keynote speech he delivered some years ago, the one-time New York Knick and former U.S. senator Bill Bradley used alliteration when he told audience members: "For too long, American leadership has waffled and wiggled and wavered."[18]

Antithesis, another means of adding vividness to a speech, achieves its objective by presenting opposites within the same or adjoining sentences. By juxtaposing contrasting ideas, the speaker can sharpen the message and clarify a point. Urban League spokesperson Whitney M. Young Jr. relied on antithesis to carry his message to his audience:

> We seek not to weaken American but to strengthen it; not to decry America, but to purify it; not to separate America but to become part of it.[19]

By pointing out opposites, antithesis increases the dramatic impact of a speaker's message.

Onomatopoeia, a word or words imitating natural sounds, also enhances vividness. For instance, in a speech on impending water shortages, one student asked her audience what they would do if the water from their shower was never a splash, but just a slow *drip, drip, drip.*

Hyperbole is the use of extreme exaggeration for effect. One speaker, for example, used hyperbole to indicate the effects of corporate outsourcing: "If we don't stop it," she noted, "everyone in this country will be unemployed." Although hyperbole can help a speaker to make his or her point, some believe that because it requires the speaker to exaggerate the audience may perceive the speaker to be lying. However, when used for emphasis or to spur the imagination of receivers, hyperbole can be effective.

Understatement is hyperbole's opposite, drawing attention to an idea by minimizing its importance. For example, in a speech on how God has been depicted in popular culture, a speaker referred to a scene in the film *Bruce Almighty* in which a room virtually explodes with light when God enters. The film's main character, Bruce, however, describes the room as being only "kinda bright." Bruce's words, spoken upon his meeting God for the first time, are an example of understatement.

When used appropriately, each of these speechmaking devices can make your message more striking, your ideas more intense, and your presentation more vivid. So remember, choose your words carefully and arrange your phrases and sentences creatively, and you will bring your speech to life.

13.4e Keep It Personal

Use the personal pronouns *I, us, me, we,* and *you* in your speech. The audience wants to know what you think and what you feel. They want to know you are including them in your thoughts, relating your ideas to them. After all, your speech is for them. Melinda Gates, the wife and partner of Microsoft founder Bill Gates, personalized a speech she gave at Duke University this way:

> Some people assume that Bill and I are too rich to make a connection with someone who's poor, even if our intentions are good. But adjectives like rich and poor don't define who any of us truly are as human beings. And they don't make any one individual less human than the next. The universe is like computer code in that way. Binary. There is life, and there is everything else. Zeroes and ones. I'm a one. You're a one. My friend in the Himalayas is a one.[20]

Despite having great wealth, Melissa Gates succeeded in establishing a personal connection with her audience.

section

13.5

Use Oral Style

When you create a speech, you write it to be heard, not read. Therefore, you should use an oral rather than a written style. Written and oral styles differ from each other in a number of important ways. Consider the following oral style characteristics:

- Oral style is more personal than written style. When delivering a speech, you are able to talk directly to your audience and invite participation in ways a writer cannot.
- Oral style is more repetitive than a written style. Because listeners cannot rehear what you have said, as they can reread a page of text, you'll use more repetition and reinforcement. By repeating and restating your ideas, you let listeners know what is important and what they need to remember.
- Oral style is much *less formal* than written style. While written discourse often contains abstract ideas, complex phrases, and a sophisticated vocabulary, simpler sentences and shorter words and phrases characterize the oral style.
- Oral style is *more adaptive* than written style. You can get immediate feedback and respond in turn.

The language of public speaking is less like the language of an essayist and more like the language of a skilled conversationalist. Listeners better retain and more easily recall a speech when it is filled with everyday colloquial expressions, clear transitions, personal pronouns, and questions that invite participation, than when it is composed of abstract language, complex sentences, and impersonal references. If you want your audience to remember what you say, make them feel more comfortable by using an oral style. A speech is not mailed to an audience; it is delivered aloud.

GAME PLAN

Choosing Your Words

- ☐ I have researched my topic and reviewed my notes for any words that may cause confusion or misunderstanding among members of my audience.
- ☐ I have used plain, unbiased, and respectful language that makes my message clear for my audience to understand.
- ☐ I have chosen words that reflect my views of political correctness, but I have also taken into account the need to avoid being sexist, racist, or ageist.
- ☐ In choosing my words, I have used figurative language in ways that make my ideas clearer yet more evocative.
- ☐ While practicing my speech, I listened for the sound and rhythm of my words, adjusting the wording to use one or more of the following techniques: parallelism, alliteration, antithesis, onomatopoeia, hyperbole, and understatement.
- ☐ Finally, while practicing my speech, I paid attention to and developed my own oral style, translating my sentence outline into an extemporaneous one that utilizes repetition and a certain degree of informality.

Exercises

WORD MATTERS

Mastering the ability to use words to create speechmaking power plays is integral to your success as a speechmaker.

1. Weave a Word Tapestry

Just as war, defensive response, and massacre can be words that indicate the same event to different people, consider the ten words below. Create a figure of speech for each one that evokes fresh images in the minds of different audiences. Decide which choice of word would work best for you and might elicit the response you want from listeners.

1. a distinctive speech
2. immigration
3. a high-school education
4. a dream job
5. birth
6. marriage
7. racism
8. this text
9. football
10. your speechmaking ability

2. Be Word Wise

You have been asked to give a speech on a newer technology—perhaps Instagram, Snapchat, Periscope, Twitter, or another of your choice. What words would you think appropriate to describe this medium in a speech to your class? How would your word choices change were you to deliver the speech to an audience of grandparents? What adaptations would be needed and why?

3. Analyze the Words Used

When giving a speech entitled "Campus Sexual Harassment Policies," a student speaker used a number of hypothetical examples. Featured in the examples were two fictional characters the speaker called Dave Stud and Diane Sex Object. Though a number of students laughed when they heard the names, others were offended and objected vocally at the speech's conclusion, noting that the speaker's word choices were sexist.

- Consider your own response. Even if you understand that the speaker didn't mean to offend, would you advise that he cut these words from his next delivery of the speech?
- Is there another way to achieve the same goals of the speech with different words? If so, which words would you choose?

4. Approach the Speaker's Stand

Choose a controversial current event as a subject. Develop two 2-minute speeches that express very different positions—the first containing words and figures of speech that are likely to bias listeners in favor of the subject, the second containing words and figures of speech that are likely to bias them against it.

Deliver both speeches in class. Ask class members which version they find more effective and why.

RECAP AND REVIEW

1. **Explain how words work.** The Triangle of Meaning—a model of the relationships among words, thoughts, and things—depicts how words work. Its primary message is that words and things are only indirectly related to each other through the thoughts of people. Words are symbols.
2. **Use words that connect with receivers.** Both the message a speaker communicates to an audience and the meaning receivers extract are a result of the words used by the speaker. When words are used effectively, they have the power to unite, evoke fresh images, and encourage a desired response.
3. **Use words that demonstrate your consideration of the audience.** Denotative meaning is a word's dictionary meaning. Connotative meaning is subjective and includes the feelings and personal associations that a word stimulates. The meaning we give to words changes through time and based on geographical location. Speakers need to be sensitive to how people from different generations and different parts of the world use language.
4. **Make strategic word choices.** This is accomplished by adhering to the following word choice guidelines: keep it simple, keep it concrete, keep it appropriate, and keep it vivid. In addition to facilitating an oral style, these guidelines also enable receivers to share the meanings a speaker has in mind.
5. **Adopt an oral style.** An oral style usually contains short sentences, colloquial expressions, clear transitions, and simpler words than writing. It is also more informal, more inviting of participation, more personal, more concrete, and more repetitive.

KEY TERMS

Ageist language 231
Alliteration 234
Antithesis 234
Connotative meaning 224
Denotative meaning 224
Euphemism 230
Figurative language 232
Hyperbole 235
Jargon and technospeak 228
Metaphor 233
Onomatopoeia 234
Political correctness 231
Racist language 231
Sexist language 231
Simile 233
Spotlighting 231
Triangle of Meaning 222
Understatement 235

© iStockphoto.com/Christian J. Stewart

14 Styles of Delivery

UPON COMPLETING THIS CHAPTER'S TRAINING, YOU WILL BE ABLE TO

1. Explain how a speaker's delivery style can enhance or detract from the speech
2. Distinguish among the following delivery modes: memorization, manuscript, extemporaneous, impromptu, and sound bite
3. Determine the best method of delivery for a speech

Poor delivery kills good ideas. Having something to say is only half the battle. The other half is conveying your message effectively and with sincerity.[1]

Good delivery connects you and the audience. A well-delivered speech convinces your audience that you care about both your topic and them. It helps your audience interpret your message appropriately, and it closes whatever gap may exist between you. Because good delivery feels natural, and because it is conversational in tone, it also sounds as if you are talking *with* rather than *at* audience members. In other words, good delivery makes you sound spontaneous, as though you were speaking the words in your presentation for the very first time.[2]

To accomplish this, you need to master whatever mode of delivery you choose to use. You need to learn the options for delivery, set a goal, and monitor your progress—just as an elite athlete does when preparing for game day.

COACHING TIP

"Public speaking is a perfectly normal act . . . which calls . . . only for an extension and development of that most familiar act, conversation."

—James Albert Winans

Be natural. Be positive. Be prepared. Be real. You should not sound phony or overrehearsed when giving your speech. Use a conversational tone, and you will be better able to connect with and relate directly to the members of your audience.

Contents

section

14.1 Choose a Delivery Mode

How do you choose an appropriate delivery style? Take the following three factors into account:

1. The nature of the speaking occasion
2. The purpose of the presentation
3. Your strengths and abilities

Decide whether it is best to deliver a speech from memory, read it from a manuscript, make a few impromptu remarks, speak extemporaneously, or present a sound bite for media consumption.

Whichever method you choose, the mode of delivery should not call attention to itself. Listeners need to be free to concentrate on your ideas, not your mode of delivery. Each of the styles is appropriate for different occasions, purposes, and speakers.

TABLE 14.1 DELIVERY MODES AND LIKELY USES

DELIVERY MODE	LIKELY USE
Memorization	When delivering a brief special occasion speech such as a toast or speech of introduction; when no lengthy quotations or statistical proof are required
Manuscript	When precise wording is crucial; when you need to avoid being misquoted
Extemporaneous	When you are given sufficient time to prepare, develop a working outline or speaker's notes, and practice
Impromptu	When you are asked to speak on a moment's notice
Sound bite/Twitter speak	When you need to provide a quotable, tweetable statement

14.1a Speaking From Memory

When you write your speech out in full, commit it to memory, and then recite it word for word for an audience without using a manuscript, outline, or speaker's notes, you are speaking from memory. **Speaking from memory**, also known as oratory, requires considerable skill and speaking expertise. For one thing, the pressures brought about by the actual presentation could cause you to draw a blank at any point during the speech. Should that occur, instead of listening to you speak, your audience faces a stunning silence as you grope for the words you lost. When you speak from memory, you attempt to deliver your speech word for word, and that makes it even more difficult for you to recover if you make a mistake.

The tension you feel when delivering a memorized speech could affect your delivery in other ways as well. Your delivery could come off as stiff, stilted, and unnatural rather than flexible, friendly, and relaxed. Because you are afraid to deviate from your memorized text for fear of forgetting something, your ability to respond easily to audience feedback might also be inhibited. The danger for some speakers is that they come off sounding mechanical, making this a technique they should not rely on unless absolutely necessary.

Memorizing a speech does, however, offer certain advantages. It is much easier to establish and sustain eye contact with the members of the audience when you don't have to continually look down at a manuscript or notes. Your hands also are freer to gesture and support the meaning of your message.

Although there certainly are a number of speaking occasions that lend themselves to speaking from memory, including toasts and testimonials, acceptance speeches, speeches of introduction, and eulogies, the bulk of your speechmaking experiences will be a composite of the remaining delivery methods. Of course, even when using these, you might find it useful to memorize some sections of your speech such as the introduction, conclusion, or a particularly effective quotation.

When delivering a speech, or even a section of a speech, from memory, keep these techniques in mind:

1. Rehearse sufficiently to sound natural.
2. Keep your energy high.
3. Use appropriate nonverbal cues to reinforce the spoken words.

© iStockphoto.com/vm

Officially speaking. Formal speaking occasions, such as official proclamations, may require speaking from a manuscript.

14.1b Manuscript Reading

When running for president in 2008, John McCain was criticized for his inability to use the teleprompter. More comfortable in "give-and-take" impromptu settings and town meetings, Senator McCain found it difficult to meet the challenge of more formal speaking demands, often sounding like he was reading his lines, and creating the impression that he was overscripted.[3] Yet, if McCain misread a line, he was accused of being unprepared—with his misstatements becoming fodder for YouTube. In contrast to McCain, president Barack Obama was very comfortable using the teleprompter, turning to it not only for his most important speeches but also for routine announcements and the opening statements at news conferences. For President Obama, the teleprompter was a means of ensuring that he stuck to his intended message.[4]

Like speaking from memory, **manuscript reading** requires that you write a manuscript in full and deliver it word for word, but you need not commit the text to memory. At the same time, because reading aloud well requires every bit as much skill as mastering a script and delivering it expressively, manuscript reading is not as easy as it sounds. If you do not invest a lot of time practicing reading your manuscript aloud, you could end up *eye-* and *hand-tied* to your manuscript, and deprive your audience of meaningful eye contact and gesturing.

Bringing the printed page to life for listeners requires that you take your eyes off the manuscript and close the communicative gap between you and your audience. If you read in a monotone, you will bore receivers. The reading of your speech needs to sound like conversation to your listeners. It needs to sound as though you are speaking rather than reading it, or it will not have the impact you desire. This requires that vocal cues (delivering lines with ease) and physical cues (no poorly timed gestures or inappropriate smiles) also support delivery (see Chapters 15 and 16).

Because the manuscript directs the speaker, it also becomes virtually impossible to go off script and adapt it, changing a word or phrase as needed. Thus, a manuscript affords a speaker less flexibility. This can be a downside, but is beneficial when a speaker needs to be especially careful about the phrasing of a problem or policy. Presidential, foreign policy, and political addresses; official proclamations; and presentations at business, trade, and stockholder meetings—occasions where a slip of the tongue could be disastrous—are appropriate settings for a manuscript speech. In addition, when time is strictly limited, a manuscript speech may be the right choice.

When the demands of the occasion make manuscript delivery necessary, remember the following:

- ☐ Write the speech to be listened to; the audience will not be reading along with you.
- ☐ Be sure to use a font that is easy to read and large enough to see.
- ☐ Mark up the manuscript with delivery cues. Focus on communicating ideas, not words.
- ☐ Practice reading it aloud so your words sound fresh.
- ☐ Become so familiar with the manuscript that you are able to maintain eye contact and integrate appropriate gestures.

14.1c Impromptu Speaking

How did you feel the last time you were put on the spot and asked to say a few words? Perhaps someone asked you to describe yourself in an interview, answer a question in class, or explain your position during a meeting. Were you ready to respond without extensive time to plan, prepare, or practice? You are likely to give at least one, if not many, impromptu speeches daily, and a majority of the public speaking you will do during your business or professional life will probably be unplanned.[5]

Unlike memorization and manuscript reading, **impromptu speaking** requires that you be able to think on your feet. All you really have to rely on when delivering an impromptu talk is your knowledge and previous experience.

If you are adept at gathering your thoughts quickly and summarizing them succinctly, then you will always be prepared to deliver an impromptu speech. You can apply all the lessons you've learned about delivering planned speeches—the principles of effective structure, support, and delivery—to the impromptu situation. Though unplanned speaking may seem unnatural or awkward to you, it offers you both flexibility and the opportunity to demonstrate your speaking versatility. Perhaps more than any other speechmaking style, delivering an impromptu speech helps you reveal to others who you are, what you are like, and what genuinely concerns you.[6]

When called on to deliver an impromptu speech, remember the following guidelines:

- ☐ Compose yourself.
- ☐ Think about your purpose.
- ☐ Relate the subject to what you know and have experienced and receiver interests.
- ☐ Organize your talk—connect your ideas to each other, and be certain to use an introduction, body, and conclusion.
- ☐ Don't ramble. Keep it brief, covering just two to three points.
- ☐ Stay on message.

© iStockphoto.com/Bronwyn8

Take note. Extemporaneous speeches are delivered conversationally with the support of speaker's notes.

14.1d Extemporaneous Speaking

When a speech is prepared and practiced in advance but is neither written out word for word nor memorized, it is most likely an example of **extemporaneous speaking**. The extemporaneous speaker delivers a speech using only speaker's notes as a reminder. Partly because the speaker selects the exact words virtually at the moment of their delivery, the language seems more natural and spontaneous. When the speech is not memorized, the speaker can exhibit a more conversational quality; when it is not read from a script, the speaker can maintain generous eye contact. This facilitates the monitoring of audience reactions and adjusting to the feedback received. As a result, the extemporaneous speaker establishes a more direct connection with audience members.

The emphasis in extemporaneous speaking is on communication, not recitation or memorization. It requires that the speaker be flexible enough to adapt to the audience and demands extensive planning, organization, and practice. Because it connects well with audiences and because it builds speaker confidence, extemporaneous speaking is the method preferred by most public speaking teachers and experienced speakers alike.

To prepare a good extemporaneous speech, remember to:

- ☐ Research the topic thoroughly.
- ☐ Create an outline and speaker's notes.
- ☐ Rehearse, familiarizing yourself with the organizational pattern, including the introduction and conclusion.
- ☐ Speak conversationally.
- ☐ Become so comfortable with the topic that you are able to adjust your speech, adapting to the audience as needed.

14.1e Sound Bite Speaking (Twitter Speak)

According to political media adviser, communications consultant, and former Fox chairman Roger Ailes, contemporary speakers should respond to our "headline society."[7] Ailes reasoned, "In today's society, long-winded people will soon be as extinct as the dinosaur."[8] Although most instructors of speech want students to avoid **sound bite speaking** (or what we might refer to as **Twitter speak**) in the classroom, there are some speaking situations in which it is now seen as required.

During political conventions or events, after the delivery of speeches by public figures, or in the course of introducing new policies or programs, spokespersons, pundits, and politicians "spin their messages," frequently using sound bites—short, memorable statements that can be tweeted after being delivered aurally. Because audiences today are impatient for information, speakers need to be able to distill their messages effectively. Notice in the table below how speakers can hold or lose the attention of receivers by the way they package a thought:[9]

Keep these techniques in mind when delivering a sound bite or Twitter speak:

- ☐ Develop a sentence that captures your subject's essence.
- ☐ Make your comments memorable.
- ☐ Abbreviate the speech until it is tweet-size—140 characters. You might also create a 6-second video to accompany it, using Vine.

TABLE 14.2

DULL	MORE INTERESTING
The two leading ways to achieve success are improving upon existing technology and diminishing the larger obligation.	The two leading recipes for success are building a better mousetrap and finding a bigger loophole. —Edgar A. Schoaff
To construct an amalgam, you have to be willing to split open its component parts.	To make an omelet, you have to be willing to break a few eggs. —Robert Penn Warren
Capital will not produce great pleasure, but it will remunerate a large research staff to examine the questions proposed for a solution.	Money won't buy happiness, but it will pay the salaries of a large research staff to study the problem. —Bill Vaughan

section 14.2

Plan and Practice

"If I'm supposed to sound spontaneous and natural, as if I'm giving my speech for the first time, why do I need to rehearse it?" asks the novice speechmaker. This question has several answers.

Just as an athlete practices a play until it is second nature, so a speechmaker needs to rehearse his or her part until it becomes "one" with him or her. For athletes, every move matters. Once they know a play cold—so they don't need to think about where they should be on the field—they are free to focus their attention on what the other team does. For speakers and athletes, it is thinking ahead and practicing that get them to that point.

Finally, the old adage "Practice makes perfect" has merit—if you practice correctly. Aspirants to political office know this well. Prior to the presidential debates, for example, candidates typically spend weeks preparing, including listening to audiotapes of their past performances and engaging in mock debates that are videotaped and reviewed.

How often and in what sequence should you practice? As much as it takes to succeed. Although rehearsal is a highly individual matter, we can provide you with some basic practice advice to ensure you practice right.

Digital Vision/Photodisc/Thinkstock

Practice makes perfect. Like athletes and actors, speakers need to practice regularly to improve performance.

14.2a Schedule Multiple Early Practices

© iStockphoto.com/baona

Scheduling. Plan your practice times in advance to make sure you don't get stuck memorizing a lot in a little amount of time.

Don't make time your enemy. Begin practicing at least half a week before you will deliver the speech. Do not wait for the night before. Practicing well ahead of the delivery date lets you master the message.

In early practice sessions, repeatedly read through your notes, outline, or manuscript. If you will be delivering a manuscript speech or a speech from memory, rehearse using a triple-spaced manuscript with large and easy-to-read fonts that you mark up to indicate which words and phrases to stress, when to speed up and slow down, and when to pause.

If you will be delivering an extemporaneous speech, this is your opportunity to refine your outline into speaker's notes. Begin by reading it over a number of times before you speak it aloud. As you rehearse, develop a list of key words and phrases from that outline and place them on no more than a handful of note cards. Write on one side of the card only. From then on, use the cards to spark your memory. Be sure to print quotations and statistics in large letters on separate cards, but do not reproduce complete paragraphs or the entire speech on these cards. Also, be sure to number the cards to avoid fumbling through them when you are in front of the audience.

Keep in mind that, though many students use note cards, most professional speakers do not, preferring instead to use a single sheet of paper containing their key words and phrases, quotations, expert testimony, and key statistics. When used alone or together with any visual aids the speaker plans to use, this page usually suffices.

14.2b Verbalize Everything

Practice your delivery of every example and illustration, recite every quotation, and say aloud every statistic you plan to use. Familiarity begets clarity and comfort in public speaking. Without sufficient practice, you won't build the self-confidence you need to deliver an effective presentation.

14.2c Prepare and Practice With Your Visual, Audio, and Memory Aids

If you will be using visual, audio, or memory aids during the speech, work with them during your practice sessions. This will help you work out any kinks, electronic or otherwise, and will make your delivery of the speech smoother and more natural.

14.2d Check Your Time

Time your presentation. If it is too long, cut out nonessential information and redundant examples. Tighten your phrasing. You might even need to eliminate one of your key points. If your speech is too short, make it more substantial. You might add another main point, or include another illustration or example.

14.2e Replicate Actual Speechmaking Conditions

Do your best to mirror the actual conditions and setting you will experience when giving your speech. Although sitting down and running through the speech in your head is useful early on in your preparation to increase your familiarity with your speech's content, standing in front of an audience is different. Make sure you practice the speech standing up and hold a realistic dress rehearsal, ideally in a room as much as possible like the one in which you actually deliver the speech. And run through the entire speech rather than continually stopping.

14.2f Watch and Listen to Yourself Alone and With Others

It is important to monitor your progress. During your preparation, you should seek feedback before doing your final polishing and running a last dress rehearsal. Get feedback while you still have time to make and master changes.

Audio or video record your rehearsal and play it back for self-evaluation. Rehearse in front of friends and family and get feedback from them. Practicing in front of other people has been shown to improve the actual performance.[10]

14.2g Give Yourself a Preliminary Evaluation

Pay attention to what works and what needs work. As you review your performance, ask yourself whether you are expressing your ideas as clearly as you would like to. Do you have an attention-getter? Is your language understandable to audience members? Is the support you used adequate? Is the organization easy to follow? Does your conclusion contain both a summary and a psychological appeal? Keep in mind that an organized speech will be easier to to remember because it will flow logically.

14.2h Refine, Practice, and Refine

In your last stage of practicing, the focus is on refining, not dramatically altering the speech. Practice. Practice. Practice. Make your final rehearsal as realistic as possible.

14.2i Work on Nonverbal Aspects of Delivery

Pay attention to your use of nonverbal cues during your practice sessions. Ask your rehearsal audiences whether you make enough eye contact, employ meaningful gestures, and use your voice and appearance to advantage (techniques we cover in more detail in Chapters 15 and 16).

14.2j Hold a Mock Q&A Session

While not all speeches are followed with a question and answer (Q&A) session, knowing how to handle one can be just as important as preparing yourself to deliver the speech. Though the Q&A has much in common with the impromptu speech, there are things you can do to prepare yourself. You can:

- ☐ Anticipate some of the questions audience members will ask, and prepare answers to them in advance.
- ☐ Think about questions you hope audience members won't ask, and prepare answers for them.
- ☐ Prepare a "Tip Sheet" with points to remember when answering particularly complex questions.
- ☐ Have someone rehearse you by asking you the potential questions you've brainstormed as well as others designed to unnerve you.
- ☐ Repeat a question aloud if it is phrased in a neutral manner, before answering it; if necessary, you can rephrase it to remove any venomous or loaded words.
- ☐ Practice saying, "I don't know," if you don't know. You still have time to find out the answers prior to the delivery day. And if you have to answer a question with an "I don't know" on delivery day, promise to find out the answer and get back to the person who posed the question.
- ☐ Remember, you don't need to answer more than is asked.

(We cover the Q&A session in more depth in Chapter 27.)

section
14.3 Avoid Common Delivery Bloopers

Your goal is to be fully ready to deliver a peak performance. To ensure you are, don't commit any of these training fouls:

- ***Preparing mentally does not replace preparing aurally.*** Though thinking through your speech is helpful, it should never replace live practice sessions in which you rehearse your speech aloud.
- ***Don't wait to be given feedback.*** It's important to seek feedback, not count on others to give it on their own. Ask your mock audience(s) what they think and feel about your speech.
- ***Don't skip practice sessions.*** Skipping practice is a sign of overconfidence. Telling yourself you have it down when the truth is you need to continue working does a disservice to yourself and your audience.

GAME PLAN

Refining My Speech Delivery

- ☐ After considering my speech topic, the occasion, and my own level of comfort, I have chosen a style of delivery that will enable me to really connect with the audience.
- ☐ Given the delivery style I've chosen to use, my speaking notes are clear, easy to follow, and marked with delivery cues such as "refer to slide," "slow down for impact," or "stress this word."
- ☐ I've practiced my speech several times; at this point, I know the organization and my notes so well that I can adjust to different audience reactions.
- ☐ The idea of a question-and-answer session makes me a little nervous so I held a mock Q&A in which I answered some of the questions I anticipate will be asked.
- ☐ To control any anxiety I may experience, I've reviewed some of the confidence-building techniques from Chapter 1.
- ☐ I've reviewed video of other accomplished speakers, and through my practice sessions, I have a sense of what will work for me and what won't in reaching my audience.

Exercises

DELIVERY

Prepare and practice so that when you present you're confident and professional.

1. Get More Comfortable in Front of Others

Prepare a manuscript or notes for a two-minute talk on one of the following topics: A Time My Beliefs Were Challenged; A Space or Environment Where I Felt Out of Place; To Tweet or Not to Tweet; The Best Advice I Ever Received; or My Favorite Things About My Hometown.[11] Deliver your talk in three ways: (1) read it word for word once, (2) speak from memory, (3) speak using notes. It's okay if it's not perfect; just get a feel for the difference in styles and practice. Remember to refer back to the guidelines for each speaking style.

2. Getting to Know You: Introducing the Q&A

Choose something to "show" that tells others about you—perhaps something personal that you use to distinguish yourself from others such as your phone's ringtone(s), a favorite pair of shoes, an unusual necklace, a special photo from Facebook or Instagram. Your audience will ask you questions about why you chose the item you did, what your choice means, why you think it distinguishes you, and so on. Be prepared to give impromptu answers.

3. How Talk Show Talents Do It

Compare and contrast the opening monologues of two late-night talk show hosts; for example, you might compare Jimmy Fallon with Jimmy Kimmel. Explain what distinguishes one performer's style from the other.

4. Analyze a Politician's Delivery

View a video of former president Bill Clinton's speech given at the 2016 Democratic Convention. Then do the following:

1. Identify and evaluate the effectiveness of the style(s) of delivery Clinton used, providing specific examples of his ability to build rapport, make an argument, and forcefully make his case.
2. Compare and contrast Clinton's speech with the one given by Melania Trump at the 2016 Republican Convention.
   - Which of the two do you think more quickly established rapport with the audience?
   - Which of the two came across as more natural and personable?
   - Which of the two made you feel as if she or he was speaking directly to you?
   - Which of the two had better eye contact?
   - Which of the two used his or her voice more effectively?
   - How did both use gestures to underscore their messages?
3. Discuss the extent to which mode and manner of delivery influence the speaker's ability to personalize a speech and connect with the audience.

5. Approach the Speaker's Stand

First, deliver an impromptu speech on a favorite recreational activity. Once this is done, write out and deliver the speech using a manuscript. Then revise your notes and deliver the speech extemporaneously.

- How different were these experiences for you? For the audience?
- Which means of delivery do you think had more conversational appeal?
- Which delivery mode was easier for the audience to listen to?

RECAP AND REVIEW

1. **Explain how a speaker's delivery style can enhance or detract from the speech.** Speakers who deliver their speeches as if they mean them are better able to connect with the audience. A well-delivered speech helps the audience interpret the message appropriately, closing whatever gap may exist between them and the speaker.
2. **Distinguish among the following delivery modes: memorization, manuscript, extemporaneous, impromptu, and sound bite.** When you speak from memory, you attempt to deliver your speech word for word without using a manuscript or notes. Manuscript reading requires that you be able to bring the printed page to life, making your words sound like conversation rather than like reading. When you speak in an impromptu manner, you deliver a speech off the cuff. In contrast, an extemporaneous speech is prepared and delivered in a conversational manner from speaker's notes. Sound bites are brief packaged thoughts offering simple solutions that appeal to our "headline society" as well as the Twittersphere.
3. **Determine the best method of delivery for a speech.** The best method depends on the nature of the speaking occasion, the purpose of the presentation, and the speaker's strengths and abilities.

KEY TERMS

Extemporaneous speaking 246
Impromptu speaking 245
Manuscript reading 244
Sound bite speaking 247
Speaking from memory 243
Twitter speak 247

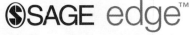

© iStockphoto.com/[joshblake]

15 The Speaker's Voice

UPON COMPLETING THIS CHAPTER'S TRAINING, YOU WILL BE ABLE TO

1. Describe how vocal cues can facilitate communication between the speaker and the audience
2. Explain how culture affects the use and interpretation of vocal cues
3. Effectively give voice to a speech

Think of award-winning performers such as Nicole Kidman or Alan Cumming. Like the rest of us, actors attempt to use their voices to reflect the state of being of the character they are portraying. For Kidman, who hails from Australia, and Cumming, who is from Scotland, this can mean concealing the sound of their normal speaking voice and adopting an American accent instead. They do this so naturally that unless we knew they were not born in the United States, we would not be able to tell. Their manner of speaking does not call attention to itself

The voice of the accomplished speaker enhances the expression of ideas *without* calling undue attention to itself or distracting receivers. When audience members are attracted, not distracted, by the sound of your voice, they are better able to concentrate on what you have to say. When listening to an effective presentation, an audience senses a speaker's enthusiasm, feels the force inherent in the speaker's voicing of ideas, and senses the speaker's desire to communicate.

Researchers have discovered that the bulk of a message's personal and connotative meaning is communicated via its nonverbal delivery. According to one study, words carry only some 7 percent of the meaning, with 38 percent of meaning attributed to vocal cues, and the remaining 55 percent attributed to the speaker's body language.[1] Audiences tend to trust the nonverbal level of communication. Deliver your speech honestly and effectively, and your audience members are likely to find you credible and believe you.

Contents

section

15.1 Control the Sound of Your Speech

How would you describe your voice? When you hear it, does it sound pleasant to you? How do others respond to it? While we would all like to have a voice that others refer to as "golden," many an effective speaker has a voice that is undistinguished. Consider, for example, that president Abraham Lincoln's voice has been called high pitched and wavering and prime minister Margaret Thatcher's as shrill and grating.[2] Each of these speakers, however, mastered the art of vocal control.

When used to advantage, your voice is a powerfully expressive tool[3] that plays an important role in your audience's response both to you and your speech.[4] Audiences form impressions of speakers based on vocal cues alone, making inferences about the speaker's age, status, ethnicity, and occupation, just to name a few. We stereotype others based on how they sound (see Table 15.1).

Keeping all this in mind, answer these questions honestly:

- Does my voice help me convey the meaning of my speech clearly?
- If I were in my audience, would I want to listen to me for an extended period of time?
- Does my voice enhance or detract from the impression I make?

In the next few sections, we look at the **paralinguistic**, or vocal cues—pitch, volume, rate, and articulation—that play a part in creating the impression you make on an audience.

TABLE 15.1 VOCAL CUES AND PERSONALITY STEREOTYPES

VOCAL CUES	SPEAKERS	STEREOTYPES
Breathiness	Males Females	Young, artistic Feminine, pretty, effervescent, high-strung, shallow
Thinness	Males Females	No effect on listener's image of speaker Social, physical, emotional, and mental immaturity; sense of humor and sensitivity
Flatness	Males Females	Masculine, sluggish, cold, withdrawn Masculine, sluggish, cold, withdrawn
Nasality	Males Females	Wide array of socially undesirable characteristics Wide array of socially undesirable characteristics
Tenseness	Males Females	Old, unyielding cantankerous Young, emotional, feminine, high-strung, less intelligent
Throatiness	Males Females	Old, realistic, mature, sophisticated, well-adjusted Less intelligent, masculine, lazy, boorish, unemotional, ugly, sickly, careless, inartistic, humble, uninteresting, neurotic, apathetic
Orotundity (fullness/ richness)	Males Females	Energetic, healthy, artistic, sophisticated, proud, interesting, enthusiastic Lively, gregarious, aesthetically sensitive, proud
Increased rate	Males Females	Animated and extroverted Animated and extroverted
Increased pitch variety	Males Females	Dynamic, feminine, aesthetic Dynamic and extroverted

Sources: Based on Dudley Knight, *Speaking With Skill: A Skills Based Approach to Speech Training* (New York: Bloomsbury Publishing, 2012); Kate DeVore, *The Voice Book: Caring for, Protecting, and Improving Your Voice* (Chicago: Chicago Review Press, 2009); and Paul Heinberg, *Voice Training for Speaking and Reading Aloud* (New York: Ronald Press, 1964).

Pitch Your Voice Properly

section
15.2

15.2a Vary Pitch

15.2b Consider the Effects of Stereotypes

Pitch is the highness or lowness of your voice on a tonal scale; it is your voice's upward or downward inflection. Like a pitcher varies location and speed when he or she throws a baseball, hoping to make it difficult for the batter to anticipate the coming pitch, we vary our voices to avoid talking in a monotone and to add expressiveness to our words. Audiences judge a speaker who varies his or her pitch to be livelier, animated, and interesting.

15.2a Vary Pitch

Our *habitual pitch,* the level at which we speak most often, may or may not be our *optimal pitch,* which is where our voice functions best and where we have extensive vocal variation up and down the scale. Varying your pitch increases the communicative value of your words. It also helps convey your message's meaning. For example, can you use pitch to change the meaning of these words?

I'm so happy to be here.

With rising and/or falling intonation, you can give that sentence very different meanings from genuinely expressing happiness, to sarcasm, to distain. Saying those words in a monotone, for instance, would mean you are not happy. Your pitch also reveals whether you are making a statement or asking a question. It conveys your emotion and can make you sound angry or annoyed, patient or tolerant. Speakers who are able to vary their pitch to reflect the mood they are expressing are more persuasive than those who use a repetitive pitch pattern.[5]

Fine tuning. How can you use the sound of your voice and other vocal cues to impact the meaning of your speech?

15.2b Consider the Effects of Stereotypes

Audiences tend to stereotype speakers on the basis of their voices. Lower-pitched voices are considered more mature, sexier, and stronger than higher-pitched voices, which are frequently associated with helplessness, nervousness, and tension. When we are nervous or scared, the pitch of our voice tends to rise because the muscles around our vocal cords constrict. To keep your pitch natural, remember to use the stress relaxation exercises discussed in Chapter 1.

section
15.3

Adjust Volume

Volume is the loudness or softness of the voice, its intensity. Aim to speak with enough force that everyone in attendance is able to hear you comfortably, but don't overwhelm your audience. Good breath control lets you vary your volume as needed. Breathe deeply from the diaphragm rather than take shallow, vocal cord–level breaths. Even when speaking your lowest, audience members in the very last row should still be able hear you.

15.3a Adapt to the Situation

Regulate your volume to reflect the size and acoustics of the room, the size of the audience, and any competing background noises. Increasing your volume at particular points can help you emphasize specific words and ideas, add emotional intensity, and energize the room. In contrast, decreasing your volume can also help you gain or sustain audience attention, convey a contrasting emotion, or even add suspense.

15.3b Consider Cultural Adaptations

Generally, in the United States we consider a voice that is too loud to be intrusive and aggressive, and a voice that is too low to be meek, hesitant, and less credible.

The volume the members of one culture judge to be appropriate may be unacceptable to and misinterpreted by the members of another culture. In general, Latinos, Arabs, Israelis, and Italians tend to speak more loudly than Anglo Americans and East Asians.[6] For Arabs, loudness connotes strength and sincerity, whereas speaking too softly implies that one lacks confidence or is timid.[7] For Asians, a gentle, soothing voice is reflective of good manners.[8]

Volume control. Listen to the room and adjust your volume accordingly.

Regulate Rate

section
15.4

15.4a Reflect Mood

15.4b Use Silent Pauses

15.4c Avoid Verbal Fillers

Rate is the speed at which you speak. Most of us speak between 125 and 175 words per minute. Speaking too quickly communicates a desire to get the speech over with in record time and audience members may find it difficult to keep up. Speaking too slowly communicates tentativeness and lack of confidence and may bore the audience.

15.4a Reflect Mood

Your rate should vary to reflect any change in the speech's mood: slow when you want to express thoughtfulness, solemnity, concern, or are relaying serious and complex material; quicker when you want to convey excitement, a sense of urgency, eagerness, happiness, or when sharing lighter contents or heading toward a climax.

For example, Martin Luther King Jr. began his "I Have a Dream" speech uttering words at approximately 92 words per minute; he finished it at a rate of approximately 145 words per minute. King's rate of speech quickened as he headed toward his speech's emotional conclusion. Think of rate as the pulse of your speech. It should quicken to convey agitation, excitement, and happiness, and fall to convey seriousness of purpose, serenity, or sadness.

© iStockphoto.com/SunChan

Like a rollercoaster. Build up the rate of your words or slow it down to match what you're trying to convey and take the audience on a ride.

COACHING TIP

"Words mean more than what is set down on paper. It takes the human voice to infuse them with meaning."

—Maya Angelou

Your voice can help or hurt your speech. When it helps, it communicates to the audience how much you care about your topic. When it hurts, it hinders your ability to connect with the audience or sustain their attention. Play your voice like you would an instrument.

15.4b Use Silent Pauses

To slow the rate of speech . . . *pause.* You can pause to emphasize your meaning, underscore the importance of an idea, lend dramatic impact to a statement, give your listeners time to reflect on what you have said, and signal the end of a thought. In fact, according to *60 Minutes* producer Don Hewitt, "The pauses tell the story. They are as important to us as commas and periods are to the *New York Times*."[9] Pauses help the speaker maintain control. Use the following pause pointers to enhance your effectiveness:

Pause . . .

- ☐ Before starting. Some speakers begin speaking even before getting to the front of the room. This demonstrates a lack of control. Instead, once in position, pause, scan the audience, and then begin.
- ☐ After posing a rhetorical question. Give members of the audience time to contemplate the question.
- ☐ When you are about to make an important point. Silence signals the significance of what will come next.
- ☐ When transitioning from one part of the speech to another. This gives receivers time to adjust psychologically.
- ☐ After delivering your final words. Don't leave your position while still speaking, demonstrating your desire to remove yourself from being the audience's focus. Instead, pause, scan the audience as you did at the outset, and then walk back to your seat at a comfortable pace.

Red light. Pauses help signal important points to the audience, and they help slow down the rate of a speech.

As with other cues, culture intervenes in our perception of the pause. Among European Americans, for example, too extended a pause can cause receivers discomfort, making them feel tense and anxious. In Japan and India, however, long pauses are natural and a sign that one is collecting one's thoughts.

15.4c Avoid Verbal Fillers

One thing you want to be certain *not* to do is fill a meaningful pause with meaningless sounds and phrases such as *er, uh, um, okay,* or *you know.* Such extraneous vocal fillers disrupt the natural flow of your presentation, diminishing your credibility. Here's an example of how verbal fillers impede effective delivery:

> Um . . . I was, uh, hoping, you . . . um, would step up, ah . . . you know, and . . . um, sign this . . . petition, um, because, you know, it is a matter . . . uh, of life, and uh . . . death.

Not very persuasive, is it? Make a conscious effort to notice when you use vocal fillers (ask a friend or family member to point out each use), and focus on eliminating them from your repertoire of spoken sounds.

© iStockphoto.com/hnrahalbey

Er, um. Aim to eliminate verbal fillers that detract from your message.

COACHING TIP

"We often refuse to accept an idea merely because the tone of voice in which it has been expressed is unsympathetic to us."

—Friedrich Nietzsche

Match your voice to your message's mood. Speaking too loudly or too softly may convey the wrong impression to receivers, especially if they are used to listening to speakers whose habitual volume intensity is different from yours.

section

15.5 Pay Attention to Articulation and Pronunciation

Articulation is the way you pronounce individual sounds. Ideally, you speak the sounds of speech sharply and distinctly. When you fail to utter a final sound (a final *t* or *d*, for example); fail to produce the sounds of words properly (substituting or adding a sound where it doesn't belong, like *idear*); or voice a sound in an unclear, imprecise, or incorrect way (*come wimme* instead of *come with me*), then you are guilty of faulty articulation. As a speaker, your responsibility is to say your words so your audience can understand them. If your listeners can't understand you, they can't respond appropriately, and they may simply conclude you either don't know what you are talking about or are an inept speaker.

While the focus of articulation is on the production of speech sounds, the focus of **pronunciation** is on whether the words themselves are said correctly. Have you ever stressed the wrong syllable in a word or pronounced sounds that should stay silent? Among common mispronunciation errors are adding unnecessary sounds, omitting necessary sounds, reversing sounds, or misplacing an accent (see Table 15.2).

To avoid problems with pronunciation, use a dictionary or check a reputable pronunciation guide online to learn how a word should be said. Because mispronouncing a word can cause a loss in credibility, it is something you want to avoid. Don't wait for an audience member to point out an error in pronunciation to you.

TABLE 15.2 FREQUENTLY MISPRONOUNCED WORDS

Some words in the English language are frequently mispronounced. We identify a number of commonly mispronounced words here with their correct pronunciations and most common mispronunciations.

	CORRECT	INCORRECT
athlete	(ATH-leet)	(ATH-a-leet)
Arctic	(ARC-tic)	(AR-tic)
comfortable	(COM-fort-a-ble)	(COMF-ter-ble)
espresso	(ess-PRESS-oh)	(ex-PRESS-oh)
figure	(FIG-yer)	(fig-er)
forte	(FORT)	(for-TAY)—correct only as a music term
lambaste	(lam-BASTE)	(lam-BAST)
menstruation	(men-stroo-A-shun)	(men-STRAY-shun)
nuclear	(NUKE-lee-ar)	(NUKE-yoo-lar)

	CORRECT	INCORRECT
nuptial	(NUP-shul)	(NUP-shoo-al)
often	(OFF-en)	(OFT-en)
probably	(PROB-ab-ly)	(PRAH-bal-ly, PROB-ly)
realtor	(RE-al-tor)	(REAL-a-tor)
supposedly	(sup-POSE-ed-ly)	(sup-POSE-ab-ly)
taut	(TAUT)	(TAUNT)
toward	(TOW-ward)	(TOR-ward)

Source: Used by permission of Samuel Stoddard, RinkWorks, www.rinkworks.com/words/mispronounced.shtml.

Be Aware of Dialects and Regionalisms

section
15.6

A **dialect** is a speech pattern characteristic of a group of people from a particular area or of a specific ethnicity. Although there is no one area or group whose dialect is right or wrong, people do have preferences regarding the appropriate use of language and may even stereotype others on the basis of their dialects. For example, people in the South may perceive those in the Northeast as brusque and abrasive, whereas Northeasterners may perceive Southerners as slow and surface-sweet. Midwestern speech patterns, in contrast, are frequently held up as a standard to emulate, and they characterize the dialects exhibited by many television news anchors. Most people have grown accustomed to Midwestern speech and prefer to listen either to it or to someone who sounds just like they themselves do.

If you don't have a neutral dialect, this doesn't mean your dialect is "bad" or inferior. Still, ask yourself whether your dialect could prevent understanding in your audience. If the answer is yes, then you will want to take some action to overcome the prejudices your listeners hold about your dialect. At the same time, each audience member should keep in mind that she or he should not prejudge a speech based on the speaker's dialect.

Despite this, it may be that audience members will perceive you as more credible if you adapt your dialect, making it more in line with the one they prefer to listen to, which in many cases will be Standard English. Adjusting your dialect (not abandoning it altogether) based on the situation is known as "code switching." Just as you might not use the same words when speaking to a supervisor, professor, or elder as you would when speaking with your friends, so you might use one dialect when interacting with others informally and another when delivering a speech in public.

GAME PLAN

Maximizing My Vocal Effectiveness

- ☐ I have identified my vocal strengths and will build on them to convey the meaning of my words clearly to the audience.
- ☐ I will use my optimal pitch rather than my habitual pitch to make listening to me easier and to ensure I have sufficient vocal range.
- ☐ I've practiced my speech to ensure everyone will be able to hear me.
- ☐ I've identified where in my speech to raise and lower my volume and where to pause to stress an important point.
- ☐ I've done my best to eliminate verbal fillers and articulation and pronunciation errors.
- ☐ I've reviewed video of how other accomplished speakers use their voices to connect with the audience.

Exercises

USING YOUR VOICE

Mastering the ability to use vocal cues to enhance delivery demonstrates speechmaking acumen. To increase your ability, participate in these activities.

1. Vocal Stretchers

Take time to conduct an examination of your voice in order to expand your vocal comfort zone. Start by "playing your voice" like an instrument, using different pitches to express your ideas, and varying your volume and rate dramatically. If you typically speak softly, now project your words with more force. If you usually speak loudly, lower your volume but still be understandable. Similarly, if you are a "fast talker," deliberately slow the flow of your words, and if you are a "slow talker," speed up without sacrificing clarity.

2. Can You Hear Me Now?

Using the sentence, "I am so happy to be here with you," pair up and take turns speaking it in a large classroom or empty auditorium, with one of you speaking from the front of the room and the other sitting in the last row. How loud do you need to speak in order to be heard? Aside from being heard, what do you need to do with your voice to make the other person believe you, doubt your sincerity, laugh at the remark, or feel compassion for you?

3. Analyze This: The Sound of Speech

Search for "speeches that inspire" or "speeches by famous people" on YouTube and listen to two. Choose one delivered by a speaker from your own culture and another by a speaker from a different culture. Take notes on each speaker's use of vocal cues, including pitch, volume, rate, articulation, and pronunciation, listening for differences as well as similarities, and discuss your impressions of their effectiveness.

4. Approach the Speaker's Stand

Make a video of yourself delivering a one-minute speech on the importance of vocal cues or another topic of your choice. Review the video and evaluate its vocal aspects, being sure to focus on those elements covered in this chapter.

RECAP AND REVIEW

1. **Describe how vocal cues can facilitate communication between the speaker and the audience.** Receivers tend to evaluate speakers based on use of pitch (the highness or lowness of the voice on a tonal scale), volume (the loudness or softness of the voice), rate (the speed of speech), articulation (the production of individual speech sounds), and pronunciation (whether the words are correctly said). When these elements of vocal delivery are used effectively, the audience views the speaker more positively.
2. **Explain how culture affects the use and interpretation of vocal cues.** Effective speakers and audiences are aware of vocal preferences or proclivities influenced by culture, recognizing that the cultural norms of others may differ from their own. By becoming aware of how people from different cultures use their voices, audience members decrease chances for misinterpreting and misjudging a speaker's intentions.
3. **Effectively give voice to a speech.** Eliminating distracting vocal qualities improves speaking habits. By identifying and then correcting vocal problems, you enhance your ability to express yourself effectively.

KEY TERMS

Articulation 264
Dialect 265
Paralinguistics 258
Pitch 259
Pronunciation 264
Rate 261
Volume 260

© iStockphoto.com/Klubovy

16

Physical Aspects of Delivery

UPON COMPLETING THIS CHAPTER'S TRAINING, YOU WILL BE ABLE TO

1. Describe how a speaker's physical cues can enhance or detract from his or her message
2. Use physical cues effectively
3. Show how kinesic and proxemic cues can help speakers communicate with receivers

Contents

Picture the mythical boxer Rocky moving down the aisle of an arena on the way to the ring. He almost dances down the aisle with a menacing posture and appearance, arms bobbing and weaving—sending a message that the other fighter better watch out.

What does an audience see when they look at you when you're about to give a speech? Your posture, facial expression, eye contact, and gestures, all of which add to or detract from the impact of your words.[1] You affect audience members not only by what you say but also by what you do and how you look when speaking. In this chapter, our focus is on what audience members see when you deliver a speech,[2] how you use **kinesics** (body language) and proxemics (space and distance) to promote the understanding and acceptance of your message.

Even when you are silent, your appearance, facial expression, eyes, posture, and movements continue talking to the audience, suggesting to them what you are thinking and feeling.[3] Like your voice, your body should not call attention to itself. It should help receivers focus on and respond to your speech.

An adept public communicator knows how to use physical cues to enhance the impact of his or her words.[4] Your goal is to project an image of vitality, so that you command attention. Do the physical cues you emit encourage the audience to respond positively?

Audience members also will communicate with you using body language. Your ability to adjust your presentation based on their reactions depends on your picking up a host of cues—smiles, frowns, eyes looking at you or away, heads nodding in agreement or disagreement, rigid or relaxed postures. When you respond to these cues appropriately, you help build a better relationship with the audience.

COACHING TIP

"People trust their ears less than their eyes."

—Herodotus

Talk to the audience not just with words but with your body. Your eyes, gestures, and physical demeanor provide audience members clues they can use to assess your sincerity and believability, likeability, and competence. They either underscore or undermine audience judgments of your authenticity and credibility. Make your appearance count, and the audience will count on you.

section

16.1 Approach the Audience With Confidence

A Chinese proverb says, "Let me see you walk, and I'll tell you what you're like." Even as you approach the speaker's stand, you are sending nonverbal messages to your audience. You have not yet spoken a word, yet by your manner of dress, rate of movement, the forcefulness in your step, the way you carry yourself and move your arms, the directness or indirectness of your gaze, your facial expression, and how and where you stand before them, listeners form opinions of you.

On the day you give your speech, be sure to walk deliberately to the front of the room, moving your arms naturally as you do so. Don't make any silly faces or nervous sounds as you approach your speaking location. Once there, pause, and let your eyes address your receivers.

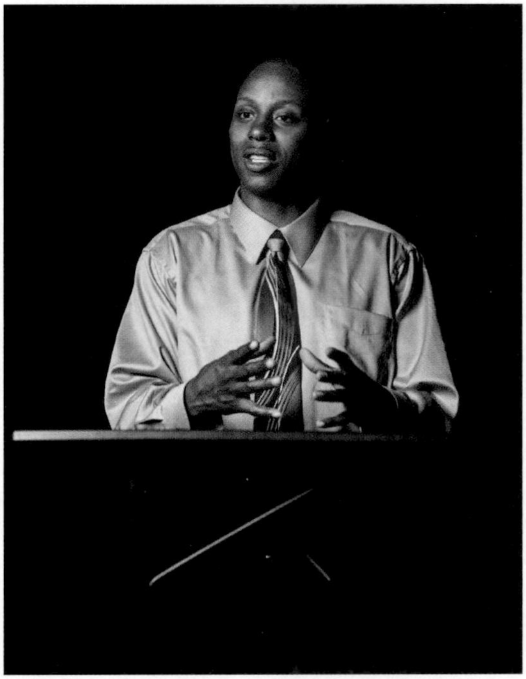

© iStockphoto.com/adamkaz

Poised for success. Manage your nonverbal communication to build a positive relationship with your audience.

Make the Most of the Speaker's Setting

section
16.2

Knowledge of **proxemics**—the use of space and distance in communication—can also benefit speakers.

16.2a Aim for Immediacy

16.2b Decide Where You Will Speak From

16.2a Aim for Immediacy

The amount of space between presenter and receivers can create a sense of **immediacy** or suggest instead that a great distance exists between them. The goal is for you to use space in a way that enhances delivery. For example, compare the demeanor of an orchestra's conductor with an actor appearing in a one-person show. The actor is able to create greater intimacy with the audience simply by approaching the front of the stage—visibly symbolizing his connection to and identification with audience members. In contrast, until the last note sounds in a concert, the conductor looks directly at the orchestra, facing away from the audience—establishing a closer relationship with the orchestra than the audience.

Similarly, the speaker's position in relationship to an audience matters. Stand too close to audience members and they may feel that their personal space is being invaded, but stand too far away, and they could perceive you as uninterested or dispassionate.

© iStockphoto.com/Abel Mitja Varela

Location matters. How can where you're standing and what's around you affect the speech's impact?

16.2b Decide Where You Will Speak From

It is important to be aware of the space given you. Unless the occasion is a formal or serious one, don't feel stuck to the lectern, which if used ineffectively creates a barrier between you and the audience. Coming out from behind it helps to establish immediacy in much the same way a smile and eye contact do, making you seem more approachable.[5] If comfortable doing so, you could even move among the audience. Whatever your choice, your movement should be purposeful.

section

16.3

Coordinate Your Body Language With Your Words

16.3a Know Your Gestures

16.3b Remember, Posture Matters

16.3c Use Facial Expressions and Eye Contact

16.3d Use Appearance to Support Performance

If what you do with your body is inconsistent with what you say, your listeners will tend to believe your body language more than your words. And they are right to do so, because that is probably where the truth lies. Thus you must use physical cues to make it easier, not harder, for your listeners to believe and listen to you.

In addition, your body movements should be purposeful. Continually pacing like a caged lion, moving randomly or perpetually like a wind-up toy, or standing rigid and expressionless like a statue are attention distracters; by calling undue attention to your movement (or lack of), you subvert the message.

16.3a Know Your Gestures

A speaker who gestures meaningfully comes across as natural, relaxed, and in touch with his or her thoughts, whereas a speaker whose gestures are stiff and unnatural may be perceived as uptight, undynamic, and unsure. The following stances and motions convey these messages.

TABLE 16.1

IF YOU . . .	YOU MAY APPEAR TO BE . . .
Clutch one arm with the other or stand in a figleaf pose	Nervous and uptight
Hold your hands stiffly at your sides	Tense and uncomfortable
Cross your arms and legs	Distant and closed off
Place your hands on your hips	Combative and giving orders
Clasp your hands behind your back	Overly confident and too self-assured
Let your arms hang naturally and loosely at your sides	Relaxed and composed

In addition to these, some of us have annoying habits that audience members could find distracting. Gestures like playing with hair, jiggling bracelets or pocket change, cracking knuckles, or tapping a foot interfere with rather than clarify your message. Become aware of whether you have any distracting mannerisms, get feedback and help from others, and work to eliminate them.

Illustrators

Use gestures to reinforce, clarify, describe, and demonstrate the meaning of your words. You can, for example, signal when about to hit a main point with one, two, or three fingers. Such a gesture is called an **illustrator**—it illustrates your content. If you held a finger up vertically over your mouth, that would substitute for saying "Quiet please." If you shook a finger at receivers while talking about the shame involved in not being an organ donor, that gesture would be emphasizing your message. You should avoid using contradicting gestures—ones that conflict with your words, negating your spoken message—unless you use it purposefully to make a point or a joke. It would not be effective to speak of the death of a hero with a smile on your face.

Emblems

Emblems are nonverbal symbols that have a direct verbal translation and are widely understood by the members of a culture. Be aware that a gesture's meaning may differ across cultures. In Japan and Korea what Americans know as the "okay" sign symbolizes "money," and among Arabs, when accompanied by a baring of teeth, it signifies extreme hostility.[6]

© iStockphoto.com/PeopleImages

OK? If you're going to employ a certain emblem or sign during your speech, make sure it's appropriate for the crowd.

Vary Gestures

Don't limit yourself to a single, all-purpose gesture. Instead, your movements should flow naturally with your words.[7] Under most conditions, gestures should coincide with, not precede or follow, verbal content.

Ask yourself these questions about your gestures:

- Are my gestures natural and spontaneous, rather than exaggerated, too patterned, or uncertain?
- Do they support my words?
- Are they varied appropriately?

16.3b Remember, Posture Matters

Posture is the position of your body in space. The posture you display conveys a lot about how you are feeling. Because you will likely stand when giving a speech, we focus on your standing posture. A public speaker who stands tall with shoulders squared sends a message of strength to audiences, whereas a speaker whose shoulders are either raised or stooped sends a message of stress or submissiveness, respectively. A speaker who leans toward an audience is usually perceived more positively than one who leans away or appears to withdraw from the audience.[8] If using a lectern, don't drape yourself over it, slouch, or rock back and forth.

When you are ready to speak, ask yourself these posture-related questions:

- Does my posture convey my command of the speech experience?
- Does it express my interest in the audience?
- Does it demonstrate my comfort with speaking before others?

Hemera Technologies/AbleStock.com/Thinkstock

Good posture. Consider the message that your body position sends to the audience.

16.3c Use Facial Expressions and Eye Contact

Audience members rely on a speaker's facial cues to reveal what's behind the speaker's words.

Put on Your Game Face

Putting on a game face doesn't mean you are going to act tough or phony; it means you use your face to set the emotional tone for your speech, beginning when the audience sees you for the first time. Then, once you begin, guide your listeners by using facial expressions that match your verbal message. Use the following facial management techniques as needed to intensify, deintensify, neutralize, or mask what you are feeling:

- When you *intensify* an emotion you exaggerate your facial expressions to reflect the degree of expression you believe audience members expect you to exhibit. For example, you may communicate more excitement than you actually feel in an effort to generate excitement among listeners.
- When you *deintensify* an emotion, you diminish your facial expressions so that audience members will judge your behavior as more acceptable. Thus, you may downplay the rage you feel in an effort to temper audience member reactions.
- When you *neutralize* an emotion, you suppress your real feelings so as to suggest greater inner strength and resilience to listeners. Thus, you attempt to hide any fears, nerves, or sadness.
- And when you *mask* an emotion, you try to replace one emotion with another to which you believe audience members will respond more favorably. You might, for example, choose to conceal feelings of outrage, anger, jealousy, or anxiety if you believe audience members would find them unacceptable.

Inappropriate facial expressions can undermine your efforts. If you smile, for instance, when discussing a serious issue, that behavior contradicts your verbal message and will diminish whatever bond exists between you and your audience.

If your face is expressionless, it will also work against you by failing to communicate your interest in your audience and your involvement in your topic.

In preparation for speaking, ask yourself these questions relevant to your facial expressiveness:

- Are my facial expressions conveying the proper emotions?
- Do my facial expressions support my thoughts and feelings?

Maintain Eye Contact

Of all the facial cues you exhibit, none affects your relationship with your audience as much as the presence or absence of eye contact. Making effective eye contact early and often with an audience serves a number of important functions:

1. Eye contact signals that the lines of communication are open between speaker and listeners. It is easier for audience members to ignore a speaker who has not established eye contact with them.
2. Eye contact psychologically reduces the distance between speaker and listeners, helping to cement their bond.
3. It allows the speaker to obtain valuable feedback from audience members regarding how the speech is coming across, enabling the speaker to adjust his or her delivery as needed.
4. It communicates the speaker's confidence, conviction, concern, and interest.

Keep these guidelines in mind when speaking to an audience:

- Begin by looking audience members in the eye.
- Keep your gaze steady and personal as you distribute it evenly about the room or auditorium; in this way you visually demonstrate your interest in everyone present.
- Do not stare blankly. A blank stare can be mistaken for a hostile glower or a sign of a blank mind.
- Maintain eye contact with your listeners for at least three seconds after you conclude your speech. Let your final words sink in before you leave the lectern.

Ned Frisk Photography/Stockbyte/Thinkstock

Look for attention. Audience members are more likely to listen to a speaker who has made eye contact.

16.3d Use Appearance to Support Performance

Your clothing and grooming are important in creating a good first impression with your audience members and in influencing their perceptions of your competence and trustworthiness.[9] Because you want audience members to accept and retain your message, you need to present yourself as positively as possible. This means that your appearance, like your gestures, should be unobtrusive and should not isolate you from your receivers. Your words should not have to compete with your appearance for the attention of your listeners. The way you dress will help make both you and your message more appealing to listeners if you keep in mind that your physical appearance needs to reflect both the occasion and the nature of your speech. For instance, if you were giving a speech on surfing, it might be fitting for you to wear shorts or a T-shirt, but a suit would be appropriate when giving a business speech.

Use these questions to assess your appearance:

- Am I well groomed?
- Am I dressed appropriately?
- Does my appearance support both the content and mood of my speech?
- Am I wearing anything that might distract the audience's attention?

GAME PLAN

Improving Your Speech Stance

- ☐ I've practiced my speech in front of a full-length mirror more than once to get an idea of my own habits when it comes to stance—for example, I like to pace, and standing still in a natural pose takes some effort.
- ☐ I can envision where in the room I'll be standing in relation to my audience.
- ☐ I've tried a few relaxed poses, and I've chosen one that feels right to me; I know where to place my hands, and I have a variety of gestures that work to engage the audience.
- ☐ I know the content of my speech so well that I feel comfortable expressing the right emotions at the right times.
- ☐ I've practiced maintaining eye contact with audience members.
- ☐ I've picked out an outfit that is comfortable and works with my speech as well as the context in which I'll be presenting.

Exercises

USING YOUR BODY

Mastering the ability to use your body and physical cues to enhance delivery will help you build a secure and positive relationship with the audience.

1. Put Your Best Face Forward

When speaking in public, your face should match the emotion inherent in your words. Explain your plan for putting your best speech-face forward. For example, you might coach yourself to approach the front of the room confidently and meet the eyes of the members of your audience before beginning to speak.

2. Register Emotion

Select an emotion—surprise, happiness, or anger—and picture it increasing and decreasing in intensity, say moving from the most subtle indication of the emotion to the most intense and back. Experienced speakers use their bodies to demonstrate such changes. Try it. Explain why being able to express such emotional distinctions can benefit you as a speaker.

3. Analyze the Speaker's Physical Stance and Delivery

Physical delivery distinguishes one speaker from another. Using examples you discover online, compare the physical speaking styles of a pair of speakers: Steve Jobs and Bill Gates, Oprah Winfrey and Ellen DeGeneres, or another pair of your own choosing. In your comparison, note the following:

- Which of the speakers engenders more trust and why
- What you specifically like or dislike about each of the speaker's styles
- Whether the speaker gestures too forcefully or not forcefully enough
- If the speaker's smile comes across as sincere or fake and why
- When the speaker leans toward and away from the audience
- When the speaker's eye contact is sustained or intermittent

4. Approach the Speaker's Stand

Prepare a two- to three-minute speech on a topic of your choice of which your instructor approves.

During your presentation, picture each member of your audience as an individual, and one at a time, have five seconds of sustained eye contact with each one while you speak. At the end of your presentation, ask audience members to assess how your eye contact made them feel. Also ask them to critique other aspects of your delivery including your use of voice, gestures, and movement.

RECAP AND REVIEW

1. **Describe how a speaker's physical cues can enhance or detract from his or her message.** What a speaker does when delivering a speech affects the audience's perception of his or her credibility. By taking time to explore how to use physical cues more effectively, a speaker can work to enhance the understanding and acceptance of ideas by audience members.
2. **Use physical cues effectively.** Physical behavior carries meaning. If a speaker displays effective gestures, body movements, facial expressions, eye contact, and posture, then it is easier to create a good relationship with receivers.
3. **Show how kinesic and proxemic cues can help speakers communicate with receivers.** The way that speakers use space and distance influences the audience–speaker relationship. An understanding of proxemics can bridge distance, create a connection, and enhance delivery.

KEY TERMS

Emblems 273

Illustrators 273

Immediacy 271

Kinesics 269

Proxemics 271

SAGE edge™

Sharpen your skills with SAGE edge at edge.sagepub.com/gamblepsp2e.

SAGE edge for students provides a personalized approach to help you accomplish your coursework goals in an easy-to-use learning environment.

© iStockphoto.com/PinkBadger

17 Using Presentation Aids

UPON COMPLETING THIS CHAPTER'S TRAINING, YOU WILL BE ABLE TO

1. Discuss the functions served by presentation aids
2. Assess the strengths of the presentation aids discussed in this chapter
3. Choose an appropriate slide presentation software program
4. Select, prepare, and integrate the most appropriate presentation aids into a speech

Whenever we view a sports event, election night results, coverage of a trial, or even the weather, we see the commentators use presentation aids to augment their reporting. In football, a yellow line indicates the first-down line. During a presidential election, maps are coded red and blue. Criminal trials feature crime scene visuals. Visuals help tell each story.

Many of us think of a public speech as filled with words. But words are not always enough. As in broadcast sports, you may discover that **presentation aids**—graphics, a photo or film segment, or maybe dramatic music—can supplement your words. Consider this observation by presidential adviser and communication and media relations specialist Merrie Spaeth:

> When Moses came down from the mountain with clay tablets bearing the Ten Commandments, it was perhaps history's first example of a speaker using props to reinforce his message. It wouldn't have had the same impact if Moses had simply announced: "God just told me 10 things, and I'm going to relay them to you."[1]

Today's audiences are more attuned to messages that have visual appeal than to ones appealing solely to their ears. Because of our immersion in a culture saturated with media and new technology, we expect speakers to stimulate our sight as well as our hearing. Thus, by effectively integrating visual and audio materials into your speech, you can make a significant difference in how your audience responds.

Contents

COACHING TIP

"I use many props. The props act as cue cards reminding me of what to say next."

—Tom Ogden

Presentation aids not only prop up your speech, they prop up your memory of what comes next, helping you segue from one important point to another. Because they enable you to speak with greater fluency and confidence, and help the audience remember your message, visual and audio evidence help to achieve the goals of your speech.

section

17.1 Use Presentation Aids Strategically

Presentation aids are often clearer than speech itself. When audiences see and hear your message, they understand and retain more of it. Keep in mind, however, that the purpose of using presentation aids is to reinforce, not replace, your spoken words. When used to advantage by a speaker, presentation aids fulfill the following functions:

- **Increase comprehension.** Humans process more than 80 percent of all information we receive through our sense of sight.[2]
- **Promote memory and recall.** We remember only 10 percent of what we read, 20 percent of what we hear, and 30 percent of what we see. But we remember more than 50 percent of what we see and hear simultaneously.[3]
- **Facilitate organization.** By displaying main ideas visually, you help your listeners follow your speech's structure and better understand your presentation.
- **Direct attention and control interest.** A dramatic photograph, object, or graph holds a listener's attention more compellingly than words alone.
- **Increase persuasiveness.** Speakers who make visuals an inherent part of their presentations are perceived as better communicators and are 43 percent more likely to persuade their audiences than were speakers who relied exclusively on spoken words.[4]
- **Communicate concisely.** Effective presentation aids help you share information that might otherwise be too complex or take up too much time. An effective chart, for example, can eloquently convey a message.

I can see clearly. There are numerous benefits for both you and your audience of using some type of visual aid.

- **Create an aura of professionalism.** When prepared with care, visual and audio aids demonstrate a professional approach, increasing credibility and your ability to communicate your message.
- **Reduce apprehension.** When using presentation aids you have something to focus on other than the fear of speaking.
- **Manage time.** Visual aids tied to specific moments in your speech can help you keep on pace and end on time.

Effective presentation aids make achieving your goal more likely. Media- and technology-savvy audiences are comfortable processing information from multiple sources simultaneously. Adept at reading pictures, they gravitate to the visual.

FIGURE 17.1
Visual Aids and Retention

	Retention After Three Hours	Retention After Three Days
Speech Alone	70%	10%
Visual Alone	72%	20%
Speech and Visual	85%	65%

When used in concert with speech, visual aids enhance message retention.

Source: Elena P. Zayas-Baya, "Instructional Media in the Total Language Picture," *International Journal of Instructional Media* 5 (1977–1978): 145–50.

section

17.2

Know How to Work With Presentation Aids

Imagine going to a presentation on why you should visit national parks and finding yourself seated in the middle of a pitch-black auditorium. The speaker holds up photos of the parks, but you cannot see them well. She then delivers a ten-minute slide show designed to present highlights of each park. The speaker, however, positions herself in front of the screen, leaving you with an obstructed view. As she talks about each slide, she uses a laser pointer, twirling it about randomly when she isn't using it. She spins it so wildly that you actually become dizzy. You fight the urge to leave.

A more successful speaker might begin by telling you a story about how she came to visit these national treasures and why you would enjoy visiting them, too. She would not obscure pertinent information with her body, but stand out of the way. She would use the laser pointer to guide you through each of the park's highlights, but turn it off when not actively using it. And she would ensure that the room had enough ambient light so that you could take notes. The speaker might end by asking you to visualize yourself standing in front of Old Faithful. The last visual you see depicts the geyser with the following words splashed across the slide: "It's time to experience the spray for yourself."

Visual interest. Compelling visuals and other presentation aids should enhance audience interest in the presentation topic.

Select the Best Aids

section 17.3

Presentation aids come in all shapes, sizes, and sounds and include people, models, objects, photographs, graphs, charts, drawings, slides, DVDs, music, and computer-generated materials. When planning on integrating visual or audio aids into a speech, consider these key questions:

1. What can I do to make my presentation more visually and aurally alive for my listeners?
2. Which presentation aids are most appropriate given the situation or setting for my speech? What kinds of presentation aids will the location of the speech allow?
3. Which presentation aids best suit the purpose of my speech?

17.3a Real People

A **human visual aid** can be effective if her role is well planned and she is not allowed to distract audience members. A student speaking on self-defense could bring along two people trained in martial arts, but they should not show off their skills until the appropriate moment. When using a human visual aid, follow these coaching pointers:

1. **Be certain your "human visual" is willing and committed to helping you accomplish your objectives.**
2. **Be sure to rehearse with this person prior to the big day.** Lack of preparation can be risky and can inhibit the smooth integration of the aide into your presentation.
3. **Any human visual aid is subordinate to your speech.** Do not have the aide share the speaker's area with you until his or her participation is required. Once the person's role is complete, move him or her back into the audience or out of sight.

You, too, serve as a visual aid. You might demonstrate the proper stance for fencing or model the dress of your native country.

17.3b Props and Models

Props and models also can enliven a presentation. When effectively used, both add clarity, interest, and drama to your ideas.

Props

A *prop* is an object that has the power to compel listeners to focus their attention on your message and better understand your subject. To be effective, the object should be large enough for everyone to see, but small enough so you can carry it to your presentation and handle it with ease. For example, a tennis racquet, a native costume, a musical instrument, food, or a toy can show your listeners what you are talking about or demonstrate how to do something. Although they can enhance interest and increase retention, props can also distract the audience. Therefore, the visual aids should be kept out of sight until needed. Otherwise, instead of concentrating on you, your listeners may focus on the object, speculating about what it is and what you are going to do with it.

Consider in advance the kinds of problems a prop could create. Animate props must be stored and treated humanely prior to, during, and after the speech. During a speech about how to handle a snake, one student placed the snake on a display table at the front of the room; much to her surprise, as she was turning to make a point, the snake slithered out of her reach and was on its way into the audience when she finally recaptured it. Remember, the visual aid should add credibility and drama to your presentation, not create fear or chaos.

Prop yourself up. Employed effectively, props can really enhance a speech's message.

Models

If you conclude that your visual aid is too large to bring to your presentation, too small to be seen, or too dangerous, valuable, or fragile to carry around, then you might use a *model* in its place. Effective models can aid in comprehension and retention by increasing the amount of audience engagement and interest. For example, one student who delivered a speech on the human heart used a larger-than-life replica that opened to reveal its chambers. The model helped clarify the information while also keeping the audience's interest.

Tips to Remember

Keep these coaching pointers in mind when using both props and models:

1. Be sure the prop or model illustrates and reinforces an important point.
2. Be sure it's visible from anywhere in the audience.
3. Keep it hidden until ready to use it.
4. Put it away when finished using it.
5. Practice so you can use it without difficulty or calling undue attention to yourself.

17.3c Photographs

Photographs also make effective visual aids. Rather than delivering the all-too-common apology, "I know you can't see this well, but . . . ," make sure audience members *can* see it well. Select your photos with care, and enlarge them sufficiently.

Try not to pass photographs around the room, because doing so diverts attention from you. The person waiting to look at the photograph, the person looking at it, and the person who has just looked at it are not with you because they are concentrating on something else.

Whatever the nature of a photo, color pictures are usually more effective than black-and-white, but it is most important that the photo's central features be clearly visible.[5]

17.3d Graphs

Well-designed **graphs** can help speakers communicate statistical information, illustrate trends, and demonstrate patterns. Among the most commonly used are line graphs, bar graphs, pie graphs, and pictographs and infographics.[6]

Line Graphs

Line graphs show trends over time. Figure 17.2 is one such graph a student used in a speech on why diet is a better way to control obesity than exercise. Referring to the visual, the student said "As you can see from this graph derived from information in the April 2016 issue of *The Atlantic,* between the years 1988 and 2006 the amount women exercised doubled while men increased their workouts by approximately 50 percent." The speaker then went on to tell her audience that despite the increase in exercise, during this time period the obesity epidemic among Americans actually worsened, increasing from 23 percent to 35 percent. The student's visual helped document that increased exercise on its own did not reduce obesity. Not only does this line graph reveal a trend over time, it enables the speaker to make and show important comparisons. In addition, notice how the lines in the graph are color-coded for clarity. When designed well, the line graph is one of the easiest types of visuals for audiences to follow. When

FIGURE 17.2

Line Graphs Foster Comparisons: Men and Women Are Working Out More

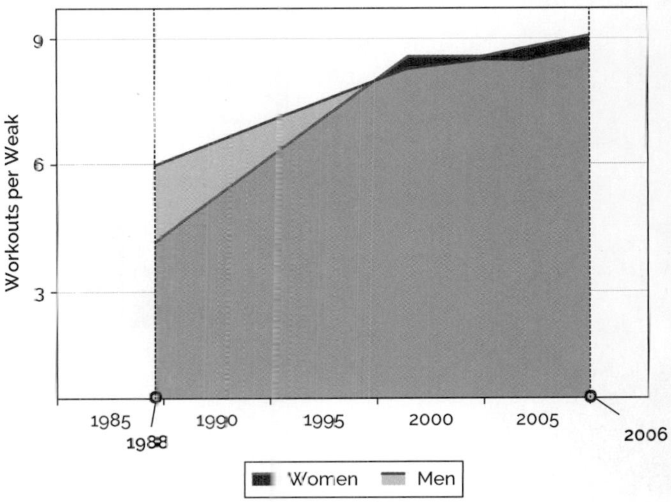

Source: Olga Khazan, "Exercise in Futility," *The Atlantic* (April 2016): 30.

FIGURE 17.3

Poorly Designed Line Graph

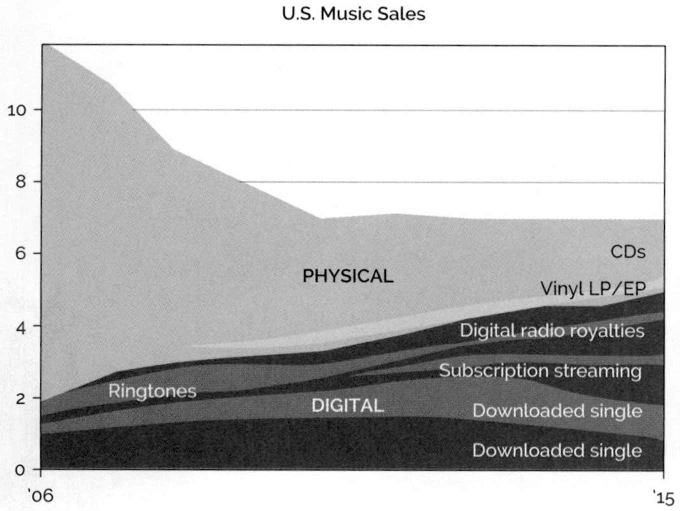

Source: Data from Recording Industry Association of America.

designed poorly, it can become confusing, as revealed by the line graph in Figure 17.3, which is complex, poorly color-coded, and difficult for an audience to read easily and quickly.

Bar Graphs

Like the line graph, the **bar graph** is useful for comparing or contrasting two or more items or groups. Bar graphs can be either horizontal or vertical. While they vary in length, the bars should be of equal widths. When prepared properly, the bar graph is usually easy for the uninitiated to read and interpret and makes the data more meaningful and dramatic for receivers. Figure 17.4 is a bar graph that shows an increase in mass shootings over a 14-year period.

FIGURE 17.4

Bar Graph Illustrates Mass Shootings on the Rise

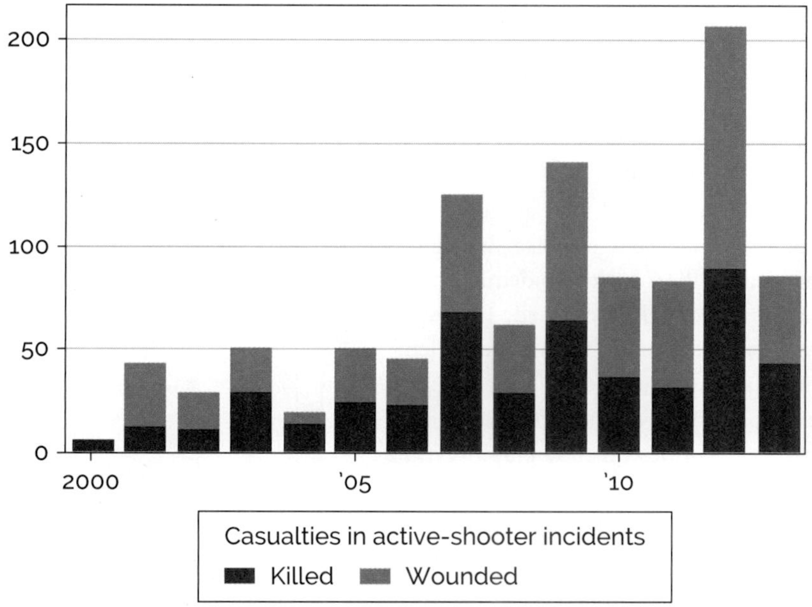

Source: Based on Federal Bureau of Investigation, "Mass Shootings on the Rise," *Wall Street Journal,* September 25, 2014, p. A1; permission conveyed through Copyright Clearance Center, Inc.

Pie Graphs

In contrast to line and bar graphs, **pie graphs** (or circle graphs) illustrate percentages of a whole or distribution patterns. Ideally, pie graphs should contain from two to five clearly labeled "slices" or divisions. Figure 17.5 shows a pie graph with slices representing the top six sports played by Division I female athletes and a seventh slice representing all other sports these athletes play. A separate tiny slice for each of the many other sports would make the graph too cluttered. Do you see any way the speaker might have reduced the slices in Figure 17.5 to 5?

FIGURE 17.5

Pie Chart Illustrates Women's Participation in Division I Athletics, by Sport in 2012–2013

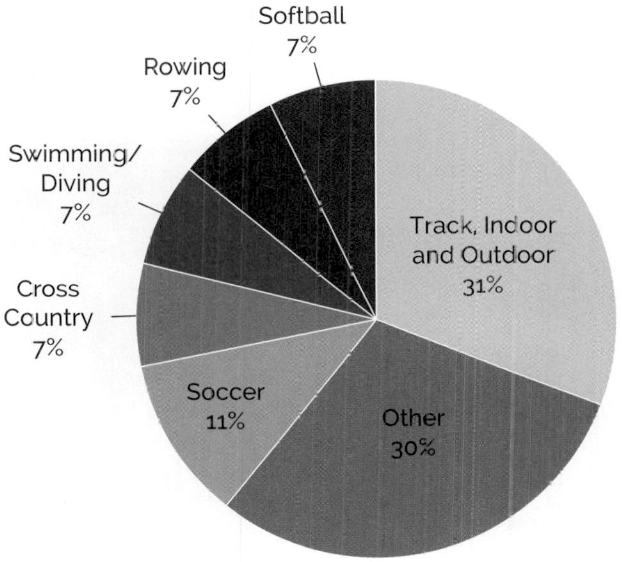

Source: NCAA (National Collegiate Athletic Association), "Sport-by-Sport Participation and Sponsorship Women's Sport 2012–2013 (Division 1)," https://www.ncaa.org/sites/default/files/Participation%20Rates%20Final.pdf.

Infographics

Composites of information, illustration, and design, **infographics** help speakers relay information in more interesting ways. Infographics are particularly useful in helping audience members visualize data.[7] A **pictograph**—a graphic representation of the subject—is a simplified version of an infographic. For example, the graph in Figure 17.6, describing the number of multiple-generation households in the United States, has visual appeal that makes it a little less formal than a bar graph. Figure 17.7 is an example of a more sophisticated infographic that one student used in a speech about online dating relationships.

FIGURE 17.6
Infographics Add Interest and Visual Appeal

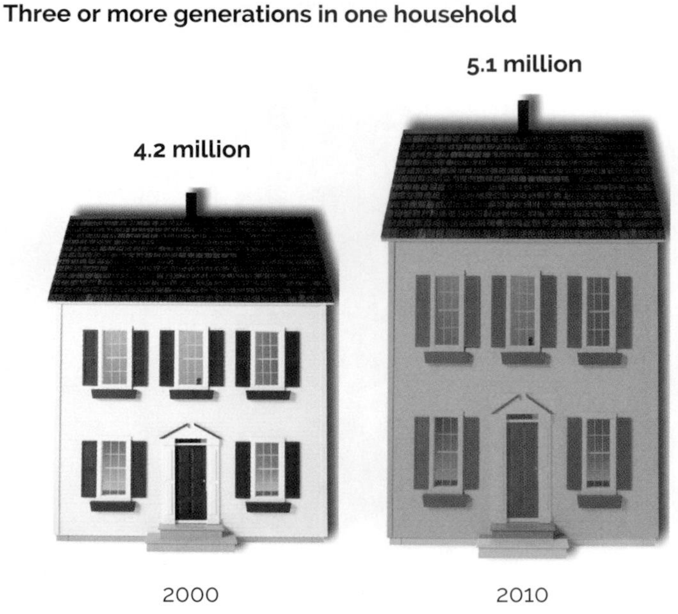

Source: U.S. Census Bureau.

See Table 17.1 to review the best uses of each type of graph.

Whatever types of graphs you use, keep in mind the following guidelines:

1. Clearly title the graph.
2. Keep the graph as simple as possible. Too many graphs or too much information contributes to information overload.
3. Help receivers with the interpretation process. Don't assume they will read the graph the way you expect them to.
4. Make sure the graph is large enough for the audience to see everything written on it and contains colors that are distinguishable. Clear graphs facilitate clear speech.

FIGURE 17.7

Dating Data Infographic

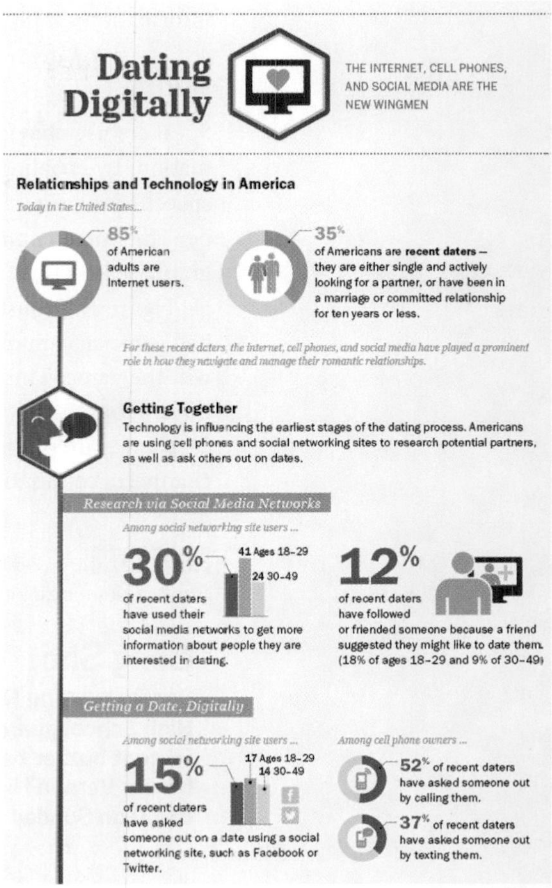

Source: Pew Research Center, "Online Dating & Relationships" [infographic], October 21, 2013, http://www.pewinternet.org/2013/10/21/online-dating-relationships.

TABLE 17.1 BEST GRAPH PRACTICES

TYPE OF GRAPH	FUNCTION
Line	To demonstrate trends or changes over time; to reveal how one thing affects another
Bar	To show comparisons and contrasts; to show differences in amount or frequency
Pie	To reveal relationships between parts and the whole; to indicate relative proportions. percentages, or distribution patterns
Infographic	To use pictorial representations to decrease the formality of a graph and enhance its appeal

17.3e Charts, Drawings, and Maps

Charts, drawings, and maps are resources speakers rely on to convey complex information simply and visually.

Charts

Speakers use **charts** to help compress or summarize large amounts of information. By enabling listeners to organize their own thoughts and follow your speech's progress, charts also simplify note taking and help audiences remember. The most commonly used chart is one that combines descriptions with graphics.

Figure 17.8 illustrates how, with a tenth of a second left to play in a basketball game, a team managed against long odds to inbound the ball and score to win the game. This chart helped a speaker to explain the play and make his point about the importance of not giving up until a game is over.

Charts are particularly useful for speakers who want to discuss a process, channel of communication, or chain of command, as Figure 17.9 demonstrates.

FIGURE 17.8

Charts Summarize Information

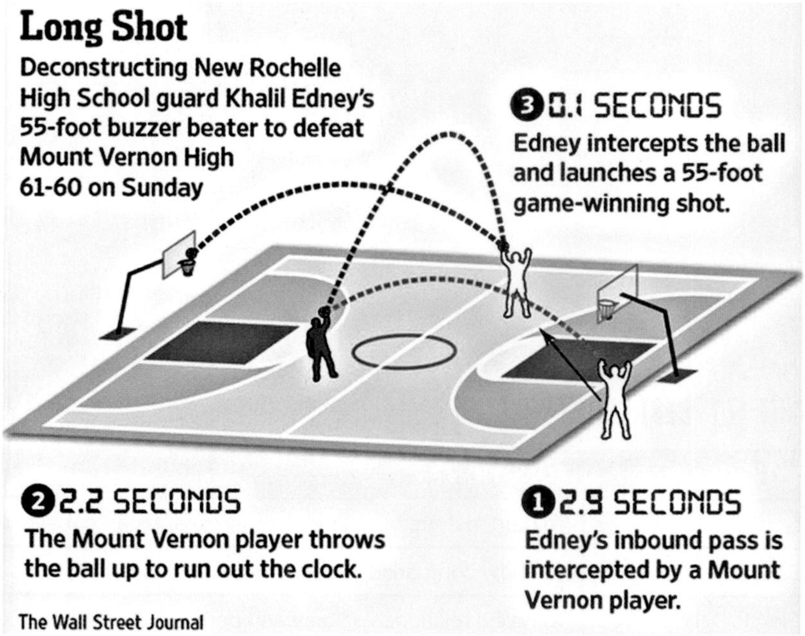

Long Shot
Deconstructing New Rochelle High School guard Khalil Edney's 55-foot buzzer beater to defeat Mount Vernon High 61-60 on Sunday
3 0.1 SECONDS
Edney intercepts the ball and launches a 55-foot game-winning shot.
2 2.2 SECONDS
The Mount Vernon player throws the ball up to run out the clock.
1 2.9 SECONDS
Edney's inbound pass is intercepted by a Mount Vernon player.
The Wall Street Journal

Source: Reprinted with permission of the *Wall Street Journal,* Copyright © 2013. Dow Jones & Company, Inc. All rights reserved worldwide.

FIGURE 17.9

Organizational Charts Reveal Chains of Command

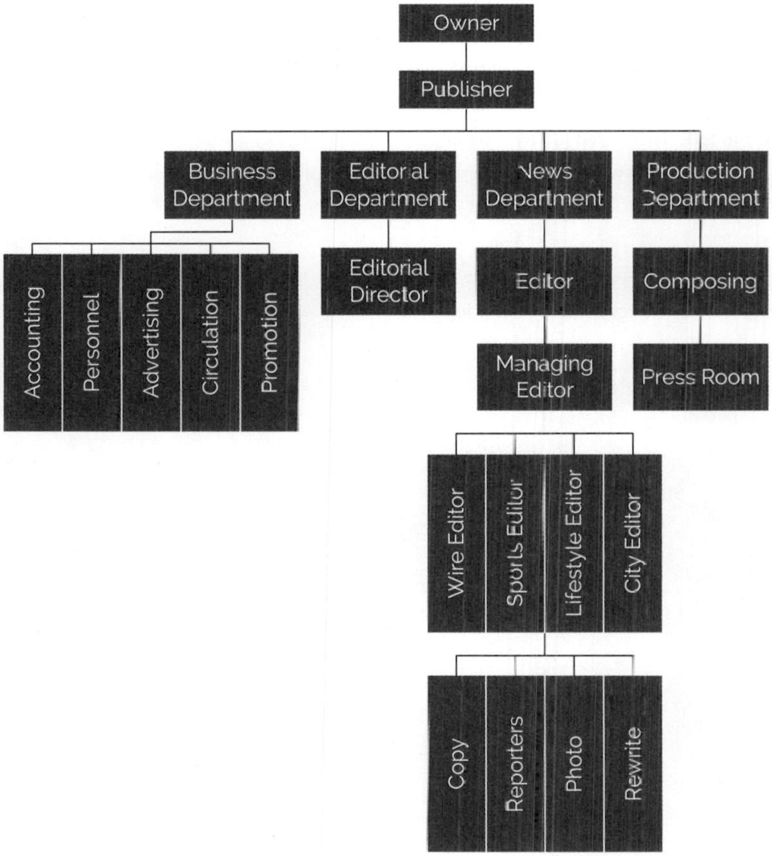

Drawings and Maps

Drawings and maps help illustrate key differences, movements, or geographic information. These visuals translate complex information into a format that receivers can grasp readily. A speaker compared different swim strokes using Figure 17.10. As she spoke, she revealed only the portion of the drawing to which she was referring; other sections were covered until she mentioned them.

FIGURE 17.10

Drawings Help Share Meaning

Source: Dorling Kindersley/Thinkstock.

Maps also make versatile visual aids. One speaker used the map in Figure 17.11 when delivering a speech on the nature of well-being. As you can see, communities in states scored higher or lower according to where they fell on the Well-Being Index, a measure of health, happiness, job satisfaction, and other factors determining quality of life.

Prepare drawings and maps in advance. Drawing them while your audience is watching consumes valuable speaking time, causes audience members to lose patience with you, and produces art that is less suitable for use.

FIGURE 17.11

Maps Illustrate Geographic Information

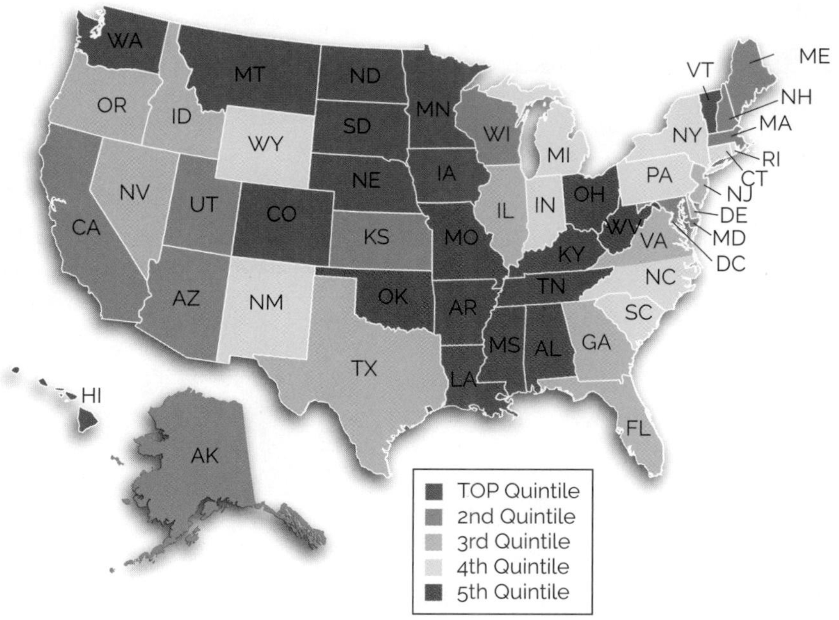

Source: Gallup-Healthways Well-Being Index, "State of American Well-Being, 2013 State Rankings and Analysis," in *State, Community, and Congressional District Analysis Report,* 7.

17.3f Audio and Video Clips

Audio and video clips can help make a speech more dynamic, involving, and exciting for receivers. Because they allow a speaker to custom design more sophisticated examples of presentation support, they can be extremely effective tools to use with today's mediawise audiences.

Though these visual aids require speakers to use more complicated equipment and may be more difficult to rehearse and set up, the vividness they provide is difficult to beat.

Video Clips

Using brief video clips in a speech can establish your credibility as well as increase audiences' interest, memory, and understanding. Imagine speaking about football and the risk of injury and then showing a video of a player being tackled during a game and suffering a concussion. Showing the segment during your speech provides an immediate dramatic impact.

You can find videos at YouTube, Vimeo, MetaCafe.com, and DailyMotion.com, among other sources. To be effective, the clip you use needs to be short—usually consuming no more than 30 seconds of a five-minute speech. You want your audience to remember your words, not just the video. It also needs to be cued up or downloaded prior to your presentation's start. If you will be using your own computer to show the clip, be sure you have compatible files and/or cables to connect to the classroom projector. And remember, double-check that the video will transfer well to a bigger screen. A video that is of low quality or too pixelated will not enhance your presentation. Think carefully about the audience and other constraints before selecting a clip. You don't want to isolate or offend the audience by using a clip that is too violent or generally in poor taste. Whatever you select, be sure to introduce the clip to the audience, preparing them for what they are about to see. Video clips work best when you are able to integrate them smoothly and without interruption into your speech.

Audio Clips

Though the majority of aids used by speakers are visual, audio also merits attention. A recording of music, sound, or speech can make your presentation more interesting and memorable. Were you speaking on the purpose of folk music, for example, playing snippets of songs or the recorded words of a musician could help you convey your message.

Audio is readily available and easy to use in your presentation, using either a computer or a CD player. Just be sure to cue the CD player to the precise point at which you want to begin before you begin your presentation. And, as with video, introduce the audio segment before using it to orient the audience to what they will be hearing.

Of note is the effectiveness of mixing visual and audio aids together—creating a fully integrated multimedia experience for the audience. Visual clips and computer images when paired with sound and text have the potential to make your speech one the audience will remember.

COACHING TIP

"The power of sound to put an audience in a certain psychological state is vastly undervalued."

—Mike Figgis

Appropriately integrated audio and video clips add drama to your speech. Use them to set, reflect, or amplify a mood. Because they strike a chord with the audience, they will make your words more interesting, involving, and memorable.

section

17.4

Be Familiar With Presentation Software

Because they are professional looking and easy to create, visual slides created using presentation software such as Prezi, Google Docs Presentation, Microsoft PowerPoint, GoAnimate, or SlideRocket can add contemporary flair, drama, professionalism, and credibility to a speech.[8] Using one of these software options also enables you to give visual shape to your arguments. In the words of Harvard psychology professor Steven Pinker, "Language is a linear medium: one word after another. But ideas are multi-dimensional. . . . When properly employed, PowerPoint makes the logical structure of an argument more transparent. Two channels sending the same information are better than one."

Presentation software also makes it easy to include a graph or chart, as most programs provide templates and tutorials explaining how to use them.[9] Recent versions of presentation software also make it easy for you to create three-dimensional artwork and incorporate sound, music, or video clips into your presentation (see Table 17.2).

TABLE 17.2 A GUIDE TO PRESENTATION SOFTWARE

SOFTWARE	PROS	CONS
Microsoft PowerPoint	+ The most widely used presentation software[a] + The program is easy to use, particularly for Microsoft Word users. + PowerPoint comes with multiple slide design options and additional templates can be downloaded directly from Microsoft.	◊ To utilize this software, students must purchase a license. ◊ Linear format is not as dynamic for presentations.
Apple Keynote	+ Can be accessed from any Mac or iOS compatible device. + Easy to share presentation files with others. Users can save Keynote documents as PowerPoint files. + Apple Keynote comes with multiple slide design options and additional templates can be downloaded directly from Apple.	◊ To utilize this software, students must purchase a license. ◊ Designed specifically for Mac and iOS devices, so some formatting may be lost when converting Keynote files to PowerPoint to present on a Windows computer. ◊ Linear format is not as dynamic for presentations.

(Continued)

TABLE 17.2 (continued)

SOFTWARE	PROS	CONS
Prezi	+ Users can access the program online; there's no need to have access to a computer with the program installed. + No fee for basic usage. + More dynamic and interactive format; presentation is on a single canvas that allows the user to create his or her own organizational structure.	◊ User must pay an annual fee to edit presentations offline and make files private. Dynamic format not ideal for content-heavy presentations. ◊ Not all information is spatially related; the canvas format can force a spatial relationship where none exists.
Google Slides	+ Free, Web-based presentation program. + Users can edit presentations when they're offline. + Collaborative; user can create and edit slides with others in real time. + Program automatically saves changes.	◊ Must have access to a Gmail account. ◊ Not as many customization options as PowerPoint or Keynote.

a. Bob Parks, "Death to Powerpoint," August 30, 2012, http://www.bloomberg.com/news/articles/2012-08-30/death-to-powerpoint.

With the advent of **computer-generated graphics** (see Figure 17.12), technology is helping transform ordinary presentations into extraordinary speechmaking events, but you need to be selective when deciding whether or not to use presentation software. If your presentation is not prepared with care, the slides may upstage you, overpower your message, or drain your speech of its vitality.[10] Or you may be tempted to use dazzling PowerPoint slides to cover up weak content.[11]

Plan out how to use each of your aids, and practice integrating each one. Unless a presentation aid is going to enhance your presentation, don't use it. Just because you can use a glitzy visual doesn't mean you should.

FIGURE 17.12

Sample Slides From a Computer-Generated Graphic Presentation

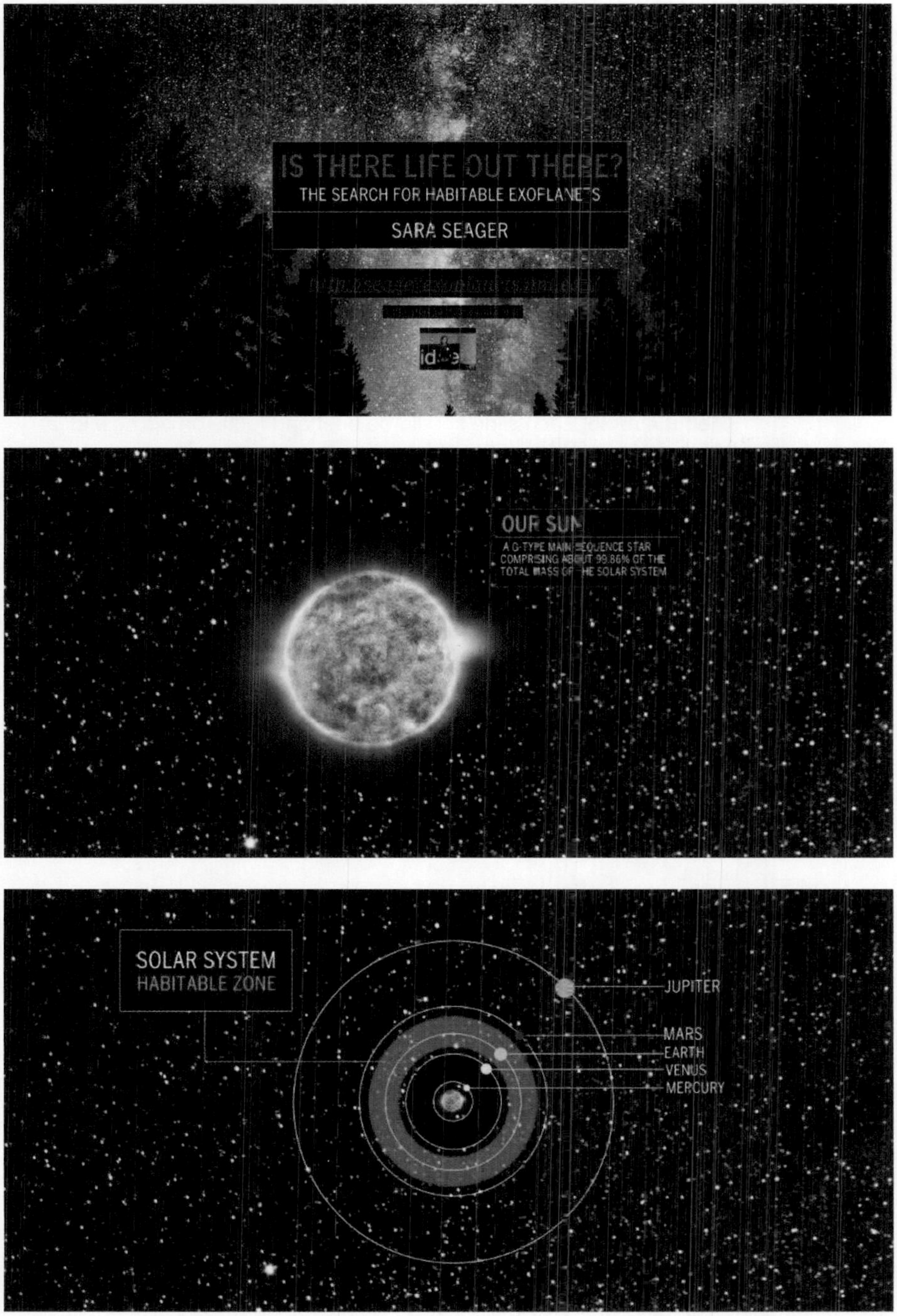

Source: "A Real Search for Alien Life," Sara Seager's presentation for TEDxCambridge 2013, September 25, 2013, http://www.youtube.com/watch?v=NnM4SaGc8R0.

section

17.5

Get the Most From Your Presentation Aids

17.5a Devise the Content and Design the Look

17.5b Choose the Right Presentation Aids

17.5c Use Presentation Aids During Your Speech

Your visuals should be large enough, clear enough, and dramatic enough to enhance the informative and persuasive power of your presentations. Like any other skill, however, selecting, designing, integrating, and using visuals take patience, persistence, and practice.

17.5a Devise the Content and Design the Look

Follow these content and design pointers to help craft effective slides.

- **Keep it simple.** Each slide should be brief and focus on a single idea.
- **Keep it short.** The fewer words, the better!
- **Use bullets.** Bulleted lists increase readability and help you organize your ideas.
- **Avoid clutter.** Minimize purely decorative design elements that distract viewers from your message.
- **Be direct.** Use active wording and parallel sentence structure.
- **Be design wise.** Keep slides consistent, to avoid distracting the audience with jarring colors or fonts.
- **Use a readable font.** Common fonts are common for a reason: They are the easiest to read. Avoid decorative or handwriting fonts, and don't mix more than two font types on a single slide. Use the same fonts on all slides.
- **Use a suitable text size.** Use 36- to 44-point type for main headings, 24 to 36 for subheads, and 18 to 24 for text. Type projected on a screen should never be smaller than 18 point. Use upper and lower case to increase legibility.
- **Be color cautious.** Using the right color enhances readership, receptivity, and retention.[12] But using color requires care. You want the color(s) you use to set the right mood and render your message readable and attractive. Keep the background color consistent. Use no more than two text colors. Differentiate background from text.
- **Be creative.** Rely on images and sounds more than text. Insert tables, art, very brief video clips, and sound directly into your slides.
- **Be in control.** Direct your audience's attention before you start a video. If you're going to talk during the video clip, mute the sound. When not referring to a slide, use a blank slide or cover the lens to bring the focus of the audience back to you.

- **Remember you are a speaker first.** You're delivering a speech, not merely a multimedia presentation. You are not replaceable!
- **Maintain eye contact.** Keep your eyes on the audience, not on the slide. Talk to the audience, not to the screen.
- **Always rehearse.** To make the most of your visual and audio aids and incorporate them seamlessly, rehearse in advance and up to your presentation.
- **Be prepared.** Have a contingency plan in case the equipment fails.

17.5b Choose the Right Presentation Aids

How do you choose a presentation aid? Start by considering your topic, your audience, and your options. For example, topics related to health and human services typically include graphs and charts to simplify the communication of complex information. Consider these criteria when deciding whether to use a presentation aid:

1. Is it worth its cost?

   Will the amount of time and effort you expend preparing the aid pay off in audience interest and response?

2. Does it "talk" to receivers?

   Will the visual or audio aid facilitate your task by saving you words? Will your listeners be able to understand and relate to it? Might anyone in your audience find the visuals or sounds you are using inappropriate or distracting?

3. Am I skilled enough and equipped to use it effectively?

   Is equipment on site? Will you have the opportunity to practice with the equipment? Unrealistic expectations regarding the time it will take you to master using a piece of equipment could leave you with too little time to rehearse your speech. Remember, using visual and audio aids well takes practice too.

Finally, when determining the presentation aids to use, keep the objectives of your speech uppermost in your mind, and limit each visual to one main point. Simplicity should lead the way. Every visual you use should be clear and concise, large and legible, and simple and straightforward. Don Keough of the Coca-Cola Company said it best: "Some pictures may be worth a thousand words, but a picture of a thousand words isn't worth much."

17.5c Use Presentation Aids During Your Speech

For maximum effectiveness, presentation aids need to be skillfully integrated into your speech and not create awkward moments for you. Here are some tips:

1. Be sure your visual and audio aids are in place before starting.
2. Present and explain each one.
3. Stand to one side of the visual and talk to the audience, making sure everyone can see the visual.
4. Keep physical possession and control of your visual.
5. Put the visual away when you are finished referring to it.

GAME PLAN

Integrating a Presentation Aid Into Your Speech

- ☐ I've spoken to my instructor about the equipment I'll need in the classroom for my speech.
- ☐ I've made sure that classroom equipment is compatible with my own.
- ☐ I've prepared a presentation aid that will be clear to eyes and ears in the front *and* back of the classroom.
- ☐ I've rehearsed how I will introduce my presentation aid and I'm comfortable making the transition.
- ☐ Setup of my equipment prior to my speech is easy.
- ☐ After my speech, I can close down and quickly remove my presentation aid to make room for the next presenter's needs.

Exercises

PRESENTATION AIDS

Mastering the ability to create and use visual and audio aids will enhance your ability to interest and involve audiences. Participating in these activities will build your skills.

1. Interpreting Visuals

Consider this: Is there more to the graphs than meets the eye in Figures 17.13 and 17.14, displaying the average test scores of four English classes on achievement exams.[13] Looking at both graphs, which one do you think displays better results and why?

Although the graph pictured in Figure 17.14 shows the same information as the graph in 17.13, why do we perceive the results differently? Why does showing the bars full length instead of cut short as in Figure 17.13 change our impression of the information?[14]

As a speaker, you should never present information in such a way that it seems to mean one thing but on closer inspection means something else.

FIGURE 17.13

Evaluating What You See, I

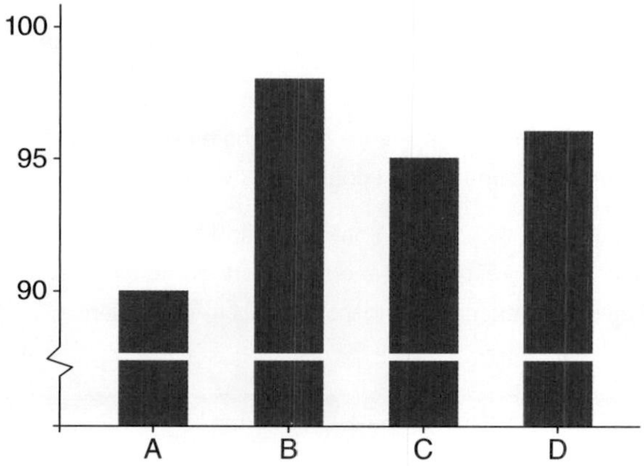

Source: Robert Boostrom, *Developing Creative and Critical Thinking: An Integrated Approach* (Lincolnwood, IL: National Textbook Co, 1992), 231.

FIGURE 17.14

Evaluating What You See, II

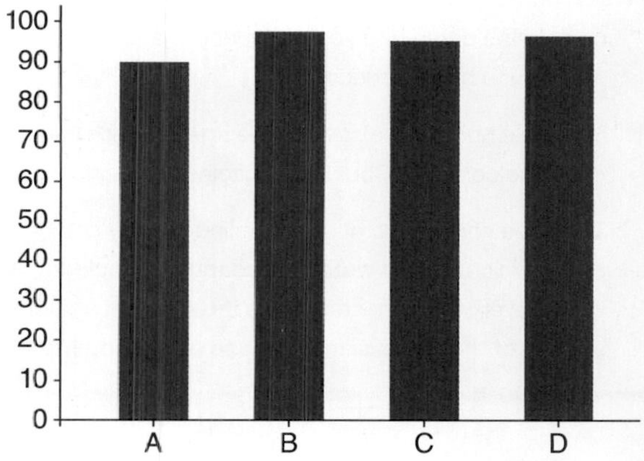

Source: Robert Boostrom, *Developing Creative and Critical Thinking: An Integrated Approach* (Lincolnwood, IL: National Textbook Co, 1992), 231.

2. Props and Models

Identify a prop or model you could use when giving a speech on each of the following topics:

- Medical Training in the United States
- Altruism
- Snowboarding
- The Value of Discipline

3. Analyze This: A Speaker's Use of Visual and Audio Aids

One student, Jim Eae, added both credibility and drama to his speech entitled "Equality" by using four apples as visual aids in the introduction of his speech and its body, and then a stone during the conclusion. Selected excerpts of his speech appear below. Read them and then answer the questions that follow.

- In your opinion, to what extent was the speaker's use of visual aids effective? Explain.
- Do you believe audience members would find the visual aids distracting or helpful? Why?
- If you were the speaker, would you have thrown a stone at your audience? Why or why not?
- What audio aids, if any, do you believe the speaker could have used to advantage?

[From the introduction] *[In turn, the speaker selects and holds up one of four apples for the audience to see]* Four apples—similar by their outer appearance, almost identical by their insides, and yet their flavors are worlds apart. This one right here, it's a sweet one, really sweet. This one right here, it's kind of sour. This one is bitter, and the last is a combination of all. Four apples—two red and two green—similar, but very different.

I'm not just talking about the differences between apples. I'm also talking about the differences between people. Color you may say is only skin-deep, but it is much more than that. Some believe it determines where you come from, what you believe, where your social interests lie, and even whom you fall in love with. Your color helps determine your uniqueness and your individuality. It helps mold you into the person you are and the person you hope to become.

[From the body of the speech] George F. Snyder, author of *Black No More,* imagined a world where everyone was the same color. . . . Could you imagine this world if everyone was the same color? I could, and I would hate it.

The hope some have of a color-blind society brings up the question: If everyone conformed and became the same, which culture would we adapt to? Would the Japanese society of respect and hard work be dominant? Would everyone choose to have the strength and endurance of the African Americans? Would the conquering attitude of the Caucasian American reign supreme? . . .

[Once again picking up an apple] My favorite apple is this green one right here. It is colored but not too colored. It is sweet, yet still sour, but best of all, it is different from every other apple. If someone were to come up with the perfect medium for the taste and color of apples, I would object because I would not have the variety to choose from anymore. I would have to settle for a bland color and a bland taste. I pray this never happens.

A great man once said, "If any of you are without fault, then let him be the first to cast a stone." It is time we stop casting stones and accept people for who they are, color and all. . . .

[From the conclusion] *[The speaker holds up a stone]* Let the man without any fault cast the first stone. During the civil rights era even police were casting stones at peaceful protesters. I, myself, have been hit with several stones of a color-blind society. For example, there were times when I wanted to speak up as a black man and not just a human, but I have to forfeit my thoughts, my ideas, and my feelings for you. Equality—that's the solution.

Alexander Kremble, a black nationalist who spent twenty years as a missionary in Liberia and founded the first organization for African American intellectuals, said the race problem is a moral one, and like all other great battles of humanity, its solution will be fought with weapons of truth. Here it is, the first stone of equality, and I cast it to you. Not because I am without fault, but because I know it is the best solution for both you and me. The solution is equality, and now the solution is no longer in my hands, but yours. So I ask, "What are you going to do with it?"

4. Approach the Speaker's Stand

1. You're giving a speech on one of the following topics:

   - The Electoral College
   - Hang Gliding
   - CPR
   - The American Foster Care System
   - Copyright Law

   Consider how you could include visual and audio aids in the speech.

2. Select a speech from YouTube, TED Talks, or *Vital Speeches of the Day* and brainstorm in class how one or more visual or audio aids either were or could be used to clarify or amplify the speaker's message.

3. Next, prepare a three- to five-minute presentation in which you use at least two visual aids and one audio aid.

RECAP AND REVIEW

1. **Discuss the functions served by presentation aids.** The right presentation aids increase listener understanding, enhance memory and recall, facilitate message organization, and help the speaker control audience attention and interest. They add impact, reduce speech apprehension, enhance speaker credibility, and increase the persuasiveness of the speaker and message.
2. **Assess the strengths of the presentation aids discussed in this chapter.** Human beings, objects, and models focus the audience's attention on the speaker's message. Photographs add realism, drama, and impact to a presentation. Graphs help receivers interpret statistical data and trends. Charts, drawings, and maps summarize large amounts of information. Graphics and sound add contemporary flair, professionalism, and credibility to a speech. Used effectively, all presentation aids add appeal and help illustrate the key points of a speech.
3. **Choose an appropriate slide presentation software program.** Prezi, Google Docs Presentation, Microsoft PowerPoint, and SlideRocket are among the software programs available. Consider the goals of the speech, constraints, and the actual audience before selecting a program.
4. **Select, prepare, and integrate the most appropriate presentation aids into a speech.** A visual or audio aid should strengthen points, connect to audience members, or enhance credibility. Content and design should be simple, straight to the point, and creative. Rehearse introducing the aids with words, and make sure all equipment and cables are in place before approaching the podium. Check the clarity and volume of the visual or audio clip so that all audience members can see and hear the content.

KEY TERMS

PART SIX

Speak to Inform

© iStockphoto.com/poba

18

Speak to Inform

UPON COMPLETING THIS CHAPTER'S TRAINING, YOU WILL BE ABLE TO

1. Define informative speaking and explain its purposes
2. Compare and contrast the following: a speech about objects and ideas; a speech about events and people; and a speech about processes and procedures
3. Deliver an informative speech that is organized and communicates as simply and directly as possible, creates information hunger in receivers by relating ideas directly to them, and is memorable

There are a nearly unlimited number of topics about which we can share information and develop understanding. Whether you are an employee, a parent, or a student, speaking informatively is part of daily life. You likely describe, demonstrate, or explain something to others every day. For organizational purposes, we divide **informative speech** into the following categories: speeches about (1) objects and ideas, (2) events and people, and (3) processes and procedures. Though these categories are far from exhaustive, they represent the most common ways public speakers package information (see Table 18.1).

COACHING TIP

The main purpose of an informative speech is to educate, not advocate.

Help audience members learn new information, and you help them grow. Knowledge that is applicable to life is power. Power up your audience with information they can understand and use, and you set them on a path unburdened by confusion.

Contents

section

18.1

Speeches About Objects and Ideas

18.1a Speaking About an Object

18.1b Speaking About an Idea

When speaking of an object, animate or inanimate, we usually describe it and tell about its uses. When we speak of an **idea or concept**, we typically define and explain it.

TABLE 18.1 INFORMATIVE SPEECH TYPES AND TOPICS

SPEECH TYPE	SAMPLE TOPICS
Objects/Ideas	Self-Driving Cars Gene Therapy Instagram September 11 Memorial The Tomb of Tutankhamun Privacy Flight Sustainable Energy Yoga
Events/People	The Repair of the Hubble Space Telescope The Publication of *Go Set a Watchman* San Diego ComiCon The Cannes Film Festival Harvey Milk J. K. Rowling Kanye West
Processes/ Procedures	How to Change the Oil in Your Car How to Speed Read How to Prepare for a Job Interview How to Perform the Heimlich Maneuver

18.1a Speaking About an Object

An **object speech** can cover anything tangible—a machine, building, structure, place, or phenomenon (see Table 18.1 for examples). The selected object may be animate or inanimate, moving or still, visible to the naked eye or beyond its scope. Whatever your object, the goal remains the same: to paint an accurate and information-rich picture.

Once you select an object for your topic, the next step is to create a specific purpose that identifies the particular aspect on which you will focus. The following are sample purpose statements for informative speeches about objects:

To inform my audience about Florida's Everglades

To inform my audience about the anatomy of the human brain

To inform my audience about the design of Roman aqueducts

To inform my audience about prehistoric tools

Frameworks for Speaking About Objects

Speeches about objects lend themselves to topical, spatial, and chronological organizational formats. A topical format allows you to divide your subject into groups or major categories, as when speaking about volcanoes, for example, focusing first on extinct volcanoes, second on dormant volcanoes, and third on active ones. A spatial or physical framework enables you to discuss one major component of the object at a time, as you might do when discussing the entrance, antechamber, and burial chamber of an Egyptian pyramid. And finally, a chronological format is most appropriate if you are going to stress how a design or phenomenon evolved over time (for example, the formation of the Hawaiian Islands).

Object lesson. Like a tour guide, an informative speaker focuses the audience's attention on what is most important to know about a speech topic.

Whatever the organizational method you choose, be sure to adhere to the guidelines discussed in greater detail in Chapter 9.

18.1b Speaking About an Idea

What does the word *existentialism* mean? What is *bullying?* How do we clarify the nature of *common law, double jeopardy,* or an *iatrogenic injury?* In a speech about an idea, also known as a concept speech, your goal is to explain it in such a way that audience members agree on two things:

1. The idea has relevance and importance for them, and
2. They want you to clarify or elaborate on it.

Ryan McVay/Photodisc/Thinkstock

Abstract ideas. What are some concepts you'd be interested in learning or talking about?

General or abstract ideas generally work best for concept speeches, as they allow for the most creative analysis and interpretation. For example, you might discuss free speech, Buddhism, or inequality (see Table 18.1 for more suggestions).

When we talk about ideas, audience members may have different interpretations of the concepts or words we use—primarily because personal experience influences meaning. This is particularly likely for nontangible topics such as injustice, religion, and responsible citizenship.

Let's look at a few of the general topics we've identified and create some specific purpose statements for each:

To inform my audience about the meaning of injustice

To inform my audience about different philosophies of religion

To inform my audience about basic tenets of responsible citizenship

Frameworks for Speaking of Ideas

You can easily develop a speech about an idea using a topical order, enumerating and discussing, in turn, key aspects of the idea, for instance explaining the ways racial prejudice affects its victims economically, politically, and socially.

Speeches about ideas also lend themselves to chronological development. When speaking about sexual harassment you might explain how our understanding of the term has changed through the years. See Chapter 9 for more on organizational formats.

Speeches About Events and People

section **18.2**

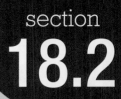

Many of us are interested in the remarkable people and events of our time and history. **Events and people** make solid informative speech topics.

18.2a Speaking of Events

A speech about an event focuses on something that happens regularly (a holiday, a birthday), or something that happened once (D-Day, the first moon landing), something that marked our lives (graduations, funerals), or something that left us with a lasting impression (the Sandy Hook shooting, the 2011 earthquake and tsunami in Japan). The event you discuss might be one you personally witnessed (a political rally), or one you choose to research (the Constitutional Convention, Rosa Parks's arrest, or the passage of the 19th Amendment, which gave women the vote). Whatever your topic, your goal is to bring the event to life so your audience can visualize and experience it.

18.2b Speaking of People

If instead of an event you tell about the life of a person—someone famous or someone you know personally, someone living or dead, someone admired by or abhorrent to all—your goal is to make that person come alive for audience members, to enable them to appreciate the person's unique qualities, and to help them understand the impact the individual has had. In other words, you seek to answer this question: Why is the person worthy of our attention?

A speech on Jeffrey Dahmer would become interesting if the speaker used it to explore the mind of a mass murderer. A speech on Louis C.K. could develop an understanding of comedic originality, and a speech on Princeton's Ann-Marie Slaughter, the author of *Unfinished Business: Women Men Work Family,* could help audiences comprehend the challenges caregivers face balancing work and family life.

18.2c Frameworks for Speaking of Events and People

Speeches on events and people lend themselves to a variety of organizational approaches; chronological, topical, and causal patterns are especially useful. Look to the purpose of your speech to help you choose. For example, if your speech aims to explain the history of an event or person—say, Hurricane Katrina—you would probably choose a chronological sequence. In contrast, if you want to approach your subject from a different angle and discuss, for instance, the social, economic, and political effects of Hurricane Katrina, a topical organization would better suit your needs. And if you want to inform your audience why Hurricane Katrina proved so destructive to the city of New Orleans, you would choose a causal order.

section

18.3

Speeches About Processes and Procedures

18.3a Frameworks for Speaking of Processes and Procedures

How do you do that? Why does this work? Can I make one too? When we answer questions like these, we share our understanding about **processes and procedures**, the third category of informative speeches.

Here are examples of purpose statements about processes and procedures:

To inform my audience about how photosynthesis works

To inform my audience about the workings of the Electoral College

To inform my audience how to change a car's oil

If you are delivering a "how" speech, then your primary goal is to increase audience understanding of your subject:

How the Kidneys Work	How Colleges Select Students
How Tornados Develop	How the Jet Stream Works

If, however, you are delivering a "how-to" speech, then your primary goal is to communicate not only information but specific skills so audience members can learn how to do something:

How to Cut Your Own Hair	How to Housebreak a Dog
How to Avoid Email Scams	How to Lobby Your Legislators

There is virtually no end to the list of processes and procedures about which you can speak.

Jupiterimages/Goodshoot/Thinkstock

Chicken stew. How to cook a certain dish is one of numerous different processes and procedures speeches you could give.

18.3a Frameworks for Speaking of Processes and Procedures

When delivering a speech that focuses on a process or procedure, you will probably find it most useful to arrange your ideas in either chronological or topical order. Chronological order works well because it naturally reflects the sequence, approach, or series of steps used from start to finish in making or doing something. For instance, in a speech on how scientists may save Earth from collision with a comet, you might detail four key steps in the process, from detecting the comet, determining when contact will occur, sending a spacecraft to intercept it, and lastly, blowing it up. But other times, you might find it more useful to discuss the major principles, techniques, or methods listeners need to understand to master the process or procedure. Then topical order is your best choice. For instance, you could focus your speech on how scientists prepare for a potential comet on a collision course with Earth, beginning with their researching the effects of past comet impacts and then describing what they are doing to improve comet-detection technology.

Keep your speech clear and comprehensible. One that contains too many main points, or step after step after step with no logical categorization, is usually too difficult for receivers to interpret and remember, making it unlikely they will be able to follow what you are sharing. By keeping your main points manageable, you facilitate better understanding of the process or procedure.

Fork in the road. What are the benefits and disadvantages of topical order or chronological development for a speech?

section

18.4 Achieving Informative Speaking Goals

Sharing information involves transferring an idea or a skill to others, with the hope that you will accomplish at least one of the following two goals:

1. Expand your audience's knowledge, or
2. Clarify what your audience knows by reducing their confusion or uncertainty, or providing a fresh way of perceiving.

To accomplish either goal, you need to deliver a speech that

1. conveys information that is well organized, clear, and accurate;
2. delivers the right amount of content, avoiding **information overload** or **underload**;
3. creates information hunger; and
4. is memorable.

18.4a Be Organized, Clear, and Accurate

A speech is clear if audience members are able to identify its specific purpose and central idea or thesis as well as comprehend, follow, and accept its main points.

Make the Information Easy to Follow

A speaker's message is easier to follow if the presentation has a discernable structure, related facts are grouped together, and oral signposts are used to help receivers follow the progression of ideas. For example, a speaker discussing the nature of secondhand smoke would be more effective if he organized the speech's main ideas around a clear definition and then an examination of the key effects of secondhand smoke, than if he confused receivers by intermingling into the speech an analysis of the effects of smoking on health care costs.

Avoid Jargon

To facilitate audience understanding, keep your speech free of unnecessary jargon—special or technical terms used primarily by those who share a profession or trade. Define unfamiliar words and concepts, use everyday language, and compare new information you are trying to convey with information already familiar to them. For example, if you used the word *sabadilla* in a speech on insecticides, you would need to explain that sabadella is a Mexican plant that chemical companies use to make a variety of insecticides. If you select and explain your words carefully, then others will listen to and learn from you.

Use Concrete Language

When you are **concrete**, you enhance your message with sufficient specificity and detail for audience members to form clear mental pictures, grounding your ideas in specific references rather than vague **abstractions**. Avoid using general words like "thing" or "it." Put your subject directly where it belongs—into receivers' minds.

Be Accurate

Clarity and accuracy go hand in hand. If your message contains inaccurate figures, if your facts are based on rumor or hearsay, and if your ideas are not supported by either primary or secondary research, then your receivers have every right to question your honesty and integrity. For example, in the fall of 2013, New Jersey governor Chris Christie repeatedly denied that his administration had intentionally created a massive traffic jam in Fort Lee, New Jersey, as political payback for the Democratic mayor of Fort Lee's refusal to endorse Christie's candidacy for reelection. Then in January 2014, texts surfaced proving that members of Christie's staff had been complicit in creating the Fort Lee traffic crisis. On January 9, 2014, Christie held a press conference to apologize to the mayor and citizens of Fort Lee and to report the firing of the members of his staff whose behavior he termed "completely unacceptable." The embarrassment and humiliation Christie admitted to experiencing could have been avoided if the governor had conducted the necessary research himself instead of defending the manufactured traffic jams as part of a "traffic study." Make it your business to do your own fact checking prior to delivering your message. Take the time you need to verify all the facts and figures you intend to share with receivers; base your message on a solid foundation of well-documented research.

18.4b Convey the Right Amount of Information

Ensure you give the audience neither too little nor too much information.

Pace, Don't Race

When you're delivering an informative speech, your job is to communicate your ideas so audience members understand them, not to race to see how much new information you can cram into their brains in five or ten minutes. Develop the main ideas of the speech carefully and clearly. Take enough time to let each point you are making stand out and register with the audience. Integrate supporting information that relates directly, not tangentially, to your main ideas. Reiterate what it is you want receivers to remember. Pace the information you deliver during the speech—being careful to make the information digestible. A challenge is to know not only what to include, but what *not* to include as well.

Don't Take Knowledge for Granted

Work to communicate even the most sophisticated ideas as simply and clearly as possible. The more you assume audience members know, the greater are your chances of being misunderstood. Instead, respect the intelligence of your receivers, but work hard to clarify the complex. Show your audience how you are building on to what they already know. When you relate new information to old and use creative analogies to help receivers make connections, you will make the unfamiliar more familiar. For example, one student compared the pending legalization of recreational marijuana to eating a box of candy, telling receivers that it may be tempting, but hidden dangers await them if they consume too much.

Repeat, but Don't Retreat

Help audience members process new content by using **repetition** (reusing the exact same words) and **restatement** (rephrasing an idea in different words to more fully explain it). But you must strike a delicate balance between these and newness, so as not to bore your audience.

Pace yourself. Don't cram too much into your speech; strike a balance between new information and clear explanations.

18.4c Create Information Hunger

How do you motivate your audience to learn a new body of content? You create information hunger by convincing them that they have a personal need to know what you are about to convey. If your audience believes your speech's content is somehow vital to them, then they are much more likely to listen carefully and act on your recommendation. For example, to create information hunger for a speech on how to lobby a legislator to support school breakfasts for impoverished students, you might ask receivers to imagine how they would feel if they had had neither dinner the night before nor breakfast today before coming to school. What would they be concentrating on—their empty stomachs or learning? Remind them that a relationship exists between filling a stomach and filling a mind.

Capture and Sustain Attention

You must first capture and then sustain the audience's interest so that they want to hear what you will say next throughout your speech. One faculty member created information hunger in a new cohort of first-year college students with these introductory words:

> This event is a formal way of marking the start of the school year, and for you, the start of your college career. Each year, a faculty member shares some ideas with your class. This year, that person is me. And I have these ideas to share with you.
>
> The first idea is pretty simple: you're screwed. Your generation is screwed.[1]

Adapt to Your Audience

Most subjects become interesting if well adapted to the audience. From the outset, receivers need to believe that your speech will benefit them—that you are about to add to their knowledge, satisfy their curiosity, or show them how what you know can help them enjoy or improve their lives. For example, if you were talking to a group of career women about the management styles of women and men, your speech would probably interest them because of its potential to affect them directly.

Use the material covered in Chapters 5 and 8 to help you adapt to and customize your content for your particular audience.

18.4d Be Memorable

In order for your speech to remain with your audience after you have finished speaking, you must convey the enthusiasm you have for your subject to your listeners, and make it memorable. To do this, you can

- ☐ Let them know what you think is important for them to retain.
- ☐ Stress those points via verbal and nonverbal means, using repetition, pauses, vocal emphasis, and gestures.
- ☐ Build in audience participation.

By helping the audience use the information you give them during or immediately following your speech—building in audience participation or asking for a behavioral response—you increase the chances of their assimilating and using the information you provide them.

Remember, although your goal may be to share ideas, people are interested in other people. Nothing enhances the communication of information more than the integration of personal anecdotes, examples, and illustration. The drama of human interest makes a speaker's information memorable by helping it come alive.

GAME PLAN

Preparing an Informative Speech

- ☐ I have chosen an organizational framework that works for my topic.
- ☐ I have determined the specific purpose of my speech, and it is clearly stated.
- ☐ I've reviewed and revised my organization so that main points clearly support main ideas.
- ☐ I've established my topic's importance and relevance in a way that suits my audience.
- ☐ I've edited the amount of information I provide so that it is accurate and complete.
- ☐ Overall, I believe my speech educates receivers on the topic, but does not overwhelm them.

Exercises

INFORMATIVE SPEAKING

Building on your skills, the following activities help enhance your understanding of informative speaking while providing the extra information savvy needed for you to convey information in interesting and involving ways.

1. Topic Frameworks

Develop a framework that includes a specific purpose, a central idea, and main points for giving an informative speech on one of the following topics:

- Planned Parenthood
- Sikhism
- The Design of Washington, D.C.
- The Koch Brothers

2. Huh? (Unclear) Versus Aha! (Clear)

Following are a number of highly technical words or phrases that would probably need to be revised using jargon-free words or phrases that audiences readily understand.

Unclear	**Clear**
Cephalagia	Headache
Agrypnia	Insomnia
Precipitous	Steep
Nil desperandum	"It ain't over till it's over."

Based on your understanding of unclear and clear words, listen to one of the following speeches and locate five examples of words or phrases that you believe need to be simplified in order to enhance clarity or five examples of words or phrases that you believe are perfectly clear.

- Madeline Albright's speech commemorating International Women's Day 2010 on YouTube
- Bill Gates's speech on creative capitalism on YouTube, or read a transcript of the speech at http://www.gatesfoundation.org/media-center/speeches/2008/01/bill-gates-2008-world-economic-forum

3. Analyze the Speech: What It Means to Be Deaf

Because informative speaking is a prime means of sharing what you know with others, it is essential for the speaker to recognize diversity and adapt to difference.

In the speech that follows, student Andi Lane addresses a diversity issue when she shares her understanding of what it means to be hearing impaired. Notice how she uses her own experiences as a starting point.

Read the transcript below and answer these questions:

1. Think about the speech's introduction and its conclusion. To what extent did the introduction succeed in getting your attention? To what extent was the speaker successful in tying her introduction and conclusion together?
2. What means did the speaker use to establish and maintain her credibility? Which kinds of information were most useful? Most memorable?
3. Are you now able to understand what it means to be deaf? If so, what did the speaker do to help you internalize such an understanding? If not, what could the speaker have done to promote better understanding?
4. Were the supporting materials the speaker used effective? How many different kinds of supporting materials did the speaker use? In what ways did they facilitate your understanding? Your emotional involvement?
5. Focus on the speaker's use of transitions. How effectively did the speaker move from one point to the next? To what extent was it easy to identify the speaker's main points?
6. What did the speaker do to help widen receiver appreciation of diversity issues?
7. What might the speaker change to enhance her speech?
8. Based on this transcript, pretend you are the speaker and develop speaker's notes to use when delivering the speech.

WHAT IT MEANS TO BE DEAF

At the beginning of this year I moved into an apartment.

When I arrived at my new place, my roommate was there to greet me, and she saw my stereo. She got really excited, and she said, "Great you have a stereo for us to listen to." I laughed and told her that was a pretty funny joke, as I turned and ran up the stairs. But Sarah never knew I said that. You see, Sarah is profoundly deaf and relies upon lip reading as her primary source of communication. Living with Sarah has taught me many things.

SN 1 Beginning with this personal anecdote is a fine way to start. The speaker builds credibility and audience interest simultaneously.

Prime among them is this: the deaf and hearing impaired face many problems on a daily basis. My interest in this subject led me to take a basic sign language and communication with the hearing impaired course. In the course I discovered that understanding the deaf culture, learning to communicate with them, and accepting them can alleviate many of the problems that deaf and hearing-impaired people face. Let's explore these points together.

SN 2 The speaker reveals her thesis and previews the speech's content.

continued

continued

SN 3 The speaker moves into the first main point of her speech. She defines deaf culture for the audience. Because she has only limited experience with the subject, the use of an authoritative source enhances her credibility.

"What exactly is deaf culture?" you might ask. This is a legitimate question, since even those who are deaf and involved in the deaf culture have a difficult time explaining it. In his book, *Sign Language and the Deaf Community,* William Stokes says that there are several characteristics that can help us define the deaf culture. The deaf culture is closed and limited only to those who are deaf. Members have a common language that they share and common beliefs about others who are deaf and also those who are hearing. They also have shared goals; one of their primary goals is a goal of acceptance—acceptance in employment, politics, and every aspect of life.

SN 4 The speaker introduces her second main point and uses comparison and contrast to help clarify for receivers the differences in communication among members of the deaf and hearing cultures. Her use of specific examples adds interest and promotes understanding.

It's also interesting to compare the hearing world to the deaf culture. In deaf culture there's less emphasis on personal space; people have to be close together in order to read each other's signs. There's also less importance placed on time. People are not always punctual; there's a more relaxed feeling in the deaf culture.

Eye contact is lengthy, necessary, and polite in the deaf culture. Also when you do introductions—we usually greet each other; we meet each other; we exchange names. In the deaf culture, you exchange first names, last names, and where you attended school.

And my final point, the difference between the hearing world and the deaf culture, is that the hearing world is more reserved where the deaf culture is more tactile. An illustration of this is that in the hearing world we shake hands. In the deaf culture—usually they exchange hugs. These are just some of the important differences that Dr. Kenya Taylor, an audiologist, points out.

SN 5 The speaker explores the third main point of the speech by explaining the nature of sign language. Again, she is careful to identify the source of her information.

Daily life is, of course, very different for those who have a hearing problem. Communication is the main distinguishing factor. Sign language is usually taught to children at a very early age to provide them with a sense of vocabulary—a way to communicate their thoughts and ideas.

There are many different types of sign language, and these vary from area to area much as spoken language does, much like a dialect. The two most common types are signed English and the American Sign Language. Sign language, basic sign, is usually taught to beginners and follows the main sentence structure as spoken English does. ASL is used by those who are hearing impaired. It's a shortened, more abbreviated form. While the same signs are used, it's the format that differs according to Greenburg in his book, *Endless Sign.*

As mentioned before, children are usually taught sign language at a very early age. It is later that they acquire lip reading or speech skills, if they acquire them at all. Most deaf people can lip read to some extent. Now, of course, this presents special problems for the person. They must always be alert and aware of what's going on. And imagine being in a dimly lit room or trying to talk to a person who has a habit of looking away. Also, when you are talking to a deaf person they can't hear the sarcasm in your voice; you need to say what you mean.

SN 6 The speaker uses specific instances to clarify the problems the hearing impaired and hearing face as they attempt to communicate with each other.

Nonverbals are important; they pick up information any way they can get it. It's funny, because now I have a habit of flipping on the interior light when I get in my car at night. This is because I'm accustomed to riding with Sarah. Even when she's not in the car, the light's on, because it's impossible for us to communicate without the interior light on.

SN 7 The speaker draws on her personal experiences to make a point. Notice how doing this adds credibility to her presentation.

Right now, I'm going to paint a hypothetical situation for you, and I would like for you to put yourself in it. And it's a situation where you will be trying to communicate with a deaf person. Let's say you're at a restaurant; you're working there. It's a real busy place, the most popular place in town. One night a man comes in, alone, and is seated in the back corner, which is dimly lit. You're in a rush, and you go over to him, and you pour his water. And as you're pouring his water, you say: "May I take your order?" And you look up, and he doesn't say anything. First of all, he doesn't know you are addressing him, and second of all, he has no idea what you said. So you repeat yourself, "May I take your order?" And the man says, "I am deaf." But you don't know what he said because you don't know sign language. He speaks, and you can't understand him, and you're about to panic. In this situation, what you don't need to do is panic. You need to remember that the only difference between you and him is that you can hear and he can't. Communication is always possible, even if you have to point at the menu or write notes.

SN 8 The speaker uses a hypothetical illustration or narrative to involve receivers directly, increase their interest, and facilitate their understanding.

This leads me into my final point, the importance of accepting those with hearing problems. The more aware we are of the problems faced by the deaf and the greater our understanding, the less prejudiced we are going to be. The main difference, the only difference, in fact, between us—those who can hear—and people who can't hear is that we hear sounds with our ears, while they hear words and expressions with their eyes. And they feel with their hearts just like we do. We can't measure a person's intelligence by the degree of a hearing loss or the way that they speak. They are our equals.

SN 9 A transition at the start of this paragraph paves the way for the speaker to introduce her final main point.

continued

continued

SN 10 Notice how the speaker cites an authoritative source prior to offering tips.

I have a few tips from *The Hearing Instruments,* Volume 36, which will help us become more sensitive when we're talking to a deaf person. First of all, you talk in a normal fashion; don't shout at them because they can't hear you anyway. Try to keep your hands away from your mouth, because, of course, if they're trying to read your lips and your hands are over your mouth, they're not going to be able to understand you. Chewing, eating, and smoking are considered rude. You want to get the person's attention before you begin to talk to them, and it's perfectly acceptable to lightly touch their arm or wrist—somewhere along there. And finally, make sure that the hearing impaired person is not facing the light. That's something that we probably wouldn't think of. But if they're facing the light, they're not going to be able to concentrate on communication.

SN 11 The speaker summarizes her message. In addition, by again using personal experiences as well as reviewing what she's learned from them, she gives her speech a sense of closure.

Today I've shared with you some background information about the deaf culture, ways in which deaf people are able to communicate, and the importance of accepting deaf people for who they are. In the short time I've lived with Sarah, I've learned so much. I learned that you don't talk to her when your back is turned or when you're in another room. I've learned that I can scream as loud as I want to in the apartment, and it wouldn't make any difference at all. I can achieve the same end result by just telling her I'm upset. And I've learned that one of my most dear friends has a profound hearing loss, but I still love her.

4. Approach the Speaker's Stand

Prepare and deliver a five- to seven-minute informative speech on one of the following topics or another of your own selection: Insomnia, Celiac Disease, Lead Poisoning, the History of Organ Transplants, Diwali, the Witness Protection Program, Bullying, or Birthday Traditions.

In developing your speech, (1) clearly state its specific purpose, (2) identify the central idea of the speech, (3) develop each main point in the speech, integrating research and supporting materials, and (4) use both an organizational format and language that facilitate audience understanding.

Prepare an outline and speaker's notes, and include a bibliography of the sources you consulted.

RECAP AND REVIEW

1. **Define informative speaking and explain its purposes.** Informative speaking involves the sharing or transfer of information from speaker to receivers. As a result of an informative speech, the speaker expands or clarifies what receivers know by adding to their knowledge and skills or reducing their confusion.
2. **Compare and contrast the following: a speech about objects and ideas, a speech about events and people, and a speech about processes and procedures.** Speeches about objects cover anything tangible, while speeches about ideas explain concepts or definitions. Speeches about events or people focus on the compelling events or people of our time or history. Process or procedure speeches explore how something is done, works, or is made, or why something happens.
3. **Deliver an informative speech that is organized and communicates as simply and directly as possible, creates information hunger in receivers by relating ideas directly to them, and is memorable.** Like any other good speech, clearly develop the main points of a speech by offering receivers concrete support and using language that is neither overly complex nor vague. A well-crafted, informative speech also avoids over- or underloading them with information. Finally, remember to link the ideas of your speech with the interests or goals of receivers, as audience members need to be drawn into and become involved with the speech's main ideas.

KEY TERMS

Abstraction 317
Concrete 317
Event/person speech 313
Idea/concept speech 310
Information overload 316
Information underload 316
Informative speech 309
Object speech 311
Process/procedure speech 314
Repetition 318
Restatement 318

PART SEVEN

Speak to Persuade

© iStockphoto.com/Groomes Photography

19

Prepare to Persuade

UPON COMPLETING THIS CHAPTER'S TRAINING, YOU WILL BE ABLE TO

1. Define persuasion
2. Distinguish the differences among attitudes, beliefs, and values
3. Identify and define your persuasive goal, particularly the change you seek in receivers
4. Compare and contrast the following types of persuasive speeches: a question of fact, a question of value, and a question of policy
5. Explain and use Monroe's Motivated Sequence

Can you imagine yourself speaking in favor of opening U.S. borders to increased numbers of immigrants, or do you see yourself advocating for closing our borders? Would you speak in support of a woman's right to choose, or are you a proponent of the right to life movement? Would you speak against the death penalty, or do you believe in capital punishment?

Choice and change characterize our lives.[1] The positions we take on the issues of the day and our efforts to convince others of our correctness can have a real and meaningful impact. In this chapter, we focus on persuasion and its purposes. In Chapter 20, we explore persuasive speaking techniques. Mastering the contents of these chapters will make you a more effective persuader and consumer of persuasion.

Contents

section

19.1

We All Practice Persuasion

Persuasion is the deliberate attempt to change or reinforce attitudes, beliefs, values, or behaviors.[2] Persuasion permeates society, but when we engage in it we must do so ethically and successfully by avoiding coercion and manipulation.[3] Let's look closely at attitudes, beliefs, and values and their relationship to persuasion to see how to use them to achieve persuasive goals.

19.1a Assess Attitudes

An attitude is a mental set or predisposition that leads us to respond to or evaluate people, places, things, or events positively or negatively. The attitudes we hold reflect our likes and dislikes. Attitudes are classified along a continuum ranging from positive to negative, with neutrality at the midpoint.

The more you know about audience members' attitudes and why they feel as they do, the better you can tailor your message to speak directly to them.[4] If you and the audience share similar attitudes toward a topic, the task is simplified. Fortunately, audience attitudes tend to cluster at a particular point along the attitude continuum. If you can identify where that point is—that is, what the general audience attitude is—then you can build an approach that takes it into account.

For example, let's assume most people in your audience are neutral toward your topic, perhaps because they know very little about it. Your primary need, in such a case, is to supply them with reasons to care and evidence that substantiates your position. If, however, most audience members oppose your proposition, your task changes. In this case, you need to offer arguments that reduce hostility or negativity and provide information to redirect audience attitudes.

When giving a speech, you have the potential to instill, change, or intensify attitudes. Attitudes differ not only in *direction* (Are they positive or negative?) and *intensity* (How strong is the positive or negative attitude?), but also in *salience*—how important and relevant the attitude is to its holders. For example, though the audience may have a positive attitude toward affirmative action programs and feel strongly about the need to correct previous inequities, if they do not believe it affects them, it will not have salience.

Among the forces shaping attitudes are family, religion, schooling, social class, and culture. These also shape beliefs, which we look at next.[5]

19.1b Build on Beliefs

We measure attitudes along a favorable–unfavorable continuum, and beliefs along a probable–improbable one. Our beliefs determine whether we accept something as true or false. Upbringing, past experiences, and evidence work together to convince us of the truth or falsity of statements of belief.

Attitudes and beliefs work in concert. If you have a positive attitude toward someone or something, you are more likely to believe good things about it and vice versa. For example, if you hold a negative attitude toward television, you might well believe that television encourages laziness in children, precipitates reading problems in young learners, and contributes to childhood obesity. In contrast, if you started out with a positive attitude toward television, then you would be more apt to believe such views were either exaggerated or untrue.

19.1c Validate Values

Values, sometimes referred to as core beliefs, are enduring and deeply ingrained indicators of what we each feel is good or bad, right or wrong. If we value honesty over deception, for example, we would classify honesty as desirable. Values motivate behavior. They guide conduct by reminding us what we find most important. They also guide our decisions about what is worth trying to change or influence.

The top five values identified by Americans in one Gallup poll were good family, good self-image, being healthy, having a sense of accomplishment, and working for a better America.[6] Speakers can use such findings to show how what they advocate supports the values important to audience members.

Jupiterimages/Photos.com/Thinkstock

Tough call. Persuading another person to change his or her view can be challenging without the right approach.

19.1d Integrate Attitudes, Beliefs, and Values

When delivering a persuasive speech, use your own values, beliefs, and attitudes to select your subject.

First, identify strong attitudes you hold about five controversial issues. For example, are you for or against granting citizenship to undocumented immigrants currently working in the United States? Next, identify the beliefs you hold that help explain your attitude on each issue, for example, "I believe undocumented immigrants are taking jobs that U.S. citizens would not take," or "I believe that undocumented immigrants are taking jobs away from U.S. citizens." Then, identify the values that support your beliefs, for example, "I value rewarding hard work," or "I value the legal process." Finally, review your list, and determine which of your strong attitudes, beliefs, or values you could successfully turn into a persuasive speech.

section
19.2

Goals and Purposes of Persuasive Speech

19.2a Identify a Goal

19.2b Specify the Change You Seek

Persuasive speakers seek change that usually results in one or more of the following goals:

- Reinforcement of a position
- Shift in a position
- Adoption of a behavior
- Elimination of a behavior

19.2a Identify a Goal

The persuasive speaker aims to influence the audience's response so that receivers feel, think, or act differently than they did before the speech. To succeed, the persuasive speaker must be able to identify his or her objectives succinctly and, more specifically, be able to answer the following two questions:

1. What exactly am I trying to reinforce or change in my receivers?
2. How must the members of my audience alter their attitudes, beliefs, values, or behaviors for them to respond as I desire?

To the extent that you change the ideas and behaviors of one or more of your receivers, obtaining a commitment or eliciting a desired action from them, you are being persuasive, and you are changing the world—presumably for the better.

19.2b Specify the Change You Seek

Once you establish your persuasive goal, you must next decide on the type and the direction of the change you seek and on how to motivate your audience to respond appropriately. For example, which of the following do you want audience members to do?

- *Adopt* a new way of thinking or behaving, such as . . .
  - Donate money to assist wounded veterans
  - March to protest racial injustice
  - Write their legislators to support strict gun control
- *Sustain* or *reinforce* a way of thinking or behaving, such as . . .
  - Reaffirm their belief in freedom of the press
  - Recommit to supporting public education
  - Strengthen their willingness to vote regularly
- *Discontinue* or *extinguish* a way of thinking or behaving, such as . . .
  - Stop sexting
  - Discontinue support for the death penalty
  - Limit fast food consumption
- *Avoid* a particular way of thinking or behaving, such as . . .
  - Not binge drink
  - Not think of academic cheating as harmless
  - Not exceed the speed limit

Those who seek to persuade also assume substantial ethical obligations. It is up to you to ensure that any changes you seek are sound and in the best interests of receivers. You need to stimulate your receivers to think or do as you desire without harming them or the public.

section

19.3

Categorize and Organize the Persuasive Speech

Persuasive speaking is categorized according to whether it focuses on a *question of fact*, a *question of value*, or a *question of policy*. Whichever you choose, your claim represents your **proposition**, that is, the relationship you wish to establish between accepted facts and your desired conclusions. Each kind of proposition requires you to use particular types of evidence, motivational appeals, and methods of organization.

19.3a Speak on a Question of Fact

Propositions of fact are statements asserting that something does or does not exist or is or is not true. The following are typical propositions of fact:

- Self-driving cars make driving safer.
- The current U.S. immigration policy is a failure.
- Ghosts exist.
- A high-fiber diet promotes longevity.
- Sustained exposure to products used in nail salons poses substantial health risks.
- The harmfulness of high fructose corn syrup is exaggerated.
- The criminal justice system discriminates against racial and ethnic minorities.
- The federal deficit is a threat to our economic security.

Your goal is to persuade receivers of the truth of your proposition with an array of evidence and argument that convinces the audience that your interpretation of a situation is valid, and thus your assertion is true and accurate, and your conclusion undeniable.

Organize the Question of Fact Speech

When speaking on a proposition of fact, part of the challenge is to convince the audience that your conclusion is based on objective evidence. At the same time, you need to present the facts as persuasively as possible.

It is common to use a *topical organization* to organize speeches on questions of fact, with each main point offering listeners a reason they should agree with the speaker.

TOPICAL ORGANIZATION

Specific Purpose: To persuade my audience that the homeless lack the resources to regain a place in American society

Proposition: The homeless lack the resources to regain a place in American society.

Main Points:

I. The homeless do not have permanent residences, so they are forced to drift from place to place.

II. The homeless have no place in the economic system.

III. The homeless suffer from conditions of hunger, and physical and mental illnesses.

However, if you believe that you can best achieve the goals of your persuasive presentation by describing an issue as worsening over time, or by describing a subject spatially—for example, how a specific issue under consideration has global implications—then instead of using a topical organizational format you might choose to use *chronological* or *spatial organization*.

19.3b Speak on a Question of Value

A **proposition of value** provides an answer to questions like these: What is bad? What is right? What is moral? A proposition of value represents your assertion of a statement's worth.

When you are speaking on a proposition of value, your task is to justify your belief or opinion so that your receivers accept it too. The following statements are propositions of value:

- Discrimination against transgender people is wrong.
- Eating animal meat is improper.
- Euthanasia is immoral.
- War is morally justifiable.
- Solitary confinement is cruel and unusual punishment.
- A fetus's right to life is more important than a woman's right to choose.
- It is unethical to have more than two children.

© iStockphoto.com/TheaDesign

Factual. A proposition of fact, such as one about U.S. immigration, requires you to strike a balance between objectiveness and persuasiveness.

How do you convince your listeners to arrive at the same conclusion as you? By offering information, evidence, and appeals, as well as by establishing standards or criteria that you hope will compel them to agree with your value judgment. In order to analyze a proposition of value, you must do two things:

☐ Define the object of evaluation and support that definition.

☐ Provide value criteria for determining what the evaluative term means, that is, how do you define what is "proper," what is "wrong," or what is "immoral"?

In the next example, the speaker explains why she believes it is immoral to fund research to clone human beings. By referring to the work of Father Richard A. McCormick, a professor of Christian ethics at the University of Notre Dame, she hopes to build support for her stance.

> Cloning would tempt people to try to create humans with certain physical or intellectual characteristics. It would elevate mere aspects of human beings above what University of Notre Dame Reverend Richard A. McCormick says is the "beautiful whole that is the human person." But who among us should decide what the desirable traits are, what the acceptable traits are? Might this practice lead to the enslavement of humans by humans?

Organizing the Question of Value Speech

Speeches on propositions of value often use a **reasons approach**, a type of topical organization, in which each reason in support of the position is presented as a main point. One student used this kind of format to explain why she believes that keeping the detention center at Guantanamo Bay open is contrary to the country's values.

REASONS FORMAT

Specific Purpose: To convince my audience that keeping Guantanamo Bay open is morally wrong because keeping it fails to advance our national security, it runs counter to our values, and it hurts our standing in the world.

Proposition: It is morally wrong to keep the detention center at Guantanamo Bay open.

Main Points:

I. Keeping Guantanamo Bay open fails to advance our national security.

II. Keeping Guantanamo Bay open runs counter to our values.

III. Keeping Guantanamo Bay open hurts our standing in the world.

Note that each reason provides a "because," or justification for the speaker's position.

After hearing that speech, another student was motivated to deliver one supporting an opposing set of values, which calls for a **refutation format**. When arguing against a previously espoused position, you first note the stance being refuted, state your position, support it, and demonstrate why your position undermines the one previously stated. In this case, the student defended the proposition, "It is morally right to keep the detention facility at Guantanamo Bay open."

19.3c Speak on a Question of Policy

A **proposition of policy** asks receivers to support a change in policy and/or to take action to remedy an existing situation or solve a perceived problem. You can probably identify countless instances in which you have observed propositions of policy. When a legislator recommends the passage of a mandatory sentencing bill or when a social activist urges the elimination of discriminatory hiring practices, each is petitioning for a particular policy because he or she believes it is both needed and desirable (hence the traditional inclusion of the word *should* in the proposition).

When speaking on a question of policy, your job is to convince the audience that your stance is right. You accomplish this first with reasons, and second by proposing practical action or a solution. Propositions of policy usually build on both propositions of fact and propositions of value. In order for you to persuade your audience that action is merited, you first have to establish a proposition of fact and convince them to accept a proposition of value. Unless you can show a need for a policy, there is no point in arguing for it. Once you demonstrate that a need exists, it is then incumbent on you to suggest a solution and illustrate how that solution would help alleviate the problem.

The following are typical propositions for policy topics:

- To be culturally literate, all college students should study a foreign language.
- Childhood immunizations should be mandatory.
- College education should be free for all.
- Artificial sweeteners should be banned.
- Sex education should not be taught in schools.
- College athletes should be paid.
- Standardized testing should be ended.

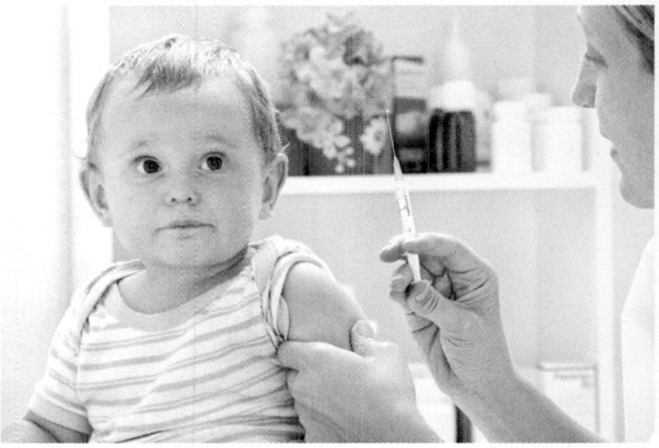

© iStockphoto.com/ Miodrag Gajic

Bare necessities. The burden of proof is on you to establish the need for the proposition of policy before you can argue the solution.

Organize the Question of Policy Speech

Individuals may agree about the facts surrounding an issue and even share a similar value orientation. Despite agreeing, however, they may disagree regarding what to do. For example, an entire community may agree that homelessness among children is a serious problem, and they may share the value that holds that we are responsible for all children, not just our own flesh and blood. Yet some might argue that we should place homeless children in foster homes; others might propose spending more money to house the homeless; still others might contend that we should view homelessness as a natural disaster and mount a mammoth effort to rid society of homelessness altogether.

Whatever the nature of the policy disagreement, there are four aspects of any controversy that advocates usually address:

- ☐ Is there a problem with the status quo?
- ☐ Is it fixable?
- ☐ Will the proposed solution work?
- ☐ Will the costs of fixing the problem outweigh the benefits of fixing the problem—that is, will the proposed solution help, or will it create new and more serious problems?[7]

Among the most popular formats for speeches on questions of policy are problem–causes–solution, comparative advantages, and Monroe's Motivated Sequence, all of which are variants of topical organization.

Often, a proposition of policy speech divides naturally into a *problem–causes–solution* organizational framework. The speech's first main point describes the nature and seriousness of the problem, the second main point explains the problem's causes, and the third main point proposes the solution and describes its practicality and benefits.

If your listeners are well informed about the problem you are discussing and convinced of a need for action, you should spend the bulk of your time explaining your plan and its viability. In this case, a *comparative advantages* format works well. In this structure, you use each main point to explain how your plan is better than the alternative. For example, in a speech opposed to online education, your main points might be that in-person classes are more effective learning environments, that they better foster social skills, and that they are more effective at preventing cheating than online classes.

section 19.4

Understand Monroe's Motivated Sequence

Monroe's Motivated Sequence is another organizational framework that speakers on propositions of policy find particularly effective in motivating receivers to act. Alan Monroe, a professor of speech at Purdue University, developed the framework more than 50 years ago. Based on the psychology of persuasion, Monroe's Motivated Sequence has five phases that move listeners toward accepting and acting on a proposition of policy.

Phase One: Attention. At the speech's outset, you must arouse the interest of your audience.

Phase Two: Need. Show your receivers that there is a serious problem with a present situation by explicitly stating the need and illustrating it with an array of supporting materials, and by relating it to their interests and desires.

Phase Three: Satisfaction. After you show your audience that there is a need, you must satisfy their desire for a solution. Present your plan and explain it fully. Help them understand that alleviating the problem will also satisfy their interests and desires.

Phase Four: Visualization. Show receivers how your proposal will both benefit them and improve the situation. Asking receivers to visualize what the world will be like if they fail to act as you request can also be effective.

Phase Five: Action. Tell audience members specifically what you would like them to do and conclude with an appeal that reinforces their commitment.

The following outline illustrates how one educator used the motivational sequence as a guide when organizing her ideas for a speech on why public schools should promote multiculturalism.

INTRODUCTION

Phase One: ATTENTION

I. Hate crimes attributed to ethnocentrism have become too prevalent in our schools.

II. Racial, ethnic, and religious biases drive students apart.

III. Today I would like to explain to you why the greatest concern of educators should be to promote multiculturalism in our schools.

Phase Two: NEED

I. We need to promote multiculturalism in schools so students feel safe.

   A. Children in U.S. classrooms represent all the world's races, religions, and ethnic groups.

   B. We must educate all children so they can learn tolerance and acceptance.

Phase Three: SATISFACTION

II. We would alleviate racial, ethnic, and religious tensions by promoting a curriculum that is pluralistic rather than ethnocentric.

   A. The pluralist approach prepares children to live in a world of competing ideas and values, to be able to live and work with people from different backgrounds, and to learn to examine their own beliefs.

      1. Pluralism teaches children that they are part of a multiracial, multiethnic, multireligious world.

      2. Pluralism teaches that we are all part of a cultural mosaic.

      3. Pluralism stresses critical thinking.

   B. The ethnocentric approach to American culture insists that we must identify only with people who have the same skin color or ethnicity.

      1. Ethnocentrism immerses children in a prideful version of their own race, ethnicity, and religion.

      2. Ethnocentrism teaches children to respect only those who are part of their own group.

      3. Ethnocentrism teaches children not to raise doubts.

Phase Four: VISUALIZATION

III. The public schools must prepare the younger generation to live in a world of differences.

   A. Imagine the history curriculum not as a tool to build ethnic pride, but as a subject in which we learn about our society.

   B. Imagine if differences were not grounds for hatred, but grounds for respect.

(Continued)

(Continued)

Phase Five: ACTION

IV. A program on multiculturalism has been proposed to the school board.

  A. You can help ensure its passage by attending a school board meeting, offering to speak at the event, and circulating petitions I will give you after my speech.

  B. If we all support these changes, we can build a better-balanced school curriculum.

CONCLUSION

I. I urge you to help rid our schools of ethnocentrism.

II. It is time to teach respect for those who are different.[8]

Using Monroe's Motivated Sequence enables a speaker to anticipate the questions and concerns audience members want addressed as they listen to the speech. Observe how the preceding outline established the topic's relevance, isolated the issue, identified a solution, helped receivers visualize the positive outcomes resulting from the solution, and appealed to them to act accordingly.

GAME PLAN

Using Monroe's Motivated Sequence

- ☐ I developed an attention getter to pique the audience's interest by connecting my topic to their concerns.
- ☐ Early in my speech, I showed receivers that there is a serious problem or issue confronting us that we must address.
- ☐ I proposed a satisfying solution to the problem or issue, supporting it with appropriate evidence.
- ☐ I prompted my audience to visualize how what I'm proposing will improve the situation.
- ☐ Finally, I laid out a concrete plan for my audience members, calling on them to take action.

Exercises

PERSUASION PREPARATION

Becoming an accomplished persuasive speaker, one who is ethical and a critical thinker, takes practice. So does processing the persuasive efforts of others. Use the following persuasive exercise to improve your skills at both.

1. Be a Fact, Value, and Policy Checker

Let's say that you decide to speak about the effects of corporate influence on the foreign policy of the United States, and you have the option of delivering a speech using a proposition of fact, value, or policy. Your propositions for each option might read as follows:

FACT	Corporate influence on the foreign policy of the United States is excessive.
VALUE	It is wrong for corporations to influence the foreign policy of the United States.
POLICY	Congress should act to reduce corporate influence over the foreign policy of the United States.

Now, to enhance your ability to create propositions of fact, value, and policy, choose two controversial topics such as "sexting" or "single-payer health care" and write a proposition of fact, value, and policy for each.

2. Incorporate Counterarguments Into Your Speech

In the book *Age of Propaganda,* psychologists Anthony Pratkanis and Elliot Aronson assert that well-informed members of an audience are more likely to be persuaded if a speaker introduces them to opposing arguments that the speaker refutes than they are by a speaker's presentation of a one-sided argument. Why is this? Because the more well informed audience members are, the greater their awareness of an issue's many sides—including arguments that run counter to the speaker's position. If the speaker ignores these, receivers may assume that the speaker is either unaware of them or unable to refute them.

In contrast, less-informed receivers are easier to persuade while leaving opposing arguments unaddressed. In fact, introducing a counterargument to an uninformed audience could result in confusion.[9]

- Consider this question: When a speaker on a controversial topic limits his or her discussion to just one side of the issue, what judgment is the speaker making about the intelligence of the audience, and how do you feel about that?
- Using one of the propositions you wrote for the previous exercise, brainstorm and jot down some of the opposing arguments that those who have knowledge about the issue might offer.

3. The Motivation Sequence

Identify a television ad or infomercial that illustrates Monroe's Motivated Sequence in action. Draft an outline that explains how the selected commercial fulfills each step in the sequence.

4. Analyze the Speech

In the speech that follows, the goal was to persuade the audience that people need to be careful to not spread misinformation and to engage in informed sharing instead. As you review the speech, consider whether the speech succeeds.

Respond to these questions:

1. To what extent, if any, do you find the speech's introduction and conclusion fulfilled their functions?
2. Was the proposition of the speech clearly stated? What action was the speaker encouraging the receivers to take?
3. What evidence is there that the speaker considered the attitudes, beliefs, and values of receivers?
4. Did the speaker demonstrate that there was a problem with the status quo?
5. Was the solution proposed by the speaker to fix the existing problem viable?
6. Was the organizational framework of the speech effective?

INFORMED SHARING

SN 1 The speaker uses a surprising piece of information and a series of rhetorical questions to introduce the speech and capture the audience's attention. The speaker immediately involves the audience in looking at a problem that is far from under control, the sharing of misinformation.

In 2010 a story broke reporting that the Los Angeles Police Department had ordered 10,000 jet packs for their officers. Pretty cool right? Until you realize that they cost 1 million dollars each. Not cool. Especially for a police force that couldn't even buy new squad cars. The story becomes a little less cool when you learn that it isn't even true. The fact that the article exists, however, is true. The story caught on like wildfire, and according to Cracked.com, was even picked up by national news outlets. While this anecdote is amusing, it isn't that important is it? I mean who cares about a story now-and-then that isn't true? However, there are more lies on the internet than you may realize. And I'm not just talking about articles from *The Onion,* or the *Babylon Bee.* Even trusted news sources get it wrong all the time.

SN 2 The speaker previews the contents of the speech for the audience.

Today we will first look at the importance of knowing the truth behind the articles that we read and share, and then we will look at how we can vet the information we take in, and finally examine the benefits of what I call informed sharing.

According to the World Economic Forum, the 2014 10th most important issue facing the world is the "rapid spread of misinformation." In 2014 and 2015, the BBC published an article of 7 news events that were not real. Eighteen more were reported by Politifact, and the *Washington Post* highlighted 15 stories that were lies, including one that nude photos of Emma Watson were leaked. Not that it couldn't happen, but it didn't. Saul Eslake writes in a 2006 paper that "Accurate, reliable and timely information is vital to effective decision-making in almost every aspect of human endeavor." This should be the goal of every article we crack open: to educate ourselves in order to improve our decision-making process, and ultimately our lives.

SN 3 The speaker establishes the topic's importance.

The concern here is that every time we get on Facebook or Twitter, we are bombarded with news stories from all kinds of sources written by all kinds of people, and many of them are not true. And then we click "share" spreading the lies to all our friends, who likely do the same. This makes it imperative for us, as consumers of media, active or passive, to know the truth behind an article before we share it with others. Plus, there is also the possibility you will embarrass yourself later when you reference a story you thought was true, but that everyone else knows was fake.

SN 4 The speaker draws the audience further into the speech.

In a social web that is woven with posts, stories, articles, and memes, how is any sane person supposed to cipher through all the material they encounter? Well, you can't. But that just means that the things you *do* choose to read or share need to be taken seriously. The first thing I do when I see a headline that catches my attention is look at the source. If it's not one I know or trust, I am likely to skim over it. Especially if it's from *The Onion.*

SN 5 The speaker uses another rhetorical question to involve receivers in coming up with possible solutions for the problem.

Secondly, Melanie McManus suggests—in her article titled, appropriately, *10 Ways to Spot a Fake News Story*—that you check other news sources. This will not only legitimize the article, but cross check the details. If multiple sources are coming to similar conclusions on an issue, then it is probably safe to say that it's legitimate. The headline itself can also be very telling. McManus lists several types of headlines that are almost always a hoax, or at the least unverifiable. End of

SN 6 The speaker relies on research that reveals how receivers can spot misinformation.

continued

continued

the world announcements, or claims to have found cures to major illnesses often fall into this category. Other types of headlines that can be "internet garbage" are those that invoke a deep emotion. When the author uses loaded language that automatically makes you angry, it's possible that they are playing with your emotions just to get you to read their article.

Other ways we can avoid sharing bad information is by simply reading the article in its entirety. Most people who have any common sense can tell that a story lacks validity just by reading it. It is when we read a headline, and immediately share the story without reading the article itself that we can be contributing to the rapid spread of misinformation.

SN 7 The speaker incorporates a reliable source to explain the importance and nature of informed sharing, effectively emphasizing its benefits for receivers.

This informed sharing can stop the spread of internet garbage. By checking our facts, reading entire articles, and reading other articles on the topic, we can reduce the amount of misinformation that is shared. Fact checking may not be important to everyone, but according to Larry Margasak of the News Literacy Project, it is for those "who want to base their decisions on accurate information." And that *should* be important to everyone. By checking your facts, both those that you read, and those that you share, you add another layer of validity to the information on the web. Finally, by calling out authors or advocates of false stories you find, you not only make yourself look smart, but you educate others.

SN 8 By reiterating a theme originally broached during the speech's introduction in the conclusion, the speaker achieves closure. The speaker also reiterates why it is important for receivers to get on board.

The spread of misinformation goes beyond the LAPD spending 10 million dollars on jet packs. It reaches into the fabric of our lives in the political, social, religious, and even personal arenas. Lies and false stories permeate the media, and it's up to you to evaluate the sources and determine the validity of the things you believe and share with others. By understanding the dangers of misinformation, doing your part to be informed, and recognizing the benefits of informed sharing, hopefully together we can make the world a smarter place.

5. Approach the Speaker's Stand

Prepare an outline for a five- to seven-minute persuasive speech on a proposition of fact, value, or policy. Be sure to use an organizational format and integrate supporting materials that help you accomplish your persuasive goal. Include a bibliography of the sources you consulted.

RECAP AND REVIEW

1. **Define persuasion.** Persuasion is the attempt to change or reinforce the attitudes, beliefs, values, or behaviors of others.
2. **Distinguish the differences among attitudes, beliefs, and values.** An attitude is a mental set or predisposition to respond to or evaluate stimuli positively or negatively. A belief is that which determines whether you accept something as probable or improbable, true or false. A value is an enduring and deeply ingrained indicator of what we feel is good or bad, right or wrong.
3. **Identify and define your persuasive goal, particularly the change you seek in receivers.** Among the goals persuasive speakers seek in receivers are for them to adopt a new way of thinking or behaving, sustain or reinforce a way of thinking or behaving, discontinue a way of thinking or behaving, or avoid a particular way of thinking or behaving.
4. **Compare and contrast the following types of persuasive speeches: a question of fact, a question of value, and a question of policy.** When speaking on a proposition of fact, you argue that something is or is not true. A proposition of value speech focuses on the worth of a given statement. In a proposition of policy speech, you argue for what you believe should be done to solve an existing problem.
5. **Explain and use Monroe's Motivated Sequence.** Monroe's Motivated Sequence contains five key phases designed to move listeners toward accepting and acting on a proposition of policy: attention, need, satisfaction, visualization, and action.

KEY TERMS

Monroe's Motivated Sequence 338
Persuasion 330
Proposition 334
Proposition of fact 334
Proposition of policy 336
Proposition of value 335
Reasons approach 336
Refutation format 336

© iStockphoto.com/GlobalStock

20

Methods of Persuasion

UPON COMPLETING THIS CHAPTER'S TRAINING, YOU WILL BE ABLE TO

1. Use sound evidence
2. Apply Toulmin's Reasonable Argument Model
3. Use deductive, inductive, and causal reasoning, as well as reasoning from analogy
4. Arouse emotion
5. Name the three tenets of persuasive speaking
6. Avoid common logical fallacies
7. Design and deliver a persuasive speech

What makes one person more persuasive than another? According to the Greek philosopher Aristotle, it is **ethos**, the ability to convince the audience of your competence, good character, and charisma—your credibility; together with **logos**, the ability to use logical proof to demonstrate the reasonableness of argument(s); and **pathos**, the ability to develop empathy and passion in others. Whom have you attempted to persuade recently? Were you successful? What did you say that enabled your audience to perceive both you and your message positively? Of course, no one is successful at persuading all people all the time no matter how high their credibility or how skillful their persuasive techniques. However, if you use the strategies discussed in this chapter, you will increase both your credibility and persuasive potential.

COACHING TIP

"Don't raise your voice; improve your argument."

—Desmond Tutu

Yelling at those who do not share your views rarely succeeds in changing their minds. Use reason and emotion instead. Convince—don't chastize. Give your audience solid evidence, effective appeals, and reason to trust you, and you'll be on your way to achieving your goal.

Contents

section

20.1

Varying Viewpoints and Your Target Audience

Audience members are not necessarily unified in their thinking about controversial issues. For example, some members of the audience may hold a position diametrically opposed to yours. With this segment, you have little, if any, chance of changing their minds with a single speech.[1] You may, however, be able to move them closer to where you stand. Others in the audience may already accept your stance. You can assume they will stay with you. A third group will be undecided. Provide this segment of the audience with reasons to care, solid evidence, and effective appeals because they are your *target audience.* It is their needs, their values, their concerns, and their interests that you need to consider most (without ignoring the others) when designing your presentation.

Change, for most people, occurs over time. If you strive to create small changes in audience members and not instant conversions, your chances for success increase. Being able to address the same audience members more than once also improves the likelihood you will succeed.

Jupiterimages/liquidlibrary/Thinkstock

Take aim. Tailor your message directly for your target audience.

Build Persuasive Credibility

section **20.2**

An effective persuasive speaker is someone audience members perceive as qualified. The more **credibility** receivers feel you have, the more likely they are to believe what you say, and think and do as you advocate. Three major factors affect the audience's judgment of your credibility: (1) their perception of your competence, (2) their perception of your character, and (3) their opinion of whether you are charismatic.

We can divide credibility into its three constituent parts: **initial credibility**, how receivers perceive you before you speak; **derived credibility**, how they perceive you while you are speaking; and **terminal credibility**, how they perceive you after your speech. Having high initial credibility gives a persuasive speaker an advantage, as audience members are more likely to give your ideas a receptive hearing. But that's just the beginning. Your message and delivery style enhance *or* weaken your initial credibility in their eyes. The opinion audience members have of you at the end of one speech could also affect their view of you at the beginning of another. You are only as credible as your receivers perceive you to be—at the moment. Employ the techniques in Section 11.2 to establish your credibility.

section

20.3 Use Evidence

As we noted, perceived credibility, or what Aristotle labeled *ethos*, is helpful in realizing your persuasive goal. However, only when you unite credibility with evidence and reasoning, or what Aristotle called *logos*, will you have created a message that has believability. Because listeners are skeptical of unsupported generalizations, back your positions with strong **evidence**. Use facts and statistics to lay the groundwork for persuasion and validate the conclusions you are asking receivers to accept. Use detailed examples to create human interest and motivate receivers to respond as you desire. Expert testimony from sources that receivers respect also adds credence to the positions you advocate. When incorporated into a speech, these will change audience judgments of your initial, derived, and terminal credibility.

Review Chapters 7 and 8 for more on research and evidence, as we revisit the key types of evidence and establish guideposts you can use to test the strength and validity of each form of persuasive support.

- ***Facts.*** A *fact* is a statement that direct observation can prove true or false. Once proven, facts are noncontroversial and readily verifiable. Some common assertions aren't facts because there isn't enough information. For instance, we don't know that cellular phones cause cancer. Still, people may claim that such statements are true. To confirm the validity of the facts you use in support of a persuasive argument, make sure that there is little, if any, controversy regarding whether the statement made is true and that the statement is based on a report by someone who directly observed the situation or event.

Be a sleuth. Track down evidence to support your claims.

- ***Statistics.*** We can often summarize a group of observations with statistics. They are helpful in comparing observed data and in emphasizing and magnifying distinctive patterns and significant differences. Make sure your statistics are recent, unbiased, noncontroversial, and from a reliable source.
- ***Examples and illustrations.*** Both real and hypothetical examples and **illustrations** are used to support facts a speaker wants audience members to accept. Longer illustrations add more drama and emotional involvement to a message and help the speaker build a case that encourages audience members to draw desired conclusions. Only use examples that are typical, significant, noncontroversial, and from a reliable source.
- ***Testimony.*** Speakers use the opinions of respected individuals to add credibility to the conclusions they draw. Testimony should be fair, unbiased, appropriate, and from a recognized expert.

In addition to helping you prove the validity of your proposition, evidence helps "inoculate" your receivers against arguments made by those who disagree with you.[2] The most persuasive evidence is that which the audience was not aware of, that makes each listener question his or her position if it's different from yours, and that anticipates the questions and doubts of receivers and puts them firmly to rest.

© iStockphoto.com/luoman

Facts are facts. Research is crucial in preparing your argument and presenting your case.

section

20.4 Make Inferences

An *inference* is a conclusion we draw *based on a fact*. They connect the dots for your audience, demonstrating how the facts you've presented support your position. But you must assess the validity of your inferences—to ensure they have a high probability of being true.

When George E. Curry of the National Newspaper Publishers Association spoke before that organization and BlackPressUSA.com, he contended that though the *Brown v. Board of Education* Supreme Court decision may have changed the course of history, racism is not a thing of the past. He used a series of facts to support his contention, telling his audience the following:

> Society still has not adequately addressed the gap between the haves and have-nots in this country.
>
> According to *The State of the Dream 2004,* a report published by United for a Fair Economy in Boston,
>
> 1. One out of every nine African Americans cannot find a job;
> 2. The unemployment rate for African Americans is more than twice the unemployment rate of Whites;
> 3. In 1968, for every dollar of White per-capita income, African Americans earned 55 cents. More than three decades later, that gap was closed by two cents. At the rate we're going, it will take African Americans another 581 years to get to the remaining forty-three cents;
> 4. Almost a third of African American children live in poverty—32.1 percent in 2002. At the rate we're going, we will not reach parity until 2212—another 208 years;
> 5. The high school dropout rate has improved dramatically, now to the point where 79 percent of all African Americans at least 25 years old have high school diplomas;
> 6. In 1968, only 4.3 percent of African Americans had completed college; today it's 17.2 percent, which is still less than 29.4 percent of Whites.
>
> Even when we become educated, the typical African American high school graduate working full-time will earn $300,000 less than his or her White counterpart over a 30-year period. An African American college graduate will earn $500,000 less and the African American worker with an advanced degree will earn $600,000 less.[3]

To confirm the validity of the inferences you use in support of a persuasive argument, apply these two criteria:

1. There is little, if any, controversy regarding whether the statement made is true, or
2. The statement is based on a report by someone who directly observed the situation or event.

Appeal to Reason

section **20.5**

Cable news hosts are known for taking social or political issues and turning them into arguments with guests. Though this may be entertaining, when we analyze them critically, the arguments often lack logic and sound principles of reasoning.

Effective persuaders reason with their audiences by presenting evidence and arguments that help move receivers closer to the speaker's view. In *The Uses of Argument,* Stephen Toulmin shows that effective reasoning has the following components:

1. ***A claim.*** The proposition or thesis you hope to prove, for example, *College football should be banned.*[4]
2. ***Data.*** Reasons, facts, and evidence for making the claim, for example, *College football should be banned because it has no academic purpose.*
3. ***A warrant.*** A logical and persuasive relationship that explains how you get to your claim from the data you offer, for example, *The primary purpose of higher education is academics.*
4. ***The backing.*** Supporting information that answers other questions of concern and strengthens the warrant when it is controversial, for example, *Football is a distraction benefiting alumni and coaches, but not students or players. Coaches make obscene millions while players receive no compensation. The majority of the student body receives no benefit because tuition costs continue to rise while colleges continue to slash budgets.*
5. ***The qualifier.*** Limitations placed on the connection between the data and the warrant, usually symbolized by words such as *often, rarely,* or *always,* for example, *Colleges often lose money on their football programs.*
6. ***Rebuttal.*** Potential counterarguments, at times proffered during the initial argument, for example, *The student-athlete is a false concept. Any Division I college player will tell you the demands of the game make the student aspect superfluous.*

In diagram form, the **Toulmin Reasonable Argument Model** shown in Figure 20.1, suggests that if you state your claim clearly and qualify it so as not to overgeneralize an issue, support it with reasons, and connect it to the evidence you offer via the warrant, you improve your chances of persuading others to accept it. You should also anticipate opposing arguments and prepare counterarguments that rebut them.

Persuaders rely on four key methods of reasoning to move receivers to affirm or act on their goal: (1) deductive reasoning, (2) inductive reasoning, (3) causal reasoning, and (4) analogical reasoning.[5]

20.5a Deductive Reasoning

When you use **deductive reasoning**, you offer general evidence that leads to a specific conclusion.

Deductive reasons take the form of **syllogisms**, which are patterns to structure arguments. A syllogism has three parts:

1. A major premise, that is, a general statement or truth; for example, *we must condemn speech that precipitates violence.*
2. A minor premise, which is a more specific statement that describes a claim made about a related object; for example, *a speech by the grand wizard of the Ku Klux Klan will precipitate violence.*
3. A conclusion derived from both the major premise and the minor premise; for example, *therefore we must condemn this speech.*

FIGURE 20.1
The Toulmin Reasonable Argument Model

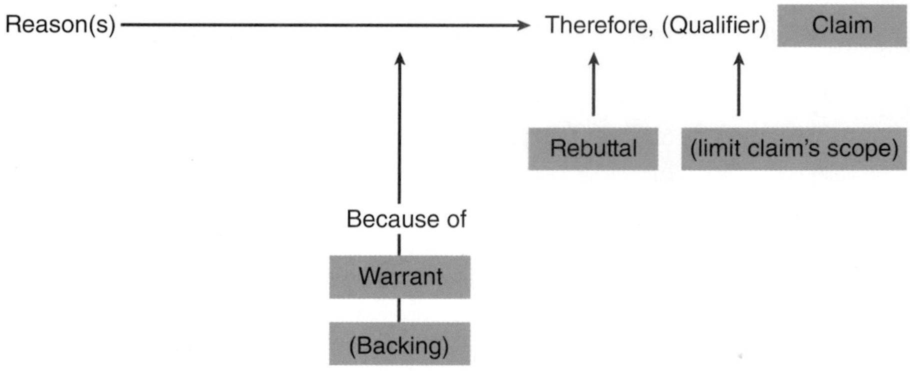

Source: Stephen Toulmin, *The Uses of Argument*. Cambridge, UK: Cambridge University Press, 1958/2003.

You can evaluate examples of deductive reasoning with these criteria:

- ☐ Both the major premise and the minor premise must be true.
- ☐ The conclusion must follow logically from the premise.

When you use deductive reasoning, you introduce your receivers to your general claim first. One of the potential disadvantages of the deductive approach is that receivers who oppose your claim may tune out and not pay attention to the specifics you offer in the minor premise. Instead of giving you the opportunity to provide them with reasons to accept your conclusion, they may be too busy rebutting your initial contention in their own minds. Of course, if you are addressing an audience that favors your proposal and merely needs reinforcing, then deductive reasoning works well.

In this example from a speech entitled "Sacred Rights: Preserving Reproductive Freedom," Faye Wattleton, then president of Planned Parenthood, defended legal protection for reproductive choice. Notice how she uses deductive reasoning to make a point:

> We've already seen some bizarre legal outcomes of this religious definition of human life *[Major Premise]*. Lawsuits have cropped up claiming fetuses as dependents for tax purposes—or claiming "illegal imprisonment" of the fetuses of pregnant inmates—or seeking to reclassify juvenile offenders as adults by tacking an extra nine months onto their age *[Minor Premise]*![6] *[Wattleton's conclusion is that we need to defend legal protection for reproductive choice by avoiding using the religious definition of human life.]*

20.5b Inductive Reasoning

When you use **inductive reasoning**, you progress from a series of specific observations to a more general claim or conclusion. You offer audience members particular reasons why they should support your generalization. For example,

FACT 1: People who live in poorer countries experience less depression.

FACT 2: Non-modern countries have the lowest rates of depression.

FACT 3: The Amish have one-tenth the depression of other Americans.

CONCLUSION: Depression is a disease of modernity and affluence.[7]

You can evaluate whether a speaker's use of inductive reasoning is effective by asking and answering these two questions:

- ☐ Are enough reasons given to justify the conclusion drawn?
- ☐ Are the instances cited typical and representative?

20.5c Causal Reasoning

When using **causal reasoning**—that is, reasoning that unites two or more events to prove that one or more of them caused the other—a speaker either cites observed causes and infers effects, or cites observed effects and infers causes. We use causal reasoning daily. Something takes place and we ask, "Why?" Similarly, we hypothesize about the effects of certain actions. The next series of statements illustrates causal reasoning from effect to cause:

EFFECT: Women are discriminated against in the workplace.

CAUSE 1: Women earn less than men in virtually every occupation.

CAUSE 2: Women are not offered the same training opportunities as men.

CAUSE 3: Society expects women but not men to put family before their jobs.

The next series of statements illustrates causal reasoning from cause to effect:

CAUSE 1: Too much of the food children eat is low in nutritional content but high in sugar, carbs, and fats.

CAUSE 2: Too many of the activities children engage in are sedentary.

EFFECT: Childhood obesity rates are rising.

Of course, causal reasoning can be problematic. Just because one thing happens and another follows does not necessarily mean that the first event was the cause. You can evaluate the soundness of causal reasoning by asking:

- ☐ Is the cause cited real or actual?
- ☐ Is the cause cited an oversimplification?

Remember, causal reasoning associates events that *precede* an occurrence with events that follow. It shows us that antecedents lead to consequences.

Make the connection. Explain the linkages between evidence and your argument. How does a caterpillar become a butterfly?

20.5d Reasoning From Analogy

When **reasoning from analogy**, we compare like things and conclude that because they are comparable in a number of ways, they also are comparable in another, new respect. For instance, if you propose that the strategies used to decrease welfare fraud in San Francisco would also work in your city, you would first have to establish that your city was like the other city in a number of important ways—perhaps the number of persons on welfare, the number of social service workers, and the financial resources. If you can convince audience members that the two cities are alike, except for the fact that your city does not yet have such a system in place, then you would be reasoning by analogy.

Use these two questions to check the validity of an analogy:

1. Are the objects of comparison in the speech alike in essential respects? That is, are they more alike than they are different?
2. Are the differences between them significant?

© iStockphoto.com/Vishwanath Bhat

Like apples and oranges. Use analogies to make new information easier to understand.

The best speakers combine several kinds of reasoning to justify the positions they are taking. Thus, your reasoning options are open. If you are going to speak ethically, however, you do not have the option of becoming unreasonable—that is, of using an argument that has only the appearance of valid reasoning without the substance.

section
20.6 Arouse Emotions

We react most strongly when we feel angry, anxious, excited, concerned, or guilty. Speakers use *pathos,* which Aristotle defines as appeals to the emotions of the audience, to instill the audience with attitudes and beliefs similar to their own and elicit a desired action. The greater your understanding of what members of your audience need, fear, and aspire to achieve, the greater your chances of gaining their attention and persuading them to accept what you are advocating.

Abraham H. Maslow, a psychologist, developed a classic theory to explain human motivation. His theory is now referred to as **Maslow's Hierarchy of Needs**.[8] Maslow depicted motivation as a pyramid, with our most basic needs at the pyramid's base and our most sophisticated needs at its apex (see Figure 20.2).

According to Maslow, basic necessities of life are physiological: air, shelter, food, water, and procreation. Next, we need to feel safe and secure, and to know that those we care about are protected as well. Our need for love and belonging is located at the third level of the hierarchy; there also lies our need for social contact and to fit into a group. The fourth tier focuses on esteem needs—our need for self-respect and to feel that others respect and value us. Finally, at the pyramid's apex is our need for self-actualization, defined as our need to realize our full potential and to accomplish everything we are capable of. By focusing on audience members' relevant need levels, speakers have in their possession the keys to unlock audience attention, involvement, and receptivity.

FIGURE 20.2
Maslow's Hierarchy of Needs

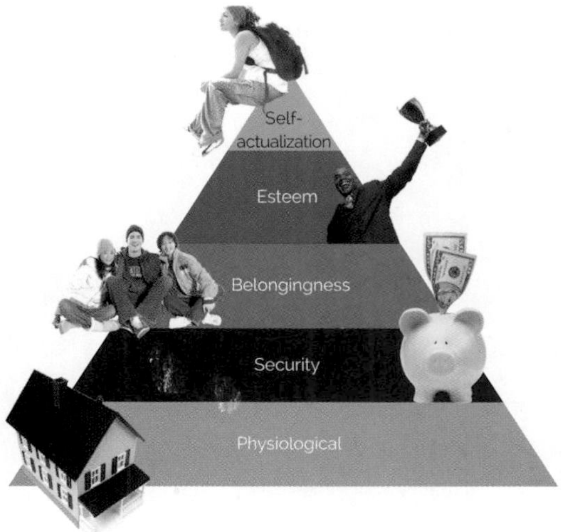

Source: Abraham Maslow, *Toward a Psychology of Being* (New York: John Wiley, 1962); images courtesy of Digital Vision/Digital Vision/Thinkstock; George Doyle/Stockbyte/Thinkstock; Thomas Northcut/Photodisc/Thinkstock; Stockbyte/Stockbyte/Thinkstock.

As a persuader, you should realize that unless audience members have their lower order needs met, you will rarely be able to motivate them by appealing to higher order needs. For instance, an appeal to esteem needs will likely fail unless the audience's physiological, security, and belongingness needs have been met. A speech on the importance of, say, achieving one's goals through higher education is unlikely to be successful if your receiver is homeless or hungry.

You can motivate the members of your audience using both positive and negative appeals. In a positive motivational appeal, you note how your proposal benefits audience members and improves their quality of life. However, a negative motivational appeal, such as a fear appeal, attempts to reach receivers by using the possibility that something dire will happen if they do not support what the speaker advocates.

In order for a fear appeal to work, audience members must believe

- ☐ You are a credible source.
- ☐ The threat you describe is real.
- ☐ Taking action to remove the threat will restore them to a state of balance.[9]

Keep in mind that your message must reveal how receivers can remove the threat. For example, one speaker attempted to persuade receivers that it was only a matter of time before a tsunami hit the United States—an appeal to fear with little if any means for receivers to do something to reduce it.[10] Once you induce fear in audience members, you have an ethical responsibility to explain to them how your proposal will free them of it.

section

20.7

Use Three Tenets of Persuasion

20.7a Think Small to Avoid a Big Fall

20.7b Use the Desire for Consistency

20.7c Don't Put the Best in the Middle

Here are three principles to guide you as you prepare to deliver a persuasive speech.

20.7a Think Small to Avoid a Big Fall

Persuasion is traditionally a step-by-step process, so keep your expectations realistic. If you try to skip too many steps, or if you expect too much from your receivers, then you may be disappointed in your results. Your receivers will be much more apt to change their way of thinking and/or behaving if the change you request is small.

20.7b Use the Desire for Consistency

One way to convince audience members to accept or act on your proposition is to demonstrate for them that a current situation has created an inconsistency in their lives and that you can help them restore their lives to a balanced state. When we feel that what a speaker is asking us to believe, think, or do contradicts our current beliefs, we are unlikely to be persuaded by them. However, if that speaker can show us why what we currently believe, think, or do is out of sync with other attitudes or beliefs we hold or goals we value, then we are more likely to change as requested to restore our comfort or well-being.

20.7c Don't Put the Best in the Middle

Use both primacy and recency theories as guides when positioning key persuasive points. Either put your strongest point up front to win audience members to your side early in your presentation, or put your strongest argument last to build momentum as you approach the end of your speech. The middle position is weakest. Your best and strongest argument certainly does not belong there. By positioning your arguments appropriately, you can be more persuasive.

Strategize. Don't bury your most important point in the middle of your speech. Either start your speech with it or bring it out at the very end.

Ethical Persuasion: Avoid Fallacies

section
20.8

A **logical fallacy** is a flawed reason. It is unethical to offer audience members reasoning marred by fallacies. In addition to not using fallacious reasons yourself, you also want to be able to spot them when other speakers use them. Among the reasoning fallacies are

- ***Hasty generalizations.*** You make a **hasty generalization** (in Latin, *dicto simplicito)* when you jump to a conclusion based on too little evidence. To avoid this reasoning defect, you need to review enough typical cases to validate your claim.
- ***Post hoc ergo propter hoc.*** This phrase is Latin for "after this; therefore, because of this." Reasoning suffers from this fallacy when you assume that merely because one event preceded another, the first event caused the second event to happen. The sunrise is not caused by a rooster crowing, nor did it rain because you washed your car. Reading scores in a school did not necessarily decline because (or only because) the curriculum was changed.
- ***Slippery slope.*** You find yourself on a **slippery slope** when asserting that one action will set in motion a chain of events. Though all choices have consequences, they rarely are as serious as users of slippery slope reasoning would have you conclude. Because once unwanted things happen, others do not certainly or even probably follow.
- ***Red herring.*** When you put a **red herring** in your speech, you lead your audience to consider an irrelevant issue instead of the subject actually under discussion. In an effort to defend the right of individuals to smoke in public places, for example, one speaker tried to deflect his listeners' concerns by focusing instead on the dangers of automobile emissions.
- ***False dichotomy.*** When you employ a **false dichotomy**, you require your audience to choose between two options, usually polar extremes, when in reality there are many in between. This polarizes receivers and reduces a complicated issue to a simple choice that all too often obscures other legitimate options. "America: Love it or leave it" and "If you are not part of the solution, you are part of the problem" are examples of the false dichotomy at work.
- ***False division.*** A **false division** infers that if something is true of the whole, it is also true of one or more of its parts. For example, just because a boat can float on water doesn't mean its motor can and an organization may not be corrupt because one of its members was convicted of embezzlement. What is true of the whole may not be true of its constituent parts.

- ***Personal attacks.*** When you engage in name-calling, you give an idea, a group, or a person a bad name ("un-American," "neo-Nazi") so that others will condemn your target without thinking critically or examining the evidence.
- ***Glittering generalities.*** A **glittering generality** is the opposite of a personal attack. Here the speaker associates an idea with things that the audience values highly (such as democracy and fairness). Again, however, the aim is to cause audience members to ignore or gloss over the evidence.
- ***Ad hominem attacks.*** When you present your audience with an **argument *ad hominem*** (literally, an argument "against the man"), you ask your audience to reject an idea because of a flaw in a person associated with that idea. "She's just a member of Generation X." An argument *ad hominem* places the focus on the person rather than on the veracity of the argument.
- ***Bandwagon appeals.*** If everyone jumps off a cliff, would you jump off a cliff too? Also known as the appeal to popular opinion, the **bandwagon appeal** tells receivers that because "everyone is doing it" they should as well. Just because many believe something, however, does not make it true.
- ***Appeal to fear.*** A speaker who makes receivers feel overly fearful in order to accomplish his or her goals often ends up pandering to prejudices or escalating the legitimate fears of receivers. Once receivers find themselves "running scared" because the dangers alluded to by the speaker have been exaggerated beyond what is likely to occur, they are rarely able to think critically and rationally about the issue.
- ***Appeal to tradition.*** When appealing to tradition, you ask the members of your audience to accept your idea or plan because that's the way it's always been done, or to reject a new idea because the old way of doing things is better. But because it was or is that way today does not necessarily make it better or best.
- ***Appeal to misplaced authority.*** When a speaker asks us to endorse an idea because a well-liked personality who is not an expert on the subject has endorsed it, we should question the request critically. Name recognition does not necessarily equal expertise.
- ***Straw man.*** When you respond to another's position by distorting, exaggerating, or misrepresenting their argument, you are depending on a "straw man" in an attempt to create the illusion that you refuted the other's stance successfully. Effectively, you misrepresent the other's position to make it easier to attack.

Such fallacies are dishonest and undermine reason and rational debate. Because they distort truth, logical fallacies are inherently invalid, and when detected, cause receivers to question the speaker's ethics.

GAME PLAN

Persuading an Audience

- ☐ I've considered my target audience and tailored my arguments to address them.
- ☐ I've reviewed the power of Maslow's Hierarchy of Needs and have included appeals to the audience's chief concerns such as safety, security, and quality of life.
- ☐ I've researched and used the most effective forms of evidence, including facts, statistics, examples/illustrations, or testimony.
- ☐ I've applied Toulmin's Reasonable Argument Model to test the integrity of my reasoning.
- ☐ I've reviewed my speech to be sure I haven't relied on any logical fallacies, and my reasoning is airtight.

Exercises

MASTERING METHODS

Understanding audience positions, building credibility, using solid evidence, and helping the audience feel that the change you call for is necessary are integral to achieving your goals. Completing these exercises will help you accomplish that.

1. Find the Fallacy

Select the transcript of a show from CNN.com, MSNBC.com, or FOXNews.com in which the host and one or more guests discuss a timely controversial issue. Analyze the claims made, the evidence offered, and the warrants used by each party. To what extent, if any, do you think the arguments made are defensible on the basis of logic and sound principles of reasoning? Support your answer.

2. The Hierarchy of Needs

Use Maslow's Hierarchy of Needs to target the types of needs you will appeal to in the following situations:

- You want to persuade an audience of high school seniors not to text and drive.
- You want to convince parents that sex offender registries are too strict.
- You want to persuade an audience of college students to get involved in local politics.
- You want to convince veterans that they should not support the passing of an amendment to ban flag burning.
- You want to convince Congress to pass a law prohibiting former members of Congress from ever becoming lobbyists.

3. Analyze the Speech: Football Is in Trouble

The focus of the speech that follows is CTE, a brain disease endangering football's future. As you read it, assess whether the speech succeeds in sparking your interest in the topic, explains why the subject ought to concern you, builds your belief in the speaker's credibility, and contains both solid reasoning and arguments designed to win your support.

Are you a fan of high-school and college football? Do you ever watch Sunday night football? How about Monday night football? What about the Super Bowl? Football is America's game, but it's in trouble, very serious trouble. Why is football in danger? As a result of the National Football League's refusal to be honest with the players and the public, football, America's sport, has been put under a microscope—literally—and what researchers have discovered is alarming and threatens the game's future. Football is in trouble.

SN 1 The speaker's opening questions are designed to involve the audience and demonstrate the popularity of football. The statement that follows the questions is simple but direct, designed to capture the audience's attention and foreshadow the speech's end. The speaker also introduces a speech motif, a refrain underscoring the speaker's message.

One reason football is in trouble is because an increasing number of football players are opting to retire early. Why are they choosing retirement over playing? They're retiring not because of bruises and broken ribs, but because they are experiencing life-altering injuries, and they fear what the game is doing to their brains and nervous systems. Not until 2013, after being pressured by physicians, the press, and league players, did the National Football League agree to a $765 million settlement of a lawsuit filed by retired players that had accused league officials of covering up the health risks players faced from repeated concussions. In April of 2016, despite player's complaints that the settlement did not go far enough, an appeals court upheld the agreement. The fund created by the league, however, fails to solve the real problem. Football is in trouble.

SN 2 The speaker identifies a reason for football's troubles.

SN 3 The speaker echoes the refrain motif.

What disease is driving football's troubles? It is CTE, chronic traumatic encephalopathy—a degenerative brain disease resulting from repeated blows to the head. The term encephalopathy derives from the ancient Greek—with *en* meaning in, *kephale* meaning head, and *patheia* meaning suffering—in head suffering. According to an op-ed piece published in the May 1, 2016 issue of *USA Today,* scientific studies have connected the repetitive head injuries of football with player depression, memory loss and worse. Dr. Bennet Omalu, the discoverer of CTE, and the subject of the film *Concussion*, believes that there is absolutely

SN 4 The speaker defines the problem threatening football players.

continued

continued

no way for the human brain to undergo hundreds, if not thousands of hits over time, and not be damaged. After he voiced this belief, the NFL tried to discredit Dr. Omalu as a quack. Sadly, many football players suffer from irreparable brain damage, without even knowing for certain if they have the disease. You see, doctors have to wait until after a player dies to determine if CTE was a contributing factor. Only once a person dies and their brains can be dissected can the doctor see the telltale brain scars or lesions and diagnose CTE.

SN 5 The speaker explains another reason why football is in trouble and why CTE research is being focused on the sport.

Sadly, professional football players are not alone in facing CTE. Since the 1920s, we have known that boxers experience brain damage. CTE also is found in hockey players, is feared by soccer players, and has been determined to afflict military veterans. Football, America's game, however, remains the prime focus of research, probably because of its potential to affect so many. It is impossible for players to play football for a long time and not have it affect their brains. As far back as the fall of 2009, this realization was the subject of an October *New York Times* editorial, but the NFL paid scant attention to it. For too long, the league simply refused to concede a link between playing football and brain disease, According to league officials, the *Times* was exaggerating the problem, blowing the topic up into something it was not. In fact, NFL Commissioner, Roger Goodell, insisted that the game of football was safer to play than it had ever been and that only a minority of players suffered from brain damage. For years, the NFL persisted in ignoring the real risks of playing the game. According to the March 25, 2016 *New York Times,* for 13 years, the league stood by research which they said was based on a full accounting of all concussions diagnosed by team doctors.

SN 6 The speaker exposes the league's neglect, supplying research supporting the speech's proposition.

Investigations by the *Times*, however, revealed that more than 100 diagnosed concussions were not included in those studies. The NFL did this even though CBS sports radio's John Feinstein reported that a league study already had revealed that 28 percent of players would suffer from CTE by the time they turned 65. Let's do the math together. There's close to 1,700 players on league rosters. So that's almost 500 current NFL players who will be afflicted with the disease. And because football is a contact sport, the elevated risk of brain trauma that players face cannot be avoided. Football and violence to the brain are inseparable. As a result, according to *60 Minutes* reporter Steve Croft, the concussion problem can be catastrophic for the NFL. The Centers for Disease Control affirms that concussions from football are an epidemic with the resulting brain damage leading to permanent brain damage.

How does CTE happen? Let me explain it this way. (The speaker picks up a jar containing an orange.) Look at the orange in this jar. Watch what happens to the orange as I turn the jar back and forth, and upside down, giving it a good shaking. You can see the orange repeatedly hitting into the ends of the jar. That's what happens to a player's brain with each blow to the head. Imagine your brain being hit again and again with such force that it slams into your skull. The impact felt by colliding football players is almost unimaginable. Picture two players of very substantial size and weight running at each other at a speed of almost 20 miles per hour. When they meet, it feels like a car crashing into a brick wall at 40–45 miles per hour. According to a study conducted at the University of North Carolina, there is a significant correlation between the number of concussions that a player experiences and the onset of dementia and depression. Multiple concussions have ended the careers of many players, among them Steve Young, Troy Aikman, Junior Seau, Ken Stabler, and Ted Johnson. Johnson was so physical that when he ran into one opponent, he cracked his helmet in two. In the past, however, though they were concussed, players often kept playing. They didn't know any better. While you can't see the brain damage, life after a series of concussions often is not very good. Many players and their widows end up donating the player's brain to research. According to the May 1, 2015 issue of *USA Today,* of 79 former football players who donated their brains to medical research after their deaths, 76 had CTE. Football is in trouble.

SN 7 The speaker makes the cause and nature of CTE understandable to the audience by creatively offering a visual example of the problem.

continued

continued

SN 8 The speaker uses statistics to demonstrate CTE's seriousness—and again repeats the speech's refrain.

SN 9 The speaker uses an analogy for impact.

SN 10 Using different words, the speaker echoes the refrain motif, noting what needs to happen for football to become safer.

SN 11 The speaker notes more dangers facing football.

SN 12 The speaker concludes by summarizing and reiterating the refrain, achieving closure.

In 2016, a film about CTE and football, *Concussion,* was released. After viewing the film it is hard not to ask if we should stop watching and playing football until it is made safer. With what we now know, watching the game today is much like it must have been when Roman citizens went to a stadium to watch gladiators fight each other to the death. Not until March 2016 did the NFL admit the link between football and brain disease publicly. Speaking before Congress, the NFL's Senior Vice President for Health and Safety, Jeff Miller, acknowledged for the first time that there was no doubt that such a linkage exists. So, the link exists, but the problem persists. How can this be? The rules have not changed. The future of football depends on whether there are changes to the rules that eliminate the game's effects on the brain. Instead of working to make the game faster and more exciting, perhaps imposing weight restrictions and making the field larger can help save football and its players. But this has not happened. With the tarnishing of football's image, and little, if anything done to make it safer, it is increasingly likely that fewer parents will permit their kids to play the game. Eventually the talent pool for football could dry up.

Today I've shared with you the relationship between CTE and football. The health risks football poses for players is apparent. I have also shared with you the league's slowness to accept facts, and its failure to ameliorate the problem. Giving money to treat afflicted players is not an effective solution. It only demonstrates how much real trouble football is in. Unfortunately, as the research continues, the damage also continues. What kind of future is that?

After experiencing the speech, consider these questions:

1. How would you phrase the speaker's proposition?
2. Is the speech well organized? Is it easy to outline? Do its parts hold together? Were there sufficient transitions?
3. What, if any, other visuals might you include were you delivering the speech?

4. Which of the speaker's arguments do you find the most and least effective and why?
5. What steps did the speaker take to be perceived as credible?
6. If you were the speaker's coach, what advice would you offer to improve the speech?

4. Approach the Speaker's Stand

Deliver a five- to seven-minute persuasive speech. Be sure to buttress your presentation with evidence designed to convince your audience that your claim is sensible, as well as with emotional appeals that arouse their desire to respond as you request.

In addition, prepare an outline and include a bibliography of at least five sources you consulted.

RECAP AND REVIEW

1. **Use sound evidence.** The use of specific facts and statistics, examples and illustrations, and expert testimony increases a speaker's persuasiveness.
2. **Apply Toulmin's Reasonable Argument Model.** Toulmin's model divides an argument into three essential parts: a claim, reasons for making the claim, and a warrant that explains how one gets to the claim from the data used.
3. **Use deductive, inductive, and causal reasoning, as well as reasoning from analogy.** When a speaker reasons deductively, he moves from the general to the specific, whereas if using inductive reasoning, he moves from a series of specific observations to a general conclusion. With causal reasoning, the speaker shows that one event caused another. When reasoning from analogy, the speaker compares like things and concludes that because they are comparable in a number of ways, they are also comparable in another way.
4. **Arouse emotion.** Speakers use pathos, or appeals to emotion, to arouse our feelings, hoping to motivate us to respond as they desire.
5. **Name the three tenets of persuasive speaking.** Adhere to the following persuasive principles: (1) think small to avoid a big fall; (2) use the desire for consistency; and (3) don't put the best material in the middle.
6. **Avoid common logical fallacies.** A logical fallacy is a flawed reason that you should not use and should be able to spot should other speakers violate ethical practices and use one.
7. **Design and deliver a persuasive speech.** Speakers who build credibility, use a variety of types of evidence and sound reasoning principles, and avoid logical fallacies are more likely to deliver effective persuasive speeches that demonstrate respect for receivers.

KEY TERMS

SAGE edge™

Sharpen your skills with SAGE edge at edge.sagepub.com/gamblepsp2e.

SAGE edge for students provides a personalized approach to help you accomplish your coursework goals in an easy-to-use learning environment.

PART EIGHT

Special Topics

© iStockphoto.com/Geber86

21 Planning and Presenting in Groups

UPON COMPLETING THIS CHAPTER'S TRAINING, YOU WILL BE ABLE TO

1. Define and identify characteristics of a small group
2. Compare and contrast speaking individually with speaking and presenting as a group
3. Demonstrate how group leaders and members contribute to or detract from a group's effectiveness
4. Use the Reflective Thinking Framework
5. Use brainstorming to facilitate group problem solving
6. Participate in a group presentation

At school, at work, and in your personal life, groups are omnipresent. You may devote significant time to being part of an improv group, sports team, or a cappella group. Whatever the nature of your group, its success depends on your ability to work together and coordinate your performance. During your college and professional career, it is very likely that you will be asked to complete group projects, speak as part of a panel at an academic conference, or pitch a business proposal with a small group.

A **small group** is composed of a limited number of people who communicate over a period of time to make decisions and accomplish specific goals. Groups comprising five to seven people usually function best because members are able to communicate easily, but it is not uncommon for some to contain as few as three or as many as fifteen people. Each individual in a group has the potential to influence the others and is expected to function both as a speaker and a listener. Group members share a common objective. Each person occupies a particular role with respect to the others, and works with them, cooperating to achieve a desired end. As they interact, members develop certain attitudes toward one another and (ideally) a sense of satisfaction from belonging to and participating in the group. Members of a group are expected to adhere to group norms—the "do's and don'ts" that groups establish to regulate the behavior of members and make it possible for them to work together to attain the group's goals.

Every group defines its own objectives and establishes its own norms. Ultimately, how members relate to one another, the roles they assume, and how they exchange information and resolve problems determine the effectiveness of the group work. Member interaction—what members say and how they say it—affects both the group's health and its long-term viability.

Healthy groups exhibit five characteristics:

1. Members support one another.
2. Decisions are made together.
3. Members trust one another.
4. Communication is open and candid.
5. The group aims to excel.[1]

Whatever the specific nature of a working group's task, whether it is to develop and present a strategic campaign to a client, develop a policy to recommend to management, or discuss conflicting opinions relative to a complex social issue, knowing how to speak effectively both in the group setting and as a member of the presentation team is vital for both the personal and professional success of members.

Contents

section

21.1

Working Together

21.1a Preparing as a Group

21.1b Member Roles and Responsibilities

21.1c Leadership Defined

Although effective membership and leadership are both essential for group success, good leadership often begins with effective membership. All must participate fully and actively in the life of the group. Every member must fulfill certain responsibilities and recognize how his or her performance contributes to or detracts from the group attaining its goal.

21.1a Preparing as a Group

To work effectively together, the first thing members need to do is spend some time sharing their school and work schedules and getting to know one another. Part of this process is to figure out each member's strengths: Who, for example, is a visual artist? Who is into technology? Who is the most organized? Members also should share their expectations for working together. In other words, members need to decide how to work together to complete their task. They can designate a leader—the person the group determines it can count on to keep members focused and who will work out the logistics of and agendas for their meetings. The group can also establish a series of rules for its operation. They might decide, for example, that members must be on time and prepared for meetings and should behave appropriately when another group member is speaking.

Once this initial phase is complete, the task of preparing your group presentation has many of the same steps as any other speech, with the added job of splitting up the work to be done. As ever, you must figure out the audience for your presentation, do research, prepare your outline, and plan what you will say, but you must do all this in concert with the rest of the group.

During the planning period, members should establish how they will conduct their research and pool their findings. Once group members complete the research phase, they then need to spend time outlining the presentation to meet the demands of their assigned or selected delivery format. They also should identify any technologies that might benefit the group's presentation, being certain to develop a means for coordinating templates for presentation slides, including font size, colors, and style.

Members also need to work out the order in which group members will speak. And, of course, the group needs to practice its presentation, including the integration of technologies, many times before getting up to present.

Let's zero in on member roles and responsibilities.

21.1b Member Roles and Responsibilities

Positive group roles accomplish dual task and maintenance functions. That is, they both help meet the group's goal and contribute to the way group members interact with one another. Negative group roles limit the group's abilities to realize the group's goal. Each member can improve task performance, foster a concern for the needs and feelings of group members, or inhibit group performance by revealing an overriding concern for self instead of group success. The choice is yours.

What kind of group member are you? Consider the assets and liabilities you bring to a group experience by indicating which task-oriented, maintenance-oriented, or self-serving roles you characteristically perform (see Table 21.1). That done, consider specific instances of how your behavior either contributed to or detracted from the success of your last group.[2]

© iStockphoto.com/German-skydiver

Do you know your role? What strengths and weaknesses do you bring to groups?

TABLE 21.1 GROUP ROLES

TASK-ORIENTED ROLES		
Initiating	You defined a problem; suggested methods, goals and procedures; and started the group moving along new paths or in different directions by offering a plan.	"Rather than dwelling on problems, let's work on discovering how we can make things better."
Information seeking	You asked for facts and opinions and sought relevant information about the problem.	"Can you show me what you discovered about why this trend exists?"
Information giving	You offered ideas, suggestions, personal experiences, and/or factual data.	"The last time we experienced a drop-off in productivity, offering incentives helped."
Clarifying	You elaborated on or paraphrased the ideas of others, offered illustrations, or tried to increase clarity by decreasing confusion.	"So, what I hear you saying is that we need to take a more direct approach. Did I get that right?"
Coordinating	You summarized ideas and tried to draw various contributions together constructively.	"If we combine each of your ideas, I think we can create a win-win situation."
Evaluating	You evaluated the group's decisions or proposed solutions and helped establish critieria that solutions should meet.	"We agreed that whatever solution we select should be comprehensive, fair, and able to stand the test of time."
Consensus testing	You tested the state of agreement among members to see if the group was approaching a decision.	"Okay. Let's poll the group. In your own words, say what you believe we are agreeing to."
MAINTENANCE-ORIENTED ROLES		
Encouraging	You responded warmly, receptively, and supportively to others and their ideas.	"What a great idea!"
Gatekeeping	You sought to keep channels of communication open by helping reticent members contribute to the group and/or by working to prevent one or two members from dominating.	"Okay. Let's hear how you feel about this too."
Harmonizing	You mediated differences between members, reconciled disagreements, and sought to reduce tension by injecting humor or other forms of relief at appropriate opportunities.	"Let's agree to disagree for now. We can come back to this later."

MAINTENANCE-ORIENTED ROLES		
Compromising	You exhibited a willingness to compromise to maintain group cohesion; you were willing to modify your stance or admit an error when appropriate.	"Wow. I'll give you that one. I can see how making the change you suggest will put us in a stronger position."
Standard setting	You assessed the state of member satisfaction with group procedures and indicated the criteria set for evaluating group functioning.	"Let's see how you think we've done today. Did we all come prepared? Are we listening to one another? Are we building on ideas?"
SELF-SERVING ROLES		
Blocking	You were disagreeable and digressed so that nothing was accomplished.	"This is a waste of time. Hey, did you watch the game last night?"
Aggressing	You criticized or blamed others and sought to deflate the egos of other members as a means of enhancing your own status in the group.	"That idea is the worst idea I've ever heard. Can't you think? Can't you be creative? I'm the only one contributing anything worthwhile here."
Recognition seeking	You made yourself the center of attention; you focused attention on yourself rather than the task; you spoke loudly and exhibited unusual or outlandish behavior.	"Am I smart, or what? Did I tell you about the time I won a car?"
Withdrawing	You stopped contributing, appeared indifferent to group efforts, daydreamed, or sulked.	"Whatever you say. I don't care anymore."
Dominating	You insisted on getting your own way; you interrupted others; you sought to impose your ideas and run the group.	"Stop. My solution is the only one worth trying. We don't need to hear any more."
Joking	You engaged in horseplay or exhibited other inappropriate behavior.	"What are you wearing? You look like you just got up. What's with you? Had a late night with Robin?"
Self-confessing	You revealed personal feelings irrelevant to the work of the group.	"I haven't told anyone this. I lied on my job application."
Help-seeking	You played on and tried to elicit the sympathies of other group members.	"Come on. Help me out here. Please also research my part. I'm just overwhelmed right now."

21.1c Leadership Defined

Effective leadership is a defining quality of most successful groups. Effective leaders are versatile. They perform combinations of task and maintenance functions designed to move the group closer to its goal.

Task leadership behaviors include establishing an agenda, giving and soliciting information and opinions, offering internal summaries that describe the group's progress, helping to keep the group on track, and helping the group analyze and evaluate issues and reach a consensus.

Maintenance leadership behaviors include the expression of agreement and support, the reduction and release of group tensions, the resolution of differences of opinion and group conflicts, and the enhancement of morale and member satisfaction.

The leader also must fully comprehend the group's goals and have a clear vision of how to reach them.

Normally, when we think of a group leader, we think of someone who is in an appointed or elected position. However, leadership is not the exclusive possession of any single group member, and a group need not have a designated leader for members to exert leadership. Indeed, groups in which every member feels prepared to share leadership often work best. After all, to lead a group is to influence it. When influence is positive, the group is led toward the realization of its goal.[3]

Leader(s). A group doesn't need a designated leader to succeed; all members can share leadership and still be successful as a group.

Solving Problems in Groups

section
21.2

The dynamics of a group's interactions affect the outcomes the group is able to achieve. Although working in groups has both advantages and disadvantages, adhering to a problem-solving framework and engaging in brainstorming facilitate the group's realization of its goal(s).

21.2a The Advantages of Group Work

Working in a group has the following advantages:

- ***Group work brings in the ideas and strengths of all members.*** Instead of only one contributor, a number of people with different information and contrasting viewpoints are able to contribute to the decision-making process, so an effective solution is more likely to emerge.
- ***Groups filter out costly errors before they do any damage.*** Because everyone in a group is focused on solving a problem, errors and weaknesses are likely to be detected.
- ***A decision made by a group is usually better received than a decision proposed by an individual.*** When several people work cooperatively to explore potential solutions, they usually are able to agree on the best.
- ***Participating in decision making strengthens individuals' commitment to implement the decision.*** Participation and motivation are effective problem-solving partners.
- ***Reaching a decision in a group can be more fulfilling and personally reinforcing than reaching a decision alone.*** The feeling of belonging makes a difference.

COACHING TIP

"Never doubt that a small group of thoughtful, committed citizens can change the world; indeed, it's the only thing that ever has."

—Margaret Mead

There is strength in numbers. Working together, you often accomplish more than working on your own. A well-functioning group almost always comes up with better decisions or solutions to problems than an individual working solo.

21.2b The Disadvantages of Group Work

There are potential disadvantages inherent in group work. Unless the group's norms establish that certain counterproductive behaviors will not be tolerated, they could impede effective group functioning. These behaviors include

- ***Personal objectives at odds with the group's goals.*** As a result, the group's objectives may be sacrificed or sabotaged as we undermine them in an effort to satisfy our personal needs.
- ***Too much comfort in numbers.*** When we know other people are available to cover for us, we may slack off.
- ***More vocal, forceful, or powerful members may dominate the group.*** By steamrolling others, we make it harder for all members to participate fully or make their true feelings known.
- ***Intransigence of one or more members.*** If a member comes to the group unwilling to listen to other points of view or to compromise, the decision-making process may become deadlocked.
- ***The group experiences a risky shift.*** Groups sometimes make decisions that are riskier than an individual working alone would be comfortable making, a change in behavior known as a **risky shift.**
- ***Slower decision making.*** It takes longer for most groups to make a decision than it does individuals.

Whether the potential advantages of working in groups outweigh the potential disadvantages depends on how effectively the group is able to perform its tasks.

21.2c The Decision-Making Framework

A group's success depends on both its leadership and its membership. It also depends on the nature of the decision-making system used by the group.

Digital Vision/Photodisc/Thinkstock

Look out. What steps can you take to prevent typical conflicts that occur in group work from impacting your group?

One method that has been known to improve problem solving is the **Reflective Thinking Framework**, derived from the writings of philosopher and educator John Dewey[4] (see Figure 21.1).

The Reflective Thinking Framework consists of six basic steps and offers a logical system for group discussion. As members work their way through the framework, they must ask and answer a series of questions before advancing to the next stage in the sequence.

- ***Step 1. Define the Problem.*** Is the problem phrased as a clear and specific question that is not slanted and thus will not arouse defensiveness? Is it phrased so as to allow a wide variety of answers rather than a simple yes or no?
- ***Step 2. Analyze the Problem.*** What are the facts of the situation? What are its causes? What is its history? How severe is it? Who is affected and how?
- ***Step 3. Establish Criteria for Solutions.*** What criteria must an acceptable solution fulfill? By what objective standards should we evaluate a solution? What requirements must a solution meet? How critical is each criterion?
- ***Step 4. Generate Potential Solutions.*** How will each possible solution remedy the problem? How well does each solution meet the established criteria? What advantages or disadvantages does each solution present?

- ***Step 5. Select the Best Solution.*** How would you rank each solution? Which solution offers the greatest number of advantages and the fewest disadvantages? How can we combine solutions to produce an even better one?
- ***Step 6. Suggest Strategies for Implementation.*** How can the solution be implemented? What steps should we take to put the solution into effect?

By systematically working through this framework and suspending judgment as they do so, group members can keep the discussion on track and improve the quality of decision making. The Reflective Thinking Framework helps group members avoid **early concurrence**—the tendency to conclude discussion prematurely. By requiring members to explore all data and evaluate alternative courses of action methodically, and by opening them to new information rather than encouraging them to base decisions on what they know at the moment, the system also helps guard against **groupthink**—the tendency to let the desire for consensus override careful analysis and reasoned decision making.[5]

In order for the Reflective Thinking Framework to function effectively for your group, ask yourself the following questions as you work your way through it:

- ☐ Are the resources of all group members being well used?
- ☐ Is the group using its time wisely?
- ☐ Is the group emphasizing fact finding and inquiry?
- ☐ Are members listening to and respecting the ideas and feelings of other members?
- ☐ Is pressure to conform deemphasized and pressure to search for diverse viewpoints emphasized?
- ☐ Is the group's atmosphere supportive, trusting, and cooperative?

Decision-making effectiveness depends on the degree to which group members feel free to speak up, maintain open minds, and exhibit a willingness to search for new information.

FIGURE 21.1
Reflective Thinking Framework

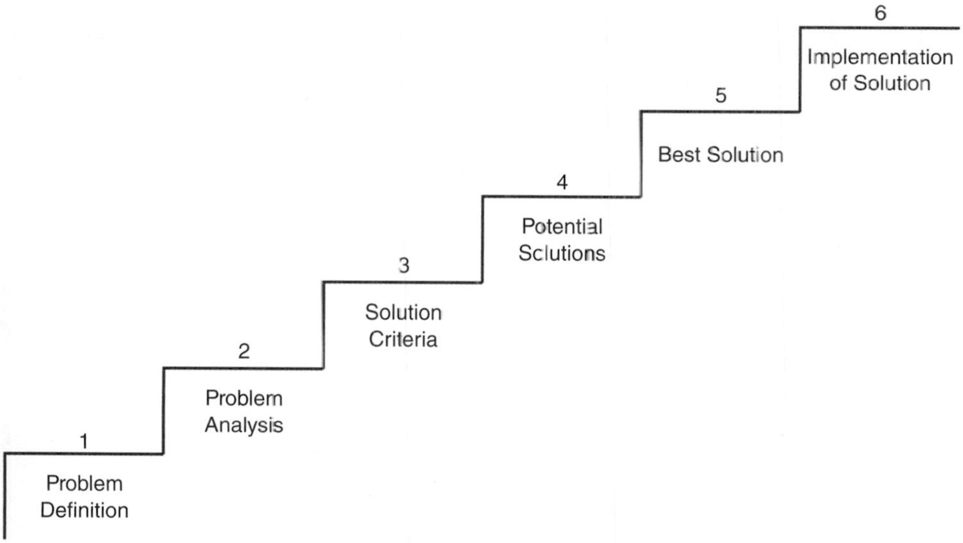

Source: Adapted from John Dewey, *How We Think* (Boston: Heath, 1910).

© iStockphoto.com/Yuri_Arcurs

Let it flow. No matter how wild or crazy your ideas may be, get as many on paper with your group and analyze them later.

21.2d Brainstorming

Fresh ideas help solve both old and new problems. Fresh ideas come from encouraging new avenues of thought. *Brainstorming*, a system of idea generation devised by Alex Osborn, allows this to happen.[6] During a brainstorming session, all members of a group spontaneously contribute ideas. The group's goal is to collect as many ideas as possible in a short time without interrupting the thought process or stopping to evaluate ideas during the brainstorming process.

Although brainstorming is most frequently incorporated in the solution phase of the Reflective Thinking Framework, it can prompt creative inquiry during any of its stages.

To ensure a successful brainstorming session, follow these guidelines:

- ☐ ***Suspend judgment.*** Brainstorming is not the time to evaluate or criticize ideas.
- ☐ ***Encourage freewheeling.*** Brainstorming is not the time to consider an idea's practicality. You can tame or tone down wild ideas later if necessary.
- ☐ ***Aim for quantity.*** Brainstorming is not the time to concentrate on idea quality, nor is it the time to censor your contributions. The more ideas you generate, the greater your chances of coming up with a good one.
- ☐ ***Record all ideas.*** Brainstorming is not the time to eliminate possibilities.
- ☐ ***Evaluate only when brainstorming is concluded.*** Only after the brainstorming process is over should you evaluate the ideas you proposed.

COACHING TIP

"There are two kinds of people, those who do the work and those who take the credit. Try to be in the first group; there is less competition there."

—Indira Ghandi

Don't expect others to do your work and give you credit for their accomplishments. Slackers need to shape up or risk being the target of other group member complaints or even being asked to leave the group.

Presenting the Group's Work

section
21.3

Your group works its way through the Reflective Thinking Framework and comes to a decision through a series of private group meetings and without an audience present. The group's next task is likely to report its findings to an audience—to inform them of the group's decision, to advocate for the adoption of the group's proposals, or both. Most often, the group presents its findings or recommendations to an audience through an oral report, a panel discussion, a symposium, or a forum. Let us explore each of these formats in turn.

21.3a The Oral Group Report

Approach the oral report of group work as you would any other speech. Your report should contain an introduction, body, and conclusion. Consider your audience and your goal when deciding whether one or more group members or all members of the group should participate in delivering the oral report, perhaps dividing it up by topic or section. If more than one member speaks, make sure you incorporate transitions, not just between sections of the speech, but also between speakers. Like any speech, in addition to being well organized, an oral report must be adapted to reflect the needs, concerns, and interests of the people you are addressing, contain an array of supporting materials and evidence (including visual aids, if appropriate), use language that accurately and effectively communicates its content, and, of course, be well rehearsed. All group members should be prepared to respond to queries.

21.3b The Panel Discussion

A panel discussion requires group members to talk through an issue in front of an audience. The positive and negative aspects are debated, usually without the direct involvement of the audience.

In effect, the group replays in public the problem-solving discussion it had in private. While neither memorized nor scripted, the panel discussion is carefully planned so that all important points are made and all group members are able to participate.

Most panel discussions also include a moderator whose role is to introduce the topic and panelists and to ensure that the topic is explored adequately. Panel discussions are held on controversial topics, where panelists may disagree.

21.3c The Symposium

A symposium is a discussion in which a number of individuals present individual speeches of approximately the same length on a central subject before an audience. Because a symposium's speakers address members of the audience directly, there usually is little, if any, interaction among the speakers during their presentations; however, participants may afterward discuss their reactions with each other as well as field questions from the audience.

Symposia are designed to (1) shed light on or explore different aspects of a problem, (2) provide material for subsequent discussion, or (3) review different steps covered during a group's problem-solving experience. Ideally, each speaker is aware of what others will present, so there is little, if any, duplication of information. Speakers are typically not in opposition to each other, but rather frame their contributions based on their focus and interests.

21.3d The Forum Presentation

The purpose of a forum is to provide a medium for an open and interactive discussion between the group and an audience. Unlike the other formats, a forum is a discussion requiring full audience participation. After a moderator and/or each speaker make a brief opening statement, audience members then are free to question the participants, who answer their queries with brief impromptu responses. A town meeting is one example of the forum in action.

A forum works best when there is a moderator to introduce the program and the speakers, as well as to clarify and summarize the program's progress as needed. It also helps when group members are aware of which issues will be discussed during the forum and are knowledgeable about the subject, because they can then prepare themselves to respond to questions quickly and thoroughly.

Assess Your Group's Development

section
21.4

If you consider how your group conducted its work, you will realize that its development moved through five stages:[7]

1. ***Forming.*** In the first stage, the members of your group probably experienced some confusion or uncertainty about how the group would function and the roles they would play in it. As the group identified who was in charge and figured out its goal, members probably sought to fit in and be perceived as likeable.
2. ***Storming.*** Next, members likely experienced some task and relational conflicts as work began. Members were focused on communicating their ideas and opinions and securing their position in the group's power structure.
3. ***Norming.*** After early conflicts, the group's structure emerged. Leaders surfaced, and roles were firmed up. Behavior in the group had more predictability as members recognized their interdependence but also their need to cooperate.
4. ***Performing.*** The focus of the group then transitioned to problem solving to accomplish the task. Members built on their skills and knowledge and surmounted hurdles in the effort to realize the group's goals.
5. ***Adjourning.*** Finally members reviewed and reflected on what they did and did not accomplish and determined whether and how to end the group.

As you consider each stage, ask yourself how your group did, and what you could have done better.

GAME PLAN

Presenting in Groups

- ☐ While we may have designated one of our members as the leader who will coordinate the order in which we speak, we are all prepared to exert leadership.
- ☐ I understand the goal of our presentation, and I understand my own role within the group.
- ☐ I know who will speak before and after me, and I am prepared to transition from and to those individuals.
- ☐ Our group worked well together, and we tackled our topic using the Reflective Thinking Framework.

Exercises

PLANNING AND PRESENTING IN A GROUP

Planning and presenting in a group poses unique challenges. By participating in the following activities you can further develop the skills and understandings needed to succeed as both group member and leader.

1. Getting to Know You

Building on this opening line, "Once upon a time, there was a group of college students who decided to get to know each other better by sharing their work habits and strengths," reveal something about yourself that others in your group should know in order for you to perform your best when working with them.

2. Assessing Group Interaction in the Media

Mediated forms of group discourse have grown in popularity over the years. The increasing number of hours devoted to talk radio programs, as well as to opinion and interview shows, testifies to this. But instead of engaging in reasoned debate, hosts and guests on some programs engage in uncivil wars characterized by escalating levels of conflict. What lessons can we learn from such programs? How can we use them to help us develop into more effective discussion group members?

Just as you need to evaluate the effectiveness of your own **fact-finding** and **decision-making groups**, so you also need to evaluate mediated discussion groups as a receiver by assessing both their methods and their conclusions. Using any mediated discussion offering of your choice, answer the following questions:

1. Was the program's topic well analyzed by participants?
2. Were both host and guests free to share ideas and feelings?
3. Did guests or host monopolize discussion?
4. Did host or guests become aggressive or abusive?
5. What did the program's host and guests do to handle any conflicts that developed?
6. Were claims made by the host or guests supported by evidence?
7. What norms appeared to govern the discussion?
8. What were the program's outcomes? Did a consensus emerge?
9. What was learned?
10. What recommendations would you make to the show's host and guests regarding their on-air behavior? What communication skills would both host and guests need to possess in order to put your recommendations into practice?

3. Brainstorming Your Way to Consensus

First read the research findings summarized following these instructions. Then brainstorm possible rationales for the statistics presented. Attempt to reach consensus as to which rationale is most likely. Once discussion is over, appoint a member to present the group's conclusions to the class:

> Despite commonly held belief, chivalry does not appear to rule at sea. According to a recent study, in sixteen maritime shipwrecks dating from 1852 to 2011 two times as many men have survived the disasters as women. What is more, 18.7 percent more crew survived than passengers.[8]

Use the following checklist to analyze how effective your group was in discussing its task.

- ☐ Did the group define the problem?
- ☐ Did the group thoroughly analyze the problem?
- ☐ Did the group brainstorm to generate a wide range of possible rationales in support of the statistical findings?
- ☐ Did the group evaluate each rationale carefully?
- ☐ Did the group succeed in reaching a consensus with regard to the most likely rationale?

4. Analyze a Group Presentation

Attend a panel discussion, symposium, or forum on campus or in the community. Evaluate how well the moderator and group participants fulfilled their respective functions.

5. Approach the Speaker's Stand

Your instructor will divide you into small groups. Your assignment is to identify and formulate a question of fact, value, or policy for your group to discuss. Then, using the Reflective Thinking Framework, conduct a group discussion on your chosen question. Be sure to outline exactly what you hope to accomplish during each stage of the sequence.

After you complete your discussion, prepare a brief paper explaining your group's accomplishments and identifying obstacles to overcome while completing your task. Also analyze the quality of leadership, membership, and decision making displayed by your group.

Finally, your instructor will ask you to use one or more of the following formats to present your findings to the class: a panel discussion, an oral report, a symposium, or a forum presentation.

RECAP AND REVIEW

1. **Define and identify characteristics of a small group.** A small group contains a limited number of people who communicate with each other over a period of time, usually face to face, to make decisions and accomplish specific goals. All members of a group have the potential to influence all other members and are expected to function as both speaker and receiver.
2. **Compare and contrast speaking individually with speaking and presenting as a group.** In contrast to an individual speech in which the audience is focused on a solo speaker, a group presentation involves interaction among multiple speakers and listeners. As part of a group, members need to organize themselves and their information to present their findings to an audience.
3. **Demonstrate how group leaders and members contribute to or detract from a group's effectiveness.** Every group defines its own objectives, norms, and operating climate. More successful groups have a number of major attributes that distinguish them: in particular, these are effective leadership, effective membership, and effective implementation of a decision-making system.
4. **Use the Reflective Thinking Framework.** The Reflective Thinking Framework involves six steps: (1) problem definition, (2) problem analysis, (3) the establishment of solution criteria, (4) the generation of solutions, (5) the selection of the best solution, and (6) strategies for implementation.
5. **Use brainstorming to facilitate group problem solving.** Brainstorming is an idea generation system during which group members suspend judgment, encourage freewheeling, aim for quantity of ideas, and record all ideas. Group members evaluate ideas produced during brainstorming after the brainstorming session concludes.
6. **Participate in a group presentation.** In many instances, after a group reaches a decision or solves a problem, the group presents its findings to others through an oral report, a panel discussion, a symposium, or a forum.

KEY TERMS

Decision-making group 386
Early concurrence 381
Fact-finding group 386
Groupthink 381
Healthy group 373
Maintenance leadership behaviors 378
Reflective Thinking Framework 380
Risky shift 380
Small group 373
Task leadership behaviors 378

AP Photo/Susan Walsh

22 Special Occasion Speeches

UPON COMPLETING THIS CHAPTER'S TRAINING, YOU WILL BE ABLE TO

1. Explain the goals and functions of special occasion speeches
2. Define and distinguish the similarities and differences between speeches of introduction, presentation, and acceptance
3. Explain the functions of the commencement address and a keynote address
4. Define the goals and distinguish the differences between a speech of tribute and a eulogy
5. Explain the key characteristics of the after-dinner speech

"Four score and seven years ago" begins one of the most famous special occasion speeches ever delivered in the history of the United States. Abraham Lincoln's address at the dedication of the national cemetery at Gettysburg was designed to reflect the needs of a very special occasion. When delivering that speech, now referred to as the "Gettysburg Address," Lincoln's purpose was not only to pay tribute to those who died during the Civil War but also to help bring the nation together. As a special occasion speaker, you too may be called on to mark an event that is important to a particular group or community, to celebrate, commemorate, entertain, or inspire an audience.

The speeches we deliver to recognize life's special moments distinguish themselves from other kinds of speeches. Though special occasion speeches may also inform or persuade, this is rarely their primary function. Instead, they acknowledge the special occasion that has brought the audience together.

Contents

section

22.1 Goals and Functions of Special Occasion Speeches

Speeches on special occasions serve two important functions. First, they help magnify the significance of the event or person being honored, and second, they help unify the audience by affirming the common values exhibited through the celebration of this person or event. To accomplish these objectives, the speaker must fully understand both the nature of the special occasion and the role he or she is to play in it.

For example, commencement speakers frequently reinforce the value of education and try to spur graduates on to achieve greatness. Whatever the occasion, it is the speaker's obligation to deliver a speech appropriate to that specific situation. Audiences come to such events with particular expectations, and the speaker's success depends on his or her ability to conform to established norms (see Table 22.1).

TABLE 22.1 TYPES OF SPECIAL OCCASION SPEECHES

TYPE	PURPOSE
1. Speech of introduction	To introduce a featured speaker to the audience
2. Speech of presentation	To present an award or special recognition
3. Speech of acceptance	To accept an award or special recognition
4. Commencement address	To praise and congratulate a graduating class
5. Keynote address	To motivate and inspire an audience at a meeting or special event
6. Tribute speech	To honor or praise a person or event
7. Eulogy	To pay tribute to a person who has died
8. After-dinner speech	To entertain after a dinner event

Types of Ceremonial Speeches

section
22.2

In the years ahead, you will be part of a number of special occasions that may require you to deliver a ceremonial speech. Perhaps you will be asked to offer a toast to celebrate the wedding or anniversary of a relative or friend, the birth of a baby, the graduation of a son or daughter, or the success of a business venture. Although such toasts are composed of only a few brief sentences and are positive in tone, they typically are also very personal and made by someone who knows the subjects very well, and who is able to share insight about them. Now and again, however, you may be called upon to deliver an impromptu and more generic kind of toast like this Irish blessing: "May you have warm words on a cold evening, a full moon on a dark night, and a road downhill all the way to your door." When you are presented with such a need, both the audience and the occasion should function as your guides.

In this chapter we explore those kinds of special occasion speeches you will be most likely to give: the speech of introduction, award presentation, award acceptance, the commencement address, the keynote address, the tribute, the euology, and the after-dinner speech.

© iStockphoto.com/Neustockimages

Be kind. It's a wedding toast, not a roast!

section

22.3

The Speech of Introduction

When you deliver a **speech of introduction**, your task is to create a desire among audience members to listen to the featured speaker. By serving, in effect, as a "warm-up" for the main speaker, you pave the way and psychologically prepare receivers for that speaker's presentation.

22.3a Your Responsibilities as an Introducer

During your brief introductory remarks, your goal is to

- Identify why the speaker is to speak
- Enhance the speaker's credibility with receivers
- Stress the importance and timeliness of the speech

Though your speech of introduction should be short, lasting no more than two to three minutes, your job is to tell receivers who will be addressing them, what the subject of that person's speech will be, and why they should pay careful attention to it. Your role, though limited in scope (after all, you are not presenting the featured speech yourself), is nonetheless very important. The way you introduce the speaker will affect the reception given him or her.

Be sure your remarks are in keeping with the tone the main speaker will set. Focus a spotlight on the speaker, but avoid creating expectations he or she will be unable to fulfill.

The more renowned the featured speaker is, the briefer the introduction needed. For example, the president of a country is usually introduced with, "Ladies and gentleman, the president of . . ." And though brief remarks suffice to introduce Bill Gates, the founder of Microsoft, a longer introduction would be used to present an executive of lesser stature.

22.3b Sample Speech of Introduction

The following speech of introduction was used by a student to introduce Russel Taylor, the founder of the Taylor Study Abroad Scholarship at the College of New Rochelle.

Over the course of his teaching career at the college, a career that spans more than 35 years, Dr. Russel Taylor has had a significant impact on the study abroad program. In addition to serving as an unofficial advisor to aspiring entrepreneurs, Dr. Taylor also spearheaded the study abroad program—generously donating and raising funds to ensure that each year students like yourselves are able to secure the financial resources needed to spend a semester or a summer studying in another country. Because of Dr. Taylor's efforts, a number of you here tonight will also be able to live that dream.

Formerly a CEO and then a professor of business, Dr. Taylor is now a devoted mentor who makes it his mission to raise awareness about our need to be "global citizens," individuals armed with the cultural experiences and knowledge we will need to connect with others, not only in business, but in life.

I am very pleased to present to you the originator of the Taylor Study Abroad Scholarship, Dr. Russel Taylor, my mentor and friend.

COACHING TIP

"The more you praise and celebrate your life, the more there is in life to celebrate."

—Oprah Winfrey

Life itself is a special occasion. When giving a special occasion speech, be sure to affirm that. Speak the right words, and you bind those listening together. Acknowledge the events that mark our lives. Make the experience powerful!

section
22.4

The Speech of Presentation

The **speech of presentation** is another common form of ceremonial speaking. The occasion for this kind of speech is the presentation of an award such as the Nobel Prize, or a teaching award at your school. Like the speech of introduction, the speech of presentation is usually brief, but it often contains somewhat more formal praise for its subject.

22.4a Your Responsibilities as a Presenter

When delivering a speech of presentation, you are not just recognizing an individual, you are also honoring an ideal. You have three goals to achieve:

1. To summarize the purpose of the award or gift, including its history, its sponsor, the ideals it represents, and the criteria used to select the recipient
2. To discuss the accomplishments of the person being honored, including what the individual specifically did to achieve the award
3. To introduce and present the award winner to the audience. When possible, leave identifying the recipient to the very end; it adds drama to the announcement.

As with the speech of introduction, you are not the star of the occasion; the audience did not come to listen to you, but rather to celebrate the winner.

Avoid overpraising the recipient. Instead, express sincere appreciation for his or her accomplishments, and highlight the behavior, values, and ideals that led to his or her receiving the award. After listening to your speech, there should be no question among audience members that the individual being honored deserves the award.

22.4b Sample Speech of Presentation

Peter Hero, president of the Community Foundation of Silicon Valley, delivered the speech of presentation when he presented Bill Gates, then chairman of Microsoft, with the foundation's 50th anniversary Spirit of Philanthropy Award. Notice how by focusing on the special contributions Gates made, Hero explains the reasons for bestowing the honor on him.

While most recognize Bill Gates for his global business acumen, it's his passion for philanthropy that has touched lives throughout the world. The Bill & Melinda Gates Foundation has awarded more than $4 billion—that's billion with a "b"—since it was created in 2000.

SN 1 The speaker discusses the generosity of the honoree.

The Gates Foundation efforts in education, its libraries initiatives and its efforts to eradicate disease in our world's poorest nations are innovative and bold. . . .

Last year alone Microsoft contributed more than $79 million in cash and $367 million in software to nearly 5,000 schools and nonprofit organizations. . . .

I first met Bill Gates in 1999 when he stopped in San Francisco and met with a group of us responding to a call from one of our board members . . . Steve Kirsch. . . . Steve had sent out an e-mail urging high-tech CEOs to join him in each giving $1 million to help resolve the unexpected $11 million shortfall at our United Way in Silicon Valley. Bill Gates and the Gates Foundation responded with a $5 million gift, more than any of our local donors. This visit gave me a preview of the generosity of both Microsoft and the Gates Foundation and for this we want to recognize and honor Bill Gates today.

SN 2 The speaker summarizes the purpose of the award and presents the award winner to the audience.

So Bill, on behalf of the board of directors, the advisory council, the entire Community Foundation of Silicon Valley, I'm honored to present you with our 50th anniversary Spirit of Philanthropy Award.

section 22.5

The Speech of Acceptance

22.5a Your Responsibilities Giving an Acceptance Speech

22.5b Sample Acceptance Speech

The **speech of acceptance** is given in response to a speech of presentation. It is usually brief and gives the person being recognized the opportunity to formally accept the award or praise being given to him or her.

22.5a Your Responsibilities Giving an Acceptance Speech

In an acceptance speech, the recipient thanks, recognizes, and gives credit to both those who bestowed the honor and those who helped him or her attain it; reflects on the values represented by the award; explains, in particular, what the award means to him or her; and graciously accepts it. Speeches of acceptance, though usually brief, are often inspirational in tone, and when well done leave no doubt in the minds of audience members that the award was given to the right person.

22.5b Sample Acceptance Speech

In the following acceptance speech excerpts, notice how the late Elie Wiesel, World War II Holocaust survivor and human rights activist, upon receiving the Nobel Peace Prize helped receivers understand the meaning of the award and the ideals it honors. By pledging to continue his efforts and by using language in keeping with the dignity of the occasion, Wiesel also communicated the deeper meaning inherent in the award.

ELIE WIESEL ACCEPTS AWARD

SN 1 The speaker accepts the award.

It is with a profound sense of humility that I accept the honor you have chosen to bestow upon me. I know: your choice transcends me. This both frightens and pleases me.

It frightens me because I wonder: do I have the right to represent the multitudes who have perished? Do I have the right to accept this great honor on their behalf? I do not. That would be presumptuous. No one may speak for the dead, no one may interpret their mutilated dreams and visions.

SN 2 The speaker credits those who helped him attain the award, and through an extended narrative reflects on the values the award represents.

It pleases me because I may say that this honor belongs to all the survivors and their children, and through us, to the Jewish people with whose destiny I have always identified.

I remember: It happened yesterday or eternities ago. A young Jewish boy discovered the kingdom of the night. I remember his bewilderment. I remember his anguish. It all happened to fast. The ghetto. The deportation. The sealed cattle car.

The fiery altar upon which the history of our people and the future of mankind were meant to be sacrificed.

I remember: He asked his father, "Can this be true? This is the 20th century, not the Middle Ages. Who would allow such crimes to be committed? How could the world remain silent?"

And now the boy is turning to me: "Tell me," he asks, "what have you done with my future? What have you done with your life?"

And I tell him that I have tried. That I have tried to keep memory alive, that I have tried to fight those who would forget. Because if we forget, we are guilty, we are accomplices. . . .

SN 3 The speaker explains the personal meaning the award has for him.

And that is why I swore never to be silent whenever and wherever human beings endure suffering and humiliation. We must always take sides. . . . There is so much injustice and suffering crying out for our attention: victims of hunger, or racism and political persecution, writers and poets, prisoners in so many lands governed by the left and by the right. Human rights are being violated on every continent. More people are oppressed than are free. . . . One person—a Raoul Wallenberg, an Albert Schweitzer, one person of integrity, can make a difference, a difference of life and death. . . .

This is what I say to the young Jewish boy wondering what I have done with his years. It is in his name that I speak to you and that I express to you my deepest gratitude. No one is as capable of gratitude as one who has emerged from the kingdom of the night.

SN 4 The speaker accepts the award graciously and with humility.

We know that every moment is a moment of grace, every hour an offering; not to share them would mean to betray them. Our lives no longer belong to us alone; they belong to all those who need us desperately.

Thank you Chairman Aarvik. Thank you members of the Nobel Committee. Thank you, people of Norway, for declaring on this singular occasion that our survival has a meaning for mankind.[1]

section

22.6

The Commencement Address

22.6a Your Responsibilities as a Commencement Speaker

22.6b Sample Commencement Address

The **commencement address** speaker praises and congratulates a graduating class. All sorts of people deliver commencement addresses, including politicians, distinguished alumni, actors, educators, and notable citizens.

22.6a Your Responsibilities as a Commencement Speaker

Because the commencement audience is predominantly composed of the families and friends of the graduates, commencement speakers usually acknowledge how both the graduates and the members of the audience contributed to the success being recognized that day.

Most commencement addresses do not stop with celebrating the recent achievements of graduates, however; they also challenge the graduates to focus on the future and the roles they will play in the months and years ahead. Commencement addresses that avoid clichés while emphasizing the accomplishments and promise of the graduates are the most effective.

22.6b Sample Commencement Address

President Obama delivered the following commencement address to Howard University's graduating class of 2016.

SN 1 The speaker recognizes, praises, and celebrates all those in attendance.

To President Frederick, the Board of Trustees, faculty and staff, fellow recipients of honorary degrees, thank you for the honor of spending this day with you. And congratulations to the Class of 2016! . . . To the parents, the grandparents, aunts, uncles, brothers, sisters, all the family and friends who stood by this class, cheered them on, helped them get here today—this is your day, as well. . . .

But seeing all of you here gives me some perspective. It makes me reflect on the changes that I've seen over my own lifetime. So let me begin with what may sound like a controversial statement—a hot take. . . . America is a better place today than it was when I graduated from college. [*Applause.*] Let me repeat: America is by almost every measure better than it was when I graduated from college. . . .

But think about it. I graduated in 1983. . . . Since that year, . . . the poverty rate is down. Americans with college degrees, that rate is up. Crime rates are down. . . . We've cut teen pregnancy in half. We've slashed the African American dropout rate by almost 60 percent, and all of you have a computer in your pocket that gives you the world at the touch of a button. In 1983, I was part of fewer than 10 percent of African Americans who graduated with a bachelor's degree. Today, you're part of the more than 20 percent who will. And more than half of blacks say we're better off than our parents were at our age—and that our kids will be better off, too.

SN 2 The speaker identifies challenges that have been overcome.

So America is better. And the world is better, too . . . .

Yes, our economy has recovered from crisis stronger than almost any other in the world. But there are folks of all races who are still hurting—who still can't find work that pays enough to keep the lights on, who still can't save for retirement. We've still got a big racial gap in economic opportunity. . . .

We've got a justice gap when too many black boys and girls pass through a pipeline from underfunded schools to overcrowded jails. This is one area where things have gotten worse. When I was in college, about half a million people in America were behind bars. Today, there are about 2.2 million. Black men are about six times likelier to be in prison right now than white men.

SN 3 The speaker identifies a series of challenges that the graduates will need to face.

Around the world, we've still got challenges to solve that threaten everybody in the 21st century—old scourges like disease and conflict, but also new challenges, from terrorism and climate change.

So make no mistake, Class of 2016—you've got plenty of work to do. But as complicated and sometimes intractable as these challenges may seem, the truth is that your generation is better positioned than any before you to meet those challenges, to flip the script.

continued

SN 4 The speaker reviews the graduates' experiences and their preparation for meeting the future and the challenges facing them head-on.

continued

Now, how you do that, how you meet these challenges, how you bring about change will ultimately be up to you. . . . With the rest of my time, I'd like to offer some suggestions for how young leaders like you can fulfill your destiny and shape our collective future—bend it in the direction of justice and equality and freedom.

First of all, . . . be confident in your heritage. [*Applause*.] Be confident in your blackness. One of the great changes that's occurred in our country since I was your age is the realization there's no one way to be black. . . . There's no straitjacket, there's no constraints, there's no litmus test for authenticity.

. . . Second, even as we each embrace our own beautiful, unique, and valid versions of our blackness, remember the tie that does bind us as African Americans—and that is our particular awareness of injustice and unfairness and struggle. That means we cannot sleepwalk through life. We cannot be ignorant of history. [*Applause*.] We can't meet the world with a sense of entitlement. . . .

. . . Number three: You have to go through life with more than just passion for change; you need a strategy. I'll repeat that. I want you to have passion, but you have to have a strategy. Not just awareness, but action. Not just hashtags, but votes. . . . And your plan better include voting—not just some of the time, but all the time. [*Applause*.] . . .

And finally, change requires more than just speaking out—it requires listening, as well. In particular, it requires listening to those with whom you disagree, and being prepared to compromise. . . .

So don't try to shut folks out, don't try to shut them down, no matter how much you might disagree with them. . . . That doesn't mean you shouldn't challenge them. Have the confidence to challenge them, the confidence in the rightness of your position. There will be times when you shouldn't compromise your core values, your integrity, and you will have the responsibility to speak up in the face of injustice. But listen. Engage. If the other side has a point, learn from them. If they're wrong, rebut them. Teach them. Beat them on the battlefield of ideas. . . .

So that's my advice. That's how you change things. Change isn't something that happens every four years or eight years; change is not placing your faith in any particular politician and then just putting your feet up and saying, okay, go. Change is the effort of committed citizens who hitch their wagons to something bigger than themselves and fight for it every single day.

. . . Now it's your turn. And the good news is, you're ready. And when your journey seems too hard, and when you run into a chorus of cynics who tell you that you're being foolish to keep believing or that you can't do something, or that you should just give up, or you should just settle—you might say to yourself a little phrase that I've found handy these last eight years: Yes, we can.

Congratulations, Class of 2016! [*Applause*.] Good luck! God bless you. God bless the United States of America. I'm proud of you.

SN 5 The speaker ends by reminding the graduates that the future is in their capable hands.

section
22.7 The Keynote Address

22.7a Your Responsibilities as a Keynote Speaker

22.7b Sample Keynote Address

The purpose of the **keynote address** is to get a meeting or conference off to a good start by establishing the right tone or mood.

22.7a Your Responsibilities as a Keynote Speaker

The functions of the keynoter vary. Some keynote speeches challenge receivers to act or achieve a goal, while others outline a problem or series of problems for them to solve. Some keynote speeches are designed to generate enthusiasm and commitment, while others are designed to demonstrate the importance of a theme or outcome.

The best keynote speakers are adept at focusing audience attention on common goals, communicating the central focus of those gathered, and setting a tone that arouses interest and encourages commitment.

22.7b Sample Keynote Address

The functions of the keynote speech are illustrated in excerpts from this keynote address delivered by Monica Morgan at the National Conference on Racism held in Sydney, Australia.

SN 1 The speaker establishes the purpose of the occasion.

I am an indigenous Woman of the Yorta Yorta people, situated in South Eastern Australia. I facilitate the activities of the Yorta Yorta Nation Aboriginal Corporation, a non-governmental representative body. Our charter is to advance our sovereignty and self-determination—to be the authoritative voice responsible to advance our sovereignty and self-determination. . . .

I am the sixth generation to "Undarnying," a Yorta Yorta woman who was present at the time of colonization of our territory by the English in the early 1800s. Since that time until today, our people have struggled to survive the attempt at genocide by all the instruments of oppression made possible by the colonizer, men who held a self-righteous, ethnocentric, possessive and controlled view of the world. The suppression of Yorta Yorta people, occurred by way of massacres, poisoned water holes, introduced diseases, dispersal, the abduction and systematic rape and torture of women and children. . . . This theft is today entrenched within Australian law. Before contact with European settlers, mounted police, missionaries and convicts, the Yorta Yorta population was estimated to be in the thousands. Our population, by the close of the 1800s was less than 100 persons. Today we number over 4,000. . . .

Today my people live in a state of trauma; this is the result of the collective effect of racism over the last 214 years. Many generations of my people have witnessed the emergence of policies that legalized the forced removal of over 100,000 children from their indigenous families in Australia; children known as the "Stolen Generation." Incarceration rates for indigenous persons is twelve times higher than that of the rest of Australia. . . . The prevalence of substance abuse, mental illness, and family breakdowns together with a life expectancy twenty years below the national average are all indicators of the racism and marginalization we continue to endure.

SN 2 The speaker focuses audience attention on the problems they need to face.

The real solution rests with the Federal Government taking real leadership, leadership that can acknowledge the past not to evoke guilt but to advance real reconciliation outcomes that will lead to the special measures designed to achieve equality for indigenous Peoples. . . .

SN 3 The speaker's inspirational tone reminds audience members of the importance of action.

I speak not only for my ancestors and my people, but also peoples who are denied their inherent right to land and an identity.[3]

section 22.8

The Speech of Tribute

A form of commemorative speaking, whether delivered to honor a living or dead person or an event, the purpose of the **speech of tribute** is to acknowledge and praise the honoree.

22.8a Your Responsibilities Giving a Speech of Tribute

The tribute speaker's job is to inform the audience of the accomplishments of a person or the importance of an event, but it is also to heighten the audience's awareness of and appreciation for the contributions or values of the honoree.

To achieve this, the tribute speaker needs to involve the audience members by making those contributions relevant to their lives. He or she also needs to clearly explain why the individual or event is being celebrated or recognized, tell stories that show why the honor is merited, and honestly praise the honoree.

Success in delivering a tribute speech depends on using the right words to convey the thoughts and emotions inherent in the occasion. Sincerity and knowledge are key. The tribute speaker's focus is on creating vivid, specific images of accomplishments that demonstrate the influence and importance of the honoree.

Three main features characterize the speech of tribute:

1. A section that describes what makes the subject of the speech worthy of special recognition
2. A section that explains in more depth what the subject accomplished
3. A section urging the audience to be inspired by the honoree's accomplishments, so that they will seek new and greater goals

22.8b Sample Speech of Tribute

Although sometimes the subject of a tribute speech is a well-known figure, the person being singled out for special recognition does not need to be famous. In fact, each of us probably can think of one or more individuals who are neither famous nor public figures but who still deserve special praise, as did student Dolores Bandow. In her speech, "A Bird Outside Your Window," Bandow pays tribute to her daughter Elizabeth, who was born with a genetic anomaly.

SN 1 The speaker introduces receivers to the subject of the tribute.

I am here today to celebrate life. I am here to celebrate a particular life which began nine years ago. . . . The day I gave birth to our third child . . . I thought was the bleakest day one could experience. . . . Of two children born at the hospital that hour, both had birth defects. The other child died. For one dreadful, fleeting moment, I thought it would be easier if ours had.

To admit such a transient thought . . . is sobering. How selfish; how self-pitying; how wrong I was. I had wanted a "perfect" baby. But by shattering our illusion of perfection with her birth, she has been perfecting our reality with her life.

Elizabeth's life has taught me compassion, unconditional love, humility; and has set me on a path to wisdom. . . . I thought I knew sadness; I hadn't. I thought I knew happiness; I thought I knew love; not all kinds. I thought I knew compassion; I thought I knew humility; I hadn't. . . .

SN 2 The speaker explores what the tribute's subject taught her and explains how the subject's achievements helped her realize life's value.

As I lay in the hospital . . . following her birth, reading medical genetics textbooks . . . I learned that humans need 46 chromosomes—precisely. Any more or any fewer can result in abnormalities of every cell. Overwhelmed by the data . . . I would steal down to the nursery. . . . Elizabeth was caged in an isolet with tubes and wires reaching out from every orifice. . . . But when my hands found their way through the maze to stroke her face, she nuzzled against me in her suckling instinct. At that moment, I saw her not as a syndrome but as my infant daughter. She made me peer beyond the "accidentals" to the "essence" of human life.

Later, at the age of seven months, Elizabeth was in heart failure, fighting for her life. Before I took her to the hospital for heart surgery, I prepared to say "good-bye" to her. Unable to make myself cross the threshold with her, I turned around and saw the flowers. I carried her over and let her breathe the fragrance. I pointed up to the clouds; I lifted her up to the trees and told her to look at it all—see it. But it was I who was seeing it as never before. . . . Sunshine is indeed what Elizabeth brought us in the form of illumination and enlightenment. She still casts her light.

Recently I've been grumpy over turning 40. When I was bemoaning my greying hair, sagging skin, and aching joints, Elizabeth said, "Mom, you should be glad to be living a long, long time. Celebrate!" . . .

SN 3 The speaker shares stories that vivify the subject's triumphs.

continued

continued

Elizabeth has been to me the bird that sings too early outside your window and rouses you from that dream state. . . . She sang her song to me. And like that bird's tune, I harked, heard, and hummed it back.

My song is this: keep in mind that children with birth anomalies are not the pitiful. Not they, but we with our attitude, ignorance, and insensitivities are pitiful. . . .

Yes, there was a brief moment at her birth when her unwelcome song jarred me awake. Sometimes the thing we welcome least is a blessing which, disguised, knocks boldly on our door; then rejected, sneaks quietly in the back door of the heart and establishes residence before being recognized—quietly working magic—quietly transforming.

SN 4 The speaker reminds receivers of what they need to be thankful for.

So Elizabeth, I thank you for singing your song outside my window and forcing me to look through that window beyond the "accidentals" to the "essence." Thank you for allowing me to glimpse through that window and see the flowers through your eyes. Thank you for showing me my reflection in that window—for making me realize that the alternative to growing old is not being alive. And thank you, Elizabeth, for making growing old worthwhile.

To you, Elizabeth: L'Chaim.[4]

The Eulogy

section **22.9**

A special form of tribute speech is the **eulogy**. When delivering a eulogy, you pay tribute to a person who has died. A eulogy is usually presented graveside or at a memorial service. Though some are very brief, lasting only a minute or two, others are more lengthy, lasting 10 or 20 minutes.

22.9a Your Responsibilities Delivering a Eulogy

When delivering a eulogy, your goal is to comfort the members of your audience without letting your own grief overwhelm you. This sometimes becomes difficult because of the emotional nature of the speech and occasion. The following qualities characterize the eulogy:

1. The speaker begins by acknowledging the special loss suffered by the family of the deceased and/or society.
2. The speaker celebrates the life of the deceased by acknowledging the legacy of the individual.
3. The speaker emphasizes the uniqueness or essence of the subject with honest emotion, anecdotes, personal recollections, and quotations from others. He or she brings the group together to share and ease their sense of loss by concentrating instead on how fortunate they were to have known the deceased and what they have learned from his or her life.

22.9b Sample Eulogy

President Barack Obama penned this eulogy for the late world champion boxer and humanitarian, Muhammad Ali.

Muhammad Ali was The Greatest. Period. If you just asked him, he'd tell you. He'd tell you he was the double greatest; that he'd "handcuffed lightning, thrown thunder into jail."

But what made The Champ the greatest—what truly separated him from everyone else—is that everyone else would tell you pretty much the same thing.

SN 1 The speaker begins by acknowledging the loss of the subject and the legacy he left.

Like everyone else on the planet, Michelle and I mourn his passing. But we're also grateful to God for how fortunate we are to have known him, if just for a while; for how fortunate we all are that The Greatest chose to grace our time.

In my private study, just off the Oval Office, I keep a pair of his gloves on display, just under that iconic photograph of him—the young champ, just 22 years old, roaring like a lion over a fallen Sonny Liston. I was too young when it was taken to understand who he was—still Cassius Clay, already an Olympic Gold Medal winner, yet to set out on a spiritual journey that would lead him to his Muslim faith,

continued

continued

exile him at the peak of his power, and set the stage for his return to greatness with a name as familiar to the downtrodden in the slums of Southeast Asia and the villages of Africa as it was to cheering crowds in Madison Square Garden.

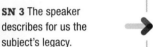

SN 2 The speaker celebrates the subject's life and talents, identifying the qualities that made him special.

"I am America," he once declared. "I am the part you won't recognize. But get used to me—black, confident, cocky; my name, not yours; my religion, not yours; my goals, my own. Get used to me."

That's the Ali I came to know as I came of age—not just as skilled a poet on the mic as he was a fighter in the ring, but a man who fought for what was right. A man who fought for us. He stood with King and Mandela; stood up when it was hard; spoke out when others wouldn't. His fight outside the ring would cost him his title and his public standing. It would earn him enemies on the left and the right, make him reviled, and nearly send him to jail. But Ali stood his ground. And his victory helped us get used to the America we recognize today.

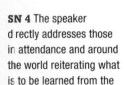

SN 3 The speaker describes for us the subject's legacy.

He wasn't perfect, of course. For all his magic in the ring, he could be careless with his words, and full of contradictions as his faith evolved. But his wonderful, infectious, even innocent spirit ultimately won him more fans than foes—maybe because in him, we hoped to see something of ourselves. Later, as his physical powers ebbed, he became an even more powerful force for peace and reconciliation around the world. We saw a man who said he was so mean he'd make medicine sick reveal a soft spot, visiting children with illness and disability around the world, telling them they, too, could become the greatest. We watched a hero light a torch, and fight his greatest fight of all on the world stage once again; a battle against the disease that ravaged his body, but couldn't take the spark from his eyes.

SN 4 The speaker directly addresses those in attendance and around the world reiterating what is to be learned from the subject's life.

Muhammad Ali shook up the world. And the world is better for it. We are all better for it. Michelle and I send our deepest condolences to his family, and we pray that the greatest fighter of them all finally rests in peace.[5]

The After-Dinner Speech

section **22.10**

Generally designed to be entertaining, the **after-dinner speech** is a common form of public address. Neither overly technical nor filled with ponderous details or complex information, the after-dinner speech is usually upbeat and takes a good-natured, sometimes humorous, whimsical, or mildly satirical look at a topic of interest and relevance to the audience.

22.10a Your Responsibilities Delivering an After-Dinner Speech

If you are asked to give an after-dinner speech, you'll probably want to choose a lighthearted topic that allows you to inject humor into your presentation. Humor, when used appropriately, helps relieve tension and relax receivers. It also helps receivers remember your presentation.[6] However, humor should be functional, not forced, and help you make a point.

The after-dinner speech depends on your ability to make a point while maintaining a sense of decorum and good taste. Remember, after-dinner speeches are usually delivered when audience members are in a mood for entertainment, and therefore must be easy to digest . . . as desserts usually are.

22.10b Sample After-Dinner Speech

The following are excerpts from an after-dinner speech, titled "Artificial Intelligence," that was delivered by Massachusetts Institute of Technology professor Marvin Minsky at a personal computer forum.

I've heard people explaining from time to time that there really wasn't any such thing, that artificial intelligence was just programs. And they were right, of course, because everything is just programs. That's called "nothing buttery." A program is nothing but a sequence of instructions, and a living thing is nothing but a bunch of atoms with various chemical bonds, and a machine is nothing but parts, and so forth. And that's a very important idea. People who don't believe that eventually get into very serious trouble, because then they end up believing that something comes from nowhere. . . .

SN 1 The speaker sets a light tone.

continued

SN 2 The speaker's good nature and appropriately humorous examples help receivers process the content.

continued

Have you ever had lunch with a writer and asked them how they write? They're always fidgety and embarrassed. Isaac Asimov is the master of this. He says that you sit in front of the typewriter and move your fingers. He's willing to face the whole mystery of that in its completeness and not pretend to know what to do. . . .

You see, you can be skeptical of artificial intelligence because it doesn't write Beethoven quartets. But the real reason to be skeptical of artificial intelligence is that it doesn't know how to eat with a fork or chopsticks, or dress itself, or walk across the room. . . . Nobody has the foggiest idea, really, of how that stuff is programmed. . . .

The number of pieces of brain that actually do anything like move your finger is very small. You'd be surprised at the number of people who think that the gift of playing the piano is in your hands. That's a joke. The hands are just I/O devices, and there's no difference between the nerves and muscles of a pianist and anyone else, except that pianists are stronger, you can believe. Never get into a fight with a pianist. They have terribly powerful arms.[7]

GAME PLAN

Giving a Special Occasion Speech

- ☐ I understand the occasion for my speech, my speech's purpose, and the audience attending my speech
- ☐ I have considered and fulfilled the responsibilities and goals of the speech.
- ☐ I have crafted a unique approach to the topic.
- ☐ Based on what I've learned in previous chapters of the playbook, I have prepared for and practiced my speech.

Exercises

SPEAKING ON SPECIAL OCCASIONS

By developing the skills necessary to fulfill the responsibilities of a special occasion speaker, you prepare yourself to speak effectively throughout the life span. Participating in the following activities will help hone your understandings and abilities.

1. Family Introductions

Introduce a family member by specifying two of his or her defining characteristics and explain why the relationship you share is meaningful.

2. And the Award Goes to . . .

Select a historical figure, artist, author, athlete, or coach. Your selected person is to receive an award (silly or serious) that you create specifically for him or her.

1. Name the award and its purpose.
2. Outline the accomplishments of the person as they relate to the award.

3. Paying Tribute

Imagine being given the opportunity to compose a tribute speech for someone you believe instrumental in helping you grow as a person. What words would you use to celebrate that person and let him or her understand the role he or she has played in your life. Try your hand at writing such a speech.

4. Analyze a Commencement Address

Search for and watch Anthony Corvino's commencement address at Binghamton University, titled "Average Is the New Exceptional," on YouTube. Identify the specific techniques that Corvino used to connect with and inspire the students graduating.

1. How did Anthony establish his own credibility at the beginning of his speech?
2. How did he use humor to reach out to audience members?
3. How did he acknowledge the efforts of the graduating students and their families?
4. How did Anthony challenge other graduates to achieve more in their future work?
5. How did he craft a new and unique approach to his commencement address?
6. Had Anthony practiced his speech with you before the big day, what kind of critiques might you have offered?

5. Approach the Speaker's Stand: Let's Toast

You are giving a toast to celebrate a special occasion such as a birthday, a housewarming, or a wedding anniversary. What steps will you take to ensure the tone of your toast reflects the person(s) or event being celebrated? Specifically, think about the following:

1. What factors do you need to consider as you prepare the speech?
2. What will you do to build rapport with your audience?
3. What will you speak about?
4. What effect do you hope your speech has?

RECAP AND REVIEW

1. **Explain the goals and functions of special occasion speeches.** Special occasion speeches help punctuate the high-water marks of our lives. They are part of the rituals that draw us together. Speeches of celebration are designed to reflect the nature and needs of the occasions that prompted their delivery.
2. **Define and distinguish the similarities and differences between speeches of introduction, presentation, and acceptance.** An introduction functions as a "warm-up" for a featured speaker, whereas presenting an award to a recipient usually includes more formal accolades. An acceptance speech is given in response to a speech of presentation, affording the honoree the opportunity to describe how much receiving such an award means.
3. **Explain the functions of the commencement address and a keynote address.** Like a coach, the commencement speech praises and congratulates a graduating class for their accomplishments. The keynote speech gets a meeting off to a good start, establishing an appropriate mood and helping attendees focus on the challenges ahead of them.
4. **Define the goals and distinguish the differences between a speech of tribute and a eulogy.** A tribute is given to acknowledge and praise a living or dead honoree, whereas a eulogy, a special form of tribute, pays homage to a person who has died.
5. **Explain the key characteristics of the after-dinner speech.** The after-dinner speech is usually lighthearted and takes a humorous or satirical look at a topic of interest.

KEY TERMS

After-dinner speech 411
Commencement address 400
Eulogy 409
Keynote address 404
Speech of acceptance 398
Speech of introduction 394
Speech of presentation 396
Speech of tribute 406

SAGE edge™

Sharpen your skills with SAGE edge at edge.sagepub.com/gamblepsp2e.

SAGE edge for students provides a personalized approach to help you accomplish your coursework goals in an easy-to-use learning environment.

Siri Stafford/Photodisc/Thinkstock

23

Business and Professional Speaking

UPON COMPLETING THIS CHAPTER'S TRAINING, YOU WILL BE ABLE TO

1. Participate proactively in an employment interview
2. Interact effectively in a meeting
3. Pitch an idea
4. Deliver a briefing
5. Present a report
6. Conduct a training session

What does speaking have to do with work? Everything! Much of your work life depends on how effectively you construct your professional image and build relationships. Speaking ability influences whether you get the job you want, hold onto the position, and advance in your field. Success at work depends on knowing how to present yourself and your ideas to others.

Contents

section

23.1

First, Get the Job: How to Handle a Job Interview

An interview with the hiring manager is often a key part of landing a job. Think of the answers you give in the interview as a series of impromptu speeches. Do the work to prepare and set yourself up for success.

23.1a Research the Job and the Position

A key part of preparing for an interview is to research both the job and the hiring organization as thoroughly as possible. If you know someone within the organization, speak with her or him. Search the Internet for the specifics of the job you seek, including typical employee responsibilities, assignments, advancement opportunities, and average salaries. Read what has been written about the company. Acquaint yourself with its successes and failures, products, and opportunities.

Compile a list of potential questions the interviewer might ask you and rehearse your answers. Possible questions include

- Why are you interested in working with us?
- How would you describe your greatest strength and weakness?
- How has your background prepared you for this job?
- Provide an example of when you convinced your supervisor to implement your idea. What was the outcome?
- Describe a time when you had to balance multiple assignments. How did you do?

Of course, in addition to preparing for potential questions, you also need to prepare yourself for the fact that you likely will be asked some questions that you have not anticipated. It is also likely that the interviewer will ask you if you have any questions for her or him. Thus, your role is not only to be able to respond seemingly spontaneously to questions you are asked, but also to come prepared to ask questions. Before arriving, compile a list of questions you want to ask the interviewer. The following are among the questions you might ask:

- What qualities are you seeking in the candidate you hire?
- How do you gauge an employee's value?
- What do you like best about the organization's culture?

Finally, be sure to review your application, and your résumé, updating each as needed.

23.1b An Interview Is a Planned Conversation

The conversation during an **interview** distinguishes itself from casual conversation in that it is planned and designed to achieve specific objectives. In an interview, you and your interviewer have opportunities to share information. Based on what is said, each of you is then left to decide whether continued association will be positive and productive.

Just as with a speech, to succeed in an interview you need to prepare, gain control of any nerves, establish rapport, communicate your confidence and competence, inform about yourself, and answer questions asked forthrightly. It is assumed that how you behave during an interview reveals how you behave in general. Potential employers rely on a number of interview formats. They may interview you using the traditional one-on-one format, have a panel of interviewers question you, or place you in a simulation giving you the opportunity to demonstrate your skills.

Well-planned interviews are structured, divided into stages. The interview's opening is an orientation to the interview process. It is also the stage during which rapport is built, figuratively breaking the ice between interviewer and interviewee. The middle or interview body is the longest interview segment. During this stage, participants get down to business. They discuss the interviewee's educational and work experiences, seeking to establish the applicant's strengths, weaknesses, accomplishments, and goals. The interview's close finds the parties reviewing the main points covered, offering final statements, and taking leave of one another.

Let's get down to business. Like any speech, planning ahead is the key to interview success.

COACHING TIP

"Before a job interview, I think, What color tie best represents me as a person this company would be interested in?"

—Jarod Kintz

Professional image is critical. Work on yours! Knowing how to present yourself and your ideas is a ticket to success. Relationship building begins with the first impression others form of you. Make yours a good one!

23.1c Get to the Heart of the Questions

Remember, questions are key in gathering the information needed to make a decision. Most interviews contain different kinds of questions. **Closed questions** can be answered with a few words. The following are closed questions: Where do you live? What was your major area of interest? What are your compensation expectations?

Open questions are broader, offering more freedom in answering them: Would you tell me about yourself?[1] How has your background prepared you for this position? What would you like to know about our firm? Please describe your greatest success and failure. Open questions like these foster the expression of feelings, attitudes, and values.

Open and closed questions can be either primary or secondary. **Primary questions** introduce a topic or area for exploration. **Secondary questions**, also known as probing questions, follow up on primary questions. Thus, the following is a primary question: What is your favorite assignment? And these are secondary questions used to follow up: What specifically did you like about that assignment? What does that mean? Can you give me an example?

Once the interviewer begins asking questions, use the following acronym to guide you in answering: **S.T.A.R.** (situation, task, action, result).[2] For example, let's say that the interviewer asks you what others would say when asked what it's like to work with you. Using the S.T.A.R. system, you would answer the question by revealing a *situation* you faced when working with another person ("My coworker fell behind in completing an assigned project"), how you assessed the *task* needing to be completed ("I realized that if he didn't complete the project on time, the promotion he had recently been promised could be in jeopardy"), the *action* you took ("I'm a team player, so I stepped up, and did some of the research myself, which enabled him to complete his analysis"), and the *results* you achieved ("When he was promoted to regional director, he asked me to be his assistant. He knew he could count on me"). "So I think if asked what it's like to work with me, others would say I always have their back. I do whatever I can to help."

FIGURE 23.1
Common Interview Questions

Tell me a little about yourself.
Why did you apply for this position?
What makes you qualified for this position? Why should we hire you?
What are your strengths? What are your weaknesses?
What would your former employer (professor, friend) say about you?
What are three words that describe you?
What are your short-term goals? What are your long-term goals?
Do you have any questions for us?

Source: Kelly M. Quintanilla and Shawn T. Whal, *Business and Professional Communication: KEYS for Workplace Excellence*, 2nd ed. (Thousand Oaks, CA: SAGE, 2014).

23.1d Be an Active Participant in the Interview

During the interview, you seek to present yourself well and answer questions clearly, providing the interviewer with sufficient information to determine whether you are the right person for the job. But you also need to ask questions that will help you decide whether to accept the job should an offer of employment be made.[3] Asking, not just answering, questions demonstrates your enthusiasm for the job. In addition to asking the questions you prepared in advance, make sure that you ask secondary questions to follow up on what the interviewer says, which shows interest and engagement.

Interestingly, successful job applicants speak for some 55 percent of the total time allotted for the interview, and initiate 56 percent of the comments made, in comparison with unsuccessful applicants who initiate only 37 percent of the comments made and speak for only 37 percent of the time.

23.1e Make a Positive Impression

When you give a formal speech, you must consider not just what you will say, but how you will present yourself. The same is true in a job interview. Assuming you want the job, one of your goals is to help an interviewer perceive you in a positive light.[4] Looking, sounding, and acting professionally throughout the interview facilitate this. If you can answer each of the following questions with a "yes," you are on track:

- ☐ Am I dressed appropriately for the interview?
- ☐ Am I familiar with the company, its competition, and industry trends?
- ☐ Am I conveying enthusiasm and energy?
- ☐ Am I communicating my happiness at being interviewed?
- ☐ Does my nonverbal behavior send the right messages, underscoring my confidence, competence, and trustworthiness?

In contrast, the following interviewee behaviors turn off interviewers:

- ☐ Arrogance
- ☐ Lack of enthusiasm
- ☐ Immaturity
- ☐ Poor communication
- ☐ Unclear goals
- ☐ Unwillingness to travel or relocate
- ☐ Deficient preparation
- ☐ Unprofessional appearance[5]

To communicate professionalism, never inquire about vacation, personal days, or benefits on your first interview. Always end the interview affirming your interest in the position. Always follow up sending a thank you note to each person with whom you interviewed.[6]

section

23.2

Speaking in a Meeting

23.2a Participating in the Meeting

23.2b Leading the Meeting

Meetings are commonplace at work and in most professional arenas. Whether you will be the meeting leader or a participant, adequate preparation is essential. So too are understanding the meeting's purpose, reviewing its agenda, engaging actively in the exchanging of information, and ensuring the meeting does not veer off topic.

Again, how you come across counts. As with other kinds of communication at work, what you say and do during a meeting affects others' impressions of you and builds, maintains, or detracts from your professional image. Ability to relate to others interpersonally in big and small groups, large and small meetings, is essential for your professional growth.

23.2a Participating in the Meeting

Every participant shares responsibility for a meeting with the meeting's leader. When participating in a meeting, be sure to follow these guidelines:

- ☐ Review the reasons for meeting ahead of time and suggest items for the agenda if requested.
- ☐ Give yourself time to prepare by reading the agenda as much in advance of the meeting as possible, and considering the concerns and questions you have regarding each agenda item.
- ☐ Participate enthusiastically, but be certain to avoid interrupting when others speak and refrain from denigrating others' input.
- ☐ Praise others' comments when appropriate.
- ☐ Keep your contributions relevant by building on and responding to others' ideas.
- ☐ Solicit feedback, ask questions, and keep track of accomplishments and responsibilities.

When a meeting is effective, members seamlessly perform task and maintenance roles, but avoid performing self-serving roles—roles focused exclusively on a member's needs but not helpful to or in the best interests of others in the meeting. In contrast to selfish, self-centered roles, task roles facilitate the meeting and the realization of its goal. Maintenance roles facilitate interaction between members.

Meetings tend to be most effective when their working atmosphere is informal, comfortable, and relaxed; there is time for ample discussion with all members participating, listening to one another and expressing ideas and feelings freely; disagreement is not suppressed; decisions are reached by consensus; no one is personally attacked; and neither the leader nor any single member dominates.

23.2b Leading the Meeting

Although at this stage in your work life, you most likely will be a meeting participant, preparing yourself to lead a meeting can be a career builder. When leading a meeting, taking the following steps will help ensure it is a positive experience and productive:

- ☐ Formulate and share the meeting's purpose in advance with those who will be attending. When called to a meeting with no clear goal, employees worry that their time will be wasted.
- ☐ Develop an agenda and circulate it in advance.
- ☐ Arrive early to ask and answer questions, chat and/or talk off topic with others (saves doing it during the meeting), and build rapport to help others feel comfortable.
- ☐ Turn off your cell phone; have others do the same.
- ☐ Introduce any guests or new attendees.
- ☐ Provide a meeting orientation—referring to the agenda and your goals.
- ☐ Maintain control of the meeting. Seek to engage all present. Take steps to ensure that no one member monopolizes discussion. Focus on covering agenda items.
- ☐ Summarize results, reviewing what was covered, reminding members of their responsibilities, and affirming accomplishments or goals met.
- ☐ Answer any questions.
- ☐ Thank members for their attendance and input, and if needed, schedule the next meeting date.

An effective leader facilitates a meeting's start and contributes to its ultimate success. The leader sets the meeting's tone, which when constructive encourages everyone to participate, precipitating high-quality interaction and a positive and productive outcome.

Team leader. When leading a meeting, make sure it has defined goals and objectives so as not to waste time.

section
23.3 The Pitch

A few years ago, Workman Publishing, an independent publishing house, held a "Pitchapalooza" session during which a few dozen aspiring authors were given one minute each to describe their book idea before a panel of publishing professionals.[7] This kind of brief, highly prepared persuasive presentation of a new idea or product is known as **a pitch.** Many workplaces provide similar opportunities for you to sell your ideas to higher-ups on a regular basis.

When pitching, your goal is to convince the people holding the power that what you propose is worthy of their money, time, or energy. Promotional pitches are usually made in person or increasingly via video or video conferencing. Formulating an effective pitch is difficult work.

A pitch is a persuasive presentation in a business setting. Some pitches are very brief—we call them "elevator pitches"—and basically depend on you distilling your idea into a few words that can be conveyed to an audience within 5 to 10 seconds. If given the luxury of 30 seconds, you can also speak to the benefits of your proposal. If given 5 minutes to pitch, you have time to present your idea, the problem it solves, its benefits, supporting evidence, the challenges you face, and the resources you require to make it happen.

Whether your pitch is 5 seconds, 30 seconds, or 5 minutes, you need to do your homework if your words are going to excite those listening. You will need to decide how to involve your audience, connect your pitch with the organization's mission, and get receivers to imagine the possibilities. A 5-minute presentation is enough time to use technology—PowerPoint or Prezi and presentation aids—that transforms your proposal into an "aha" moment.

The following are typical pitch components:

- Identify a need or opportunity.
- State your proposal simply and clearly; tell what you do.
- Explain your rationale (the needs and benefits fulfilled) and strategy.
- Communicate your USP (unique selling proposition)—reveal what makes your idea unique.
- Engage with your audience; make it easy for them to respond affirmatively.
- Review the timeline, costs, and challenges.
- Integrate presentation aids to make your vision come alive.
- End by reiterating the benefits of your proposal, linking it again with the goals of decision makers, and appealing in your close for them to give you the go-ahead.

Sometimes it is better to pitch with a partner or a team. When presenting with others, prepare a detailed outline specifying each person's role and responsibilities. Be sure to hold one another accountable as you work to coordinate the presentation's parts. You are aiming for a coherent whole, not several individual little speeches.

As when preparing a speech, research thoroughly, know your audience, and rehearse, rehearse, rehearse! Anticipate possible questions and practice responses. Remember, you need to make it easy for those making the decision to say yes.

Thomas Northcut/Photodisc/Thinkstock

Down the middle. Make your pitches clear and easy to understand for your audience so they don't get overwhelmed, bored, or forget them.

Briefings and Reports

section 23.4

Briefings and reports are informative presentations commonly delivered in organizations.

A **briefing** is a brief talk that provides information needed to complete a task or make a decision. Briefings may focus on the past to bring others up to date, letting them know what was accomplished in their absence or since their last briefing. Briefings can also be future oriented, focusing on client interests and needs. Whatever their purpose, briefings have the following in common:

- They are short, typically one to three minutes in length.
- They are simply organized, usually topically or chronologically.
- They concisely summarize what has been done and/or what needs to be done.
- They may utilize simple presentation aids.
- They are delivered conversationally.

A **report** provides a summary of what you have learned or accomplished. Status reports, feasibility studies, and investigative reports are presented regularly in organizations. Each of these reports informs decision makers or team members on goals that have been reached and remaining obstacles. Such information may be communicated to your boss, a project team, other committees or boards, clients, and the general public. An organization's culture influences the nature of the reports, including whether they are formal or informal, include presentation aids or not, and allow for question-and-answer (Q&A) follow-ups. The following guidelines will serve you in preparing and delivering a report:

- Begin by providing an overview or summary of the project's purpose.
- Describe the current status of the project, providing a brief summation of progress made relative to each of the project's goals.
- Be open and forthright, explaining hurdles overcome, reasons for any delays, detailing what is yet to be accomplished, and requesting assistance, if needed.
- Conclude by sharing a realistic assessment of the project's future.
- Ask for and answer questions, being careful not to become defensive.
- Thank those listening for their attention.

Like pitches, reports can be presented with a team, requiring that members divide up responsibilities, agree on a timeline, and coordinate the preparation, rehearsal, and delivery of information. Members of a successful team formulate the report's purpose, craft its outline, and collaborate to answer the following questions:

- ☐ How do we introduce the information so those in attendance will listen attentively?
- ☐ What are the report's main points?
- ☐ How should we present its central message?
- ☐ At what point are transitions most appropriate?
- ☐ How do we conclude so that all aspects are summarized and the presentation ends on a high note?
- ☐ What presentation aids should we use?
- ☐ How should we prepare for the Q&A that follows?
- ☐ How do we approach and learn from the rehearsal period?

After the presentation, the group holds a debriefing session to assess its effectiveness. Keep in mind that when reporting, you are building on skills and knowledge gained in preparing other kinds of speeches.

section
23.5 The Training Session

Trainers teach their audience members how to do something. Although the content of a training session is similar to a "how-to" speech, both the purpose and method of delivery are substantially different.

Trainers give workshops on virtually any subject: how to develop sales or interpersonal skills, how to avoid a lawsuit, how to handle cultural diversity, or how to run a meeting. Sometimes training is conducted informally and involves relatively direct advice—such as appropriate business-casual dress or what to wear on casual Fridays. Other times, training is highly sophisticated and coordinated. For example, the Disney organization has an entire training institute devoted to running courses related to custom business solutions and professional development.

Although what follows is a prescription for adult learning, it applies to college students and others as well:

- ☐ Demonstrate the relevance of the training to those in attendance. Help them understand and be able to explain how they will use the material.
- ☐ Plan activities to ensure attendees are actively involved in the session. Avoid the lecture format. The session you lead should involve active learning so that those in it are given ample opportunities to apply and practice skills, experiencing for themselves the session's content.
- ☐ Understand what attendees do and do not know. Aim the session "where they are," not above or below their knowledge level.
- ☐ Pace the session appropriately. Spaced learning tends to work—learn, apply, learn, apply.

© iStockphoto.com/zoranm

Hands-on. Training should differ from any other speech because it should have interactive elements allowing staff members to practice their skills.

GAME PLAN

Preparing for an Interview

- ☐ I know the exact location of the interview and how long it takes me to get there, so I am certain to arrive on time.
- ☐ I will dress appropriately, choosing what I wear so that it does not distract from the professional impression I hope to make.
- ☐ I've practiced my handshake and greeting before a mirror or with another person.
- ☐ I've thoroughly researched the company as well as the position I seek.
- ☐ I've prepared a professional-looking résumé and considered what aspects of my experience the interviewer will likely question me about.
- ☐ I've practiced answering both common and challenging questions.
- ☐ I'm prepared to ask the interviewer questions.

Exercises

SPEAKING ON THE JOB

Mastering the ability to prepare and deliver different kinds of work-related presentations is a professional image enhancer. Participating in these activities will help you increase the value you bring to your employer.

1. Research the Employer You Want

Review the careers page on the website of a company or an organization where you would like to work. Based on your research, answer these questions:

- What values does the company promote?
- What is the company looking for in an employee?
- What benefits does the company offer in return?
- Do you imagine you would be happy working for this company? Why?

Based on your exploration of the company's job postings and their descriptions, prepare a list of three personal traits you possess that you believe an interviewer at that company would value.

2. Practice Your Response

Review the following interview questions. Then pair up and practice answering them:

- Why do you want this job?
- How would you describe yourself?
- Would you tell me about a past experience that reveals you can handle pressure and are resilient?
- What was your greatest success in college?
- This job requires creativity. What have you done that demonstrates your creativity?
- What do you think would be your greatest challenge were we to hire you?
- If I were to Google you, what would I find out that we haven't discussed?
- What questions do you have for me?

3. Plan It

Develop a plan to interview for an on-campus position and brief your professor on progress, or develop a pitch to persuade the dean of students to grant club status and funding to a group you create.

4. Analyze the Pitch

Watch an episode of *Shark Tank,* a television show in which wealthy venture capitalists—the "sharks" —interview aspiring entrepreneurs who each deliver a pitch designed to persuade the sharks to invest in them and their business. Analyze the effectiveness of each entrepreneur's pitch, and evaluate the extent to which the individuals seeking funding effectively answered the questions posed by the sharks.

5. Approach the Speaker's Stand

1. *The Pitch.* Develop and deliver a pitch to persuade a loan officer at a bank in your community to lend you money for one of the following: a proposed business venture, to travel abroad, or to go to graduate school.
2. *The S.T.A.R.* You are being interviewed. The interviewer asks, "What do you think others would say if I asked them if you were dependable?" Answer the question using the S (situation); T (task); A (action); R (result) strategy.

RECAP AND REVIEW

1. **Participate proactively in an employment interview.** You need to prepare yourself to interview. Research the company, anticipate questions, answer questions knowledgeably and honestly, and present yourself as professionally as possible.
2. **Interact effectively in a meeting.** Leaders and members work collaboratively to ensure the success of a meeting. Both need to prepare for the meeting, review its agenda, and participate enthusiastically.
3. **Pitch an idea.** Pitches are persuasive in nature and are planned to convince others that an investment in what is being asked for promotes the organization's mission, and is worth the time, money, and energy that needs to be expended.
4. **Deliver a briefing.** Briefings, though very short, make sure everyone is on the same page, reviewing or previewing what has or needs to be done.
5. **Present a report.** A report summarizes the status of a project or other undertaking, letting others know what you have accomplished, what remains to be completed, and what it means for the organization.
6. **Conduct a training session.** Training sessions are held on a wide range of topics related to the specific needs and goals of an organization and the specific audiences addressed.

KEY TERMS

SAGE edge™

Sharpen your skills with SAGE edge at edge.sagepub.com/gamblepsp2e.

SAGE edge for students provides a personalized approach to help you accomplish your coursework goals in an easy-to-use learning environment.

© iStockphoto.com/skynesher

24

Storytelling

UPON COMPLETING THIS CHAPTER'S TRAINING, YOU WILL BE ABLE TO

1. Identify stories from your life to share when giving talks to others
2. Explain the ingredients integral to a story
3. Demonstrate ability in using a variety of language tools
4. Create narratives that motivate and involve others

Contents

About a year ago, Suki Kim delivered a TED Talk titled "This Is What It's Like to Go Undercover in North Korea."[1] She started her presentation with these words, using pauses to punctuate her story:

In 2011, [pause]

during the final six months of Kim Jong-Il's life, [pause]

I lived undercover in North Korea. [pause]

I was born and raised in South Korea, their enemy. [pause]

I live in America, their other enemy. [pause]

Since 2002, I had visited North Korea a few times. [pause]

And I had come to realize that to write about it with any meaning, [pause]

or to understand the place beyond the regime's propaganda, [pause]

the only option was total immersion. [pause]

Suki's story fascinated the audience. In this chapter, we explore how to tell stories that lead audiences to enter the speaker's world. Are you prepared to tell stories that pass on understandings and dreams, bridge barriers, take hold of others, engender positive feelings, bring people psychologically closer, and help them adapt and engage?[2] Doing so will strengthen your presentation.

COACHING TIP

"Those who tell the stories rule society."

—Plato

Tell a story and change the world. Good stories embody powerful messages. Tell one at the right time and you build a connection that will last.

section

24.1 Discover Your Inner Storyteller

Effective speechmakers tell a wide range of stories, some based on difficult experiences, others on formative ones. Your goal is to reframe your experiences, learn how to embody and perform them, and then create stories, articulating powerful messages that surmount boredom, inspiring and guiding others, fostering their participation. The more personal and authentic your stories, the easier it becomes for others to identify with and latch onto their themes and the more likely they are to take the action you advocate.

It's time to meet your inner storyteller. Begin with some self-reflection: Using a scale of 1 to 10 with 1 representing "Never," and 10 representing "Always," award yourself the number of points you believe you deserve for each of the following statements:

I speak to build connections with others.	______	My words are an apt reflection of me.	______
Most of the time, I tell a story to make my point.	______	Others remember my words.	______
Others respond favorably to the stories I tell.	______	Others find my words motivating.	______
I find it easy to speak in metaphorical language.	______	I repeat what I think is important.	______
I reach others on an emotional level.	______	When presenting ideas, I invite audience interaction.	______

The more points you award yourself on each item, the more proficient you believe your storytelling skill to be. What do your scores suggest about your readiness to use words to inspire and lead others to a new understanding?

24.1a Find Your Voice

What is a real voice? It is the voice we use when we are being genuine and true to ourselves. To discover this voice, we first figure out who we are and what of our life story can be shared with others. Our potential to affect and influence others emerges from this act. In fact, as the author John Barth noted, "The story of your life is not your life. It is your story."[3]

To be an effective storyteller, you need to be adept at using words to tell stories that demonstrate goals. To make an impression that lasts, you'll want to share the history and motivations of your life, because you convey your identity and beliefs as you do so.[4] Because one of the speaker's tasks is to instill, describe, and communicate a vision, your success depends upon your ability to tell stories that capture your essence, create meanings, and shape others' expectations—motivating their positive response. If you can use words and narration that resonate with receivers, helping them to imagine new perspectives, then you have a valuable tool in facilitating your personal connection with others.[5]

24.1b Give Voice to Your Goals

Whether our goal is to share knowledge, inspire, remind others of the past or prepare them for the future, build credibility, or enhance brand recognition, the stories we tell help determine our success.

Storytelling is perhaps the most significant act anyone hoping to influence others can perform. Being able to translate thoughts and ideas into words that others understand and respond to is an essential speaking skill. Through the stories you tell, receivers reflect on experiences designed to capture their hearts and minds, or as executive coaches Richard Maxell and Robert Dickman assert, "A story is a fact, wrapped in an emotion that compels us to take an action that transforms our world."[6] Stories engage and inspire audiences. They help you shape the reality you seek others to imagine.

For example, if your goal were to convince your audience to take action against bullying, you might consider sharing with them the tragic story of two girls, ages 12 and 14, who were charged with committing a felony—aggravated stalking—because of their relentless bullying of another 12-year-old girl. The target of their bullying, Rebecca Sedwick, ultimately committed suicide by jumping off a tower.[7]

24.1c Use a Narrative to Frame Your Goals

A *narrative* describes what people are doing and why. It is an organized story of a sequence of events, characters or agents, a thesis or theme, and an outcome. Narratives enable you to personalize your speech's message, provide it with a frame, and reveal an outcome that offers a lesson we can learn from. Such stories reveal your perspective. We all present events in a way that suits our personal interests.

To influence others with a story, first reflect on the purpose(s) you want your story to serve. Consider how to reach and tap into the experiences of those whom you seek to influence, how you can build connections that impart information, facilitate learning, and spark the insights you desire.

Five key elements give a story legs.

1. A good story reflects your passion or a sense of purpose, rallying others to participate with you in creating a better future.
2. A good story supplies a source of conflict—something (or someone) that everyone is able to agree threatens the future.
3. A good story offers up a hero or protagonist who will conquer the villain or offer a solution to the problem.
4. A good story creates an awakening in the hero and audience—an "aha" moment—one that, once taken to heart, will make the world a better place.
5. And a good story reveals a need for change or an opportunity for transformation.

Let's try it. Pick one of the following story starters, and use it to tell a story from your experience that will teach others a lesson you learned. Tell us who the hero and villain are, describe them and the situation they face, explain the conflict, and reveal the solution or "aha" moment and its impact.

© iStockphoto.com/lmgorthand

Grandma's house. Stories can help personalize your speech and make it more memorable for your audience.

- Once upon a time . . .
- I'll never forget the first time . . .
- It was the scariest day of my life . . .
- It was the best day of my life . . .
- When I was growing up, my (grandma, grandpa, mom, dad, sister, brother, best friend) told me . . .
- What if . . . ?[8]

After telling your story and actively listening to the stories others tell, reflect on how the experience enhanced your awareness and understanding of self and others. According to Peter Senge, when people understand one another, it is easier for a commonality of direction to emerge.[9] By sharing stories, we are able to see through each other's eyes.

24.1d Remember That Timing Matters

When telling a story, timing matters. When you tell the right story at the right time, it's as though your words and actions are magical, causing others to respond to and follow you, taking your words to heart. Two examples come to mind:

First, picture this. Soon after the terrorist attacks of September 11, 2001, president George W. Bush traveled to Ground Zero in New York City. Handed a bullhorn, the president stood on a pile of rubble, placed his arm around a fireman, and addressed the crowd. That image is implanted in the minds of those who experienced it in person or via the media. It represented the right story at the right time, offering the public a protagonist who was set on conquering those who attacked the United States.

Then, picture the following. President Bush now is standing on the deck of a Navy aircraft carrier wearing a flight jacket, declaring the war against Iraq over and claiming victory. Though this story also was compelling and has shown its staying power, we learned soon after the president's appearance on the carrier that it was far too early for the leader to be telling this story. The hero had not yet vanquished the enemy. The war would endure for many years more.

When a speaker tells the wrong story or tells a story at the wrong time, it causes us to pause, question the speaker's performance, and look elsewhere for inspiration.[10]

24.1e Lead With Stories

What kinds of stories do effective speakers tell? According to Stephen Denning, stories can spark action, reveal who the speaker is, transmit ideas, communicate the nature of the speaker's cause, share knowledge, and lead the audience into the future. For example, if your goal is to spark action, you might tell a story describing a successful change, yet leave room for the listener to imagine. You might even say, "Just imagine . . . " or "What if . . . ?" If your objective is to share knowledge, your story might focus on a mistake made, how it was corrected, and why the solution was effective. Those listening to you will benefit from thinking, "We'd better look out for that too."[11]

By using and telling stories others identify with, you engage receivers, inspiring them to accept your message, follow your lead, and act.

section
24.2 Use Language to Connect

- 24.2a Develop Language Sensitivity
- 24.2b Keep It Simple
- 24.2c Strategize About Word Choices
- 24.2d Use Word Pictures
- 24.2e Repeat/Repeat/Repeat
- 24.2f Speak of "I" and "We"
- 24.2g Generate Involvement and Participation

When worded effectively, stories cement speaker–audience connection. When ineffectively worded, however, they precipitate questions and concerns threatening to sever those ties. Should this occur, you are left to clean up the mess made with words.

To be effective and enhance your ability to inspire, heighten your sensitivity to language. Choose words that (1) add vividness and force to ideas, (2) steer others toward your goal, and (3) strengthen a positive image among audience members. Language should function as a credibility enhancer. Your words can help others perceive you as confident and trustworthy or cause them to question your competence and confidence. Though there is no set formula that will ensure your storytelling success—we can't tell you to add two similes, one metaphor, a moving illustration, and a startling example to a presentation to get others to accept your ideas—we can review some of the language tools at your disposal and how to use them in the stories you tell.

24.2a Develop Language Sensitivity

Avoid using words or expressions that insult, anger, demean, or devalue others. Calling others derogatory names, intimidating them, or using profanity typically produces negative outcomes. For example, calling environmentalists "tree huggers" or labeling people with conservative social and political values "country club fat cats" could reflect badly on a speaker among those who disagree with his or her assessment.

You would also be wise to avoid using clichés—words or phrases that at one time were effective but due to overuse have now lost their impact. For example, asking others to "think outside of the box" has now become cliché; it would be better to ask receivers to view the situation from an alternative perspective.

AP Photo/Shizuo Kambayashi

Short and sweet. Don't complicate your message with complex, intricate, and confusing language.

24.2b Keep It Simple

When insecure, speakers fall back on complex language. The most effective ones, however, forsake "word armor" or speech that cloaks thought or appeals to narrow audiences. Clear speakers use focused and jargon-free language and short sentences.

24.2c Strategize About Word Choices

Remember that audience members are not walking dictionaries. Avoid using words that confuse and alienate. Most will respond to the connotative or subjective meaning of words, not their denotative or dictionary meanings. So recognize the feelings and personal associations that your words might stimulate in others. This enables you to control the perceptions, conceptions, and reflections of receivers so you can steer them toward the response you desire.

24.2d Use Word Pictures

Visionary stories—stories that paint a compelling picture of what things will look and feel like in the future—are powerful and motivating. You can harness visionary language by using metaphors. According to **framing theory**, when we compare two unlike things in a figure of speech, the comparison influences us on an unconscious level. The metaphor causes us to make an association. Change the metaphor and you change how others think about the subject.[12] Complex metaphors form the basis for narratives or stories. For example, one student compared Twitter to a tracking device when speaking about the hidden dangers of the service:

Worth a thousand words. Invoking visionary language through metaphors will help your audience make strong connections.

> Using Twitter is an easy way to share information and thoughts. Sounds harmless, doesn't it? I don't think it is harmless. Like GPS, Twitter is one big tracking device. Hit the tweet button on websites, and Twitter knows what websites you visit. Tweet a link or share what you like via Twitter, and Twitter knows who you follow, your location, and what you usually tweet about.

24.2e Repeat/Repeat/Repeat

Ideas fight for attention. They rarely get through the first time. They rely on restatement and repetition. The more you repeat an idea, the more receivers remember it. One of the most famous examples of successful use of repetition is the speech Martin Luther King Jr. delivered in 1963 at the Lincoln Memorial:

> I say to you today, my friends, so even though we face the difficulties of today and tomorrow, I still have a dream. It is a dream deeply rooted in the American dream. I have a dream that one day this nation will rise up, live out the true meaning of its creed: "We hold these truths to be self-evident: that all men are created equal." . . .
>
> I have a dream that my four little children will one day live in a nation where they will not be judged by the color of their skin but by the content of their character. I have a dream today. . . .
>
> I have a dream that one day every valley shall be exalted, and every hill and mountain shall be made low, the rough places shall be made plain, and the crooked places shall be made straight, and the glory of the Lord will be revealed, and all flesh shall see it together.[13]

Because of the repetition of "I have a dream," the speech has a rhythm that enhanced its memorability and staying power.

24.2f Speak of "I" and "We"

"I" language finds you taking responsibility for or ownership of your story. You assume responsibility for your thoughts, feelings, and actions. **"We" language** indicates shared responsibility.

For example, one student speaking about how to respond when you see someone being bullied told the story of freshman goalie Daniel Cui, who was publicly bullied on Facebook in 2011 after allowing the winning goal in a soccer game. But Cui's teammates rallied behind him, posting a photo of him making a winning save in another game. The student told the audience, "We can make the difference. We can't be bystanders to another's bullying. We need to fight back. We can't let the bullies have the last word."

By using "we" language, you build a collaborative climate—a kind of "We're in this together" story. When receivers feel this sentiment, they won't forget it.

24.2g Generate Involvement and Participation

A speaker who creates an emotionally charged event captures our interest. Inviting participation accomplishes this. When you connect with audience members, they are more likely to become involved. When you also ask them to do something during your presentation, their engagement increases.

For example, here's how one student used audience participation to demonstrate the prevalence of lying:

> How important is honesty to you? Let's conduct a class survey to find out. I'd like to start with everyone on his or her feet, so please stand up. I'm going to ask some questions now. If you answer "yes" to any question, please sit down and remain seated.
>
> Have you ever had to lie or cheat?
>
> According to an NBC poll on lying, some 39 percent of those surveyed reported that they never had to lie or cheat. I wonder if they were telling the truth.
>
> Have you lied to anyone in the past week?
>
> According to the NBC poll, only 25 percent of those surveyed admitted having told at least one lie in the past week. I wonder if they understood the question.
>
> Do you think that you can ever justify lying to another person?
>
> According to the NBC poll, 52 percent of those surveyed believe that lying can never be justified.
>
> Have you ever lied to someone to avoid hurting his or her feelings?
>
> The NBC poll reveals that 65 percent of those surveyed have done just that.
>
> Look around. How many members of our class are still standing?[14] What does that tell us about the role lying really plays in our lives?

The speaker drew receivers in by asking them questions that physically involved them in the speech. The speaker's visual depiction of the prevalence of lying added impact to the speaker's message.

GAME PLAN

I Know a Story Is a Good One When . . .

- ☐ It is delivered in simple language and is easy to understand.
- ☐ It contains rich visual imagery.
- ☐ The goal of the speech is easy to discern.
- ☐ The goal of the speech is delivered in compelling language.
- ☐ The speech engages listeners and encourages them to be involved and participate.

Exercises

STORYTELLING

Though we have told stories to our families, friends, and teachers all our lives, we can become better at telling them to members of different audiences—especially those we hope will follow our lead. The following activities prepare you to do that.

1. Your Day

Pair up with a partner and prepare a short outline that describes a day in your life. Instead of merely listing your schedule of events, tell a story about them. Using the guidelines from this chapter, describe in detail what you had hoped to accomplish, whom you worked with, what you did to motivate or energize yourself and them, and how you felt about the results achieved at day's end.

2. Unifying Metaphors

Suppose you had to give a speech on what it means to think globally. First, identify the specific points you would make in your talk. Next, identify a unifying metaphor, explaining how you will use it to relate to the audience. Last, choose three additional language tools and describe how you will integrate them into the five ingredients of a story.

3. Analyze the Speech: What Separates Us From Chimpanzees

View Jane Goodall's speech "What Separates Us From Chimpanzees" on TED Talks. Focus on Goodall's use of props, sound effects, and stories in the speech.

1. How did Goodall establish a connection with the audience?
2. What purpose do you think that Goodall's imitation of a chimpanzee's voice served?
3. To what extent, if any, did Goodall's integration of stories influence your reaction to the speech?

4. Approach the Speaker's Stand

According to Marshall Ganz, an expert on public policy at Harvard's John F. Kennedy School of Government, a social movement emerges as a result of the efforts of purposeful actors who assert new public values, form new relationships rooted in those values, and mobilize followers to translate the values into action by telling a new story.[15]

For example, in 1962 Rachel Carson published *Silent Spring,* a book that is widely acknowledged to have launched the American environmental movement. Craft a speech that focuses on a story about a movement of your choice in one of the following ways:

- Make your story a story of *self:* a moment when you or someone else faced a challenge
- A story of *us:* a story that expresses shared values
- A story of *now:* a story articulating an urgent challenge that demands immediate action

RECAP AND REVIEW

1. **Identify stories from your life to share when giving talks to others.** Finding your authentic voice and sharing stories that motivate others to join you in seeking a goal will make you a more effective speaker and help you bring about the transformations you seek.
2. **Explain the ingredients integral to a story.** Stories reflect the speaker's passion or sense of purpose. They supply antagonists or villains that threaten the future. They offer up heroes or protagonists who offer solutions. They create an awakening or "aha" moment. They reveal a need for change or a transformation opportunity.
3. **Demonstrate ability in using a variety of language tools.** Effective storytellers have language sensitivity. They make strategic word choices, use word pictures or figures of speech, understand the value of repetition and restatement, employ both "I" and "we" language, and generate audience involvement and participation.
4. **Create narratives that motivate and involve others.** Stories make words memorable. They challenge us to make the speaker's dream of the future a reality.

KEY TERMS

Framing theory 437

"I" language 438

Storytelling 433

"We" language 438

© iStockphoto.com/Chris Schmidt

25

Speaking in College Courses

UPON COMPLETING THIS CHAPTER'S TRAINING, YOU WILL BE ABLE TO

1. Discuss dimensions of presenting orally in courses across the curriculum
2. Adapt oral presentations to specific educational contexts and audiences
3. Prepare and deliver a report on a professional or scholarly article, poster presentation, position presentation or debate, and service learning or internship report

The skills needed to speak in a public speaking course share much in common with the skills needed to speak before any audience. In academic settings, students are often given assignments in which they must develop a topic and communicate findings to their instructors and fellow students. In every class in which an oral presentation is assigned, students need to define the purpose of the assignment, the professor's expectations, and their fellow students' needs. Not much different from giving a speech in speech class, is it?

COACHING TIP

"There is no such thing as presentation talent; it is called presentation skills."

—David JP Phillips

This book gives you the skills you need to speak well and purposefully in every course, not just speech class. Use these skills to your advantage. Apply your skills across the curriculum and you expand your reach. Presentation skills make a difference.

Contents

section
25.1

Presenting Across the Curriculum

25.1a Communicate Your Ideas to Others

25.1b Pay Attention to Context

Speech class offers you numerous opportunities to practice presenting to an audience. However, such a course probably is not the only college course in which you will give oral presentations.

25.1a Communicate Your Ideas to Others

Oral presentations are a staple in many courses across the college curriculum. Engineering students are expected to present their designs. Art students are expected to explain their approaches to a piece and critique the work of others. No matter your major, it is important for you to be adept at communicating your ideas to your peers.

25.1b Pay Attention to Context

Class presentations strike a happy balance. They tend to be less formal than public speeches but more formal than daily conversations. Class audiences tend to be more homogenous than public audiences because receivers usually have a knowledge base similar to that of the presenter. It is probably safe to assume that your classmates have retained the information covered in the course to date, but beyond that it is still wise to double-check your receivers' level of understanding. Some members of the audience will match your expertise, others will surpass it or not measure up, and others will have no special expertise at all.

Although you will speak less formally before an audience of your peers than to a general audience, demonstrating your respect for everyone present remains essential.

© iStockphoto.com/kristian sekulic

You cannot hide. No matter your field, communicating with others and presenting your ideas well are essential skills to develop.

Speaking Assignments in Every Course

section **25.2**

The nature of the presentations assigned to you in courses other than speech class may involve alternative topics and formats such as reviewing a scholarly or professional article, delivering a poster presentation, debating a stance on a controversial issue, or reporting on a service learning or internship experience.

25.2a Review a Scholarly or Professional Article

Part of the learning process in any college course is to become conversant in the scholarly and professional literature of the field. Sometimes, an instructor will assign a student to read and review an article in class. To do so, follow this outline:

- ☐ Introduce the article by identifying its author(s), title, the issue, date, and pages of the journal in which it appeared. Next, summarize its purpose, the thesis, or hypothesis it advanced, and your understanding of the author's theoretical perspective.
- ☐ Describe the research methods the author(s) used, identifying subjects, instruments, and procedures.
- ☐ Discuss findings, specifying what the author(s) concluded and the implications of the conclusions drawn.
- ☐ Evaluate the article, summarizing its weaknesses, strengths, and significance.
- ☐ Discuss the author's credibility based on the work completed and sources consulted, and the validity or reliability of the study.
- ☐ Explain how you and others can apply the article to your own lives.
- ☐ Offer suggestions for further research.

© iStockphoto.com/Chris Schmidt

20 percent of your grade. While perhaps a little less formal, a class presentation still necessitates following the other rules of speaking.

FIGURE 25.1
Sample Poster Layout

Conventional layout for a poster. Long panel at top center is title/author banner. Individual panels can be connected by numbers and arrows. Also, note the use of space between panels to achieve visual appeal.

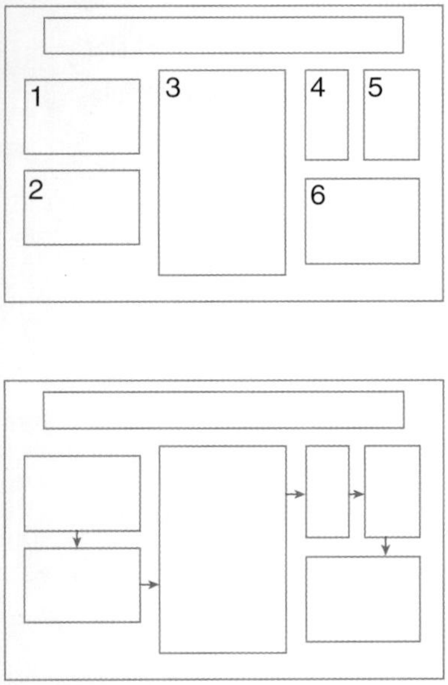

Source: Carol Waite Connor, "The Poster Session: A Guide for Preparation" (U. S. Geological Survey Open-File Report 88–667), 1992.

25.2b Deliver a Poster Presentation

A **poster presentation** is a graphical approach to presenting information. A poster shows and tells a story on virtually any subject.

When preparing a poster, simplicity is key. In poster text sections, headings should be bold and the body kept brief, with any text block typically not exceeding 50 words. Those looking at your poster should be able to read it from a distance of five feet. Thus, lettering should be at least 24 point with heads a minimum of 36 point. Use bold visuals to augment the text with two or three colors. Both the poster's text sections and visuals should be given titles.

The poster's layout should be visually creative. Open layouts help maintain interest. The poster should pull the viewer from its top to the bottom and from left to right. Text and visuals should be balanced with white (empty) space defining the information flow. Sample layouts appear in Figure 25.1.

Offer a short abstract to orient the poster viewer. On the poster, summarize your message clearly. Design the poster to cut through jargon and get at the heart of a topic—its central message. Objectives and main points should be crystal clear and well organized with graphs and images doing much of the work. The goal is to engage others in conversation about the poster. While you may have prepared a brief oral summary of your work, as others ask you questions about your poster, you may find yourself delivering what are actually a series of brief impromptu speeches. In fact, as you prepare the poster, it is good practice to anticipate the questions others might ask you.

When well prepared and presented, a poster fulfills one or more of the following objectives:

- It is a source of information.
- It begins a conversation.
- It advertises your work.
- It summarizes your work.

Use the following suggestions to guide you in creating and presenting a poster:

- ☐ Consider the message you want your poster to communicate before starting it.
- ☐ Give the poster a short but informative title.
- ☐ Keep the message focused and simple—identifying what the audience should come away knowing.
- ☐ Use a logical and easy-to-follow layout.
- ☐ Use headings to orient viewers and establish main points.
- ☐ Edit text judiciously.
- ☐ Emphasize graphics.
- ☐ Use color to attract and appropriate font sizes to make it easy to read.
- ☐ Prepare to discuss and answer questions about the poster by rehearsing.
- ☐ When presenting, explain your work succinctly, speaking clearly and establishing eye contact with receivers.

25.2c Present or Debate a Position

Position presentations and **debates** are also used across a variety of disciplines. Both call upon you to use your persuasive skills to argue an issue.

When giving a position presentation, you deliver a persuasive argument on a controversial issue. In a debate, two sides take turns presenting pro and con positions, with each side competing to win over the audience.

En garde. Be ready to both defend your side and attack the other in a debate.

The "pro" side of a debate is called the **affirmative side**. The role of the affirmative side is to support a resolution calling for change, such as: "Resolved: Congress should increase the inheritance tax." In contrast, the "con" or **negative side**, seeks to convince the judges and/or members of the audience that change is not needed, working to defeat the resolution and maintain the status quo.

Whether you are debating solo or as part of a team, your role is to develop and present arguments to support your stance. Throughout the course of a debate, you will have the opportunity to refute the arguments the opposing side presents. This phase—known as refutation—involves pointing out the flaws of the other side's arguments and rebuilding the arguments you presented yourself. This may require you to point out their errors in reasoning, demonstrate their use of weak evidence, and offer new evidence in support of your claims.

Think of a debate like a fencing match: You need to attack the other side while defending your own arguments and position. If you ignore an argument or error made by the other side, you weaken your ability to win. Thus, it is important to keep track of everything the other side says and every argument they put forth, being certain to effectively refute or weaken them.

To prevail in a debate, be sure to

- Present an organized speech.
- Communicate your passion for your position.
- Identify and present credible and convincing evidence in support of your side's position.
- Either tell the judges and receivers what they should decide or, if your position is an unpopular one, ask them to suspend judgment until hearing both sides' arguments.
- Stress your side's strong points.
- Emphasize the opposing side's weaknesses.
- Think quickly and creatively.

25.2d Report on a Service Learning or Internship Experience

Reporting on a service learning project or internship requires that you reflect on what you gained from participating in the experience.

When first engaged in **service learning**—a project that addresses a community or public agency need—or an internship, keep a weekly timetable and daily log of your experiences. Keep notes on the meetings you attended, conversations you had, challenges you faced, and any relevant interactions and relationships.

Begin by providing the audience with background information on the organization, agency, or group you served and your specific department or assignment in it. Then share your expectations going into the experience. Review the kinds of tasks you performed, telling stories about the nature of particular days as appropriate. Describe how the tasks affected you, explaining what you learned both personally and professionally, and reflecting on how your work contributed to the organization. End by sharing whether your expectations were fulfilled, identifying how you will apply new skills, qualifications, and understandings you were able to acquire during the experience, and offer your recommendations for future service learning volunteers or interns at the same site.

Because both service learning and internships are learning experiences, reflection and analysis play integral parts in your report for either.

GAME PLAN

Debating

- ☐ Whether or not I personally believe in the pro/con stance I've been asked to take, I've prepared to deliver an argument that is passionate in defending my assigned position.
- ☐ As part of my research, I have examined and read up on both sides of the issue. Doing so helps me prepare refutations.
- ☐ I've researched the opposing side's arguments to find flaws that expose the other side's weaknesses.
- ☐ I've practiced delivering a defense of the strongest points of my position.
- ☐ I've practiced my opening and closing statements.

Exercises

SPEAKING ACROSS THE CURRICULUM

Good presentations, whatever the course, can be informative, persuasive, and entertaining. Every presentation helps the audience think and learn. Participating in the following activities will help you develop the skills needed to present in different classes and to different audiences.

1. The List

Opportunities for oral assignments, group or individual, include more than podium speeches, especially in courses other than speech class. Identify courses you are currently taking in which you can apply the skills learned in this chapter. Be specific in detailing the skills learned that benefited you the most.

2. Student Observation

Observe a student delivering an oral presentation in a course other than speech. Note the following:

1. What was the course? What was the assignment?
2. How did the speaker approach the assignment?

Then, depending on the type of presentation the speaker completed, explain the extent to which the speaker succeeded in doing one or more of the following:

- Effectively provided the background of the scholarly article
- Presented a clear poster presentation
- Convinced or left you undecided by the debate
- Demonstrated the meaningfulness of the service learning or internship experience

3. Analyze the Speech

In this excerpt from a debate on the following question: "Should states repeal felon disenfranchisement laws?" the student taking the affirmative position offered the following argument.

SN 1 The speaker clearly states the affirmative position.

States should repeal felon disenfranchisement laws because having a right to vote is essential to the functioning of our democracy. Despite this, 6 million of our fellow American citizens have had that right taken away—many of them forever—because they have been found guilty of committing crimes and put in prison. In some states, more than 7 percent of the state's adult citizens have been disenfranchised in this manner—with a disproportionate number of them minorities. In Florida, Kentucky, and Virginia, 20 percent of African Americans cannot vote because of having formerly been convicted of a crime.

SN 2 The speaker uses statistics to explain the problem's magnitude.

According to Eric Holder Jr., attorney general of the United States, this system of disenfranchisement is both outdated and counterproductive. Here's why.

SN 3 The speaker references a credible source.

Once a convicted felon serves out a sentence, that person should be considered rehabilitated. Instead, in states with disenfranchisement policies, former convicts are stigmatized and isolated, which only increases the probability of their committing crimes in the future.

SN 4 The speaker explains the dangers of not supporting the affirmative position.

Additionally, disenfranchisement may be affecting the outcome of elections. Remember presidential elections can end up being decided by one states' voters. For example, when George W. Bush won the state of Florida by 537 votes in 2000, some attribute it to the fact that more than 800,000 Floridians who had criminal records were not allowed to vote.

In order not to undermine the citizenship of those who have paid their debt to society, and to preserve the integrity of our democracy, we need to make it easier for former convicts to regain the right to vote.

SN 5 The speaker closes the argument's presentation by affirming what is to be gained if receivers support it.

1. Do you think the student's argument was effective? Why or why not?
2. How do you imagine the negative side refuted the argument?

4. Approach the Speaker's Stand

Select and deliver a position statement on one of the following belief statements, or one of your own choosing:

- Anyone in the United States can make it if he or she works hard.
- Shakespeare is the most influential writer of all time.
- Actors are role models whether they want to be or not.
- A parliamentary system is a superior form of government.

RECAP AND REVIEW

1. **Discuss dimensions of presenting orally in courses across the curriculum.** Although oral presentations differ from class to class, you can apply the skills you have acquired in planning and preparing public speeches to presentations assigned in other classes.
2. **Adapt oral presentations to specific educational contexts and audiences.** Every audience is different, requiring different information and the application of a different skill set. Although some audiences you address will share your knowledge level, others will match it, surpass it, or not measure up.
3. **Prepare and deliver a report on a professional or scholarly article, poster presentation, position presentation or debate, and service learning or internship report.** One format differs from another, requiring you to master the requirements for each kind of presentation. Reviews need to be thorough, posters need to tell a cogent story, the arguments you use in a debate need to be persuasive, and in a service learning or internship report you need to demonstrate what you have accomplished and how you have profited from the experience.

KEY TERMS

Affirmative side 448

Debate 448

Negative side 448

Position presentation 448

Poster presentation 446

Service learning 449

SAGE edge™

Sharpen your skills with SAGE edge at edge.sagepub.com/gamblepsp2e.

SAGE edge for students provides a personalized approach to help you accomplish your coursework goals in an easy-to-use learning environment.

© iStockphoto.com/vm

26

Presenting Online

UPON COMPLETING THIS CHAPTER'S TRAINING, YOU WILL BE ABLE TO

1. Compare and contrast presenting online and off-line
2. Distinguish among online formats
3. Distinguish among online platforms
4. Develop and deliver an online presentation

Recording a presentation and posting it online extends its life—disconnecting it from time, place, and audience constraints. Online presentations also have the potential to reach a wider audience. Whether used during webinars, voice or video Internet conferences, or streamed events, recorded presentations are playing increasingly common roles in the digital and real world.

Contents

section

26.1

The Technological Difference

- 26.1a Technology-Dependent Delivery
- 26.1b Presentation Cues for Online Speeches

You need to plan, prepare, and deliver your online presentation, just as you would in person. Despite these similarities, the online format is distinct in several ways.

26.1a Technology-Dependent Delivery

Although face-to-face presentations may use technology to support the speaker's delivery, online presentations are totally dependent on technology for their delivery. The speaker must be trained in using the technology and the audience requires Internet connectivity and the skills to view and respond online.

The items on the following list constitute the equipment essential for creating online presentations. Both presenters and users must be proficient in understanding the technology and its requirements.

- A computer with sufficient memory
- A hard drive with sufficient space
- Recording and editing software
- Webcam, high-quality smartphone, or video camera
- A microphone
- A broadband Internet connection

26.1b Presentation Cues for Online Speeches

Video accentuates facial cues. As a result, the speaker needs to adjust as an actor might when transitioning from stage to television. Though live theater calls for larger gestures and exaggerated facial expressions, mediated screens call for more nuanced nonverbal expressions and require speakers to tone down their gestures and face work. To be considered genuine, body language in the virtual world should connect presenter and receiver without seeming forced or unnatural.

Comstock/Stockbyte/Thinkstock

Loud and clear. Having a firm grasp on technology is obviously essential for an online presentation but also for many other speeches.

Formats for Online Presentations

section 26.2

Like live presenters, online presenters have an array of formats to choose from, including but not limited to the single-speaker presentation (interactive or not), the panel presentation (moderated or not), the interview, and the digital story. No matter the content's nature or format, you will need to practice until you own the material and the technology.

26.2a Choose a Synchronous or Asynchronous Format

Online presentations can be streamed (presented live) or recorded and presented at a later time. Presentations delivered in real-time are **synchronous**. Presentations recorded and played back at another time are **asynchronous**. A synchronous webinar, like a face-to-face presentation, for example, allows for audience participation and questions, is conversational in tone and precipitates more of a connection between speaker(s) and receiver(s). As a result, synchronous online speakers are able to interact with and receive immediate feedback from their audiences, which can be a significant advantage. But there are also disadvantages. For example, the synchronous speaker has just one chance to achieve his or her goals. Once the webinar begins, the speaker cannot start over without adversely affecting his or her credibility with members of the audience. In addition, since a synchronous presentation is given at a set time, some members of the audience can be unavailable simply because the presentation begins very late or very early in their time zone.

In comparison, a talk delivered asynchronously has other challenges and benefits. One benefit is that audiences can view asynchronous presentations as many times as they want and whenever it is convenient for them to do so. For this reason, speeches delivered synchronously are sometimes saved and posted online. Another advantage is that the speaker has the ability to refine the final performance before it is released to the audience. The speaker can stop and start over as many times as needed to produce a polished final product without adversely affecting the speaker's credibility. Recording too many times, however, may result in the speaker appearing less natural to the audience. Similarly, the lack of immediate feedback and the loss of direct interaction between the speaker and audience are additional challenges associated with asynchronous presentations.

© iStockphoto.com/Rawpixel Ltd

Concerned with delivery? Like most speeches, you get one chance with a synchronous presentation, while an asynchronous one gives you multiple chances to nail your delivery.

26.2b When It's Just You

Like public presentations, online presentations may rely on a single speaker communicating content. When the camera is focused on a single person, it is essential to offer a compelling visual that won't distract your audience. Get ready for your close-up, and keep these suggestions in mind:

- ***Make sure you have good lighting.*** If the audience can't see you, they're less likely to absorb your message. Check that the light is bright and even.
- ***Present in front of a neat background.*** Consider what's behind and above you. A simple background is best.
- ***Wear colors, clothing, and jewelry that are technology friendly.*** Avoid loud clothing patterns. Blue is a safe color for the screen, while green can be tricky. Pastels and shades of brown are generally acceptable, but consider the color of your background, so you don't blend in. Avoid wearing jewelry that moves (like long earrings) or makes noise (such as bangle bracelets) to minimize distractions.
- ***Keep your energy up.*** Demonstrate your enthusiasm, but be sure to modulate your voice, pausing for emphasis.
- ***Refrain from fidgeting.*** Unnecessary movement can be distracting. If your whole body is on camera, gesture naturally. If you are sitting, gesture sparingly. If the chair you are seated in swivels, avoid spinning or switch to a chair that is stationary.
- ***Know where to look.*** Don't look up at the ceiling or down at your notes for more than a couple of seconds. Your eyes should not wander aimlessly. Look at the camera as if it is a person. When presenting online, the camera is your substitute audience.
- ***Avoid slideshow speak.*** Use photos, graphics, and video clips to capture and maintain interest, but don't read slides aloud. You should remain the key source of information.

Where's Waldo? Make sure that what the viewer sees online is clear and not distracting.

Most single-person online presentations are kept brief because of the tendency of the audience to become bored if the speaker delivers a monologue lacking in dynamism. As with face-to-face presentations, delivery matters.

26.2c When It's You With Others

Some topics benefit from having multiple speakers involved. Panel presentations find you and usually three to four others discussing a subject, with a moderator also present to ensure that you stay on topic and that no one member monopolizes the discussion. The moderator plays an important role. She or he is present to guide the conversation—not to outshine the participants. The best moderators have a good sense of pacing, making sure that no one panelist talks too long on any one aspect, redirecting when a panelist strays from the topic, weaving questions from the audience seamlessly into the conversation, and following up when appropriate by asking a more probing question.

The advantage of a panel is that different views are shared and commented upon. As with the single-speaker presentation, a panel presentation can be interactive and media rich or not. Synchronous online panels mirror their face-to-face counterparts. Software programs such as Adobe Presenter allow members of the audience to interact with the panelists by asking questions or providing commentary during or after each presentation. If the panel discussion will be recorded and shared, panels may request that the asynchronous audience email comments and questions to the presenters or moderator.

As with a solo online speech, consider the visual aspect of the presentation. Make sure the participants' apparel and manner, as well as the physical space, do not distract from the message.

26.2d When It's an Interview

Sometimes the delivery of information is made more interesting if one person questions or interviews another person about a preselected subject. Just as with face-to-face interviews, the online interview format works best when the interviewee is a credible source and the interviewer is well prepared. During interactive, synchronous interviews, audience members are sometimes able to submit questions they would like the interviewer to ask, often via email, Twitter, or text. Interviews conducted in a conversational manner usually appeal more to audience members than strictly Q&A interviews, and remember not to distract your audience from your message with your apparel or setting.

Video chat. Interviews online can be just as effective as in person, and multiple people can usually submit questions.

26.2e When It's a Digital Story

Storytelling is a powerful promotional tool. With technology, speakers can integrate audio, video, verbal content, and narration to create story-based presentations. Digital storytelling can highlight the importance of an event or communicate the essence of a particular individual. Featuring such a presentation on YouTube, LinkedIn, or on a personal website increases its reach.

To prepare a digital story, first outline the story's components, describing its plot, characters, setting, and theme or moral. Then prepare a storyboard or structured presentation blueprint detailing the audio, video, and any other illustrative support to be included to enhance dramatic interest. Consider using narrative infographics, which convey more information than typical stylized data presentations because they take full advantage of the capabilities of the visual medium, including its capacity for animation.[1]

A special kind of digital story is a digital portfolio. A digital portfolio is designed to showcase or market you, demonstrating your skills and highlighting what you can do. It is particularly helpful in interviewing and other competitive situations. Among the contents of your digital portfolio might be a discussion of who you are, what you hope to accomplish professionally, successes you have experienced, the best thing about working with you, sample reports you are proud of, a training session you designed and/or conducted, and sample letters or testimonials of recognition or praise—all reinforcing and building your personal brand.

COACHING TIP

"Whether speaking online or face to face, the best way to sound like you know what you're talking about is to know what you're talking about."

—Author unknown

Prepare yourself! Though presenting a speech online doesn't change the basics of speechmaking, you now also need to adapt to the demands of whatever technology platform you use. Choose your platform based on its ability to support your presentation goals and keep your audience engaged.

Online Platforms for Presenting

section **26.3**

Among the online platforms you should be familiar with are video, podcasts, webinars, and PowerPoint or other graphical presentation software. Let us look at each in turn.

26.3a Video

A well-made or well-chosen video adds impact to a presentation. A site like YouTube is populated with a plethora of presentations including how-to speeches, political statements, civic appeals, and tributes, ranging from amateur videos produced using webcams or cell phones to professionally-produced presentations created using high-definition digital video equipment. Both unsophisticated and sophisticated videos can go viral and spread rapidly across the Internet.

As we have discussed, video can be used successfully for presentations involving any number of people. The greater the number of people involved, however, the more complex the shoot. Users may record directly from a video camera or webcam or use programs such as Vimeo and Panopto, which can record the presentation directly from a computer or other device that has a video camera. Such programs are designed to capture the user as well as what appears on a computer screen, making it easy to incorporate video and other visuals or provide voice-over. Once the recording has been completed, the user can save the file and upload it to YouTube or another distribution platform to share with others.

26.3b Podcast

When video is unavailable, unaffordable, or unnecessary, the online presenter(s) may rely solely on audio for message delivery. A popular audio format is called a **podcast**, a digital audio recording that is made accessible online. The Library of Congress, iTunes, and Stitcher are three of many podcast repositories. Podcasts can feature a single speaker, two speakers, perhaps using the interview format, or a panel. Most news organizations, such as National Public Radio, offer podcast versions of their programs for download. Following this model, you might create a podcast that the members of your class can download. Speakers presenting via podcast can use a script or speak extemporaneously.

Podcasts are relatively easy to create, requiring only a computer with a built-in or plugged-in microphone, free audio-recording software such as Audacity, the ability to save the recording as an audio file or mp3, and a website from which it can be downloaded.

You might also make the podcast part of your rehearsal regimen. Simply record one of your rehearsal sessions, send it to a few friends and family members, and solicit their feedback.

26.3c Webinar

A **webinar** is a conference held online that is viewable by invited guests with a Web connection. Though initially delivered synchronously, webinars can also be saved for later viewing. Webinars can present a single speaker, panel, or group collaborating in real time across time zones. They are especially useful for training seminars when participants are geographically dispersed. An advantage of a webinar is that the facilitator or presenter can obtain feedback from participants, respond to questions, and adjust the webinar content and presentation during the session.

For your presentation you need access to a webinar hosting platform such as GoToMeeting that will provide a Web link or phone number for audience members to use to access the event. Most webinar software also allows you to show slides, incorporate videos, and moderate audience participation. Creating a chat window for participants or encouraging participants to share, tweet, or blog reactions during the online event fosters engagement. Periodically integrating polls, chats, and instant feedback increases interactivity while also letting you gauge the pulse of the remote audience.

© iStockphoto.com/aydinynr

Come together. Webinars are a great way to hold classes online for people spread far apart.

26.3d PowerPoint/Graphical Presentation

Wisely used, slides help maintain a presentation's momentum and help the speaker move through his or her points smoothly. Online presenters often use more visual aids than live presenters in an effort to keep participants fully engaged. PowerPoint presentations can be synchronous or asynchronous. You can record a voice-over to accompany the slides that are saved and given to an audience. Speakers can also use PowerPoint live during the online presentation.

Though PowerPoint has become a presentation staple (sometimes overused in face-to-face presentations), it also may stand alone as a graphic-rich online presentation—with or without audio or video enhancements. Prezi (prezi.com), another Web-based resource for creating dramatic online graphic presentations, offers a free basic version that is easy to use. Many graphical platforms offer user tutorials.

Prezi.com

Text overload. When using PowerPoint or a similar program, be sure not to overwhelm your audience with heavy text paragraphs on your slides.

GAME PLAN

Preparing for a Webinar Presentation

- ☐ I've identified the format for my webinar.
- ☐ I've organized my information to fit the time constraints.
- ☐ I've planned for interactivity and a means by which audience members can ask questions or respond to a poll.
- ☐ I've prepared visuals to integrate into the webinar.
- ☐ I've prepared an introduction for myself and any other presenters.
- ☐ I've prepared an explanation of how a webinar works, its interactive nature, and how the audience can participate by asking questions.
- ☐ I've rehearsed and held dry runs prior to holding the webinar.
- ☐ I've made a plan to record the webinar to make it available for those unable to participate in real time.

Exercises

PRESENTING ONLINE

Developing your understanding of online presentations and the skills needed to present online will increase your breadth and depth as a speaker.

1. Know What You Need

Using the equipment list in Section 26.1, review the technology available to you. Explore the equipment in your classroom and the media center. Does your classroom feature a Smart Board? If not, does it have a projector and screen? Is there a DVD player? Can you easily stream video? Do you have whatever cables are required or do you need to have them delivered from the media center?

Troubleshoot technology well before you present. Try to anticipate anything that can go wrong during your presentation. The goal is to solve a potential problem before it presents itself.

2. Know Your Options

Explore and discuss the merits of various media platforms or software for the following formats:

- Podcasting: SoundCloud versus iTunes
- Video sharing: YouTube versus Vimeo
- Webinars: GoToMeeting versus WebEx

3. Analyze This

View an online presentation of your choosing, such as a how-to video on YouTube, a TED Talk, or a training video for software. Using a 10-point scale ranging from 1 (totally ineffective) to 10 (totally effective) and the following criteria, evaluate the selected speech or presentation:

1. Adaptation of content for online platform ________
2. Adaptation of speaker to online platform ________
3. Speaker's ability to sustain interest ________
4. Organization of presentation ________
5. Language ________
6. Timeliness of content ________
7. Integration of audio, video, graphical support ________
8. Speaker's physical and vocal delivery ________
9. Quality of recording ________
10. Overall effectiveness ________

4. Approach the Speaker's Stand

Prepare and post online a how-to speech on a technology topic such as "How to Prepare a Podcast" or "How to Post a Video Online." Each speech should include the following steps:

1. Identification of equipment required
2. Review of software and platform used
3. Clear instructions on preparation and presentation
4. Anything more you believe necessary

RECAP AND REVIEW

1. **Compare and contrast presenting online and offline.** Online presentations have fewer time, place, and audience constraints than face-to-face speeches, as well as the potential to reach a global audience. An online speech is dependent on technology and the speaker must be aware of his or her facial and body language cues.
2. **Distinguish among online formats.** Among popular online formats are the single presenter, the panel of presenters, the interview, and digital storytelling. Online speeches can be presented live or be prerecorded.
3. **Distinguish among online platforms.** The most popular online platforms regularly used for presentations include video, podcasts, and webinars.
4. **Develop and deliver an online presentation.** Online presentations require many of the same skills, abilities, and preparation as presentations made before live audiences. However, the online presenter must also be versed in the demands and requirements of the technology being used.

KEY TERMS

SAGE edge™

Sharpen your skills with SAGE edge at edge.sagepub.com/gamblepsp2e.

SAGE edge for students provides a personalized approach to help you accomplish your coursework goals in an easy-to-use learning environment.

27

Answering Questions

UPON COMPLETING THIS CHAPTER'S TRAINING, YOU WILL BE ABLE TO

1. Explain the purpose of the question-and-answer (Q&A) session
2. Determine how best to schedule a Q&A session
3. Use guidelines to manage the Q&A session

The question-and-answer (**Q&A**) session plays an integral role in most business and professional talks. It can be enjoyable as well as challenging. Q&A sessions give audience members a voice, affording them the opportunity to ask the speaker questions about his or her remarks and to share their reactions. From both the speaker's and the audience's perspectives, these are real advantages. The Q&A gives the speaker one more crack at winning over the audience and gives the audience another opportunity to assess the speaker's preparedness and expertise. For example, if a speaker's answers leave receivers confused or unconvinced, the speaker may lose ground. Thus, speakers need to be able to voice skillful responses to the questions audience members ask.

COACHING TIP

"Questions are great, but only if you know the answers."

—Laurell K. Hamilton

Be a mind reader! Anticipate the questions audience members will ask you after listening to your speech. Answer questions clearly and competently and receivers will conclude you were prepared, knowledgeable, and confident. Take control of the Q&A session. Keep your focus on the question asked you. Relate every question asked to your goal.

Contents

section

27.1 The Timing of the Q&A Session

At what point(s) during your talk should questions from the audience be asked and answered? Should they be asked before, during, or after your presentation? Should they be separate from or part of the presentation itself? The answer to each of these questions is, it depends.

27.1a Before Presenting

Sometimes a speaker solicits questions from the audience in advance, perhaps passing out note cards and asking potential receivers to jot down and submit questions they would like answered. Doing this prior to speaking lets the speaker adapt the talk so it covers the key concerns of receivers.

Other times, to demonstrate their expertise and confidence, speakers solicit questions personally from the audience at the outset of a presentation. If the speaker has prepared effectively, many of the questions asked will be ones the speaker anticipated, and he or she can assure receivers that all their questions will soon be answered.

Raise your hand. Getting questions from the audience prior to your speech can be an effective way to tailor the speech to the crowd's needs.

27.1b While Presenting

A speaker can also allow questions during a presentation. If you are giving a business presentation, for example, your boss may interrupt with a question at any point—and you likely have no choice but to stop and answer it. Although such questions may disrupt your presentation's flow, you can respond immediately to any concerns, which can keep receivers focused on your message instead of fixating on their objection. However, audience members may ask questions prematurely about points you intend to cover later. When this happens, you have a choice: You can answer the question, or you can tell the audience that you will answer it shortly if they will just be patient for a few moments. For example, you might respond, "Great question. In fact, I'm going to cover that in just a minute."

What if during your talk a listener raises an irrelevant question—one that could throw your presentation off track? When this happens, you need to take control, by reframing the question to focus on your goal. For example, if you were asked about the effects of diet on childhood diabetes during a speech on Type II diabetes, you could reframe the question noting, "Childhood diabetes is Type 1 diabetes; diet, however, is also consequential for Type II diabetes. . . . "

27.1c After Presenting

Questions can also be held until the presentation's end. This has a number of benefits:

- You control how and when you share your presentation's content.
- You avoid being distracted by poorly timed or irrelevant queries.
- You avoid the objection-finder or rude questioner whose goal it is to demonstrate how much she or he knows and focus attention on her- or himself.
- It helps ensure you will complete your talk on time.
- It helps audience members to focus on what you are saying, instead of being preoccupied with formulating questions while you speak—thereby missing key content.

This is not to suggest that saving questions to the end does not also have its drawbacks. Sometimes, for example, if a question occurs to you as an audience member, you find it difficult to maintain your concentration on what the speaker is saying. Another drawback has to do with how receivers remember—or the **primacy-recency factor**. We tend to remember what we hear first and last—losing much of the middle over time. Thus, saving questions to the end makes it more likely receivers will remember how you answered a question, rather than the points you made during your talk.

section 27.2

Managing the Q&A

Whenever questions are asked, they can pose challenges for you. Some questions may attack your position. Others may be stated so poorly that you have difficulty understanding them. And others may be completely off topic. Whatever their nature, by giving the questioner your full attention while she or he is speaking, and following these guidelines, you will be able to handle most questions posed.

27.2a Anticipate Questions—Especially Hard Ones

Empathy is a speaker's ally. Being able to put yourself in the shoes of audience members will enable you to look at your presentation through their eyes and anticipate questions they will likely ask. For example, what aspects of your remarks might they find confusing? Which might they find objectionable? Which of your points might they like to know more about? Preparing your responses to potential questions is just as important as preparing the presentation itself.

27.2b Don't Pontificate

Every question deserves an answer that demonstrates your respect for the questioner. An answer should never be a put-down. If you belittle or embarrass a questioner, even if the question she or he posed was demeaning, hostile, or has an answer obvious to many in the audience, you lose. Instead of pontificating and attempting to one-up the questioner, work to build support by taking the question seriously and answering politely. You might even offer the questioner a compliment: "I understand why you find this point troublesome. We did too. However, the more we researched, the more evidence we uncovered that told us we were on the right track. Let me share some of that evidence with you."

27.2c Understand Every Question Asked

Rather than multiply confusion, **paraphrase** each question asked you to confirm you understand. "What I hear you asking is . . . Am I correct?" In addition to uncovering if you "get the question," or heard it correctly, restating a question in your own words also helps you provide a frame or context for the question that makes it easier for you to answer and easier for the audience to understand.

27.2d Give Audience Members the Green Light

Adhere to protocol when fielding questions: The first hand up or first question submitted should be the first you answer. But be prepared. Audience members sometimes hesitate to ask questions, fearing asking a question that you or others might consider stupid. Let receivers know that there is no such thing as a stupid question. Help them understand that you hope they will ask questions because your goal is to ensure their understanding. If they still hesitate, ask yourself a question you believe they might want answered, saying something such as "A question you probably have is . . . ." Receivers will be pleased you opened the channel.

27.2e Stay on Course

When off track, a question can sidetrack you and your talk, defeating your purpose for speaking. Instead of being drawn off target, respond to every question in a way reflective and supportive of your ultimate goal. You might say, "Let me approach the question this way . . . ." If the questioner objects, agree either to meet with the questioner later to discuss the issue or promise to send him information clarifying your position.

27.2f Think Through Your Answer

Use caution, pausing before answering a question, especially a question you find particularly challenging. First, repeat or paraphrase the question asked, and then ask the questioner how she or he might answer the question him- or herself. If needed, you might also defer to another audience member prior to responding yourself. If you don't know or can't come up with a good answer, don't bluff or say "No comment." Simply respond, "That's a question I would like to look into. Let me have your contact information, and I will get back to you."

Control the traffic. What methods can you use to manage hostile and inappropriate questions while maintaining a healthy dialogue?

27.2g Keep Defensiveness at Bay

Some members of the audience may ask you questions that you don't like. If this happens and you are asked a hostile question, don't be put off or get defensive. Maintain your composure, expressing your respect for the questioner, rephrasing the question more appropriately, and responding politely. This will earn you the respect of the audience.

27.2h Address Answers to Both the Questioner and the Audience

Though a specific individual asked you a question, address your answer to the entire audience. Make initial eye contact with the questioner, but then widen your gaze to encompass everyone in the room. This will connect you to the audience, keep everyone interested and involved, and make it less likely that the person asking the question will become hostile if she or he does not like your answer. It will also decrease the likelihood of the questioner trying to engage you in a one-on-one debate.

Graceful finish. Smoothly transition toward the end of the Q&A, and let the audience know you're coming to a close.

27.2i Gracefully Bring the Q&A Session to a Close

A Q&A session should not terminate without warning. Rather than ending abruptly, tell the audience when the Q&A session is about to end. You might say, "I will take two more questions, and then we will have to call it a day." Take the two questions, closing with a statement that reinforces your message: "It has been a pleasure spending time with you today. I'm glad for the opportunity to answer your questions. I appreciate your willingness to share your thoughts with me."

GAME PLAN

Prepping for a Q&A Session

- ☐ While preparing for and researching my speech, I kept a running list of my own questions, taking note of the ones that were left unanswered.
- ☐ I've reviewed my speech for potentially confusing language.
- ☐ I've reviewed all of my research and notes (even material that did not make it into my final draft), so I would have the information needed to answer potential questions.
- ☐ I've reviewed the guidelines in this chapter and have reserved enough time to conduct a Q&A session, confident in my ability to come up with reliable answers to questions asked.

Exercises

THE QUESTION-AND-ANSWER SESSION

Developing skill in handling the question-and-answer session helps build a speaker's comfort, expertise, and overall credibility. Maintaining composure while handling challenges and clearing up confusion helps receivers view you as confident, competent, and trustworthy. Completing these exercises will pave the way to a more productive Q&A.

1. Vital Questions

Select a recent TED Talk at www.ted.com. Imagine you are a member of the audience. What questions would you want to ask the speaker? Were you the speaker, how would you answer the questions you posed?

2. Anticipate and Prepare

The topic you have been assigned is "Mental Health in the National Football League." Develop a list of five questions to ask about the subject. After creating your five questions, prepare an information sheet containing details you could consult if asked any one of the five questions.

3. Analyze the Speech: The Interview

Search for a prerecorded interview with a person you admire—a scholar, politician, musician, artist, writer, or actor. Write down the names of the interviewer and interviewee, and assess the effectiveness of the questions asked by the interviewer and the responses given by the interviewee. To what extent did the interviewee do the following?

1. Have facts needed to answer the questions asked
2. Answer questions courteously
3. Display good will
4. Exhibit a lack of defensiveness
5. Acknowledge respect for the interviewer
6. Avoid answering impulsively
7. Communicate credibly

4. Approach the Speaker's Stand

Attend a presentation at your school. After listening to the speaker(s) present, ask at least one question plus a follow-up question. Using the questions in the previous exercise, critique the speaker's response to your questions. In a report to the class, share your evaluation, explaining your expectations about how the speaker ought to have answered. Role-play how you would have responded to one of the questions you posed.

RECAP AND REVIEW

1. **Explain the purpose of the question-and-answer (Q&A) session.** The purpose of the question-and-answer session is to clear up any confusion or misperceptions on the part of members of the audience. It is the also the speaker's final opportunity to demonstrate topic mastery and credibility.
2. **Determine how best to schedule a Q&A session.** Though usually held at the end of a presentation, the speaker may also field questions prior to or during a speech.
3. **Use guidelines to manage the Q&A session.** Effective speakers anticipate tough questions and adhere to certain guidelines when providing answers. They call on questioners in the order that hands were raised or questions were submitted and they don't shy away from answering difficult questions. Good speakers demonstrate their respect for questions. They think through questions to avoid inappropriate responses and keep defensiveness in check. They address answers to the questioner and the audience as a whole. They gracefully close the Q&A session.

KEY TERMS

Paraphrase 470

Primacy-recency factor 469

Q&A 467

SAGE edge™

Sharpen your skills with SAGE edge at edge.sagepub.com/gamblepsp2e.

SAGE edge for students provides a personalized approach to help you accomplish your coursework goals in an easy-to-use learning environment.

Glossary

Abstraction Something that is vague; language that is neither concrete nor specific

Affirmative side The pro side in a debate; the side speaking in support of a resolution calling for change

After-dinner speech A speech that is relevant to the occasion and designed to entertain

Ageist language Language that discriminates on the basis of age

Alliteration Repetition of the initial consonant sounds in nearby words

Antithesis The presence of opposites within the same or adjoining sentences; the juxtaposition of opposing ideas

Argument *ad hominem* Name-calling; the use of offensive and insulting words to win an argument

Articulation The act of producing individual sounds

Asynchronous presentation An online presentation that is recorded and then viewed at another time

Attending The listening stage during which an individual selects to pay attention to one or more specific aural stimuli

Attitude A mental set or predisposition to respond to something favorably or unfavorably; a readiness to respond positively or negatively

Audience analysis The systematic identification of the demographic and psychographic characteristics of an audience to determine member interests and motivation

Bandwagon appeal An appeal to popular opinion

Bar graph A type of graph used to compare or contrast two or more items or groups

Behavioral objective A desired specific speech outcome; a desired observable and measurable audience response

Belief That which one holds to be true or false, probable or improbable

Body of the speech That portion of the speech made up of and elaborated by the speech's main points

Brainstorming A system of idea generation devised by Alex Osborne

Briefing A short talk providing those with a stake in the outcome a summary of what has been done or still needs to be done to complete a project

Causal reasoning Reasoning that unites two or more events to prove that one or more of them caused the other

Causal transitions Transitions that help show the cause-and-effect relationships between ideas

Cause-and-effect order An organizational pattern in which information is categorized according to whether it is related to a problem's causes or effects

Centering The directing of thoughts internally via a deep or centering breath

Centering breath A deep breath followed by a strong exhalation

Central idea The topic statement of a speech

Channel A pathway through which a message passes

Chart A visual aid used to compress or summarize a large amount of information

Chronological order An organizational format based around time or the order in which things happen

Chronological transitions Transitions that help in understanding the time relationship between ideas

Claim An assertion made in arguing; a debatable conclusion

Closed-ended questions Highly structured questions requiring only that the respondent indicate which of the provided responses most accurately reflects his or her answer to a question

Closed question A highly structured question seeking a short and precise answer such as yes or no

Closure A technique designed to achieve psychological symmetry or balance; the speaker refers in the conclusion of a speech to the same ideas explored during the speech's beginning

Co-culture A group of people who share a culture outside of the dominant culture

Cognitive restructuring A technique designed to redirect thinking away from body sensations and irrational beliefs to beliefs that promote growth

Commencement address A speech given to a graduating class

Common ground The concerns and interests shared by the speaker and the audience

Communication A process that involves the attempted sharing of information; the means by which people generate meaning

Complementary transitions Transitions that help the speaker add one idea to the next

Computer-generated graphics The use of technology in creating graphics

Concrete A description attributed to words that evoke precise meaning; language that is free of jargon

Conclusion The ending of a speech; designed to reinforce the central idea or thesis, motivate an appropriate audience response, and achieve closure

Configural formats Listener-responsible organizational formats in which examples and stories carry the crux of a message

Connotative meaning Personal meaning; meaning that is subjective and variable

Contrasting transitions Transitions that show how the idea that follows differs from the ones that precede it

Coordinate points Points in an outline that are of equal weight or substance

Coordination The principle establishing that main points should be relatively equal in importance

Covert lie An unspoken lie; a lie designed to conceal sensitive information that needs to be said but isn't

Credibility Audience judgments of a speaker's competence, character, and charisma

Critical thinking The process of arriving at a judgment only after an honest evaluation of alternatives; the exhibiting of careful and deliberate evaluation of a claim

Cultural diversity The recognition and valuing of difference

Cultural identity The internalization of culturally appropriate beliefs, values, and roles acquired through interacting with members of a cultural group; a product of group membership

Culture The system of knowledge, beliefs, values, attitudes, behavior, and artifacts that the members of a society learn, accept, and use in daily life

Debate A form of argument in which two sides take turns presenting pro and con positions, with each side competing to win adherents

Decision-making group A group whose members seek a consensus regarding what the group should or should not do to solve a problem

Deductive reasoning Reasoning that takes a known idea or principle and applies it to a situation; reasoning that moves from the general to the specific

Deferred-thesis pattern A kind of configural format in which the main points of a speech gradually build to the speaker's thesis

Definitions Statements used to clarify the meaning of words and concepts

Demographic profile A composite of audience characteristics including age; gender; educational level; racial, ethnic or cultural ties; group affiliations; and socioeconomic background

Denotative meaning The dictionary meaning of a word

Derived credibility Audience perception of a speaker's credibility during the giving of a speech

Descriptions Words that evoke fresh imagery or sensory response

Dialect A speech pattern characteristic of a group of people from a particular area or of a specific ethnicity

Drawings and maps Visual aids used to illustrate differences, movements, or geographic information

Early concurrence The tendency to conclude discussion prematurely

Effects of communication Communication outcomes

Emblems Nonverbal symbols with direct translations that are culturally learned

Ethical communication Communication that presents ideas fairly; the revealing of information receivers need to assess both the message and speaker critically

Ethical speechmaking Speech that involves the responsible handling of information and an awareness of the outcomes or consequences of a speech

Ethics An exploration of how values distinguish actions; a society's notions about the rightness and wrongness of behavior

Ethnocentricity A belief that one's culture is better than others

Ethnocentrism Judging another culture solely by the standards of your own culture

Ethos The ability to convince the audience of your good character or credibility

Eulogy A special form of tribute speech that pays tribute to a deceased person, usually given at a gravesite or at a memorial service

Euphemism An indirect expression that makes it easier to handle unpleasant subjects

Evaluating The process of using critical thinking skills to weigh a message's worth

Event/person speech A speech designed around a remarkable person or compelling event

Evidence Material used to validate a claim

Expert testimony Testimony provided by sources recognized as authorities on the topic

Explanations Clarifying words

Extemporaneous outline An outline containing brief notes, also known as speaker notes, to remind the speaker of key parts of the speech and references

Extemporaneous speaking Speaking that is planned and rehearsed but delivered using only a few notes

Fact-finding group A group whose members share thoughts and information to enhance understanding and learning

False dichotomy A proposition that requires the audience to choose between two options when in reality there are many

False division A false division suggesting that if something is true of the whole, it is also true of one or more of the parts

Feedback Information received in response to a sent message

Field of experience The sum of all experiences; the attitudes, values, and lessons one brings to a situation

Figurative analogy An analogy comparing two things that are distinctively dissimilar

Figurative language Words that facilitate the picturing of meaning

Framing theory A theory focusing on the shaping of experience to promote an interpretation

General purpose The overall purpose of a speech, such as to inform, persuade, or entertain

Glittering generality The use of positive association designed to encourage idea acceptance

Graphs Visual aids that are designed to communicate statistical information, illustrate trends, and/or demonstrate patterns

Groupthink The tendency to let a desire for consensus override careful analysis and reasoned decision making

Hasty generalization The act of being too quick to draw an inference; jumping to a conclusion on the basis of too little evidence

Healthy group A group in which members support one another, make decisions together, trust one another, have open communication, and aim to excel

Hearing An involuntary physiological process

Heterogeneous audience An audience whose members possess dissimilar characteristics, rich in age, attitude, value, and knowledge diversity

High-context communication Communication that avoids confrontation; communication that relies on indirect messages

Homogeneous audience An audience whose members possess similar characteristics such as age, attitude, value, and knowledge similarity

Human visual aid The use of a real person as a visual or audio aid

Hyperbole Extreme exaggeration

Hypothetical examples Examples that have not actually occurred, but might

Idea/concept speech A speech given to explain or define something intangible or abstract

"I" language Language of responsibility and ownership

Illustrations Extended examples or narratives

Illustrators Gestures to reinforce, clarify, describe, and demonstrate the meaning of your words

Immediacy A sense of closeness

Impromptu speaking Speaking that is "off the cuff" and accomplished with little or no notice

Inductive reasoning Reasoning that relies on observation and specific instances to build an argument; reasoning progressing from specific observations to a conclusion

Infographic A composite of information, illustration, and design

Information overload Being given too much information to process or handle

Information underload Being given too little information; underestimating the amount of information needed

Informative speech A speech designed to impart new information, a new skill, or a fresh way of thinking about something

Initial credibility The receiver's perception of a speaker's credibility prior to his or her speaking

Internal preview A speech segment that helps the speaker hold a speech together by indicating what to look for as a speech progresses

Internal summary A speech segment that helps the speaker clarify or emphasize what was said

Interpreting A listening stage during which the focus is on meaning and the decoding of the speaker's message

Interview A meeting during which questions are asked and answered by both interviewer and interviewee

Introduction The opening of a speech; designed to capture the audience's attention, build credibility, orient receivers to what is to follow

Jargon and technospeak Types of specialized language clear only to people with specific knowledge

Keynote address A speech usually given at a conference and designed to generate enthusiasm for and commitment to a desired outcome

Kinesics The study of body language or human body motion, including gestures, body movements, facial expressions, eye behavior, and posture

Lay testimony Peer testimony, the opinions of "ordinary people"

Linear formats Speech formats by which the main points relate to the topic sentence

Line graph A graph that shows trends over time

Listening A voluntary mental process occurring in stages

Literal analogy An analogy comparing two things from similar classes

Logical fallacy A flawed reason

Logos Logical proof demonstrating the reasonableness of argument(s)

Low-context communication Communication that is direct and addresses issues head-on

Main points The central themes of a speech; the key ideas that serve as the outline's framework; the subtopics directly supporting the thesis

Maintenance leadership behaviors Roles focused on maintaining the group, including expressing agreement and support

Manuscript reading A speech in which the speaker delivers a written manuscript word for word

Marginalized group A group whose members feel like outsiders

Maslow's Hierarchy of Needs A pyramid progressing from the most basic to the most sophisticated human needs

Message The content of communication

Metaphor A direct comparison between two things or ideas

Monroe's Motivated Sequence An organizational framework particularly effective in moving receivers toward accepting and acting on a proposition of policy

Narrative An extended example or illustration; a story describing what people are doing and why

Narrative pattern A configural format in which the speaker tells a story or series of stories without stating a thesis or identifying main points

Negative side The side in a debate seeking to maintain the status quo

Noise Anything that interferes with the ability to send or receive a message

Object speech A speech about something tangible

One-sided presentation A presentation offering only a single perspective on an issue

Onomatopoeia A word or words that imitate natural sounds

Open-ended questions Questions allowing a respondent to answer fully and in his or her own words

Open question A question offering freedom in answering by calling for more than a one-word response

Outline A speech skeleton on which main ideas and support are hung

Overt lie A deliberate lie; a distortion of the facts

Paralinguistics The study of messages sent using vocal cues

Parallelism Words, phrases, or sentences that parallel or balance each other; repetition of words, phrases, or sentences

Paraphrase Restating material in your own words

Pathos The ability to develop empathy and passion in others

Peer testimony Testimony provided by lay or ordinary people who possess firsthand experience on a subject

Performance anxiety A variant of communication anxiety; fear of presenting a speech

Persuasion The deliberate attempt to change or reinforce attitudes, beliefs, values, or behavior

Pictograph A simplified infographic; a pictorial representation of a graph's subject

Pie graph A graph used to illustrate percentages of a whole or distribution patterns

Pitch The highness or lowness of the voice on a tonal scale; a voice's upward or downward inflection

Pitch, a A kind of persuasive or sales presentation during which the speaker attempts to obtain an endorsement for a proposal

Plagiarism The deliberate or accidental claiming of another's words or ideas as one's own

Podcast A digital audio recording accessible to Web users

Political correctness The act of using words that are polite and convey respect for the needs and interests of different groups

Position presentation A presentation in which the speaker delivers a persuasive argument on a controversial issue

Poster presentation A graphically based approach to presenting information or research

Post hoc ergo propter hoc A logical fallacy asserting that because one event preceded another, it caused it

Presentation aids Audio and visual stimuli that support and enhance speech content

Primacy-recency factor The tendency to remember information that is placed at the beginning and end of a speech better than the information that is placed in the middle of the speech

Primary question A question that introduces a topic or area for exploration

Primary research Original research involving the collection of firsthand data

Probing question A question that seeks more information

Problem–solution order An organizational format that divides information into two main parts, the problem and its solution

Process anxiety Fear of preparing a speech

Process/procedure speech A speech designed to convey how something works or how to do something

Pronunciation The accepted way to sound a word; identifying whether the production of the individual sounds used to form a word is correct

Proposition The relationship the speaker wishes to establish between accepted facts and his or her desired conclusions

Proposition of fact An assertion that something does or does not exist, is or is not true, or is or not of value; an effort to prove something factual

Proposition of policy A recommendation for change or no change; a type of persuasive speech focusing on what speaker thinks should be done

Proposition of value An assertion of a statement's worth; a type of persuasive speech rendering a judgment about something

Proxemics The study of space and distance in communication

Psychographics A description of values, beliefs, and interests, including how members of an audience see themselves, their attitudes, and motives

Public speaking anxiety A variant of communication anxiety, made up of process and performance anxiety

Q&A A question-and-answer session

Racist language Language discriminatory toward the members of a race; words that express bigoted views

Rate The speed at which words are spoken

Reasoning from analogy The process of comparing like things and concluding that because they are comparable in a number of ways, they also are comparable in another, new respect

Reasons approach The presentation of reasons to justify a speech's goal

Receiver The recipient of a message; a party to communication

Red herring A distraction; the process of leading the audience to consider an irrelevant issue

Reflective Thinking Framework A problem-solving system advanced by John Dewey

Refutation format The style of debate when one side points out the flaws in the other side's arguments and offers new evidence to support its own claim

Remembering The mental saving of a message for further use

Repetition Restatement of the exact same words

Report A summary of what you have learned or accomplished

Responding The process of replying and providing feedback

Restatement Rephrasing an idea in different words to more fully explain it

Rhetorical questions Questions requiring no overt answer or response

Risky shift A group phenomenon in which a group makes a decision that is riskier than an individual would make if working alone

Scaled questions Questions enabling respondents to indicate their views along a continuum or scale

Secondary question A probing question; a question following up on a primary question

Secondary research Research carried out with existing data such as published statistics, texts, and articles by experts together with media and personal documents

Self-analysis A means of identifying what is important to you by using a series of self-investigation strategies

Self-talk Internal communication; intrapersonal communication

Service learning A learning project addressing a community or public agency need

Sexist language Language that suggests the sexes are unequal and that one gender has more status and value and is more capable than another

Signposts Signaling cues designed to help focus the attention of receivers

Simile An indirect comparison of dissimilar things usually with the words *like* or *as*

Situational/cultural context The setting for communication; the communication environment

Slippery slope An erroneous assertion that one action will set in motion a chain of events

Small group A limited number of people who communicate over time to make decisions and accomplish goals

Sound bite speaking A short clip of speech promoting or spinning a perspective

Source The message originator

Spatial order An organizational framework that uses space as the means of arrangement

Speaking from memory Making a speech that is committed to memory and then spoken without using any notes

Specific purpose A single sentence or infinitive phrase identifying the speaker's goal

Speech of acceptance A speech given in response to a speech of presentation

Speech of introduction A speech designed to create a desire among audience members to listen to a featured speaker

Speech of presentation A speech presenting an award

Speech of tribute A form of commemorative speaking honoring a living or dead person or an event

Speech–thought differential The difference between speaking speed and thinking speed

Spotlighting A sexist language practice used to reinforce inequality

S.T.A.R. An acronym for answering interview questions; the letters in S.T.A.R. stand for situation, task, action, and result

Statistics Numbers summarizing a group of observations

Storytelling A means of communicating a complex idea clearly and powerfully through words and images

Subordinate points Information supportive of the main points in a speech; the foundation on which larger ideas are constructed

Subordination The support underlying an outline's main points

Syllogism A form of deductive reasoning containing a major premise, minor premise, and claim

Synchronous presentation An online presentation delivered in real time

Task leadership behaviors Roles that advance the group's completion of its task

Terminal credibility The audience's perception of a speaker's credibility after listening to his or her speech

Testimony The use of opinions of others to support positions the speaker is taking or to reinforce claims the speaker is making

Thesis A clear statement or claim about a topic; a means of dividing a speech into its major components

Thesis statement The expression of a speech's central idea; the claim or core idea of a speech

Thought stopping A technique designed to control speech anxiety; an example of cognitive restructuring

Topical order An organizational pattern composed of a series of topics related to the subject

Toulmin's Reasonable Argument Model A model describing the parts of an argument

Transitions Words that bridge ideas

Triangle of Meaning The model depicting the relationship that exists among words, things, and thoughts

Twitter speak A sound bite containing no more than 140 characters

Two-sided presentation A presentation containing two alternative perspectives

Understanding A stage in listening

Understatement Drawing attention to an idea by minimizing its importance

Values Core beliefs; the standards we use to judge that which is good and bad, worthwhile and worthless, ethical and unethical, right and wrong

Volume The loudness or softness of the voice; vocal intensity

Webinar An online conference

Web pattern A configural format in which threads of thought refer back to the speaker's central purpose

"We" language Language indicating shared responsibility

Wiki A collaborative website whose content is composed and edited by members of the public

Notes

Chapter 1

1. John Wooden and Jay Carty, *Coach Wooden's Pyramid of Success Playbook* (New York: Regal Publishers, 2005): 11.
2. See, for example, *Raising the Bar: Employers' Views on College Learning in the Wake of the Economic Downturn* (Washington, DC: Hart Research Associates, 2010); "Communication Top Skills Sought by Employers," *Training,* October 11, 2010, www.training.com; Peter D. Hart Research Associates, "How Should Colleges Prepare Students to Succeed in Today's Global Economy?" a survey conducted for the Association of American Colleges and Universities (2006); Randal S. Hansen and Katharine Handson, "What Do Employers Really Want? Top Skills and Values Employers Seek From Job-Seekers," June 4, 2007, www.quintcareers.com/job_skills_values.html; and Dee-Ann Durbin, "Study: Plenty of Jobs for Graduates in 2000," *Austin American-Statesman,* December 5, 1999, A28.
3. "Job Outlook," a survey conducted by the National Association of Colleges and Employers (2014).
4. See, for example, Rainer Martens, *Coaches Guide to Sport Psychology* (Champaign, IL: Human Kinetics, 1987); Don Greene, *Fight Your Fear and Win* (New York: Random House, 2001); A. Ville and J. Biggs, *Grace Under Pressure* (United Kingdom: Lulu Press, 2004); and B. Hale, *Imagery Training* (Leeds, UK: Coachwise, 1998).
5. Richard H. Cox, *Sport Psychology: Concepts and Applications,* 7th ed. (New York: McGraw-Hill, 2012).
6. See, for example, R. R. Behnke, A. N. Finn, and C. R. Sawyer, "Audience Perceived Anxiety Patterns of Public Speakers," *Communication Quarterly* 51, no. 4 (2003): 470–81; R. R. Behnke and C. R. Sawyer, "Milestones of Anticipatory Public Speaking Anxiety," *Communication Education* 48 (1999): 165–72; M. B. Stein, J. R. Walker, and D. R. Forde, "Public Speaking Fears in a Community Sample: Prevalence, Impact on Functioning, and Diagnostic Classification," *Archives of General Psychiatry* (February 1996): 169–74; and Roper Starch, "How Americans Communicate," a poll commissioned by the National Communication Association (1999).
7. Amy M. Bippus and John A. Daly, "What Do People Think Causes Stage Fright? Native Attributions About the Reasons for Public Speaking Anxiety," *Communication Education* 48 (April 1999): 63–72.
8. David Wallechinsky, Irving Wallace, and Amy Wallace, *The Book of Lists* (New York: William Morrow, 1977): 469.
9. Joe Ayres, "Perception of Speaking Ability: An Explanation for Speech Fright," *Communication Education* (July 1986) 275–87.
10. See, for example, Bernardo J. Carducci with Philip G. Zimbardo, "Are You Shy?" *Psychology Today,* (November–December 1995): 34–41, 64–70, 78–82.
11. For a summary of these studies, see D. W. Klopf, "Cross Cultural Apprehension Research: A Summary of Pacific Basin Studies," in J. A. Daly and J. A. McCroskey, eds., *Avoiding Communication: Shyness, Reticence, and Communication Apprehension* (Beverly Hills, CA: Sage, 1984): 157–69; D. W. Klopf and R. E. Cambra, "Communication Apprehension Among College Students in America, Australia, Japan, and Korea," *Journal of Psychology* 102 (1979): 27–31; and S. M. Ralston, R. Ambler, and J. N. Scudder, "Reconsidering the Impact of Racial Differences in the College Public Speaking Classroom on Minority Student Communication Anxiety," *Communication Reports* 4 (1991): 43–50.
12. Virginia P. Richmond and James P. McCroskey, *Communication: Apprehension, Avoidance, and Effectiveness,* 3rd ed. (Scottsdale, AZ: Gorsuch Scarisbrick, 1992).
13. See Sue Shellenbarger, "Strike a Powerful Pose," *Wall Street Journal,* August 21, 2013, D1, D2.
14. See Barbara G. Markway, Cheryl N. Carmin, C. Alex Pollard, and Teresa Flynn, *Dying of Embarrassment: Help for Social Anxiety and Phobia* (Oakland, CA: New Harbinger 1992).
15. See, for example, K. Haddad and P. Tremayne, "The Effects of Centering on the Free-Throw Shooting Performance of Young Athletes," *Sport Psychologist* 23 (2009): 118–36.

16. See, for example, L. Kelly, "Social Skills Training as a Mode of Treatment for Social Communication Problems," in J. A. Daly and J. C. McCroskey, eds., *Avoiding Communication: Shyness, Reticence, and Communication Apprehension* (Beverly Hills, CA: Sage, 1984), 189–207; and G. M. Phillips, "Rhetoritherapy Versus the Medical Model: Dealing with Reticence," *Communication Education* 26 (1977): 34–43.
17. Eric Finzi, *Face of Emotion: How Botox Affects Our Mood and Relationships* (New York: Palgrave Macmillan, 2013).
18. Karen Weintraub, "Turning a Frown Upside-Down May Help Lessen Depression," *USA Today,* January 29, 2013, 6D.
19. Theodore Clevenger Jr., "A Synthesis of Experimental Research in Stage Fright," *Quarterly Journal of Speech* 45 (April 1959): 136.
20. J. A. Daly, A. L. Vangelisti, H. L. Neel, and P. D. Cavanaugh, "Pre-Performance Concerns Associated With Public Speaking Anxiety," *Communication Quarterly* 37 (1989): 39–53.

Chapter 2

1. See, for example, Sarah Murray, "Know Thyself," in *FT.Com/Business Education* (January 28, 2013): 50–54.
2. Developed as part of an exercise in a public speaking class at the New York Institute of Technology. Students examined an online site, "Welcome to Lily's Hometown: Shanghai, China," http://linguistlist.org/fund-drive/2008/hometown-tour/lily/index.htm and were then asked to create a speech as if Shanghai was their hometown. New York Institute of Technology offers degrees in New York, China, and the Middle East.

Chapter 3

1. See, for example, Gail L. Thompson, "Teachers' Cultural Ignorance Imperils Student Success," *USA Today,* May 29, 2002, 13A.
2. U.S. Census Bureau; Haya El Nasser, "39 Million Make Hispanics Largest Minority Group," *USA Today,* June 19, 2003, 1A, 2A.
3. Wendy Griswold, *Cultures and Societies in a Changing World* (Thousand Oaks, CA: Pine Forge Press, 1994): 1.
4. Ibid.
5. See Larry A. Samovar, Richard E. Porter, Edwin R. McDaniel, and Carolyn S. Roy, *Communication Between Cultures,* 8th ed. (Boston, MA: Wadsworth, 2013): 201–3.
6. Robert R. Harris and Robert T. Moran, *Managing Cultural Differences,* 3rd ed. (Houston, TX: Gulf, 1991).
7. D. Tannen, *You Just Don't Understand: Women and Men in Conversation* (New York: Morrow, 1990).
8. Anna Marie Chavez, "Why Girls Matter," *Vital Speeches of the Day,* March 2016, 85–7.
9. Sarah Maslin Nir, "In Diverse City, Audiences Where Every Joke Translates," *New York Times,* March 5, 2013, A20, A22.
10. Louis A. Day, *Ethics in Media Communications: Cases and Controversies,* 2nd ed. (Belmont, CA: Wadsworth, 1991), 2. See also the 5th ed. (2006).
11. Melissa Korn, "Does an 'A' in Ethics Have Any Value?" *Wall Street Journal,* February 7, 2013, B4.
12. See Sissela Bok, *Lying* (New York: Pantheon, 1978); Sissela Bok, *Secrets* (New York: Random House, 1989); and Steven A. McCormack and Timothy R. Levine, "When Lies Are Uncovered: Emotional and Relational Outcomes of Discovered Deception," *Communication Monographs* 57 (June 1990): 119.
13. Adetokunbo F. Knowles-Borishade, "Paradigm for Classical African Orature," in Christine Kelly et al., eds., *Diversity in Public Communication: A Reader* (Dubuque, IA: Kendall-Hunt, 1995), 100.
14. Larry A. Samovar, Richard E. Porter, Edwin R. McDaniel, and Carolyn S. Roy, *Communication Between Cultures* (Boston, MA: Cengage, 2012).
15. See, for example, Vincent Ryan Ruggiero, *Thinking Critically About Ethical Issues,* 7th ed. (New York: McGraw-Hill, 2008); Barbara Warnick and Edward S. Inch, *Critical Thinking and Communication* (New York: Macmillan, 1994), 11.
16. Donald Hatcher, "Critical Thinking: A New Definition and Defense," *Inquiry* 20, no. 1 (June 28, 2000): 3–8.
17. Holger Kluge, "Reflections on Diversity," *Vital Speeches of the Day,* January 1997, 171.

Chapter 4

1. Daniel Ames, Lily Benjamin Maissen, and Joel Brockner, "The Role of Listening in Interpersonal Influence," *Journal of Research in Personality* 46 (2012): 345–49.
2. See, for example, Virginia Q. Tilley and Kevin C. Dunn, "Hobart and William Smith Professors Give Powell's Speech a Failing Grade," Hobart and William Smith

Colleges, February 15–17, 2003; and Alexander Cockburn, "Colin Powell and The Great 'Intelligence Fraud,'" *The Nation,* March 3, 2003, http://www.counterpunch.org/2003/02/15/colin-powell-and-the-great-quot-intelligence-fraud-quot/.

3. Judi Brownell, *Listening: Attitudes, Principles, and Skills,* 3rd ed. (Boston: Allyn & Bacon, 2006).
4. William B. Gudykunst, *Bridging Differences,* 14th ed. (Thousand Oaks, CA: SAGE, 2004), 196–97.
5. See Richard Paul, *Critical Thinking: What Every Person Needs to Survive in a Rapidly Changing World* (Rohnert Park, CA: Center for Critical Thinking, 1990).
6. See, for example, R. Emanuel, J. Adams, K. Baker, E. K. Daufin, C. Ellington, E. Fitts, J. Himsel, L. Holladay, and D. Okeowo, "How College Students Spend Their Time Communicating," *International Journal of Listening* 22 (2008): 13–28; William Pauk, *How to Study in College* (Boston: Houghton Mifflin, 1989), 121–33.
7. Ralph G. Nichols and Leonard A. Stevens, *Are You Listening?* (New York: McGraw-Hill, 1957).
8. See, for example, David Glenn, "Divided Attention: In an Age of Classroom Multitasking, Scholars Probe the Nature of Learning and Memory," *Chronicle of Higher Education,* February 28, 2010, http://chronicle.com/article/Scholars-Turn-Their-Attention/63746; Faith Brynie, "The Madness of Multitasking," *Psychology Today,* Brain Sense blog, August 24, 2009, https://www.psychologytoday.com/blog/brain-sense/200908/the-madness-multitasking.
9. For more information on the relationship between note taking and listening see Robert Bostrom and D. Bruce Searle, "Encoding Media, Affect and Gender," in Robert Bostrom, ed., *Listening Behavior: Measurement and Application* (New York: Guilford, 1990), 28–30; and Florence L. Wolff, Nadine C. Marsnik, William Tacey, and Ralph Nichols, *Perceptive Listening* (Englewood Cliffs, NJ: Prentice Hall, 1983), 88–97.

Chapter 5

1. Lane Cooper, *The Rhetoric of Aristotle: An Expanded Translation With Supplementary Examples for Students of Composition and Public Speaking* (New York: Appleton-Century-Crofts, 1960), 136.
2. See, for example, Jonathan R. Alger, "The Educational Value of Diversity," *Academe* (January–February 1997): 20–22.
3. Peggy Noonan, *What I Saw at the Revolution* (New York: Ivy Books, 1990), 70–72.
4. Ellen DeGeneris, Tulane commencement speech (2009), www.goodnet.org/articles/1087.
5. Lynne C. Lancaster and David Stillman, *When Generations Collide* (New York: Harper, 2002), 1–32.
6. See Pew Research Center, "Millennials. Confident. Connected. Open to Change," executive summary, http://www.pewsocialtrends.org/2010/02/24/millennials-confident-connected-open-to-change.
7. Deborah Tannen, *You Just Don't Understand* (New York: Ballantine, 1992), 42.
8. See Carl Iver Hovland, Irving Lester Janis, and Harold H. Kelley, *Communication and Persuasion* (New Haven, CT: Yale University Press, 1961), 183.
9. See William J. McGuire, "Persuasion, Resistance and Attitude Change," in I. Pool et al., eds., *Handbook of Communication* (Skokie, IL: Rand McNally, 1973), 216–52.
10. Richard D. Lewis, *When Cultures Collide: Leading Across Cultures,* 3rd ed. (Boston: Intercultural Press, 2005).
11. Roger Ailes, *You Are the Message* (New York: Doubleday, 1988), 51.

Chapter 6

1. For an analysis of topics used in speeches by leaders of the largest corporations in the United States, see Robert J. Meyers and Martha Stout Kessler, "Business Speeches: A Study of the Themes in Speeches by America's Corporate Leaders," *Journal of Business Communication* 17, no. 3 (1980): 5–17.
2. For a discussion on brainstorming by a key developer of the process, see Alex F. Osborn, *Applied Imagination* (New York: Scribner, 1962).
3. James Endrst, "'On Looking' Peers Into Our Attention-Deficient Lives," *USA Today,* January 29, 2013, 2D.
4. For a variation on this technique, see R. R. Allen and Ray E. McKerron, *The Pragmatics of Public Communication,* 3rd ed. (Dubuque, IA: Kendall-Hunt, 1985), 42–44.
5. David Livermore, *Leading With Cultural Intelligence* (New York: AMACOM, 2010).
6. See also Richard D. Lewis, *When Cultures Collide* (London: Nicholas Brealey, 1996).
7. See, for example, B. Kirchner, "Mind-Map Your Way to an Idea: Here Is One Approach to Rooting Out

Workable Topics That Move You," *Writer* 122, no. 3 (2009): 28–29.

8. Dan Shuey, "Untitled," *Winning Orations* (Mankato, MN: Interstate Oratorical Association, 2004).

Chapter 7

1. We thank the reference librarians at both the College of New Rochelle and the New York Institute of Technology for their invaluable input for this section.
2. H. Fleshler, J. Ilardo, and J. Demorectsky, "The Influence of Field Dependence, Speaker Credibility Set, and Message Documentation on Evaluations of Speaker and Message Credibility," *Southern Speech Communication Journal* 39 (Summer 1974): 389–402.
3. Dethia Ricks and Roni Rabin, "Panel's Ties to Drugmakers Not Cited in New Cholesterol Guidelines," *Newsday.com,* July 15, 2004.
4. To learn more about citation formats, see the *Publication Manual of the American Psychological Association,* 6th ed. (2010), and *The MLA Handbook for Writers of Research Papers,* 7th ed. (2009).

Chapter 8

1. Nancy Duarte, *Resonate: Present Visual Stories That Transform Audiences* (New York: Wiley, 2010).
2. Barack Obama, excerpted from his speech given before the Democratic National Convention, July 27, 2004, Boston, MA.
3. Ron Reagan, excerpt from his speech delivered before the Democratic National Convention, July 27, 2004, Boston, MA.
4. See Kara Yorio, "Everyone Can Benefit From Understanding Tourette's," *The Record,* May 26, 2015, BL 1–2.
5. Joan Didion, "Why I Write," *New York Times Book Review,* December 5, 1976.
6. William G. Durden, "Just Do Science," *Vital Speeches of the Day,* March 2013, 69.
7. Andrea S. Libresco, "We Are All Public Officials," *Vital Speeches of the Day,* November 2012, 350.
8. Aamer Madhani, "Clinton Touts Leadership Record in Farewell Speech," *USA Today,* February 1, 2013, 4A.
9. See Hans Hoeken and Lettica Hustinx, "When Is Statistical Evidence Superior to Anecdotal Evidence in Supporting Probability Claims? The Role of Argument Type," *Human Communication Research* 35 (2009): 491–510; Neil J. Salkind, *Statistics for People Who (Think They) Hate Statistics,* 4th ed. (Thousand Oaks, CA: Sage, 2011).
10. James Williams, "Race and the Gun Debate," *Wall Street Journal,* March 27, 2013, A17.
11. See, for example, Cynthia Crossen, *Tainted Truth: The Manipulation of Fact in America* (New York: Simon & Schuster, 1994).
12. G. Cowley, "Can Sunshine Save Your Life," *Newsweek,* December 30, 1991, 56.
13. John Foubert, Special to CNN: "'Rapebait' E-mail Reveals Dark Side of Frat Culture," October 9, 2013, www.cnn.com/2013/10/09/opinion/foubert-fraternities-rape/.
14. Becky McKay, "Homeless Children: A National Crisis," in *Winning Orations, 1990* (Mankato, MN: Interstate Oratorical Association, 1990), 42.
15. Gordon Smith, "What If This Is Broadcasting's New Moment to Flourish?" *Vital Speeches of the Day,* June 2012, 196–98.

Chapter 9

1. Ernest C. Thompson, "An Experimental Investigation of the Relative Effectiveness of Organizational Structure in Oral Communication," *Southern Speech Journal* 26 (1960): 59–69. Though conducted more than a half-century ago, this study is still relevant.
2. To increase understanding of how the arrangement of information affects message reception, see Dacia Charlesworth, "Re-presenting Subversive Songs: Applying Strategies for Invention and Arrangement to Nontraditional Speech Texts," *Communication Teacher* 24, no. 3 (July 2010): 122–26.
3. Christopher Spicer and Ronald Bassett, "The Effect of Organization Learning From an Informative Message," *Southern Speech Communication Journal* 41 (Spring 1976): 290–99; for a scholarly discussion of what we can learn about organization from an orderly universe, see Margaret J. Wheatley, *Leadership and the New Science* (San Francisco: Berrett-Koehler, 1994).
4. See, for example, J. Hinds, "Reader Versus Writer Responsibility: A New Typology," in Ulla Connor and Robert B. Kapan, eds., *Writing Across Languages: Analysis of 1.2 Written Text* (Reading, MA: Addison-Wesley, 1986), 141–52.
5. See, for example, Arran Gare, "Narratives and Culture: The Role of Stories in Self-Creation," *Telos* (Winter

2002); and Jessica Lee Shumake, "Reconceptualizing Communication and Rhetoric From a Feminist Perspective," *Guidance & Counseling* (Summer 2002).
6. Richard Nisbett, *The Geography of Thought: How Asians and Westerners Think Differently . . . and Why* (New York: Free Press, 2003).
7. National Public Radio, "Analysis: Geography of Thought," *Talk of the Nation* broadcast of interview of Richard Nisbett by Neal Conan, March 3, 2003.
8. Ibid.

Chapter 10

1. Alternative approaches to outlining abound. For one such alternative, see Christina G. Paxman, "Map Your Way to Speech Success! Employing Mind Mapping as a Speech Preparation Technique," *Communication Teacher* 25, no. 1 (January 2011): 7–11.

Chapter 11

1. Stephen C. Rafe, *How to Be Prepared to Speak on Your Feet* (New York: Harper Business, 1990), 89.
2. William M. Jennings, "The Story of the Lost Corpse," *Vital Speeches of the Day,* November 2012, 359.
3. See, for example, Steven D. Cohen, "The Art of Public Narrative: Teaching Students How to Construct Memorable Anecdotes," *Communication Teacher* 25, no. 4 (October 2011): 197–204.
4. Kurstin Finch, "Are the Stakes Too High?" in *Winning Orations, 1995* (Northfield, MN: Interstate Oratorical Association, 1995), 88.
5. Cathy Frisinger, "Eye-Opening Discoveries About a Good Night's Sleep," *The Record,* May 20, 2008, F3.
6. Barack Obama, "Anti-Semitism Is on the Rise. We Cannot Deny It," *Vital Speeches of the Day,* March 2016, 87–89.
7. See Charles R. Gruner, "Advice to the Beginning Speaker on Using Humor—What the Research Tells Us," *Communication Education* 34 (April 1988): 142–47.
8. Conan O'Brien, commencement address at Dartmouth, https://www.dartmouth.edu/~commence/news/speeches/2011/obrien-speech.html.
9. Theresa McGuiness, "Greeks in Crisis," in *Winning Orations, 1991* (Mankato, MN: Interstate Oratorical Association, 1991), 73.
10. Michael Eisner, "Managing a Creative Organization," *Vital Speeches of the Day,* June 1996, 502.
11. Ann Marie Ursini, "Subtitle Nation," *Winning Orations* (Mankato, MN: Interstate Oratorical Association, 2003).
12. John M. Murphy, "Inventing Authority: Bill Clinton, Martin Luther King, Jr., and the Orchestration of Rhetorical Traditions," *Quarterly Journal of Speech* 83 (1997): 71–89.
13. William J. Clinton, "Remarks to the Eighth Annual Holy Convocation of the Church of God in Christ," in *Selected Speeches of President William Jefferson Clinton* (Washington, DC: President of the United States, 1991), 21.
14. Ibid.
15. Alicia Croshal, "Gossip: It's Worth Talking About," in *Winning Orations, 1991* (Mankato, MN: Interstate Oratorical Association, 1991), 1.

Chapter 12

1. Sharon Bower, *Painless Public Speaking* (London: Thorsons Publishers, 1990), 96–97.
2. Stephen C. Rafe, *How to Be Prepared to Speak on Your Feet* (New York: Harper Business, 1990), 78.
3. See Daniel Rose, "Message. Messenger. Audience," *Vital Speeches of the Day,* December 2012, 392.
4. From a speech developed by students in 2014 during a workshop in the basic course at the New York Institute of Technology.
5. Talbot D'Alemberte, "Civil Justice Reform," *Vital Speeches of the Day,* March 1992, 308.
6. John F. McDonnell, "PaxPacifica," *Vital Speeches of the Day,* April 1992, 372.
7. Denalie Silha, "Rediscovering a Lost Resource," in *Winning Orations, 1991* (Mankato, MN: Interstate Oratorical Association, 1991), 81.
8. Marilyn Moore, "What We Can Do," *Vital Speeches of the Day,* March 2016, 90–92.
9. See Roger Cohen, "For Coke, World Is Its Oyster," *New York Times,* November 21, 1991, D5; Michael Lev, "Advertisers Seek Global Messages," *New York Times,* November 18, 1991; and Indra Nooyi, "Short Term Demands vs. Long-Term Responsibilities," *Vital Speeches of the Day,* June 2010, 250.

Chapter 13

1. See Teri Kwal Gamble and Michael Gamble, *Communication Works,* 11th ed. (New York: McGraw-Hill, 2013).
2. See John McCrone, *The Ape That Spoke: Language and the Evolution of the Human Mind* (New York: Marroni, 1991).

3. Richard Breslin and Tomoko Yoshida, *Intercultural Communication Training: An Introduction* (Thousand Oaks, CA: Sage, 1994).
4. Larry A. Samovar, Richard E. Porter, and Edwin R. McDaniel, *Communication Between Cultures,* 7th ed. (Boston, MA: Wadsworth, 2010).
5. Larry A. Samovar and Richard E. Porter, *Communication Between Cultures,* 1st ed. (Belmont, CA: Wordsworth, 1991), 152.
6. See, for example, R. S. Zaharna, "Bridging Cultural Differences: American Public Relations Practices and Arab Communication Patterns," *Public Relations Review* 21 (1995): 241–55.
7. Christopher Engholm, *When Business East Meets Business West* (New York: Wiley, 1991), 106.
8. See, for example, R. L. De Mente, *Japan Unmasked: The Character and Culture of the Japanese* (Tokyo: Tuttle, 2005), 179.
9. M. Hecht, M. S. Collier, and S. Ribeau, *African American Communication: Ethnic Identity and Cultural Interpretation* (Thousand Oaks, CA: Sage, 1993).
10. See, for example, David Schuman and Dick Olufs, *Diversity on Campus* (Boston: Allyn & Bacon, 1995).
11. For a discussion of age discrimination in the workplace, see Marianne Lavelle, "On the Edge of Age Discrimination," *New York Times Magazine,* March 9, 1997, 66–69.
12. William B. Gudykunst, *Bridging Differences,* 4th ed. (Thousand Oaks, CA: Sage, 2004).
13. Jesse Jackson, "Common Ground and Common Sense," *Vital Speeches of the Day,* August 1988, 649–53.
14. See James Geary, *I Is an Other: The Secret Life of Metaphor and How It Shapes the Way We See the World* (New York: Harper, 2011).
15. Chief Seattle, "The Indian's Night Promises to Be Dark," in *Indian Oratory: Famous Speeches by Noted Indian Chieftains,* W. C. Vanderwerth, ed. (Norman: University of Oklahoma Press, 1971).
16. Wayne Dyer, *Everyday Wisdom,* rev. ed. (New York: Hay House, 2005).
17. Reprinted by arrangement with the Heirs to the Estate of Martin Luther King, Jr., c/o Writers House as agent for the proprietor, New York, NY.
18. Bill Bradley, keynote speech presented to the Democratic National Convention, July 13, 1992.
19. W. J. Banach, "In Search of an Eloquent Thank You," *Vital Speeches of the Day,* October 1991, 63.
20. See "Melinda Gates: Creating a Brotherhood," *Duke Today,* May 12, 2013, today.duke.edu/2013/05/gatestalk

Chapter 14

1. R. Jay Magill Jr., *Sincerity* (New York: Norton, 2012).
2. See, for example, Rebecca K. Ivic and Robert J. Green, "Developing Charismatic Delivery Through Transformational Presentations: Modeling the Persona of Steve Jobs," *Communication Teacher* 26, no. 2 (April 2012): 65–68.
3. Mark Leibovich, "McCain Battles a Nemesis, the Teleprompter," *New York Times,* July 6, 2008, A1, A19.
4. Peter Baker, "President Sticks to the Script, With a Little Help," *New York Times,* March 6, 2009, A14.
5. See "The Public Course: Is It Preparing Students With Work Related Skills?" *Communication Education* 36 (1987): 131–37.
6. Daniel Akst, "Say It As If You Mean It," *Wall Street Journal,* July 9, 2012, A13.
7. Roger Ailes, *You Are the Message* (New York: Doubleday, 1989), 17.
8. Ibid.
9. Ibid.
10. T. E. Smith and A. B. Frymier, "Get 'Real': Does Practicing Speeches Before an Audience Improve Performance?" *Communication Quarterly* 54 (2006): 111–25.
11. These topics appeared in Michael Smerconish, "College Essay Questions Make for Spirited Conversations," *The Record,* December 25, 2013, A23.

Chapter 15

1. See, for example, Robert Rivlin and Karen Gravelle, *Deciphering the Senses: The Expanding World of Human Perception* (New York: Simon & Schuster, 1998), 98; A. Warfield, "Do You Speak Body Language?" *Training and Development* 55, no. 4 (2001): 60; Ray Birdwhistell, *Kinesics and Context* (Philadelphia: University of Pennsylvania Press, 1970); and Albert Mehrabian, *Silent Messages* (Belmont, CA: Wadsworth, 1971).
2. See, for example, Megan Gambino, "Ask an Expert: What Did Abraham Lincoln's Voice Sound Like?" Smithsonian .com, http://www.smithsonianmag.com/history/ask-an-expert-what-did-abraham-lincolns-voice-sound-like-13446201/.
3. Bert Decker, *You've Got to Be Believed to Be Heard* (New York: St. Martin's Press, 1992), 31.

4. For an interesting discussion of nonverbal cues, lying, and judgments of speaker credibility, see Paul Ekman, *Telling Lies* (New York: Norton, 1992).
5. Judith A. Hall, "Voice Tone and Persuasiveness," *Journal of Personality and Social Psychology* 38 (1980): 924–34.
6. Rosita Daskel Albert and Gayle L. Nelson, "Hispanic/Anglo-American Differences in Attributions to Paralinguistic Behavior," *International Journal of Intercultural Relations* 17 (1993): 19–40.
7. Larry A. Samovar, Richard E. Porter, Edwin R. McDaniel, and Carolyn S. Roy, *Communication Between Cultures,* 9th ed. (Boston: Cengage, 2017), 321.
8. Ibid.
9. Leon Fletcher, "Polishing Your Silent Languages," *The Toastmaster,* March 1990, 15.

Chapter 16

1. Bert Decker, *You've Got to Be Believed to Be Heard* (New York: St. Martin's Press, 1992), 31.
2. See Vernon B. Harper, "Walking the Walk: Understanding Nonverbal Communication Through Walking," *Communication Teacher* 18, no. 1 (January 2004): 17–19.
3. See, for example, M. Bowden, *Winning Body Language: Control the Conversation, Command Attention, and Convey the Right Message Without Saying a Word* (New York: McGraw-Hill, 2011).
4. See Garr Reynolds, *The Naked Presented* (Berkeley, CA: New Riders, 2011). For a more scholarly discussion of what happens when a speaker's body language is inconsistent with his or her words, see James B. Stiff and Gerald R. Miller, "Come to Think of It . . . Interrogative Probes, Deceptive Communication and Deception Detection," *Human Communication Research* 12 (1986): 339–57.
5. See Virginia P. Richmond, Derek R. Lange, and James C. McCroskey, "Teacher Immediacy and the Teacher–Student Relationship," in Timothy P. Mottet, Virginia P. Richmond, and James C. McCroskey, eds., *Handbook of Instructional Communication: Rhetorical and Relational Perspectives* (Boston: Allyn & Bacon, 2006), 167–93.
6. Robert G. Harper, Arthur N. Wiens, and Joseph D. Matarazzo, *Nonverbal Communication: The State of the Art* (New York: Wiley, 1978), 164.
7. See A. Melinger and W. M. Levelt, "Gesture and the Communicative Intention of the Speaker," *Gesture* 4 (2004): 119–41.
8. See Nancy Henley, *Body Politics* (Englewood Cliffs, NJ: Prentice Hall, 1977).
9. Shelly Chiden, "Communication of Physical Attractiveness and Persuasion," *Journal of Personality and Social Psychology* 37 (1979): 1387–97.

Chapter 17

1. Merrie Spaeth, "'Prop' Up Your Speaking Skills," *Wall Street Journal,* July 1, 1996, A14.
2. See Richard E. Mayer, ed., *Multimedia Learning* (New York: Cambridge University Press, 2009); Dale Cyphert, "PowerPoint and the Evolution of Electronic Evidence From the Contemporary Business Presentation," *American Communication Journal* 11, no. 2 (Summer 2009): 1–20; Dale Cyphert, "Presentation Technology in the Age of Electronic Eloquence: From Visual Aid to Visual Rhetoric," *Communication Education* 56, no. 2 (2007): 168–92; Alan L. Brown, *Power Pitches* (Chicago: Irwin, 1997); and Virginia Johnson, "Picture-Perfect Presentations," *Training and Development Journal* 43 (1989): 45.
3. See Elena P. Zayas-Baya, "Instructional Media in the Total Language Picture," *International Journal of Instructional Media* 5 (1977–1978): 145–50.
4. See Garr Reyonds, *Presentation Zen,* 2nd ed. (Berkeley, CA: New Riders, 2012); "Presenting Effective Presentations With Visual Aids," United States Department of Labor, Occupational Safety & Health Administration (May 1996), http://www.rufwork.com/110/mats/osha VisualAids.html; "Thriving in Academe: A Rationale for Visual Communication," National Education Association Advocate Online (December 2001); Donald R. Vogel, Gary W. Dickson, and John A. Lehman, "Persuasion and the Role of Visual Presentation Support: The UM/3M Study," commissioned by Visual Systems Division of 3M (1986).
5. Todd T. Holm, "A Cheap and Easy Way to Mount Visual Aids," *The Forensic of Pi Kappa Delta* 96 (Summer 2011): 21–24.
6. See Tom Mucciolo, "Driving Data With Charts," *Speechwriter's Newsletter,* January 1, 1997, 6.
7. See, for example, Drew Skau, "11 Infographics About Infographics," February 18, 2013, http://www

.scribblelive.com/blog/2013/02/18/11-infographics-about-infographics/.

8. See R. Larson, "Enhancing the Recall of Presented Material," *Computers and Education* 53, no. 4 (2009): 1278–84; Nancy Duarte, *Slideology: The Art and Science of Creating Great Presentations* (Sebastopol, CA: O'Reilly, 2008); Tom Mucciolo and Rich Mucciolo, *Purpose, Movement, Color: A Strategy for Effective Presentations* (New York: MediaNet, 1994).
9. See, for example, D. D. Booher, *Speak With Confidence: Powerful Presentations That Inform, Inspire, and Persuade* (New York: McGraw-Hill, 2003).
10. L. Zuckerman, "Words Go Right to the Brain, But Can They Stir the Heart?" *New York Times,* April 17, 1999, A17–A19.
11. See Dale Cypert, "The Problem of PowerPoint: Visual Aid or Visual Rhetoric?" *Business Communication Quarterly* (March 2004): 80–84; June Kronholz, "PowerPoint Goes to School," *Wall Street Journal,* November 12, 2002, B1, B6.
12. See Virginia Johnson, "Picture Perfect Presentations," *The Toastmaster,* February 1990, 7.
13. From Robert Boostrom, *Developing Creative and Critical Thinking: An Integrated Approach* (Lincolnwood, IL: National Textbook Company, 1992), 231.
14. Ibid.

Chapter 18

1. Jeffrey Bosworth, "Hunting for Hope in Modern America," *Vital Speeches of the Day,* October 2013, 332.

Chapter 19

1. Robert B. Cialdini, *Influence: Science and Practice,* 4th ed. (Boston: Allyn & Bacon, 2001), 239.
2. See, for example, Gerald R. Miller, "On Being Persuaded: Some Basic Distinctions," in James Price Dillard and Michael Pfau, eds., *The Persuasive Handbook: Developments in Theory and Practice* (Thousand Oaks, CA: SAGE, 2002), 3–16.
3. See Herbert W. Simons and Jean G. Jones, *Persuasion in Society,* 2nd ed. (New York: Routledge, 2011).
4. See, for example, Richard M. Perloff, *The Dynamics of Persuasion: Communication and Attitudes in the 21st Century,* 4th ed. (New York: Routledge, 2010).
5. A framework for understanding both attitudes and beliefs is offered by Martin Fishbein and Icek Ajzen, *Belief, Attitude, Intention and Behavior: An Introduction to Theory and Research* (Reading, MA: Addison-Wesley, 1975).
6. See, for example, "Most in U.S. Say Americans Are Divided on Important Values," Gallup.com, December 14, 2012, http://www.gallup.com/poll/159257/say-americans-divided-important-values.aspx; and "Social Values: Public Values Intangible Assets More Than Material Possessions," *Gallup Report* (March/April 1989): 35–44.
7. See Martha Cooper, *Analyzing Public Discourse* (Prospect Heights, IL: Waveland, 1989), 46.
8. This outline is based in part on a speech by Diane Ravitch, delivered on November 2, 1990, entitled "Multiculturalism in the Public Schools." It is included in Richard L. Johannesen, R. R. Allen, and Wil A. Linkugel, eds., *Contemporary American Speeches* (Dubuque, IA: Kendall Hunt, 1992), 257–62.
9. Anthony Pratkanis and Eliot Aronson, *Age of Propaganda* (New York: W. H. Freeman, 1991), 154–55.

Chapter 20

1. See, for example, John A. Banas and Stephen A. Rains, "A Meta-Analysis of Research on Inoculation Theory," *Communication Monographs* 77 (2010): 282–311.
2. See John C. Reinard, "The Empirical Study of the Persuasive Effects of Evidence: The Status After Fifty Years of Research," *Human Communication Research* 15 (1988): 3–59.
3. From George E. Curry, "*Brown v. Board of Education*—50 Years Later," *Vital Speeches of the Day,* March 2004, 315.
4. See Buzz Bissinger, "Why College Football Should Be Banned," *Wall Street Journal,* May 5–6, 2012, C3.
5. See, for example, Nancy M. Cavender and Howard Kahane, *Logic and Contemporary Rhetoric: The Use of Reason in Everyday Life,* 11th ed. (Belmont, CA: Wadsworth, 2010).
6. Faye Wattleton, "Sacred Rights: Preserving Reproductive Freedom for Women," in Richard L. Johannesen, R. R. Allen, and Wil A. Linkugel, eds., *Contemporary American Speeches,* 7th ed. (Dubuque, IA: Kendall Hunt, 1992), 269–73.
7. See Andrew Weil, "Don't Let Chaos Get You Down," *Newsweek,* November 7 and 14, 2011, 9.

8. See Abraham H. Maslow, *Motivation and Personality,* 2nd ed. (New York: Harper & Row, 1970).
9. See F. J. Boster and P. Mongeau, "Fear Arousing Persuasive Messages," in R. N. Bostrom, ed., *Communication Yearbook* (Beverly Hills, CA: SAGE, 1984), 330–75.
10. See, for example, Frank Rich, "Decision 2004: Fear Fatigue vs. Sheer Fatigue," *New York Times,* October 31, 2004, sec. 2, 1, 34.

Chapter 21

1. Charles Redding, *Communication Within the Organization* (New York: Industrial Communication Council, 1972).
2. See Kenneth Benne and Paul Sheats, "Functional Roles of Group Members," *Journal of Social Issues* 4 (1948): 41–49.
3. See Teri Gamble and Michael Gamble, *Leading With Communication* (Thousand Oaks, CA: SAGE, 2013); Michael Z. Hackman and Craig E. Johnson, *Leadership: A Communication Perspective,* 4th ed. (Long Grove, IL: Waveland, 2004); and Kevin Barge, "Leadership as Medium: A Leaderless Group Discussion Model," *Communication Quarterly* 37, no. 4 (Fall 1989): 237–47.
4. See John Dewey, *How We Think* (Boston: MA: Heath, 1910).
5. See Irving Janis, *Victims of Groupthink: A Psychological Study of Foreign Policy Decisions and Fiascos* (Boston: Houghton Mifflin, 1972).
6. Alex Osborn, *Applied Imagination* (New York: Scribner, 1957).
7. B. Tuchman, "Developmental Sequence in Small Groups," *Psychological Bulletin* 63 (1965): 384–99; and S. A. Wheelen and J. M. Hockberger, "Validation Studies of the Group Development Questionnaire," *Small Group Research* 27, no. 1 (1996): 143–70.
8. Christopher Shea, "Altruism: Every Man for Himself," *Wall Street Journal,* Saturday/Sunday, May 19–20, 2012, C4.

Chapter 22

1. Elie Wiesel acceptance of the 1986 Nobel Peace Prize, *New York Times,* December 11, 1986, 8.
2. Remarks by the president at Howard University Commencement Ceremony, President Barack Obama, https://www.whitehouse.gov/the-press-office/2016/05/07/remarks-president-howard-university-commencement-ceremony, licensed under CC BY 3.0 US, https://creativecommons.org/licenses/by/3.0/us/legalcode. Excerpted from the original. Notes added by Teri Kwal Gamble and Michael W. Gamble.
3. Monica Morgan, keynote speech, National Conference on Racism, Sydney, Australia, March 12, 2002, https://www.humanrights.gov.au/news/speeches/beyond-tolerance-national-conference-racism-speeches.
4. Dolores M. Bandow, "A Bird Outside Your Window," in Richard L. Johannessen et al., eds., *Contemporary American Speeches* (Dubuque, IA: Kendall Hunt, 1992), 402–4. *L'Chaim* means "to life."
5. Barack Obama, remarks by President Obama at memorial service for former South African president Nelson Mandela, December 10, 2013, https://www.whitehouse.gov/the-press-office/2013/12/10/remarks-president-obama-memorial-service-former-south-african-president-. For a eulogy given by Russel Brand, celebrating the life of Amy Winehouse, see http://www.russellbrand.com/for-amy/ or www.theguardian.com/music/2011/jul/24/russell-brand-amy-winehouse-woman.
6. Robert M. Kaplan and Gregory C. Pascoe, "Humorous Lectures and Humorous Examples: Some Effects Upon Comprehension and Retention," *Journal of Educational Psychology* 69 (1977): 61–65.
7. "Marvin Minsky Speaks," http://zhurnaly.com/cgi-bin/wiki/MarvinMinskySpeaks.

Chapter 23

1. Arlene Hirsch, "Tell Me About Yourself Doesn't Mean 'Tell It All,'" *The Record,* November 28, 2004, J1, J2; and Anthony DePalma, "Preparing for 'Tell Us About Yourself,'" *New York Times,* July 27, 2003, NJ1.
2. Eli Amdur, "Train Yourself to Be a S.T.A.R. During the Job Interview," *The Record,* September 4, 2005, J1.
3. Eli Amdur, "An Interview Is a Two-Way Deal, so Ask Questions," *The Record,* April 17, 2005, J1, J2.
4. Eli Amdur, "Be the Person Companies Will Want to Hire," *The Record,* October 24, 2004, J1, J2; "Initial Minutes of Job Interview Are Critical," *USA Today,* January 1, 2000, 8.
5. See, for example, Malcolm Gladwell, "What Do Job Interviews Really Tell Us?" *New Yorker,* May 29, 2000, 84.
6. See Allison Doyle, "How to Write an Interview Thank You Letter," thebalance.com, updated May 16, 2016, http://jobsearch.about.com/b/2013/07/31/thank-you-letter-after-interview.htm; and Joann S. Lublin, "Notes to

Interviewers Should Go Beyond a Simple Thank You," *Wall Street Journal,* February 5, 2008, B1.

7. David Shapiro Jr., "Finding Niches for Authors' Pitches," *Wall Street Journal,* July 1, 2013, A21.

Chapter 24

1. See Suki Kim, "This Is What It's Like to Go Undercover in North Korea," TED Talk, June 2015, https://www.ted.com/talks/suki_kim_this_is_what_it_s_like_to_go_undercover_in_north_korea/transcript?language=en.
2. T. T. Barker and K. Gower, "Strategic Application of Storytelling in Organizations," *Journal of Business Communication* 4, no. 73 (2010): 295–312.
3. See Bill George, Peter Sims, Andrew N. McLean, and Diana Mayer, "Discovering Your Authentic Leadership," *Harvard Business Review,* February 2007, www.HBR.org.
4. K. B. Boal and P. I. Schultz, "Storytelling, Time, and Evolution: The Role of Strategic Leadership in Complex Adaptive Systems," *Leadership Quarterly* 18, no. 4 (2007): 411–28.
5. T. Mohan, H. McGregor, S. Saunders, and R. Archee, *Communicating as Professionals* (Melbourne: Thomson, 2008).
6. Richard Maxell and Robert Dickman, *The Elements of Persuasion* (New York: HarperCollins, 2007), 5.
7. See, for example, "Today's Debate: Digital Harassment," *USA Today,* October 24, 2013, 8A.
8. C. M. Phoel, "Leading Words: How to Use Stories to Change Minds and Ignite Action," *Harvard Management Communication Letter* 3, no. 2 (Spring 2006): 3–5.
9. M. K. Smith, "Peter Senge and the Learning Organization," *Encyclopedia of Informal Education* (2001), http://infed.org/mobi/petersenge-and-the-learning-organization/.
10. Steven Pinker, *The Stuff of Thought: Language as a Window Into Human Nature* (New York: Viking, 2007).
11. Stephen Denning, *The Secret Language of Leadership* (San Francisco: Jossey-Bass, 2007); also see Stephen Denning, *The Leader's Guide to Storytelling: Mastering the Art and Discipline of Business Narrative* (San Francisco: Jossey-Bass, 2011).
12. See, for example, G. Lakoff, "Framing the Dems," *American Prospect,* August 1, 2003; and G. Lakoff and M. Johnson, *Metaphors We Live By* (Chicago: University of Chicago Press, 1980).
13. Martin Luther King Jr., "I Have a Dream," presented at Lincoln Memorial in Washington, DC, August 28, 1963. Reprinted by arrangement with the Heirs to the Estate of Martin Luther King Jr., c/o Writers House as agent for the proprietor New York, NY.
14. NBC News, "Lying Survey Results at a Glance, updated July 11, 2006, www.nbcnews.com/id/13819955/ns/us_news-life/t/lying-survey-results-glance/.
15. Marshall Ganz, "Leading Change: Leadership, Organization, and Social Movements, in Nitin Nohria and Rakesh Khurana, *Handbook of Leadership Theory and Practice* (Boston: Harvard Business Press, 2010), 527–68.

Chapter 26

1. For more information on narrative infographics, see "Teaching Storytelling Through Narrative Infographics" on Bovee & Thill's Business Communication blog, http://blog.businesscommunicationnetwork.com/.

Index

PEARSON ALWAYS LEARNING

GO! With Microsoft® Office 2010

A Custom Edition for Moberly Area Community College

Taken from:
GO! With Microsoft® Office 2010 Volume 1
by Shelley Gaskin, Robert L. Ferrett, Alicia Vargas, and Carolyn McLellan

Cover Art: Courtesy of Photodisc, Stockbyte, Glow Images/Getty

Taken from:

GO! With Microsoft® Office 2010 Volume 1
by Shelley Gaskin, Robert L. Ferrett, Alicia Vargas, and Carolyn McLellan

Published by Prentice Hall
Upper Saddle River, New Jersey 07458

This special edition published in cooperation with Pearson Learning Solutions.

Pearson Learning Solutions, 501 Boylston Street, Suite 900, Boston, MA 02116
A Pearson Education Company
www.pearsoned.com

Printed in the United States of America

2 3 4 5 6 7 8 9 10 V0ZN 16 15 14 13 12 11

000200010270760445

SW

PEARSON

ISBN 10: 1-256-15076-2
ISBN 13: 978-1-256-15076-3

Brief Contents

PowerPoint

Integrated Projects

Contents

Word

Chapter 2 Using Tables and Templates to Create Resumes and Cover Letters

Chapter 3 Analyzing Data with Pie Charts, Line Charts, and What-If Analysis Tools 353

PowerPoint

Chapter 1 Getting Started with Microsoft Office PowerPoint 621

Chapter 2 Formatting PowerPoint Presentations 679

GO! System Contributors

We thank the following people for their hard work and support in making the *GO!* System all that it is!

Instructor Resource Authors

Adickes, Erich	Parkland College
Baray, Carrie	Ivy Tech Community College
Clausen, Jane	Western Iowa Tech Community College
Crossley, Connie	Cincinnati State Technical and Community College
Emrich, Stefanie	Metropolitan Community College of Omaha, Nebraska
Faix, Dennis	Harrisburg Area Community College
Hadden, Karen	Western Iowa Tech Community College
Hammerle, Patricia	Indiana University/Purdue University at Indianapolis
Hines, James	Tidewater Community College
Holland, Susan	Southeast Community College-Nebraska
Landenberger, Toni	Southeast Community College-Nebraska
McMahon, Richard	University of Houston—Downtown
Miller, Sandra	Wenatchee Valley College
Niebur, Katherine	Dakota County Technical College
Nowakowski, Anthony	Buffalo State
Pierce, Tonya	Ivy Tech Community College
Roselli, Diane	Harrisburg Area Community College
St. John, Steve	Tulsa Community College
Sterr, Jody	Blackhawk Technical College
Thompson, Joyce	Lehigh Carbon Community College
Tucker, William	Austin Community College

Technical Editors

Matthew Bisi
Mary Corcoran
Lori Damanti
Barbara Edington
Sarah Evans
Adam Layne
Joyce Nielsen
Janet Pickard
Sean Portnoy
Jan Snyder
Mara Zebest

Student Reviewers

Albinda, Sarah Evangeline	Phoenix College
Allen, John	Asheville-Buncombe Tech Community College
Alexander, Steven	St. Johns River Community College
Alexander, Melissa	Tulsa Community College
Bolz, Stephanie	Northern Michigan University
Berner, Ashley	Central Washington University
Boomer, Michelle	Northern Michigan University
Busse, Brennan	Northern Michigan University
Butkey, Maura	Central Washington University
Cates, Concita	Phoenix College
Charles, Marvin	Harrisburg Area Community College
Christensen, Kaylie	Northern Michigan University
Clark, Glen D. III	Harrisburg Area Community College
Cobble, Jan N.	Greenville Technical College
Connally, Brianna	Central Washington University
Davis, Brandon	Northern Michigan University
Davis, Christen	Central Washington University
De Jesus Garcia, Maria	Phoenix College
Den Boer, Lance	Central Washington University
Dix, Jessica	Central Washington University
Moeller, Jeffrey	Northern Michigan University
Downs, Elizabeth	Central Washington University
Elser, Julie	Harrisburg Area Community College
Erickson, Mike	Ball State University
Frye, Alicia	Phoenix College
Gadomski, Amanda	Northern Michigan University
Gassert, Jennifer	Harrisburg Area Community College
Gross, Mary Jo	Kirkwood Community College
Gyselinck, Craig	Central Washington University
Harrison, Margo	Central Washington University
Hatt, Patrick	Harrisburg Area Community College
Heacox, Kate	Central Washington University
Hedgman, Shaina	Tidewater College
Hill, Cheretta	Northwestern State University
Hochstedler, Bethany	Harrisburg Area Community College Lancaster
Homer, Jean	Greenville Technical College
Innis, Tim	Tulsa Community College
Jarboe, Aaron	Central Washington University
Key, Penny	Greenville Technical College
Klein, Colleen	Northern Michigan University
Lloyd, Kasey	Ivy Tech Bloomington
Moeller, Jeffrey	Northern Michigan University
Mullen, Sharita	Tidewater Community College
Nelson, Cody	Texas Tech University
Nicholson, Regina	Athens Tech College
Niehaus, Kristina	Northern Michigan University
Nisa, Zaibun	Santa Rosa Community College
Nunez, Nohelia	Santa Rosa Community College
Oak, Samantha	Central Washington University
Oberly, Sara	Harrisburg Area Community College Lancaster
Oertii, Monica	Central Washington University
Palenshus, Juliet	Central Washington University
Pohl, Amanda	Northern Michigan University
Presnell, Randy	Central Washington University
Reed, Kailee	Texas Tech University
Ritner, April	Northern Michigan University
Roberts, Corey	Tulsa Community College
Rodgers, Spencer	Texas Tech University
Rodriguez, Flavia	Northwestern State University
Rogers, A.	Tidewater Community College
Rossi, Jessica Ann	Central Washington University
Rothbauer, Taylor	Trident Technical College
Rozelle, Lauren	Texas Tech University
Schmadeke, Kimberly	Kirkwood Community College
Shafapay, Natasha	Central Washington University
Shanahan, Megan	Northern Michigan University
Sullivan, Alexandra Nicole	Greenville Technical College
Teska, Erika	Hawaii Pacific University
Torrenti, Natalie	Harrisburg Area Community College
Traub, Amy	Northern Michigan University
Underwood, Katie	Central Washington University
Walters, Kim	Central Washington University
Warren, Jennifer L.	Greenville Technical College
Wilson, Kelsie	Central Washington University
Wilson, Amanda	Green River Community College
Wylie, Jimmy	Texas Tech University

Series Reviewers

Abraham, Reni	Houston Community College
Addison, Paul	Ivy Tech Community College
Agatston, Ann	Agatston Consulting Technical College
Akuna, Valeria, Ph.D.	Estrella Mountain Community College
Alexander, Melody	Ball Sate University
Alejandro, Manuel	Southwest Texas Junior College
Alger, David	Tidewater Community College Chesapeake Campus
Allen, Jackie	Rowan-Cabarrus Community College
Ali, Farha	Lander University
Amici, Penny	Harrisburg Area Community College
Anderson, Patty A.	Lake City Community College
Andrews, Wilma	Virginia Commonwealth College, Nebraska University
Anik, Mazhar	Tiffin University
Armstrong, Gary	Shippensburg University
Arnold, Linda L.	Harrisburg Area Community College
Ashby, Tom	Oklahoma City Community College
Atkins, Bonnie	Delaware Technical Community College
Aukland, Cherie	Thomas Nelson Community College
Bachand, LaDonna	Santa Rosa Community College
Bagui, Sikha	University of West Florida
Beecroft, Anita	Kwantlen University College
Bell, Paula	Lock Haven College
Belton, Linda	Springfield Tech. Community College
Bennett, Judith	Sam Houston State University
Bhatia, Sai	Riverside Community College
Bishop, Frances	DeVry Institute—Alpharetta (ATL)
Blaszkiewicz, Holly	Ivy Tech Community College/Region 1
Boito, Nancy	HACC Central Pennsylvania's Community College
Borger-Boglin, Grietje L.	San Antonio College/Northeast Lakeview College
Branigan, Dave	DeVry University
Bray, Patricia	Allegany College of Maryland
Britt, Brenda K.	Fayetteville Technical Community College
Brotherton, Cathy	Riverside Community College
Brown, Judy	Western Illinois University
Buehler, Lesley	Ohlone College
Buell, C	Central Oregon Community College
Burns, Christine	Central New Mexico Community College
Byars, Pat	Brookhaven College
Byrd, Julie	Ivy Tech Community College
Byrd, Lynn	Delta State University, Cleveland, Mississippi
Cacace, Richard N.	Pensacola Junior College
Cadenhead, Charles	Brookhaven College
Calhoun, Ric	Gordon College
Cameron, Eric	Passaic Community College
Canine, Jill	Ivy Tech Community College of Indiana
Cannamore, Madie	Kennedy King
Cannon, Kim	Greenville Technical College
Carreon, Cleda	Indiana University—Purdue University, Indianapolis
Carriker, Sandra	North Shore Community College
Casey, Patricia	Trident Technical College
Cates, Wally	Central New Mexico Community College
Chaffin, Catherine	Shawnee State University
Chauvin, Marg	Palm Beach Community College, Boca Raton
Challa, Chandrashekar	Virginia State University
Chamlou, Afsaneh	NOVA Alexandria
Chapman, Pam	Wabaunsee Community College
Christensen, Dan	Iowa Western Community College
Clay, Betty	Southeastern Oklahoma State University
Collins, Linda D.	Mesa Community College
Cone, Bill	Northern Arizona University
Conroy-Link, Janet	Holy Family College
Conway, Ronald	Bowling Green State University
Cornforth, Carol G.	WVNCC
Cosgrove, Janet	Northwestern CT Community
Courtney, Kevin	Hillsborough Community College
Coverdale, John	Riverside Community College
Cox, Rollie	Madison Area Technical College
Crawford, Hiram	Olive Harvey College
Crawford, Sonia	Central New Mexico Community College
Crawford, Thomasina	Miami-Dade College, Kendall Campus
Credico, Grace	Lethbridge Community College
Crenshaw, Richard	Miami Dade Community College, North
Crespo, Beverly	Mt. San Antonio College
Crooks, Steven	Texas Tech University
Crossley, Connie	Cincinnati State Technical Community College
Curik, Mary	Central New Mexico Community College
De Arazoza, Ralph	Miami Dade Community College
Danno, John	DeVry University/Keller Graduate School
Davis, Phillip	Del Mar College
Davis, Richard	Trinity Valley Community College
Davis, Sandra	Baker College of Allen Park
Dees, Stephanie D.	Wharton County Junior College
DeHerrera, Laurie	Pikes Peak Community College
Delk, Dr. K. Kay	Seminole Community College
Denton, Bree	Texas Tech University
Dix, Jeanette	Ivy Tech Community College
Dooly, Veronica P.	Asheville-Buncombe Technical Community College
Doroshow, Mike	Eastfield College
Douglas, Gretchen	SUNYCortland
Dove, Carol	Community College of Allegheny
Dozier, Susan	Tidewater Community College, Virginia Beach Campus
Driskel, Loretta	Niagara Community College
Duckwiler, Carol	Wabaunsee Community College
Duhon, David	Baker College
Duncan, Mimi	University of Missouri-St. Louis
Duthie, Judy	Green River Community College
Duvall, Annette	Central New Mexico Community College

Ecklund, Paula	Duke University
Eilers, Albert	Cincinnati State Technical and Community College
Eng, Bernice	Brookdale Community College
Epperson, Arlin	Columbia College
Evans, Billie	Vance-Granville Community College
Evans, Jean	Brevard Community College
Feuerbach, Lisa	Ivy Tech East Chicago
Finley, Jean	ABTCC
Fisher, Fred	Florida State University
Foster, Nancy	Baker College
Foster-Shriver, Penny L.	Anne Arundel Community College
Foster-Turpen, Linda	CNM
Foszcz, Russ	McHenry County College
Fry, Susan	Boise State University
Fustos, Janos	Metro State
Gallup, Jeanette	Blinn College
Gelb, Janet	Grossmont College
Gentry, Barb	Parkland College
Gerace, Karin	St. Angela Merici School
Gerace, Tom	Tulane University
Ghajar, Homa	Oklahoma State University
Gifford, Steve	Northwest Iowa Community College
Glazer, Ellen	Broward Community College
Gordon, Robert	Hofstra University
Gramlich, Steven	Pasco-Hernando Community College
Graviett, Nancy M.	St. Charles Community College, St. Peters, Missouri
Greene, Rich	Community College of Allegheny County
Gregoryk, Kerry	Virginia Commonwealth State
Griggs, Debra	Bellevue Community College
Grimm, Carol	Palm Beach Community College
Guthrie, Rose	Fox Valley Technical College
Hahn, Norm	Thomas Nelson Community College
Haley-Hunter, Deb	Bluefield State College
Hall, Linnea	Northwest Mississippi Community College
Hammerschlag, Dr. Bill	Brookhaven College
Hansen, Michelle	Davenport University
Hayden, Nancy	Indiana University—Purdue University, Indianapolis
Hayes, Theresa	Broward Community College
Headrick, Betsy	Chattanooga State
Helfand, Terri	Chaffey College
Helms, Liz	Columbus State Community College
Hernandez, Leticia	TCI College of Technology
Hibbert, Marilyn	Salt Lake Community College
Hinds, Cheryl	Norfolk State University
Hines, James	Tidewater Community College
Hoffman, Joan	Milwaukee Area Technical College
Hogan, Pat	Cape Fear Community College
Holland, Susan	Southeast Community College
Holliday, Mardi	Community College of Philadelphia
Hollingsworth, Mary Carole	Georgia Perimeter College
Hopson, Bonnie	Athens Technical College
Horvath, Carrie	Albertus Magnus College
Horwitz, Steve	Community College of Philadelphia
Hotta, Barbara	Leeward Community College
Howard, Bunny	St. Johns River Community
Howard, Chris	DeVry University
Huckabay, Jamie	Austin Community College
Hudgins, Susan	East Central University
Hulett, Michelle J.	Missouri State University
Humphrey, John	Asheville Buncombe Technical Community College
Hunt, Darla A.	Morehead State University, Morehead, Kentucky
Hunt, Laura	Tulsa Community College
Ivey, Joan M.	Lanier Technical College
Jacob, Sherry	Jefferson Community College
Jacobs, Duane	Salt Lake Community College
Jauken, Barb	Southeastern Community
Jerry, Gina	Santa Monica College
Johnson, Deborah S.	Edison State College
Johnson, Kathy	Wright College
Johnson, Mary	Kingwood College
Johnson, Mary	Mt. San Antonio College
Jones, Stacey	Benedict College
Jones, Warren	University of Alabama, Birmingham
Jordan, Cheryl	San Juan College
Kapoor, Bhushan	California State University, Fullerton
Kasai, Susumu	Salt Lake Community College
Kates, Hazel	Miami Dade Community College, Kendall
Keen, Debby	University of Kentucky
Keeter, Sandy	Seminole Community College
Kern-Blystone, Dorothy Jean	Bowling Green State
Kerwin, Annette	College of DuPage
Keskin, Ilknur	The University of South Dakota
Kinney, Mark B.	Baker College
Kirk, Colleen	Mercy College
Kisling, Eric	East Carolina University
Kleckner, Michelle	Elon University
Kliston, Linda	Broward Community College, North Campus
Knuth, Toni	Baker College of Auburn Hills
Kochis, Dennis	Suffolk County Community College
Kominek, Kurt	Northeast State Technical Community College
Kramer, Ed	Northern Virginia Community College
Kretz, Daniel	Fox Valley Technical College
Laird, Jeff	Northeast State Community College
Lamoureaux, Jackie	Central New Mexico Community College
Lange, David	Grand Valley State
LaPointe, Deb	Central New Mexico Community College
Larsen, Jacqueline Anne	A-B Tech
Larson, Donna	Louisville Technical Institute
Laspina, Kathy	Vance-Granville Community College
Le Grand, Dr. Kate	Broward Community College
Lenhart, Sheryl	Terra Community College
Leonard, Yvonne	Coastal Carolina Community College
Letavec, Chris	University of Cincinnati
Lewis, Daphne L, Ed.D.	Wayland Baptist University
Lewis, Julie	Baker College-Allen Park
Liefert, Jane	Everett Community College

Lindaman, Linda	Black Hawk Community College
Lindberg, Martha	Minnesota State University
Lightner, Renee	Broward Community College
Lindberg, Martha	Minnesota State University
Linge, Richard	Arizona Western College
Logan, Mary G.	Delgado Community College
Loizeaux, Barbara	Westchester Community College
Lombardi, John	South University
Lopez, Don	Clovis-State Center Community College District
Lopez, Lisa	Spartanburg Community College
Lord, Alexandria	Asheville Buncombe Tech
Lovering, LeAnne	Augusta Technical College
Lowe, Rita	Harold Washington College
Low, Willy Hui	Joliet Junior College
Lucas, Vickie	Broward Community College
Luna, Debbie	El Paso Community College
Luoma, Jean	Davenport University
Luse, Steven P.	Horry Georgetown Technical College
Lynam, Linda	Central Missouri State University
Lyon, Lynne	Durham College
Lyon, Pat Rajski	Tomball College
Macarty, Matthew	University of New Hampshire
MacKinnon, Ruth	Georgia Southern University
Macon, Lisa	Valencia Community College, West Campus
Machuca, Wayne	College of the Sequoias
Mack, Sherri	Butler County Community College
Madison, Dana	Clarion University
Maguire, Trish	Eastern New Mexico University
Malkan, Rajiv	Montgomery College
Manning, David	Northern Kentucky University
Marcus, Jacquie	Niagara Community College
Marghitu, Daniela	Auburn University
Marks, Suzanne	Bellevue Community College
Marquez, Juanita	El Centro College
Marquez, Juan	Mesa Community College
Martin, Carol	Harrisburg Area Community College
Martin, Paul C.	Harrisburg Area Community College
Martyn, Margie	Baldwin-Wallace College
Marucco, Toni	Lincoln Land Community College
Mason, Lynn	Lubbock Christian University
Matutis, Audrone	Houston Community College
Matkin, Marie	University of Lethbridge
Maurel, Trina	Odessa College
May, Karen	Blinn College
McCain, Evelynn	Boise State University
McCannon, Melinda	Gordon College
McCarthy, Marguerite	Northwestern Business College
McCaskill, Matt L.	Brevard Community College
McClellan, Carolyn	Tidewater Community College
McClure, Darlean	College of Sequoias
McCrory, Sue A.	Missouri State University
McCue, Stacy	Harrisburg Area Community College
McEntire-Orbach, Teresa	Middlesex County College
McKinley, Lee	Georgia Perimeter College
McLeod, Todd	Fresno City College
McManus, Illyana	Grossmont College
McPherson, Dori	Schoolcraft College
Meck, Kari	HACC
Meiklejohn, Nancy	Pikes Peak Community College
Menking, Rick	Hardin-Simmons University
Meredith, Mary	University of Louisiana at Lafayette
Mermelstein, Lisa	Baruch College
Metos, Linda	Salt Lake Community College
Meurer, Daniel	University of Cincinnati
Meyer, Colleen	Cincinnati State Technical and Community College
Meyer, Marian	Central New Mexico Community College
Miller, Cindy	Ivy Tech Community College, Lafayette, Indiana
Mills, Robert E.	Tidewater Community College, Portsmouth Campus
Mitchell, Susan	Davenport University
Mohle, Dennis	Fresno Community College
Molki, Saeed	South Texas College
Monk, Ellen	University of Delaware
Moore, Rodney	Holland College
Morris, Mike	Southeastern Oklahoma State University
Morris, Nancy	Hudson Valley Community College
Moseler, Dan	Harrisburg Area Community College
Nabors, Brent	Reedley College, Clovis Center
Nadas, Erika	Wright College
Nadelman, Cindi	New England College
Nademlynsky, Lisa	Johnson & Wales University
Nagengast, Joseph	Florida Career College
Nason, Scott	Rowan Cabarrus Community College
Ncube, Cathy	University of West Florida
Newsome, Eloise	Northern Virginia Community College Woodbridge
Nicholls, Doreen	Mohawk Valley Community College
Nicholson, John R.	Johnson County Community College
Nielson, Phil	Salt Lake Community College
Nunan, Karen L.	Northeast State Technical Community College
O'Neal, Lois Ann	Rogers State University
Odegard, Teri	Edmonds Community College
Ogle, Gregory	North Community College
Orr, Dr. Claudia	Northern Michigan University South
Orsburn, Glen	Fox Valley Technical College
Otieno, Derek	DeVry University
Otton, Diana Hill	Chesapeake College
Oxendale, Lucia	West Virginia Institute of Technology
Paiano, Frank	Southwestern College
Pannell, Dr. Elizabeth	Collin College
Patrick, Tanya	Clackamas Community College
Paul, Anindya	Daytona State College
Peairs, Deb	Clark State Community College
Perez, Kimberly	Tidewater Community College
Porter, Joyce	Weber State University
Prince, Lisa	Missouri State University-Springfield Campus
Proietti, Kathleen	Northern Essex Community College
Puopolo, Mike	Bunker Hill Community College
Pusins, Delores	HCCC
Putnam, Darlene	Thomas Nelson Community College

Raghuraman, Ram	Joliet Junior College
Rani, Chigurupati	BMCC/CUNY
Reasoner, Ted Allen	Indiana University—Purdue
Reeves, Karen	High Point University
Remillard, Debbie	New Hampshire Technical Institute
Rhue, Shelly	DeVry University
Richards, Karen	Maplewoods Community College
Richardson, Mary	Albany Technical College
Rodgers, Gwen	Southern Nazarene University
Rodie, Karla	Pikes Peak Community College
Roselli, Diane Maie	Harrisburg Area Community College
Ross, Dianne	University of Louisiana in Lafayette
Rousseau, Mary	Broward Community College, South
Rovetto, Ann	Horry-Georgetown Technical College
Rusin, Iwona	Baker College
Sahabi, Ahmad	Baker College of Clinton Township
Samson, Dolly	Hawaii Pacific University
Sams, Todd	University of Cincinnati
Sandoval, Everett	Reedley College
Santiago, Diana	Central New Mexico Community College
Sardone, Nancy	Seton Hall University
Scafide, Jean	Mississippi Gulf Coast Community College
Scheeren, Judy	Westmoreland County Community College
Scheiwe, Adolph	Joliet Junior College
Schneider, Sol	Sam Houston State University
Schweitzer, John	Central New Mexico Community College
Scroggins, Michael	Southwest Missouri State University
Sedlacek, Brenda	Tidewater Community College
Sell, Kelly	Anne Arundel Community College
Sever, Suzanne	Northwest Arkansas Community College
Sewell, John	Florida Career College
Sheridan, Rick	California State University-Chico
Silvers, Pamela	Asheville Buncombe Tech
Sindt, Robert G.	Johnson County Community College
Singer, Noah	Tulsa Community College
Singer, Steven A.	University of Hawai'i, Kapi'olani Community College
Sinha, Atin	Albany State University
Skolnick, Martin	Florida Atlantic University
Smith, Kristi	Allegany College of Maryland
Smith, Patrick	Marshall Community and Technical College
Smith, Stella A.	Georgia Gwinnett College
Smith, T. Michael	Austin Community College
Smith, Tammy	Tompkins Cortland Community Collge
Smolenski, Bob	Delaware County Community College
Smolenski, Robert	Delaware Community College
Southwell, Donald	Delta College
Spangler, Candice	Columbus State
Spangler, Candice	Columbus State Community College
Stark, Diane	Phoenix College
Stedham, Vicki	St. Petersburg College, Clearwater
Stefanelli, Greg	Carroll Community College
Steiner, Ester	New Mexico State University
Stenlund, Neal	Northern Virginia Community College, Alexandria
St. John, Steve	Tulsa Community College
Sterling, Janet	Houston Community College
Stoughton, Catherine	Laramie County Community College
Sullivan, Angela	Joliet Junior College
Sullivan, Denise	Westchester Community College
Sullivan, Joseph	Joliet Junior College
Swart, John	Louisiana Tech University
Szurek, Joseph	University of Pittsburgh at Greensburg
Taff, Ann	Tulsa Community College
Taggart, James	Atlantic Cape Community College
Tarver, Mary Beth	Northwestern State University
Taylor, Michael	Seattle Central Community College
Terrell, Robert L.	Carson-Newman College
Terry, Daniel	Northern Virginia Community College
Thangiah, Sam	Slippery Rock University
Thayer, Paul	Austin Community College
Thompson, Joyce	Lehigh Carbon Community College
Thompson-Sellers, Ingrid	Georgia Perimeter College
Tomasi, Erik	Baruch College
Toreson, Karen	Shoreline Community College
Townsend, Cynthia	Baker College
Trifiletti, John J.	Florida Community College at Jacksonville
Trivedi, Charulata	Quinsigamond Community College, Woodbridge
Tucker, William	Austin Community College
Turgeon, Cheryl	Asnuntuck Community College
Turpen, Linda	Central New Mexico Community College
Upshaw, Susan	Del Mar College
Unruh, Angela	Central Washington University
Vanderhoof, Dr. Glenna	Missouri State University-Springfield Campus
Vargas, Tony	El Paso Community College
Vicars, Mitzi	Hampton University
Villarreal, Kathleen	Fresno
Vitrano, Mary Ellen	Palm Beach Community College
Vlaich-Lee, Michelle	Greenville Technical College
Volker, Bonita	Tidewater Community College
Waddell, Karen	Butler Community College
Wahila, Lori (Mindy)	Tompkins Cortland Community College
Wallace, Melissa	Lanier Technical College
Walters, Gary B.	Central New Mexico Community College
Waswick, Kim	Southeast Community College, Nebraska
Wavle, Sharon M.	Tompkins Cortland Community College
Webb, Nancy	City College of San Francisco
Webb, Rebecca	Northwest Arkansas Community College
Weber, Sandy	Gateway Technical College
Weissman, Jonathan	Finger Lakes Community College
Wells, Barbara E.	Central Carolina Technical College
Wells, Lorna	Salt Lake Community College
Welsh, Jean	Lansing Community College Nebraska
White, Bruce	Quinnipiac University
Willer, Ann	Solano Community College
Williams, Mark	Lane Community College
Williams, Ronald D.	Central Piedmont Community College
Wilms, Dr. G. Jan	Union University
Wilson, Kit	Red River College
Wilson, MaryLou	Piedmont Technical College
Wilson, Roger	Fairmont State University
Wimberly, Leanne	International Academy of Design and Technology

Winters, Floyd	Manatee Community College
Worthington, Paula	Northern Virginia Community College
Wright, Darrell	Shelton State Community College
Wright, Julie	Baker College
Yauney, Annette	Herkimer County Community College
Yip, Thomas	Passaic Community College
Zavala, Ben	Webster Tech
Zaboski, Maureen	University of Scranton
Zlotow, Mary Ann	College of DuPage
Zudeck, Steve	Broward Community College, North
Zullo, Matthew D.	Wake Technical Community College

About the Authors

Shelley Gaskin, Series Editor, is a professor in the Business and Computer Technology Division at Pasadena City College in Pasadena, California. She holds a bachelor's degree in Business Administration from Robert Morris College (Pennsylvania), a master's degree in Business from Northern Illinois University, and a doctorate in Adult and Community Education from Ball State University. Before joining Pasadena City College, she spent 12 years in the computer industry where she was a systems analyst, sales representative, and Director of Customer Education with Unisys Corporation. She also worked for Ernst & Young on the development of large systems applications for their clients. She has written and developed training materials for custom systems applications in both the public and private sector, and has written and edited numerous computer application textbooks.

This book is dedicated to my students, who inspire me every day.

Robert L. Ferrett recently retired as the Director of the Center for Instructional Computing at Eastern Michigan University, where he provided computer training and support to faculty. He has authored or co-authored more than 70 books on Access, PowerPoint, Excel, Publisher, WordPerfect, Windows, Word, OpenOffice, and Computer Fundamentals. He has been designing, developing, and delivering computer workshops for more than three decades. Before writing for the *GO! Series*, Bob was a series editor for the Learn Series. He has a bachelor's degree in Psychology, a master's degree in Geography, and a master's degree in Interdisciplinary Technology from Eastern Michigan University. His doctoral studies were in Instructional Technology at Wayne State University.

I'd like to dedicate this book to my wife Mary Jane, whose constant support has been so important all these years.

Alicia Vargas is a faculty member in Business Information Technology at Pasadena City College. She holds a master's and a bachelor's degree in business education from California State University, Los Angeles, and has authored several textbooks and training manuals on Microsoft Word, Microsoft Excel, and Microsoft PowerPoint.

This book is dedicated with all my love to my husband Vic, who makes everything possible; and to my children Victor, Phil, and Emmy, who are an unending source of inspiration and who make everything worthwhile.

Carolyn McLellan is the Dean of the Division of Information Technology and Business at Tidewater Community College in Virginia Beach, Virginia. She has a master's degree in Secondary Education from Regent University and a bachelor's degree in Business Education from Old Dominion University. She taught for Norfolk Public Schools for 17 years in Business Education and served as a faculty member at Tidewater Community College for eight years teaching networking, where she developed over 23 new courses and earned the Microsoft Certified Trainer and Microsoft Certified System Engineer industry certifications. In addition to teaching, Carolyn loves to play volleyball, boogie board at the beach, bicycle, crochet, cook, and read.

This book is dedicated to my daughters, Megan and Mandy, who have my eternal love; to my mother, Jean, who always believes in me and encouraged me to become a teacher; to my sister Debbie, who was my first student and who inspires me with her strength in overcoming hardships; to my niece Jenna, for her bravery, composure, and beauty; to my grandsons, Damon and Jordan, who bring me happiness and a renewed joie de vie; and to the students and IT faculty at Tidewater Community College.

Teach the Course You Want in Less Time

A Microsoft® Office textbook designed for student success!

GO!

- **Project-Based** – Students learn by creating projects that they will use in the real world.
- **Microsoft Procedural Syntax** – Steps are written to put students in the right place at the right time.
- **Teachable Moment** – Expository text is woven into the steps—at the moment students need to know it—not chunked together in a block of text that will go unread.
- **Sequential Pagination** – Students have actual page numbers instead of confusing letters and abbreviations.

Student Outcomes and Learning Objectives – Objectives are clustered around projects that result in student outcomes.

Project Activities – A project summary stated clearly and quickly.

Project Files – Clearly shows students which files are needed for the project and the names they will use to save their documents.

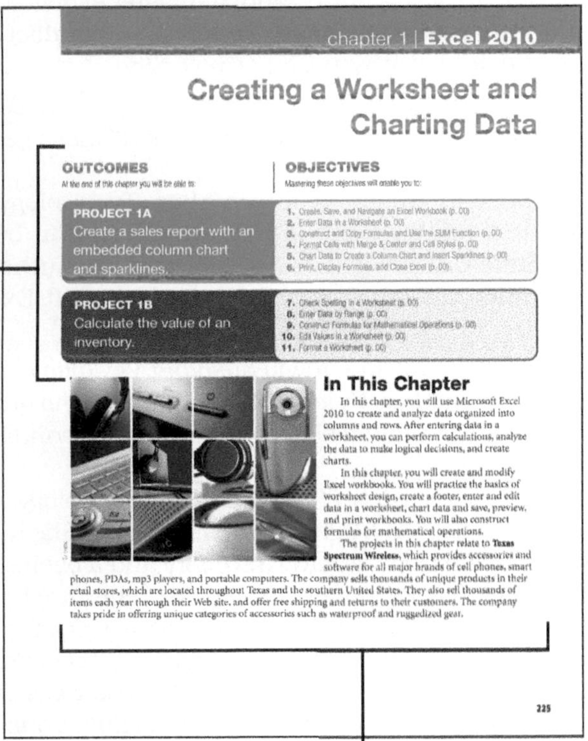

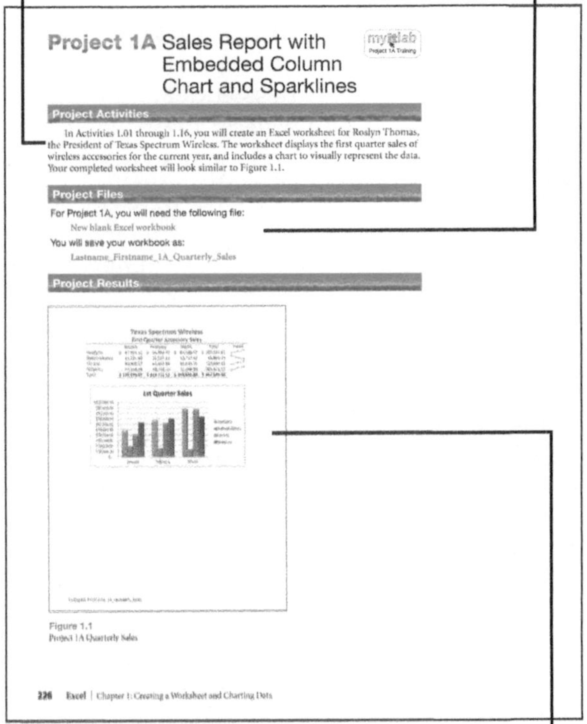

Scenario – Each chapter opens with a story that sets the stage for the projects the student will create.

Project Results – Shows students how their final outcome will appear.

Key Feature

Microsoft Procedural Syntax – Steps are written to put the student in the right place at the right time.

Color Coding – Color variations between the two projects in each chapter make it easy to identify which project students are working on.

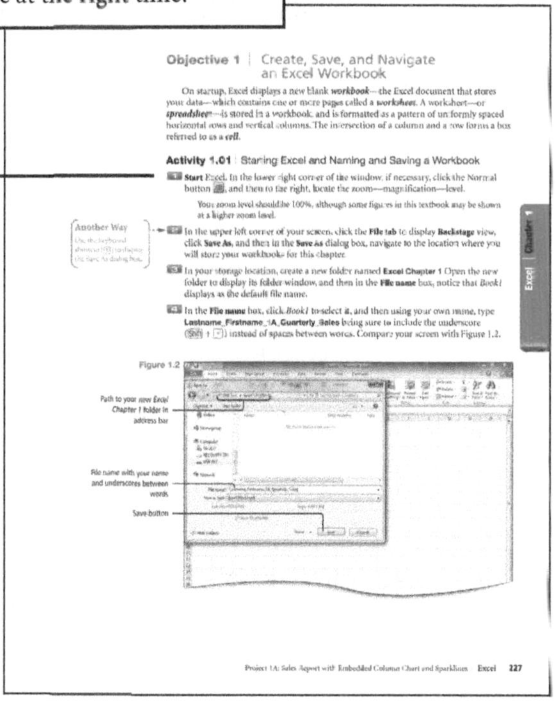

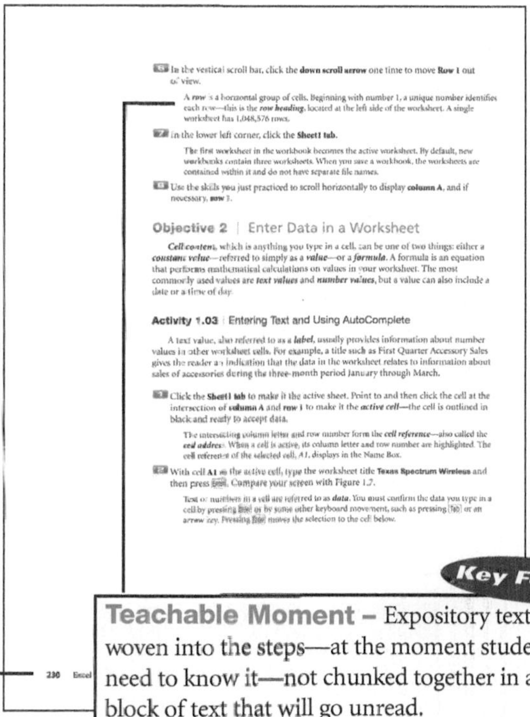

Key Feature

Sequential Pagination – Students are given actual page numbers to navigate through the textbook instead of confusing letters and abbreviations.

Key Feature

Teachable Moment – Expository text is woven into the steps—at the moment students need to know it—not chunked together in a block of text that will go unread.

End-of-Chapter

Content-Based Assessments – Assessments with defined solutions.

Objective List - Every project includes a listing of covered objectives from Projects A and B.

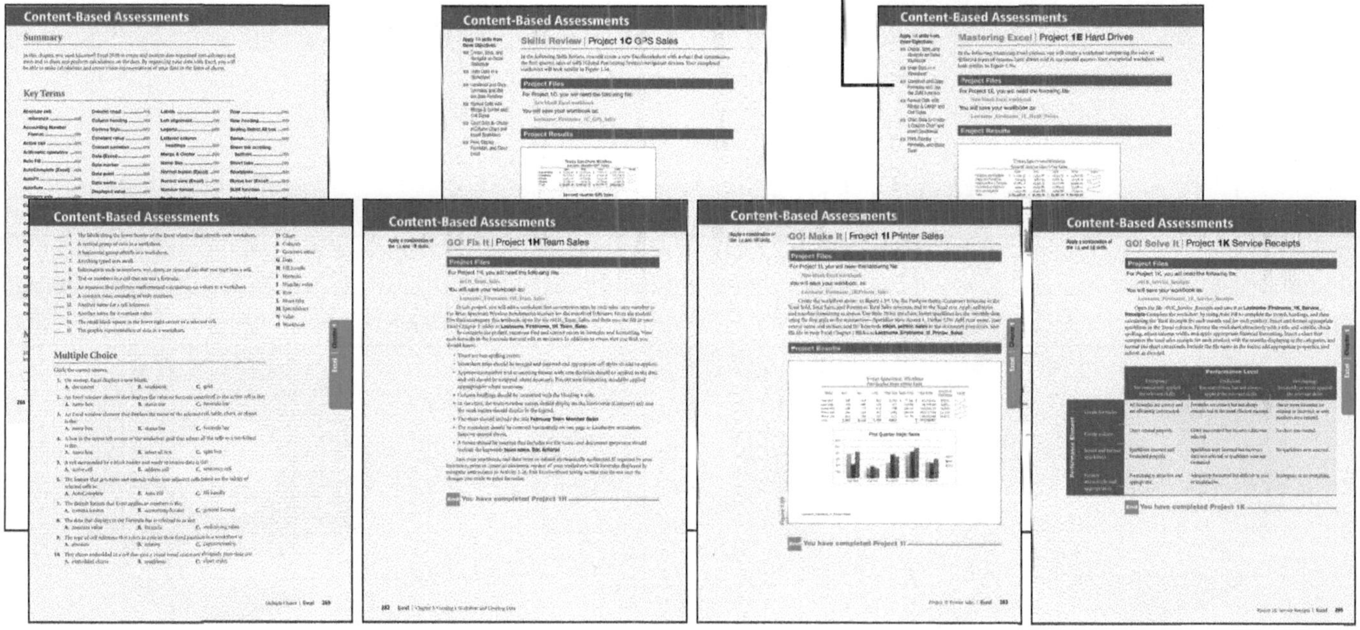

End-of-Chapter

Outcomes-Based Assessments – Assessments with open-ended solutions.

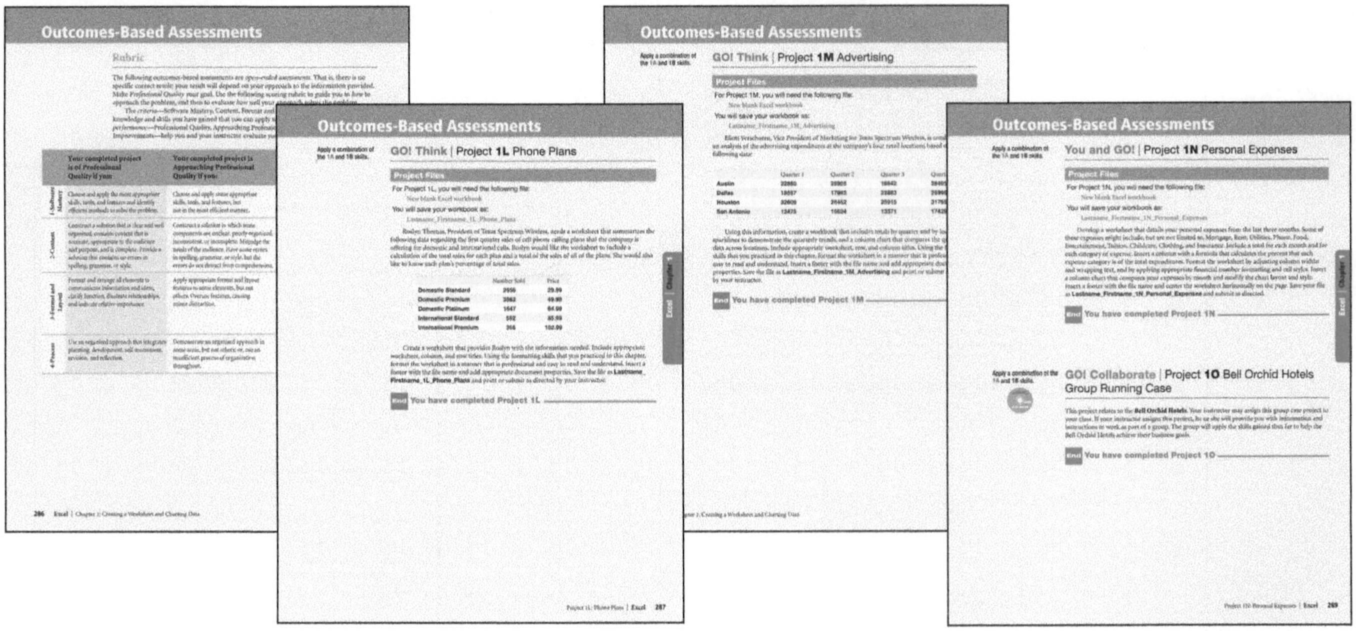

Task-Specific Rubric – A matrix specific to the **GO! Solve It** projects that states the criteria and standards for grading these defined-solution projects.

Outcomes Rubric – A matrix specific to the **GO! Think** projects that states the criteria and standards for grading these open-ended assessments.

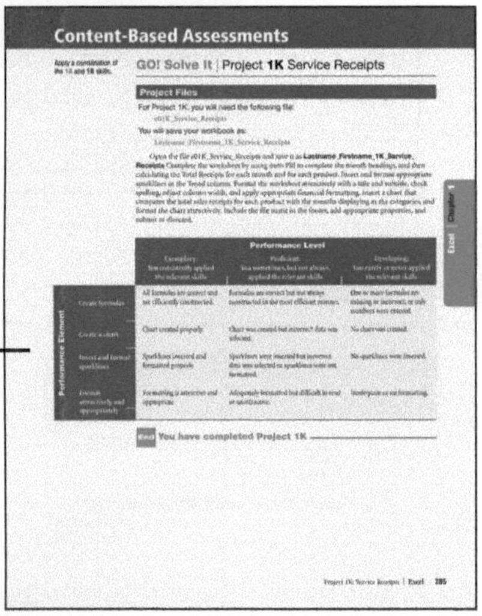

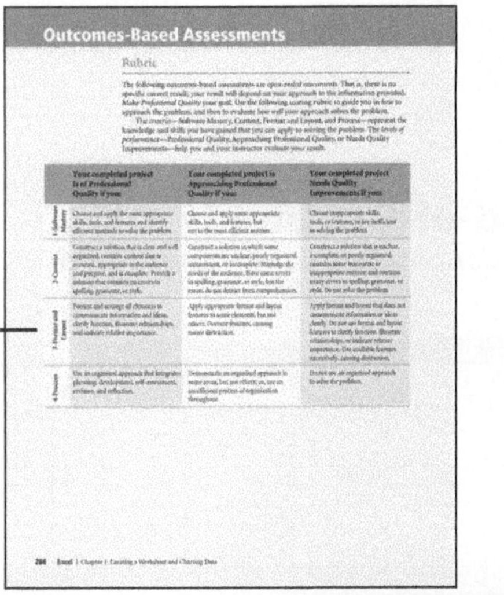

Student CD – All student data files readily available on a CD that comes with the book.

Podcasts – Videos that teach some of the more difficult topics when working with Microsoft applications.

Student Videos – A visual and audio walk-through of every A and B project in the book (see sample images on following page).

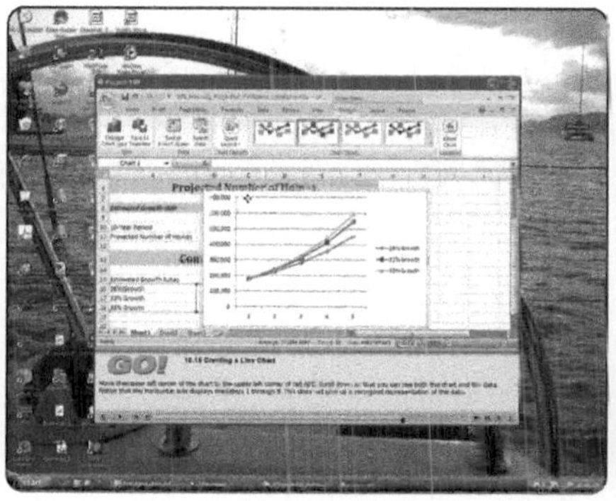

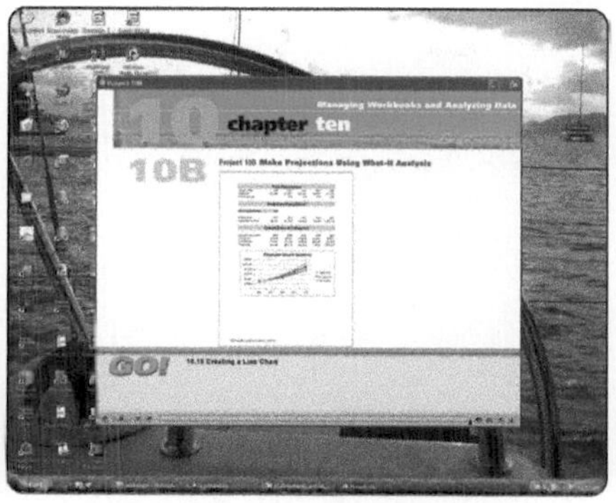

Student Videos! – Each chapter comes with two videos that include audio, demonstrating the objectives and activities taught in the chapter.

All Instructor materials available on the IRCD

Instructor Materials

Annotated Instructor Edition - An instructor tool includes a full copy of the student textbook annotated with teaching tips, discussion topics, and other useful pieces for teaching each chapter.

Assignment Sheets – Lists all the assignments for the chapter. Just add in the course information, due dates, and points. Providing these to students ensures they will know what is due and when.

Scripted Lectures – Classroom lectures prepared for you.

Annotated Solution Files – Coupled with the assignment tags, these create a grading and scoring system that makes grading so much easier for you.

PowerPoint Lectures – PowerPoint presentations for each chapter.

Scoring Rubrics – Can be used either by students to check their work or by you as a quick check-off for the items that need to be corrected.

Syllabus Templates - For 8-week, 12-week, and 16-week courses.

Test Bank – Includes a variety of test questions for each chapter.

Companion Website – Online content such as the Online Study Guide, Glossary, and Student Data Files are all at **www.pearsonhighered.com/go**.

Using the Common Features of Microsoft Office 2010

OUTCOMES

At the end of this chapter you will be able to:

OBJECTIVES

Mastering these objectives will enable you to:

PROJECT 1A

Create, save, and print a Microsoft Office 2010 file.

1. Use Windows Explorer to Locate Files and Folders (p. 3)
2. Locate and Start a Microsoft Office 2010 Program (p. 6)
3. Enter and Edit Text in an Office 2010 Program (p. 9)
4. Perform Commands from a Dialog Box (p. 11)
5. Create a Folder, Save a File, and Close a Program (p. 13)
6. Add Document Properties and Print a File (p. 18)

PROJECT 1B

Use the Ribbon and dialog boxes to perform common commands in a Microsoft Office 2010 file.

7. Open an Existing File and Save It with a New Name (p. 22)
8. Explore Options for an Application (p. 25)
9. Perform Commands from the Ribbon (p. 26)
10. Apply Formatting in Office Programs (p. 32)
11. Use the Microsoft Office 2010 Help System (p. 43)
12. Compress Files (p. 44)

olly/Shutterstock

In This Chapter

In this chapter, you will use Windows Explorer to navigate the Windows folder structure, create a folder, and save files in Microsoft Office 2010 programs. You will also practice using the features of Microsoft Office 2010 that are common across the major programs that comprise the Microsoft Office 2010 suite. These common features include creating, saving, and printing files.

Common features also include the new Paste Preview and Microsoft Office Backstage view. You will apply formatting, perform commands, and compress files. You will see that creating professional-quality documents is easy and quick in Microsoft Office 2010, and that finding your way around is fast and efficient.

The projects in this chapter relate to **Oceana Palm Grill**, which is a chain of 25 casual, full-service restaurants based in Austin, Texas. The Oceana Palm Grill owners plan an aggressive expansion program. To expand by 15 additional restaurants in North Carolina and Florida by 2018, the company must attract new investors, develop new menus, and recruit new employees, all while adhering to the company's quality guidelines and maintaining its reputation for excellent service. To succeed, the company plans to build on its past success and maintain its quality elements.

Project 1A PowerPoint File

myitlab Project 1A Training

Project Activities

In Activities 1.01 through 1.06, you will create a PowerPoint file, save it in a folder that you create by using Windows Explorer, and then print the file or submit it electronically as directed by your instructor. Your completed PowerPoint slide will look similar to Figure 1.1.

Project Files

For Project 1A, you will need the following file:

New blank PowerPoint presentation

You will save your file as:

Lastname_Firstname_1A_Menu_Plan

Project Results

Figure 1.1
Project 1A Menu Plan

Objective 1 | Use Windows Explorer to Locate Files and Folders

A ***file*** is a collection of information stored on a computer under a single name, for example, a Word document or a PowerPoint presentation. Every file is stored in a ***folder***—a container in which you store files—or a ***subfolder***, which is a folder within a folder. Your Windows operating system stores and organizes your files and folders, which is a primary task of an operating system.

You ***navigate***—explore within the organizing structure of Windows—to create, save, and find your files and folders by using the ***Windows Explorer*** program. Windows Explorer displays the files and folders on your computer, and is at work anytime you are viewing the contents of files and folders in a ***window***. A window is a rectangular area on a computer screen in which programs and content appear; a window can be moved, resized, minimized, or closed.

Activity 1.01 | Using Windows Explorer to Locate Files and Folders

1. Turn on your computer and display the Windows ***desktop***—the opening screen in Windows that simulates your work area.

> **Note | Comparing Your Screen with the Figures in This Textbook**
>
> Your screen will match the figures shown in this textbook if you set your screen resolution to 1024 × 768. At other resolutions, your screen will closely resemble, but not match, the figures shown. To view your screen's resolution, on the Windows 7 desktop, right-click in a blank area, and then click Screen resolution. In Windows Vista, right-click a blank area, click Personalize, and then click Display Settings. In Windows XP, right-click the desktop, click Properties, and then click the Settings tab.

2. In your CD/DVD tray, insert the **Student CD** that accompanies this textbook. Wait a few moments for an **AutoPlay** window to display. Compare your screen with Figure 1.2.

   AutoPlay is a Windows feature that lets you choose which program to use to start different kinds of media, such as music CDs, or CDs and DVDs containing photos; it displays when you plug in or insert media or storage devices.

> **Note | If You Do Not Have the Student CD**
>
> If you do not have the Student CD, consult the inside back flap of this textbook for instructions on how to download the files from the Pearson Web site.

Figure 1.2

3 In the upper right corner of the **AutoPlay** window, move your mouse over—***point*** to—the **Close** button, and then ***click***—press the left button on your mouse pointing device one time.

4 On the left side of the **Windows taskbar**, click the **Start** button to display the **Start menu**. Compare your screen with Figure 1.3.

The ***Windows taskbar*** is the area along the lower edge of the desktop that contains the ***Start button*** and an area to display buttons for open programs. The Start button displays the ***Start menu***, which provides a list of choices and is the main gateway to your computer's programs, folders, and settings.

Figure 1.3

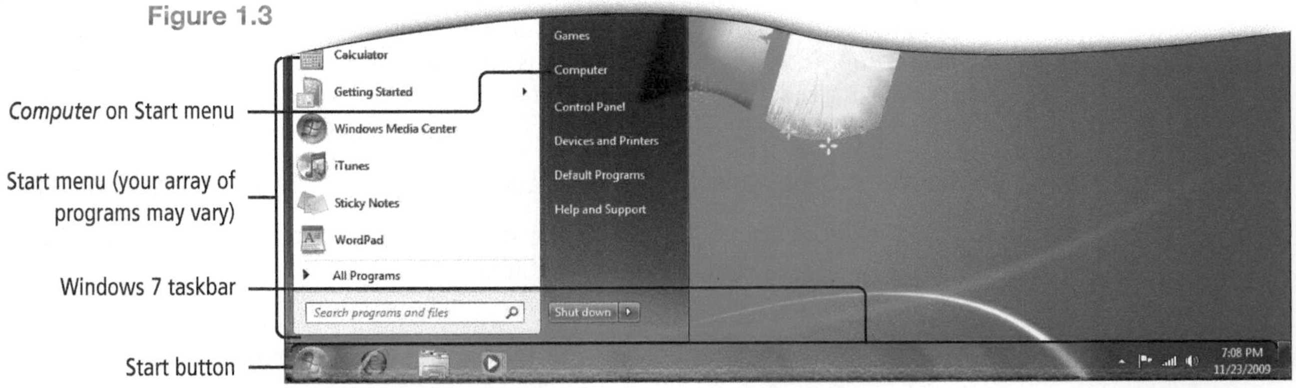

5 On the right side of the **Start menu**, click **Computer** to see the disk drives and other hardware connected to your computer. Compare your screen with Figure 1.4, and then take a moment to study the table in Figure 1.5.

The ***folder window*** for *Computer* displays. A folder window displays the contents of the current folder, ***library***, or device, and contains helpful parts so that you can navigate within Windows.

In Windows 7, a library is a collection of items, such as files and folders, assembled from *various locations*; the locations might be on your computer, an external hard drive, removable media, or someone else's computer.

The difference between a folder and a library is that a library can include files stored in *different locations*—any disk drive, folder, or other place that you can store files and folders.

Figure 1.4

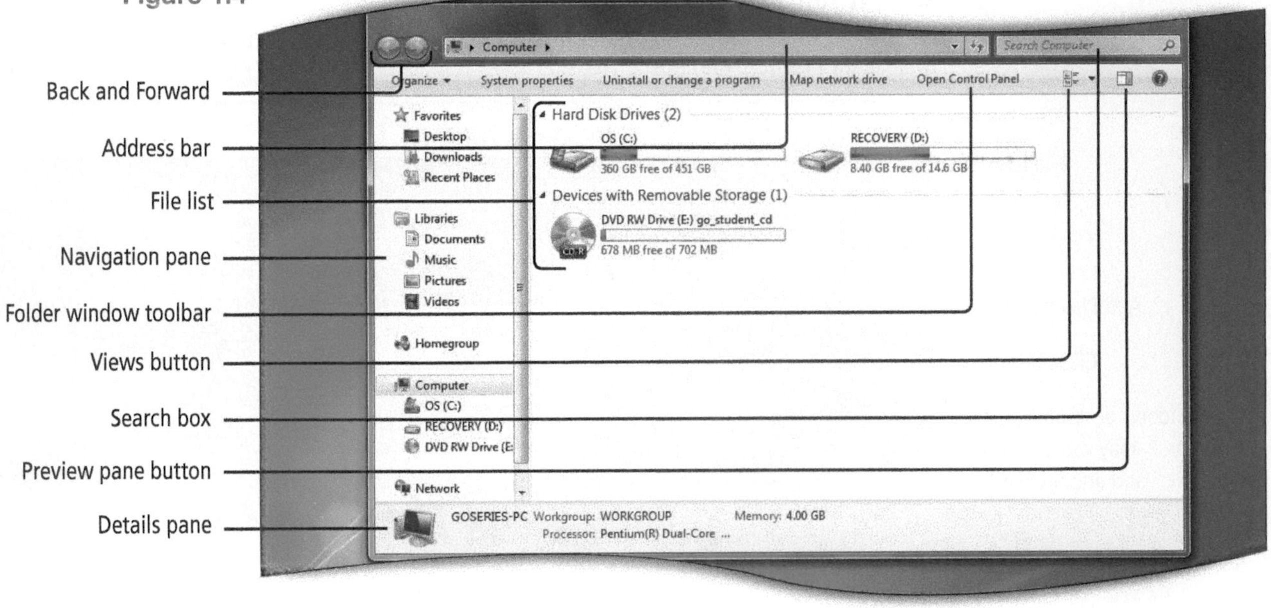

Window Part	Use to:
Address bar	Navigate to a different folder or library, or go back to a previous one.
Back and Forward buttons	Navigate to other folders or libraries you have already opened without closing the current window. These buttons work in conjunction with the address bar; that is, after you use the address bar to change folders, you can use the Back button to return to the previous folder.
Details pane	Display the most common file properties—information about a file, such as the author, the date you last changed the file, and any descriptive ***tags***, which are custom file properties that you create to help find and organize your files.
File list	Display the contents of the current folder or library. In Computer, the file list displays the disk drives.
Folder window for *Computer*	Display the contents of the current folder, library, or device. The Folder window contains helpful features so that you can navigate within Windows.
Folder window toolbar	Perform common tasks, such as changing the view of your files and folders or burning files to a CD. The buttons available change to display only relevant tasks.
Navigation pane	Navigate to, open, and display favorites, libraries, folders, saved searches, and an expandable list of drives.
Preview pane button	Display (if you have chosen to open this pane) the contents of most files without opening them in a program. To open the preview pane, click the Preview pane button on the toolbar to turn it on and off.
Search box	Look for an item in the current folder or library by typing a word or phrase in the search box.
Views button	Choose how to view the contents of the current location.

Figure 1.5

6 On the toolbar of the **Computer** folder window, click the **Views button arrow** —the small arrow to the right of the Views button—to display a list of views that you can apply to the file list. If necessary, on the list, click **Tiles**.

The Views button is a ***split button***; clicking the main part of the button performs a ***command*** and clicking the arrow opens a menu or list. A command is an instruction to a computer program that causes an action to be carried out.

When you open a folder or a library, you can change how the files display in the file list. For example, you might prefer to see large or small ***icons***—pictures that represent a program, a file, a folder, or some other object—or an arrangement that lets you see various types of information about each file. Each time you click the Views button, the window changes, cycling through several views—additional view options are available by clicking the Views button arrow.

Another Way

Point to the CD/DVD drive, right-click, and then click Open.

7 In the **file list**, under **Devices with Removable Storage**, point to your **CD/DVD Drive**, and then ***double-click***—click the left mouse button two times in rapid succession—to display the list of folders on the CD. Compare your screen with Figure 1.6.

When double-clicking, keep your hand steady between clicks; this is more important than the speed of the two clicks.

Figure 1.6

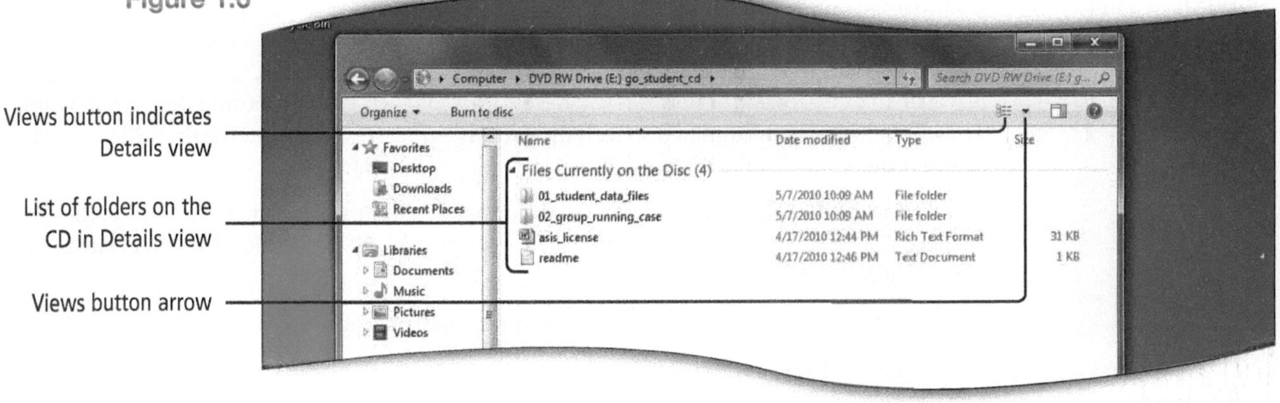

8 In the **file list**, point to the folder **01_student_data_files** and double-click to display the list of subfolders in the folder. Double-click to open the folder **01_common_features.** Compare your screen with Figure 1.7.

The Student Resource CD includes files that you will use to complete the projects in this textbook. If you prefer, you can also copy the **01_student_data_files** folder to a location on your computer's hard drive or to a removable device such as a ***USB flash drive***, which is a small storage device that plugs into a computer USB port. Your instructor might direct you to other locations where these files are located; for example, on your learning management system.

Figure 1.7

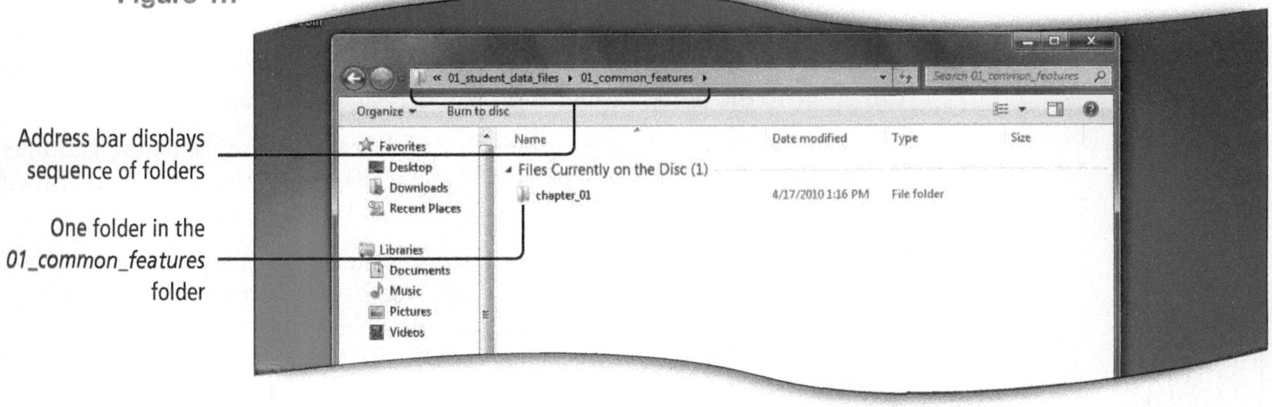

9 In the upper right corner of the **Computer** window, click the **Close** button to redisplay your desktop.

Objective 2 | Locate and Start a Microsoft Office 2010 Program

Microsoft Office 2010 includes programs, servers, and services for individuals, small organizations, and large enterprises. A ***program***, also referred to as an ***application***, is a set of instructions used by a computer to perform a task, such as word processing or accounting.

Activity 1.02 | Locating and Starting a Microsoft Office 2010 Program

1 On the **Windows taskbar**, click the **Start** button to display the **Start** menu.

2 From the displayed **Start** menu, locate the group of **Microsoft Office 2010** programs on your computer—the Office program icons from which you can start the program may be located on your Start menu, in a Microsoft Office folder on the **All Programs** list, on your desktop, or any combination of these locations; the location will vary depending on how your computer is configured.

All Programs is an area of the Start menu that displays all the available programs on your computer system.

3 Examine Figure 1.8, and notice the programs that are included in the Microsoft Office Professional Plus 2010 group of programs. (Your group of programs may vary.)

Microsoft Word is a word processing program, with which you create and share documents by using its writing tools.

Microsoft Excel is a spreadsheet program, with which you calculate and analyze numbers and create charts.

Microsoft Access is a database program, with which you can collect, track, and report data.

Microsoft PowerPoint is a presentation program, with which you can communicate information with high-impact graphics and video.

Additional popular Office programs include ***Microsoft Outlook*** to manage e-mail and organizational activities, ***Microsoft Publisher*** to create desktop publishing documents such as brochures, and ***Microsoft OneNote*** to manage notes that you make at meetings or in classes and to share notes with others on the Web.

The Professional Plus version of Office 2010 also includes ***Microsoft SharePoint Workspace*** to share information with others in a team environment and ***Microsoft InfoPath Designer and Filler*** to create forms and gather data.

Figure 1.8

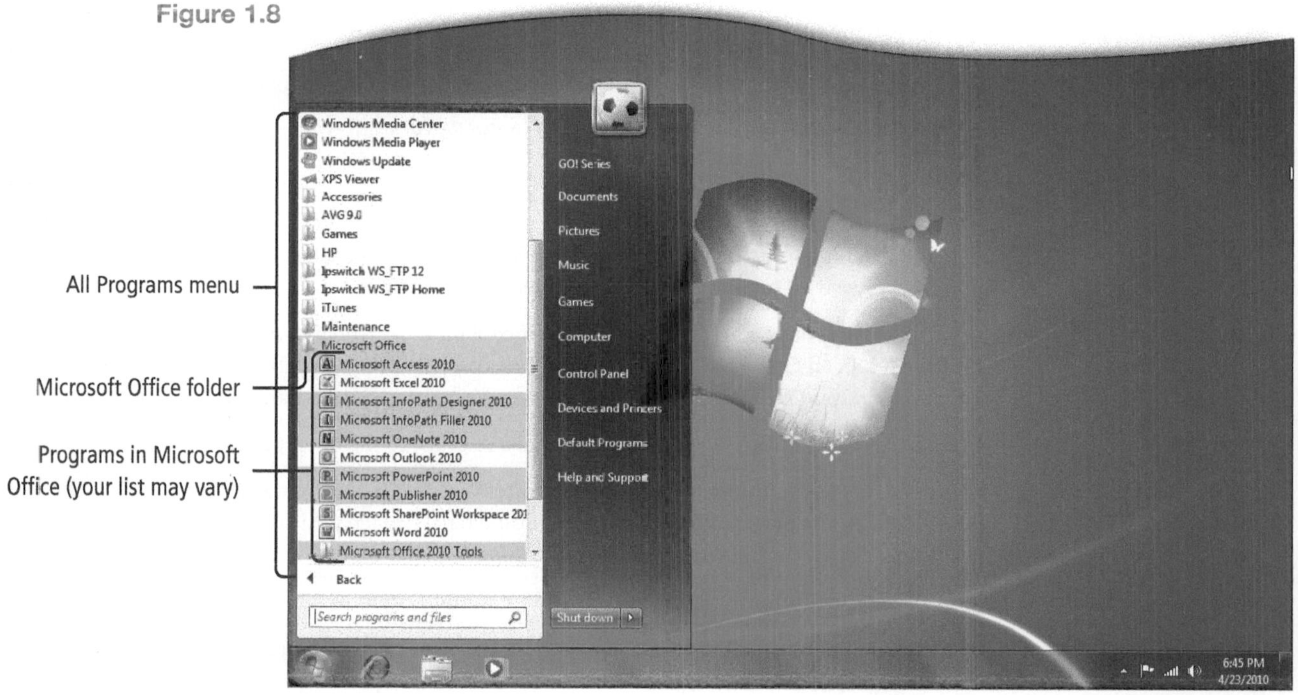

4 Click to open the program **Microsoft PowerPoint 2010.** Compare your screen with Figure 1.9, and then take a moment to study the description of these screen elements in the table in Figure 1.10.

Figure 1.9

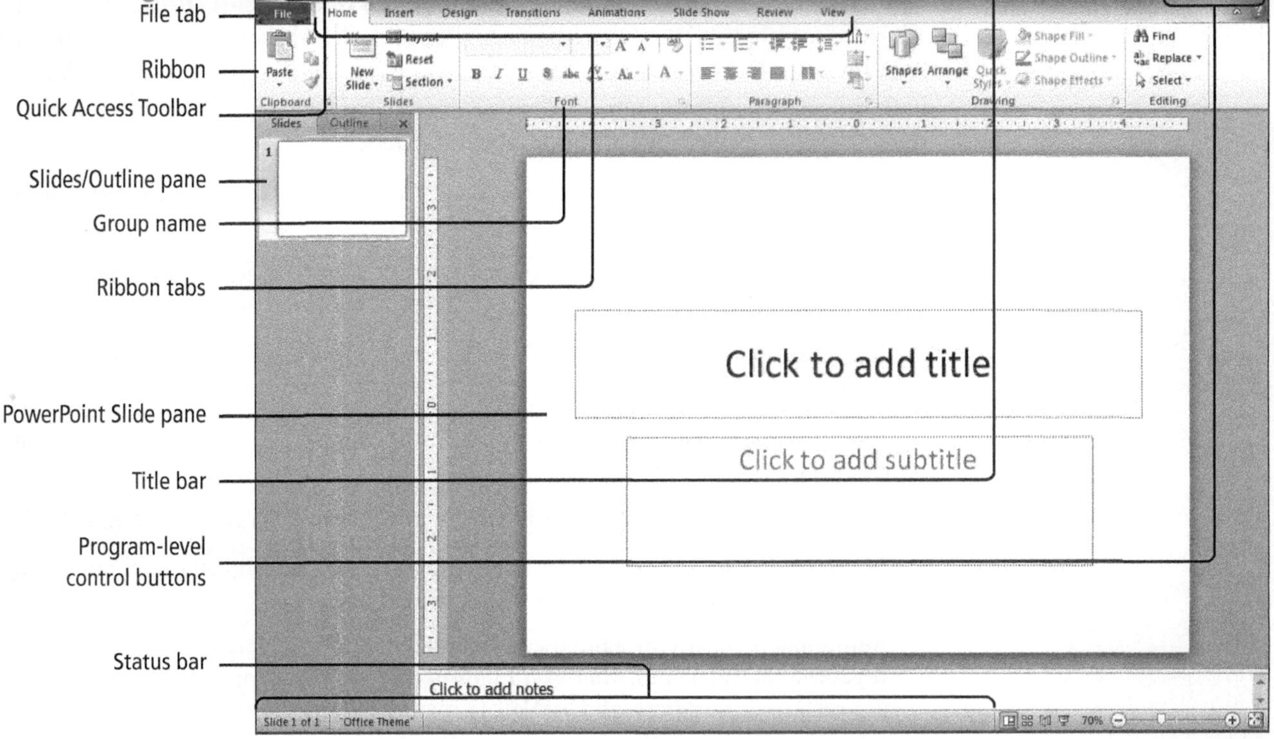

Screen Element	Description
File tab	Displays Microsoft Office Backstage view, which is a centralized space for all of your file management tasks such as opening, saving, printing, publishing, or sharing a file—all the things you can do *with* a file.
Group names	Indicate the name of the groups of related commands on the displayed tab.
PowerPoint Slide pane	Displays a large image of the active slide in the PowerPoint program.
Program-level control buttons	Minimizes, restores, or closes the program window.
Quick Access Toolbar	Displays buttons to perform frequently used commands and resources with a single click. The default commands include Save, Undo, and Redo. You can add and delete buttons to customize the Quick Access Toolbar for your convenience.
Ribbon	Displays a group of task-oriented tabs that contain the commands, styles, and resources you need to work in an Office 2010 program. The look of your Ribbon depends on your screen resolution. A high resolution will display more individual items and button names on the Ribbon.
Ribbon tabs	Display the names of the task-oriented tabs relevant to the open program.
Slides/Outline pane	Displays either thumbnails of the slides in a PowerPoint presentation (Slides tab) or the outline of the presentation's content (Outline tab). In each Office 2010 program, different panes display in different ways to assist you.
Status bar	Displays file information on the left and View and Zoom on the right.
Title bar	Displays the name of the file and the name of the program. The program window control buttons—Minimize, Maximize/Restore Down, and Close—are grouped on the right side of the title bar.

Figure 1.10

Objective 3 | Enter and Edit Text in an Office 2010 Program

All of the programs in Office 2010 require some typed text. Your keyboard is still the primary method of entering information into your computer. Techniques to ***edit***—make changes to—text are similar among all of the Office 2010 programs.

Activity 1.03 | Entering and Editing Text in an Office 2010 Program

1. In the middle of the PowerPoint Slide pane, point to the text *Click to add title* to display the [I] pointer, and then click one time.

   The ***insertion point***—a blinking vertical line that indicates where text or graphics will be inserted—displays.

   In Office 2010 programs, the mouse ***pointer***—any symbol that displays on your screen in response to moving your mouse device—displays in different shapes depending on the task you are performing and the area of the screen to which you are pointing.

2. Type **Oceana Grille Info** and notice how the insertion point moves to the right as you type. Point slightly to the right of the letter *e* in *Grille* and click to place the insertion point there. Compare your screen with Figure 1.11.

Figure 1.11

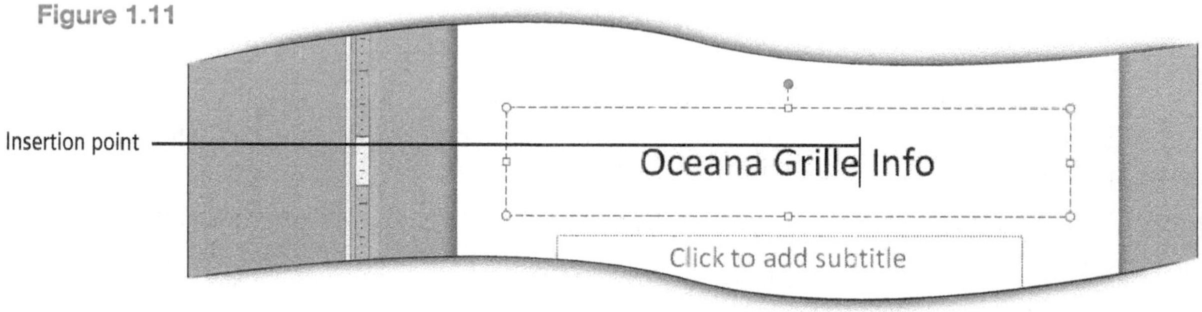

3. On your keyboard, locate and press the [Backspace] key to delete the letter *e*.

   Pressing [Backspace] removes a character to the left of the insertion point.

4. Point slightly to the left of the *I* in *Info* and click one time to place the insertion point there. Type **Menu** and then press [Spacebar] one time. Compare your screen with Figure 1.12.

   By ***default***, when you type text in an Office program, existing text moves to the right to make space for new typing. Default refers to the current selection or setting that is automatically used by a program unless you specify otherwise.

Figure 1.12

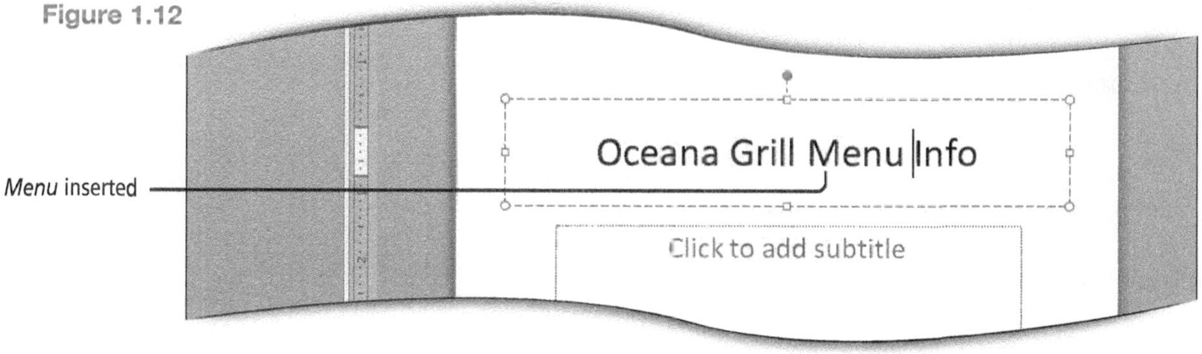

5 Press [Del] four times to delete *Info* and then type **Plan**

Pressing [Del] removes—deletes—a character to the right of the insertion point.

6 With your insertion point blinking after the word *Plan*, on your keyboard, hold down the [Ctrl] key. While holding down [Ctrl], press [←] three times to move the insertion point to the beginning of the word *Grill*.

This is a ***keyboard shortcut***—a key or combination of keys that performs a task that would otherwise require a mouse. This keyboard shortcut moves the insertion point to the beginning of the previous word.

A keyboard shortcut is commonly indicated as [Ctrl] + [←] (or some other combination of keys) to indicate that you hold down the first key while pressing the second key. A keyboard shortcut can also include three keys, in which case you hold down the first two and then press the third. For example, [Ctrl] + [Shift] + [←] selects one word to the left.

7 With the insertion point blinking at the beginning of the word *Grill*, type **Palm** and press [Spacebar].

8 Click anywhere in the text *Click to add subtitle*. With the insertion point blinking, type the following and include the spelling error: **Prepered by Annabel Dunham**

9 With your mouse, point slightly to the left of the *A* in *Annabel*, hold down the left mouse button, and then ***drag***—hold down the left mouse button while moving your mouse—to the right to select the text *Annabel Dunham*, and then release the mouse button. Compare your screen with Figure 1.13.

The ***Mini toolbar*** displays commands that are commonly used with the selected object, which places common commands close to your pointer. When you move the pointer away from the Mini toolbar, it fades from view.

To ***select*** refers to highlighting, by dragging with your mouse, areas of text or data or graphics so that the selection can be edited, formatted, copied, or moved. The action of dragging includes releasing the left mouse button at the end of the area you want to select. The Office programs recognize a selected area as one unit, to which you can make changes. Selecting text may require some practice. If you are not satisfied with your result, click anywhere outside of the selection, and then begin again.

Figure 1.13

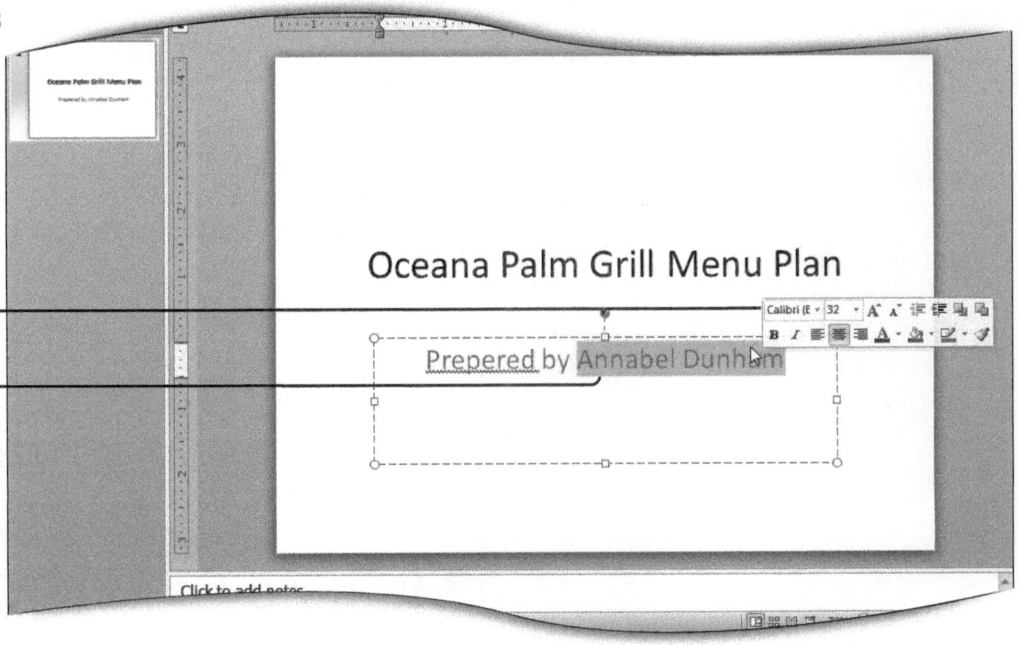

Mini toolbar displays

Annabel Dunham selected

10 With the text *Annabel Dunham* selected, type your own firstname and lastname.

In any Windows-based program, such as the Microsoft Office 2010 programs, selected text is deleted and then replaced when you begin to type new text. You will save time by developing good techniques to select and then edit or replace selected text, which is easier than pressing the Del key numerous times to delete text that you do not want.

11 Notice that the misspelled word *Prepered* displays with a wavy red underline; additionally, all or part of your name might display with a wavy red underline.

Office 2010 has a dictionary of words against which all entered text is checked. In Word and PowerPoint, words that are *not* in the dictionary display a wavy red line, indicating a possible misspelled word or a proper name or an unusual word—none of which are in the Office 2010 dictionary.

In Excel and Access, you can initiate a check of the spelling, but wavy red underlines do not display.

12 Point to *Prepered* and then ***right-click***—click your right mouse button one time.

The Mini toolbar and a ***shortcut menu*** display. A shortcut menu displays commands and options relevant to the selected text or object—known as ***context-sensitive commands*** because they relate to the item you right-clicked.

Here, the shortcut menu displays commands related to the misspelled word. You can click the suggested correct spelling *Prepared*, click Ignore All to ignore the misspelling, add the word to the Office dictionary, or click Spelling to display a ***dialog box***. A dialog box is a small window that contains options for completing a task. Whenever you see a command followed by an ***ellipsis*** (...), which is a set of three dots indicating incompleteness, clicking the command will always display a dialog box.

13 On the displayed shortcut menu, click **Prepared** to correct the misspelled word. If necessary, point to any parts of your name that display a wavy red underline, right-click, and then on the shortcut menu, click Ignore All so that Office will no longer mark your name with a wavy underline in this file.

More Knowledge | Adding to the Office Dictionary

The main dictionary contains the most common words, but does not include all proper names, technical terms, or acronyms. You can add words, acronyms, and proper names to the Office dictionary by clicking Add to Dictionary when they are flagged, and you might want to do so for your own name and other proper names and terms that you type often.

Objective 4 | Perform Commands from a Dialog Box

In a dialog box, you make decisions about an individual object or topic. A dialog box also offers a way to adjust a number of settings at one time.

Activity 1.04 | Performing Commands from a Dialog Box

1 Point anywhere in the blank area above the title *Oceana Palm Grill Menu Plan* to display the pointer.

2 Right-click to display a shortcut menu. Notice the command *Format Background* followed by an ellipsis (...). Compare your screen with Figure 1.14.

Recall that a command followed by an ellipsis indicates that a dialog box will display if you click the command.

Figure 1.14

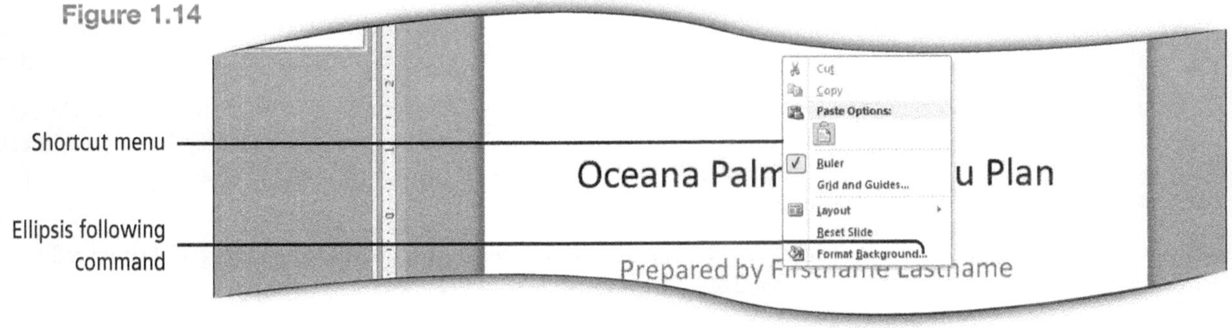

3 Click **Format Background** to display the **Format Background** dialog box, and then compare your screen with Figure 1.15.

Figure 1.15

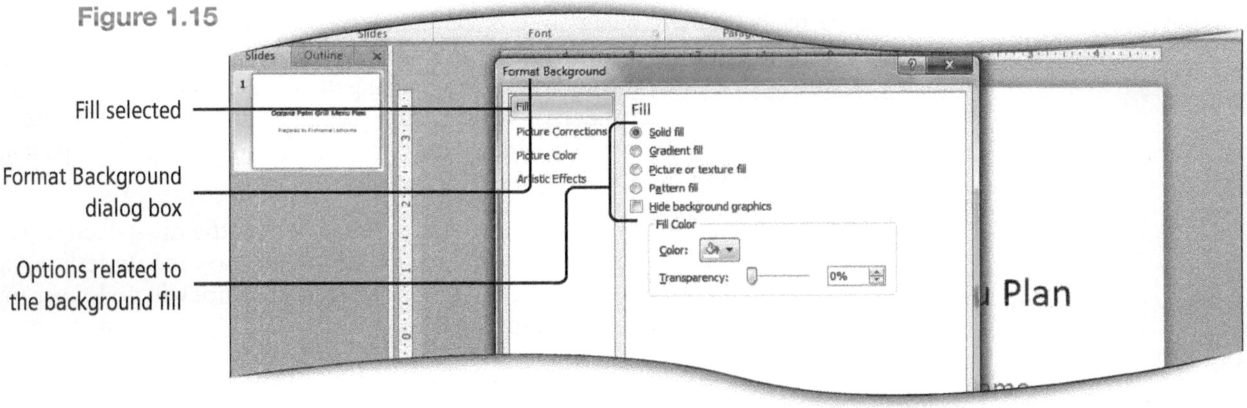

4 On the left, if necessary, click **Fill** to display the **Fill** options.

Fill is the inside color of an object. Here, the dialog box displays the option group names on the left; some dialog boxes provide a set of tabs across the top from which you can display different sets of options.

5 On the right, under **Fill**, click the **Gradient fill** option button.

The dialog box displays additional settings related to the gradient fill option. An ***option button*** is a round button that enables you to make one choice among two or more options. In a gradient fill, one color fades into another.

6 Click the **Preset colors arrow**—the arrow in the box to the right of the text *Preset colors*—and then in the gallery, in the second row, point to the fifth fill color to display the ScreenTip *Fog*.

A ***gallery*** is an Office feature that displays a list of potential results. A ***ScreenTip*** displays useful information about mouse actions, such as pointing to screen elements or dragging.

7 Click **Fog**, and then notice that the fill color is applied to your slide. Click the **Type arrow**, and then click **Rectangular** to change the pattern of the fill color. Compare your screen with Figure 1.16.

Figure 1.16

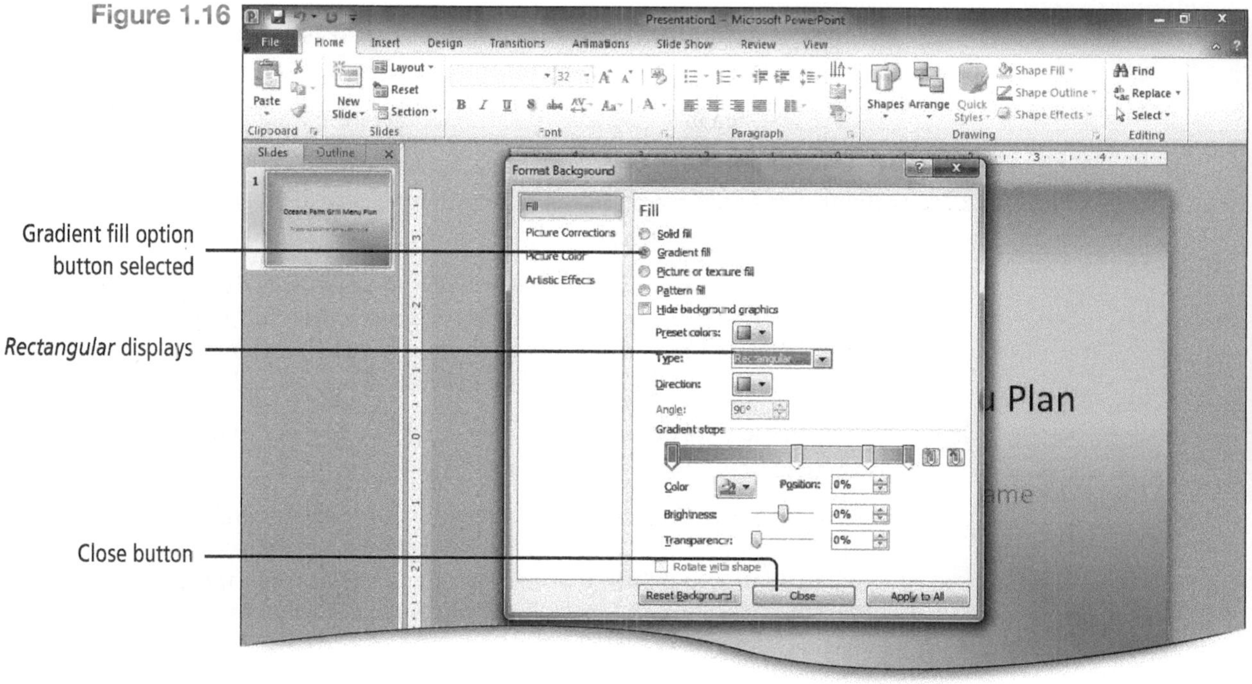

8 At the bottom of the dialog box, click **Close**.

As you progress in your study of Microsoft Office, you will practice using many dialog boxes and applying dramatic effects such as this to your Word documents, Excel spreadsheets, Access databases, and PowerPoint slides.

Objective 5 | Create a Folder, Save a File, and Close a Program

A ***location*** is any disk drive, folder, or other place in which you can store files and folders. Where you store your files depends on how and where you use your data. For example, for your classes, you might decide to store primarily on a removable USB flash drive so that you can carry your files to different locations and access your files on different computers.

If you do most of your work on a single computer, for example your home desktop system or your laptop computer that you take with you to school or work, store your files in one of the Libraries—Documents, Music, Pictures, or Videos—provided by your Windows operating system.

Although the Windows operating system helps you to create and maintain a logical folder structure, take the time to name your files and folders in a consistent manner.

Activity 1.05 | Creating a Folder, Saving a File, and Closing a Program

A PowerPoint presentation is an example of a file. Office 2010 programs use a common dialog box provided by the Windows operating system to assist you in saving files. In this activity, you will create a folder on a USB flash drive in which to store files. If you prefer to store on your hard drive, you can use similar steps to store files in your My Documents folder in your Documents library.

1 Insert a USB flash drive into your computer, and if necessary, **Close** the **AutoPlay** dialog box. If you are not using a USB flash drive, go to Step 2.

As the first step in saving a file, determine where you want to save the file, and if necessary, insert a storage device.

2 At the top of your screen, in the title bar, notice that *Presentation1 – Microsoft PowerPoint* displays.

Most Office 2010 programs open with a new unsaved file with a default name—*Presentation1*, *Document1*, and so on. As you create your file, your work is temporarily stored in the computer's memory until you initiate a Save command, at which time you must choose a file name and location in which to save your file.

3 In the upper left corner of your screen, click the **File tab** to display **Microsoft Office Backstage** view. Compare your screen with Figure 1.17.

Microsoft Office ***Backstage view*** is a centralized space for tasks related to *file* management; that is why the tab is labeled *File*. File management tasks include, for example, opening, saving, printing, publishing, or sharing a file. The ***Backstage tabs***—*Info*, *Recent*, *New*, *Print*, *Save & Send*, and *Help*—display along the left side. The tabs group file-related tasks together.

Above the Backstage tabs, ***Quick Commands***—*Save*, *Save As*, *Open*, and *Close*—display for quick access to these commands. When you click any of these commands, Backstage view closes and either a dialog box displays or the active file closes.

Here, the ***Info tab*** displays information—*info*—about the current file. In the center panel, various file management tasks are available in groups. For example, if you click the Protect Presentation button, a list of options that you can set for this file that relate to who can open or edit the presentation displays.

On the Info tab, in the right panel, you can also examine the ***document properties***. Document properties, also known as ***metadata***, are details about a file that describe or identify it, such as the title, author name, subject, and keywords that identify the document's topic or contents. On the Info page, a thumbnail image of the current file displays in the upper right corner, which you can click to close Backstage view and return to the document.

More Knowledge | Deciding Where to Store Your Files

Where should you store your files? In the libraries created by Windows 7 (Documents, Pictures, and so on)? On a removable device like a flash drive or external hard drive? In Windows 7, it is easy to find your files, especially if you use the libraries. Regardless of where you save a file, Windows 7 will make it easy to find the file again, even if you are not certain where it might be.

In Windows 7, storing all of your files within a library makes sense. If you perform most of your work on your desktop system or your laptop that travels with you, you can store your files in the libraries created by Windows 7 for your user account—Documents, Pictures, Music, and so on. Within these libraries, you can create folders and subfolders to organize your data. These libraries are a good choice for storing your files because:

- From the Windows Explorer button on the taskbar, your libraries are always just one click away.
- The libraries are designed for their contents; for example, the Pictures folder displays small images of your digital photos.
- You can add new locations to a library; for example, an external hard drive, or a network drive. Locations added to a library behave just like they are on your hard drive.
- Other users of your computer cannot access your libraries.
- The libraries are the default location for opening and saving files within an application, so you will find that you can open and save files with fewer navigation clicks.

Figure 1.17

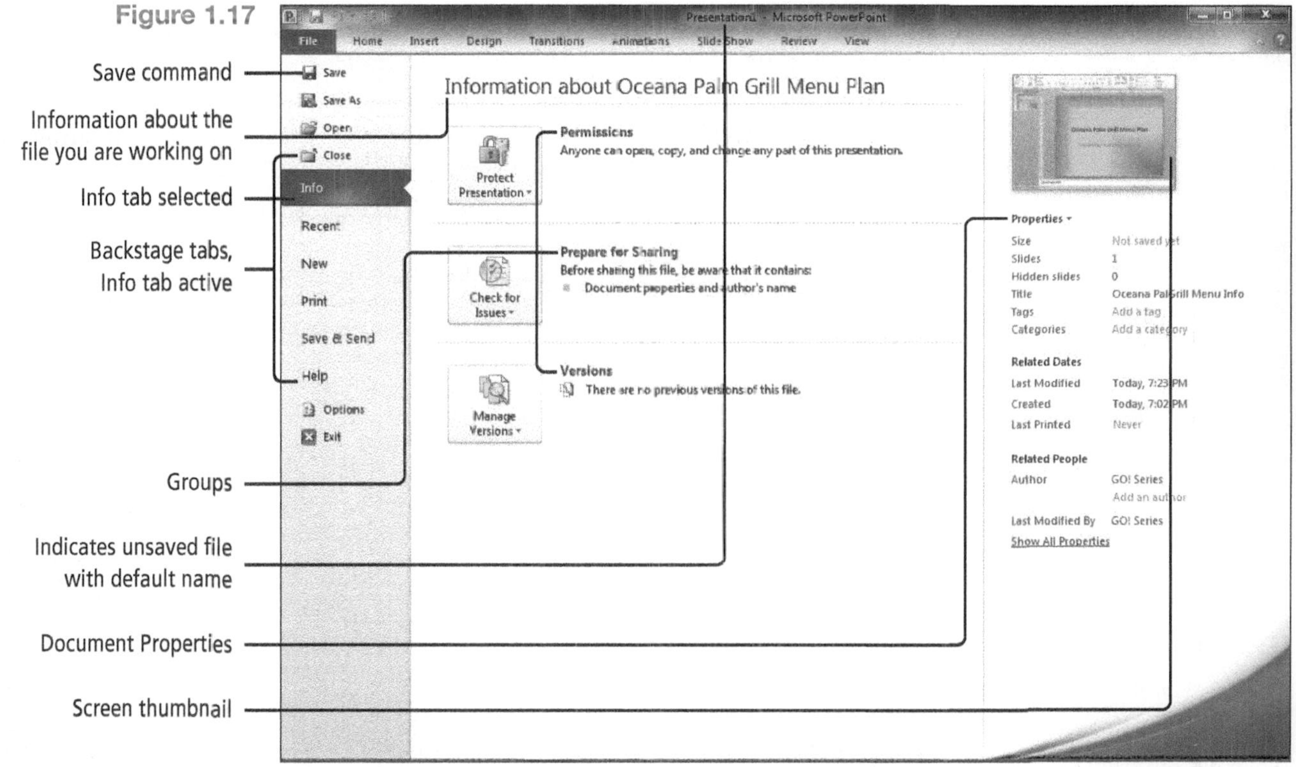

4 Above the **Backstage tabs**, click **Save** to display the **Save As** dialog box.

Backstage view closes and the Save As dialog box, which includes a folder window and an area at the bottom to name the file and set the file type, displays.

When you are saving something for the first time, for example a new PowerPoint presentation, the Save and Save As commands are identical. That is, the Save As dialog box will display if you click Save or if you click Save As.

Note | Saving Your File

After you have named a file and saved it in your desired location, the Save command saves any changes you make to the file without displaying any dialog box. The Save As command will display the Save As dialog box and let you name and save a new file based on the current one—in a location that you choose. After you name and save the new document, the original document closes, and the new document—based on the original one—displays.

5 In the **Save As** dialog box, on the left, locate the **navigation pane**; compare your screen with Figure 1.18.

By default, the Save command opens the Documents library unless your default file location has been changed.

Figure 1.18

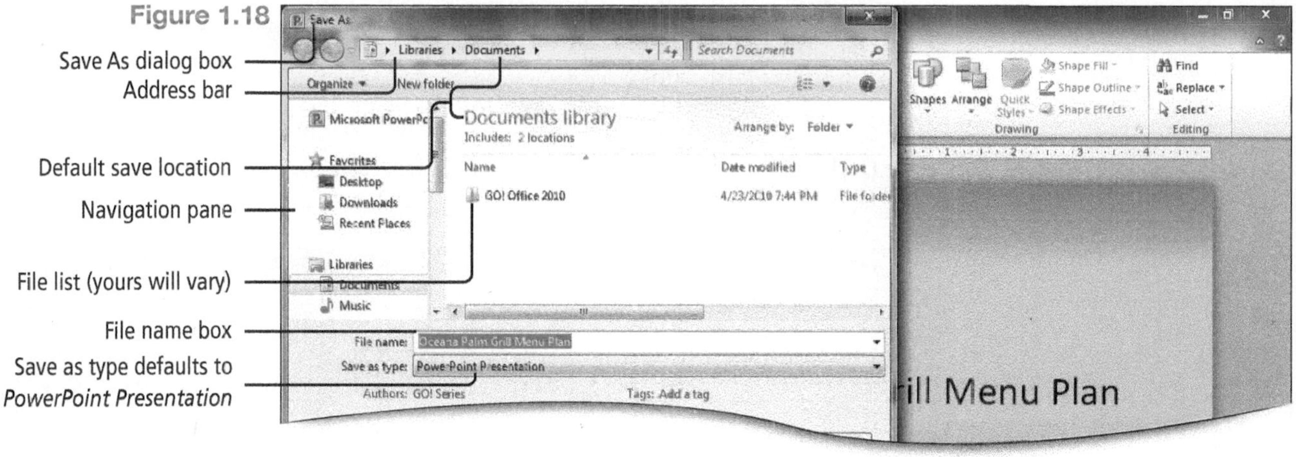

6 On the right side of the **navigation pane**, point to the **scroll bar**. Compare your screen with Figure 1.19.

A ***scroll bar*** displays when a window, or a pane within a window, has information that is not in view. You can click the up or down scroll arrows—or the left and right scroll arrows in a horizontal scroll bar—to scroll the contents up or down or left and right in small increments.

You can also drag the ***scroll box***—the box within the scroll bar—to scroll the window in either direction.

Figure 1.19

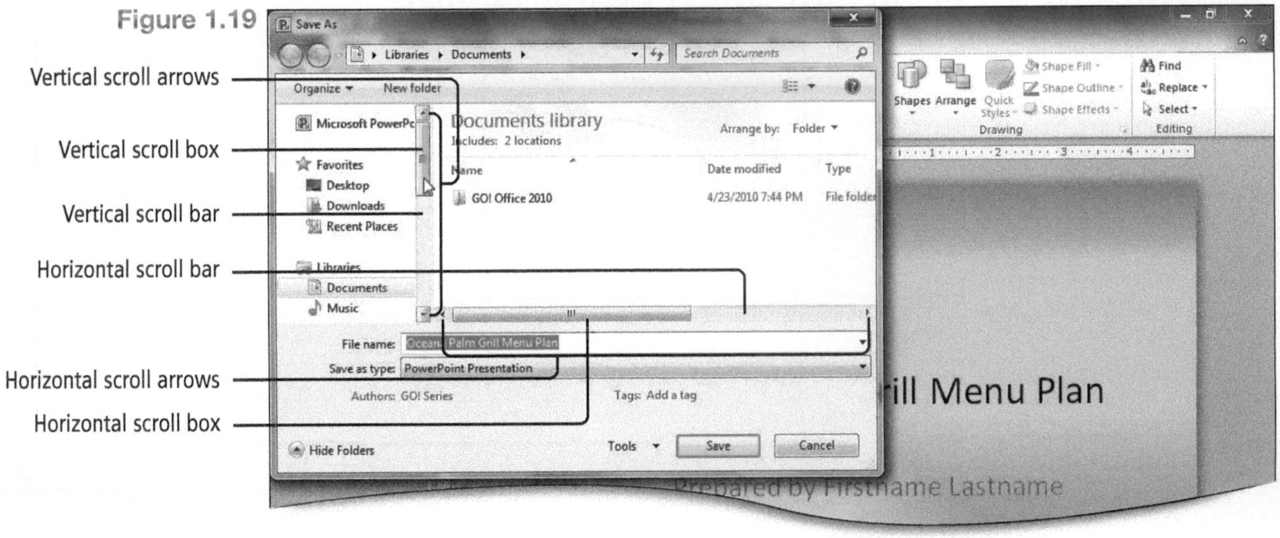

7 Click the **down scroll arrow** as necessary so that you can view the lower portion of the **navigation pane**, and then click the icon for your USB flash drive. Compare your screen with Figure 1.20. (If you prefer to store on your computer's hard drive instead of a USB flash drive, in the navigation pane, click Documents.)

Figure 1.20

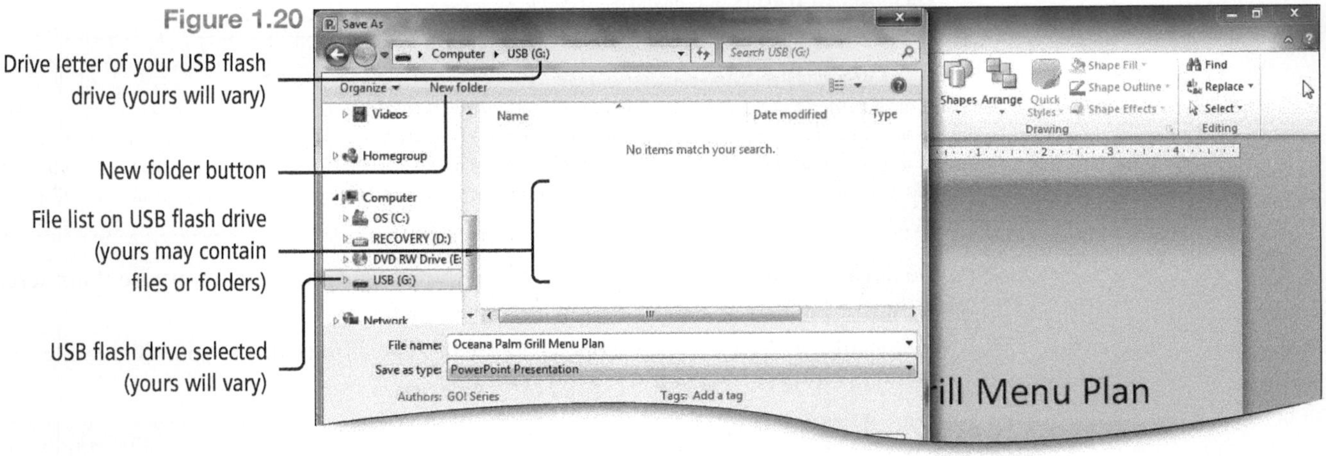

8 On the toolbar, click the **New folder** button.

In the file list, a new folder is created, and the text *New folder* is selected.

9 Type **Common Features Chapter 1** and press Enter. Compare your screen with Figure 1.21.

In Windows-based programs, the Enter key confirms an action.

Figure 1.21

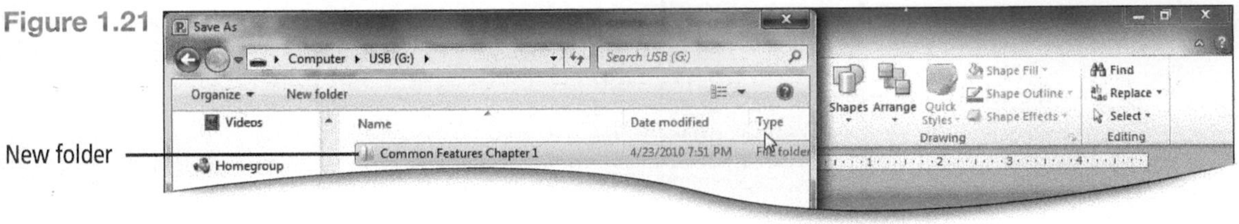

10 In the **file list**, double-click the name of your new folder to open it and display its name in the **address bar**.

11 In the lower portion of the dialog box, click in the **File name** box to select the existing text. Notice that Office inserts the text at the beginning of the presentation as a suggested file name.

12 On your keyboard, locate the [-] key. Notice that the Shift of this key produces the underscore character. With the text still selected, type **Lastname_Firstname_1A_Menu_Plan** Compare your screen with Figure 1.22.

You can use spaces in file names, however some individuals prefer not to use spaces. Some programs, especially when transferring files over the Internet, may not work well with spaces in file names. In general, however, unless you encounter a problem, it is OK to use spaces. In this textbook, underscores are used instead of spaces in file names.

Figure 1.22

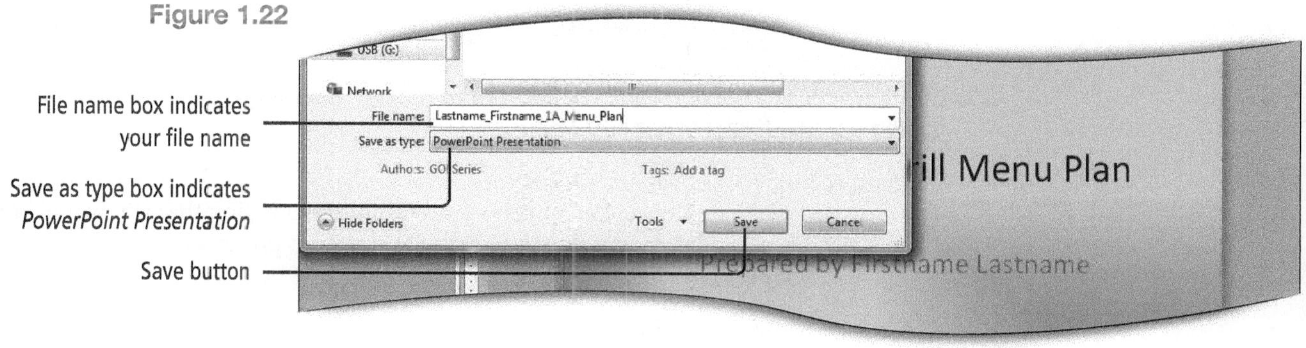

13 In the lower right corner, click **Save**; or press [Enter]. See Figure 1.23.

Your new file name displays in the title bar, indicating that the file has been saved to a location that you have specified.

Figure 1.23

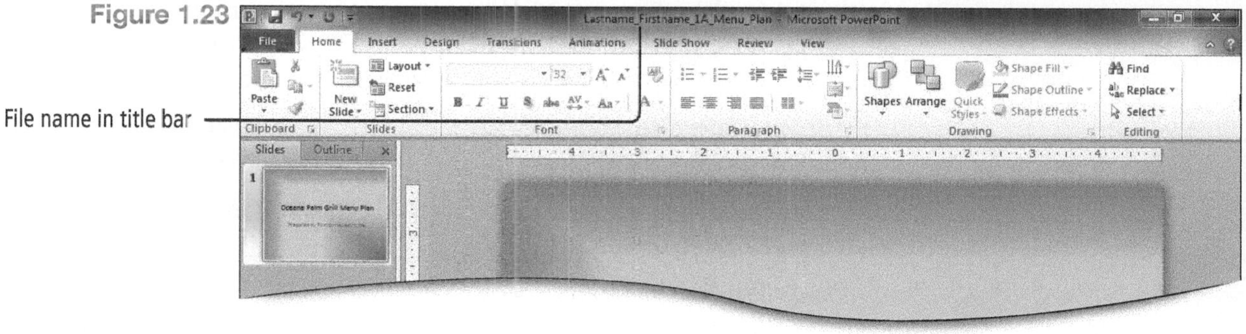

14 In the text that begins *Prepared by*, click to position the insertion point at the end of your name, and then press [Enter] to move to a new line. Type **For Laura Hernandez**

15 Click the **File tab** to display **Backstage** view. At the top of the center panel, notice that the path where your file is stored displays. Above the Backstage tabs, click **Close** to close the file. In the message box, click **Save** to save the changes you made and close the file. Leave PowerPoint open.

PowerPoint displays a message asking if you want to save the changes you have made. Because you have made additional changes to the file since your last Save operation, an Office program will always prompt you to save so that you do not lose any new data.

Objective 6 | Add Document Properties and Print a File

The process of printing a file is similar in all of the Office applications. There are differences in the types of options you can select. For example, in PowerPoint, you have the option of printing the full slide, with each slide printing on a full sheet of paper, or of printing handouts with small pictures of slides on a page.

Activity 1.06 | Adding Document Properties and Printing a File

> **Alert! | Are You Printing or Submitting Your Files Electronically?**
>
> If you are submitting your files electronically only, or have no printer attached, you can still complete this activity. Complete Steps 1-9, and then submit your file electronically as directed by your instructor.

1. In the upper left corner, click the **File tab** to display **Backstage** view. Notice that the **Recent tab** displays.

   Because no file was open in PowerPoint, Office applies predictive logic to determine that your most likely action will be to open a PowerPoint presentation that you worked on recently. Thus, the Recent tab displays a list of PowerPoint presentations that were recently open on your system.

2. At the top of the **Recent Presentations** list, click your **Lastname_Firstname_1A_Menu_Plan** file to open it.

3. Click the **File tab** to redisplay **Backstage** view. On the right, under the screen thumbnail, click **Properties**, and then click **Show Document Panel**. In the **Author** box, delete the existing text, and then type your firstname and lastname. Notice that in PowerPoint, some variation of the slide title is automatically inserted in the Title box. In the **Subject** box, type your Course name and section number. In the **Keywords** box, type **menu plan** and then in the upper right corner of the **Document Properties** panel, click the **Close the Document Information Panel** button [×].

   Adding properties to your documents will make them easier to search for in systems such as Microsoft SharePoint.

> **Another Way**
>
> Press Ctrl + P or Ctrl + F2 to display the Print tab in Backstage view.

4. Redisplay **Backstage** view, and then click the **Print tab.** Compare your screen with Figure 1.24.

   On the Print tab in Backstage view, in the center panel, three groups of printing-related tasks display—Print, Printer, and Settings. In the right panel, the ***Print Preview*** displays, which is a view of a document as it will appear on the paper when you print it.

   At the bottom of the Print Preview area, on the left, the number of pages and arrows with which you can move among the pages in Print Preview display. On the right, ***Zoom*** settings enable you to shrink or enlarge the Print Preview. Zoom is the action of increasing or decreasing the viewing area of the screen.

Figure 1.24

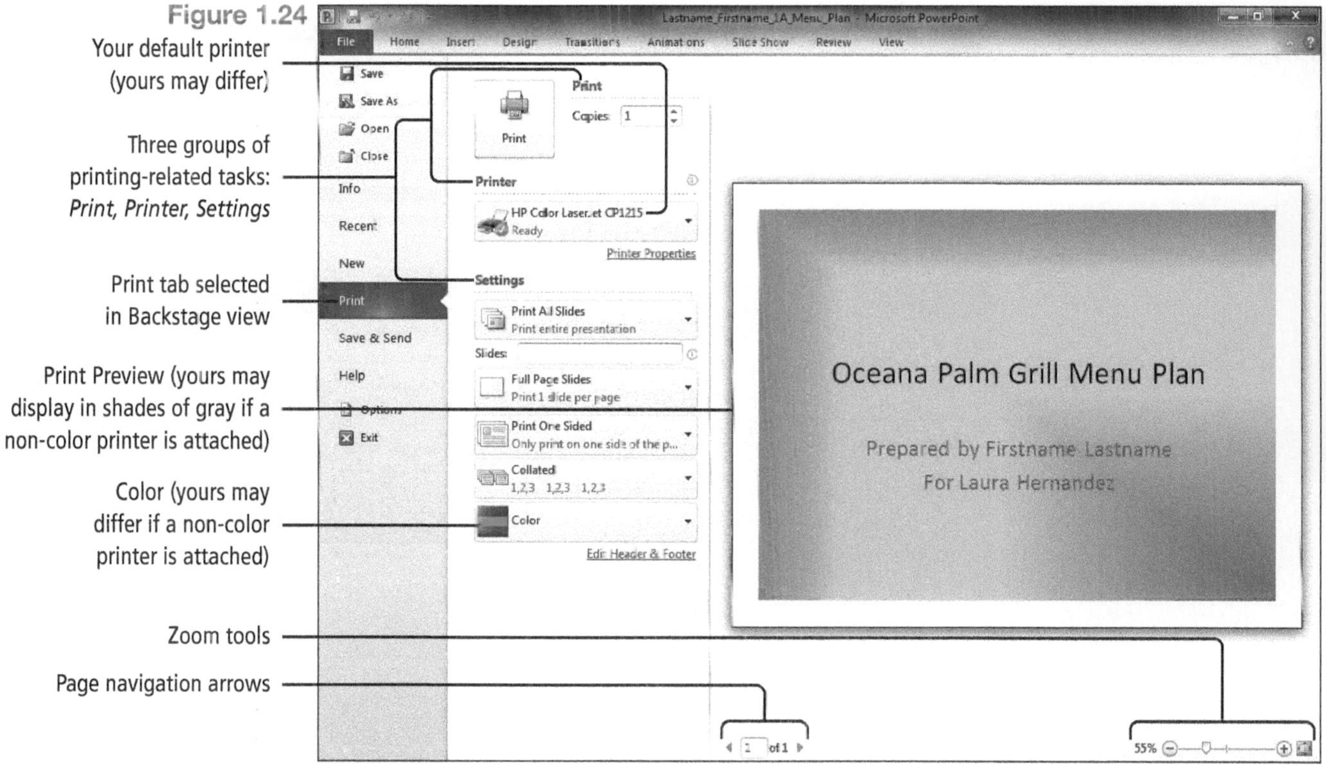

1. Locate the **Settings group**, and notice that the default setting is to **Print All Slides** and to print **Full Page Slides**—each slide on a full sheet of paper.
2. Point to **Full Page Slides**, notice that the button glows orange, and then click the button to display a gallery of print arrangements. Compare your screen with Figure 1.25.

Figure 1.25

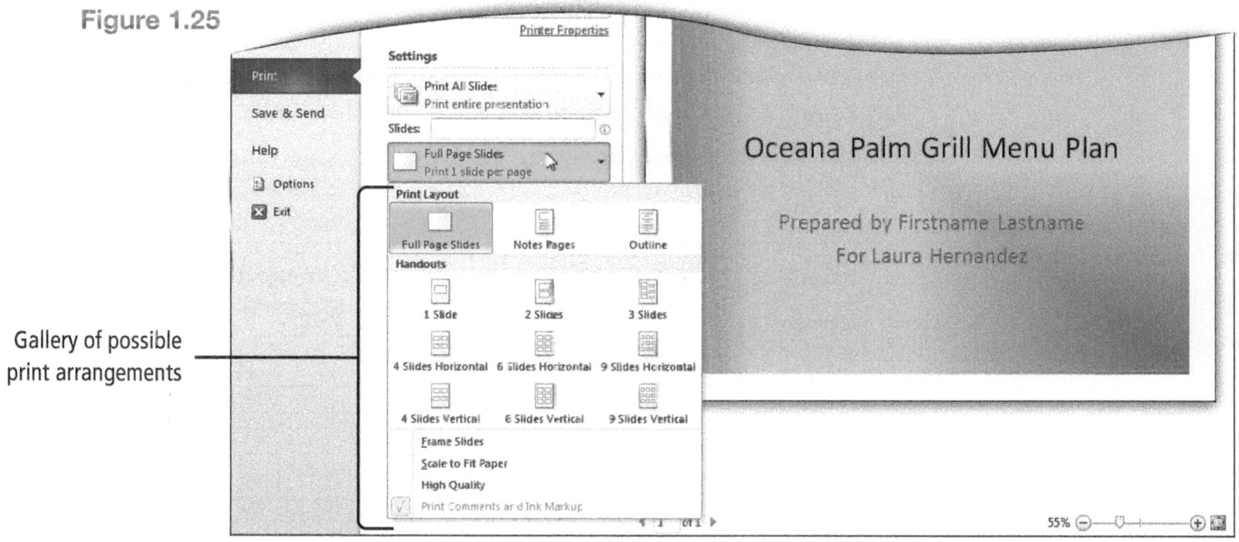

3. In the displayed gallery, under **Handouts**, click **1 Slide**, and then compare your screen with Figure 1.26.

   The Print Preview changes to show how your slide will print on the paper in this arrangement.

Figure 1.26

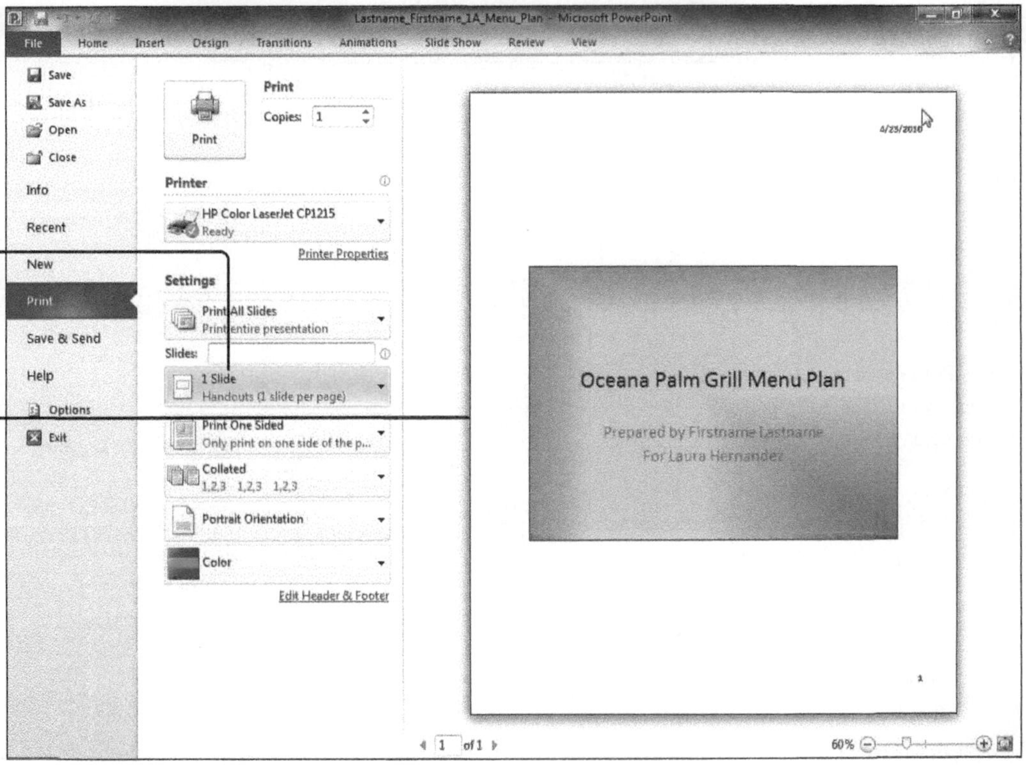

Handouts selected

Print Preview displays the 1 slide printed as handouts setting

8 To submit your file electronically, skip this step and move to Step 9. To print your slide, be sure your system is connected to a printer, and then in the **Print group**, click the **Print** button. On the Quick Access Toolbar, click **Save**, and then move to Step 10.

The handout will print on your default printer—on a black and white printer, the colors will print in shades of gray. Backstage view closes and your file redisplays in the PowerPoint window.

9 To submit your file electronically, above the **Backstage tabs**, click **Close** to close the file and close **Backstage** view, click **Save** in the displayed message, and then follow the instructions provided by your instructor to submit your file electronically.

10 Display **Backstage** view, and then below the **Backstage tabs**, click **Exit** to close your file and close PowerPoint.

Another Way

In the upper right corner of your PowerPoint window, click the red Close button.

More Knowledge | Creating a PDF as an Electronic Printout

From Backstage view, you can save an Office file as a ***PDF file. Portable Document Format*** (PDF) creates an image of your file that preserves the look of your file, but that cannot be easily changed. This is a popular format for sending documents electronically, because the document will display on most computers. From Backstage view, click Save & Send, and then in the File Types group, click Create PDF/XPS Document. Then in the third panel, click the Create PDF/XPS button, navigate to your chapter folder, and then in the lower right corner, click Publish.

End You have completed Project 1A

Project 1B Word File

myitlab Project 1B Training

Project Activities

In Activities 1.07 through 1.16, you will open, edit, save, and then compress a Word file. Your completed document will look similar to Figure 1.27.

Project Files

For Project 1B, you will need the following file:

cf01B_Cheese_Promotion

You will save your Word document as:

Lastname_Firstname_1B_Cheese_Promotion

Project Results

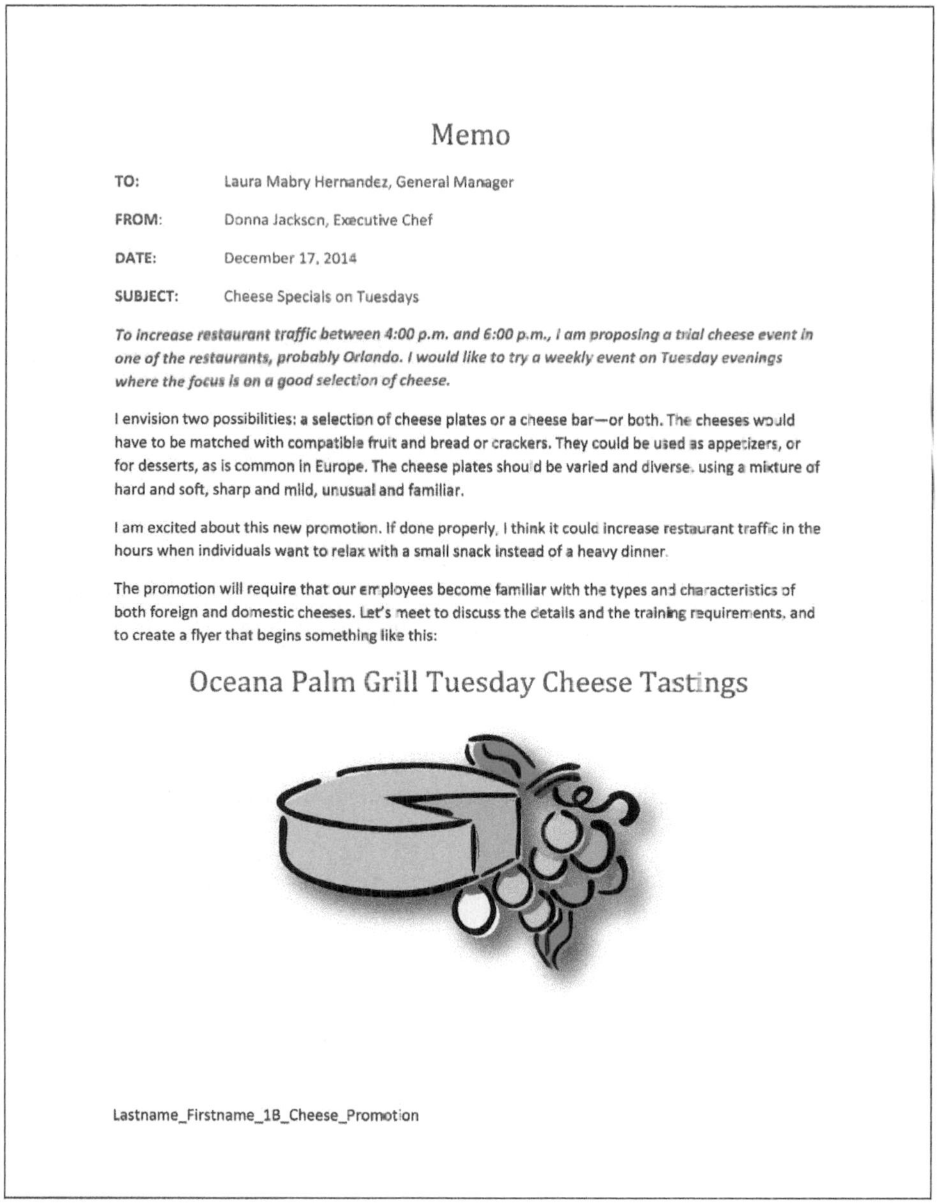

Memo

TO: Laura Mabry Hernandez, General Manager

FROM: Donna Jackson, Executive Chef

DATE: December 17, 2014

SUBJECT: Cheese Specials on Tuesdays

To increase restaurant traffic between 4:00 p.m. and 6:00 p.m., I am proposing a trial cheese event in one of the restaurants, probably Orlando. I would like to try a weekly event on Tuesday evenings where the focus is on a good selection of cheese.

I envision two possibilities: a selection of cheese plates or a cheese bar—or both. The cheeses would have to be matched with compatible fruit and bread or crackers. They could be used as appetizers, or for desserts, as is common in Europe. The cheese plates should be varied and diverse, using a mixture of hard and soft, sharp and mild, unusual and familiar.

I am excited about this new promotion. If done properly, I think it could increase restaurant traffic in the hours when individuals want to relax with a small snack instead of a heavy dinner.

The promotion will require that our employees become familiar with the types and characteristics of both foreign and domestic cheeses. Let's meet to discuss the details and the training requirements, and to create a flyer that begins something like this:

Oceana Palm Grill Tuesday Cheese Tastings

Lastname_Firstname_1B_Cheese_Promotion

Figure 1.27
Project 1B Cheese Promotion

Objective 7 | Open an Existing File and Save It with a New Name

In any Office program, use the Open command to display the ***Open dialog box***, from which you can navigate to and then open an existing file that was created in that same program.

The Open dialog box, along with the Save and Save As dialog boxes, are referred to as ***common dialog boxes***. These dialog boxes, which are provided by the Windows programming interface, display in all of the Office programs in the same manner. Thus, the Open, Save, and Save As dialog boxes will all look and perform the same in each Office program.

Activity 1.07 | Opening an Existing File and Saving it with a New Name

In this activity, you will display the Open dialog box, open an existing Word document, and then save it in your storage location with a new name.

1 Determine the location of the student data files that accompany this textbook, and be sure you can access these files.

For example:

If you are accessing the files from the Student CD that came with this textbook, insert the CD now.

If you copied the files from the Student CD or from the Pearson Web site to a USB flash drive that you are using for this course, insert the flash drive in your computer now.

If you copied the files to the hard drive of your computer, for example in your Documents library, be sure you can locate the files on the hard drive.

2 Determine the location of your **Common Features Chapter 1** folder you created in Activity 1.05, in which you will store your work from this chapter, and then be sure you can access that folder.

For example:

If you created your chapter folder on a USB flash drive, insert the flash drive in your computer now. This can be the same flash drive where you have stored the student data files; just be sure to use the chapter folder you created.

If you created your chapter folder in the Documents library on your computer, be sure you can locate the folder. Otherwise, create a new folder at the computer at which you are working, or on a USB flash drive.

3 Using the technique you practiced in Activity 1.02, locate and then start the **Microsoft Word 2010** program on your system.

Another Way

In the Word (or other program) window, press Ctrl + F12 to display the Open dialog box.

4 On the Ribbon, click the **File tab** to display **Backstage** view, and then click **Open** to display the **Open** dialog box.

5 In the **navigation pane** on the left, use the scroll bar to scroll as necessary, and then click the location of your student data files to display the location's contents in the **file list**. Compare your screen with Figure 1.28.

For example:

If you are accessing the files from the Student CD that came with your book, under Computer, click the CD/DVD.

If you are accessing the files from a USB flash drive, under Computer, click the flash drive name.

If you are accessing the files from the Documents library of your computer, under Libraries, click Documents.

Figure 1.28

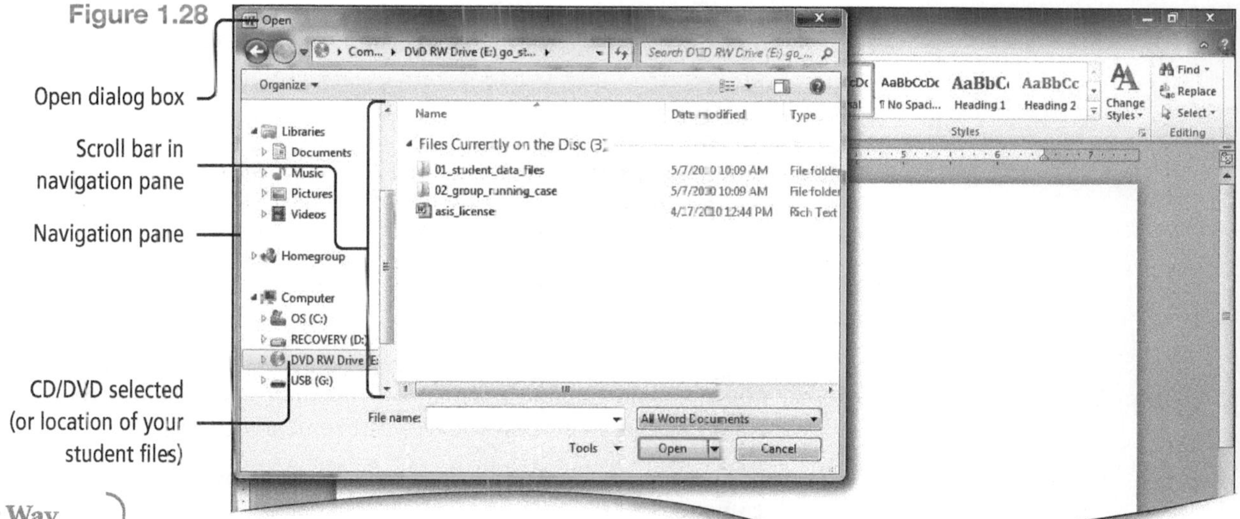

> **Another Way**
> Point to a folder name, right-click, and then from the shortcut menu, click Open.

6 Point to the folder **01_student_data_files** and double-click to open the folder. Point to the subfolder **01_common_features**, double-click, and then compare your screen with Figure 1.29.

Figure 1.29

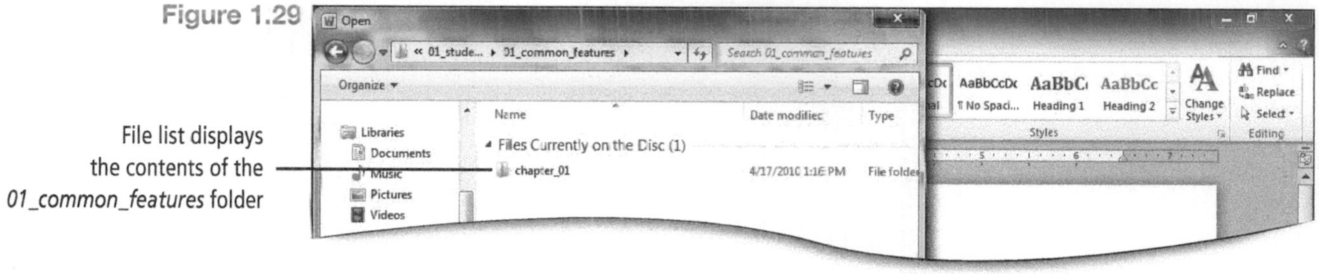

> **Another Way**
> Click one time to select the file, and then press Enter or click the Open button in the lower right corner of the dialog box.

7 In the **file list**, point to the **chapter_01** subfolder and double-click to open it. In the **file list**, point to Word file **cf01B_Cheese_Promotion** and then double-click to open and display the file in the Word window. On the Ribbon, on the **Home tab**, in the **Paragraph group**, if necessary, click the **Show/Hide** button ¶ so that it is active—glowing orange. Compare your screen with Figure 1.30.

On the title bar at the top of the screen, the file name displays. If you opened the document from the Student CD, (*Read-Only*) will display. If you opened the document from another source to which the files were copied, (*Read-Only*) might not display. ***Read-Only*** is a property assigned to a file that prevents the file from being modified or deleted; it indicates that you cannot save any changes to the displayed document unless you first save it with a new name.

Figure 1.30

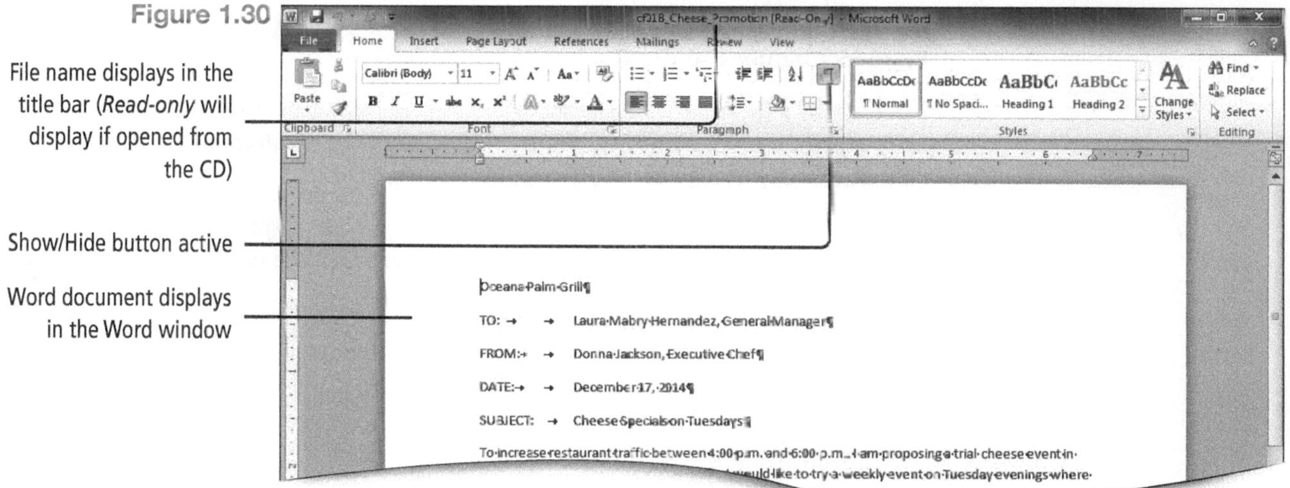

Alert! | Do You See a Message to Enable Editing or Enable Content?

In Office 2010, some files open in ***Protected View*** if the file appears to be from a potentially risky location, such as the Internet. Protected View is a new security feature in Office 2010 that protects your computer from malicious files by opening them in a restricted environment until you enable them. ***Trusted Documents*** is another security feature that remembers which files you have already enabled. You might encounter these security features if you open a file from an e-mail or download files from the Internet; for example, from your college's learning management system or from the Pearson Web site. So long as you trust the source of the file, click Enable Editing or Enable Content—depending on the type of file you receive—and then go ahead and work with the file.

Another Way

Press F12 to display the Save As dialog box.

8 Click the **File tab** to display **Backstage** view, and then click the **Save As** command to display the **Save As** dialog box. Compare your screen with Figure 1.31.

The Save As command displays the Save As dialog box where you can name and save a *new* document based on the currently displayed document. After you name and save the new document, the original document closes, and the new document—based on the original one—displays.

Figure 1.31

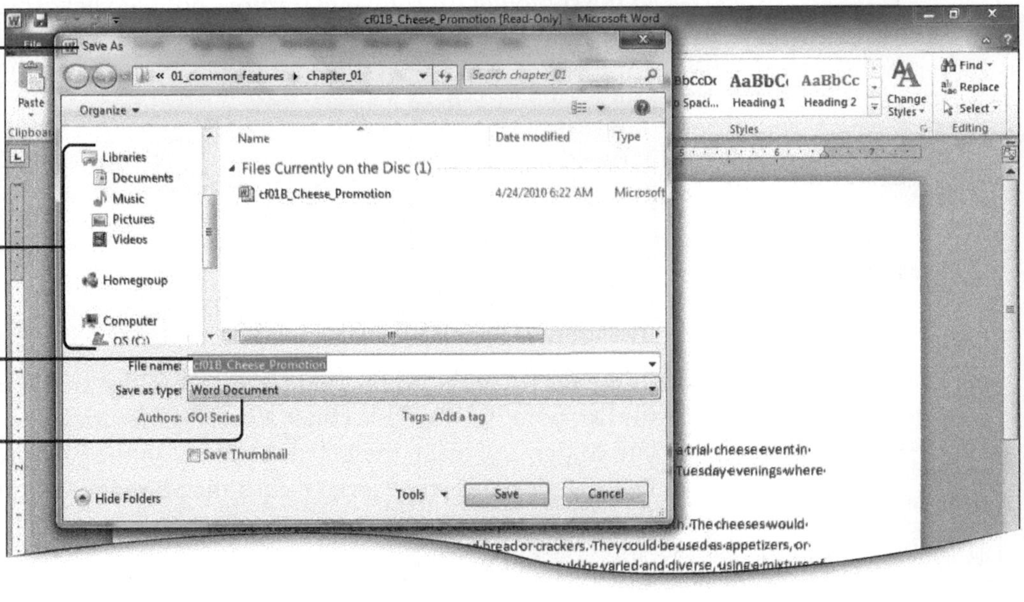

9 In the **navigation pane**, click the location in which you are storing your projects for this chapter—the location where you created your **Common Features Chapter 1** folder; for example, your USB flash drive or the Documents library.

10 In the **file list**, double-click the necessary folders and subfolders until your **Common Features Chapter 1** folder displays in the **address bar**.

11 Click in the **File name** box to select the existing file name, or drag to select the existing text, and then using your own name, type **Lastname_Firstname_1B_Cheese_Promotion** Compare your screen with Figure 1.32.

As you type, the file name from your 1A project might display briefly. Because your 1A project file is stored in this location and you began the new file name with the same text, Office predicts that you might want the same or similar file name. As you type new characters, the suggestion is removed.

Figure 1.32

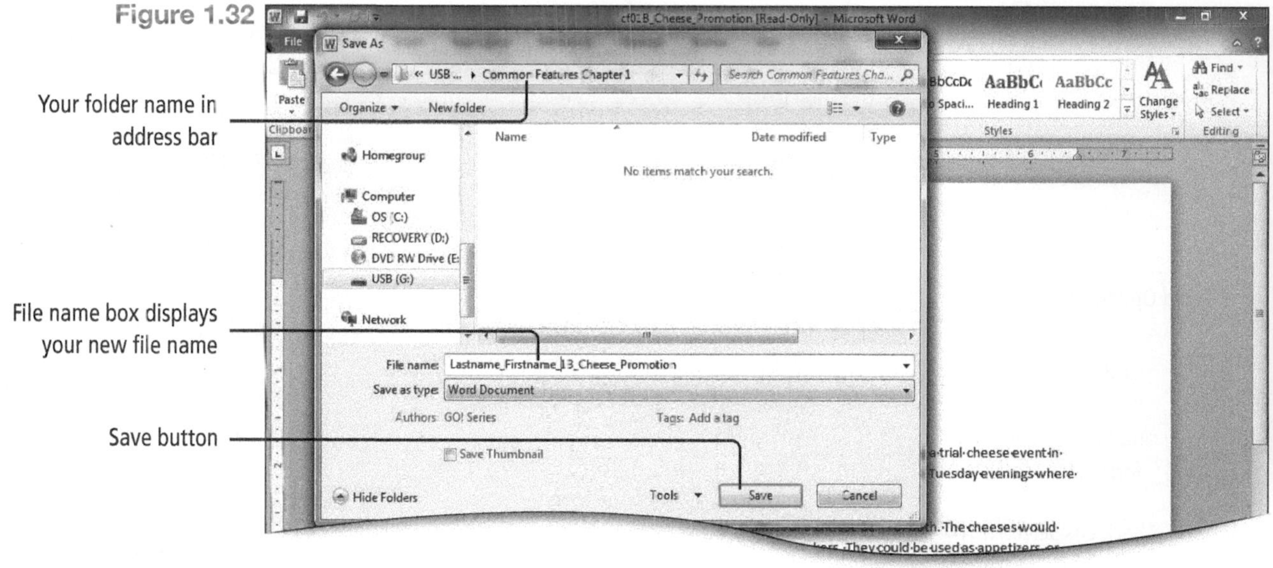

12 In the lower right corner of the **Save As** dialog box, click **Save**; or press Enter. Compare your screen with Figure 1.33.

The original document closes, and your new document, based on the original, displays with the name in the title bar.

Figure 1.33

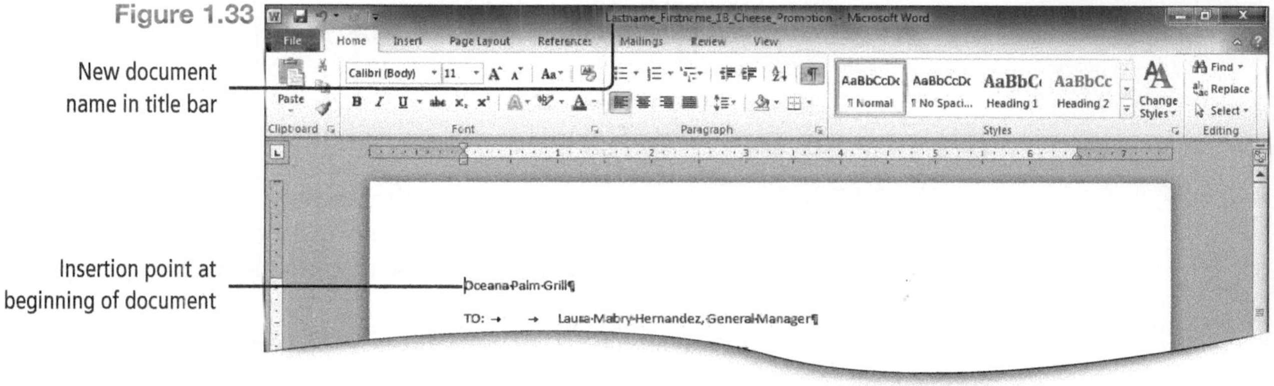

Objective 8 | Explore Options for an Application

Within each Office application, you can open an ***Options dialog box*** where you can select program settings and other options and preferences. For example, you can set preferences for viewing and editing files.

Activity 1.08 | Viewing Application Options

1 Click the **File tab** to display **Backstage** view. Under the **Help tab**, click **Options**.

2 In the displayed **Word Options** dialog box, on the left, click **Display**, and then on the right, locate the information under **Always show these formatting marks on the screen**.

When you press Enter, Spacebar, or Tab on your keyboard, characters display to represent these keystrokes. These screen characters do not print, and are referred to as ***formatting marks*** or ***nonprinting characters***.

3 Under **Always show these formatting marks on the screen**, be sure the last check box, **Show all formatting marks**, is selected—select it if necessary. Compare your screen with Figure 1.34.

Figure 1.34

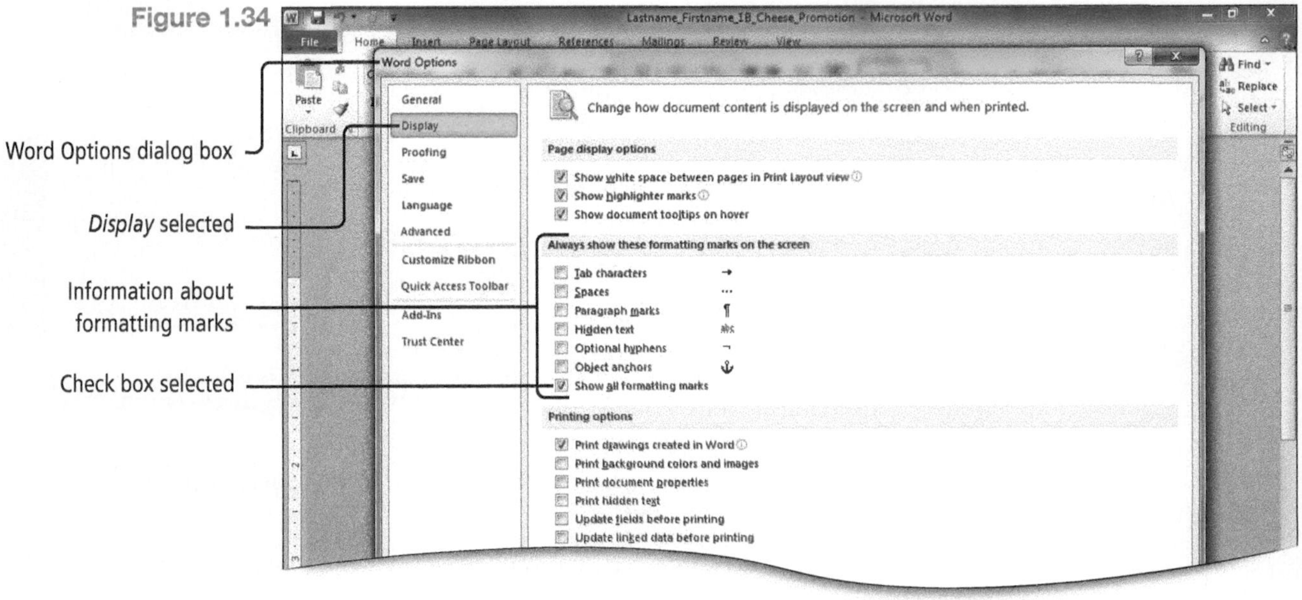

4 In the lower right corner of the dialog box, click **OK**.

Objective 9 | Perform Commands from the Ribbon

The ***Ribbon***, which displays across the top of the program window, groups commands and features in a manner that you would most logically use them. Each Office program's Ribbon is slightly different, but all contain the same three elements: ***tabs***, ***groups***, and ***commands***.

Tabs display across the top of the Ribbon, and each tab relates to a type of activity; for example, laying out a page. Groups are sets of related commands for specific tasks. Commands—instructions to computer programs—are arranged in groups, and might display as a button, a menu, or a box in which you type information.

You can also minimize the Ribbon so only the tab names display. In the minimized Ribbon view, when you click a tab the Ribbon expands to show the groups and commands, and then when you click a command, the Ribbon returns to its minimized view. Most Office users, however, prefer to leave the complete Ribbon in view at all times.

Activity 1.09 | Performing Commands from the Ribbon

1 Take a moment to examine the document on your screen.

This document is a memo from the Executive Chef to the General Manager regarding a new restaurant promotion.

2 On the Ribbon, click the **View tab**. In the **Show group**, if necessary, click to place a check mark in the **Ruler** check box, and then compare your screen with Figure 1.35.

When working in Word, display the rulers so that you can see how margin settings affect your document and how text aligns. Additionally, if you set a tab stop or an indent, its location is visible on the ruler.

Figure 1.35

3 On the Ribbon, click the **Home tab**. In the **Paragraph group**, if necessary, click the **Show/Hide** button [¶] so that it glows orange and formatting marks display in your document. Point to the button to display information about the button, and then compare your screen with Figure 1.36.

When the Show/Hide button is active—glowing orange—formatting marks display. Because formatting marks guide your eye in a document—like a map and road signs guide you along a highway—these marks will display throughout this instruction. Many expert Word users keep these marks displayed while creating documents.

Figure 1.36

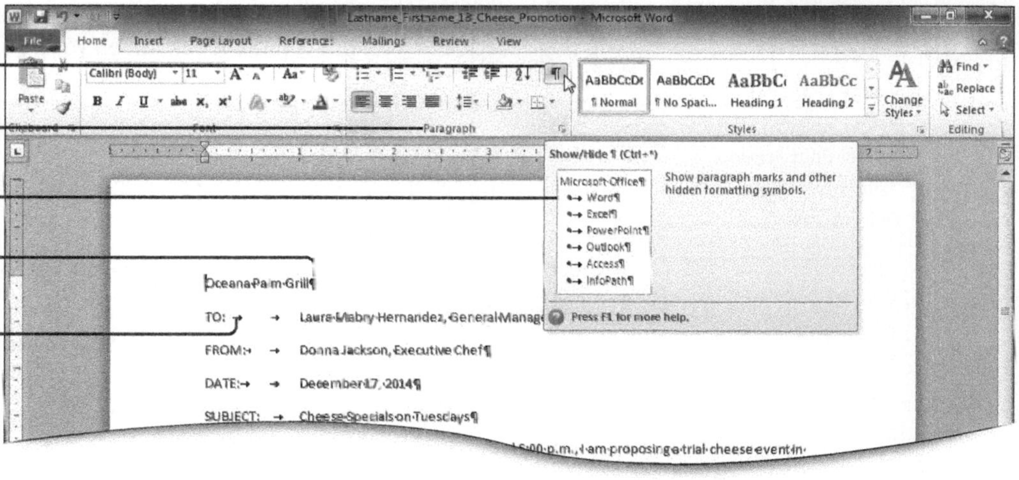

4 In the upper left corner of your screen, above the Ribbon, locate the **Quick Access Toolbar**.

The ***Quick Access Toolbar*** contains commands that you use frequently. By default, only the commands Save, Undo, and Redo display, but you can add and delete commands to suit your needs. Possibly the computer at which you are working already has additional commands added to the Quick Access Toolbar.

5 At the end of the Quick Access Toolbar, click the **Customize Quick Access Toolbar** button [▾].

6 Compare your screen with Figure 1.37.

A list of commands that Office users commonly add to their Quick Access Toolbar displays, including *Open*, *E-mail*, and *Print Preview and Print*. Commands already on the Quick Access Toolbar display a check mark. Commands that you add to the Quick Access Toolbar are always just one click away.

Here you can also display the More Commands dialog box, from which you can select any command from any tab to add to the Quick Access Toolbar.

Figure 1.37

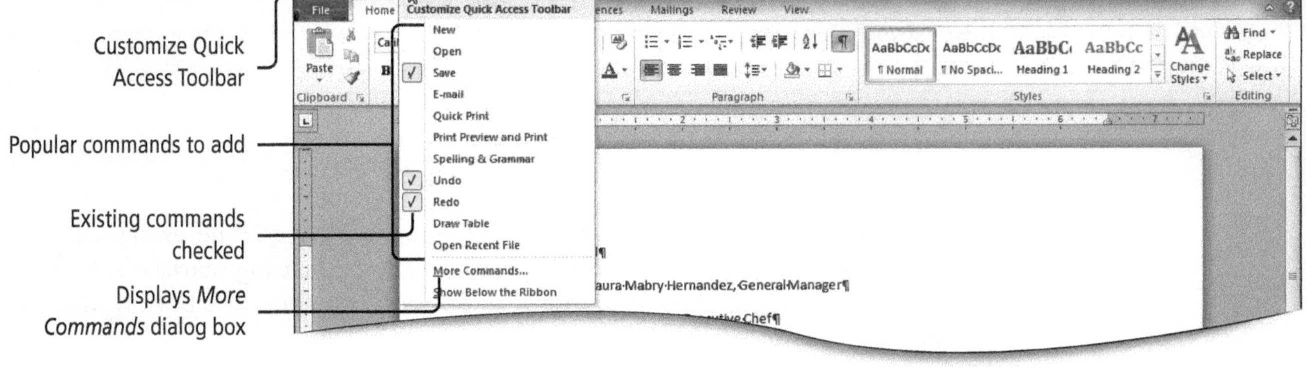

> **Another Way**
>
> Right-click any command on the Ribbon, and then on the shortcut menu, click Add to Quick Access Toolbar.

7 On the displayed list, click **Print Preview and Print**, and then notice that the icon is added to the **Quick Access Toolbar**. Compare your screen with Figure 1.38.

The icon that represents the Print Preview command displays on the Quick Access Toolbar. Because this is a command that you will use frequently while building Office documents, you might decide to have this command remain on your Quick Access Toolbar.

Figure 1.38

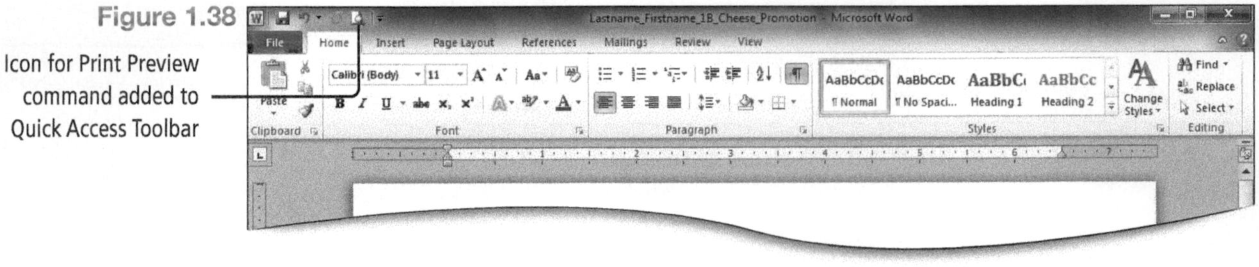

8 In the first line of the document, be sure your insertion point is blinking to the left of the *O* in *Oceana*. Press Enter one time to insert a blank paragraph, and then click to the left of the new paragraph mark (¶) in the new line.

The ***paragraph symbol*** is a formatting mark that displays each time you press Enter.

9 On the Ribbon, click the **Insert tab**. In the **Illustrations group**, point to the **Clip Art** button to display its ScreenTip.

Many buttons on the Ribbon have this type of ***enhanced ScreenTip***, which displays more descriptive text than a normal ScreenTip.

10 Click the **Clip Art** button.

The Clip Art ***task pane*** displays. A task pane is a window within a Microsoft Office application that enables you to enter options for completing a command.

11 In the **Clip Art** task pane, click in the **Search for** box, delete any existing text, and then type **cheese grapes** Under **Results should be:**, click the arrow at the right, if necessary click to *clear* the check mark for **All media types** so that no check boxes are selected, and then click the check box for **Illustrations**. Compare your screen with Figure 1.39.

Figure 1.39

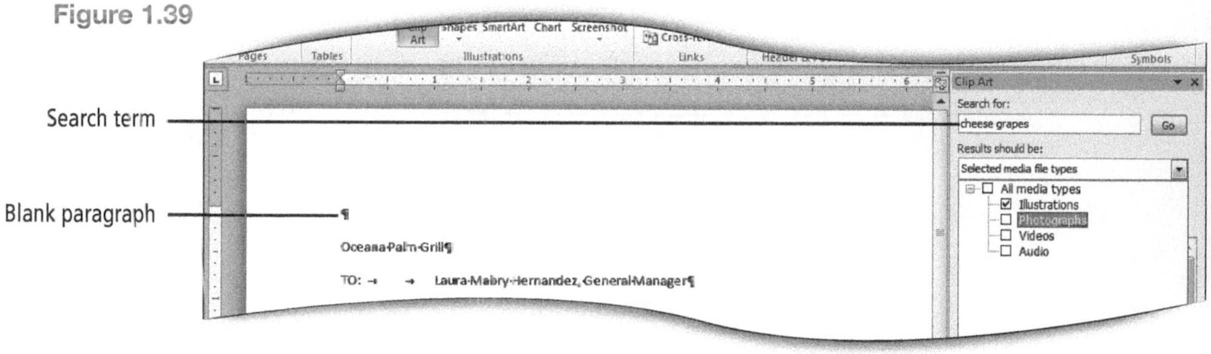

12 Click the **Results should be arrow** again to close the list, and then if necessary, click to place a check mark in the **Include Office.com content** check box.

By selecting this check box, the search for clip art images will include those from Microsoft's online collections of clip art at www.office.com.

13 At the top of the **Clip Art** task pane, click **Go**. Wait a moment for clips to display, and then locate the clip indicated in Figure 1.40.

Figure 1.40

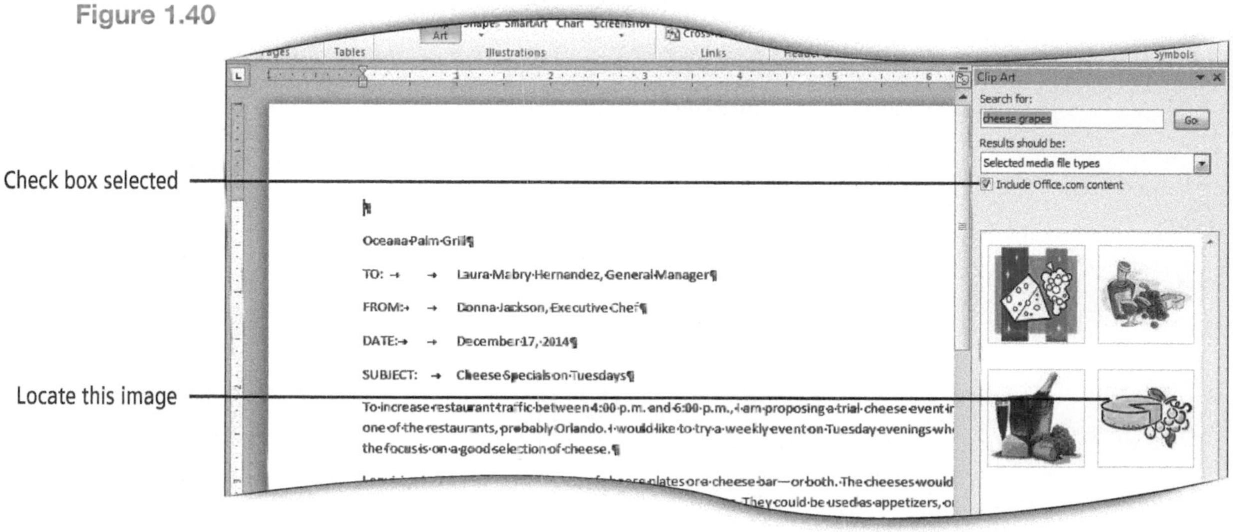

14 Click the image indicated in Figure 1.40 one time to insert it at the insertion point, and then in the upper right corner of the **Clip Art** task pane, click the **Close** [X] button.

> **Alert! | If You Cannot Locate the Image**
>
> If the image shown in Figure 1.40 is unavailable, select a different cheese image that is appropriate.

15 With the image selected—surrounded by a border—on the Ribbon, click the **Home tab**, and then in the **Paragraph group**, click the **Center** button. Click anywhere outside of the bordered picture to ***deselect***—cancel the selection. Compare your screen with Figure 1.41.

Figure 1.41

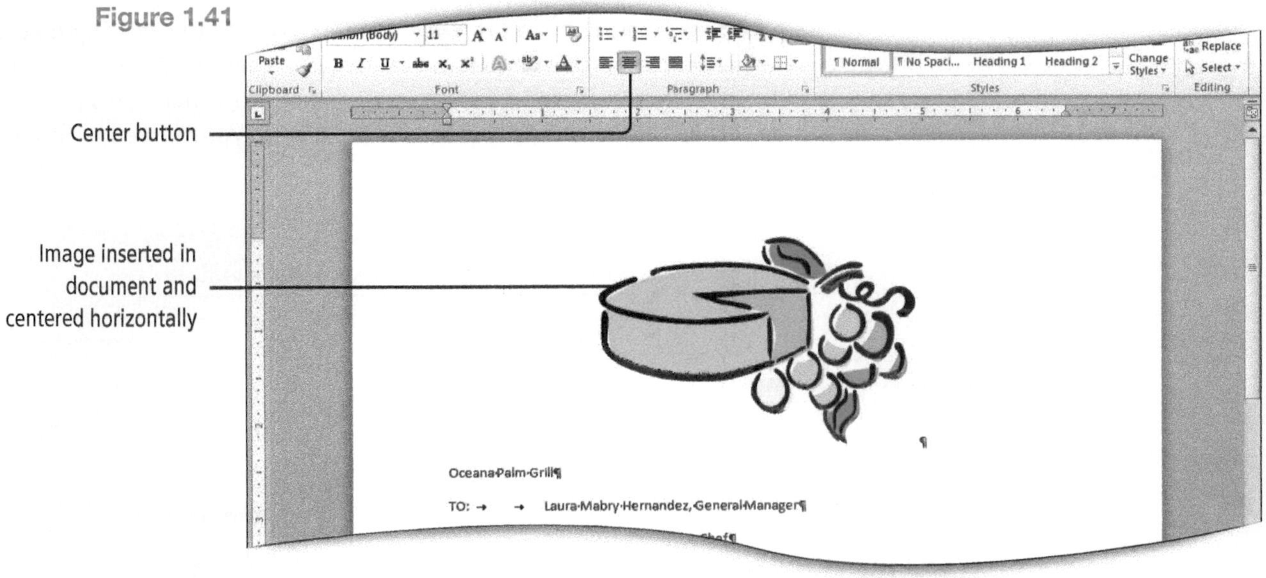

16 Point to the inserted clip art image, and then watch the last tab of the Ribbon as you click the image one time to select it.

The *Picture Tools* display and an additional tab—the *Format* tab—is added to the Ribbon. The Ribbon adapts to your work and will display additional tabs—referred to as ***contextual tabs***—when you need them.

17 On the Ribbon, under **Picture Tools**, click the **Format tab**.

Alert! | The Size of Groups on the Ribbon Varies with Screen Resolution

Your monitor's screen resolution might be set higher than the resolution used to capture the figures in this book. In Figure 1.42 below, the resolution is set to 1024 × 768, which is used for all of the figures in this book. Compare that with Figure 1.43 below, where the screen resolution is set to 1280 × 1024.

At a higher resolution, the Ribbon expands some groups to show more commands than are available with a single click, such as those in the Picture Styles group. Or, the group expands to add descriptive text to some buttons, such as those in the Arrange group. Regardless of your screen resolution, all Office commands are available to you. In higher resolutions, you will have a more robust view of the commands.

Figure 1.42

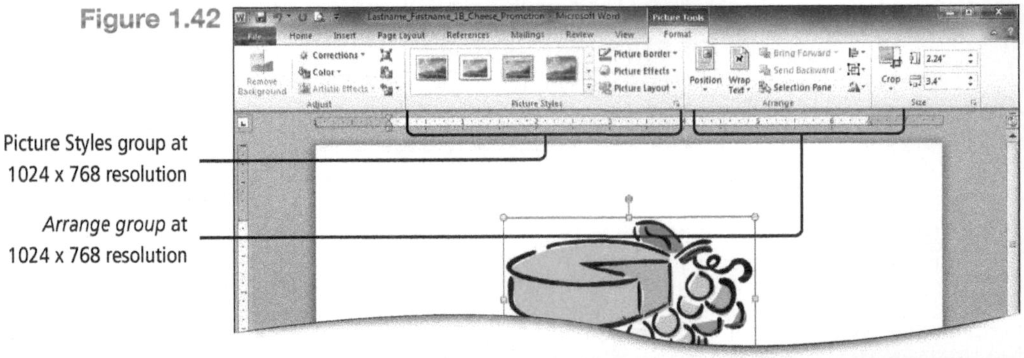

Figure 1.43

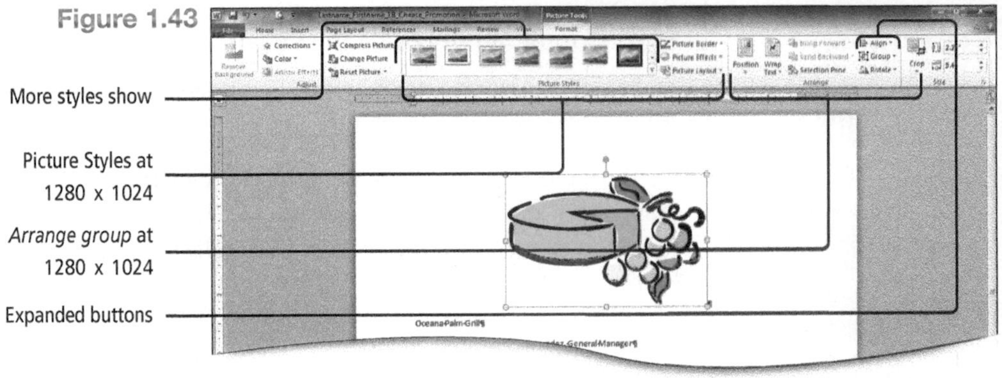

18 In the **Picture Styles group**, point to the first style to display the ScreenTip *Simple Frame, White*, and notice that the image displays with a white frame.

19 Watch the image as you point to the second picture style, and then to the third, and then to the fourth.

This is ***Live Preview***, a technology that shows the result of applying an editing or formatting change as you point to possible results—*before* you actually apply it.

20 In the **Picture Styles group**, click the fourth style—**Drop Shadow Rectangle**—and then click anywhere outside of the image to deselect it. Notice that the Picture Tools no longer display on the Ribbon. Compare your screen with Figure 1.44.

Contextual tabs display only when you need them.

Figure 1.44

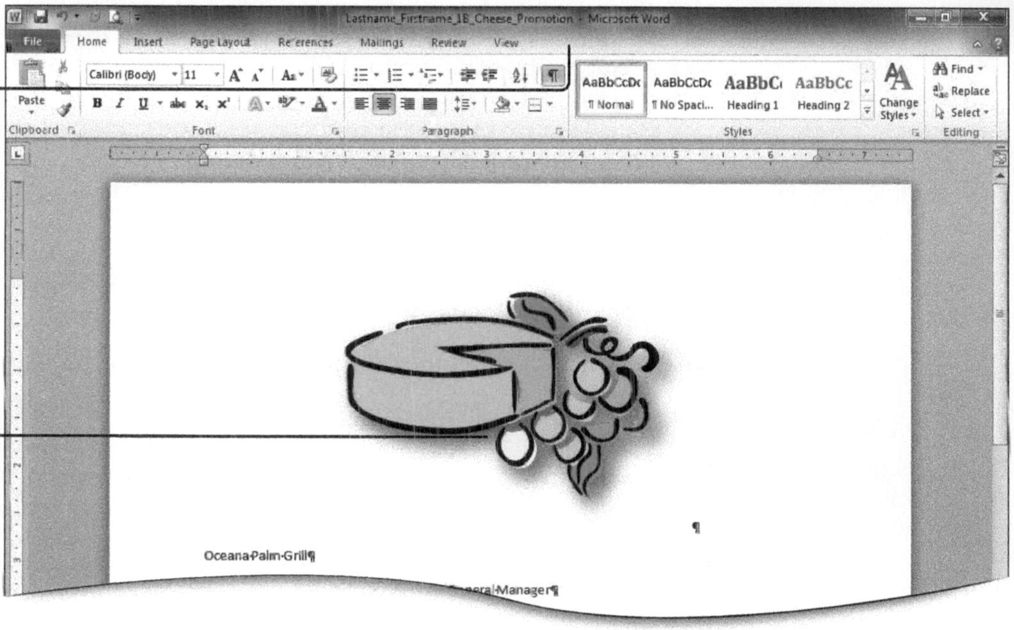

21 In the upper left corner of your screen, on the Quick Access Toolbar, click the **Save** button to save the changes you have made.

Activity 1.10 | Minimizing and Using the Keyboard to Control the Ribbon

Instead of a mouse, some individuals prefer to navigate the Ribbon by using keys on the keyboard. You can activate keyboard control of the Ribbon by pressing the Alt key. You can also minimize the Ribbon to maximize your available screen space.

1 On your keyboard, press the Alt key, and then on the Ribbon, notice that small labels display. Press N to activate the commands on the **Insert tab**, and then compare your screen with Figure 1.45.

Each label represents a ***KeyTip***—an indication of the key that you can press to activate the command. For example, on the Insert tab, you can press F to activate the Clip Art task pane.

Figure 1.45

KeyTips indicate that keyboard control of the Ribbon is active

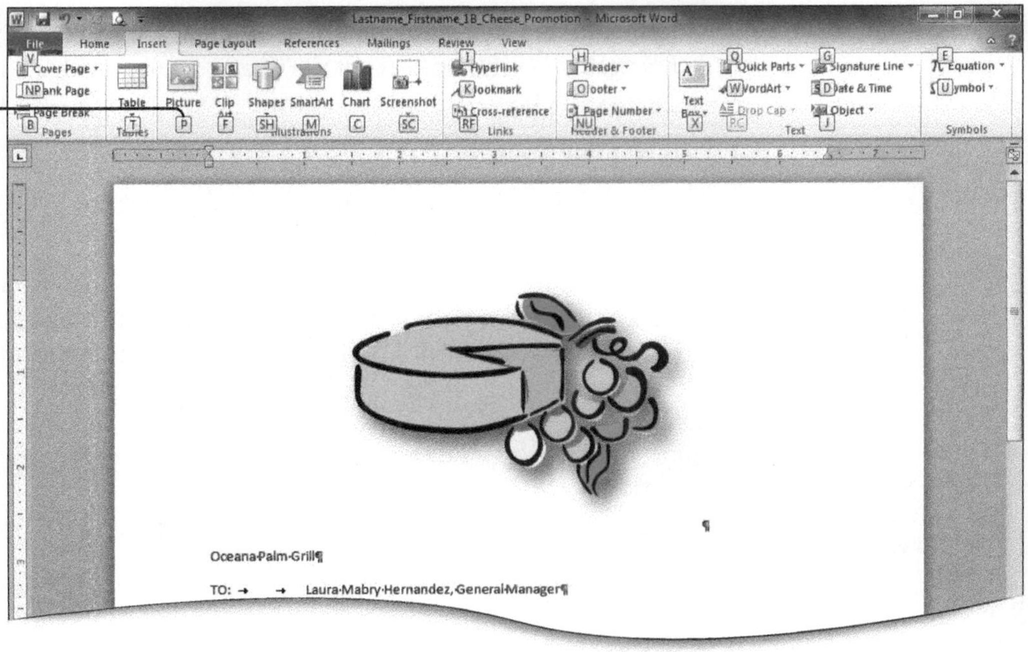

2 Press Esc to redisplay the KeyTips for the tabs. Then, press Alt again to turn off keyboard control of the Ribbon.

3 Point to any tab on the Ribbon and right-click to display a shortcut menu.

Here you can choose to display the Quick Access Toolbar below the Ribbon or minimize the Ribbon to maximize screen space. You can also customize the Ribbon by adding, removing, renaming, or reordering tabs, groups, and commands on the Ribbon, although this is not recommended until you become an expert Office user.

> **Another Way**
> Double-click the active tab; or, click the Minimize the Ribbon button at the right end of the Ribbon.

4 Click **Minimize the Ribbon**. Notice that only the Ribbon tabs display. Click the **Home tab** to display the commands. Click anywhere in the document, and notice that the Ribbon reverts to its minimized view.

> **Another Way**
> Double-click any tab to redisplay the full Ribbon.

5 Right-click any Ribbon tab, and then click **Minimize the Ribbon** again to turn the minimize feature off.

Most expert Office users prefer to have the full Ribbon display at all times.

6 Point to any tab on the Ribbon, and then on your mouse device, roll the mouse wheel. Notice that different tabs become active as your roll the mouse wheel.

You can make a tab active by using this technique, instead of clicking the tab.

Objective 10 | Apply Formatting in Office Programs

Formatting is the process of establishing the overall appearance of text, graphics, and pages in an Office file—for example, in a Word document.

Activity 1.11 | Formatting and Viewing Pages

In this activity, you will practice common formatting techniques used in Office applications.

1 On the Ribbon, click the **Insert tab**, and then in the **Header & Footer group**, click the **Footer** button.

Another Way

On the Design tab, in the Insert group, click Quick Parts, click Field, and then under Field names, click FileName.

2 At the top of the displayed gallery, under **Built-In**, click **Blank**. At the bottom of your document, with *Type text* highlighted in blue, using your own name type the file name of this document **Lastname_Firstname_1B_Cheese_Promotion** and then compare your screen with Figure 1.46.

Header & Footer Tools are added to the Ribbon. A ***footer*** is a reserved area for text or graphics that displays at the bottom of each page in a document. Likewise, a ***header*** is a reserved area for text or graphics that displays at the top of each page in a document. When the footer (or header) area is active, the document area is inactive (dimmed).

Figure 1.46

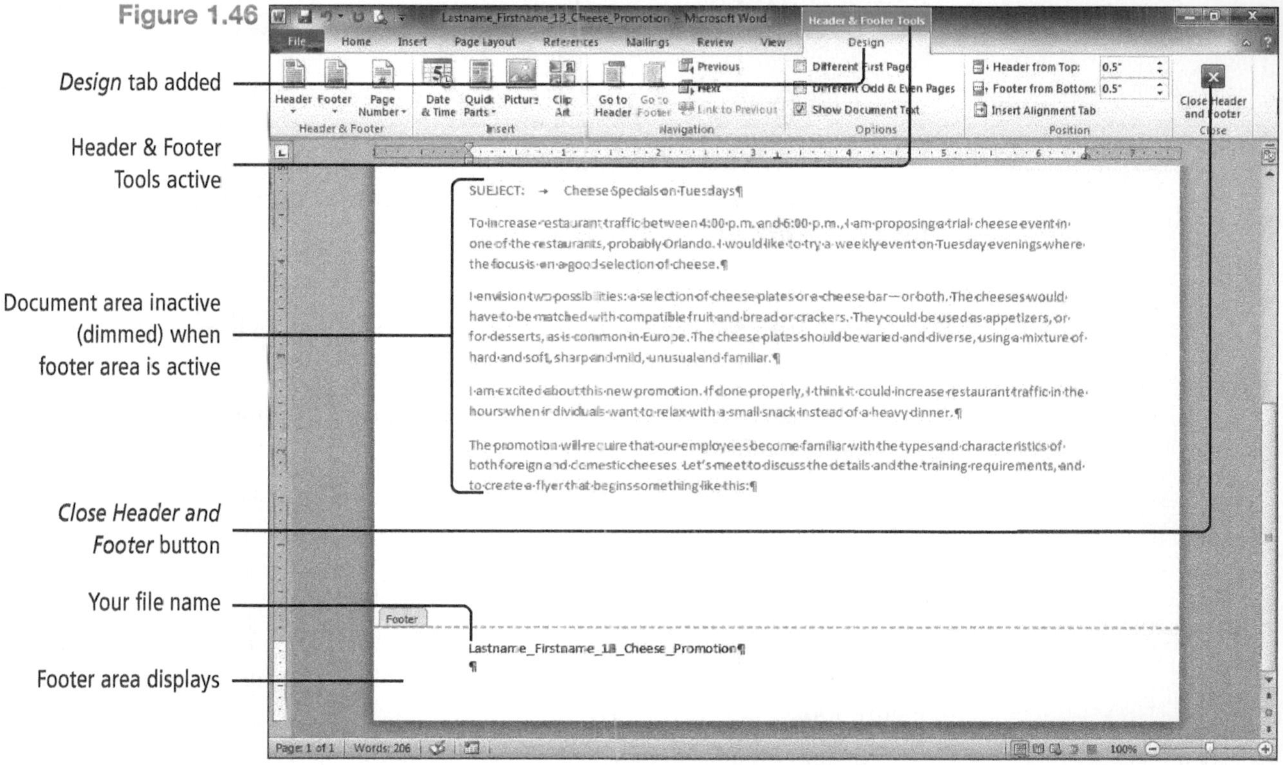

3 On the Ribbon, on the **Design tab**, in the **Close group**, click the **Close Header and Footer** button.

4 On the Ribbon, click the **Page Layout tab**. In the **Page Setup group**, click the **Orientation** button, and notice that two orientations display—*Portrait* and *Landscape*. Click **Landscape**.

In ***portrait orientation***, the paper is taller than it is wide. In ***landscape orientation***, the paper is wider than it is tall.

5 In the lower right corner of the screen, locate the **Zoom control** buttons .

To ***zoom*** means to increase or decrease the viewing area. You can zoom in to look closely at a section of a document, and then zoom out to see an entire page on the screen. You can also zoom to view multiple pages on the screen.

6 Drag the **Zoom slider**  to the left until you have zoomed to approximately *60%*. Compare your screen with Figure 1.47.

Figure 1.47

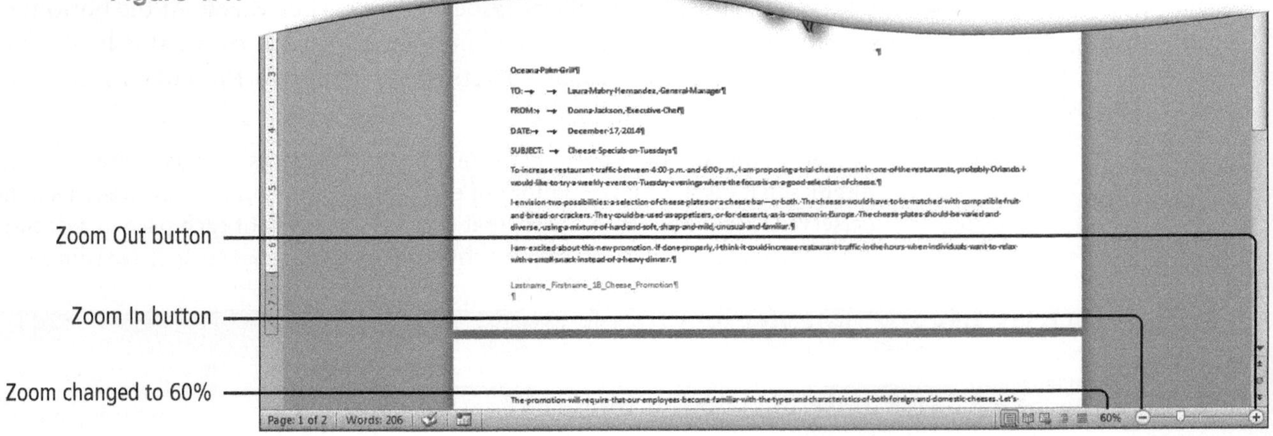

7 On the **Page Layout tab**, in the **Page Setup group**, click the **Orientation** button, and then click **Portrait.**

Portrait orientation is commonly used for business documents such as letters and memos.

8 In the lower right corner of your screen, click the **Zoom In** button [⊕] as many times as necessary to return to the **100%** zoom setting.

Use the zoom feature to adjust the view of your document for editing and for your viewing comfort.

9 On the Quick Access Toolbar, click the **Save** button [Save] to save the changes you have made to your document.

Activity 1.12 | Formatting Text

1 To the left of *Oceana Palm Grill*, point in the margin area to display the [pointer] pointer and click one time to select the entire paragraph. Compare your screen with Figure 1.48.

Use this technique to select complete paragraphs from the margin area. Additionally, with this technique you can drag downward to select multiple-line paragraphs—which is faster and more efficient than dragging through text.

Figure 1.48

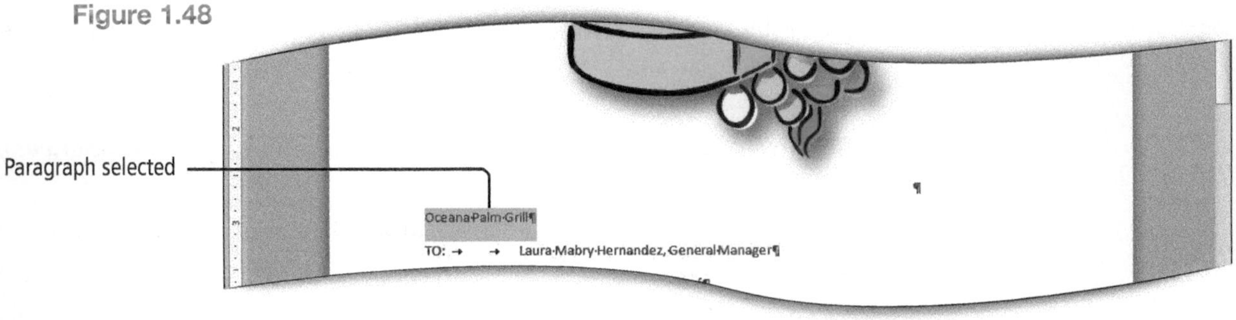

2 On the Ribbon, click the **Home tab**, and then in the **Paragraph group**, click the **Center** button [Center] to center the paragraph.

Alignment refers to the placement of paragraph text relative to the left and right margins. ***Center alignment*** refers to text that is centered horizontally between the left and right margins. You can also align text at the left margin, which is the default alignment for text in Word, or at the right margin.

3 On the **Home tab**, in the **Font group**, click the **Font button arrow** Calibri (Body). At the top of the list, point to **Cambria**, and as you do so, notice that the selected text previews in the Cambria font.

A ***font*** is a set of characters with the same design and shape. The default font in a Word document is Calibri, which is a ***sans serif*** font—a font design with no lines or extensions on the ends of characters.

The Cambria font is a ***serif*** font—a font design that includes small line extensions on the ends of the letters to guide the eye in reading from left to right.

The list of fonts displays as a gallery showing potential results. For example, in the Font gallery, you can see the actual design and format of each font as it would look if applied to text.

4 Point to several other fonts and observe the effect on the selected text. Then, at the top of the **Font** gallery, under **Theme Fonts**, click **Cambria**.

A ***theme*** is a predesigned set of colors, fonts, lines, and fill effects that look good together and that can be applied to your entire document or to specific items.

A theme combines two sets of fonts—one for text and one for headings. In the default Office theme, Cambria is the suggested font for headings.

5 With the paragraph *Oceana Palm Grill* still selected, on the **Home tab**, in the **Font group**, click the **Font Size button arrow** 11, point to **36**, and then notice how Live Preview displays the text in the font size to which you are pointing. Compare your screen with Figure 1.49.

Figure 1.49

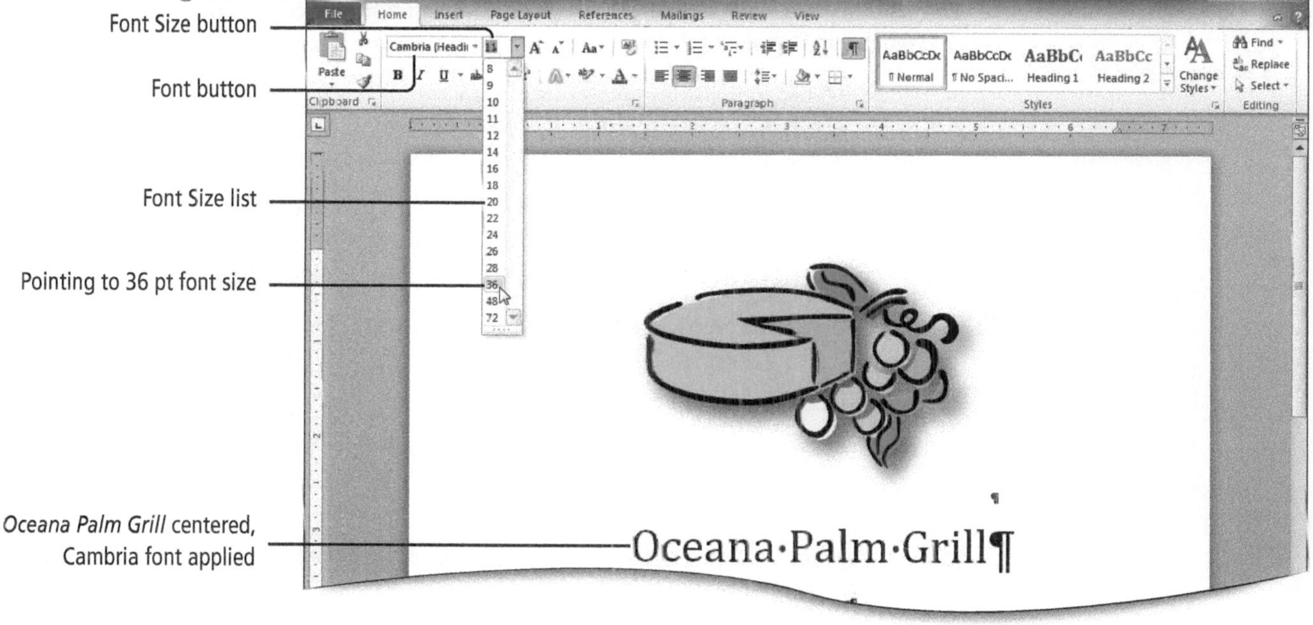

6 On the displayed list of font sizes, click **20**.

Fonts are measured in ***points***, with one point equal to 1/72 of an inch. A higher point size indicates a larger font size. Headings and titles are often formatted by using a larger font size. The word *point* is abbreviated as ***pt***.

7 With *Oceana Palm Grill* still selected, on the **Home tab**, in the **Font group**, click the **Font Color button arrow** A. Under **Theme Colors**, in the seventh column, click the last color—**Olive Green, Accent 3, Darker 50%**. Click anywhere to deselect the text.

8 To the left of *TO:*, point in the left margin area to display the [pointer icon] pointer, hold down the left mouse button, and then drag down to select the four memo headings. Compare your screen with Figure 1.50.

Use this technique to select complete paragraphs from the margin area—dragging downward to select multiple-line paragraphs—which is faster and more efficient than dragging through text.

Figure 1.50

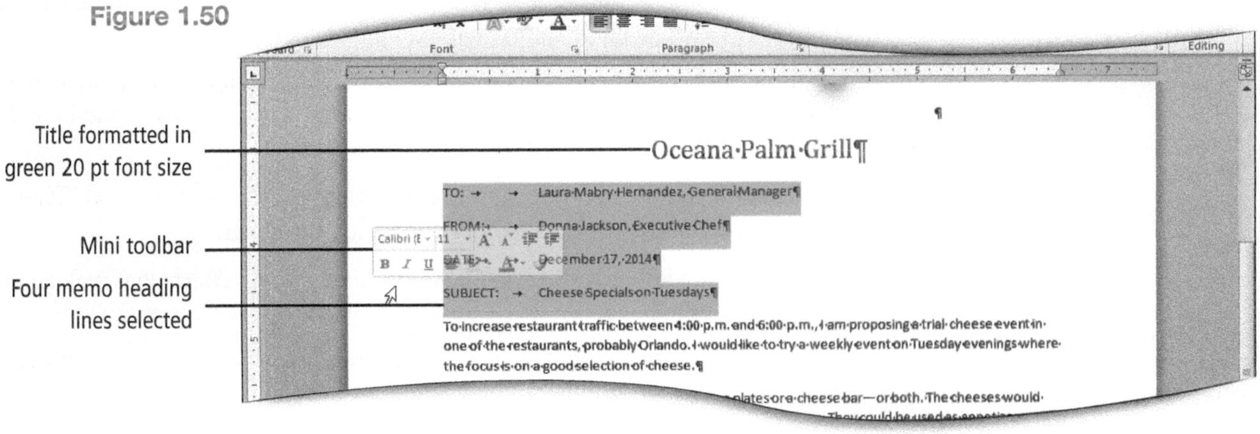

9 With the four paragraphs selected, on the Mini toolbar, click the **Font Color** button [A], which now displays a dark green bar instead of a red bar.

The font color button retains its most recently used color—Olive Green, Accent 3, Darker 50%. As you progress in your study of Microsoft Office, you will use other buttons that behave in this manner; that is, they retain their most recently used format.

The purpose of the Mini toolbar is to place commonly used commands close to text or objects that you select. By selecting a command on the Mini toolbar, you reduce the distance that you must move your mouse to access a command.

10 Click anywhere in the paragraph that begins *To increase*, and then ***triple-click***—click the left mouse button three times—to select the entire paragraph. If the entire paragraph is not selected, click in the paragraph and begin again.

11 With the entire paragraph selected, on the Mini toolbar, click the **Font Color button arrow** [A], and then under **Theme Colors**, in the sixth column, click the first color—**Red, Accent 2**.

It is convenient to have commonly used commands display on the Mini toolbar so that you do not have to move your mouse to the top of the screen to access the command from the Ribbon.

12 Select the text *TO:* and then on the displayed Mini toolbar, click the **Bold** button [B] and the **Italic** button [I].

Font styles include bold, italic, and underline. Font styles emphasize text and are a visual cue to draw the reader's eye to important text.

13 On the displayed Mini toolbar, click the **Italic** button [I] again to turn off the Italic formatting. Notice that the Italic button no longer glows orange.

A button that behaves in this manner is referred to as a ***toggle button***, which means it can be turned on by clicking it once, and then turned off by clicking it again.

14 With *TO:* still selected, on the Mini toolbar, click the **Format Painter** button [icon]. Then, move your mouse under the word *Laura*, and notice the [icon] mouse pointer. Compare your screen with Figure 1.51.

You can use the ***Format Painter*** to copy the formatting of specific text or of a paragraph and then apply it in other locations in your document.

The pointer takes the shape of a paintbrush, and contains the formatting information from the paragraph where the insertion point is positioned. Information about the Format Painter and how to turn it off displays in the status bar.

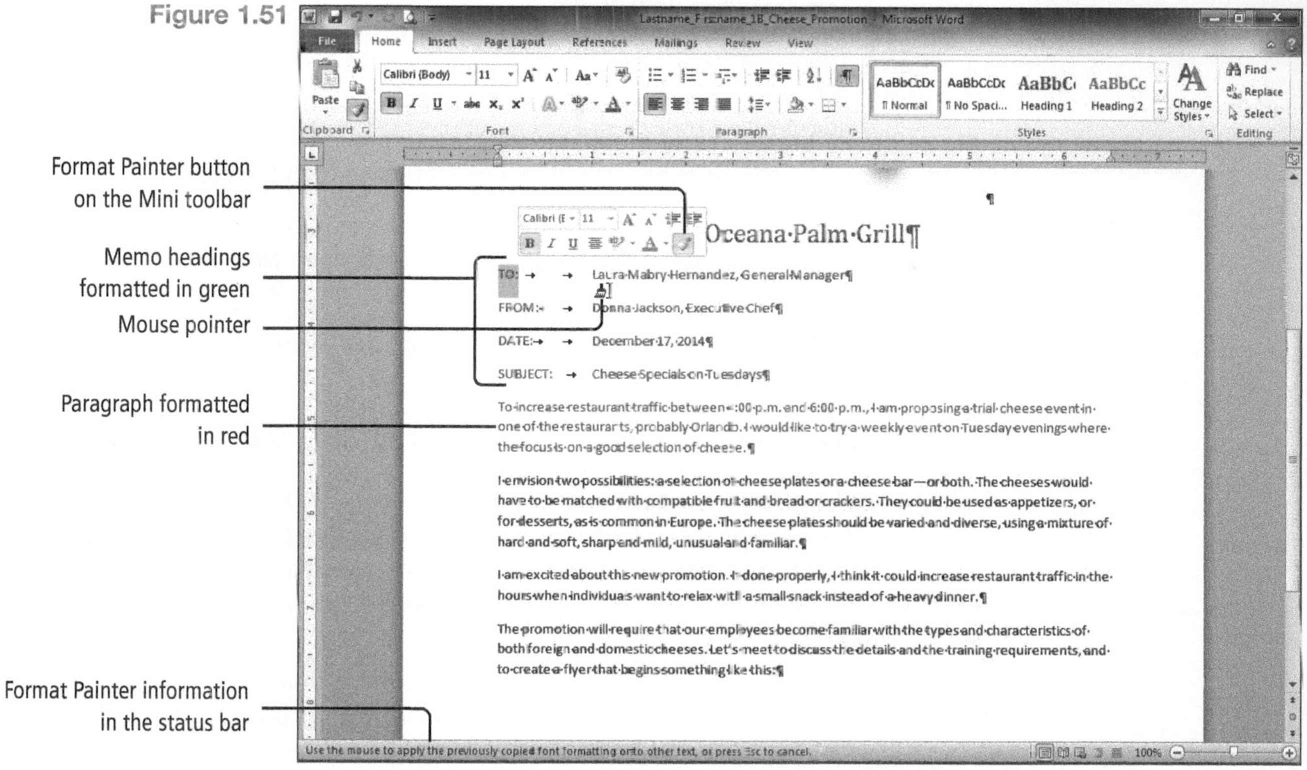

Figure 1.51

15 With the [icon] pointer, drag to select the text *FROM:* and notice that the Bold formatting is applied. Then, point to the selected text *FROM:* and on the Mini toolbar, *double-click* the **Format Painter** button [icon].

16 Select the text *DATE:* to copy the Bold formatting, and notice that the pointer retains the [icon] shape.

When you *double-click* the Format Painter button, the Format Painter feature remains active until you either click the Format Painter button again, or press Esc to cancel it—as indicated on the status bar.

17 With Format Painter still active, select the text *SUBJECT:*, and then on the Ribbon, on the **Home tab**, in the **Clipboard group**, notice that the **Format Painter** button [icon] is glowing orange, indicating that it is active. Compare your screen with Figure 1.52.

Figure 1.52

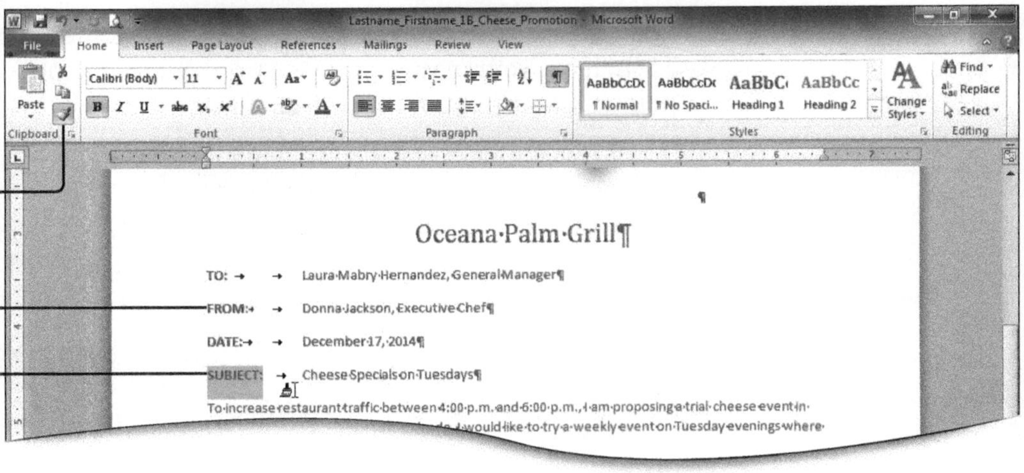

18 Click the **Format Painter** button on the Ribbon to turn the command off.

19 In the paragraph that begins *To increase*, triple-click again to select the entire paragraph. On the displayed Mini toolbar, click the **Bold** button and the **Italic** button. Click anywhere to deselect.

20 On the Quick Access Toolbar, click the **Save** button to save the changes you have made to your document.

Activity 1.13 | Using the Office Clipboard to Cut, Copy, and Paste

The ***Office Clipboard*** is a temporary storage area that holds text or graphics that you select and then cut or copy. When you ***copy*** text or graphics, a copy is placed on the Office Clipboard and the original text or graphic remains in place. When you ***cut*** text or graphics, a copy is placed on the Office Clipboard, and the original text or graphic is removed—cut—from the document.

After cutting or copying, the contents of the Office Clipboard are available for you to ***paste***—insert—in a new location in the current document, or into another Office file.

1 Hold down Ctrl and press Home to move to the beginning of your document, and then take a moment to study the table in Figure 1.53, which describes similar keyboard shortcuts with which you can navigate quickly in a document.

To Move	Press
To the beginning of a document	Ctrl + Home
To the end of a document	Ctrl + End
To the beginning of a line	Home
To the end of a line	End
To the beginning of the previous word	Ctrl + ←
To the beginning of the next word	Ctrl + →
To the beginning of the current word (if insertion point is in the middle of a word)	Ctrl + ←
To the beginning of a paragraph	Ctrl + ↑
To the beginning of the next paragraph	Ctrl + ↓
To the beginning of the current paragraph (if insertion point is in the middle of a paragraph)	Ctrl + ↑
Up one screen	PgUp
Down one screen	PageDown

Figure 1.53

Another Way

Right-click the selection, and then click Copy on the shortcut menu; or, use the keyboard shortcut Ctrl + C.

2 To the left of *Oceana Palm Grill*, point in the left margin area to display the [pointer] pointer, and then click one time to select the entire paragraph. On the **Home tab**, in the **Clipboard group**, click the **Copy** button [Copy].

Because anything that you select and then copy—or cut—is placed on the Office Clipboard, the Copy command and the Cut command display in the Clipboard group of commands on the Ribbon.

There is no visible indication that your copied selection has been placed on the Office Clipboard.

3 On the **Home tab**, in the **Clipboard group**, to the right of the group name *Clipboard*, click the **Dialog Box Launcher** button [launcher], and then compare your screen with Figure 1.54.

The Clipboard task pane displays with your copied text. In any Ribbon group, the ***Dialog Box Launcher*** displays either a dialog box or a task pane related to the group of commands.

It is not necessary to display the Office Clipboard in this manner, although sometimes it is useful to do so. The Office Clipboard can hold 24 items.

Figure 1.54

Copy button

Dialog Box Launcher in Clipboard group

Clipboard task pane displays

Selected text on the Office Clipboard

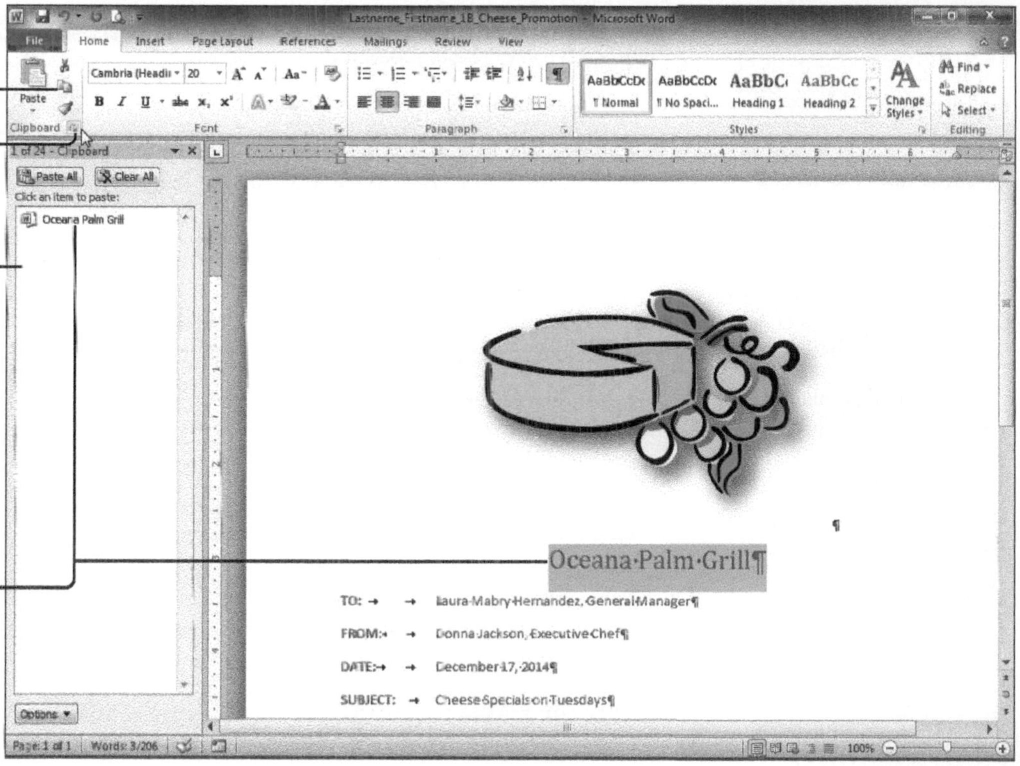

4 In the upper right corner of the **Clipboard** task pane, click the **Close** button [X].

Another Way

Right-click, on the shortcut menu under Paste Options, click the desired option button.

5 Press Ctrl + End to move to the end of your document. Press Enter one time to create a new blank paragraph. On the **Home tab**, in the **Clipboard group**, point to the **Paste** button, and then click the *upper* portion of this split button.

The Paste command pastes the most recently copied item on the Office Clipboard at the insertion point location. If you click the lower portion of the Paste button, a gallery of Paste Options displays.

6 Click the **Paste Options** button that displays below the pasted text as shown in Figure 1.55.

Here you can view and apply various formatting options for pasting your copied or cut text. Typically you will click Paste on the Ribbon and paste the item in its original format. If you want some other format for the pasted item, you can do so from the ***Paste Options gallery***.

The Paste Options gallery provides a Live Preview of the various options for changing the format of the pasted item with a single click. The Paste Options gallery is available in three places: on the Ribbon by clicking the lower portion of the Paste button—the Paste button arrow; from the Paste Options button that displays below the pasted item following the paste operation; or, on the shortcut menu if you right-click the pasted item.

Figure 1.55

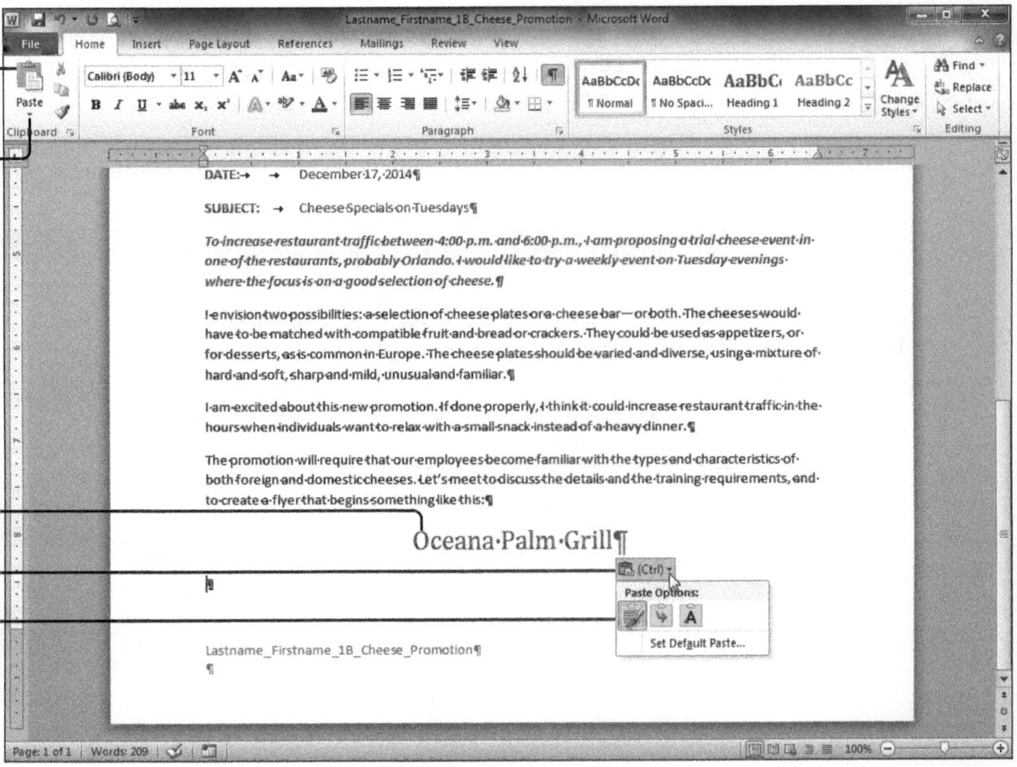

7 In the displayed **Paste Options** gallery, *point* to each option to see the Live Preview of the format that would be applied if you clicked the button.

The contents of the Paste Options gallery are contextual; that is, they change based on what you copied and where you are pasting.

8 Press Esc to close the gallery; the button will remain displayed until you take some other screen action.

> **Another Way**
>
> On the Home tab, in the Clipboard group, click the Cut button; or, use the keyboard shortcut Ctrl + X.

9 Press Ctrl + Home to move to the top of the document, and then click the **cheese image** one time to select it. While pointing to the selected image, right-click, and then on the shortcut menu, click **Cut**.

Recall that the Cut command cuts—removes—the selection from the document and places it on the Office Clipboard.

10 Press [Del] one time to remove the blank paragraph from the top of the document, and then press [Ctrl] + [End] to move to the end of the document.

11 With the insertion point blinking in the blank paragraph at the end of the document, right-click, and notice that the **Paste Options** gallery displays on the shortcut menu. Compare your screen with Figure 1.56.

Figure 1.56

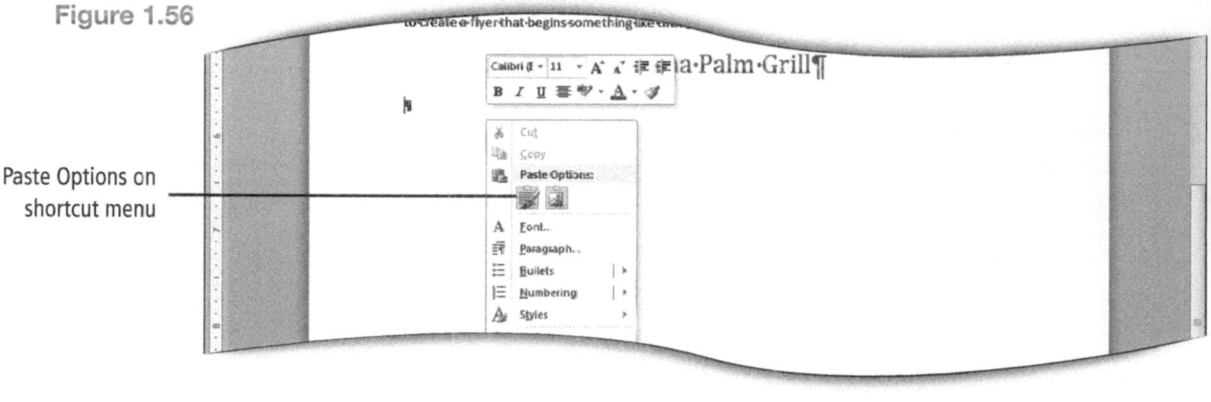

12 On the shortcut menu, under **Paste Options**, click the first button—**Keep Source Formatting**.

13 Click the picture to select it. On the **Home tab**, in the **Paragraph group**, click the **Center** button.

14 Above the cheese picture, click to position the insertion point at the end of the word *Grill*, press [Spacebar] one time, and then type **Tuesday Cheese Tastings** Compare your screen with Figure 1.57.

Figure 1.57

Activity 1.14 | Viewing Print Preview and Printing a Word Document

1 Press [Ctrl] + [Home] to move to the top of your document. Select the text *Oceana Palm Grill*, and then replace the selected text by typing **Memo**

2 Display **Backstage** view, on the right, click **Properties**, and then click **Show Document Panel**. Replace the existing author name with your first and last name. In the **Subject** box, type your course name and section number, and then in the **Keywords** box, type **cheese promotion** and then **Close** [×] the **Document Information Panel**.

> **Another Way**
>
> Press Ctrl + F2 to display Print Preview.

3 On the Quick Access Toolbar, click **Save** to save the changes you have made to your document.

4 On the Quick Access Toolbar, click the **Print Preview** button that you added. Compare your screen with Figure 1.58.

Figure 1.58

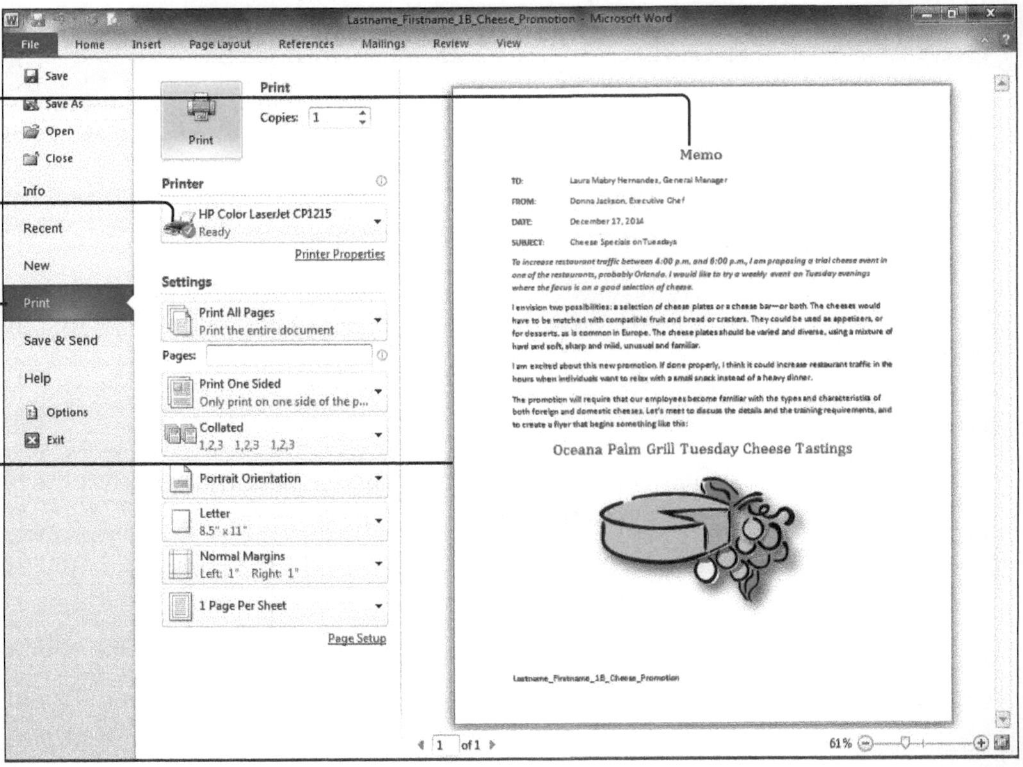

Memo typed
If no printer is attached to your system, OneNote is the default printer
Print tab active in Backstage view
Print Preview (if you have a non-color printer as your default printer, the preview may display in shades of gray)

5 Examine the **Print Preview**. Under **Settings**, notice that in **Backstage** view, several of the same commands that are available on the Page Layout tab of the Ribbon also display.

For convenience, common adjustments to Page Layout display here, so that you can make last-minute adjustments without closing Backstage view.

6 If you need to make any corrections, click the Home tab to return to the document and make any necessary changes.

It is good practice to examine the Print Preview before printing or submitting your work electronically. Then, make any necessary corrections, re-save, and redisplay Print Preview.

7 If you are directed to do so, click Print to print the document; or, above the Info tab, click Close, and then submit your file electronically according to the directions provided by your instructor.

If you click the Print button, Backstage view closes and the Word window redisplays.

8 On the Quick Access Toolbar, point to the **Print Preview icon** you placed there, right-click, and then click **Remove from Quick Access Toolbar**.

If you are working on your own computer and you want to do so, you can leave the icon on the toolbar; in a lab setting, you should return the software to its original settings.

9 At the right end of the title bar, click the program **Close** button [x] .

10 If a message displays asking if you want the text on the Clipboard to be available after you quit Word, click **No**.

This message most often displays if you have copied some type of image to the Clipboard. If you click Yes, the items on the Clipboard will remain for you to use.

Objective 11 | Use the Microsoft Office 2010 Help System

Within each Office program, the Help feature provides information about all of the program's features and displays step-by-step instructions for performing many tasks.

Activity 1.15 | Using the Microsoft Office 2010 Help System in Excel

In this activity, you will use the Microsoft Help feature to find information about formatting numbers in Excel.

> **Another Way**
> Press F1 to display Help.

1 **Start** the **Microsoft Excel 2010** program. In the upper right corner of your screen, click the **Microsoft Excel Help** button [?].

2 In the **Excel Help** window, click in the white box in upper left corner, type **formatting numbers** and then click **Search** or press Enter.

3 On the list of results, click **Display numbers as currency**. Compare your screen with Figure 1.59.

Figure 1.59

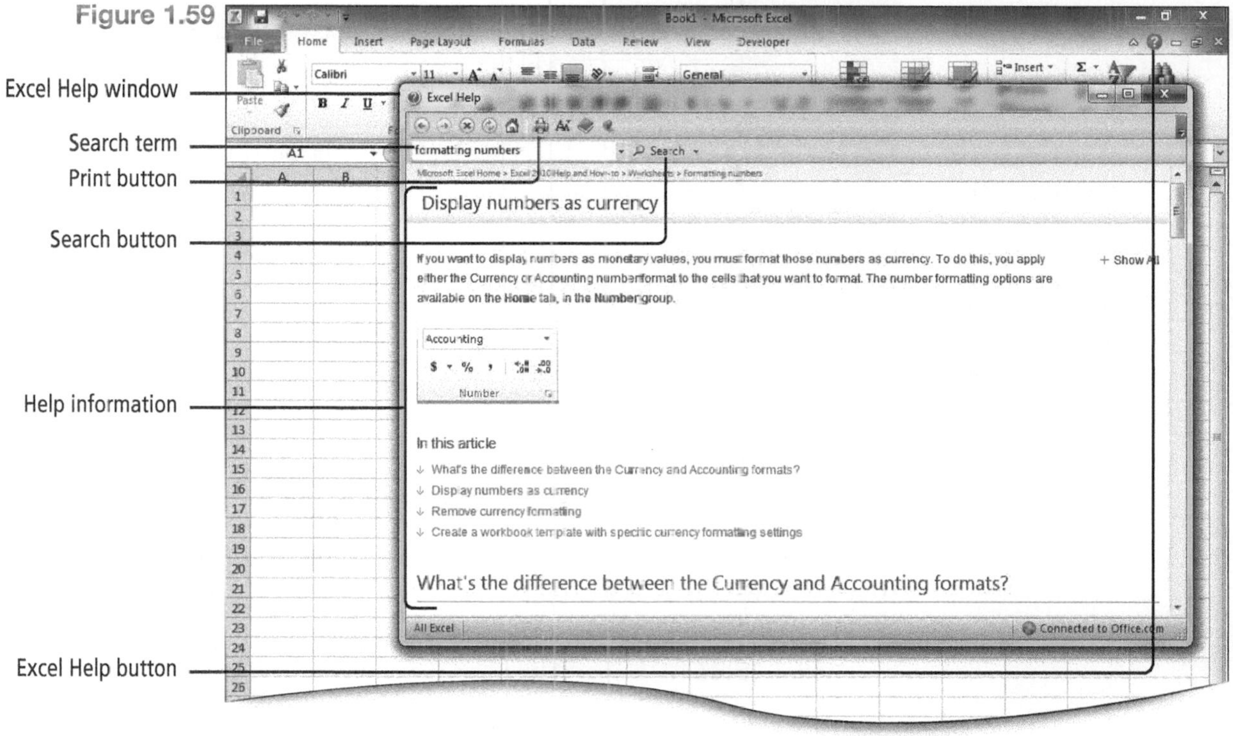

4 If you want to do so, on the toolbar at the top of the **Excel Help** window, click the Print [print] button to print a copy of this information for your reference.

5 On the title bar of the Excel Help window, click the **Close** button . On the right side of the Microsoft Excel title bar, click the **Close** button to close Excel.

Objective 12 | Compress Files

A ***compressed file*** is a file that has been reduced in size. Compressed files take up less storage space and can be transferred to other computers faster than uncompressed files. You can also combine a group of files into one compressed folder, which makes it easier to share a group of files.

Activity 1.16 | Compressing Files

In this activity, you will combine the two files you created in this chapter into one compressed file.

1 On the Windows taskbar, click the **Start** button, and then on the right, click **Computer**.

2 On the left, in the **navigation pane**, click the location of your two files from this chapter—your USB flash drive or other location—and display the folder window for your **Common Features Chapter 1** folder. Compare your screen with Figure 1.60.

Figure 1.60

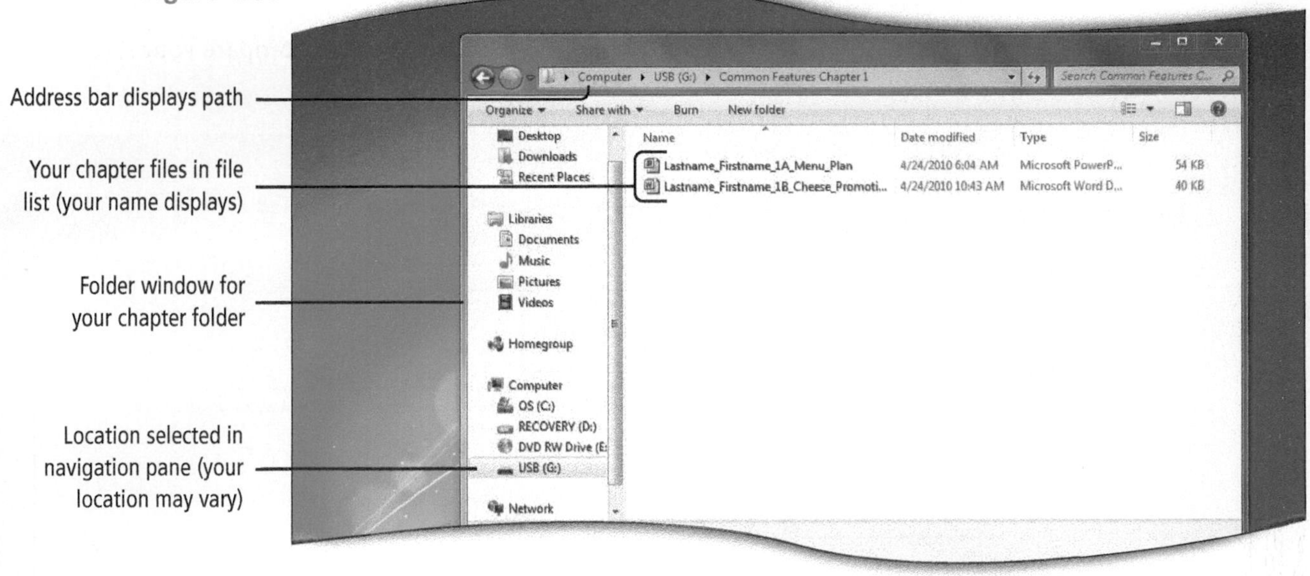

3 In the **file list**, click your **Lastname_Firstname_1A_Menu_Plan** file one time to select it.

4 Hold down Ctrl, and then click your **Lastname_Firstname_1B_Cheese_Promotion** file to select both files. Release Ctrl.

In any Windows-based program, holding down Ctrl while selecting enables you to select multiple items.

5 Point anywhere over the two selected files and right-click. On the shortcut menu, point to **Send to**, and then compare your screen with Figure 1.61.

Figure 1.61

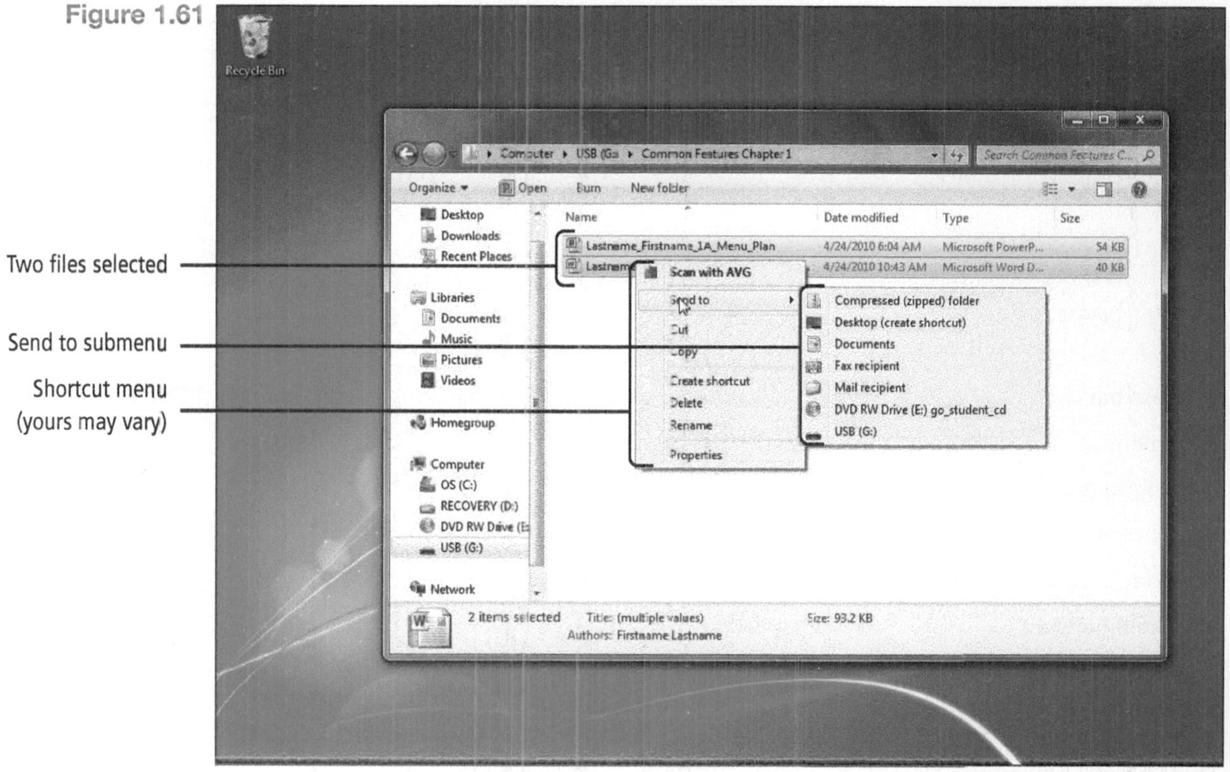

6 On the shortcut submenu, click **Compressed (zipped) folder**.

Windows creates a compressed folder containing a *copy* of each of the selected files. The folder name is the name of the file or folder to which you were pointing, and is selected—highlighted in blue—so that you can rename it.

7 Using your own name, type **Lastname_Firstname_Common_Features_Ch1** and press Enter.

The compressed folder is now ready to attach to an e-mail or share in some other electronic format.

8 **Close** [x] the folder window. If directed to do so by your instructor, submit your compressed folder electronically.

> **More Knowledge | Extracting Compressed Files**
>
> ***Extract*** means to decompress, or pull out, files from a compressed form. When you extract a file, an uncompressed copy is placed in the folder that you specify. The original file remains in the compressed folder.

End **You have completed Project 1B**

Content-Based Assessments

Summary

In this chapter, you used Windows Explorer to navigate the Windows file structure. You also used features that are common across the Microsoft Office 2010 programs.

Key Terms

Address bar 5
Alignment 34
All Programs 7
Application 6
AutoPlay 3
Back and Forward buttons 5
Backstage tabs 14
Backstage view 14
Center alignment 34
Click 4
Command 5
Common dialog boxes 22
Compressed file 44
Context sensitive command 11
Contextual tabs 30
Copy 38
Cut 38
Default 9
Deselect 29
Desktop 3
Details pane 5
Dialog box 11
Dialog Box Launcher 39
Document properties 14
Double-click 5
Drag 10
Edit 9
Ellipsis 11
Enhanced ScreenTip 28
Extract 45
File 3
File list 5
Fill 12
Folder 3
Folder window 4
Font 35
Font styles 36
Footer 33
Format Painter 37
Formatting 32
Formatting marks 25
Gallery 12
Groups 26
Header 33
Icons 5
Info tab 14
Insertion point 9
Keyboard shortcut 10
KeyTip 31
Landscape orientation 33
Library 4
Live Preview 31
Location 13
Metadata 14
Microsoft Access 7
Microsoft Excel 7
Microsoft InfoPath 7
Microsoft Office 2010 6
Microsoft OneNote 7
Microsoft Outlook 7
Microsoft PowerPoint 7
Microsoft Publisher 7
Microsoft SharePoint Workspace 7
Microsoft Word 7
Mini toolbar 10
Navigate 3
Navigation pane 5
Nonprinting characters 25
Office Clipboard 38
Open dialog box 22
Option button 12
Options dialog box 25
Paragraph symbol 28
Paste 38
Paste Options 40
PDF (Portable Document Format) file 20
Point 4
Pointer 9
Points 35
Portrait orientation 33
Preview pane button 5
Print Preview 18
Program 6
Program-level control buttons 8
Protected View 24
Pt 35
Quick Access Toolbar 27
Quick Commands 14
Read-Only 23
Ribbon 26
Ribbon tabs 8
Right-click 11
Sans serif 35
ScreenTip 12
Scroll bar 16
Scroll box 16
Search box 5
Select 10
Serif 35
Shortcut menu 11
Split button 5
Start button 4
Start menu 4
Status bar 8
Subfolder 3
Tabs 26
Tags 5
Task pane 28
Theme 35
Title bar 8
Toggle button 36
Triple-click 36
Trusted Documents 24
USB flash drive 6
Views button 5
Window 3
Windows Explorer 3
Windows taskbar 4
Zoom 18

Content-Based Assessments

Matching

Match each term in the second column with its correct definition in the first column by writing the letter of the term on the blank line in front of the correct definition.

A Address bar
B Command
C File
D Folder
E Folder window
F Icons
G Keyboard shortcut
H Library
I Microsoft Excel
J Program
K Ribbon
L Start menu
M Subfolder
N Title bar
O Windows Explorer

____ 1. A collection of information stored on a computer under a single name.

____ 2. A container in which you store files.

____ 3. A folder within a folder.

____ 4. The program that displays the files and folders on your computer.

____ 5. The Windows menu that is the main gateway to your computer.

____ 6. In Windows 7, a window that displays the contents of the current folder, library, or device, and contains helpful parts so that you can navigate

____ 7. In Windows, a collection of items, such as files and folders, assembled from various locations that might be on your computer.

____ 8. The bar at the top of a folder window with which you can navigate to a different folder or library, or go back to a previous one.

____ 9. An instruction to a computer program that carries out an action.

____ 10. Small pictures that represent a program, a file, a folder, or an object.

____ 11. A set of instructions that a computer uses to perform a specific task.

____ 12. A spreadsheet program used to calculate numbers and create charts.

____ 13. The user interface that groups commands on tabs at the top of the program window.

____ 14. A bar at the top of the program window displaying the current file and program name.

____ 15. One or more keys pressed to perform a task that would otherwise require a mouse.

Multiple Choice

Circle the correct answer.

1. A small toolbar with frequently used commands that displays when selecting text or objects is the:
A. Quick Access Toolbar **B.** Mini toolbar **C.** Document toolbar

2. In Office 2010, a centralized space for file management tasks is:
A. a task pane **B.** a dialog box **C.** Backstage view

3. The commands Save, Save As, Open, and Close in Backstage view are located:
A. above the Backstage tabs **B.** below the Backstage tabs **C.** under the screen thumbnail

4. The tab in Backstage view that displays information about the current file is the:
A. Recent tab **B.** Info tab **C.** Options tab

5. Details about a file, including the title, author name, subject, and keywords are known as:
A. document properties **B.** formatting marks **C.** KeyTips

6. An Office feature that displays a list of potential results is:
A. Live Preview **B.** a contextual tab **C.** a gallery

7. A type of formatting emphasis applied to text such as bold, italic, and underline, is called:
   A. a font style **B.** a KeyTip **C.** a tag

8. A technology showing the result of applying formatting as you point to possible results is called:
   A. Live Preview **B.** Backstage view **C.** gallery view

9. A temporary storage area that holds text or graphics that you select and then cut or copy is the:
   A. paste options gallery **B.** ribbon **C.** Office clipboard

10. A file that has been reduced in size is:
    A. a compressed file **B.** an extracted file **C.** a PDF file

Creating Documents with Microsoft Word 2010

OUTCOMES

At the end of this chapter you will be able to:

OBJECTIVES

Mastering these objectives will enable you to:

PROJECT 1A
Create a flyer with a picture.

1. Create a New Document and Insert Text (p. 51)
2. Insert and Format Graphics (p. 53)
3. Insert and Modify Text Boxes and Shapes (p. 58)
4. Preview and Print a Document (p. 62)

PROJECT 1B
Format text, paragraphs, and documents.

5. Change Document and Paragraph Layout (p. 67)
6. Create and Modify Lists (p. 73)
7. Set and Modify Tab Stops (p. 78)
8. Insert a SmartArt Graphic (p. 80)

Joy Brown/Shutterstock

In This Chapter

In this chapter, you will use Microsoft Word, which is one of the most common programs found on computers and one that almost everyone has a reason to use. You will use many of the new tools found in Word 2010. When you learn word processing, you are also learning skills and techniques that you need to work efficiently on a computer. You can use Microsoft Word to perform basic word processing tasks such as writing a memo, a report, or a letter. You can also use Word to complete complex word processing tasks, such as creating sophisticated tables, embedding graphics, writing blogs, creating publications, and inserting links into other documents and the Internet. Word is a program that you can learn gradually, and then add more advanced skills one at a time.

The projects in this chapter relate to **Laurel College**. The college offers this diverse geographic area a wide range of academic and career programs, including associate degrees, certificate programs, and non-credit continuing education and personal development courses. The college makes positive contributions to the community through cultural and athletic programs and partnerships with businesses and nonprofit organizations. The college also provides industry-specific training programs for local businesses through its growing Economic Development Center.

Project 1A Flyer

myitlab Project 1A Training

Project Activities

In Activities 1.01 through 1.12, you will create a flyer announcing a new rock climbing class offered by the Physical Education Department at Laurel College. Your completed document will look similar to Figure 1.1.

Project Files

For Project 1A, you will need the following files:

New blank Word document
w01A_Fitness_Flyer
w01A_Rock_Climber

You will save your document as:

Lastname_Firstname_1A_Fitness_Flyer

Project Results

Rock Climbing 101

Meets Tuesday and Thursdays, 7-9 p.m.

Begins September 13, ends December 16

College Gymnasium, Room 104

Increase your fitness level by learning basic rock climbing using the new Laurel College Gymnasium rock climbing wall. The Physical Education Department is offering Rock Climbing 101 as part of its Recreational Fitness Program.

You will participate in a challenging class that will help you burn calories and increase your strength. Rock climbing results in an exciting and sometimes strenuous workout. The class will help you relieve stress, and you may notice increased flexibility, improved posture, and better muscle tone.

Register for Rock Climbing 101 on the first night of class. Wear comfortable clothing, and bring a bottle of water. Before enrolling in this or any other exercise class, discuss your plan with your physician.

Improve your strength, balance, and coordination

Lastname_Firstname_1A_Fitness_Flyer

Figure 1.1
Project 1A Fitness Flyer

Objective 1 | Create a New Document and Insert Text

When you create a new document, you can type all of the text, or you can type some of the text and then insert additional text from another source.

Activity 1.01 | Starting a New Word Document and Inserting Text

1. **Start** Word and display a new blank document. On the **Home tab**, in the **Paragraph group**, if necessary click the Show/Hide button ¶ so that it is active (glows orange) to display the formatting marks. If the rulers do not display, click the View tab, and then in the Show group, select the Ruler check box.

2. Type **Rock Climbing 101** and then press Enter two times. As you type the following text, press the Spacebar only one time at the end of a sentence: **Increase your fitness level by learning basic rock climbing using the new Laurel College Gymnasium rock climbing wall. The Physical Education Department is offering Rock Climbing 101 as part of its Recreational Fitness Program.**

   As you type, the insertion point moves to the right, and when it approaches the right margin, Word determines whether the next word in the line will fit within the established right margin. If the word does not fit, Word moves the entire word down to the next line. This feature is called ***wordwrap*** and means that you press Enter *only* when you reach the end of a paragraph—it is not necessary to press Enter at the end of each line of text.

> **Note** | Spacing Between Sentences
>
> Although you might have learned to add two spaces following end-of-sentence punctuation, the common practice now is to space only one time at the end of a sentence.

3. Press Enter one time. Take a moment to study the table in Figure 1.2 to become familiar with the default document settings in Microsoft Word, and then compare your screen with Figure 1.3.

   When you press Enter, Spacebar, or Tab on your keyboard, characters display in your document to represent these keystrokes. These characters do not print and are referred to as ***formatting marks*** or ***nonprinting characters***. These marks will display throughout this instruction.

Default Document Settings in a New Word Document

Setting	Default format
Font and font size	The default font is Calibri and the default font size is 11.
Margins	The default left, right, top, and bottom page margins are 1 inch.
Line spacing	The default line spacing is 1.15, which provides slightly more space between lines than single spacing does—an extra 1/6 of a line added between lines than single spacing.
Paragraph spacing	The default spacing after a paragraph is 10 points, which is slightly less than the height of one blank line of text.
View	The default view is Print Layout view, which displays the page borders and displays the document as it will appear when printed.

Figure 1.2

Figure 1.3

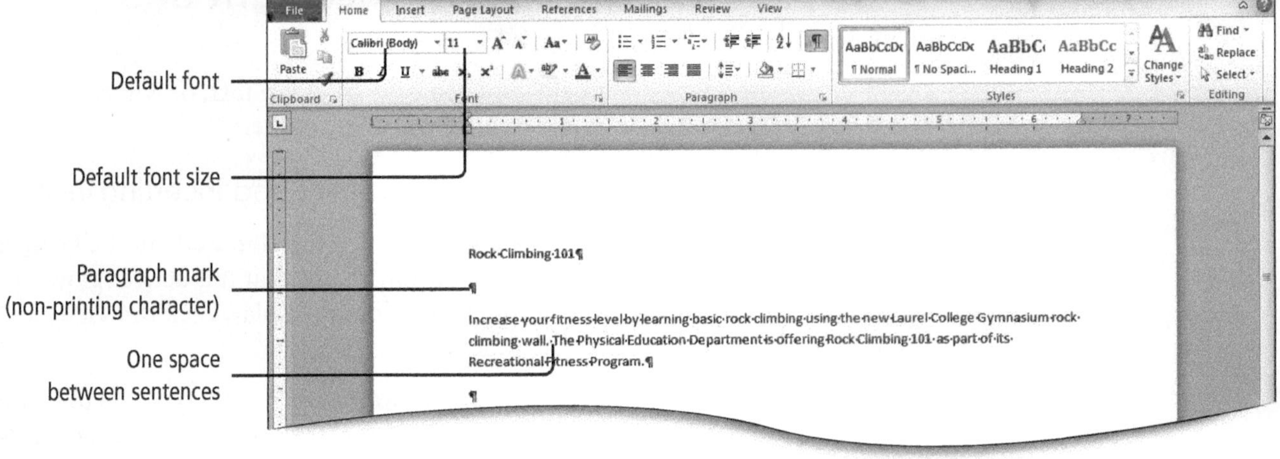

4 On the Ribbon, click the **Insert tab**. In the **Text group**, click the **Object button arrow**, and then click **Text from File**.

> **Alert! | Does the Object Dialog Box Display?**
>
> If the Object dialog box displays, you probably clicked the Object *button* instead of the Object *button arrow*. Close the Object dialog box, and then in the Text group, click the Object button arrow, as shown in Figure 1.4. Click *Text from File*, and then continue with Step 5.

> **Another Way**
>
> Open the file, copy the required text, close the file, and then paste the text into the current document.

5 In the **Insert File** dialog box, navigate to the student files that accompany this textbook, locate and select **w01A_Fitness_Flyer**, and then click **Insert**. Compare your screen with Figure 1.4.

A *copy* of the text from the w01A_Fitness_Flyer file displays at the insertion point location; the text is not removed from the original file.

Figure 1.4

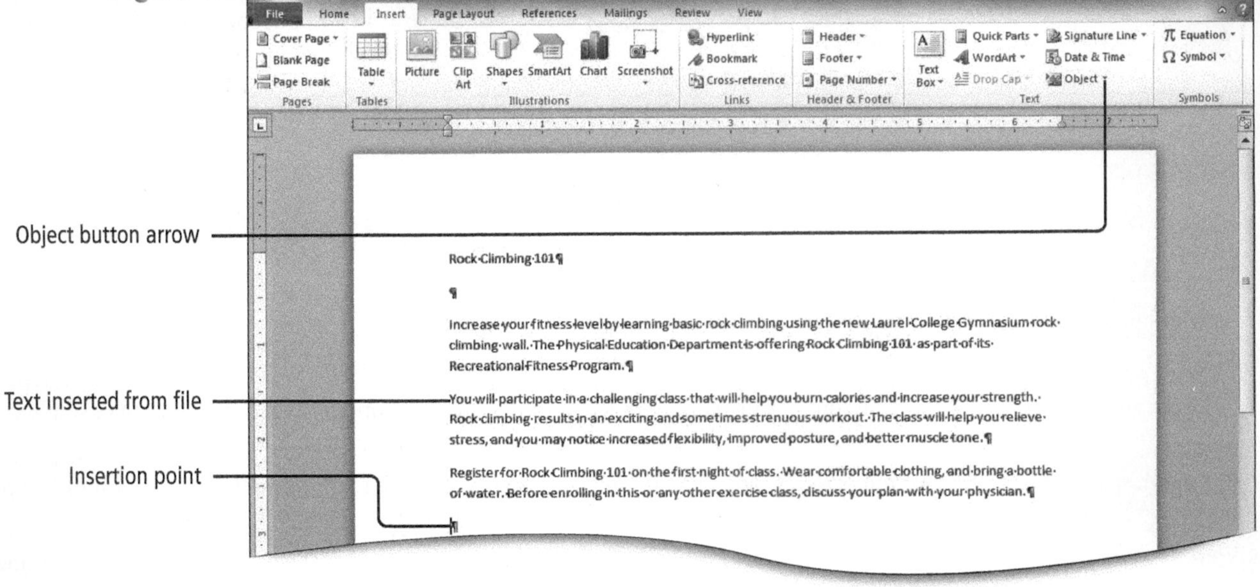

6 On the **Quick Access Toolbar**, click the **Save** button. In the **Save As** dialog box, navigate to the location where you are saving your files for this chapter, and then create and open a new folder named **Word Chapter 1** In the **File name** box, replace the existing text with **Lastname_Firstname_1A_Fitness_Flyer** and then click **Save**.

> **More Knowledge | Word's Default Settings Are Easier to Read Online**
>
> Until just a few years ago, word processing programs used single spacing, an extra blank paragraph to separate paragraphs, and 12 pt Times New Roman as the default formats. Now, studies show that individuals find the Word default formats described in Figure 1.2 to be easier to read online, where many documents are now viewed and read.

Objective 2 | Insert and Format Graphics

To add visual interest to a document, insert ***graphics***. Graphics include pictures, clip art, charts, and ***drawing objects***—shapes, diagrams, lines, and so on. For additional visual interest, you can convert text to an attractive graphic format; add, resize, move, and format pictures; and add an attractive page border.

Activity 1.02 | Formatting Text Using Text Effects

Text effects are decorative formats, such as shadowed or mirrored text, text glow, 3-D effects, and colors that make text stand out.

1. Including the paragraph mark, select the first paragraph of text—*Rock Climbing 101*. On the **Home tab**, in the **Font group**, click the **Text Effects** button [A▾].
2. In the displayed **Text Effects** gallery, in the first row, point to the second effect to display the ScreenTip *Fill - None, Outline - Accent 2* and then click this effect.
3. With the text still selected, in the **Font group**, click in the **Font Size** box [11▾] to select the existing font size. Type **60** and then press Enter.

   When you want to change the font size of selected text to a size that does not display in the Font Size list, type the number in the Font Size button box and press Enter to confirm the new font size.
4. With the text still selected, in the **Paragraph group**, click the **Center** button [≡] to center the text. Compare your screen with Figure 1.5.

Figure 1.5

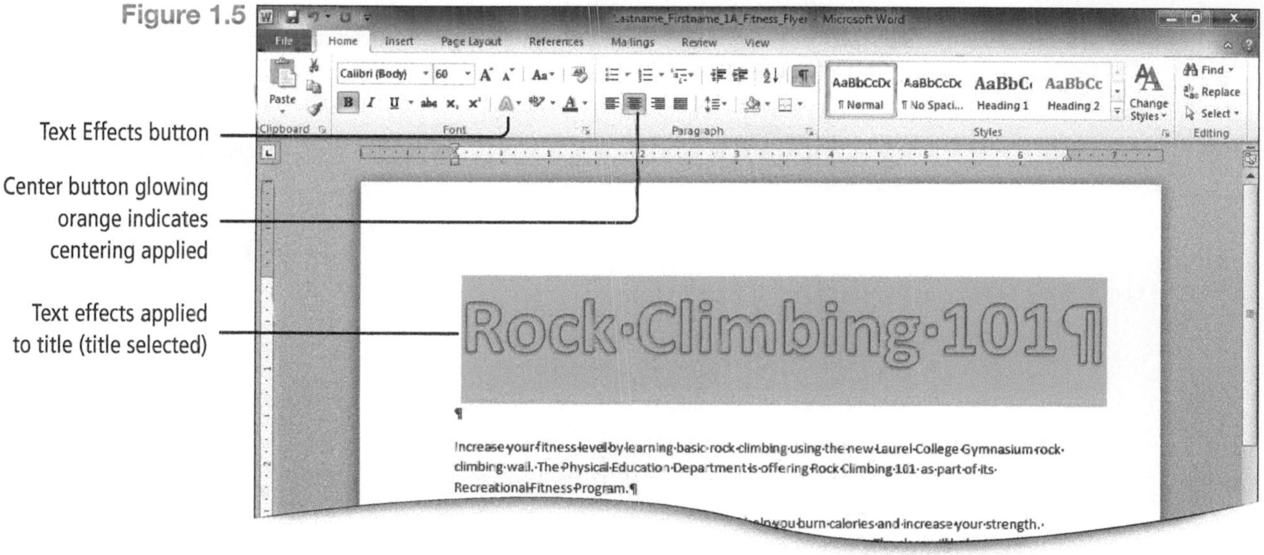

5. With the text still selected, in the **Font group**, click the **Text Effects** button [A▾]. Point to **Shadow**, and then under **Outer**, in the second row, click the third style—**Offset Left.**
6. With the text still selected, in the **Font group**, click the **Font Color button arrow** [A▾]. Under **Theme Colors**, in the fourth column, click the first color—**Dark Blue, Text 2.**

7 Click anywhere in the document to deselect the text, and then compare your screen with Figure 1.6.

Figure 1.6

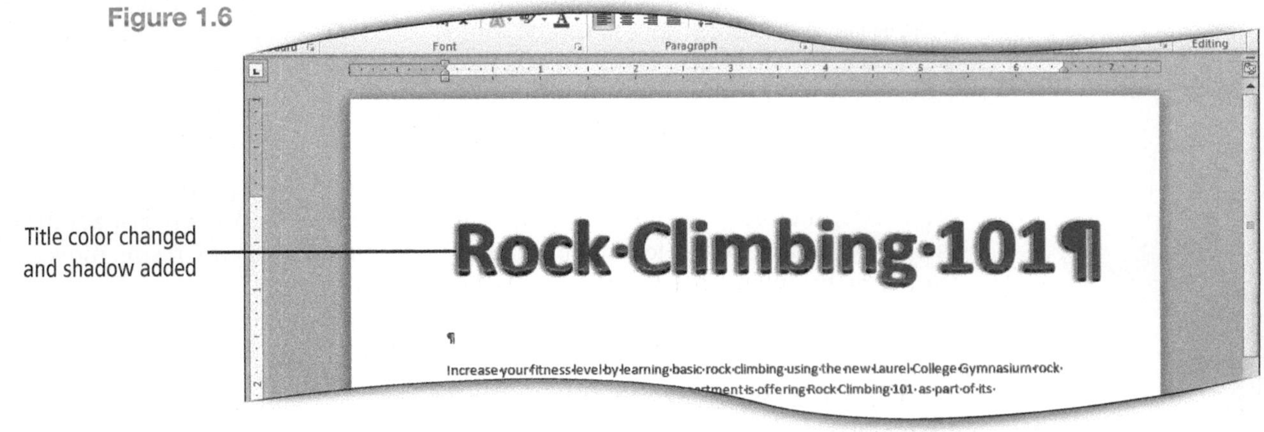

8 **Save** your document.

Activity 1.03 | Inserting and Resizing Pictures

1 In the paragraph that begins *Increase your fitness*, click to position the insertion point at the beginning of the paragraph.

2 On the **Insert tab**, in the **Illustrations group**, click the **Picture** button. In the **Insert Picture** dialog box, navigate to your student data files, locate and click **w01A_Rock_Climber**, and then click **Insert**.

Word inserts the picture as an ***inline object***; that is, the picture is positioned directly in the text at the insertion point, just like a character in a sentence. Sizing handles surround the picture indicating it is selected.

3 If necessary, scroll to view the entire picture. Notice the round and square sizing handles around the border of the selected picture, as shown in Figure 1.7.

The round corner sizing handles resize the graphic proportionally. The square sizing handles resize a graphic vertically or horizontally only; however, sizing with these will distort the graphic. A green rotate handle, with which you can rotate the graphic to any angle, displays above the top center sizing handle.

Figure 1.7

4 At the lower right corner of the picture, point to the round sizing handle until the pointer displays. Drag upward and to the left until the bottom of the graphic is aligned at approximately **4 inches on the vertical ruler**. Compare your screen with Figure 1.8. Notice that the graphic is proportionally resized.

Figure 1.8

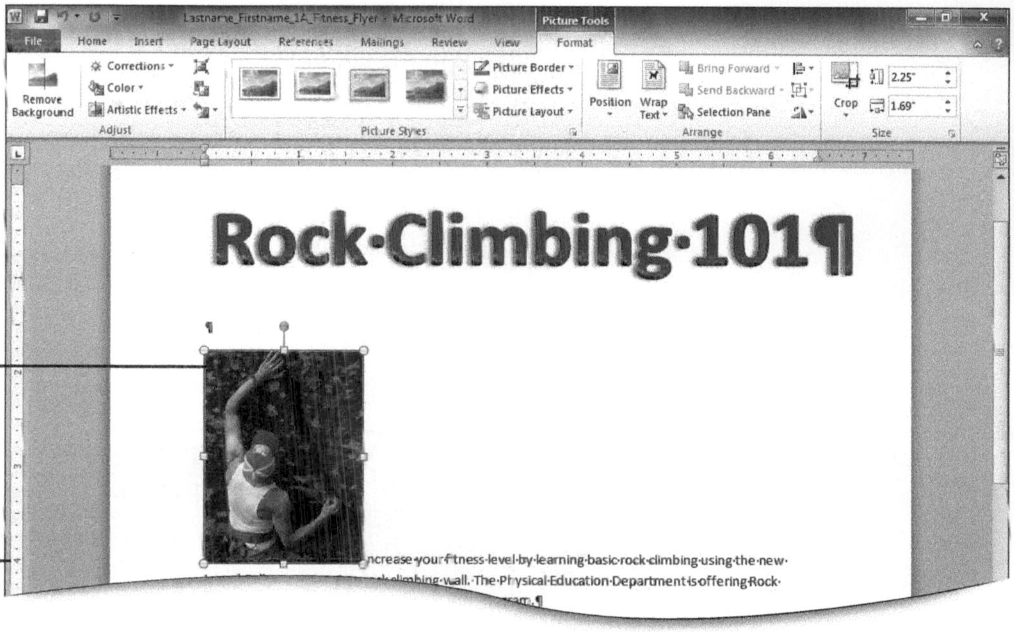

Picture resized

4-inch mark on the vertical ruler

> **Another Way**
> Click the Undo button to undo the change.

5 On the **Format tab**, in the **Adjust group**, click the **Reset Picture button arrow**, and then click **Reset Picture & Size.**

6 In the **Size group**, click the **Shape Height spin box up arrow** as necessary to change the height of the picture to **4.5"**. Scroll down to view the entire picture on your screen, compare your screen with Figure 1.9, and then **Save** your document.

When you use the Height and Width ***spin boxes*** to change the size of a graphic, the graphic will always resize proportionally; that is, the width adjusts as you change the height and vice versa.

Figure 1.9

Picture height increased to 4.5 inches

Activity 1.04 | Wrapping Text Around a Picture

Graphics inserted as inline objects are treated like characters in a sentence, which can result in unattractive spacing. You can change an inline object to a ***floating object***—a graphic that can be moved independently of the surrounding text characters.

1. Be sure the picture is selected—you know it is selected if the sizing handles display.
2. On the **Format tab**, in the **Arrange group**, click the **Wrap Text** button to display a gallery of text wrapping arrangements.

   Text wrapping refers to the manner in which text displays around an object.

3. From the gallery, click **Square** to wrap the text around the graphic, and then notice the ***anchor*** symbol to the left of the first line of the paragraph. Compare your screen with Figure 1.10.

   Select square text wrapping when you want to wrap the text to the left or right of the image. When you apply text wrapping, the object is always associated with—anchored to—a specific paragraph.

Figure 1.10

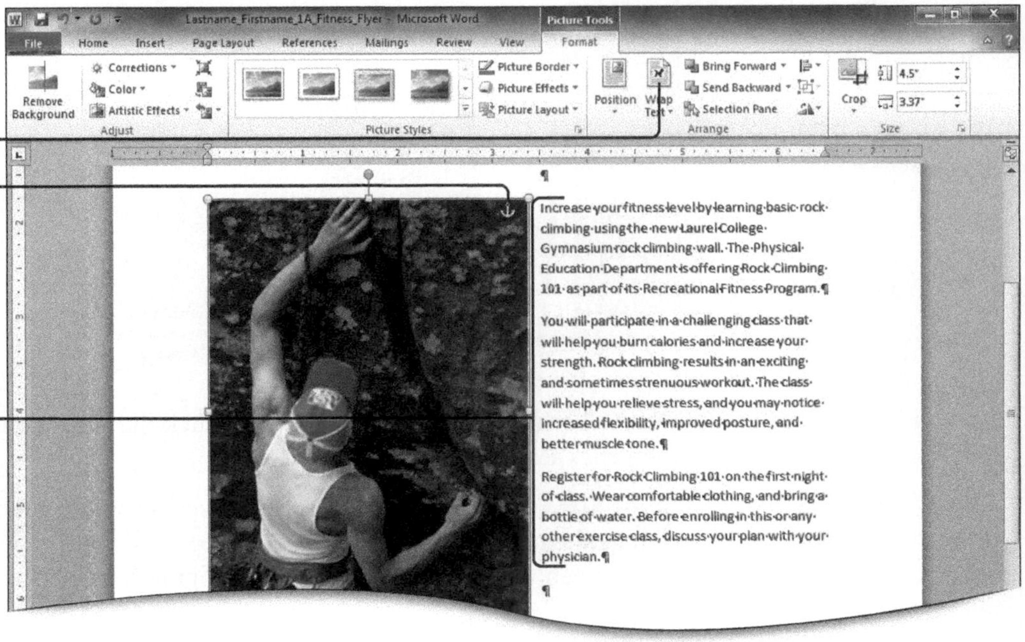

4. **Save** your document.

Activity 1.05 | Moving a Picture

1. Point to the rock climber picture to display the pointer.
2. Hold down Shift and drag the picture to the right until the right edge of the picture aligns at approximately **6.5 inches on the horizontal ruler**. Notice that the picture moves in a straight line when you hold down Shift. Compare your screen with Figure 1.11.

Figure 1.11

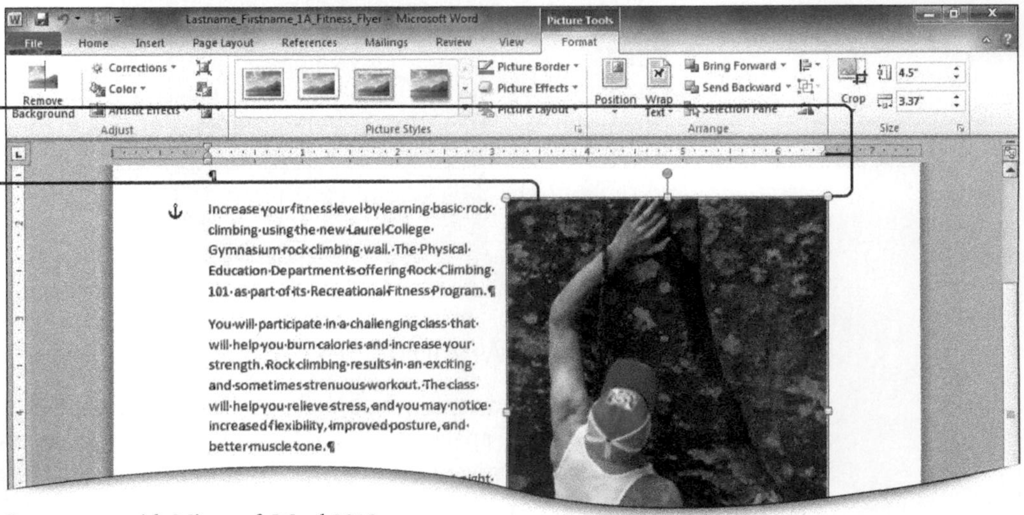

3 If necessary, press any of the arrow keys on your keyboard to ***nudge***—move in small increments—the picture in any direction so that the text wraps to match Figure 1.11. **Save** your document.

Activity 1.06 | Applying Picture Styles and Artistic Effects

Picture styles include shapes, shadows, frames, borders, and other special effects with which you can stylize an image. ***Artistic effects*** are formats that make pictures look more like sketches or paintings.

1 Be sure the rock climber picture is selected. On the **Format tab**, in the **Picture Styles group**, click the **Picture Effects** button. Point to **Soft Edges**, and then click **5 Point**.

The Soft Edges feature fades the edges of the picture. The number of points you choose determines how far the fade goes inward from the edges of the picture.

2 On the **Format tab**, in the **Adjust group**, click the **Artistic Effects** button. In the first row of the gallery, point to, but do not click, the third effect—**Pencil Grayscale**.

Live Preview displays the picture with the *Pencil Grayscale* effect added.

3 In the second row of the gallery, click the third effect—**Paint Brush**. Notice that the picture looks like a painting, rather than a photograph, as shown in Figure 1.12. **Save** your document.

Figure 1.12

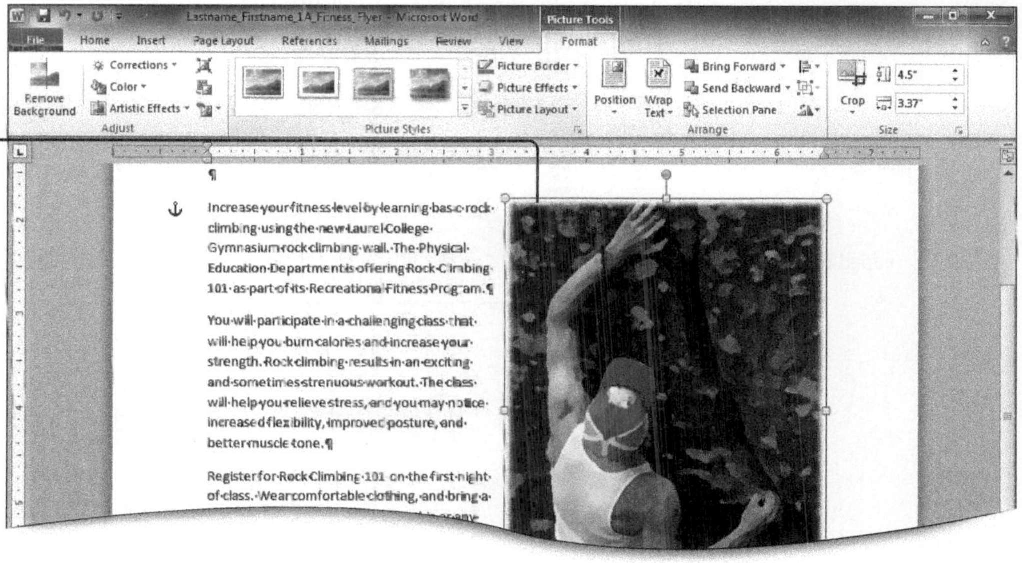

Paint Brush artistic effect applied to picture

Activity 1.07 | Adding a Page Border

Page borders frame a page and help to focus the information on the page.

1 Click anywhere outside the picture to deselect it. On the **Page Layout tab**, in the **Page Background group**, click the **Page Borders** button.

2 In the **Borders and Shading** dialog box, under **Setting**, click **Box**. Under **Style**, scroll down the list about a third of the way and click the heavy top line with the thin bottom line—check the **Preview** area to be sure the heavier line is the nearest to the edges of the page.

3 Click the **Color arrow**, and then in the fourth column, click the first color—**Dark Blue, Text 2**.

4 Under **Apply to**, be sure *Whole document* is selected, and then compare your screen with Figure 1.13.

Figure 1.13

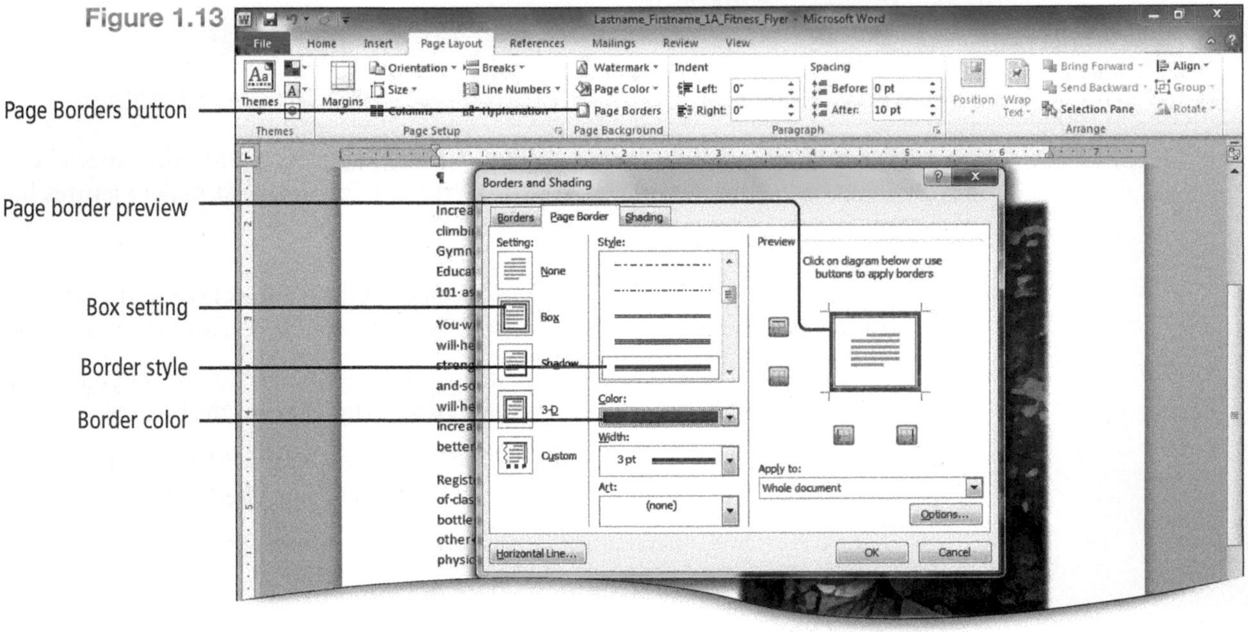

5 At the bottom of the **Borders and Shading** dialog box, click **OK**.

6 Press Ctrl + Home to move to the top of the document, and then compare your page border with Figure 1.14. **Save** your document.

Figure 1.14

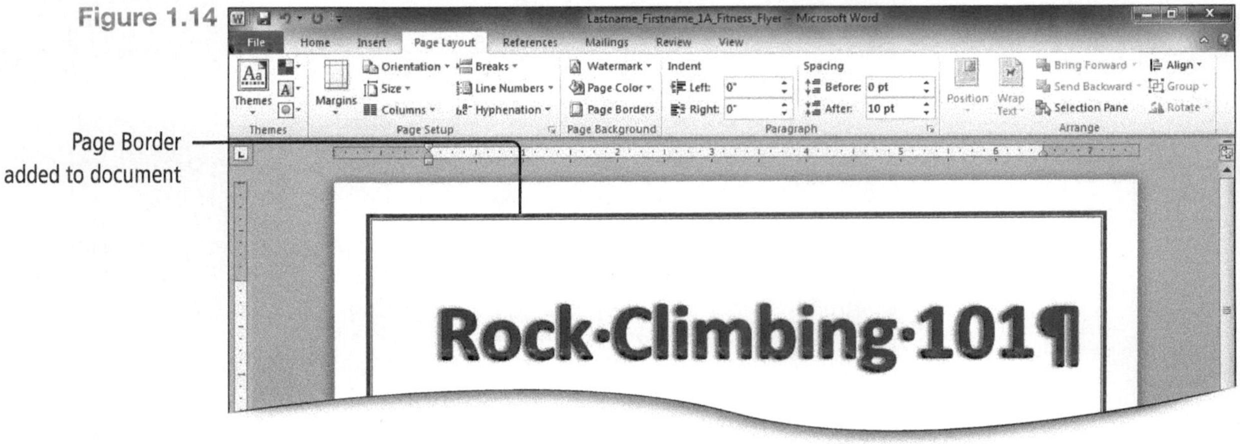

Objective 3 | Insert and Modify Text Boxes and Shapes

Word provides predefined ***shapes*** and ***text boxes*** that you can add to your documents. A shape is an object such as a line, arrow, box, callout, or banner. A text box is a movable, resizable container for text or graphics. Use these objects to add visual interest to your document.

Activity 1.08 | Inserting a Shape

1 Press ↓ one time to move to the blank paragraph below the title. Press Enter four times to make space for a text box, and notice that the picture anchored to the paragraph moves with the text.

2 Press Ctrl + End to move to the bottom of the document, and notice that your insertion point is positioned in the empty paragraph at the end of the document.

3 Click the **Insert tab**, and then in the **Illustrations group**, click the **Shapes** button to display the gallery. Compare your screen with Figure 1.15.

Figure 1.15

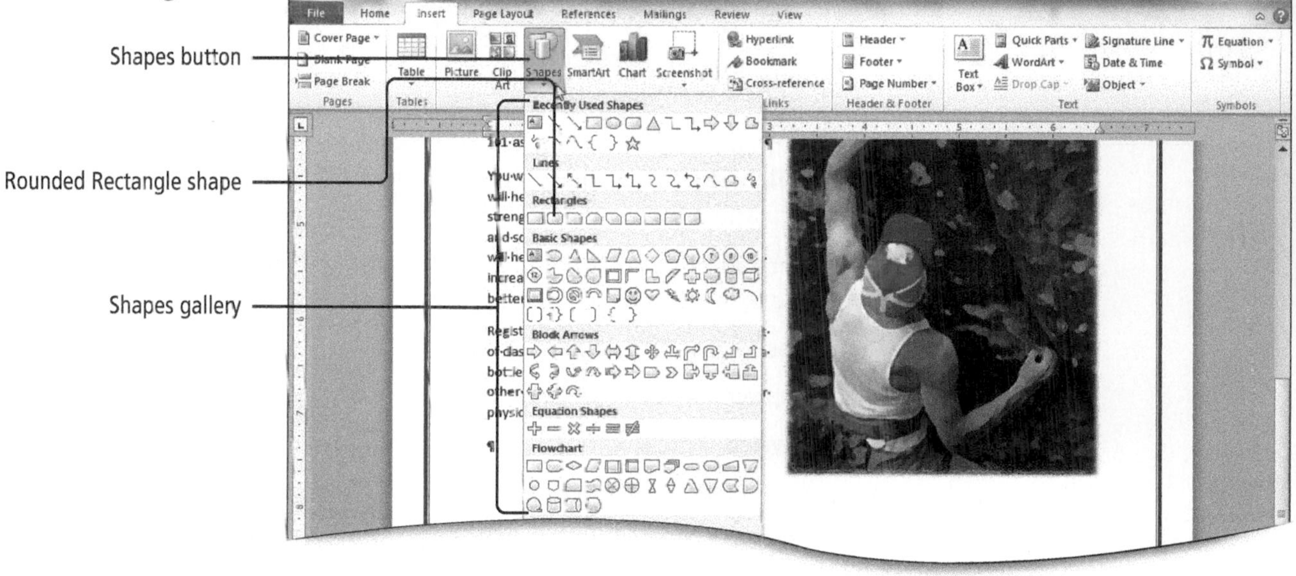

4 Under **Rectangles**, click the second shape—**Rounded Rectangle**, and then move your pointer. Notice that the [+] pointer displays.

5 Position the [+] pointer just under the lower left corner of the picture, and then drag down approximately **1 inch** and to the right edge of the picture.

6 Point to the shape and right-click, and then from the shortcut menu, click **Add Text**.

7 With the insertion point blinking inside the shape, point inside the shape and right-click, and then on the Mini toolbar, change the **Font Size** to **16**, and be sure **Center** alignment is selected.

8 Click inside the shape again, and then type **Improve your strength, balance, and coordination** If necessary, use the lower middle sizing handle to enlarge the shape to view your text. Compare your screen with Figure 1.16. **Save** your document.

Figure 1.16

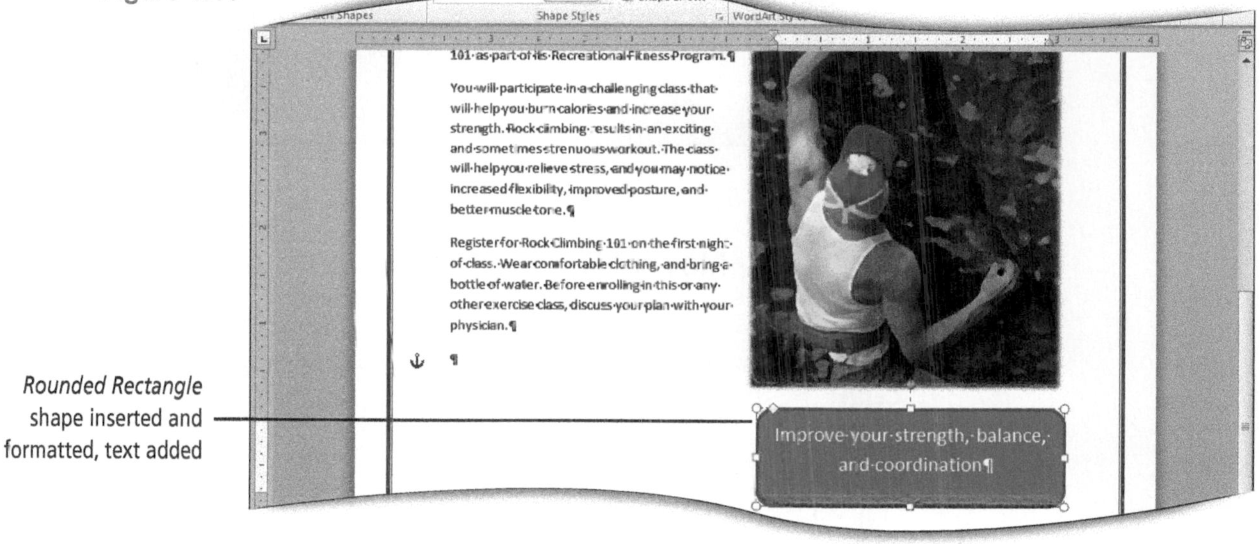

Activity 1.09 | Inserting a Text Box

A text box is useful to differentiate portions of text from other text on the page. You can move a text box anywhere on the page.

1. Press Ctrl + Home to move to the top of the document.
2. On the **Insert tab**, in the **Text group**, click the **Text Box** button. At the bottom of the gallery, click **Draw Text Box**.
3. Position the ⊞ pointer below the letter *k* in *Rock*—at approximately **1.5 inches on the vertical ruler**. Drag down and to the right to create a text box approximately **1.5 inches** high and **3 inches** wide—the exact size and location need not be precise.
4. With the insertion point blinking in the text box, type the following, pressing Enter after each line to create a new paragraph:

   Meets Tuesdays and Thursdays, 7-9 p.m.

   Begins September 13, ends December 16

   College Gymnasium, Room 104
5. Compare your screen with Figure 1.17.

Figure 1.17

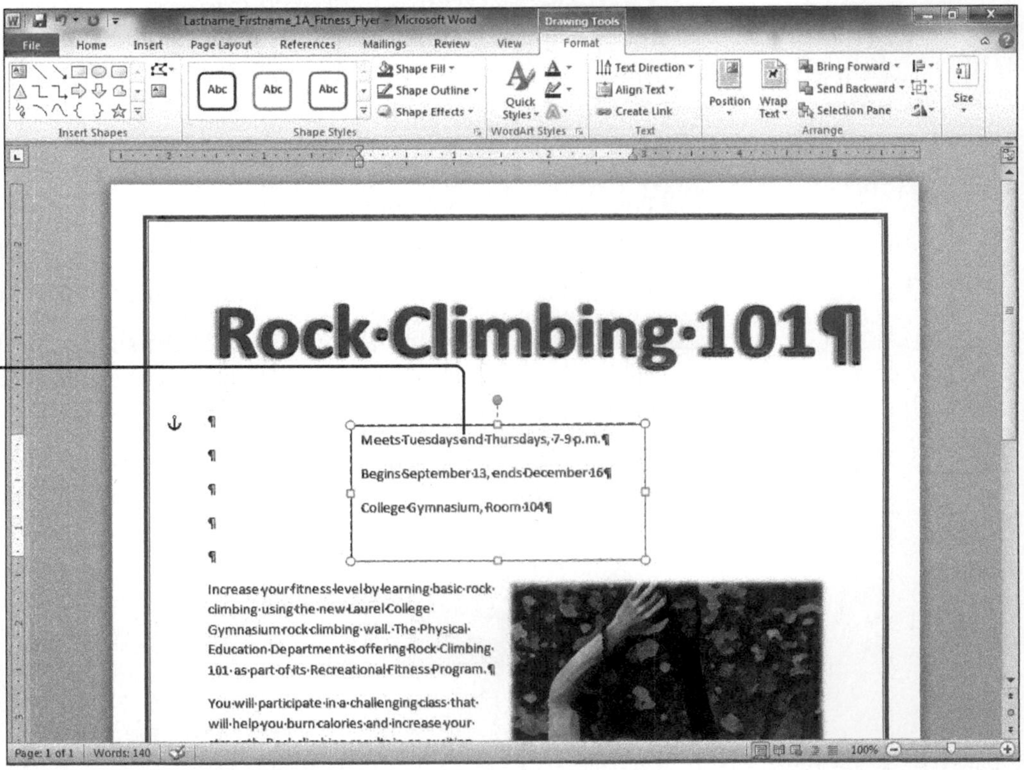

6. **Save** your document.

Activity 1.10 | Moving, Resizing, and Formatting Shapes and Text Boxes

1. In the text box you just created in the upper portion of the flyer, select all of the text. From the Mini toolbar, change the **Font Size** to **14**, apply **Bold** B, and then **Center** ≡ the text.

2. On the **Format tab**, in the **Size group**, if necessary, click the **Size** button. Click the **Shape Height spin arrows** [1.5"] as necessary to set the height of the text box to **1.2"**. Click the **Shape Width spin arrows** [1.37"] as necessary to set the width of the text box to **4"**.

3. In the **Shape Styles group**, click the **Shape Effects** button. Point to **Shadow**, and then under **Outer**, in the first row, click the first style—**Offset Diagonal Bottom Right**.

4. In the **Shape Styles group**, click the **Shape Outline button arrow**. In the fourth column, click the first color—**Dark Blue, Text 2** to change the color of the text box border.

5. Click the **Shape Outline button arrow** again, point to **Weight**, and then click **3 pt**.

6. Click anywhere in the document to deselect the text box. Notice that with the text box deselected, you can see all the measurements on the horizontal ruler.

7. Click anywhere in the text box and point to the text box border to display the [move] pointer. By dragging, visually center the text box vertically and horizontally in the space below the *Rock Climbing 101* title. Then, if necessary, press any of the arrow keys on your keyboard to nudge the text box in precise increments to match Figure 1.18.

Figure 1.18

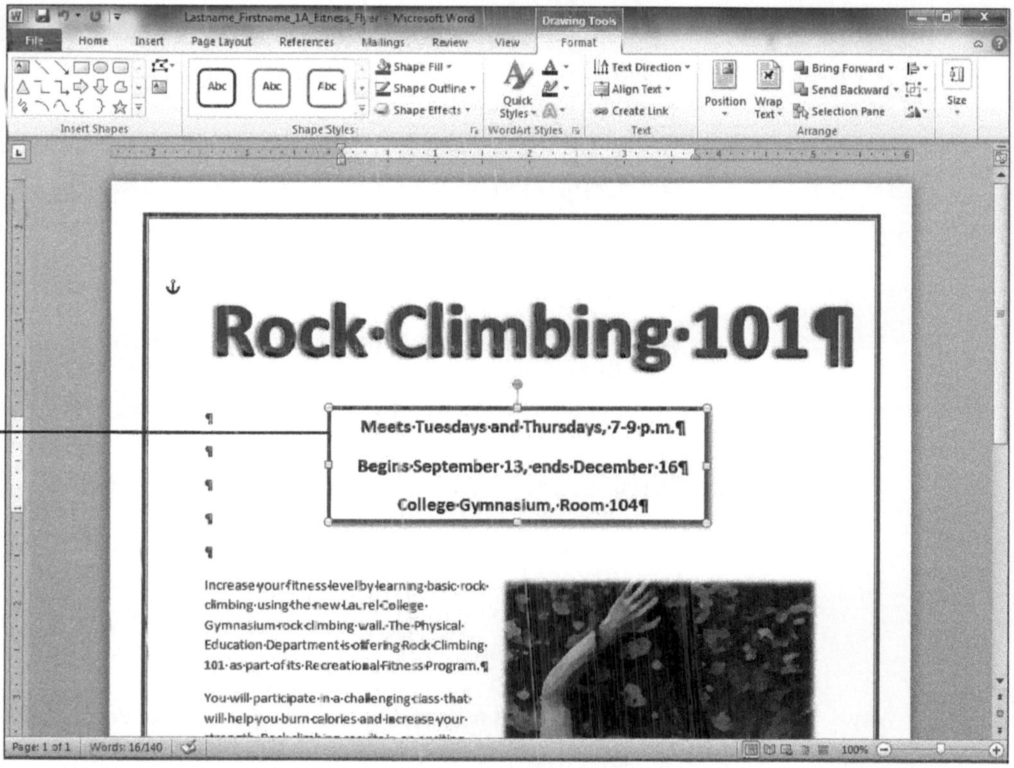

Text formatted and centered in text box, shadow added, border color and weight changed

8. Press Ctrl + End to move to the bottom of the document. Click on the border of the rounded rectangular shape to select it.

9. On the **Format tab**, in the **Size group**, if necessary, click the **Size** button. Click the **Shape Height spin arrows** [1.5"] as necessary to change the height of the shape to **0.8"**.

10. In the **Shape Styles group**, click the **Shape Fill button arrow**, and then at the bottom of the gallery, point to **Gradient.** Under **Dark Variations**, in the third row click the first gradient—**Linear Diagonal - Bottom Left to Top Right.**

11. In the **Shape Styles group**, click the **Shape Outline button arrow**. In the sixth column, click the first color—**Red, Accent 2**.

12 Click the **Shape Outline button arrow** again, point to **Weight**, and then click **1 1/2 pt**. Click anywhere in the document to deselect the shape. Compare your screen with Figure 1.19, and then **Save** your document.

Figure 1.19

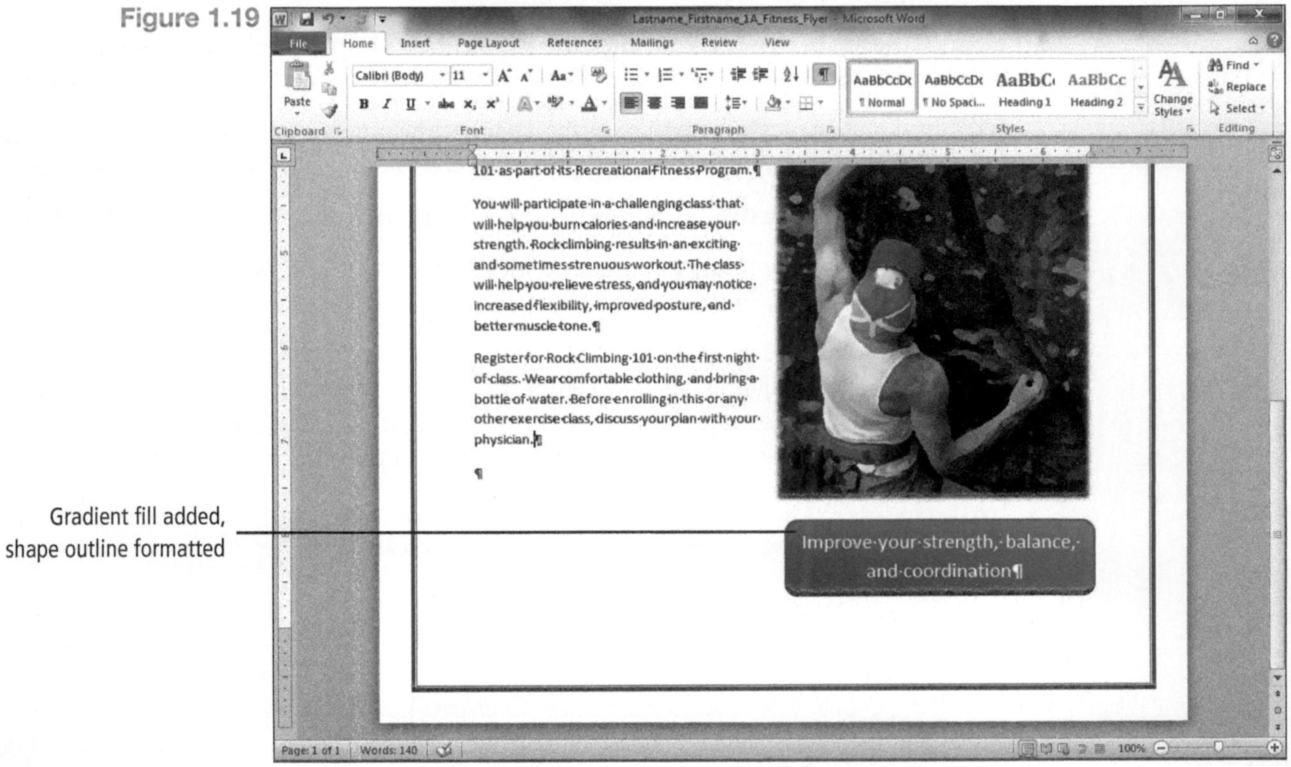

Objective 4 | Preview and Print a Document

While you are creating your document, it is useful to preview your document periodically to be sure that you are getting the result you want. Then, before printing, make a final preview to be sure the document layout is what you intended.

Activity 1.11 | Adding a File Name to the Footer

Information in headers and footers helps to identify a document when it is printed or displayed electronically. Recall that a header is information that prints at the top of every page; a footer is information that prints at the bottom of every page. In this textbook, you will insert the file name in the footer of every Word document.

Another Way

At the bottom edge of the page, right-click; from the shortcut menu, click Edit Footer.

1 Click the **Insert tab**, and then, in the **Header & Footer group**, click the **Footer** button.

2 At the bottom of the **Footer** gallery, click **Edit Footer**.

The footer area displays with the insertion point blinking at the left edge, and on the Ribbon, the Header & Footer Tools display and add the Design tab.

3 On the **Design tab**, in the **Insert group**, click the **Quick Parts** button, and then click **Field**. In the **Field** dialog box, under **Field names**, use the vertical scroll bar to examine the items that you can insert in a header or footer.

A ***field*** is a placeholder that displays preset content such as the current date, the file name, a page number, or other stored information.

4 In the **Field names** list, scroll as necessary to locate and then click **FileName**. Compare your screen with Figure 1.20.

Figure 1.20

Quick Parts button

Field dialog box

FileName field

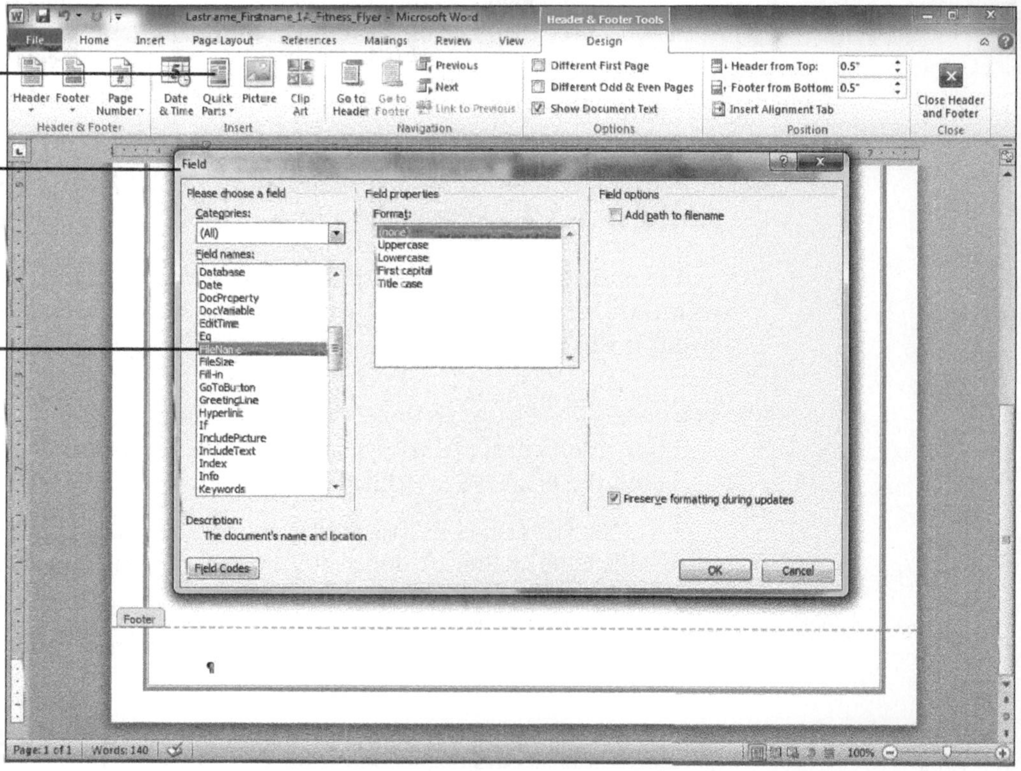

5 In the lower right corner of the **Field** dialog box, click **OK**, and then compare your screen with Figure 1.21.

Figure 1.21

Document text and image dimmed when footer is open

File name in footer

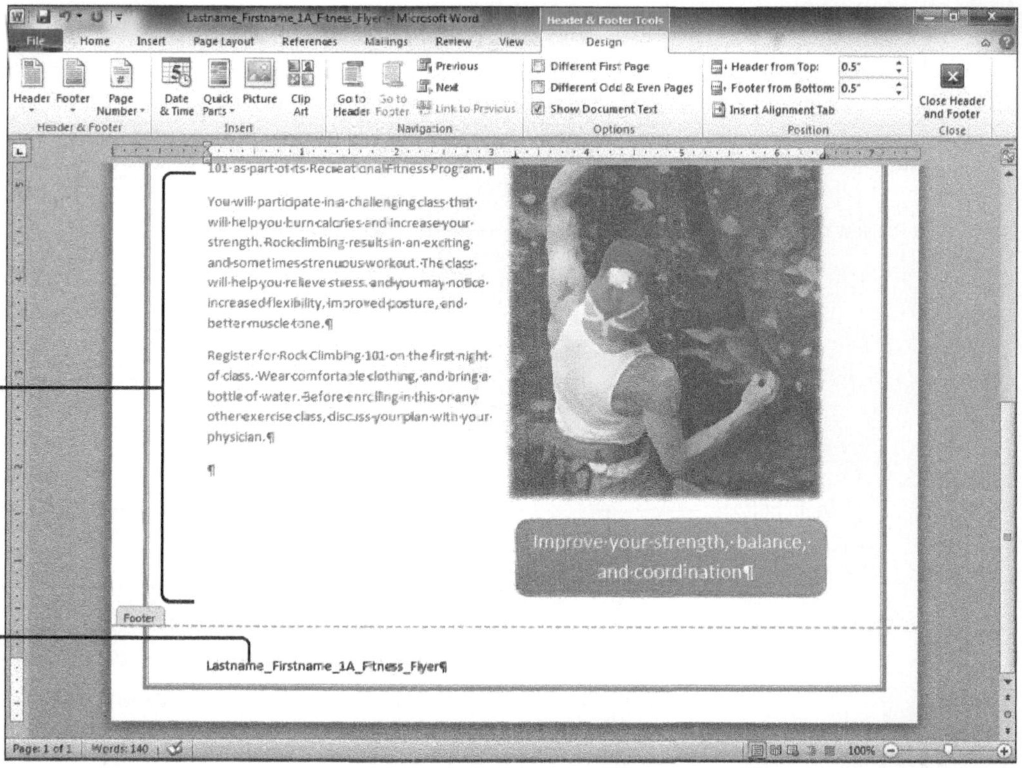

Another Way

Double-click anywhere in the document to close the footer area.

6 On the **Design tab**, at the far right in the **Close group**, click the **Close Header and Footer** button.

When the body of the document is active, the footer text is dimmed—displays in gray. Conversely, when the footer area is active, the footer text is not dimmed; instead, the document text is dimmed.

7 **Save** your document.

Activity 1.12 | Previewing and Printing a Document

To ensure that you are getting the result you want, it is useful to periodically preview your document. Then, before printing, make a final preview to be sure the document layout is what you intended.

Another Way

Press Ctrl + F2 to display Print Preview.

1 Press Ctrl + Home to move the insertion point to the top of the document. In the upper left corner of your screen, click the **File tab** to display **Backstage** view, and then click the **Print tab** to display the **Print Preview**.

The Print tab in Backstage view displays the tools you need to select your settings. On the right, Print Preview displays your document exactly as it will print; the formatting marks do not display.

2 In the lower right corner of the **Print Preview**, notice the zoom buttons that display. Compare your screen with Figure 1.22.

Figure 1.22

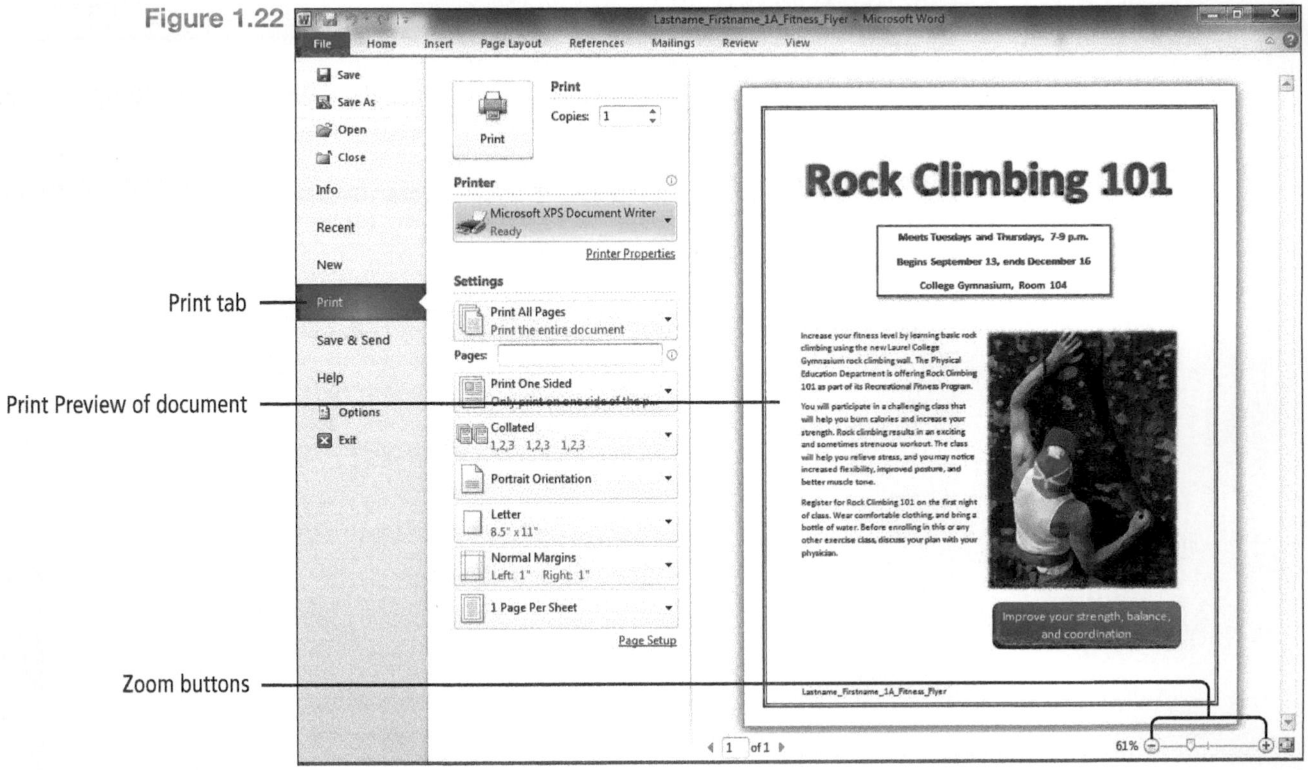

3 Click the **Zoom In** button to view the document at full size, and notice that a larger preview is easier to read. Click the **Zoom Out** button to view the entire page.

4 Click the **Info tab**. On the right, under the screen thumbnail, click **Properties**, and then click **Show Document Panel**.

Here you can adjust the document properties.

5 In the **Author** box, delete any text and then type your firstname and lastname. In the **Subject** box type your course name and section number, and in the **Keywords** box type **fitness, rock climbing** **Close** the Document Panel.

6 **Save** your document. To print, display **Backstage** view, and then on the **navigation bar**, click **Print**. In the **Settings** group, be sure the correct printer is selected, and then in the **Print group**, click the **Print** button. Or, submit your document electronically as directed by your instructor.

7 In **Backstage** view, click **Exit** to close the document and exit Word.

End **You have completed Project 1A**

Project 1B Information Handout

myitlab
Project 1B Training

Project Activities

In Activities 1.13 through 1.23, you will format and add lists to an information handout that describes student activities at Laurel College. Your completed document will look similar to Figure 1.23.

Project Files

For Project 1B, you will need the following file:

w01B_Student_Activities

You will save your document as:

Lastname_Firstname_1B_Student_Activities

Project Results

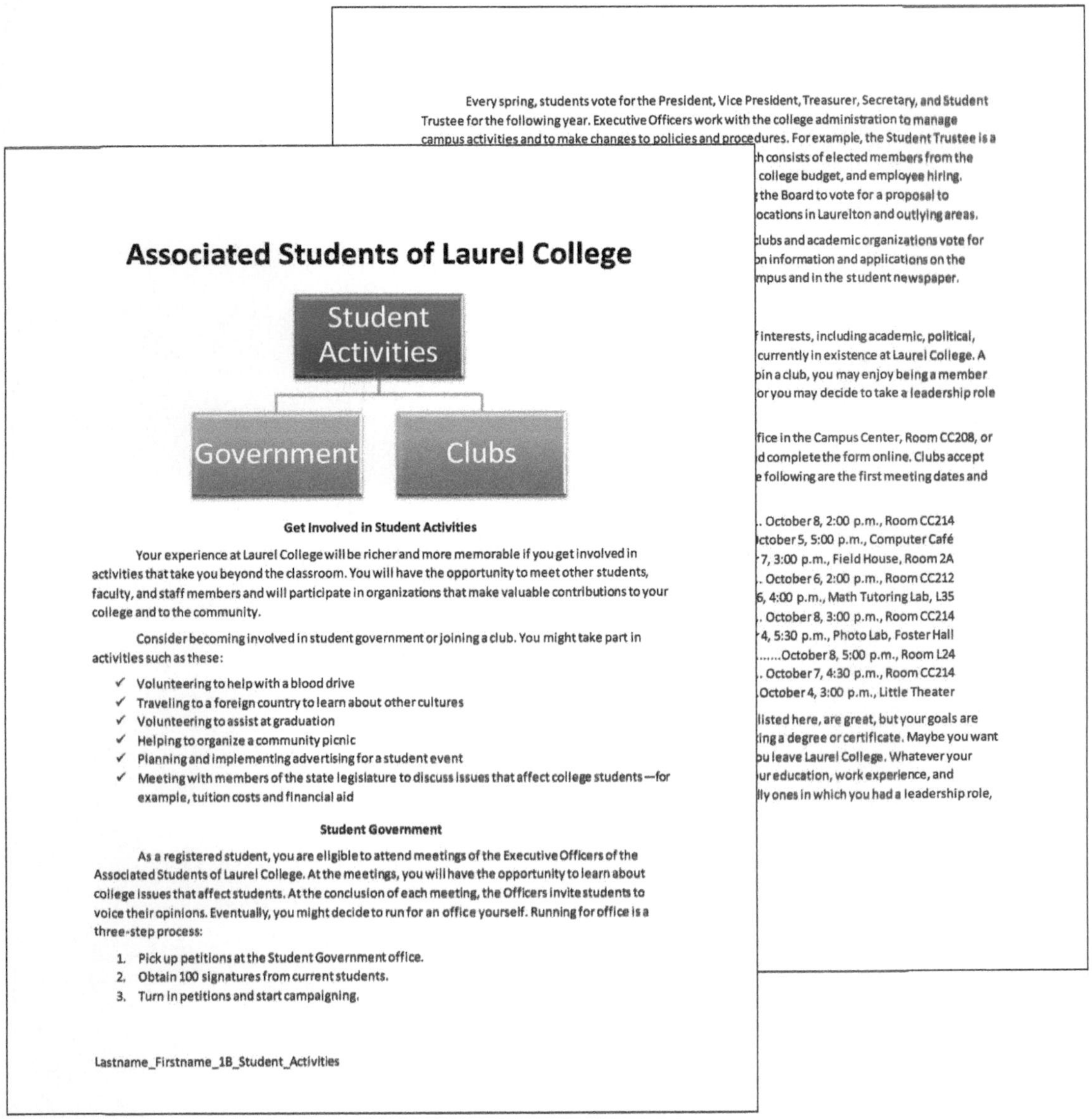
Every spring, students vote for the President, Vice President, Treasurer, Secretary, and Student Trustee for the following year. Executive Officers work with the college administration to manage campus activities and to make changes to policies and procedures. For example, the Student Trustee is a

Associated Students of Laurel College

Get Involved in Student Activities

Your experience at Laurel College will be richer and more memorable if you get involved in activities that take you beyond the classroom. You will have the opportunity to meet other students, faculty, and staff members and will participate in organizations that make valuable contributions to your college and to the community.

Consider becoming involved in student government or joining a club. You might take part in activities such as these:

- ✓ Volunteering to help with a blood drive
- ✓ Traveling to a foreign country to learn about other cultures
- ✓ Volunteering to assist at graduation
- ✓ Helping to organize a community picnic
- ✓ Planning and implementing advertising for a student event
- ✓ Meeting with members of the state legislature to discuss issues that affect college students—for example, tuition costs and financial aid

Student Government

As a registered student, you are eligible to attend meetings of the Executive Officers of the Associated Students of Laurel College. At the meetings, you will have the opportunity to learn about college issues that affect students. At the conclusion of each meeting, the Officers invite students to voice their opinions. Eventually, you might decide to run for an office yourself. Running for office is a three-step process:

1. Pick up petitions at the Student Government office.
2. Obtain 100 signatures from current students.
3. Turn in petitions and start campaigning.

Lastname_Firstname_1B_Student_Activities

Figure 1.23
Project 1B Student Activities

Objective 5 | Change Document and Paragraph Layout

Document layout includes ***margins***—the space between the text and the top, bottom, left, and right edges of the paper. Paragraph layout includes line spacing, indents, and tabs. In Word, the information about paragraph formats is stored in the paragraph mark at the end of a paragraph. When you press the Enter, the new paragraph mark contains the formatting of the previous paragraph, unless you take steps to change it.

Activity 1.13 | Setting Margins

1. **Start** Word. From **Backstage** view, display the **Open** dialog box. From your student files, locate and open the document **w01B_Student_Activities**. On the **Home tab**, in the **Paragraph group**, be sure the **Show/Hide** button ¶ is active—glows orange—so that you can view the formatting marks.

2. From **Backstage** view, display the **Save As** dialog box. Navigate to your **Word Chapter 1** folder, and then **Save** the document as **Lastname_Firstname_1B_Student_Activities**

3. Click the **Page Layout tab**. In the **Page Setup group**, click the **Margins** button, and then take a moment to study the buttons in the Margins gallery.

   The top button displays the most recent custom margin settings, while the other buttons display commonly used margin settings.

4. At the bottom of the **Margins** gallery, click **Custom Margins**.

5. In the **Page Setup** dialog box, press Tab as necessary to select the value in the **Left** box, and then, with *1.25"* selected, type **1**

   This action will change the left margin to 1 inch on all pages of the document. You do not need to type the inch (") mark.

6. Press Tab to select the margin in the **Right** box, and then type **1** At the bottom of the dialog box, notice that the new margins will apply to the **Whole document**. Compare your screen with Figure 1.24.

Figure 1.24

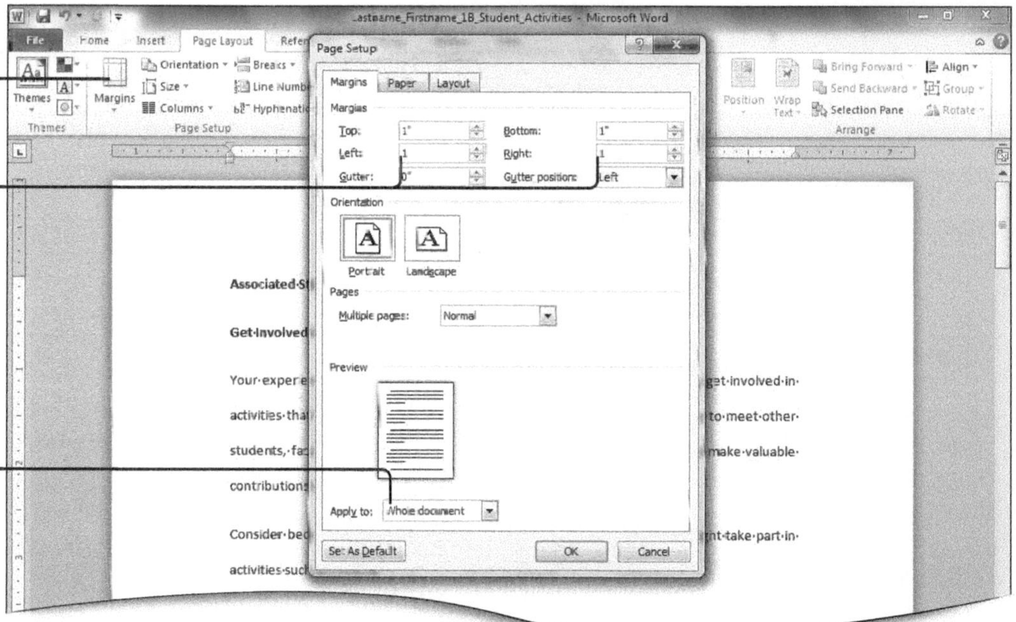

Another Way

Click the View tab, and then in the Show group, select the Ruler check box.

7 Click **OK** to apply the new margins and close the dialog box. If the ruler below the Ribbon is not displayed, at the top of the vertical scroll bar, click the View Ruler button.

8 Scroll to view the bottom of **Page 1** and the top of **Page 2**. Notice that the page edges display, and the page number and total number of pages display on the left side of the status bar.

9 Near the bottom edge of **Page 1**, point anywhere in the margin area, right-click, and then click **Edit Footer** to display the footer area.

10 On the **Design tab**, in the **Insert group**, click the **Quick Parts** button, and then click **Field**. In the **Field** dialog box, under **Field names**, locate and click **FileName**, and then click **OK**.

11 Double-click anywhere in the document to close the footer area, and then **Save** your document.

Activity 1.14 | Aligning Text

Alignment refers to the placement of paragraph text relative to the left and right margins. Most paragraph text uses ***left alignment***—aligned at the left margin, leaving the right margin uneven. Three other types of paragraph alignment are: ***center alignment***—centered between the left and right margins; ***right alignment***—aligned at the right margin with an uneven left margin; and ***justified alignment***—text aligned evenly at both the left and right margins. See the table in Figure 1.25.

Paragraph Alignment Options

Alignment	Button	Description and Example
Align Text Left		Align Text Left is the default paragraph alignment in Word. Text in the paragraph aligns at the left margin, and the right margin is uneven.
Center		Center alignment aligns text in the paragraph so that it is centered between the left and right margins.
Align Text Right		Align Text Right aligns text at the right margin. Using Align Text Right, the left margin, which is normally even, is uneven.
Justify		The Justify alignment option adds additional space between words so that both the left and right margins are even. Justify is often used when formatting newspaper-style columns.

Figure 1.25

1 Scroll to position the middle of **Page 2** on your screen, look at the left and right margins, and notice that the text is justified—both the right and left margins of multiple-line paragraphs are aligned evenly at the margins. On the **Home tab**, in the **Paragraph group**, notice that the **Justify** button is active.

2 In the paragraph that begins *Every spring, students vote*, in the first line, look at the space following the word *Every*, and then compare it with the space following the word *Trustee* in the second line. Notice how some of the spaces between words are larger than others.

To achieve a justified right margin, Word adjusts the size of spaces between words in this manner, which can result in unattractive spacing in a document that spans the width of a page. Many individuals find such spacing difficult to read.

> **Another Way**
>
> On the Home tab, in the Editing group, click the Select button, and then click Select All.

3. Press Ctrl + A to select all of the text in the document, and then on the **Home tab**, in the **Paragraph group**, click the **Align Text Left** button.

4. Press Ctrl + Home. At the top of the document, in the left margin area, point to the left of the first paragraph—*Associated Students of Laurel College*—until the pointer displays, and then click one time to select the paragraph. On the Mini toolbar, change the **Font Size** to **26**.

   Use this technique to select entire lines of text.

5. Point to the left of the first paragraph—*Associated Students of Laurel College*—to display the pointer again, and then drag down to select the first two paragraphs, which form the title and subtitle of the document.

6. On the Mini toolbar, click the **Center** button to center the title and subtitle between the left and right margins, and then compare your screen with Figure 1.26.

Figure 1.26

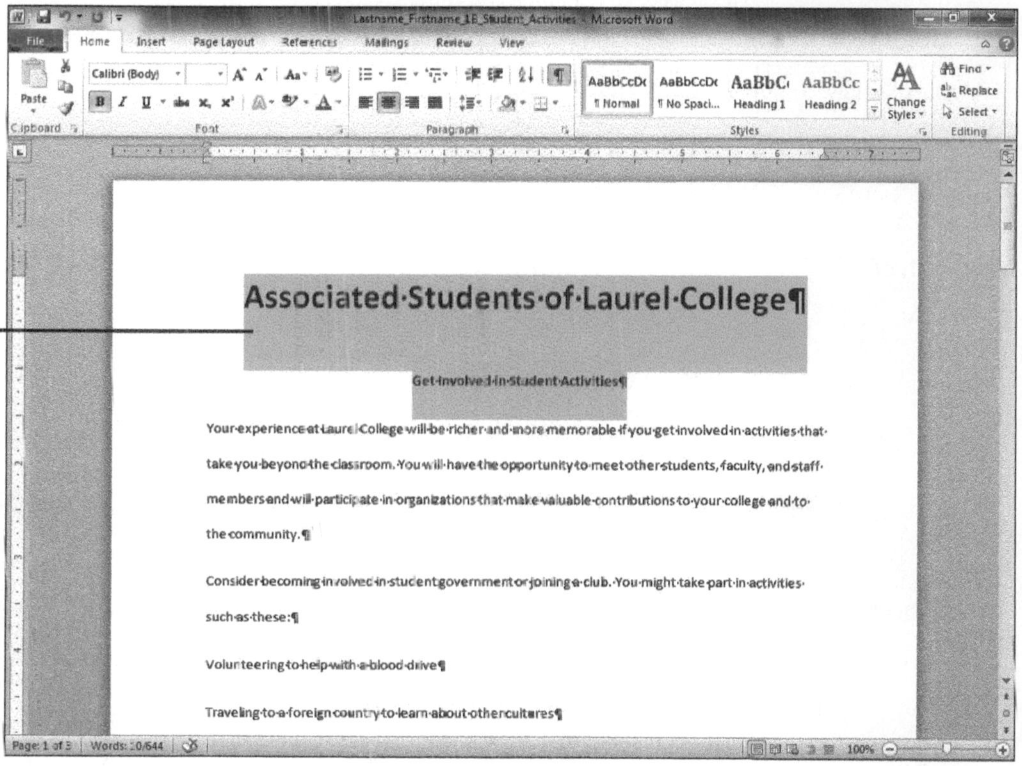

Title centered and font size set to 26

7. Scroll down to view the bottom of **Page 1**, and then locate the first bold subheading—*Student Government*. Point to the left of the paragraph to display the pointer, and then click one time.

8. With *Student Government* selected, use your mouse wheel or the vertical scroll bar to bring the lower portion of **Page 2** into view. Locate the subheading *Clubs*. Move the pointer to the left of the paragraph to display the pointer, hold down Ctrl, and then click one time.

   Two subheadings are selected; in Windows-based programs, you can hold down Ctrl to select multiple items.

9. On the Mini toolbar, click the **Center** button to center both subheadings, and then click **Save**.

Activity 1.15 | Changing Line Spacing

Line spacing is the distance between lines of text in a paragraph. Three of the most commonly used line spacing options are shown in the table in Figure 1.27.

Line Spacing Options

Alignment	Description, Example, and Information
Single spacing	**This text in this example uses single spacing.** Single spacing was once the most commonly used spacing in business documents. Now, because so many documents are read on a computer screen rather than on paper, single spacing is becoming less popular.
Multiple 1.15 spacing	**This text in this example uses multiple 1.15 spacing.** The default line spacing in Microsoft Word 2010 is 1.15, which is equivalent to single spacing with an extra 1/6 line added between lines to make the text easier to read on a computer screen. Many individuals now prefer this spacing, even on paper, because the lines of text appear less crowded.
Double spacing	**This text in this example uses double spacing.** College research papers and draft documents that need space for notes are commonly double-spaced; there is space for a full line of text between each document line.

Figure 1.27

1. Press Ctrl + Home to move to the beginning of the document. Press Ctrl + A to select all of the text in the document.
2. With all of the text in the document selected, on the **Home tab**, in the **Paragraph group**, click the **Line Spacing** button, and notice that the text in the document is double spaced—**2.0** is checked. Compare your screen with Figure 1.28.

Figure 1.28

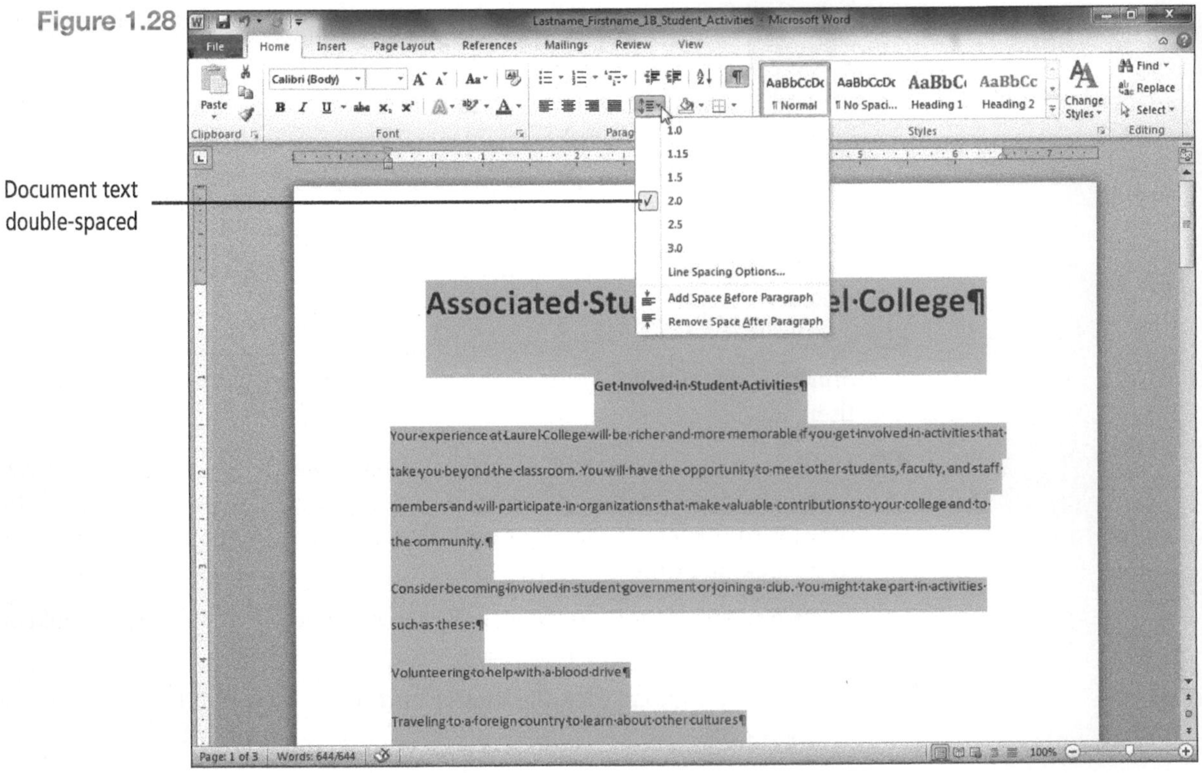

3 On the **Line Spacing** menu, click the *second* setting—**1.15**—and then click anywhere in the document. Compare your screen with Figure 1.29, and then **Save** your document.

Double spacing is most commonly used in research papers and rough draft documents. Recall that 1.15 is the default line spacing for new Word documents. Line spacing of 1.15 has slightly more space between the lines than single spacing. On a computer screen, spacing of 1.15 is easier to read than single spacing. Because a large percentage of Word documents are read on a computer screen, 1.15 is the default spacing for a new Word document.

Figure 1.29

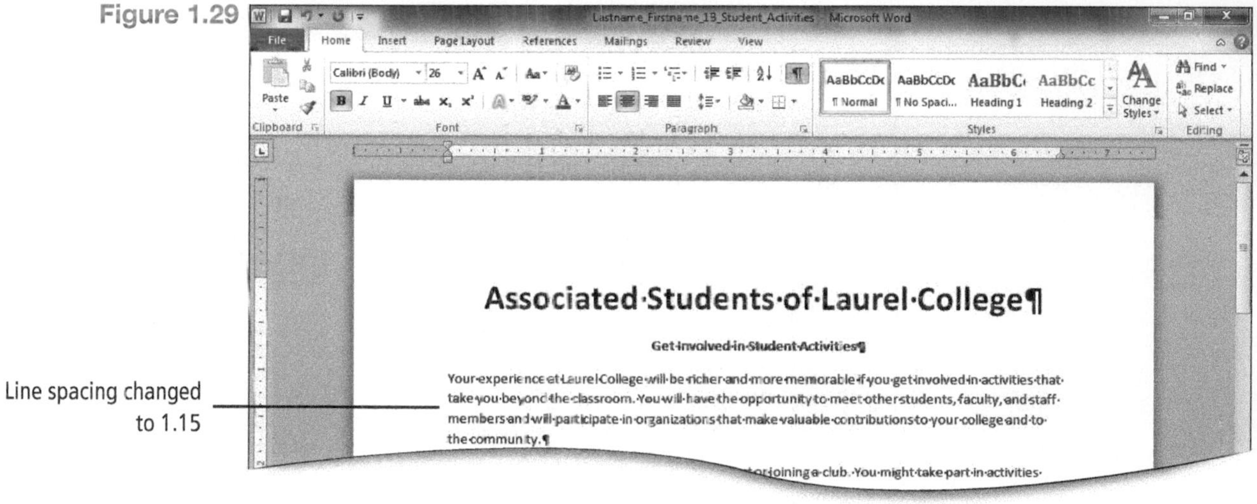

Activity 1.16 | Indenting Text and Adding Space After Paragraphs

Common techniques to distinguish paragraphs include adding space after each paragraph, indenting the first line of each paragraph, or both.

1 Below the title and subtitle of the document, click anywhere in the paragraph that begins *Your experience.*

2 On the **Home tab**, in the **Paragraph group**, click the **Dialog Box Launcher**.

3 In the **Paragraph** dialog box, on the **Indents and Spacing tab**, under **Indentation**, click the **Special arrow**, and then click **First line** to indent the first line by 0.5″, which is the default indent setting. Compare your screen with Figure 1.30.

Figure 1.30

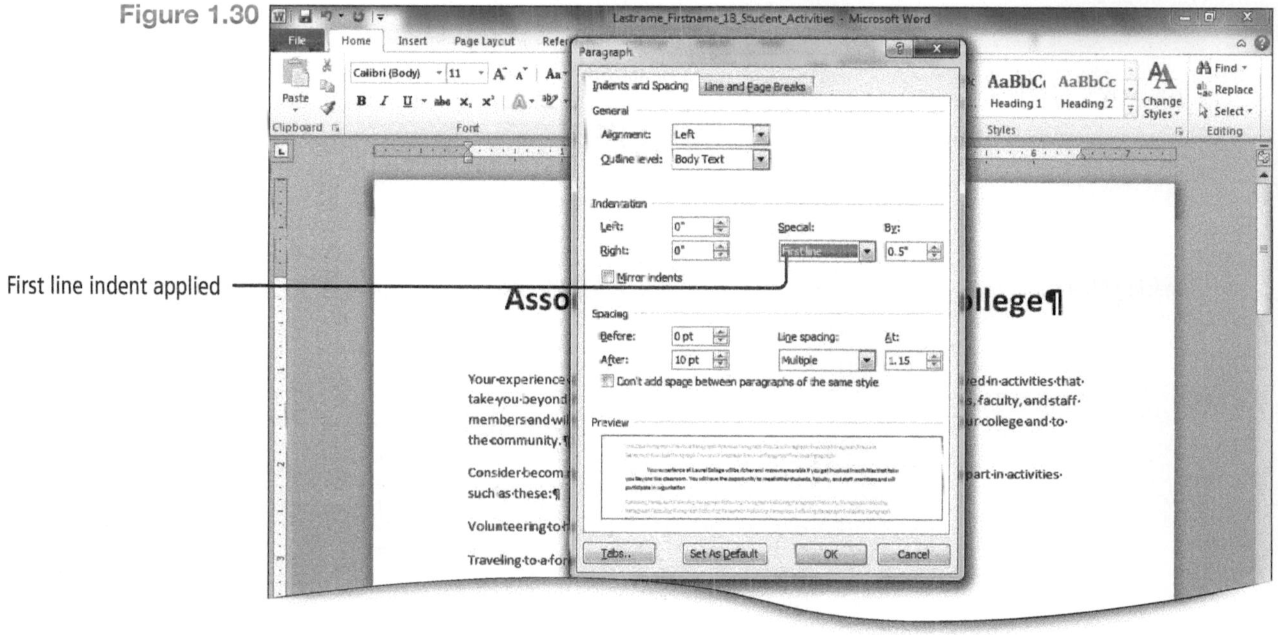

4 Click **OK**, and then click anywhere in the next paragraph, which begins *Consider becoming*. On the ruler under the Ribbon, drag the **First Line Indent** button to **0.5 inches on the horizontal ruler**, and then compare your screen with Figure 1.31.

Figure 1.31

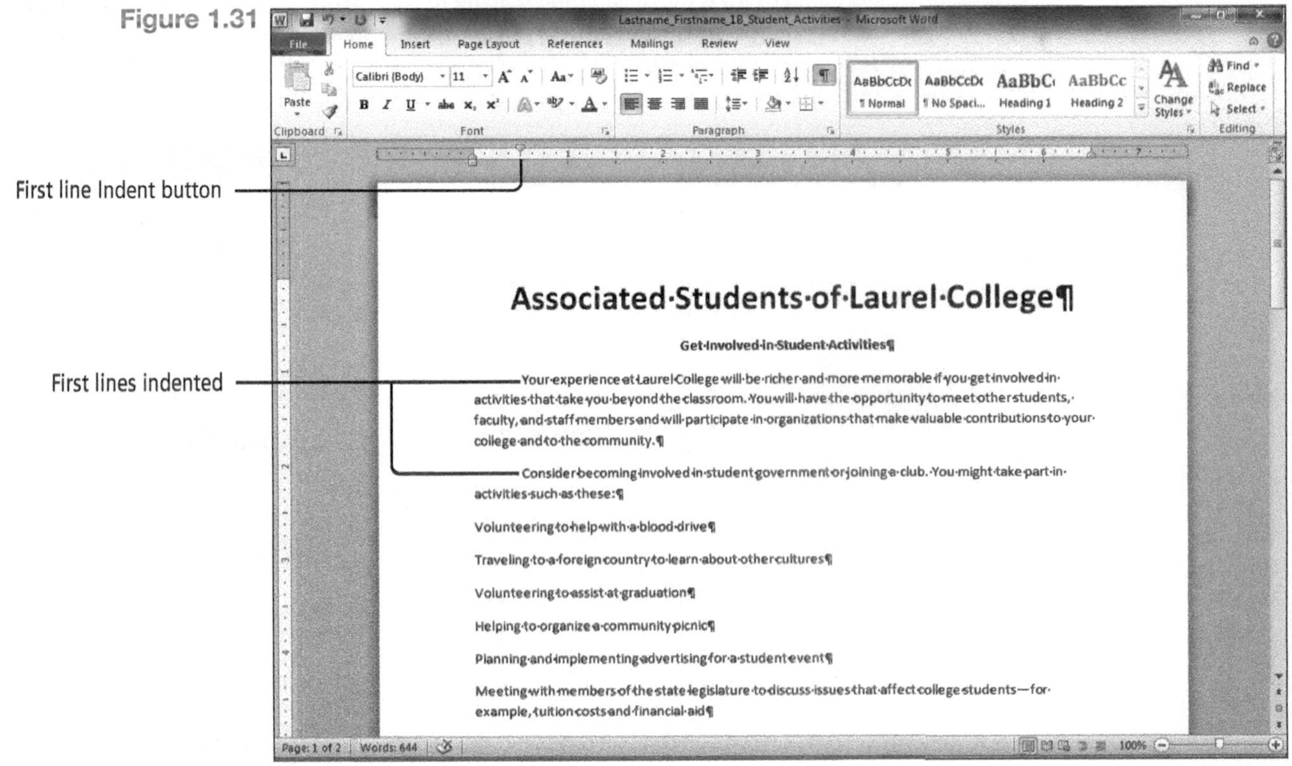

Another Way

On either the Home tab or the Page Layout tab, display the Paragraph dialog box from the Paragraph group, and then under Spacing, click the spin box arrows as necessary.

5 By using either of the techniques you just practiced, or by using the Format Painter, apply a first line indent of **0.5″** in the paragraph that begins *As a registered* to match the indent of the remaining paragraphs in the document.

6 Press Ctrl + A to select all of the text in the document. Click the **Page Layout tab**, and then in the **Paragraph group**, under **Spacing**, click the **After spin box down arrow** one time to change the value to **6 pt**.

To change the value in the box, you can also select the existing number, type a new number, and then press Enter. This document will use 6 pt spacing after paragraphs.

7 Press Ctrl + Home, and then compare your screen with Figure 1.32.

Figure 1.32

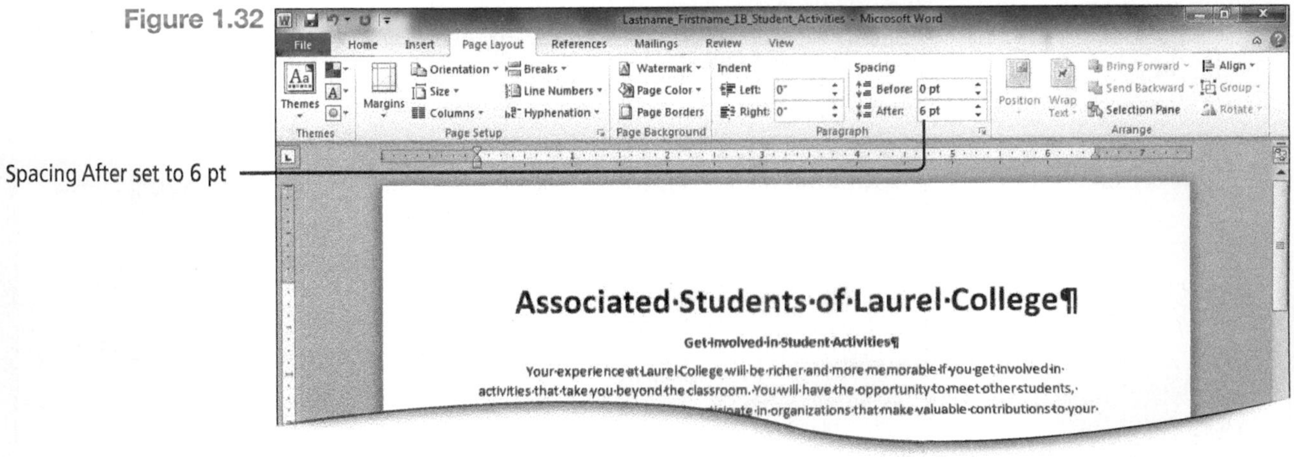

8 Scroll to view the lower portion of **Page 1**. Select the subheading *Student Government*, including the paragraph mark following it, hold down Ctrl, and then select the subheading *Clubs*.

9 With both subheadings selected, in the **Paragraph group**, under **Spacing**, click the **Before up spin box arrow** two times to set the **Spacing Before** to **12 pt**. Compare your screen with Figure 1.33, and then **Save** your document.

This action increases the amount of space above each of the two subheadings, which will make them easy to distinguish in the document. The formatting is applied only to the two selected paragraphs.

Figure 1.33

Spacing before set to 12 pt.

12-point spacing before paragraphs

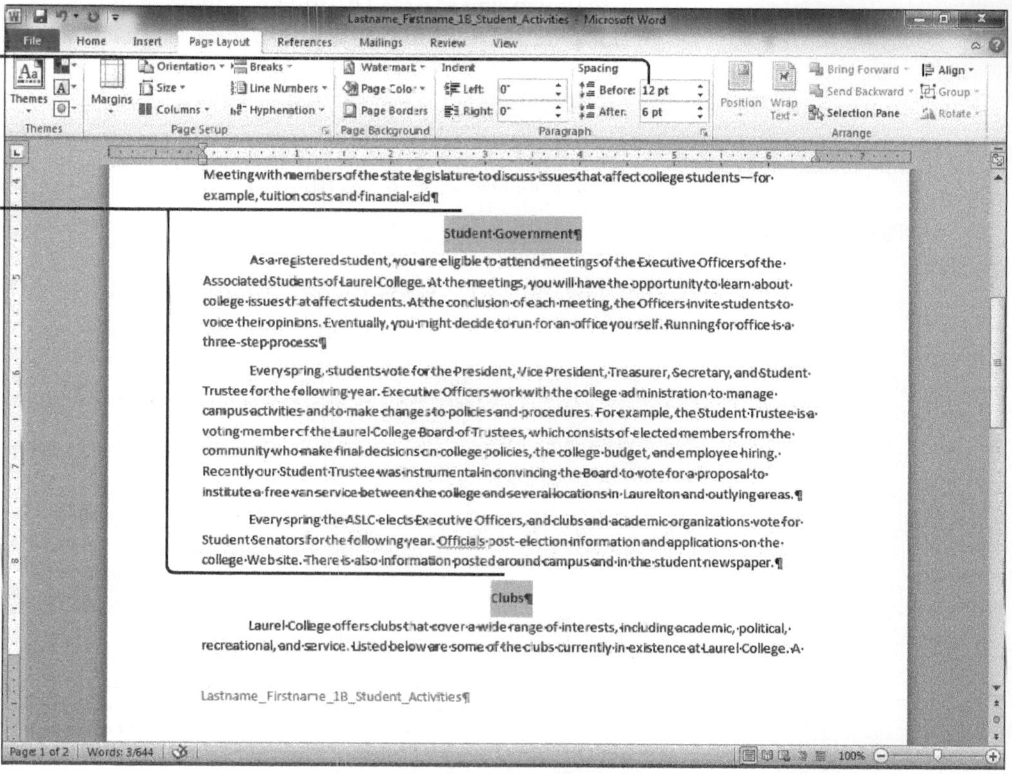

Objective 6 | Create and Modify Lists

To display a list of information, you can choose a ***bulleted list***, which uses ***bullets***—text symbols such as small circles or check marks—to introduce each item in a list. You can also choose a ***numbered list***, which uses consecutive numbers or letters to introduce each item in a list.

Use a bulleted list if the items in the list can be introduced in any order; use a numbered list for items that have definite steps, a sequence of actions, or are in chronological order.

Activity 1.17 | Creating a Bulleted List

1 In the upper portion of **Page 1**, locate the paragraph that begins *Volunteering to help*, and then point to this paragraph from the left margin area to display the pointer. Drag down to select this paragraph and the next five paragraphs.

2 On the **Home tab**, in the **Paragraph group**, click the **Bullets** button to change the selected text to a bulleted list.

The spacing between each of the bulleted points changes to the spacing between lines in a paragraph—in this instance, 1.15 line spacing. The spacing after the last item in the list is the same as the spacing after each paragraph—in this instance, 6 pt. Each bulleted item is automatically indented.

3 On the ruler, point to the **First Line Indent** button and read the ScreenTip, and then point to the **Hanging Indent** button. Compare your screen with Figure 1.34.

By default, Word formats bulleted items with a first line indent of 0.25″ and adds a Hanging Indent at 0.5″. The hanging indent maintains the alignment of text when a bulleted item is more than one line, for example, the last bulleted item in this list.

Figure 1.34

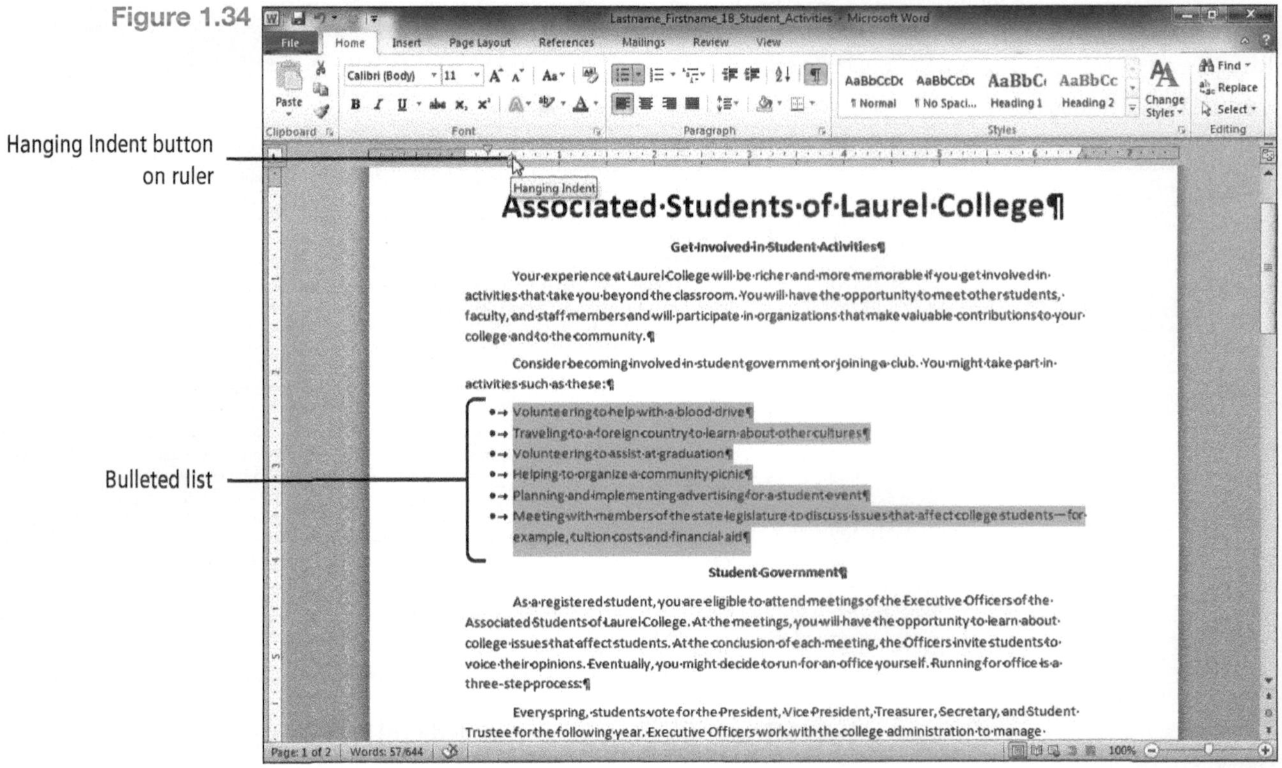

4 Scroll down to view **Page 2**. By using the pointer from the left margin area, select all of the paragraphs that indicate the club names and meeting dates, beginning with *Chess Club* and ending with *Theater Club*.

5 In the **Paragraph group**, click the **Bullets** button, and then **Save** your document.

Activity 1.18 | Creating a Numbered List

1 Scroll to view **Page 1**, and then under the subheading *Student Government*, in the paragraph that begins *As a registered student*, click to position the insertion point at the *end* of the paragraph following the colon. Press Enter to create a blank paragraph.

2 Notice that the paragraph is indented, because the First Line Indent from the previous paragraph carried over to the new paragraph.

3 To change the indent formatting for this paragraph, on the ruler, drag the **First Line Indent** button [icon] to the left so that it is positioned directly above the lower button. Compare your screen with Figure 1.35.

Figure 1.35

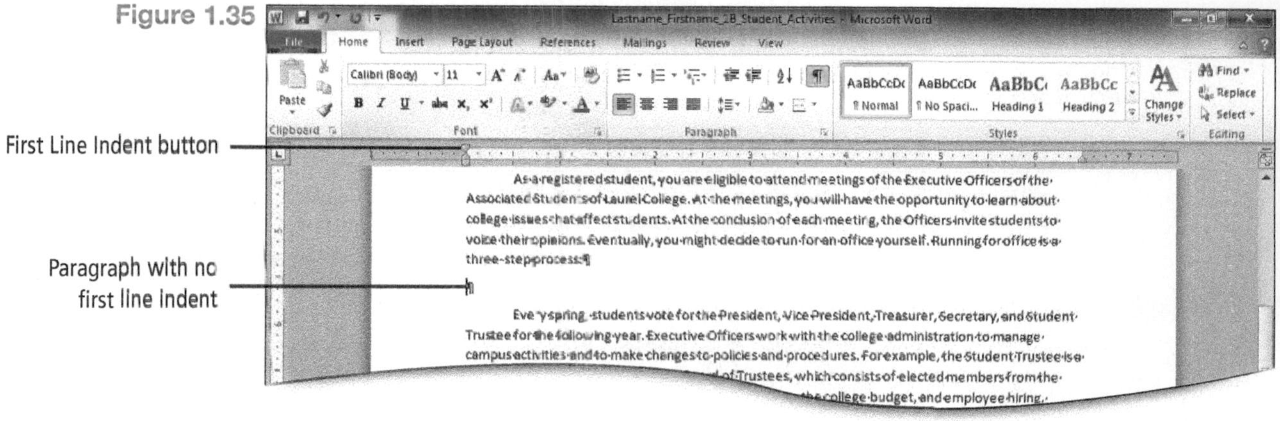

4 Being sure to include the period, type **1.** and press Spacebar.

Word determines that this paragraph is the first item in a numbered list and formats the new paragraph accordingly, indenting the list in the same manner as the bulleted list. The space after the number changes to a tab, and the AutoCorrect Options button displays to the left of the list item. The tab is indicated by a right arrow formatting mark.

> **Alert! | Activating Automatic Numbered Lists**
>
> If a numbered list does not begin automatically, display Backstage view, and then click the Options tab. On the left side of the Word Options dialog box, click Proofing. Under AutoCorrect options, click the AutoCorrect Options button. In the AutoCorrect dialog box, click the AutoFormat As You Type tab. Under *Apply as you type*, select the *Automatic numbered lists* check box, and then click OK two times to close both dialog boxes.

5 Click the **AutoCorrect Options** button [icon], and then compare your screen with Figure 1.36.

From the displayed list, you can remove the automatic formatting here, or stop using the automatic numbered lists option in this document. You also have the option to open the AutoCorrect dialog box to *Control AutoFormat Options*.

Figure 1.36

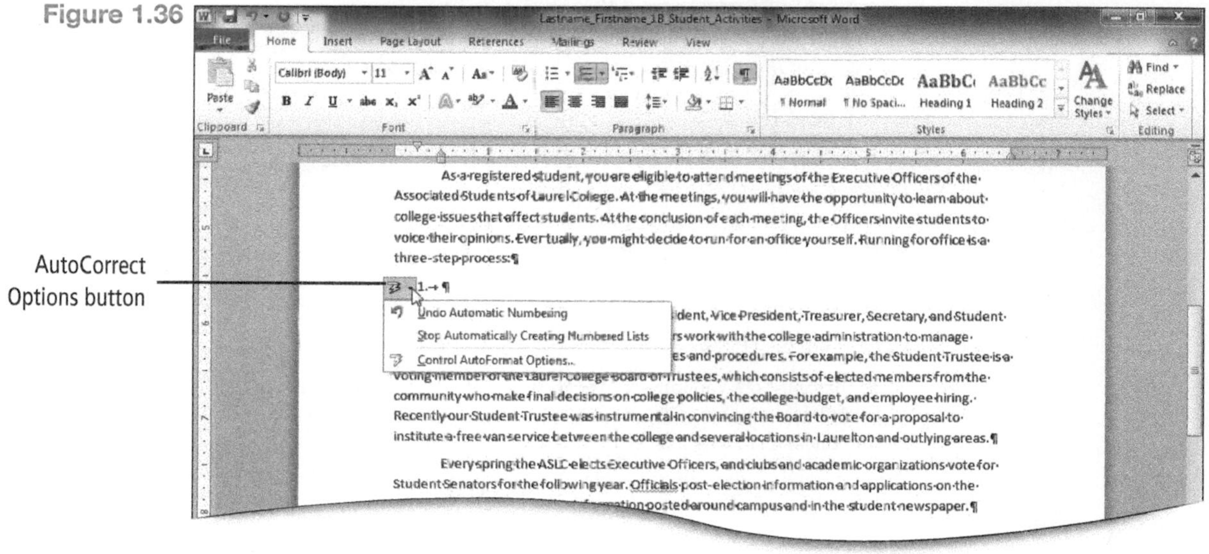

6 Click the **AutoCorrect Options** button again to close the menu without selecting any of the commands. Type **Pick up petitions at the Student Government office.** and press Enter. Notice that the second number and a tab are added to the next line.

7 Type **Obtain 100 signatures from current students.** and press Enter. Type **Turn in petitions and start campaigning.** and press Enter. Compare your screen with Figure 1.37.

Figure 1.37

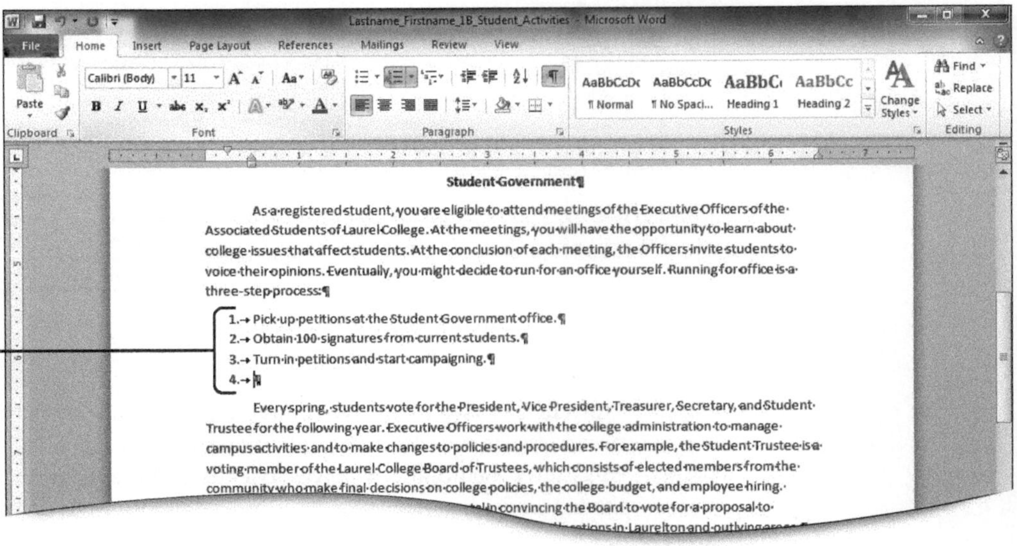

Numbered list

8 Press ←Bksp to turn off the list numbering. Then, press ←Bksp three more times to remove the blank paragraph. Compare your screen with Figure 1.38.

Figure 1.38

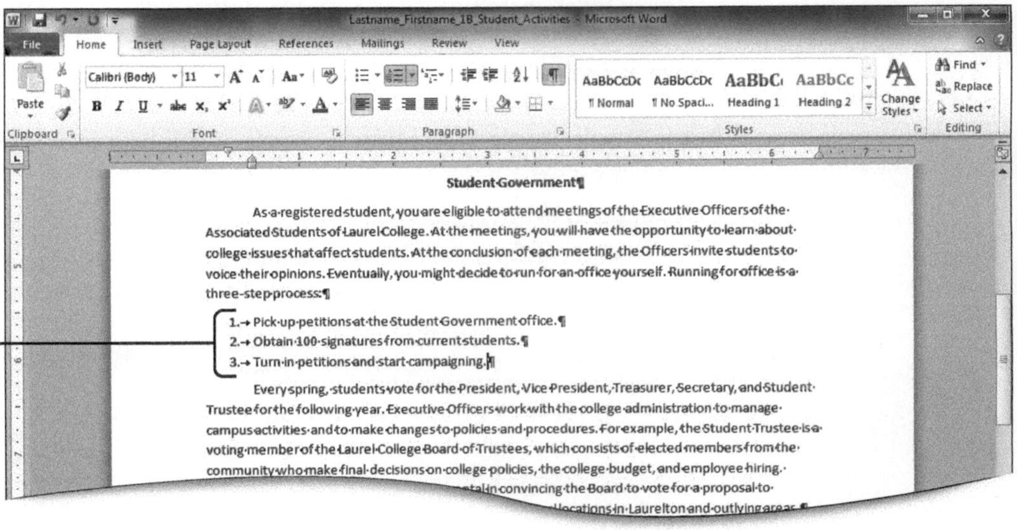

Three items in the list, item 4 deleted

9 **Save** your document.

More Knowledge | To End a List

To turn a list off, you can press ←Bksp, click the Numbering or Bullets button, or press Enter a second time. Both list buttons—Numbering and Bullets—act as ***toggle buttons***; that is, clicking the button one time turns the feature on, and clicking the button again turns the feature off.

Activity 1.19 | Customizing Bullets

1 Press Ctrl + End to move to the end of the document, and then scroll up as necessary to display the bulleted list containing the list of clubs.

2 Point to the left of the first list item to display the [pointer icon] pointer, and then drag down to select all the clubs in the list—the bullet symbols are not highlighted.

3 Point to the selected list and right-click. From the shortcut menu, point to **Bullets**, and then compare your screen with Figure 1.39.

Figure 1.39

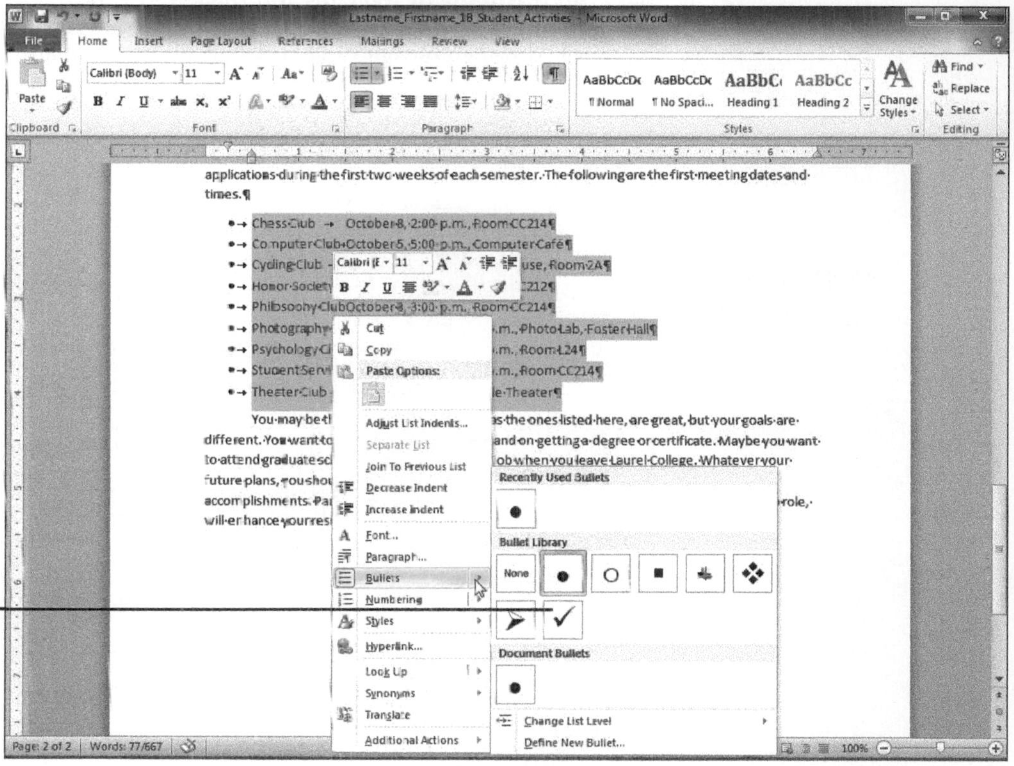

Check mark bullet

4 Under **Bullet Library**, click the **check mark** symbol. If the check mark is not available, choose another bullet symbol.

> **Another Way**
>
> On the Home tab, in the Clipboard group, click the Format Painter button.

5 With the bulleted list still selected, right-click over the list, and then on the Mini toolbar, click the **Format Painter** button [Format Painter icon].

6 Use the vertical scroll bar or your mouse wheel to scroll to view **Page 1**. Move the pointer to the left of the first item in the bulleted list to display the [pointer icon] pointer, and then drag down to select all of the items in the list and to apply the format of the second bulleted list to this list. Compare your screen with Figure 1.40, and then **Save** [Save icon] your document.

Figure 1.40

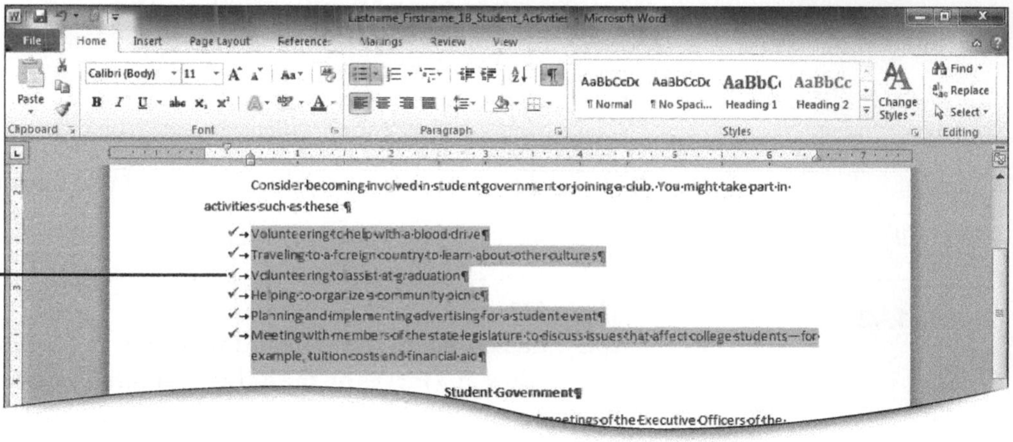

Bullet symbol changed

Objective 7 | Set and Modify Tab Stops

Tab stops mark specific locations on a line of text. Use tab stops to indent and align text, and use the [Tab] key to move to tab stops.

Activity 1.20 | Setting Tab Stops

1 Scroll to view the middle of **Page 2**, and then by using the ⬚ pointer at the left of the first item, select all of the items in the bulleted list. Notice that there is a tab mark between the name of the club and the date.

> The arrow that indicates a tab is a nonprinting formatting mark.

2 To the left of the horizontal ruler, point to the **Tab Alignment** button ⬚ to display the *Left Tab* ScreenTip, and then compare your screen with Figure 1.41.

Figure 1.41

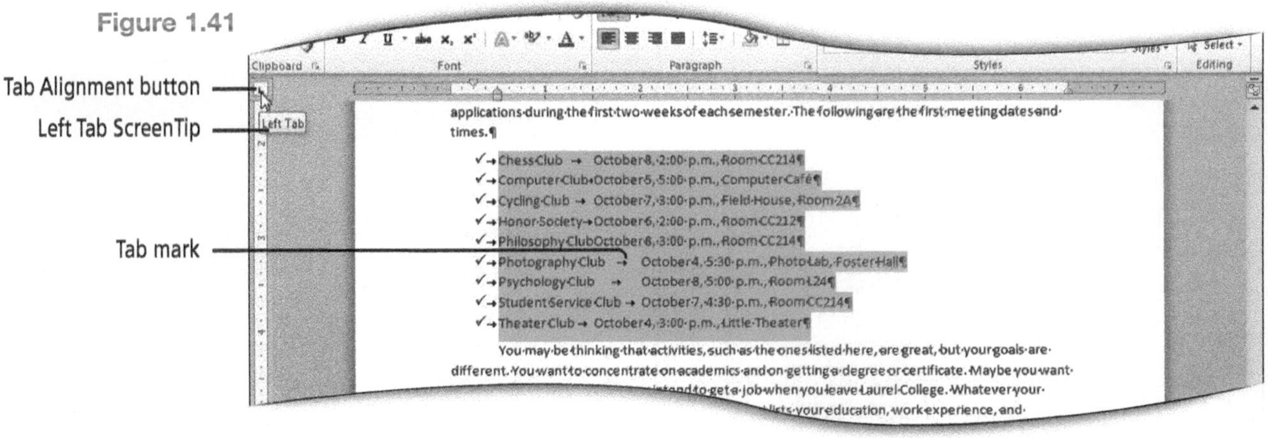

Tab Alignment button
Left Tab ScreenTip
Tab mark

3 Click the **Tab Alignment** button ⬚ several times to view the tab alignment options shown in the table in Figure 1.42.

Tab Alignment Options

Type	Tab Alignment Button Displays This Marker	Description
Left	⬚	Text is left aligned at the tab stop and extends to the right.
Center	⬚	Text is centered around the tab stop.
Right	⬚	Text is right aligned at the tab stop and extends to the left.
Decimal	⬚	The decimal point aligns at the tab stop.
Bar	⬚	A vertical bar displays at the tab stop.
First Line Indent	▽	Text in the first line of a paragraph indents.
Hanging Indent	△	Text in all lines except the first line in the paragraph indents.
Left Indent	⬚	Moves both the First Line Indent and Hanging Indent buttons.

Figure 1.42

4 Display the **Left Tab** button ⬚. Along the lower edge of the horizontal ruler, point to and then click at **3 inches on the horizontal ruler**. Notice that all of the dates left align at the new tab stop location, and the right edge of the column is uneven.

5 Compare your screen with Figure 1.43, and then **Save** your document.

Figure 1.43

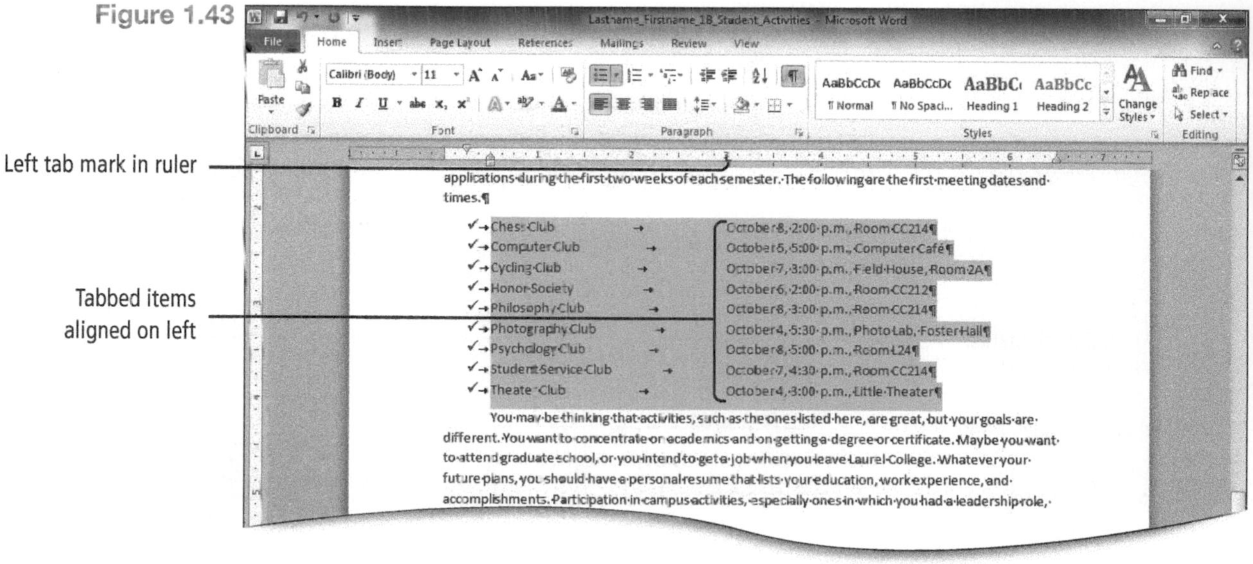

Activity 1.21 | Modifying Tab Stops

Tab stops are a form of paragraph formatting, and thus, the information about tab stops is stored in the paragraph mark in the paragraphs to which they were applied.

1 With the bulleted list still selected, on the ruler, point to the new tab marker, and then when the *Left Tab* ScreenTip displays, drag the tab marker to **3.5 inches on the horizontal ruler.**

In all of the selected lines, the text at the tab stop left aligns at 3.5 inches.

> **Another Way**
>
> On the Home tab, in the Paragraph group, click the Dialog Box Launcher. At the bottom of the Paragraph dialog box, click the Tabs button.

2 On the ruler, point to the tab marker to display the ScreenTip, and then double-click to display the **Tabs** dialog box.

3 In the **Tabs** dialog box, under **Tab stop position**, if necessary select *3.5″* and then type **6**

4 Under **Alignment**, click the **Right** option button. Under **Leader**, click the **2** option button. Near the bottom of the **Tabs** dialog box, click **Set**.

Because the Right tab will be used to align the items in the list, the tab stop at 3.5″ is no longer necessary.

5 In the **Tabs** dialog box, in the **Tab stop position** box, click **3.5″** to select this tab stop, and then in the lower portion of the **Tabs** dialog box, click the **Clear** button to delete this tab stop, which is no longer necessary. Compare your screen with Figure 1.44.

Figure 1.44

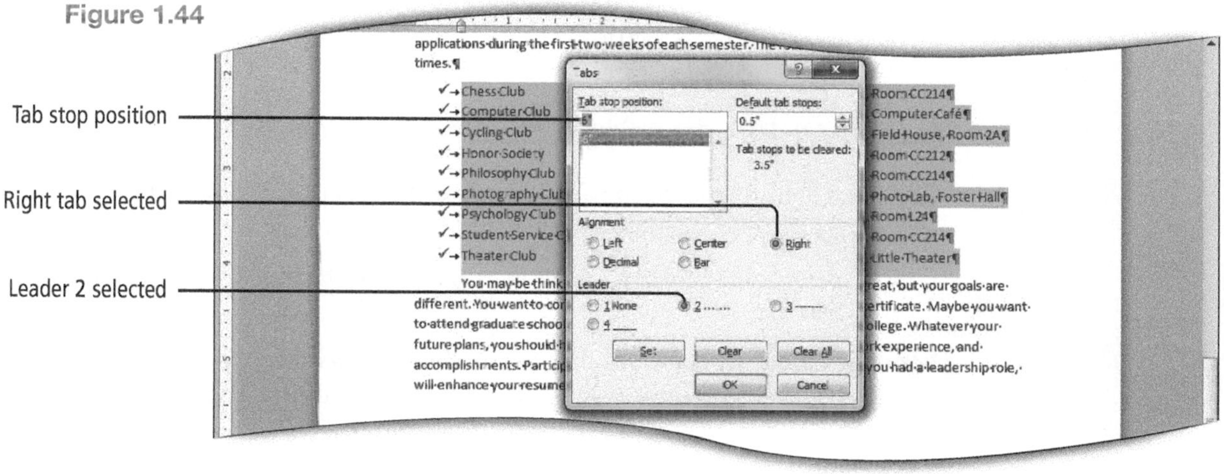

6 Click **OK**. On the ruler, notice that the left tab marker at *3.5″* no longer displays, a right tab marker displays at *6″*, and a series of dots—a ***dot leader***—displays between the columns of the list. Notice also that the right edge of the column is even. Compare your screen with Figure 1.45.

A ***leader character*** creates a solid, dotted, or dashed line that fills the space to the left of a tab character and draws the reader's eyes across the page from one item to the next. When the character used for the leader is a dot, it is commonly referred to as a dot leader.

Figure 1.45

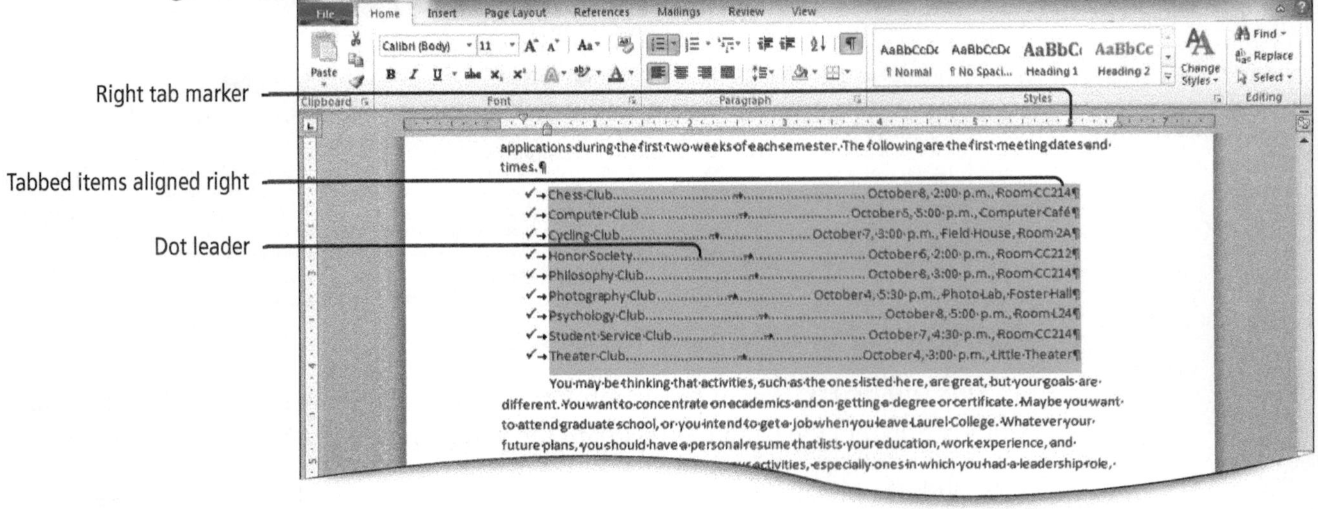

7 In the bulleted list that uses dot leaders, locate the *Honor Society* item, and then click to position the insertion point at the end of that line. Press Enter to create a new blank bullet item.

8 Type **Math Club** and press Tab. Notice that a dot leader fills the space to the tab marker location.

9 Type **October 6, 4:00 p.m., Math Tutoring Lab, L35** and notice that the text moves to the left to maintain the right alignment of the tab stop.

10 **Save** your document.

Objective 8 | Insert a SmartArt Graphic

SmartArt graphics are designer-quality visual representations of information, and Word provides many different layouts from which you can choose. A SmartArt graphic can communicate your messages or ideas more effectively than plain text and adds visual interest to a document or Web page.

Activity 1.22 | Inserting a SmartArt Graphic

1 Press Ctrl + Home to move to the top of the document. Press End to move to the end of the first paragraph—the title—and then press Enter to create a blank paragraph.

Because the paragraph above is 26 pt font size, the new paragraph mark displays in that size.

2 Click the **Insert tab**, and then in the **Illustrations group**, point to the **SmartArt** button to display its ScreenTip. Read the ScreenTip, and then click the button.

3 In the center portion of the **Choose a SmartArt Graphic** dialog box, scroll down and examine the numerous types of SmartArt graphics available.

4 On the left, click **Hierarchy**, and then in the first row, click the first graphic—**Organization Chart.**

At the right of the dialog box, a preview and description of the graphic displays.

5 Compare your screen with Figure 1.46.

Figure 1.46

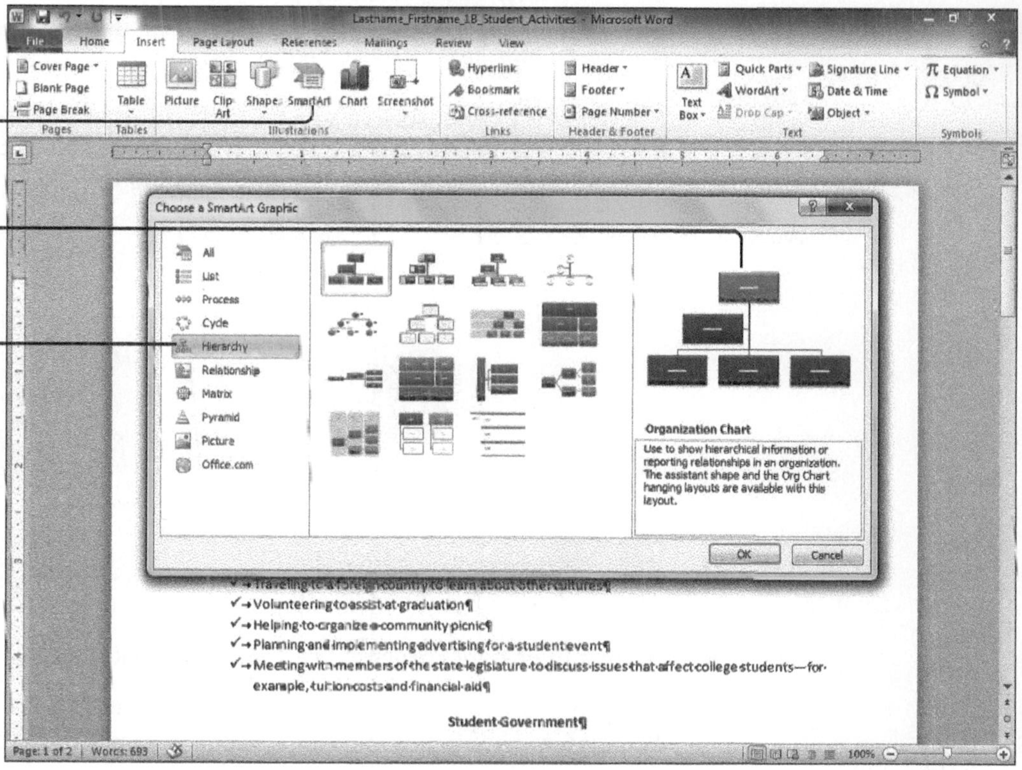

6 Click **OK**. If the pane indicating *Type your text here* does not display on the left side of the graphic, on the Design tab, in the Create Graphic group, click the Text Pane button. **Save** your document.

The SmartArt graphic displays at the insertion point location and consists of two parts—the graphic itself, and the Text Pane. On the Ribbon, the SmartArt Tools add the Design tab and the Format tab. You can type directly into the graphics, or type in the Text Pane. By typing in the Text Pane, you might find it easier to organize your layout.

Activity 1.23 | Modifying a SmartArt Graphic

1 In the SmartArt graphic, in the second row, click the border of the *[Text]* box to display a *solid* border and sizing handles, and then press Del. Repeat this procedure in the bottom row to delete the middle *[Text]* box.

Another Way

Close the Text Pane and type the text directly in the SmartArt boxes.

2 In the **Text Pane**, click in the top bulleted point, and then type **Student Activities** Notice that the first bulleted point aligns further to the left than the other points.

The ***top-level points*** are the main points in a SmartArt graphic. ***Subpoints*** are indented second-level bullet points.

3 Press [↓]. Type **Government** and then press [↓] again. Type **Clubs** and then compare your screen with Figure 1.47.

Figure 1.47

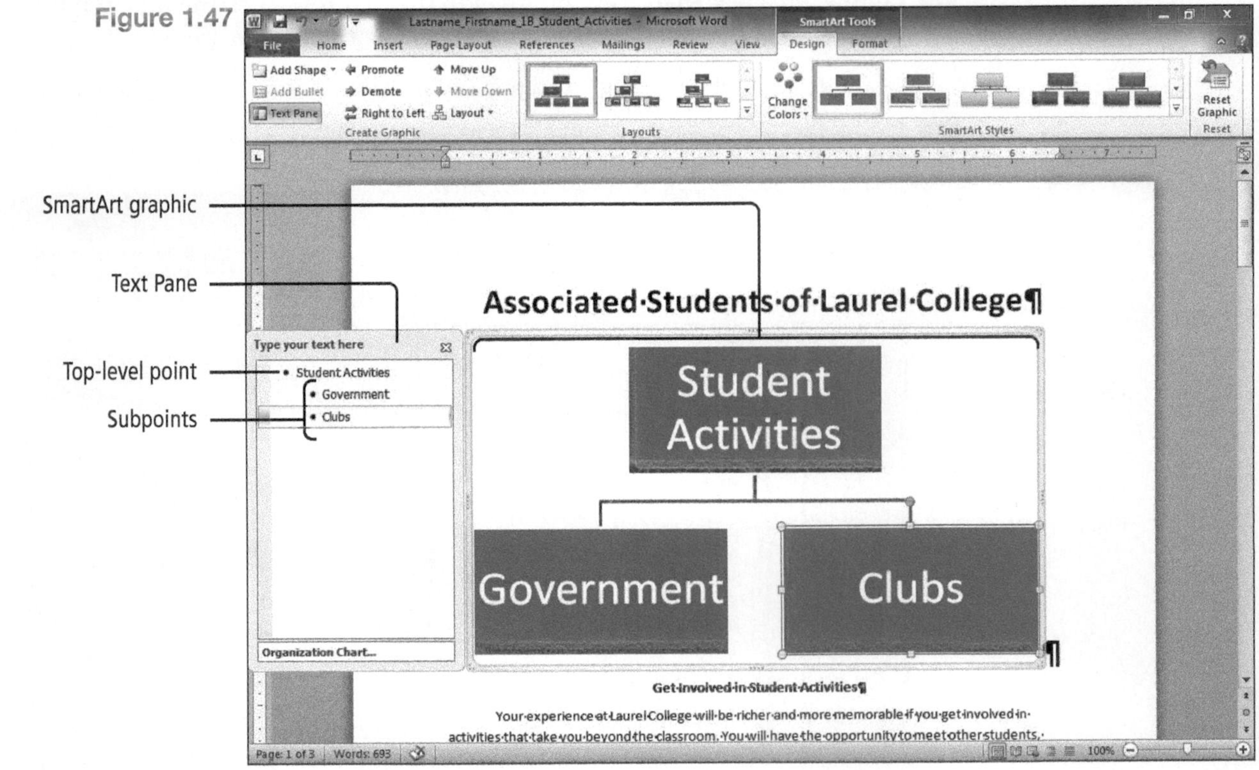

4 In the upper right corner of the **Text Pane**, click the **Close** button [⊠].

5 Click the border of the SmartArt graphic—a pale border surrounds it. Click the **Format tab**, and then in the **Size group**, if necessary click the **Size** button to display the **Shape Height** and **Shape Width** boxes.

6 Set the **Height** to **2.5″** and the **Width** to **4.2″**, and then compare your screen with Figure 1.48.

Figure 1.48

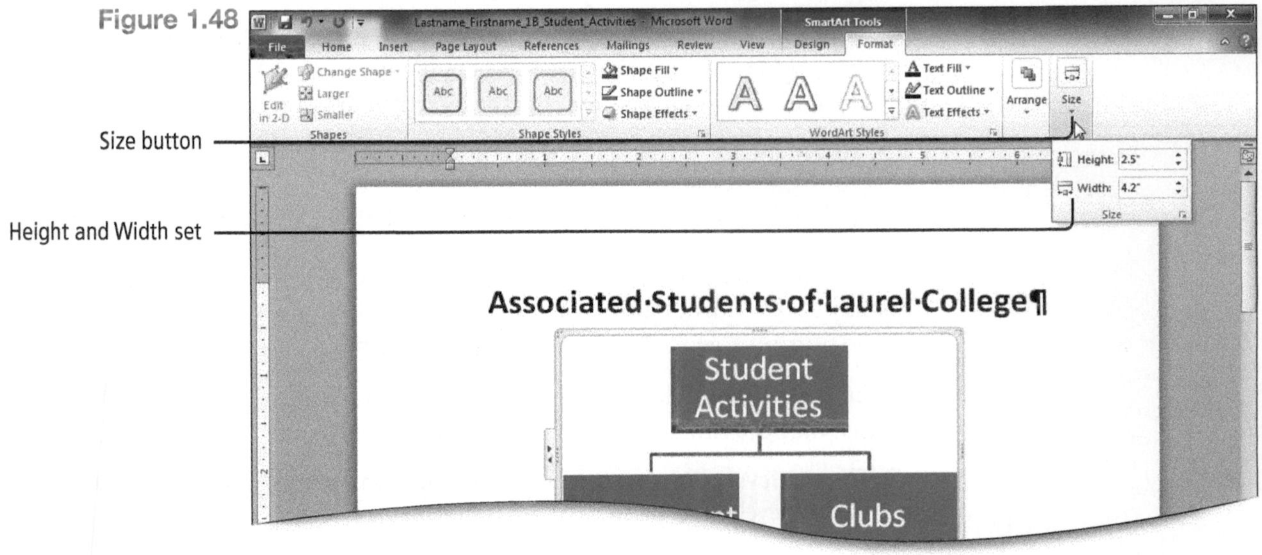

7 With the SmartArt graphic still selected, click the **Design tab**, and then in the **SmartArt Styles group**, click the **Change Colors** button. Under **Colorful**, click the second style—**Colorful Range - Accent Colors 2 to 3**.

8 On the **Design tab**, in the **SmartArt Styles group**, click the **More** button. Under **3-D**, click the first style—**Polished**. Compare your screen with Figure 1.49.

Figure 1.49

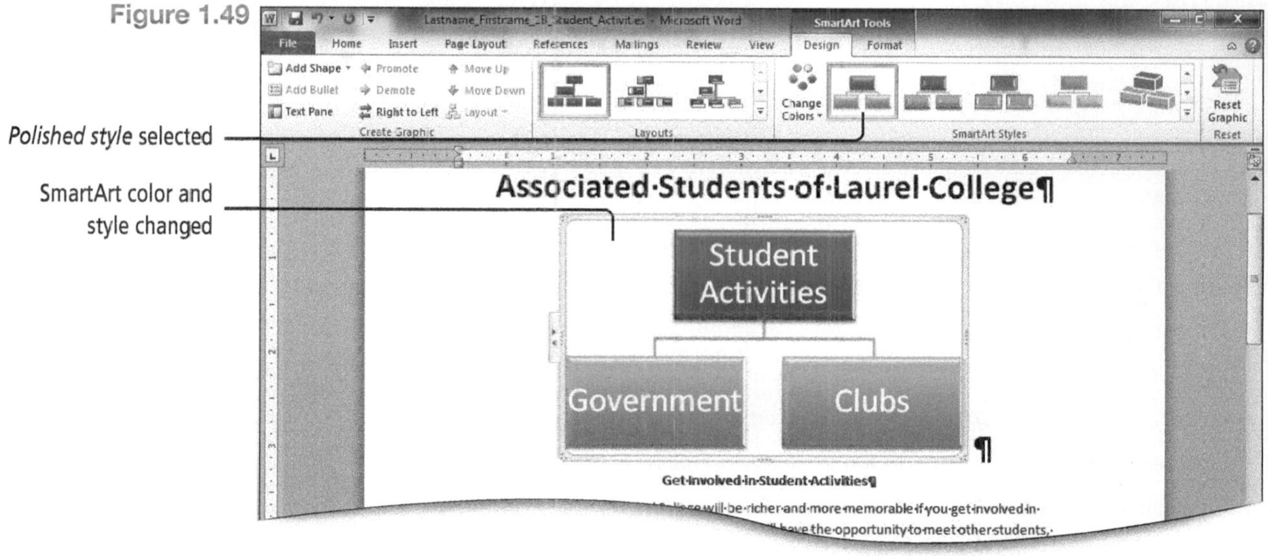

9 Click outside of the graphic to deselect it. Display **Backstage** view. On the right, under the screen thumbnail, click **Properties**, and then click **Show Document Panel**. In the **Author** box, delete any text and then type your firstname and lastname. In the **Subject** box, type your course name and section number, and in the **Keywords** box type **Student Activities, Associated Students** **Close** the Document Panel and **Save** your document.

10 Display **Backstage** view, and then click **Print** to display **Print Preview**. At the bottom of the preview, click the **Next Page** and **Previous Page** buttons to move between pages. If necessary, return to the document and make any necessary changes.

11 As directed by your instructor, print your document or submit it electronically. **Close** Word.

More Knowledge | Changing the Bullet Level in a SmartArt Graphic

To increase or decrease the level of an item, on the Design tab, in the Create Graphic group, click either the Promote or the Demote button.

End You have completed Project 1B

Content-Based Assessments

Summary

In this chapter, you created and formatted documents using Microsoft Word 2010. You inserted and formatted graphics, created and formatted bulleted and numbered lists, and created and formatted text boxes. You also created lists using tab stops with dot leaders, and created and modified a SmartArt graphic.

Key Terms

Matching

Match each term in the second column with its correct definition in the first column by writing the letter of the term on the blank line in front of the correct definition.

____ 1. Formats that make pictures look more like sketches or paintings.

____ 2. A small box with an upward- and downward-pointing arrow that enables you to move rapidly through a set of values by clicking.

____ 3. Small circles in the corners of a selected graphic with which you can resize the graphic proportionally.

____ 4. The manner in which text displays around an object.

____ 5. An object or graphic that can be moved independently of the surrounding text.

____ 6. The process of using the arrow keys to move an object in small precise increments.

____ 7. An object or graphic inserted in a document that acts like a character in a sentence.

____ 8. Frames, shapes, shadows, borders, and other special effects that can be added to an image to create an overall visual style for the image.

____ 9. Predefined drawing objects, such as stars, banners, arrows, and callouts, included with Microsoft Office, and that can be inserted into documents.

A Artistic effects
B Bullets
C Floating object
D Inline object
E Justified alignment
F Left alignment
G Line spacing
H Nudge
I Picture styles
J Shapes
K Sizing handles
L SmartArt
M Spin box
N Tab stop
O Text wrapping

_____ 10. A commonly used alignment of text in which text is aligned at the left margin, leaving the right margin uneven.

_____ 11. An alignment of text in which the text is evenly aligned on both the left and right margins.

_____ 12. The distance between lines of text in a paragraph.

_____ 13. Text symbols such as small circles or check marks that introduce items in a list.

_____ 14. A mark on the ruler that indicates the location where the insertion point will be placed when you press the Tab key.

_____ 15. A designer-quality graphic used to create a visual representation of information.

Multiple Choice

Circle the correct answer.

1. Characters that display on the screen to show the location of paragraphs, tabs, and spaces, but that do not print, are called:
A. text effects **B.** bullets **C.** formatting marks

2. The placement of paragraph text relative to the left and right margins is referred to as:
A. alignment **B.** spacing **C.** indents

3. The symbol that indicates to which paragraph an image is attached is:
A. a small arrow **B.** an anchor **C.** a paragraph mark

4. A movable, resizable container for text or graphics is a:
A. text box **B.** dialog box **C.** SmartArt graphic

5. A banner is an example of a predefined:
A. paragraph **B.** format **C.** shape

6. A placeholder that displays preset content, such as the current date, the file name, a page number, or other stored information is:
A. a leader **B.** a field **C.** a tab

7. The space between the text and the top, bottom, left, and right edges of the paper are referred to as:
A. alignment **B.** margins **C.** spacing

8. A group of items in which items are displayed in order to indicate definite steps, a sequence of actions, or chronological order is a:
A. numbered list **B.** bulleted list **C.** outline list

9. A series of dots following a tab that serve to guide the reader's eye is a:
A. leader **B.** field **C.** shape

10. Tab stops are a form of:
A. line formatting **B.** document formatting **C.** paragraph formatting

Apply 1A skills from these Objectives:

1. Create a New Document and Insert Text
2. Insert and Format Graphics
3. Insert and Modify Text Boxes and Shapes
4. Preview and Print a Document

Skills Review | Project 1C Welcome Week

In the following Skills Review, you will create and edit a flyer for the Laurel College New Student Welcome Week. Your completed document will look similar to Figure 1.50.

Project Files

For Project 1C, you will need the following files:

New blank Word document
w01C_Welcome_Text
w01C_Welcome_Picture

You will save your document as:

Lastname_Firstname_1C_Welcome_Week

Project Results

Welcome Week

The Laurel College Student Government Association is sponsoring a week of special activities for new students. This is your opportunity to meet the people and learn about the programs that will help you succeed at Laurel College.

Attend as many days as you would like—activities begin on Tuesday, September 7—to get an orientation to the campus, meet students and faculty, and get helpful information about the college. When your classes begin on September 13, you will know your way around and recognize friendly faces.

Welcome Week Highlights

Tuesday: Campus tour and meeting with administrators

Wednesday: Open house in all academic departments

Thursday: Club meetings to recruit members

Friday: Student Government-hosted barbecue

Enjoy!

Lastname_Firstname_1C_Welcome_Week

Figure 1.50

(Project 1C Welcome Week continues on the next page)

Skills Review | Project 1C Welcome Week (continued)

1 **Start** Word and display a new blank document. On the **Home tab**, in the **Paragraph group**, be sure the **Show/Hide ¶** button is active so that you can view formatting marks. In the **Quick Access Toolbar**, click the **Save** button, navigate to your **Word Chapter 1** folder, and then **Save** the document as **Lastname_Firstname_1C_Welcome_Week**

a. Type **Welcome Week** and then press Enter two times.

b. Type **The Laurel College Student Government Association is sponsoring a week of special activities for new students. This is your opportunity to meet the people and learn about the programs that will help you succeed at Laurel College.**

c. Press Enter one time. Click the **Insert tab**. In the **Text group**, click the **Object button arrow**, and then click **Text from File**. Navigate to your student files, select the file **w01C_Welcome_Text**, and then at the bottom of the **Insert File** dialog box, click **Insert**. **Save** your document.

2 At the top of the document, in the left margin area, point to the left of the first paragraph—*Welcome Week*—until the pointer displays, and then click one time to select the paragraph. On the **Home tab**, in the **Font group**, click the **Text Effects** button. In the displayed **Text Effects** gallery, in the first row, click the fourth effect—**Fill - White, Outline - Accent 1**.

a. With the text still selected, in the **Font group**, click the **Font Size button arrow**, and then click **72**. In the **Paragraph group**, click the **Center** button.

b. With the text still selected, in the **Font group**, click the **Text Effects** button. Point to **Shadow**, and then under **Outer**, in the first row click the third style—**Offset Diagonal Bottom Left**. In the **Font group**, click the **Font Color button arrow**. Under **Theme Colors**, in the fourth column, click the first color—**Dark Blue, Text 2**.

c. In the paragraph that begins *The Laurel College*, click to position the insertion point at the beginning of the paragraph. On the **Insert tab**, in the **Illustrations group**, click the **Picture** button. From your student data files, **Insert** the file **w01C_Welcome_Picture**. On the **Format tab**, in the **Size group**, click the **Shape Height down spin arrow** as necessary to change the height of the picture to **2″**.

d. With the picture still selected, on the **Format tab**, in the **Arrange group**, click the **Wrap Text** button. From the **Wrap Text** gallery, click **Square**.

e. Hold down Shift and point anywhere in the picture to display the pointer. Drag the picture to align the right edge of the picture just to the left of the right margin.

f. On the **Format tab**, in the **Picture Styles group**, click the **Picture Effects** button. Point to **Glow**, and then under **Glow Variations**, in the third row, click the first style—**Blue, 11 pt glow, Accent color 1**. Nudge as necessary to match the picture position shown in Figure 1.50.

g. Click anywhere to deselect the picture. Click the **Page Layout tab**, and then in the **Page Background group**, click the **Page Borders** button. In the **Borders and Shading** dialog box, under **Setting**, click **Box**. Under **Style**, scroll down the list. About two-thirds down the list, click the style with a thin top and bottom line and a slightly thicker middle line.

h. Click the **Color arrow**, and then under **Theme Colors**, in the fourth column, click the first color—**Dark Blue, Text 2**. Click **OK**, and then **Save** your document.

3 Press Ctrl + End to move to the bottom of the document. On the **Insert tab**, in the **Text group**, click the **Text Box** button. At the bottom of the **Text Box** gallery, click **Draw Text Box**.

a. At the bottom of the document, position the pointer in an open area near the left margin, and then drag down and to the right to create a text box approximately **2.5 inches** high and **5.5 inches** wide; you need not be precise.

b. With the insertion point positioned in the text box, type the following:

Welcome Week Highlights

Tuesday: Campus tour and meeting with administrators

Wednesday: Open house in all academic departments

Thursday: Club meetings to recruit members

Friday: Student Government-hosted barbecue

(Project 1C Welcome Week continues on the next page)

Skills Review | Project 1C Welcome Week (continued)

c. In the text box, select all of the text. On the Mini toolbar, click the **Font Size button arrow**, and then click **14**. Click the **Bold** button, and then click the **Center** button.

d. On the **Format tab**, in the **Size group**, if necessary click the **Size** button. Click the **Shape Height spin arrows** as necessary to change the height of the text box to **2.5″**. Click the **Shape Width button up spin arrow** as necessary to widen the text box to **5.5″**.

e. In the **Shape Styles group**, click the **Shape Effects** button. Point to **Shadow**, and then under **Outer**, in the second row, click the second style—**Offset Center**. In the **Shape Styles group**, click the **Shape Outline button arrow**. Under **Theme Colors**, in the fourth column, click the first color—**Dark Blue, Text 2**.

f. If necessary, click anywhere inside the text box. Point to the text box border to display the [move] pointer. Drag the text box to align the left edge at approximately **0.5 inches on the horizontal ruler** and to align the top edge at approximately **5.5 inches on the vertical ruler**. You may have to click outside the text box several times to see the exact location on the rulers.

g. On the **Insert tab**, in the **Illustrations group**, click the **Shapes** button. Under **Basic Shapes**, in the first row, click the seventh shape—**Diamond**.

h. Position the [+] pointer slightly under the text box and at approximately **2 inches on the horizontal ruler**. Drag down approximately **1 inch** and to the right approximately **2 inches**. On the **Format tab**, in the **Size group**, adjust the **Shape Height** to **0.9″** and the **Shape Width** to **2″**.

i. Right-click the new shape, and then click **Add Text**. Type **Enjoy!** and then select the text you typed. On the Mini toolbar, click the **Font Size button arrow**, and then click **20**. Click the **Bold** button, and then if necessary, click the **Center** button.

j. On the **Format tab**, in the **Shape Styles group**, click the **Shape Fill button arrow**, and then under **Theme Colors**, in the fourth column, click the first color—**Dark Blue, Text 2**.

k. Point to the shape border until the [move] pointer displays, and then position the shape with its widest points aligned with the lower edge of the text box and approximately centered. As necessary, move the shape in small increments by pressing the arrow keys on your keyboard. Refer to Figure 1.50 for approximate placement. **Save** your document.

4 Click the **Insert tab**, and then, in the **Header & Footer group**, click the **Footer** button. At the bottom of the **Footer** gallery, click **Edit Footer**.

a. On the **Design tab**, in the **Insert group**, click the **Quick Parts** button, and then click **Field**. In the **Field names** list, scroll as necessary to locate and click **FileName**. Click **OK**, and then double-click anywhere in the document.

b. Press Ctrl + Home to move the insertion point to the beginning of the document. Display **Backstage** view. On the right, under the screen thumbnail, click **Properties**, and then click **Show Document Panel**. In the **Author** box, delete any text and then type your firstname and lastname. In the **Subject** box, type your course name and section number, and in the **Keywords** box type **Welcome Week**

c. **Close** the Document Panel. In **Backstage** view, click the **Print tab** to display the **Print Preview**. If necessary, return to the document to make any corrections or adjustments.

d. **Save** your document, print or submit electronically as directed by your instructor, and then **Close** Word.

End **You have completed Project 1C**

Apply 1B skills from these Objectives:

- 5 Change Document and Paragraph Layout
- 6 Create and Modify Lists
- 7 Set and Modify Tab Stops
- 8 Insert a SmartArt Graphic

Skills Review | Project 1D Constitution

In the following Skills Review, you will edit the constitution of the Associated Students of Laurel College. Your completed document will look similar to Figure 1.51.

Project Files

For Project 1D, you will need the following file:

w01D_Constitution

You will save your document as:

Lastname_Firstname_1D_Constitution

Project Results

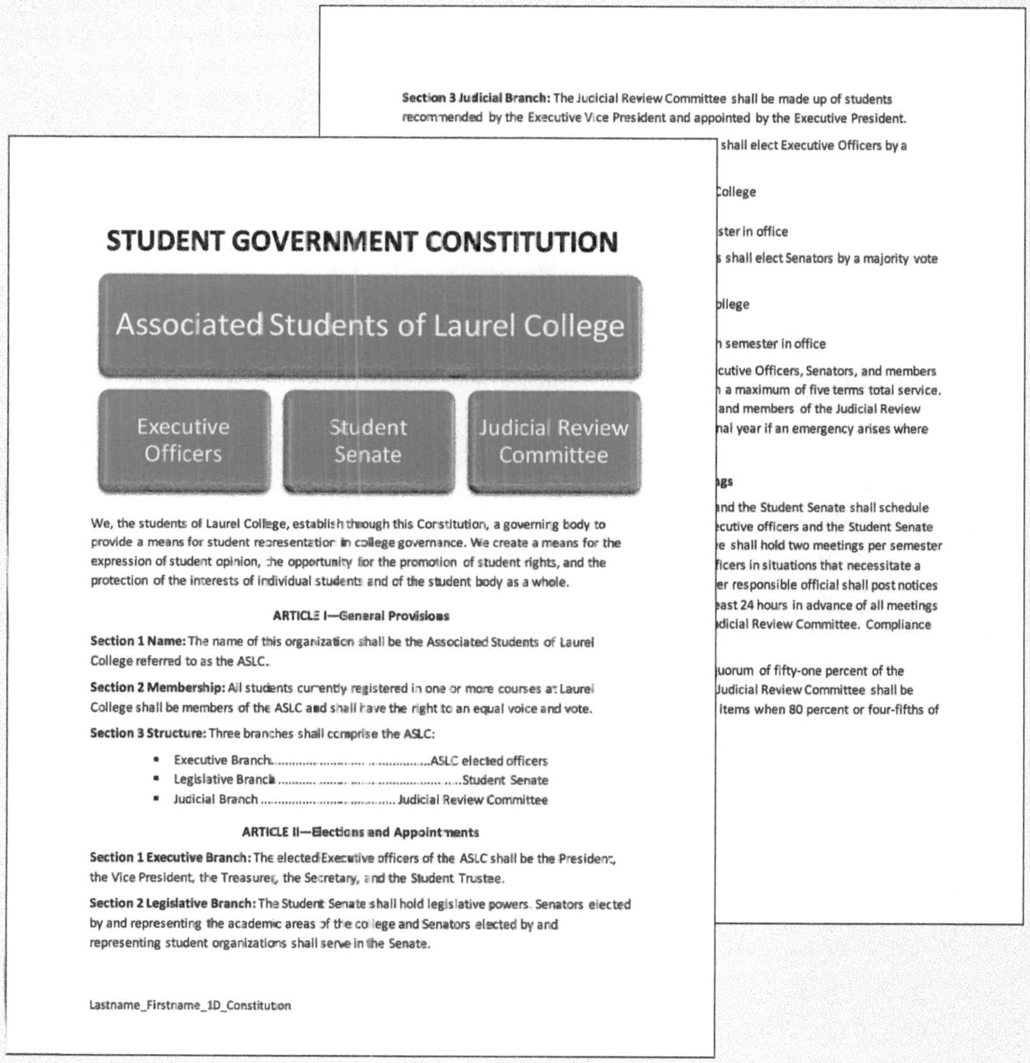
Section 3 Judicial Branch: The Judicial Review Committee shall be made up of students recommended by the Executive Vice President and appointed by the Executive President.

shall elect Executive Officers by a

College

ster in office

s shall elect Senators by a majority vote

ollege

h semester in office

cutive Officers, Senators, and members

a maximum of five terms total service.

and members of the Judicial Review

nal year if an emergency arises where

gs

nd the Student Senate shall schedule

cutive officers and the Student Senate

e shall hold two meetings per semester

ficers in situations that necessitate a

er responsible official shall post notices

east 24 hours in advance of all meetings

dicial Review Committee. Compliance

uorum of fifty-one percent of the

Judicial Review Committee shall be

items when 80 percent or four-fifths of

STUDENT GOVERNMENT CONSTITUTION

We, the students of Laurel College, establish through this Constitution, a governing body to provide a means for student representation in college governance. We create a means for the expression of student opinion, the opportunity for the promotion of student rights, and the protection of the interests of individual students and of the student body as a whole.

ARTICLE I—General Provisions

Section 1 Name: The name of this organization shall be the Associated Students of Laurel College referred to as the ASLC.

Section 2 Membership: All students currently registered in one or more courses at Laurel College shall be members of the ASLC and shall have the right to an equal voice and vote.

Section 3 Structure: Three branches shall comprise the ASLC:

- Executive Branch..ASLC elected officers
- Legislative Branch..Student Senate
- Judicial Branch..Judicial Review Committee

ARTICLE II—Elections and Appointments

Section 1 Executive Branch: The elected Executive officers of the ASLC shall be the President, the Vice President, the Treasurer, the Secretary, and the Student Trustee.

Section 2 Legislative Branch: The Student Senate shall hold legislative powers. Senators elected by and representing the academic areas of the college and Senators elected by and representing student organizations shall serve in the Senate.

Lastname_Firstname_1D_Constitution

Figure 1.51

(Project 1D Constitution continues on the next page)

Skills Review | Project 1D Constitution (continued)

1 **Start** Word. From your student files, locate and open the document **w01D_Constitution.** Display **Backstage** view, click **Save As**, and then navigate to your **Word Chapter 1** folder. **Save** the document as **Lastname_Firstname_1D_Constitution**

a. On the **Home tab**, in the **Paragraph group**, be sure the **Show/Hide** button is active so you can view formatting marks. Click the **Page Layout tab**. In the **Page Setup group**, click the **Margins** button, and then at the bottom of the **Margins** gallery, at the bottom of the list, click **Custom Margins**. In the **Page Setup** dialog box, in the **Top** box, type **1** Press Tab as necessary to select the values in the **Bottom**, **Left**, and **Right** boxes and change all margins to **1**. Click **OK**.

b. Press Ctrl + A to select all of the text in the document. On the **Home tab**, in the **Paragraph group**, click the **Align Text Left** button to change the alignment from justified to left aligned.

c. With all of the text still selected, on the **Home tab**, in the **Paragraph group**, click the **Line Spacing** button, and then click **1.15**. Click the **Page Layout tab**, and then in the **Paragraph group**, under **Spacing**, set **After** to **6 pt** spacing after each paragraph.

d. At the top of the document, click anywhere in the title, right-click, and then on the Mini toolbar, click **Center**. Near the top of **Page 1**, locate and select the paragraph that begins *ARTICLE 1*. Hold down Ctrl, and then use the vertical scroll bar to scroll through the document, and then select the other two paragraphs that begin *ARTICLE*. On the Mini toolbar, click **Center**.

e. With the three subheadings that begin *ARTICLE* still selected, on the **Page Layout tab**, in the **Paragraph group**, under **Spacing**, set **Before** to **12 pt**.

f. Scroll to view the bottom of **Page 1**, point anywhere in the bottom margin area, right-click, and then click **Edit Footer**. On the **Design tab**, in the **Insert group**, click the **Quick Parts** button, and then click **Field**. In the **Field names** list, scroll as necessary to locate and click **FileName**. Click **OK**, and then double-click anywhere in the document to exit the footer area.

2 Near the middle of **Page 1**, *above* the *ARTICLE II* subheading, locate the paragraph that begins *Executive Branch*, and then move the pointer into the left margin area to display the pointer. Drag down to select this paragraph and the next two paragraphs. On the **Home tab**, in the **Paragraph group**, click the **Bullets** button.

a. Scroll to view the bottom of **Page 1**, and then locate the paragraph that begins *Completion of at least*. Select that paragraph and the next two paragraphs. On the **Home tab**, in the **Paragraph group**, click the **Numbering** button.

b. Locate the paragraph that begins *Section 4 Elections*. Click to position the insertion point at the *end* of that paragraph after the colon, and then press Enter.

c. Type **1.** and press Spacebar. Type **Completion of at least 12 credit hours at Laurel College** and then press Enter. Type the following text for items 2 and 3 in the list:

Minimum GPA of 2.75

Enrollment in at least six credit hours each semester in office

d. Near the middle of **Page 1**, select the three items in the bulleted list, right-click the list, and then point to **Bullets**. Under **Bullet Library**, click the **black square** symbol. If the black square is not available, choose another bullet symbol. **Save** your document.

3 Be sure the bulleted list is still selected. Point to the left tab marker at **2″ on the horizontal ruler**. When the *Left Tab* ScreenTip displays, double-click to open the **Tabs** dialog box.

a. Under **Tab stop position**, with *2″* selected, at the bottom of the dialog box, click **Clear** to delete this tab stop. Then, type **5.5** in the **Tab stop position** box.

b. Under **Alignment**, click the **Right** option button. Under **Leader**, click the **2** option button. At the bottom of the **Tabs** dialog box, click the **Set** button, and then click **OK**.

4 Press Ctrl + Home to move to the top of the document. Click at the end of the title, and then press Enter to insert a blank paragraph. Click the **Insert tab**, and then in the **Illustrations group**, click the **SmartArt** button.

a. In the **Choose a SmartArt Graphic** dialog box, on the left, click **Hierarchy**, and in the second row, click the fourth style—**Table Hierarchy**. At the bottom of the **Choose a SmartArt Graphic** dialog box, click **OK**. If necessary, on the Design tab, in the Create Graphic group, activate the Text Pane button.

(Project 1D Constitution continues on the next page)

Skills Review | Project 1D Constitution (continued)

b. In the SmartArt graphic, in the second row, click the border of the first *[Text]* box, and then press Del. Press Del again to delete a second *[Text]* box. In the **Text Pane**, under **Type your text here** box, click in the last bulleted point. On the **Design tab**, in the **Create Graphic group**, click the **Promote** button to move the list item up one level.

c. In the **Text Pane**, click in the top bulleted point, type **Associated Students of Laurel College** and then press ↓. Type the following in the three remaining boxes:

Executive Officers

Student Senate

Judicial Review Committee

d. In the upper right corner of the **Text Pane**, click the **Close** button. Be sure the graphic is selected—a pale border surrounds the entire graphic, and then click the outside border one time. Click the **Format tab**, and then in the **Size group**, if necessary click the **Size** button. By clicking the spin box arrows, change the **Shape Height** to **2.6″** and the **Shape Width** to **6.5″**.

e. With the SmartArt graphic still selected, on the **Design tab**, in the **SmartArt Styles group**, click the **Change Colors** button. Scroll down, and then under **Accent 5**, click the second style—**Colored Fill - Accent 5**.

f. On the **Design tab**, in the **SmartArt Styles group**, click the **More** button. Under **3-D**, click the second style—**Inset**. Click anywhere in the document to deselect the graphic. Press Ctrl + Home to move the insertion point to the beginning of the document.

g. Display **Backstage** view, on the right, under the screen thumbnail, click **Properties**, and then click **Show Document Panel**. In the **Author** box, type your firstname and lastname. In the **Subject** box type your course name and section number, and in the **Keywords** box type **student constitution**

h. **Close** the Document Panel. Click **Save**. Display **Backstage** view and click the **Print tab**. Examine the **Print Preview**. Print or submit electronically as directed. **Close** Word.

End **You have completed Project 1D**

Apply 1A skills from these Objectives:

1. Create a New Document and Insert Text
2. Insert and Format Graphics
3. Insert and Modify Text Boxes and Shapes
4. Preview and Print a Document

Mastering Word | Project 1E Retreat

In the following Mastering Word project, you will create a flyer announcing a retreat for the Associated Students of Laurel College Board. Your completed document will look similar to Figure 1.52.

Project Files

For Project 1E, you will need the following files:

New blank Word document
w01E_Retreat_Text
w01E_Retreat_Picture

You will save your document as:

Lastname_Firstname_1E_Retreat

Project Results

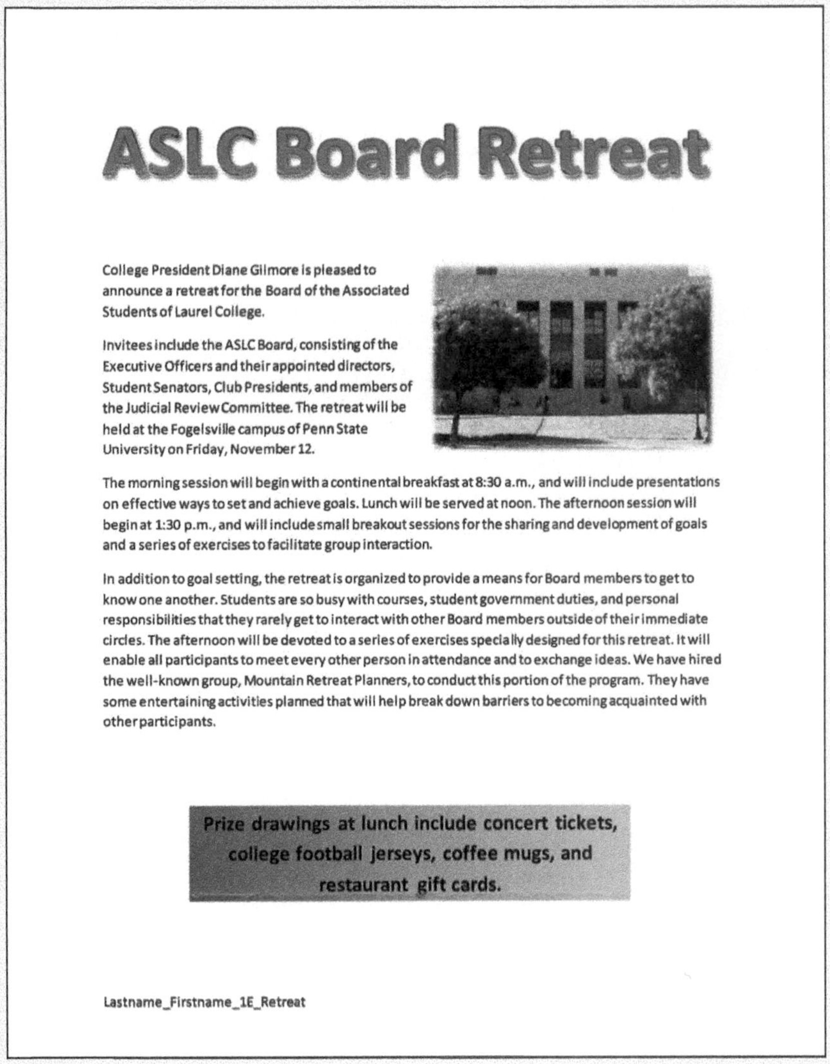

ASLC Board Retreat

College President Diane Gilmore is pleased to announce a retreat for the Board of the Associated Students of Laurel College.

Invitees include the ASLC Board, consisting of the Executive Officers and their appointed directors, Student Senators, Club Presidents, and members of the Judicial Review Committee. The retreat will be held at the Fogelsville campus of Penn State University on Friday, November 12.

The morning session will begin with a continental breakfast at 8:30 a.m., and will include presentations on effective ways to set and achieve goals. Lunch will be served at noon. The afternoon session will begin at 1:30 p.m., and will include small breakout sessions for the sharing and development of goals and a series of exercises to facilitate group interaction.

In addition to goal setting, the retreat is organized to provide a means for Board members to get to know one another. Students are so busy with courses, student government duties, and personal responsibilities that they rarely get to interact with other Board members outside of their immediate circles. The afternoon will be devoted to a series of exercises specially designed for this retreat. It will enable all participants to meet every other person in attendance and to exchange ideas. We have hired the well-known group, Mountain Retreat Planners, to conduct this portion of the program. They have some entertaining activities planned that will help break down barriers to becoming acquainted with other participants.

Prize drawings at lunch include concert tickets, college football jerseys, coffee mugs, and restaurant gift cards.

Lastname_Firstname_1E_Retreat

Figure 1.52

(Project 1E Retreat continues on the next page)

Mastering Word | Project 1E Retreat (continued)

1 **Start** Word and display a new blank document. **Save** the document in your **Word Chapter 1** folder as **Lastname_Firstname_1E_Retreat** and then add the file name to the footer. Be sure the formatting marks and rulers display.

2 Type **ASLC Board Retreat** and press Enter two times. Type **College President Diane Gilmore is pleased to announce a retreat for the Board of the Associated Students of Laurel College.** Press Enter one time. **Insert** the file **w01E_Retreat_Text**.

3 Select the title *ASLC Board Retreat*. On the **Home tab**, in the **Font group**, display the **Text Effects** gallery, and then in the third row, apply the first effect—**Fill - White, Gradient Outline - Accent 1**. Change the **Font Size** to **56** pt. Apply a **Shadow** text effect using the first effect under **Outer—Offset Diagonal Bottom Right**. Change the **Font Color** to **Olive Green, Accent 3, Darker 25%**—in the seventh column, the fifth color.

4 Click to position the insertion point at the beginning of the paragraph that begins *College President*, and then from your student files, **Insert** the picture **w01E_Retreat_Picture**. Change the **Shape Height** of the picture to **2″**, and then set the **Wrap Text** to **Square**. Move the picture so that the right edge aligns with the right margin, and the top edge aligns with the top edge of the text that begins *College President*. Apply a **Film Grain Artistic Effect**—the third effect in the third row. From **Picture Effects**, add a **5 Point Soft Edge**.

5 Scroll to view the lower portion of the page. **Insert** a **Text Box** beginning at the left margin and at approximately **7 inches on the vertical ruler** that is approximately 1″ high and 4.5″ wide. Then, in the **Size group**, make the measurements exact by setting the **Height** to **1″** and the **Width** to **4.6″**. Type the following text in the text box:

> **Prize drawings at lunch include concert tickets, college football jerseys, coffee mugs, and restaurant gift cards.**

6 Select the text in the text box. Change the **Font Size** to **16** pt, apply **Bold**, and **Center** the text. Add a **Shape Fill** to the text box using the theme color **Olive Green, Accent 3, Lighter 40%**. Then apply a **Gradient** fill using the **Linear Right** gradient. Change the **Shape Outline** color to **White, Background 1**. Drag the text box as necessary to center it horizontally between the left and right margins, and vertically between the last line of text and the footer.

7 Display the **Document Panel**. Type your firstname and lastname in the **Author** box, your course name and section number in the **Subject** box, and then in the **Keywords** box type **retreat, ASLC**

8 **Close** the Document Panel. **Save** and preview your document, make any necessary adjustments, and then print your document or submit it electronically as directed. **Close** Word.

End **You have completed Project 1E**

Apply 1B skills from these Objectives:

- 5 Change Document and Paragraph Layout
- 6 Create and Modify Lists
- 7 Set and Modify Tab Stops
- 8 Insert a SmartArt Graphic

Mastering Word | Project 1F Cycling Trip

In the following Mastering Word project, you will create an informational handout about a planned trip by the Laurel College Cycling Club. Your completed document will look similar to Figure 1.53.

Project Files

For Project 1F, you will need the following file:

w01F_Cycling_Trip

You will save your document as:

Lastname_Firstname_1F_Cycling_Trip

Project Results

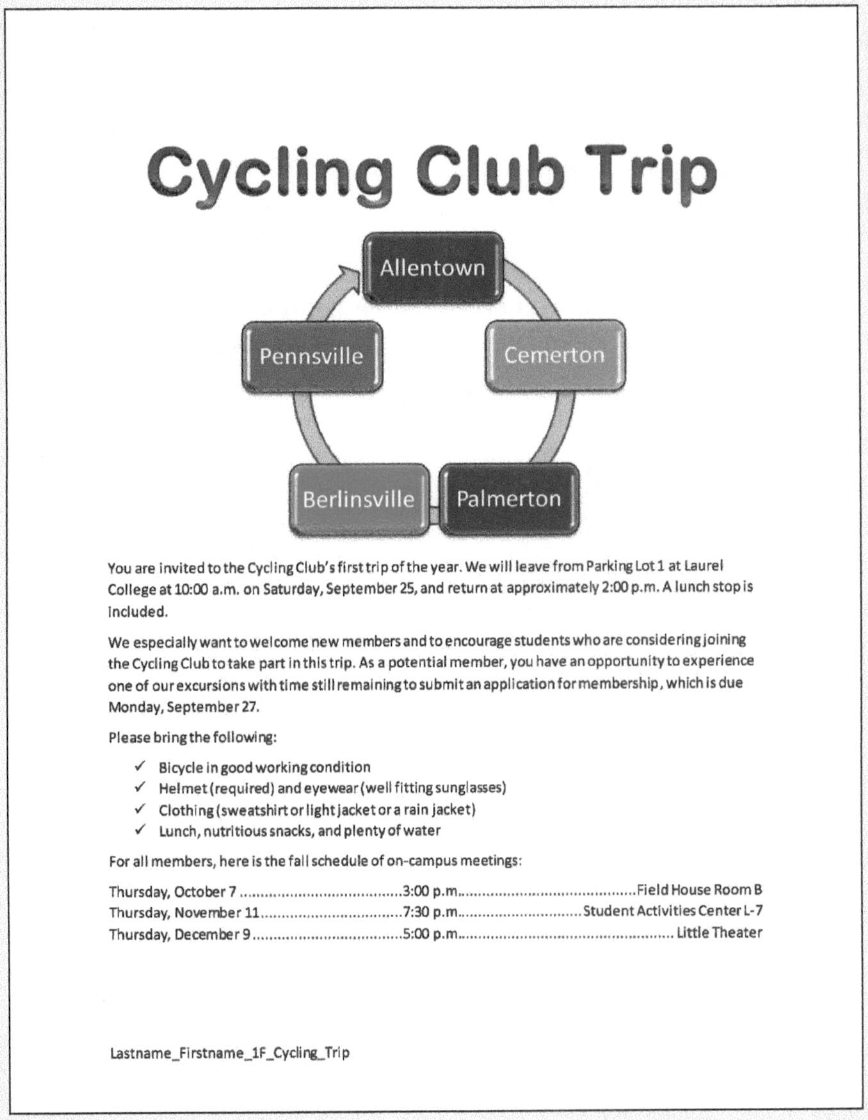

Cycling Club Trip

You are invited to the Cycling Club's first trip of the year. We will leave from Parking Lot 1 at Laurel College at 10:00 a.m. on Saturday, September 25, and return at approximately 2:00 p.m. A lunch stop is included.

We especially want to welcome new members and to encourage students who are considering joining the Cycling Club to take part in this trip. As a potential member, you have an opportunity to experience one of our excursions with time still remaining to submit an application for membership, which is due Monday, September 27.

Please bring the following:

- ✓ Bicycle in good working condition
- ✓ Helmet (required) and eyewear (well fitting sunglasses)
- ✓ Clothing (sweatshirt or light jacket or a rain jacket)
- ✓ Lunch, nutritious snacks, and plenty of water

For all members, here is the fall schedule of on-campus meetings:

Thursday, October 7	3:00 p.m.	Field House Room B
Thursday, November 11	7:30 p.m.	Student Activities Center L-7
Thursday, December 9	5:00 p.m.	Little Theater

Lastname_Firstname_1F_Cycling_Trip

Figure 1.53

(Project 1F Cycling Trip continues on the next page)

Mastering Word | Project 1F Cycling Trip (continued)

1 **Start** Word. From your student files open the document **w01F_Cycling_Trip**. **Save** the document in your **Word Chapter 1** folder as **Lastname_Firstname_1F_Cycling_Trip** Add the file name to the footer. Display formatting marks.

2 Display the **Page Setup** dialog box. Set the **Top** margin to **1.25″** and the other three margins to **1″**. Select all of the text in the document, including the title. Add **6 pt** spacing after all paragraphs. Change the **Line Spacing** to **1.15**. Change the alignment to **Align Text Left**. **Center** the document title—*Cycling Club Trip*.

3 Locate the paragraph that begins *Bicycle in good*. Select that paragraph and the three paragraphs that follow it. Create a bulleted list from the selected text. Use the shortcut menu to display bullet options, and change the bullet character to a **check mark** or another symbol if the check mark is unavailable.

4 Position the insertion point in the blank paragraph at the end of the document. Add a **Right** tab stop at **3.5″**. Display the **Tabs** dialog box and add a dot leader. **Set** the tab stop, and then add and **Set** another **Right** tab stop with a dot leader at **6.5″**.

5 Type the text shown in **Table 1**, pressing Tab between columns and Enter at the end of each line. Refer to Figure 1.53.

6 Select the first two lines in the tabbed list and change the **Space After** to **0 pt**. Near the top of the document, position the insertion point in the blank line below the title. Display the **Choose a SmartArt Graphic** dialog box, select the **Cycle** category, and then in the second row, select the first style—**Continuous Cycle**.

7 Display the **Text Pane**. Add the following cities in this order: **Allentown** and **Cemerton** and **Palmerton** and **Berlinsville** and **Pennsville**

8 **Close** the Text Pane. Click the SmartArt border. On the **Format tab**, set the **Shape Width** of the SmartArt graphic to **6.5″** and the **Shape Height** to **3″**. On the **Design tab**, from the **SmartArt Styles** gallery, apply the **Cartoon 3-D** style, and change the colors to the first color under **Colorful—Colorful – Accent Colors**.

9 Display the **Document Panel**, type your firstname and lastname in the **Author** box, your course name and section number in the **Subject** box, and then in the **Keywords** box type **cycling, cycling club**

10 **Close** the Document Panel. **Save** your document. Preview your document, check for and make any adjustments, and then print your document or submit it electronically as directed. **Close** Word.

Table 1

Thursday, October 7	3:00 p.m.	Field House Room B
Thursday, November 11	7:30 p.m.	Student Activities Center L-7
Thursday, December 9	5:00 p.m.	Little Theater

(Return to Step 6)

End **You have completed Project 1F**

Apply a combination of **1A** and **1B** skills:

1. Create a New Document and Insert Text
2. Insert and Format Graphics
3. Insert and Modify Text Boxes and Shapes
4. Preview and Print a Document
5. Change Document and Paragraph Layout
6. Create and Modify Lists
7. Set and Modify Tab Stops
8. Insert a SmartArt Graphic

myitlab grader

Mastering Word | Project 1G Web Sites

In the following Mastering Word project, you will edit guidelines for club Web sites at Laurel College. Your completed document will look similar to Figure 1.54.

Project Files

For Project 1G, you will need the following files:

New blank Word document
w01G_Chess_Club_Picture
w01G_Web_Sites_Text

You will save your document as:

Lastname_Firstname_1G_Web_Sites

Project Results

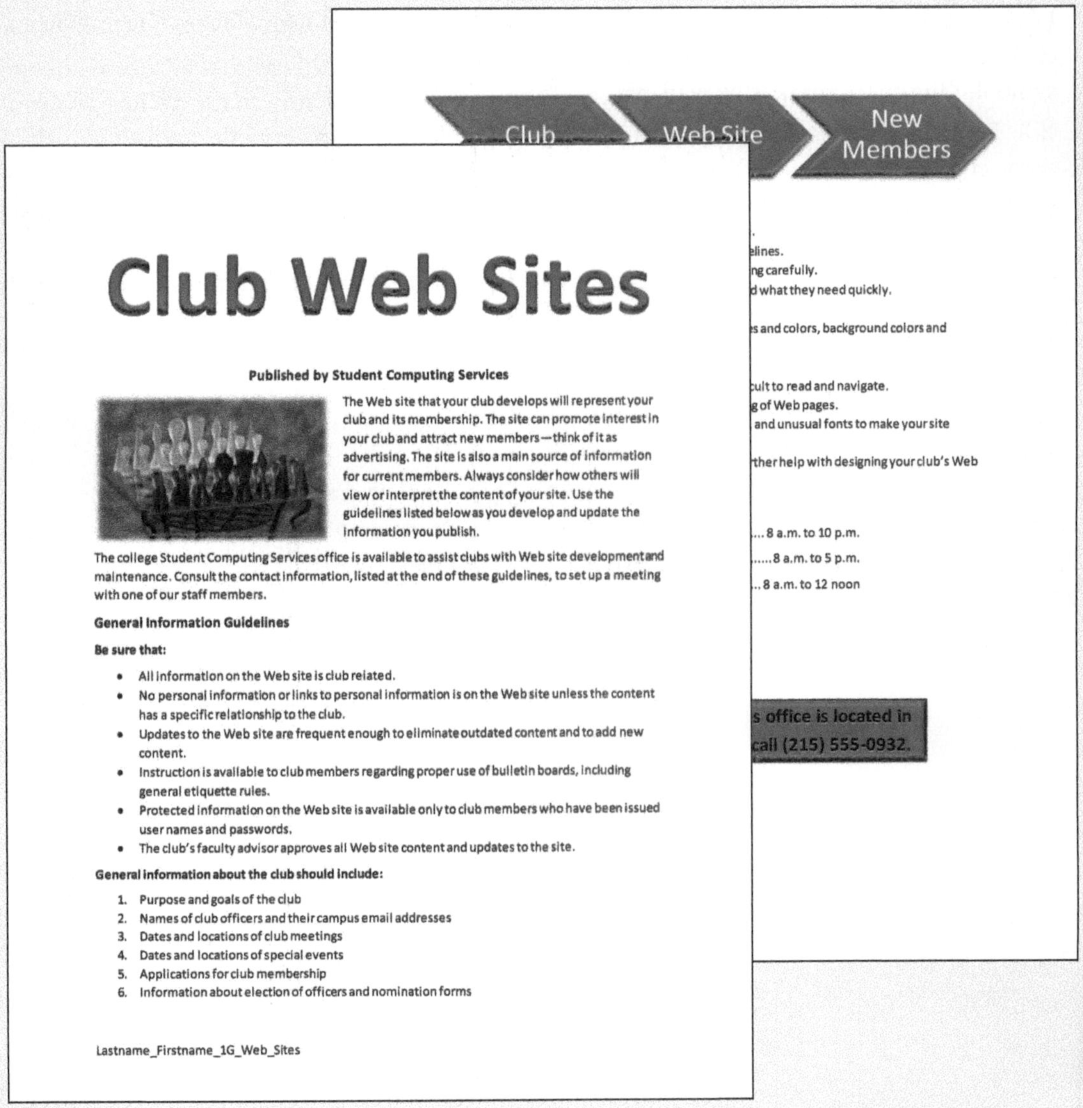
Club
Web Site
New Members
lines.
ng carefully.
d what they need quickly.
s and colors, background colors and
ult to read and navigate.
g of Web pages.
and unusual fonts to make your site
rther help with designing your club's Web
... 8 a.m. to 10 p.m.
..... 8 a.m. to 5 p.m.
.. 8 a.m. to 12 noon
s office is located in
call (215) 555-0932.
Club Web Sites
Published by Student Computing Services
The Web site that your club develops will represent your club and its membership. The site can promote interest in your club and attract new members—think of it as advertising. The site is also a main source of information for current members. Always consider how others will view or interpret the content of your site. Use the guidelines listed below as you develop and update the information you publish.
The college Student Computing Services office is available to assist clubs with Web site development and maintenance. Consult the contact information, listed at the end of these guidelines, to set up a meeting with one of our staff members.
General Information Guidelines
Be sure that:
• All information on the Web site is club related.
• No personal information or links to personal information is on the Web site unless the content has a specific relationship to the club.
• Updates to the Web site are frequent enough to eliminate outdated content and to add new content.
• Instruction is available to club members regarding proper use of bulletin boards, including general etiquette rules.
• Protected information on the Web site is available only to club members who have been issued user names and passwords.
• The club's faculty advisor approves all Web site content and updates to the site.
General information about the club should include:
1. Purpose and goals of the club
2. Names of club officers and their campus email addresses
3. Dates and locations of club meetings
4. Dates and locations of special events
5. Applications for club membership
6. Information about election of officers and nomination forms
Lastname_Firstname_1G_Web_Sites

Figure 1.54

(Project 1G Web Sites continues on the next page)

Mastering Word | Project 1G Web Sites (continued)

1 **Start** Word and display a new blank document. Display formatting marks and rulers. **Save** the document in your **Word Chapter 1** folder as **Lastname_Firstname_1G_Web_Sites** Add the file name to the footer.

Type **Club Web Sites** and then press Enter. Select the title you just typed. From the **Text Effects** gallery, in the fourth row, apply the second effect—**Gradient Fill - Orange, Accent 6, Inner Shadow**, change the **Font Size** to **72** pt, and **Center** the title.

2 Click in the blank line below the title. Locate and insert the file **w01G_Web_Sites_Text**. *Except* for the document title, select all of the document text. **Align Text Left**, change the **Line Spacing** to **1.15**, and change the **Spacing After** to **6 pt**. Locate and **Center** the document subtitle that begins *Published by*.

3 In the middle of **Page 1**, under the subheading *Be sure that*, select the six paragraphs down to, but not including, the *General information* subheading. Format the selected text as a bulleted list. Near the bottom of **Page 1** and the top of **Page 2**, under the *Web Site Design Guidelines* subheading, select all of the paragraphs to the end of the document—not including the blank paragraph mark—and create another bulleted list.

4 Under the subheading that begins *General information*, select the six paragraphs and apply **Numbering** to create a numbered list.

Near the top of the document, position the insertion point to the left of the paragraph that begins The Web site. **Insert** the picture **w01G_Chess_Club_Picture**. Set the **Wrap Text** to **Square**. Decrease the picture **Width** to **2.7"**. From the **Picture Effects** gallery, apply the **Soft Edges** effect using **5 Point**.

5 Press Ctrl + End to move to the blank line at the end of the document. Type **For assistance, Student Computing Services hours are:** and then press Enter. Set a **Left** tab stop at **1.5"**. Display the **Tabs** dialog box. At **5"** add a **Right** tab stop with a **dot leader** and click **Set**. Click **OK** to close the dialog box, press Tab to begin, and then type the following information; be sure to press Tab to begin each line and press Tab between the days and the times and press Enter at the end of each line:

Monday–Thursday	8 a.m. to 10 p.m.
Friday	8 a.m. to 5 p.m.
Saturday	8 a.m. to 12 noon

6 At the top of **Page 2**, position the insertion point to the left of the subheading *Web Site Design Guidelines*. Press Enter one time, and then click in the blank paragraph you just created. **Insert** a **SmartArt** graphic, and then from the **Process** group, select the **Basic Chevron Process**—in the fourth row, the third graphic. Click the border of the graphic, and then on the **Format tab**, set the **Shape Height** of the graphic to **1"** and the **Shape Width** of the graphic to **6.5"**. From the **Design tab**, display the **Text Pane**, and then type **Club** and **Web Site** and **New Members Close** the **Text Pane**. Change style to **3-D Inset** and the colors to **Colored Fill – Accent 6**, which is in the last set of colors.

7 At the bottom of **Page 2**, **Insert** a **Text Box** and set the height to **0.7"** and the width to **5"**. In the text box, type: **The Student Computing Services office is located in the Cedar Building, Room 114, call (215) 555-0932.**

Select the text in the text box. From the Mini toolbar, change the **Font Size** to **16** pt, apply **Bold**, and **Center** the text. Change the **Shape Fill** to **Orange, Accent 6, Darker 25%**. From the **Shape Effects** gallery, apply a **Circle Bevel**. By using the pointer, visually center the text box horizontally between the left and right margins and vertically between the tabbed list and the footer.

8 As the document properties, type your firstname and lastname in the **Author** box, your course name and section number in the **Subject** box, and then in the **Keywords** box type **Web sites, guidelines, Student Computing Services** **Save** your document, examine the Print Preview, check for and make any adjustments, and then print your document or submit it electronically as directed. **Close** Word.

End **You have completed Project 1G**

Apply a combination of the 1A and 1B skills.

GO! Fix It | Project 1H Guidelines

Project Files

For Project 1H, you will need the following file:

w01H_Guidelines

You will save your document as:

Lastname_Firstname_1H_Guidelines

From the student files that accompany this textbook, locate and open the file w01H_More_Guidelines, and then save the file in your Word Chapter 1 folder as **Lastname_Firstname_1H_Guidelines**

This document contains errors that you must find and correct. Read and examine the document, and then edit to correct any errors that you find and to improve the overall document format. Types of errors could include, but are not restricted to:

- Wasted space due to text not wrapping around pictures
- Inconsistent line spacing in paragraphs
- Inconsistent spacing between paragraphs
- Inconsistent paragraph indents
- Inconsistent indenting of lists
- Titles that do not extend across the page
- Text boxes that are too small
- Tabbed lists with wide spaces that do not contain leaders
- Spaces between paragraphs created using empty paragraphs rather than space after paragraphs

Things you should know to complete this project:

- Displaying formatting marks will assist in locating spacing errors.
- There are no errors in the fonts, although the title font size is too small.
- The final flyer should fit on one page.

Save your document and add the file name to the footer. In the Document Panel, type your firstname and lastname in the Author box and your course name and section number in the Subject box. In the Keywords box type **Web site guidelines** and then save your document and submit as directed.

End You have completed Project 1H

Content-Based Assessments

Apply a combination of the 1A and 1B skills.

GO! Make It | Project 1I Flyer

Project Files

For Project 1I, you will need the following files:

w01I_Team_Building w01I_Park_Picture

You will save your document as:

Lastname_Firstname_1I_Team_Building

From the student files that accompany this textbook, locate and open the file w01I_Team_Building, and then save the file in your chapter folder as **Lastname_Firstname_1I_Team_Building**

Use the skills you have practiced, create the document shown in Figure 1.55. The title uses Gradient Fill – Blue, Accent 1, 48 pt. The SmartArt graphic uses the Radial Cycle with an Intense Effect style, is 3″ high and 6.5″ wide, has the Colorful Range – Accent Colors 2 to 3 applied. The w01I_Park_Picture picture has a 2.5 pt soft edge, and is 2.5″ wide. The page border uses Dark Blue, Text 2.

Add the file name to the footer; in the Document Panel, add your name and course information and the Keywords **team building**; save your document; and then submit as directed.

Project Results

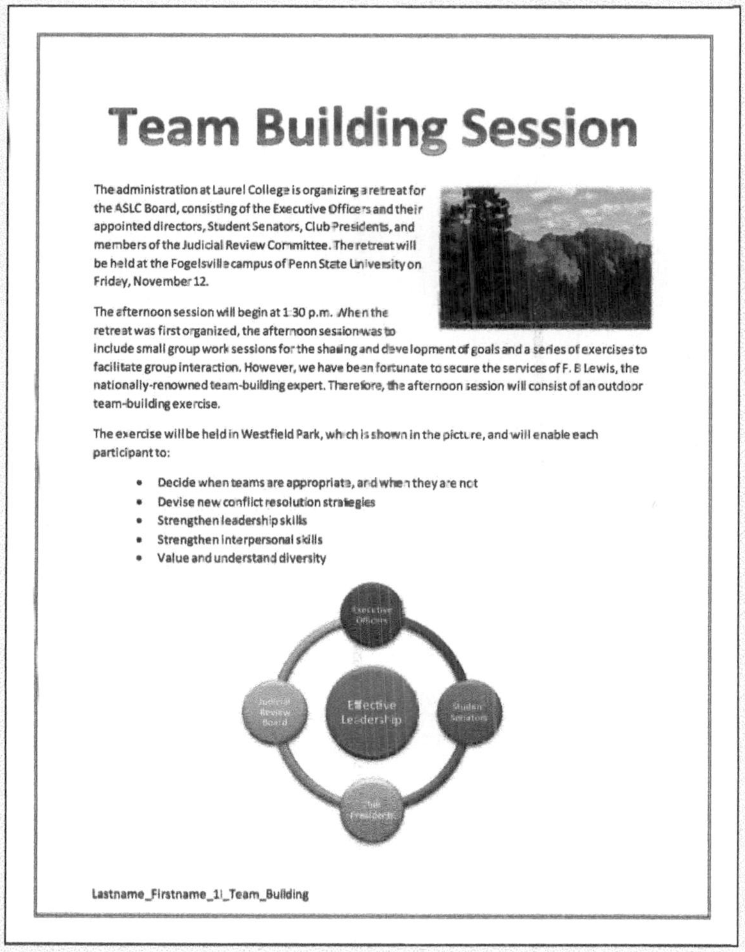

Team Building Session

The administration at Laurel College is organizing a retreat for the ASLC Board, consisting of the Executive Officers and their appointed directors, Student Senators, Club Presidents, and members of the Judicial Review Committee. The retreat will be held at the Fogelsville campus of Penn State University on Friday, November 12.

The afternoon session will begin at 1:30 p.m. When the retreat was first organized, the afternoon session was to include small group work sessions for the sharing and development of goals and a series of exercises to facilitate group interaction. However, we have been fortunate to secure the services of F. B Lewis, the nationally-renowned team-building expert. Therefore, the afternoon session will consist of an outdoor team-building exercise.

The exercise will be held in Westfield Park, which is shown in the picture, and will enable each participant to:

- Decide when teams are appropriate, and when they are not
- Devise new conflict resolution strategies
- Strengthen leadership skills
- Strengthen interpersonal skills
- Value and understand diversity

Lastname_Firstname_1I_Team_Building

Figure 1.55

End You have completed Project 1I

Apply a combination of the 1A and 1B skills.

GO! Solve It | Project 1J Food Drive

Project Files

For Project 1J, you will need the following file:

New blank Word document
w01J_Food_Drive

You will save your document as:

Lastname_Firstname_1J_Food_Drive

Create a new document and save it in your Word Chapter 1 folder as **Lastname_Firstname_1J_Food_Drive** Use the following information to create a flyer that includes a title that uses Text Effects, introductory text, two lists of an appropriate type, one text box, and a picture with appropriate formatting and text wrapping. Use your own picture or w01J_Food_Drive.

This Thanksgiving, the Associated Students of Laurel College is sponsoring a food drive for the local community. All college clubs are invited to participate. Results will be adjusted for club membership by measuring the results in pounds of food per member. Three kinds of food are acceptable: canned goods, non-perishable dry goods, and boxed or canned dry drink mixes, such as coffee, tea, or lemonade.

To participate, a club must follow this procedure: fill out a competition form, collect the goods, and then turn the food in on November 13. The address and telephone number for the ASLC is the Cedar Building, Room 222, Laurelton, PA 19100, (215) 555-0902.

Add the file name to the footer. To the Properties area, add your name, your course name and section number, and the keywords **food drive, clubs**

Performance Criteria	Performance Level		
	Exemplary: You consistently applied the relevant skills	Proficient: You sometimes, but not always, applied the relevant skills	Developing: You rarely or never applied the relevant skills
Create and format lists	Both lists use the proper list type and are formatted correctly.	One of the lists is formatted correctly.	Neither of the lists are formatted correctly.
Insert and format a picture	The picture is inserted and positioned correctly, and text is wrapped around the picture.	The picture is inserted but not formatted properly.	No picture is inserted.
Insert a text box	A text box with appropriate information is inserted and formatted.	A text box is adequately formatted but is difficult to read or unattractive.	No text box is inserted.
Insert introductory text	Introductory text explains the reason for the flyer, with no spelling or grammar errors.	Some introductory text is included, but does not contain sufficient information and/or includes spelling or grammar errors.	No introductory text, or insufficient introductory text.
Insert title using Text Effects	Text Effects title inserted and centered on the page.	Text Effects title is inserted, but not centered or formatted attractively on the page.	No Text Effects title is included.

End **You have completed Project 1J**

Apply a combination of the 1A and 1B skills..

GO! Solve It | Project 1K Fitness Services

Project Files

For Project 1K, you will need the following files:

New blank Word document
w01K_Volleyball

You will save your document as:

Lastname_Firstname_1K_Fitness_Services

Create a new file and save it as **Lastname_Firstname_1K_Fitness Services** Use the following information to create a flyer that includes introductory text, a SmartArt graphic, a title that uses Text Effects, and a picture that has an artistic effect applied and uses text wrapping. Use your own picture or w01K_Volleyball.

The Associated Students of Laurel College sponsors fitness activities. These take place both on campus and off campus. The activities fall into two categories: Fitness Services and Intramural Sports. Fitness Services are noncompetitive activities, with the most popular being Kickboxing, Jogging, and Aerobics. The most popular Intramural Sports activities—which include competitive team and club sports—are Field Hockey, Volleyball, and Basketball.

Add the file name to the footer, and add your name, your course name and section number, and the keywords **fitness, sports** to the Properties area.

		Performance Level		
		Exemplary: You consistently applied the relevant skills	Proficient: You sometimes, but not always, applied the relevant skills	Developing: You rarely or never applied the relevant skills
Performance Criteria	Insert title using Text Effects	Text Effects title inserted and centered on the page.	Text Effects title is inserted, but not centered on the page.	No Text Effects title is included.
	Insert introductory text	Introductory text explains the reason for the flyer, with no spelling or grammar errors.	Some introductory text is included, but does not sufficiently explain the topic and/or includes spelling or grammar errors.	No or insufficient introductory text is included.
	Insert and format a picture	The picture is inserted and positioned correctly, an artistic effect is applied, and text is wrapped around the picture.	The picture is inserted but not formatted properly.	No picture is inserted in the document.
	Insert and format SmartArt	The SmartArt graphic displays both categories of fitness activities and examples of each type.	The SmartArt graphic does not display fitness activities by category.	No SmartArt graphic inserted.

End **You have completed Project 1K**

Outcomes-Based Assessments

Rubric

The following outcomes-based assessments are *open-ended assessments*. That is, there is no specific correct result; your result will depend on your approach to the information provided. Make *Professional Quality* your goal. Use the following scoring rubric to guide you in *how* to approach the problem and then to evaluate *how well* your approach solves the problem.

The *criteria*—Software Mastery, Content, Format and Layout, and Process—represent the knowledge and skills you have gained that you can apply to solving the problem. The *levels of performance*—Professional Quality, Approaching Professional Quality, or Needs Quality Improvements—help you and your instructor evaluate your result.

	Your completed project is of Professional Quality if you:	Your completed project is Approaching Professional Quality if you:	Your completed project Needs Quality Improvements if you:
1-Software Mastery	Choose and apply the most appropriate skills, tools, and features and identify efficient methods to solve the problem.	Choose and apply some appropriate skills, tools, and features, but not in the most efficient manner.	Choose inappropriate skills, tools, or features, or are inefficient in solving the problem.
2-Content	Construct a solution that is clear and well organized, contains content that is accurate, appropriate to the audience and purpose, and is complete. Provide a solution that contains no errors in spelling, grammar, or style.	Construct a solution in which some components are unclear, poorly organized, inconsistent, or incomplete. Misjudge the needs of the audience. Have some errors in spelling, grammar, or style, but the errors do not detract from comprehension.	Construct a solution that is unclear, incomplete, or poorly organized; contains some inaccurate or inappropriate content; and contains many errors in spelling, grammar, or style. Do not solve the problem.
3-Format and Layout	Format and arrange all elements to communicate information and ideas, clarify function, illustrate relationships, and indicate relative importance.	Apply appropriate format and layout features to some elements, but not others. Overuses features, causing minor distraction.	Apply format and layout that does not communicate information or ideas clearly. Do not use format and layout features to clarify function, illustrate relationships, or indicate relative importance. Use available features excessively, causing distraction.
4-Process	Use an organized approach that integrates planning, development, self-assessment, revision, and reflection.	Demonstrate an organized approach in some areas, but not others; or, uses an insufficient process of organization throughout.	Do not use an organized approach to solve the problem.

Outcomes-Based Assessments

Apply a combination of the **1A** and **1B** skills..

GO! Think | Project 1L Academic Services

Project Files

For Project 1L, you will need the following file:

New blank Word document

You will save your document as:

Lastname_Firstname_1L_Academic_Services

The Services Coordinator of the Associated Students of Laurel College needs to create a flyer to inform students of academic services available at the ASLC office. Referrals are available for medical, legal, and counseling services, as well as tutoring and volunteer organizations. Among the services offered at the ASLC office are free printing (up to 250 pages per semester), help with minor legal issues, housing information, bicycle repair, minor computer repair, and help placing students with volunteer organizations.

Create a flyer with basic information about the services provided. Be sure the flyer is easy to read and understand and has an attractive design. If you need more information about student services available at other colleges, search the Web for **student government** and add whatever services you think might be (or should be) available at your college. Add appropriate information to the Document Panel. Save the document as **Lastname_Firstname_1L_Academic_Services** and submit it as directed.

End **You have completed Project 1L**

Apply a combination of the **1A** and **1B** skills.

GO! Think | Project 1M Campus Bookstore

Project Files

For Project 1M, you will need the following files:

New blank Word document
w01L_Campus_Bookstore

You will save your document as:

Lastname_Firstname_1M_Campus_Bookstore

The manager of the Laurel College Bookstore needs to create a flyer that can be handed out by the ASLC to students during Welcome Week. The bookstore gives students attending Welcome Week a discount of 20% on special items such as sweatshirts and other college-related clothing, coffee mugs, calendars, and similar items. Door prizes will also be awarded. The bookstore is open Monday and Thursday from 8 a.m. to 10 p.m., Tuesday and Wednesday from 8 a.m. to 8 p.m., and Friday from 8 a.m. to 5 p.m.

Using your own campus bookstore as an example, create a flyer that gives general information about the bookstore, provides one or more lists of items that are on sale, displays the picture w01M_ Campus_Bookstore, and has a highlighted area that gives the store hours.

Add appropriate information to the Document Panel. Save the document as **Lastname_Firstname_1M_Campus_Bookstore** and submit it as directed.

End **You have completed Project 1M**

Outcomes-Based Assessments

Apply a combination of the 1A and 1B skills.

You and GO! | Project 1N Family Flyer

Project Files

For Project 1N, you will need the following file:

New blank Word document

You will save your document as

Lastname_Firstname_1N_Family_Flyer

In this project, you will create a one-page flyer that you can send to your family. Include any information that may interest your family members, such as work-related news, school events, vacation plans, and the activities and accomplishments of you, your spouse, your friends, or other family members. Choose any writing style that suits you—chatty, newsy, entertaining, or humorous.

To complete the assignment, be sure to include a title, at least one list, a picture, and either a SmartArt graphic or a text box or shape. Before you submit the flyer, be sure to check it for grammar and spelling errors, and also be sure to format the document in an attractive manner, using the skills you practiced in this chapter.

Save the file as **Lastname_Firstname_1N_Family_Flyer** Add the file name to the footer, and add your name, your course name and section number, and the keywords **flyer** and **family** to the Properties area. Submit your file as directed.

End **You have completed Project 1N**

Apply a combination of the 1A and 1B skills.

GO! CD-ROM

GO! Collaborate | Project 1O Bell Orchid Hotels Group Running Case

This project relates to the **Bell Orchid Hotels**. Your instructor may assign this group case project to your class. If your instructor assigns this project, he or she will provide you with information and instructions to work as part of a group. The group will apply the skills gained thus far to help the Bell Orchid Hotels achieve their business goals.

End **You have completed Project 1O**

Using Tables and Templates to Create Resumes and Cover Letters

OUTCOMES

At the end of this chapter you will be able to:

OBJECTIVES

Mastering these objectives will enable you to:

PROJECT 2A
Create a resume by using a Word table.

1. Create a Table (p. 107)
2. Add Text to a Table (p. 108)
3. Format a Table (p. 111)

PROJECT 2B
Create a cover letter and resume by using a template.

4. Create a New Document from an Existing Document (p. 120)
5. Change and Reorganize Text (p. 123)
6. Use the Proofing Options (p. 130)
7. Create a Document Using a Template (p. 134)

James Thew/Shutterstock

In This Chapter

Tables are useful for organizing and presenting data. Because a table is so easy to use, many individuals prefer to arrange tabular information in a Word table rather than setting a series of tabs. Use a table when you want to present rows and columns of information or to create a structure for a document such as a resume.

When using Word to write business or personal letters, use a commonly approved letter format. You will make a good impression on prospective employers if you use a standard business letter style when you are writing a cover letter for a resume. You can create a resume using one of the Microsoft resume templates included with Microsoft Office or available online.

The projects in this chapter relate to **Madison Staffing Services**. Many companies prefer to hire employees through a staffing service, so that both the employer and the employee can determine if the match is a good fit. Madison Staffing Services takes care of the details of recruiting, testing, hiring, and paying the employee. At the end of the employment assignment, neither the employer nor the employee is required to make a permanent commitment. Many individuals find full-time jobs with an employer for whom they initially worked through a staffing agency.

Project 2A Resume

myitlab
Project 2A Training

Project Activities

In Activities 2.01 through 2.09, you will create a table to use as the structure for a resume for one of Madison Staffing Services' clients. Your completed document will look similar to Figure 2.1.

Project Files

For Project 2A, you will need the following file:

w02A_Experience

You will save your document as:

Lastname_Firstname_2A_Resume

Project Results

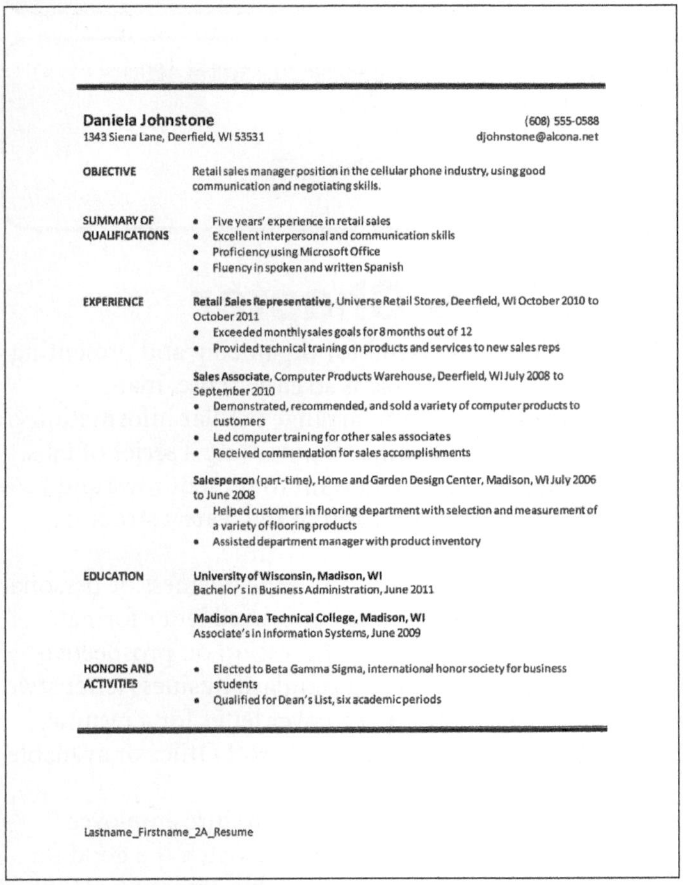

Daniela Johnstone (608) 555-0588
1343 Siena Lane, Deerfield, WI 53531 djohnstone@alcona.net

OBJECTIVE	Retail sales manager position in the cellular phone industry, using good communication and negotiating skills.
SUMMARY OF QUALIFICATIONS	• Five years' experience in retail sales • Excellent interpersonal and communication skills • Proficiency using Microsoft Office • Fluency in spoken and written Spanish
EXPERIENCE	**Retail Sales Representative,** Universe Retail Stores, Deerfield, WI October 2010 to October 2011 • Exceeded monthly sales goals for 8 months out of 12 • Provided technical training on products and services to new sales reps **Sales Associate,** Computer Products Warehouse, Deerfield, WI July 2008 to September 2010 • Demonstrated, recommended, and sold a variety of computer products to customers • Led computer training for other sales associates • Received commendation for sales accomplishments **Salesperson** (part-time), Home and Garden Design Center, Madison, WI July 2006 to June 2008 • Helped customers in flooring department with selection and measurement of a variety of flooring products • Assisted department manager with product inventory
EDUCATION	**University of Wisconsin, Madison, WI** Bachelor's in Business Administration, June 2011 **Madison Area Technical College, Madison, WI** Associate's in Information Systems, June 2009
HONORS AND ACTIVITIES	• Elected to Beta Gamma Sigma, international honor society for business students • Qualified for Dean's List, six academic periods

Lastname_Firstname_2A_Resume

Figure 2.1
Project 2A Resume

Objective 1 | Create a Table

A ***table*** is an arrangement of information organized into rows and columns. The intersection of a row and a column in a table creates a box called a ***cell*** into which you can type. Tables are useful to present information in a logical and orderly manner.

Activity 2.01 | Creating a Table

1. Start **Word**, and in the new blank document, display formatting marks and rulers.
2. Click the **File tab**, and then in **Backstage** view, click **Save As**. In the **Save As** dialog box, navigate to the location where you are storing your projects for this chapter. Create a new folder named **Word Chapter 2**
3. **Save** the file in the **Word Chapter 2** folder as **Lastname_Firstname_2A_Resume**
4. Scroll to the end of the document, right-click near the bottom of the page, and then click **Edit Footer**. On the **Design tab**, in the **Insert group**, click the **Quick Parts** button, and then click **Field**.
5. Under **Field names**, scroll down, click **FileName**, and then click **OK. Close** the footer area.
6. On the **Insert tab**, in the **Tables group**, click the **Table** button. In the **Table** grid, in the fourth row, point to the second square, and notice that the cells display in orange and *2 × 4 Table* displays at the top of the grid. Compare your screen with Figure 2.2.

Figure 2.2

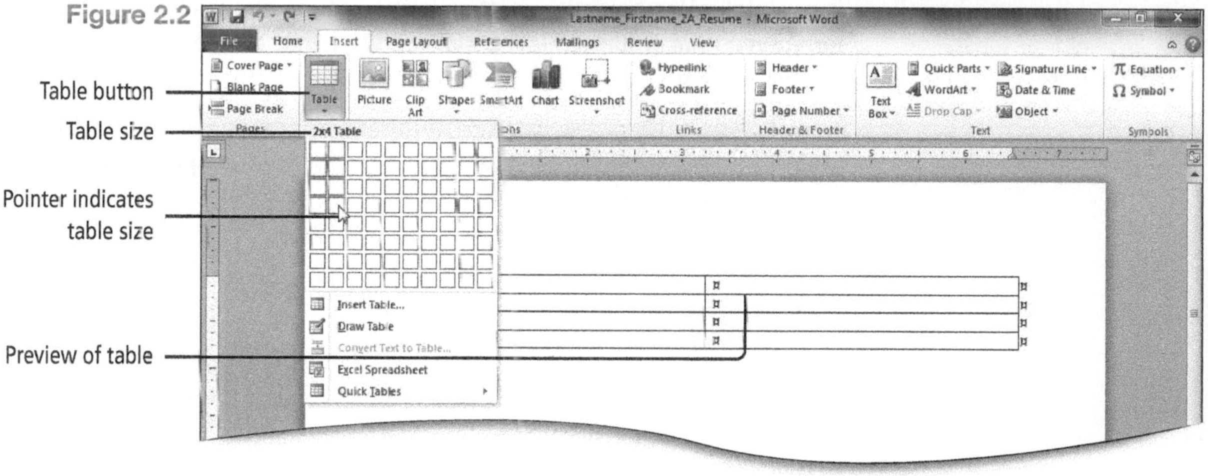

7. Click one time to create the table. Notice that formatting marks in each cell indicate the end of the contents of each cell and the mark to the right of each *row* indicates the row end. **Save** your document, and then compare your screen with Figure 2.3.

   A table with four rows and two columns displays at the insertion point location, and the insertion point displays in the upper left cell. The table fills the width of the page, from the left margin to the right margin. On the Ribbon, Table Tools display and add two tabs—*Design* and *Layout*. Borders display around each cell in the table.

Figure 2.3

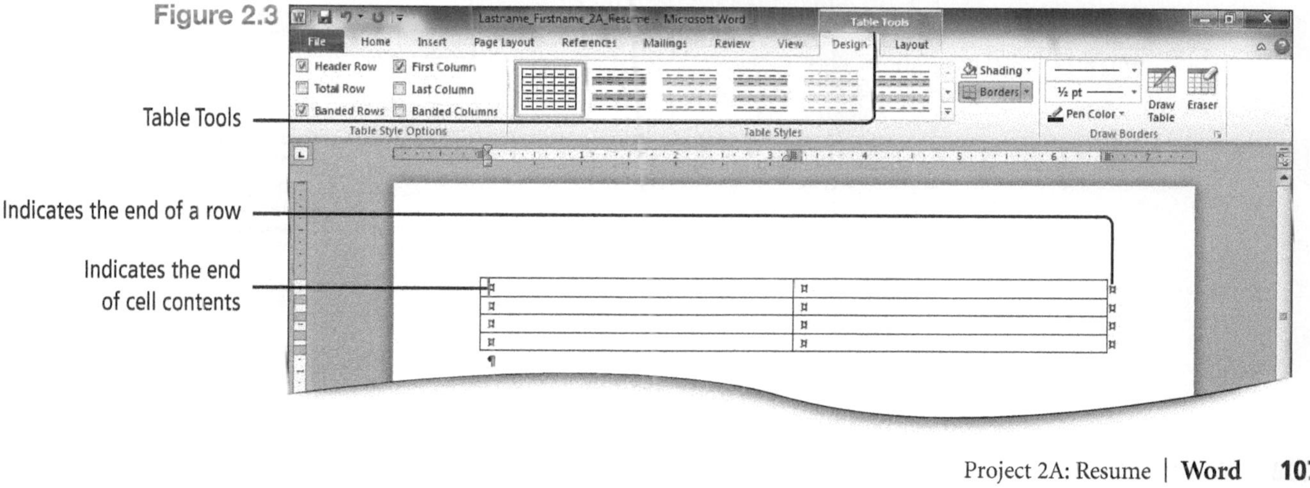

Objective 2 | Add Text to a Table

In a Word table, each cell behaves similarly to a document. For example, as you type in a cell, when you reach the right border of the cell, wordwrap moves the text to the next line. When you press Enter, the insertion point moves down to a new paragraph in the same cell. You can also insert text from another document into a table cell.

Activity 2.02 | Adding Text to a Table

There are numerous acceptable formats for resumes, many of which can be found in Business Communications textbooks. The layout used in this project is suitable for a recent college graduate and places topics in the left column and details in the right column.

1. Scroll up to view the top of the document. With the insertion point blinking in the first cell in the first row, type **OBJECTIVE** and then press Tab.

   Pressing Tab moves the insertion point to the next cell in the row, or, if the insertion point is already in the last cell in the row, pressing Tab moves the insertion point to the first cell in the following row.

2. Type **Retail sales manager position in the cellular phone industry, using good communication and negotiating skills.** Notice that the text wraps in the cell and the height of the row adjusts to fit the text.

3. Press Tab to move to the first cell in the second row. Type **SUMMARY OF QUALIFICATIONS** and then press Tab. Type the following, pressing Enter at the end of each line *except* the last line:

   Five years' experience in retail sales

   Excellent interpersonal and communication skills

   Proficiency using Microsoft Office

   Fluency in spoken and written Spanish

   The default font and font size in a table are the same as for a document—Calibri 11 pt. The default line spacing in a table is single spacing with no space before or after paragraphs, which differs from the defaults for a document.

4. **Save** your document, and then compare your screen with Figure 2.4.

Figure 2.4

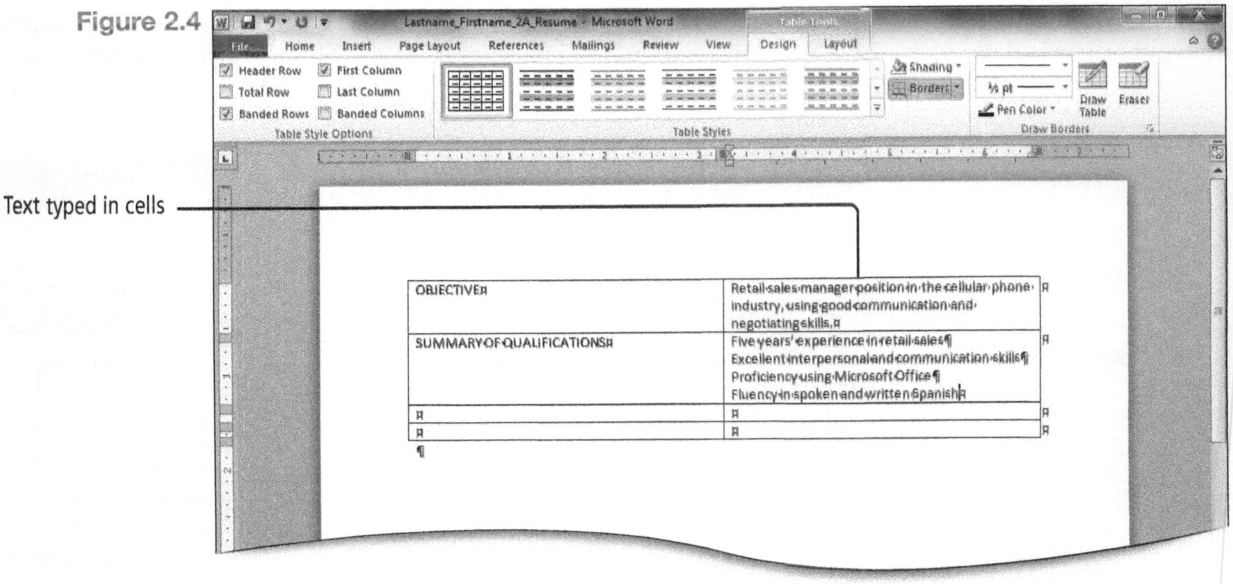

Activity 2.03 | Inserting Existing Text into a Table Cell

1 Press [Tab] to move to the first cell in the third row. Type **EXPERIENCE** and then press [Tab].

2 Type the following, pressing [Enter] after each line:

> **Retail Sales Representative, Universe Retail Stores, Deerfield, WI October 2010 to October 2011**
>
> **Exceeded monthly sales goals for 8 months out of 12**
>
> **Provided technical training on products and services to new sales reps**

3 Be sure your insertion point is positioned in the second column to the left of the cell marker below *sales reps*. Compare your screen with Figure 2.5.

Figure 2.5

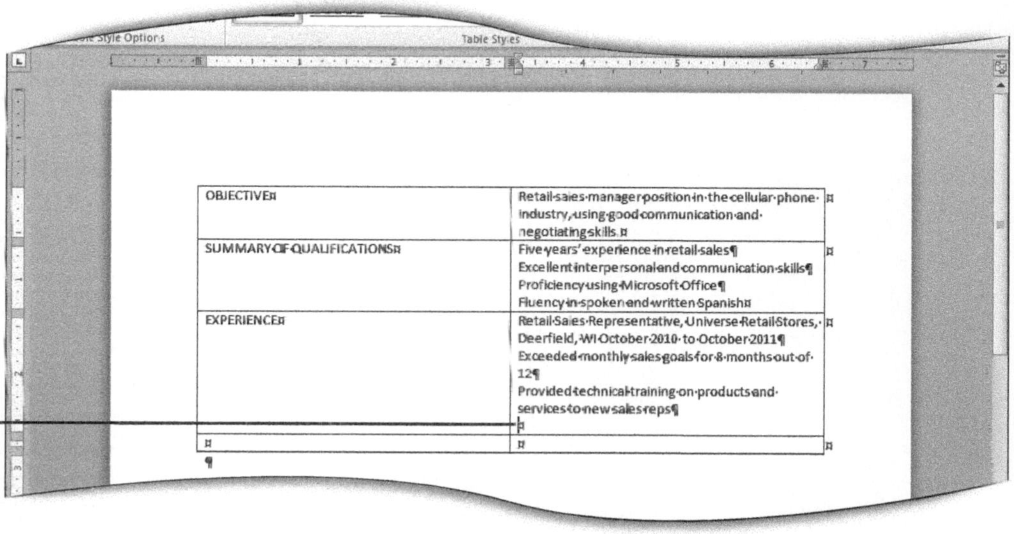

> **Another Way**
>
> Open the second document and select the text you want. Copy the text, and then paste at the desired location.

4 On the **Insert tab**, in the **Text group**, click the **Object button arrow**, and then click **Text from File**. Navigate to your student files, select **w02A_Experience**, and then click **Insert**.

5 Press [Backspace] one time to remove the blank line at the end of the inserted text, and then compare your screen with Figure 2.6.

Figure 2.6

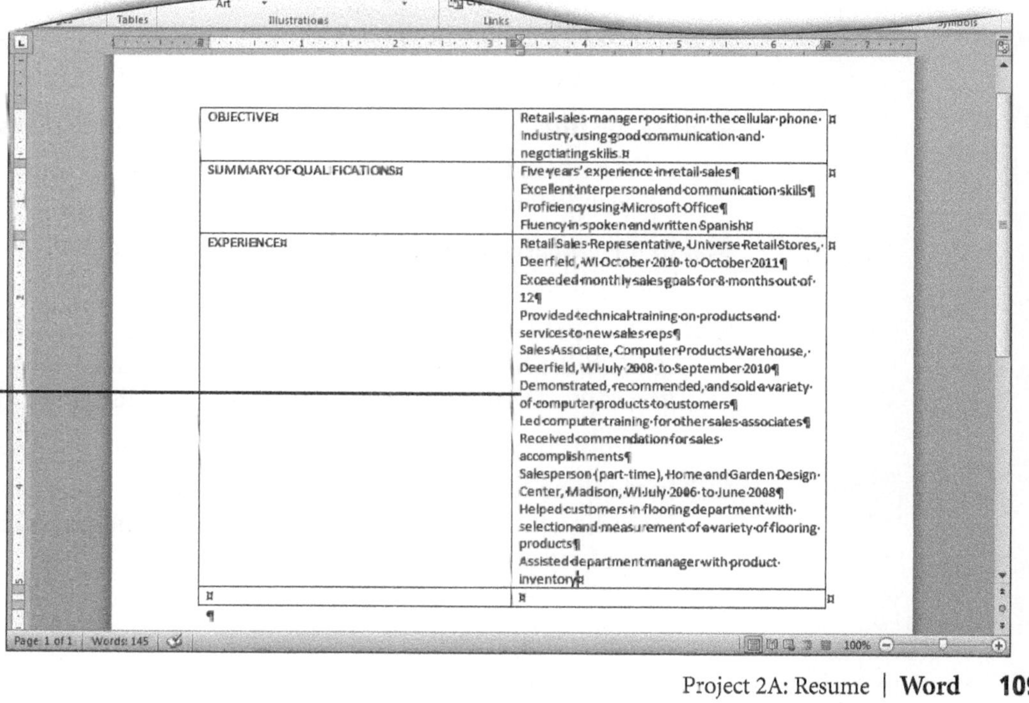

6 Press Tab to move to the first cell in the fourth row. Type **EDUCATION** and then press Tab.

7 Type the following, pressing Enter at the end of each item *except* the last one:

University of Wisconsin, Madison, WI

Bachelor's in Business Administration, June 2011

Madison Area Technical College, Madison, WI

Associate's in Information Systems, June 2009

8 Compare your screen with Figure 2.7.

Figure 2.7

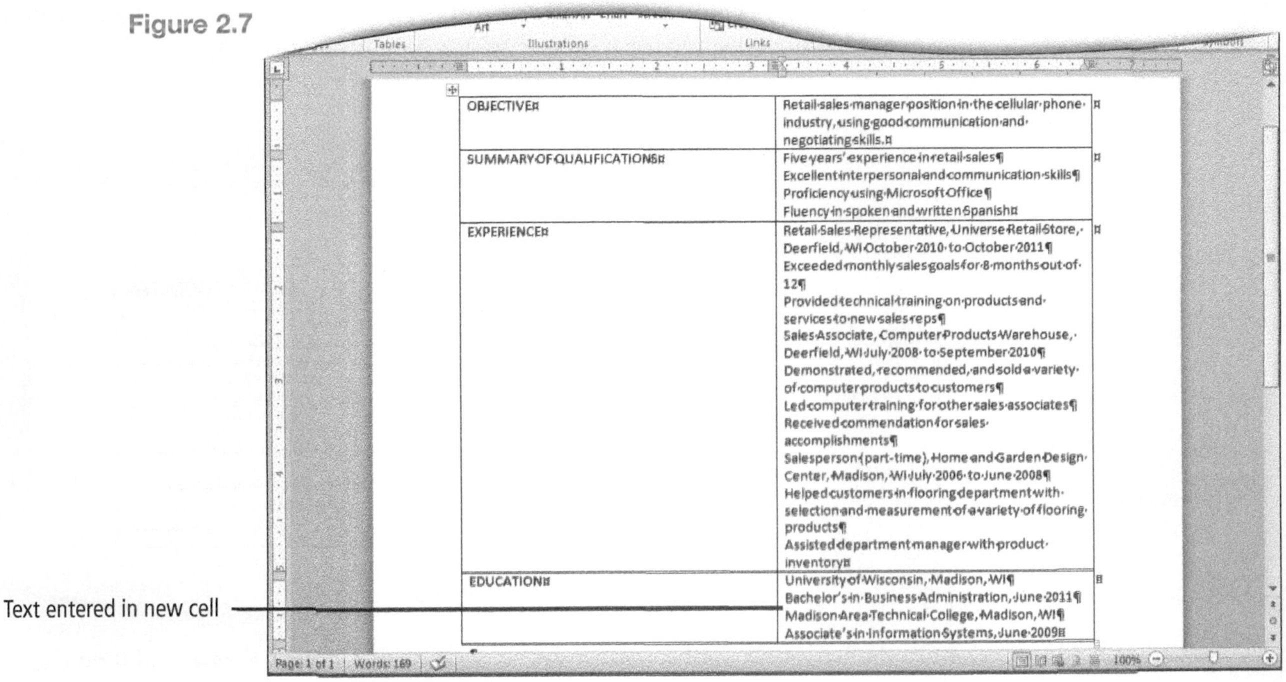

9 **Save** your document.

Activity 2.04 | Creating Bulleted Lists in a Table

1 Scroll to view the top of your document, and then in the cell to the right of *SUMMARY OF QUALIFICATIONS*, select all of the text.

2 On the **Home tab**, in the **Paragraph group**, click the **Bullets** button.

The selected text displays as a bulleted list. Using a bulleted list in this manner makes each qualification more distinctive.

3 In the **Paragraph group**, click the **Decrease Indent** button one time to align the bullets at the left edge of the cell.

4 In the **Clipboard group**, double-click the **Format Painter** button. In the cell to the right of *EXPERIENCE*, select the second and third paragraphs—beginning *Exceeded* and *Provided*—to create the same style of bulleted list as you did in the previous step.

When you double-click the Format Painter button, it remains active until you turn it off.

5 In the same cell, under *Sales Associate*, select the three paragraphs that begin *Demonstrated* and *Led* and *Received* to create another bulleted list aligned at the left edge of the cell.

> **Another Way**
>
> Click the Format Painter again.

6 With the Format Painter pointer still active, in the same cell, select the paragraphs that begin *Helped* and *Assisted* to create the same type of bulleted list.

7 Press Esc to turn off the Format Painter. Click anywhere in the table to deselect the text, and then compare your screen with Figure 2.8.

Figure 2.8

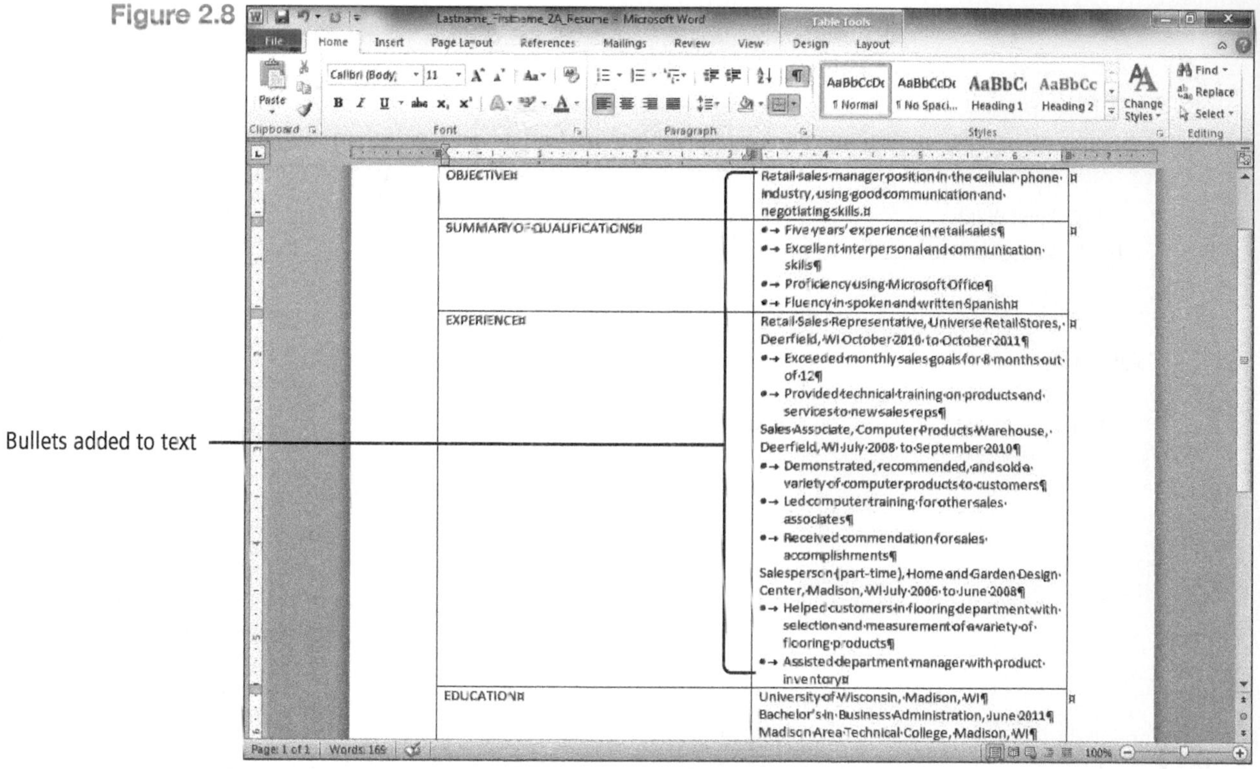

8 **Save** your document.

Objective 3 | Format a Table

Use Word's formatting tools to make your tables attractive and easy to read. Types of formatting you can add to a table include changing the row height and the column width, removing or adding borders, increasing or decreasing the paragraph or line spacing, or enhancing the text.

Activity 2.05 | Changing the Width of Table Columns

When you create a table, all of the columns are of equal width. In this activity, you will change the width of the columns.

1 In any row, point to the vertical border between the two columns to display the pointer.

2 Drag the column border to the left to approximately **1.25 inches on the horizontal ruler.**

3 Scroll to the top of the document. Notice that in the second row, the text *SUMMARY OF QUALIFICATIONS* wraps to two lines to accommodate the new column width.

4 If necessary, in the left column, click in any cell. On the Ribbon, under **Table Tools**, click the **Layout tab**.

5 In the **Cell Size group**, click the **Table Column Width button spin arrows** as necessary to change the width of the first column to **1.4"**. Compare your screen with Figure 2.9.

After dragging a border with your mouse, use the Width button to set a precise measurement if necessary.

Figure 2.9

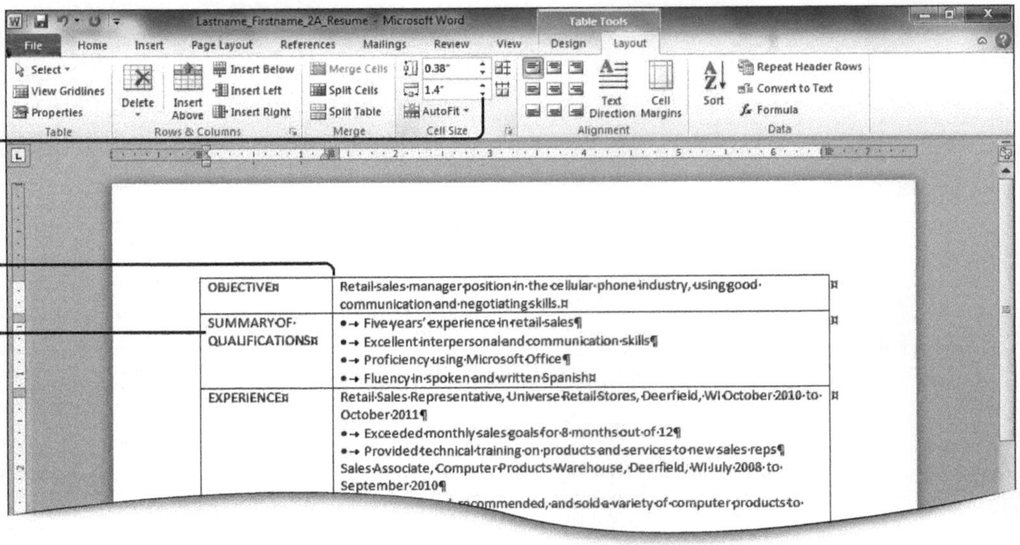

6 **Save** your document.

> **More Knowledge | Changing Column Widths**
>
> You will typically get the best results if you change the column widths starting at the left side of the table, especially in tables with three or more columns. Word can also calculate the best column widths for you. To do this, select the table. Then, on the Layout tab, in the Cell Size group, click the AutoFit button and click AutoFit Contents.

Activity 2.06 | Adding Rows to a Table

You can add rows or columns anywhere in a table.

1 Scroll to view the lower portion of the table. In the last row of the table, click anywhere in the *second* cell that contains the educational information, and then press Tab.

A new row displays at the bottom of the table. When the insertion point is in the last cell in the bottom row of a table, you can add a row by pressing the Tab key; the insertion point will display in the first cell of the new row.

2 Type **HONORS AND ACTIVITIES** and then press Tab.

3 Type the following, pressing Enter after the first item but not the second item:

Elected to Beta Gamma Sigma, international honor society for business students

Qualified for Dean's List, six academic periods

4 Select the text you typed in the last cell of the bottom row. On the **Home tab**, in the **Paragraph group**, click the **Bullets** button, and then click the **Decrease Indent** button one time to align the bullets at the left edge of the cell.

5 Scroll up to view the entire table, click anywhere in the table to deselect the text, and then compare your screen with Figure 2.10.

Figure 2.10

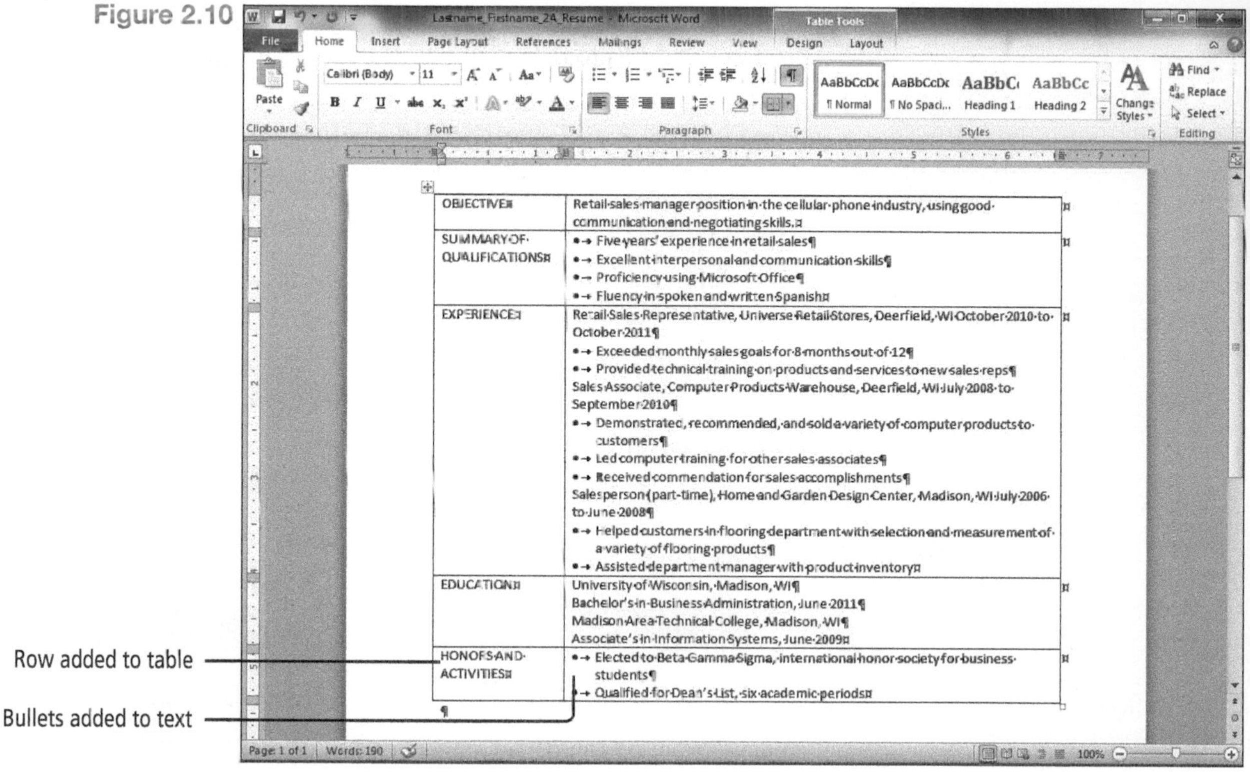

> **Another Way**
> Right-click in the top row, point to Insert, and then click Insert Rows Above.

6 Click anywhere in the top row of the table.

7 On the **Layout tab**, in the **Rows & Columns group**, click the **Insert Above** button. Compare your screen with Figure 2.11.

A new row displays above the row that contained the insertion point, and the new row is selected.

Figure 2.11

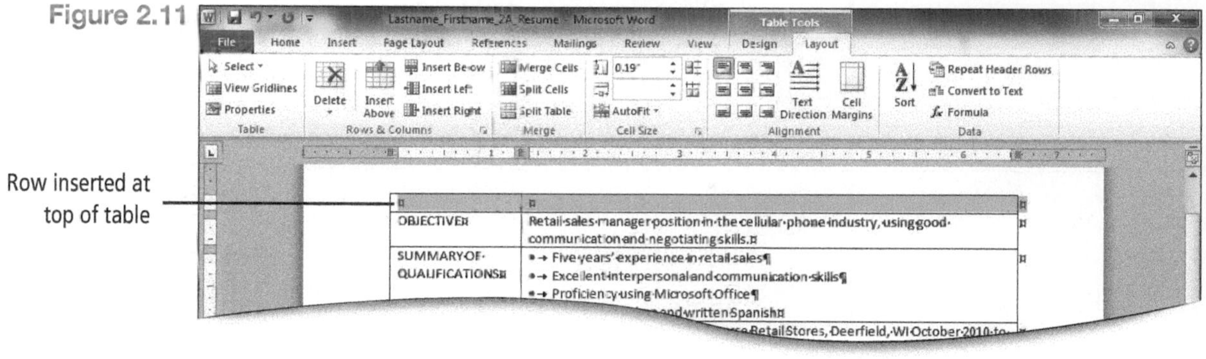

8 **Save** your document.

Activity 2.07 | Merging Cells

The title of a table typically spans all of the columns. In this activity, you will merge cells so that you can position the personal information across both columns.

1 Be sure the two cells in the top row are selected; if necessary, drag across both cells to select them.

> **Another Way**
>
> Right-click the selected row and click Merge Cells on the shortcut menu.

2 On the **Layout tab**, in the **Merge group**, click the **Merge Cells** button.

The cell border between the two cells no longer displays.

3 With the merged cell still selected, on the **Home tab**, in the **Paragraph group**, click the **Dialog Box Launcher** to display the **Paragraph** dialog box.

4 In the **Paragraph** dialog box, on the **Indents and Spacing tab**, in the lower left corner, click the **Tabs** button to display the **Tabs** dialog box.

5 In the **Tabs** dialog box, under **Tab stop position**, type **6.5** and then under **Alignment**, click the **Right** option button. Click **Set**, and then click **OK** to close the dialog box.

6 Type **Daniela Johnstone** Hold down Ctrl and then press Tab. Notice that the insertion point moves to the right-aligned tab stop at 6.5".

In a Word table, you must use Ctrl + Tab to move to a tab stop, because pressing Tab is reserved for moving the insertion point from cell to cell.

7 Type **(608) 555-0588** and then press Enter.

8 Type **1343 Siena Lane, Deerfield, WI 53531** Hold down Ctrl and then press Tab.

9 Type **djohnstone@alcona.net** and then compare your screen with Figure 2.12.

Figure 2.12

Right tab stop added to ruler

Cells merged in top row

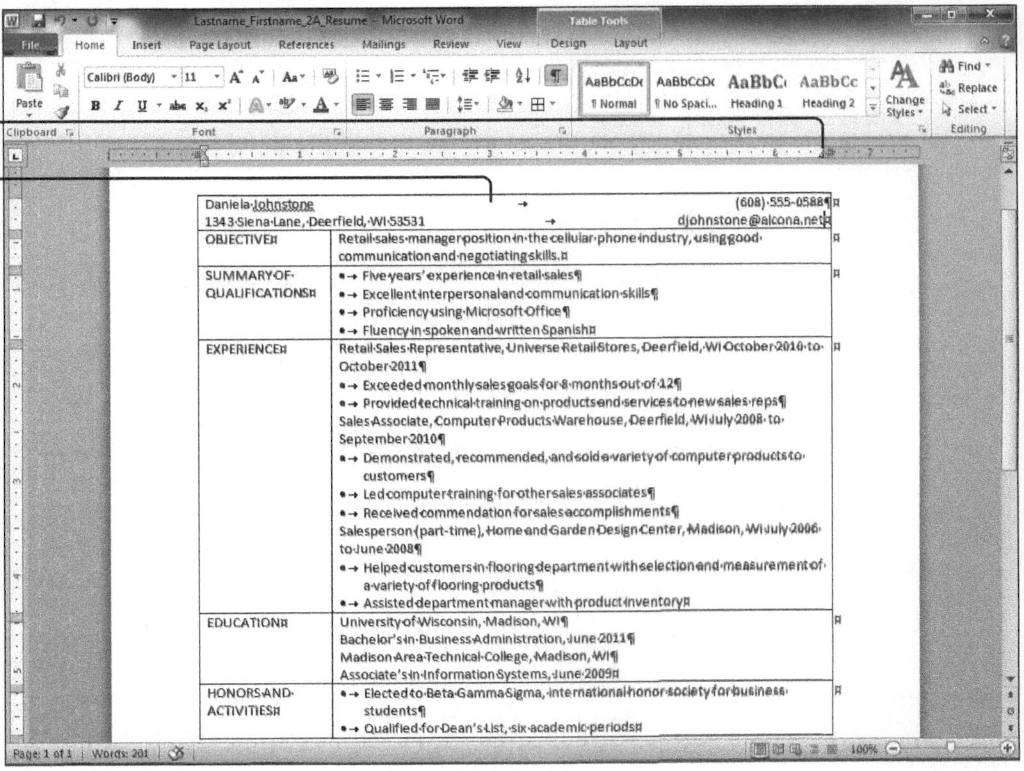

10 **Save** your document.

Activity 2.08 | Formatting Text in Cells

1 In the first row of the table, select the name *Daniela Johnstone*, and then on the Mini toolbar, apply **Bold** and change the **Font Size** to **16**.

2 Under *Daniela Johnstone*, click anywhere in the second line of text, which contains the address and e-mail address.

3 On the **Page Layout tab**, in the **Paragraph group**, click the **Spacing After up spin arrow** three times to add **18 pt** spacing between the first row of the table and the second row. Compare your screen with Figure 2.13.

These actions separate the personal information from the body of the resume and adds focus to the applicant's name.

Figure 2.13

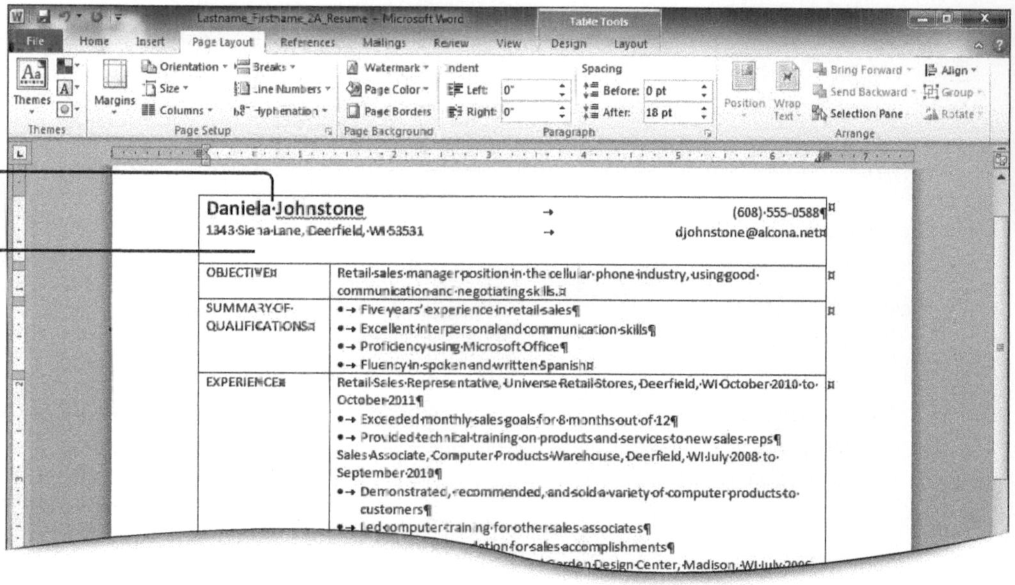

4 Using the technique you just practiced, in the second column, click in the last paragraph of every cell and add **18 pt Spacing After** the last paragraph of all rows including the last row; a border will be added to the bottom of the table, and spacing will be needed between the last row and the border.

5 In the second row, point to the word *OBJECTIVE*, hold down the left mouse button, and then drag downward in the first column only to select all the headings in uppercase letters. On the Mini toolbar, click the **Bold** button **B**.

> **Note | Selecting Only One Column**
>
> When you drag downward to select the first column, a fast mouse might also begin to select the second column when you reach the bottom. If this happens, drag upward slightly to deselect the second column and select only the first column.

6 In the cell to the right of *EXPERIENCE*, without selecting the following comma, select *Retail Sales Representative* and then on the Mini toolbar, click the **Bold** button **B**.

7 In the same cell, apply **Bold** **B** to the other job titles—*Sales Associate* and *Salesperson*—but do not bold *(part time)*.

8 In the cell to the right of *EDUCATION*, apply **Bold** **B** to *University of Wisconsin, Madison, WI* and *Madison Area Technical College, Madison, WI*.

9 In the same cell, click anywhere in the line beginning *Bachelor's*. On the **Page Layout tab**, in the **Paragraph group**, click the **Spacing After up spin arrow** two times to add **12 pt** spacing after the paragraph.

10 In the cell to the right of *EXPERIENCE*, under *Retail Sales Representative*, click anywhere in the second bulleted item, and then add **12 pt Spacing After** the item.

11 In the same cell, repeat this process for the last bulleted item under *Sales Associate.*

12 Scroll to the top of the screen, and then compare your screen with Figure 2.14.

Figure 2.14

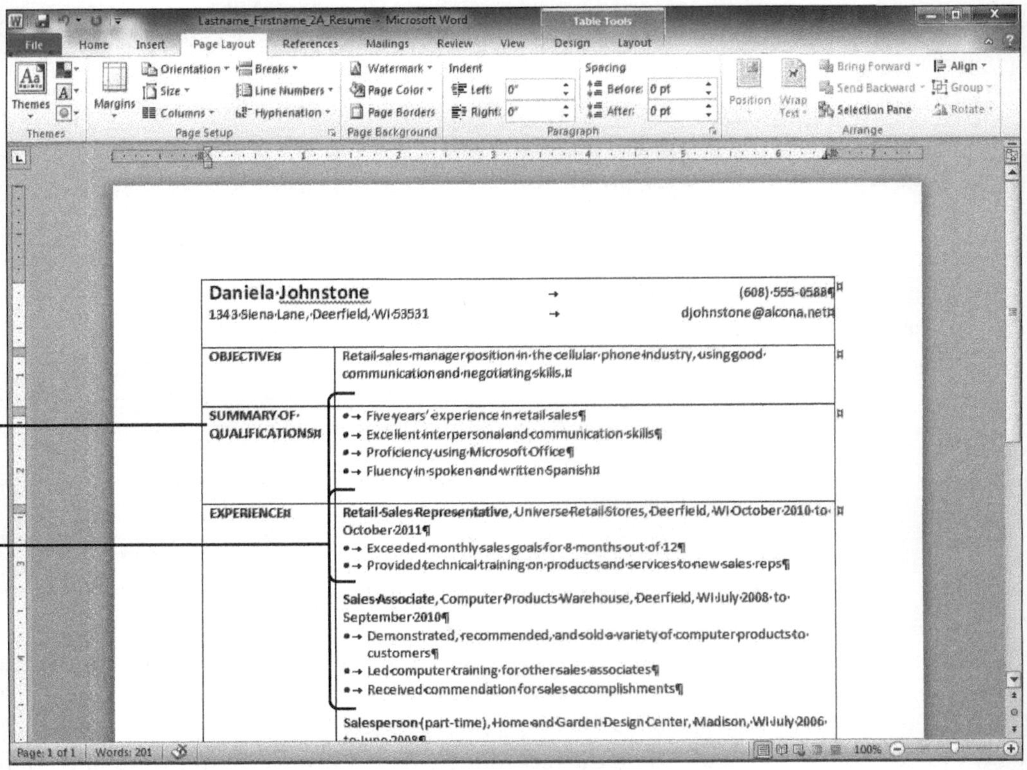

Bold emphasis added to first column

Space added after paragraphs in second column

13 **Save** your document.

Activity 2.09 | Changing the Table Borders

When you create a table, all of the cells have black borders. Most resumes do not display any cell borders. A border at the top and bottom of the resume, however, is attractive and adds a professional look to the document.

1 If necessary, press Ctrl + Home to move the insertion point to the top of the table, and then point slightly outside of the upper left corner of the table to display the **table move handle**.

2 With the pointer, click one time to select the entire table, and notice that the row markers at the end of each row are also selected.

Shaded row markers indicate that the entire row is selected.

3 Click the **Design tab**. In the **Table Styles group**, click the **Borders button arrow**, and then click **No Border**.

The black borders no longer display; instead, depending on your setup, either no borders—the default setting—or nonprinting blue dashed borders display.

4 Click the **File tab** to display **Backstage** view, and then click the **Print tab** to preview the table. Notice that no borders display in the preview, as shown in Figure 2.15.

Figure 2.15

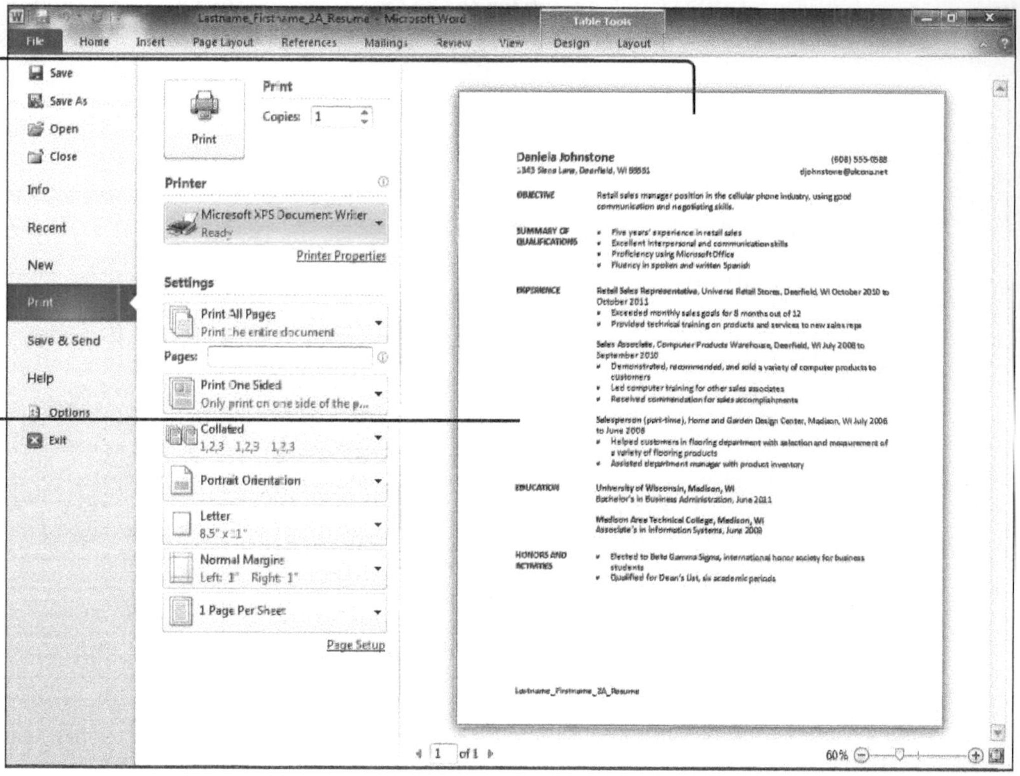

> **Another Way**
>
> Right-click the selected table, click Borders and Shading, and then click the Borders tab.

5 Click the **Design tab**; be sure the table is still selected. In the **Table Styles group**, click the **Borders button arrow**, and then at the bottom of the **Borders** gallery, click **Borders and Shading**.

6 Under **Setting**, click the **Custom** button. Under **Style**, scroll down about a third of the way and click the style with the thick upper line and the thin lower line.

> **Another Way**
>
> Click the top border button, which is one of the buttons that surround the Preview.

7 In the **Preview** box at the right, point to the *top* border of the small preview and click one time.

8 Under **Style**, click the style with the thin upper line and the thick lower line, and then in the **Preview** box, click the *bottom* border of the preview. Compare your screen with Figure 2.16.

Figure 2.16

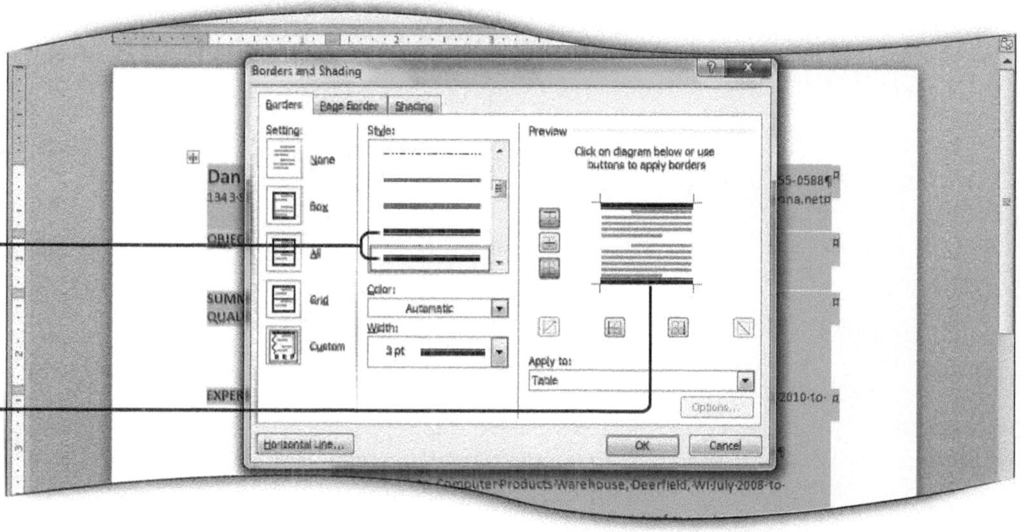

9 Click **OK**, click anywhere to cancel the selection, and then notice that there is only a small amount of space between the upper border and the first line of text.

10 Click anywhere in the text *Daniela Johnstone*, and then on the **Page Layout tab**, in the **Paragraph group**, click the **Spacing Before up spin arrow** as necessary to add **18 pt** spacing before the first paragraph.

11 Display **Backstage** view. Click the **Print tab** to preview the table. Compare your screen with Figure 2.17.

Figure 2.17

Top border

Spacing added above first paragraph

Bottom border

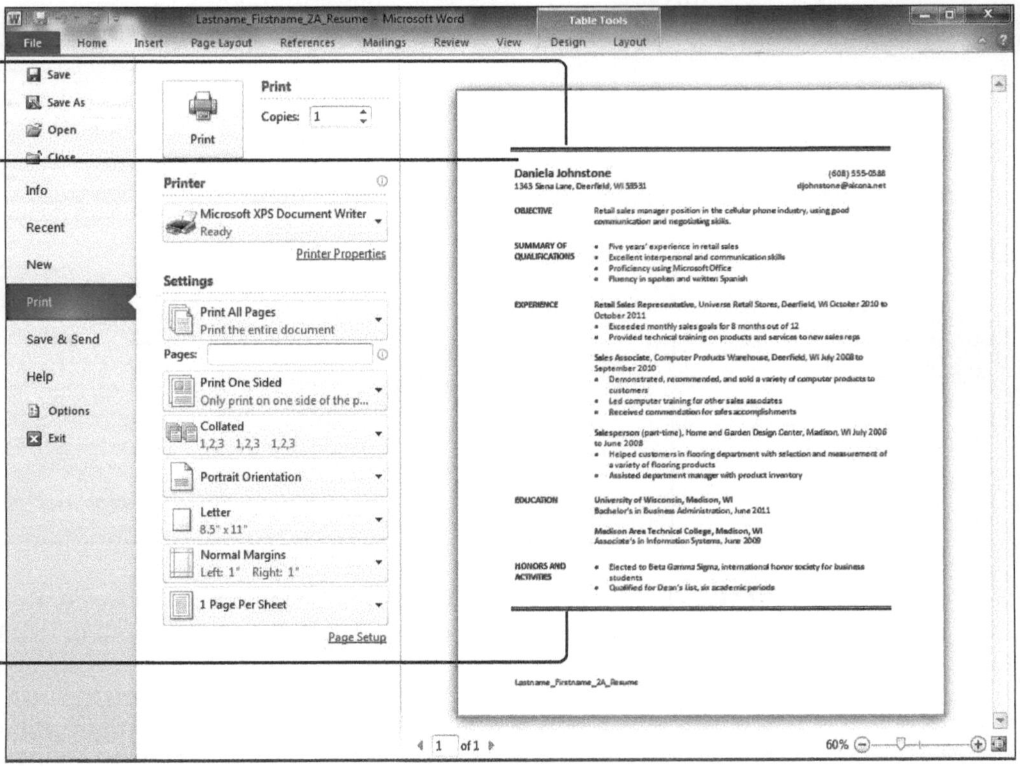

12 In **Backstage** view, click the **Info tab**. On the right, under the document thumbnail, click **Properties**, and then click **Show Document Panel**. In the **Author** box, delete any text and then type your firstname and lastname. In the **Subject** box, type your course name and section number, and in the **Keywords** box type **resume, Word table**

13 **Close** [×] the **Document Panel**. **Save** [save icon] and then print your document, or submit it electronically, as directed by your instructor. **Exit** Word.

End **You have completed Project 2A**

Project 2B Cover Letter and Resume

myitlab
Project 2B Training

Project Activities

In Activities 2.10 through 2.22, you will create a letterhead, and then use the letterhead to create a cover letter. You will also create a short resume using a Microsoft template and save it as a Web page. Your completed documents will look similar to Figure 2.18.

Project Files

For Project 2B, you will need the following file:

w02B_Cover_Letter_Text

You will save your documents as:

Lastname_Firstname_2B_Letterhead
Lastname_Firstname_2B_Cover_Letter
Lastname_Firstname_2B_Brief_Resume
Lastname_Firstname_2B_HTML_Resume

Project Results

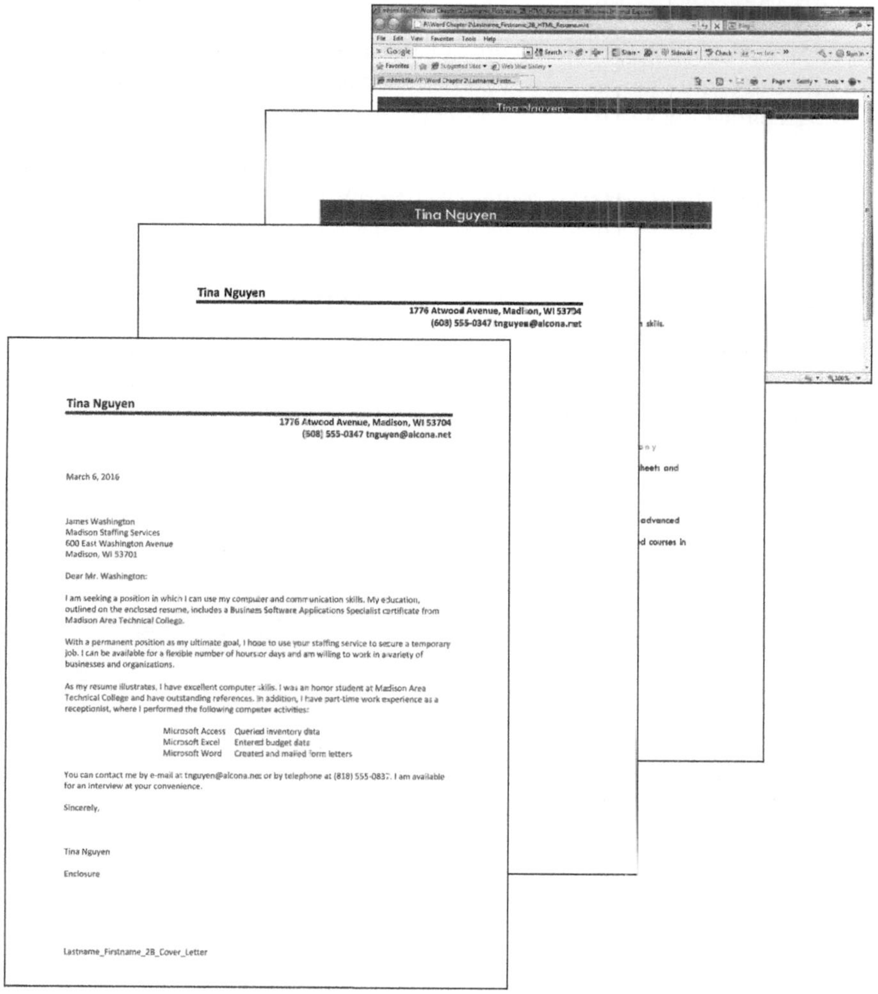

Figure 2.18
Project 2B Cover Letter and Resume

Objective 4 | Create a New Document from an Existing Document

A ***template*** is an *existing* document that you use as a starting point for a *new* document. The template document opens a copy of itself, unnamed, and then you use the structure—and possibly some content, such as headings—as the starting point for a new document.

All documents are based on a template. When you create a new blank document, it is based on Word's ***Normal template***, which serves as the starting point for all new Word documents.

Activity 2.10 | Creating a Letterhead

A ***letterhead*** is the personal or company information that displays at the top of a letter, and which commonly includes a name, address, and contact information. The term also refers to a piece of paper imprinted with such information at the top.

1. **Start** Word, and in the new blank document, be sure that formatting marks and rulers display.

2. On the **Home tab**, in the **Styles group**, click the **More** button. In the displayed gallery, click the **No Spacing** button.

   Recall that the default spacing for a new Word document is 10 points of blank space following a paragraph and line spacing of 1.15. The ***No Spacing style*** inserts *no* extra space following a paragraph and uses single spacing.

   By using the No Spacing style, you will be able to follow the prescribed format of a letter, which Business Communications texts commonly describe in terms of single spacing.

3. Type **Tina Nguyen** and then press Enter.

4. Type **1776 Atwood Avenue, Madison, WI 53704** and then press Enter.

5. Type **(608) 555-0347 tnguyen@alcona.net** and then press Enter. If the e-mail address changes to blue text, right-click the e-mail address, and then from the shortcut menu, click **Remove Hyperlink**. Compare your screen with Figure 2.19.

Figure 2.19

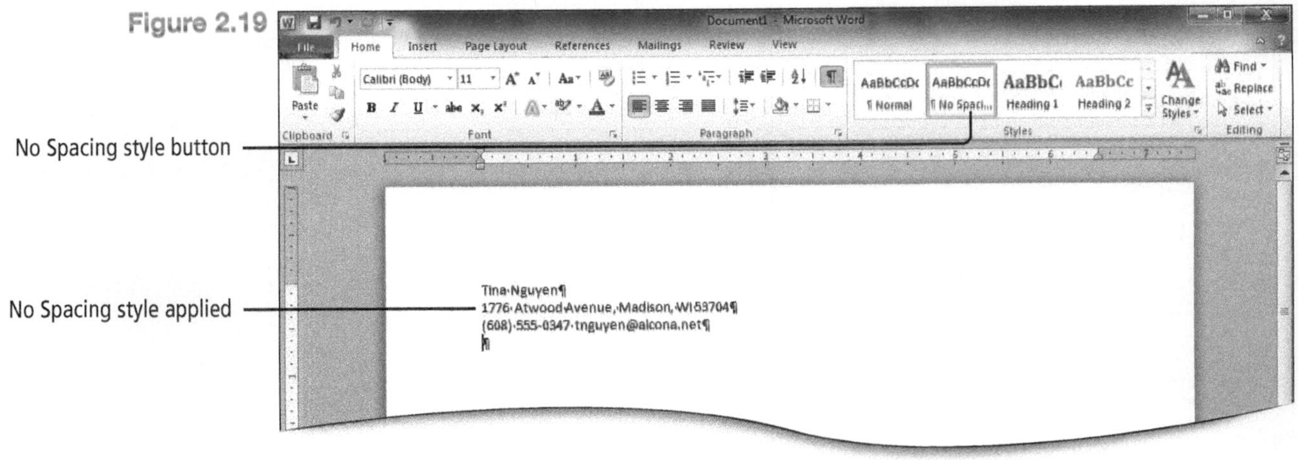

6. Select the first paragraph—*Tina Nguyen*—and then on the Mini toolbar, apply **Bold** and change the **Font Size** to **16**.

7 Select the second and third paragraphs. On the Mini toolbar, apply **Bold** [B] and change the **Font Size** to **12**.

> **Another Way**
> Press Ctrl + R to align text to the right.

8 With the two paragraphs still selected, on the **Home tab**, in the **Paragraph group**, click the **Align Text Right** button.

9 Click anywhere in the first paragraph—*Tina Nguyen*. In the **Paragraph group**, click the **Borders button arrow**, and then at the bottom, click **Borders and Shading**.

10 In the **Borders and Shading** dialog box, under **Style**, be sure the first style—a single solid line—is selected.

> **Another Way**
> Alternatively, click the bottom border button.

11 Click the **Width arrow**, and then click **3 pt**. To the right, under **Preview**, click the bottom border of the diagram. Under **Apply to**, be sure *Paragraph* displays. Compare your screen with Figure 2.20.

Figure 2.20

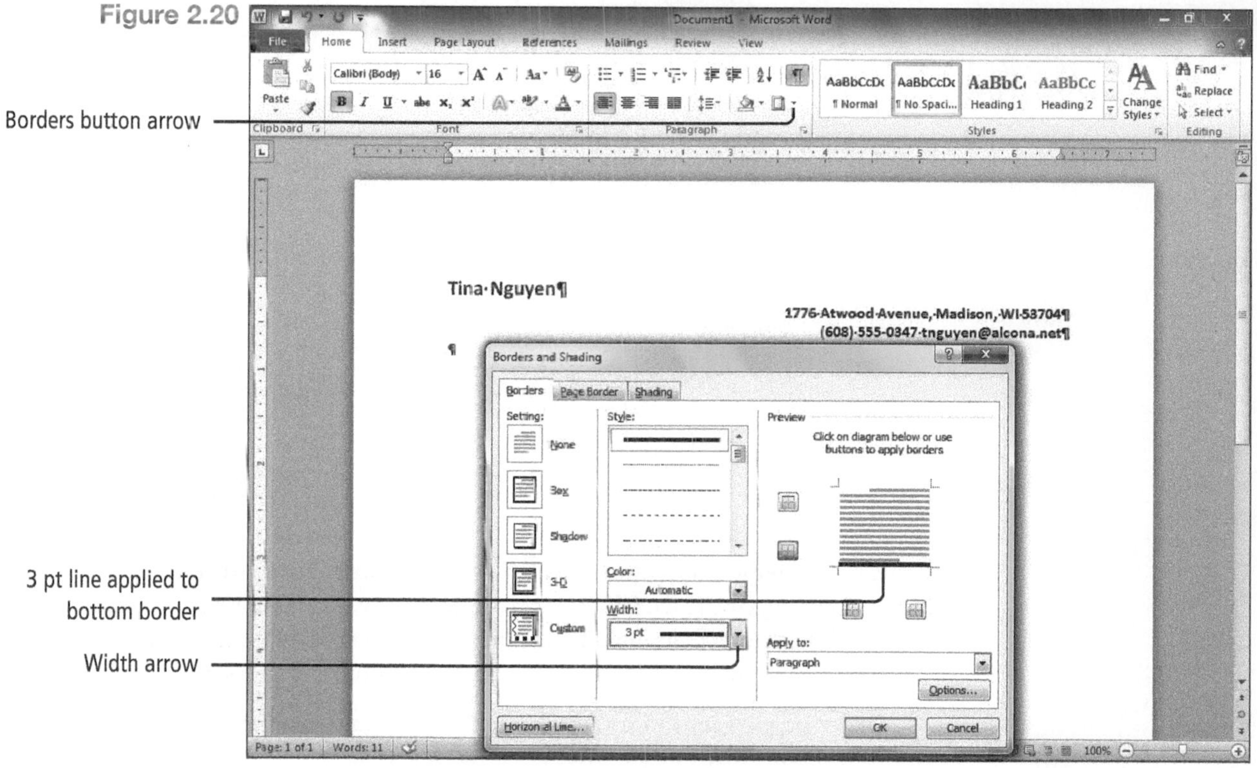

12 Click **OK** to display a 3 pt line below *Tina Nguyen*, which extends from the left margin to the right margin.

13 Display **Save As** dialog box, **Save** the document in your **Word Chapter 2** folder as **Lastname_Firstname_2B_Letterhead** and then add the file name to the footer.

14 Display **Backstage** view, click the **Info tab**, and then on the right, under the document thumbnail, click **Properties**. Click **Show Document Panel**. In the **Author** box, delete any text and then type your firstname and lastname. In the **Subject** box, type your course name and section number, and in the **Keywords** box type **personal letterhead**

15 **Close** [×] the **Document Panel**.

16 **Save** your document. Display **Backstage** view, and then click **Close** to close the document but leave Word open. Hold this file until you complete this project.

Activity 2.11 | Creating a Document from an Existing Document

To use an existing document as the starting point for a new document, Word provides the *New from existing* command.

1 Click the **File tab** to display **Backstage** view, and then click **New** to display the new document options. Compare your screen with Figure 2.21.

Here you can create a new document in a variety of ways, including from an existing document.

Figure 2.21

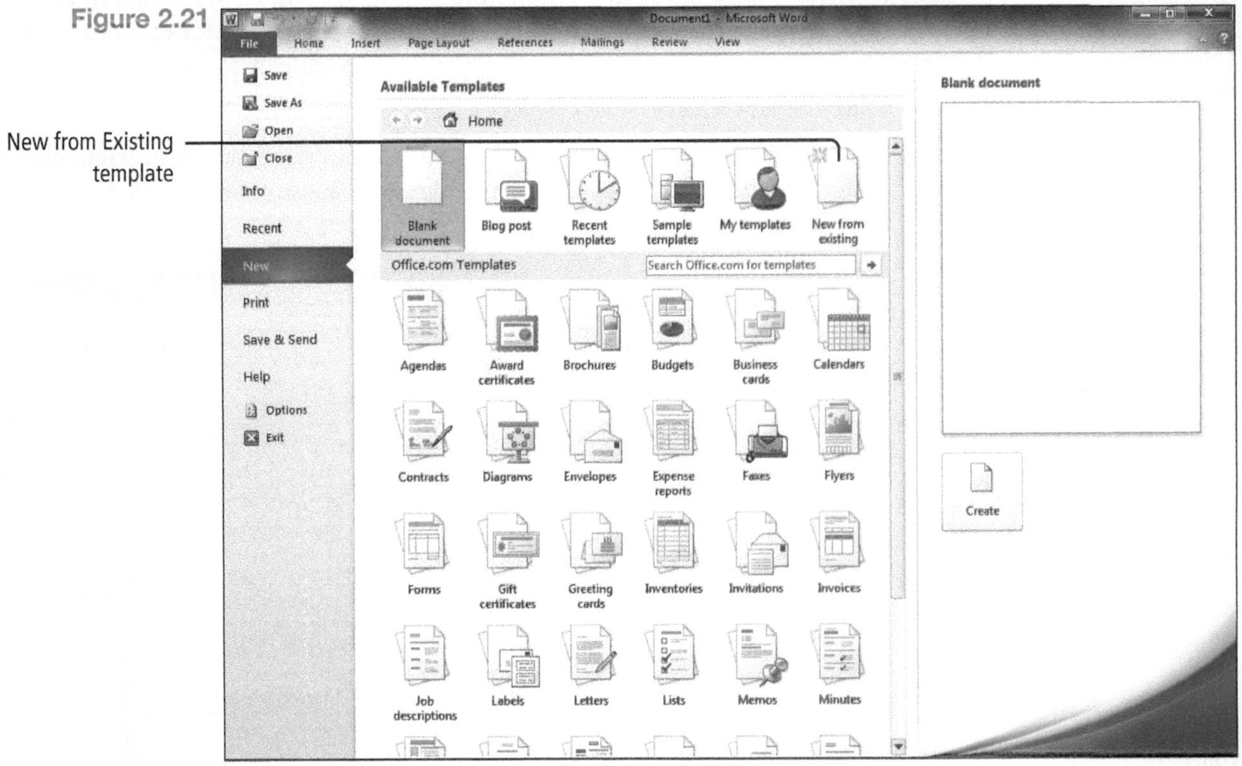

2 Under **Available Templates**, click the **New from existing** button. In the displayed **New from Existing Document** dialog box, if necessary, navigate to your **Word Chapter 2** folder, click your **Lastname_Firstname_2B_Letterhead** document to select it, and then in the lower right corner, click **Create New**. Compare your screen with Figure 2.22.

Word opens a copy of your 2B_Letterhead document in the form of a new Word document—the title bar indicates *Document* followed by a number. You are not opening the original document, and changes that you make to this new document will not affect the contents of your 2B_Letterhead document.

Figure 2.22

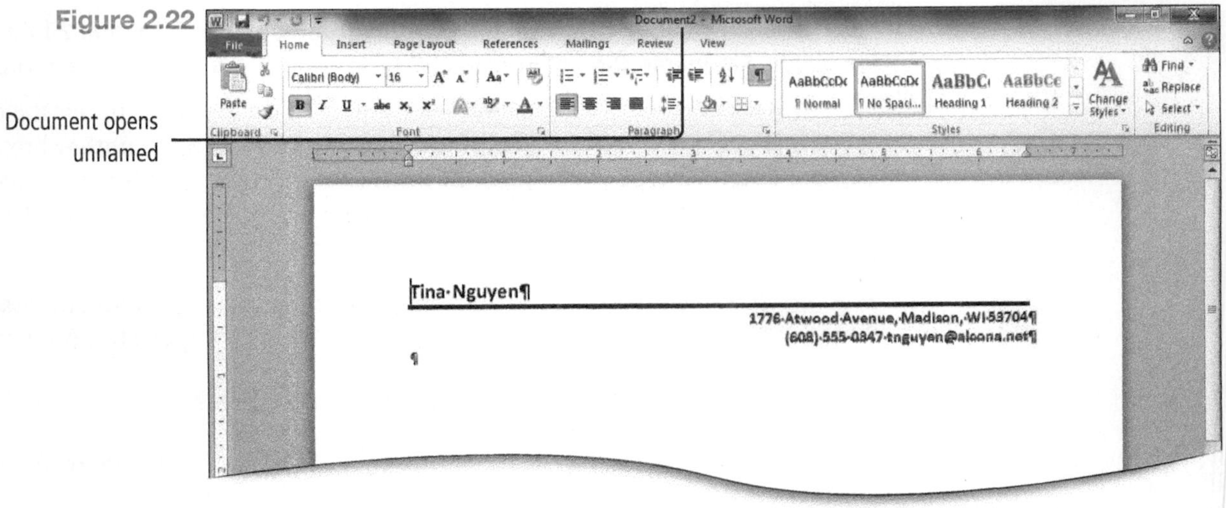

3 Display the **Save As** dialog box, and then navigate to your **Word Chapter 2** folder. **Save** the file as **Lastname_Firstname_2B_Cover_Letter**

The personal information that you typed in the 2B_Letterhead Document Panel remains in the new document.

4 Scroll down to view the footer area, and notice that a footer displays.

The footer displays because it was included in the document that you saved as a template. The *FileName* field does not automatically update to the new file name.

5 Point to the footer and right-click, and then click **Edit Footer**. Point to the highlighted footer text, right-click, and then from the shortcut menu, click **Update Field**. At the far right end of the Ribbon, click the **Close Header and Footer** button.

6 **Save** your document.

> **More Knowledge | Creating a Template File**
>
> You can also identify an original document so that your Windows operating system always knows that you want to create a new unnamed copy. To do so, save your document as a template file instead of a document. Word will then attach the dotx extension to the file, instead of the docx extension that is applied for a document, and will store the template file in a special location with other templates. Then, you can open the template from the New Document dialog box by clicking *My templates*.

Objective 5 | Change and Reorganize Text

Business letters follow a standard format and contain the following parts: the current date, referred to as the ***date line***; the name and address of the person receiving the letter, referred to as the ***inside address***; a greeting, referred to as the ***salutation***; the text of the letter, usually referred to as the ***body*** of the letter; a closing line, referred to as the ***complimentary closing***; and the ***writer's identification***, which includes the name or job title (or both) of the writer, and which is also referred to as the ***writer's signature block***.

Some letters also include the initials of the person who prepared the letter, an optional ***subject line*** that describes the purpose of the letter, or a list of ***enclosures***—documents included with the letter.

Activity 2.12 | Recording AutoCorrect Entries

You can correct commonly misspelled words automatically by using Word's ***AutoCorrect*** feature. Commonly misspelled words—such as *teh* instead of *the*—are corrected using a built-in list that is installed with Office. If you have words that you frequently misspell, you can add them to the list for automatic correction.

1 Click the **File tab** to display **Backstage** view. On the **Help tab**, click **Options** to display the **Word Options** dialog box.

2 On the left side of the **Word Options** dialog box, click **Proofing**, and then under **AutoCorrect options**, click the **AutoCorrect Options** button.

3 In the **AutoCorrect** dialog box, click the **AutoCorrect tab**. Under **Replace**, type **resumee** and under **With**, type **resume**

If another student has already added this AutoCorrect entry, a Replace button will display.

4 Click **Add**. If the entry already exists, click Replace instead, and then click Yes.

5 In the **AutoCorrect** dialog box, under **Replace**, type **computr** and under **With**, type **computer** and then compare your screen with Figure 2.23.

Figure 2.23

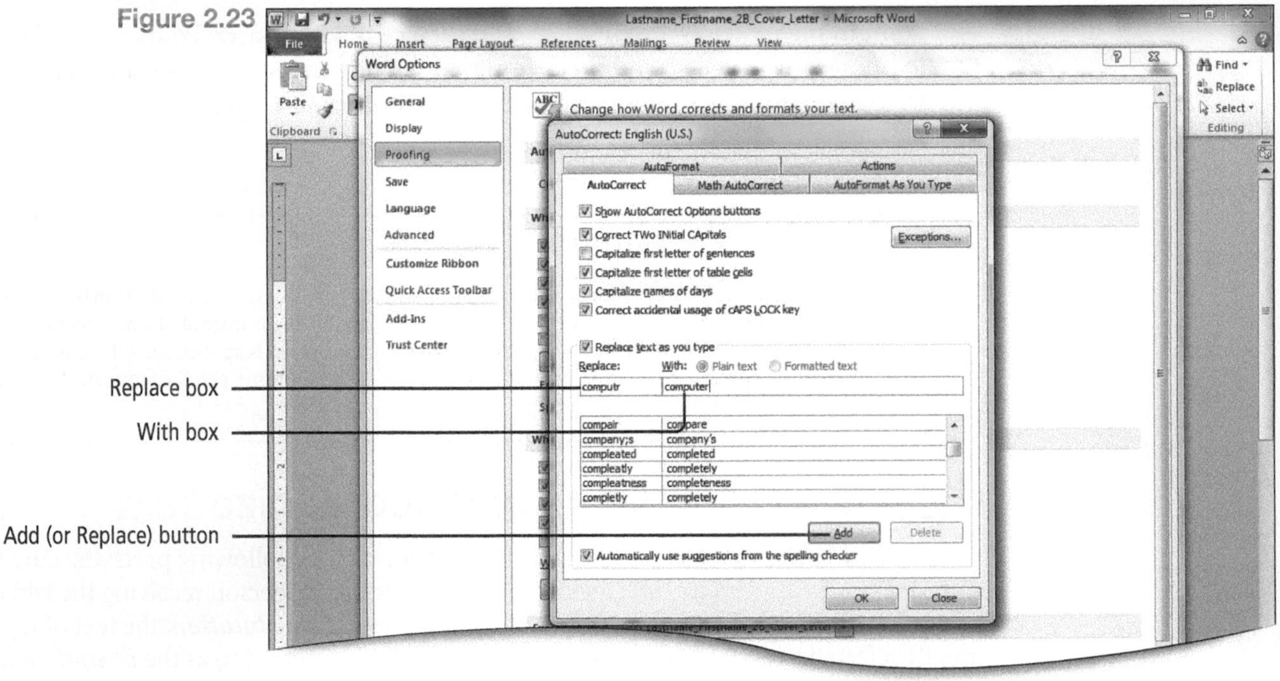

6 Click **Add** (or Replace) and then click **OK** two times to close the dialog boxes.

Activity 2.13 | Creating a Cover Letter

There are a variety of accepted letter formats that you will see in reference manuals and Business Communication texts. The one used in this chapter is a block style cover letter taken from *Business Communication Today*.

1 Press Ctrl + End to move the insertion point to the blank line below the letterhead. Press Enter three times, and then type **March 16, 2016** to create the dateline.

Most Business Communication texts recommend that the dateline be positioned at least 0.5 inch (3 blank lines) below the letterhead; or, position the dateline approximately 2 inches from the top edge of the paper.

2 Press Enter four times, which leaves three blank lines. Type the following inside address on four lines, but do not press Enter following the last line:

James Washington

Madison Staffing Services

600 East Washington Avenue

Madison, WI 53701

The recommended space between the dateline and inside address varies slightly among Business Communication texts and office reference manuals. However, all indicate that the space can be from one to 10 blank lines depending on the length of your letter.

3 Press Enter two times to leave one blank line. Compare your screen with Figure 2.24.

Figure 2.24

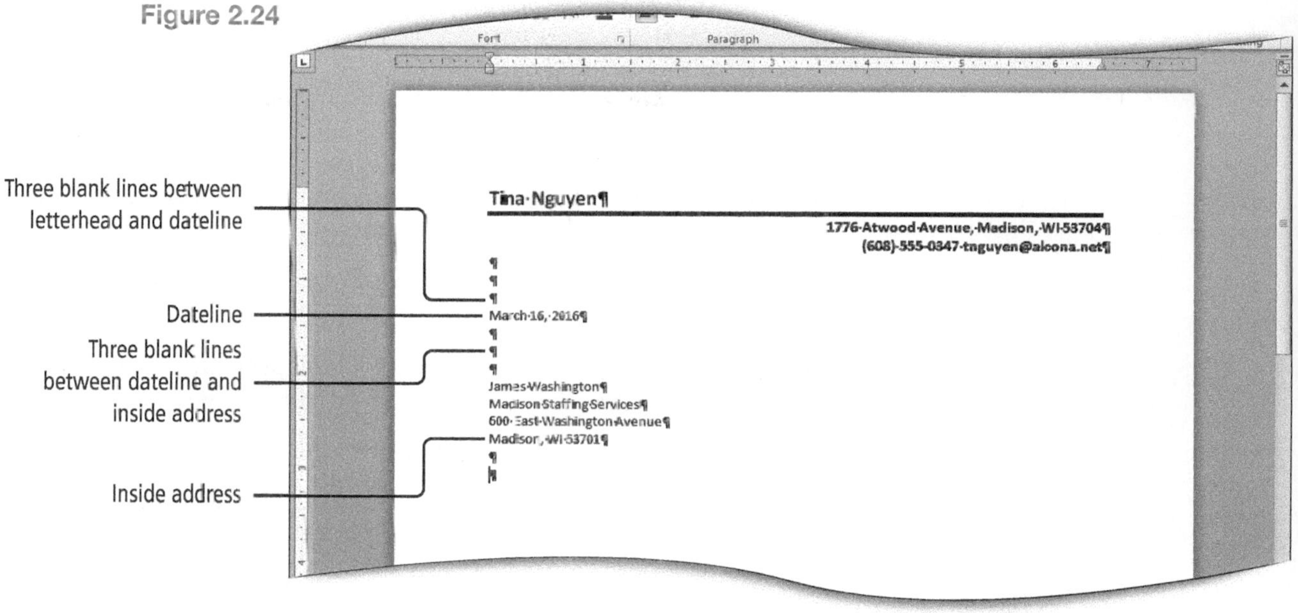

4 Type the salutation **Dear Mr. Washington:** and then press Enter two times.

Always leave one blank line above and below the salutation.

5 Type, exactly as shown, the following opening paragraph that includes an intentional word usage error: **I am seeking a position in witch I can use my** and press Spacebar. Type, exactly as shown, **computr** and then watch *computr* as you press Spacebar.

The AutoCorrect feature recognizes the misspelled word, and then changes *computr* to *computer* when you press Spacebar, Enter, or a punctuation mark.

6 Type the following, including the misspelled last word: **and communication skills. My education, outlined on the enclosed resumee** and then type **,** (a comma). Notice that when you type the comma, AutoCorrect replaces *resumee* with *resume.*

7 Press Spacebar. Complete the paragraph by typing **includes a Business Software Applications Specialist certificate from MATC.** Compare your screen with Figure 2.25.

Figure 2.25

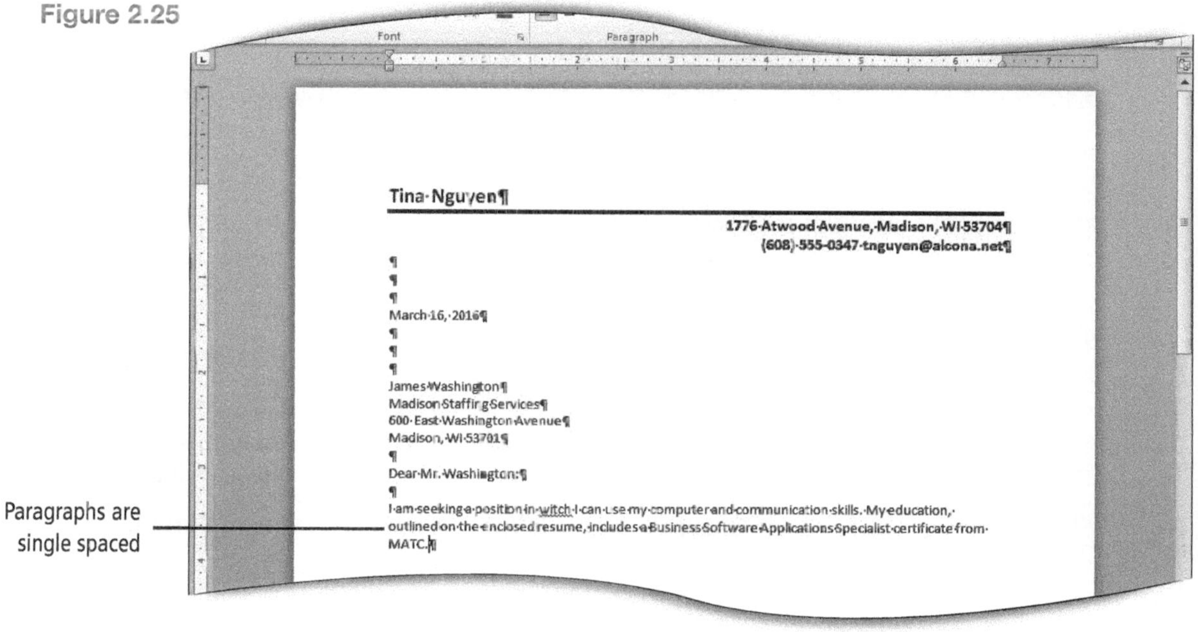

8 Press Enter two times. On the **Insert tab**, in the **Text group**, click the **Object button arrow**, and then click **Text from File**. From your student files, locate and **Insert** the file **w02B_Cover_Letter_Text**.

Some of the words in the cover letter text display red, green, or blue wavy underlines. These indicate potential spelling, grammar, or word usage errors, and you will correct them before the end of this project.

9 Scroll as necessary to display the lower half of the letter on your screen, and be sure your insertion point is positioned in the blank paragraph at the end of the document.

10 Press Enter one time to leave one blank line between the last paragraph of the letter and the complimentary closing.

11 Type **Sincerely,** as the complimentary closing, and then press Enter four times to leave three blank lines between the complimentary closing and the writer's identification.

12 Type **Tina Nguyen** as the writer's identification, and then press Enter two times.

13 Type **Enclosure** to indicate that a document is included with the letter. **Save** your document, and then compare your screen with Figure 2.26.

Figure 2.26

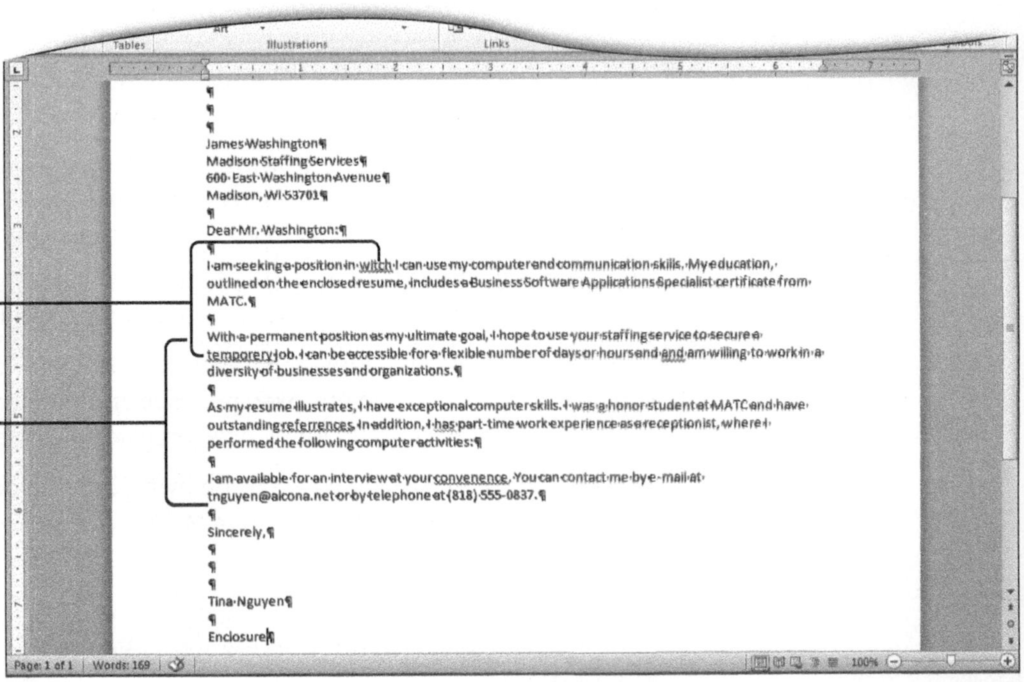

Activity 2.14 | Finding and Replacing Text

Use the Find command to locate text in a document quickly. Use the Find and Replace command to make the same change, or to make more than one change at a time, in a document.

1 Press Ctrl + Home to position the insertion point at the beginning of the document.

Because a find operation—or a find and replace operation—begins from the location of the insertion point and proceeds to the end of the document, it is good practice to position the insertion point at the beginning of the document before initiating the command.

Another Way

Hold down Ctrl and press F.

2 On the **Home tab**, in the **Editing group**, click the **Find** button.

The Navigation Pane displays on the left side of the screen, with a search box at the top of the pane.

3 In the search box, type **ac** If necessary, scroll down slightly in your document to view the entire body text of the letter, and then compare your screen with Figure 2.27.

In the document, the search letters *ac* are selected and highlighted in yellow for all three words that contain the letters *ac* together. In the Navigation Pane, the three instances are shown in context—*ac* displays in bold.

Figure 2.27

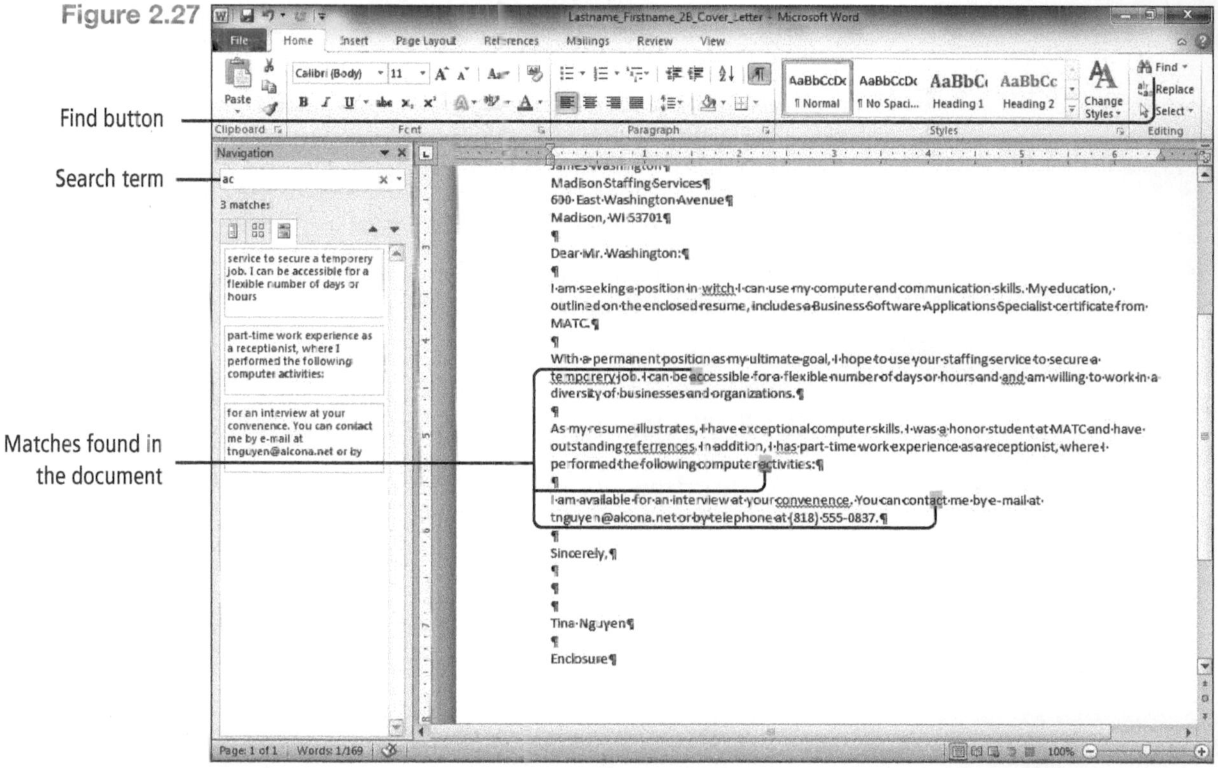

4 In the search box, complete the word **accessible**.

One match for the search term displays in context in the Navigation Pane and is highlighted in the document.

5 In the document, point to the yellow highlighted word *accessible*, double-click, and then type **available** to replace the word. Notice that the list of results is now empty.

6 **Close** the **Navigation Pane**, and then on the **Home tab**, in the **Editing group**, click the **Replace** button.

7 In the **Find and Replace** dialog box, in the **Find what** box, replace the existing text by typing **MATC** In the **Replace with** box, type **Madison Area Technical College** and then compare your screen with Figure 2.28

Figure 2.28

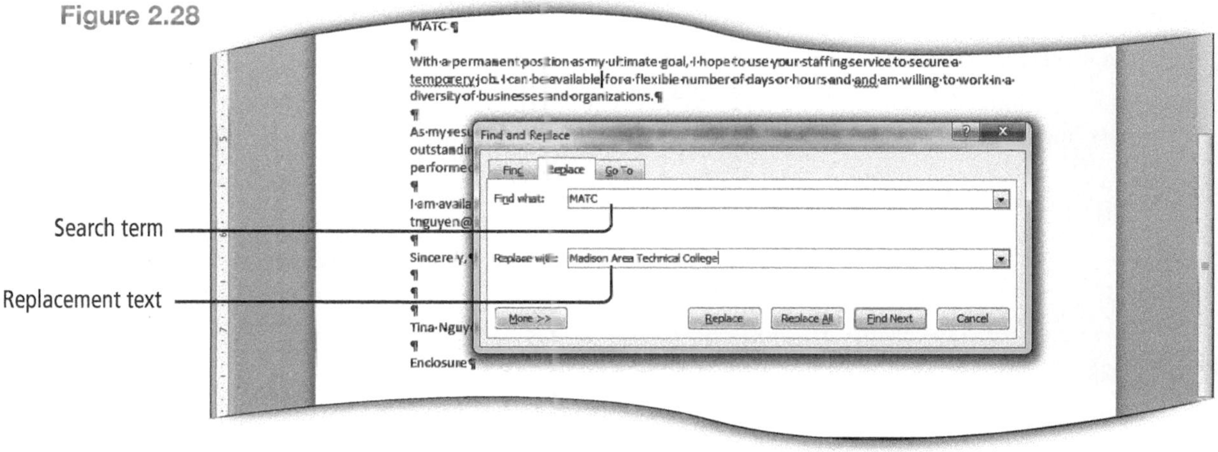

8 In the lower left corner of the dialog box, click the **More** button to expand the dialog box, and then under **Search Options**, select the **Match case** check box.

The acronym *MATC* appears in the document two times. In a formal letter, the reader may not know what the acronym means, so you should include the full text instead of an acronym. In this instance, you must select the *Match case* check box so that the replaced text will match the case you typed in the Replace with box, and *not* display in all uppercase letters in the manner of *MATC*.

9 In the **Find and Replace** dialog box, click the **Replace All** button to replace both instances of *MATC*. Click **OK** to close the message box.

10 In the **Find and Replace** dialog box, clear the **Match case** check box, click the **Less** button, and then **Close** the dialog box.

The Find and Replace dialog box opens with the settings used the last time it was open. Thus, it is good practice to reset this dialog box to its default settings each time you use it.

11 **Save** your document.

Activity 2.15 | Selecting and Moving Text to a New Location

By using Word's ***drag-and-drop*** feature, you can use the mouse to drag selected text from one location to another. Drag-and-drop is most effective when the text to be moved and the destination are on the same screen.

1 Take a moment to study the table in Figure 2.29 to become familiar with the techniques you can use to select text in a document quickly.

Selecting Text in a Document

To Select	Do This
A portion of text	Click to position the insertion point at the beginning of the text you want to select, hold down Shift, and then click at the end of the text you want to select. Alternatively, hold down the left mouse button and drag from the beginning to the end of the text you want to select.
A word	Double-click the word.
A sentence	Hold down Ctrl and click anywhere in the sentence.
A paragraph	Triple-click anywhere in the paragraph; or, move the pointer to the left of the line, into the margin area. When the pointer displays, double-click.
A line	Move the pointer to the left of the line. When the pointer displays, click one time.
One character at a time	Position the insertion point to the left of the first character, hold down Shift, and press ← or → as many times as desired.
A string of words	Position the insertion point to the left of the first word, hold down Shift and Ctrl, and then press ← or → as many times as desired.
Consecutive lines	Position the insertion point to the left of the first word, hold down Shift and press ↑ or ↓.
Consecutive paragraphs	Position the insertion point to the left of the first word, hold down Shift and Ctrl and press ↑ or ↓.
The entire document	Hold down Ctrl and press A. Alternatively, move the pointer to the left of any line in the document. When the pointer displays, triple-click.

Figure 2.29

2 Be sure you can view the entire body of the letter on your screen. In the paragraph that begins *With a permanent position*, in the second line, locate and double-click *days*.

3 Point to the selected word to display the [pointer icon] pointer.

4 Drag to the right until the dotted vertical line that floats next to the pointer is positioned to the right of the word *hours* in the same line, as shown in Figure 2.30.

Figure 2.30

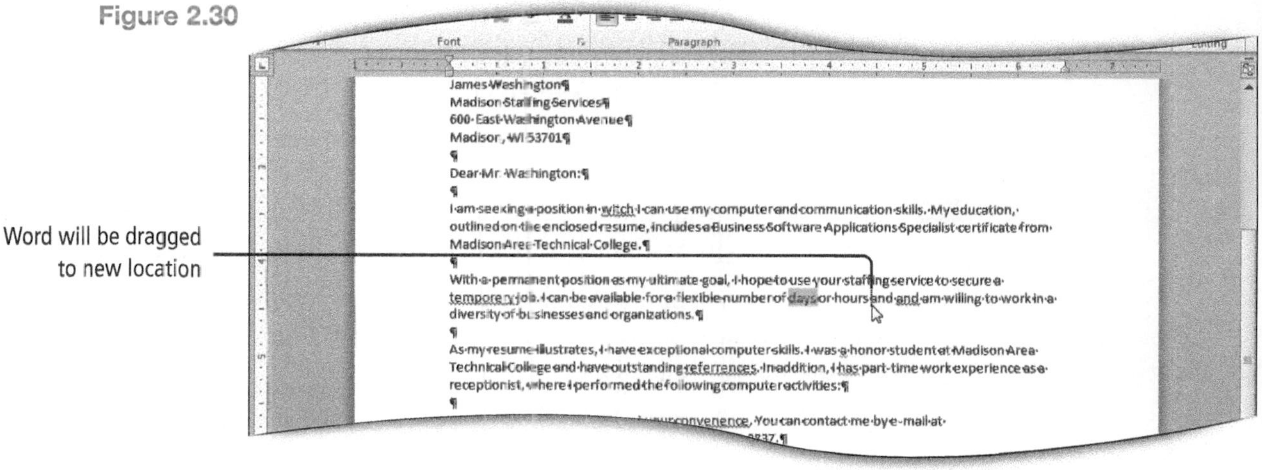

5 Release the mouse button to move the text. Select the word *hours* and drag it to the left of the word *or*—the previous location of the word *days*. Click anywhere in the document to deselect the text.

6 Examine the text that you moved, and add or remove spaces as necessary.

7 Hold down Ctrl, and then in the paragraph that begins *I am available*, click anywhere in the first sentence to select the entire sentence.

8 Drag the selected sentence to the end of the paragraph by positioning the small vertical line that floats with the pointer to the left of the paragraph mark. Compare your screen with Figure 2.31.

Figure 2.31

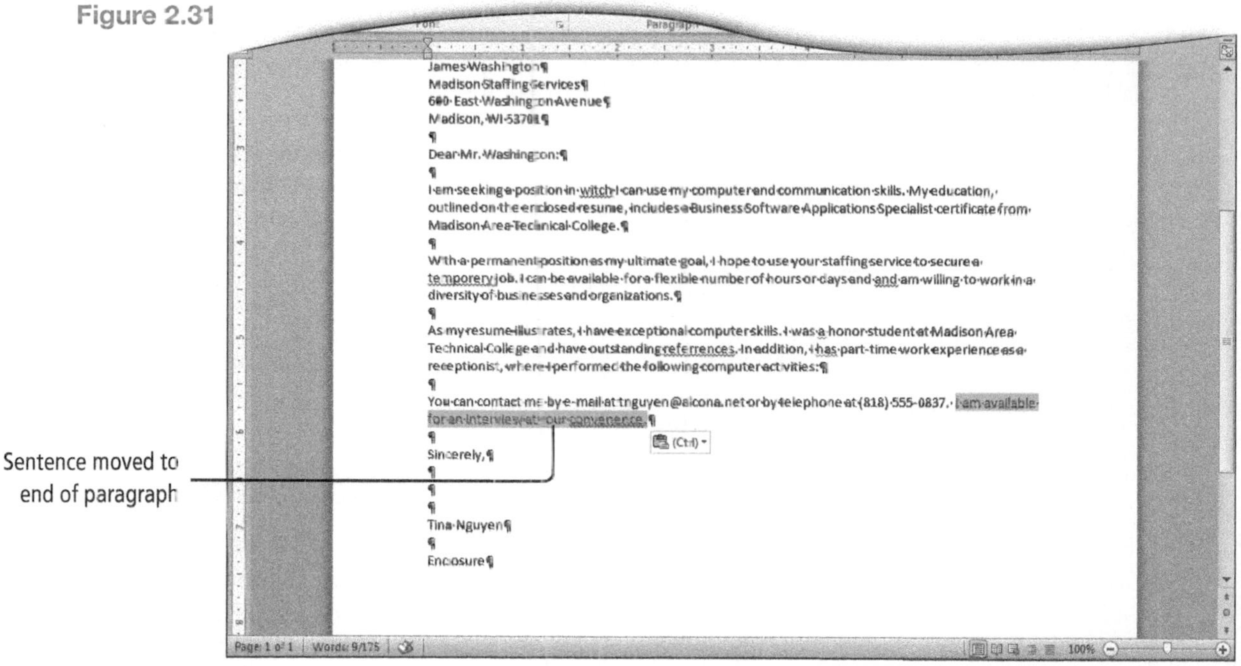

9 **Save** [Save icon] your document.

Activity 2.16 | Inserting and Formatting a Table in a Document

1 Locate the paragraph that begins *As my resume*, and then click to position the insertion point in the blank line below that paragraph. Press Enter one time.

2 On the **Insert tab**, in the **Tables group**, click the **Table** button. In the **Table** grid, in the third row, click the second square to insert a 2 × 3 table.

3 In the first cell of the table, type **Microsoft Access** and then press Tab. Type **Queried inventory data** and then press Tab. Complete the table using the following information:

Microsoft Excel	**Entered budget data**
Microsoft Word	**Created and mailed form letters**

4 Point slightly outside of the upper left corner of the table to display the **table move handle** button. With the pointer, click one time to select the entire table.

5 On the **Layout tab**, in the **Cell Size group**, click the **AutoFit** button, and then click **AutoFit Contents** to have Word choose the best column widths for the two columns based on the text you entered.

6 On the **Home tab**, in the **Paragraph group**, click the **Center** button to center the table between the left and right margins.

7 On the **Design tab**, in the **Table Styles group**, click the **Borders button arrow**, and then click **No Border**. Click anywhere to cancel the selection of the table, and then compare your screen with Figure 2.32.

A light dashed line may display in place of the original table borders if your default settings have been changed.

Figure 2.32

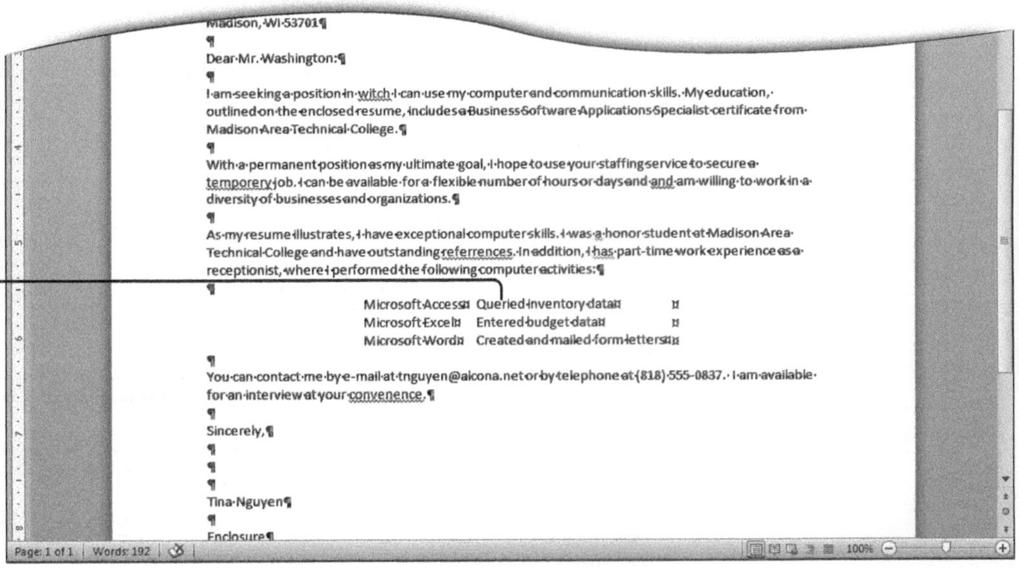

8 **Save** your document.

Objective 6 | Use the Proofing Options

Word compares your typing to words in the Office dictionary and compares your phrases and punctuation to a list of grammar rules. This automatic proofing is set by default. Words that are not in the dictionary are marked with a wavy red underline. Phrases and punctuation that differ from the grammar rules are marked with a wavy green underline.

Word also compares commonly misused words with a set of word usage rules, and marks misused words with a wavy blue underline; for example the misuse of *their*, *there*, and *they're*. However, Word will not flag the word *sign* as misspelled even though you intended to type *sing a song* rather than *sign a song*, because both are words contained within Word's dictionary. Your own knowledge and proofreading skills are still required, even when using a sophisticated Word processing program like Word.

Activity 2.17 | Checking Spelling and Grammar Errors

There are two ways to respond to spelling and grammar errors flagged by Word. You can right-click a flagged word or phrase, and then from the shortcut menu choose a correction or action. Or, you can initiate the Spelling and Grammar command to display the Spelling and Grammar dialog box, which provides more options than the shortcut menus.

> **Alert! | Spelling and Grammar Checking**
>
> If you do not see any wavy red, green, or blue lines under words, the automatic spelling and/or grammar checking has been turned off on your system. To activate the spelling and grammar checking, display Backstage view, on the Help tab, click Options, click Proofing, and then under *When correcting spelling in Microsoft Office programs*, select the first four check boxes. Under *When correcting spelling and grammar in Word*, select the first four check boxes, and then click the Writing Style arrow and click Grammar Only. Under *Exceptions for*, clear both check boxes. To display the flagged spelling and grammar errors, click the Recheck Document button, and then close the dialog box.

1 Position the body of the letter on your screen, and then examine the text to locate green, red, and blue wavy underlines. Compare your screen with Figure 2.33.

A list of grammar rules applied by a computer program like Word can never be exact, and a computer dictionary cannot contain all known words and proper names. Thus, you will need to check any words flagged by Word with wavy underlines, and you will also need to proofread for content errors.

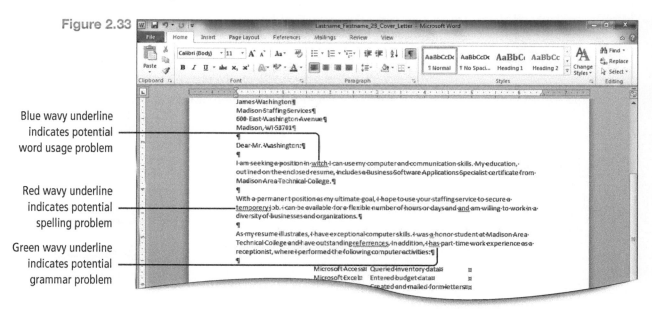

Figure 2.33

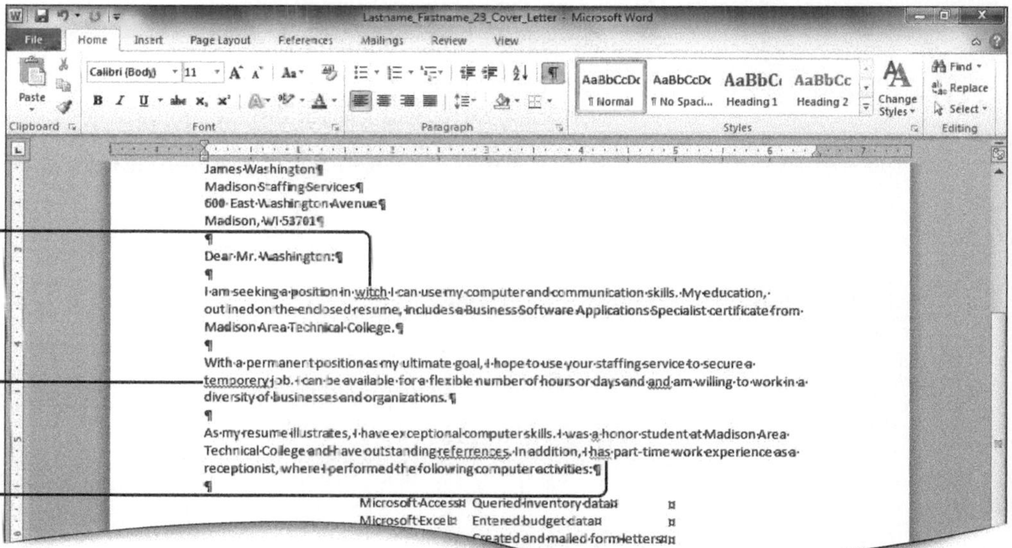

Blue wavy underline indicates potential word usage problem

Red wavy underline indicates potential spelling problem

Green wavy underline indicates potential grammar problem

2 In the lower left corner of your screen, in the status bar, locate and point to the icon to display the ScreenTip *Proofing errors were found. Click to correct.*

If this button displays, you know there are potential errors identified in the document.

3 In the paragraph that begins *With a permanent*, locate the word *temporery* with the wavy red underline. Point to the word and right-click to display the shortcut menu, and then compare your screen with Figure 2.34.

Figure 2.34

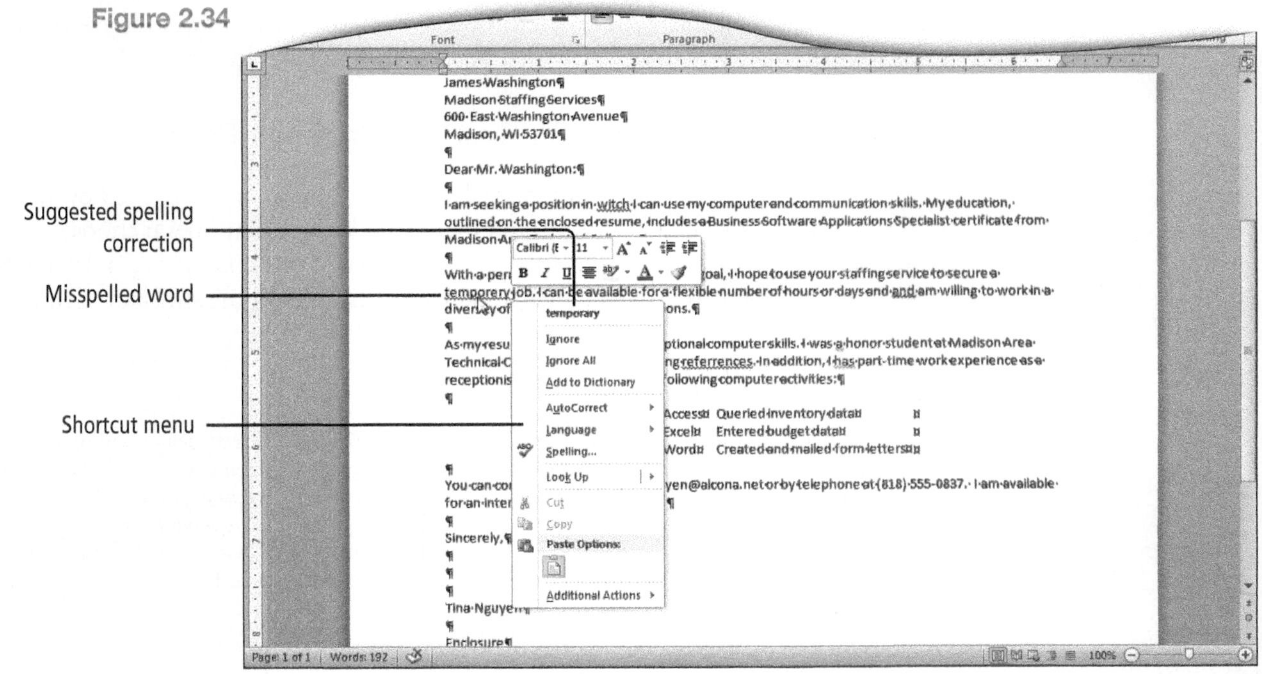

4 On the shortcut menu, click **temporary** to correct the spelling error.

5 In the next line, locate the word *and* that displays with a wavy red underline, point to word and right-click, and then from the shortcut menu, click **Delete Repeated Word** to delete the duplicate word.

> **Another Way**
>
> Press F7 to start the Spelling & Grammar command.

6 Press Ctrl + Home to move the insertion point to the beginning of the document. Click the **Review tab**, and then in the **Proofing group**, click the **Spelling & Grammar** button to check the spelling and grammar of the text in the document. Compare your screen with Figure 2.35.

The word *witch* is highlighted—a *Possible Word Choice Error*—and the sentence containing the potential error displays in the dialog box. A suggested change also displays.

Figure 2.35

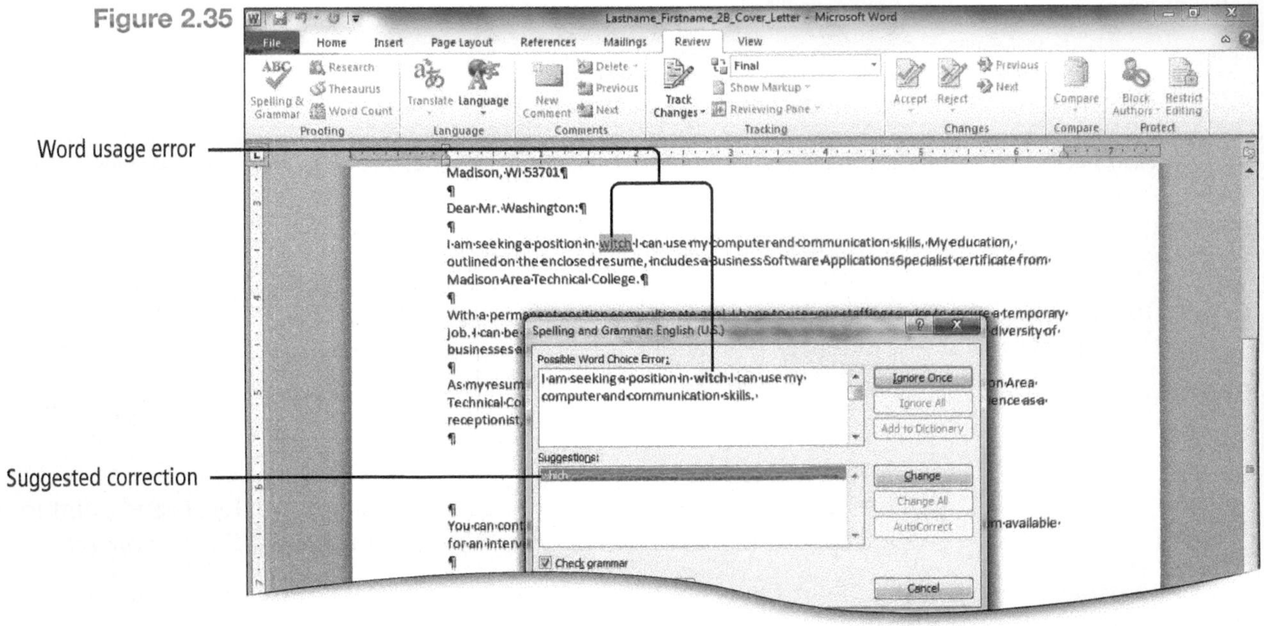

7 In the **Spelling and Grammar** dialog box, click the **Change** button to change to the correct usage *which*.

The next marked word—a possible spelling error—displays.

8 Click the **Change** button to change *referrences* to *references*. Notice that the next error is a possible grammar error.

9 Click the **Change** button to change *a* to *an*. Continue the spelling and grammar check and change *has* to *have* and correct the spelling of *convenence*.

10 When Word indicates *The spelling and grammar check is complete*, click **OK**.

11 **Save** your document.

Activity 2.18 | Using the Thesaurus

A ***thesaurus*** is a research tool that lists ***synonyms***—words that have the same or similar meaning to the word you selected.

1 Scroll so that you can view the body of the letter. In the paragraph that begins *With a permanent*, at the end of the second line, locate and right-click the word *diversity*.

2 On the shortcut menu, point to **Synonyms**, and then compare your screen with Figure 2.36.

A list of synonyms displays; the list will vary in length depending on the selected word.

Figure 2.36

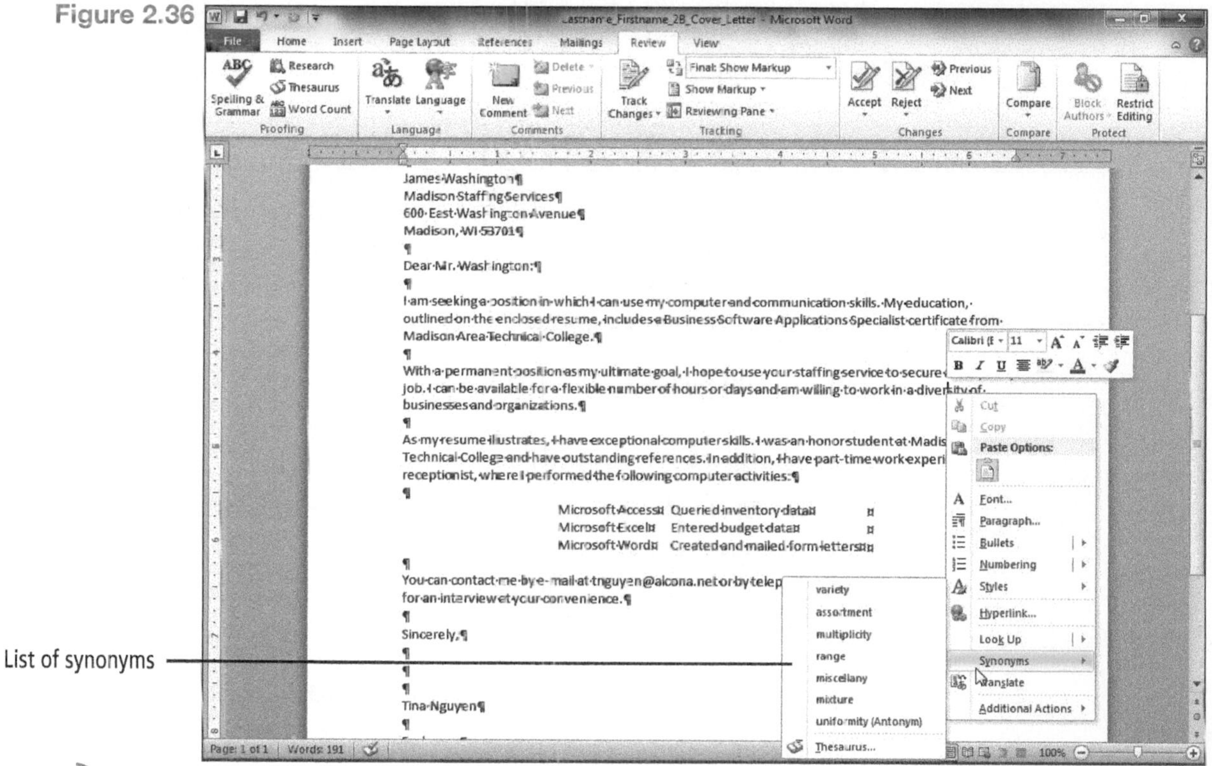

> **Another Way**
>
> Click the word, and then on the Review tab, in the Proofing group, click the Thesaurus button.

3 From the list of synonyms, click **variety** to replace *diversity* with *variety*.

4 In the paragraph that begins *As my resume*, point to the word *exceptional*, right-click, point to **Synonyms**, and then at the bottom of the shortcut menu, click **Thesaurus** to display the **Research** task pane.

5 In the **Research** task pane, under **Thesaurus**, point to the non-bold word *excellent*, and then click the **arrow**. Compare your screen with Figure 2.37.

Figure 2.37

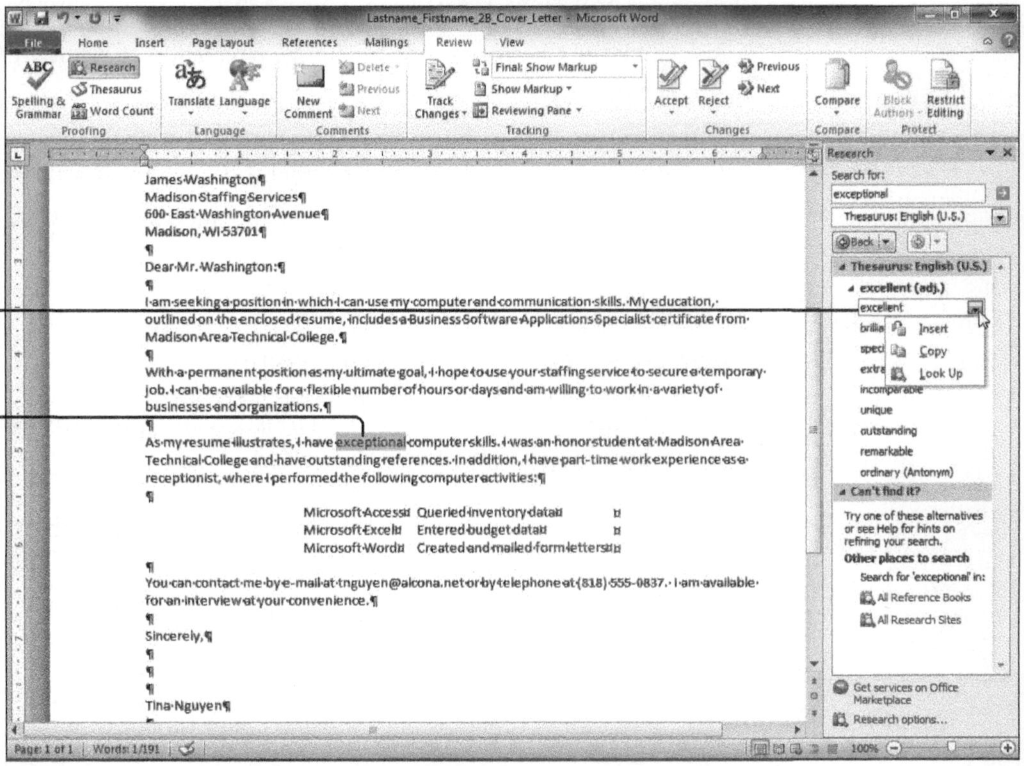

Synonym

Selected word

6 On the menu, click **Insert**, and then **Close** [X] the **Research** task pane.

excellent replaces the word *exceptional*.

7 Display **Backstage** view and click the **Info tab**. On the right, under the document thumbnail, click **Properties**, and then click **Show Document Panel**. In the **Author** box, type your firstname and lastname. Be sure your course name and section number display in the **Subject** box, and as the **Keywords**, replace any existing text with **cover letter**

8 **Close** [X] the **Document Panel**.

9 **Save** [Save], and then display **Backstage** view. Click **Close** to close the document but leave Word open. Hold this file until you complete this project.

Objective 7 | Create a Document Using a Template

Microsoft provides pre-designed templates for letters, resumes, invoices, and other types of documents. Recall that when you open a template, it opens unnamed so that you can reuse it as often as you need to do so.

Activity 2.19 | Locating and Opening a Template

If you need to create a short resume quickly, or if you need ideas about how to format your resume, Microsoft Word provides pre-designed resume templates. Some templates are available on your computer; many more are available online. After opening a template, you can add text as indicated, modify the layout and design, and add or remove resume elements.

1 Close any open documents, and then from **Backstage** view, click **New**.

2 Under **Available Templates**, click **Sample templates**.

3 Under **Available Templates**, scroll toward the bottom of the window, and then click **Median Resume.** Notice that a preview of the *Median Resume* template displays on the right. Compare your screen with Figure 2.38.

Figure 2.38

Preview of template

Selected template

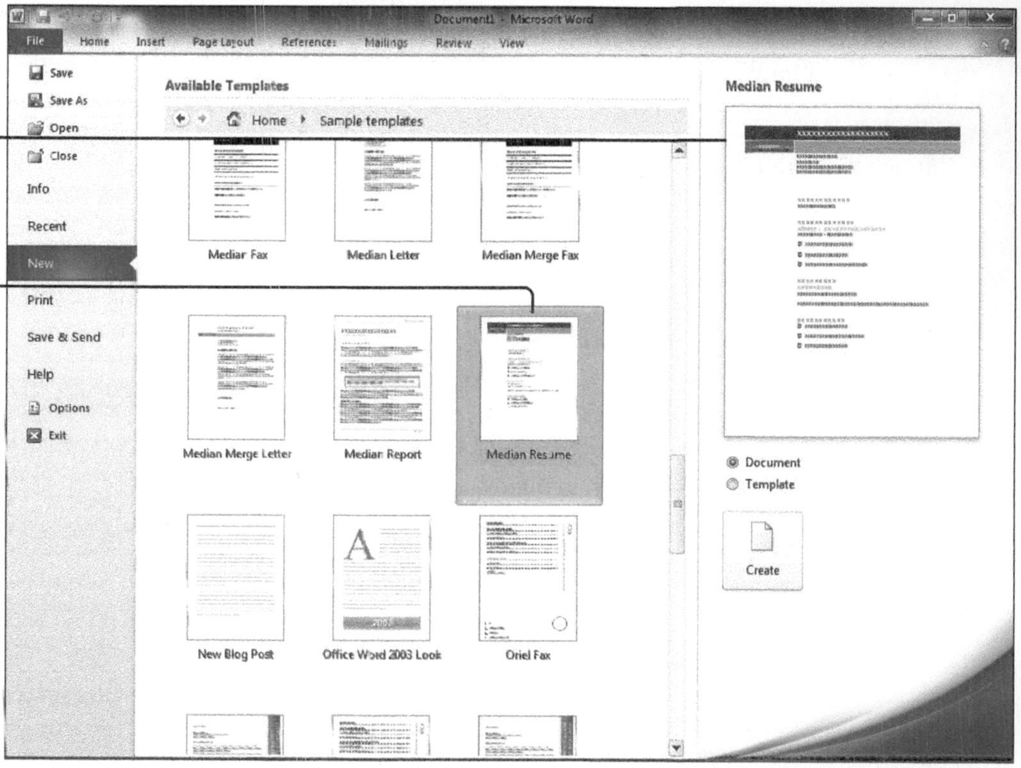

4 In the lower right corner, click the **Create** button.

The template opens a copy of itself in the form of a new Word document—the title bar indicates *Document* followed by a number. Recall that you are not opening the template itself, and that changes you make to this new document will not affect the contents of the template file.

5 Display the **Save As** dialog box. **Save** the document in your **Word Chapter 2** folder as **Lastname_Firstname_2B_Brief_Resume** and then add the file name to the footer—called the *First Page Footer* in this template.

6 **Save** your document.

Activity 2.20 | Replacing Template Placeholder Text

After you save the template file as a Word document, you can begin to substitute your own information in the indicated locations. You can also remove unneeded resume elements that are included with the template.

1 Click on the picture, and notice that a Picture Tool tab is added to the Ribbon.

2 Click the **Layout tab**, and then in the **Table group**, click the **View Gridlines** button to display non-printing table borders.

This template consists of two Word tables, and the name in the first row of the upper table displays either the user name or the text *[Type your name]* in square brackets.

3 At the top of the upper table, click the **Resume Name tab arrow**, and then compare your screen with Figure 2.39.

There are two styles available with the Median template—with or without a photo. You should not include a picture on a resume unless physical appearance is directly related to the job for which you are applying—for example, for a job as an actor or a model.

Figure 2.39

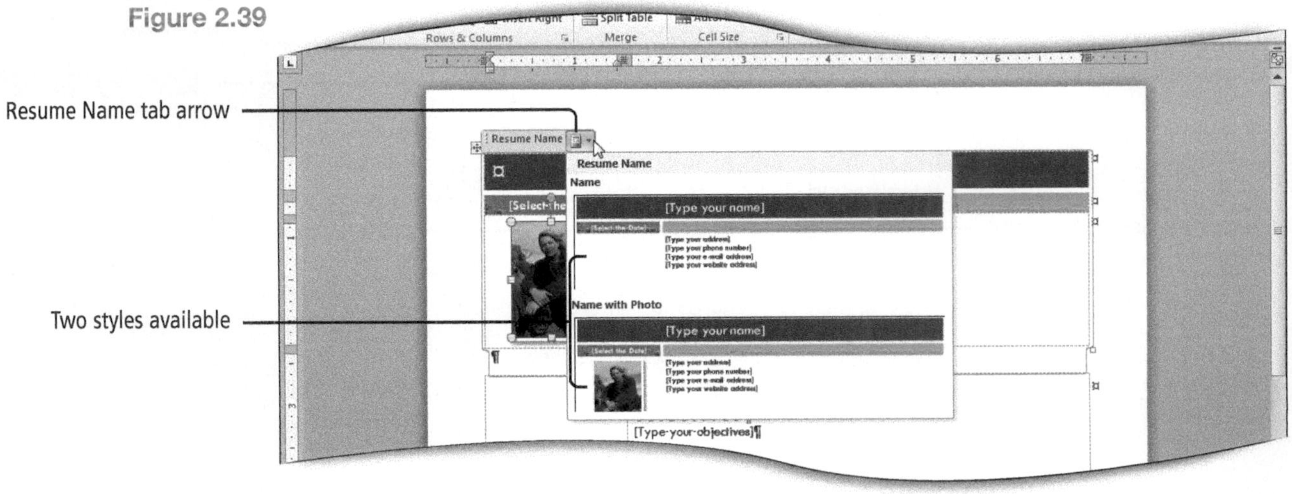

4 In the **Resume Name** gallery, click the first style—**Name**—to switch to the style with no picture.

5 In the first row of the table, select the displayed text—typically the name of your computer as indicated in your Windows operating system—and replace the text by typing **Tina Nguyen**

Another Way

Select the entire row, right-click, and then from the shortcut menu, click Delete Rows.

6 In the second row, click anywhere in the date control *[Select the Date]*. On the Ribbon, click the **Layout tab**. In the **Rows & Columns group**, click the **Delete** button, and then click **Delete Rows**.

Text surrounded by brackets is called a ***content control***. There are several different types of content controls, including date, picture, and ***text controls***. Most of the controls in this template are text controls. Because resumes do not typically include a date, you can delete this row.

7 Click anywhere in the content control *[Type your address]*. Compare your screen with Figure 2.40.

For the name and address at the top of the document, all of the text controls are grouped together. Each control has ***placeholder text***, text that indicates the type of information to be entered. The name in the first row may also be a content control with placeholder text.

Figure 2.40

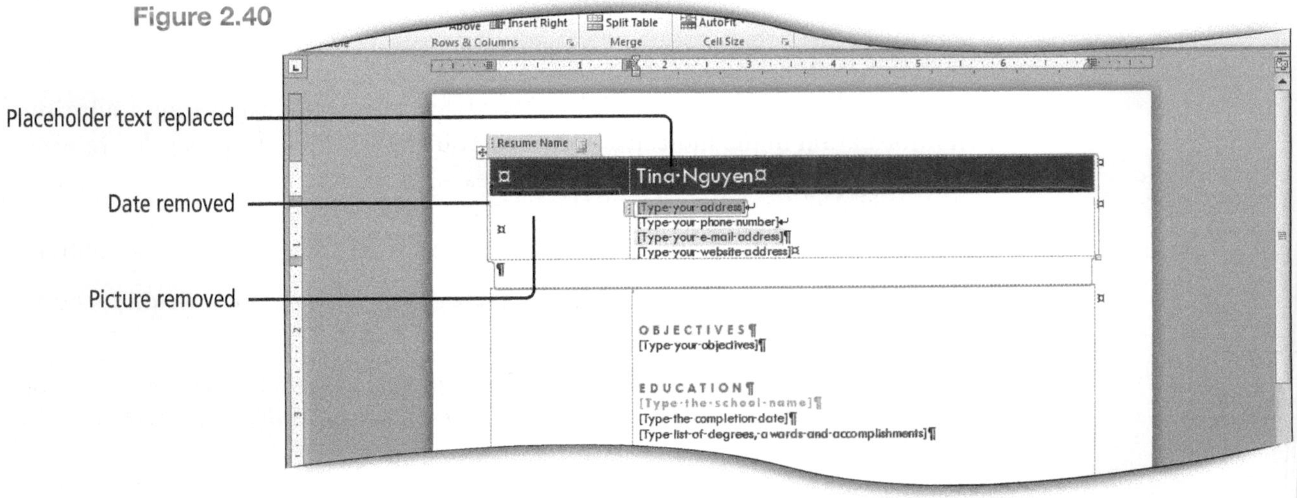

8 Complete the personal information by using the following information:

[Type your address]	**1776 Atwood Avenue, Madison, WI 53704**
[Type your phone number]	**(608) 555-0347**
[Type your e-mail address]	**tnguyen@alcona.net**
[Type your website address]	(leave this blank)

9 In the lower table, click in the *[Type your objectives]* control, and then type **To obtain a position using my computer and communications skills.**

10 Complete the **Education** section by using the following information:

[Type the school name]	**Madison Area Technical College**
[Type the completion date]	**June 2015**
[Type list of degrees, awards and accomplishments] *(type three separate lines)*	**Business Computing Specialist certificate** **Dean's List, four semesters** **President, Community Service Club**

11 Complete the **Experience** section by using the following information:

[Type the job title]	**Office Assistant (part-time)**
[Type the company name]	**The Robinson Company**
[Type the start date]	**September 2014**
[Type the end date]	**present**
[Type list of job responsibilities]	**Data entry and report generation using company spreadsheets and databases.**

12 Click in the *[Type list of skills]* control, type **Proficiency using Word, Excel, and Access (completed advanced courses in Microsoft Office programs)** and then press Enter.

13 As the second bulleted point, type **Excellent written and verbal communications (completed courses in Business Communications, PowerPoint, and Speech)** and then compare your screen with Figure 2.41. **Save** your document.

Figure 2.41

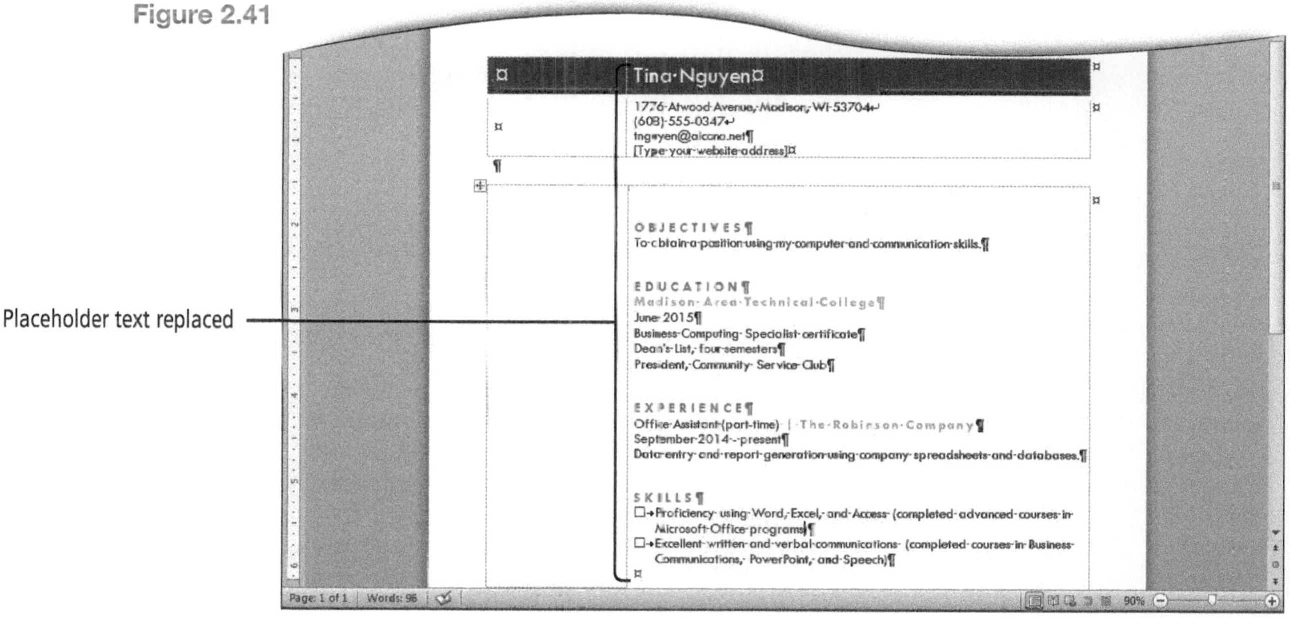

Activity 2.21 | Removing Template Controls and Formatting the Resume

1 Near the top of the document, point to the text control that you did not use—*[Type your website address]*. Right-click the control, and then from the shortcut menu, click **Remove Content Control**. Press Backspace as necessary to position the insertion point at the end of the e-mail address. Select the three lines with the address, phone, and e-mail information. On the Mini toolbar, notice that the text size is *11.5*. Click the **Font Size button arrow**, and then click **12**.

2 Click anywhere in lower table—the table with the *Objectives* row at the top—and then point to the upper left corner of the active table to display the **move table handle**. Click one time to select the lower table.

3 On the Mini toolbar, change the **Font Size** to **12** to match the table above.

4 Click anywhere to cancel the selection. On the **Page Layout tab**, in the **Page Setup group**, click the **Margins** button, and then click **Custom Margins**. Change the **Top** margin to **1.5** and the **Left** and **Right** margins to **1** to make this short resume better fill the page. Compare your screen with Figure 2.42.

Figure 2.42

New margins

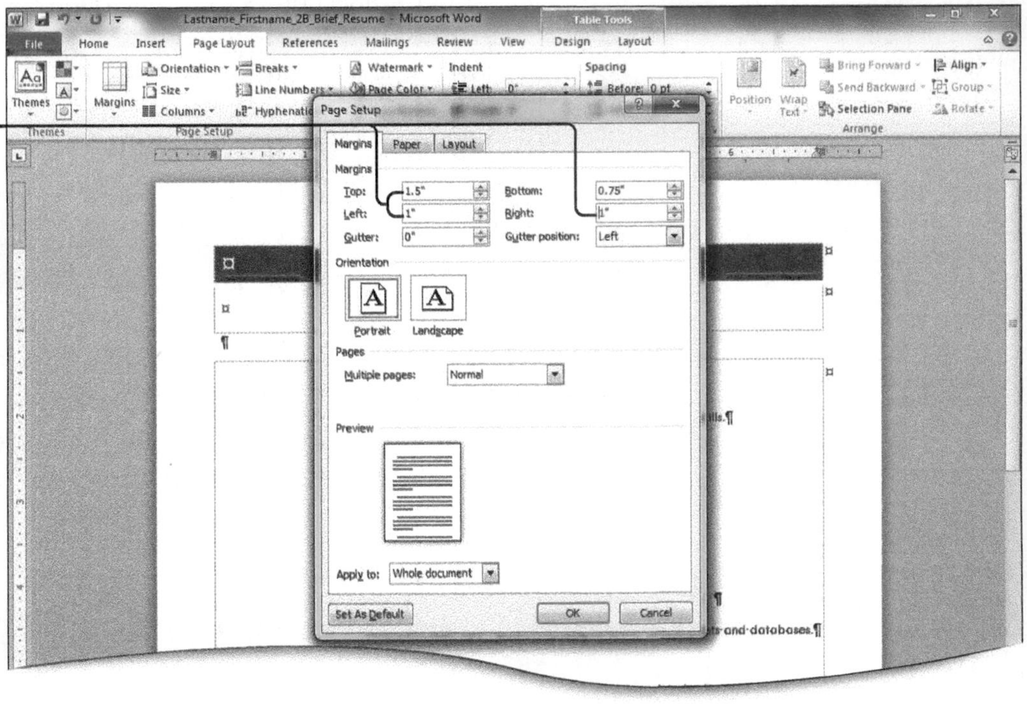

5 Click **OK** to close the **Page Setup** dialog box and apply the new margins. If the name at the top of the document changes back to a placeholder, click the control and type **Tina Nguyen**

6 Right-click the name at the top of the document—*Tina Nguyen*—and then from the shortcut menu, click **Remove Content Control**.

This action will leave the name but remove the control. Remove the control if the Document Properties will have an author other than the name in this control. If you do *not* remove the content control, when you add document properties, the name will change to the name you type in the Author box.

7 Press Ctrl + F2 to display the Print Preview in **Backstage** view. Click the **Info tab**. On the right, under the document thumbnail, click **Properties**, and then click **Show Document Panel**. In the **Author** box, delete any text and then type your firstname and lastname. In the **Subject** box, type your course name and section number, and in the **Keywords** box, type **short resume, template**

8 **Close** the **Document Panel**. **Save** your document, and then hold this file until you complete this project. Leave the resume displayed on your screen.

Activity 2.22 | Saving a Resume as a Web Page

You can save your resume as a Web page. This enables you to post the Web page on your own Web site or on Web space provided by your college. It also enables you to send the resume as an e-mail attachment that can be opened using any Web browser.

1 With your **2B_Brief_Resume** still open on your screen, click **Save** to be sure the current version of the document is saved.

2 Display the **Save As** dialog box. In the lower portion of the **Save As** dialog box, click the **Save as type arrow**, and then click **Single File Web Page**.

A ***Single File Web Page*** is a document saved using the ***Hypertext Markup Language (HTML)***. HTML is the language used to format documents that can be opened using a Web browser such as Internet Explorer.

3 In the **Save As** dialog box, in the **File name** box, type **Lastname_Firstname_2B_HTML_Resume** Click **Save**, and then click **Yes** if a message box displays. Notice that the Web page displays in Word.

4 Display **Backstage** view. On the right, click **Properties**, and then click **Advanced Properties**. In the **Properties** dialog box, on the **Summary tab**, in the **Subject** box, be sure your course name and section number display. In the **Author** box, be sure your first and last names display. In the **Keywords** box, replace the existing text with **HTML** Click **OK**, and then click the **Home tab**. **Save** the document; print or submit electronically as directed.

5 **Exit** Word. From the **Start** menu, click **Computer**. Navigate to your **Word Chapter 2** folder, and then double-click your **Lastname_Firstname_2B_HTML_Resume** file to open the resume in your Web browser. Compare your screen with Figure 2.43.

Figure 2.43

Resume displayed in a Web browser

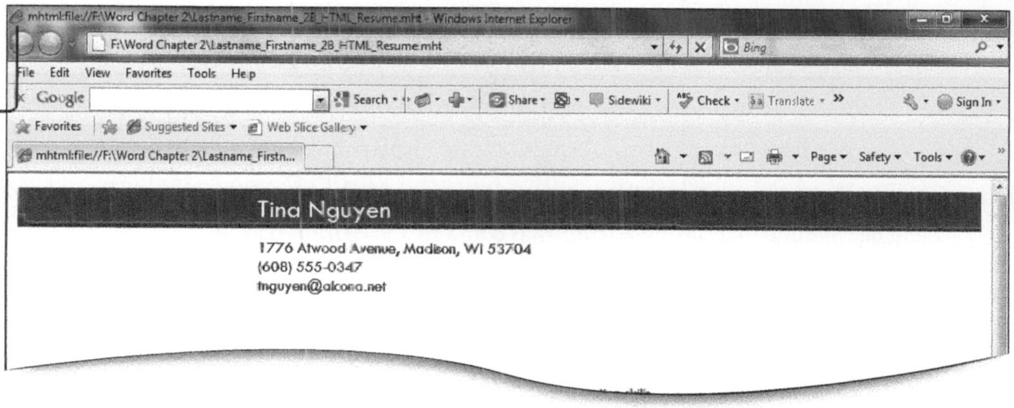

6 **Close** your Web browser. As directed by your instructor, print or submit electronically the four files from this project—2B_Letterhead, 2B_Cover_Letter, 2B_Brief_Resume, and 2B_HTML_Resume.

End **You have completed Project 2B**

Content-Based Assessments

Summary

In this chapter, you created a table, and then used the table to create a resume. You created a letterhead template, and then created a document using a copy of the letterhead template. You created a cover letter for the resume, moved text, corrected spelling and grammar, and used the built-in thesaurus. Finally, you created a short resume using a template, and also saved the resume as a Web page.

Key Terms

- **AutoCorrect** 123
- **Body** 123
- **Cell** 107
- **Complimentary closing** 123
- **Content control** 136
- **Date line** 123
- **Drag and drop** 128
- **Enclosures** 123
- **HTML** 139
- **Hypertext Markup Language (HTML)** 139
- **Inside address** 123
- **Letterhead** 120
- **New from existing** 121
- **No Spacing style** 120
- **Normal template** 120
- **Placeholder text** 136
- **Salutation** 123
- **Single File Web Page** 139
- **Subject line** 123
- **Synonyms** 133
- **Table** 107
- **Template** 120
- **Text control** 136
- **Thesaurus** 133
- **Writer's identification** 123
- **Writer's signature block** 123

Matching

Match each term in the second column with its correct definition in the first column by writing the letter of the term on the blank line in front of the correct definition.

____ 1. An arrangement of information organized into rows and columns.

____ 2. The box at the intersection of a row and column in a table.

____ 3. A document structure that opens a copy of itself, opens unnamed, and is used as the starting point for another document.

____ 4. The template that serves as a basis for all new Word documents.

____ 5. The personal or company information that displays at the top of a letter.

____ 6. The Word style that inserts no extra space following a paragraph and uses single spacing.

____ 7. The first line in a business letter that contains the current date and that is positioned just below the letterhead if a letterhead is used.

____ 8. The name and address of the person receiving a letter and positioned below the date line.

____ 9. The greeting line of a letter.

____ 10. A parting farewell in a letter.

____ 11. The name and title of the author of a letter, placed near the bottom of the letter under the complimentary closing.

____ 12. The optional line following the inside address in a business letter that states the purpose of the letter.

A AutoCorrect
B Cell
C Complimentary closing
D Date line
E Drag and drop
F Enclosures
G Inside address
H Letterhead
I No Spacing
J Normal template
K Salutation
L Subject line
M Table
N Template
O Writer's identification

_____ 13. Additional documents included with a business letter.

_____ 14. A Word feature that corrects common spelling errors as you type, for example changing *teh* to *the*.

_____ 15. A technique by which you can move, by dragging, selected text from one location in a document to another.

Multiple Choice

Circle the correct answer.

1. When you create a table, the width of all of cells in the table is:
A. equal **B.** proportional **C.** 1 inch

2. To indicate words that might be misspelled because they are not in Word's dictionary, Word flags text with:
A. blue wavy underlines **B.** green wavy underlines **C.** red wavy underlines

3. To indicate possible grammar errors, Word flags text with:
A. blue wavy underlines **B.** green wavy underlines **C.** red wavy underlines

4. To indicate possible errors in word usage, Word flags text with:
A. blue wavy underlines **B.** green wavy underlines **C.** red wavy underlines

5. A research tool that provides a list of words with similar meanings is:
A. a thesaurus **B.** a dictionary **C.** an encyclopedia

6. A word with the same or similar meaning as another word is:
A. an acronym **B.** a search term **C.** a synonym

7. In a template, an area indicated by placeholder text into which you can add text, pictures, dates, or lists is a:
A. text control **B.** content control **C.** quick control

8. A document saved in HTML, which can be opened using a Web browser, is a:
A. Web page **B.** template **C.** resume

9. Using drag-and-drop to move text is most useful when both the text and the destination are on the same:
A. document **B.** section **C.** screen

10. To locate specific text in a document quickly, use the:
A. Find command **B.** Replace command **C.** Locate command

Apply 2A skills from these Objectives:

1. Create a Table
2. Add Text to a Table
3. Format a Table

Skills Review | Project 2C Student Resume

In the following Skills Review, you will use a table to create a resume for Joshua Green. Your completed resume will look similar to Figure 2.44.

Project Files

For Project 2C, you will need the following files:

New blank Word document
w02C_Skills
w02C_Experience

You will save your document as:

Lastname_Firstname_2C_Student_Resume

Project Results

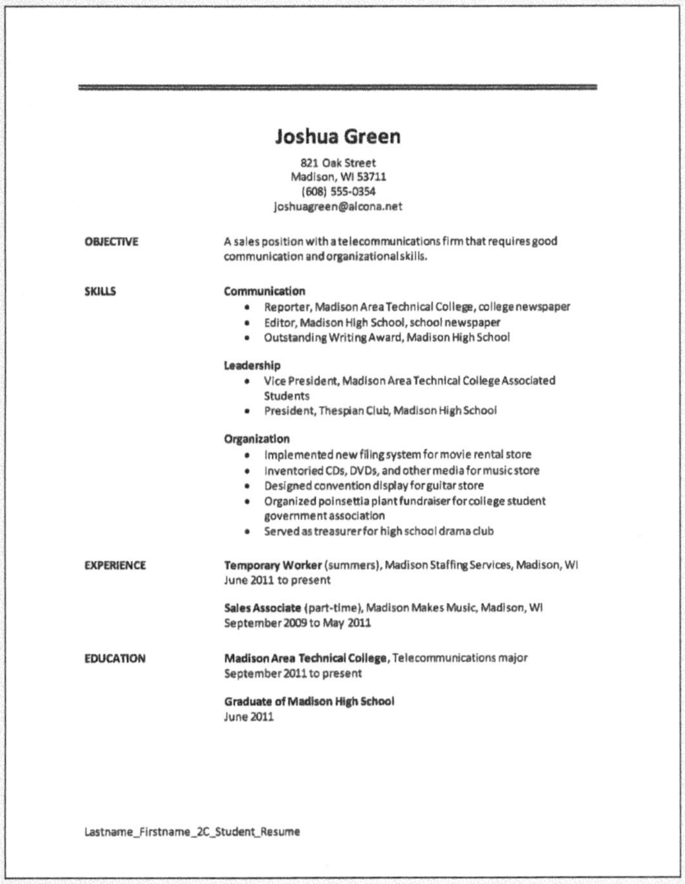

Joshua Green
821 Oak Street
Madison, WI 53711
(608) 555-0354
joshuagreen@alcona.net

OBJECTIVE	A sales position with a telecommunications firm that requires good communication and organizational skills.
SKILLS	**Communication** • Reporter, Madison Area Technical College, college newspaper • Editor, Madison High School, school newspaper • Outstanding Writing Award, Madison High School **Leadership** • Vice President, Madison Area Technical College Associated Students • President, Thespian Club, Madison High School **Organization** • Implemented new filing system for movie rental store • Inventoried CDs, DVDs, and other media for music store • Designed convention display for guitar store • Organized poinsettia plant fundraiser for college student government association • Served as treasurer for high school drama club
EXPERIENCE	**Temporary Worker** (summers), Madison Staffing Services, Madison, WI June 2011 to present **Sales Associate** (part-time), Madison Makes Music, Madison, WI September 2009 to May 2011
EDUCATION	**Madison Area Technical College**, Telecommunications major September 2011 to present **Graduate of Madison High School** June 2011

Lastname_Firstname_2C_Student_Resume

Figure 2.44

(Project 2C Student Resume continues on the next page)

Skills Review | Project 2C Student Resume (continued)

1 **Start** Word. In the new blank document, be sure that formatting marks and rulers display. **Save** the document in your **Word Chapter 2** folder as **Lastname_Firstname_2C_Student_Resume**

a. Add the file name to the footer, and then close the footer area. Click the **Insert tab**, and then in the **Tables group**, click the **Table** button. In the **Table** grid, in the fourth row, click the second square to insert a **2 × 4** table.

b. In the first cell of the table, type **Joshua Green** and then press Enter. Type the following text, pressing Enter after each line *except* the last line:

821 Oak Street

Madison, WI 53711

(608) 555-0354

joshuagreen@alcona.net

c. Press ↓ to move to the first cell in the second row. Type **SKILLS** and then press ↓ to move to the first cell in the third row.

d. Type **EXPERIENCE** and then press ↓. Type **EDUCATION**

e. In the first cell, if the e-mail address displays in blue, right-click the e-mail address, and then from the shortcut menu, click **Remove Hyperlink**. **Save** your document

2 Click in the cell to the right of *SKILLS*, and then type the following, pressing Enter after each item:

Communication
Reporter, Madison Area Technical College, college newspaper
Editor, Madison High School, school newspaper
Outstanding Writing Award, Madison High School

a. With the insertion point in the new line at the end of the cell, click the **Insert tab**. In the **Text group**, click the **Object button arrow**, and then click **Text from File**.

b. Navigate to your student files, select **w02C_Skills**, and then click **Insert**. Press Backspace one time to remove the blank line.

c. Click in the cell to the right of *EXPERIENCE*, and then insert the file **w02C_Experience**. Press Backspace one time to remove the blank line.

d. Click in the cell to the right of *EDUCATION*, and then type the following, pressing Enter after all *except* the last item:

Madison Area Technical College, Telecommunications major

September 2011 to present

Graduate of Madison High School

June 2011

3 Click anywhere in the top row of the table. Click the **Layout tab**, and then in the **Rows & Columns group**, click the **Insert Below** button. Type **OBJECTIVE** and then press Tab.

a. Type **A sales position with a telecommunications firm that requires good communication and organizational skills.**

b. In any row, point to the vertical border between the two columns to display the ⟷ pointer. Drag the column border to the left to approximately **1.75 inches on the horizontal ruler.**

c. Click anywhere in the left column. Click the **Layout tab**. In the **Cell Size group**, in the **Table Column Width** box, if necessary, type **1.75** and press Enter.

d. In the first row of the document, drag across both cells to select them. On the **Layout tab**, in the **Merge group**, click the **Merge Cells** button. Right-click the selected cell, and then from the Mini toolbar, click the **Center** button.

e. In the top row, select the first paragraph of text—*Joshua Green*. From the Mini toolbar, increase the **Font Size** to **20** and apply **Bold**.

f. In the second row, point to the word *OBJECTIVE*, hold down the left mouse button, and then drag down to select the row headings in uppercase letters. On the Mini toolbar, click the **Bold** button. **Save** your document.

4 Click in the cell to the right of *OBJECTIVE*. On the **Page Layout tab**, in the **Paragraph group**, click the **Spacing After up spin arrow** three times to change the spacing to **18 pt**.

a. In the cell to the right of *SKILLS*, apply **Bold** to the words *Communication*, *Leadership*, and *Organization*. Then, under each bold heading in the cell, select the lines of text, and create a bulleted list.

b. In the first two bulleted lists, click in the last bullet item, and then on the **Page Layout tab**, in the **Paragraph group**, set the **Spacing After** to **12 pt**.

(Project 2C Student Resume continues on the next page)

Content-Based Assessments

Skills Review | Project 2C Student Resume (continued)

c. In the last bulleted list, click in the last bullet item, and then set the **Spacing After** to **18 pt**.

d. In the cell to the right of *EXPERIENCE*, apply **Bold** to *Temporary Worker* and *Sales Associate*. Click in the line *June 2011 to present* and apply **Spacing After** of **12 pt**. Click in the line *September 2009 to May 2011* and apply **Spacing After** of **18 pt**.

e. In the cell to the right of *EDUCATION*, apply **Bold** to *Madison Area Technical College* and *Graduate of Madison High School*.

f. In the same cell, click in the line *September 2011 to present* and apply **Spacing After** of **12 pt**.

g. In the first row, click in the last line—*joshuagreen@alcona.net*—and then change the **Spacing After** to **18 pt**. Click in the first line—*Joshua Green*—and set the **Spacing Before** to **30 pt** and the **Spacing After** to **6 pt**.

5 Point to the upper left corner of the table, and then click the displayed **table move handle** button [⊞] to select the entire table. On the **Design tab**, in the **Table Styles group**, click the **Borders button arrow**, and then click **No Border**.

a. On the **Design tab**, in the **Table Styles group**, click the **Borders button arrow** again, and then at the bottom of the gallery, click **Borders and Shading**. In the **Borders and Shading** dialog box, under **Setting**, click **Custom**. Under **Style**, scroll down slightly, and then click the style with two equal lines.

b. Click the **Width arrow**, and then click **1 1/2 pt**. Under **Preview**, click the top border of the preview box, and then click **OK**.

c. Click the **File tab** to display **Backstage** view, and then click the **Print tab** to display the Print Preview.

d. Click the **Info tab**. On the right side, under the document thumbnail, click **Properties**, and then click **Show Document Panel**.

e. In the **Author** box, delete any text and then type your firstname and lastname. In the **Subject** box, type your course name and section number, and in the **Keywords** box type **resume, table**

f. **Close** the **Document Panel**. **Save** [💾] and then, as directed by your instructor, print your document or submit it electronically. **Exit** Word.

End **You have completed Project 2C**

Content-Based Assessments

Apply 2B skills from these Objectives:

4 Create a New Document from an Existing Document
5 Change and Reorganize Text
6 Use the Proofing Options
7 Create a Document Using a Template

Skills Review | Project 2D Ross Letter

In the following Skills Review, you will create a letterhead, and then create a new document from the letterhead to create a resume cover letter. You will also create a short resume using a Microsoft template and save it as a Web page. Your completed documents will look similar to Figure 2.45.

Project Files

For Project 2D, you will need the following files:

New blank Word document
w02D_Letter_Text
Equity Resume Template from Word's installed templates

You will save your documents as:

Lastname_Firstname_2D_Ross_Letterhead
Lastname_Firstname_2D_Ross_Letter
Lastname_Firstname_2D_Resume
Lastname_Firstname_2D_Web_Resume

Project Results

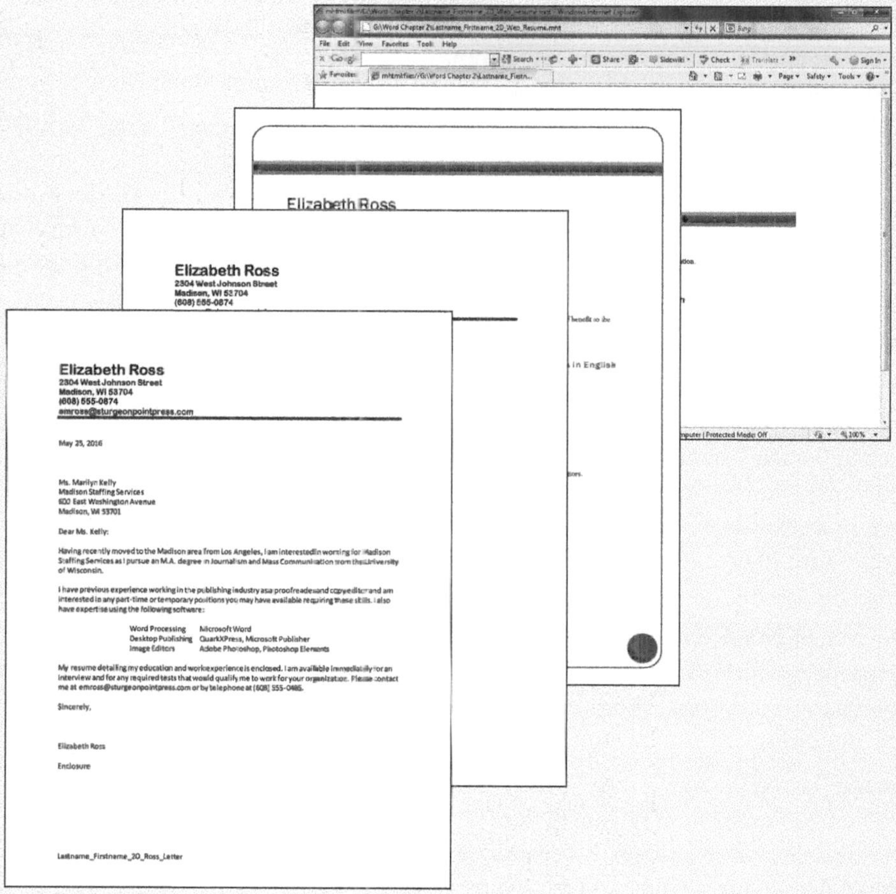

Figure 2.45

(Project 2D Ross Letter continues on the next page)

Skills Review | Project 2D Ross Letter (continued)

1 **Start** Word. In the new blank document, be sure that formatting marks and rulers display. On the **Home tab**, in the **Styles group**, click the **No Spacing** button.

a. Type **Elizabeth Ross** and then press Enter. Type **2304 West Johnson Street** and press Enter. Type **Madison, WI 53704** and then press Enter.

b. Type **(608) 555-0874** and then press Enter. Type **emross@sturgeonpointpress.com** and then press Enter three times. If the e-mail address changes to blue text, right-click the e-mail address, and then click Remove Hyperlink.

c. Select all five lines of the personal information, but do not select the blank paragraphs. From the Mini toolbar, change the **Font** to **Arial Rounded MT Bold**. Select the first paragraph—*Elizabeth Ross*—and then on the Mini toolbar, apply **Bold** and change the **Font Size** to **20**.

d. Click anywhere in the fifth line of text—the e-mail address. On the **Home tab**, in the **Paragraph group**, click the **Borders button arrow**, and then click **Borders and Shading**. Under **Style**, click the first style—a single solid line. Click the **Width arrow**, and then click **3 pt**. In the **Preview** area, click the bottom border, and then click **OK**.

e. Display **Backstage** view, and then click **Save As**. Save the document in your **Word Chapter 2** folder as **Lastname_Firstname_2D_Ross_Letterhead**

f. Add the file name to the footer, and then close the footer area. Display **Backstage** view, click **Properties**, and then click **Show Document Panel**. In the **Author** box, delete any text and then type your firstname and lastname. In the **Subject** box, type your course name and section number, and in the **Keywords** box, type **personal letterhead**

g. **Close** the **Document Panel**. **Save** your document. From **Backstage** view, click **Close** to close the document but leave Word open. Hold this file until you complete the project.

2 From **Backstage** view, click **New**. Under **Available Templates**, click **New from existing**. Navigate to your **Word Chapter 2** folder, click your **Lastname_Firstname_2D_Ross_Letterhead** document, and then in the lower right corner, click **Create New**. From **Backstage** view, click **Save As**. Navigate to your **Word Chapter 2** folder, and **Save** the file as **Lastname_Firstname_2D_Ross_Letter** Double-click the footer, right-click the file name, and then click **Update Field**. Close the footer area.

a. From **Backstage** view, display the **Word Options** dialog box. In the **Word Options** list, click **Proofing**, and then under **AutoCorrect options**, click the **AutoCorrect Options** button.

b. In the **AutoCorrect** dialog box, click the **AutoCorrect tab**. Under **Replace**, type **expereince** and under **With**, type **experience** Click **Add**. If the entry already exists, click Replace instead, and then click Yes. Click **OK** two times to close the dialog boxes.

c. Press Ctrl + End, type **May 25, 2016** and then press Enter four times. Type the following inside address using four lines:

Ms. Marilyn Kelly

Madison Staffing Services

600 East Washington Avenue

Madison, WI 53701

d. Press Enter two times, type **Dear Ms. Kelly:** and then press Enter two times. On the **Insert tab**, in the **Text group**, click the **Object button arrow**, and then click **Text from File**. From your student files, locate and insert the file **w02D_Letter_Text**.

e. Scroll to view the lower portion of the page, and be sure your insertion point is in the empty paragraph mark at the end. Press Enter, type **Sincerely,** and then press Enter four times. Type **Elizabeth Ross** and press Enter two times. Type **Enclosure** and then **Save** your document.

f. Near the bottom of the document, locate the paragraph that begins *I am available* and click to position the insertion point at the beginning of the paragraph. Type **My resume detailing my education and work** Press Spacebar and then type the misspelled word **expereince** Press Spacebar and notice that AutoCorrect corrects the misspelling. Type **is enclosed.** and then press Spacebar.

g. Press Ctrl + Home. On the **Home tab**, in the **Editing group**, click the **Replace** button. In the **Find what** box, type **association** In the **Replace with** box, type **organization** and then click **Replace All**. Click **OK** to close the message box, and then **Close** the **Find and Replace** dialog box.

(Project 2D Ross Letter continues on the next page)

Skills Review | Project 2D Ross Letter (continued)

h. In the paragraph that begins *I have previous*, double-click *experience*. Point to the selected word to display the [pointer icon] pointer, and then drag the word to the left of *working*. Adjust spacing as necessary.

i. Below the paragraph that begins *I have previous*, position the insertion point in the second blank line. On the **Insert tab**, in the **Tables group**, click the **Table** button. In the **Table** grid, in the third row, click the second square to insert a 2 × 3 table. Type the following information in the table:

Word Processing	Microsoft Word
Desktop Publishing	QuarkXPress, Microsoft Publisher
Image Editors	Adobe Photoshop, Photoshop Elements

j. Point outside of the upper left corner and click the **table move handle** button to select the entire table. On the **Layout tab**, in the **Cell Size group**, click the **AutoFit** button, and then click **AutoFit Contents.** On the **Home tab**, in the **Paragraph group**, click the **Center** button. On the **Design tab**, in the **Table Styles group**, click the **Borders button arrow**, and then click **No Border**. **Save** your document.

3 If you do not see any wavy red and green lines under words, refer to the Alert in Activity 2.17 to enable the default settings for automatic proofing.

a. In the paragraph that begins *Having lately*, in the second line, locate and right-click the phrase *an M.A. degrees*, and then from the shortcut menu, click *an M.A. degree*. In the same paragraph, locate and right-click *Journlism*. From the shortcut menu, click *Journalism*.

b. Press Ctrl + Home. On the **Review tab**, in the **Proofing group**, click the **Spelling & Grammar** button. In the **Spelling and Grammar** dialog box, click the **Change** button to change *are* to *am*. For the misspelled word *expertis*, under **Suggestions**, be sure *expertise* is selected, and then click **Change**.

c. **Change** *qualifie* to *qualify*, and then click **OK** to close the message box.

d. Near the top of the document, in the paragraph that begins *Having lately*, right-click *lately*. In the shortcut menu, point to **Synonyms**, and then click *recently*. In the same line, right-click *region*, and replace it with the synonym *area*.

e. Display **Backstage** view, click **Properties**, and then click **Show Document Panel**. Type your firstname and lastname as the **Author** and your course number and section as the **Subject**. In the **Keywords** box, replace any existing text with **cover letter Close** the **Document Panel**. **Save** your document. From **Backstage** view, **Close** the document but leave Word open. Hold this file until you complete the project.

4 Display **Backstage** view, and then click **New**. Under **Available Templates**, click **Sample templates**. Locate and click **Equity Resume**. In the lower right corner, click **Create**.

a. **Save** the document in your **Word Chapter 2** folder as **Lastname_Firstname_2D_Resume** and then add the file name to the footer—called *First Page Footer* in this template. At the top of the resume, select the text in the first control, which displays the name of the computer at which you are working. Replace this text by typing **Elizabeth Ross** Right-click the name, and then from the shortcut menu, click **Remove Content Control**.

b. Click the *[Type your phone number]* control, and then type **(608) 555-0874** Click the *[Type your address]* control, type **2304 West Johnson Street** and press Enter. Type **Madison, WI 53703**

c. Click the *[Type your e-mail address]* control, and then type **emross@sturgeonpointpress.com** Right-click the *[Type your website]* control, and then from the shortcut menu, click **Remove Content Control**. Press Backspace to remove the *website* line.

d. Click the *[Type the objectives]* control, and then type **A copy editing or proofreading position where my editing and advanced computer skills will be of benefit to the organization.**

e. Under *Education*, click the *[Type the completion date]* control, and then type **University of Wisconsin-Milwaukee, May 2015** Click the *[Type the degree]* control, and then type **Bachelor of Arts in English** For the *[Type list of accomplishments]* bulleted list, type:

Dean's list, six terms

Harriet McArthur Creative Writing Award

(Project 2D Ross Letter continues on the next page)

Skills Review | Project 2D Ross Letter (continued)

Assistant Editor of college newspaper

3.8 GPA

f. Under *Experience*, enter the text shown in **Table 1** below.

g. Click the *[Type list of skills]* control and type **Word** Press Enter, and then type two additional bullet points with **QuarkXPress** and **Adobe Photoshop**

h. Display **Backstage** view, click **Properties**, and then click **Show Document Panel**. Type your firstname and lastname as the **Author**. In the **Subject** box, type your course and section number. In the **Keywords** box, **resume, template Close** the **Document Panel**.

i. **Save** your document.

j. Display **Backstage** view, click **Save As**, and then in the **Save as type** box, click **Single File Web Page**. Navigate to your **Word Chapter 2** folder. In the **File name** box, type **Lastname_Firstname_2D_Web_Resume** Click **Save**.

k. Display **Backstage** view, click **Properties**, and then click **Advanced Properties**. In the **Properties** dialog box, be sure your name displays in the *Author* box, and then in the **Keywords** box, add **HTML** to the list of keywords. Click **OK** and **Save** your document.

l. **Exit** Word. From the **Start** menu, click **Computer** (or My Computer). Navigate to your **Word Chapter 2** folder, and then double-click your **2D_Web_Resume** file to open the resume in your Web browser. **Close** the Web browser. As directed by your instructor, print or submit electronically the four files that are the results of this project—2D_Ross_Letterhead, 2D_Ross_Letter, 2D_Resume, and 2D_Web_Resume.

Table 1

[Type the start date]	**May 2012**
[Type the end date]	**Present-**
[Type the job title]	**Senior Copy Editor**
[Type the company name]	**Sturgeon Point Press**
[Type the company address]	**Milwaukee, WI**
[Type job responsibilities]	**Produced final edited copy of books, technical manuals, and pamphlets; supervised three copy editors.**

(Return to Step 4-g)

End You have completed Project 2D

Content-Based Assessments

Apply **2A** skills from these Objectives:

1. Create a Table
2. Add Text to a Table
3. Format a Table

Mastering Word | Project 2E Job Listings

In the following Mastering Word project, you will create an announcement for new job postings at Madison Staffing Services. Your completed document will look similar to Figure 2.46.

Project Files

For Project 2E, you will need the following files:

New blank Word document
w02E_New_Jobs

You will save your document as:

Lastname_Firstname_2E_Job_Listings

Project Results

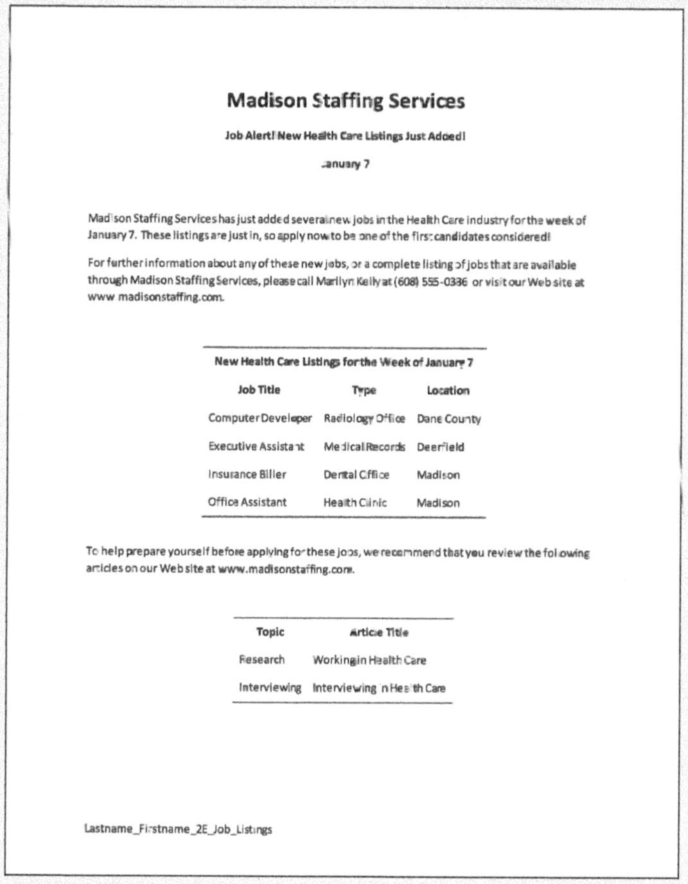

Madison Staffing Services

Job Alert! New Health Care Listings Just Added!

January 7

Madison Staffing Services has just added several new jobs in the Health Care industry for the week of January 7. These listings are just in, so apply now to be one of the first candidates considered!

For further information about any of these new jobs, or a complete listing of jobs that are available through Madison Staffing Services, please call Marilyn Kelly at (608) 555-0336 or visit our Web site at www.madisonstaffing.com.

New Health Care Listings for the Week of January 7		
Job Title	**Type**	**Location**
Computer Developer	Radiology Office	Dane County
Executive Assistant	Medical Records	Deerfield
Insurance Biller	Dental Office	Madison
Office Assistant	Health Clinic	Madison

To help prepare yourself before applying for these jobs, we recommend that you review the following articles on our Web site at www.madisonstaffing.com.

Topic	**Article Title**
Research	Working in Health Care
Interviewing	Interviewing in Health Care

Lastname_Firstname_2E_Job_Listings

Figure 2.46

(Project 2E Job Listings continues on the next page)

Mastering Word | Project 2E Job Listings (continued)

1 **Start** Word and display a new blank document; display formatting marks and rulers. **Save** the document in your **Word Chapter 2** folder as **Lastname_Firstname_2E_Job_Listings** and then add the file name to the footer.

2 Type **Madison Staffing Services** and press Enter. Type **Job Alert! New Health Care Listings Just Added!** and press Enter. Type **January 7** and press Enter two times. **Insert** the file **w02E_New_Jobs**.

3 At the top of the document, select and **Center** the three title lines. Select the title *Madison Staffing Services* and change the **Font Size** to **20** pt and apply **Bold**. Apply **Bold** to the second and third title lines. Locate the paragraph that begins *For further information*, and then below that paragraph, click to position the insertion point in the second blank paragraph. **Insert** a **3 × 4** table. Enter the following:

Job Title	Type	Location
Executive Assistant	Medical Records	Deerfield
Insurance Biller	Dental Office	Madison
Office Assistant	Health Clinic	Madison

4 In the table, click anywhere in the second row, and then insert a row above. Add the following information so that the job titles remain in alphabetic order:

Computer Developer	Radiology Office	Dane County

5 Select the entire table. On the **Layout tab**, in the **Cell Size group**, use the **AutoFit** button to **AutoFit Contents**. With the table still selected, **Center** the table. With the table still selected, on the **Page Layout tab**, add **6 pt Spacing Before** and **6 pt Spacing After**.

6 With the table still selected, remove all table borders, and then add a **Custom 1 pt** solid line top border and bottom border. Select all three cells in the first row, apply **Bold**, and then **Center** the text. Click anywhere in the first row, and then insert a new row above. Merge the three cells in the new top row, and then type **New Health Care Listings for the Week of January 7** Notice that the new row keeps the formatting of the row from which it was created.

7 At the bottom of the document, **Insert** a **2 × 3** table. Enter the following:

Topic	Article Title
Research	Working in Health Care
Interviewing	Interviewing in Health Care

8 Select the entire table. On the **Layout tab**, in the **Cell Size group**, use the **AutoFit** button to **AutoFit Contents**. On the **Home tab**, **Center** the table. On the **Page Layout tab**, add **6 pt Spacing Before** and **6 pt Spacing After**.

9 With the table still selected, remove all table borders, and then add a **Custom 1 pt** solid line top border and bottom border. Select the cells in the first row, apply **Bold**, and then **Center** the text.

10 In the **Document Panel**, add your name and course information and the **Keywords new listings, health care** **Save** and then print or submit the document electronically as directed. **Exit** Word.

End **You have completed Project 2E**

Content-Based Assessments

Apply 2B skills from these Objectives:

- 4 Create a New Document from an Existing Document
- 5 Change and Reorganize Text
- 6 Use the Proofing Options
- 7 Create a Document Using a Template

Mastering Word | Project 2F Job Tips

In the following Mastering Word project, you will create a fax and a memo that includes job tips for Madison Staffing Services employees. Your completed documents will look similar to Figure 2.47.

Project Files

For Project 2F, you will need the following files:

w02F_Memo_Heading
w02F_Memo_Text
Origin Fax template from Word's installed templates

You will save your documents as:

Lastname_Firstname_2F_Job_Tips
Lastname_Firstname_2F_Fax

Project Results

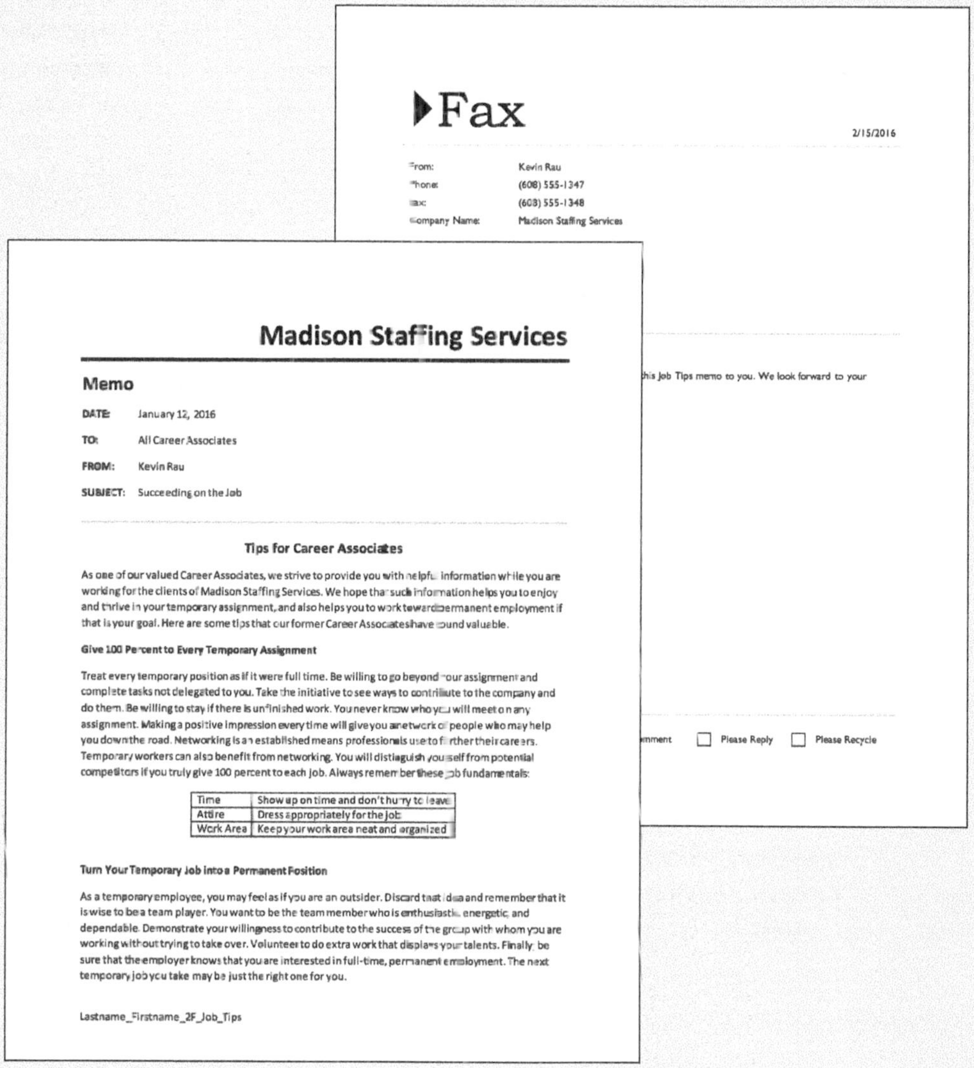

Figure 2.47

(Project 2F Job Tips continues on the next page)

Mastering Word | Project 2F Job Tips (continued)

1 **Start** Word; display rulers and formatting marks. In **Backstage** view, create a **New** document using the **New from existing** template. In the **New from Existing Document** dialog box, navigate to your student files, click **w02F_Memo_Heading**, and then click **Create New**.

2 Display the **Document Panel**, add your name and course information and the **Keywords memo, associates**

3 **Save** the document in your **Word Chapter 2** folder as **Lastname_Firstname_2F_Job_Tips** Add the file name to the footer.

4 At the top of your document, in the *DATE* paragraph, click to the right of the tab formatting mark, and then type **January 12, 2016** Use a similar technique to add the following information:

TO:	**All Career Associates**
FROM:	**Kevin Rau**
SUBJECT:	**Succeeding on the Job**

5 Position the insertion point in the blank paragraph below the memo heading. **Insert** the file **w02F_Memo_Text** and press Backspace to remove the blank line at the end of the selected text.

6 Select and **Center** the title *Tips for Career Associates.* By using either the **Spelling and Grammar** dialog box, or by right-clicking selected words, correct all spelling, grammar, and word usage errors.

7 In the first line of the paragraph that begins *Treat every*, locate and right-click *provisional.* Use the shortcut menu to change the word to the synonym *temporary*. In the second line of the same paragraph, change *donate* to the synonym *contribute.*

8 At the end of the paragraph that begins *Treat every temporary*, create a blank paragraph. **Insert** at **2** × **3** table, and then type the following information:

Time	**Show up on time and don't hurry to leave**
Attire	**Dress appropriately for the job**
Work Area	**Keep your work area neat and organized**

9 Select the entire table. **AutoFit Contents** and **Center** the table. Display **Backstage** view and preview the document. **Save** and **Close** the document but leave Word open. Hold this file until you complete this project.

10 From **Sample templates**, create a document based on the **Origin Fax** template. Save the document in your **Word Chapter 2** folder as **Lastname_Firstname_2F_Fax** and then add the file name to the footer—called the *First Page Footer* in this template.

11 Click the *Pick a date* placeholder, type **2/15/2016** and then type the following for the remaining controls:

From:	**Kevin Rau**
Phone:	**(608) 555-1347**
Fax:	**(608) 555-1348**
Company Name:	**Madison Staffing Services**
To:	**Jane Westerfield**
Phone:	**(608) 555-0034**
Fax:	**(608) 555-0035**

12 Locate and right-click *Kevin Rau*; remove the content control. Delete the lower *Company Name* text and remove the control to its right. In the *Type comments* control, type **Jane: I know you are on leave, so I thought I would fax this Job Tips memo to you. We look forward to your return.**

13 In the **Document Panel**, add your name and course information and the **Keywords job tips, fax Save** the document.

14 As directed by your instructor, print or submit electronically the two files that are the results of this project. **Exit** Word.

End You have completed Project 2F

Content-Based Assessments

Apply 2A and 2B skills from these Objectives:

1. Create a Table
2. Add Text to a Table
3. Format a Table
4. Create a New Document from an Existing Document
5. Change and Reorganize Text
6. Use the Proofing Options
7. Create a Document Using a Template

myitlab grader

Mastering Word | Project 2G Job Letter

In the following Mastering Word project, you will create a new document from an existing document, format a table, and then create a fax cover using a template. Your completed documents will look similar to Figure 2.48.

Project Files

For Project 2G, you will need the following files:

w02G_Letter_Text
w02G_Letterhead
w02G_Resume
Equity Fax template from Word's installed templates

You will save your documents as:

Lastname_Firstname_2G_Job_Letter
Lastname_Firstname_2G_Resume
Lastname_Firstname_2G_Fax

Project Results

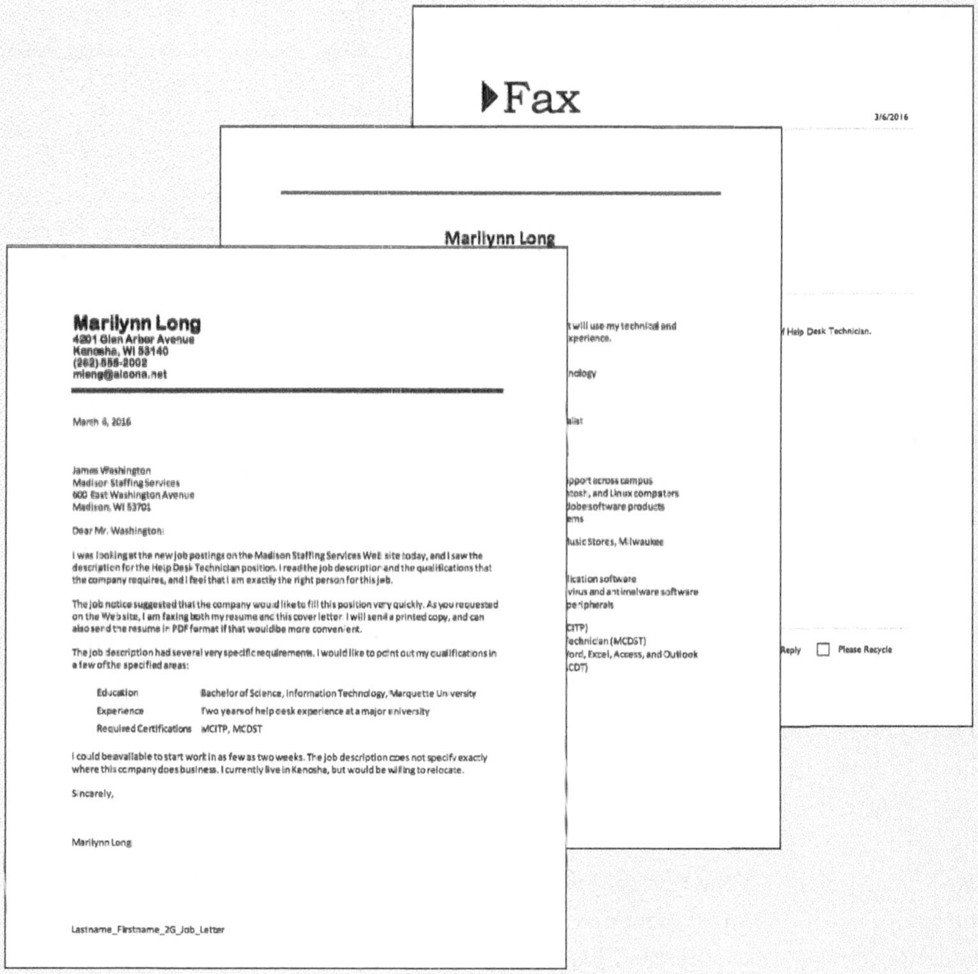

Figure 2.48

(Project 2G Job Letter continues on the next page)

Mastering Word | Project 2G Job Letter (continued)

1 **Start** Word and display rulers and formatting marks. By using the **New from existing** template, create a document from the file **w02G_Letterhead**. **Save** the document in your **Word Chapter 2** folder as **Lastname_Firstname_2G_Job_Letter** Add the file name to the footer. Move to the end of the document, and then on the **Home tab**, apply the **No Spacing** style. Type **March 6, 2016** and then press Enter four times. Type the following:

James Washington
Madison Staffing Services
600 East Washington Avenue
Madison, WI 53701

2 Press Enter two times, type **Dear Mr. Washington:** and press Enter two times. **Insert** the text from the file **w02G_Letter_Text** and remove the blank line at the bottom of the selected text.

3 Move to the top of the document, and then by using either the **Spelling and Grammar** dialog box, or by right-clicking selected words, correct spelling, grammar, and word usage errors. In the paragraph that begins *I was looking*, in the third line, locate and right-click *corporation*. Use the shortcut menu to open the **Thesaurus** and change the word to the synonym *company*. In the same line, change *correct* to the synonym *right*.

4 In the paragraph that begins *I currently*, select the first sentence of the paragraph and drag it to the end of the same paragraph. In the second blank line below the paragraph that begins *The job description*, **Insert** a **2 × 3** table, and then type the text shown in **Table 1** below.

5 Select the entire table. **AutoFit Contents**, **Center** the table, remove the table borders, and then add **3 pt** spacing before and after by typing **3** in the **Spacing** boxes and pressing Enter.

6 In the **Document Panel**, add your name and course information and the **Keywords job letter** Preview the document. **Save** and **Close** the document but leave Word open. Hold the file until you complete this project.

7 From your student files, open **w02G_Resume**. **Save** the document in your **Word Chapter 2** folder as **Lastname_Firstname_2G_Resume** Add the file name to the footer.

8 **Insert** a new second row in the table. In the first cell of the new row, type **OBJECTIVE** and then press Tab. Type **To obtain a Help Desk Technician position that will use my technical and communication skills and computer support experience.** In the same cell, add **12 pt Spacing After**.

9 Select the entire table. On the **Layout tab**, **AutoFit Contents**. Remove the table borders, and then display the **Borders and Shading** dialog box. With the table selected, create a **Custom** single solid line **1 1/2 pt** top border.

10 In the first row of the table, select both cells and then **Merge Cells**. **Center** the five lines and apply **Bold**. In the first row, select *Marilynn Long* and change the **Font Size** to **20 pt** and add **36 pt Spacing Before**. In the e-mail address at the bottom of the first row, add **24 pt Spacing After**.

11 In the first column, apply **Bold** to the four headings. In the cell to the right of *EDUCATION*, **Bold** the names of the two schools, and add **12 pt Spacing After** the two lines that begin *September*. In the cell to the right of *RELEVANT EXPERIENCE*, bold the names of the two jobs—*IT Help Desk Specialist* and *Computer Technician*. In the same cell, below the line that begins *January 2014*, apply bullets to the four lines that comprise the job duties. Create a similar bulleted list for the duties as a Computer Technician. Add **12 pt Spacing After** to the last line of each of the bulleted lists.

12 In the cell to the right of *CERTIFICATIONS*, select all four lines and create a bulleted list. In the **Document Panel**, add your name and course information and the **Keywords help desk resume** and then submit your document as directed. **Save** and **Close** the document but leave Word open.

13 From **Sample templates**, create a document based on the **Origin Fax** template. **Save** the document in your **Word**

Table 1

Education	Bachelor of Science, Information Technology, Marquette University
Experience	Two years of help desk experience at a major university
Required Certifications	MCITP, MCDST

(Return to Step 5)

(Project 2G Job Letter continues on the next page)

Mastering Word | Project 2G Job Letter (continued)

Chapter 2 folder as **Lastname_Firstname_2G_Fax** and then add the file name to the footer—called a *First Page Footer* in this template.

14 Type the text shown in **Table 2** for the content controls.

15 Locate and right-click *Marilynn Long*; remove the content control. In the **Document Panel**, add your name and course information and the **Keywords fax cover page** As directed by your instructor, print or submit electronically the three files from this project. **Exit** Word.

Table 2

Pick a date	**3/6/2016**
From:	**Marilynn Long**
Phone:	**(608) 555-0967**
Fax:	**(608) 555-0966**
Company Name:	Remove this content control and row heading
To:	**James Washington, Recruiter**
Phone:	**(608) 555-0034**
Fax:	**(608) 555-0035**
Company Name	**Madison Staffing Services**
Comments:	**Two pages to follow that include my resume and a cover letter for the position of Help Desk Technician.**

(Return to Step 15)

End **You have completed Project 2G**

Apply a combination of the 2A and 2B skills.

GO! Fix It | Project **2H** New Jobs

In this project, you will construct a solution by applying any combination of the skills you practiced from the Objectives in Projects 2A and 2B.

Project Files

For Project 2H, you will need the following file:

w02H_New_Jobs

You will save your document as:

Lastname_Firstname_2H_New_Jobs

From the student files that accompany this textbook, locate and open the file w02H_New_Jobs, and then save the file in your Word Chapter 2 folder as **Lastname_Firstname_2H_New_Jobs**

This document contains errors that you must find and correct. Read and examine the document, and then edit to correct the errors that you find and to improve the overall document format. Types of errors could include, but are not restricted to:

- Spelling errors
- Grammar errors
- Word choice errors
- Duplicate words
- Unattractive table column widths
- Title not merged across the top row of the table
- Inconsistent spacing before and after paragraphs in the table

Things you should know to complete this project:

- Viewing the document in Print Preview will help identify some of the problems
- The Spelling and Grammar checker will be useful
- Adjust the column widths *before* merging the title

Save your document and add the file name to the footer. In the Document Panel, type your firstname and lastname in the Author box and your course name and section number in the Subject box. In the Keywords box type **job listings** and then save your document and submit as directed.

End You have completed Project 2H

Apply a combination of the 2A and 2B skills.

GO! Make It | Project 2I Training

Project Files

For Project 2I, you will need the following file:

New blank Word document

You will save your document as:

Lastname_Firstname_2I_Training

Start Word, and then save the file in your Word Chapter 2 folder as **Lastname_Firstname_2I_Training**

Use the skills you practiced in this chapter to create the table shown in Figure 2.49. The first row font is Cambria 16 pt, the remainder is Cambria 14 pt. The spacing after the first row is 36 pt, the spacing at the bottom of the rows is 12 pt.

Add the file name to the footer; in the Document Panel, add your name and course information and the Keywords **online training** Save your document, and then submit as directed.

Project Results

Selected Training Programs Available Online

Software	Program Title
Microsoft Word	• Create your first Word document I • Getting started with Word 2010 • Use the Navigation Pane to search and move around in your document • Create your first Word document II
Microsoft Excel	• Get to know Excel 2010: Create your first workbook • Charts I: How to create a chart in Excel • Get to know Excel 2010: Enter formulas • Sort data in a range or table

Lastname_Firstname_2I_Training

Figure 2.49

End You have completed Project 2I

Apply a combination of the 2A and 2B skills.

GO! Solve It | Project 2J Job Postings

Project Files

For Project 2J, you will need the following files:

New blank Word document
w02J_Job_Postings

You will save your documents as:

Lastname_Firstname_2J_Letterhead
Lastname_Firstname_2J_Job_Postings

Print the w02J_Job_Postings document, and use the information to complete this project. Create a new company letterhead and save it in your Word Chapter 2 folder as **Lastname_Firstname_2J_Letterhead** Add the file name to the footer. Add your name, your course name and section number, and the keyword **letterhead** to the Properties area.

Create a new document based on the existing document you just created. The new document will be a list of new jobs posted by Madison Staffing Services. The job posting should include the letterhead, introductory text, and a table that includes the information about the new jobs that are currently available. The job list should be in table format. Use either two or three columns, and label the columns appropriately. Format the table, the table borders, and the text in an attractive, readable manner.

Save the document as **Lastname_Firstname_2J_Job_Postings** Add the file name to the footer, and add your name, your course name and section number, and the keywords **new jobs** to the Properties area. Submit your two files as directed.

Performance Element	Performance Level		
	Exemplary: You consistently applied the relevant skills	Proficient: You sometimes, but not always, applied the relevant skills	Developing: You rarely or never applied the relevant skills
Create and format a letterhead template	The text in the letterhead is appropriately formatted, the company name stands out, and the spacing between paragraphs is attractive.	The letterhead is complete, but the line spacing or text formatting is not appropriate for a letterhead.	The spacing and formatting is not appropriate for a letterhead.
Insert a table	The inserted table has the appropriate number of columns and rows to display the information.	The table is not structured to effectively display the information.	No table is inserted in the document.
Format the table structure	Table column widths fit the information, extra space is added between the rows, and borders are attractively formatted.	The column widths do not reflect the amount of information in the column, and the spacing between the cells is insufficient.	Table displays only default column widths and spacing.
Format the text in the table	Important text is highlighted and formatted appropriately, making the text easy to read and interpret.	Some text formatting is added, but the formatting does not highlight the important information.	No text formatting is included.

End You have completed Project 2J

Apply a combination of the 2A and 2B skills.

GO! Solve It | Project 2K Agenda

Project Files

For Project 2K, you will need the following file:
Agenda template from Word's Online templates

You will save your document as:
Lastname_Firstname_2K_Agenda

Create a new document based on an agenda template—such as the *Formal meeting agenda* template—from the Agenda templates at Microsoft Office Online. Save the agenda as **Lastname_Firstname_2K_Agenda** Use the following information to prepare an agenda for a Madison Staffing Services meeting.

The meeting will be chaired by Marilyn Kelly and will be the monthly meeting of the company administrators—Kevin Rau, Marilyn Kelly, Andre Randolph, Susan Nguyen, and Charles James. The meeting will be held on March 15, 2016, at 3:00 p.m. The old business (open issues) include 1) expanding services into the printing and food service industries; 2) recruitment at the UW-Madison and MATC campuses; and 3) the addition of a part-time trainer. The new business will include 1) recruitment at the University of Wisconsin, Milwaukee; 2) rental of office space in or around Milwaukee; 3) purchase of new computers for the training room; and 4) renewal of snow removal service contract.

Add the file name to the footer, and add your name, your course name and section number, and the keywords **agenda, monthly administrative meeting** to the Properties area. Submit as directed.

	Performance Level		
	Exemplary: You consistently applied the relevant skills	Proficient: You sometimes, but not always, applied the relevant skills	Developing: You rarely or never applied the relevant skills
Performance Element: Select an agenda template	Agenda template is appropriate for the information provided for the meeting.	Agenda template is used, but does not fit the information provided.	No template is used for the agenda.
Add appropriate information to the template	All information is inserted in the appropriate places. All unused controls are removed.	All information is included, but not in the appropriate places, and not all of the unused controls are removed.	Information is missing and unused placeholders are not removed.
Format template information	All text in the template is properly aligned and formatted.	All text is included, but alignment or formatting is inconsistent.	No additional formatting has been added.

End **You have completed Project 2K**

Outcomes-Based Assessments

Rubric

The following outcomes-based assessments are *open-ended assessments*. That is, there is no specific correct result; your result will depend on your approach to the information provided. Make *Professional Quality* your goal. Use the following scoring rubric to guide you in *how* to approach the problem and then to evaluate *how well* your approach solves the problem.

The *criteria*—Software Mastery, Content, Format and Layout, and Process—represent the knowledge and skills you have gained that you can apply to solving the problem. The *levels of performance*—Professional Quality, Approaching Professional Quality, or Needs Quality Improvements—help you and your instructor evaluate your result.

	Your completed project is of Professional Quality if you:	**Your completed project is Approaching Professional Quality if you:**	**Your completed project Needs Quality Improvements if you:**
1-Software Mastery	Choose and apply the most appropriate skills, tools, and features and identify efficient methods to solve the problem.	Choose and apply some appropriate skills, tools, and features, but not in the most efficient manner.	Choose inappropriate skills, tools, or features, or are inefficient in solving the problem.
2-Content	Construct a solution that is clear and well organized, contains content that is accurate, appropriate to the audience and purpose, and is complete. Provide a solution that contains no errors in spelling, grammar, or style.	Construct a solution in which some components are unclear, poorly organized, inconsistent, or incomplete. Misjudge the needs of the audience. Have some errors in spelling, grammar, or style, but the errors do not detract from comprehension.	Construct a solution that is unclear, incomplete, or poorly organized; contains some inaccurate or inappropriate content; and contains many errors in spelling, grammar, or style. Do not solve the problem.
3-Format and Layout	Format and arrange all elements to communicate information and ideas, clarify function, illustrate relationships, and indicate relative importance.	Apply appropriate format and layout features to some elements, but not others. Overuse features, causing minor distraction.	Apply format and layout that does not communicate information or ideas clearly. Do not use format and layout features to clarify function, illustrate relationships, or indicate relative importance. Use available features excessively, causing distraction.
4-Process	Use an organized approach that integrates planning, development, self-assessment, revision, and reflection.	Demonstrate an organized approach in some areas, but not others; or, use an insufficient process of organization throughout.	Do not use an organized approach to solve the problem.

Apply a combination of the 2A and 2B skills.

GO! Think | Project 2L Workshops

Project Files

For Project 2L, you will need the following files:

New blank Word document
w02L_Workshop_Information

You will save your document as:

Lastname_Firstname_2L_Workshops

Madison Staffing Services offers a series of workshops for its employee-clients. Any temporary employee who is available during the workshop hours can attend the workshops and there is no fee. Currently, the company offers three-session workshops covering Excel and Word, a two-session workshop covering Business Communication, and a one-session workshop covering *Creating a Resume*.

Print the w02L_Workshop_Information file and use the information to complete this project. Create an announcement with a title, an introductory paragraph, and a table listing the workshops and the topics covered in each workshop. Use the file w02L_Workshop_Information for help with the topics covered in each workshop. Format the table cells appropriately. Add an appropriate footer and information to the Document Panel. Save the document as **Lastname_Firstname_2L_Workshops** and submit it as directed.

End **You have completed Project 2L**

Apply a combination of the 2A and 2B skills.

GO! Think | Project 2M Planner

Project Files

For Project 2M, you will need the following files:

Weekly appointment sheet template from Word's Online templates
w02M_Workshop_Information

You will save your document as:

Lastname_Firstname_2M_Planner

To keep track of workshops provided to employees, the trainer fills out a weekly schedule. Each workshop lasts two hours. Print the w02M_Workshop_Information file and use part or all of the information to complete this project.

Create a new document using a template, for example the *Weekly appointment sheet* template found in the Planners category in the online template list. Create a template for a week, and include the first part of each workshop series, along with the Creating a Resume workshop. Customize the template as necessary to include *Room* and *Workshop* titles for each day of the week. The computer skills workshops are held in the Lab, the others are held in Room 104. The trainer always schedules the hour before each workshop for preparation. Fill out the workshop schedule and use your choice of formatting to indicate that the workshops cover a two-hour period. Add appropriate information to the Document Panel. Save the document as **Lastname_Firstname_2M_Planner** and submit it as directed.

End **You have completed Project 2M**

Apply a combination of the 2A and 2B skills.

You and GO! | Project 2N Personal Resume

Project Files

For Project 2N, you will need the following file:

New blank Word document

You will save your documents as

Lastname_Firstname_2N_Personal_Resume
Lastname_Firstname_2N_Cover_Letter

Locate and print the information for a job for which you would like to apply, and then create your own personal resume using a table and a cover letter. Include any information that is appropriate, including your objective for a specific job, your experience, skills, education, honors, or awards. Create your own letterhead and cover letter, using the cover letter you created in Project 2B as a guide.

To complete the assignment, be sure to format the text appropriately, resize the table columns in the resume to best display the information, and check both documents for spelling and grammar errors.

Save the resume as **Lastname_Firstname_2N_Personal_Resume** and the cover letter as **Lastname_Firstname_2N_Personal_Cover_Letter** Add the file name to the footer, and add your name, your course name and section number, and the keywords **my resume** and **cover letter** to the Properties area. Submit your file as directed.

End You have completed Project 2N

Apply a combination of the 2A and 2B skills.

GO! CD-ROM

GO! Collaborate | Project 2O Bell Orchid Hotels Group Running Case

Your instructor may assign this group case project to your class. If your instructor assigns this project, he or she will provide you with information and instructions to work as part of a group. The group will apply the skills gained thus far to help the Bell Orchid Hotel Group achieve its business goals.

End You have completed Project 2O

Creating Research Papers, Newsletters, and Merged Mailing Labels

OUTCOMES

At the end of this chapter you will be able to:

OBJECTIVES

Mastering these objectives will enable you to:

PROJECT 3A

Create a research paper that includes citations and a bibliography.

1. Create a Research Paper (p. 165)
2. Insert Footnotes in a Research Paper (p. 167)
3. Create Citations and a Bibliography in a Research Paper (p. 172)

PROJECT 3B

Create a multiple-column newsletter and merged mailing labels.

4. Format a Multiple-Column Newsletter (p. 181)
5. Use Special Character and Paragraph Formatting (p. 186)
6. Create Mailing Labels Using Mail Merge (p. 189)

Shutterstock

In This Chapter

Microsoft Word provides many tools for creating complex documents. For example, Word has tools that enable you to create a research paper that includes citations, footnotes, and a bibliography. You can also create multiple-column newsletters, format the nameplate at the top of the newsletter, use special character formatting to create distinctive title text, and add borders and shading to paragraphs to highlight important information.

In this chapter, you will edit and format a research paper, create a two-column newsletter, and then create a set of mailing labels to mail the newsletter to multiple recipients.

The projects in this chapter relate to **Memphis Primary Materials** located in the Memphis area. In addition to collecting common recyclable materials, the company collects and recycles computers, monitors, copiers and fax machines, cell phones, wood pallets, and compostable materials. The company's name comes from the process of capturing the "primary materials" of used items for reuse. Memphis Primary Materials ensures that its clients comply with all state and local regulations. They also provide training to clients on the process and benefits of recycling.

Project 3A Research Paper

myitlab
Project 3A Training

Project Activities

In Activities 3.01 through 3.07, you will edit and format a research paper that contains an overview of recycling activities in which businesses can engage. This paper was created by Elizabeth Freeman, a student intern working for Memphis Primary Metals, and will be included in a customer information packet. Your completed document will look similar to Figure 3.1.

Project Files

For Project 3A, you will need the following file:

w03A_Green_Business

You will save your document as:

Lastname_Firstname_3A_Green_Business

Project Results

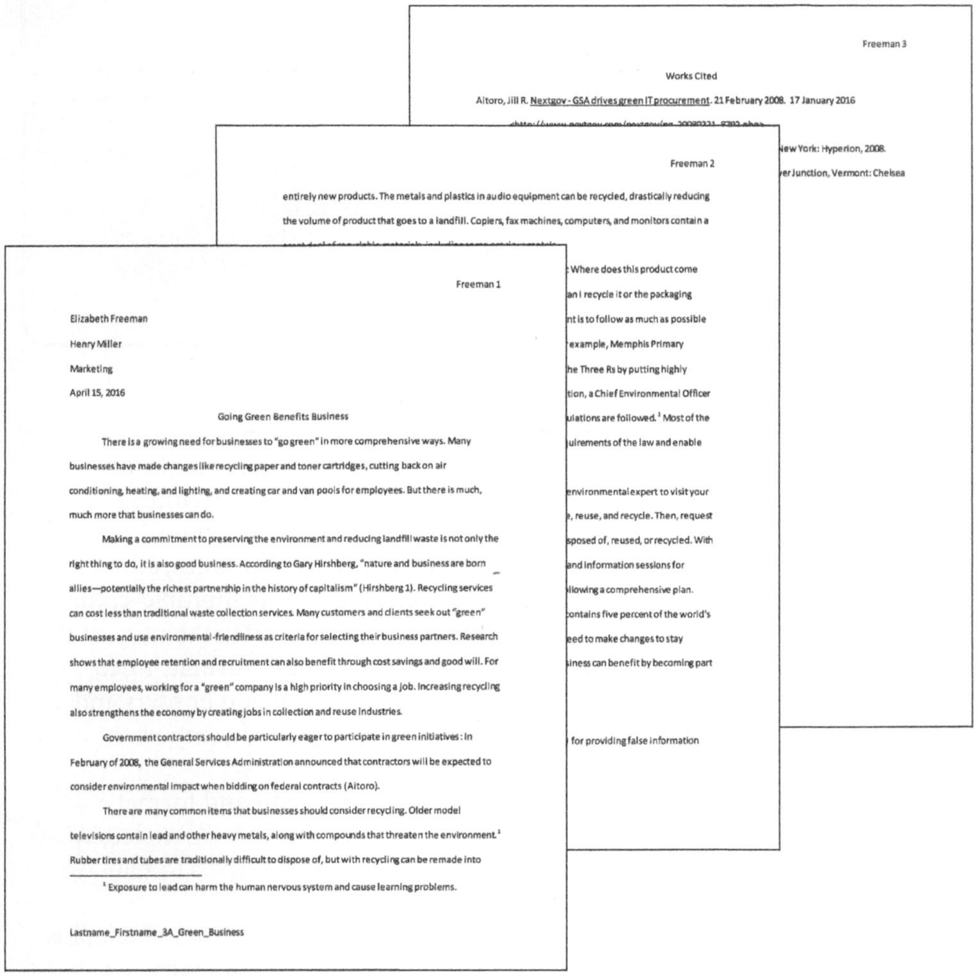

Freeman 3

Works Cited

Aitoro, Jill R. Nextgov - GSA drives green IT procurement. 21 February 2008. 17 January 2016

Freeman 2

entirely new products. The metals and plastics in audio equipment can be recycled, drastically reducing the volume of product that goes to a landfill. Copiers, fax machines, computers, and monitors contain a

Freeman 1

Elizabeth Freeman

Henry Miller

Marketing

April 15, 2016

Going Green Benefits Business

There is a growing need for businesses to "go green" in more comprehensive ways. Many businesses have made changes like recycling paper and toner cartridges, cutting back on air conditioning, heating, and lighting, and creating car and van pools for employees. But there is much, much more that businesses can do.

Making a commitment to preserving the environment and reducing landfill waste is not only the right thing to do, it is also good business. According to Gary Hirshberg, "nature and business are born allies—potentially the richest partnership in the history of capitalism" (Hirshberg 1). Recycling services can cost less than traditional waste collection services. Many customers and clients seek out "green" businesses and use environmental-friendliness as criteria for selecting their business partners. Research shows that employee retention and recruitment can also benefit through cost savings and good will. For many employees, working for a "green" company is a high priority in choosing a job. Increasing recycling also strengthens the economy by creating jobs in collection and reuse industries.

Government contractors should be particularly eager to participate in green initiatives: In February of 2008, the General Services Administration announced that contractors will be expected to consider environmental impact when bidding on federal contracts (Aitoro).

There are many common items that businesses should consider recycling. Older model televisions contain lead and other heavy metals, along with compounds that threaten the environment.[1] Rubber tires and tubes are traditionally difficult to dispose of, but with recycling can be remade into

[1] Exposure to lead can harm the human nervous system and cause learning problems.

Lastname_Firstname_3A_Green_Business

Figure 3.1
Project 3A Green Business

Objective 1 | Create a Research Paper

When you write a research paper or a report for college or business, follow a format prescribed by one of the standard ***style guides***—a manual that contains standards for the design and writing of documents. The two most commonly used styles for research papers are those created by the ***Modern Language Association (MLA)*** and the ***American Psychological Association (APA)***; there are several others.

Activity 3.01 | Formatting Text and Page Numbers in a Research Paper

When formatting the text for your research paper, refer to the standards for the style guide that you have chosen. In this activity, you will create a research paper using the MLA style. The MLA style uses 1-inch margins, a 0.5″ first line indent, and double spacing throughout the body of the document, with no extra space above or below paragraphs.

1. **Start** Word. From your student files, locate and open the document **w03A_Green_Business.** If necessary, display the formatting marks and rulers. In the location where you are storing your projects for this chapter, create a new folder named **Word Chapter 3** and then save the file in the folder as **Lastname_Firstname_3A_Green_Business**

2. Press Ctrl + A to select the entire document. On the **Home tab**, in the **Paragraph group**, click the **Line and Paragraph Spacing** button, and then change the line spacing to **2.0.** On the **Page Layout tab**, in the **Paragraph group**, change the **Spacing After** to **0 pt**.

3. Press Ctrl + Home to deselect and move to the top of the document. Press Enter one time to create a blank line at the top of the document, and then click to position the insertion point in the blank line. Type **Elizabeth Freeman** and press Enter.

4. Type **Henry Miller** and press Enter. Type **Marketing** and press Enter. Type **April 15, 2016** and press Enter. Type **Going Green Benefits Business** Right-click anywhere in the line you just typed, and then on the Mini toolbar, click the **Center** button. Compare your screen with Figure 3.2.

Figure 3.2

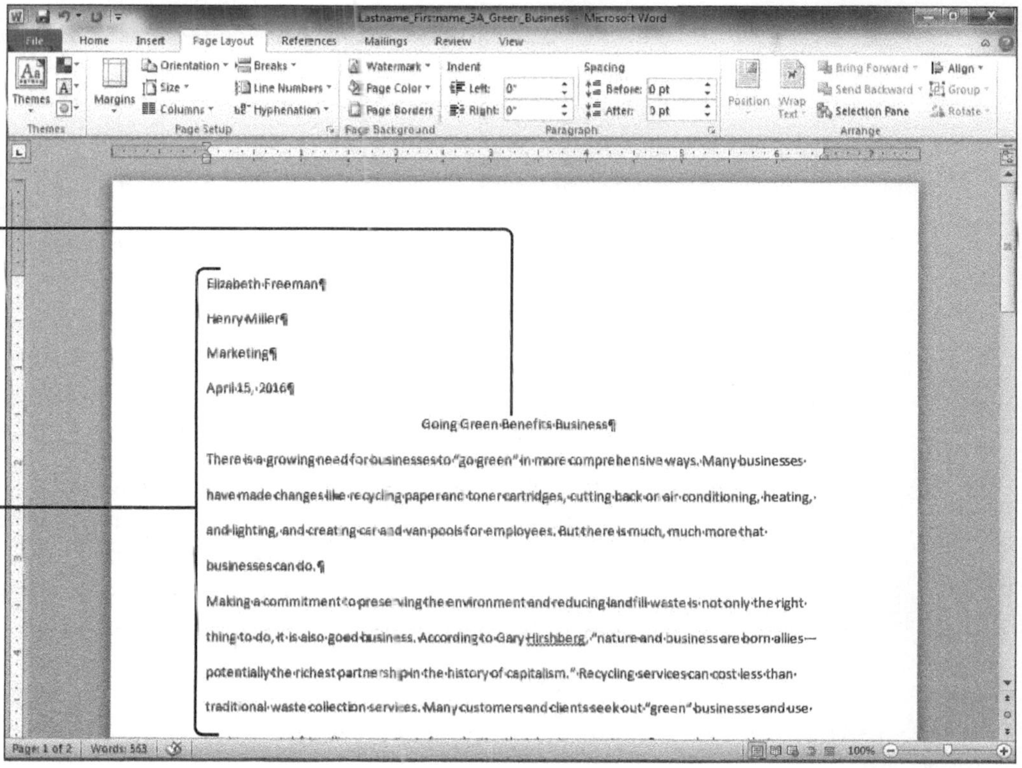

Title centered

Text double-spaced

> **More Knowledge | Creating a Document Heading for a Research Paper**
>
> On the first page of an MLA-style research paper, on the first line, type the report author. On the second line, type the person for whom the report is prepared—for example, your professor or supervisor. On the third line, type the name of the class or department or organization. On the fourth line, type the date. On the fifth line type the report title and center it.

5. At the top of the **Page 1**, point anywhere in the white top margin area, right-click, and then click **Edit Header**. In the header area, type **Freeman** and then press Spacebar.

   Recall that the text you insert into a header or footer displays on every page of a document. Within a header or footer, you can insert many different types of information; for example, automatic page numbers, the date, the time, the file name, or pictures.

6. On the **Design tab**, in the **Header & Footer group**, click the **Page Number** button, and then point to **Current Position**. In the displayed gallery, under **Simple**, click **Plain Number**. Compare your screen with Figure 3.3.

   Word will automatically number the pages using this number format.

Figure 3.3

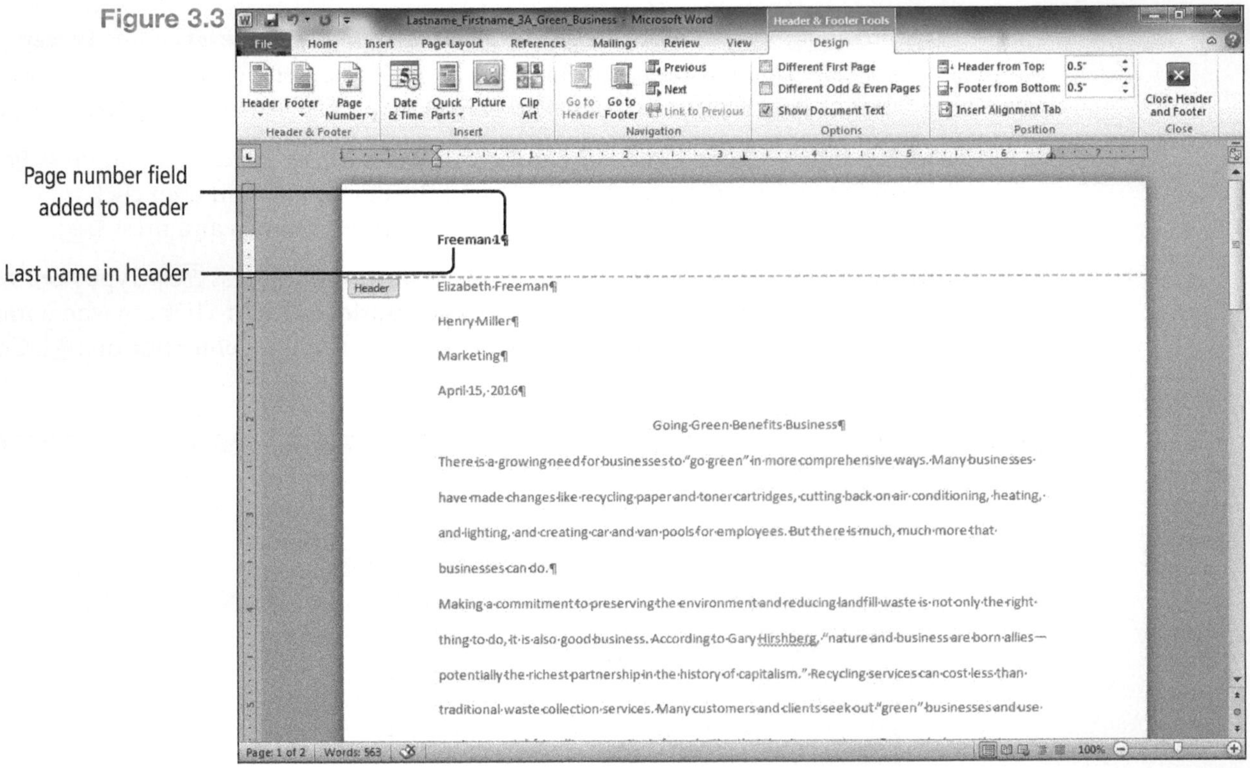

7. On the **Home tab**, in the **Paragraph group**, click the **Align Text Right** button. Double-click anywhere in the document to close the header area.

8. Near the top of **Page 1**, locate the paragraph beginning *There is a growing*, and then click to position the insertion point at the beginning of the paragraph. By moving the vertical scroll bar, scroll to the end of the document, hold down Shift, and then click to right of the last paragraph mark to select all of the text from the insertion point to the end of the document. Release Shift.

Another Way

Right-click the selected text, click Paragraph, on the Indents and Spacing tab, under Indentation, click the Special arrow, and then click First line. Under Indentation, in the By box, be sure 0.5" displays.

9 With the text selected, on the ruler, point to the **First Line Indent** button, and then drag the button to **0.5" on the horizontal ruler**. Compare your screen with Figure 3.4.

The MLA style uses 0.5-inch indents at the beginning of the first line of every paragraph. Indenting—moving the beginning of the first line of a paragraph to the right or left of the rest of the paragraph—provides visual cues to the reader to help divide the document text and make it easier to read.

Figure 3.4

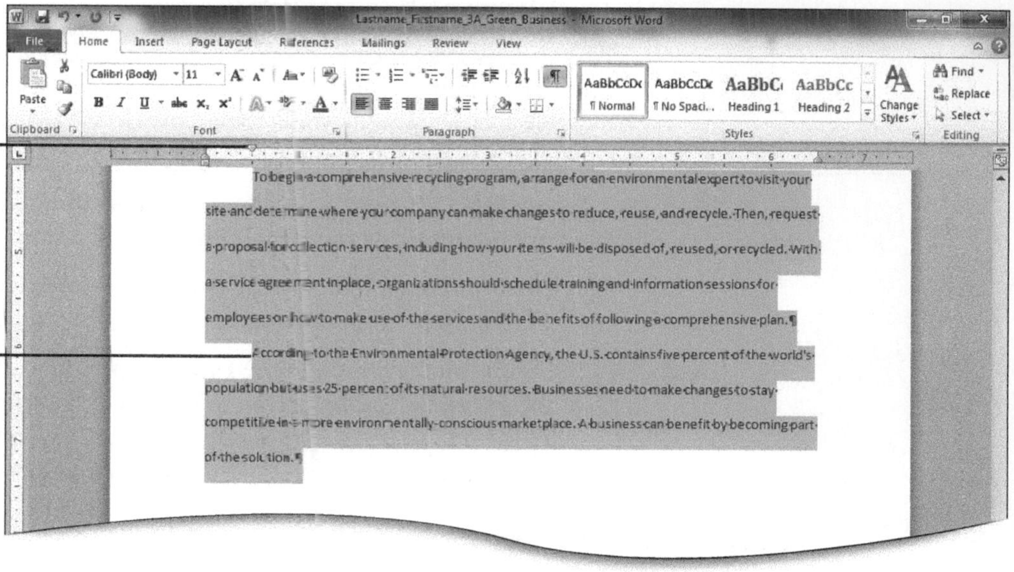

10 Click anywhere to deselect the text. Scroll to view the bottom of **Page 1**, point anywhere in the bottom white margin area, right-click, and then click **Edit Footer**. On the **Design tab**, in the **Insert group**, click the **Quick Parts** button, and then click **Field**. In the **Field** dialog box, under **Field names**, locate and click **FileName**, and then click **OK**.

The file name in the footer is *not* part of the research report format, but it is included in projects in this textbook so that you and your instructor can identify your work.

11 Double-click anywhere in the document to close the Footer area, and then **Save** your document.

> **More Knowledge | Suppressing the Page Number on the First Page**
>
> Some style guidelines require that the page number and other header and footer information on the first page be hidden from view—*suppressed*. To hide the information contained in the header and footer areas on Page 1 of a document, double-click in the header or footer area. Then, on the Design tab, in the Options group, select the Different First Page check box.

Objective 2 | Insert Footnotes in a Research Paper

Reports and research papers typically include information that you find in other sources, and these must be credited. Within report text, numbers mark the location of ***notes***—information that expands on the topic being discussed but that does not fit well in the document text. The numbers refer to ***footnotes***—notes placed at the bottom of the page containing the note, or to ***endnotes***—notes placed at the end of a document or chapter.

Activity 3.02 | Inserting Footnotes

Footnotes can be added as you type the document or after the document is complete. Word renumbers the footnotes automatically, so footnotes do not need to be entered in order, and if one footnote is removed, the remaining footnotes renumber automatically.

1 Scroll to view the top of **Page 2**. Locate the paragraph that begins *Consumers and businesses*. In the seventh line of text, toward the end of the line, click to position the insertion point to the right of the period after *followed*.

2 On the **References tab**, in the **Footnotes group**, click the **Insert Footnote** button.

Word creates space for a footnote in the footnote area at the bottom of the page and adds a footnote number to the text at the insertion point location. Footnote *1* displays in the footnote area, and the insertion point moves to the right of the number. A short black line is added just above the footnote area. You do not need to type the footnote number.

3 Type **Tennessee, for example, imposes penalties of up to $10,000 for providing false information regarding the recycling of hazardous waste.**

This is an explanatory footnote; the footnote provides additional information that does not fit well in the body of the report.

4 Click the **Home tab**, and then in the **Font group**, notice that the font size of the footer is *10 pt*. In the **Paragraph group**, click the **Line and Paragraph Spacing** button, and notice that the line spacing is *1.0*—single-spaced—even though the font size of the document text is 11 pt and the text is double-spaced, as shown in Figure 3.5.

Figure 3.5

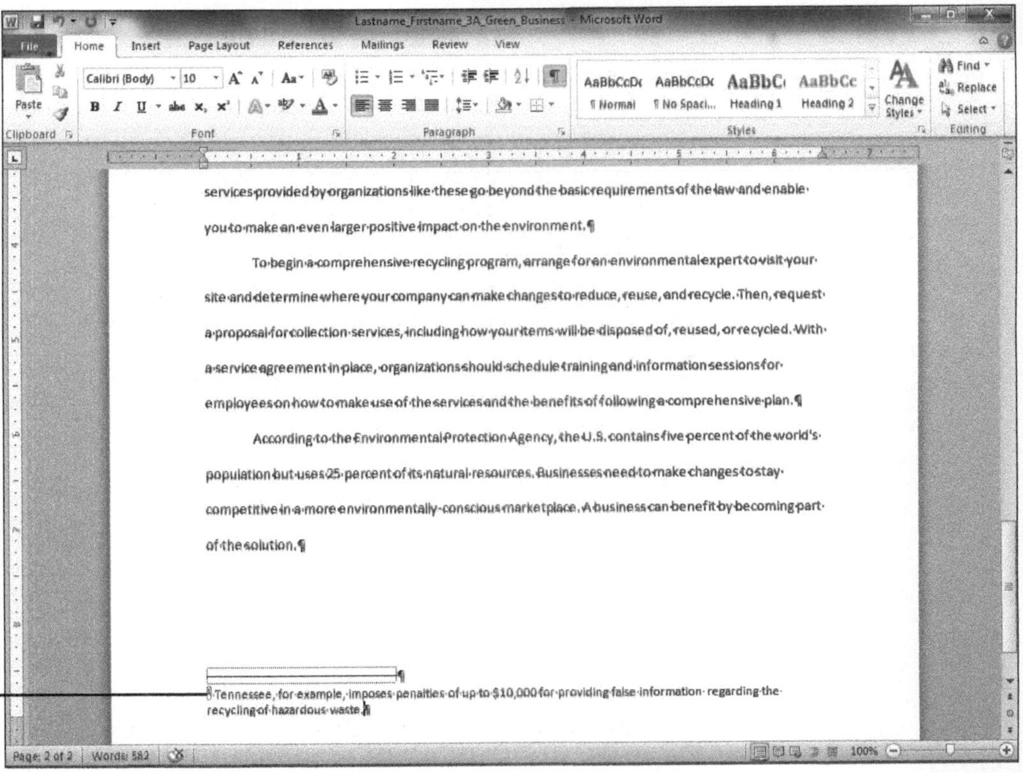

Footnote text, single-spaced and 10 pt. font size

5 Scroll to view the bottom of **Page 1**, and then locate the paragraph that begins *There are many common*. At the end of the second line of text, click to position the insertion point to the right of the period following *environment*.

6 On the **References tab**, in the **Footnotes group**, click the **Insert Footnote** button. Type **Exposure to lead can harm the human nervous system and cause learning problems.** Notice that the footnote you just added becomes the new footnote *1*, as shown in Figure 3.6.

The first footnote is renumbered as footnote *2*.

Figure 3.6

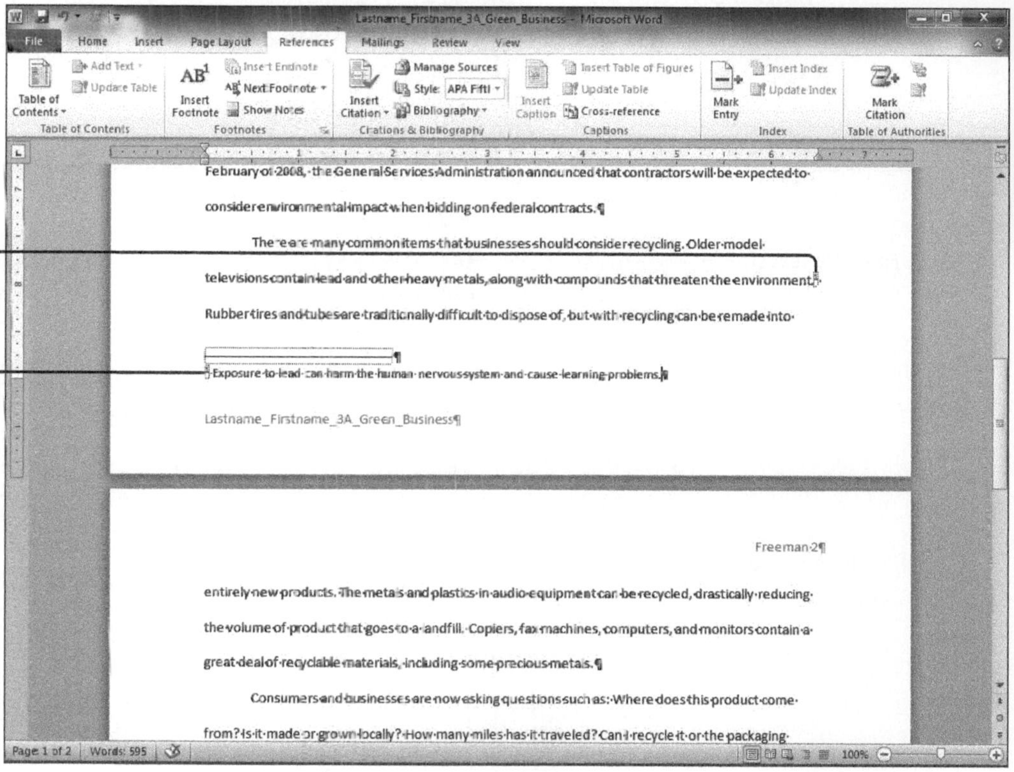

7 **Save** your document.

More Knowledge | Using Symbols Rather Than Numbers for Notes

Instead of using numbers to designate footnotes, you can use standard footnote symbols. The seven traditional symbols, available from the Footnote and Endnote dialog box, in order, are * (asterisk), † (dagger), ‡ (double dagger), § (section mark), || (parallels), ¶ (paragraph mark), and # (number or pound sign). This sequence can be continuous (this is the default setting), or can begin anew with each page.

Activity 3.03 | Modifying a Footnote Style

Microsoft Word contains built-in paragraph formats called ***styles***—groups of formatting commands, such as font, font size, font color, paragraph alignment, and line spacing—which can be applied to a paragraph with one command.

The default style for footnote text is a single-spaced paragraph that uses a 10-point Calibri font and no paragraph indents. MLA style specifies double-spaced text in all areas of a research paper—including footnotes. According to the MLA style, first lines of footnotes must also be indented 0.5 inch and use the same font size as the report text.

1 Scroll to view the bottom of **Page 2**. Point anywhere in the footnote text and right-click, and then from the shortcut menu, click **Style**. Compare your screen with Figure 3.7.

The Style dialog box displays, listing the styles currently in use in the document, in addition to some of the word processing elements that come with special built-in styles. Because you right-clicked on the footnote text, the selected style is the Footnote Text style.

Figure 3.7

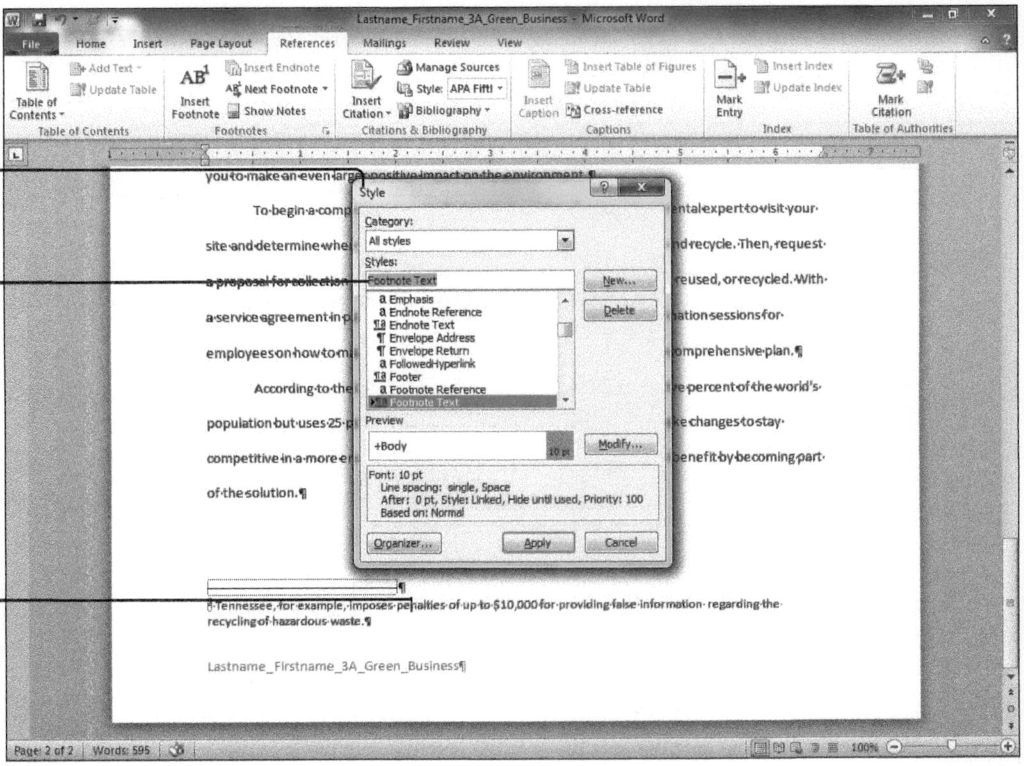

2 In the **Style** dialog box, click the **Modify** button to display the **Modify Style** dialog box.

3 In the **Modify Style** dialog box, locate the small **Formatting** toolbar in the center of the dialog box, click the **Font Size button arrow**, click **11**, and then compare your screen with Figure 3.8.

Figure 3.8

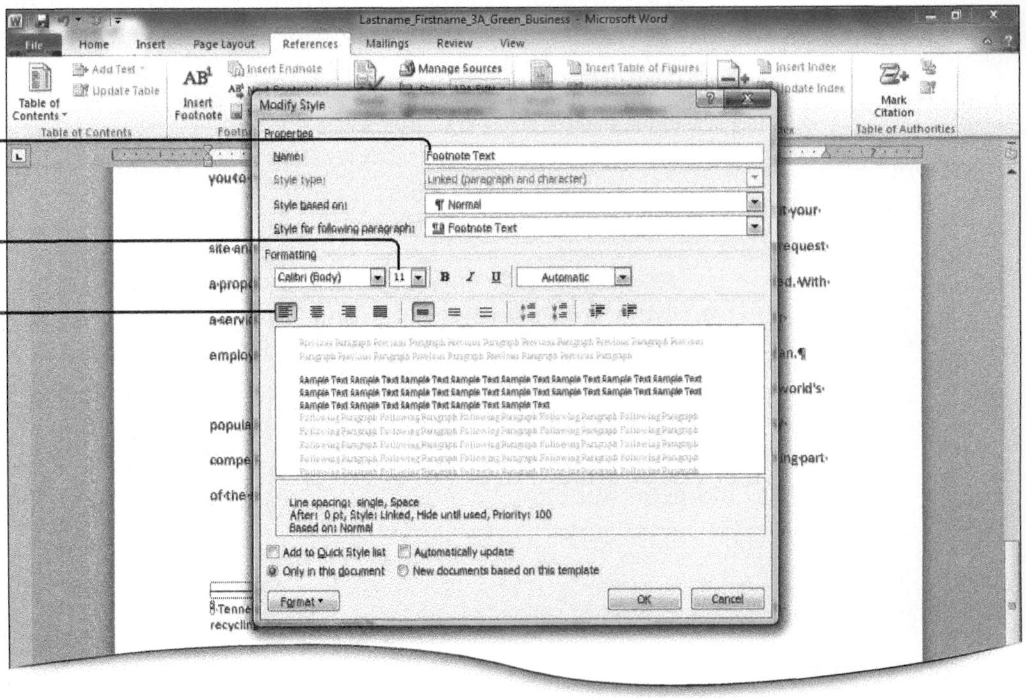

4. In the lower left corner of the dialog box, click the **Format** button, and then click **Paragraph**. In the **Paragraph** dialog box, under **Indentation**, click the **Special arrow**, and then click **First line**.

5. Under **Spacing**, click the **Line spacing** button arrow, and then click **Double**. Compare your dialog box with Figure 3.9.

Figure 3.9

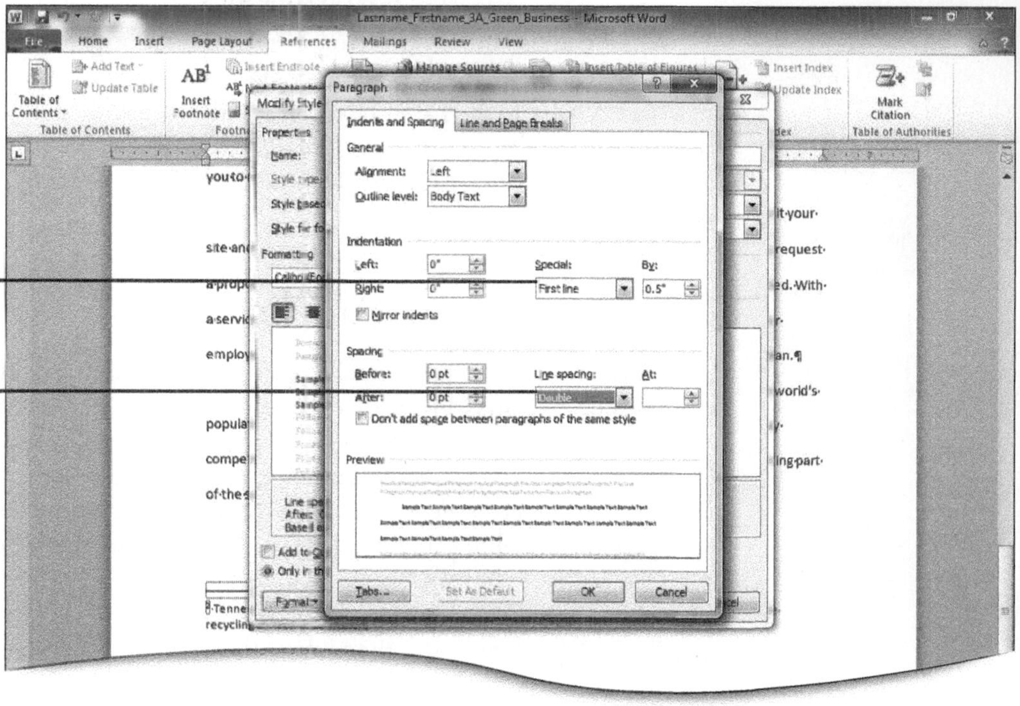

6. Click **OK** to close the **Paragraph** dialog box, click **OK** to close the **Modify Style** dialog box, and then click **Apply** to apply the new style. Notice that when you click Apply, the Style dialog box closes. Compare your screen with Figure 3.10.

   Your inserted footnotes are formatted with the new Footnote Text paragraph style; any new footnotes that you insert will also use this format.

Figure 3.10

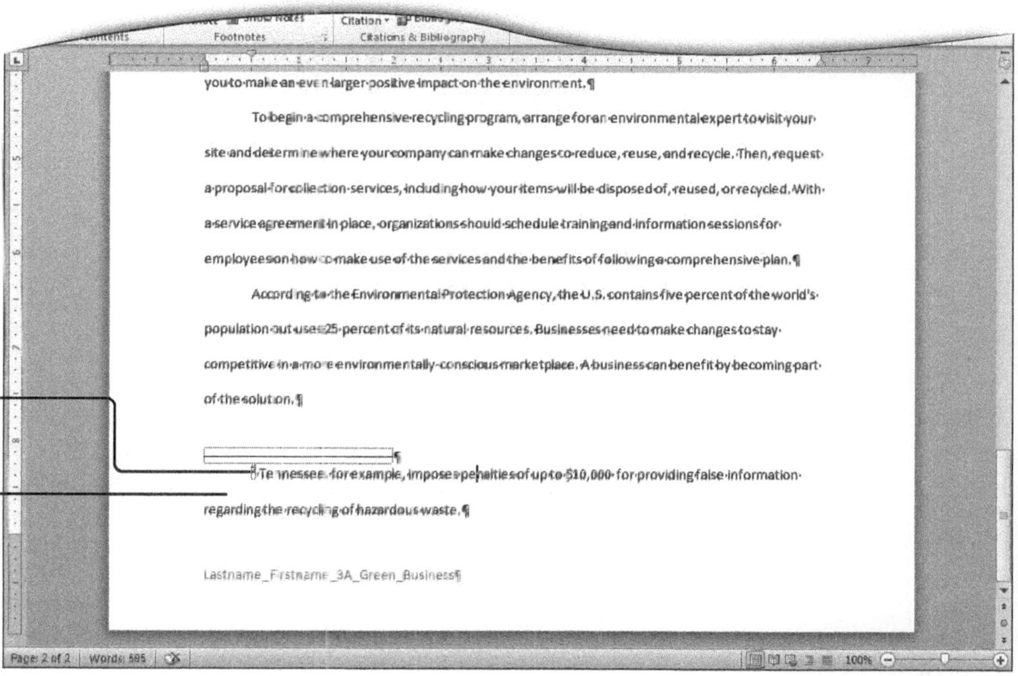

7 Scroll to view the bottom of **Page 1** to confirm that the new format was also applied to the first footnote, and then **Save** your document.

Objective 3 | Create Citations and a Bibliography in a Research Paper

When you use quotations from, or detailed summaries of, other people's work, you must specify the source of the information. A ***citation*** is a note inserted into the text of a report or research paper that refers the reader to a source in the bibliography. Create a ***bibliography*** at the end of a document to list the sources referred to in the document. Such a list is typically titled ***Works Cited*** (in MLA style), *Bibliography*, *Sources*, or *References*.

Activity 3.04 | Adding Citations

When writing a long research paper, you will likely reference numerous books, articles, and Web sites. Some of your research sources may be referenced many times, others only one time. References to sources within the text of your research paper are indicated in an *abbreviated* manner. However, as you enter a citation for the first time, you can also enter the *complete* information about the source. Then, when you have finished your paper, you will be able to automatically generate the list of sources that must be included at the end of your research paper.

1 Press Ctrl + Home, and then locate the paragraph that begins *Making a commitment.* In the third line, following the word *capitalism*, click to position the insertion point to the right of the quotation mark.

The citation in the document points to the full source information in the bibliography, which typically includes the name of the author, the full title of the work, the year of publication, and other publication information.

2 On the **References tab**, in the **Citations & Bibliography group**, click the **Style button arrow**, and then click **MLA Sixth Edition** (or the latest edition) to insert a reference using MLA style.

3 Click the **Insert Citation** button, and then click **Add New Source.** Be sure *Book* is selected as the **Type of Source**. Add the following information, and then compare your screen with Figure 3.11:

Author:	**Hirshberg, Gary**
Title:	**Stirring it Up: How to Make Money and Save the World**
Year:	**2008**
City:	**New York**
Publisher:	**Hyperion**

In the MLA style, citations that refer to items on the *Works Cited* page are placed in parentheses and are referred to as ***parenthetical references***—references that include the last name of the author or authors and the page number in the referenced source, which you add to the reference. No year is indicated, and there is no comma between the name and the page number.

Figure 3.11

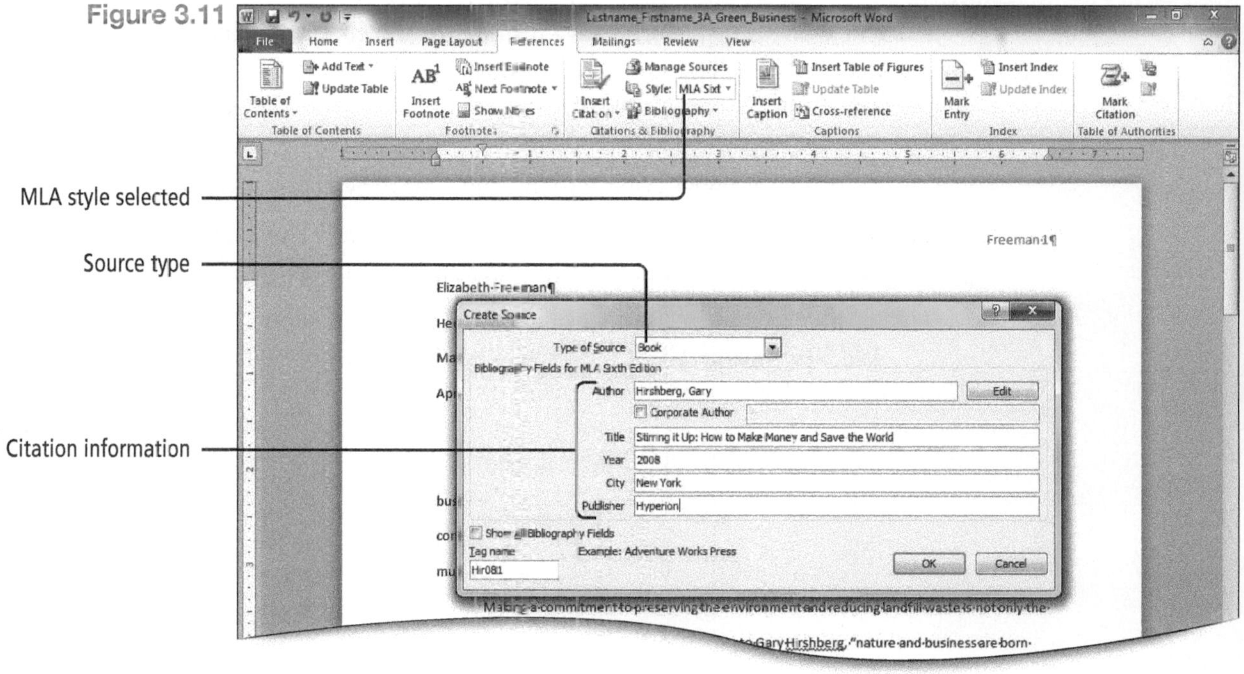

Note | Citing Corporate Authors

If the author of a document is identified as the name of an organization only, select the Corporate Author check box and type the name of the organization in the Corporate Author box.

4 Click **OK** to insert the citation. In the paragraph, point to *(Hirshberg)* and click one time to select the citation.

5 In the lower right corner of the box that surrounds the reference, point to the small arrow to display the ScreenTip *Citation Options*. Click this **Citation Options arrow**, and then from the list of options, click **Edit Citation**.

6 In the **Edit Citation** dialog box, under **Add**, in the **Pages** box, type **1** to indicate that you are citing from page 1 of this source. Compare your screen with Figure 3.12.

Figure 3.12

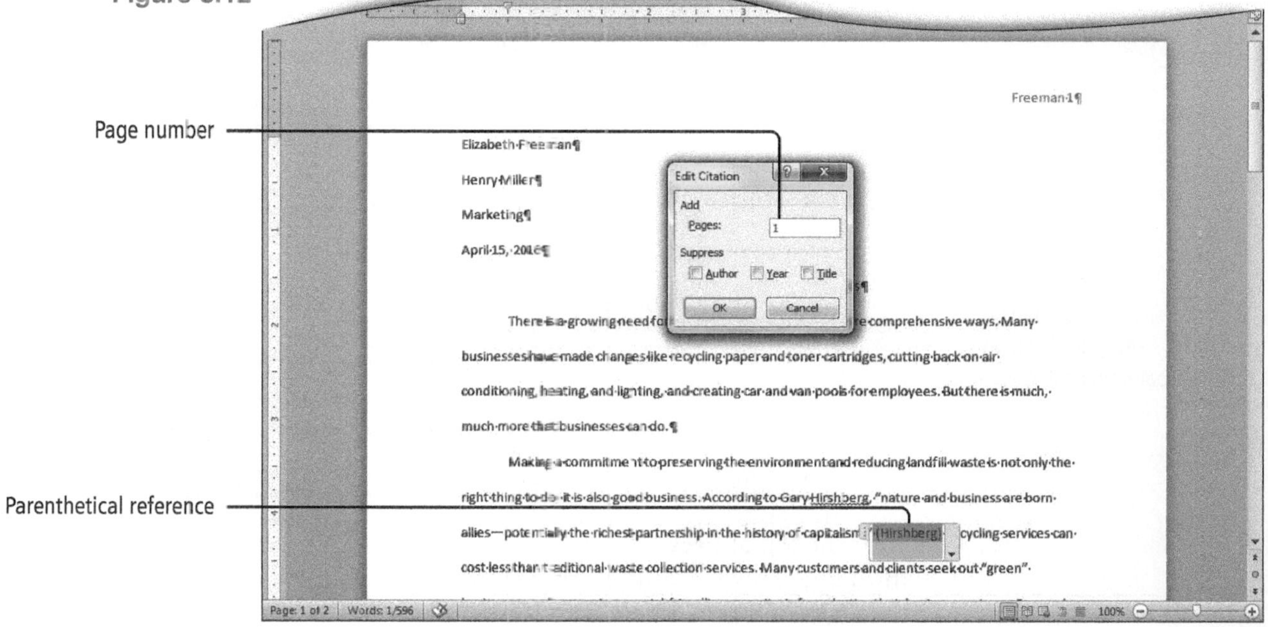

7 Click **OK** to display the page number of the citation. Click outside of the citation box to deselect it. Then type a period to the right of the citation, and delete the period to the left of the quotation mark.

In the MLA style, if the reference occurs at the end of a sentence, the parenthetical reference always displays to the left of the punctuation mark that ends the sentence.

8 In the next paragraph, which begins *Government contractors*, click to position the insertion point at the end of the paragraph, but before the period.

9 In the **Citations & Bibliography group**, click the **Insert Citation** button, and then click **Add New Source**. Click the **Type of Source arrow**, scroll down as necessary, and then click **Web site**. Add the following information:

Author:	**Aitoro, Jill R.**
Name of Web Page:	**Nextgov - GSA drives green IT procurement**
Year:	**2008**
Month:	**February**
Day:	**21**
Year Accessed:	**2016**
Month Accessed:	**January**
Day Accessed:	**17**
URL:	**http://www.nextgov.com/nextgov/ng_20080221_8792.php**

10 Compare your screen with Figure 3.13, and then click **OK** to close the **Create Source** dialog box and add the citation.

A parenthetical reference is added. Because the cited Web page has no page numbers, only the author name is used in the parenthetical reference.

Figure 3.13

Web site citation

Insertion point indicates location of parenthetical reference

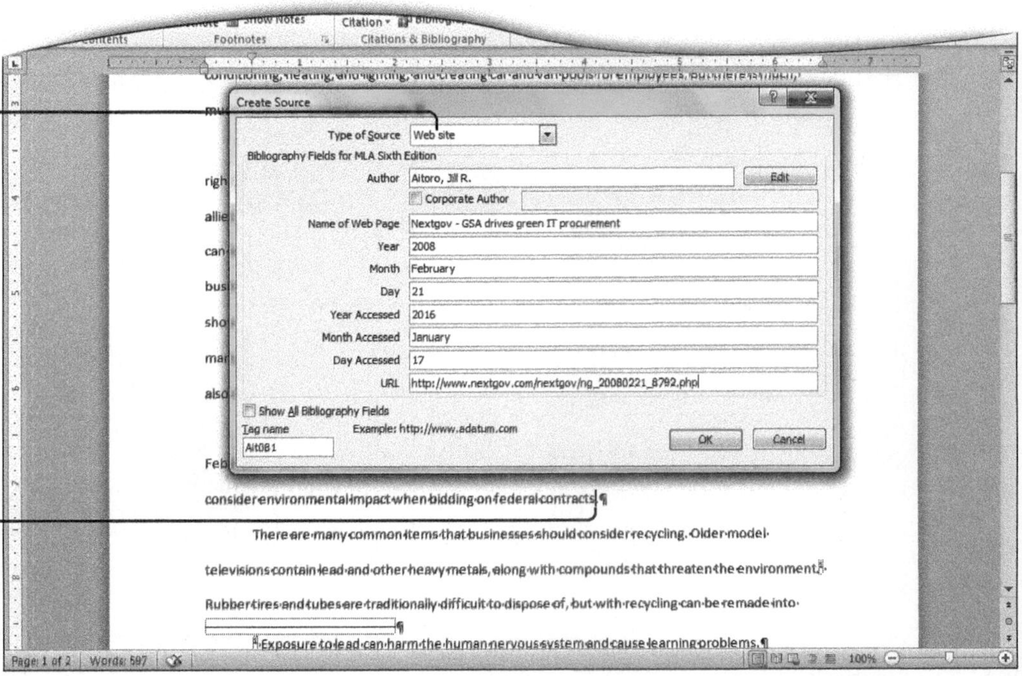

11 Near the top of **Page 2**, in the paragraph that begins *Consumers and businesses*, in the third line, click to position the insertion point following the word *toxic* to the left of the question mark.

12 In the **Citations & Bibliography group**, click the **Insert Citation** button, and then click **Add New Source**. Click the **Type of Source arrow**, if necessary scroll to the top of the list, click **Book**, and then add the following information:

Author:	**Scott, Nicky**
Title:	**Reduce, Reuse, Recycle: An Easy Household Guide**
Year:	**2007**
City:	**White River Junction, Vermont**
Publisher:	**Chelsea Green Publishing**

13 Click **OK**. Click the inserted citation to select it, click the **Citation Options arrow**, and then click **Edit Citation**.

14 In the **Edit Citation** dialog box, under **Add**, in the **Pages** box, type **7** to indicate that you are citing from page 7 of this source. Click **OK**.

15 On the **References tab**, in the **Citations & Bibliography group**, click the **Manage Sources** button. In the **Source Manager** dialog box, under **Current List**, click the third source and then compare your screen with Figure 3.14.

The Source Manager dialog box displays. Other citations on your computer display in the Master List box. The citations for the current document display in the Current List box. Word maintains the Master List so that if you use the same sources regularly, you can copy sources from your Master List to the current document. A preview of the selected bibliography entry also displays at the bottom of the dialog box.

Figure 3.14

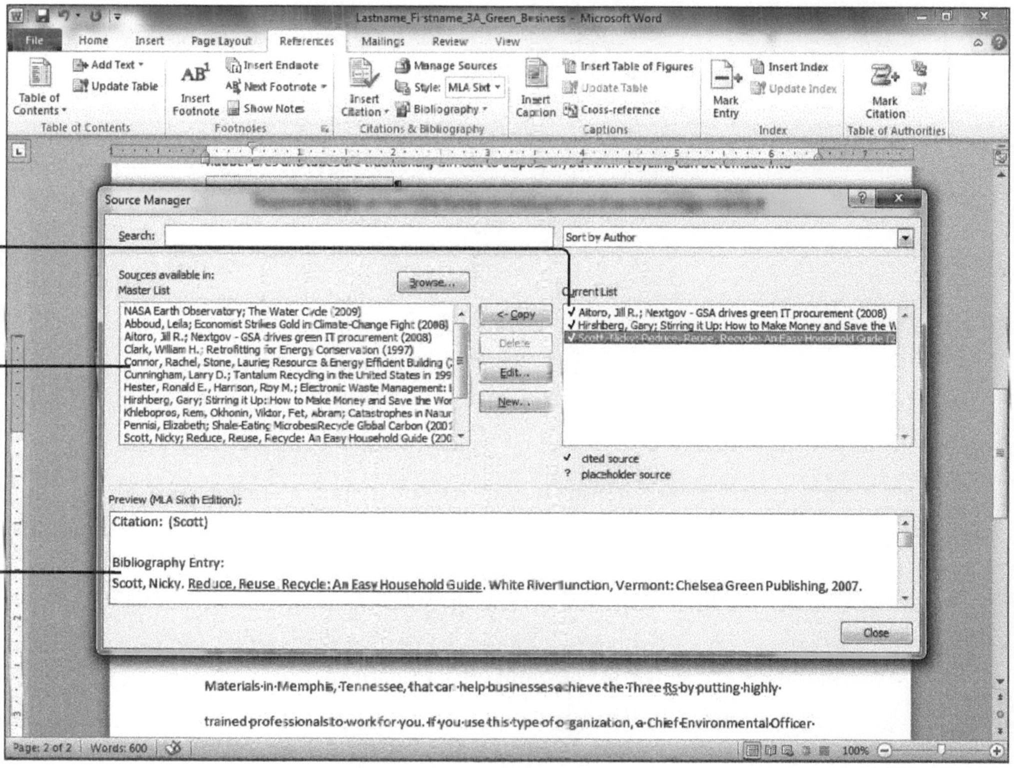

16 At the bottom of the **Source Manager** dialog box, click **Close**. Click anywhere in the document to deselect the parenthetical reference, and then **Save** your document.

Activity 3.05 | Inserting Page Breaks

In this activity you will insert a manual page break so that you can begin your bibliography on a new page.

1. Press Ctrl + End to move the insertion point to the end of the document. Notice that the insertion point displays at the end of the final paragraph, but above the footnote—the footnote is always associated with the page that contains the citation.

2. Press Ctrl + Enter to insert a manual page break.

   A ***manual page break*** forces a page to end at the insertion point location, and then places any subsequent text at the top of the next page. Recall that the new paragraph retains the formatting of the previous paragraph, so the first line is indented.

3. On the ruler, point to the **First Line Indent** button, and then drag the **First Line Indent** button to the left to **0 inches on the horizontal ruler**.

4. Scroll as necessary to position the bottom of **Page 2** and the top of **Page 3** on your screen.

5. Compare your screen with Figure 3.15, and then **Save** your document.

   A ***page break indicator***, which shows where a manual page break was inserted, displays at the bottom of the Page 2, and the footnote remains on the page that contains the citation, even though it displays below the page break indicator.

Figure 3.15

First Line Indent button at 0 inches

Page Break indicator shows manual page break inserted

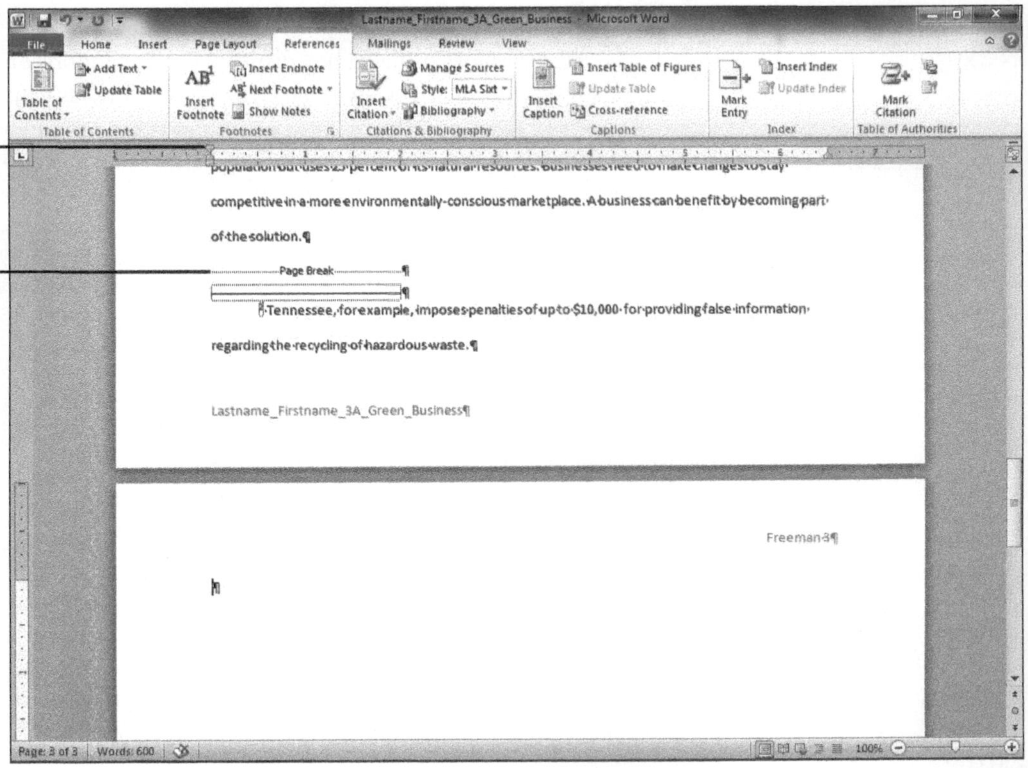

Activity 3.06 | Creating a Reference Page

At the end of a report or research paper, include a list of each source referenced. *Works Cited* is the reference page heading used in the MLA style guidelines. Other styles may refer to this page as a *Bibliography* (Business Style) or *References* (APA Style). This information is always displayed on a separate page.

1. With the insertion point blinking in the first line of **Page 3**, type **Works Cited** and then press Enter. On the **References tab**, in the **Citations & Bibliography group**, in the **Style** box, be sure *MLA* displays.

2. In the **Citations & Bibliography group**, click the **Bibliography** button, and then near the bottom of the list, click **Insert Bibliography**.

3 Scroll as necessary to view the entire list of three references, and then click anywhere in the inserted text.

The bibliography entries that you created display as a field, which is indicated by the gray shading when you click in the text. The field links to the Source Manager for the citations. The references display alphabetically by the author's last name.

4 In the bibliography, point to the left of the first entry—beginning *Aitoro, Jill*—to display the [pointer] pointer. Drag down to select all three references.

> **Another Way**
>
> Display the Paragraph dialog box. Under Spacing, click the Line spacing arrow, and then click Double. Under Spacing, in the After box, type 0.

5 On the **Home tab**, in the **Paragraph group**, change the **Line spacing** to **2.0**, and then on the **Page Layout tab**, in the **Paragraph group**, change the **Spacing After** to **0 pt**.

The entries display according to MLA guidelines; the text is double-spaced, the extra space between paragraphs is removed, and each entry uses a ***hanging indent***—the first line of each entry extends 0.5 inch to the left of the remaining lines of the entry.

6 At the top of **Page 3**, right-click the *Works Cited* title, and then click the **Center** button [Center]. Compare your screen with Figure 3.16, and then **Save** [Save] your document.

In MLA style, the *Works Cited* title is centered.

Figure 3.16

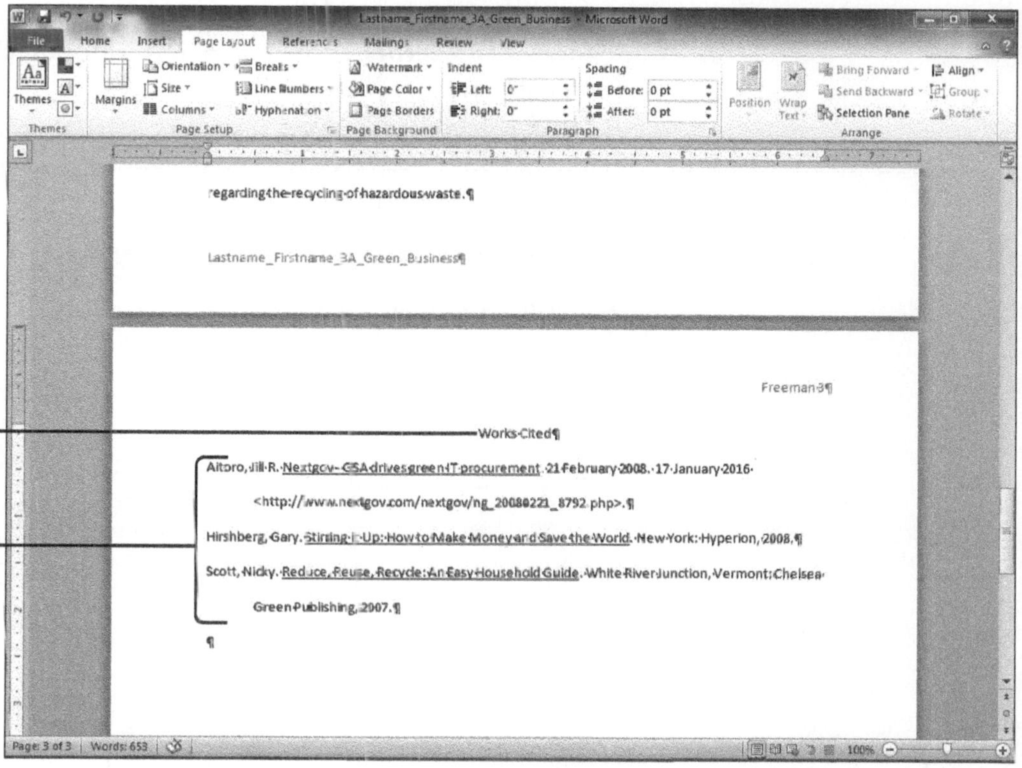

Activity 3.07 | Managing Document Properties

Recall that document property information is stored in the Document Panel. An additional group of property categories is also available.

1 Display **Backstage** view. On the right, under the document thumbnail, click **Properties**, and then click **Show Document Panel** to display the **Document Panel**.

2 Type your name and course information, and then add the keywords **green business, research paper**

3 In the upper left corner of the **Document Panel**, click the **Document Properties** button, and then compare your screen with Figure 3.17.

Figure 3.17

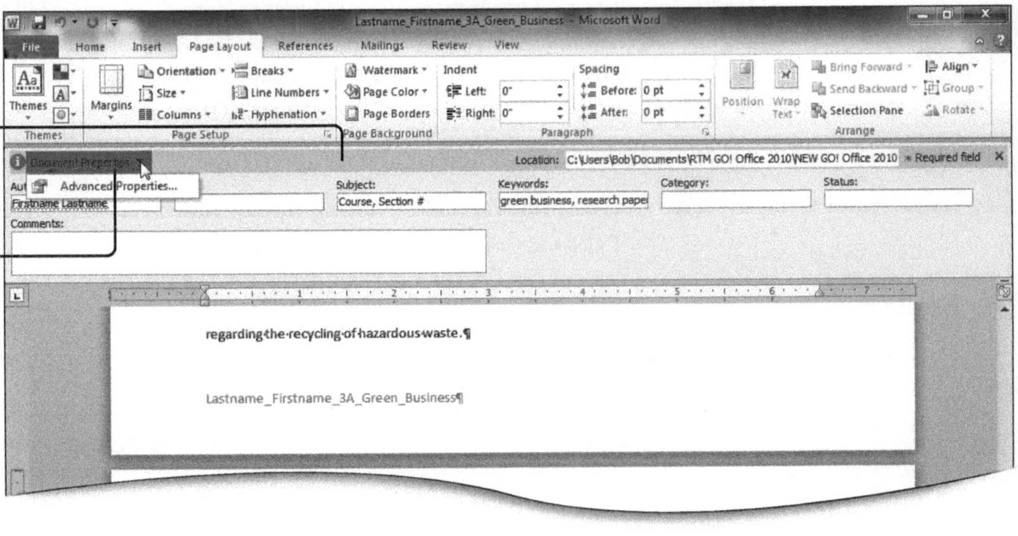

4 Click **Advanced Properties**. In the **Properties** dialog box, click the **Statistics tab**, and then compare your screen with Figure 3.18.

The document statistics show the number of revisions made to the document, the last time the document was edited, and the number of paragraphs, lines, words, and characters in the document.

Figure 3.18

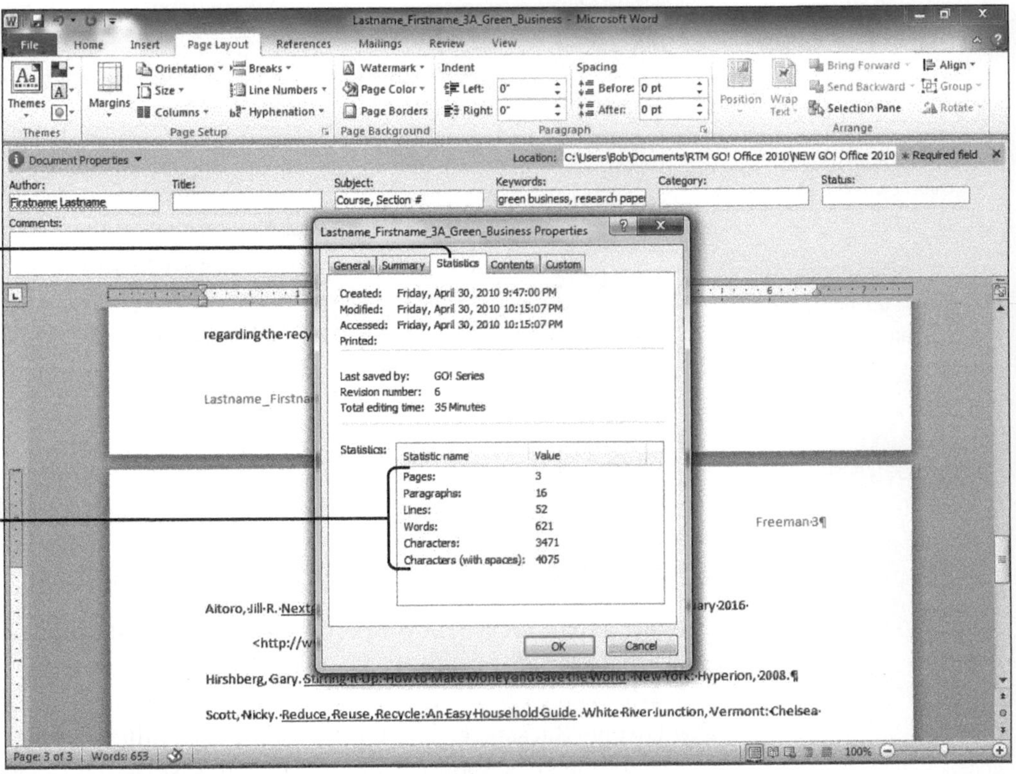

5 In the **Properties** dialog box, click the **Summary tab**. Notice that not all of the categories are filled in, and also notice that there are categories on this tab that are not found in the Document Panel.

Some of the boxes may contain information from your computer system.

6 In the **Properties** dialog box, click in the **Title** box and type **Going Green Benefits Business**

7 Click in the **Manager** box and type **Henry Miller**

8 In the **Company** box, select and delete any existing text, and then type **Memphis Primary Materials**

9 Click in the **Category** box and type **Marketing Documents**

10 Click in the **Comments** box and type **Draft copy of a research report that will be included in the marketing materials packet**

Additional information categories are available by clicking the Custom tab.

11 Compare your screen with Figure 3.19, and then at the bottom of the **Properties** dialog box, click **OK**.

Figure 3.19

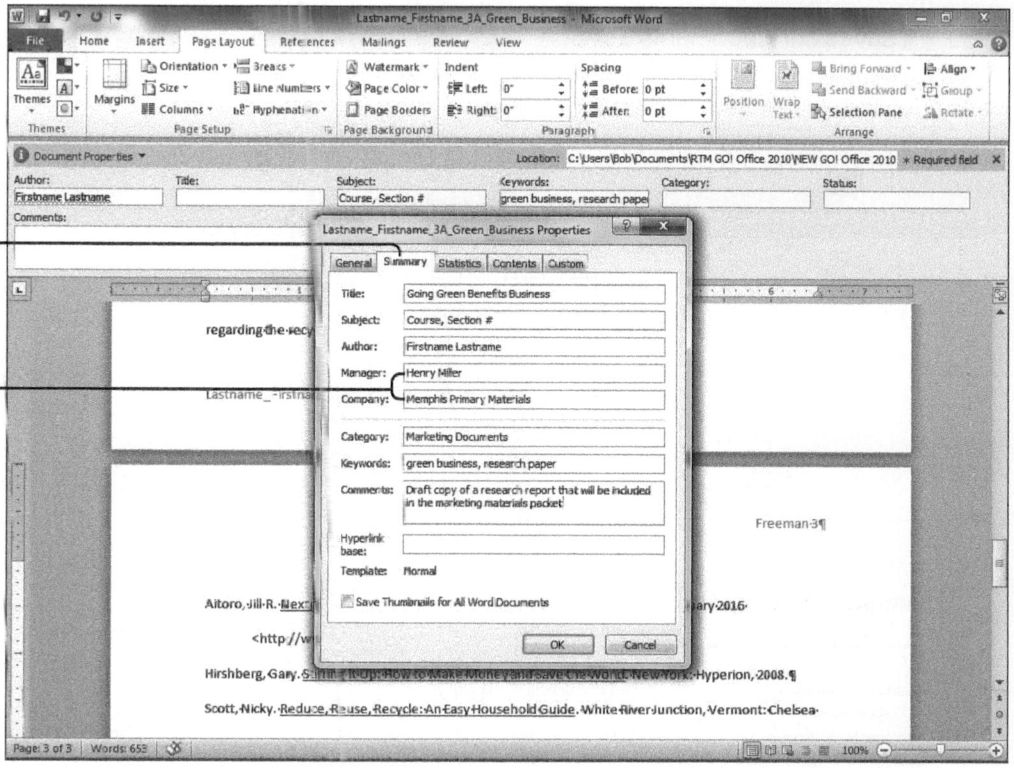

12 **Close** the **Document Panel**. Press Ctrl + F2, and then examine the three pages of your document in **Print Preview**. Redisplay your document.
If necessary, make any corrections or adjustments.

13 **Save** your document, and then print or submit electronically as directed by your instructor. **Exit** Word.

End **You have completed Project 3A**

Project 3B Newsletter with Mailing Labels

myitlab
Project 3B Training

Project Activities

In Activities 3.08 through 3.17, you will edit a newsletter that Memphis Primary Materials sends to its list of customers and subscribers. Your completed documents will look similar to Figure 3.20.

Project Files

For Project 3B, you will need the following files:

New blank Word document
w03B_Memphis_Newsletter
w03B_Addresses

You will save your documents as:

Lastname_Firstname_3B_Memphis_Newsletter
Lastname_Firstname_3B_Mailing_Labels
Lastname_Firstname_3B_Addresses

Project Results

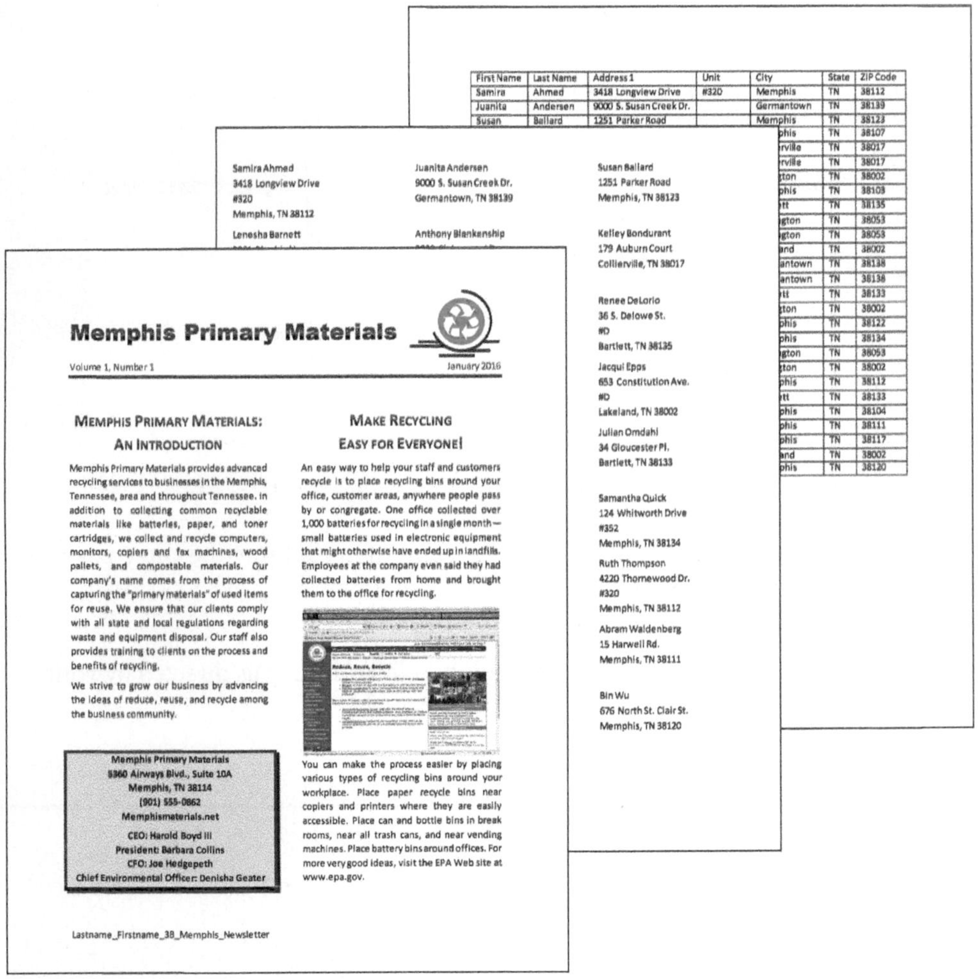

Figure 3.20
Project 3B Memphis Newsletter

Objective 4 | Format a Multiple-Column Newsletter

All newspapers and most magazines and newsletters use multiple columns for articles because text in narrower columns is easier to read than text that stretches across a page. Word has a tool with which you can change a single column of text into two or more columns, and then format the columns. If a column does not end where you want it to, you can end the column at a location of your choice by inserting a ***manual column break.***

Activity 3.08 | Changing One Column of Text to Two Columns

Newsletters are usually two or three columns wide. When using 8.5 × 11-inch paper in portrait orientation, avoid creating four or more columns because they are so narrow that word spacing looks awkward, often resulting in one long word on a line by itself.

1. **Start** Word. From your student files, locate and open the document **w03B_Memphis_Newsletter**. If necessary, display the formatting marks and rulers. **Save** the file in your **Word Chapter 3** folder as **Lastname_Firstname_3B_Memphis_Newsletter** and then add the file name to the footer.

2. Select the first paragraph of text—*Memphis Primary Materials*. From the Mini toolbar, change the **Font** to **Arial Black** and the **Font Size** to **24**.

3. Select the first two paragraphs—the title and the Volume information and date. From the Mini toolbar, click the **Font Color button arrow**, and then under **Theme Colors**, in the fifth column, click the last color—**Blue, Accent 1, Darker 50%**.

4. With the text still selected, on the **Home tab**, in the **Paragraph group**, click the **Borders button arrow**, and then at the bottom, click **Borders and Shading**.

5. In the **Borders and Shading** dialog box, on the **Borders tab**, click the **Color arrow**, and then under **Theme Colors**, in the fifth column, click the last color—**Blue, Accent 1, Darker 50%**.

Another Way

In the Preview area, click the Bottom Border button.

6. Click the **Width arrow**, and then click **3 pt**. In the **Preview** box at the right, point to the *bottom* border of the small preview and click one time. Compare your screen with Figure 3.21.

Figure 3.21

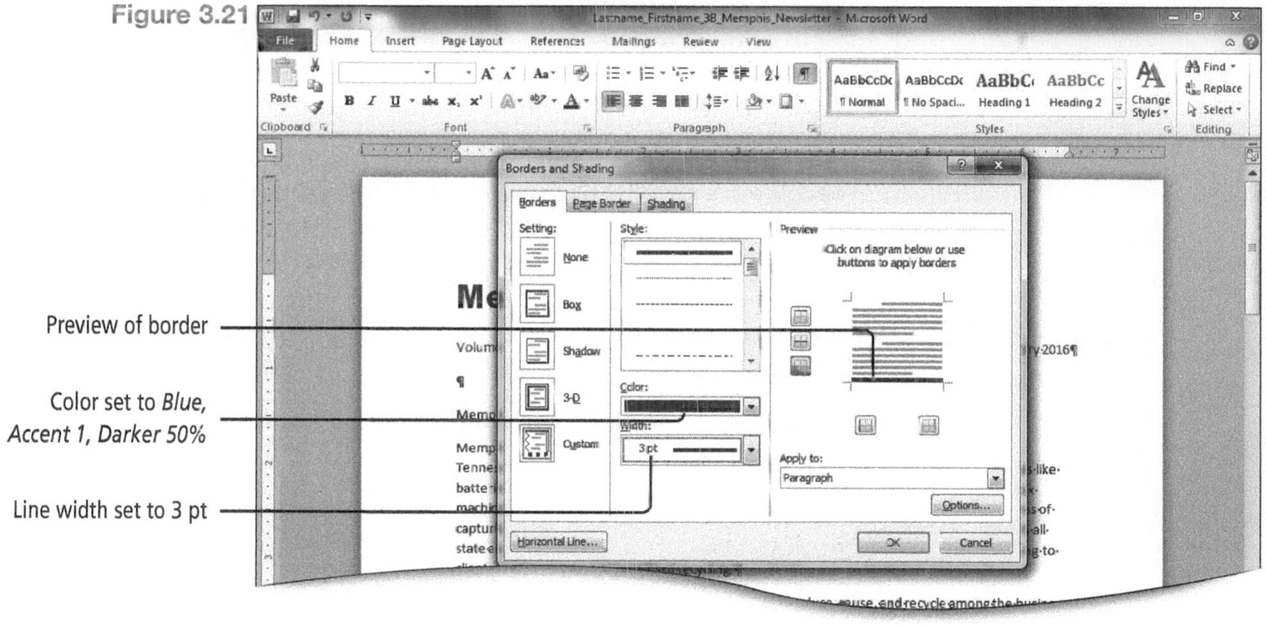

7 In the **Borders and Shading** dialog box, click **OK**.

The line visually defines the newsletter ***nameplate***—the banner on the front page of a newsletter that identifies the publication.

8 Below the nameplate, beginning with the paragraph *Memphis Primary Materials: An Introduction*, select all of the text to the end of the document, which extends to two pages.

9 On the **Page Layout tab**, in the **Page Setup group**, click the **Columns** button. From the **Columns** gallery, click **Two**.

10 Scroll up to view the top of **Page 1**, and then compare your screen with Figure 3.22, and then **Save** the document.

Word divides the text into two columns, and inserts a ***section break*** below the nameplate, dividing the one-column section of the document from the two-column section of the document. A ***section*** is a portion of a document that can be formatted differently from the rest of the document. A section break marks the end of one section and the beginning of another section. Do not be concerned if your columns do not break at the same line as shown in the figure.

Figure 3.22

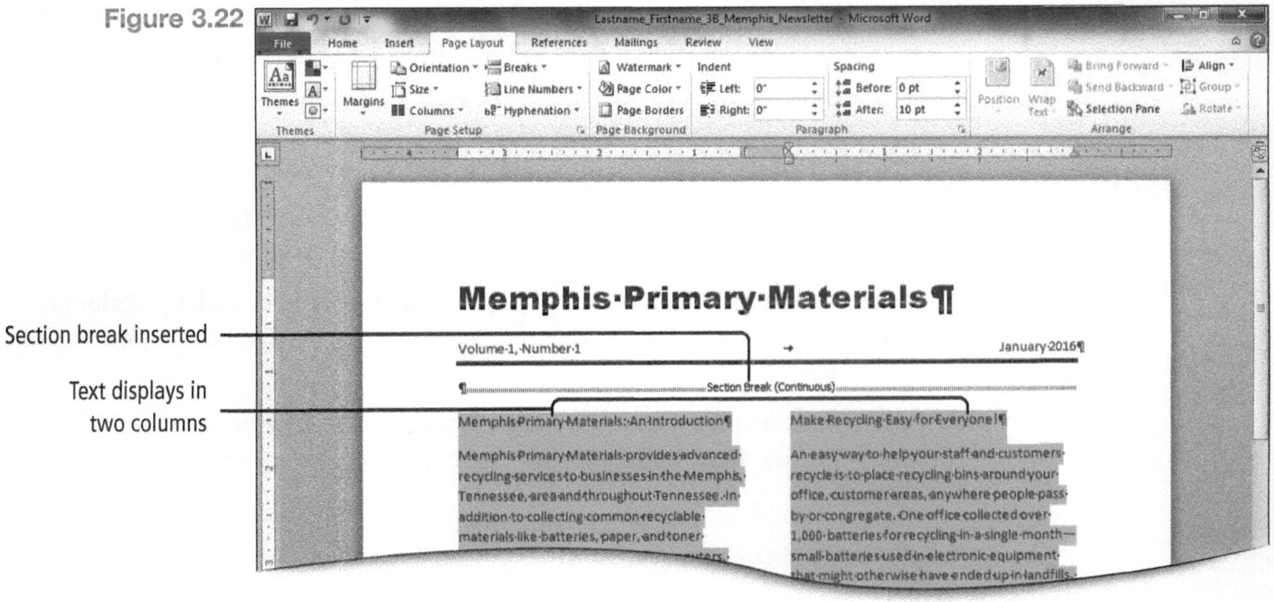

Activity 3.09 | Formatting Multiple Columns

The uneven right margin of a single page-width column is easy to read. When you create narrow columns, justified text is sometimes preferable. Depending on the design and layout of your newsletter, you might decide to reduce extra space between paragraphs and between columns to improve the readability of the document.

1 With the two columns of text still selected, on the **Page Layout tab**, in the **Paragraph group**, click the **Spacing After down spin arrow** one time to change the spacing after to **6 pt**.

2 On the **Home tab**, in the **Paragraph group**, click the **Justify** button.

3 Click anywhere in the document to deselect the text, and then compare your screen with Figure 3.23. **Save** the document.

Figure 3.23

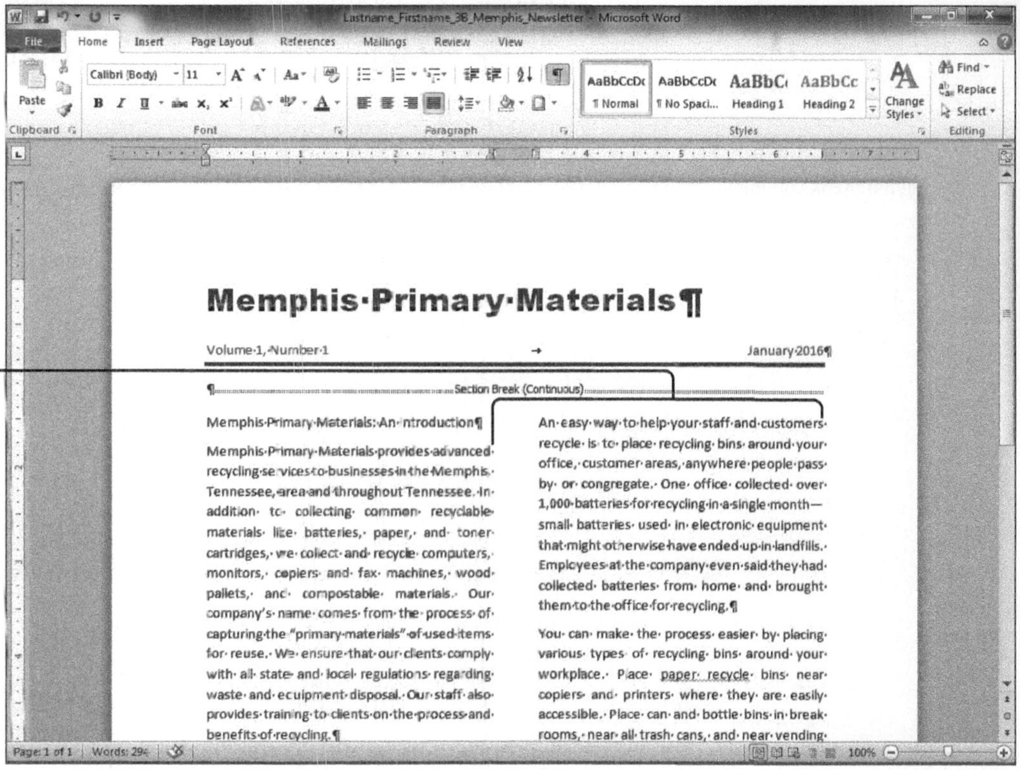

Column text justified

> **More Knowledge | Justifying Column Text**
>
> Although many magazines and newspapers still justify text in columns, there are a variety of opinions about whether to justify the columns, or to use left alignment and leave the right edge uneven. Justified text tends to look more formal and cleaner, but in a word processing document, it also results in uneven spacing between words. It is the opinion of some authorities that justified text is more difficult to read, especially in a page-width document. Let the overall look and feel of your newsletter be your guide.

Activity 3.10 | Inserting a Column Break

1 Scroll down to view the lower portion of the page. In the first column, locate the company address that begins with the paragraph *Memphis Primary Materials*, and then select that paragraph and the three following paragraphs, ending with the telephone number.

2 On the **Page Layout tab**, in the **Paragraph group**, click the **Spacing After down spin arrow** one time to change the spacing after to **0 pt**.

3 Select the three paragraphs that begin with *CEO* and end with *CFO*, and then in the **Paragraph group**, change the **Spacing After** to **0 pt**.

4 Near the bottom of the first column, click to position the insertion point at the beginning of the line that begins *Make Recycling*.

5 On the **Page Layout tab**, in the **Page Setup group**, click the **Breaks** button to display the gallery of Page Breaks and Section Breaks. Compare your screen with Figure 3.24.

Figure 3.24

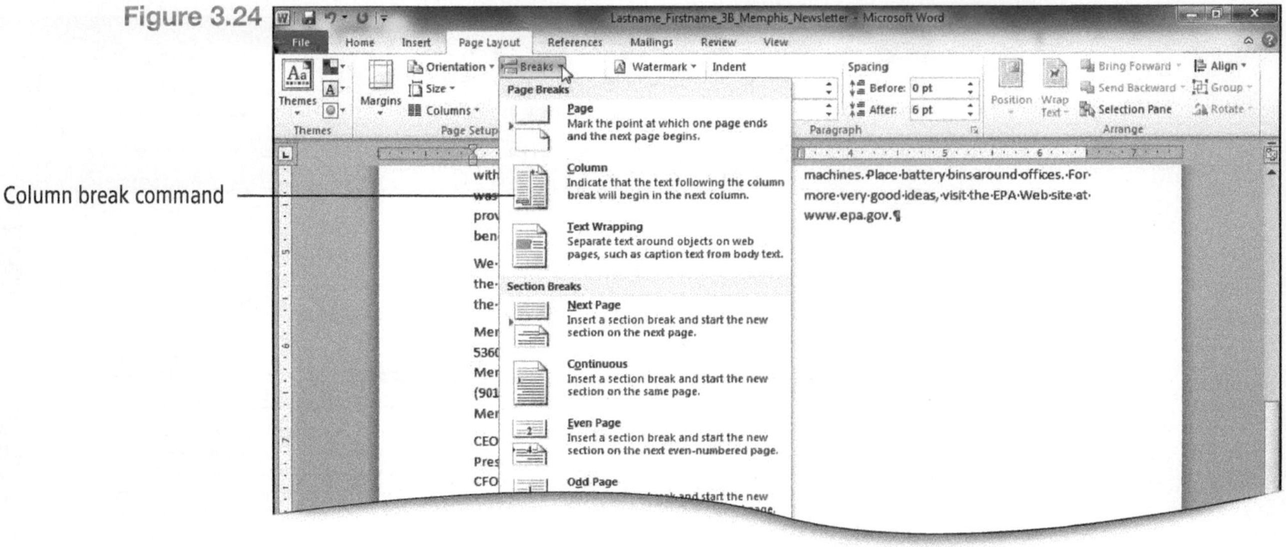

6 Under **Page Breaks**, click **Column**. Scroll to view the bottom of the first column.

A column break displays at the insertion point; text to the right of the insertion point moves to the top of the next column.

7 Compare your screen with Figure 3.25, and then **Save** the document.

A ***column break indicator***—a dotted line containing the words *Column Break*—displays at the bottom of the column.

Figure 3.25

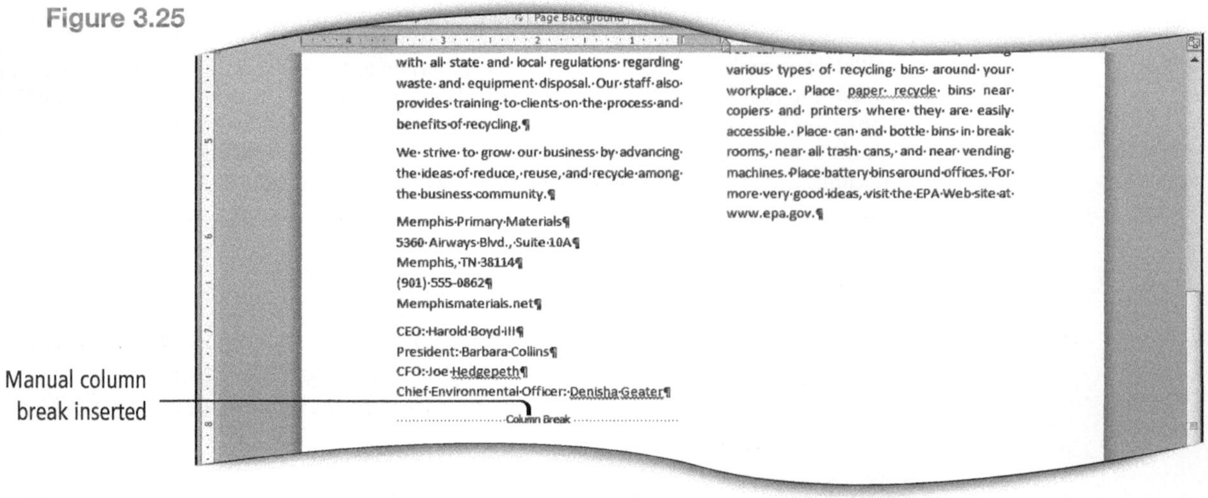

Activity 3.11 | Inserting a Clip Art Image

Clip art images—predefined graphics included with Microsoft Office or downloaded from the Web—can make your document visually appealing and more interesting.

1 Press Ctrl + Home. On the **Insert tab**, in the **Illustrations group**, click the **Clip Art** button to display the **Clip Art** task pane on the right of your screen.

2 In the **Clip Art** task pane, click in the **Search for** box, and then replace any existing text with **environmental awareness** so that Word can search for images that contain the keywords *environmental* and *awareness*.

3 In the **Clip Art** task pane, click the **Results should be arrow**. Be sure the **Illustrations** check box is selected, and then click as necessary to clear the *Photographs*, *Videos*, and *Audio* check boxes. Click the **Results should be** arrow again to collapse the list. Be sure the **Include Office.com content** check box is selected.

4 In the **Clip Art** task pane, click the **Go** button. Locate the image of the three white arrows in a blue circle. Click on the image to insert it, and then compare your screen with Figure 3.26.

Recall that when you insert a graphic, it is inserted as an inline object; that is, it is treated as a character in a line of text. Here, the inserted clip art becomes the first character in the nameplate.

Figure 3.26

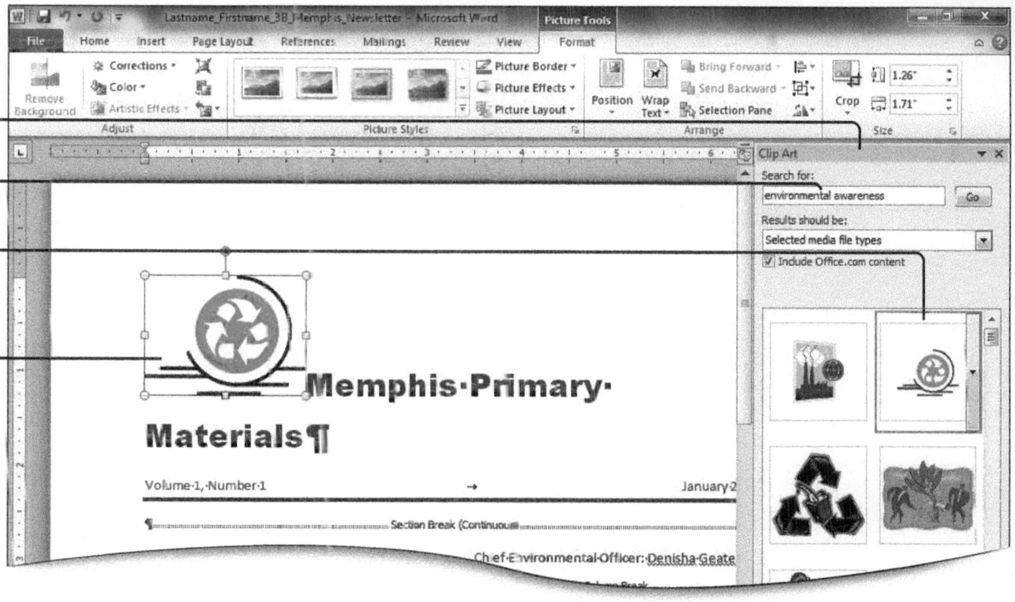

5 **Close** [X] the **Clip Art** task pane. With the image still selected, on the **Format tab**, in the **Size group**, click in the **Shape Height** box, type **1** and then press Enter. In the **Arrange group**, click the **Wrap Text** button, and then click **Square**.

6 Point to the image to display the [move] pointer, and then drag the image to the right so that the bottom edge aligns slightly above *January 2016*, and the right side aligns with the right margin. Recall that you can press the arrow keys as necessary to move the image in small, precise increments.

7 Compare your screen with Figure 3.27, and then **Save** [save] the document.

Figure 3.27

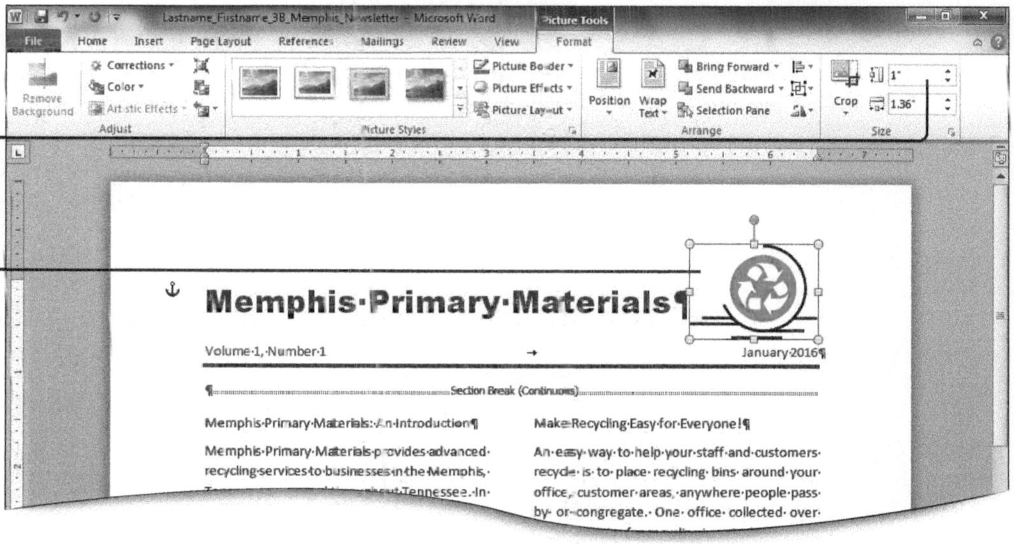

Activity 3.12 | Inserting a Screenshot

A ***screenshot*** is an image of an active window on your computer that you can paste into a document. Screenshots are especially useful when you want to insert an image of a Web site into a document you are creating in Word. You can insert a screenshot of any open window on your computer.

1 In the second column, click to position the insertion point at the beginning of the paragraph that begins *You can make*. Open your Internet browser, and then in the address bar type **www.epa.gov/osw/conserve/rrr** and press Enter. Maximize the browser window, if necessary.

2 From the taskbar, redisplay your **3B_Memphis_Newletter** document.

3 On the **Insert tab**, in the **Illustrations group**, click the **Screenshot** button.

All of your open windows display in the Available Windows gallery and are available to paste into the document.

4 In the **Screenshot** gallery, click the browser window that contains the EPA site to insert the screenshot at the insertion point, and notice that the image resizes to fit between the column margins. Compare your screen with Figure 3.28. **Save** the document.

Figure 3.28

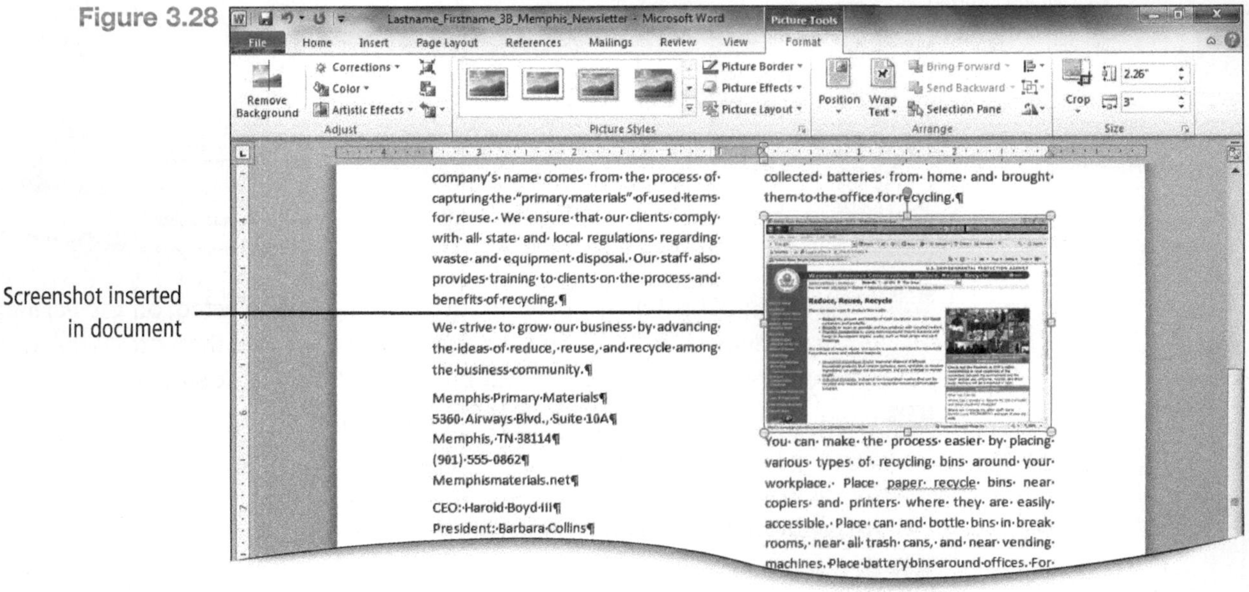

Objective 5 | Use Special Character and Paragraph Formatting

Special text and paragraph formatting is useful to emphasize text, and it makes your newsletter look more professional. For example, you can place a border around one or more paragraphs or add shading to a paragraph. When adding shading, use light colors; dark shading can make the text difficult to read.

Activity 3.13 | Applying the Small Caps Font Effect

For headlines and titles, ***small caps*** is an attractive font effect. The effect changes lowercase letters to uppercase letters, but with the height of lowercase letters.

1 At the top of the first column, select the paragraph *Memphis Primary Materials: An Introduction* including the paragraph mark.

2 Right-click the selected text, and then from the shortcut menu, click **Font**. In the **Font** dialog box, click the **Font color arrow**, and then under **Theme Colors**, in the fifth column, click the last color—**Blue, Accent 1, Darker 50%**.

3 Under **Font style**, click **Bold**. Under **Size**, click **18**. Under **Effects**, select the **Small caps** check box. Compare your screen with Figure 3.29.

The Font dialog box provides more options than are available on the Ribbon and enables you to make several changes at the same time. In the Preview box, the text displays with the selected formatting options applied.

Figure 3.29

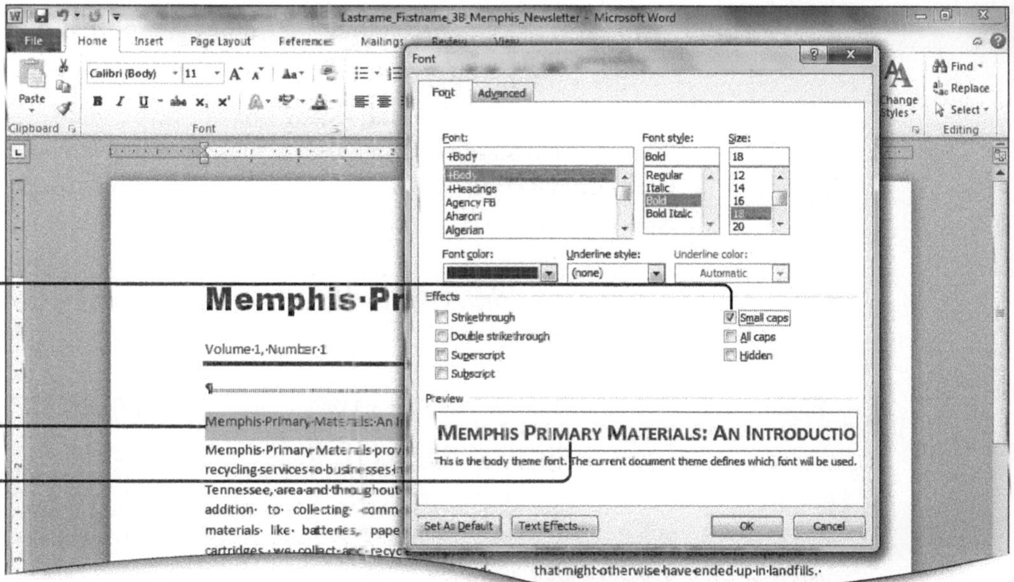

4 Click **OK**. Right-click the selected text, and then on the Mini toolbar, click **Center** [icon].

5 With the text still selected, right-click, and then on the Mini toolbar, click the **Format Painter** button [icon]. Then, with the [icon] pointer, at the top of the second column, select the paragraph *Make Recycling Easy for Everyone!* to apply the same formats. Notice that the column title wraps placing a single word on the second line.

6 Position the insertion point to the right of the word *Recycling*, and then press Del to remove the space. Hold down Shift and then press Enter.

Holding down Shift while pressing Enter inserts a ***manual line break***, which moves the text to the right of the insertion point to a new line while keeping the text in the same paragraph. A ***line break indicator***, in the shape of a bent arrow, indicates that a manual line break was inserted.

7 Compare your screen with Figure 3.30, and then **Save** [icon] the document.

Figure 3.30

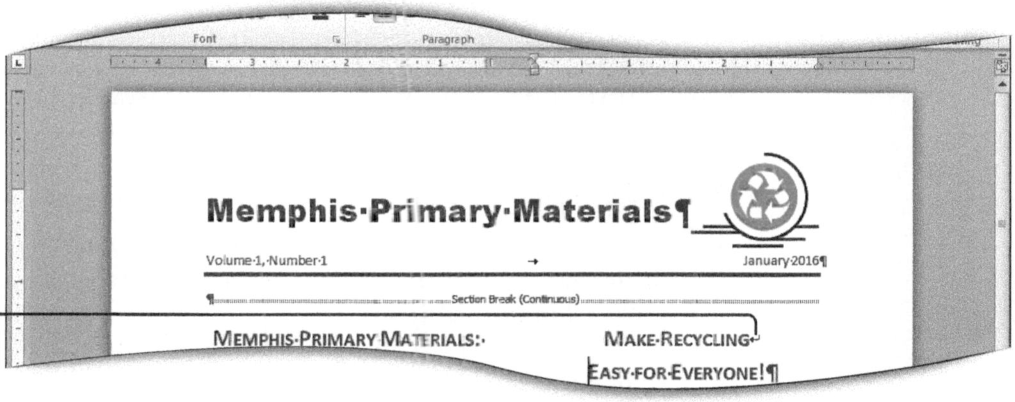

Activity 3.14 | Adding a Border and Shading to a Paragraph

Paragraph borders provide strong visual cues to the reader. Paragraph shading can be used with or without borders. When used with a border, light shading can be very effective in drawing the reader's eye to the text.

1 In the first column, in the paragraph that begins *We strive to grow*, click to position the insertion point at the end of the paragraph, and then press Enter one time.

2 At the bottom of the column, select the nine lines of company information, beginning with *Memphis Primary Materials* and ending with the paragraph that begins *Chief Environmental*. On the Mini toolbar, apply **Bold** and **Center**.

3 With the text still selected, on the **Home tab**, in the **Paragraph group**, click the **Borders button arrow**, and then click **Borders and Shading**.

4 In the **Borders and Shading** dialog box, be sure the **Borders tab** is selected. Under **Setting**, click **Shadow**. If necessary, click the **Color arrow**, and then in the fifth column, click the last color—**Blue, Accent 1, Darker 50%**. Click the **Width arrow**, and then click **3 pt**. Compare your screen with Figure 3.31.

In the lower right portion of the Borders and Shading dialog box, the *Apply to* box displays *Paragraph*. The *Apply to* box directs where the border will be applied—in this instance, the border will be applied only to the selected paragraphs.

Figure 3.31

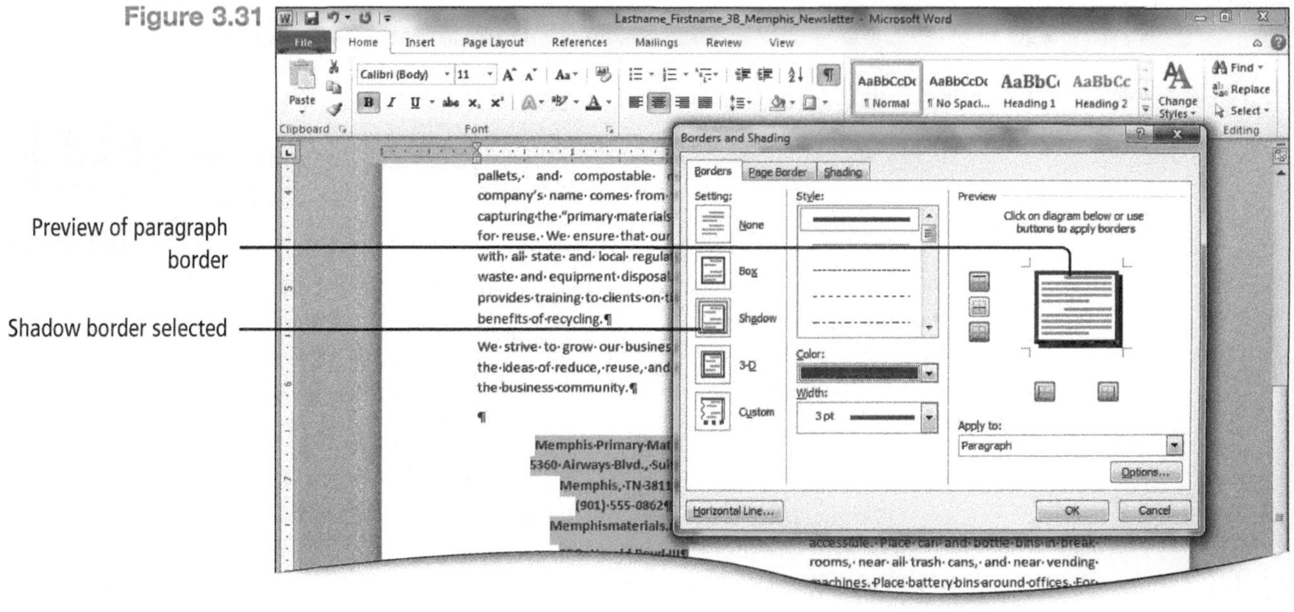

Note | Adding Simple Borders to Text

You can add simple borders from the Borders button gallery, located in the Paragraph group. This button offers less control over the border appearance, however, because the line thickness and color applied will match whatever was last used on this computer. The Borders and Shading dialog box enables you to make your own custom selections.

5 At the top of the **Borders and Shading** dialog box, click the **Shading tab**.

6 Click the **Fill arrow**, and then in the fifth column, click the second color—**Blue, Accent 1, Lighter 80%**. Notice that the shading change is reflected in the Preview area on the right side of the dialog box.

7 At the bottom of the **Borders and Shading** dialog box, click **OK**. Click anywhere in the document to deselect the text, and then compare your screen with Figure 3.32.

Figure 3.32

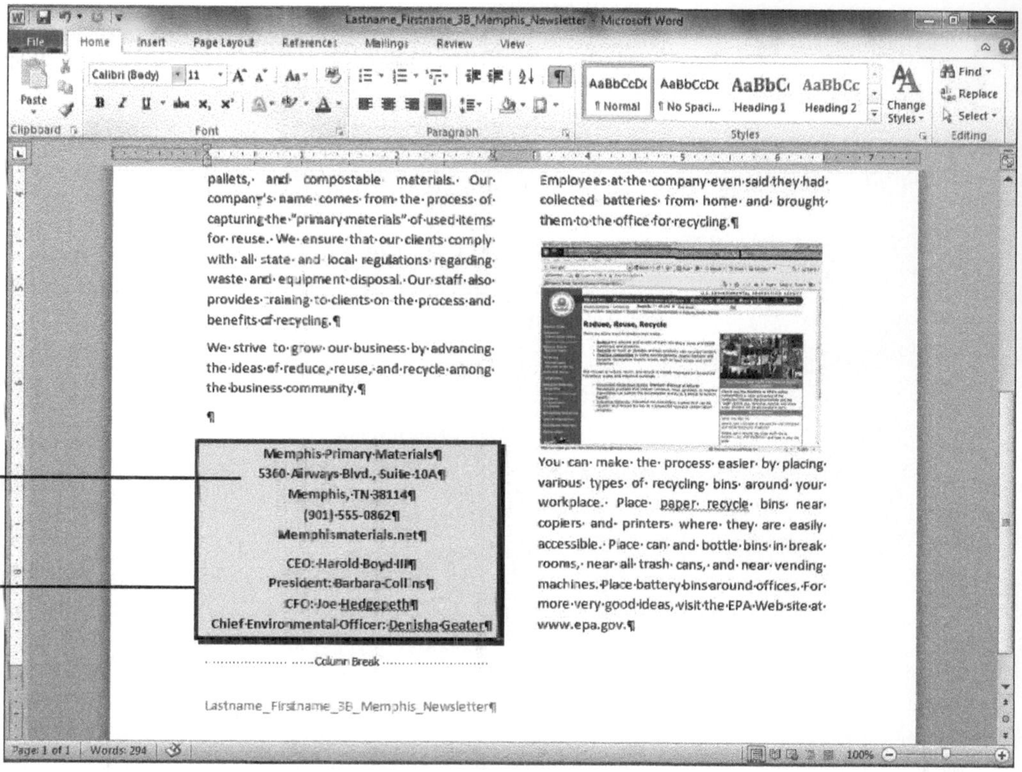

Lastname_Firstname_3B_Memphis_Newsletter - Microsoft Word
pallets, and compostable materials. Our company's name comes from the process of capturing the "primary materials" of used items for reuse. We ensure that our clients comply with all state and local regulations regarding waste and equipment disposal. Our staff also provides training to clients on the process and benefits of recycling.
We strive to grow our business by advancing the ideas of reduce, reuse, and recycle among the business community.
Memphis Primary Materials
5360 Airways Blvd., Suite 10A
Memphis, TN 38114
(901) 555-0862
MemphisMaterials.net
CEO: Harold Boyd III
President: Barbara Collins
CFO: Joe Hedgepeth
Chief Environmental Officer: Denisha Geater
Column Break
Lastname_Firstname_3B_Memphis_Newsletter
Employees at the company even said they had collected batteries from home and brought them to the office for recycling.
You can make the process easier by placing various types of recycling bins around your workplace. Place paper recycle bins near copiers and printers where they are easily accessible. Place can and bottle bins in break rooms, near all trash cans, and near vending machines. Place battery bins around offices. For more very good ideas, visit the EPA Web site at www.epa.gov.
Page: 1 of 1
Words: 294
100%
Shading applied to paragraph text
Shadowed border applied to selected paragraphs

8 From **Backstage** view, display the **Document Panel**.

9 In the **Author** box, delete any text and then type your firstname and lastname. In the **Subject** box, type your course name and section number, and in the **Keywords** box, type **newsletter, January Close** [X] the **Document Panel**.

10 Press Ctrl + F2 to view the **Print Preview**. **Close** the preview, make any necessary corrections, and then click **Save** [icon]. **Exit** Word; hold this file until you complete this Project.

Objective 6 | Create Mailing Labels Using Mail Merge

Word's ***mail merge*** feature joins a ***main document*** and a ***data source*** to create customized letters or labels. The main document contains the text or formatting that remains constant. For labels, the main document contains the formatting for a specific label size. The data source contains information including the names and addresses of the individuals for whom the labels are being created. Names and addresses in a data source might come from a Word table, an Excel spreadsheet, or an Access database.

The easiest way to perform a mail merge is to use the Mail Merge Wizard, which asks you questions and, based on your answers, walks you step by step through the mail merge process.

Activity 3.15 | Opening the Mail Merge Wizard Template

In this activity, you will open the data source for the mail merge, which is a Word table containing names and addresses.

1 **Start** Word and display a new blank document. Display formatting marks and rulers. **Save** the document in your **Word Chapter 3** folder as **Lastname_Firstname_3B_Mailing_Labels**

2 With your new document open on the screen, **Open** the file **w03B_Addresses**. **Save** the address file in your **Word Chapter 3** folder as **Lastname_Firstname_3B_Addresses** and then add the file name to the footer.

This document contains a table of addresses. The first row contains the column names. The remaining rows contain the names and addresses.

3 Click to position the insertion point in the last cell in the table, and then press Tab to create a new row. Enter the following information, and then compare your table with Figure 3.33:

First Name	**John**
Last Name	**Wisniewski**
Address 1	**1226 Snow Road**
Address 2	**#234**
City	**Lakeland**
State	**TN**
ZIP Code	**38002**

Figure 3.33

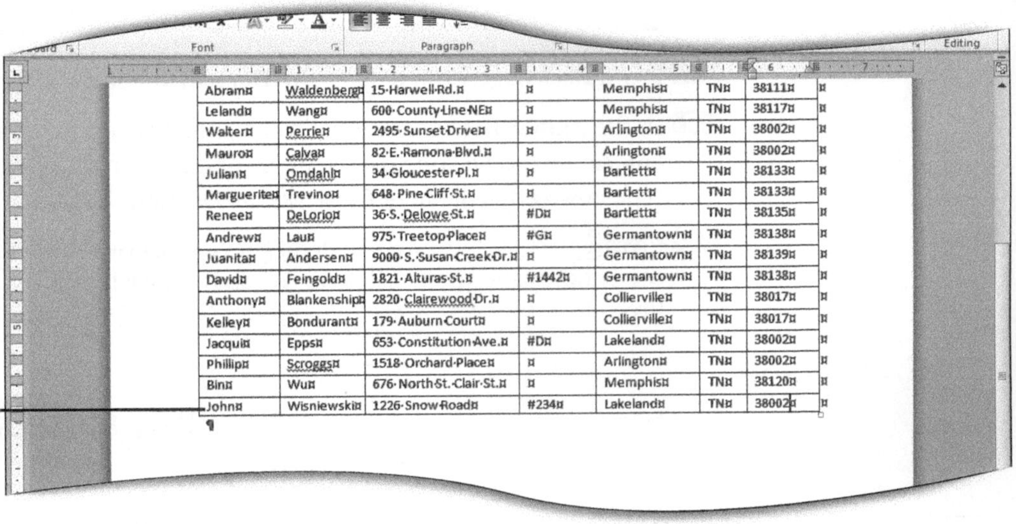

Abram	Waldenberg	15 Harwell Rd.		Memphis	TN	38111
Leland	Wang	600 County Line NE		Memphis	TN	38117
Walter	Perrie	2495 Sunset Drive		Arlington	TN	38002
Mauro	Calva	82 E. Ramona Blvd.		Arlington	TN	38002
Julian	Omdahl	34 Gloucester Pl.		Bartlett	TN	38133
Marguerite	Trevino	648 Pine Cliff St.		Bartlett	TN	38133
Renee	DeLorio	36 S. Delowe St.	#D	Bartlett	TN	38135
Andrew	Lau	975 Treetop Place	#G	Germantown	TN	38138
Juanita	Andersen	9000 S. Susan Creek Dr.		Germantown	TN	38139
David	Feingold	1821 Alturas St.	#1442	Germantown	TN	38138
Anthony	Blankenship	2820 Clairewood Dr.		Collierville	TN	38017
Kelley	Bondurant	179 Auburn Court		Collierville	TN	38017
Jacqui	Epps	653 Constitution Ave.	#D	Lakeland	TN	38002
Phillip	Scroggs	1518 Orchard Place		Arlington	TN	38002
Bin	Wu	676 North St. Clair St.		Memphis	TN	38120
John	Wisniewski	1226 Snow Road	#234	Lakeland	TN	38002

New record added to address list

4 **Save**, and then **Close** the table of addresses. Be sure your blank **Lastname_Firstname_3B_Mailing_Labels** document displays.

5 Click the **Mailings tab**. In the **Start Mail Merge group**, click the **Start Mail Merge** button, and then click **Step by Step Mail Merge Wizard** to display the **Mail Merge** task pane.

6 Under **Select document type**, click the **Labels** option button. At the bottom of the task pane, click **Next: Starting document** to display Step 2 of 6 of the Mail Merge Wizard.

7 Under **Select starting document**, be sure **Change document layout** is selected, and then under **Change document layout**, click **Label options**.

8 In the **Label Options** dialog box, under **Printer information**, click the **Tray arrow**, and then click **Default tray (Automatically Select)**—the exact wording may vary depending on your printer, but select the *Default* or *Automatic* option—to print the labels on regular paper rather than manually inserting labels in the printer.

9 Under **Label information**, click the **Label vendors arrow**, and then click **Avery US Letter**. Under **Product number**, scroll about halfway down the list, and then click **5160 Easy Peel Address Labels**. Compare your screen with Figure 3.34.

The Avery 5160 address label is a commonly used label. The precut sheets contain three columns of 10 labels each—for a total of 30 labels per sheet.

Figure 3.34

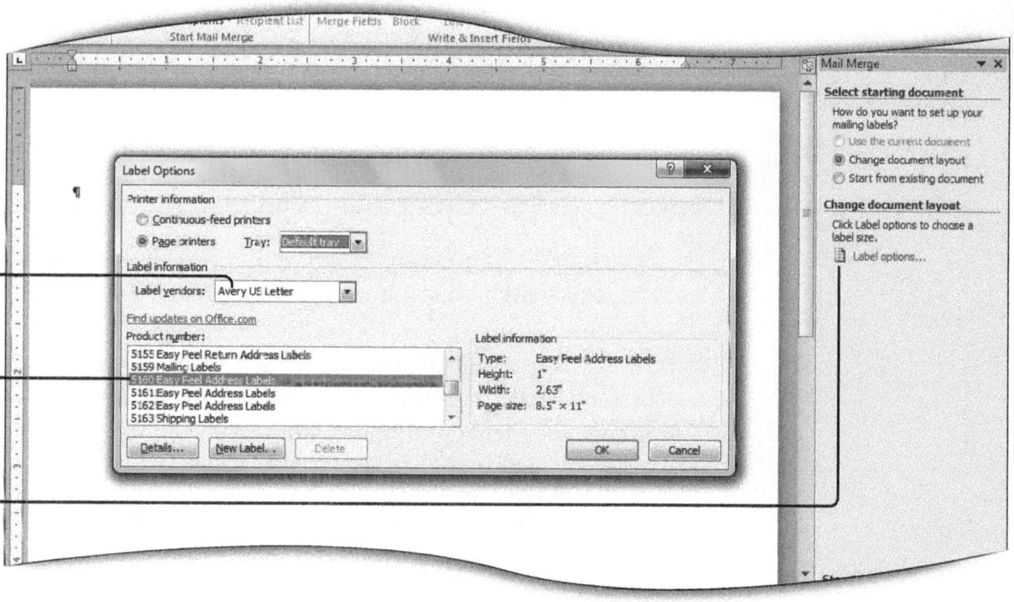

10 At the bottom of the **Label Options** dialog box, click **OK**. If a message box displays, click OK to set up the labels. At the bottom of the task pane, click **Next: Select recipients**.

The label page is set up with three columns and ten rows. The label borders may or may not display on your screen, depending on your settings. Here in Step 3 of the Mail Merge Wizard, you must identify the recipients—the data source. For your recipient data source, you can choose to use an existing list—for example, a list of names and addresses that you have in an Access database, an Excel worksheet, a Word table, or your Outlook contacts list. If you do not have an existing data source, you can type a new list at this point in the wizard.

11 If gridlines do not display, click the **Layout tab**. In the **Table group**, click the **View Gridlines** button, and then notice that each label is outlined with a dashed line. If you cannot see the right and left edges of the page, in the status bar, click the **Zoom Out** button as necessary to see the right and left edges of the label sheet on your screen.

12 Under **Select recipients**, be sure the **Use an existing list** option button is selected. Under **Use an existing list**, click **Browse**.

13 Navigate to your **Word Chapter 3** folder, select your **Lastname_Firstname_3B_Addresses** file, and then click **Open** to display the **Mail Merge Recipients** dialog box.

In the Mail Merge Recipients dialog box, the column headings are formed from the text in the first row of your Word table of addresses. Each row of information that contains data for one person is referred to as a ***record***. The column headings—for example, *Last_Name* and *First_Name*—are referred to as ***fields***. An underscore replaces the spaces between words in the field name headings.

14 Compare your screen with Figure 3.35.

Figure 3.35

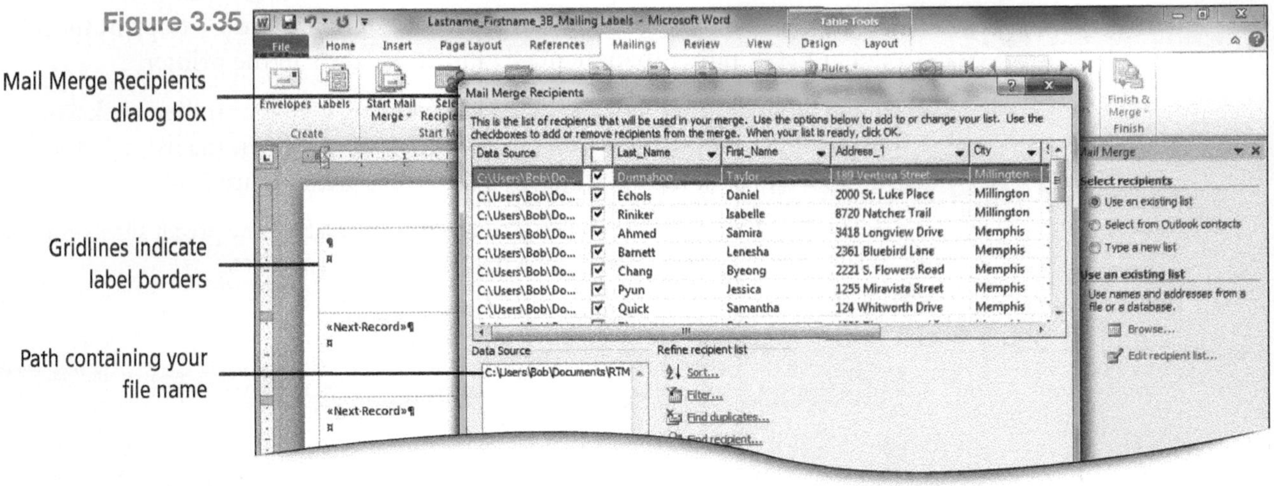

Activity 3.16 | Completing the Mail Merge Wizard

You can add or edit names and addresses while completing the Mail Merge Wizard. You can also match your column names with preset names used in Mail Merge.

1 In the lower left portion of the **Mail Merge Recipients** dialog box, in the **Data Source** box, click the path that contains your file name. Then, at the bottom of the **Mail Merge Recipients** dialog box, click **Edit**.

2 In the upper right corner of the **Data Form** dialog box, click **Add New**. In the blank record, type the following, pressing Tab to move from field to field, and then compare your **Data Form** dialog box with Figure 3.36.

First_Name	**Susan**
Last_Name	**Ballard**
Address_1	**1251 Parker Road**
Unit:	
City	**Memphis**
State	**TN**
ZIP_Code	**38123**

Figure 3.36

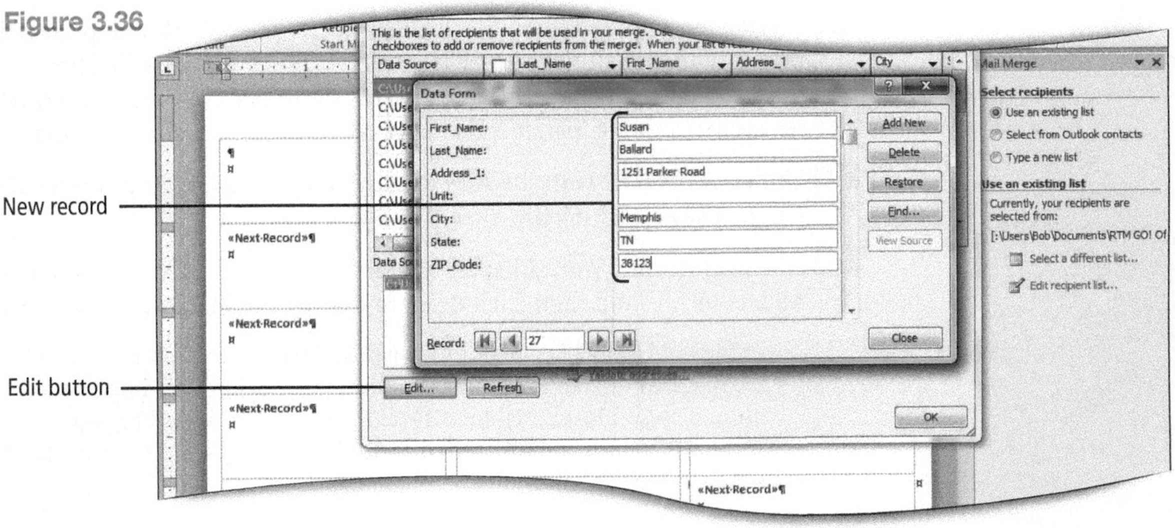

3 In the lower right corner of the **Data Form** dialog box, click **Close**. Scroll to the end of the recipient list to confirm that the record for *Susan Ballard* that you just added is in the list. At the bottom of the **Mail Merge Recipients** dialog box, click **OK**.

4 At the bottom of the **Mail Merge** task pane, click **Next: Arrange your labels.**

5 Under **Arrange your labels**, click **Address block**. In the **Insert Address Block** dialog box, under **Specify address elements**, examine the various formats for names. If necessary, under *Insert recipient's name in this format*, select the *Joshua Randall Jr.* format. Compare your dialog box with Figure 3.37.

Figure 3.37

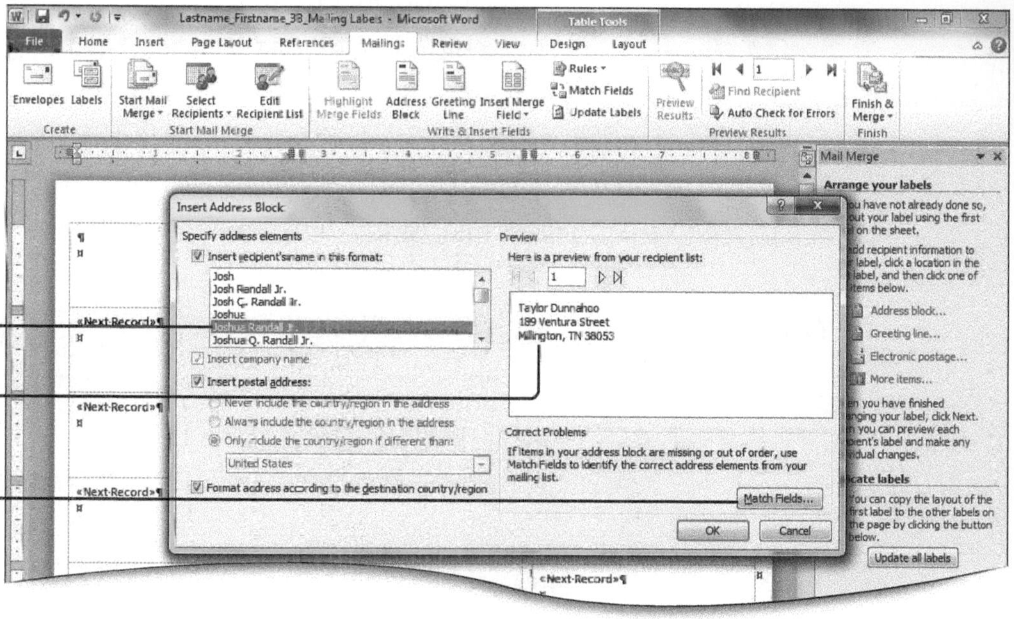

6 In the lower right corner of the **Insert Address Block** dialog box, click **Match Fields.**

If your field names are descriptive, the Mail Merge program will identify them correctly, as is the case with most of the information in the *Required for Address Block* section. However, the Address 2 field is unmatched—in the source file, this column is named *Unit*.

7 Scroll down and examine the dialog box, and then compare your screen with Figure 3.38.

Figure 3.38

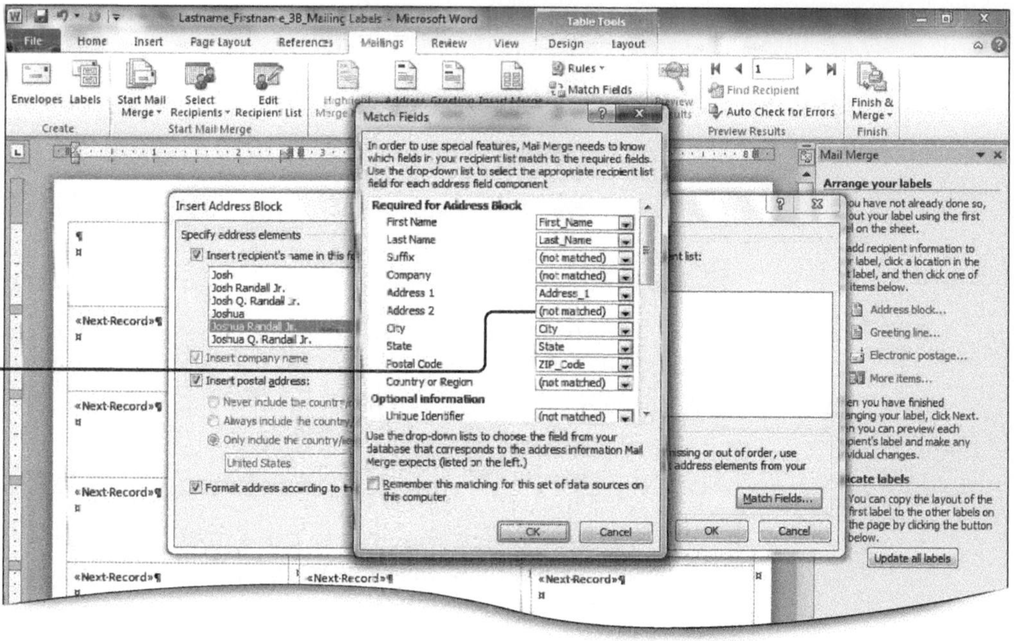

8 Click the **Address 2 arrow**, and then from the list of available fields, click **Unit** to match the Mail Merge field with the field in your data source.

9 At the bottom of the **Match Fields** dialog box, click **OK**. At the bottom of the **Insert Address Block** dialog box, click **OK**.

Word inserts the Address block in the first label space surrounded by double angle brackets. The *AddressBlock* field name displays, which represents the address block you saw in the Preview area of the Insert Address Block dialog box.

10 In the task pane, under **Replicate labels**, click **Update all labels** to insert an address block in each label space for each subsequent record.

11 At the bottom of the task pane, click **Next: Preview your labels**. Notice that for addresses with four lines, the last line of the address is cut off.

12 Press Ctrl + A to select all of the label text, click the **Page Layout tab**, and then in the **Paragraph group**, click in the **Spacing Before** box. Type **3** and press Enter.

13 Click in any label to deselect, and notice that 4-line addresses are no longer cut off. Compare your screen with Figure 3.39.

Figure 3.39

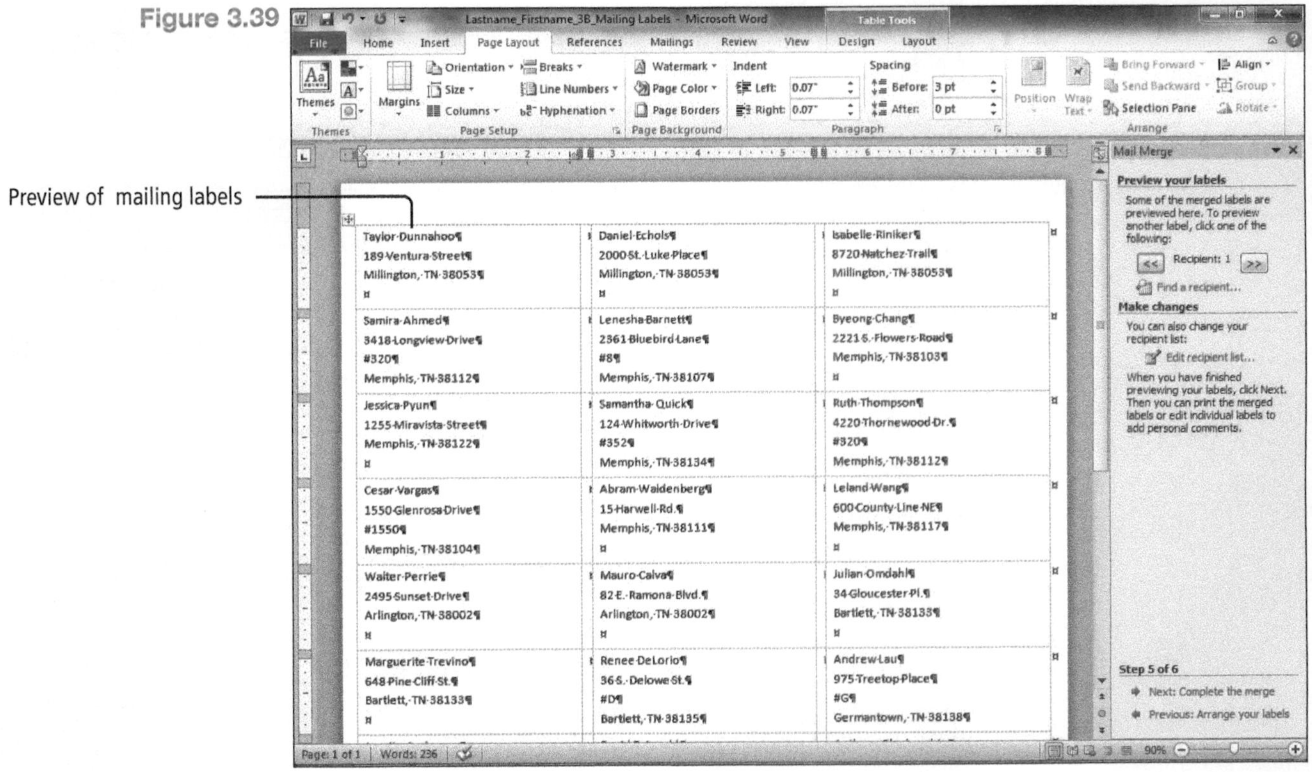

14 At the bottom of the task pane, click **Next: Complete the merge**.

Step 6 of the Mail Merge task pane displays. At this point you can print or edit your labels, although this is done more easily in the document window.

15 **Save** your labels, and then **Close** the **Mail Merge** task pane.

Activity 3.17 | Previewing and Printing the Mail Merge Document

If you discover that you need to make further changes to your labels, you can still make them even though the Mail Merge task pane is closed.

1 Add the file name to the footer, close the footer area, and then move to the top of Page 2. Click anywhere in the empty table row, click the **Layout tab**, in the **Rows & Columns group**, click the **Delete** button, and then click **Delete Rows**.

Adding footer text to a label sheet replaces the last row of labels on a page with the footer text, and moves the last row of labels to the top of the next page. In this instance, a blank second page is created, which you can delete by deleting the blank row.

2 Press Ctrl + F2 to display the **Print Preview**. Notice that the labels do not display in alphabetical order.

3 Click the **Mailings tab**, and then in the **Start Mail Merge group**, click the **Edit Recipient List** button to display the list of names and addresses.

4 In the **Mail Merge Recipients** dialog box, click the **Last_Name** field heading, and notice that the names are sorted alphabetically by the recipient's last name.

Mailing labels are often sorted by either last name or by ZIP Code.

5 Click the **Last_Name** field heading again, and notice that the last names are sorted in descending order. Click the **Last_Name** field one more time to return to ascending order, and then click **OK**. Press Ctrl + Home, and then compare your screen with Figure 3.40.

Figure 3.40

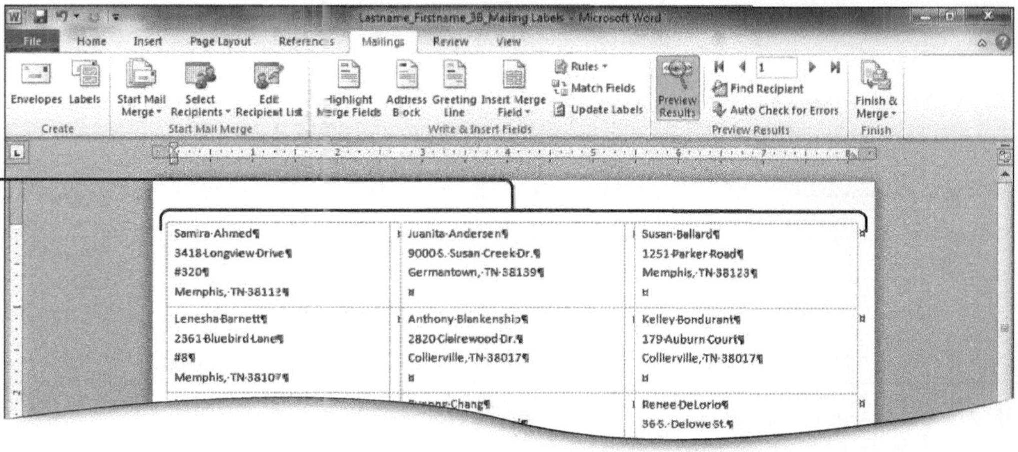

6 From **Backstage** view, display the **Document Panel**. In the **Author** box, delete any text and then type your firstname and lastname. In the **Subject** box, type your course name and section number, and in the **Keywords** box type **newsletter mailing labels** **Close** the **Document Panel**.

7 Click **Save**. Display **Backstage** view, and then click the **Print tab**. Examine the **Print Preview** on the right side of the window.

8 As directed by your instructor, print or submit electronically.

If you print, the labels will print on whatever paper is in the printer; unless you have preformatted labels available, the labels will print on a sheet of paper. Printing the labels on plain paper enables you to proofread the labels before you print them on more expensive label sheets.

9 **Close** the document, click **Yes** to save the data source, and then if necessary, click **Save** to save the labels.

10 In addition to your labels and address document, print or submit your **3B_Memphis_Newsletter** document as directed. **Exit** Word.

End **You have completed Project 3B**

Content-Based Assessments

Summary

In this chapter, you created a research paper using the MLA style. You added a header, footnotes, citations, and a bibliography, and changed the footnote style. You created a newsletter that used multiple columns. You added a column break, a page break, and a manual line break. You added special font effects, and added a border and shading to a paragraph. Finally, you used the Mail Merge Wizard to create a set of mailing labels for the newsletter.

Key Terms

Matching

Match each term in the second column with its correct definition in the first column by writing the letter of the term on the blank line in front of the correct definition.

_____ 1. A manual that contains standards for the design and writing of documents.

_____ 2. One of two commonly used style guides for formatting research papers.

_____ 3. An image of an active window on your computer that you can paste into a document.

_____ 4. In a research paper, information that expands on the topic, but that does not fit well in the document text.

_____ 5. In a research paper, a note placed at the bottom of the page.

_____ 6. In a research paper, a note placed at the end of a document or chapter.

_____ 7. A list of cited works in a report or research paper, also referred to as *Works Cited*, *Sources*, or *References*, depending upon the report style.

_____ 8. In the MLA style, a list of cited works placed at the end of a research paper or report.

_____ 9. A group of formatting commands, such as font, font size, font color, paragraph alignment, and line spacing that can be applied to a paragraph with one command.

_____ 10. A note, inserted into the text of a research paper that refers the reader to a source in the bibliography.

_____ 11. In the MLA style, a citation that refers to items on the *Works Cited* page, and which is placed in parentheses; the citation includes the last name of the author or authors, and the page number in the referenced source.

A American Psychological Association (APA)
B Bibliography
C Citation
D Endnote
E Footnote
F Hanging indent
G Manual column break
H Manual page break
I Note
J Page break indicator
K Parenthetical reference
L Screenshot
M Style
N Style guide
O Works Cited

_____ 12. The action of forcing a page to end and placing subsequent text at the top of the next page.

_____ 13. A dotted line with the text *Page Break* that indicates where a manual page break was inserted.

_____ 14. An indent style in which the first line of a paragraph extends to the left of the remaining lines, and that is commonly used for bibliographic entries.

_____ 15. An artificial end to a column to balance columns or to provide space for the insertion of other objects.

Multiple Choice

Circle the correct answer.

1. Column text that is aligned to both the left and right margins is referred to as:
A. centered **B.** justified **C.** indented

2. The banner on the front page of a newsletter that identifies the publication is the:
A. heading **B.** nameplate **C.** title

3. A portion of a document that can be formatted differently from the rest of the document is a:
A. tabbed list **B.** paragraph **C.** section

4. A font effect, commonly used in titles, that changes lowercase text into uppercase letters using a reduced font size is:
A. Small Caps **B.** Level 2 Head **C.** Bevel

5. To end a line before the normal end of the line, without creating a new paragraph, hold down the Shift key while pressing the:
A. Enter key **B.** Ctrl key **C.** Alt key

6. The nonprinting symbol that displays where a manual line break is inserted is the:
A. short arrow **B.** bent arrow **C.** anchor

7. In mail merge, the document that contains the text or formatting that remains constant is the:
A. data source **B.** mailing list **C.** main document

8. In mail merge, the list of variable information, such as names and addresses, that is merged with a main document to create customized form letters or labels is the:
A. data source **B.** mailing list **C.** main document

9. In mail merge, a row of information that contains data for one person is a:
A. record **B.** field **C.** label

10. To perform a mail merge using Word's step-by-step guided process, use the:
A. Mail Merge Template **B.** Mail Merge Management Source **C.** Mail Merge Wizard

Content-Based Assessments

Apply 3A skills from these Objectives:

1. Create a Research Paper
2. Insert Footnotes in a Research Paper
3. Create Citations and a Bibliography in a Research Paper

Skills Review | Project 3C Recycling Report

In the following Skills Review, you will format and edit a research paper for Memphis Primary Materials. The research topic is recycling in the natural environment. Your completed document will look similar to Figure 3.41.

Project Files

For Project 3C, you will need the following file:

w03C_Recycling_Report

You will save your document as:

Lastname_Firstname_3C_Recycling_Report

Project Results

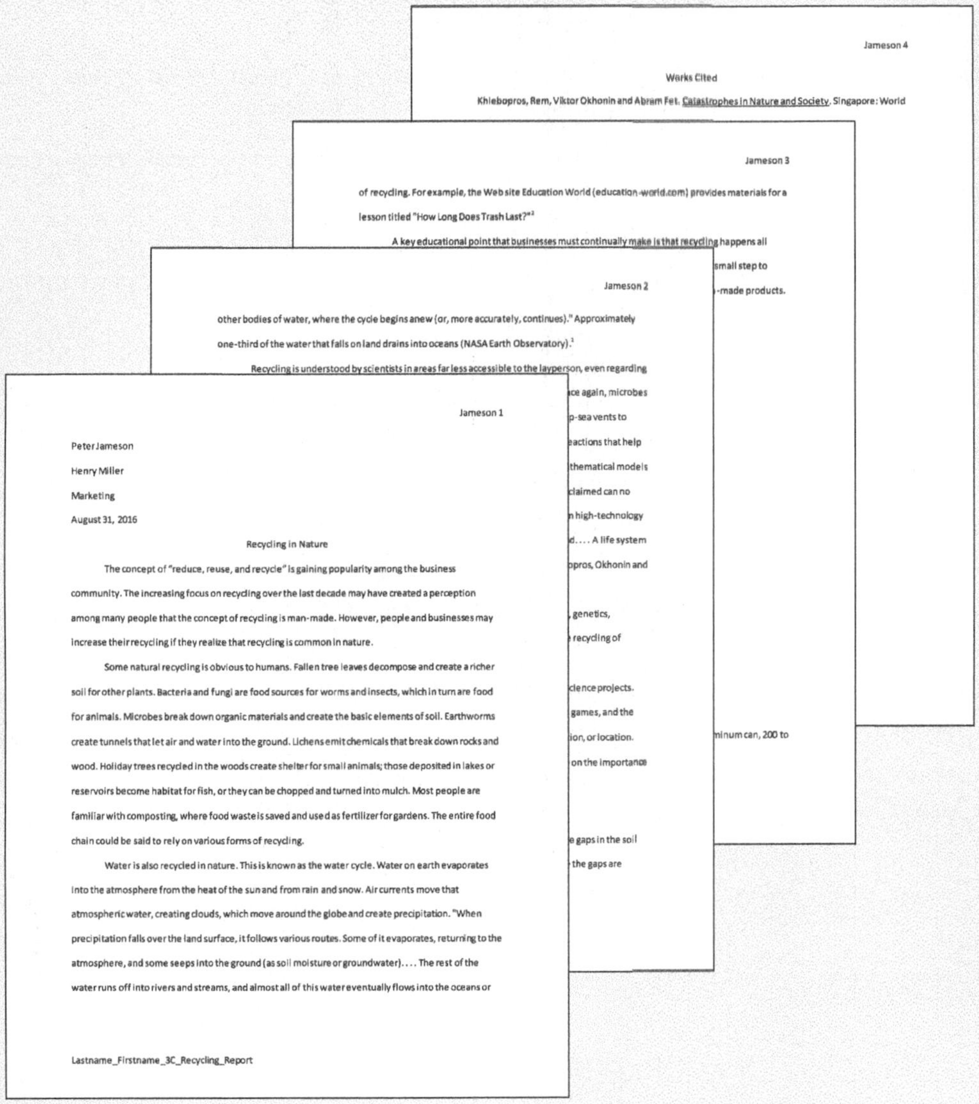

Figure 3.41

(Project 3C Recycling Report continues on the next page)

Content-Based Assessments

Skills Review

Start Word. From ...r student files, locate and open the document w03...cling_Report. Display the formatting marks ...lers. Save the file in your Word Chapter 3 folder ...name_Firstname_3C_Recycling_Report

On the Home tab, in the Paragraph

a. Press ... Line spacing button, and then change ...g to 2.0. On the Page Layout tab, in the ...oup, change the Spacing After to 0 pt.

b. ... Home, press Enter to create a blank line at the document, and then click to position ...ion point in the blank line. Type Peter ...n and then press Enter. Type Henry Miller and ...ress Enter. Type Marketing and then press Enter. August 31, 2016 and then press Enter.

... Recycling in Nature and then right-click ...where in the title you just typed. From the Mini ...olbar, Center the title.

... Near the top of **Page 1**, locate the paragraph beginning *The concept of*, and then click to position the insertion point at the beginning of the paragraph. Scroll to the end of the document, hold down Shift, and then click to the right of the last paragraph mark to select all of the text from the insertion point to the end of the document. On the horizontal ruler, drag the **First Line Indent** button to **0.5"**.

e. On **Page 1**, point to the top margin area and right-click. Click **Edit Header**. In the header area, type **Jameson** and then press Spacebar.

f. On the **Design tab**, in the **Header & Footer group**, click the **Page Number** button, and then point to **Current Position**. In the displayed gallery, under **Simple**, click **Plain Number**. On the **Home tab**, in the **Paragraph group**, click the **Align Text Right** button.

g. Click the **Design tab**, and then in the **Navigation group**, click the **Go to Footer** button. In the **Insert group**, click the **Quick Parts** button, and then click **Field**. In the **Field** dialog box, under **Field names**, locate and click **FileName**, and then click **OK**.

h. Double-click anywhere outside the footer area. **Save** your document.

2 Scroll to view the top of **Page 2**, locate the paragraph that ends *drains into oceans*, and then click to position the insertion point to the right of the period following *oceans*. On the **References tab**, in the **Footnotes group**, click the **Insert Footnote** button.

a. Type **Groundwater is found in two layers of the soil, the "zone of aeration," where gaps in the soil are filled with both air and water, and, further down, the "zone of saturation," where the gaps are completely filled with water.**

b. In the lower half of **Page 2**, locate the paragraph that begins *School students*. Click to position the insertion point at the end of the paragraph and insert a footnote.

c. As the footnote text, type **A wool sock will last one year in a landfill; a soup can, 80 to 100 years; an aluminum can, 200 to 500 years; and plastic rings from a six-pack of cans, 450 years. Save** your document.

d. At the bottom of **Page 2**, right-click anywhere in either footnote. From the shortcut menu, click **Style**. In the **Style** dialog box, click the **Modify** button. In the **Modify Style** dialog box, locate the small Formatting toolbar in the center of the dialog box, click the **Font Size button arrow**, and then click **11**.

e. In the lower left corner of the dialog box, click the **Format** button, and then click **Paragraph**. In the **Paragraph** dialog box, under **Indentation**, click the **Special arrow**, and then click **First line**. Under **Spacing**, click the **Line spacing button arrow**, and then click **Double**.

f. Click **OK** to close the **Paragraph** dialog box, click **OK** to close the **Modify Style** dialog box, and then click **Apply** to apply the new style. Notice that the second footnote moves to **Page 3**. **Save** your document.

3 Scroll to view the top of **Page 2**, and then locate the footnote marker at the end of the second line of text. Click to position the insertion point to the left of the period at the end of the paragraph.

a. On the **References tab**, in the **Citations & Bibliography group**, click the **Style button arrow**, and then click **MLA** to insert a reference using MLA style. Click the **Insert Citation** button, and then click **Add New Source**. Click the **Type of Source arrow**,

(Project 3C Recycling Report continues on the next page)

Skills Review | Project 3C Recycling Report (continued)

and then click **Web site**. Select the **Corporate Author** check box, and then add the following information (type the URL on one line):

Corporate Author:	**NASA Earth Observatory**
Name of Web Page:	**The Water Cycle**
Year:	**2009**
Month:	**March**
Day:	**3**
Year Accessed:	**2016**
Month Accessed:	**May**
Day Accessed:	**24**
URL:	**http://earthobservatory.nasa.gov/Features/Water/water_2.php**

b. Click **OK** to insert the citation. In the next paragraph, which begins *Recycling is understood,* in the fifth line, click to position the insertion point to the right of the quotation mark. In the **Citations & Bibliography group**, click the **Insert Citation** button, and then click **Add New Source**. Click the **Type of Source arrow**, click **Journal Article**, and then add the following information (type the Title on one line):

Author:	**Pennisi, Elizabeth**
Title:	**Shale-Eating Microbes Recycle Global Carbon**
Journal Name:	**Science**
Year:	**2001**
Pages:	**1043**

c. Click **OK**. In the text, click to select the citation, click the **Citation Options arrow**, and then click **Edit Citation**. In the **Edit Citation** dialog box, under **Add**, in the **Pages** box, type **1043** and then click **OK**. Add a period to the right of the citation and delete the period to the left of the quotation mark.

d. In the same paragraph, position the insertion point at the end of the paragraph. In the **Citations & Bibliography group**, click the **Insert Citation** button, and then click **Add New Source**. Click the **Type of Source arrow**, click **Book**, and add the following information (type the Author information on one line):

Author:	**Khlebopros, Rem; Okhonin, Fet, Abram**
Title:	**Catastrophes in Nature and So**
Year:	**2007**
City:	**Singapore**
Publisher:	**World Scientific Publishing Company**

e. Click **OK**. Click to select the citation, click the **Citation Options arrow**, and then click **Edit Cita** In the **Edit Citation** dialog box, under **Add**, in the **Pages** box, type **111** Click **OK**. Add a period to the right of the citation and delete the period to the left of the quotation mark.

f. Press Ctrl + End to move the insertion point to the end of the document. Press Ctrl + Enter to insert a manual page break. On the ruler, drag the **First Line Indent** button to the left to **0 inches on the horizontal ruler**.

g. Type **Works Cited** and then press Enter. On the **References tab**, in the **Citations & Bibliography group**, be sure **MLA** displays in the **Style** box. In the **Citations & Bibliography group**, click the **Bibliography** button, and then click **Insert Bibliography**.

h. In the bibliography, move the pointer to the left of the first entry—beginning *Khlebopros*—to display the pointer. Drag down to select all three references. On the **Home tab**, in the **Paragraph group**, set the **Line spacing** to **2.0**. On the **Page Layout tab**, set the **Spacing After** to **0 pt**.

i. Right-click the *Works Cited* title, and then from the Mini toolbar, click the **Center** button. **Save** your document.

4 From **Backstage** view, display the **Document Panel**, type your name and course information, and then add the keywords **recycling, nature, research paper** In the upper left corner of the panel, click the **Document Properties** button, and then click **Advanced Properties**.

(Project 3C Recycling Report continues on the next page)

Skills Review | Project 3C Recycling Report (continued)

a. In the **Properties** dialog box, click the **Summary tab**. In the **Properties** dialog box, fill in the following information:

Title:	**Recycling in Nature**
Manager:	**Henry Miller**
Company:	**Memphis Primary Materials**
Comments:	**Draft of a new white paper research report on recycling**

b. At the bottom of the **Properties** dialog box, click **OK**. **Close** the **Document Panel**. **Save** your document. View the Print Preview, and then print or submit electronically as directed by your instructor. **Exit** Word.

End **You have completed Project 3C**

Content-Based Assessments

Apply 3B skills from these Objectives:

4 Format a Multiple-Column Newsletter

5 Use Special Character and Paragraph Formatting

6 Create Mailing Labels Using Mail Merge

Skills Review | Project 3D Company Newsletter

In the following Skills Review, you will format a newsletter for Memphis Primary Materials, and then create a set of mailing labels for the newsletter. Your completed documents will look similar to Figure 3.42.

Project Files

For Project 3D, you will need the following files:

New blank Word document
w03D_Company_Newsletter
w03D_Addresses

You will save your documents as:

Lastname_Firstname_3D_Company_Newsletter
Lastname_Firstname_3D_Addresses
Lastname_Firstname_3D_Labels

Project Results

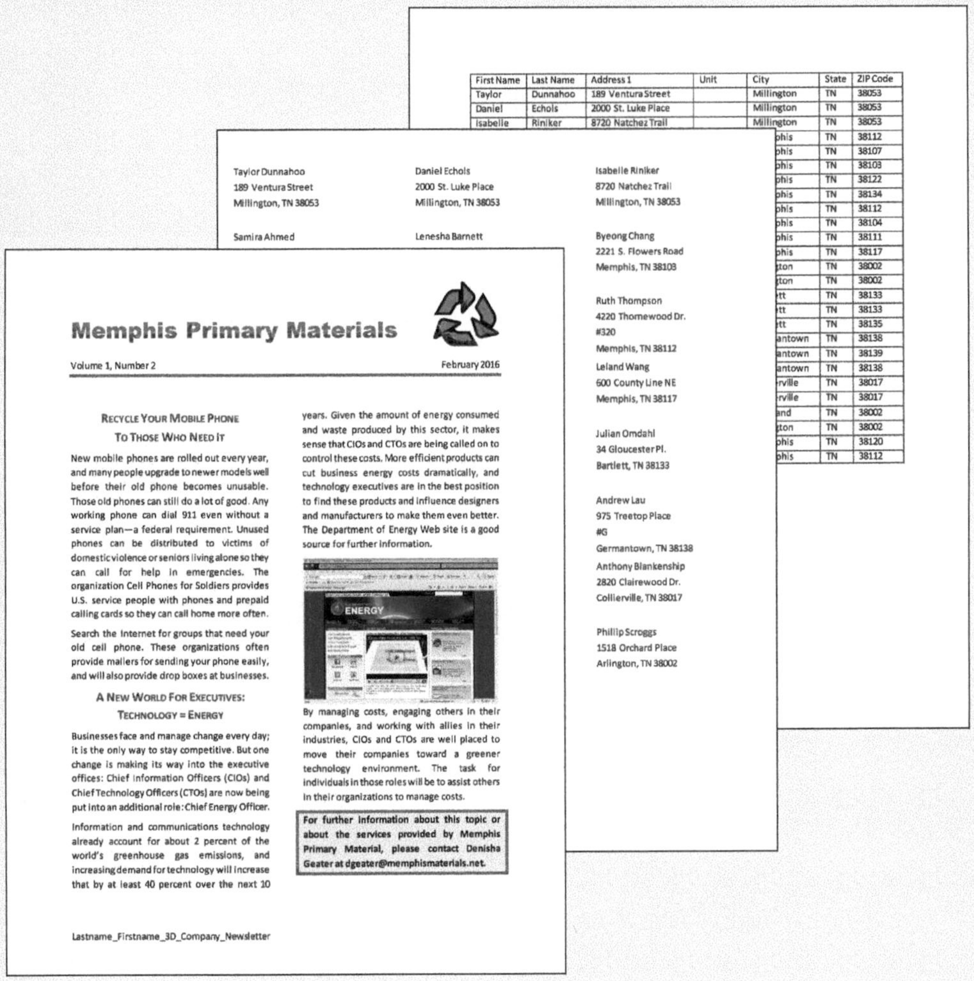

Figure 3.42

(Project 3D Company Newsletter continues on the next page)

Skills Review | Project 3D Company Newsletter (continued)

1 **Start** Word. From your student files, open the document **w03D_Company_Newsletter**. **Save** the file in your **Word Chapter 3** folder as **Lastname_Firstname_3D_Company_Newsletter** and then add the file name to the footer.

a. Select the first paragraph of text—*Memphis Primary Materials*. From the Mini toolbar, change the **Font** to **Arial Black** and the **Font Size** to **24**. Select the title you just formatted. Click the **Font Color button arrow**, and then under **Theme Colors**, in the seventh column, click the fifth color—**Olive Green, Accent 3, Darker 25%**.

b. Select the second paragraph. On the **Home tab**, in the **Paragraph group**, click the **Borders button arrow**, and then click **Borders and Shading**. In the **Borders and Shading** dialog box, click the **Color arrow**, and then under **Theme Colors**, in the seventh column, click the fifth color—**Olive Green, Accent 3, Darker 25%**. Click the **Width arrow**, and then click **3 pt**. In the **Preview** area, click the *bottom* border of the Preview and then click **OK**.

c. Below the nameplate, locate the paragraph that begins *Recycle Your Mobile*, and then select all of the text from that point to the end of the document. On the **Page Layout tab**, in the **Page Setup group**, click the **Columns** button, and then click **Two**.

d. With the text still selected, in the **Paragraph group**, set **Spacing After** to **6 pt**. On the **Home tab**, in the **Paragraph group**, click the **Justify** button. Click anywhere in the document to deselect the text, and then **Save** the newsletter.

e. Press Ctrl + Home. On the **Insert tab**, in the **Illustrations group**, click the **Clip Art** button. In the **Clip Art** task pane, click in the **Search for** box, and then type **conservation**

f. In the **Clip Art** task pane, click the **Results should be arrow**, and be sure that only the **Illustrations** check box is selected. Be sure the **Include Office.com content** check box is selected, and then click **Go**. Locate the image of three green arrows, as shown in Figure 3.42, and then click on the image.

g. On the **Format tab**, in the **Size group**, click in the **Shape Height** box, type **1** and then press Enter. In the **Arrange group**, click the **Wrap Text** button, and then click **Square**. **Close** the Clip Art task pane, and then drag the image to the location shown in Figure 3.42.

h. In the second column, position the insertion point at the beginning of the paragraph that begins *By managing costs*. Open your Web browser. In the address bar, type **www.energy.gov** and then press Enter. Maximize the browser window. Use the taskbar to return to your Word document.

i. On the **Insert tab**, in the **Illustrations group**, click the **Screenshot** button. In the gallery, click the DOE screenshot to insert it. **Close** your Web browser, and then **Save** your document.

2 At the top of the first column, select the paragraph that begins *Recycle Your Mobile*. Be sure to include the paragraph mark. Right-click the selected text, and then click **Font**. In the **Font** dialog box, click the **Font color arrow**, and then under **Theme Colors**, in the seventh column, click the last color—**Olive Green, Accent 3, Darker 50%**. Under **Font style**, click **Bold**. Under **Size**, click **14**. Under **Effects**, select the **Small caps** check box.

a. In the **Font** dialog box, click **OK**. Right-click the selected text, and then click the **Center** button. In the title you just formatted, click to position the insertion point to the right of *Phone*, and then press Del to remove the space. Hold down Shift, and then press Enter to insert a manual line break.

b. Select and right-click the title you just formatted, and then on the Mini toolbar, click the **Format Painter** button. Near the middle of the first column, select the paragraph that begins *A New World* to apply the same formatting.

c. At the bottom of the second column, in the paragraph that begins *For further*, select the entire paragraph. On the Mini toolbar, apply **Bold**.

d. With the text still selected, on the **Home tab**, in the **Paragraph group**, click the **Borders button arrow**, and then click **Borders and Shading**. In the **Borders and Shading** dialog box, be sure the **Borders tab** is selected. Under **Setting**, click **Box**. Click the **Width arrow**, and then click **3 pt**. If necessary, click the **Color arrow**, and then in the seventh column, click the fifth color—**Olive Green, Accent 3, Darker 25%**.

e. At the top of the **Borders and Shading** dialog box, click the **Shading tab**. Click the **Fill arrow**, and then in the seventh column, click the second color—**Olive Green, Accent 3, Lighter 80%**. At the bottom of the **Borders and Shading** dialog box, click **OK**. Click anywhere in the document to deselect the text.

(Project 3D Company Newsletter continues on the next page)

Skills Review | Project 3D Company Newsletter (continued)

f. Near the bottom of the first column, in the paragraph that begins *Information and communications*, click to position the insertion point at the beginning of the sixth line. On the **Page Layout tab**, in the **Page Setup group**, click the **Breaks** button. Under **Page Breaks**, click **Column**.

g. From **Backstage** view, display the **Document Panel**, type your name and course information. Add the keywords **newsletter, energy** and then **Close** the **Document Panel**. **Save** the document, view the Print Preview, and then **Exit** Word. Hold this file until you complete this project.

3 **Start** Word and display a new blank document. Display formatting marks and rulers. **Save** the document in your **Word Chapter 3** folder as **Lastname_Firstname_3D_Labels Open** the file **w03D_Addresses Save** the address file in your **Word Chapter 3** folder as **Lastname_Firstname_3D_Addresses** and then add the file name to the footer.

a. Click to position the insertion point in the last cell in the table, and then press Tab to create a new row. Enter the following new record:

First Name	**Eldon**
Last Name	**Aarons**
Address 1	**5354 Thornewood Dr.**
Unit	**#2B**
City	**Memphis**
State	**TN**
ZIP Code	**38112**

b. **Save**, and then **Close** the table of addresses; be sure your blank **Lastname_Firstname_3D_Labels** document displays. Click the **Mailings tab**. In the **Start Mail Merge group**, click the **Start Mail Merge** button, and then click **Step by Step Mail Merge Wizard**. Under **Select document type**, click the **Labels** option button.

c. At the bottom of the task pane, click **Next: Starting document**. Under **Select starting document**, be sure **Change document layout** is selected, and then under **Change document layout**, click **Label options**.

d. In the **Label Options** dialog box, under **Printer information**, click the **Tray arrow**, and then click **Default tray (Automatically Select)**.

e. Under **Label information**, click the **Label vendors arrow**, and then click **Avery US Letter**. Under **Product number**, scroll about halfway down the list, and then click **5160**. At the bottom of the **Label Options** dialog box, click **OK**. At the bottom of the task pane, click **Next: Select recipients**.

f. Under **Select recipients**, be sure the **Use an existing list** option button is selected. Under **Use an existing list**, click **Browse**. Navigate to your **Word Chapter 3** folder, select your **Lastname_Firstname_3D_Addresses** file, and then click **Open**. At the bottom of the **Mail Merge Recipients** dialog box, click **OK**, and then in the **Mail Merge** task pane, click **Next: Arrange your labels**.

g. Under **Arrange your labels**, click **Address block**. If necessary, in the **Insert Address Block** dialog box, under **Insert recipient's name in this format**, select the **Joshua Randall Jr.** format.

h. Click **Match Fields**. Click the **Address 2 arrow**, and then click **Unit**. Click **OK** two times.

i. In the task pane, under **Replicate labels**, click **Update all labels**. Click **Next: Preview your labels**. Press Ctrl + A to select all of the label text, and then on the **Page Layout tab**, click in the **Spacing Before** box, type **4** and press Enter to ensure that the four-line addresses will fit on the labels. **Save** your labels, and then **Close** the **Mail Merge** task pane.

4 Add the file name to the footer, and then close the footer area. Click in the bottom empty row of the table, click the **Layout tab**, in the **Rows & Columns group**, click **Delete**, and then click **Delete Rows**. From **Backstage** view, display the **Document Panel**, type your name and course information, and then add the keywords **newsletter mailing labels Close** the **Document Panel**.

a. Print or submit electronically your 3D_Company_Newsletter, 3D_Addresses, and 3D_Labels documents.

b. **Close** the document, click **Save** to save the labels, and then **Exit** Word.

End You have completed Project 3D

Content-Based Assessments

Apply 3A skills from these Objectives:

1. Create a Research Paper
2. Insert Footnotes in a Research Paper
3. Create Citations and a Bibliography in a Research Paper

Mastering Word | Project 3E Hazards

In the following Mastering Word project, you will edit and format a research paper for Memphis Primary Materials, the topic of which is hazardous materials in electronic waste. Your completed document will look similar to Figure 3.43.

Project Files

For Project 3E, you will need the following file:

w03E_Hazards

You will save your document as:

Lastname_Firstname_3E_Hazards

Project Results

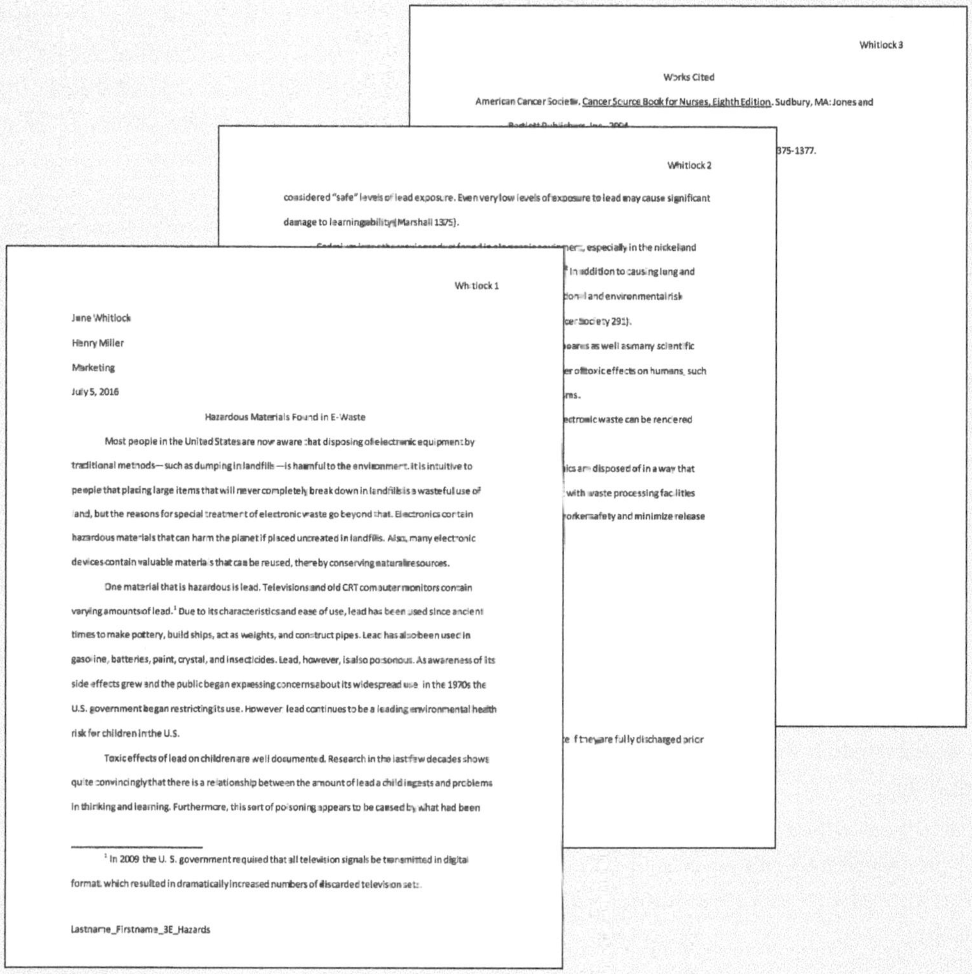

Figure 3.43

(Project 3E Hazards continues on the next page)

Mastering Word | Project 3E Hazards (continued)

1 **Start** Word. From your student files open the document **w03E_Hazards. Save** the document in your **Word Chapter 3** folder as **Lastname_Firstname_3E_Hazards** Display the header area, type **Whitlock** and then press Spacebar. Display the **Page Number gallery**, and then in the **Current Position**, add the **Plain Number** style. Apply **Align Text Right** formatting to the header. Add the file name to the footer.

2 Return to the beginning of the document, press Enter to insert a blank line, click in the blank line, type **June Whitlock** and then press Enter. Type **Henry Miller** and press Enter. Type **Marketing** and press Enter. Type **July 5, 2016**

3 Select all of the text in the document. Change the **Line Spacing** to **2.0**, and change the **Spacing After** to **0 pt**. Deselect the text, right-click anywhere in the title *Hazardous Materials Found in E-Waste*, and then **Center** the title.

Starting with the paragraph that begins *Most people*, select the text from that point to the end of the document, and then set the **First Line Indent** to **0.5"**.

4 Near the middle of **Page 1**, in the paragraph that begins *One material*, in the second line, click to position the insertion point to the right of the period following *lead*, and then add the following footnote:

> **In 2009 the U.S. government required that all television signals be transmitted in digital format, which resulted in dramatically increased numbers of discarded television sets.**

On **Page 2**, in the paragraph that begins *Cadmium is another*, in the second line, click to position the insertion point to the right of the period following *devices*, and then add the following footnote:

> **Newer lithium batteries are not considered hazardous waste if they are fully discharged prior to disposal.**

5 Right-click anywhere in the footnote, modify the **Style** to set the **Font Size** to **11**, and then change the **Format** of paragraphs to add a **First line** indent and use double-spacing.

Near the bottom of **Page 1**, locate the paragraph that begins *Toxic effects*, and then click position the insertion point to the left of the period at the end of the paragraph, which displays at the top of **Page 2**. In the **MLA** format, add the following **Journal Article** citation (type the Title on one line):

Author:	**Marshall, Eliot**
Title:	**EPA May Allow More Lead in Gasoline**
Journal Name:	**Science**
Year:	**1982**
Pages:	**1375–1377**

6 Near the top of **Page 2**, locate the paragraph that begins *Cadmium*, and then click to position the insertion point to the left of the period at the end of the paragraph. Add the following **Book** citation, using a **Corporate Author** (type the Title on one line):

Corporate Author:	**American Cancer Society**
Title:	**Cancer Source Book for Nurses, Eighth Edition**
Year:	**2004**
City:	**Sudbury, MA**
Publisher:	**Jones and Bartlett Publishers, Inc.**

Select the *Marshall* citation and add the page number **1375** At the end of the next paragraph, select the *American Cancer Society* citation and add the page number **291**

7 Move to the end of the document, and then insert a manual page break to create a new page. Change the **First Line Indent** to **0"**. Add a **Works Cited** title, and then **Insert Bibliography**. Select the two references, apply **Double** line spacing, and then remove spacing after the paragraphs. **Center** the *Works Cited* title.

Display the **Document Panel** and add your name and course information and the keywords **hazardous materials Save** your document. Display the Print Preview, make any necessary adjustments, and then print or submit electronically as directed. **Exit** Word.

End **You have completed Project 3E**

Apply 3B skills from these Objectives:

- 4 Format a Multiple-Column Newsletter
- 5 Use Special Character and Paragraph Formatting
- 6 Create Mailing Labels Using Mail Merge

Mastering Word | Project 3F Spring Newsletter

In the following Mastering Word project, you will format a newsletter for Memphis Primary Materials, and then create a set of mailing labels for the newsletter. Your completed documents will look similar to Figure 3.44.

Project Files

For Project 3F, you will need the following files:

New blank Word document
w03F_Spring_Newsletter
w03F_Addresses

You will save your documents as:

Lastname_Firstname_3F_Spring_Newsletter
Lastname_Firstname_3F_Labels

Project Results

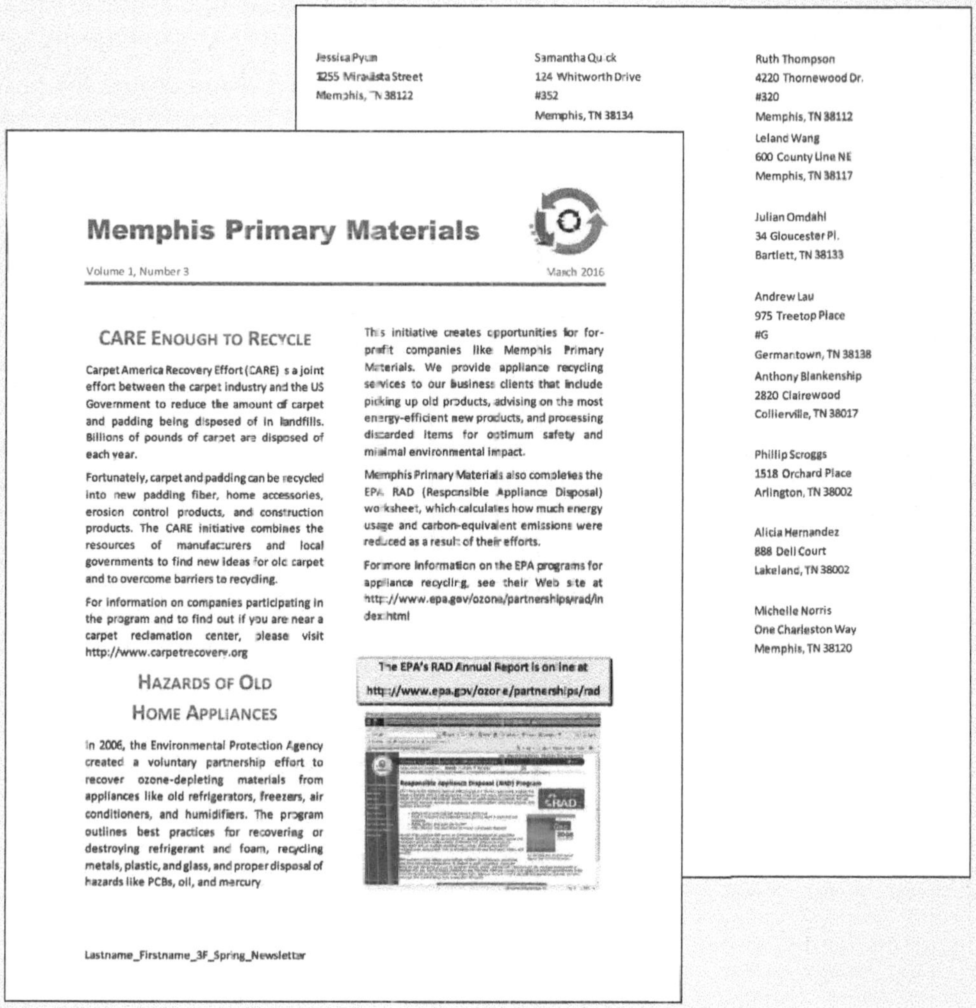

Figure 3.44

(Project 3F Spring Newsletter continues on the next page)

Mastering Word | Project 3F Spring Newsletter (continued)

1 **Start** Word. Open **w03F_Spring_Newsletter**, and then save it in your **Word Chapter 3** folder as **Lastname_Firstname_3F_Spring_Newsletter** Add the file name to the footer. Display the rulers and formatting marks.

Select the first line of text—*Memphis Primary Materials*. Change the **Font** to **Arial Black**, the **Font Size** to **24**, and the **Font Color** to **Orange, Accent 6, Darker 25%**.

Select the second line of text—the date and volume. Change the **Font Color** to **Orange, Accent 6, Darker 25%**. Display the **Borders and Shading** dialog box, and then add an **Orange, Accent 6, Darker 25%**, **3 pt** line below the selected text.

2 Click at the beginning of the newsletter title. Display the **Clip Art** task pane, search for **recycle earth** and then insert the image of the orange and tan recycle arrows. Change the **Height** to **1** and then apply **Square** text wrapping. Close the **Clip Art** task pane. Drag the image to the location shown in Figure 3.44.

Starting with the paragraph that begins *CARE enough*, select all of the text from that point to the end of the document. Change the **Spacing After** to **6 pt**, format the text in two columns, and apply the **Justify** alignment.

3 At the top of the first column, select the paragraph *CARE Enough to Recycle*. From the **Font** dialog box, change the **Font Size** to **20**, apply **Bold**, add the **Small caps** effect, and change the **Font color** to **Orange, Accent 6, Darker 25%**. **Center** the paragraph. Near the bottom of the same column, apply the same formatting to the paragraph that begins *Hazards of Old*. Add a manual line break between *Old* and *Home*.

Move to the blank line at the bottom of the second column. Open your Web browser and open the **www.epa.gov/ozone/partnerships/rad/** Web site. Maximize the browser window and return to your Word document. Insert a **Screenshot** of the EPA Web page. **Close** your Web browser.

4 Select the two lines of text above the inserted screenshot. **Center** the text and apply **Bold**. Add a **Shadow** border, change the **Color** to **Tan, Background 2, Darker 25%**, the **Width** to **1 1/2 pt**, and then on the **Shading tab** of the dialog box, apply a **Fill** of **Tan, Background 2** shading—in the third column, the first color.

Display the **Document Panel** and add your name, course information, and the **Keywords Spring newsletter** Display the **Print Preview**, return to your document and make any necessary corrections, and then **Save** and **Close** the document. Hold this document until you complete the project.

5 Display a **New** blank document. **Save** the document in your **Word Chapter 3** folder as **Lastname_Firstname_3F_Labels** On the **Mailings tab**, start the **Step by Step Mail Merge Wizard.**

In **Step 1**, select **Labels** as the document type. In **Step 2**, set **Label options** to use the **Auto default** tray (yours may vary) and **Avery US Letter 5160**.

In **Step 3**, use an existing list, browse to select **w03F_Addresses**. In **Step 4**, add an **Address block** to the labels, use the *Joshua Randall Jr.* format, and then **Match Fields** by matching *Address 2* to *Unit*.

Update all labels and **Preview**. Select all of the label text, and then on the **Page Layout tab**, click in the **Spacing Before** box, type **4** and press Enter to ensure that the four-line addresses will fit on the labels. On the **Layout tab**, in the **Table group**, if necessary click **View Gridlines** to check the alignment of the labels.

Complete the merge, and then **Close** the **Mail Merge** task pane. Delete the last two empty rows of the table, and then add the file name to the footer.

6 Display the **Document Panel**, and then add your name and course information and the keywords **mailing labels** Display the **Print Preview**, return to your document and make any necessary corrections, and then **Save**. Print or submit electronically your two files that are the results of this project—3F_Spring_Newsletter and 3F_Labels. **Exit** Word.

End **You have completed Project 3F**

Apply 3A and 3B skills from these Objectives:

1. Create a Research Paper
2. Insert Footnotes in a Research Paper
3. Create Citations and a Bibliography in a Research Paper
4. Format a Multiple-Column Newsletter
5. Use Special Character and Paragraph Formatting
6. Create Mailing Labels Using Mail Merge

myitlab grader

Mastering Word | Project 3G Economics

In the following Mastering Word project, you will edit and format a newsletter and a research paper for Memphis Primary Materials on the topic of environmental economics. Your completed documents will look similar to Figure 3.45.

Project Files

For Project 3G, you will need the following files:

New blank Word document
w03G_Economics
w03G_Addresses
w03G_April_Newsletter

You will save your documents as:

Lastname_Firstname_3G_Economics
Lastname_Firstname_3G_April_Newsletter
Lastname_Firstname_3G_Labels

Project Results

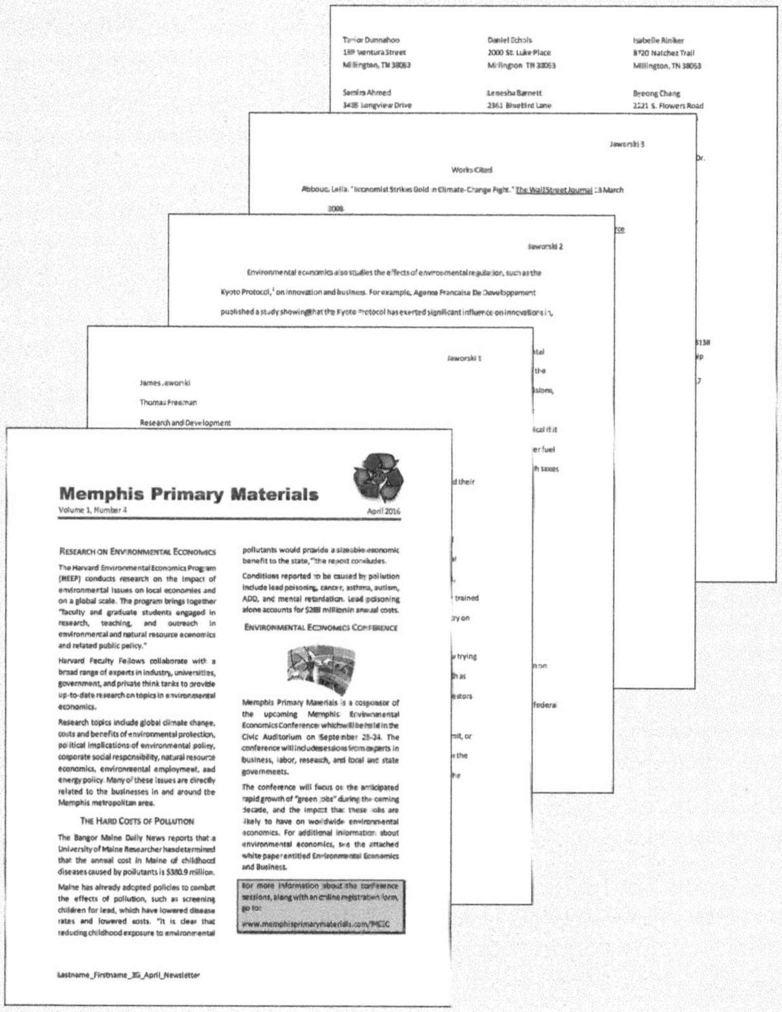

Figure 3.45

(Project 3G Economics continues on the next page)

Mastering Word | Project 3G Economics (continued)

1 **Start** Word. Open the document **w03G_April_Newsletter**, and then save the document in your **Word Chapter 3** folder as **Lastname_Firstname_3G_April_Newsletter** Add the file name to the footer. Starting with the paragraph that begins *Research on Environmental Economics*, select all of the text from that point to the end of the document—the document text extends to two pages. Set the **Spacing After** to **6 pt**, format the selected text as two columns, and set the alignment to **Justify**.

2 Near the bottom of the first column, in the paragraph that begins *Maine has already*, click to position the insertion point to the left of the sixth line, which begins *pollutants would*. Insert a column break. At the top of the first column, select the paragraph *Research on Environmental Economics*.

Display the **Font** dialog box, set the **Font Size** to **14**, apply **Bold**, set the **Font color** to **Dark Blue, Text 2**, and then add the **Small caps** effect. **Center** the paragraph. Use the Format Painter to copy the formatting and then apply the same formatting to the paragraph *The Hard Costs of Pollution* located near the bottom of the first column and to *Environmental Economics Conference* in the second column.

3 At the bottom of the second column, select the last two paragraphs of text. From the **Borders and Shading** dialog box, apply a **1 1/2 pt**, **Shadow** border using the **Dark Blue, Text 2** color, and then on the **Shading tab**, apply a **Fill** of **Dark Blue, Text 2, Lighter 80%**.

In the second column, click to position the insertion point at the beginning of the paragraph that begins *Memphis Primary Materials is a cosponsor*. Display the **Clip Art** task pane. Search for **conference** and limit your search to **Illustrations. Insert** the image shown in Figure 3.45, apply **Top and Bottom** text wrapping, decrease the **Height** of the image to **1″**, and position the image as shown. **Close** the Clip Art task pane.

Display the **Document Panel** and add your name and course information and the **Keywords April newsletter** **Save** and then **Close** the document. Hold this file until you complete this project.

4 From your student files, open the document **w03G_Economics**, and then save it in your **Word Chapter 3** folder as **Lastname_Firstname_3G_Economics** Display the header area, type **Jaworski** and then press Spacebar. In the **Header & Footer group**, add a **Plain Number** from the **Current Position** gallery. Apply **Align Text Right** formatting to the header. Move to the footer area and add the file name to the footer.

Select all of the text in the document. Change the **Line Spacing** to **2.0**, and change the **Spacing After** to **0**. Near the top of the document, **Center** the title *Environmental Economics and Business*. Beginning with the text below the centered title, select the text from that point to the end of the document, and then set a **First Line Indent** at **0.5″**.

5 At the bottom of **Page 1**, in the paragraph that begins *Environmental economics also*, in the second line, click to position the insertion point to the right of the comma following *Protocol*, and then insert the following footnote:

> **The Kyoto Protocol is an international agreement under the UN Framework Convention on Climate Change that went into effect in 2005.**

In the next paragraph, which begins *In the United States*, in the second line, position the insertion point to the right of the period following *Economics*, and then insert the following footnote:

> **The NCEE offers a centralized source of technical expertise to the EPA, as well as other federal agencies, Congress, universities, and other organizations.**

Right-click in the footnote, and then modify the style to set the **Font Size** to **11** and the format of the paragraph to include a **First line** indent and double-spacing. **Save** your document.

6 Near the bottom of **Page 1**, in the paragraph that begins *Environmental economists*, position the insertion point to the left of the period at the end of the paragraph. Using **MLA** format, add the following **Article in a Periodical** citation (type the Title on one line):

Author:	**Abboud, Leila**
Title:	**Economist Strikes Gold in Climate-Change Fight**
Periodical Title:	**The Wall Street Journal**
Year:	**2008**
Month:	**March**
Day:	**13**

(Project 3G Economics continues on the next page)

Mastering Word | Project 3G Economics (continued)

Select the *Abboud* citation and add the page number **A1** Near the middle of **Page 2**, in the paragraph that begins *In the United States*, click to position the insertion point to the left of the period at the end of the paragraph. Add the following **Book** citation in **MLA** format (type the Title on one line):

Author:	**Tietenberg, Tom; Folmer, Henk, Editors**
Title:	**The International Yearbook of Environmental Resource Economics, 2006/2007**
Year:	**2006**
City:	**Northampton, MA**
Publisher:	**Edward Elgar Publishers**

7 Select the *Tietenberg* citation and add the page number **1** Insert a manual page break at the end of the document. On the new **Page 3**, on the ruler, set the **First Line Indent** to **0"**. Type **Works Cited** and then press Enter.

On the **References tab**, in the **Citations & Bibliography group**, be sure *MLA* displays in the **Style** box. Insert the bibliography. Select the inserted references, set the **Line Spacing** to **2.0**, and then set **Spacing After** to **0 pt. Center** the *Works Cited* title.

Display the **Document Panel** and add your name and course information and the **Keywords environmental economics** Display the **Print Preview** to check your document, make any necessary adjustments, **Save**, and then **Close** the document. Hold this file until you complete this project.

8 Display a **New** blank document. **Save** the document in your **Word Chapter 3** folder as **Lastname_Firstname_3G_Labels** On the **Mailings tab**, start the **Step by Step Mail Merge Wizard**. In **Step 1**, select **Labels** as the document type. In **Step 2**, set **Label options** to use the **Auto default** tray (yours may vary) and **Avery US Letter 5160**. If you cannot see the gridlines, on the **Layout tab**, in the **Table group**, click **View Gridlines**. In **Step 3**, use an existing list, browse to select **w03G_Addresses**, and then click **OK**.

In **Step 4**, add an **Address block** to the labels, use the *Joshua Randall Jr.* format, and then **Match Fields** by matching *Address 2* to *Unit*. **Update all labels** and then **Preview**. Select all of the label text, and then on the **Page Layout tab**, click in the **Spacing Before** box, type **4** and press Enter. Complete the merge, and then **Close** the **Mail Merge** task pane. Delete the last two empty rows of the table, and then add the file name to the footer, which adds an additional page.

Display the **Document Panel**, and then add your name, course information, and the keywords **mailing labels** Click **Save**. Print or submit electronically your three files that are the results of this project—3G_Economics, 3G_April_Newsletter, and 3G_Labels. **Exit** Word.

End **You have completed Project 3G**

Apply a combination of the 3A and 3B skills.

GO! Fix It | Project 3H Metals Report

Project Files

For Project 3H, you will need the following file:

w03H_Metals_Report

You will save your document as:

Lastname_Firstname_3H_Metals_Report

From the student files that accompany this textbook, locate and open the file w03H_Metals_Report, and then save the file in your Word Chapter 3 folder as **Lastname_Firstname_3H_Metals_Report**

This document contains errors that you must find and correct. Read and examine the document, and then edit to correct any errors that you find and to improve the overall document format. Types of errors could include, but are not restricted to:

- Formatting does not match MLA style guidelines that you practiced in the chapter
- Incorrect header format
- Incorrect spacing between paragraphs
- Incorrect paragraph indents
- Incorrect line spacing
- Incorrect footnote format
- Incorrectly formatted reference page

Things you should know to complete this project:

- Displaying formatting marks will assist in locating spacing errors.
- There are no errors in the parenthetical references in the document.
- There are no errors in the information in the footnotes or bibliographical references.

Save your document and add the file name to the footer. In the Document Panel, add your name, course information, and the keywords **valuable metals, recycling** Save your document and submit as directed.

End You have completed Project 3H

Apply a combination of the 3A and 3B skills.

GO! Make It | Project 3I Green Newsletter

Project Files

For Project 3I, you will need the following files:

New blank Word document
w03I_Competition
w03I_Kids

You will save your document as:

Lastname_Firstname_3I_Green_Newsletter

Start with a new Word document, and then save the file in your chapter folder as **Lastname_Firstname_3I_Green_Newsletter** Create the document shown in Figure 3.46. Create a nameplate, and then insert the files w03I_Competition and w03I_Kids. The title is Arial Black, 24 pt, Dark Blue, Text 2. Other titles and borders are Dark Blue, Text 2. The two titles in the columns are Calibri, 16 pt. The clip art image can be found by using the search term **recycle** and the screenshot can be found at the Web address in the last line of the newsletter.

Add the file name to the footer; in the Document Panel, add your name and course information and the Keywords **green, campuses, kids** Save your document and submit as directed.

Project Results

Memphis Primary Materials

Volume 1, Number 4 April 2016

THE COMPETITIVE SPIRIT OF GREEN

One way to increase people's willingness to reuse and recycle is to invoke their spirit of competition—and prizes do not hurt either. College campuses are proving this by participating in the America's Greenest Campus competition.

America's Greenest Campus is a nationwide contest, with the goal of reducing the carbon footprint of entire campus populations across the country.

Partnering with Smart Power and the U.S. Department of Energy, the winning campus will receive a donation of $10,000. As of February 2009, the University of Maryland has reduced its CO2 emissions by 2% and George Mason University by 3%.

Students, faculty, and staff are encouraged to recycle, turn off lights, reduce heating and air conditioning, and engage in many other small and large changes that can help the environment. Treehugger.com calls the contest, "the NCAA of sustainability."

Another college competition for environmentalism is RecycleMania. Designed to encourage colleges and universities to reduce waste, the competition collects reports on recycling and trash over a 10-week period. This competition thinks of colleges and universities as small cities that consume large amounts of resources and generate a lot of solid waste. Participating campuses are ranked by categories such as "least amount of waste per capita." Weekly results are distributed to the participants so they can benchmark against their competition and step up their efforts.

With growing awareness of the need to reduce, reuse, and recycle among students, expect some competition if you are part of a campus community!

CLEANUP IS FOR KIDS

Cleaning up the planet isn't just for college students. Younger students often have a desire to get involved with environmental activities, and there is no shortage of resources.

Start at the website of the Environmental Protection Agency. They provide resources like Cleanup for Kids, a Web site of the National Oceanic and Atmospheric Administration (NOAA), which makes the hazards of oil spills real through science demonstrations. The brochure, *Environmental Protection Begins With You*, outlines examples of community volunteer projects in which students can participate.

Learn more at the EPA website:
http://www.epa.gov/highschool/waste.htm

Lastname_Firstname_3I_Green_Newsletter

Figure 3.46

End You have completed Project 3I

Apply a combination of the 3A and 3B skills.

GO! Solve It | Project 3J Municipal Newsletter

Project Files

For Project 3J, you will need the following file:

New blank Word document

You will save your document as:

Lastname_Firstname_3J_Municipal_Newsletter

Memphis Primary Materials writes an informational newsletter for customers. Create a new document and save it in your Word Chapter 3 folder as **Lastname_Firstname_3J_Municipal_Newsletter** Use the following information to create a newsletter that includes a nameplate, multiple columns, at least two articles with article titles formatted so that they stand out, at least one clip art image, one screenshot, and one paragraph that includes a border and shading.

This issue (Volume 1, Number 6—June 2016) will focus on municipal solid waste—the waste generated by householders and small businesses. This category of waste does not include hazardous, industrial, or construction waste. The articles you write can be on any topic regarding municipal waste, and might include an introduction to the topic and a discussion of recycling in the U.S. or in the Memphis community. You will need to research this topic on the Web. A good place to start is www.epa.gov, which has many articles on solid municipal waste, and also provides links to further articles on the topic. You might also consider doing a Web search for the term **municipal solid waste recycling**

Add the file name to the footer. To the Document Panel, add your name, your course name and section number, and the keywords **municipal solid waste recycling**

Performance Element	Performance Level: Exemplary: You consistently applied the relevant skills	Proficient: You sometimes, but not always, applied the relevant skills	Developing: You rarely or never applied the relevant skills
Create and format nameplate	The nameplate includes both the company name and the date and volume information, and is formatted attractively.	One or more of the nameplate elements are done correctly, but other items are either omitted or not formatted properly.	The newsletter does not include a nameplate.
Insert at least two articles in multiple-column format	The newsletter contains at least two articles, displayed in multiple columns that are well written and are free of grammar and spelling errors.	The newsletter contains only one article, or the text is not divided into two columns, or there are spelling and grammar errors in the text.	The newsletter contains only one article, the article is not divided into multiple columns, and there are spelling and grammar errors.
Insert and format at least one clip art image	An appropriate clip art image is included. The image is sized and positioned appropriately.	A clip art image is inserted, but is either inappropriate, or is formatted or positioned poorly.	No clip art image is included.
Border and shading added to a paragraph	One or more paragraphs display an attractive border with shading that enables the reader to read the text.	A border or shading is displayed, but not both; or, the shading is too dark to enable the reader to easily read the text.	No border or shading is added to a paragraph.
Insert a screenshot	A screenshot is inserted in one of the columns; the screenshot is related to the content of the article.	A screenshot is inserted in the document, but does not relate to the content of the article.	No screenshot is inserted.

End You have completed Project 3J

Apply a combination of the 3A and 3B skills.

GO! Solve It | Project 3K Paper Report

Project Files

For Project 3K, you will need the following file:

New blank Word document

You will save your document as:

Lastname_Firstname_3K_Paper_Report

Create a new file and save it as **Lastname_Firstname_3K_Paper_Report** Use the following information to create a report written in the MLA format. The report should include at least two footnotes, at least two citations, and should include a *Works Cited* page.

Memphis Primary Materials writes and distributes informational reports on topics of interest to the people of Memphis. This report will be written by Sarah Stanger for the head of Marketing, Henry Miller. Information reports are provided as a public service of the company, and are distributed free of charge.

The topic of the report is recycling and reuse of paper and paper products. The report should contain an introduction, and then details about how much paper is used, what it is used for, the increase of paper recycling over time, and how paper products can be recycled or reused. A good place to start is www.epa.gov, which has many articles on paper use and recycling, and also provides links to further articles on the topic. You might also consider doing a Web search for the terms **paper recycling**

Add the file name to the footer, and add your name, your course name and section number, and the keywords **paper products, recycling** to the Document Panel.

Performance Element	Performance Level		
	Exemplary: You consistently applied the relevant skills	**Proficient:** You sometimes, but not always, applied the relevant skills	**Developing:** You rarely or never applied the relevant skills
Format the header and heading	The last name and page number are right-aligned in the header, and the report has a four-line heading and a centered title.	The header and heading are included, but are not formatted according to MLA style guidelines.	The header or heading is missing or incomplete.
Format the body of the report	The report is double-spaced, with no space after paragraphs. The first lines of paragraphs are indented 0.5″.	Some, but not all, of the report formatting is correct.	The majority of the formatting does not follow MLA guidelines.
Footnotes are included and formatted correctly	Two or more footnotes are included, and the footnote text is 11 pt, double-spaced, and the first line of each footnote is indented.	The correct number of footnotes is included, but the footnotes are not formatted properly.	No footnotes are included.
Citations and bibliography are included and formatted according to MLA guidelines	At least two citations are included in parenthetical references, with page numbers where appropriate, and the sources are included in a properly formatted Works Cited page.	Only one citation is included, or the citations and sources are not formatted correctly.	No citations or Works Cited page are included.

End You have completed Project 3K

Outcomes-Based Assessments

Rubric

The following outcomes-based assessments are *open-ended assessments*. That is, there is no specific correct result; your result will depend on your approach to the information provided. Make *Professional Quality* your goal. Use the following scoring rubric to guide you in *how* to approach the problem, and then to evaluate *how well* your approach solves the problem.

The *criteria*—Software Mastery, Content, Format and Layout, and Process—represent the knowledge and skills you have gained that you can apply to solving the problem. The *levels of performance*—Professional Quality, Approaching Professional Quality, or Needs Quality Improvements—help you and your instructor evaluate your result.

	Your completed project is of Professional Quality if you:	**Your completed project is Approaching Professional Quality if you:**	**Your completed project Needs Quality Improvements if you:**
1-Software Mastery	Choose and apply the most appropriate skills, tools, and features and identify efficient methods to solve the problem.	Choose and apply some appropriate skills, tools, and features, but not in the most efficient manner.	Choose inappropriate skills, tools, or features, or are inefficient in solving the problem.
2-Content	Construct a solution that is clear and well organized, contains content that is accurate, appropriate to the audience and purpose, and is complete. Provide a solution that contains no errors in spelling, grammar, or style.	Construct a solution in which some components are unclear, poorly organized, inconsistent, or incomplete. Misjudge the needs of the audience. Have some errors in spelling, grammar, or style, but the errors do not detract from comprehension.	Construct a solution that is unclear, incomplete, or poorly organized; contains some inaccurate or inappropriate content; and contains many errors in spelling, grammar, or style. Do not solve the problem.
3-Format and Layout	Format and arrange all elements to communicate information and ideas, clarify function, illustrate relationships, and indicate relative importance.	Apply appropriate format and layout features to some elements, but not others. Overuse features, causing minor distraction.	Apply format and layout that does not communicate information or ideas clearly. Do not use format and layout features to clarify function, illustrate relationships, or indicate relative importance. Use available features excessively, causing distraction.
4-Process	Use an organized approach that integrates planning, development, self-assessment, revision, and reflection.	Demonstrate an organized approach in some areas, but not others; or, use an insufficient process of organization throughout.	Do not use an organized approach to solve the problem.

Outcomes-Based Assessments

Apply a combination of the 3A and 3B skills.

GO! Think | Project 3L Jobs Newsletter

Project Files

For Project 3L, you will need the following file:

New blank Word document

You will save your document as:

Lastname_Firstname_3L_Jobs_Newsletter

The marketing manager of Memphis Primary Materials needs to create the next issue of the company's monthly newsletter (Volume 1, Number 7—July 2016), which will focus on "green jobs." Green jobs are jobs associated with environmentally friendly companies or are positions with firms that manufacture, sell, or install energy-saving or resource-saving products.

Use the following information to create a newsletter that includes a nameplate, multiple columns, at least two articles with article titles formatted so that they stand out, at least one clip art image, one screenshot, and one paragraph that includes a border and shading.

The articles you write can be on any topic regarding green jobs, and might include an introduction to the topic, information about a recent (or future) green job conference, and a discussion of green jobs in the United States. You will need to research this topic on the Web. A good place to start is www.epa.gov. You might also consider doing a Web search for the terms **green jobs** or **green jobs conference**

Add the file name to the footer. Add appropriate information to the Document Panel. Save the document as **Lastname_Firstname_3L_Jobs_Newsletter** and submit it as directed.

End You have completed Project 3L

Apply a combination of the 3A and 3B skills.

GO! Think | Project 3M Construction Report

Project Files

For Project 3M, you will need the following file:

New blank Word document

You will save your document as:

Lastname_Firstname_3M_Construction_Report

As part of the ongoing research provided on environment topics by the staff of Memphis Primary Materials, the Marketing Director, Henry Miller, has asked a summer intern, James Bodine, to create a report on recycling and reuse in the construction and demolition of buildings.

Create a new file and save it as **Lastname_Firstname_3M_Construction_Report** Use the following information to create a report written in the MLA format. The report should include at least two footnotes, at least two citations, and should include a *Works Cited* page.

The report should contain an introduction, and then details about, for example, how much construction material can be salvaged from existing buildings, how these materials can be reused in future buildings, and how materials can be saved and recycled on new building projects. A good place to start is www.epa.gov, which has a number of articles on recycling and reuse of materials during construction and demolition. You might also consider doing a Web search for the terms **construction recycling** or **demolition recycling** or **construction and demolition**

Add the file name to the footer Add appropriate information to the Document Panel and submit it as directed.

End You have completed Project 3M

Outcomes-Based Assessments

Apply a combination of the 3B skills.

You and GO! | Project 3N College Newsletter

Project Files

For Project 3N, you will need the following file:

New blank Word document

You will save your document as

Lastname_Firstname_3N_College_Newsletter

In this project, you will create a one-page newsletter. The newsletter should include at least one article describing your college and one article about an academic or athletic program at your college.

Be sure to include a nameplate, at least two articles, at least one clip art or screenshot image, and a bordered paragraph or paragraphs. Before you submit the newsletter, be sure to check it for grammar and spelling errors, and also be sure to format the newsletter in an attractive manner by using the skills you practiced in this chapter.

Save the file as **Lastname_Firstname_3N_College_Newsletter** Add the file name to the footer, and add your name, your course name and section number, and the keywords **newsletter** and **college** to the Document Panel. Save and submit your file as directed.

End You have completed Project 3N

Apply a combination of the 3A and 3B skills.

GO! CD-ROM

GO! Collaborate | Project 3O Bell Orchid Hotels Group Running Case

Your instructor may assign this group case project to your class. If your instructor assigns this project, he or she will provide you with information and instructions to work as part of a group. The group will apply the skills gained thus far to help the Bell Orchid Hotel Group achieve its business goals.

End You have completed Project 3O

Business Running Case

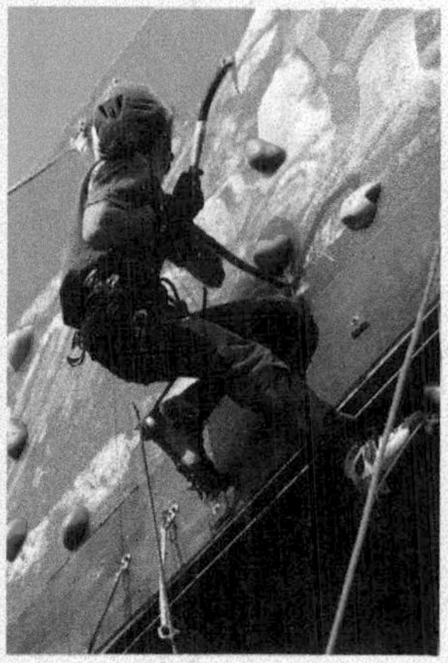

Razvan CHIRNOAGA/Shutterstock

This project relates to **Front Range Action Sports**, which is one of the country's largest retailers of sports gear and outdoor recreation merchandise. The company has large retail stores in Colorado, Washington, Oregon, California, and New Mexico, in addition to a growing online business. Major merchandise categories include fishing, camping, rock climbing, winter sports, action sports, water sports, team sports, racquet sports, fitness, golf, apparel, and footwear.

In this project, you will apply skills you practiced from the Objectives in Word Chapters 1-3. You will assist Irene Shviktar, the Vice President of Marketing, to edit and create documents for a National Sales Meeting that will precede a Winter Sports Expo sponsored by Front Range Action Sports. The first document is a cover letter from the vice president to the company president. The letter will accompany a packet of materials for the meeting and the expo, which includes a brief resume for the guest speaker, a flyer that will announce the expo, a newsletter for employees, a research paper on the history and development of skis, and a set of name tags for a group of employees attending the national sales meeting. Your completed documents will look similar to Figure 1.1.

Project Files

For Project BRC1, you will need the following files:

- New blank Word document
- wBRC1_Cover_Letter_Text
- wBRC1_Newsletter
- wBRC1_Career_Text
- wBRC1_Ski_Research
- wBRC1_Addresses
- wBRC1_Flyer_Text
- wBRC1_Downhill_Racing
- wBRC1_Powder_Skiing

You will save your documents as:

- Lastname_Firstname_BRC1_Cover_Letter
- Lastname_Firstname_BRC1_Newsletter
- Lastname_Firstname_BRC1_Resume
- Lastname_Firstname_BRC1_Ski_Research
- Lastname_Firstname_BRC1_Name_Tags
- Lastname_Firstname_BRC1_Flyer

Project Results

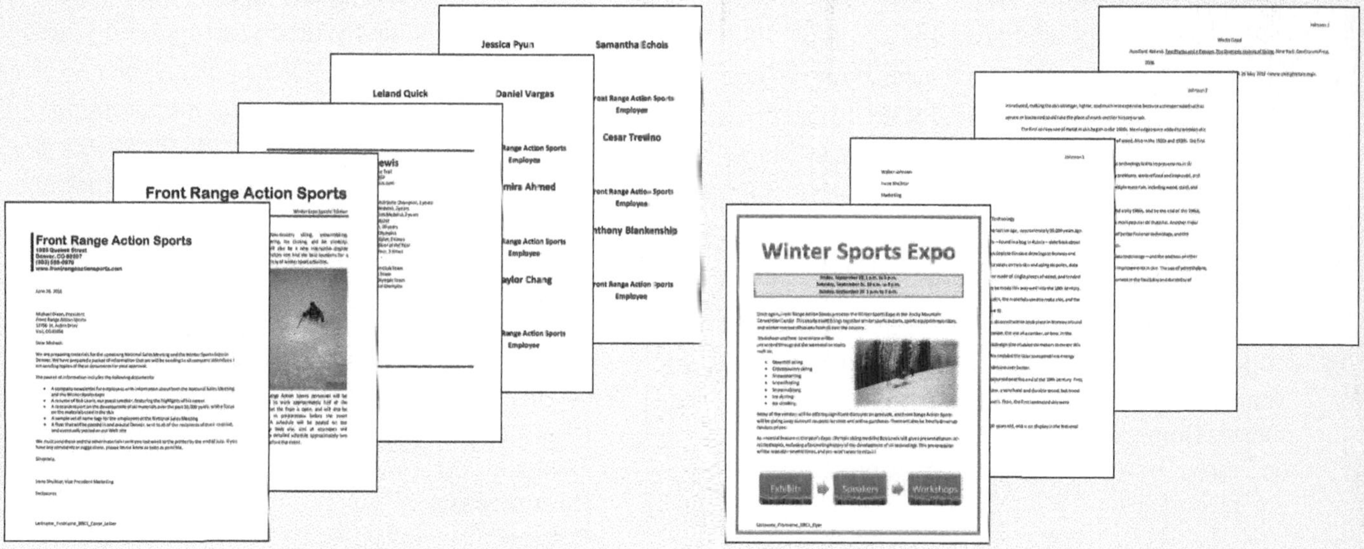

Figure 1.1

Business Running Case

Front Range Action Sports

1 **Start** Word and display a new document. Display rulers and formatting marks. In the location where you are storing your projects, create a new folder named **Front Range Action Sports** or navigate to this folder if you have already created it. **Save** the new document as **Lastname_Firstname_BRC1_Cover_Letter** Add the file name to the footer. Apply the **No Spacing** style to the document, and then type the following to form a letterhead:

Front Range Action Sports

1926 Quebec Street

Denver, CO 80207

(303) 555-0970

www.frontrangeactionsports.com

a. Press Enter to create a blank line below the letterhead. If the Web address changes to blue, right-click the address, and then from the shortcut menu, remove the hyperlink.

b. Select the letterhead text, but not the blank line. Change the **Font** to **Arial Rounded MT Bold**. Select the first line, and increase the **Font Size** to **28 pt** Change the **Font Size** of the remaining four lines to **12 pt**. Select all five lines of the letterhead, display the **Borders and Shading** dialog box, and then create a **6 pt**, **Black** border on the left side of the selected text.

c. Enter the following information using business letter format:

June 26, 2016

Michael Dixon, President

Front Range Action Sports

12756 St. Aubin Drive

Vail, CO 81658

d. Press Enter two times. With the insertion point in the second blank line below the inside address, **Insert** the text from the file **wBRC1_Cover_Letter_Text**, and then remove the blank line at the bottom of the selected text.

e. Move to the top of the document, and then by using either the **Spelling and Grammar** dialog box, or by right-clicking selected words, correct the *three* spelling, grammar, and word usage errors. Ignore proper names. In the paragraph that begins *If you have any*, select the first sentence and move it to the end of the paragraph.

f. In the middle of the document, select the five paragraphs beginning with *A company newsletter*, and create a bulleted list. In the fourth bullet, select the text *national sales meeting*, and then on the **Home tab**, in the **Font group**, click the **Change Case** button Aa, and then click **Capitalize Each Word**.

g. Display the **Document Panel**, add your name, course information, and the **Keywords expo, national sales meeting** View your document in **Print Preview,** make any necessary adjustments, **Save** and **Close** your document, and then hold this file until you complete the project.

2 From your student files, open **wBRC1_Newsletter**, and then **Save** it in your **Front Range Action Sports** folder as **Lastname_Firstname_BRC1_Newsletter** Add the file name to the footer.

a. Select the first paragraph of text—*Front Range Action Sports*. Change the **Font** to **Arial Rounded MT Bold**, the **Font Size** to **36**, and **Center** the text. Select the second paragraph of text, display the **Borders and Shading** dialog box, and then add a **Black**, **3 pt** line below the selected text.

b. Starting with the paragraph that begins *National Sales*, select all of the text from that point to the end of the document. Change the **Spacing After** to **6 pt**, format the text in two columns, and apply the **Justify** alignment.

c. At the top of the first column, select the paragraph *National Sales Meeting*. From the **Font** dialog box, change the **Font Size** to **20**, apply **Bold**, add the **Small caps** effect, and then **Center** the paragraph. Near the bottom of the same column, apply the same formatting to the paragraph *Winter Sports Expo*.

d. In the blank line above the last paragraph of the newsletter, **Insert** the picture **wBRC1_Powder_Skiing**. Set the **Width** of the picture to **3"**.

e. Display the **Document Panel**, and then add your name and course information and the **Keywords Expo newsletter** View your document in **Print Preview,** make any necessary adjustments, **Save** and **Close** your document, and then hold this file until you complete the project.

3 Display a new blank document and **Save** it in your **Front Range Action Sports** folder as **Lastname_Firstname_BRC1_Resume** Add the file name to the footer. **Insert** a **2 × 3** table.

(Business Running Case: Front Range Action Sports continues on the next page)

Front Range Action Sports (continued)

a. In the first cell of the table, type on four lines:

Robert Lewis

1227 Aspen Lake Trail

Vail, CO 81657

www.boblewisskis.com

b. In the second row, in the first cell, type **CAREER HIGHLIGHTS** In the cell to the immediate right, **Insert** the text from the file **wBRC1_Career_Text**, and then press Backspace to remove the blank line at the bottom of the inserted text.

c. In the third row, in the first cell, type **EDUCATION** In the cell to the right, type Mr. Lewis' educational information as follows:

University of Colorado

Ph.D. in Psychology

University of Colorado

M.S. in Psychology

University of Minnesota

B.S. in Psychology

d. Insert a new row at the bottom of the table. In the first cell of the new row, type **CONSULTANT** and then in the cell to the right, type the following:

U.S. Junior Ski Team

U.S. National Ski Team

Special Olympics

e. Apply **Bold** to the headings *CAREER HIGHLIGHTS*, *EDUCATION*, and *CONSULTANT*. Drag the vertical border between the two columns to approximately **1.5 inches on the horizontal ruler**.

f. In the first row, **Merge** the two cells, and then **Center** the text. Select *Robert Lewis*, increase the font size to **24 pt**, apply **Bold**, and then add **12 pt** spacing **Before** the text. If necessary, remove the hyperlink from the Web address. Select the Web address and add **18 pt** spacing after the text.

g. Create a bulleted list for the items below *SKIING* and below *COACHING*. In the cells to the right of *EDUCATION* and *CONSULTANT*, add **12 pt** spacing **After** the last item in each cell. Add **12 pt** spacing **After** *Ph.D. in Psychology* and *M.S. in Psychology*. Apply **Bold** to the three paragraphs that begin *University*.

h. Select the table, and then remove all borders. From the **Borders and Shading** dialog box, add a **3 pt** border to the top and bottom of the table. Change the top margin to **1.5"**. To the **Document Panel**, add your name, course information, and the **Keywords Robert Lewis resume** View your document in **Print Preview,** make any necessary adjustments, **Save** and then **Close** your document. Hold this file until you complete the project.

4 From your student files, open the document **wBRC1_Ski_Research**. **Save** the document in your **Front Range Action Sports** folder as **Lastname_Firstname_BRC1_Ski_Research** Display the header area, type **Johnson** and then press Spacebar. Display the **Page Number gallery**, and then in the **Current Position**, add the **Plain Number** style. Apply **Align Text Right** formatting to the header. Add the file name to the footer.

a. In the blank line at the beginning of the document, type **Walter Johnson** and then press Enter. Type **Irene Shviktar** and press Enter. Type **Marketing** and press Enter. Type **June 5, 2016**

b. Select all of the text in the document. Change the **Line Spacing** to **2.0**, and then change the **Spacing After** to **0 pt.** Click anywhere in the title that begins *The Evolution* and then **Center** the title.

c. Beginning with the paragraph that begins *The use of skis*, select the text from that point to the end of the document. Indent the first line of each selected paragraph to **0.5"**.

d. Near the top of **Page 1**, in the paragraph that begins *The use of skis*, in the third line, position the insertion point to the right of the period following *wood*, and then insert the following footnote:

The oldest known ski and pole is more than 4,000 years old, and is on display in the National Ski Hall of Fame and Museum in Ishpeming, Michigan.

e. Select the footnote text, change the **Font Size** to **11 pt**, add a **First Line Indent** of **0.5"**, and set **Line spacing** to **2.0"**.

f. In the paragraph that begins *The use of skis*, position the insertion point to the left of the period at the end of the paragraph. Using the **MLA** format, insert the following **Book** citation:

Author: **Huntford, Roland**

Title: **Two Planks and a Passion: The Dramatic History of Skiing**

Year: **2008**

City: **New York**

Publisher: **Continuum Press**

(Business Running Case: Front Range Action Sports continues on the next page)

Front Range Action Sports (continued)

g. In the text, select the *Huntford* citation and insert the page numbers **4-6** Position the insertion point to the left of the period at the end of the document. Add the following **Web site** citation:

Author:	**Lund, Morten; Masia, Seth**
Name of Web Page:	**A Short History of Skis**
Year Accessed:	**2016**
Month Accessed:	**May**
Day Accessed:	**25**
URL:	**www.skiinghistory.org**

h. At the end of the document, insert a manual page break to create a new page. Change the **First Line Indent** to **0"**. Add a **Works Cited** title, display the **Bibliography** gallery, and then at the bottom of the gallery, click **Insert Bibliography**. Select the two references, remove the space after the paragraphs, and change the line spacing to **2.0**. **Center** the *Works Cited* title.

i. Press Ctrl + A to move to the top of the document, and then on the **Review tab**, in the **Proofing group**, click **Spelling & Grammar**. Ignore proper names, change *polyethelene* to *polyethylene*, and correct the subject-verb agreement between *have* and *has* in the last paragraph. Display the **Document Panel** and add your name and course information and the **Keywords ski history, ski research** View your document in **Print Preview** and make any necessary adjustments. **Save** and **Close** your document, and hold this file until you complete the project.

5 Display a **New** blank document. Start the **Step by Step Mail Merge Wizard** and select **Labels** as the document type. In **Step 2**, set **Label options** to use the **Auto default** tray (yours may vary) and **Avery US Letter 74541 Clip Style Name Badges**. In **Step 3**, **Use an existing list**, browse to select **wBRC1_Addresses**, click **Open**, and then click **OK**. This is a Name Badge label, and the steps differ slightly from the steps for creating mailing labels.

a. In **Step 4**, on the Ribbon, in the **Write & Insert Fields group**, click the **Insert Merge Field button arrow**, click **First_Name** field, press Spacebar, and then repeat for the **Last_Name** field. Press Enter six times.

b. Type **Front Range Action Sports** and press Enter. Type **Employee** Select the first line of the label—*<<First_Name>>* *<<Last_Name>>*. Change the **Font Size** to **24**, apply **Bold**, and then **Center** the text. Select the last two lines of text, change the **Font Size** to **18**, apply **Bold**, and then **Center** the text. In the **Mail Merge** task pane, click **Update all labels**, and then move to step 5—**Preview your labels.**

c. **Complete the merge**. On the **Mailings tab**, in the **Finish group**, click the **Finish & Merge** button, and then click **Edit Individual Documents**. Merge **All** of the records. **Save** the resulting document in your **Front Range Action Sports** folder as **Lastname_Firstname_BRC1_Name_Tags** and then if necessary, close the Mail Merge task pane. Add the file name to the footer. Preview the labels in **Print Preview** and make any necessary adjustments.

d. Display the **Document Panel**, and then add your name and course information and the **Keywords name tags, expo Save** and close your label document. **Close** the original document without saving. Hold this file until you complete the project.

6 From your student files, open **wBRC1_Flyer_Text**, and then **Save** it in your **Front Range Action Sports** folder as **Lastname_Firstname_BRC1_Flyer** Add the file name to the footer.

a. Select the title *Winter Sports Expo*, and apply a **Gradient Fill - Blue, Accent 1 Text Effect**—in the third row, the fourth effect. Increase the **Font Size** to **56** point, and then **Center** the title. Select the two paragraphs below the title that begin *Friday* and *Saturday*, and then change the **Spacing After** to **0**. Select the three paragraphs below the title—the three days and times—and then **Center** and apply **Bold**.

b. With the three paragraphs still selected, display the **Borders and Shading** dialog box. Apply a **Box** border using theme color **Blue, Accent 1** and a **3 pt** border, and add **Shading** using theme color **Blue, Accent 1, Lighter 80%**. Apply a **Page Border** using the **Box** setting, and the theme color **Blue, Accent 1** with a **Weight** of **6 pt**.

c. Format the seven sport topics—beginning with *Downhill skiing*—as a bulleted list, and then click anywhere to deselect the bulleted list. **Insert** the picture **wBRC1_Downhill_Racing**. Change the **Width** of the picture to **3.5"**, and then set **Wrap Text** to **Square**. Move the picture so that the right edge

(Business Running Case: Front Range Action Sports continues on the next page)

Front Range Action Sports (continued)

aligns with the right margin, and the top edge aligns with the top edge of the text that begins *Workshops and how-to*. Apply a **Picture Effect** using the **Soft Edge** of **10 point**.

d. Move to the end of the document and press Enter two times. Display the **Choose a SmartArt Graphic** dialog box, select **Process**, and then choose the first style—**Basic Process**. Click the border of the SmartArt graphic to deselect the first box. On the **Format tab**, set the **Width** of the SmartArt graphic to **6.5"** and the **Height** to **1"**; or, drag the SmartArt graphic sizing handles to change the width to **6.5"** and the height to **1"**.

In the three boxes, add the following text in this order: **Exhibits** and **Speakers** and **Workshops** On the **Design tab**, apply the **3-D Polished** style. Click anywhere outside of the SmartArt to deselect it. Display your document in **Print Preview** and make any necessary adjustments.

e. Display the **Document Panel** and add your name and course information and the **Keywords expo, flyer** **Save** and **Close** the document. Submit the six files that you created in this project—the cover letter, newsletter, resume, research paper, name tag labels, and flyer—as directed by your instructor. **Exit** Word.

End **You have completed Business Running Case 1**

Creating a Worksheet and Charting Data

OUTCOMES

At the end of this chapter you will be able to:

OBJECTIVES

Mastering these objectives will enable you to:

PROJECT 1A

Create a sales report with an embedded column chart and sparklines.

1. Create, Save, and Navigate an Excel Workbook (p. 227)
2. Enter Data in a Worksheet (p. 230)
3. Construct and Copy Formulas and Use the SUM Function (p. 236)
4. Format Cells with Merge & Center and Cell Styles (p. 240)
5. Chart Data to Create a Column Chart and Insert Sparklines (p. 242)
6. Print, Display Formulas, and Close Excel (p. 247)

PROJECT 1B

Calculate the value of an inventory.

7. Check Spelling in a Worksheet (p. 253)
8. Enter Data by Range (p. 255)
9. Construct Formulas for Mathematical Operations (p. 256)
10. Edit Values in a Worksheet (p. 261)
11. Format a Worksheet (p. 262)

Shutterstock

In This Chapter

In this chapter, you will use Microsoft Excel 2010 to create and analyze data organized into columns and rows. After entering data in a worksheet, you can perform calculations, analyze the data to make logical decisions, and create charts.

In this chapter, you will create and modify Excel workbooks. You will practice the basics of worksheet design, create a footer, enter and edit data in a worksheet, chart data, and then save, preview, and print workbooks. You will also construct formulas for mathematical operations.

The projects in this chapter relate to **Texas Spectrum Wireless**, which provides accessories and software for all major brands of cell phones, smart phones, PDAs, mp3 players, and portable computers. The company sells thousands of unique products in their retail stores, which are located throughout Texas and the southern United States. They also sell thousands of items each year through their Web site, and offer free shipping and returns to their customers. The company takes pride in offering unique categories of accessories such as waterproof and ruggedized gear.

Project 1A Sales Report with Embedded Column Chart and Sparklines

myitlab
Project 1A Training

Project Activities

In Activities 1.01 through 1.16, you will create an Excel worksheet for Roslyn Thomas, the President of Texas Spectrum Wireless. The worksheet displays the first quarter sales of wireless accessories for the current year, and includes a chart to visually represent the data. Your completed worksheet will look similar to Figure 1.1.

Project Files

For Project 1A, you will need the following file:

New blank Excel workbook

You will save your workbook as:

Lastname_Firstname_1A_Quarterly_Sales

Project Results

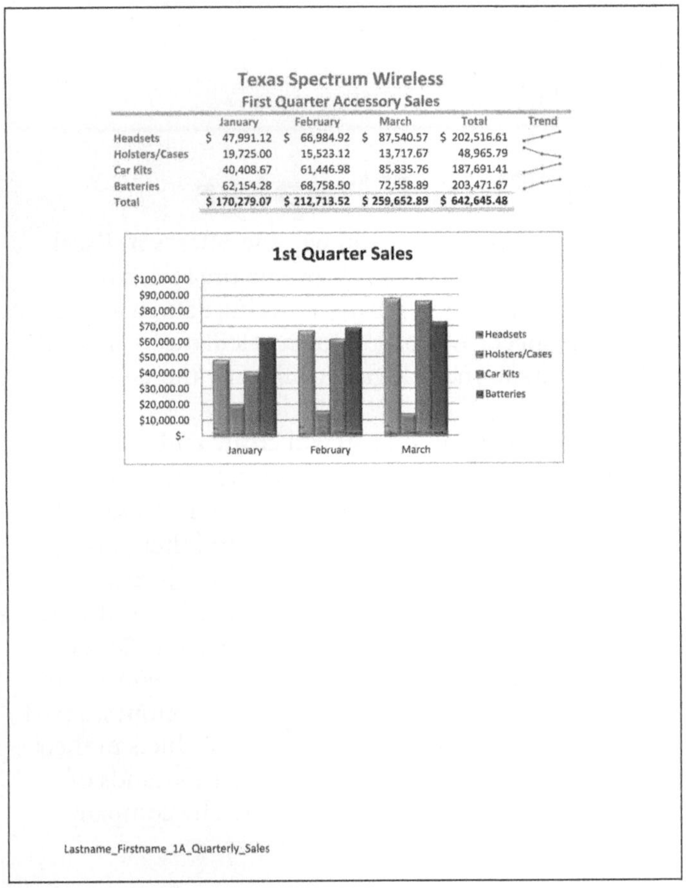

Texas Spectrum Wireless
First Quarter Accessory Sales

	January	February	March	Total	Trend
Headsets	$ 47,991.12	$ 66,984.92	$ 87,540.57	$ 202,516.61	
Holsters/Cases	19,725.00	15,523.12	13,717.67	48,965.79	
Car Kits	40,408.67	61,446.98	85,835.76	187,691.41	
Batteries	62,154.28	68,758.50	72,558.89	203,471.67	
Total	$ 170,279.07	$ 212,713.52	$ 259,652.89	$ 642,645.48	

Lastname_Firstname_1A_Quarterly_Sales

Figure 1.1
Project 1A Quarterly Sales

Objective 1 | Create, Save, and Navigate an Excel Workbook

On startup, Excel displays a new blank ***workbook***—the Excel document that stores your data—which contains one or more pages called a ***worksheet***. A worksheet—or ***spreadsheet***—is stored in a workbook, and is formatted as a pattern of uniformly spaced horizontal rows and vertical columns. The intersection of a column and a row forms a box referred to as a ***cell***.

Activity 1.01 | Starting Excel and Naming and Saving a Workbook

Another Way

Use the keyboard shortcut F12 to display the Save As dialog box.

1 **Start** Excel. In the lower right corner of the window, if necessary, click the Normal button, and then to the right, locate the zoom—magnification—level.

Your zoom level should be 100%, although some figures in this textbook may be shown at a higher zoom level.

2 In the upper left corner of your screen, click the **File tab** to display **Backstage** view, click **Save As**, and then in the **Save As** dialog box, navigate to the location where you will store your workbooks for this chapter.

3 In your storage location, create a new folder named **Excel Chapter 1** Open the new folder to display its folder window, and then in the **File name** box, notice that *Book1* displays as the default file name.

4 In the **File name** box, click *Book1* to select it, and then using your own name, type **Lastname_Firstname_1A_Quarterly_Sales** being sure to include the underscore (Shift + -) instead of spaces between words. Compare your screen with Figure 1.2.

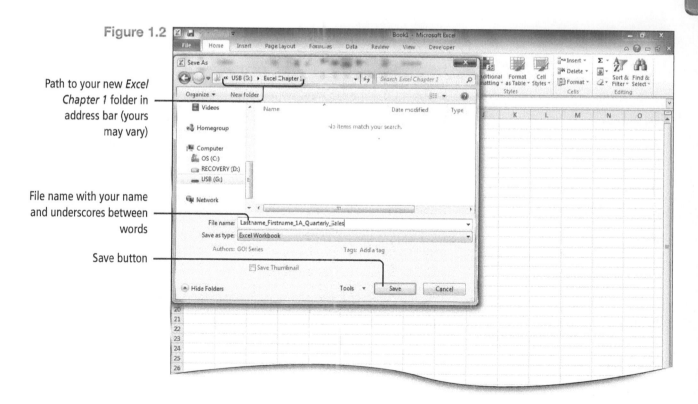

Figure 1.2

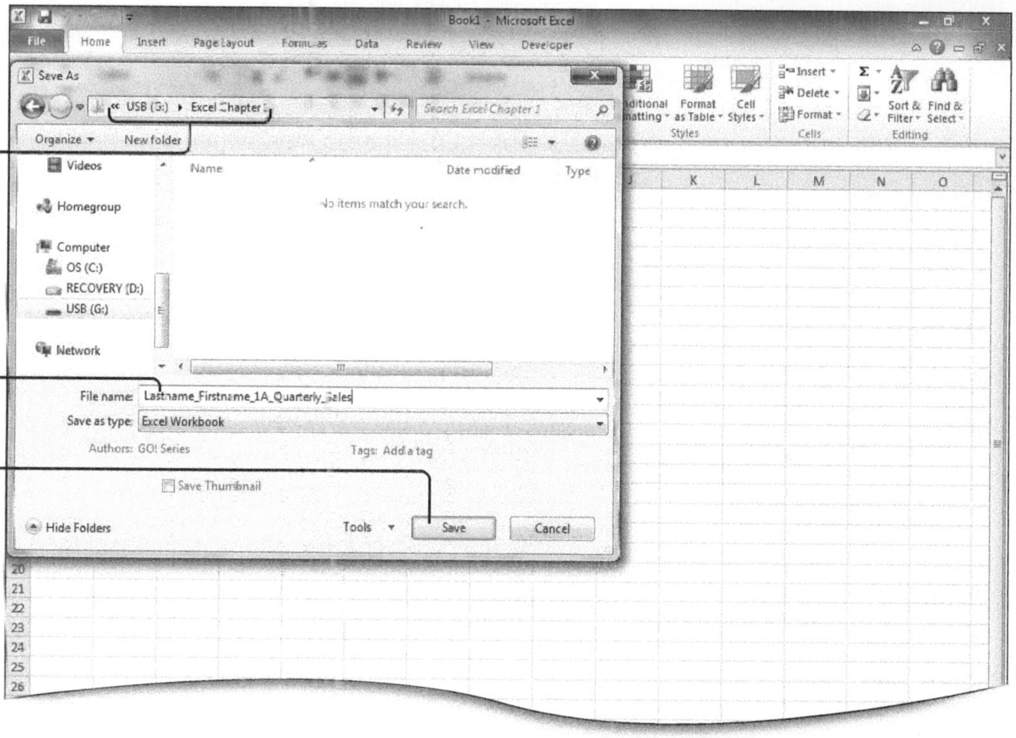

5 Click **Save**. Compare your screen with Figure 1.3, and then take a moment to study the Excel window parts in the table in Figure 1.4.

Figure 1.3

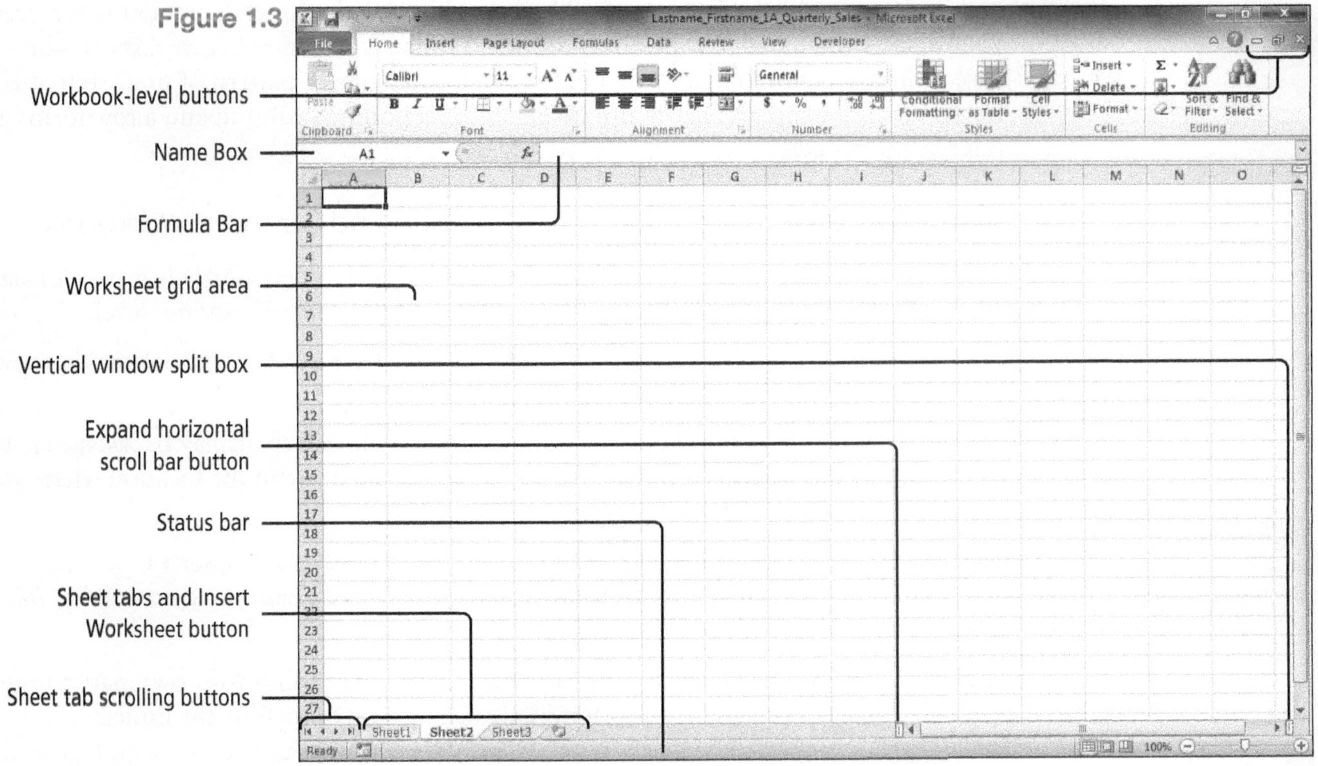

Parts of the Excel Window

Screen Part	Description
Expand horizontal scroll bar button	Increases the width of the horizontal scroll bar.
Formula Bar	Displays the value or formula contained in the active cell; also permits entry or editing.
Sheet tabs and Insert Worksheet button	Identify the worksheets in a workbook and inserts an additional worksheet.
Name Box	Displays the name of the selected cell, table, chart, or object.
Sheet tab scrolling buttons	Display sheet tabs that are not in view when there are numerous sheet tabs.
Status bar	Displays the current cell mode, page number, worksheet information, view and zoom buttons, and for numerical data, common calculations such as Sum and Average.
Vertical window split box	Splits the worksheet into two vertical views of the same worksheet.
Workbook-level buttons	Minimize, close, or restore the previous size of the displayed workbook.
Worksheet grid area	Displays the columns and rows that intersect to form the worksheet's cells.

Figure 1.4

Activity 1.02 | Navigating a Worksheet and a Workbook

1 Take a moment to study Figure 1.5 and the table in Figure 1.6 to become familiar with the Excel workbook window.

Figure 1.5

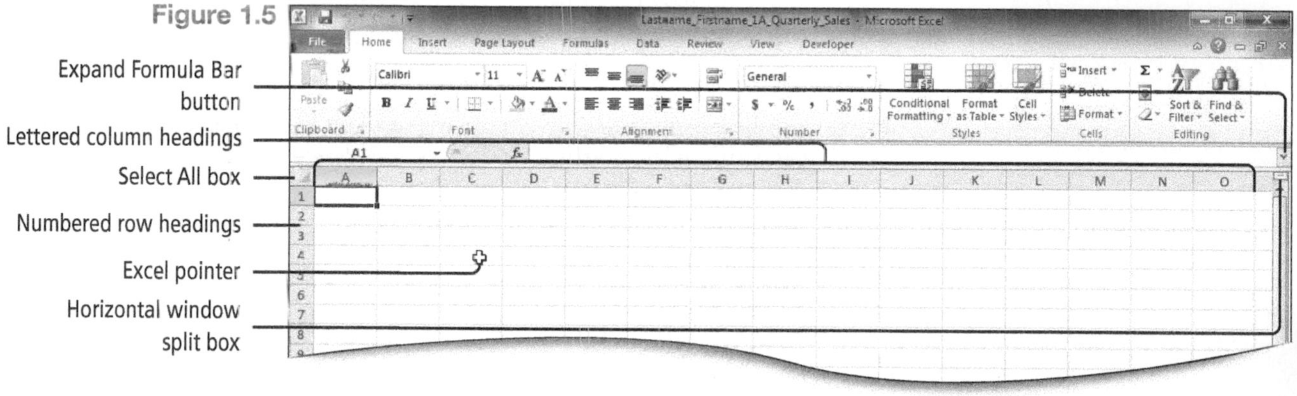

Excel Workbook Window Elements	
Workbook Window Element	**Description**
Excel pointer	Displays the pointer in Excel.
Expand Formula Bar button	Increases the height of the Formula Bar to display lengthy cell content.
Horizontal window split box	Splits the worksheet into two horizontal views of the same worksheet.
Lettered column headings	Indicate the column letter.
Numbered row headings	Indicate the row number.
Select All box	Selects all the cells in a worksheet.

Figure 1.6

2 In the lower right corner of the screen, in the horizontal scroll bar, click the **right scroll arrow** one time to shift **column A** out of view.

A ***column*** is a vertical group of cells in a worksheet. Beginning with the first letter of the alphabet, *A*, a unique letter identifies each column—this is called the ***column heading***. Clicking one of the horizontal scroll bar arrows shifts the window either left or right one column at a time.

3 Point to the **right scroll arrow**, and then hold down the left mouse button until the columns begin to scroll rapidly to the right; release the mouse button when you begin to see pairs of letters as the column headings.

4 Slowly drag the horizontal scroll box to the left, and notice that just above the scroll box, ScreenTips with the column letters display as you drag. Drag the horizontal scroll box left or right—or click the left or right scroll arrow—as necessary to position **column Z** near the center of your screen.

Column headings after column Z use two letters starting with AA, AB, and so on through ZZ. After that, columns begin with three letters beginning with AAA. This pattern provides 16,384 columns. The last column is XFD.

5 In the lower left portion of your screen, click the **Sheet2 tab**.

The second worksheet displays and is the active sheet. Column A displays at the left.

6 In the vertical scroll bar, click the **down scroll arrow** one time to move **Row 1** out of view.

A ***row*** is a horizontal group of cells. Beginning with number 1, a unique number identifies each row—this is the ***row heading***, located at the left side of the worksheet. A single worksheet has 1,048,576 rows.

7 In the lower left corner, click the **Sheet1 tab**.

The first worksheet in the workbook becomes the active worksheet. By default, new workbooks contain three worksheets. When you save a workbook, the worksheets are contained within it and do not have separate file names.

8 Use the skills you just practiced to scroll horizontally to display **column A**, and if necessary, **row 1**.

Objective 2 | Enter Data in a Worksheet

Cell content, which is anything you type in a cell, can be one of two things: either a ***constant value***—referred to simply as a ***value***—or a ***formula***. A formula is an equation that performs mathematical calculations on values in your worksheet. The most commonly used values are ***text values*** and ***number values***, but a value can also include a date or a time of day.

Activity 1.03 | Entering Text and Using AutoComplete

A text value, also referred to as a ***label***, usually provides information about number values in other worksheet cells. For example, a title such as First Quarter Accessory Sales gives the reader an indication that the data in the worksheet relates to information about sales of accessories during the three-month period January through March.

1 Click the **Sheet1 tab** to make it the active sheet. Point to and then click the cell at the intersection of **column A** and **row 1** to make it the ***active cell***—the cell is outlined in black and ready to accept data.

The intersecting column letter and row number form the ***cell reference***—also called the ***cell address***. When a cell is active, its column letter and row number are highlighted. The cell reference of the selected cell, *A1*, displays in the Name Box.

2 With cell **A1** as the active cell, type the worksheet title **Texas Spectrum Wireless** and then press Enter. Compare your screen with Figure 1.7.

Text or numbers in a cell are referred to as ***data***. You must confirm the data you type in a cell by pressing Enter or by some other keyboard movement, such as pressing Tab or an arrow key. Pressing Enter moves the selection to the cell below.

Figure 1.7

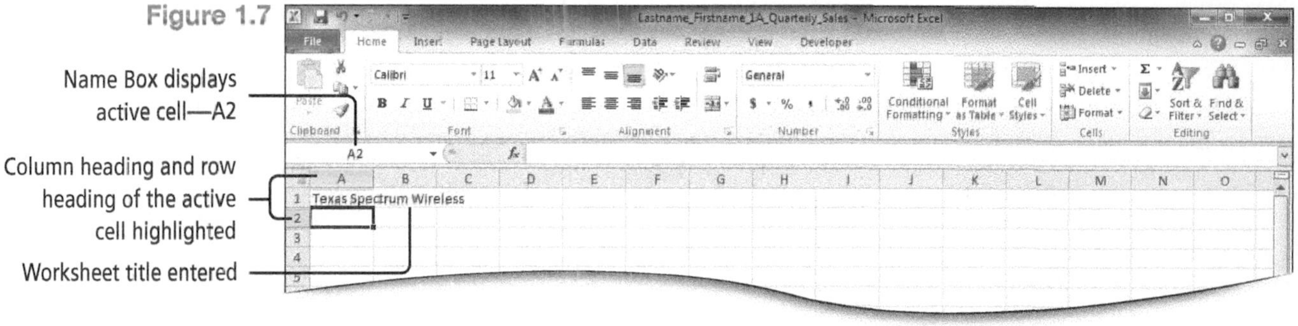

3 In cell **A1**, notice that the text does not fit; the text spills over and displays in cells **B1** and **C1** to the right.

If text is too long for a cell and cells to the right are empty, the text will display. If the cells to the right contain other data, only the text that will fit in the cell displays.

4 In cell **A2**, type the worksheet subtitle **First Quarter Accessory Sales** and then press Enter. Compare your screen with Figure 1.8.

Figure 1.8

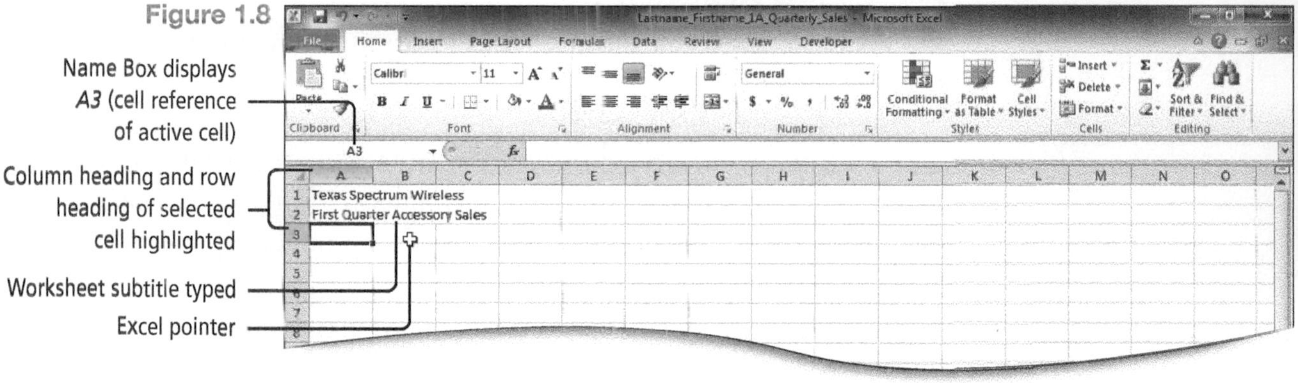

5 Press Enter again to make cell **A4** the active cell. In cell **A4**, type **Headsets** which will form the first row title, and then press Enter.

The text characters that you typed align at the left edge of the cell—referred to as ***left alignment***—and cell A5 becomes the active cell. Left alignment is the default for text values.

6 In cell **A5**, type **H** and notice the text from the previous cell displays.

If the first characters you type in a cell match an existing entry in the column, Excel fills in the remaining characters for you. This feature, called ***AutoComplete***, assists only with alphabetic values.

7 Continue typing the remainder of the row title **olsters/Cases** and press Enter.

The AutoComplete suggestion is removed when the entry you are typing differs from the previous value.

> **Another Way**
> Use the keyboard shortcut Ctrl + S to Save changes to your workbook.

8 In cell **A6**, type **Car Kits** and press Enter. In cell **A7**, type **Batteries** and press Enter. In cell **A8**, type **Total** and press Enter. On the Quick Access Toolbar, click **Save**.

Activity 1.04 | Using Auto Fill and Keyboard Shortcuts

1 Click cell **B3**. Type **J** and notice that when you begin to type in a cell, on the **Formula Bar**, the **Cancel** and **Enter** buttons become active, as shown in Figure 1.9.

Figure 1.9

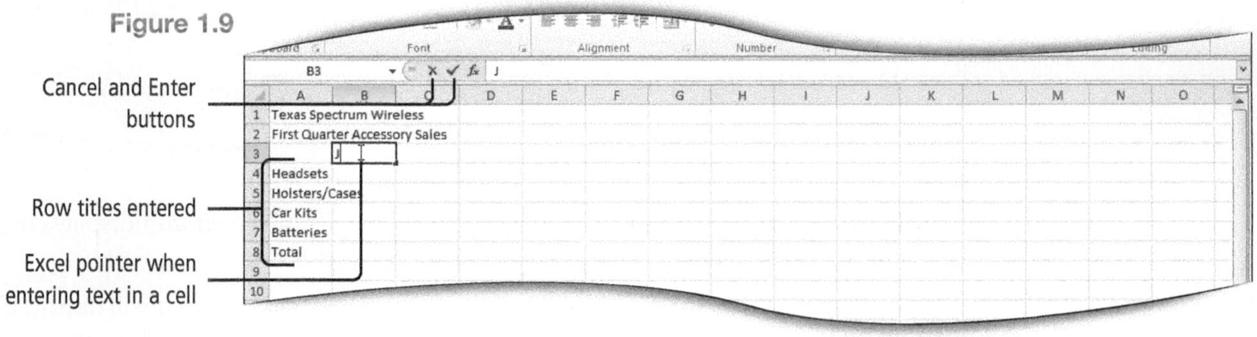

2 Continue to type **anuary** On the **Formula Bar**, notice that values you type in a cell also display there. Then, on the **Formula Bar**, click the **Enter** button to confirm the entry and keep cell **B3** active.

3 With cell **B3** active, locate the small black square in the lower right corner of the selected cell.

You can drag this ***fill handle***—the small black square in the lower right corner of a selected cell—to adjacent cells to fill the cells with values based on the first cell.

4 Point to the **fill handle** until the pointer displays, hold down the left mouse button, drag to the right to cell **D3**, and as you drag, notice the ScreenTips *February* and *March*. Release the mouse button.

5 Under the text that you just filled, click the **Auto Fill Options** button that displays, and then compare your screen with Figure 1.10.

Auto Fill generates and extends a ***series*** of values into adjacent cells based on the value of other cells. A series is a group of things that come one after another in succession; for example, *January*, *February*, *March*.

The Auto Fill Options button displays options to fill the data; options vary depending on the content and program from which you are filling, and the format of the data you are filling.

Fill Series is selected, indicating the action that was taken. Because the options are related to the current task, the button is referred to as being ***context sensitive***.

Figure 1.10

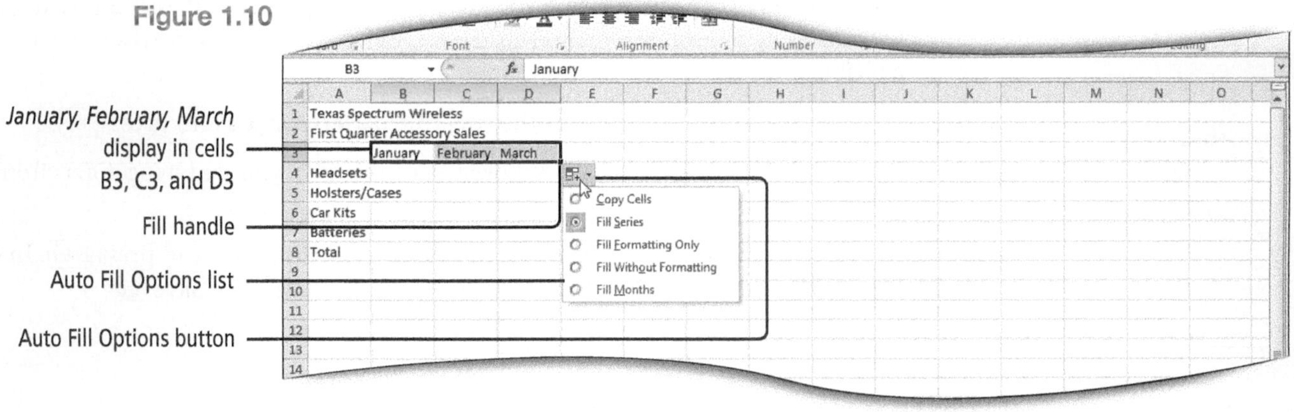

6 Click in any cell to cancel the display of the Auto Fill Options list.

The list no longer displays; the button will display until you perform some other screen action.

7 Press Ctrl + Home, which is the keyboard shortcut to make cell **A1** active.

8 On the Quick Access Toolbar, click **Save** to save the changes you have made to your workbook, and then take a moment to study the table in Figure 1.11 to become familiar with additional keyboard shortcuts with which you can navigate the Excel worksheet.

Keyboard Shortcuts to Navigate the Excel Window

To Move the Location of the Active Cell:	Press:
Up, down, right, or left one cell	↑, ↓, →, ←
Down one cell	Enter
Up one cell	Shift + Enter
Up one full screen	Page Up
Down one full screen	PageDown
To column A of the current row	Home
To the last cell in the last column of the active area (the rectangle formed by all the rows and columns in a worksheet that contain entries)	Ctrl + End
To cell A1	Ctrl + Home
Right one cell	Tab
Left one cell	Shift + Tab

Figure 1.11

Activity 1.05 | Aligning Text and Adjusting the Size of Columns

1 In the **column heading area**, point to the vertical line between **column A** and **column B** to display the pointer, press and hold down the left mouse button, and then compare your screen with Figure 1.12.

A ScreenTip displays information about the width of the column. The default width of a column is 64 ***pixels***. A pixel, short for ***picture element***, is a point of light measured in dots per square inch. Sixty-four pixels equal 8.43 characters, which is the average number of digits that will fit in a cell using the default font. The default font in Excel is Calibri and the default font size is 11.

Figure 1.12

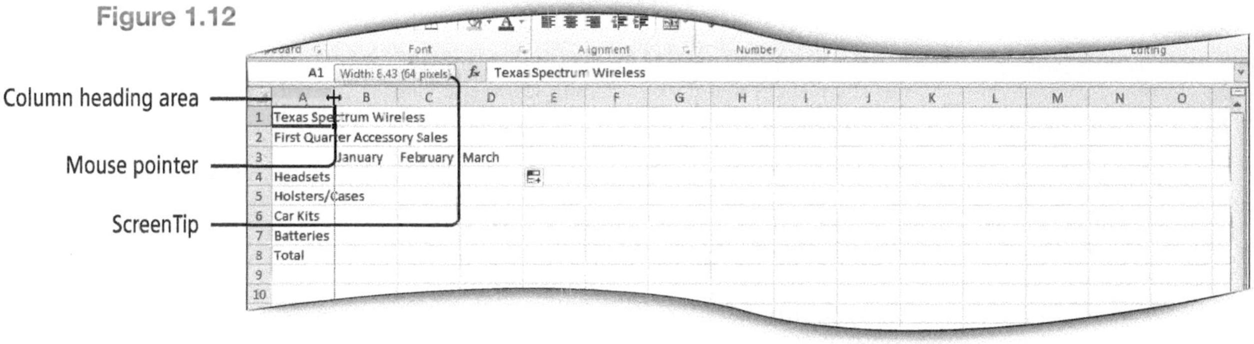

2 Drag to the right, and when the number of pixels indicated in the ScreenTip reaches **100 pixels**, release the mouse button. If you are not satisfied with your result, click Undo on the Quick Access Toolbar and begin again.

This width accommodates the longest row title in cells A4 through A8—*Holsters/Cases*. The worksheet title and subtitle in cells A1 and A2 span more than one column and still do not fit in column A.

3 Point to cell **B3** and then drag across to select cells **B3**, **C3**, and **D3**. Compare your screen with Figure 1.13; if you are not satisfied with your result, click anywhere and begin again.

The three cells, B3 through D3, are selected and form a ***range***—two or more cells on a worksheet that are adjacent (next to each other) or nonadjacent (not next to each other). This range of cells is referred to as *B3:D3*. When you see a colon (:) between two cell references, the range includes all the cells between the two cell references.

A range of cells that is selected in this manner is indicated by a dark border, and Excel treats the range as a single unit so you can make the same changes to more than one cell at a time. The selected cells in the range are highlighted except for the first cell in the range, which displays in the Name Box.

Figure 1.13

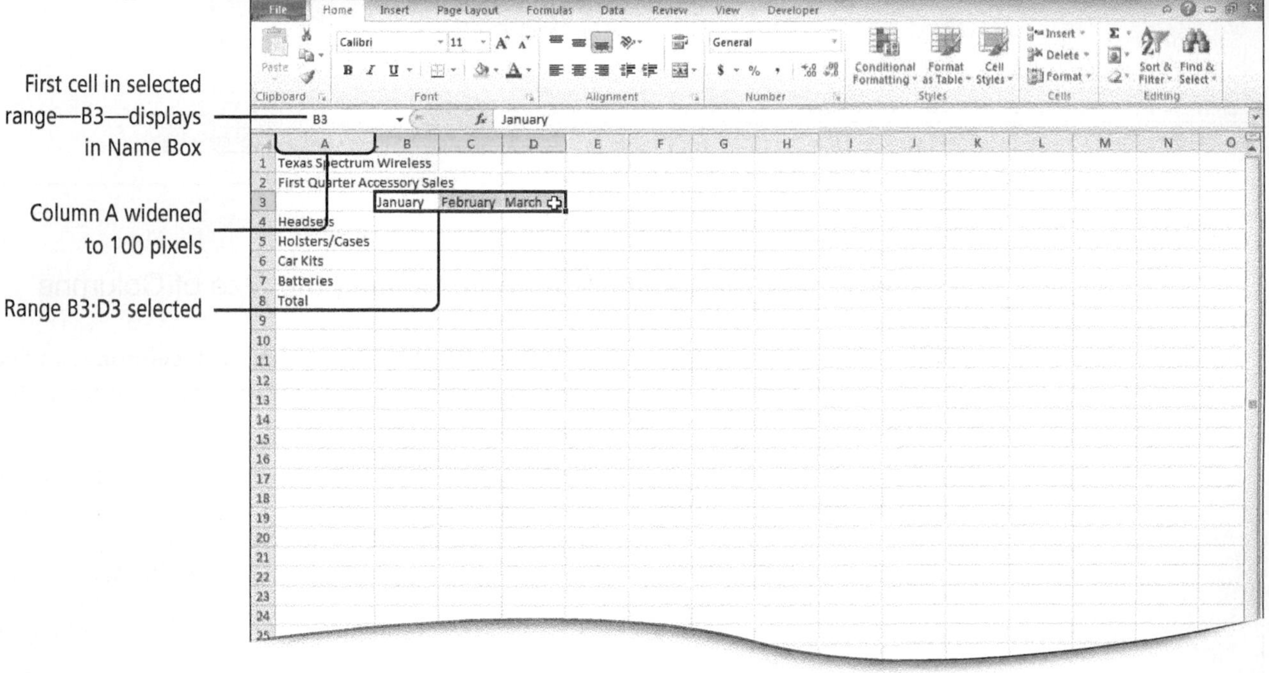

4 With the range **B3:D3** selected, point anywhere over the selected range, right-click, and then on the Mini toolbar, click the **Center** button. On the Quick Access Toolbar, click **Save**.

The column titles *January*, *February*, *March* align in the center of each cell.

Activity 1.06 | Entering Numbers

To type number values, use either the number keys across the top of your keyboard or the numeric keypad if you have one—laptop computers may not have a numeric keypad.

1 Under *January*, click cell **B4**, type **47991.12** and then on the **Formula Bar**, click the **Enter** button [✓] to maintain cell **B4** as the active cell. Compare your screen with Figure 1.14.

By default, *number* values align at the right edge of the cell. The default ***number format***—a specific way in which Excel displays numbers—is the ***general format***. In the default general format, whatever you type in the cell will display, with the exception of trailing zeros to the right of a decimal point. For example, in the number 237.50 the *0* following the *5* is a trailing zero.

Data that displays in a cell is the ***displayed value***. Data that displays in the Formula Bar is the ***underlying value***. The number of digits or characters that display in a cell—the displayed value—depends on the width of the column. Calculations on numbers will always be based on the underlying value, not the displayed value.

Figure 1.14

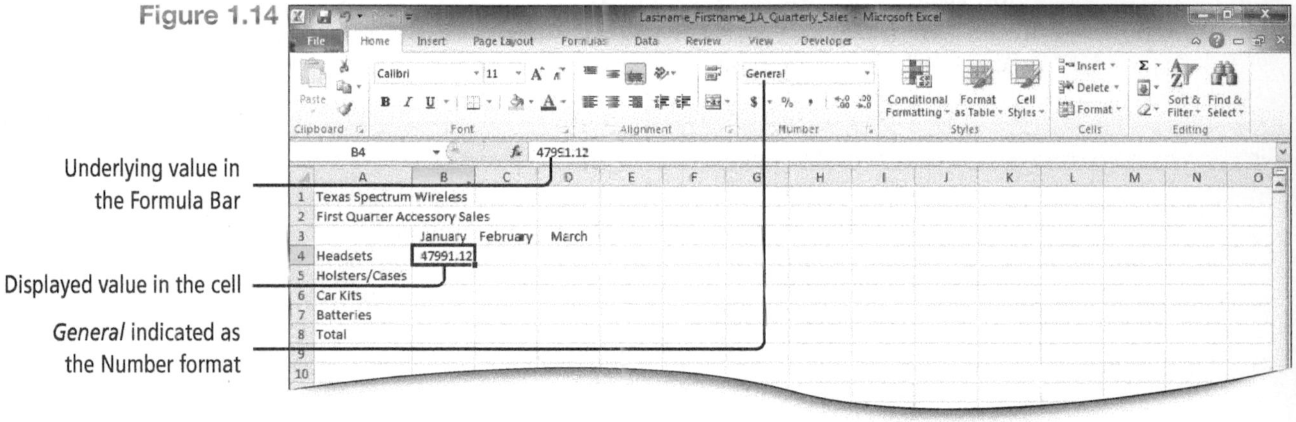

2 Press [Tab] to make cell **C4** active. Then, enter the remaining sales numbers as shown by using the following technique: Press [Tab] to confirm your entry and move across the row, and then press [Enter] at the end of a row to move to the next row.

	January	February	March
Headsets	47991.12	**66984.92**	**87540.57**
Holsters/Cases	**19725**	**15523.12**	**13717.67**
Car Kits	**40408.67**	**61446.98**	**85835.76**
Batteries	**62154.28**	**68758.50**	**72558.89**

3 Compare the numbers you entered with Figure 1.15 and then **Save** [💾] your workbook.

In the default general format, trailing zeros to the right of a decimal point will not display. For example, when you type *68758.50*, the cell displays 68758.5 instead.

Figure 1.15

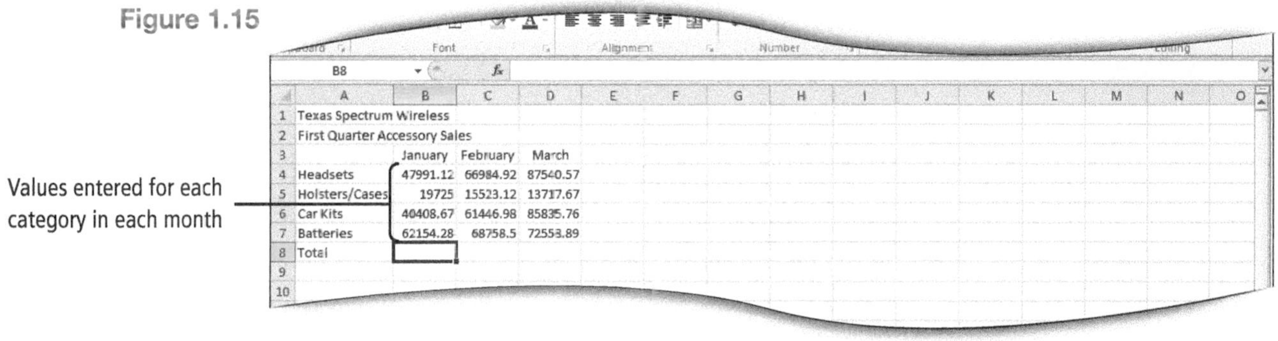

Objective 3 | Construct and Copy Formulas and Use the SUM Function

A cell contains either a constant value (text or numbers) or a formula. A formula is an equation that performs mathematical calculations on values in other cells, and then places the result in the cell containing the formula. You can create formulas or use a ***function***—a prewritten formula that looks at one or more values, performs an operation, and then returns a value.

Activity 1.07 | Constructing a Formula and Using the SUM Function

In this activity, you will practice three different ways to sum a group of numbers in Excel.

1 Click cell **B8** to make it the active cell and type **=**

The equal sign (=) displays in the cell with the insertion point blinking, ready to accept more data.

All formulas begin with the = sign, which signals Excel to begin a calculation. The Formula Bar displays the = sign, and the Formula Bar Cancel and Enter buttons display.

2 At the insertion point, type **b4** and then compare your screen with Figure 1.16.

A list of Excel functions that begin with the letter *B* may briefly display—as you progress in your study of Excel, you will use functions of this type. A blue border with small corner boxes surrounds cell B4, which indicates that the cell is part of an active formula. The color used in the box matches the color of the cell reference in the formula.

Figure 1.16

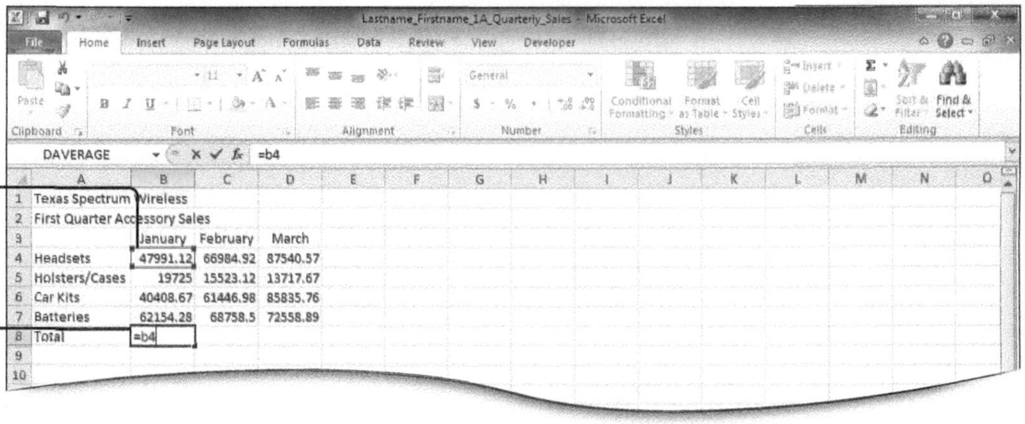

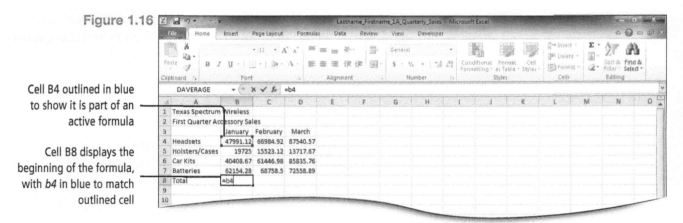

3 At the insertion point, type **+** and then type **b5**

A border of another color surrounds cell B5, and the color matches the color of the cell reference in the active formula. When typing cell references, it is not necessary to use uppercase letters.

4 At the insertion point, type **+b6+b7** and then press Enter.

The result of the formula calculation—*170279.1*—displays in the cell. Recall that in the default General format, trailing zeros do not display.

5 Click cell **B8** again, look at the **Formula Bar**, and then compare your screen with Figure 1.17.

The formula adds the values in cells B4 through B7, and the result displays in cell B8. In this manner, you can construct a formula by typing. Although cell B8 displays the *result* of the formula, the formula itself displays in the Formula Bar. This is referred to as the ***underlying formula***.

Always view the Formula Bar to be sure of the exact content of a cell—*a displayed number may actually be a formula*.

Figure 1.17

Formula displays in Formula Bar

Total of values in cells B4:B7 displays in cell B8

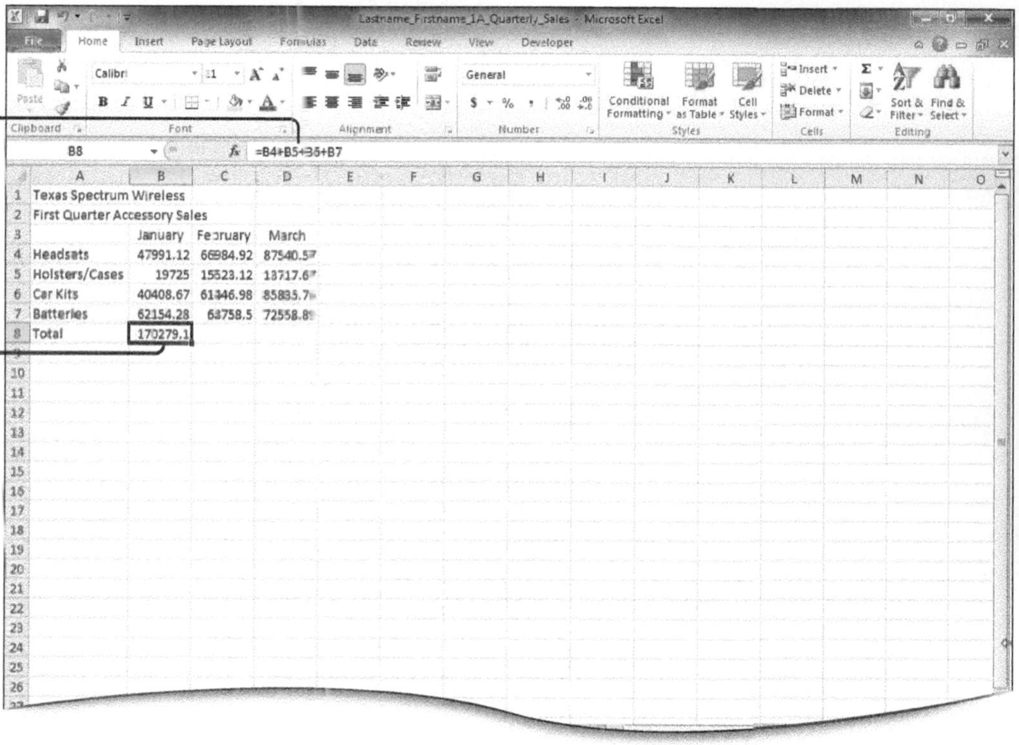

6 Click cell **C8** and type **=** to signal the beginning of a formula. Then, point to cell **C4** and click one time.

The reference to the cell C4 is added to the active formula. A moving border surrounds the referenced cell, and the border color and the color of the cell reference in the formula are color coded to match.

7 At the insertion point, type **+** and then click cell **C5**. Repeat this process to complete the formula to add cells **C4** through **C7**, and then press Enter.

The result of the formula calculation—*212713.5*—displays in the cell. This method of constructing a formula is the ***point and click method***.

Another Way

Use the keyboard shortcut Alt + =; or, on the Formulas tab, in the Function Library group, click the AutoSum button.

8 Click cell **D8**. On the **Home tab**, in the **Editing group**, click the **Sum** button Σ, and then compare your screen with Figure 1.18.

SUM is an Excel function—a prewritten formula. A moving border surrounds the range D4:D7 and =*SUM(D4:D7)* displays in cell D8.

The = sign signals the beginning of a formula, *SUM* indicates the type of calculation that will take place (addition), and *(D4:D7)* indicates the range of cells on which the sum calculation will be performed. A ScreenTip provides additional information about the action.

Figure 1.18

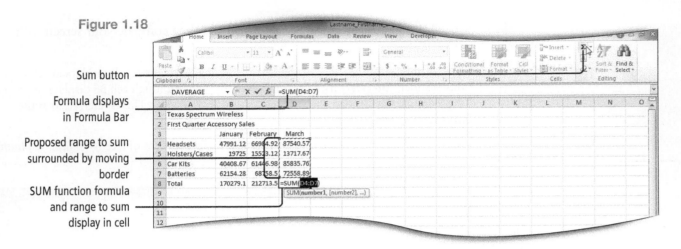

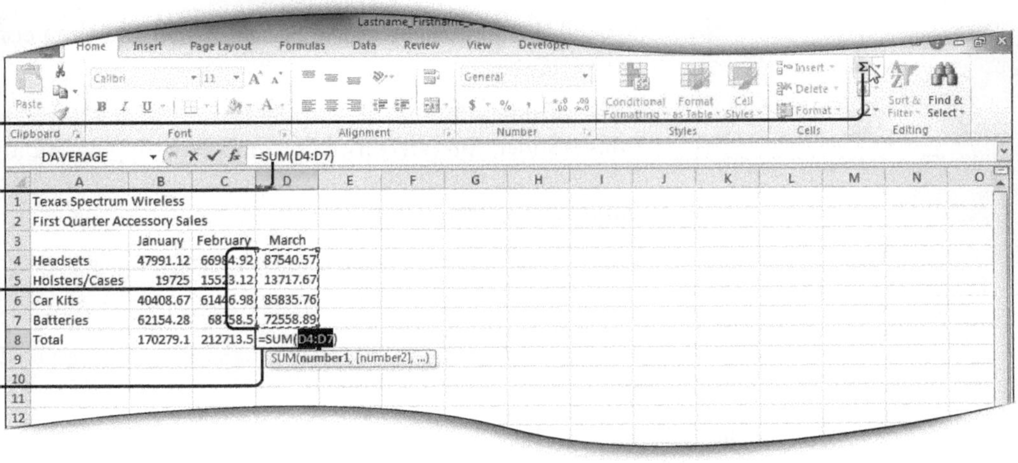

9 Look at the **Formula Bar**, and notice that the formula also displays there. Then, look again at the cells surrounded by the moving border.

When you activate the Sum function, Excel first looks *above* the active cell for a range of cells to sum. If no range is above the active cell, Excel will look to the *left* for a range of cells to sum. If the proposed range is not what you want to calculate, you can select a different group of cells.

10 Press Enter to construct a formula by using the prewritten SUM function.

Your total is *259652.9*. Because the Sum function is frequently used, it has its own button in the Editing group on the Home tab of the Ribbon. A larger version of the button also displays on the Formulas tab in the Function Library group. This button is also referred to as ***AutoSum***.

11 Notice that the totals in the range **B8:D8** display only *one* decimal place. Click **Save**.

Number values that are too long to fit in the cell do *not* spill over into the unoccupied cell to the right in the same manner as text values. Rather, Excel rounds the number to fit the space.

Rounding is a procedure that determines which digit at the right of the number will be the last digit displayed and then increases it by one if the next digit to its right is 5, 6, 7, 8, or 9.

Activity 1.08 | Copying a Formula by Using the Fill Handle

You have practiced three ways to create a formula—by typing, by using the point-and-click technique, and by using a Function button from the Ribbon. You can also copy formulas. When you copy a formula from one cell to another, Excel adjusts the cell references to fit the new location of the formula.

1 Click cell **E3**, type **Total** and then press Enter.

The text in cell E3 is centered because the centered format continues from the adjacent cell.

2 With cell **E4** as the active cell, hold down Alt, and then press =. Compare your screen with Figure 1.19.

Alt + = is the keyboard shortcut for the Sum function. Recall that Excel first looks above the selected cell for a proposed range of cells to sum, and if no data is detected, Excel looks to the left and proposes a range of cells to sum.

Figure 1.19

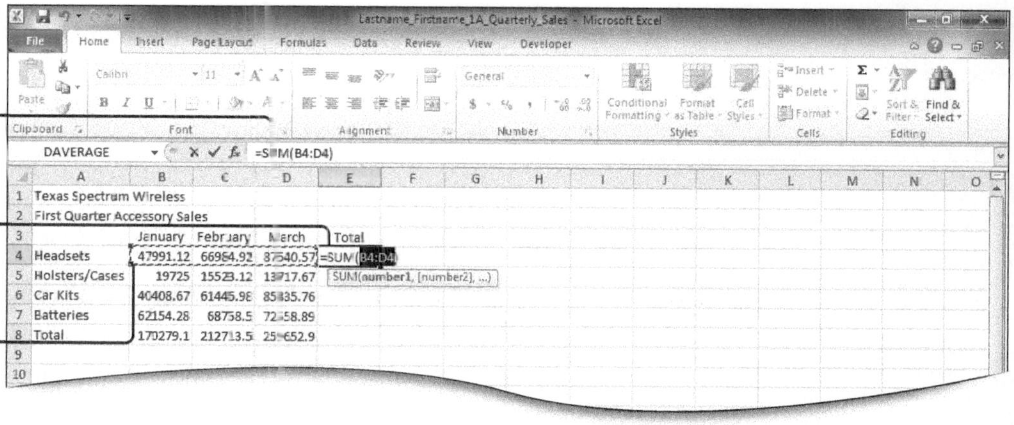

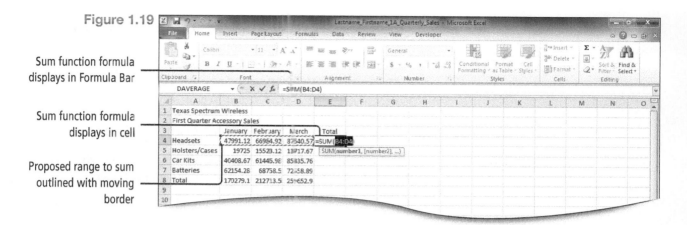

3 On the **Formula Bar**, click the **Enter** button [✓] to display the result and keep cell **E4** active.

The total dollar amount of *Headsets* sold in the quarter is *202516.6*. In cells E5:E8, you can see that you need a formula similar to the one in E4, but formulas that refer to the cells in row 5, row 6, and so on.

4 With cell **E4** active, point to the fill handle in the lower right corner of the cell until the [+] pointer displays. Then, drag down through cell **E8**; if you are not satisfied with your result, on the Quick Access Toolbar, click Undo [↶] and begin again. Compare your screen with Figure 1.20.

Figure 1.20

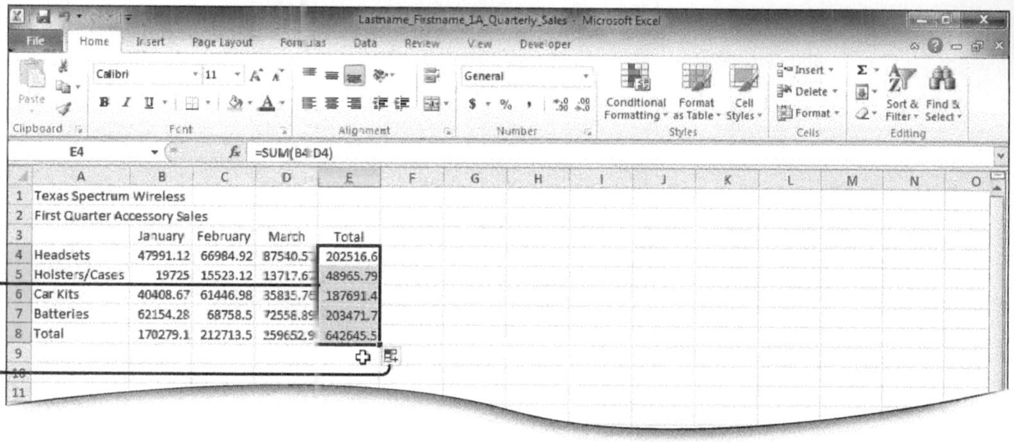

5 Click cell **E5**, look at the **Formula Bar**, and notice the formula *=SUM(B5:D5)*. Click cell **E6**, look at the **Formula Bar**, and then notice the formula *=SUM(B6:D6)*.

In each row, Excel copied the formula but adjusted the cell references *relative to* the row number. This is called a ***relative cell reference***—a cell reference based on the relative position of the cell that contains the formula and the cells referred to.

The calculation is the same, but it is performed on the cells in that particular row. Use this method to insert numerous formulas into spreadsheets quickly.

6 Click cell **F3**, type **Trend** and then press [Enter]. **Save** [💾] your workbook.

Objective 4 | Format Cells with Merge & Center and Cell Styles

Format—change the appearance of—cells to make your worksheet attractive and easy to read.

Activity 1.09 | Using Merge & Center and Applying Cell Styles

> **Another Way**
>
> Select the range, right-click over the selection, and then on the Mini toolbar, click the Merge & Center button.

1. Select the range **A1:F1**, and then in the **Alignment group**, click the **Merge & Center** button. Then, select the range **A2:F2** and click the **Merge & Center** button.

   The ***Merge & Center*** command joins selected cells into one larger cell and centers the contents in the new cell; individual cells in the range B1:F1 and B2:F2 can no longer be selected—they are merged into cell A1 and A2 respectively.

2. Click cell **A1**. In the **Styles group**, click the **Cell Styles** button, and then compare your screen with Figure 1.21.

   A ***cell style*** is a defined set of formatting characteristics, such as font, font size, font color, cell borders, and cell shading.

Figure 1.21

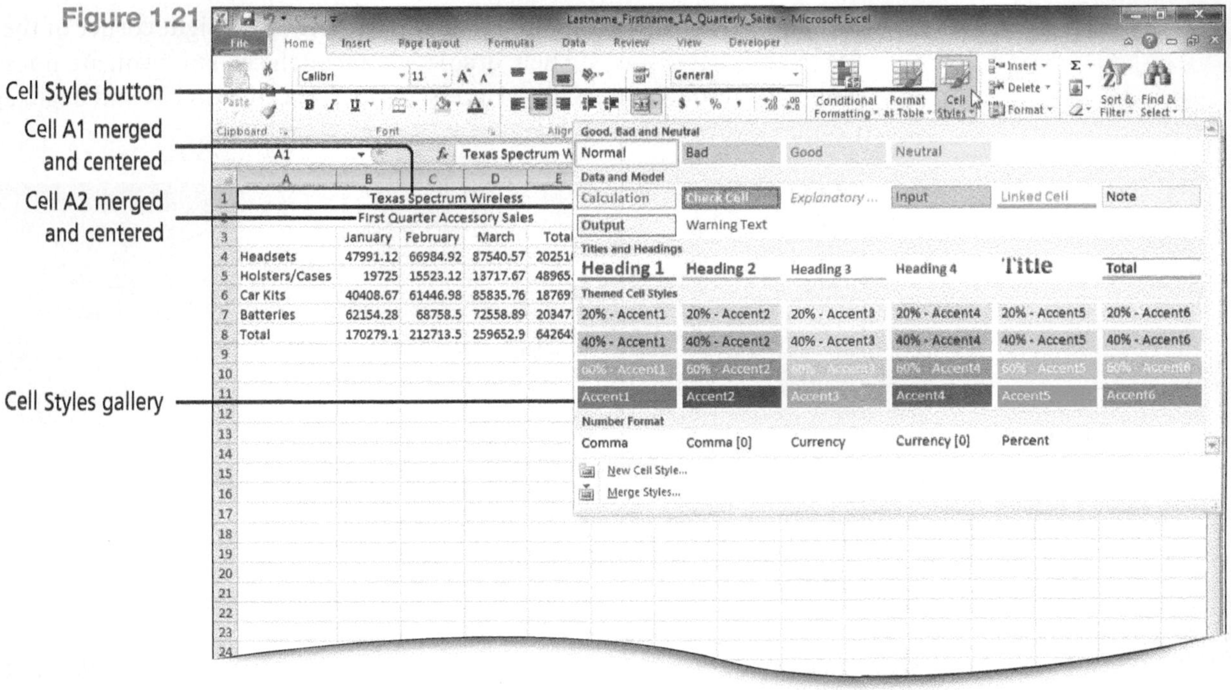

3. In the displayed gallery, under **Titles and Headings**, click **Title** and notice that the row height adjusts to accommodate this larger font size.

4. Click cell **A2**, display the **Cell Styles** gallery, and then under **Titles and Headings**, click **Heading 1**.

   Use cell styles to maintain a consistent look in a worksheet and across worksheets in a workbook.

5. Select the range **B3:F3**, hold down Ctrl, and then select the range **A4:A8** to select the column titles and the row titles.

   Use this technique to select two or more ranges that are nonadjacent—not next to each other.

6 Display the **Cell Styles** gallery, click **Heading 4** to apply this cell style to the column titles and row titles, and then **Save** your workbook.

> **Another Way**
>
> In the Name Box type b4:e4,b8:e8 and then press Enter.

Activity 1.10 | Formatting Financial Numbers

1 Select the range **B4:E4**, hold down Ctrl, and then select the range **B8:E8**.

This range is referred to as *b4:e4,b8:e8* with a comma separating the references to the two nonadjacent ranges.

> **Another Way**
>
> Display the Cell Styles gallery, and under Number Format, click Currency.

2 On the **Home tab**, in the **Number group**, click the **Accounting Number Format** button $. Compare your screen with Figure 1.22.

The ***Accounting Number Format*** applies a thousand comma separator where appropriate, inserts a fixed U.S. dollar sign aligned at the left edge of the cell, applies two decimal places, and leaves a small amount of space at the right edge of the cell to accommodate a parenthesis when negative numbers are present. Excel widens the columns to accommodate the formatted numbers.

Figure 1.22

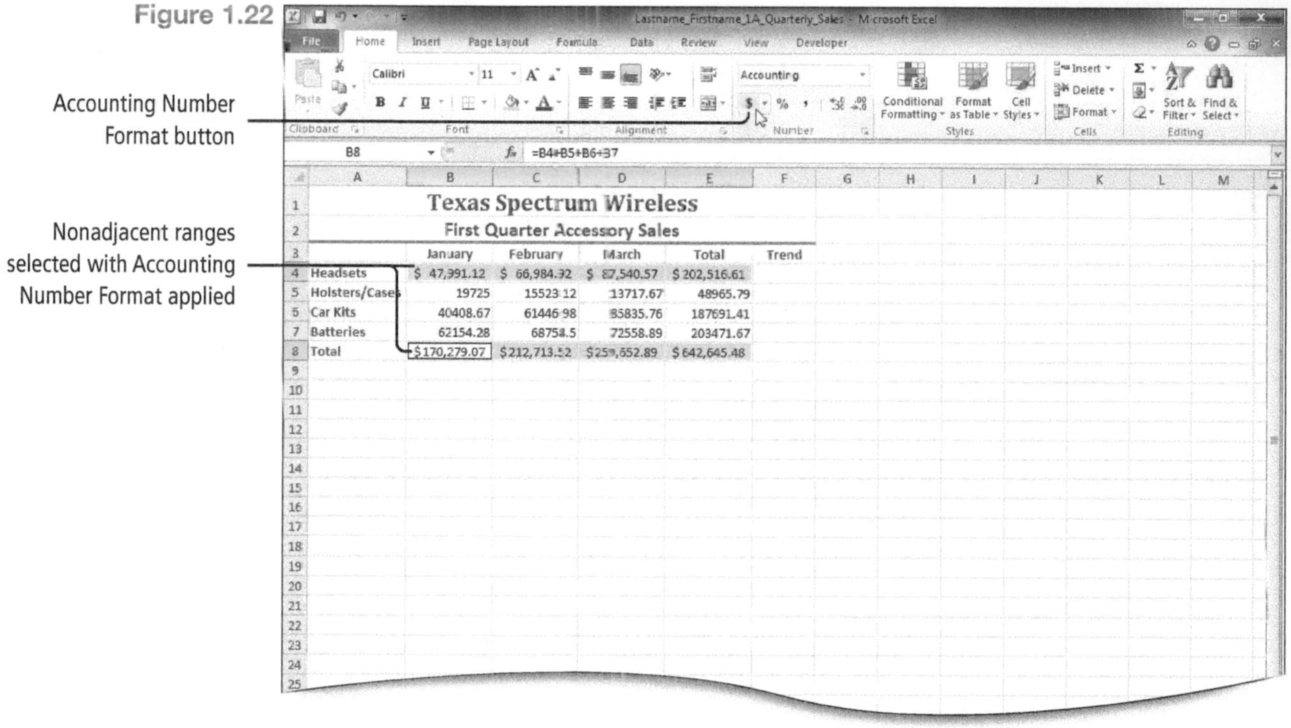

3 Select the range **B5:E7**, and then in the **Number group**, click the **Comma Style** button ,.

The ***Comma Style*** inserts thousand comma separators where appropriate and applies two decimal places. Comma Style also leaves space at the right to accommodate a parenthesis when negative numbers are present.

When preparing worksheets with financial information, the first row of dollar amounts and the total row of dollar amounts are formatted in the Accounting Number Format; that is, with thousand comma separators, dollar signs, two decimal places, and space at the right to accommodate a parenthesis for negative numbers, if any. Rows that are *not* the first row or the total row should be formatted with the Comma Style.

4 Select the range **B8:E8**. From the **Styles group**, display the **Cell Styles** gallery, and then under **Titles and Headings**, click **Total**. Click any blank cell to cancel the selection, and then compare your screen with Figure 1.23.

This is a common way to apply borders to financial information. The single border indicates that calculations were performed on the numbers above, and the double border indicates that the information is complete. Sometimes financial documents do not display values with cents; rather, the values are rounded up. You can do this by selecting the cells, and then clicking the Decrease Decimal button two times.

Figure 1.23

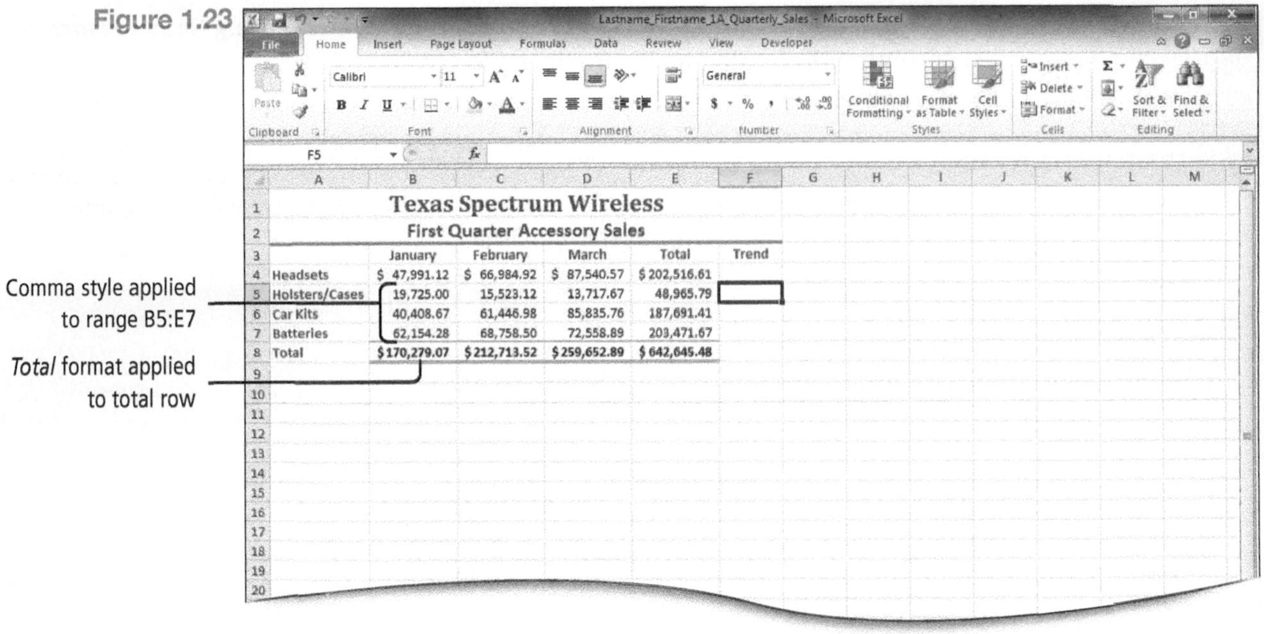

5 Click the **Page Layout tab**, and then in the **Themes group**, click **Themes**. Click the **Composite** theme, and notice that the cell styles change to match the new theme. Click **Save**.

Recall that a theme is a predefined set of colors, fonts, lines, and fill effects that look good together.

Objective 5 | Chart Data to Create a Column Chart and Insert Sparklines

A ***chart*** is a graphic representation of data in a worksheet. Data presented as a chart is easier to understand than a table of numbers. ***Sparklines*** are tiny charts embedded in a cell and give a visual trend summary alongside your data. A sparkline makes a pattern more obvious to the eye.

Activity 1.11 | Charting Data in a Column Chart

In this activity, you will create a ***column chart*** showing the monthly sales of accessories by category during the first quarter. A column chart is useful for illustrating comparisons among related numbers. The chart will enable the company president, Rosalyn Thomas, to see a pattern of overall monthly sales.

1 Select the range **A3:D7**. Click the **Insert tab**, and then in the **Charts group**, click **Column** to display a gallery of Column chart types.

When charting data, typically you should *not* include totals—include only the data you want to compare. By using different ***chart types***, you can display data in a way that is meaningful to the reader—common examples are column charts, pie charts, and line charts.

2 On the gallery of column chart types, under **2-D Column**, point to the first chart to display the ScreenTip *Clustered Column*, and then click to select it. Compare your screen with Figure 1.24.

A column chart displays in the worksheet, and the charted data is bordered by colored lines. Because the chart object is selected—surrounded by a border and displaying sizing handles—contextual tools named *Chart Tools* display and add contextual tabs next to the standard tabs on the Ribbon.

Figure 1.24

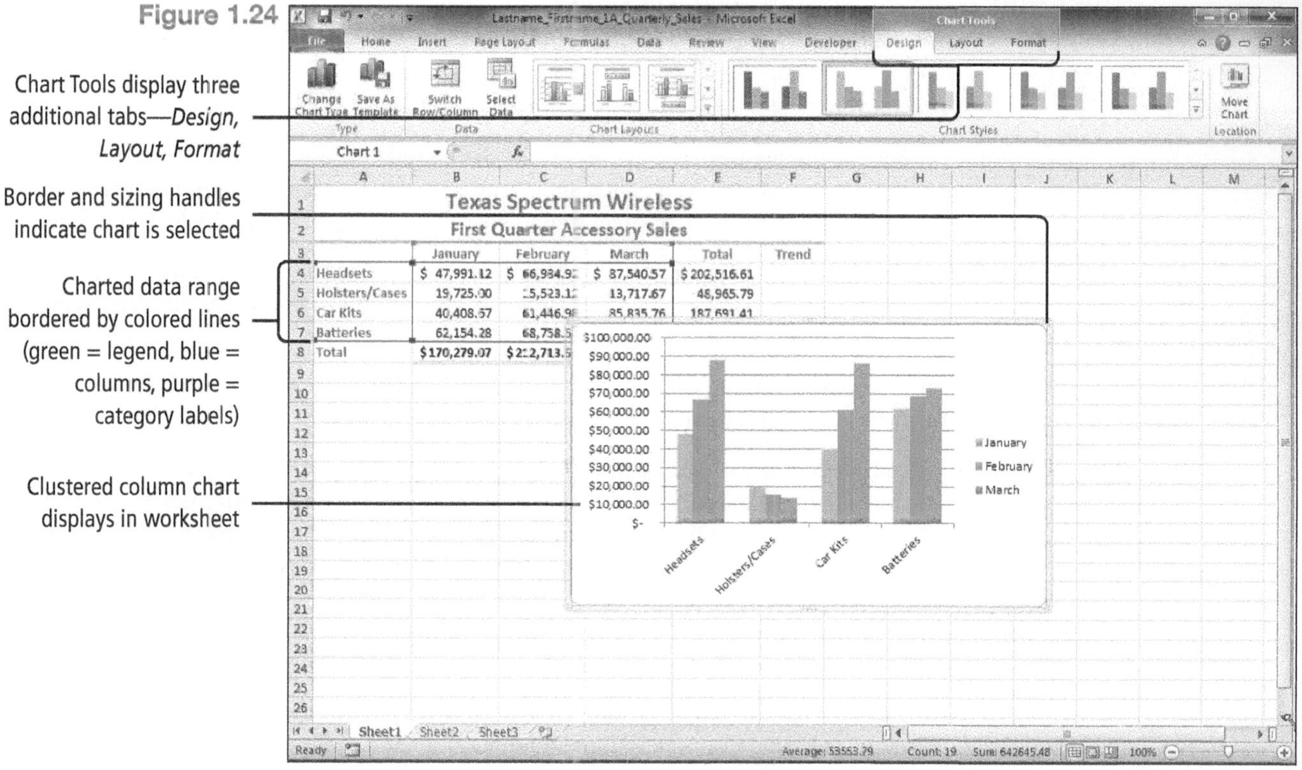

3 Point to the top border of the chart to display the pointer, and then drag the upper left corner of the chart just inside the upper left corner of cell **A10**, approximately as shown in Figure 1.25.

Based on the data you selected in your worksheet, Excel constructs a column chart and adds ***category labels***—the labels that display along the bottom of the chart to identify the category of data. This area is referred to as the ***category axis*** or the ***x-axis***. Excel uses the row titles as the category names.

On the left, Excel includes a numerical scale on which the charted data is based; this is the ***value axis*** or the ***y-axis***. On the right, a ***legend***, which identifies the patterns or colors that are assigned to the categories in the chart, displays.

Figure 1.25

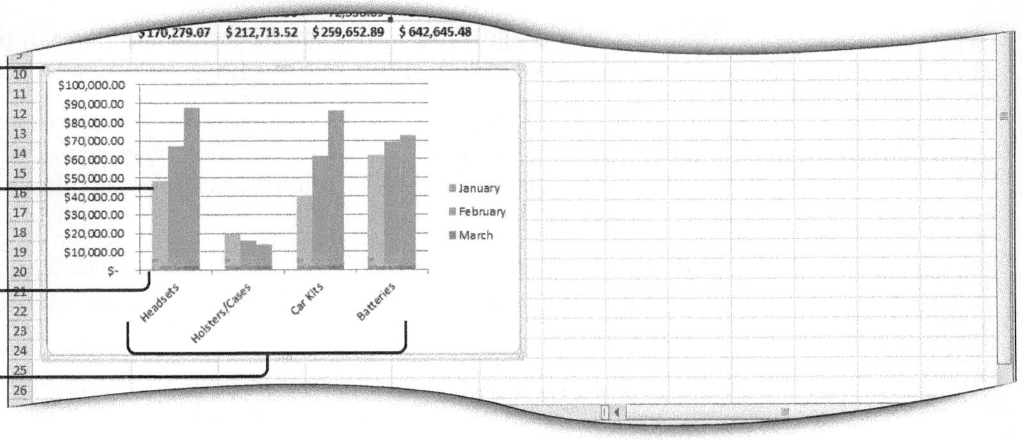

4 On the Ribbon, locate the contextual tabs under **Chart Tools—Design**, **Layout**, and **Format**.

When a chart is selected, Chart Tools become available and three tabs provide commands for working with the chart.

5 Locate the group of cells bordered in blue.

Each of the twelve cells bordered in blue is referred to as a ***data point***—a value that originates in a worksheet cell. Each data point is represented in the chart by a ***data marker***—a column, bar, area, dot, pie slice, or other symbol in a chart that represents a single data point.

Related data points form a ***data series***; for example, there is a data series for *January*, for *February*, and for *March*. Each data series has a unique color or pattern represented in the chart legend.

6 On the **Design tab** of the Ribbon, in the **Data group**, click the **Switch Row/Column** button, and then compare your chart with Figure 1.26.

In this manner, you can easily change the categories of data from the row titles, which is the default, to the column titles. Whether you use row or column titles as your category names depends on how you want to view your charted data. Here, the president wants to see monthly sales and the breakdown of product categories within each month.

Figure 1.26

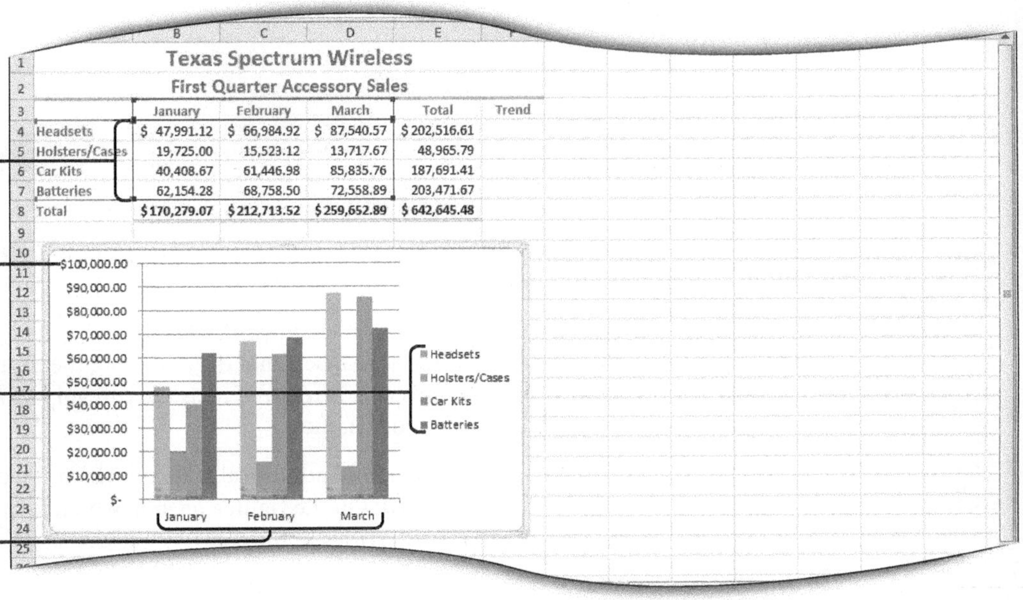

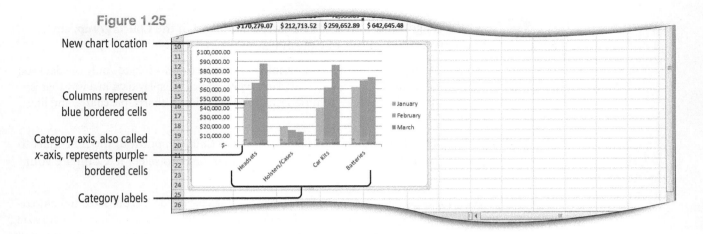

7 On the **Design tab**, in the **Chart Layouts group**, locate and click the **More** button [▾]. Compare your screen with Figure 1.27.

In the ***Chart Layouts gallery***, you can select a predesigned ***chart layout***—a combination of chart elements, which can include a title, legend, labels for the columns, and the table of charted cells.

Figure 1.27

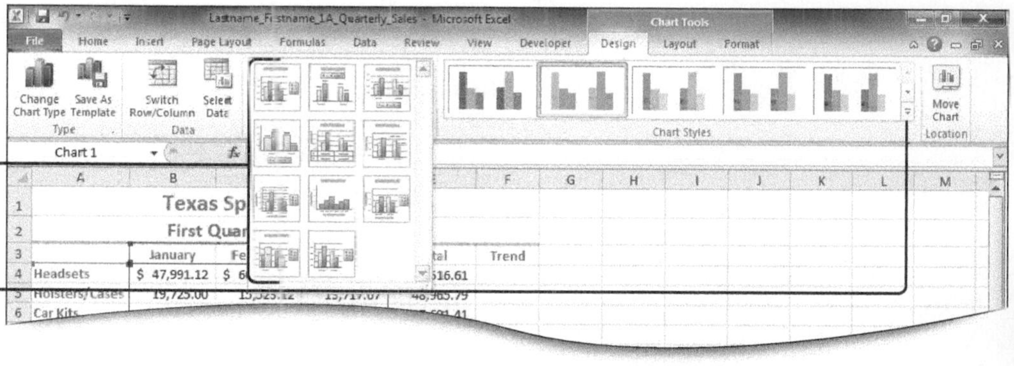

8 Click several different layouts to see the effect on your chart, and then using the ScreenTips as your guide, locate and click **Layout 1**.

9 In the chart, click anywhere in the text *Chart Title* to select the title box, watch the **Formula Bar** as you type **1st Quarter Sales** and then press Enter to display the new chart title.

10 Click in a white area just slightly *inside* the chart border to deselect the chart title. On the **Design tab**, in the **Chart Styles group**, click the **More** button [▾]. Compare your screen with Figure 1.28.

The ***Chart Styles gallery*** displays an array of pre-defined ***chart styles***—the overall visual look of the chart in terms of its colors, backgrounds, and graphic effects such as flat or beveled columns.

Figure 1.28

11 Using the ScreenTips as your guide, locate and click **Style 26**.

This style uses a white background, formats the columns with theme colors, and applies a beveled effect. With this clear visual representation of the data, the president can see the sales of all product categories in each month, and can see that the sale of headsets and car kits has risen quite markedly during the quarter.

12 Click any cell to deselect the chart, and notice that the *Chart Tools* no longer display in the Ribbon. Click **Save** [Save icon], and then compare your screen with Figure 1.29.

Contextual tabs display when an object is selected, and then are removed from view when the object is deselected.

Figure 1.29

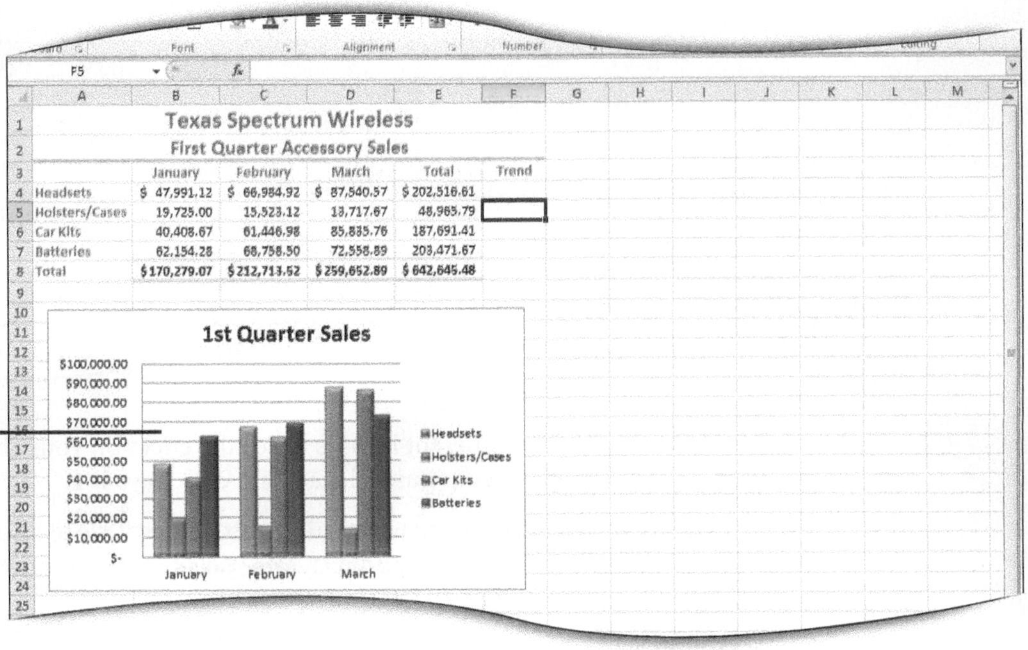

Chart Style 26 applied to the chart

Activity 1.12 | Creating and Formatting Sparklines

By creating sparklines, you provide a context for your numbers. Your readers will be able to see the relationship between a sparkline and its underlying data quickly.

> **Another Way**
>
> In the worksheet, select the range F4:F7 to insert it into the Location Range box.

1 Select the range **B4:D7**. Click the **Insert tab**, and then in the **Sparklines group**, click **Line**. In the displayed **Create Sparklines** dialog box, notice that the selected range *B4:D7* displays.

2 With the insertion point blinking in the **Location Range** box, type **f4:f7** Compare your screen with Figure 1.30.

Figure 1.30

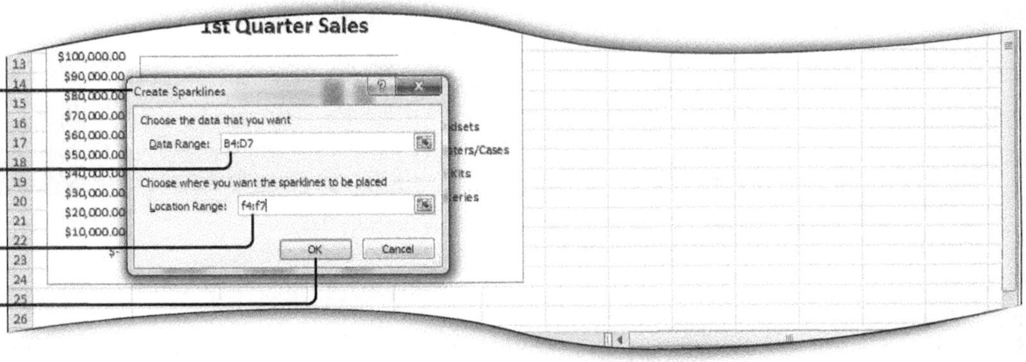

Create Sparklines dialog box

Data Range indicates your selected data

Location Range typed

OK button

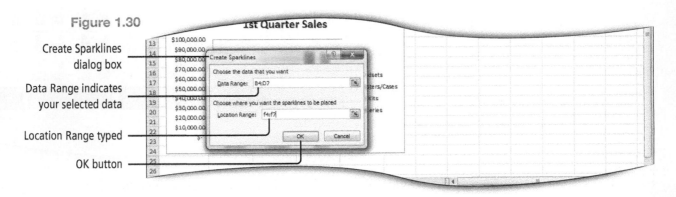

3 Click **OK** to insert the trend lines in the range F4:F7, and then on the **Design tab**, in the **Show group**, click the **Markers** check box to select it.

Alongside each row of data, the sparkline provides a quick visual trend summary for sales of each accessory item over the three-month period. For example, you can see instantly that of the four items, only Holsters/Cases had declining sales for the period.

4 In the **Style group**, click the **More** button. In the second row, click the fourth style—**Sparkline Style Accent 4, Darker 25%**. Click cell **A1** to deselect the range. Click **Save**. Compare your screen with Figure 1.31.

Use markers, colors, and styles in this manner to further enhance your sparklines.

Figure 1.31

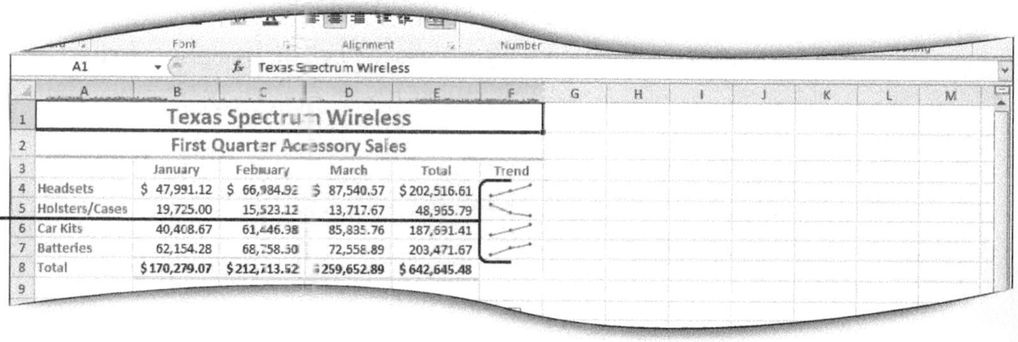

Objective 6 | Print, Display Formulas, and Close Excel

Use *Page Layout view* and the commands on the Page Layout tab to prepare for printing.

Activity 1.13 | Changing Views, Creating a Footer, and Using Print Preview

For each Excel project in this textbook, you will create a footer containing your name and the project name.

1 Be sure the chart is *not* selected. Click the **Insert tab**, and then in the **Text group**, click the **Header & Footer** button to switch to Page Layout view and open the **Header area**. Compare your screen with Figure 1.32.

In Page Layout view, you can see the edges of the paper of multiple pages, the margins, and the rulers. You can also insert a header or footer by typing in the areas indicated and use the Header & Footer Tools.

Figure 1.32

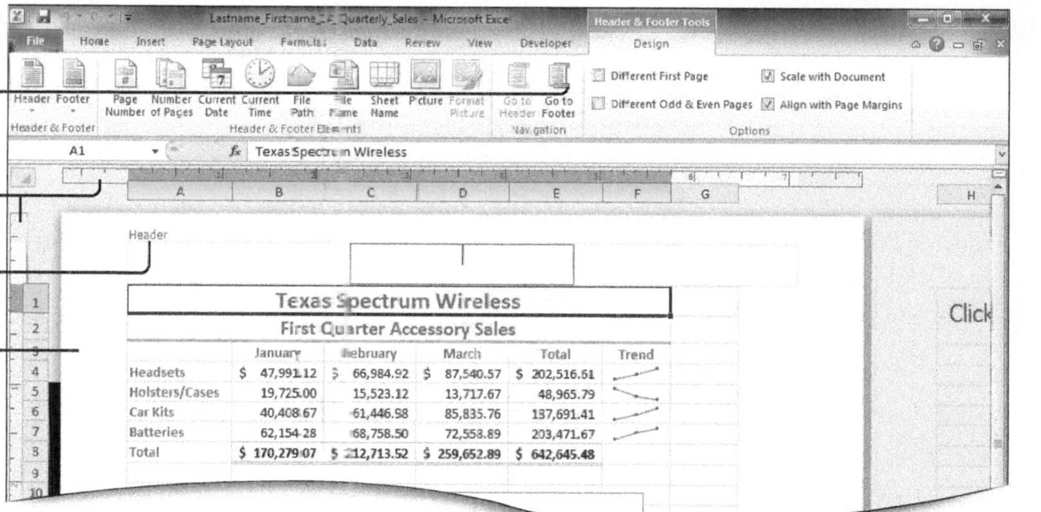

2 On the **Design tab**, in the **Navigation group**, click **Go to Footer** to open the **Footer area**, and then click just above the word *Footer* to place the insertion point in the **left section** of the **Footer area**.

3 In the **Header & Footer Elements group**, click the **File Name** button to add the name of your file to the footer—*&[File]* displays in the left section of the **Footer area**. Then, click in a cell just above the footer to exit the **Footer area** and view your file name.

4 Scroll up to see your chart, click a corner of the chart to select it, and then see if the chart is centered under the data. *Point* to the small dots on the right edge of the chart; compare your screen with Figure 1.33.

Figure 1.33

Horizontal resize pointer

Border indicates chart is selected

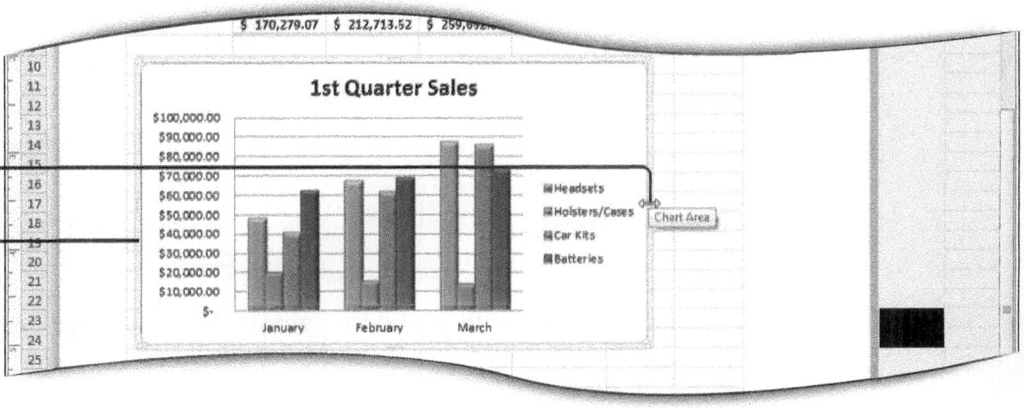

5 Drag the ↔ pointer to the right so that the right border of the chart is just inside the right border of **column F**. Be sure the left and right borders of the chart are just slightly **inside** the left border of **column A** and the right border of **column F**—adjust as necessary.

6 Click any cell to deselect the chart. Click the **Page Layout tab**, in the **Page Setup group**, click the **Margins** button, and then at the bottom of the **Margins** gallery, click **Custom Margins**. In the **Page Setup** dialog box, under **Center on page**, select the **Horizontally** check box.

This action will center the data and chart horizontally on the page, as shown in the Preview area.

7 In the lower right corner of the **Page Setup** dialog box, click **OK**. In the upper left corner of your screen, click the **File tab** to display **Backstage** view. On the **Info tab**, on the right under the screen thumbnail, click **Properties**, and then click **Show Document Panel**.

8 In the **Author** box, replace the existing text with your firstname and lastname. In the **Subject** box, type your course name and section number. In the **Keywords** box type **accessory sales** and then **Close** × the **Document Information Panel**.

> **Another Way**
>
> Press Ctrl + F2 to view the Print Preview.

9 Click the **File tab** to redisplay **Backstage** view, and then on the left, click the **Print tab** to view the Print commands and the **Print Preview**. Compare your screen with Figure 1.34.

Figure 1.34

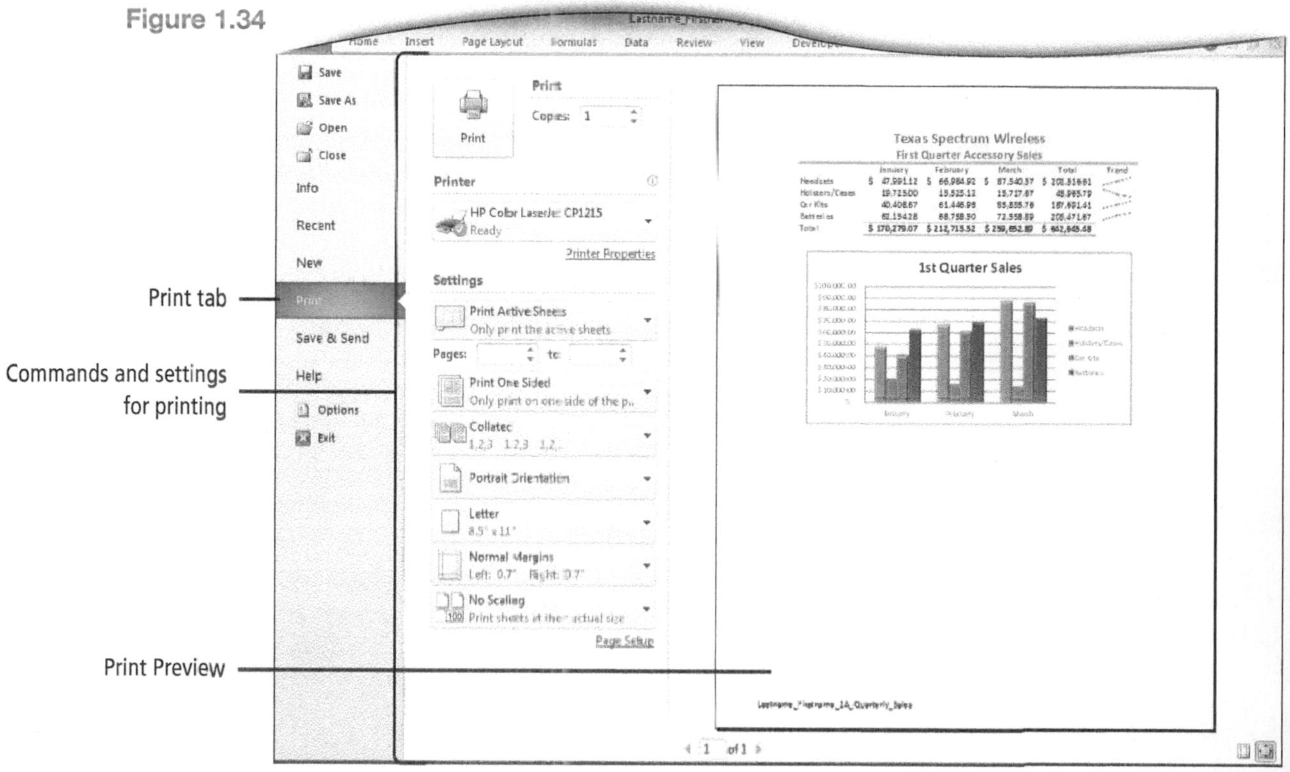

10 Note any adjustments that need to be made, and then on the Ribbon, click the **Home tab** to close Backstage view and return to the worksheet. In the lower right corner of your screen, click the **Normal** button to return to the Normal view, and then press Ctrl + Home to return to cell **A1**.

The ***Normal view*** maximizes the number of cells visible on your screen and keeps the column letters and row numbers closer. The vertical dotted line between columns indicates that as currently arranged, only the columns to the left of the dotted line will print on the first page. The exact position of the vertical line may depend on your default printer setting.

11 Make any necessary adjustments, and then **Save** your workbook.

Activity 1.14 | Deleting Unused Sheets in a Workbook

A new Excel workbook contains three blank worksheets. It is not necessary to delete unused sheets, but doing so saves storage space and removes any doubt that additional information is in the workbook.

1 At the bottom of your worksheet, click the **Sheet2 tab** to display the second worksheet in the workbook and make it active.

Another Way

On the Home tab, in the Cells group, click the Delete button arrow, and then click Delete Sheet.

2 Hold down Ctrl, and then click the **Sheet3 tab**. Release Ctrl, and then with both sheets selected (the tab background is white), point to either of the selected sheet tabs, right-click, and then on the shortcut menu, click **Delete**.

Excel deletes the two unused sheets from your workbook. If you attempt to delete a worksheet with data, Excel will display a warning and permit you to cancel the deletion. ***Sheet tabs*** are labels along the lower border of the Excel window that identify each worksheet.

Activity 1.15 | Printing a Worksheet

1 Click **Save** [Save icon].

2 Display **Backstage** view and on the left click the Print tab. Under **Print**, be sure **Copies** indicates *1*. Under **Settings**, verify that *Print Active Sheets* displays. Compare your screen with Figure 1.35.

Figure 1.35

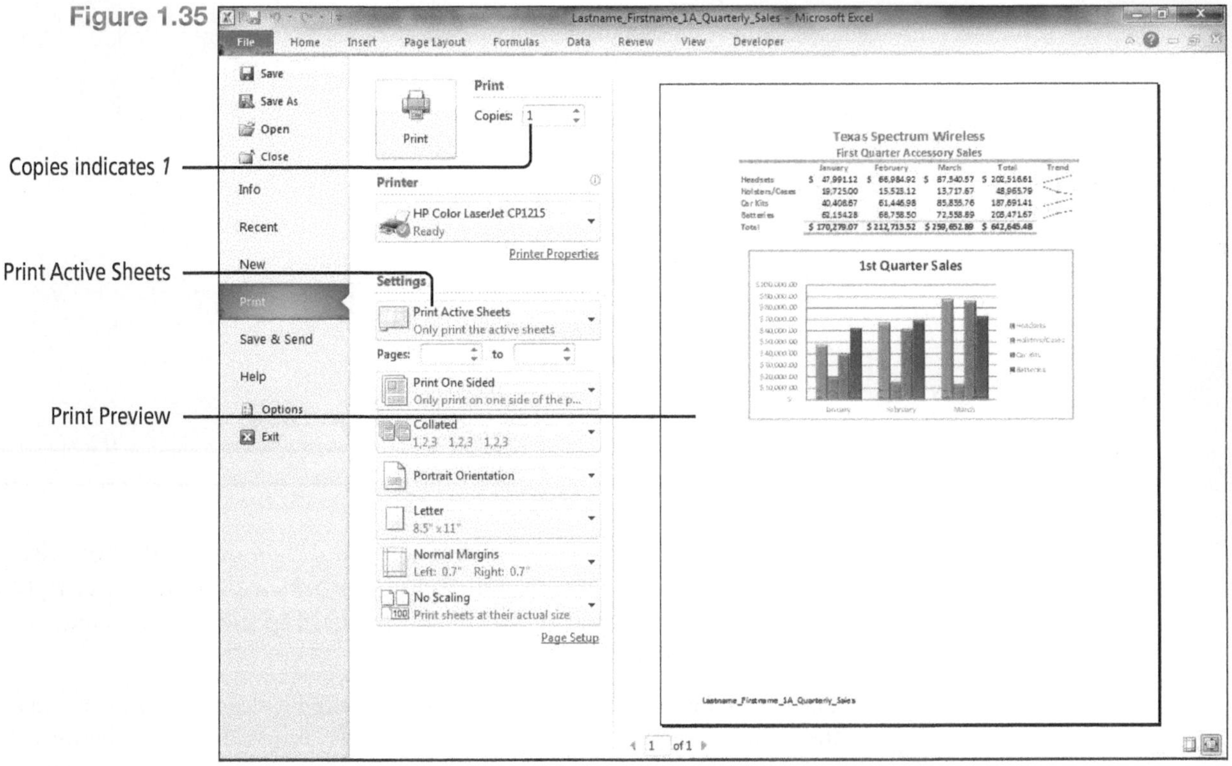

3 To print on paper, be sure that a printer is available to your system, and then in the **Print group**, click the **Print** button. To create an electronic printout, on the Backstage tabs, click the **Save & Send tab**, under **File Types** click **Create PDF/XPS Document**, and then on the right, click **Create PDF/XPS**. In the **Publish as PDF or XPS** dialog box, navigate to your storage location, and then click the **Publish** button to create the PDF file. Close the Adobe window.

Activity 1.16 | Displaying, Printing, and Hiding Formulas

When you type a formula in a cell, the cell displays the *results* of the formula calculation. Recall that this value is called the displayed value. You can view and print the underlying formulas in the cells. When you do so, a formula often takes more horizontal space to display than the result of the calculation.

1 If necessary, redisplay your worksheet. Because you will make some temporary changes to your workbook, on the Quick Access Toolbar, click **Save** [Save icon] to be sure your work is saved up to this point.

> **Another Way**
>
> Hold down Ctrl, and then press ` (usually located below Esc).

2 On the **Formulas tab**, in the **Formula Auditing group**, click the **Show Formulas** button. Then, in the **column heading area**, point to the **column A** heading to display the [↓] pointer, hold down the left mouse button, and then drag to the right to select columns **A:F**. Compare your screen with Figure 1.36.

Figure 1.36

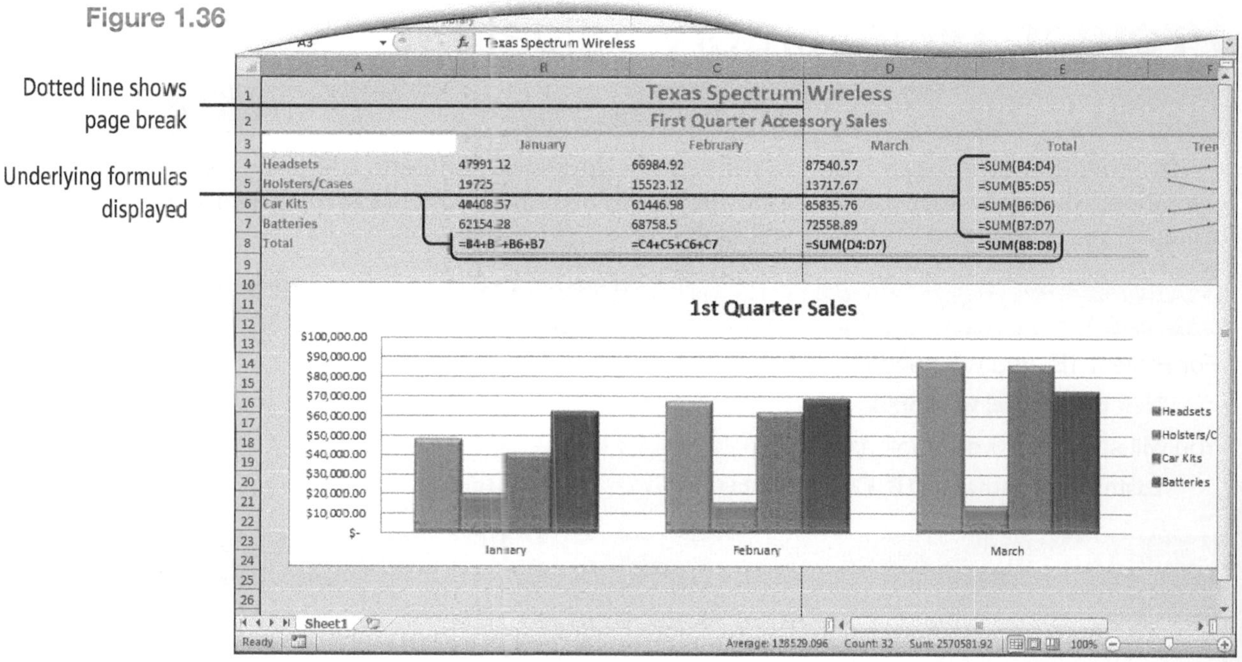

> **Note | Turning the Display of Formulas On and Off**
>
> The Show Formulas button is a toggle button. Clicking it once turns the display of formulas on—the button will glow orange. Clicking the button again turns the display of formulas off.

3 Point to the column heading boundary between any two of the selected columns to display the pointer, and then double-click to AutoFit the selected columns.

AutoFit adjusts the width of a column to fit the cell content of the *widest* cell in the column.

> **Another Way**
>
> In the Scale to Fit group, click the Dialog Box Launcher button to display the Page tab of the Page Setup dialog box. Then, under Scaling, click the Fit to option button.

4 On the **Page Layout tab**, in the **Page Setup group**, click **Orientation**, and then click **Landscape**. In the **Scale to Fit** group, click the **Width arrow**, and then click **1 page** to scale the data to fit onto one page.

Scaling shrinks the width (or height) of the printed worksheet to fit a maximum number of pages, and is convenient for printing formulas. Although it is not always the case, formulas frequently take up more space than the actual data.

> **Another Way**
>
> In the Page Setup group, click the Dialog Box Launcher button to display the Page tab of the Page Setup dialog box. Then, under Orientation, click the Landscape option button.

5 In the **Page Setup group**, click the **Dialog Box Launcher** button. In the **Page Setup** dialog box, click the **Margins tab**, and then under **Center on page**, if necessary, click to select the **Horizontally** check box.

6 Click **OK** to close the dialog box. Check to be sure your chart is centered below the data and the left and right edges are slightly inside column A and column F—drag a chart edge and then deselect the chart if necessary. Display the **Print Preview**, and then submit your worksheet with formulas displayed, either printed or electronically, as directed by your instructor.

7 Click the **File tab** to display **Backstage** view, click **Close**, and when prompted, click **Don't Save** so that you do *not* save the changes you made—displaying formulas, changing column widths and orientation, and scaling—to print your formulas.

8 In the upper right corner of your screen, click the **Close** button to exit Excel.

End You have completed Project 1A

Project 1B Inventory Valuation

myitlab
Project 1B Training

Project Activities

In Activities 1.17 through 1.24, you will create a workbook for Josette Lovrick, Operations Manager, which calculates the retail value of an inventory of car convenience products. Your completed worksheet will look similar to Figure 1.37.

Project Files

For Project 1B, you will need the following file:

New blank Excel workbook

You will save your workbook as:

Lastname_Firstname_1B_Car_Products

Project Results

Texas Spectrum Wireless
Car Products Inventory Valuation
As of December 31

	Warehouse Location	Quantity in Stock	Retail Price	Total Retail Value	Percent of Total Retail Value
Antenna Signal Booster	Dallas	1,126	$ 19.99	$ 22,508.74	8.27%
Car Power Port Adapter	Dallas	3,546	19.49	69,111.54	25.39%
Repeater Antenna	Houston	1,035	39.99	41,389.65	15.21%
SIM Card Reader and Writer	Houston	2,875	16.90	48,587.50	17.85%
Sticky Dash Pad	Houston	3,254	11.99	39,015.46	14.33%
Window Mount GPS Holder	Dallas	2,458	20.99	51,593.42	18.95%
Total Retail Value for All Products				$ 272,206.31	

Lastname_Firstname_1B_Car_Products

Figure 1.37
Project 1B Car Products

Objective 7 | Check Spelling in a Worksheet

In Excel, the spelling checker performs similarly to the other Microsoft Office programs.

Activity 1.17 | Checking Spelling in a Worksheet

1 **Start** Excel and display a new blank workbook. In cell **A1**, type **Texas Spectrum Wireless** and press Enter. In cell **A2**, type **Car Products Inventory** and press Enter.

2 On the Ribbon, click the **File tab** to display **Backstage** view, click **Save As**, and then in the **Save As** dialog box, navigate to your **Excel Chapter 1** folder. As the **File name**, type **Lastname_Firstname_1B_Car_Products** and then click **Save**.

3 Press Tab to move to cell **B3**, type **Quantity** and press Tab. In cell **C3**, type **Average Cost** and press Tab. In cell **D3**, type **Retail Price** and press Tab.

4 Click cell **C3**, and then look at the **Formula Bar**. Notice that in the cell, the displayed value is cut off; however, in the **Formula Bar**, the entire text value—the underlying value—displays. Compare your screen with Figure 1.38.

Text that is too long to fit in a cell spills over to cells on the right only if they are empty. If the cell to the right contains data, the text in the cell to the left is truncated. The entire value continues to exist, but is not completely visible.

Figure 1.38

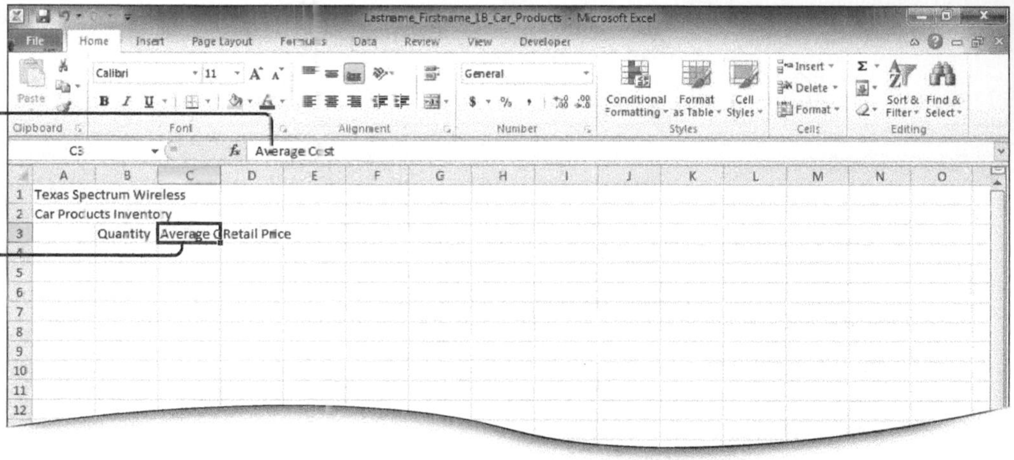

5 Click cell **E3**, type **Total Retail Value** and press Tab. In cell **F3**, type **Percent of Total Retail Value** and press Enter.

6 Click cell **A4**. *Without* correcting the spelling error, type **Antena Signal Booster** Press Enter. In the range **A5:A10**, type the remaining row titles shown below. Then compare your screen with Figure 1.39.

Car Power Port Adapter

Repeater Antenna

SIM Card Reader and Writer

Sticky Dash Pad

Window Mount GPS Holder

Total Retail Value for All Products

Figure 1.39

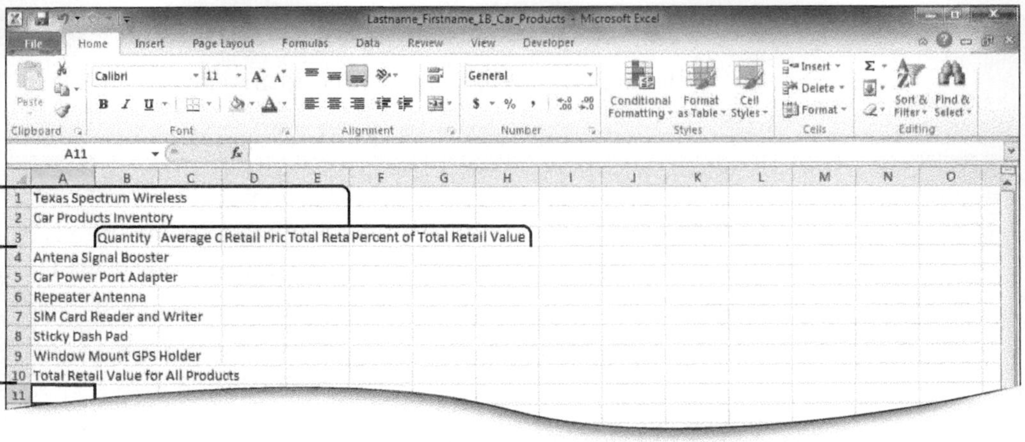

7 In the **column heading area**, point to the right boundary of **column A** to display the ⊞ pointer, and then drag to the right to widen **column A** to **215** pixels.

8 Select the range **A1:F1**, **Merge & Center** the text, and then from the **Cell Styles** gallery, apply the **Title** style.

9 Select the range **A2:F2**, **Merge & Center** the text, and then from the **Cell Styles** gallery, apply the **Heading 1** style. Press Ctrl + Home to move to the top of your worksheet.

> **Another Way**
>
> Press F7, which is the keyboard shortcut for the Spelling command.

10 With cell **A1** as the active cell, click the **Review tab**, and then in the **Proofing group**, click the **Spelling** button. Compare your screen with Figure 1.40.

Figure 1.40

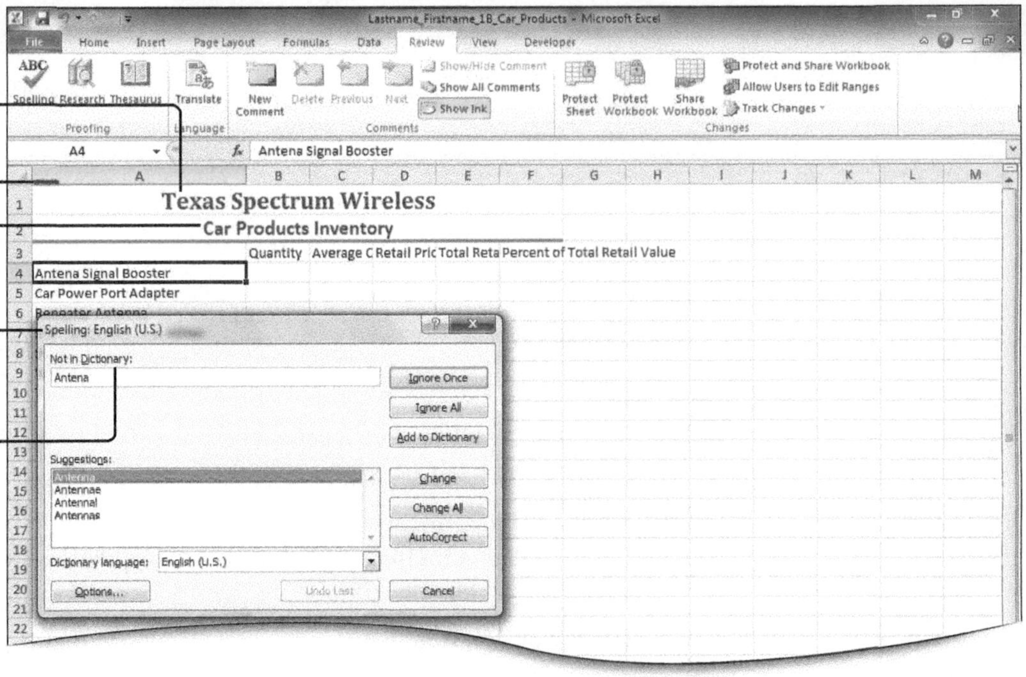

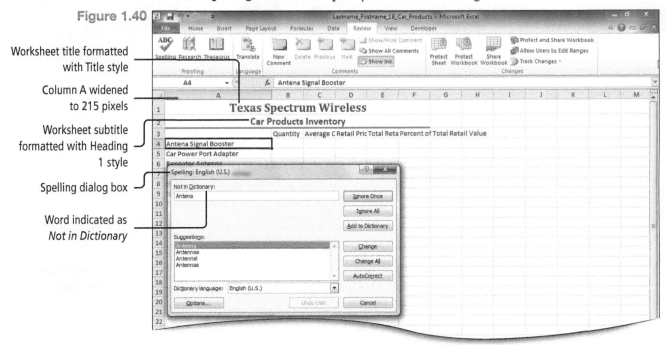

> **Alert! | Does a Message Display Asking if You Want to Continue Checking at the Beginning of the Sheet?**
>
> If a message displays asking if you want to continue checking at the beginning of the sheet, click Yes. The Spelling command begins its checking process with the currently selected cell and moves to the right and down. Thus, if your active cell was a cell after A4, this message may display.

11 In the **Spelling** dialog box, under **Not in Dictionary**, notice the word *Antena*.

The spelling tool does not have this word in its dictionary. Under *Suggestions*, Excel provides a list of suggested spellings.

12 Under **Suggestions**, click **Antenna**, and then click the **Change** button.

Antena, a typing error is changed to *Antenna*. A message box displays *The spelling check is complete for the entire sheet*—unless you have additional unrecognized words. Because the spelling check begins its checking process starting with the currently selected cell, it is good practice to return to cell A1 before starting the Spelling command.

13 Correct any other errors you may have made. When the message displays, *The spelling check is complete for the entire sheet*, click **OK**. **Save** your workbook.

Objective 8 | Enter Data by Range

You can enter data by first selecting a range of cells. This is a time-saving technique, especially if you use the numeric keypad to enter the numbers.

Activity 1.18 | Entering Data by Range

1 Select the range **B4:D9**, type **1126** and then press Enter.

The value displays in cell B4, and cell B5 becomes the active cell.

2 With cell **B5** active in the range, and pressing Enter after each entry, type the following, and then compare your screen with Figure 1.41:

4226
1035
2875
3254
2458

After you enter the last value and press Enter, the active cell moves to the top of the next column within the selected range. Although it is not required to enter data in this manner, you can see that selecting the range before you enter data saves time because it confines the movement of the active cell to the selected range.

Figure 1.41

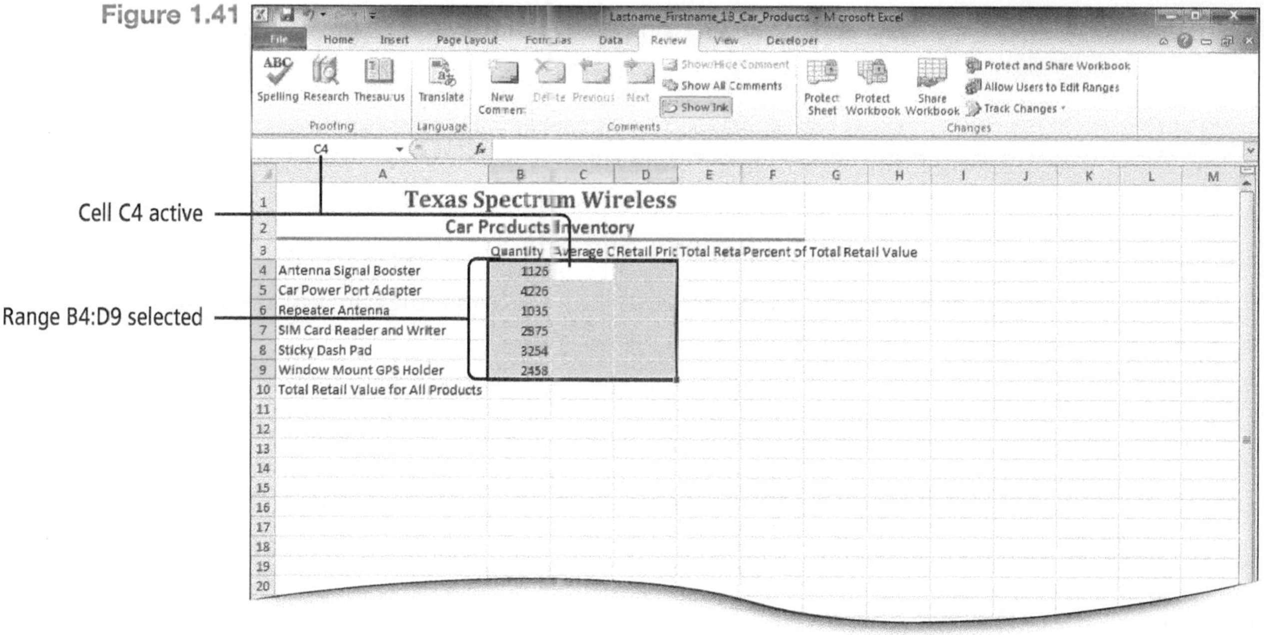

3 With the selected range still active, from the following table, beginning in cell **C4** and pressing Enter after each entry, enter the data for the **Average Cost** column and then the **Retail Price** column. If you prefer, deselect the range to enter the values—typing in a selected range is optional.

Average Cost	Retail Price
9.75	19.99
9.25	19.49
16.90	39.99
9.55	16.90
4.20	12.99
10.45	20.99

Recall that the default number format for cells is the *General* number format, in which numbers display exactly as you type them and trailing zeros do not display, even if you type them.

4 Click any blank cell, and then compare your screen with Figure 1.42. Correct any errors you may have made while entering data, and then click **Save**.

Figure 1.42

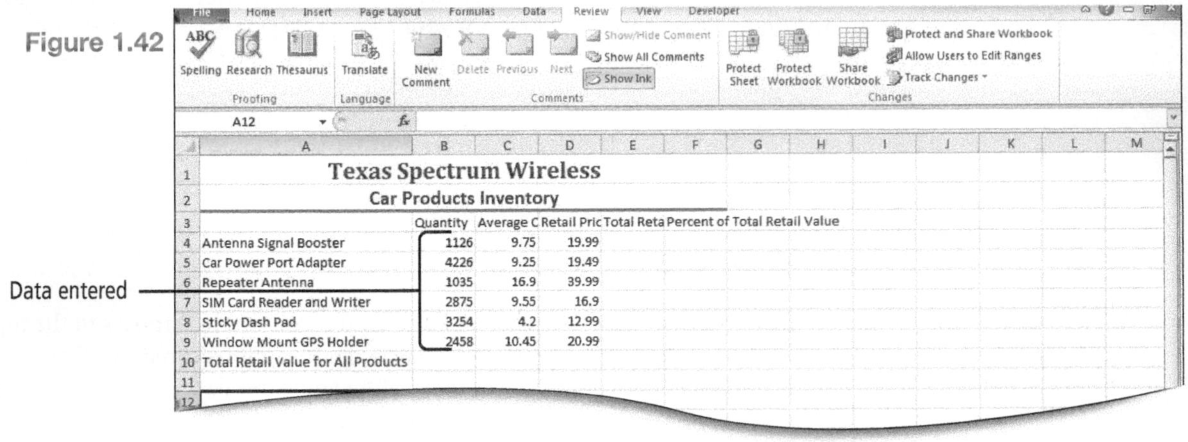

Objective 9 | Construct Formulas for Mathematical Operations

Operators are symbols with which you can specify the type of calculation you want to perform in a formula.

Activity 1.19 | Using Arithmetic Operators

1 Click cell **E4**, type **=b4*d4** and notice that the two cells are outlined as part of an active formula. Then press Enter.

The *Total Retail Value* of all *Antenna Signal Booster* items in inventory—*22508.74*—equals the *Quantity* (1,126) times the *Retail Price* (selling price) of 19.99. In Excel, the asterisk (*) indicates multiplication.

2 Take a moment to study the symbols you will use to perform basic mathematical operations in Excel, as shown in the table in Figure 1.43, which are referred to as ***arithmetic operators***.

Symbols Used in Excel for Arithmetic Operators	
Operator Symbol	**Operation**
+	Addition
-	Subtraction (also negation)
*	Multiplication
/	Division
%	Percent
^	Exponentiation

Figure 1.43

3 Click cell **E4**.

You can see that in cells E5:E9, you need a formula similar to the one in E4, but one that refers to the cells in row 5, row 6, and so forth. Recall that you can copy formulas and the cell references will change *relative to* the row number.

4 With cell **E4** selected, position your pointer over the fill handle in the lower right corner of the cell until the + pointer displays. Then, drag down through cell **E9** to copy the formula.

Another Way

Select the range, display the Cell Styles gallery, and then under Number Format, click Comma [0].

5 Select the range **B4:B9**, and then on the **Home tab**, in the **Number group**, click the **Comma Style** button ,. Then, in the **Number group**, click the **Decrease Decimal** button two times to remove the decimal places from these values.

Comma Style formats a number with two decimal places; because these are whole numbers referring to quantities, no decimal places are necessary.

6 Select the range **E4:E9**, and then at the bottom of your screen, in the status bar, notice the displayed values for **Average**, **Count**, and **Sum**—*48118.91833*, *6* and *288713.51*.

When you select numerical data, three calculations display in the status bar by default—Average, Count, and Sum. Here, Excel indicates that if you averaged the selected values, the result would be *48118.91833*, there are 6 cells in the selection that contain values, and that if you added the values the result would be 288713.51.

7 Click cell **E10**, in the **Editing group**, click the **Sum** button Σ, notice that Excel selects a range to sum, and then press Enter to display the total *288713.5*.

8 Select the range **C5:E9** and apply the **Comma Style** ,; notice that Excel widens **column E**.

9 Select the range **C4:E4**, hold down Ctrl, and then click cell **E10**. Release Ctrl and then apply the **Accounting Number Format** $. Notice that Excel widens the columns as necessary.

10 Click cell **E10**, and then from the **Cell Styles** gallery, apply the **Total** style. Click any blank cell, and then compare your screen with Figure 1.44.

Figure 1.44

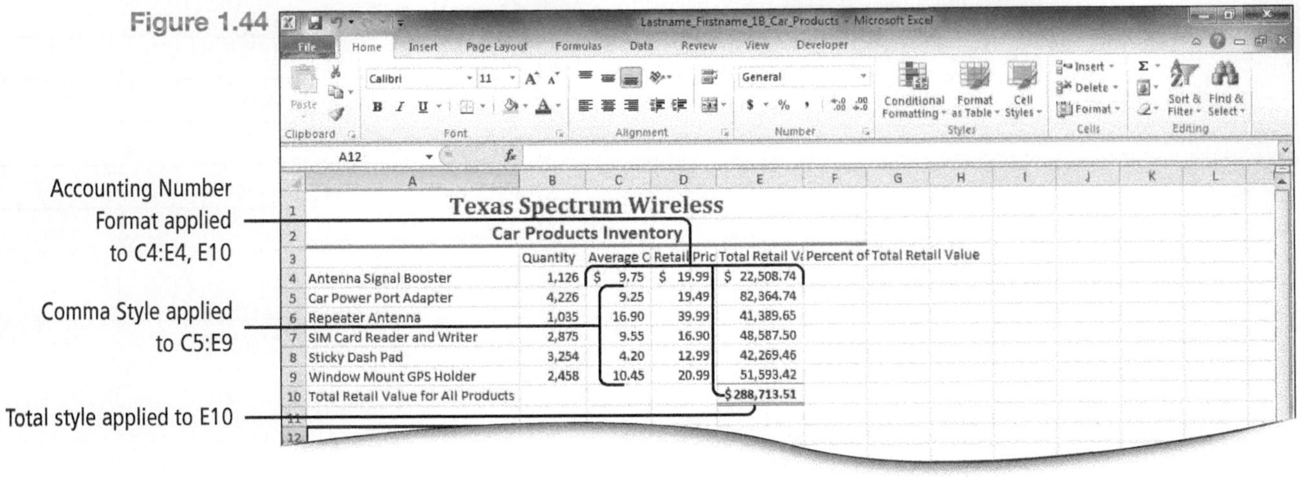

11 **Save** your workbook.

> **More Knowledge | Multiple Status Bar Calculations**
>
> You can display a total of six calculations on the status bar. To add additional calculations—Minimum, Maximum, and Numerical Count (the number of selected cells that contain a number value)—right-click on the status bar, and then click the additional calculations that you want to display.

Activity 1.20 | Copying Formulas Containing Absolute Cell References

In a formula, a relative cell reference refers to a cell by its position *in relation to* the cell that contains the formula. An ***absolute cell reference***, on the other hand, refers to a cell by its *fixed* position in the worksheet, for example, the total in cell E10.

A relative cell reference automatically adjusts when a formula is copied. In some calculations, you do *not* want the cell reference to adjust; rather, you want the cell reference to remain the same when the formula is copied.

1 Click cell **F4**, type **=** and then click cell **E4**. Type **/** and then click cell **E10**.

The formula *=E4/E10* indicates that the value in cell E4 will be *divided* by the value in cell E10. Why? Because Ms. Lovrick wants to know the percentage by which each product's Total Retail Value makes up the Total Retail Value for All Products.

Arithmetically, the percentage is computed by dividing the *Total Retail Value* for each product by the *Total Retail Value for All Products*. The result will be a percentage expressed as a decimal.

2 Press Enter. Click cell **F4** and notice that the formula displays in the **Formula Bar**. Then, point to cell **F4** and double-click.

The formula, with the two referenced cells displayed in color and bordered with the same color, displays in the cell. This feature, called the ***range finder***, is useful for verifying formulas because it visually indicates which workbook cells are included in a formula calculation.

3 Press Enter to redisplay the result of the calculation in the cell, and notice that approximately 8% of the total retail value of the inventory is made up of Antenna Signal Boosters.

4 Click cell **F4** again, and then drag the fill handle down through cell **F9**. Compare your screen with Figure 1.45.

Each cell displays an error message—*#DIV/0!* and a green triangle in the upper left corner of each cell indicates that Excel detects an error.

Like a grammar checker, Excel uses rules to check for formula errors and flags errors in this manner. Additionally, the Auto Fill Options button displays, from which you can select formatting options for the copied cells.

Figure 1.45

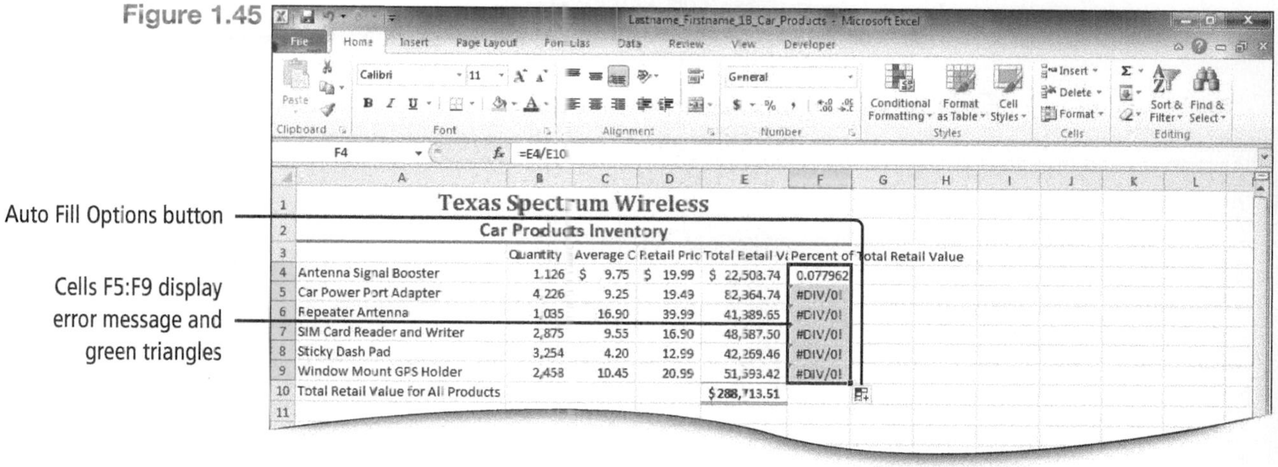

5 Click cell **F5**, and to the left of the cell, point to the **Error Checking** button to display its ScreenTip—*The formula or function used is dividing by zero or empty cells.*

In this manner, Excel suggests the cause of an error.

6 Look at the **Formula Bar** and examine the formula.

The formula is *=E5/E11*. The cell reference to *E5* is correct, but the cell reference following the division operator (/) is *E11*, and E11 is an *empty* cell.

7 Click cell **F6**, point to the **Error Checking** button, and in the **Formula Bar** examine the formula.

Because the cell references are relative, Excel builds the formulas by increasing the row number for each equation. But in this calculation, the divisor must always be the value in cell E10—the *Total Retail Value for All Products.*

8 Point to cell **F4**, and then double-click to place the insertion point within the cell.

Another Way

Edit the formula so that it indicates *=E4/$E$10*

9 Within the cell, use the arrow keys as necessary to position the insertion point to the left of *E10*, and then press F4. Compare your screen with Figure 1.46.

Dollar signs ($) display, which changes the reference to cell E10 to an absolute cell reference. The use of the dollar sign to denote an absolute reference is not related in any way to whether or not the values you are working with are currency values. It is simply the symbol that Excel uses to denote an absolute cell reference.

Figure 1.46

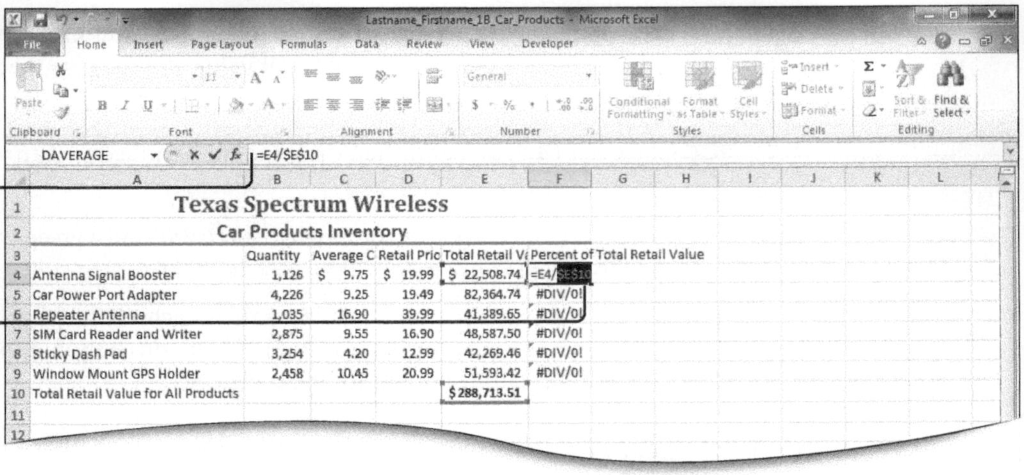

Edited formula with dollar signs denoting an absolute cell reference

10 On the **Formula Bar**, click the **Enter** button so that **F4** remains the active cell. Then, drag the fill handle to copy the new formula down through cell **F9**. Compare your screen with Figure 1.47.

Figure 1.47

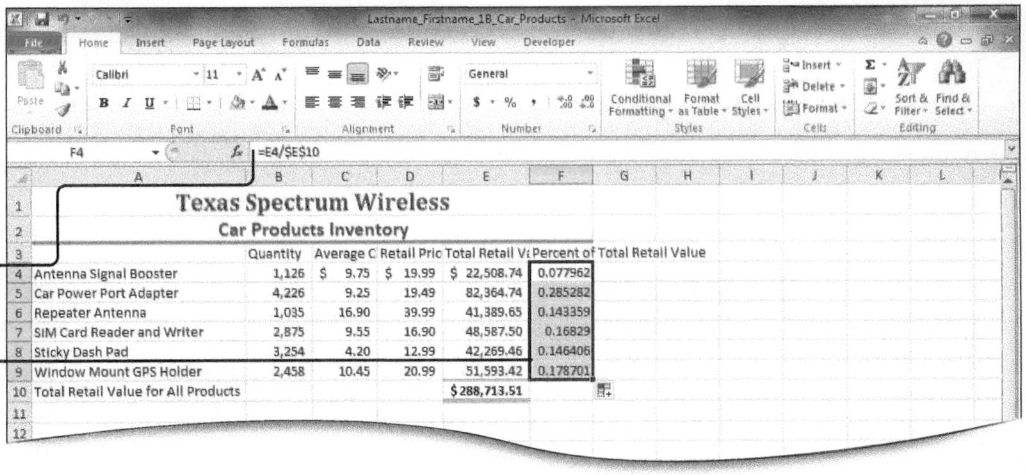

Formula containing absolute cell reference for the first cell in selected range

Percentage of total (E10) calculated for each product

11 Click cell **F5**, examine the formula in the **Formula Bar**, and then examine the formulas for cells **F6**, **F7**, **F8**, and **F9**.

For each formula, the cell reference for the *Total Retail Value* of each product changed relative to its row; however, the value used as the divisor—*Total Retail Value for All Products* in cell F10—remained absolute. Thus, using either relative or absolute cell references, it is easy to duplicate formulas without typing them.

12 **Save** your workbook.

More Knowledge | Calculate a Percentage if You Know the Total and the Amount

Using the equation *amount/total = percentage*, you can calculate the percentage by which a part makes up a total—with the percentage formatted as a decimal. For example, if on a test you score 42 points correctly out of 50, your percentage of correct answers is 42/50 = 0.84 or 84%.

Objective 10 | Edit Values in a Worksheet

Excel performs calculations on numbers; that is why you use Excel. If you make changes to the numbers, Excel automatically *re*-calculates. This is one of the most powerful and valuable features of Excel.

Activity 1.21 | Editing Values in a Worksheet

You can edit text and number values directly within a cell or on the Formula Bar.

1 In cell **E10**, notice the column total *$288,713.51*. Then, click cell **B5**, and to change its value type **3546** Watch cell **E5** and press [Enter].

Excel formulas *re-calculate* if you change the value in a cell that is referenced in a formula. It is not necessary to delete the old value in a cell; selecting the cell and typing a new value replaces the old value with your new typing.

The *Total Retail Value* of all *Car Power Port Adapters* items recalculates to *69,111.54* and the total in cell E10 recalculates to *$275,460.31*. Additionally, all of the percentages in column F recalculate.

2 Point to cell **D8**, and then double-click to place the insertion point within the cell. Use the arrow keys to move the insertion point to left or right of *2*, and use either [Del] or [Backspace] to delete *2* and then type **1** so that the new Retail Price is *11.99*.

3 Watch cell **E8** and **E10** as you press [Enter], and then notice the recalculation of the formulas in those two cells.

Excel recalculates the value in cell E8 to *39,015.46* and the value in cell E10 to *$272,206.31*. Additionally, all of the percentages in column F recalculate because the *Total Retail Value for All Products* recalculated.

4 Point to cell **A2** so that the [✥] pointer is positioned slightly to the right of the word *Inventory*, and then double-click to place the insertion point in the cell. Edit the text to add the word **Valuation** pressing [Spacebar] as necessary, and then press [Enter].

5 Click cell **B3**, and then in the **Formula Bar**, click to place the insertion point after the letter *y*. Press [Spacebar] one time, type **In Stock** and then on the **Formula Bar**, click the **Enter** button [✓]. Click **Save** [💾], and then compare your screen with Figure 1.48.

Recall that if text is too long to fit in the cell and the cell to the right contains data, the text is truncated—cut off—but the entire value still exists as the underlying value.

Figure 1.48

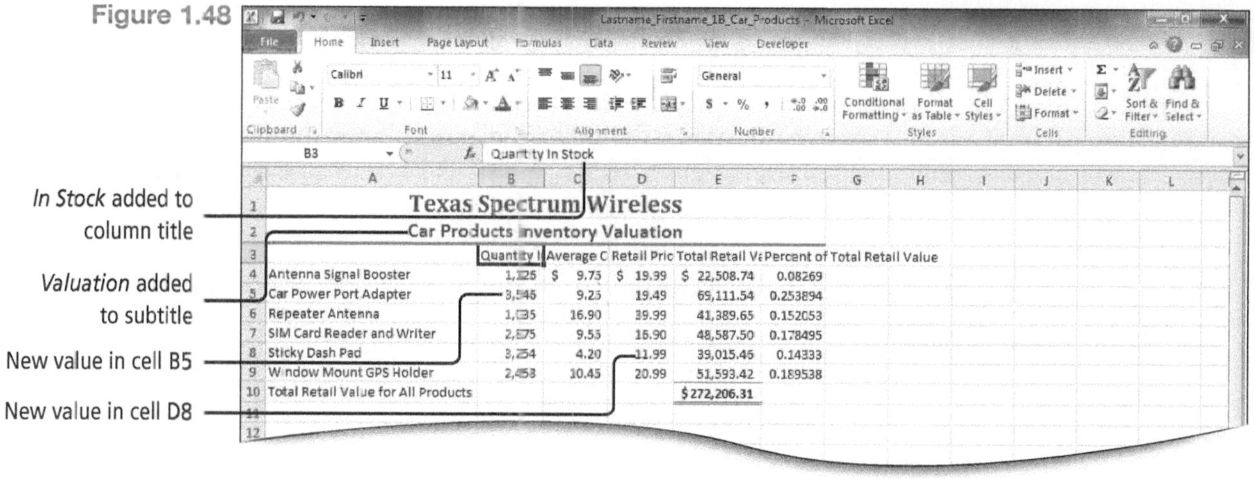

Activity 1.22 | Formatting Cells with the Percent Style

A percentage is part of a whole expressed in hundredths. For example, 75 cents is the same as 75 percent of one dollar. The Percent Style button formats the selected cell as a percentage rounded to the nearest hundredth.

1 Click cell **F4**, and then in the **Number group**, click the **Percent Style** button [%].

Your result is 8%, which is *0.08269* rounded to the nearest hundredth and expressed as a percentage. Percent Style displays the value of a cell as a percentage.

2 Select the range **F4:F9**, right-click over the selection, and then on the Mini toolbar, click the **Percent Style** button [%], click the **Increase Decimal** button [.00] two times, and then click the **Center** [≡] button.

Percent Style may not offer a percentage precise enough to analyze important financial information—adding additional decimal places to a percentage makes data more precise.

3 Click any cell to cancel the selection, **Save** [💾] your workbook, and then compare your screen with Figure 1.49.

Figure 1.49

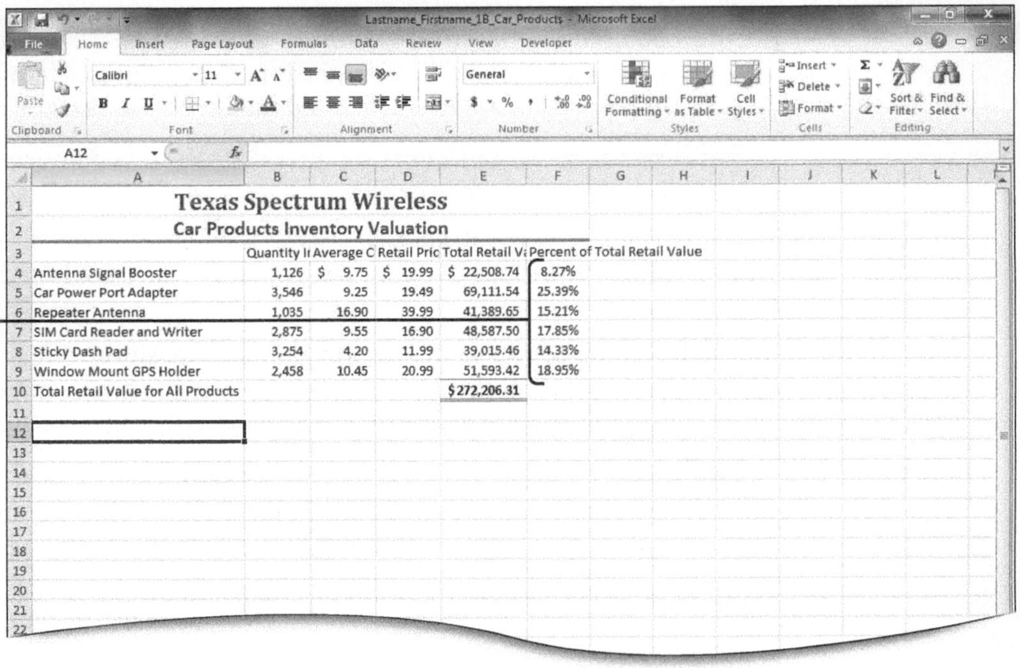

F4:F9 formatted with Percent Style and two decimal places

Objective 11 | Format a Worksheet

Formatting refers to the process of specifying the appearance of cells and the overall layout of your worksheet. Formatting is accomplished through various commands on the Ribbon, for example, applying Cell Styles, and also from shortcut menus, keyboard shortcuts, and the Format Cells dialog box.

Activity 1.23 | Inserting and Deleting Rows and Columns

1 In the **row heading area** on the left side of your screen, point to the row heading for **row 3** to display the [→] pointer, and then right-click to simultaneously select the row and display a shortcut menu.

> **Another Way**
>
> Select the row, on the Home tab, in the Cells group, click the Insert button arrow, and then click Insert Sheet Rows. Or, select the row and click the Insert button—the default setting of the button inserts a new sheet row above the selected row.

2 On the displayed shortcut menu, click **Insert** to insert a new **row 3**.

The rows below the new row 3 move down one row, and the Insert Options button displays. By default, the new row uses the formatting of the row *above*.

3 Click cell **E11**. On the **Formula Bar**, notice that the range changed to sum the new range **E5:E10**. Compare your screen with Figure 1.50.

If you move formulas by inserting additional rows or columns in your worksheet, Excel automatically adjusts the formulas. Excel adjusted all of the formulas in the worksheet that were affected by inserting this new row.

Figure 1.50

Formula Bar displays the formula in E11

New row 3 inserted

Insert Options button

Cell E11 selected

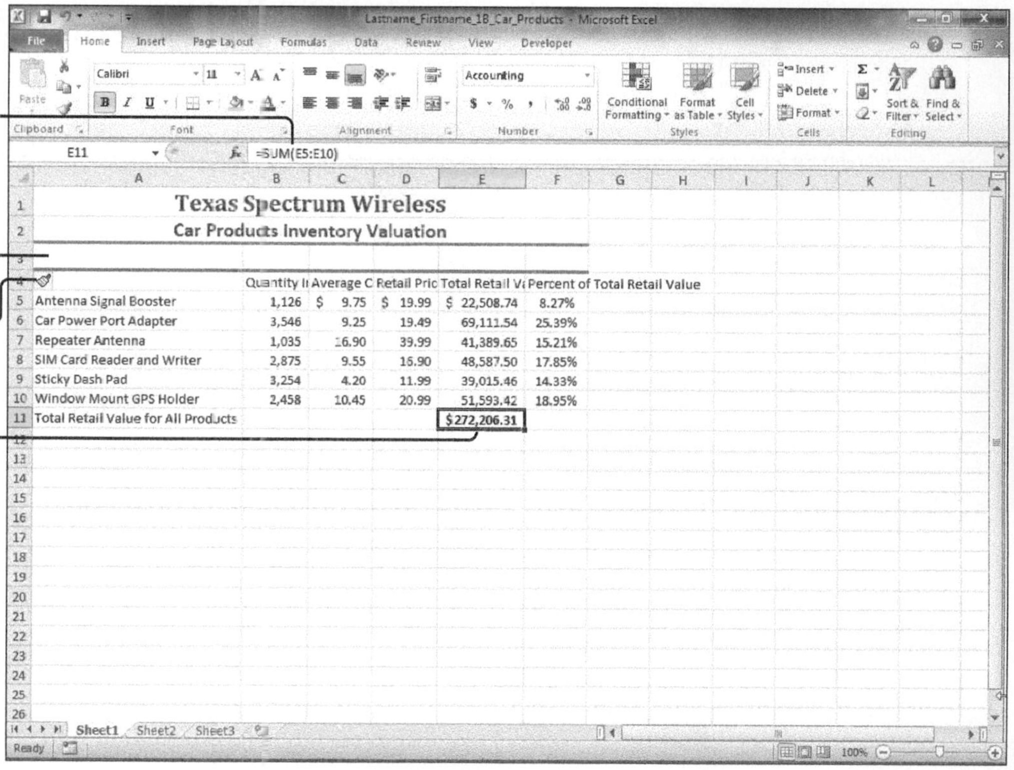

> **Another Way**
>
> Select the column, on the Home tab, in the Cells group, click the Insert button arrow, and then click Insert Sheet Columns. Or, select the column and click the Insert button—the default setting of the button inserts a new sheet column to the right of the selected column.

4 Click cell **A3**, type **As of December 31** and then on the **Formula Bar**, click the **Enter** button ✓ to maintain **A3** as the active cell. **Merge & Center** the text across the range **A3:F3**, and then apply the **Heading 2** cell style.

5 In the **column heading area**, point to **column B** to display the ⬇ pointer, right-click, and then click **Insert**.

By default, the new column uses the formatting of the column to the *left*.

6 Click cell **B4**, type **Warehouse Location** and then press Enter.

7 In cell **B5**, type **Dallas** and then type **Dallas** again in cells **B6** and **B10**. Use AutoComplete to speed your typing by pressing Enter as soon as the AutoComplete suggestion displays. In cells **B7**, **B8**, and **B9**, type **Houston**

8 In the **column heading area**, point to **column D**, right-click, and then click **Delete**.

The remaining columns shift to the left, and Excel adjusts all the formulas in the worksheet accordingly. You can use a similar technique to delete a row in a worksheet.

9 Compare your screen with Figure 1.51, and then **Save** your workbook.

Figure 1.51

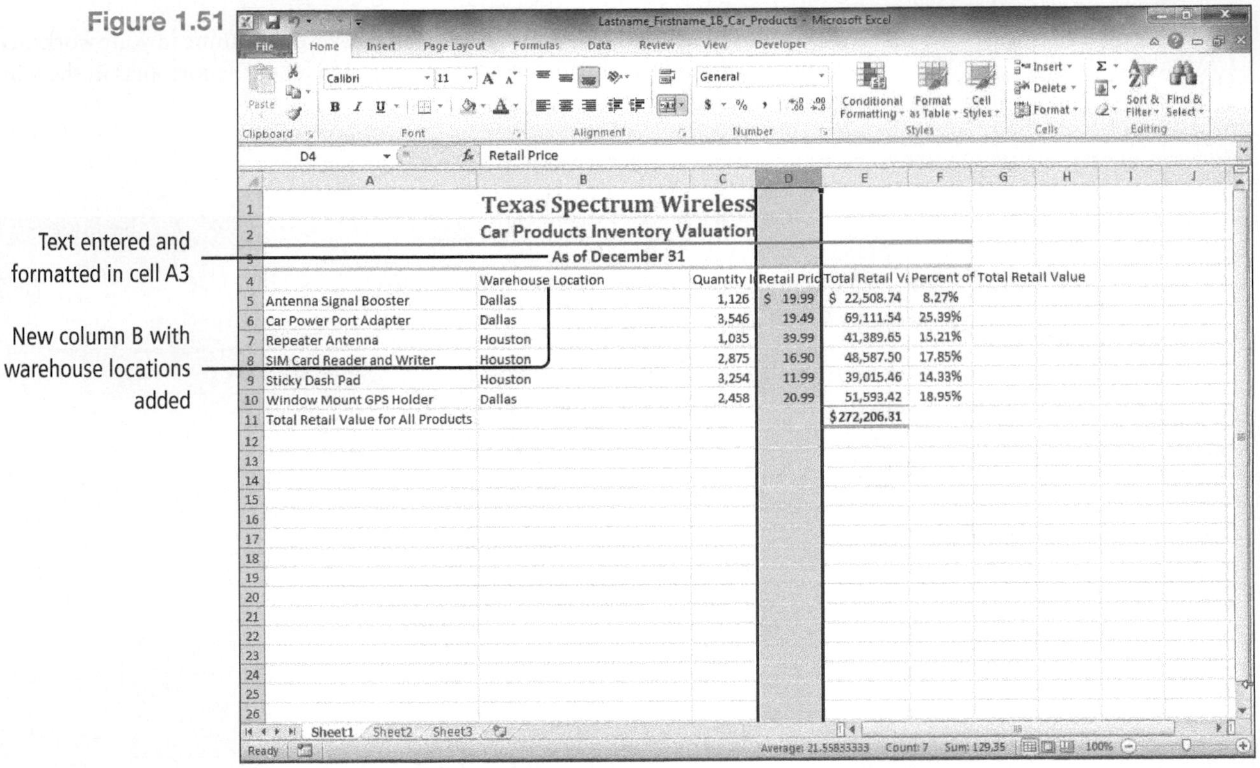

Activity 1.24 | Adjusting Column Widths and Wrapping Text

Use the Wrap Text command to display the contents of a cell on multiple lines.

1 In the **column heading area**, point to the **column B** heading to display the pointer, and then drag to the right to select **columns B:F**.

2 With the columns selected, in the **column heading area**, point to the right boundary of any of the selected columns to display the pointer, and then drag to set the width to **90 pixels**.

Use this technique to format multiple columns or rows simultaneously.

3 Select the range **B4:F4** that comprises the column headings, and then on the **Home tab**, in the **Alignment group**, click the **Wrap Text** button. Notice that the row height adjusts.

4 With the range **B4:F4** still selected, in the **Alignment group**, click the **Center** button and the **Middle Align** button. With the range **B4:F4** still selected, apply the **Heading 4** cell style.

The Middle Align command aligns text so that it is centered between the top and bottom of the cell.

5 Select the range **B5:B10**, right-click, and then on the shortcut menu, click the **Center** button [≡]. Click cell **A11**, and then from the **Cell Styles** gallery, under **Themed Cell Styles**, click **40% - Accent1**. Click any blank cell, and then compare your screen with Figure 1.52.

Figure 1.52

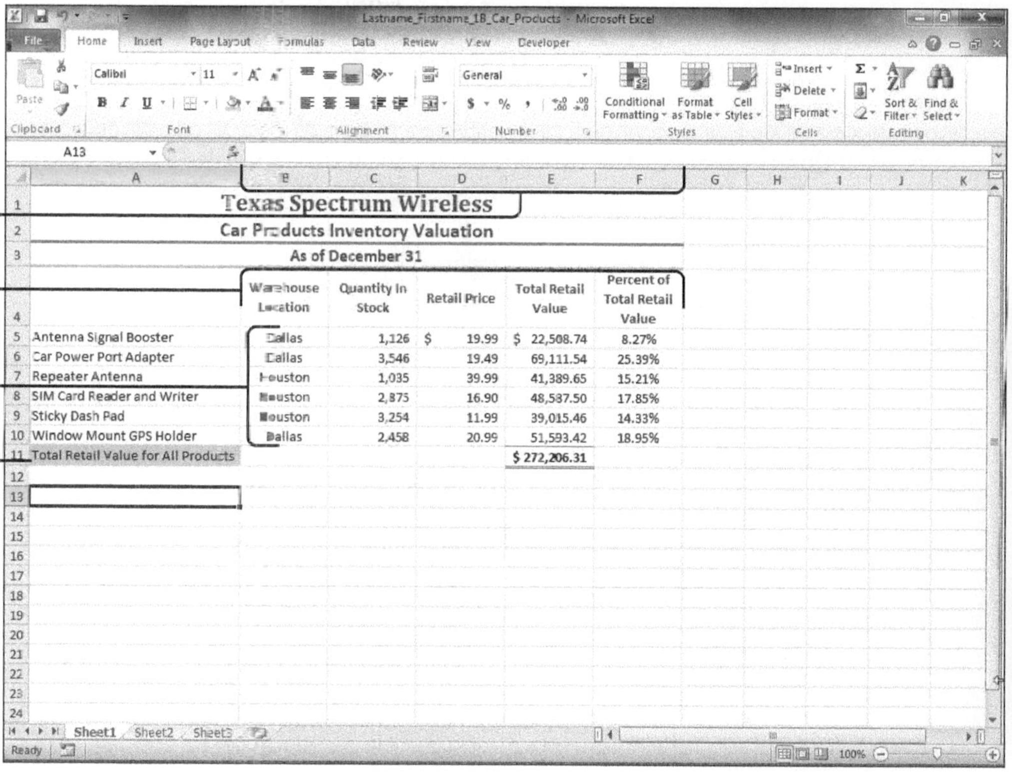

6 Click the **Insert tab**, and then in the **Text group**, click **Header & Footer** to switch to Page Layout view and open the **Header area**.

7 In the **Navigation group**, click the **Go to Footer** button to move to the bottom of the page and open the **Footer area**, and then click just above the word *Footer* to place the insertion point in the **left section** of the **Footer area**.

8 In the **Header & Footer Elements group**, click the **File Name** button to add the name of your file to the footer—*&[File]* displays in the left section of the **Footer area**. Then, click in a cell above the footer to exit the **Footer area** and view your file name.

9 Click the **Page Layout tab**, in the **Page Setup group**, click the **Margins** button, and then at the bottom of the **Margins gallery**, click **Custom Margins**. In the **Page Setup** dialog box, under **Center on page**, select the **Horizontally** check box; click **OK**.

10 In the upper left corner of your screen, click **File** to display **Backstage** view. On the **Info tab**, on the right under the screen thumbnail, click **Properties**, and then click **Show Document Panel**.

11 In the **Author** box, replace the existing text with your firstname and lastname. In the **Subject** box, type your course name and section number. In the **Keywords** box, type **car products, inventory** and then **Close** [×] the **Document Information Panel**.

12 Press Ctrl + F2 to view the **Print Preview**. At the bottom of the **Print Preview**, click the **Next Page** button ▶, and notice that as currently formatted, the worksheet occupies two pages.

13 In the center panel, under **Settings**, click **Portrait Orientation**, and then click **Landscape Orientation**. Compare your screen with Figure 1.53.

You can change the orientation on the Page Layout tab, or here, in the Print Preview. Because it is in the Print Preview that you will often see adjustments that need to be made, commonly used settings display on the Print tab in Backstage view.

Figure 1.53

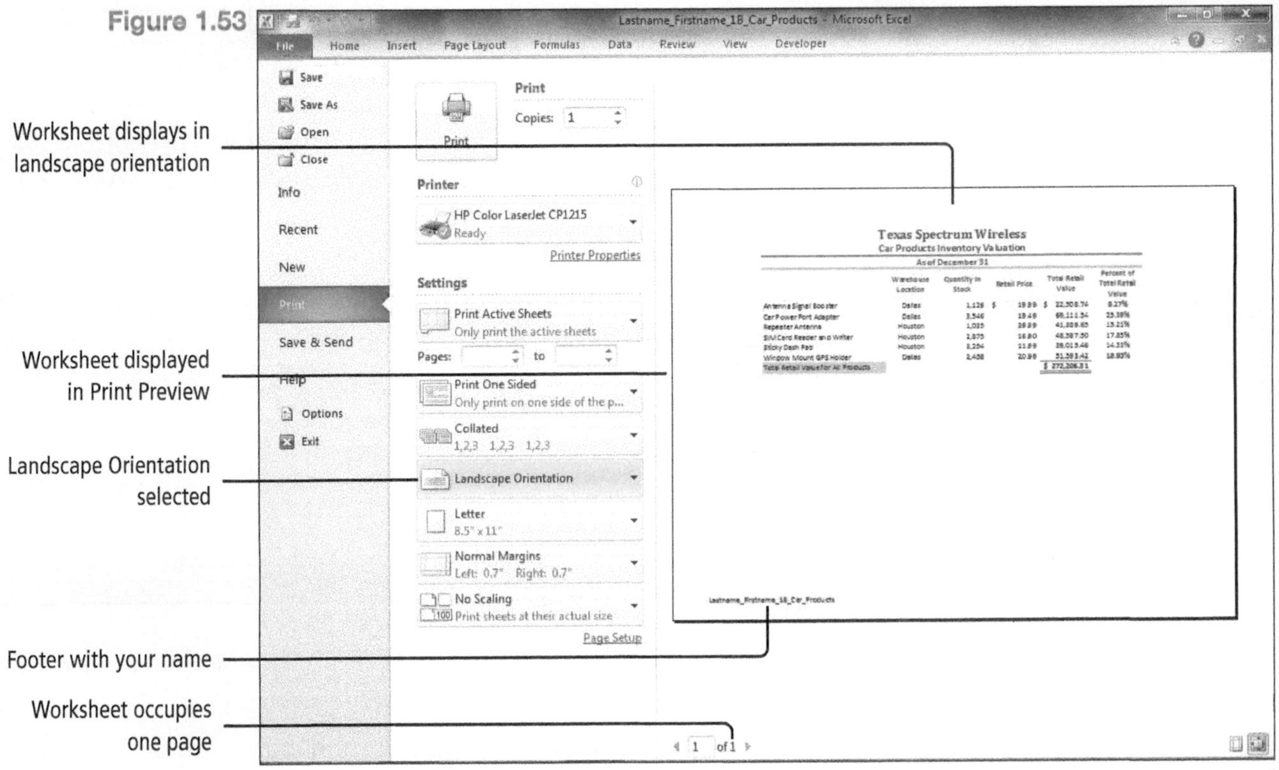

14 Note any additional adjustments or corrections that need to be made, and then on the Ribbon, click **Home** to redisplay your worksheet. In the lower right corner of your screen, on the right side of the status bar, click the **Normal** button ▦ to return to the Normal view, and then press Ctrl + Home to return to cell **A1**.

15 Make any necessary corrections. Then, at the bottom of your worksheet, click the **Sheet2 tab** to make it the active worksheet. Hold down Ctrl, and then click the **Sheet3 tab**. Release Ctrl, and then with both sheets selected (tab background is white), point to either of the selected sheet tabs, right-click, and click **Delete** to delete the unused sheets in the workbook.

16 **Save** [Save icon] your workbook.

17 Print or submit your worksheet electronically as directed by your instructor. If required by your instructor, print or create an electronic version of your worksheet with formulas displayed using the instructions in Activity 1.16 in Project 1A.

18 Close your workbook and close Excel.

End **You have completed Project 1B**

Content-Based Assessments

Summary

In this chapter, you used Microsoft Excel 2010 to create and analyze data organized into columns and rows and to chart and perform calculations on the data. By organizing your data with Excel, you will be able to make calculations and create visual representations of your data in the form of charts.

Key Terms

Matching

Match each term in the second column with its correct definition in the first column by writing the letter of the term on the blank line in front of the correct definition.

_____ 1. An Excel file that contains one or more worksheets.

_____ 2. Another name for a worksheet.

_____ 3. The intersection of a column and a row.

A Cell

B Cell address

C Cell content

_____	4.	The labels along the lower border of the Excel window that identify each worksheet.
_____	5.	A vertical group of cells in a worksheet.
_____	6.	A horizontal group of cells in a worksheet.
_____	7.	Anything typed into a cell.
_____	8.	Information such as numbers, text, dates, or times of day that you type into a cell.
_____	9.	Text or numbers in a cell that are not a formula.
_____	10.	An equation that performs mathematical calculations on values in a worksheet.
_____	11.	A constant value consisting of only numbers.
_____	12.	Another name for a cell reference.
_____	13.	Another name for a constant value.
_____	14.	The small black square in the lower right corner of a selected cell.
_____	15.	The graphic representation of data in a worksheet.

D Chart
E Column
F Constant value
G Data
H Fill handle
I Formula
J Number value
K Row
L Sheet tabs
M Spreadsheet
N Value
O Workbook

Multiple Choice

Circle the correct answer.

1. On startup, Excel displays a new blank:
A. document **B.** workbook **C.** grid

2. An Excel window element that displays the value or formula contained in the active cell is the:
A. name box **B.** status bar **C.** formula bar

3. An Excel window element that displays the name of the selected cell, table, chart, or object is the:
A. name box **B.** status bar **C.** formula bar

4. A box in the upper left corner of the worksheet grid that selects all the cells in a worksheet is the:
A. name box **B.** select all box **C.** split box

5. A cell surrounded by a black border and ready to receive data is the:
A. active cell **B.** address cell **C.** reference cell

6. The feature that generates and extends values into adjacent cells based on the values of selected cells is:
A. AutoComplete **B.** Auto Fill **C.** fill handle

7. The default format that Excel applies to numbers is the:
A. comma format **B.** accounting format **C.** general format

8. The data that displays in the Formula Bar is referred to as the:
A. constant value **B.** formula **C.** underlying value

9. The type of cell reference that refers to cells by their fixed position in a worksheet is:
A. absolute **B.** relative **C.** exponentiation

10. Tiny charts embedded in a cell that give a visual trend summary alongside your data are:
A. embedded charts **B.** sparklines **C.** chart styles

Apply 1A skills from these Objectives:

1. Create, Save, and Navigate an Excel Workbook
2. Enter Data in a Worksheet
3. Construct and Copy Formulas and Use the Sum Function
4. Format Cells with Merge & Center and Cell Styles
5. Chart Data to Create a Column Chart and Insert Sparklines
6. Print, Display Formulas, and Close Excel

Skills Review | Project 1C GPS Sales

In the following Skills Review, you will create a new Excel worksheet with a chart that summarizes the first quarter sales of GPS (Global Positioning System) navigation devices. Your completed worksheet will look similar to Figure 1.54.

Project Files

For Project 1C, you will need the following file:

New blank Excel workbook

You will save your workbook as:

Lastname_Firstname_1C_GPS_Sales

Project Results

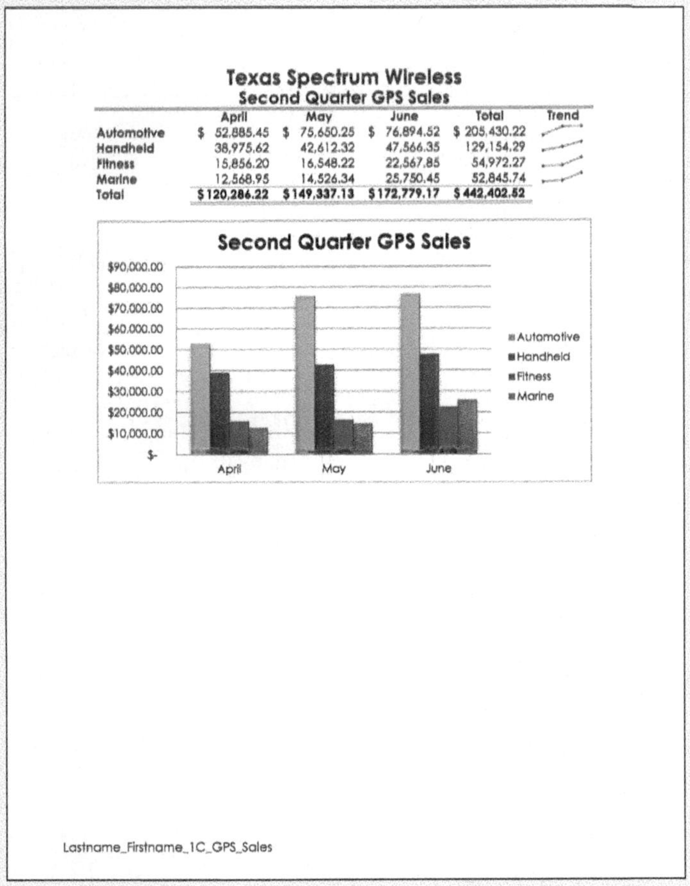

Texas Spectrum Wireless

Second Quarter GPS Sales

	April	May	June	Total	Trend
Automotive	$ 52,885.45	$ 75,650.25	$ 76,894.52	$ 205,430.22	
Handheld	38,975.62	42,612.32	47,566.35	129,154.29	
Fitness	15,856.20	16,548.22	22,567.85	54,972.27	
Marine	12,568.95	14,526.34	25,750.45	52,845.74	
Total	$ 120,286.22	$ 149,337.13	$ 172,779.17	$ 442,402.52	

Figure 1.54

(Project 1C GPS Sales continues on the next page)

Skills Review | Project 1C GPS Sales (continued)

1 **Start** Excel. Click the **File tab** to display **Backstage** view, click **Save As**, and then in the **Save As** dialog box, navigate to your **Excel Chapter 1** folder. In the **File name** box, using your own name, type **Lastname_Firstname_1C_GPS_Sales** and then press Enter.

a. With cell **A1** as the active cell, type the worksheet title **Texas Spectrum Wireless** and then press Enter. In cell **A2**, type the worksheet subtitle **Second Quarter GPS Sales** and then press Enter.

b. Click in cell **A4**, type **Automotive** and then press Enter. In cell **A5**, type **Handheld** and then press Enter. In cell **A6**, type **Fitness** and then press Enter. In cell **A7**, type **Marine** and then press Enter. In cell **A8**, type **Total** and then press Enter.

c. Click cell **B3**. Type **April** and then in the **Formula Bar**, click the **Enter** button to keep cell **B3** the active cell. With **B3** as the active cell, point to the fill handle in the lower right corner of the selected cell, drag to the right to cell **D3**, and then release the mouse button to enter the text *May* and *June*.

d. Press Ctrl + Home, to make cell **A1** the active cell. In the **column heading area**, point to the vertical line between **column A** and **column B** to display the ✛ pointer, hold down the left mouse button and drag to the right to increase the column width to **100 pixels**.

e. Point to cell **B3**, and then drag across to select cells **B3** and **C3** and **D3**. With the range **B3:D3** selected, point anywhere over the selected range, right-click, and then on the Mini toolbar, click the **Center** button.

f. Click cell **B4**, type **52885.45** and press Tab to make cell **C4** active. Enter the remaining values, as shown in **Table 1**, pressing Tab to move across the rows and Enter to move down the columns.

2 Click cell **B8** to make it the active cell and type =

a. At the insertion point, type **b4** and then type + Type **b5** and then type **+b6+b7** Press Enter. Your result is *120286.2*.

b. Click in cell **C8**. Type = and then click cell **C4**. Type + and then click cell **C5**. Repeat this process to complete the formula to add cells **C4** through **C7**, and then press Enter. Your result is *149337.1*.

c. Click cell **D8**. On the **Home tab**, in the **Editing group**, click the **Sum** button, and then press Enter to construct a formula by using the SUM function. Your result is *172779.2*. You can use any of these methods to add values; the Sum button is the most efficient.

d. In cell **E3** type **Total** and press Enter. With cell **E4** as the active cell, hold down Alt, and then press =. On the **Formula Bar**, click the **Enter** button to display the result and keep cell **E4** active.

e. With cell **E4** active, point to the fill handle in the lower right corner of the cell. Drag down through cell **E8**, and then release the mouse button to copy the formula with relative cell references down to sum each row.

3 Click cell **F3**. Type **Trend** and then press Enter.

a. Select the range **A1:F1**, and then on the **Home tab**, in the **Alignment group**, click the **Merge & Center** button. Select the range **A2:F2**, and then click the **Merge & Center** button.

b. Click cell **A1**. In the **Styles group**, click the **Cell Styles** button. Under **Titles and Headings**, click **Title**. Click cell **A2**, display the **Cell Styles** gallery, and then click **Heading 1**.

c. Select the range **B3:F3**, hold down Ctrl, and then select the range **A4:A8**. From the **Cell Styles** gallery, click **Heading 4** to apply this cell style to the column and row titles.

d. Select the range **B4:E4**, hold down Ctrl, and then select the range **B8:E8**. On the **Home tab**, in the **Number group**, click the **Accounting Number Format** button. Select the range **B5:E7**, and then in the **Number group**, click the **Comma Style** button. Select the range **B8:E8**. From the **Styles group**, display the **Cell Styles** gallery, and then under **Titles and Headings**, click **Total**.

Table 1

	April	May	June
Automotive	52885.45	75650.25	76894.52
Handheld	38975.62	42612.32	47566.35
Fitness	15856.20	16548.22	22567.85
Marine	12568.95	14526.34	25750.45

---> (Return to Step 2)

(Project 1C GPS Sales continues on the next page)

Excel | Chapter 1

Skills Review | Project 1C GPS Sales (continued)

e. On the Ribbon, click the **Page Layout tab**, and then from the **Themes group**, click the **Themes** button to display the **Themes** gallery. Click the **Austin** theme.

4 Select the range **A3:D7**. Click the **Insert tab**, and then in the **Charts group**, click **Column**. From the gallery of column chart types, under **2-D Column**, click the first chart—**Clustered Column**.

a. On the Quick Access Toolbar, click the **Save** button to be sure that you have saved your work up to this point. Point to the top border of the chart to display the pointer, and then drag to position the chart inside the upper left corner of cell **A10**.

b. On the **Design tab**, in the **Data group**, click the **Switch Row/Column** button so that the months display on the Horizontal (Category) axis and the types of GPS equipment display in the legend.

c. On the **Design tab**, in the **Chart Layouts group**, click the first layout—**Layout 1**.

d. In the chart, click anywhere in the text *Chart Title* to select the text box. Type **Second Quarter GPS Sales** and then press Enter.

e. Click anywhere in the chart so that the chart title text box is not selected. On the **Design tab**, in the **Chart Styles group**, click the **More** button. Using the ScreenTips as your guide, locate and click **Style 18**.

f. Point to the lower right corner of the chart to display the pointer, and then drag down and to the right so that the lower right border of the chart is positioned just inside the lower right corner of cell **F26**.

5 Select the range **B4:D7**. Click the **Insert tab**, and then in the **Sparklines group**, click **Line**. In the **Create Sparklines** dialog box, in the **Location Range** box, type **f4:f7** and then click **OK** to insert the sparklines.

a. On the **Design tab**, in the **Show group**, select the **Markers** check box to display markers in the sparklines.

b. On the **Design tab**, in the **Style group**, click the **More** button, and then in the second row, click the fourth style—**Sparkline Style Accent 4, Darker 25%**.

6 On the **Insert tab**, in the **Text group**, click **Header & Footer** to switch to **Page Layout** view and open the **Header** area.

a. In the **Navigation group**, click the **Go to Footer** button to open the Footer area. Click just above the word *Footer* to place the insertion point in the **left section** of the Footer.

b. In the **Header & Footer Elements group**, click the **File Name** button, and then click in a cell just above the footer to exit the Footer area.

7 On the right side of the status bar, click the **Normal** button to return to Normal view, and then press Ctrl + Home to make cell **A1** active.

a. Click the **File tab**, and then on the right, click **Properties**. Click **Show Document Panel**, and then in the **Author** box, delete any text and type your firstname and lastname. In the **Subject** box, type your course name and section number, and in the **Keywords** box, type **GPS sales Close** the Document Information Panel.

b. At the bottom of your worksheet, click the **Sheet2** tab. Hold down Ctrl, and then click the **Sheet3** tab. With both sheets selected, point to either of the selected sheet tabs, right-click, and then click **Delete** to delete the sheets.

c. Click the **Page Layout tab**. In the **Page Setup group**, click the **Margins** button, and then at the bottom of the **Margins** gallery, click **Custom Margins**. In the **Page Setup** dialog box, under **Center on page**, select the **Horizontally** check box.

d. In the lower right corner of the **Page Setup** dialog box, click **OK**. On the **File tab**, click **Print** to view the **Print Preview**. Click the **Home tab** to return to Normal view and if necessary, make any necessary corrections and resize and move your chart so that it is centered under the worksheet.

e. On the Quick Access Toolbar, click the **Save** button to be sure that you have saved your work up to this point.

f. Print or submit your workbook electronically as directed by your instructor. If required by your instructor, print or create an electronic version of your worksheets with formulas displayed by using the instructions in Activity 1.16. **Exit** Excel without saving so that you do not save the changes you made to print formulas.

End **You have completed Project 1C**

Apply 1B skills from these Objectives:

- 7 Check Spelling in a Worksheet
- 8 Enter Data by Range
- 9 Construct Formulas for Mathematical Operations
- 10 Edit Values in a Worksheet
- 11 Format a Worksheet

Skills Review | Project 1D Charger Inventory

In the following Skills Review, you will create a worksheet that summarizes the inventory of cell phone chargers. Your completed worksheet will look similar to Figure 1.55.

Project Files

For Project 1D, you will need the following file:

New blank Excel workbook

You will save your workbook as:

Lastname_Firstname_1D_Charger_Inventory

Project Results

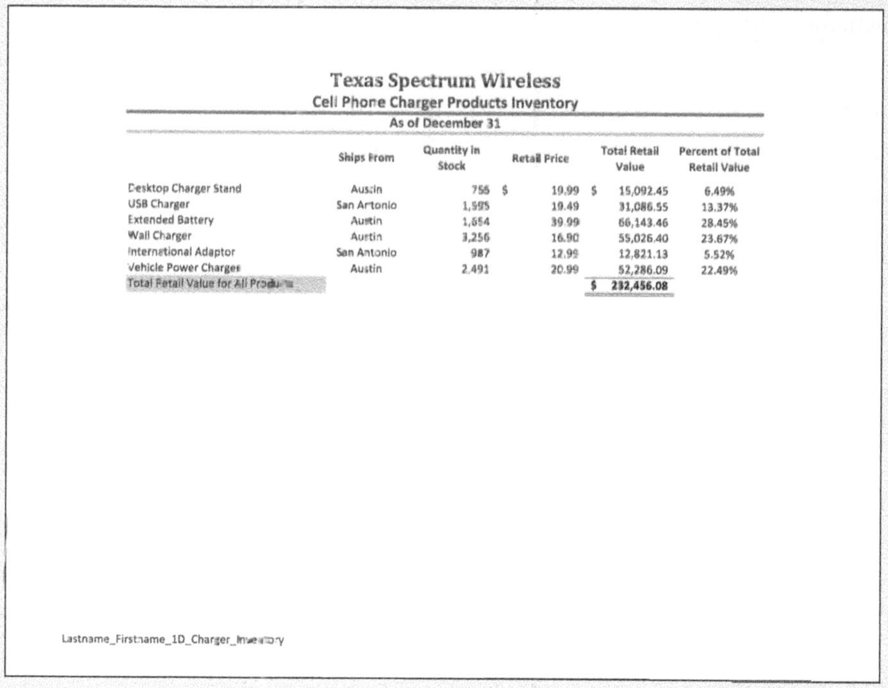

Texas Spectrum Wireless

Cell Phone Charger Products Inventory

As of December 31

	Ships From	Quantity in Stock	Retail Price	Total Retail Value	Percent of Total Retail Value
Desktop Charger Stand	Austin	755	$ 19.99	$ 15,092.45	6.49%
USB Charger	San Antonio	1,595	19.49	31,086.55	13.37%
Extended Battery	Austin	1,654	39.99	66,143.46	28.45%
Wall Charger	Austin	3,256	16.90	55,026.40	23.67%
International Adaptor	San Antonio	987	12.99	12,821.13	5.52%
Vehicle Power Charger	Austin	2,491	20.99	52,286.09	22.49%
Total Retail Value for All Produ				$ 232,456.08	

Lastname_Firstname_1D_Charger_Inventory

Figure 1.55

(Project 1D Charger Inventory continues on the next page)

Skills Review | Project 1D Charger Inventory (continued)

1 **Start** Excel and display a new blank workbook. **Save** the workbook in your **Excel Chapter 1** folder, as **Lastname_Firstname_1D_Charger_Inventory** In cell **A1** type **Texas Spectrum Wireless** and in cell **A2** type **Cell Phone Charger Products Inventory**

a. Click cell **B3**, type **Quantity in Stock** and press Tab. In cell **C3** type **Average Cost** and press Tab. In cell **D3**, type **Retail Price** and press Tab. In cell **E3**, type **Total Retail Value** and press Tab. In cell **F3** type **Percent of Total Retail Value** and press Enter.

b. Click cell **A4**, type **Desktop Charger Stand** and press Enter. In the range **A5:A10**, type the remaining row titles as shown, including the misspelled words.

USB Charger

Extended Battery

Wall Charger

International Adaptor

Vehicle Powr Charger

Total Retail Value for All Products

c. Press Ctrl + Home to move to the top of your worksheet. On the **Review tab**, in the **Proofing group**, click the **Spelling** button. Correct *Powr* to **Power** and any other spelling errors you may have made, and then when the message displays, *The spelling check is complete for the entire sheet*, click **OK**.

d. In the **column heading area**, point to the right boundary of **column A** to display the ⟷ pointer, and then drag to the right to widen **column A** to **225** pixels.

e. In the **column heading area**, point to the **column B** heading to display the ↓ pointer, and then drag to the right to select **columns B:F**.With the columns selected, in the **column heading area**, point to the right boundary of any of the selected columns, and then drag to the right to set the width to **100 pixels**.

f. Select the range **A1:F1**. On the **Home tab**, in the **Alignment group**, click the **Merge & Center** button, and then from the **Cell Styles** gallery, apply the **Title** style. Select the range **A2:F2**. **Merge & Center** the text across the selection, and then from the **Cell Styles** gallery, apply the **Heading 1** style.

2 Select the empty range **B4:D9**. With cell B4 active in the range, type **755** and then press Enter.

a. With cell **B5** active in the range, and pressing Enter after each entry, type the following data in the *Quantity in Stock* column:

1595

2654

3256

987

2491

b. With the selected range still active, from the following table, beginning in cell **C4** and pressing Enter after each entry, enter the following data for the **Average Cost** column and then the **Retail Price** column. If you prefer, type without selecting the range first; recall that this is optional.

Average Cost	Retail Price
9.75	19.99
9.25	19.49
16.90	39.99
9.55	16.90
14.20	12.99
10.45	20.99

3 In cell **E4**, type **=b4*d4** and then press Enter to construct a formula that calculates the *Total Retail Value* of the *Desktop Charger Stands* (Quantity × Retail Price).

a. Click cell **E4**, position your pointer over the fill handle, and then drag down through cell **E9** to copy the formula.

b. Select the range **B4:B9**, and then on the **Home tab**, in the **Number group**, click the **Comma Style** button. Then, in the **Number group**, click the **Decrease Decimal** button two times to remove the decimal places from these non-currency values.

c. Click cell **E10**, in the **Editing group**, click the **Sum** button, and then press Enter to calculate the *Total Retail Value for All Products*. Your result is *272446.1*.

d. Select the range **C5:E9** and apply the **Comma Style**. Select the range **C4:E4**, hold down Ctrl, and then click cell **E10**. With the nonadjacent cells selected, apply the **Accounting Number Format**. Click cell **E10**, and then from the **Cell Styles** gallery, apply the **Total** style.

(Project 1D Charger Inventory continues on the next page)

Skills Review | Project 1D Charger Inventory (continued)

e. Click cell **F4**, type = and then click cell **E4**. Type / and then click cell **E10**. Press F4 to make the reference to cell *E10* absolute, and then on the **Formula Bar**, click the **Enter** button so that **F4** remains the active cell. Drag the fill handle to copy the formula down through cell **F9**.

f. Point to cell **B6**, and then double-click to place the insertion point within the cell. Use the arrow keys to move the insertion point to left or right of *2*, and use either Del or Backspace to delete 2, and then type **1** and press Enter so that the new *Quantity in Stock* is *1654*. Notice the recalculations in the worksheet.

4 Select the range **F4:F9**, right-click over the selection, and then on the Mini toolbar, click the **Percent Style** button. Click the **Increase Decimal** button two times, and then **Center** the selection.

a. In the **row heading area** on the left side of your screen, point to **row 3** to display the → pointer, and then right-click to simultaneously select the row and display a shortcut menu. On the displayed shortcut menu, click **Insert** to insert a new **row 3**.

b. Click cell **A3**, type **As of December 31** and then on the **Formula Bar**, click the **Enter** button to keep cell **A3** as the active cell. **Merge & Center** the text across the range **A3:F3**, and then apply the **Heading 2** cell style.

5 In the **column heading area**, point to **column B**. When the ↓ pointer displays, right-click, and then click **Insert** to insert a new column.

a. Click cell **B4**, and type **Ships From** and press Enter. In cell **B5**, type **Austin** and then press Enter. In cell **B6**, type **San Antonio** and then press Enter

b. Using AutoComplete to speed your typing by pressing Enter as soon as the AutoComplete suggestion displays, in cells **B7**, **B8**, and **B10** type **Austin** and in cell **B9** type **San Antonio**

c. In the **column heading area**, point to the right boundary of **column B**, and then drag to the left and set the width to **90 pixels**. From the **column heading area**, point to **column D**, right-click, and then click **Delete**.

d. Select the range **B4:F4**, and then on the **Home tab**, in the **Alignment group**, click the **Wrap Text** button, the **Center** button, and the **Middle Align** button. With the range still selected, apply the **Heading 4** cell style.

e. Select the range **B5:B10**, right-click, and then click the **Center** button. Click cell **A11**, and then from the **Cell Styles** gallery, under **Themed Cell Styles**, click **40% - Accent1**.

6 On the **Insert tab**, in the **Text group**, click **Header & Footer**. In the **Navigation group**, click the **Go To Footer** button, and then click just above the word *Footer*. In the **Header & Footer Elements group**, click the **File Name** button to add the name of your file to the footer. Click in a cell just above the footer to exit the **Footer area**, and then return the worksheet to **Normal** view.

a. Press Ctrl + Home to move the insertion point to cell **A1**. On the **Page Layout tab**, in the **Page Setup group**, click **Orientation**, and then click **Landscape**.

b. In the **Page Setup group**, click the **Margins** button, and then at the bottom of the **Margins gallery**, click **Custom Margins**. In the **Page Setup** dialog box, under **Center on page**, select the **Horizontally** check box, and then click **OK**.

c. Click the **File tab** to display **Backstage** view, and then on the right, click **Properties**. Click **Show Document Panel**, and then in the **Author** box, delete any text and type your firstname and lastname. In the **Subject** box type your course name and section number, in the **Keywords** box type **cell phone chargers** and then **Close** the **Document Information Panel**.

d. Select **Sheet2** and **Sheet3**, and then **Delete** both sheets.

e. **Save** your file and then print or submit your workbook electronically as directed by your instructor. If required by your instructor, print or create an electronic version of your worksheet with formulas displayed by using the instructions in Activity 1.16. **Exit** Excel without saving so that you do not save the changes you made to print formulas.

End **You have completed Project 1D**

Apply 1A skills from these Objectives:

1. Create, Save, and Navigate an Excel Workbook
2. Enter Data in a Worksheet
3. Construct and Copy Formulas and Use the SUM Function
4. Format Cells with Merge & Center and Cell Styles
5. Chart Data to Create a Column Chart and Insert Sparklines
6. Print, Display Formulas, and Close Excel

Mastering Excel | Project 1E Hard Drives

In the following Mastering Excel project, you will create a worksheet comparing the sales of different types of external hard drives sold in the second quarter. Your completed worksheet will look similar to Figure 1.56.

Project Files

For Project 1E, you will need the following file:

New blank Excel workbook

You will save your workbook as:

Lastname_Firstname_1E_Hard_Drives

Project Results

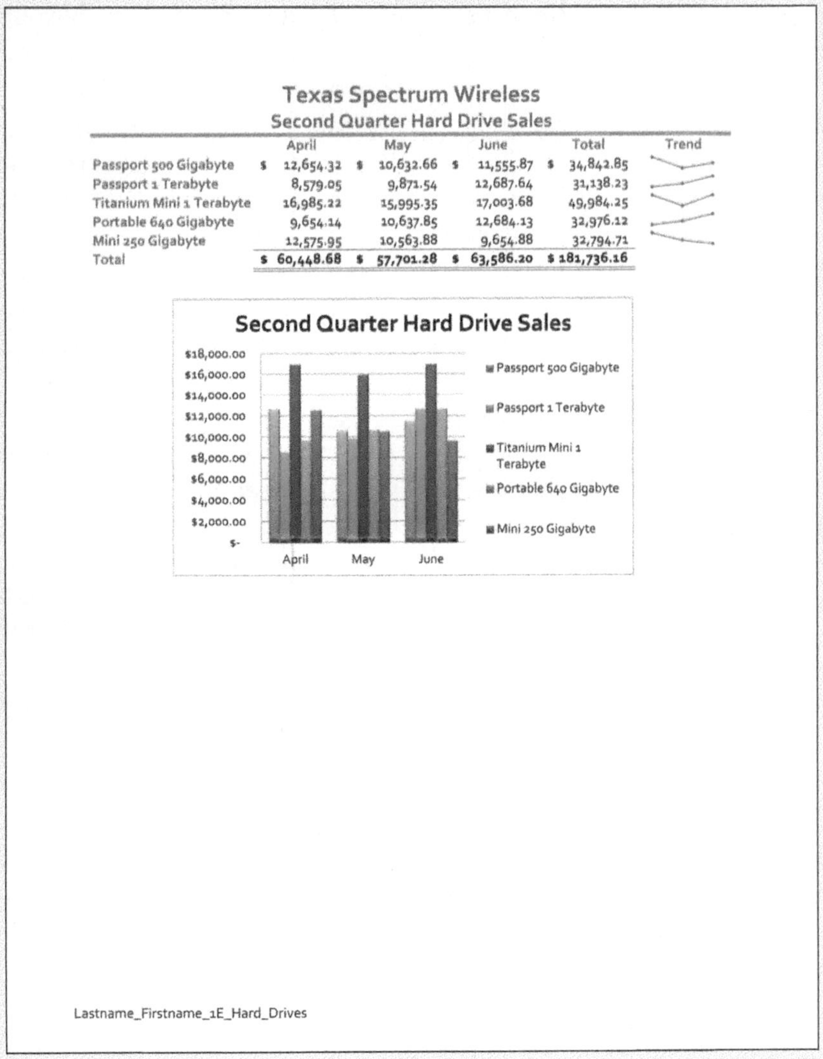
Texas Spectrum Wireless

Second Quarter Hard Drive Sales

	April	May	June	Total	Trend
Passport 500 Gigabyte	$ 12,654.32	$ 10,632.66	$ 11,555.87	$ 34,842.85	
Passport 1 Terabyte	8,579.05	9,871.54	12,687.64	31,138.23	
Titanium Mini 1 Terabyte	16,985.22	15,995.35	17,003.68	49,984.25	
Portable 640 Gigabyte	9,654.14	10,637.85	12,684.13	32,976.12	
Mini 250 Gigabyte	12,575.95	10,563.88	9,654.88	32,794.71	
Total	$ 60,448.68	$ 57,701.28	$ 63,586.20	$ 181,736.16	

Lastname_Firstname_1E_Hard_Drives

Figure 1.56

(Project 1E Hard Drives continues on the next page)

Mastering Excel | Project 1E Hard Drives (continued)

1 **Start** Excel. In cell **A1**, type **Texas Spectrum Wireless** and in cell **A2**, type **Second Quarter Hard Drive Sales** Change the **Theme** to **Module**, and then **Save** the workbook in your **Excel Chapter 1** folder as **Lastname_Firstname_1E_Hard_Drives**

2 In cell **B3**, type **April** and then use the fill handle to enter the months *May* and *June* in the range **C3:D3**. In cell **E3**, type **Total** and in cell **F3**, type **Trend**

3 **Center** the column titles in the range **B3:F3**. **Merge & Center** the title across the range **A1:F1**, and apply the **Title** cell style. **Merge & Center** the subtitle across the range **A2:F2**, and apply the **Heading 1** cell style.

4 Widen **column A** to **170 pixels**, and then in the range **A4:A9**, type the following row titles:

Passport 500 Gigabyte

Passport 1 Terabyte

Titanium Mini 1 Terabyte

Portable 640 Gigabyte

Mini 250 Gigabyte

Total

5 Widen columns **B:F** to **100 pixels**, and then in the range **B4:D8**, enter the monthly sales figures for each type of hard drive, as shown in **Table 1** at the bottom of the page.

6 In cell **B9**, **Sum** the *April* hard drive sales, and then copy the formula across to cells **C9:D9**. In cell **E4**, **Sum** the *Passport 500 Gigabyte sales*, and then copy the formula down to cells **E5:E9**.

7 Apply the **Heading 4** cell style to the row titles and the column titles. Apply the **Total** cell style to the totals in the range **B9:E9**. Apply the **Accounting Number Format** to the first row of sales figures and to the total row. Apply the **Comma Style** to the remaining sales figures.

8 To compare the monthly sales of each product visually, select the range that represents the sales figures for the three months, including the month names, and for each product name—do not include any totals in the range. With this data selected, **Insert** a **2-D Clustered Column** chart. Switch the Row/Column data so that the months display on the category axis and the types of hard drives display in the legend.

9 Position the upper left corner of the chart in the approximate center of cell **A11** so that the chart is visually centered below the worksheet, as shown in Figure 1.56. Apply **Chart Style 26**, and then modify the **Chart Layout** by applying **Layout 1**. Change the **Chart Title** to **Second Quarter Hard Drive Sales**

10 In the range **F4:F8**, insert **Line** sparklines that compare the monthly data. Do not include the totals. Show the sparkline **Markers** and apply **Sparkline Style Accent 2, Darker 50%**—in the first row, the second style.

11 Insert a **Footer** with the **File Name** in the **left section**, and then return the worksheet to **Normal** view. Display the **Document Panel**, add your name, your course name and section, and the keywords **hard drives, sales** Delete the unused sheets, and then center the worksheet **Horizontally** on the page. Check your worksheet by previewing it in **Print Preview**, and then make any necessary corrections.

12 **Save** your workbook, and then print or submit electronically as directed. If required by your instructor, print or create an electronic version of your worksheets with formulas displayed by using the instructions in Activity 1.16. **Exit** Excel without saving so that you do not save the changes you made to print formulas.

Table 1

	April	May	June
Passport 500 Gigabyte	12654.32	10632.66	11555.87
Passport 1 Terabyte	8579.05	9871.54	12687.64
Titanium Mini 1 Terabyte	16985.22	15995.35	17003.68
Portable 640 Gigabyte	9654.14	10637.85	12684.13
Mini 250 Gigabyte	12575.95	10563.88	9654.88

(Return to Step 6)

End **You have completed Project 1E**

Apply 1B skills from these Objectives:

7 Check Spelling in a Worksheet
8 Enter Data by Range
9 Construct Formulas for Mathematical Operations
10 Edit Values in a Worksheet
11 Format a Worksheet

Mastering Excel | Project 1F Camera Accessories

In the following Mastering Excel project, you will create a worksheet that summarizes the sale of digital camera accessories. Your completed worksheet will look similar to Figure 1.57.

Project Files

For Project 1F, you will need the following file:

New blank Excel workbook

You will save your workbook as:

Lastname_Firstname_1F_Camera_Accessories

Project Results

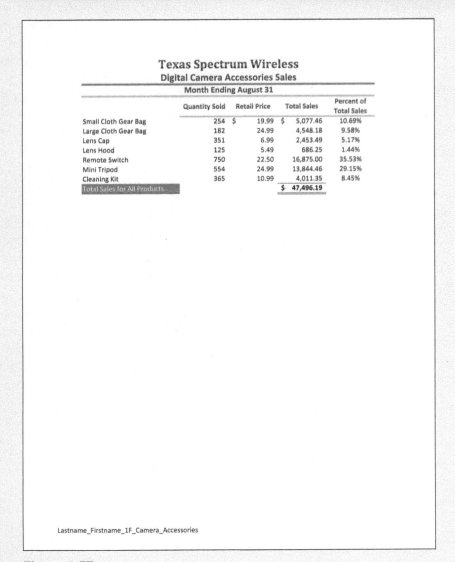

Texas Spectrum Wireless

Digital Camera Accessories Sales

Month Ending August 31

	Quantity Sold	Retail Price	Total Sales	Percent of Total Sales
Small Cloth Gear Bag	254	$ 19.99	$ 5,077.46	10.69%
Large Cloth Gear Bag	182	24.99	4,548.18	9.58%
Lens Cap	351	6.99	2,453.49	5.17%
Lens Hood	125	5.49	686.25	1.44%
Remote Switch	750	22.50	16,875.00	35.53%
Mini Tripod	554	24.99	13,844.46	29.15%
Cleaning Kit	365	10.99	4,011.35	8.45%
Total Sales for All Products			**$ 47,496.19**	

Lastname_Firstname_1F_Camera_Accessories

Figure 1.57

(Project 1F Camera Accessories continues on the next page)

Mastering Excel | Project 1F Camera Accessories (continued)

1 **Start** Excel and display a new blank workbook. **Save** the workbook in your **Excel Chapter 1** folder as **Lastname_Firstname_1F_Camera_Accessories** In cell **A1**, type **Texas Spectrum Wireless** In cell **A2**, type **Digital Camera Accessories Sales** and then **Merge & Center** the title and the subtitle across **columns A:F**. Apply the **Title** and **Heading 1** cell styles respectively.

2 Beginning in cell **B3**, type the following column titles: **Product Number** and **Quantity Sold** and **Retail Price** and **Total Sales** and **Percent of Total Sales**

3 Beginning in cell **A4**, type the following row titles, including misspelled words:

Small Cloth Gear Bag
Large Cloth Gear Bag
Lens Cap
Lens Hood
Remote Switch
Mini Tripod
Cleening Kit
Total Sales for All Products

4 Make cell **A1** the active cell, and then check spelling in your worksheet. Correct *Cleening* to **Cleaning**, and make any other necessary corrections. Widen **column A** to **180 pixels** and **columns B:F** to **90 pixels**.

5 In the range **B4:D10**, type the data shown in **Table 1** at the bottom of the page.

6 In cell **E4**, construct a formula to calculate the *Total Sales* of the *Small Cloth Gear Bags* by multiplying the *Quantity Sold* times the *Retail Price*. Copy the formula down for the remaining products. In cell **E11**, use the **SUM** function to calculate the *Total Sales for All Products*, and then apply the **Total** cell style to the cell.

7 Using absolute cell references as necessary so that you can copy the formula, in cell **F4**, construct a formula to calculate the *Percent of Total Sales* for the first product by dividing the *Total Sales* of the *Small Cloth Gear Bags* by the *Total Sales for All Products*. Copy the formula down for the remaining products. To the computed percentages, apply **Percent Style** with two decimal places, and then **Center** the percentages.

8 Apply the **Comma Style** with no decimal places to the *Quantity Sold* figures. To cells **D4**, **E4**, and **E11** apply the **Accounting Number Format**. To the range **D5:E10**, apply the **Comma Style**.

9 Change the *Retail Price* of the *Mini Tripod* to **24.99** and the *Quantity Sold* of the *Remote Switch* to **750** Delete **column B**, and then **Insert** a new **row 3**. In cell **A3**, type **Month Ending August 31** and then **Merge & Center** the text across the range **A3:E3**. Apply the **Heading 2** cell style. To cell **A12**, apply the **Accent1** cell style. Select the four column titles, apply **Wrap Text**, **Middle Align**, and **Center** formatting, and then apply the **Heading 3** cell style.

10 Insert a **Footer** with the **File Name** in the **left section**, and then return to **Normal** view. Display the **Document Panel**, add your name, your course name and section, and the keywords **digital camera accessories, sales**

11 Delete the unused sheets, and then center the worksheet **Horizontally** on the page. Preview the worksheet in **Print Preview**, and make any necessary corrections.

12 **Save** your workbook, and then print or submit electronically as directed. If required by your instructor, print or create an electronic version of your worksheets with formulas displayed by using the instructions in Activity 1.16. **Exit** Excel without saving so that you do not save the changes you made to print formulas.

Table 1

	Product Number	Quantity Sold	Retail Price
Small Cloth Gear Bag	CGB-3	254	19.99
Large Cloth Gear Bag	CGB-8	182	24.99
Lens Cap	LC-2	351	6.99
Lens Hood	LH-4	125	5.49
Remote Switch	RS-5	677	22.50
Mini Tripod	MTP-6	554	29.99
Cleaning Kit	CK-8	365	10.99

(Return to Step 6)

End **You have completed Project 1F**

Apply 1A and 1B skills from these Objectives:

1. Create, Save, and Navigate an Excel Workbook
2. Enter Data in a Worksheet
3. Construct and Copy Formulas and Use the SUM Function
4. Format Cells with Merge & Center and Cell Styles
5. Chart Data to Create a Column Chart and Insert Sparklines
6. Print, Display Formulas, and Close Excel
7. Check Spelling in a Worksheet
8. Enter Data by Range
9. Construct Formulas for Mathematical Operations
10. Edit Values in a Worksheet
11. Format a Worksheet

myitlab grader

Mastering Excel | Project 1G Sales Comparison

In the following Mastering Excel project, you will create a new worksheet that compares annual laptop sales by store location. Your completed worksheet will look similar to Figure 1.58.

Project Files

For Project 1G, you will need the following file:

New blank Excel workbook

You will save your workbook as:

Lastname_Firstname_1G_Sales_Comparison

Project Results

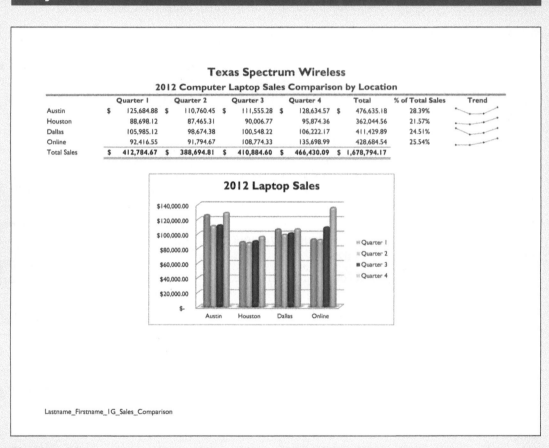

Texas Spectrum Wireless

2012 Computer Laptop Sales Comparison by Location

	Quarter 1	Quarter 2	Quarter 3	Quarter 4	Total	% of Total Sales	Trend
Austin	$ 125,684.88	$ 110,760.45	$ 111,555.28	$ 128,634.57	$ 476,635.18	28.39%	
Houston	88,698.12	87,465.31	90,006.77	95,874.36	362,044.56	21.57%	
Dallas	105,985.12	98,674.38	100,548.22	106,222.17	411,429.89	24.51%	
Online	92,416.55	91,794.67	108,774.33	135,698.99	428,684.54	25.54%	
Total Sales	**$ 412,784.67**	**$ 388,694.81**	**$ 410,884.60**	**$ 466,430.09**	**$ 1,678,794.17**		

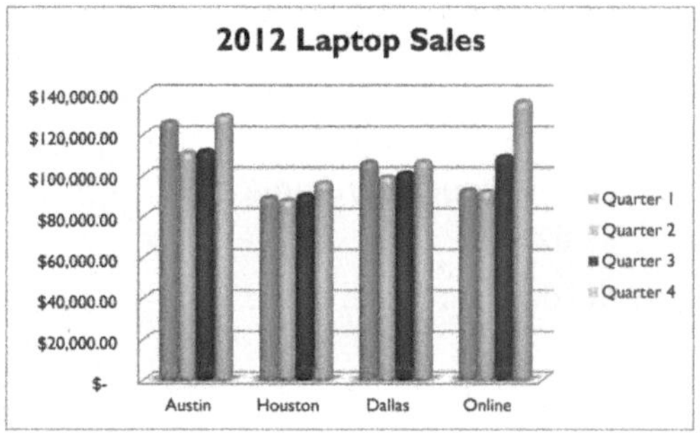

Lastname_Firstname_1G_Sales_Comparison

Figure 1.58

(Project 1G Sales Comparison continues on the next page)

Content-Based Assessments

Mastering Excel | Project 1G Sales Comparison (continued)

1 **Start** Excel. In a new blank workbook, as the worksheet title, in cell **A1**, type **Texas Spectrum Wireless** As the worksheet subtitle, in cell **A2**, type **2012 Computer Laptop Sales Comparison by Location** and then **Save** the workbook in your **Excel Chapter 1** folder as **Lastname_Firstname_1G_Sales_Comparison**

2 In cell **B3**, type **Quarter 1** and then use the fill handle to enter *Quarter 2*, *Quarter 3*, and *Quarter 4* in the range **C3:E3**. In cell **F3**, type **Total** In cell **G3**, type **% of Total Sales** In cell **H3**, type **Trend**

3 In the range **A4:A7**, type the following row titles: **Austin** and **Houston** and **Online** and **Total Sales**

4 Widen columns **A:H** to **115 pixels**. **Merge & Center** the title across the range **A1:H1**, and then apply the **Title** cell style. **Merge & Center** the subtitle across the range **A2:H2**, and then apply the **Heading 1** cell style. Select the seven column titles, apply **Center** formatting, and then apply the **Heading 4** cell style.

5 In the range **B4:E6**, enter the sales values for each Quarter as shown in **Table 1** at the bottom of the page.

6 **Sum** the *Quarter 1* sales, and then copy the formula across for the remaining Quarters. **Sum** the sales for the *Austin* location, and then copy the formula down through cell **F7**. Apply the **Accounting Number Format** to the first row of sales figures and to the total row, and the **Comma Style** to the remaining sales figures. Format the totals in **row 7** with the **Total** cell style.

7 **Insert** a new **row 6** with the row title **Dallas** and the following sales figures for each quarter: **105985.12** and **98674.38** and **100548.22** and **106222.17** Copy the formula in cell **F5** down to cell **F6** to sum the new row.

8 Using absolute cell references as necessary so that you can copy the formula, in cell **G4** construct a formula to calculate the *Percent of Total Sales* for the first location by dividing the *Total* for the *Austin* location by the *Total Sales* for all Quarters. Copy the formula down for the remaining locations. To the computed percentages, apply **Percent Style** with two decimal places, and then **Center** the percentages.

9 Insert **Line** sparklines in the range **H4:H7** that compare the quarterly data. Do not include the totals. Show the sparkline **Markers** and apply the second style in the second row—**Sparkline Style Accent 2, Darker 25%**.

10 **Save** your workbook. To compare the quarterly sales of each location visually, select the range that represents the sales figures for the four quarters, including the quarter names and each location—do not include any totals in the range. With this data selected, **Insert** a **Column, Clustered Cylinder** chart.

11 Switch the row/column data so that the locations display on the category axis. Position the top edge of the chart in **row 10** and visually center it below the worksheet data. Apply **Chart Style 26**, and then modify the **Chart Layout** by applying **Layout 1**. Change the **Chart Title** to **2012 Laptop Sales**

12 Deselect the chart. Change the **Orientation** to **Landscape**, center the worksheet **Horizontally** on the page, and then change the **Theme** to **Solstice**. Scale the worksheet so that the **Width** fits to **1 page**. Insert a **Footer** with the **File Name** in the **left section**. Return the worksheet to **Normal** view and make **A1** the active cell so that you can view the top of your worksheet.

13 Display the **Document Panel**, add your name, your course name and section, and the keywords **laptops, sales** Delete the unused sheets, preview your worksheet in **Print Preview**, and then make any necessary corrections.

14 **Save** your workbook, and then print or submit electronically as directed. If required by your instructor, print or create an electronic version of your worksheets with formulas displayed by using the instructions in Activity 1.16. **Exit** Excel without saving so that you do not save the changes you made to print formulas.

Table 1

	Quarter 1	Quarter 2	Quarter 3	Quarter 4
Austin	125684.88	110760.45	111555.28	128634.57
Houston	88698.12	87465.31	90006.77	95874.36
Online	92416.55	91794.67	108774.33	135698.99

(Return to Step 6)

End **You have completed Project 1G**

Apply a combination of the 1A and 1B skills.

GO! Fix It | Project 1H Team Sales

Project Files

For Project 1H, you will need the following file:

e01H_Team_Sales

You will save your workbook as:

Lastname_Firstname_1H_Team_Sales

In this project, you will edit a worksheet that summarizes sales by each sales team member at the Texas Spectrum Wireless San Antonio location for the month of February. From the student files that accompany this textbook, open the file e01H_Team_Sales, and then save the file in your Excel Chapter 1 folder as **Lastname_Firstname_1H_Team_Sales**

To complete the project, you must find and correct errors in formulas and formatting. View each formula in the Formula Bar and edit as necessary. In addition to errors that you find, you should know:

- There are two spelling errors.
- Worksheet titles should be merged and centered and appropriate cell styles should be applied.
- Appropriate number and accounting format with zero decimals should be applied to the data and text should be wrapped where necessary. Percent style formatting should be applied appropriately where necessary.
- Column headings should be formatted with the Heading 4 style.
- In the chart, the team member names should display on the Horizontal (Category) axis and the week names should display in the legend.
- The chart should include the title **February Team Member Sales**
- The worksheet should be centered horizontally on one page in Landscape orientation. Remove unused sheets.
- A footer should be inserted that includes the file name, and document properties should include the keywords **team sales, San Antonio**

Save your workbook, and then print or submit electronically as directed. If required by your instructor, print or create an electronic version of your worksheets with formulas displayed by using the instructions in Activity 1.16. Exit Excel without saving so that you do not save the changes you made to print formulas.

End You have completed Project 1H

Apply a combination of the 1A and 1B skills.

GO! Make It | Project 1I Printer Sales

Project Files

For Project 1I, you will need the following file:

New blank Excel workbook

You will save your workbook as:

Lastname_Firstname_1I_Printer_Sales

Create the worksheet shown in Figure 1.59. Use the Pushpin theme and change the Orientation to Landscape. Construct formulas in the Total Sold, Total Sales, and Percent of Total Sales columns, and in the Total row. Apply cell styles and number formatting as shown. Use Style 26 for the chart. Insert sparklines for the monthly data using the first style in the second row—Sparkline Style Accent 1, Darker 25%. Add your name, your course name and section, and the keywords **inkjet, printer, sales** to the document properties. Save the file in your Excel Chapter 1 folder as **Lastname_Firstname_1I_Printer_Sales**

Project Results

Texas Spectrum Wireless
First Quarter Inkjet Printer Sales

Model	April	May	June	Total Sold	Retail Price	Total Sales	Percent of Total Sales	Trend
Lear 200	390	224	421	1,035	$ 79.99	$ 82,789.65	8.50%	
Lear 355	168	186	153	507	169.99	86,184.93	8.85%	
Prima X50	250	379	339	968	199.99	193,590.32	19.88%	
Prima X90	386	423	482	1,291	249.99	322,737.09	33.15%	
Prima Z25	261	244	307	812	354.99	288,251.88	29.61%	
Total	1,455	1,456	1,702	4,613		$ 973,553.87		

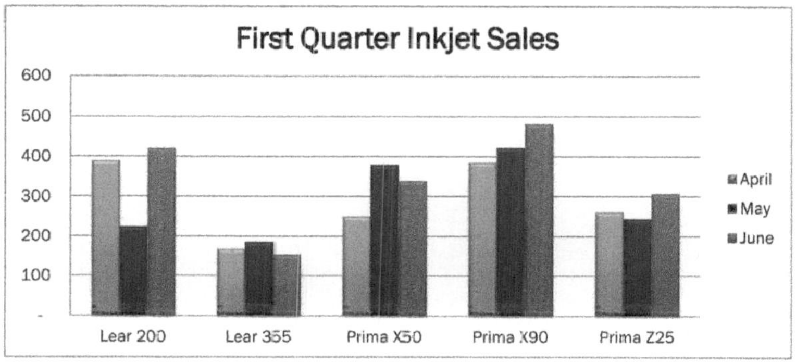

Lastname_Firstname_1I_Printer_Sales

Figure 1.59

End **You have completed Project 1I**

Apply a combination of the 1A and 1B skills.

GO! Solve It | Project 1J Warranty Sales

Project Files

For Project 1J, you will need the following file:

e01J_Warranty_Sales

You will save your workbook as:

Lastname_Firstname_1J_Warranty_Sales

Open the file e01J_Warranty_Sales and save it as **Lastname_Firstname_1J_Warranty_Sales** Complete the worksheet by using Auto Fill to enter the Quarter headings, and then calculating *Total Sold*, *Total Sales*, *Total For All Products*, and *Percent of Total Sales*. Format the worksheet attractively, and apply appropriate financial formatting. Insert a chart that compares the total number of warranties sold for each item across Quarters, and format the chart to display the information appropriately. Include the file name in the footer, add appropriate document properties, and submit as directed.

Performance Element	Performance Level Exemplary: You consistently applied the relevant skills	Proficient: You sometimes, but not always, applied the relevant skills	Developing: You rarely or never applied the relevant skills
Create formulas	All formulas are correct and are efficiently constructed.	Formulas are correct but not always constructed in the most efficient manner.	One or more formulas are missing or incorrect; or only numbers were entered.
Create a chart	Chart created properly.	Chart was created but incorrect data was selected.	No chart was created.
Format attractively and appropriately	Formatting is attractive and appropriate.	Adequately formatted but difficult to read or unattractive.	Inadequate or no formatting.

End **You have completed Project 1J**

Apply a combination of the 1A and 1B skills.

GO! Solve It | Project 1K Service Receipts

Project Files

For Project 1K, you will need the following file:

e01K_Service_Receipts

You will save your workbook as:

Lastname_Firstname_1K_Service_Receipts

Open the file e01K_Service_Receipts and save it as **Lastname_Firstname_1K_Service_Receipts** Complete the worksheet by using Auto Fill to complete the month headings, and then calculating the Total Receipts for each month and for each product. Insert and format appropriate sparklines in the Trend column. Format the worksheet attractively with a title and subtitle, check spelling, adjust column width, and apply appropriate financial formatting. Insert a chart that compares the total sales receipts for each product with the months displaying as the categories, and format the chart attractively. Include the file name in the footer, add appropriate properties, and submit as directed.

		Performance Level		
		Exemplary: You consistently applied the relevant skills	Proficient: You sometimes, but not always, applied the relevant skills	Developing: You rarely or never applied the relevant skills
Performance Element	Create formulas	All formulas are correct and are efficiently constructed.	Formulas are correct but not always constructed in the most efficient manner.	One or more formulas are missing or incorrect; or only numbers were entered.
	Create a chart	Chart created properly.	Chart was created but incorrect data was selected.	No chart was created.
	Insert and format sparklines	Sparklines inserted and formatted properly.	Sparklines were inserted but incorrect data was selected or sparklines were not formatted.	No sparklines were inserted.
	Format attractively and appropriately	Formatting is attractive and appropriate.	Adequately formatted but difficult to read or unattractive.	Inadequate or no formatting.

End You have completed Project 1K

Excel | Chapter 1

Outcomes-Based Assessments

Rubric

The following outcomes-based assessments are *open-ended assessments*. That is, there is no specific correct result; your result will depend on your approach to the information provided. Make *Professional Quality* your goal. Use the following scoring rubric to guide you in *how* to approach the problem, and then to evaluate *how well* your approach solves the problem.

The *criteria*—Software Mastery, Content, Format and Layout, and Process—represent the knowledge and skills you have gained that you can apply to solving the problem. The *levels of performance*—Professional Quality, Approaching Professional Quality, or Needs Quality Improvements—help you and your instructor evaluate your result.

	Your completed project is of Professional Quality if you:	**Your completed project is Approaching Professional Quality if you:**	**Your completed project Needs Quality Improvements if you:**
1-Software Mastery	Choose and apply the most appropriate skills, tools, and features and identify efficient methods to solve the problem.	Choose and apply some appropriate skills, tools, and features, but not in the most efficient manner.	Choose inappropriate skills, tools, or features, or are inefficient in solving the problem.
2-Content	Construct a solution that is clear and well organized, contains content that is accurate, appropriate to the audience and purpose, and is complete. Provide a solution that contains no errors in spelling, grammar, or style.	Construct a solution in which some components are unclear, poorly organized, inconsistent, or incomplete. Misjudge the needs of the audience. Have some errors in spelling, grammar, or style, but the errors do not detract from comprehension.	Construct a solution that is unclear, incomplete, or poorly organized; contains some inaccurate or inappropriate content; and contains many errors in spelling, grammar, or style. Do not solve the problem.
3-Format and Layout	Format and arrange all elements to communicate information and ideas, clarify function, illustrate relationships, and indicate relative importance.	Apply appropriate format and layout features to some elements, but not others. Overuse features, causing minor distraction.	Apply format and layout that does not communicate information or ideas clearly. Do not use format and layout features to clarify function, illustrate relationships, or indicate relative importance. Use available features excessively, causing distraction.
4-Process	Use an organized approach that integrates planning, development, self-assessment, revision, and reflection.	Demonstrate an organized approach in some areas, but not others; or, use an insufficient process of organization throughout.	Do not use an organized approach to solve the problem.

Outcomes-Based Assessments

Apply a combination of the 1A and 1B skills.

GO! Think | Project 1L Phone Plans

Project Files

For Project 1L, you will need the following file:

New blank Excel workbook

You will save your workbook as:

Lastname_Firstname_1L_Phone_Plans

Roslyn Thomas, President of Texas Spectrum Wireless, needs a worksheet that summarizes the following data regarding the first quarter sales of cell phone calling plans that the company is offering for domestic and international calls. Roslyn would like the worksheet to include a calculation of the total sales for each plan and a total of the sales of all of the plans. She would also like to know each plan's percentage of total sales.

	Number Sold	Price
Domestic Standard	2556	29.99
Domestic Premium	3982	49.99
Domestic Platinum	1647	64.99
International Standard	582	85.99
International Premium	365	102.99

Create a worksheet that provides Roslyn with the information needed. Include appropriate worksheet, column, and row titles. Using the formatting skills that you practiced in this chapter, format the worksheet in a manner that is professional and easy to read and understand. Insert a footer with the file name and add appropriate document properties. Save the file as **Lastname_Firstname_1L_Phone_Plans** and print or submit as directed by your instructor.

End **You have completed Project 1L**

Apply a combination of the 1A and 1B skills.

GO! Think | Project 1M Advertising

Project Files

For Project 1M, you will need the following file:

New blank Excel workbook

You will save your workbook as:

Lastname_Firstname_1M_Advertising

Eliott Verschoren, Vice President of Marketing for Texas Spectrum Wireless, is conducting an analysis of the advertising expenditures at the company's four retail locations based on the following data:

	Quarter 1	Quarter 2	Quarter 3	Quarter 4
Austin	22860	25905	18642	28405
Dallas	18557	17963	22883	25998
Houston	32609	28462	25915	31755
San Antonio	12475	15624	13371	17429

Using this information, create a workbook that includes totals by quarter and by location, sparklines to demonstrate the quarterly trends, and a column chart that compares the quarterly data across locations. Include appropriate worksheet, row, and column titles. Using the formatting skills that you practiced in this chapter, format the worksheet in a manner that is professional and easy to read and understand. Insert a footer with the file name and add appropriate document properties. Save the file as **Lastname_Firstname_1M_Advertising** and print or submit as directed by your instructor.

End You have completed Project 1M

Outcomes-Based Assessments

Apply a combination of the 1A and 1B skills.

You and GO! | Project 1N Personal Expenses

Project Files

For Project 1N, you will need the following file:

New blank Excel workbook

You will save your workbook as:

Lastname_Firstname_1N_Personal_Expenses

Develop a worksheet that details your personal expenses from the last three months. Some of these expenses might include, but are not limited to, Mortgage, Rent, Utilities, Phone, Food, Entertainment, Tuition, Childcare, Clothing, and Insurance. Include a total for each month and for each category of expense. Insert a column with a formula that calculates the percent that each expense category is of the total expenditures. Format the worksheet by adjusting column widths and wrapping text, and by applying appropriate financial number formatting and cell styles. Insert a column chart that compares your expenses by month and modify the chart layout and style. Insert a footer with the file name and center the worksheet horizontally on the page. Save your file as **Lastname_Firstname_1N_Personal_Expenses** and submit as directed.

End You have completed Project 1N

Apply a combination of the 1A and 1B skills.

GO! Collaborate | Project 1O Bell Orchid Hotels Group Running Case

GO! CD-ROM

This project relates to the **Bell Orchid Hotels**. Your instructor may assign this group case project to your class. If your instructor assigns this project, he or she will provide you with information and instructions to work as part of a group. The group will apply the skills gained thus far to help the Bell Orchid Hotels achieve their business goals.

End You have completed Project 1O

Using Functions, Creating Tables, and Managing Large Workbooks

OUTCOMES

At the end of this chapter you will be able to:

OBJECTIVES

Mastering these objectives will enable you to:

PROJECT 2A

Analyze inventory by applying statistical and logical calculations to data and by sorting and filtering data.

1. Use the SUM, AVERAGE, MEDIAN, MIN, and MAX Functions (p. 293)
2. Move Data, Resolve Error Messages, and Rotate Text (p. 297)
3. Use COUNTIF and IF Functions and Apply Conditional Formatting (p. 299)
4. Use Date & Time Functions and Freeze Panes (p. 304)
5. Create, Sort, and Filter an Excel Table (p. 306)
6. Format and Print a Large Worksheet (p. 309)

PROJECT 2B

Summarize the data on multiple worksheets.

7. Navigate a Workbook and Rename Worksheets (p. 314)
8. Enter Dates, Clear Contents, and Clear Formats (p. 315)
9. Copy and Paste by Using the Paste Options Gallery (p. 319)
10. Edit and Format Multiple Worksheets at the Same Time (p. 320)
11. Create a Summary Sheet with Column Sparklines (p. 326)
12. Format and Print Multiple Worksheets in a Workbook (p. 330)

Shutterstock

In This Chapter

In this chapter, you will use the Statistical functions to calculate the average of a group of numbers, and use other Logical and Date & Time functions. You will use the counting functions and apply conditional formatting to make data easy to visualize. In this chapter, you will also create a table and analyze the table's data by sorting and filtering the data. You will summarize a workbook that contains multiple worksheets.

The projects in this chapter relate to **Laurales Herbs and Spices**. After ten years as an Executive Chef, Laura Morales started her own business, which offers quality products for cooking, eating, and entertaining in retail stores and online. In addition to herbs and spices, there is a wide variety of condiments, confections, jams, sauces, oils, and vinegars. Later this year, Laura will add a line of tools, cookbooks, and gift baskets. The company name is a combination of Laura's first and last names, and also the name of an order of plants related to cinnamon.

Project 2A Inventory Status Report

myitlab
Project 2A Training

Project Activities

In Activities 2.01 through 2.15, you will edit a worksheet for Laura Morales, President, detailing the current inventory of flavor products at the Oakland production facility. Your completed worksheet will look similar to Figure 2.1.

Project Files

For Project 2A, you will need the following file:

e02A_Flavor_Inventory

You will save your workbook as:

Lastname_Firstname_2A_Flavor_Inventory

Project Results

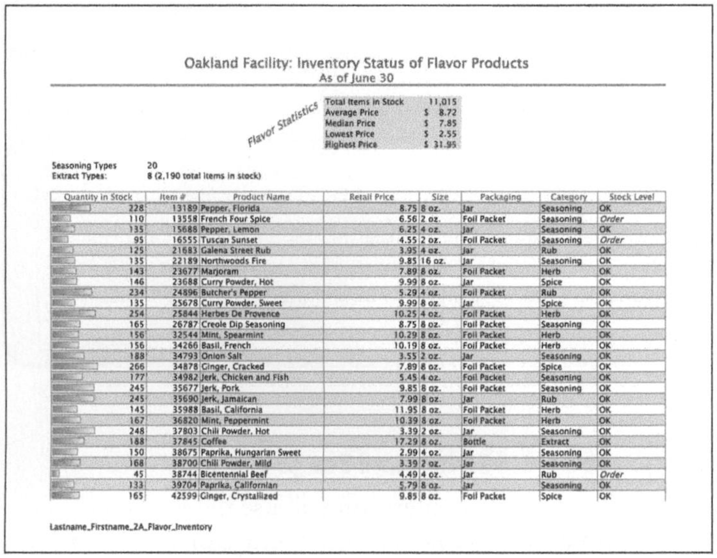

Oakland Facility: Inventory Status of Flavor Products
As of June 30

Flavor Statistics

Total Items in Stock	11,015
Average Price	$ 8.72
Median Price	$ 7.85
Lowest Price	$ 2.55
Highest Price	$ 31.95

Seasoning Types 20
Extract Types: 8 (2,190 total items in stock)

Quantity in Stock	Item #	Product Name	Retail Price	Size	Packaging	Category	Stock Level
228	13189	Pepper, Florida	8.75	8 oz.	Jar	Seasoning	OK
110	13558	French Four Spice	6.56	2 oz.	Foil Packet	Seasoning	*Order*
135	15688	Pepper, Lemon	6.25	4 oz.	Jar	Seasoning	OK
95	16555	Tuscan Sunset	4.55	2 oz.	Foil Packet	Seasoning	*Order*
125	21683	Galena Street Rub	3.95	4 oz.	Jar	Rub	OK
135	22189	Northwoods Fire	9.85	16 oz.	Jar	Seasoning	OK
143	23677	Marjoram	7.89	8 oz.	Foil Packet	Herb	OK
146	23688	Curry Powder, Hot	9.99	8 oz.	Jar	Spice	OK
234	24896	Butcher's Pepper	5.29	4 oz.	Foil Packet	Rub	OK
135	25678	Curry Powder, Sweet	9.99	8 oz.	Jar	Spice	OK
254	25844	Herbes De Provence	10.25	4 oz.	Foil Packet	Herb	OK
165	26787	Creole Dip Seasoning	8.75	8 oz.	Foil Packet	Seasoning	OK
156	32544	Mint, Spearmint	10.29	8 oz.	Foil Packet	Herb	OK
156	34266	Basil, French	10.19	8 oz.	Foil Packet	Herb	OK
188	34793	Onion Salt	3.55	2 oz.	Jar	Seasoning	OK
266	34878	Ginger, Cracked	7.89	8 oz.	Foil Packet	Spice	OK
177	34982	Jerk, Chicken and Fish	5.45	4 oz.	Foil Packet	Seasoning	OK
245	35677	Jerk, Pork	9.85	8 oz.	Foil Packet	Seasoning	OK
245	35690	Jerk, Jamaican	7.99	8 oz.	Jar	Rub	OK
145	35988	Basil, California	11.95	8 oz.	Foil Packet	Herb	OK
167	36820	Mint, Peppermint	10.39	8 oz.	Foil Packet	Herb	OK
248	37803	Chili Powder, Hot	3.39	2 oz.	Jar	Seasoning	OK
188	37845	Coffee	17.29	8 oz.	Bottle	Extract	OK
150	38675	Paprika, Hungarian Sweet	2.99	4 oz.	Jar	Seasoning	OK
168	38700	Chili Powder, Mild	3.39	2 oz.	Jar	Seasoning	OK
45	38744	Bicentennial Beef	4.49	4 oz.	Jar	Rub	*Order*
133	39704	Paprika, Californian	5.79	8 oz.	Jar	Seasoning	OK
165	42599	Ginger, Crystallized	9.85	8 oz.	Foil Packet	Spice	OK

Lastname_Firstname_2A_Flavor_Inventory

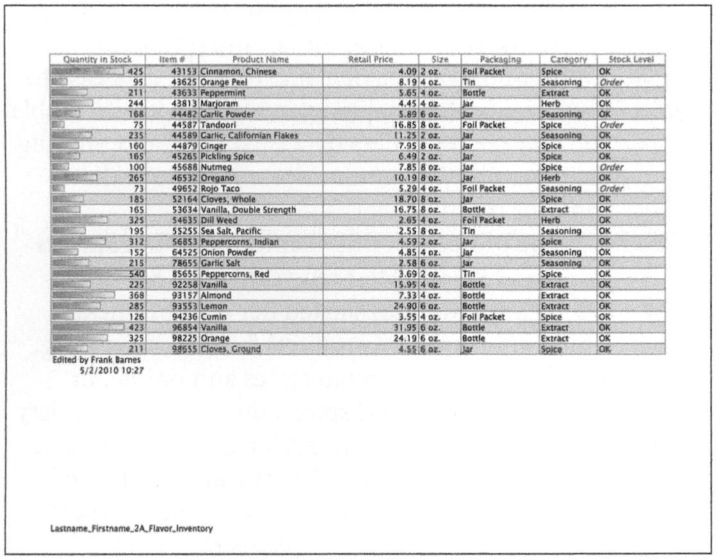

Quantity in Stock	Item #	Product Name	Retail Price	Size	Packaging	Category	Stock Level
425	43153	Cinnamon, Chinese	4.09	2 oz.	Foil Packet	Spice	OK
95	43625	Orange Peel	8.19	4 oz.	Tin	Seasoning	*Order*
211	43633	Peppermint	5.65	4 oz.	Bottle	Extract	OK
244	43813	Marjoram	4.45	4 oz.	Jar	Herb	OK
168	44482	Garlic Powder	5.89	6 oz.	Jar	Seasoning	OK
75	44587	Tandoori	16.85	8 oz.	Foil Packet	Spice	*Order*
235	44589	Garlic, Californian Flakes	11.25	2 oz.	Jar	Seasoning	OK
160	44879	Ginger	7.95	8 oz.	Jar	Spice	OK
165	45265	Pickling Spice	6.49	2 oz.	Jar	Spice	OK
100	45688	Nutmeg	7.85	8 oz.	Jar	Spice	*Order*
265	46532	Oregano	10.19	8 oz.	Jar	Herb	OK
73	49652	Rojo Taco	5.29	4 oz.	Foil Packet	Seasoning	*Order*
185	52164	Cloves, Whole	18.70	8 oz.	Jar	Spice	OK
165	53634	Vanilla, Double Strength	16.75	8 oz.	Bottle	Extract	OK
325	54635	Dill Weed	2.65	4 oz.	Foil Packet	Herb	OK
195	55255	Sea Salt, Pacific	2.55	8 oz.	Tin	Seasoning	OK
312	56853	Peppercorns, Indian	4.59	2 oz.	Jar	Spice	OK
152	64525	Onion Powder	4.85	4 oz.	Jar	Seasoning	OK
215	78655	Garlic Salt	2.58	6 oz.	Jar	Seasoning	OK
540	85655	Peppercorns, Red	3.69	2 oz.	Tin	Spice	OK
225	92258	Vanilla	15.95	4 oz.	Bottle	Extract	OK
368	93157	Almond	7.33	4 oz.	Bottle	Extract	OK
285	93553	Lemon	24.90	6 oz.	Bottle	Extract	OK
126	94236	Cumin	3.55	4 oz.	Foil Packet	Spice	OK
423	96854	Vanilla	31.95	6 oz.	Bottle	Extract	OK
325	98225	Orange	24.19	6 oz.	Bottle	Extract	OK
211	98655	Cloves, Ground	4.55	6 oz.	Jar	Spice	OK

Edited by Frank Barnes
5/2/2010 10:27

Lastname_Firstname_2A_Flavor_Inventory

Figure 2.1
Project 2A Flavor Inventory

Objective 1 | Use the SUM, AVERAGE, MEDIAN, MIN, and MAX Functions

A ***function*** is a predefined formula—a formula that Excel has already built for you—that performs calculations by using specific values in a particular order or structure. ***Statistical functions***, which include the AVERAGE, MEDIAN, MIN, and MAX functions, are useful to analyze a group of measurements.

Activity 2.01 | Using the SUM and AVERAGE Functions

Laura has a worksheet with information about the inventory of flavor product types currently in stock at the Oakland facility. In this activity, you will use the SUM and AVERAGE functions to gather information about the product inventory.

1. **Start** Excel. From **Backstage** view, display the **Open** dialog box, and then from the student files that accompany this textbook, locate and open **e02A_Flavor_Inventory**. Click the **File tab** to redisplay **Backstage** view, and then click **Save As**. In the **Save As** dialog box, navigate to the location where you are storing your projects for this chapter.

2. Create a new folder named **Excel Chapter 2** open the new folder, and then in the **File name** box, type **Lastname_Firstname_2A_Flavor_Inventory** Click **Save** or press Enter.

3. Scroll down. Notice that the worksheet contains data related to types of flavor products in inventory, including information about the *Quantity in Stock*, *Item #*, *Product Name*, *Retail Price*, *Size*, *Packaging*, and *Category*.

4. Leave row 3 blank, and then in cell **A4**, type **Total Items in Stock** In cell **A5**, type **Average Price** In cell **A6**, type **Median Price**

5. Click cell **B4**. Click the **Formulas tab**, and then in the **Function Library group**, click the **AutoSum** button. Compare your screen with Figure 2.2.

   The ***SUM function*** that you have used is a predefined formula that adds all the numbers in a selected range of cells. Because it is frequently used, there are several ways to insert the function.

   For example, you can insert the function from the Home tab's Editing group, by using the keyboard shortcut Alt + =, from the Function Library group on the Formulas tab, and also from the Math & Trig button in that group.

Figure 2.2

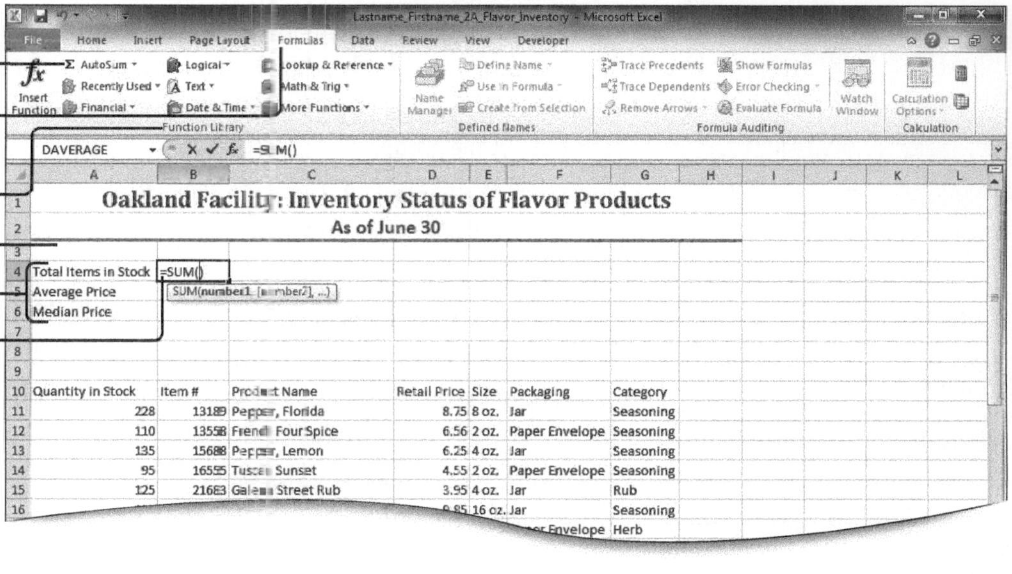

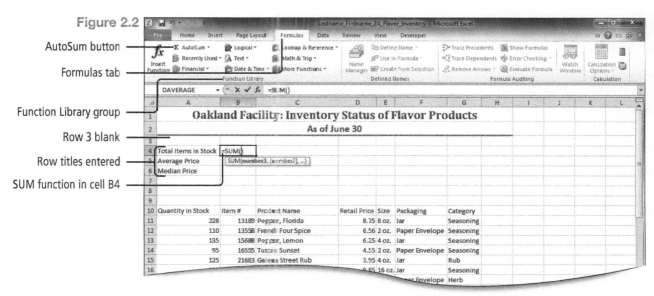

6 With the insertion point blinking in the function, select the range **A11:A65**, dragging down as necessary, and then press Enter. Scroll up to view the top of your worksheet, and notice your result in cell **B4**, *11015*.

7 Click cell **B4** and look at the **Formula Bar**: Compare your screen with Figure 2.3.

SUM is the name of the function. The values in parentheses are the ***arguments***—the values that an Excel function uses to perform calculations or operations. In this instance, the argument consists of the values in the range A11:A65.

Figure 2.3

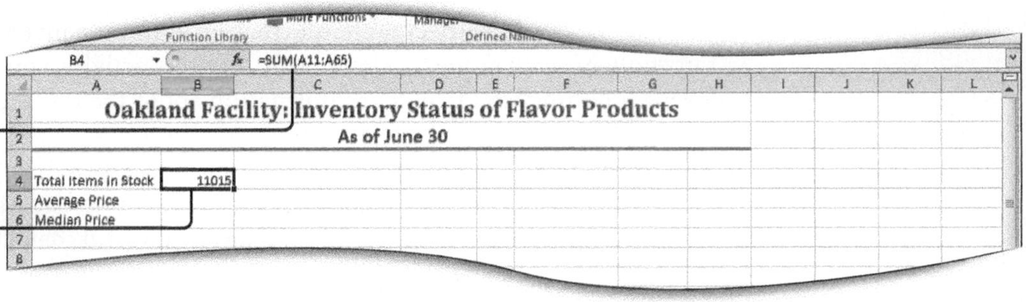

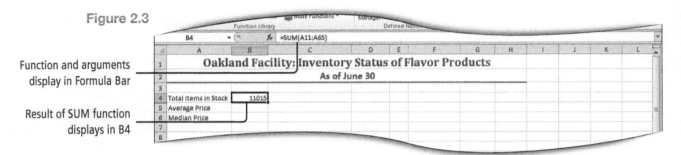

8 Click cell **B5**. In the **Function Library group**, click the **More Functions** button, point to **Statistical**, point to **AVERAGE**, and notice the ScreenTip. Compare your screen with Figure 2.4.

The ScreenTip describes how the AVERAGE function will compute the calculation.

Figure 2.4

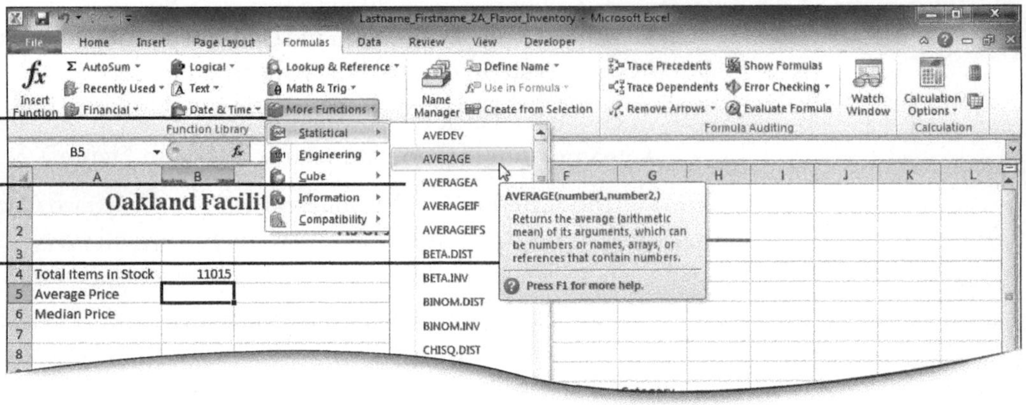

9 Click **AVERAGE**, and then if necessary, drag the title bar of the **Function Arguments** dialog box down and to the right so you can view the **Formula Bar** and cell **B5**.

The ***AVERAGE function*** adds a group of values, and then divides the result by the number of values in the group.

In the cell, the Formula Bar, and the dialog box, Excel proposes to average the value in cell B4. Recall that Excel functions will propose a range if data is above or to the left of a selected cell.

10 In the **Function Arguments** dialog box, notice that *B4* is highlighted. Press Del to delete the existing text, type **d11:d65** and then compare your screen with Figure 2.5.

Because you want to average the values in the range D11:D65—and not cell B4—you must edit the proposed range in this manner.

Another Way

Alternatively, with the existing text selected, select the range D11:D65 and press Enter.

Figure 2.5

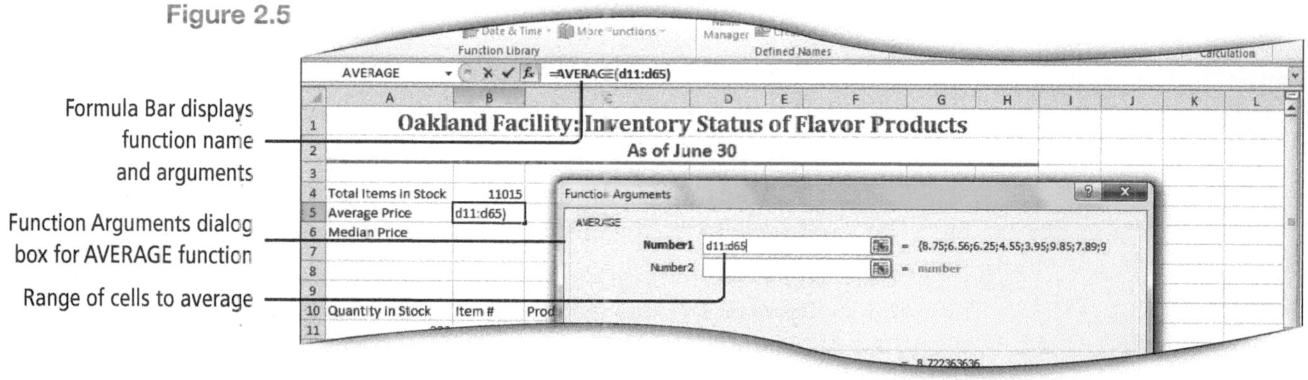

11 In the **Function Arguments** dialog box, click **OK**, and then **Save**.

The result indicates that the average Retail Price of all products is *8.72*.

Activity 2.02 | Using the MEDIAN Function

The ***MEDIAN function*** is a statistical function that describes a group of data—you may have seen it used to describe the price of houses in a particular geographical area. The MEDIAN function finds the middle value that has as many values above it in the group as are below it. It differs from AVERAGE in that the result is not affected as much by a single value that is greatly different from the others.

1 Click cell **B6**. In the **Function Library group**, click the **More Functions** button, display the list of **Statistical** functions, scroll down as necessary, and then click **MEDIAN**.

2 In the **Function Arguments** dialog box, to the right of the **Number 1** box, click the **Collapse Dialog** button.

The dialog box collapses to a small size with space only for the first argument so you can see more of your data.

3 Select the range **D11:D65**, and then compare your screen with Figure 2.6.

When indicating which cells you want to use in the function's calculation—known as *defining the arguments*—you can either select the values with your mouse or type the range of values, whichever you prefer.

Figure 2.6

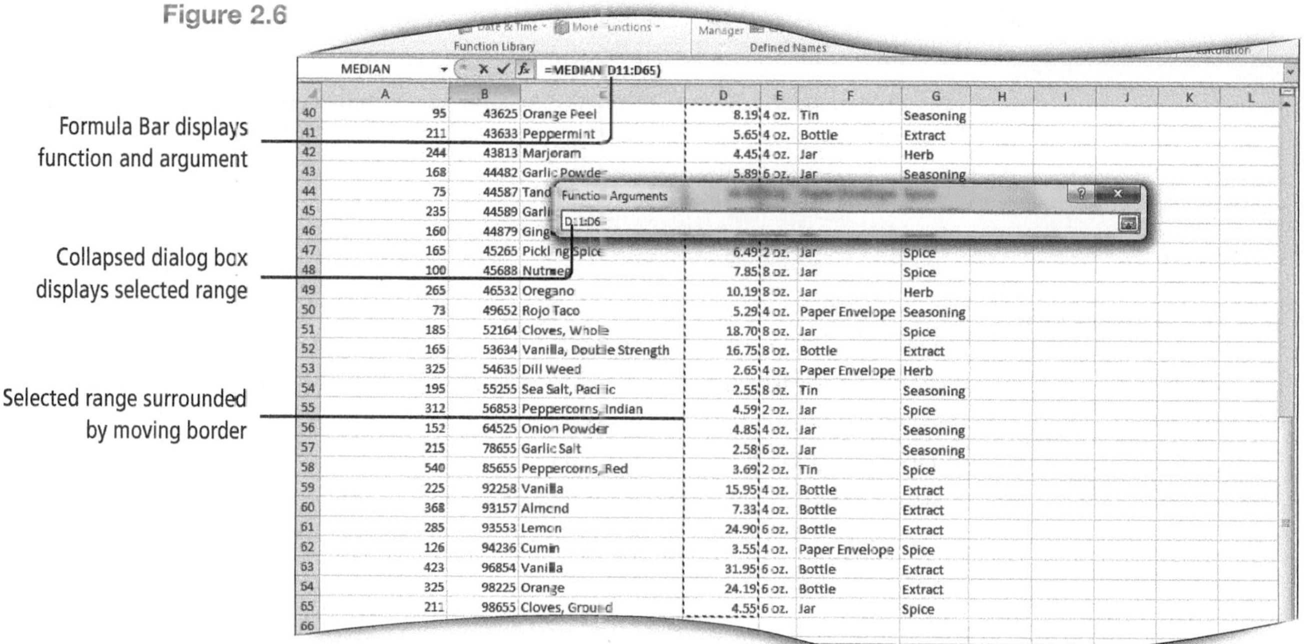

Another Way

Press Enter to expand the dialog box.

4 At the right end of the collapsed dialog box, click the **Expand Dialog** button to expand the dialog box to its original size, and then click **OK** to display *7.85*.

In the range of prices, 7.85 is the middle value. Half of all flavor products are priced *above* 7.85 and half are priced *below* 7.85.

5 Scroll up to view **row 1**. Select the range **B5:B6** and right-click over the selection. On the Mini toolbar, click the **Accounting Number Format** button.

6 Right-click cell **B4**, and then on the Mini toolbar, click the **Comma Style** button one time and the **Decrease Decimal** button two times. Click **Save** and compare your screen with Figure 2.7.

Figure 2.7

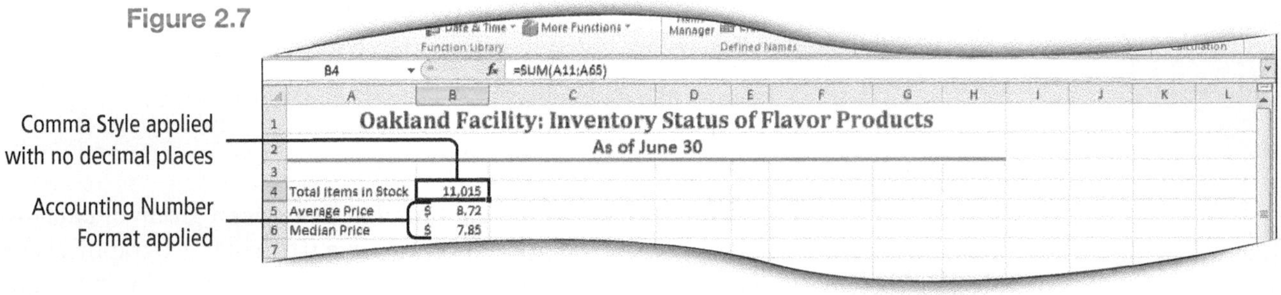

Activity 2.03 | Using the MIN and MAX Functions

The statistical ***MIN function*** determines the smallest value in a selected range of values. The statistical ***MAX function*** determines the largest value in a selected range of values.

1 In cell **A7**, type **Lowest Price** and then in cell **A8**, type **Highest Price**

2 Click cell **B7**. On the **Formulas tab**, in the **Function Library group**, click the **More Functions** button, display the list of **Statistical** functions, scroll as necessary, and then click **MIN**.

3 At the right end of the **Number1** box, click the **Collapse Dialog** button, select the range **D11:D65**, and then click the **Expand Dialog** button. Click **OK**.

The lowest Retail Price is *2.55*.

4 Click cell **B8**, and then by using a similar technique, insert the **MAX** function to determine the highest **Retail Price**—*31.95*.

5 Select the range **B7:B8** and apply the **Accounting Number Format**, click **Save**, and then compare your screen with Figure 2.8.

Figure 2.8

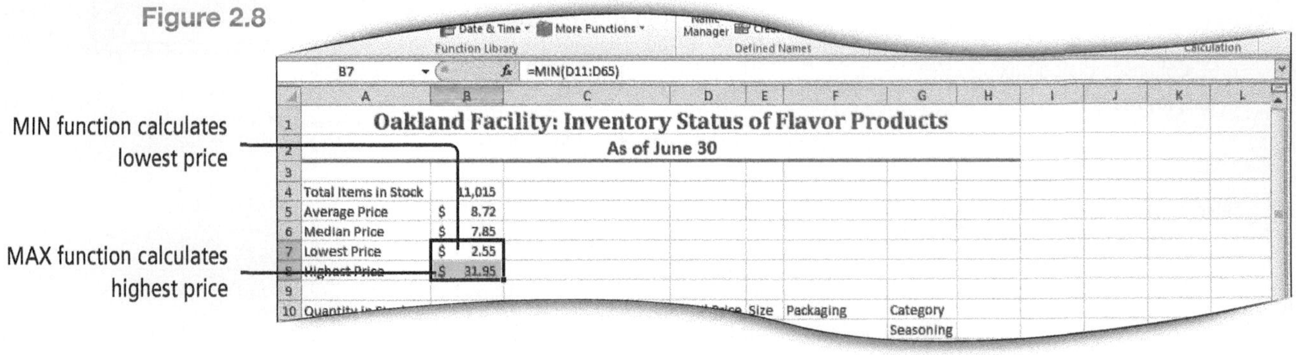

Objective 2 | Move Data, Resolve Error Messages, and Rotate Text

When you move a formula, the cell references within the formula do not change, no matter what type of cell reference you use.

If you move cells into a column that is not wide enough to display number values, Excel will display a message so that you can adjust as necessary.

You can reposition data within a cell at an angle by rotating the text.

Activity 2.04 | Moving Data and Resolving a # # # # # Error Message

1 Select the range **A4:B8**. Point to the right edge of the selected range to display the pointer, and then compare your screen with Figure 2.9.

Figure 2.9

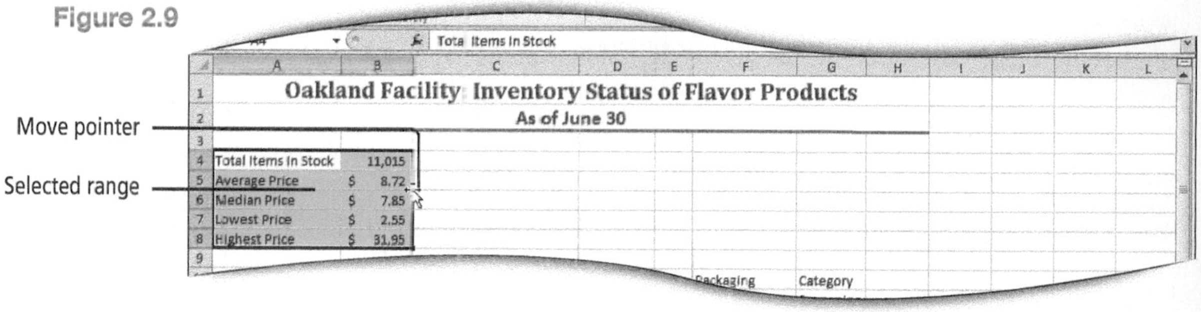

2 Drag the selected range to the right until the ScreenTip displays *D4:E8*, release the mouse button, and then notice that a series of # symbols displays in **column E**. Point to any of the cells that display # symbols, and then compare your screen with Figure 2.10.

Using this technique, cell contents can be moved from one location to another; this is referred to as ***drag and drop***.

If a cell width is too narrow to display the entire number, Excel displays the ##### error, because displaying only a portion of a number would be misleading. The underlying values remain unchanged and are displayed in the Formula Bar for the selected cell. An underlying value also displays in the ScreenTip if you point to a cell containing # symbols.

Figure 2.10

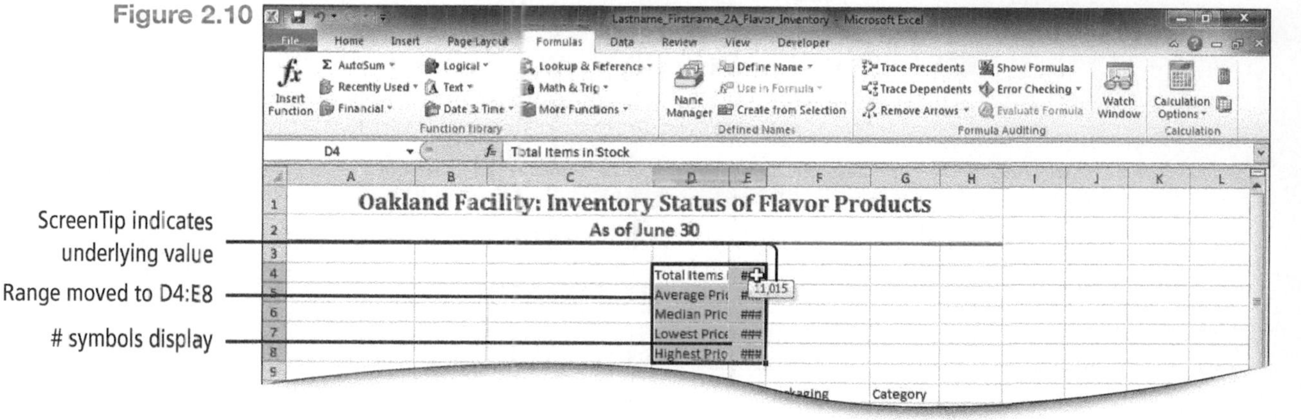

3 Select **column E** and widen it to **50** pixels, and notice that two cells are still not wide enough to display the cell contents.

4. In the **column heading area**, point to the right boundary of **column E** to display the [+] pointer. Double-click to AutoFit the column to accommodate the widest entry.

5. Using the same technique, AutoFit **column D** to accommodate the widest text entry.

6. Select the range **D4:E8**. On the **Home tab**, in the **Styles group**, display the **Cell Styles** gallery. Under **Themed Cell Styles**, click **20%-Accent1**. Click **Save** [Save].

Activity 2.05 | Rotating Text

Rotated text is useful to draw attention to data on your worksheet.

1. In cell **C6**, type **Flavor Statistics** Select the range **C4:C8**, right-click over the selection, and then on the shortcut menu, click **Format Cells.** In the **Format Cells** dialog box, click the **Alignment tab**. Under **Text control**, select the **Merge cells** check box.

> **Another Way**
> Type the number of degrees directly into the Degrees box or use the spin box arrows to set the number.

2. In the upper right portion of the dialog box, under **Orientation**, point to the **red diamond**, and then drag the diamond upward until the **Degrees** box indicates **30.** Compare your screen with Figure 2.11.

Figure 2.11

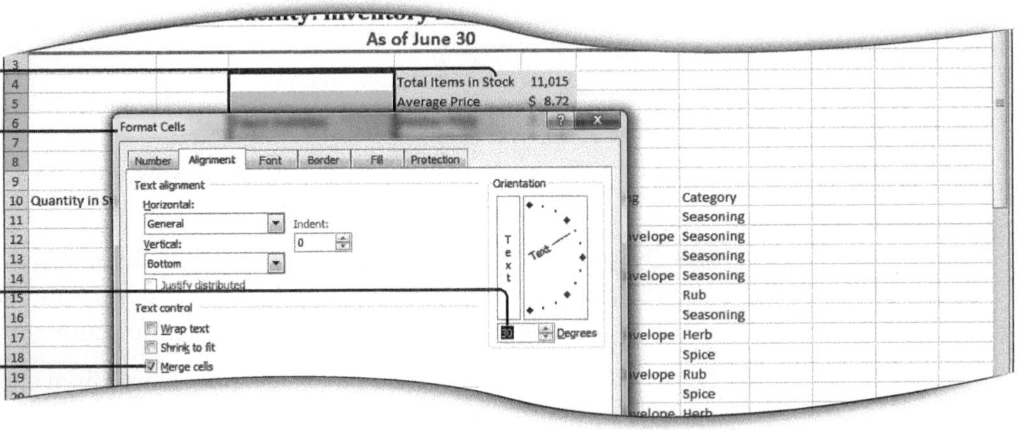

3. In the lower right corner of the **Format Cells** dialog box, click **OK.**

4. With the merged cell still selected, on the **Home tab**, in the **Font group**, change the **Font Size** [11] to **14**, and then apply **Bold** [B] and **Italic** [I]. Click the **Font Color arrow** [A], and then in the fourth column, click the first color—**Dark Blue, Text 2.**

5. In the **Alignment group**, apply **Align Text Right** [≡]. Click cell **A1**, **Save** [Save] your workbook, and then compare your screen with Figure 2.12.

Figure 2.12

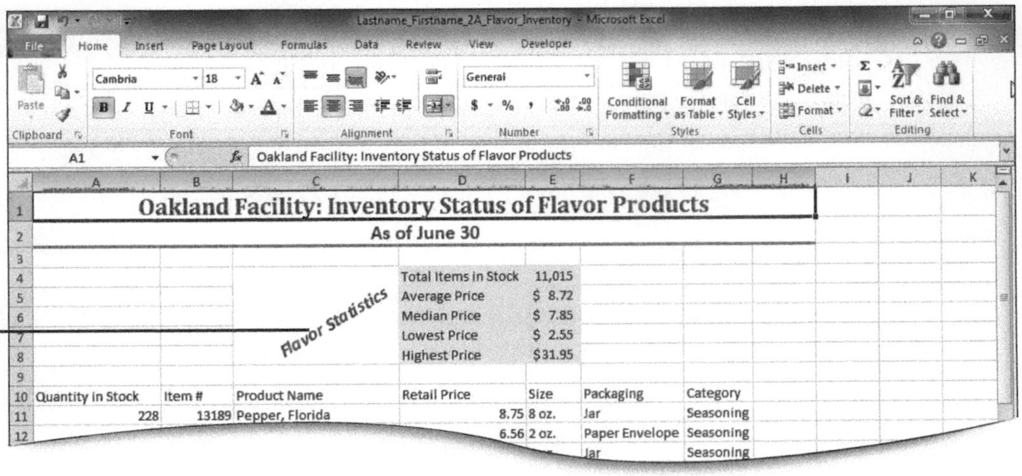

Objective 3 | Use COUNTIF and IF Functions and Apply Conditional Formatting

Recall that statistical functions analyze a group of measurements. Another group of Excel functions, referred to as ***logical functions***, test for specific conditions. Logical functions typically use conditional tests to determine whether specified conditions—called ***criteria***—are true or false.

Activity 2.06 | Using the COUNTIF Function

The ***COUNTIF function*** is a statistical function that counts the number of cells within a range that meet the given condition—the criteria that you provide. The COUNTIF function has two arguments—the range of cells to check and the criteria.

The seasonings of Laurales Herbs and Spices will be featured on an upcoming segment of a TV shopping channel. In this activity, you will use the COUNTIF function to determine the number of *seasoning* products currently available in inventory.

1. In the **row heading area**, point to **row 9** and right-click to select the row and display the shortcut menu. Click **Insert**, and then press F4 two times to repeat the last action and thus insert three blank rows.

   F4 is useful to repeat commands in Microsoft Office programs. Most commands can be repeated in this manner.

2. From the **row heading area**, select **rows 9:11**. On the **Home tab**, in the **Editing group**, click the **Clear** button, and then click **Clear Formats** to remove the blue accent color in columns D and E from the new rows.

   When you insert rows or columns, formatting from adjacent rows or columns repeats in the new cells.

3. Click cell **E4**, look at the **Formula Bar**, and then notice that the arguments of the **SUM** function adjusted and refer to the appropriate cells in rows 14:68.

   The referenced range updates to *A14:A68* after you insert the three new rows. In this manner, Excel adjusts the cell references in a formula relative to their new locations.

4. In cell **A10**, type **Seasoning Types:** and then press Tab.

5. With cell **B10** as the active cell, on the **Formulas tab**, in the **Function Library group**, click the **More Functions** button, and then display the list of **Statistical** functions. Click **COUNTIF**.

   Recall that the COUNTIF function counts the number of cells within a range that meet the given condition.

6. In the **Range** box, click the **Collapse Dialog** button, select the range **G14:G68**, and then at the right end of the collapsed dialog box, click the **Expand Dialog** button. Click in the **Criteria** box, type **Seasoning** and then compare your screen with Figure 2.13.

Figure 2.13

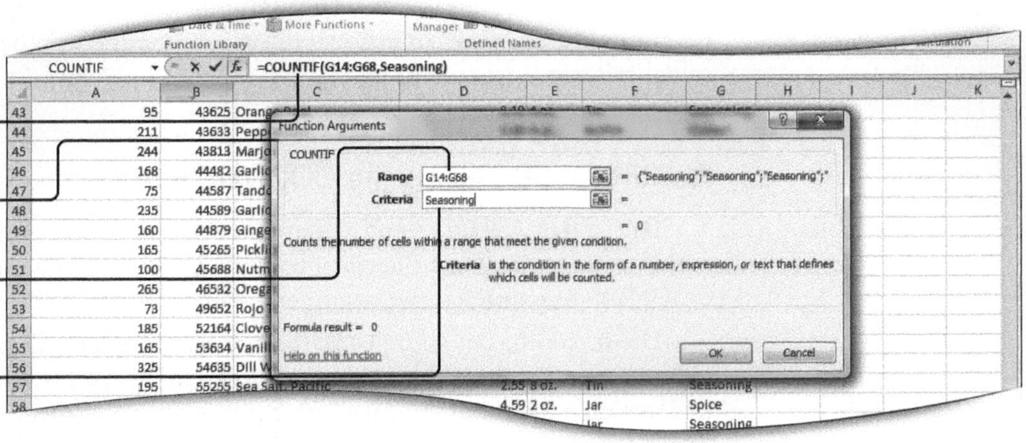

7. In the lower right corner of the **Function Arguments** dialog box, click **OK**.

   There are *20* different *Seasoning* products available to feature on the TV show.

8. On the **Home tab**, in the **Alignment group**, click **Align Text Left** to place the result closer to the row title. **Save** your workbook.

Activity 2.07 | Using the IF Function

A ***logical test*** is any value or expression that you can evaluate as being true or false. The ***IF function*** uses a logical test to check whether a condition is met, and then returns one value if true, and another value if false.

For example, *C14=228* is an expression that can be evaluated as true or false. If the value in cell C14 is equal to 228, the expression is true. If the value in cell C14 is not 228, the expression is false.

In this activity, you will use the IF function to determine the inventory levels and determine if more products should be ordered.

1. Click cell **H13**, type **Stock Level** and then press Enter.
2. In cell **H14**, on the **Formulas tab**, in the **Function Library group**, click the **Logical** button, and then in the list, click **IF**. Drag the title bar of the **Function Arguments** dialog box up or down to view **row 14** on your screen.
3. With the insertion point in the **Logical_test** box, click cell **A14**, and then type **<125**

   This logical test will look at the value in cell A14, which is *228*, and then determine if the number is less than 125. The expression *<125* includes the < ***comparison operator***, which means *less than*. Comparison operators compare values.

4. Examine the table in Figure 2.14 for a list of comparison operator symbols and their definitions.

Comparison Operators

Comparison Operator	Symbol Definition
=	Equal to
>	Greater than
<	Less than
>=	Greater than or equal to
<=	Less than or equal to
<>	Not equal to

Figure 2.14

5 Press Tab to move the insertion point to the **Value_if_true** box, and then type **Order**

If the result of the logical test is true—the Quantity in Stock is less than 125—cell H14 will display the text *Order* indicating that additional product must be ordered.

6 Click in the **Value_if_false** box, type **OK** and then compare your dialog box with Figure 2.15.

If the result of the logical test is false—the Quantity in Stock is *not* less than 125—then Excel will display *OK* in the cell.

Figure 2.15

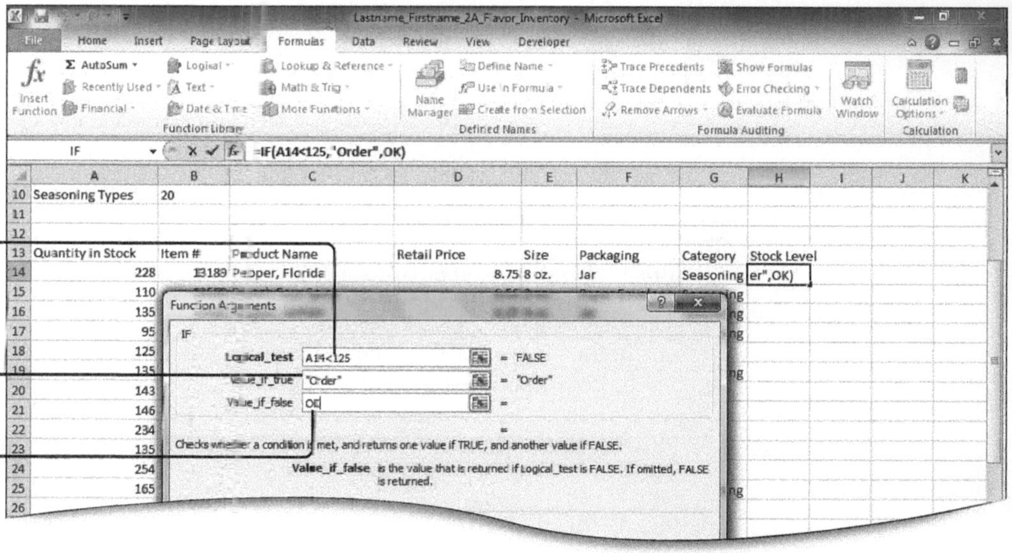
Logical test will determine if value in A14 is less than 125
Value if true (less than 125) will indicate *Order*
Value if false (125 or more) will indicate *OK*
=IF(A14<125,"Order",OK)
Function Arguments
Logical_test
Value_if_true
Value_if_false
Checks whether a condition is met, and returns one value if TRUE, and another value if FALSE.

7 Click **OK** to display the result *OK* in cell **H14**.

8 Using the fill handle, copy the function in cell **H14** down through cell **H68**. Then scroll as necessary to view cell **A18**, which indicates *125*. Look at cell **H18** and notice that the **Stock Level** is indicated as *OK*. **Save** your workbook. Compare your screen with Figure 2.16.

The comparison operator indicated <125 (less than 125) and thus a value of *exactly* 125 is indicated as OK.

Figure 2.16

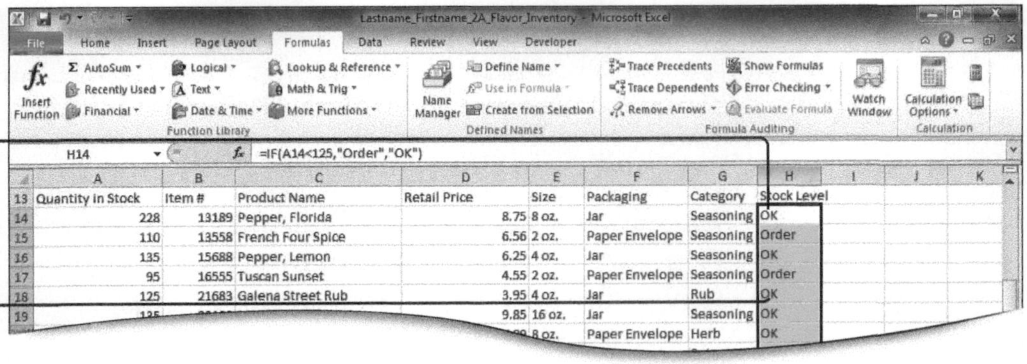

Activity 2.08 | Applying Conditional Formatting by Using Highlight Cells Rules and Data Bars

A ***conditional format*** changes the appearance of a cell based on a condition—a criteria. If the condition is true, the cell is formatted based on that condition; if the condition is false, the cell is *not* formatted. In this activity, you will use conditional formatting as another way to draw attention to the Stock Level of products.

1. Be sure the range **H14:H68** is selected. On the **Home tab**, in the **Styles group**, click the **Conditional Formatting** button. In the list, point to **Highlight Cells Rules**, and then click **Text that Contains.**

2. In the **Text That Contains** dialog box, with the insertion point blinking in the first box, type **Order** and notice that in the selected range, the text *Order* displays with the default format—Light Red Fill with Dark Red Text.

3. In the second box, click the **arrow**, and then in the list, click **Custom Format.**

   Here, in the Format Cells dialog box, you can select any combination of formats to apply to the cell if the condition is true. The custom format you specify will be applied to any cell in the selected range if it contains the text *Order*.

4. On the **Font tab**, under **Font style**, click **Bold Italic**. Click the **Color arrow**, and then under **Theme Colors**, in the sixth column, click the first color—**Red, Accent 2**. Click **OK**. Compare your screen with Figure 2.17.

   In the range, if the cell meets the condition of containing *Order*, the font color will change to Bold Italic, Red, Accent 2.

Figure 2.17

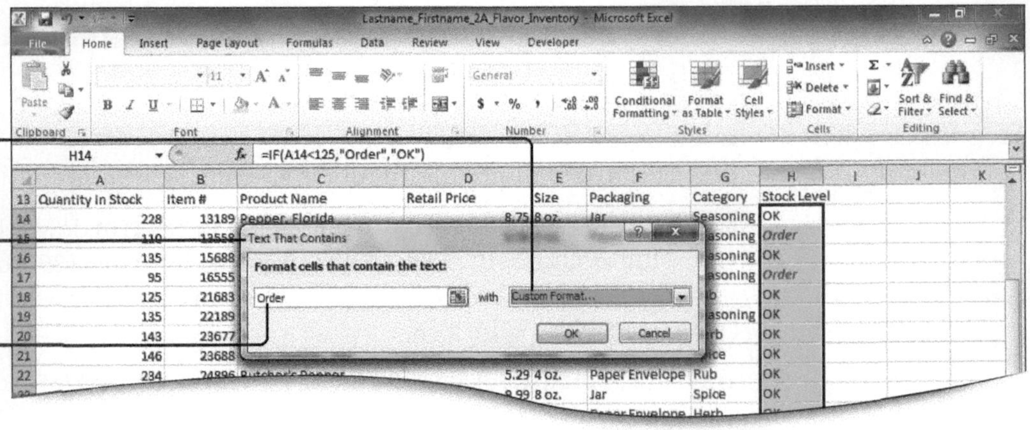

5 In the **Text That Contains** dialog box, click **OK.**

6 Select the range **A14:A68**. In the **Styles group**, click the **Conditional Formatting** button. Point to **Data Bars**, and then under **Gradient Fill**, click **Orange Data Bar**. Click anywhere to cancel the selection; click [Save]. Compare your screen with Figure 2.18.

A ***data bar*** provides a visual cue to the reader about the value of a cell relative to other cells. The length of the data bar represents the value in the cell. A longer bar represents a higher value and a shorter bar represents a lower value. Data bars are useful for identifying higher and lower numbers quickly within a large group of data, such as very high or very low levels of inventory.

Figure 2.18

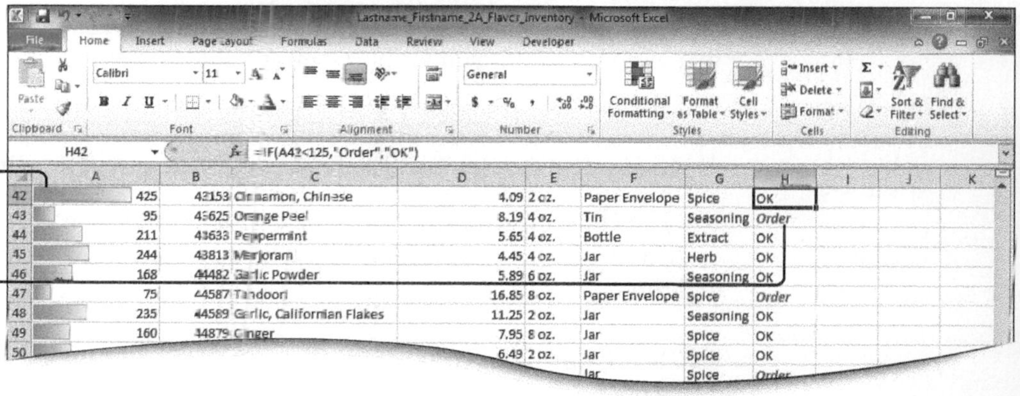

Activity 2.09 | Using Find and Replace

The ***Find and Replace*** feature searches the cells in a worksheet—or in a selected range—for matches, and then replaces each match with a replacement value of your choice.

Comments from customers on the company's blog indicate that, for dried herbs and seasonings, customers prefer a sealable foil packet rather than a paper envelope. Thus, all products of this type have been repackaged. In this activity, you will replace all occurrences of *Paper Envelope* with *Foil Packet.*

1 Select the range **F14:F68.**

Restrict the find and replace operation to a specific range in this manner, especially if there is a possibility that the name occurs elsewhere.

2 On the **Home tab**, in the **Editing group**, click the **Find & Select** button, and then click **Replace.**

3 Type **Paper Envelope** to fill in the **Find what** box. In the **Replace with** box, type **Foil Packet** and then compare your screen with Figure 2.19.

Figure 2.19

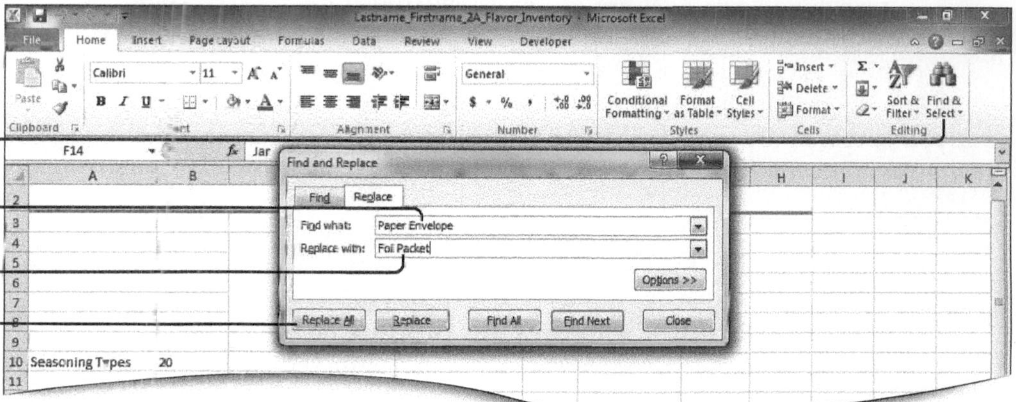

4 Click the **Replace All** button. In the message box, notice that 19 replacements were made, and then click **OK**. In the lower right corner of the **Find and Replace** dialog box, click the **Close** button. Click **Save** .

Objective 4 | Use Date & Time Functions and Freeze Panes

Excel can obtain the date and time from your computer's calendar and clock and display this information on your worksheet.

By freezing or splitting panes, you can view two areas of a worksheet and lock rows and columns in one area. When you freeze panes, you select the specific rows or columns that you want to remain visible when scrolling in your worksheet.

Activity 2.10 | Using the NOW Function to Display a System Date

The ***NOW function*** retrieves the date and time from your computer's calendar and clock and inserts the information into the selected cell. The result is formatted as a date and time.

1 Scroll down as necessary, and then click cell **A70**. Type **Edited by Frank Barnes** and then press Enter.

2 With cell **A71** as the active cell, on the **Formulas tab**, in the **Function Library group**, click the **Date & Time** button. In the list of functions, click **NOW**. Compare your screen with Figure 2.20.

Figure 2.20

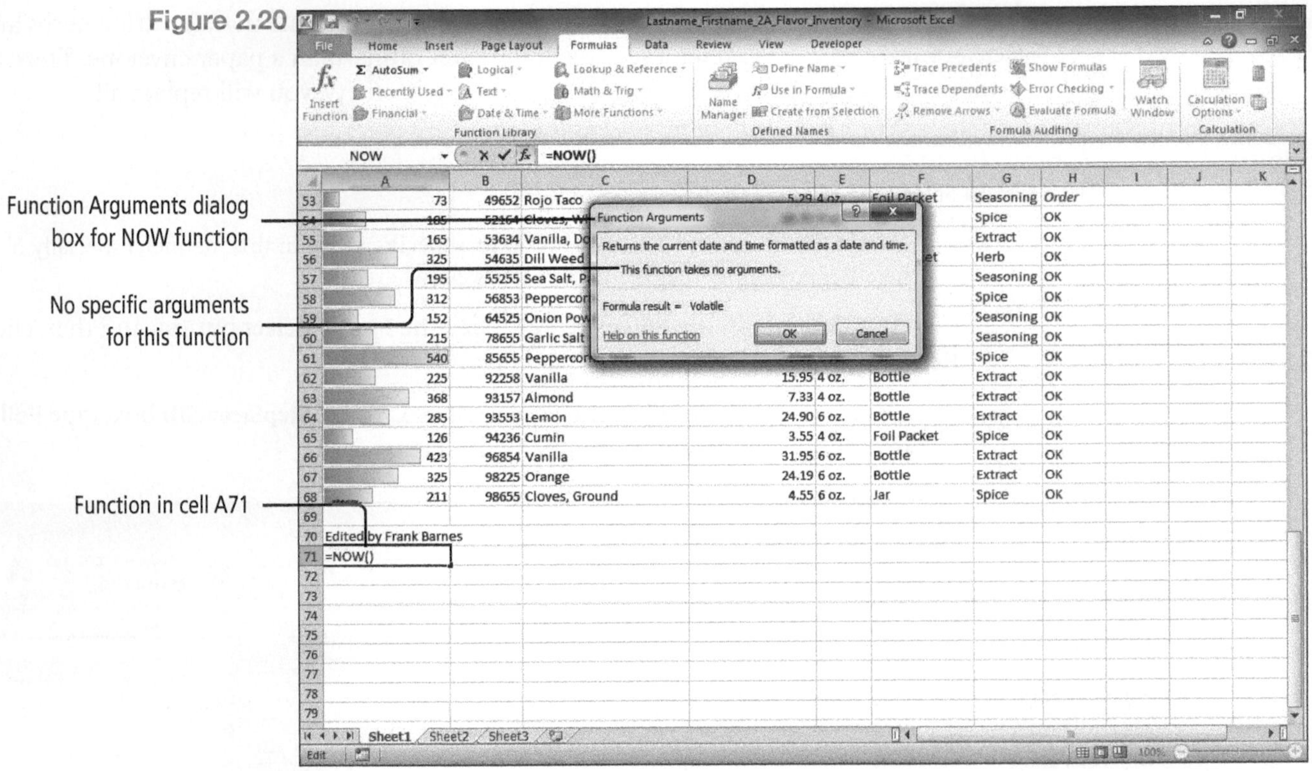

3 Read the description in the **Function Arguments** dialog box, and notice that this result is *Volatile.*

The Function Arguments dialog box displays a message indicating that this function does not require an argument. It also states that this function is ***volatile***, meaning the date and time will not remain as entered, but rather the date and time will automatically update each time you open this workbook.

4 In the **Function Arguments** dialog box, click **OK** to close the dialog box to display the current date and time in cell **A71**. **Save** your workbook.

> More Knowledge | NOW Function Recalculates Each Time a Workbook Opens
>
> The NOW function updates each time the workbook is opened. With the workbook open, you can force the NOW function to update by pressing F9, for example, to update the time.

Activity 2.11 | Freezing and Unfreezing Panes

In a large worksheet, if you scroll down more than 25 rows or scroll beyond column O (the exact row number and column letter varies, depending on your screen resolution), you will no longer see the top rows or first column of your worksheet where identifying information about the data is usually placed. You will find it easier to work with your data if you can always view the identifying row or column titles.

The ***Freeze Panes*** command enables you to select one or more rows or columns and then freeze (lock) them into place. The locked rows and columns become separate panes. A ***pane*** is a portion of a worksheet window bounded by and separated from other portions by vertical or horizontal bars.

1 Press Ctrl + Home to make cell **A1** the active cell. Scroll down until **row 40** displays at the top of your Excel window, and notice that all of the identifying information in the column titles is out of view.

2 Press Ctrl + Home again, and then from the **row heading area**, select **row 14**. Click the **View tab**, and then in the **Window group**, click the **Freeze Panes** button. In the list, click **Freeze Panes**. Click any cell to deselect the row, and then notice that a line displays along the upper border of **row 14**.

By selecting row 14, the rows above—rows 1 - 13—are frozen in place and will not move as you scroll down.

3 Watch the row numbers below **row 13**, and then begin to scroll down to bring **row 40** into view again. Notice that rows 1:13 are frozen in place. Compare your screen with Figure 2.21.

The remaining rows of data continue to scroll. Use this feature when you have long or wide worksheets.

Figure 2.21

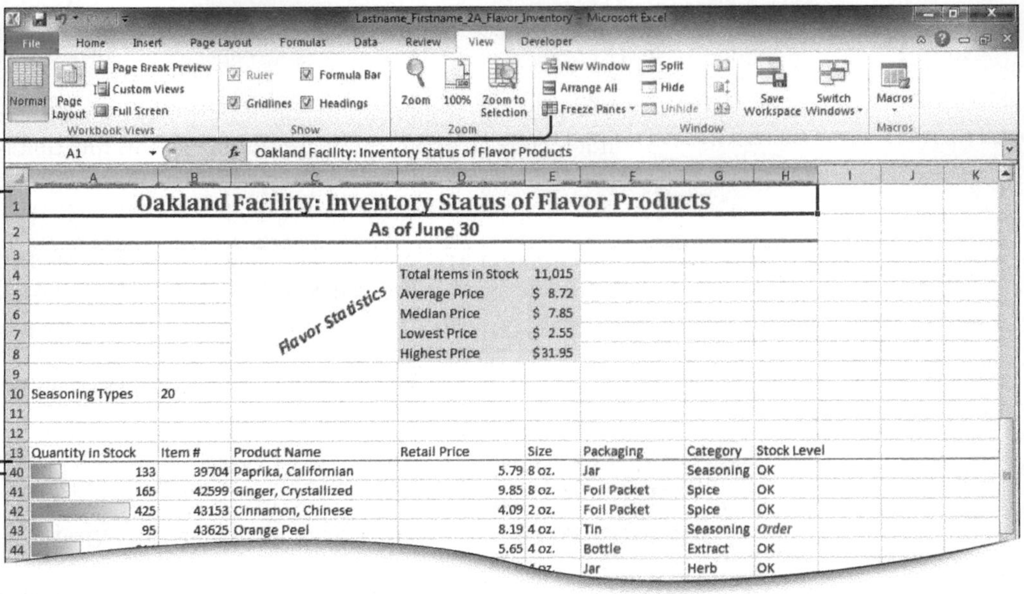

4. In the **Window group**, click the **Freeze Panes** button, and then click **Unfreeze Panes** to unlock all rows and columns. **Save** your workbook.

> **More Knowledge | Freeze Columns or Freeze both Rows and Columns**
>
> You can freeze columns that you want to remain in view on the left. Select the column to the right of the column(s) that you want to remain in view while scrolling to the right, and then click the Freeze Panes command. You can also use the command to freeze both rows and columns; click a *cell* to freeze the rows *above* the cell and the columns to the *left* of the cell.

Objective 5 | Create, Sort, and Filter an Excel Table

To analyze a group of related data, you can convert a range of cells to an ***Excel table***. An Excel table is a series of rows and columns that contains related data that is managed independently from the data in other rows and columns in the worksheet.

Activity 2.12 | Creating an Excel Table

1. Be sure that you have applied the Unfreeze Panes command—no rows on your worksheet are locked. Then, click any cell in the data below row 13.

> **Another Way**
>
> Select the range of cells that make up the table, including the header row, and then click the Table button.

2. Click the **Insert tab**. In the **Tables group**, click the **Table** button. In the **Create Table** dialog box, if necessary, click to select the **My table has headers** check box, and then compare your screen with Figure 2.22.

   The column titles in row 13 will form the table headers. By clicking in a range of contiguous data, Excel will suggest the range as the data for the table. You can adjust the range if necessary.

Figure 2.22

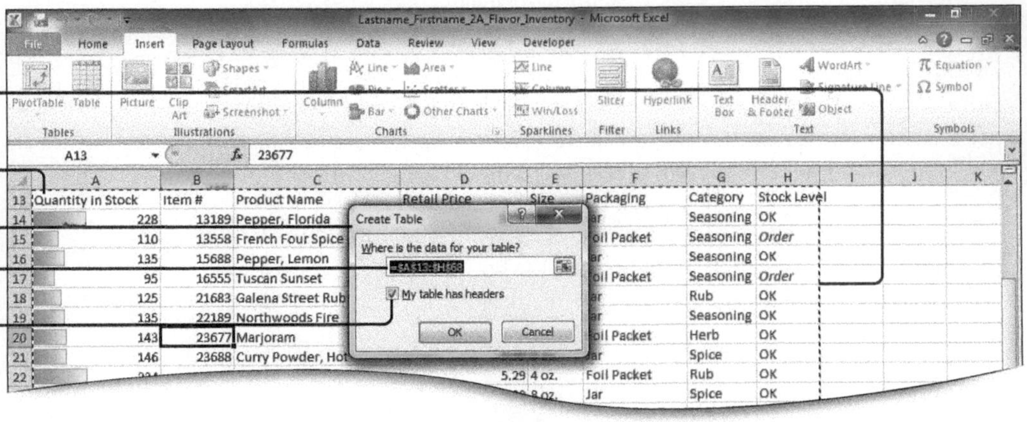

3 Click **OK**. With the range still selected, on the Ribbon notice that the **Table Tools** are active.

4 On the **Design tab**, in the **Table Styles group**, click the **More** button, and then under **Light**, locate and click **Table Style Light 16**.

5 Press Ctrl + Home. Click **Save**, and then compare your screen with Figure 2.23.

Sorting and filtering arrows display in the table's header row.

Figure 2.23

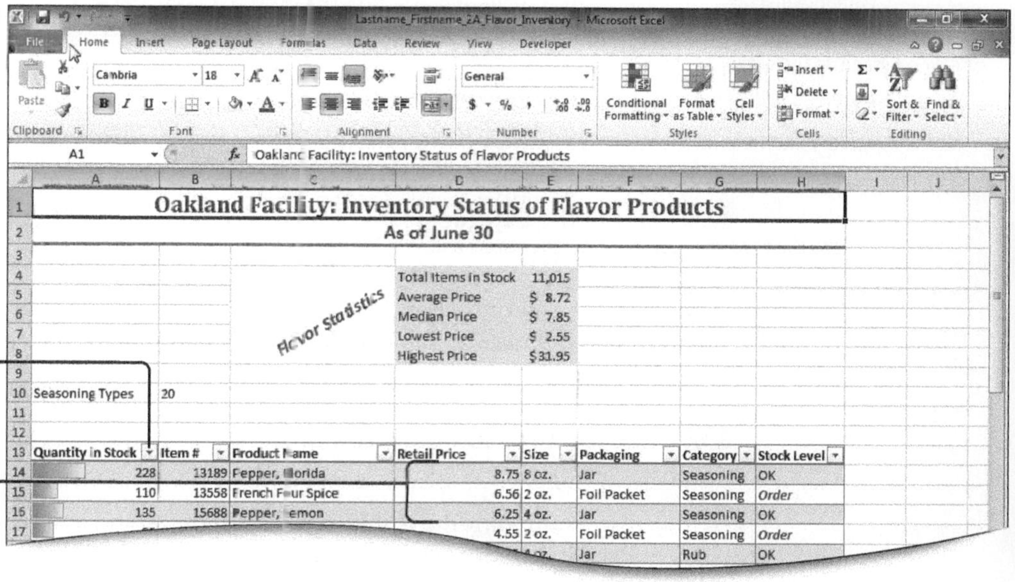

Activity 2.13 | Sorting and Filtering an Excel Table

You can ***sort*** tables—arrange all the data in a specific order—in ascending or descending order. You can ***filter*** tables—display only a portion of the data based on matching a specific value—to show only the data that meets the criteria that you specify.

1 In the header row of the table, click the **Retail Price arrow**, and then on the menu, click **Sort Smallest to Largest**. Next to the arrow, notice the small **up arrow** indicating an ascending (smallest to largest) sort.

The rows in the table are sorted from the lowest retail price to highest retail price.

2 In the table's header row, click the **Category arrow**. On the menu, click **Sort A to Z**. Next to the arrow, notice the small **up arrow** indicating an ascending (A to Z) sort.

The rows in the table are sorted alphabetically by Category.

3 Click the **Category arrow** again, and then sort from **Z to A**.

The rows in the table are sorted in reverse alphabetic order by Category name, and the small arrow points downward, indicating a descending (Z to A) sort.

4 Click the **Category arrow** again. On the menu, click the **(Select All)** check box to clear all the check boxes. Click to select only the **Extract** check box, and then click **OK**. Compare your screen with Figure 2.24.

Only the rows containing *Extract* in the Category column display—the remaining rows are hidden from view. A small funnel—the filter icon—indicates that a filter is applied to the data in the table. Additionally, the row numbers display in blue to indicate that some rows are hidden from view. A filter hides entire rows in the worksheet.

Figure 2.24

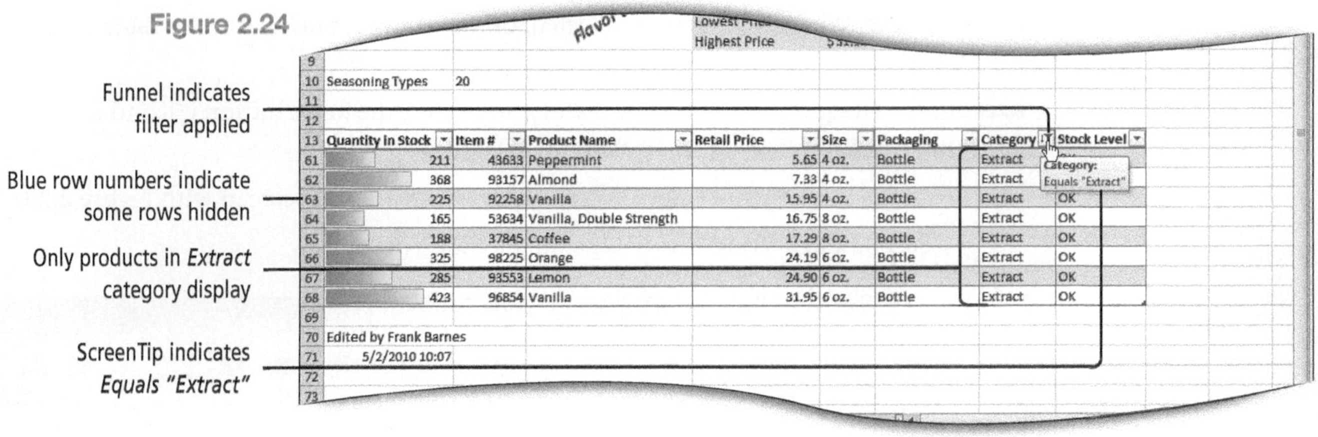

5 Point to the **Category arrow**, and notice that *Equals "Extract"* displays to indicate the filter criteria.

6 Click any cell in the table so that the table is selected. On the Ribbon, click the **Design tab**, and then in the **Table Style Options group**, select the **Total Row** check box.

Total displays in cell A69. In cell H69, the number *8* indicates that eight rows currently display.

7 Click cell **A69**, click the **arrow** that displays to the right of cell **A69**, and then in the list, click **Sum**.

Excel sums only the visible rows in Column A, and indicates that 2190 products in the Extract category are in stock. In this manner, you can use an Excel table to quickly find information about a group of data.

8 Click cell **A11**, type **Extract Types:** and press Tab. In cell **B11**, type **8 (2,190 total items in stock)** and then press Enter.

9 In the table header row, click the **Category arrow**, and then on the menu, click **Clear Filter From "Category"**.

All the rows in the table redisplay. The Z to A sort on Category remains in effect.

10 Click the **Packaging arrow**, click the **(Select All)** check box to clear all the check boxes, and then click to select the **Foil Packet** check box. Click **OK**.

11 Click the **Category arrow**, click the **(Select All)** check box to clear all the check boxes, and then click the **Herb** check box. Click **OK**, and then compare your screen with Figure 2.25.

By applying multiple filters, Laura can quickly determine that seven items in the Herb category are packaged in foil packets with a total of 1,346 such items in stock.

Figure 2.25

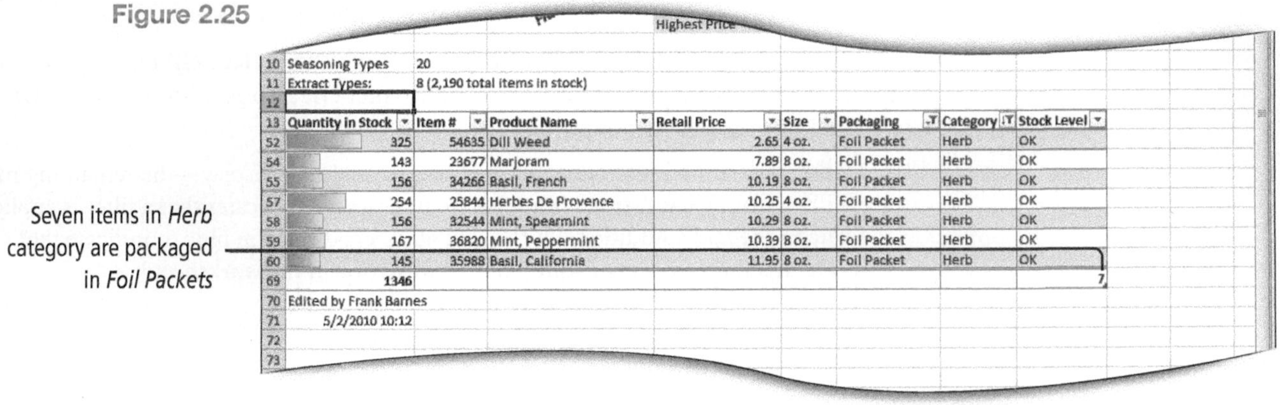
Seven items in *Herb* category are packaged in *Foil Packets*
Highest Price
10 Seasoning Types 20
11 Extract Types: 8 (2,190 total items in stock)
13 Quantity in Stock | Item # | Product Name | Retail Price | Size | Packaging | Category | Stock Level
52 325 54635 Dill Weed 2.65 4 oz. Foil Packet Herb OK
54 143 23677 Marjoram 7.89 8 oz. Foil Packet Herb OK
55 156 34266 Basil, French 10.19 8 oz. Foil Packet Herb OK
57 254 25844 Herbes De Provence 10.25 4 oz. Foil Packet Herb OK
58 156 32544 Mint, Spearmint 10.29 8 oz. Foil Packet Herb OK
59 167 36820 Mint, Peppermint 10.39 8 oz. Foil Packet Herb OK
60 145 35988 Basil, California 11.95 8 oz. Foil Packet Herb OK
69 1346 7
70 Edited by Frank Barnes
71 5/2/2010 10:12

12 Click the **Category arrow**, and then click **Clear Filter From "Category"**. Use the same technique to remove the filter from the **Packaging** column.

13 In the table header row, click the **Item# arrow**, and then click **Sort Smallest to Largest**, which will apply an ascending sort to the data using the *Item#* column. **Save** your workbook.

Activity 2.14 | Converting a Table to a Range of Data

When you are finished answering questions about the data in a table by sorting, filtering, and totaling, you can convert the table into a normal range. Doing so is useful if you want to use the feature only to apply an attractive Table Style to a range of cells. For example, you can insert a table, apply a Table Style, and then convert the table to a normal range of data but keep the formatting.

> **Another Way**
> With any table cell selected, right-click, point to Table, and then click Convert to Range.

1 Click anywhere in the table to activate the table and display the **Table Tools** on the Ribbon. On the **Design tab**, in the **Table Style Options group**, click the **Total Row** check box to clear the check mark and remove the Total row from the table.

2 On the **Design tab**, in the **Tools group**, click the **Convert to Range** button. In the message box, click **Yes**. Click **Save**, and then compare your screen with Figure 2.26.

Figure 2.26

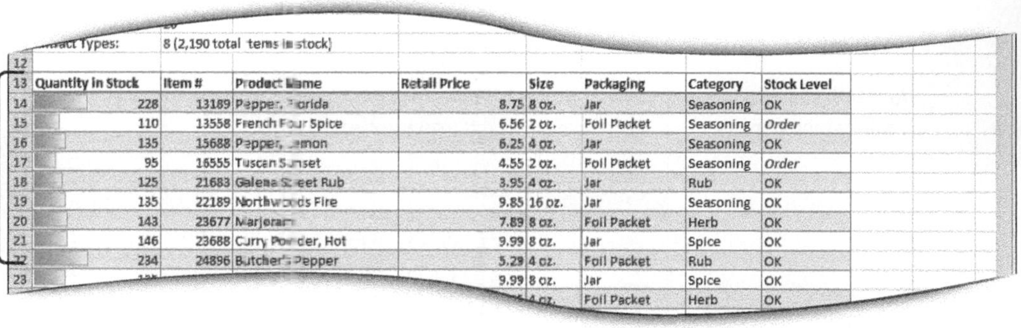

Table converted to a normal range, color and shading formats remain

Objective 6 | Format and Print a Large Worksheet

A worksheet might be too wide, too long—or both—to print on a single page. Use Excel's ***Print Titles*** and ***Scale to Fit*** commands to create pages that are attractive and easy to read.

The Print Titles command enables you to specify rows and columns to repeat on each printed page. Scale to Fit commands enable you to stretch or shrink the width, height, or both, of printed output to fit a maximum number of pages.

Activity 2.15 | Printing Titles and Scaling to Fit

1 Press Ctrl + Home to display the top of your worksheet. Select the range **A13:H13**. On the **Home tab**, from the **Styles group**, apply the **Heading 4** cell style, and then apply **Center**.

2 On the **Insert tab**, in the **Text group**, click **Header & Footer**. In the **Navigation group**, click the **Go to Footer** button, and then click just above the word *Footer*.

3 In the **Header & Footer Elements group**, click the **File Name** button to add the name of your file to the footer—*&[File]* displays. Then, click in a cell just above the footer to exit the Footer and view your file name.

4. Delete the unused sheets **Sheet2** and **Sheet3**. On the right edge of the status bar, click the **Normal** button, and then press Ctrl + Home to display the top of your worksheet.

   Dotted lines indicate where the pages would break if printed as currently formatted; these dotted lines display when you switch from Page Layout view to Normal view.

5. On the **Page Layout tab**, in the **Themes group**, click the **Themes** button, and then click **Concourse**.

6. In the **Page Setup group**, click **Margins**, and then at the bottom, click **Custom Margins**. In the **Page Setup** dialog box, under **Center on page**, select the **Horizontally** check box, and then click **OK**.

7. In the **Page Setup group**, click **Orientation**, and then click **Landscape**. Press Ctrl + F2 to display the **Print Preview**. At the bottom of the **Print Preview**, click the **Next Page** button ▶. Compare your screen with Figure 2.27.

   As currently formatted, the worksheet will print on five pages, and the columns will span multiple pages. Additionally, after Page 1, no column titles are visible to identify the data in the columns.

Figure 2.27

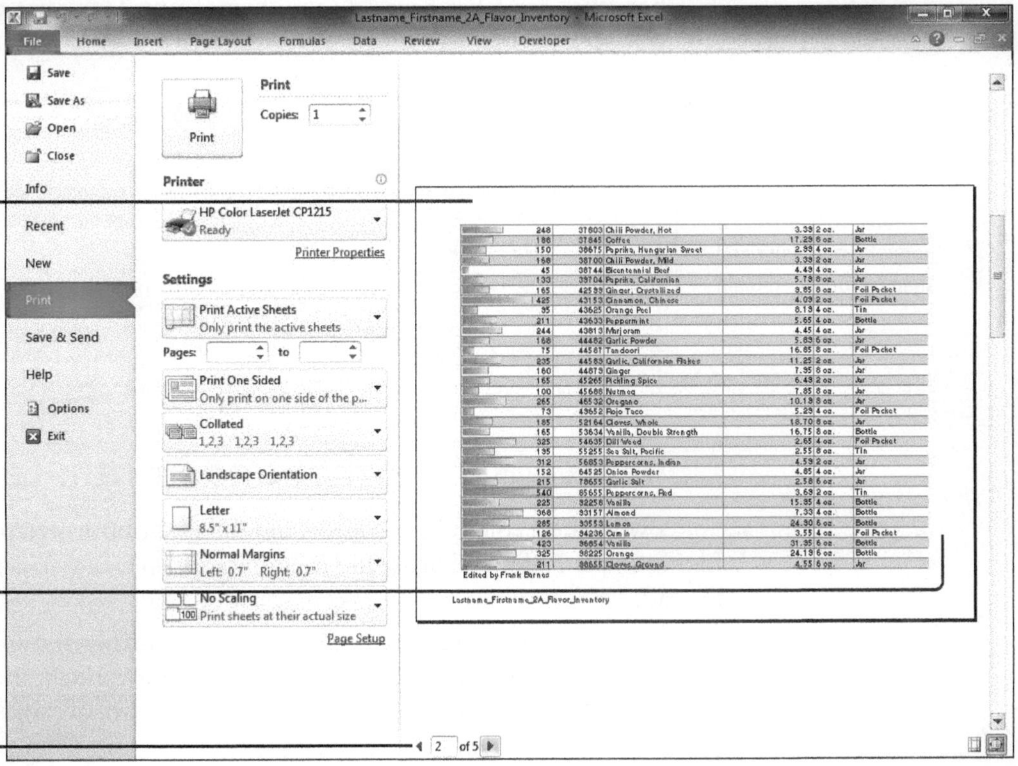

No identifying column titles at top of page

Additional columns not visible on this page

Page 2 indicated

8 Click **Next Page** [▶] two times to display **Page 4**, and notice that two columns move to an additional page.

9 On the Ribbon, click **Page Layout** to redisplay the worksheet. In the **Page Setup group**, click the **Print Titles** button. Under **Print titles**, click in the **Rows to repeat at top** box, and then at the right, click the **Collapse Dialog** button.

10 From the **row heading area**, select **row 13**, and then click the **Expand Dialog** button. Click **OK** to print the column titles in row 13 at the top of every page.

Adding the titles on each page increases the number of pages to 6.

> **Another Way**
>
> With the worksheet displayed, on the Page Layout tab, in the Scale to Fit group, click the Width button arrow, and then click 1 page.

11 Press [Ctrl] + [F2] to display the **Print Preview**. In the center panel, at the bottom of the **Settings group**, click the **Scaling** button, and then on the displayed list, point to **Fit All Columns on One Page**. Compare your screen with Figure 2.28.

This action will shrink the width of the printed output to fit all the columns on one page. You can make adjustments like this on the Page Layout tab, or here, in the Print Preview.

Figure 2.28

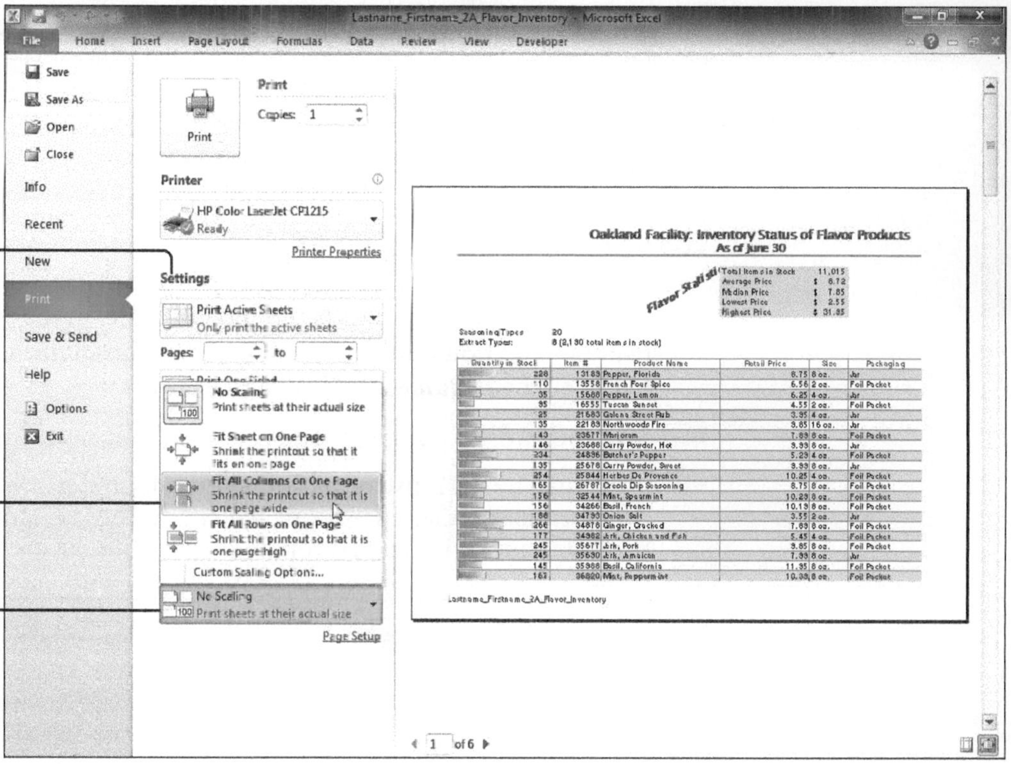

12 Click **Fit All Columns on One Page**. Notice in the **Print Preview** that all the columns display on one page.

13 At the bottom of the **Print Preview**, click the **Next Page** button [▶] one time. Notice that the output will now print on two pages and that the column titles display at the top of **Page 2**. Compare your screen with Figure 2.29.

Figure 2.29

Column titles display on Page 2

Page 2 of 2 indicated

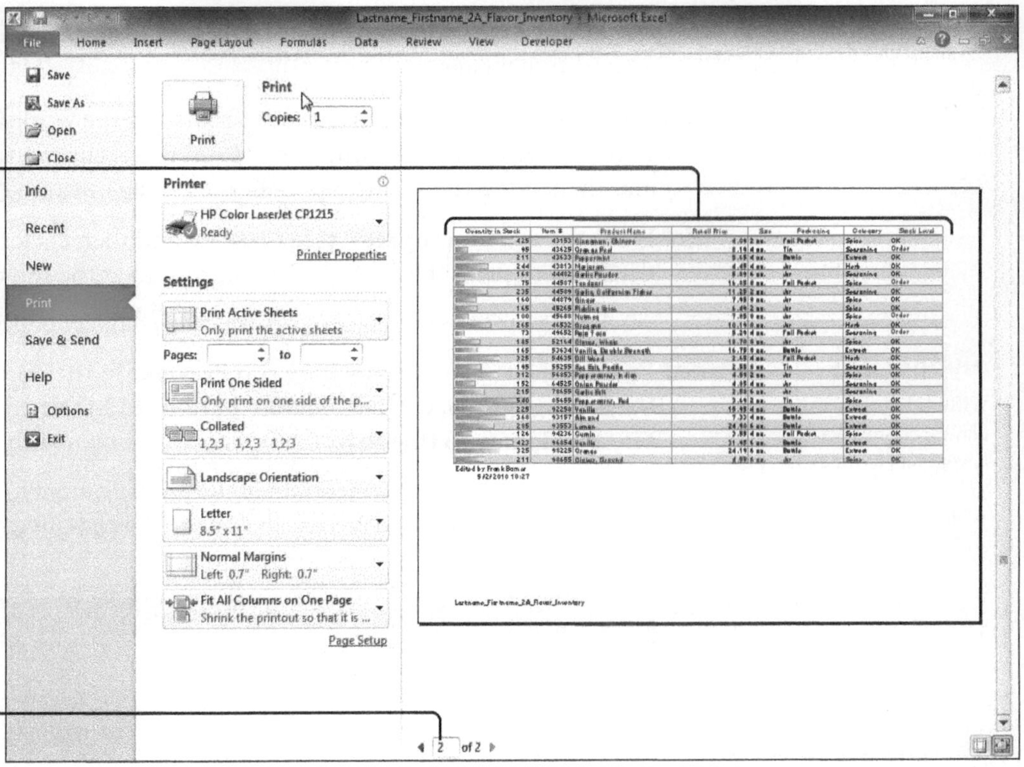

14 In **Backstage** view, click the **Info tab**. On the right, under the document thumbnail, click **Properties**, and then click **Show Document Panel**. In the **Author** box, replace the existing text with your firstname and lastname. In the **Subject** box, type your course name and section number. In the **Keywords** box, type **inventory, Oakland** and then **Close** [×] the **Document Information Panel**.

15 **Save** your workbook, and then print or submit electronically as directed.

16 If required by your instructor, print or create an electronic version of your worksheets with formulas displayed by using the instructions in Activity 1.16, and then **Close** [×] Excel without saving so that you do not save the changes you made to print formulas.

> **More Knowledge | Scaling for Data that is Slightly Larger than the Printed Page**
>
> If your data is just a little too large to fit on a printed page, you can scale the worksheet to make it fit. Scaling reduces both the width and height of the printed data to a percentage of its original size or by the number of pages that you specify. To adjust the printed output to a percentage of its actual size, for example to 80%, on the Page Layout tab, in the Scale to Fit group, click the Scale arrows to select a percentage.

End **You have completed Project 2A**

Project 2B Weekly Sales Summary

myitlab
Project 2B Training

Project Activities

In Activities 2.16 through 2.26, you will edit an existing workbook for Laura Morales. The workbook summarizes the online and in-store sales of products during a one-week period in July. The worksheets of your completed workbook will look similar to Figure 2.30.

Project Files

For Project 2B, you will need the following file:

e02B_Weekly_Sales

You will save your workbook as:

Lastname_Firstname_2B_Weekly_Sales

Project Results

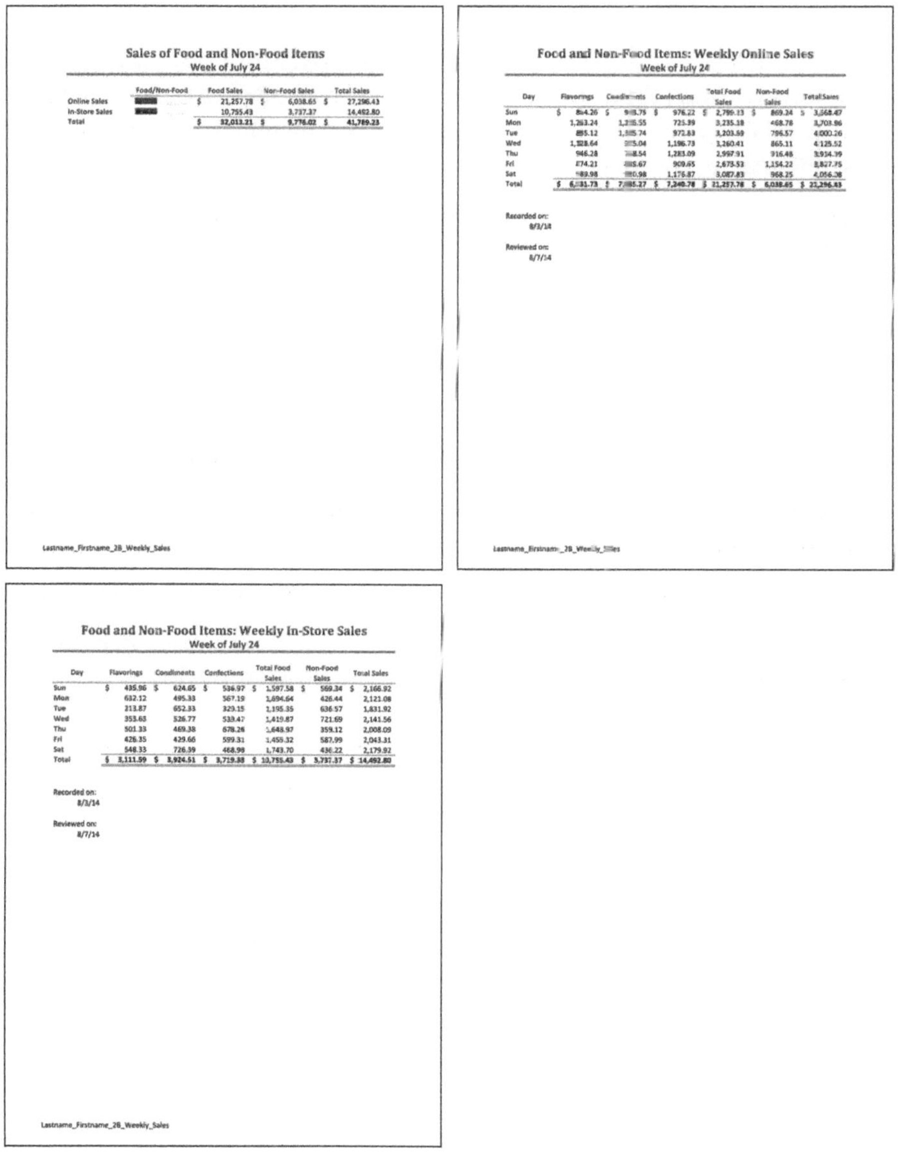

Sales of Food and Non-Food Items
Week of July 24

	Food/Non-Food	Food Sales	Non-Food Sales	Total Sales
Online Sales		$ 21,257.78	$ 6,038.65	$ 27,296.43
In-Store Sales		10,755.43	3,737.37	14,492.80
Total		$ 32,013.21	$ 9,776.02	$ 41,789.23

Lastname_Firstname_2B_Weekly_Sales

Food and Non-Food Items: Weekly Online Sales
Week of July 24

Day	Flavorings	Condiments	Confections	Total Food Sales	Non-Food Sales	Total Sales
Sun	$ [illegible]	$ [illegible]	$ 976.22	$ 2,799.13	$ 869.24	$ 3,568.47
Mon	[illegible]	[illegible]	725.39	3,235.18	468.78	3,703.96
Tue	[illegible]	[illegible]	972.83	3,203.69	796.57	4,000.26
Wed	[illegible]	[illegible]	1,196.73	3,260.41	865.11	4,125.52
Thu	946.28	[illegible]	1,283.09	2,997.91	916.48	3,914.39
Fri	[illegible]	[illegible]	909.65	2,673.53	1,154.22	3,827.75
Sat	[illegible]	[illegible]	1,176.87	3,087.83	968.25	4,056.08
Total	$ [illegible]	$ [illegible]	$ 7,240.78	$ 21,257.78	$ 6,038.65	$ 27,296.43

Recorded on:
8/3/14

Reviewed on:
8/7/14

Lastname_Firstname_2B_Weekly_Sales

Food and Non-Food Items: Weekly In-Store Sales
Week of July 24

Day	Flavorings	Condiments	Confections	Total Food Sales	Non-Food Sales	Total Sales
Sun	$ 435.96	$ 624.65	$ 536.97	$ 1,597.58	$ 569.34	$ 2,166.92
Mon	632.12	495.33	567.19	1,694.64	426.44	2,121.08
Tue	213.87	652.33	329.15	1,195.35	636.57	1,831.92
Wed	353.63	526.77	539.47	1,419.87	721.69	2,141.56
Thu	501.33	469.38	678.26	1,648.97	359.12	2,008.09
Fri	426.35	429.66	599.31	1,455.32	587.99	2,043.31
Sat	548.33	726.39	468.98	1,743.70	436.22	2,179.92
Total	$ 3,111.59	$ 3,924.51	$ 3,719.38	$ 10,755.43	$ 3,737.37	$ 14,492.80

Recorded on:
8/3/14

Reviewed on:
8/7/14

Lastname_Firstname_2B_Weekly_Sales

Figure 2.30
Project 2B Weekly Sales

Excel | Chapter 2

Objective 7 | Navigate a Workbook and Rename Worksheets

Use multiple worksheets in a workbook to organize data in a logical arrangement. When you have more than one worksheet in a workbook, you can ***navigate*** (move) among worksheets by clicking the ***sheet tabs***. Sheet tabs identify each worksheet in a workbook and are located along the lower left edge of the workbook window. When you have more worksheets in the workbook than can be displayed in the sheet tab area, use the four sheet tab scrolling buttons to move sheet tabs into and out of view.

Activity 2.16 | Navigating Among Worksheets, Renaming Worksheets, and Changing the Tab Color of Worksheets

Excel names the first worksheet in a workbook *Sheet1* and each additional worksheet in order—*Sheet2*, *Sheet3*, and so on. Most Excel users rename the worksheets with meaningful names. In this activity, you will navigate among worksheets, rename worksheets, and change the tab color of sheet tabs.

Another Way

Press Ctrl + F12 to display the Open dialog box. Press F12 to display the Save As dialog box.

1. **Start** Excel. From **Backstage** view, display the **Open** dialog box. From your student files, open **e02B_Weekly_Sales**. From **Backstage** view, display the **Save As** dialog box, navigate to your **Excel Chapter 2** folder, and then using your own name, save the file as **Lastname_Firstname_2B_Weekly_Sales**

   In the displayed workbook, there are two worksheets into which some data has already been entered. For example, on the first worksheet, the days of the week and sales data for the one-week period displays.

2. Along the bottom of the Excel window, point to and then click the **Sheet2 tab**.

   The second worksheet in the workbook displays and becomes the active worksheet. *Sheet2* displays in bold.

3. In cell **A1**, notice the text *In-Store*—this worksheet will contain data for in-store sales.

4. Click the **Sheet1 tab**. Then, point to the **Sheet1 tab**, and double-click to select the sheet tab name. Type **Online Sales** and press Enter.

   The first worksheet becomes the active worksheet, and the sheet tab displays *Online Sales*.

5. Point to the **Sheet2 tab**, right-click, and then from the shortcut menu, click **Rename**. Type **In-Store Sales** and press Enter. Compare your screen with Figure 2.31.

   You can use either of these methods to rename a sheet tab.

Figure 2.31

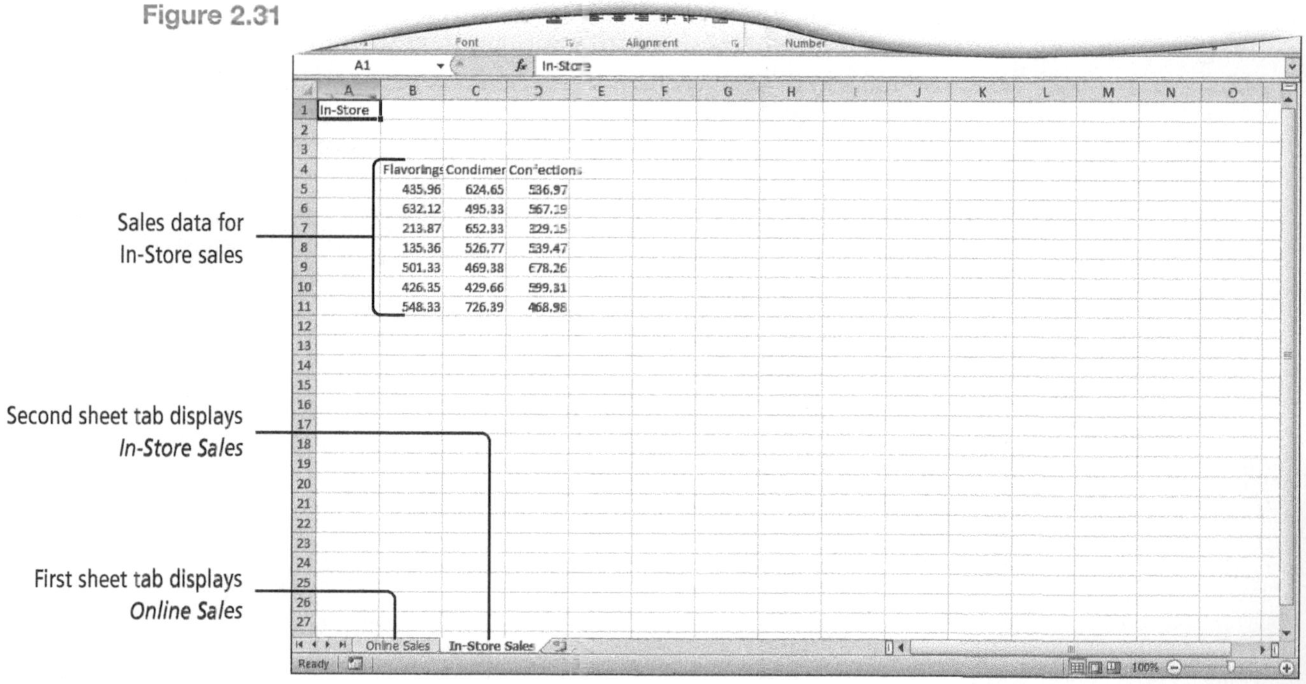

> **Another Way**
> Alternatively, on the Home tab, in the Cells group, click the Format button, and then on the displayed list, point to Tab Color.

6 Point to the **In-Store Sales sheet tab** and right-click. On the shortcut menu, point to **Tab Color**, and then in the last column, click the first color—**Orange, Accent 6**.

7 Using the technique you just practiced, change the tab color of the **Online Sales sheet tab** to **Aqua, Accent 5**—in the next to last column, the first color. **Save** your workbook.

Objective 8 | Enter Dates, Clear Contents, and Clear Formats

Dates represent a type of value that you can enter in a cell. When you enter a date, Excel assigns a serial value—a number—to the date. This makes it possible to treat dates like other numbers. For example, if two cells contain dates, you can find the number of days between the two dates by subtracting the older date from the more recent date.

Activity 2.17 | Entering and Formatting Dates

In this activity, you will examine the various ways that Excel can format dates in a cell. Date values entered in any of the following formats will be recognized by Excel as a date:

Format	Example
m/d/yy	7/4/12
d-mmm	4-Jul
d-mmm-yy	4-Jul-12
mmm-yy	Jul-12

On your keyboard, - (the hyphen key) and / (the forward slash key) function identically in any of these formats and can be used interchangeably. You can abbreviate the month name to three characters or spell it out. You can enter the year as two digits, four digits, or even leave it off. When left off, the current year is assumed but does not display in the cell.

A two-digit year value of 30 through 99 is interpreted by the Windows operating system as the four-digit years of 1930 through 1999. All other two-digit year values are assumed to be in the 21st century. If you always type year values as four digits, even though only two digits may display in the cell, you can be sure that Excel interprets the year value as you intended. Examples are shown in Figure 2.32.

How Excel Interprets Dates

Date Typed As:	Completed by Excel As:
7/4/12	7/4/2012
7-4-98	7/4/1998
7/4	4-Jul (current year assumed)
7-4	4-Jul (current year assumed)
July 4	4-Jul (current year assumed)
Jul 4	4-Jul (current year assumed)
Jul/4	4-Jul (current year assumed)
Jul-4	4-Jul (current year assumed)
July 4, 1998	4-Jul-98
July 2012	Jul-12 (first day of month assumed)
July 1998	Jul-98 (first day of month assumed)

Figure 2.32

1. On the **Online Sales** sheet, click cell **A16** and notice that the cell indicates *8/3* (August 3). In the **Formula Bar**, notice that the full date of August 3, 2014 displays in the format *8/3/2014*.

2. With cell **A16** selected, on the **Home tab**, in the **Number group**, click the **Number Format arrow**. At the bottom of the menu, click **More Number Formats** to display the **Number tab** of the **Format Cells** dialog box.

   Under Category, *Date* is selected, and under Type, *3/14* is selected. Cell A16 uses this format type; that is, only the month and day display in the cell.

3. In the displayed dialog box, under **Type**, click several other date types and watch the **Sample** area to see how applying the selected date format would format your cell. When you are finished, click the **3/14/01** type, and then compare your screen with Figure 2.33.

Figure 2.33

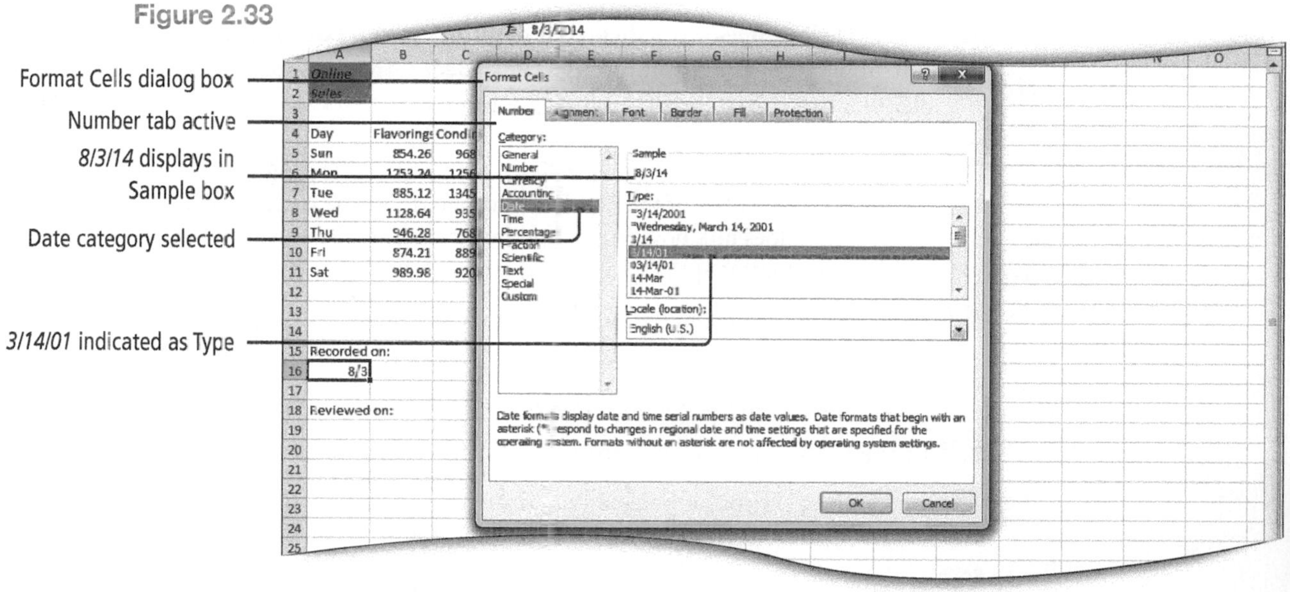

4 At the bottom of the dialog box, click **OK**. Click cell **A19**, type **8-7-14** and then press Enter.

Cell A19 has no special date formatting applied, and thus displays in the default date format *8/7/2014*.

> **Alert! | The Date Does Not Display as 8/7/2014?**
>
> Settings in your Windows operating system determine the default format for dates. If your result is different, it is likely that the formatting of the default date was adjusted on the computer at which you are working.

5 Click cell **A19** again. Hold down Ctrl and press ; (semicolon) on your keyboard. Press Enter to confirm the entry.

Excel enters the current date, obtained from your computer's internal calendar, in the selected cell using the default date format. Ctrl + ; is a quick method to enter the current date.

6 Click cell **A19** again, type **8/7/14** and then press Enter.

Because the year *14* is less than 30, Excel assumes a 21st century date and changes *14* to *2014* to complete the four-digit year. Typing *98* would result in *1998*. For two-digit years that you type that are between 30 and 99, Excel assumes a 20th century date.

7 Click cell **A16**, and then on the **Home tab**, in the **Clipboard group**, click the **Format Painter** button. Click cell **A19**, and notice that the date format from cell **A16** is copied to cell **A19**. **Save** your workbook.

Activity 2.18 | Clearing Cell Contents and Formats

A cell has *contents*—a value or a formula—and a cell may also have one or more *formats* applied, for example bold and italic font styles, fill color, font color, and so on. You can choose to clear—delete—the *contents* of a cell, the *formatting* of a cell, or both.

Clearing the contents of a cell deletes the value or formula typed there, but it does *not* clear formatting applied to a cell. In this activity, you will clear the contents of a cell and then clear the formatting of a cell that contains a date to see its underlying content.

1 In the **Online Sales** worksheet, click cell **A1**. In the **Editing group**, click the **Clear** button. On the displayed list, click **Clear Contents** and notice that the text is cleared, but the orange formatting remains.

2 Click cell **A2**, and then press Del.

You can use either of these two methods to delete the *contents* of a cell. Deleting the contents does not, however, delete the formatting of the cell; you can see that the orange fill color format applied to the two cells still displays.

3 In cell **A1**, type **Online Sales** and then on the **Formula Bar**, click the **Enter** button so that cell **A1** remains the active cell.

In addition to the orange fill color, the bold italic text formatting remains with the cell.

4 In the **Editing group**, click the **Clear** button, and then click **Clear Formats.**

Clearing the formats deletes formatting from the cell—the orange fill color and the bold and italic font styles—but does not delete the cell's contents.

5 Use the same technique to clear the orange fill color from cell **A2**. Click cell **A16**, click the **Clear** button, and then click **Clear Formats.** In the **Number group**, notice that *General* displays as the number format of the cell.

The box in the Number group indicates the current Number format of the selected cell. Clearing the date formatting from the cell displays the date's serial number. The date, August 3, 2014, is stored as a serial number that indicates the number of days since January 1, 1900. This date is the 41,854th day since the reference date of January 1, 1900.

6 On the Quick Access Toolbar, click the **Undo** button to restore the date format. **Save** your workbook, and then compare your screen with Figure 2.34.

Figure 2.34

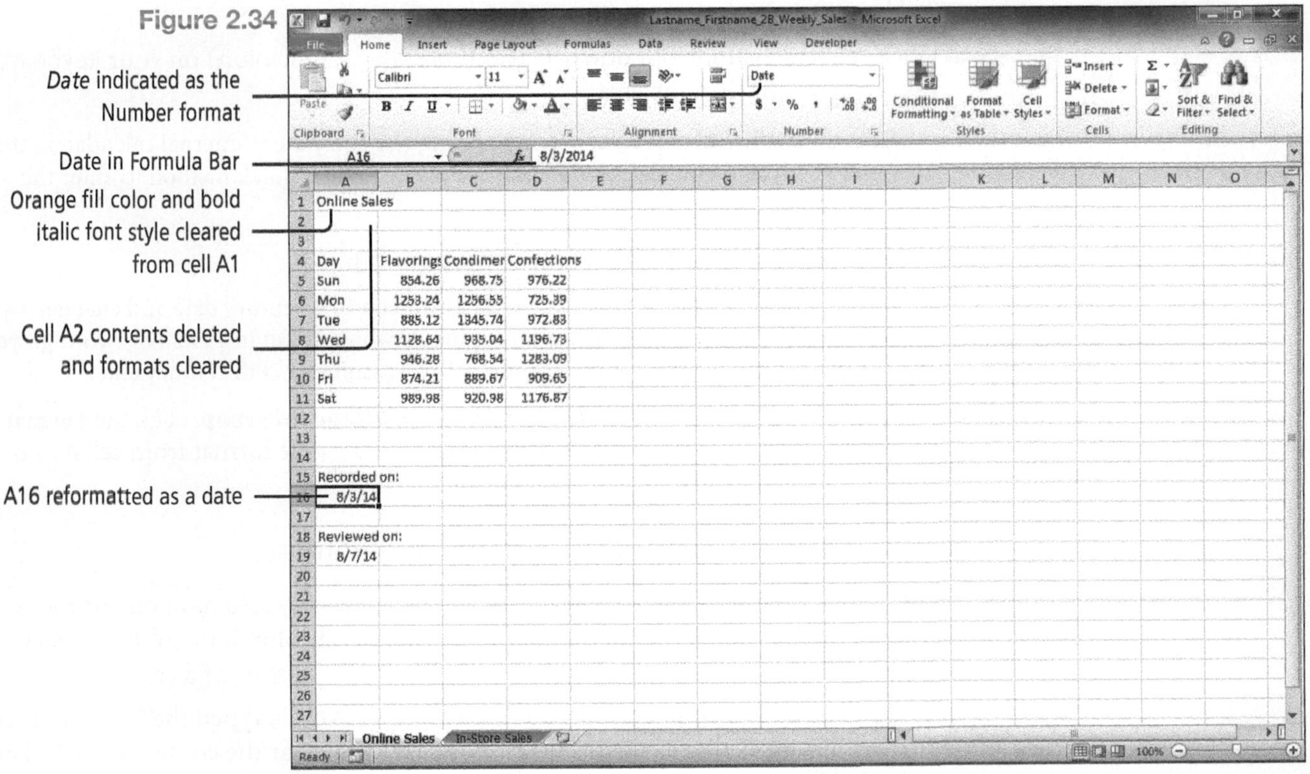

Objective 9 | Copy and Paste by Using the Paste Options Gallery

Data in cells can be copied to other cells in the same worksheet, to other sheets in the same workbook, or to sheets in another workbook. The action of placing cell contents that have been copied or moved to the Office Clipboard into another location is called ***paste***.

Activity 2.19 | Copying and Pasting by Using the Paste Options Gallery

Recall that the Office Clipboard is a temporary storage area maintained by your Windows operating system. When you select one or more cells, and then perform the Copy command or the Cut command, the selected data is placed on the Office Clipboard. From the Office Clipboard storage area, the data is available for pasting into other cells, other worksheets, other workbooks, and even into other Office programs. When you paste, the ***Paste Options gallery*** displays, which includes Live Preview to preview the Paste formatting that you want.

Excel | Chapter 2

1 With the **Online Sales** worksheet active, select the range **A4:A19**.

A range of cells identical to this one is required for the *In-Store Sales* worksheet.

> **Another Way**
> Use the keyboard shortcut for Copy, which is Ctrl + C; or click the Copy button in the Clipboard group on the Home tab.

2 Right-click over the selection, and then click **Copy** to place a copy of the cells on the Office Clipboard. Notice that the copied cells display a moving border.

3 At the bottom of the workbook window, click the **In-Store Sales sheet tab** to make it the active worksheet. Point to cell **A4**, right-click, and then on the shortcut menu, under **Paste Options**, *point* to the first button—**Paste**. Compare your screen with Figure 2.35.

Live Preview displays how the copied cells will be placed in the worksheet if you click the Paste button. In this manner, you can experiment with different paste options, and then be sure you are selecting the paste operation that you want. When pasting a range of cells, you need only point to or select the cell in the upper left corner of the ***paste area***—the target destination for data that has been cut or copied using the Office Clipboard.

Figure 2.35

Paste Options (6 option buttons)

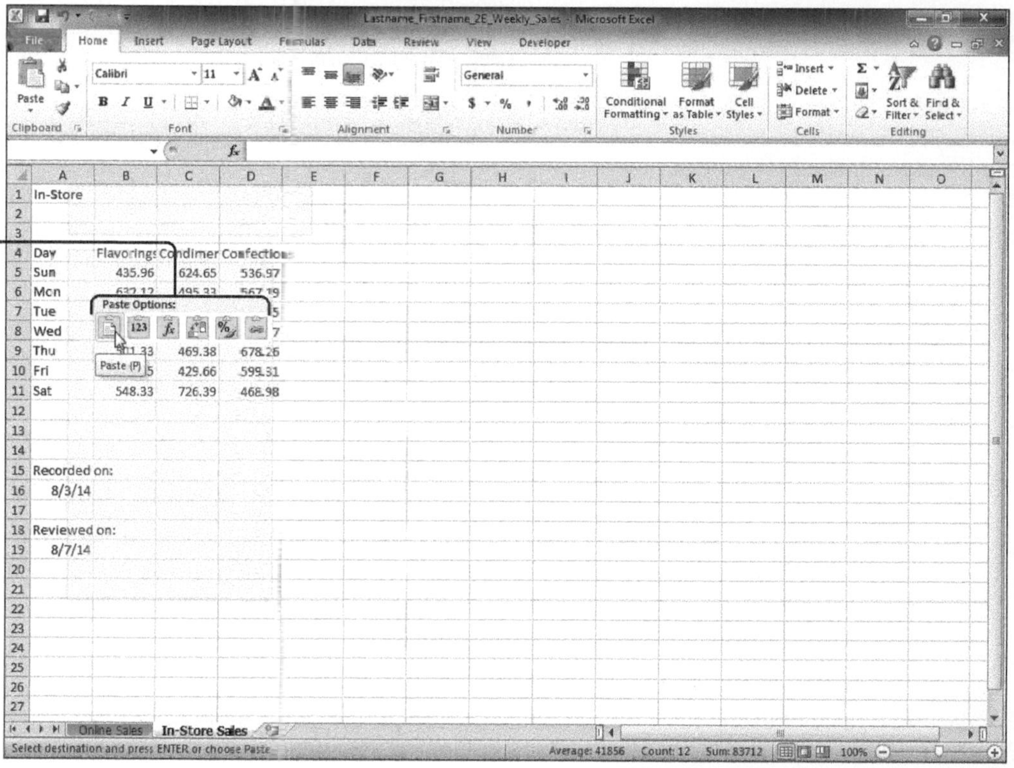

Another Way

Use the keyboard shortcut for Paste, which is Ctrl + V; or click the Paste button in the Clipboard group on the Home tab.

4 Click the first button, **Paste**. In the status bar, notice that the message still displays, indicating that your selected range remains available on the Office Clipboard.

5 Display the **Online Sales** worksheet. Press Esc to cancel the moving border. **Save** your workbook.

The status bar no longer displays the message.

Note | Pressing Enter to Complete a Paste Action

If you want to paste the same text more than one time, click the Paste button so that the copied text remains available on the Office Clipboard. Otherwise, you can press Enter to complete the Paste command.

Objective 10 | Edit and Format Multiple Worksheets at the Same Time

You can enter or edit data on several worksheets at the same time by selecting and grouping multiple worksheets. Data that you enter or edit on the active sheet is reflected in all selected sheets. If you apply color to the sheet tabs, the name of the sheet tab will be underlined in the color you selected. If the sheet tab displays with a background color, you know the sheet is not selected.

Activity 2.20 | Grouping Worksheets for Editing

In this activity, you will group the two worksheets, and then format both worksheets at the same time.

1 With the **Online Sales** sheet active, press Ctrl + Home to make cell **A1** the active cell. Point to the **Online Sales sheet tab**, right-click, and then from the shortcut menu, click **Select All Sheets**.

2 At the top of your screen, notice that *[Group]* displays in the title bar. Compare your screen with Figure 2.36.

Both worksheets are selected, as indicated by *[Group]* in the title bar and the sheet tab names underlined in the selected tab color. Data that you enter or edit on the active sheet will also be entered or edited in the same manner on all the selected sheets in the same cells.

Figure 2.36

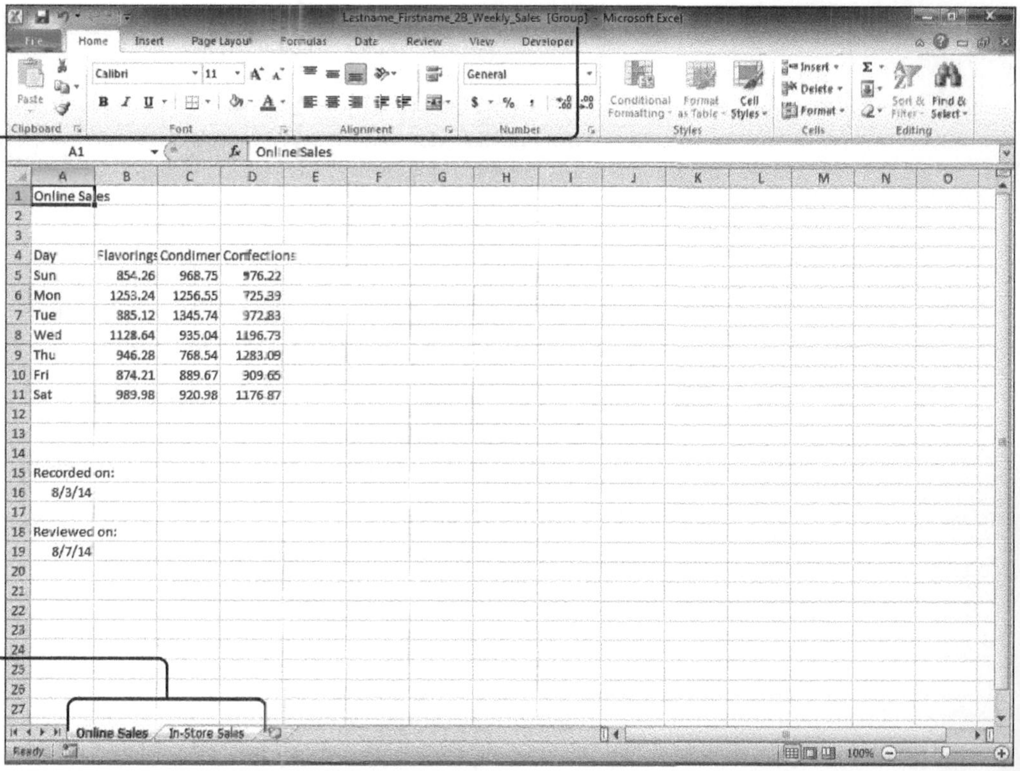

3 Select **columns A:G**, and then set their width to **85 pixels**.

4 Click cell **A2**, type **Week of July 24** and then on the **Formula Bar**, click the **Enter** button to keep cell **A2** as the active cell. **Merge & Center** the text across the range **A2:G2**, and then apply the **Heading 1** cell style.

5 Click cell **E4**, type **Total Food Sales** and then press Tab. In cell **F4**, type **Non-Food Sales** and then press Tab. In cell **G4**, type **Total Sales** and then press Enter.

6 Select the range **A4:G4**, and then apply the **Heading 3** cell style. In the **Alignment group**, click the **Center**, **Middle Align**, and **Wrap Text** buttons. **Save** your workbook.

Another Way

Right-click any sheet tab, and then click Ungroup Sheets.

7 Display the **In-Store Sales** worksheet to cancel the grouping, and then compare your screen with Figure 2.37.

As soon as you select a single sheet, the grouping of the sheets is canceled and *[Group]* no longer displays in the title bar. Because the sheets were grouped, the same new text and formatting was applied to both sheets. In this manner, you can make the same changes to all the sheets in a workbook at one time.

Figure 2.37

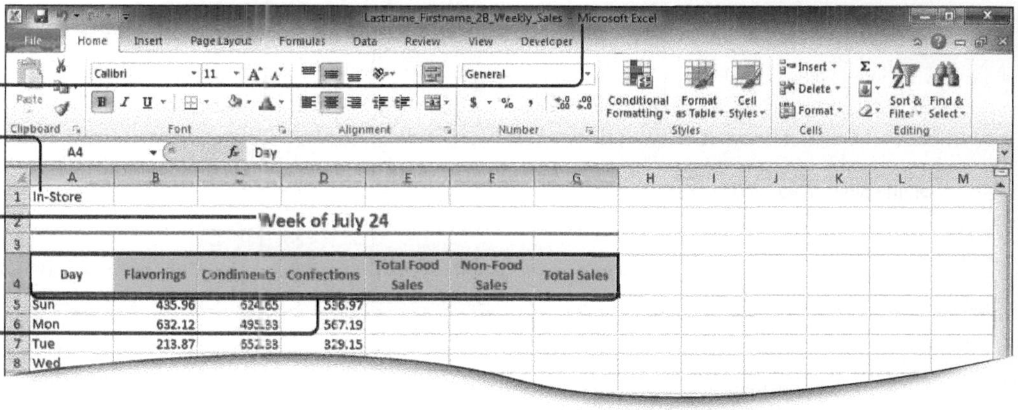

Activity 2.21 | Formatting and Constructing Formulas on Grouped Worksheets

Recall that formulas are equations that perform calculations on values in your worksheet and that a formula starts with an equal sign (=). Operators are the symbols with which you specify the type of calculation that you want to perform on the elements of a formula. In this activity, you will enter sales figures for Non-Food items from both Online and In-Store sales, and then calculate the total sales.

1 Display the **Online Sales** worksheet. Verify that the sheets are not grouped—*[Group]* does *not* display in the title bar.

2 Click cell **A1**, type **Food and Non-Food Items: Weekly Online Sales** and then on the **Formula Bar**, click the **Enter** button to keep cell **A1** as the active cell. **Merge & Center** the text across the range **A1:G1**, and then apply the **Title** cell style.

3 In the column titled *Non-Food Sales*, click cell **F5**, in the range **F5:F11**, type the following data for Non-Food Sales, and then compare your screen with Figure 2.38.

	Non-Food Sales
Sun	**869.24**
Mon	**468.78**
Tue	**796.57**
Wed	**865.11**
Thu	**916.48**
Fri	**1154.22**
Sat	**968.25**

Figure 2.38

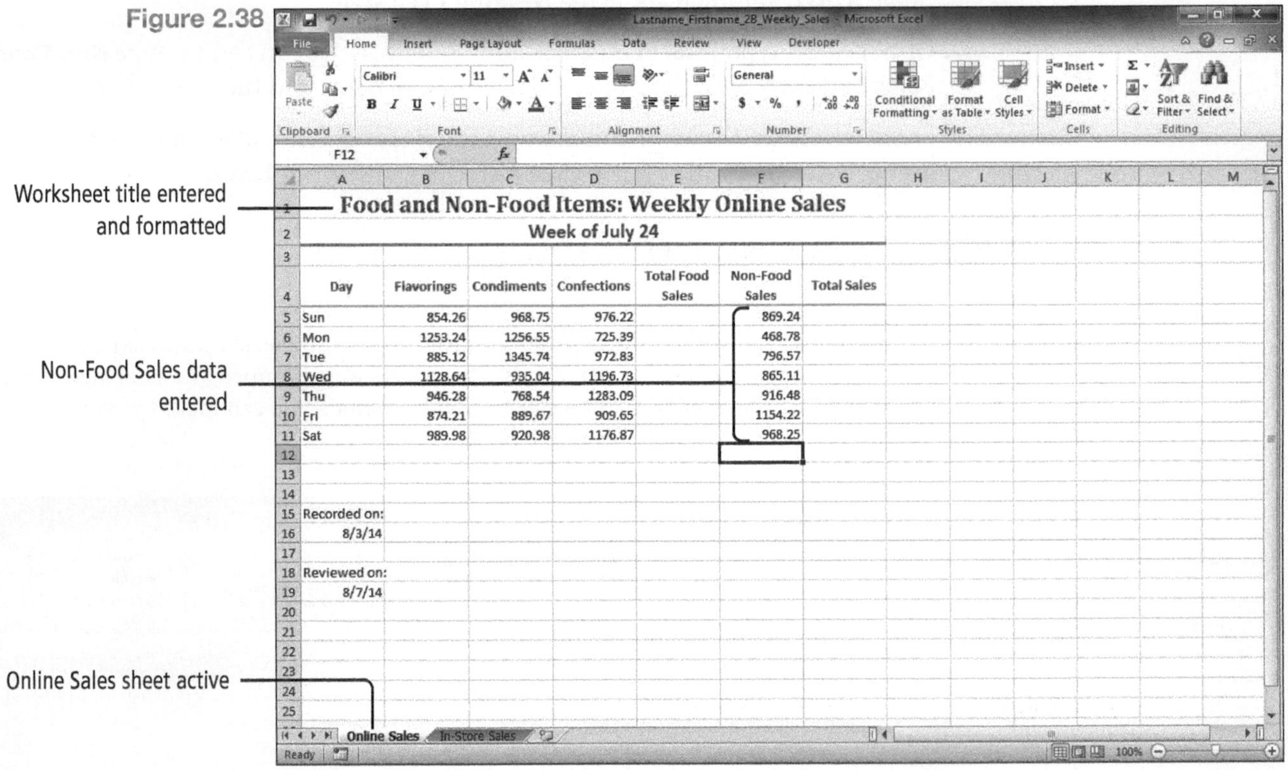

4 Display the **In-Store Sales** sheet. In cell **A1**, replace *In-Store* by typing **Food and Non-Food Items: Weekly In-Store Sales** and then on the **Formula Bar**, click the **Enter** button to keep cell **A1** as the active cell. **Merge & Center** the text across the range **A1:G1**, and then apply the **Title** cell style.

5 In the column titled *Non-Food Sales*, click cell **F5**, in the range **F5:F11**, type the following data for Non-Food Sales, and then compare your screen with Figure 2.39.

	Non-Food Sales
Sun	**569.34**
Mon	**426.44**
Tue	**636.57**
Wed	**721.69**
Thu	**359.12**
Fri	**587.99**
Sat	**436.22**

Figure 2.39

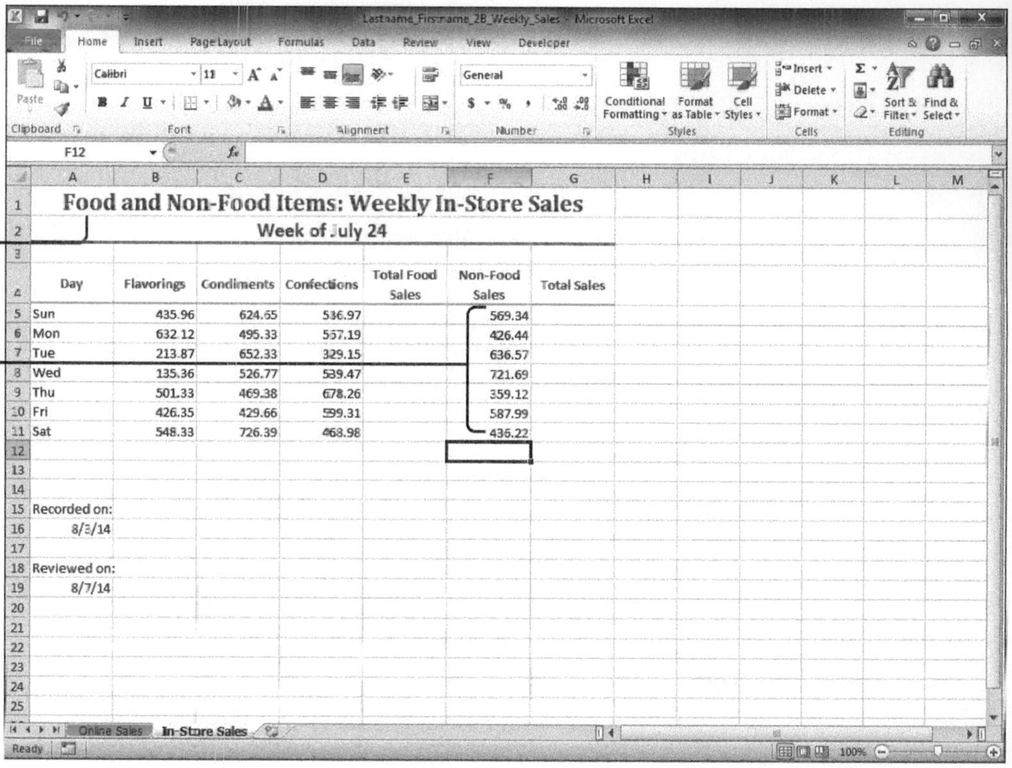

6 **Save** your workbook. Right-click the **Online Sales sheet tab**, and then from the shortcut menu, click **Select All Sheets**.

The first worksheet becomes the active sheet, and the worksheets are grouped. *[Group]* displays in the title bar, and the sheet tabs are underlined in the tab color to indicate they are selected as part of the group. Recall that when grouped, any action that you perform on the active worksheet is *also* performed on any other selected worksheets.

7 With the sheets *grouped* and the **Online Sales** sheet active, click cell **E5**. On the **Home tab**, in the **Editing group**, click the **Sum** button [Σ]. Compare your screen with Figure 2.40.

Recall that when you enter the SUM function, Excel looks first above and then left for a proposed range of cells to sum.

Figure 2.40

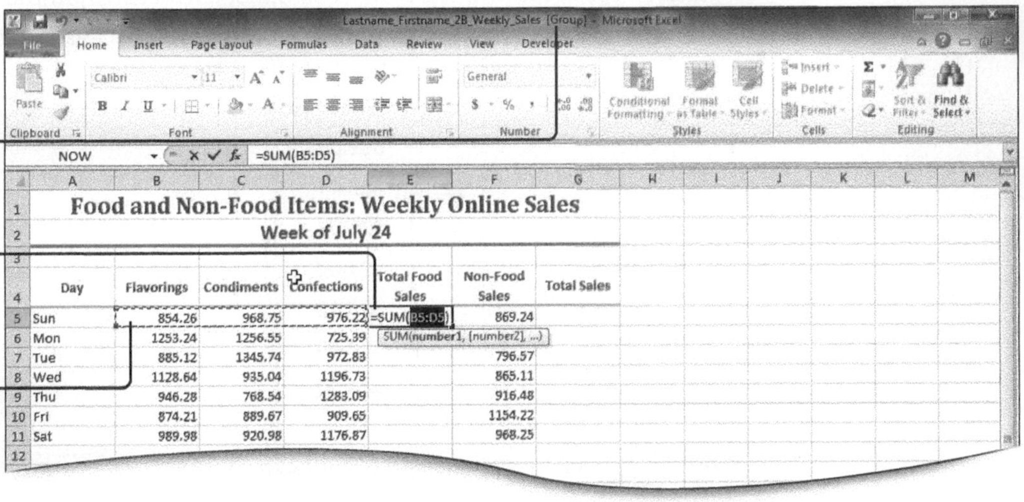

8 Press [Enter] to display Total Food Sales for Sunday, which is *2799.23*.

9 Click cell **E5**, and then drag the fill handle down to copy the formula through cell **E11**.

10 Click cell **G5**, type **=** click cell **E5**, type **+** click cell **F5**, and then compare your screen with Figure 2.41.

Using the point-and-click technique to construct this formula is only one of several techniques you can use. Alternatively, you could use any other method to enter the SUM function to add the values in these two cells.

Figure 2.41

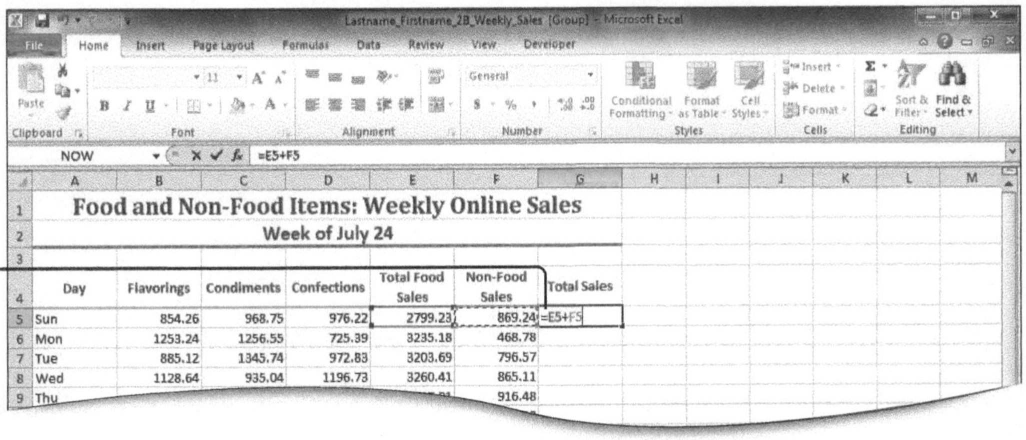

11 Press [Enter] to display the result *3668.47*, and then copy the formula down through cell **G11**.

12 In cell **A12**, type **Total** and then select the range **B5:G12**, which is all of the sales data and the empty cells at the bottom of each column of sales data.

13 With the range **B5:G12** selected, hold down [Alt] and press [=] to enter the **SUM** function in each empty cell.

Selecting a range in this manner will place the Sum function in the empty cells at the bottom of each column.

14 Select the range **A5:A12**, and then apply the **Heading 4** cell style.

15 To apply financial formatting to the worksheets, select the range **B5:G5**, hold down Ctrl, and then select the range **B12:G12**. With the nonadjacent ranges selected, apply the **Accounting Number Format** [$ ▾].

16 Select the range **B6:G11** and apply **Comma Style** [,]. Select the range **B12:G12** and apply the **Total** cell style.

17 Press Ctrl + Home to move to the top of the worksheet; compare your screen with Figure 2.42.

Figure 2.42

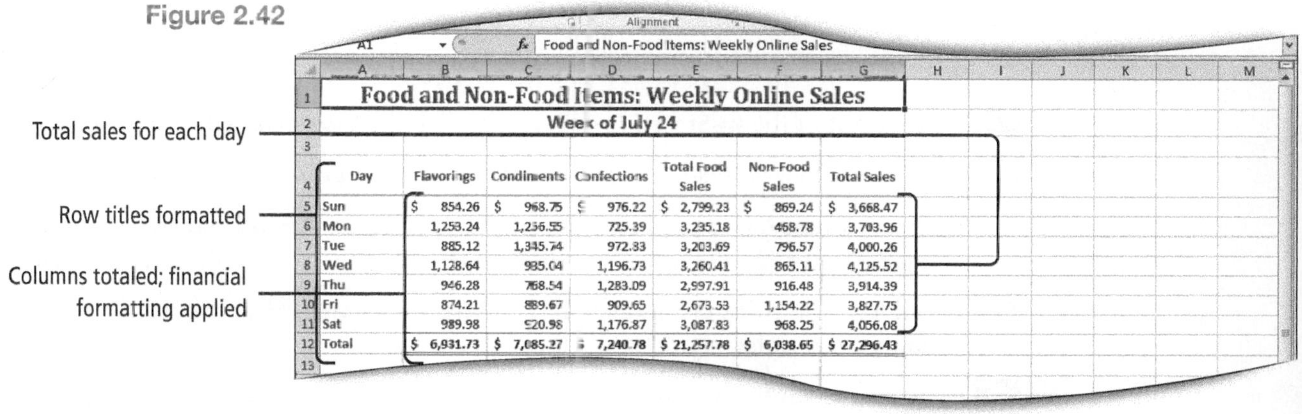

18 Click the **In-Store Sales sheet tab** to cancel the grouping and display the second worksheet. Click **Save** [💾], and then compare your screen with Figure 2.43.

With your worksheets grouped, the calculations on the first worksheet were also performed on the second worksheet.

Figure 2.43

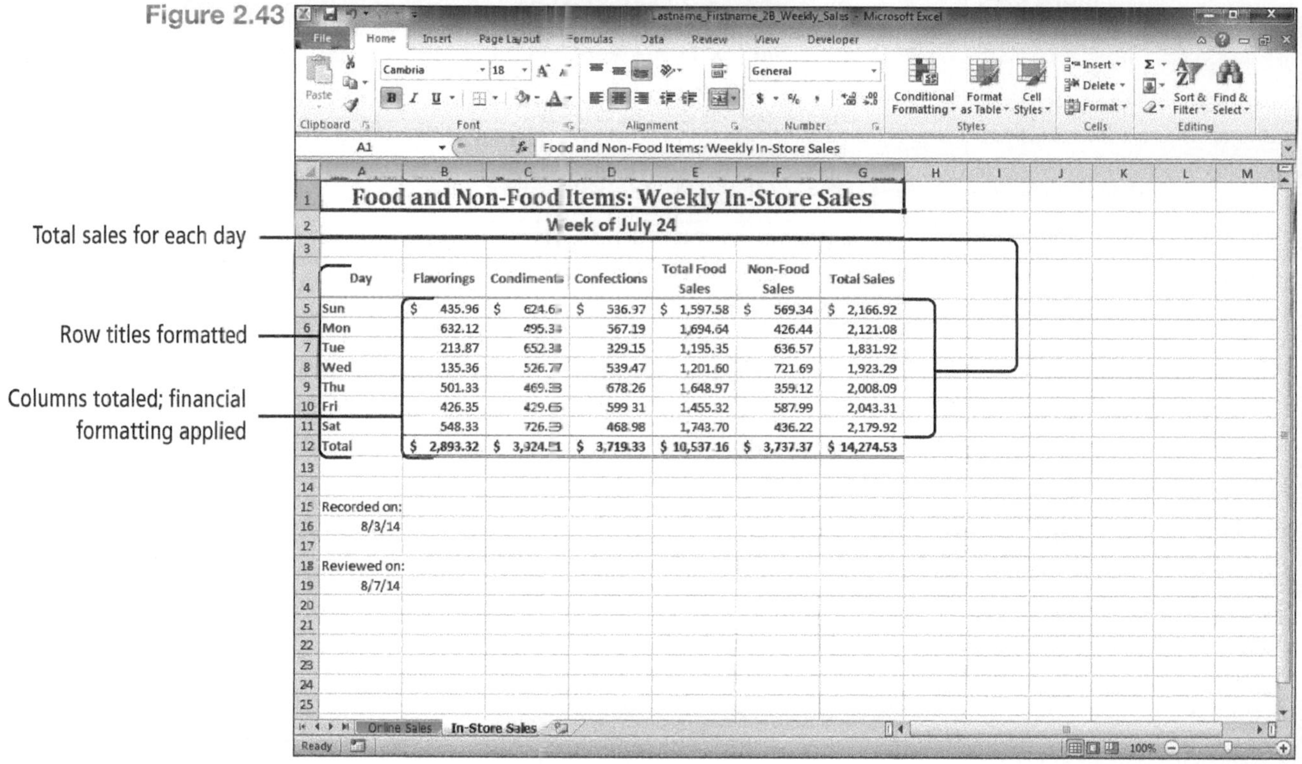

Excel | Chapter 2

Objective 11 | Create a Summary Sheet with Column Sparklines

A ***summary sheet*** is a worksheet where totals from other worksheets are displayed and summarized. Recall that sparklines are tiny charts within a single cell that show a data trend.

Activity 2.22 | Constructing Formulas that Refer to Cells in Another Worksheet

In this activity, you will insert a new worksheet in which you will place the totals from the Online Sales worksheet and the In-Store Sales worksheet. You will construct formulas in the Summary worksheet to display the total sales for both online sales and in-store sales that will update the Summary worksheet whenever changes are made to the other worksheet totals.

1 To the right of the **In-Store Sales** sheet tab, click the **Insert Worksheet** button.

2 Rename the new worksheet tab **Summary** Change the **Tab Color** to **Olive Green, Accent 3**.

3 Widen **columns A:E** to **110** pixels. In cell **A1**, type **Sales of Food and Non-Food Items** **Merge & Center** the title across the range **A1:E1**, and then apply the **Title** cell style.

4 In cell **A2**, type **Week of July 24** and then **Merge & Center** across **A2:E2**; apply the **Heading 1** cell style.

5 Leave **row 3** blank. To form column titles, in cell **B4**, type **Food/Non-Food** and press Tab. In cell **C4**, type **Food Sales** and press Tab. In cell **D4**, type **Non-Food Sales** and press Tab. In cell **E4**, type **Total Sales** Press Enter. Select the range **B4:E4**. Apply the **Heading 3** cell style and **Center**.

6 To form row titles, in cell **A5**, type **Online Sales** In cell **A6**, type **In-Store Sales** and then compare your screen with Figure 2.44.

Figure 2.44

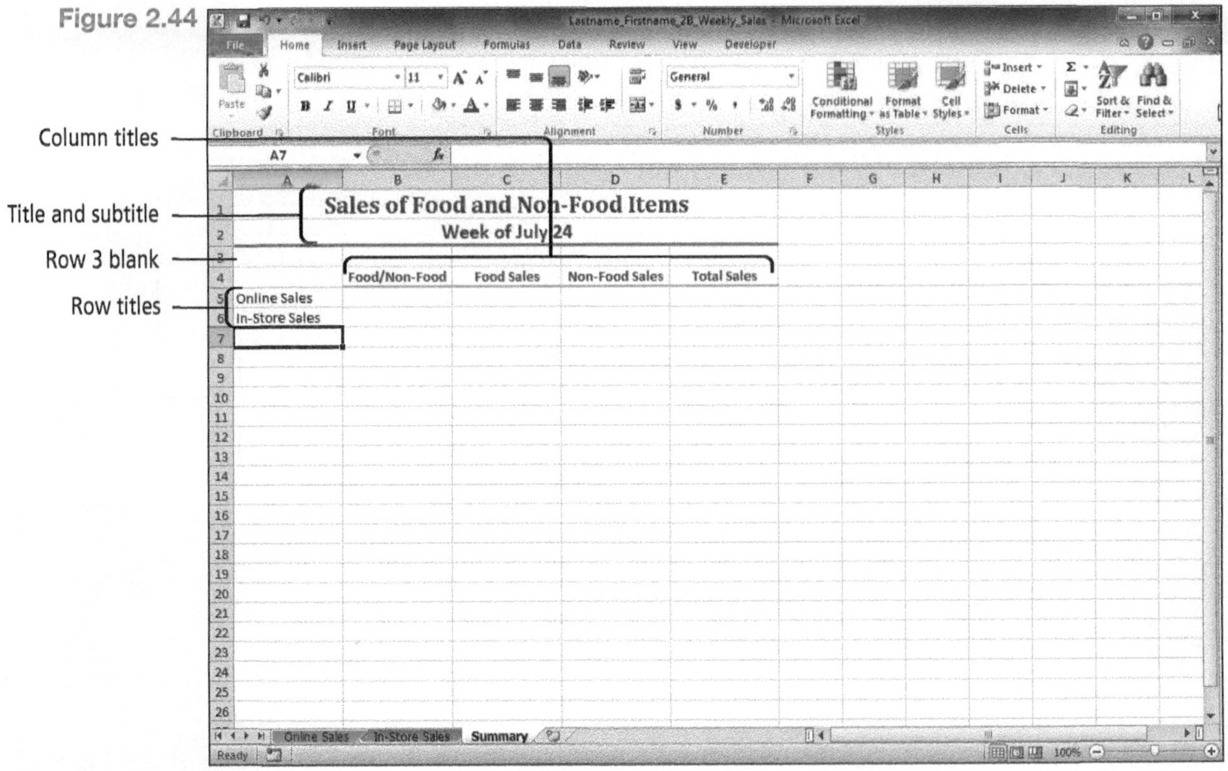

7 Click cell **C5**. Type = Click the **Online Sales sheet tab**. On the **Online Sales** worksheet, click cell **E12**, and then press Enter to redisplay the **Summary** worksheet and insert the total **Food Sales** amount of *$21,257.78*.

8 Click cell **C5** to select it again. Look at the **Formula Bar**, and notice that instead of a value, the cell contains a formula that is equal to the value in another cell in another worksheet. Compare your screen with Figure 2.45.

The value in this cell is equal to the value in cell E12 of the *Online Sales* worksheet. The Accounting Number Format applied to the referenced cell is carried over. By using a formula of this type, changes in cell E12 on the *Online Sales* worksheet will be automatically updated in this *Summary* worksheet.

Figure 2.45

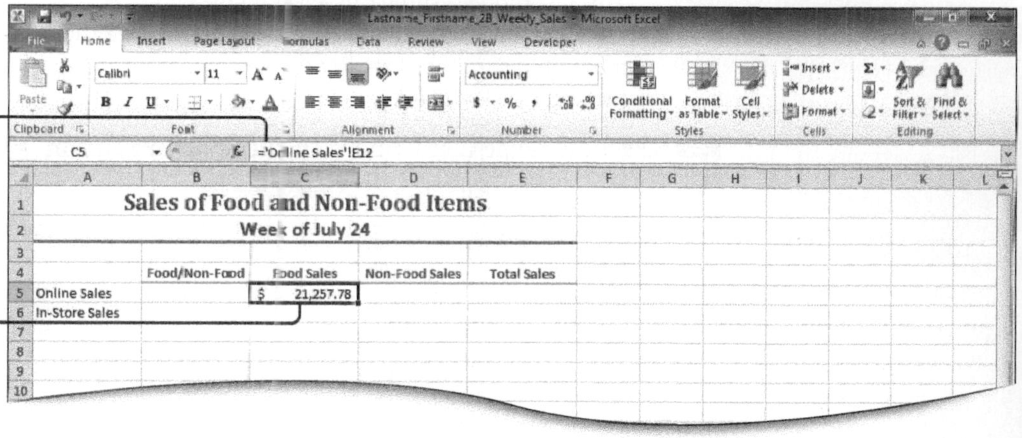

9 Click cell **D5**. Type = and then click the **Online Sales sheet tab**. Click cell **F12**, and then press Enter to redisplay the **Summary** worksheet and insert the total **Non-Food Sales** amount of *$6,038.65*.

10 By using the techniques you just practiced, in cells **C6** and **D6** insert the total **Food Sales** and **Non-Food Sales** data from the **In-Store Sales** worksheet. Click **Save**, and then compare your screen with Figure 2.46.

Figure 2.46

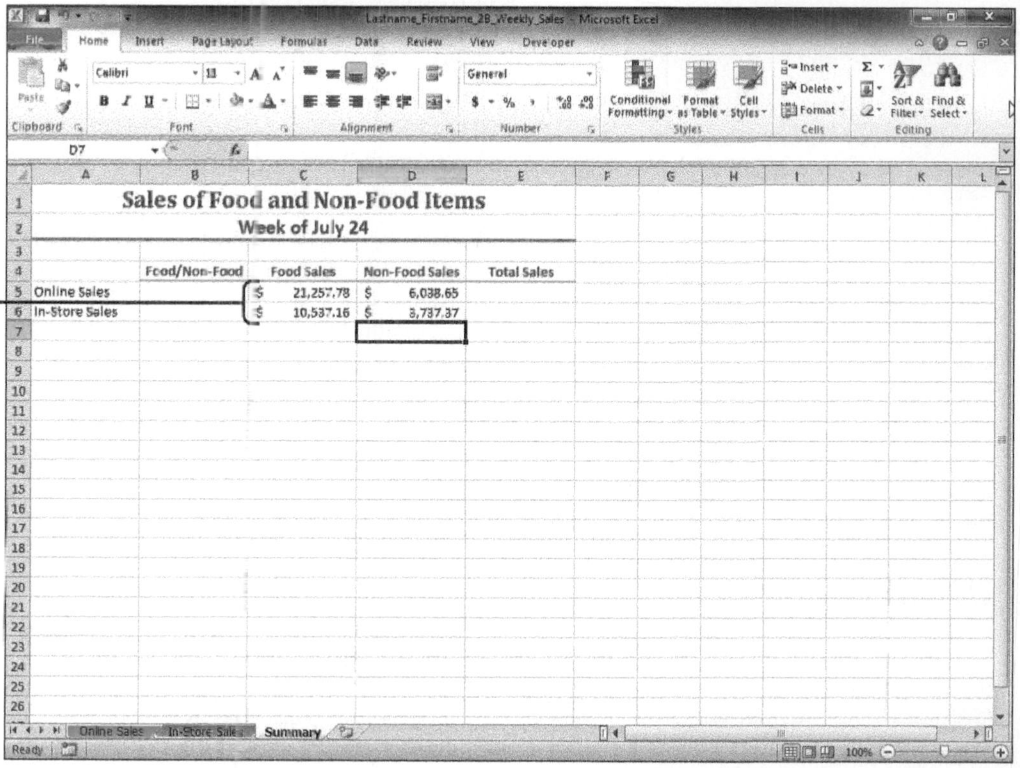

Activity 2.23 | Changing Values in a Detail Worksheet to Update a Summary Worksheet

The formulas in cells C5:D6 display the totals from the other two worksheets. Changes made to any of the other two worksheets—sometimes referred to as ***detail sheets*** because the details of the information are contained there—that affect their totals will display on this Summary worksheet. In this manner, the Summary worksheet accurately displays the current totals from the other worksheets.

1 In cell **A7**, type **Total** Select the range **C5:E6**, and then click the **Sum** button [Σ] to total the two rows.

This technique is similar to selecting the empty cells at the bottom of columns and then inserting the SUM function for each column. Alternatively, you could use any other method to sum the rows. Recall that cell formatting carries over to adjacent cells unless two cells are left blank.

2 Select the range **C5:E7**, and then click the **Sum** button [Σ] to total the three columns. Compare your screen with Figure 2.47.

Figure 2.47

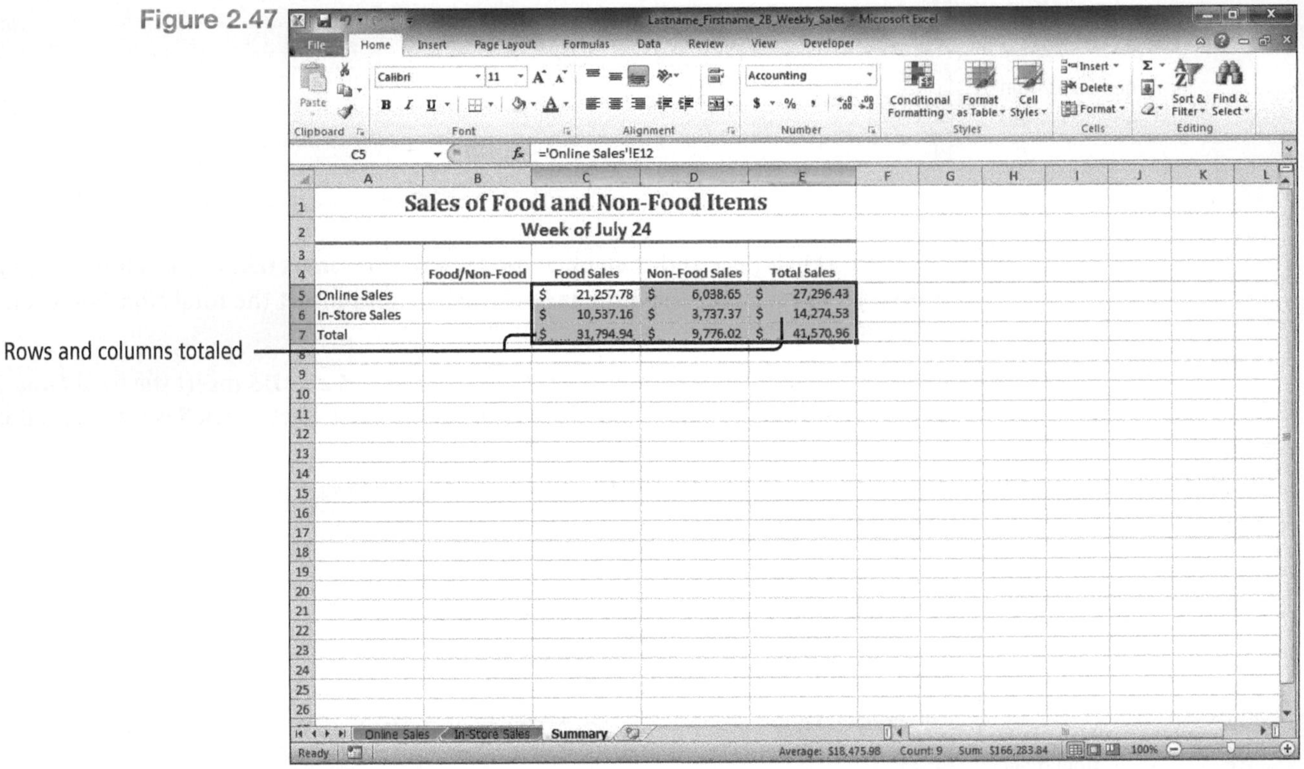

3 In cell **C6**, notice that total **Food Sales** for **In-Store Sales** is *$10,537.16*, and in cell **C7**, notice the total of *$31,794.94*.

4 Display the **In-Store Sales** worksheet, click cell **B8**, type **353.63** and then press [Enter]. Notice that the formulas in the worksheet recalculate.

5 Display the **Summary** worksheet, and notice that in the **Food Sales** column, both the total for the *In-Store Sales* location and the *Total* also recalculated.

In this manner, a Summary sheet recalculates any changes made in the other worksheets.

6 Select the range **C6:E6** and change the format to **Comma Style**. Select the range **C7:E7**, and then apply the **Total** cell style. Select the range **A5:A7** and apply the **Heading 4** cell style. **Save** [💾] your workbook. Click cell **A1**, and then compare your screen with Figure 2.48.

Figure 2.48

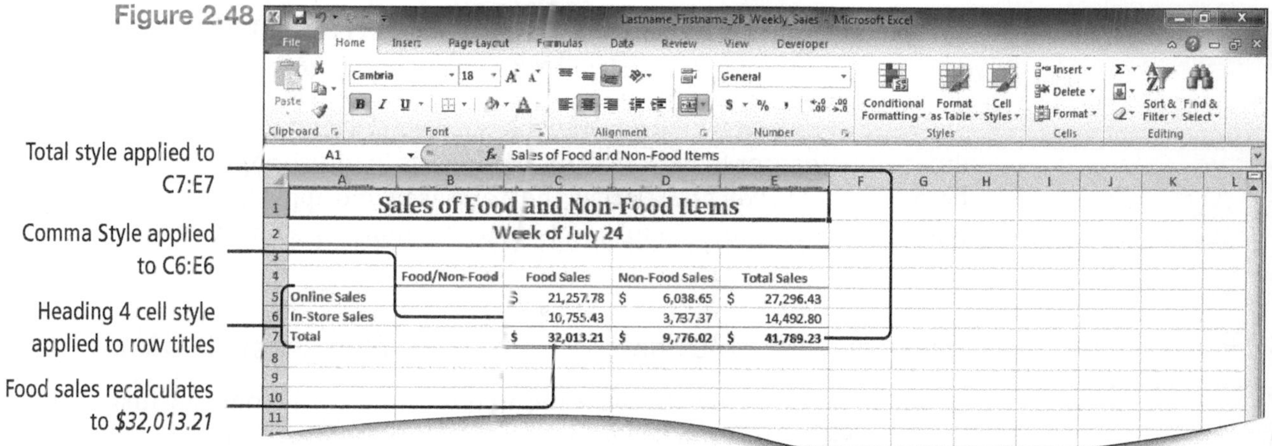

Activity 2.24 | Inserting Sparklines

In this activity, you will insert column sparklines to visualize the ratio of Food to Non-Food sales for both Online and In-Store.

1 Click cell **B5**. On the **Insert tab**, in the **Sparklines group**, click **Column**. In the **Create Sparklines** dialog box, with the insertion point blinking in the **Data Range** box, select the range **C5:D5**. Compare your screen with Figure 2.49.

Figure 2.49

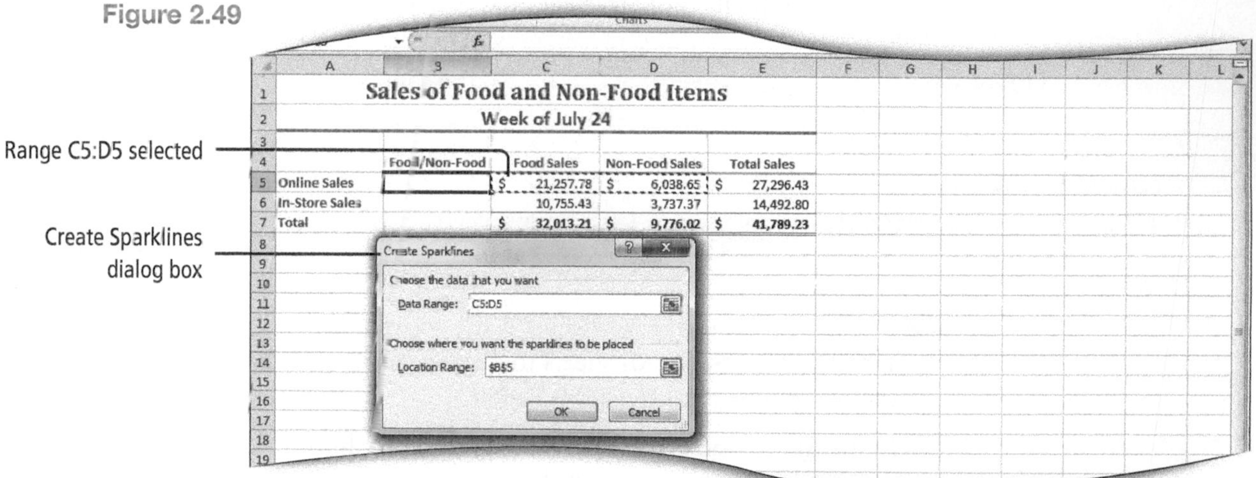

2 Click **OK**. Click cell **B6**, and then **Insert** a **Column Sparkline** for the range **C6:D6**. In the **Style group**, apply **Sparkline Style Accent 2, Darker 25%**—in the second row, the second style. Press Ctrl + Home, click **Save**, and then compare your screen with Figure 2.50.

You can see, at a glance, that for both Online and In-Store sales, Food sales are much greater than Non-Food sales.

Figure 2.50

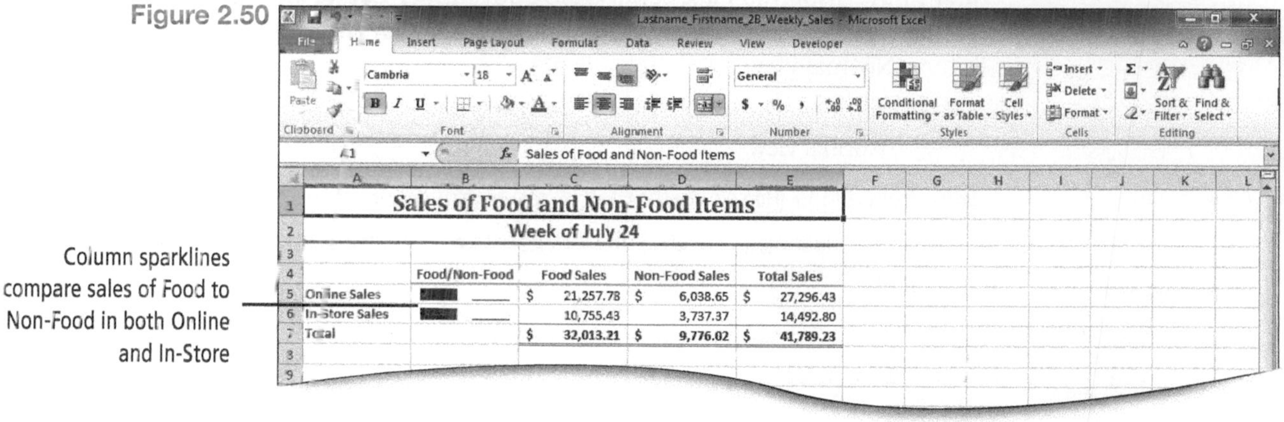

Objective 12 | Format and Print Multiple Worksheets in a Workbook

Each worksheet within a workbook can have different formatting, for example different headers or footers. If all the worksheets in the workbook will have the same header or footer, you can select all the worksheets and apply formatting common to all of the worksheets; for example, you can set the same footer in all of the worksheets.

Activity 2.25 | Moving and Formatting Worksheets in a Workbook

In this activity, you will move the Summary sheet to become the first worksheet in the workbook. Then you will format and prepare your workbook for printing. The three worksheets containing data can be formatted simultaneously.

1. Point to the **Summary sheet tab**, hold down the left mouse button to display a small black triangle—a caret—and then notice that a small paper icon attaches to the mouse pointer.
2. Drag to the left until the caret and mouse pointer are to the left of the **Online Sales sheet tab**, as shown in Figure 2.51, and then release the left mouse button.

   Use this technique to rearrange the order of worksheets within a workbook.

Figure 2.51

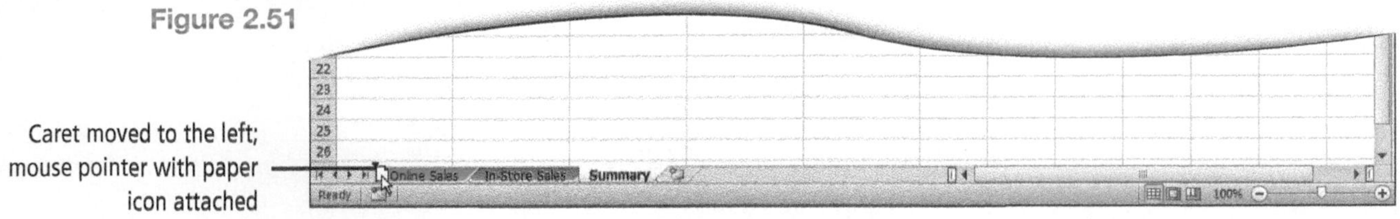

3. Be sure the **Summary** worksheet is the active sheet, point to its sheet tab, right-click, and then click **Select All Sheets** to display *[Group]* in the title bar. On the **Insert tab**, in the **Text group**, click **Header & Footer**.
4. In the **Navigation group**, click the **Go to Footer** button, click in the **left section** above the word *Footer*, and then in the **Header & Footer Elements group**, click the **File Name** button.
5. Click in a cell above the footer to deselect the **Footer area**. On the **Page Layout tab**, in the **Page Setup group**, click the **Margins** button, and then at the bottom of the **Margins** gallery, click **Custom Margins**.
6. In the displayed **Page Setup** dialog box, under **Center on page**, select the **Horizontally** check box. Click **OK**, and then on the status bar, click the **Normal** button to return to Normal view.

   After displaying worksheets in Page Layout View, dotted lines indicate the page breaks in Normal view.

7. Press Ctrl + Home; verify that *[Group]* still displays in the title bar.

   By selecting all sheets, you can apply the same formatting to all the worksheets at the same time.

8 Display **Backstage** view, show the **Document Panel**, type your firstname and lastname in the Author box, and then type your course name and section number in the **Subject** box. As the **Keywords** type **weekly sales, online, in-store** and then **Close** [×] the **Document Information Panel**.

9 Press Ctrl + F2; compare your screen with Figure 2.52.

By grouping, you can view all sheets in Print Preview. If you do not see *1 of 3* at the bottom of the Preview, click the Home tab, select all the sheets again, and then redisplay Print Preview.

Figure 2.52

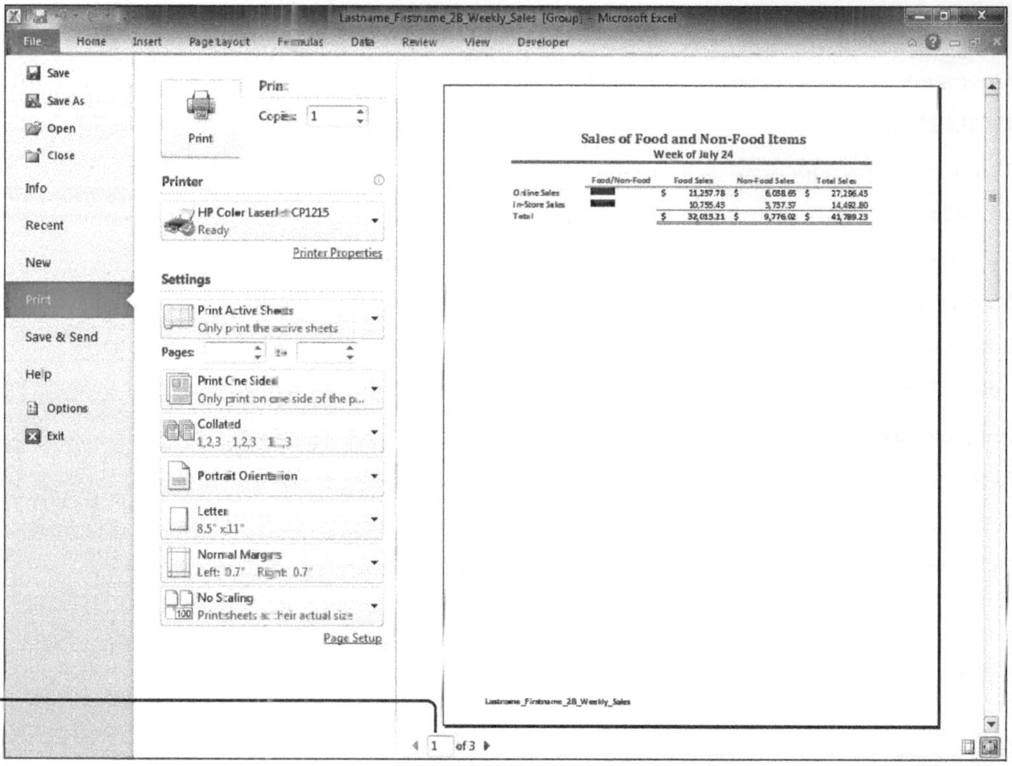

10 At the bottom of the **Print Preview**, click the **Next Page** [▶] button as necessary and take a moment to view each page of your workbook.

Activity 2.26 | Printing All the Worksheets in a Workbook

1 In **Backstage** view, click the **Save** button to save your workbook before printing. To submit your workbook electronically, follow the instructions provided by your instructor. To print your workbook, continue to Step 2.

2 Display **Backstage** view, click the **Print tab**, verify that the worksheets in your workbook are still grouped—*[Group]* displays in the title bar—and then in the center panel, in the **Print group**, click the **Print** button.

3 If required, print or create an electronic version of your worksheets with formulas displayed by using the instructions in Activity 1.16, and then **Close** [×] Excel without saving so that you do not save the changes you made to print formulas.

End **You have completed Project 2B**

Content-Based Assessments

Summary

In this chapter, you used the Statistical, Logical, and Date & Time functions from the Function Library. You created a table and analyzed the table's data by sorting and filtering. You also created a workbook with multiple worksheets, and then summarized all the worksheets on a summary worksheet.

Key Terms

Matching

Match each term in the second column with its correct definition in the first column by writing the letter of the term on the blank line in front of the correct definition.

____ 1. A predefined formula that performs calculations by using specific values in a particular order or structure.

____ 2. Excel functions such as AVERAGE that are useful to analyze a group of measurements.

____ 3. A predefined formula that adds all the numbers in a selected range.

____ 4. A function that adds a group of values, and then divides the result by the number of values in the group.

____ 5. A function that finds the middle value that has as many values above it in the group as are below it.

____ 6. A function that determines the smallest value in a range.

____ 7. A function that determines the largest value in a range.

____ 8. The action of moving a selection by dragging it to a new location.

____ 9. A group of functions that tests for specific conditions, and which typically use conditional tests to determine whether specified conditions are true or false.

____ 10. Conditions that you specify in a logical function.

____ 11. A statistical function that counts the number of cells within a range that meet the given condition and which has two arguments—the range of cells to check and the criteria.

____ 12. Any value or expression that can be evaluated as being true or false.

A AVERAGE function
B Comparison operators
C Conditional format
D COUNTIF function
E Criteria
F Drag and drop
G Function
H IF function
I Logical functions
J Logical test
K MAX function
L MEDIAN function
M MIN function
N Statistical functions
O SUM function

_____ 13. A function that uses a logical test to check whether a condition is met, and then returns one value if true, and another value if false.

_____ 14. Symbols that evaluate each value to determine if it is the same (=), greater than (>), less than (<), or in between a range of values as specified by the criteria.

_____ 15. A format that changes the appearance of a cell based on a condition.

Multiple Choice

Circle the correct answer.

1. A shaded bar that provides a visual cue about the value of a cell relative to other cells is a:
   A. data bar **B.** detail bar **C.** filter

2. The function that retrieves and then displays the date and time from your computer is the:
   A. DATE function **B.** NOW function **C.** CALENDAR function

3. The command that enables you to select one or more rows or columns and lock them into place is:
   A. drag and drop **B.** scale to fit **C.** freeze panes

4. A series of rows and columns with related data that is managed independently from other data is a:
   A. table **B.** pane **C.** detail sheet

5. The process of arranging data in a specific order based on the value in each field is called:
   A. filtering **B.** sorting **C.** scaling

6. The process of displaying only a portion of the data based on matching a specific value to show only the data that meets the criteria that you specify is called:
   A. filtering **B.** sorting **C.** scaling

7. The Excel command that enables you to specify rows and columns to repeat on each printed page is:
   A. navigate **B.** print titles **C.** conditional format

8. The labels along the lower border of the workbook window that identify each worksheet are the:
   A. data bars **B.** sheet tabs **C.** detail sheets

9. A worksheet where totals from other worksheets are displayed and summarized is a:
   A. summary sheet **B.** detail sheet **C.** table

10. The worksheets that contain the details of the information summarized on a summary sheet are called:
    A. summary sheets **B.** detail sheets **C.** tables

Apply 2A skills from these Objectives:

1. Use the SUM, AVERAGE, MEDIAN, MIN, and MAX Functions
2. Move Data, Resolve Error Messages, and Rotate Text
3. Use COUNTIF and IF Functions and Apply Conditional Formatting
4. Use Date & Time Functions and Freeze Panes
5. Create, Sort, and Filter an Excel Table
6. Format and Print a Large Worksheet

Skills Review | Project 2C Sauces Inventory

In the following Skills Review, you will edit a worksheet for Laura Morales, President, detailing the current inventory of sauces at the Portland facility. Your completed workbook will look similar to Figure 2.53.

Project Files

For Project 2C, you will need the following file:

e02C_Sauces_Inventory

You will save your workbook as:

Lastname_Firstname_2C_Sauces_Inventory

Project Results

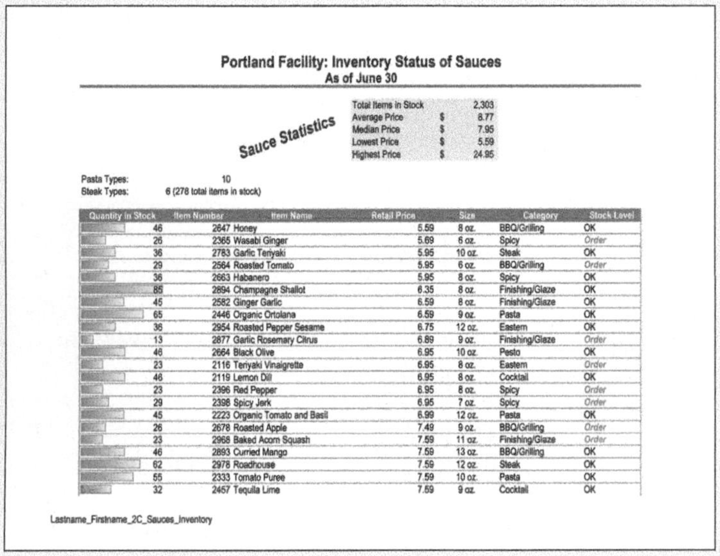

Portland Facility: Inventory Status of Sauces
As of June 30

Sauce Statistics

Total Items in Stock		2,303
Average Price	$	8.77
Median Price	$	7.95
Lowest Price	$	5.59
Highest Price	$	24.95

Pasta Types: 10
Steak Types: 6 (278 total items in stock)

Quantity in Stock	Item Number	Item Name	Retail Price	Size	Category	Stock Level
46	2647	Honey	5.59	8 oz.	BBQ/Grilling	OK
26	2365	Wasabi Ginger	5.69	6 oz.	Spicy	Order
36	2783	Garlic Teriyaki	5.95	10 oz.	Steak	OK
29	2564	Roasted Tomato	5.95	6 oz.	BBQ/Grilling	Order
36	2663	Habanero	5.95	8 oz.	Spicy	OK
85	2894	Champagne Shallot	6.35	8 oz.	Finishing/Glaze	OK
45	2582	Ginger Garlic	6.59	8 oz.	Finishing/Glaze	OK
65	2446	Organic Ortolana	6.59	9 oz.	Pasta	OK
36	2954	Roasted Pepper Sesame	6.75	12 oz.	Eastern	OK
13	2877	Garlic Rosemary Citrus	6.89	9 oz.	Finishing/Glaze	Order
46	2664	Black Olive	6.95	10 oz.	Pesto	OK
23	2116	Teriyaki Vinaigrette	6.95	8 oz.	Eastern	Order
46	2119	Lemon Dill	6.95	8 oz.	Cocktail	OK
23	2396	Red Pepper	6.95	8 oz.	Spicy	Order
29	2398	Spicy Jerk	6.95	7 oz.	Spicy	Order
45	2223	Organic Tomato and Basil	6.99	12 oz.	Pasta	OK
26	2678	Roasted Apple	7.49	9 oz.	BBQ/Grilling	Order
23	2968	Baked Acorn Squash	7.59	11 oz.	Finishing/Glaze	Order
46	2893	Curried Mango	7.59	13 oz.	BBQ/Grilling	OK
62	2978	Roadhouse	7.59	12 oz.	Steak	OK
55	2333	Tomato Puree	7.59	10 oz.	Pasta	OK
32	2457	Tequila Lime	7.59	9 oz.	Cocktail	OK

Lastname_Firstname_2C_Sauces_Inventory

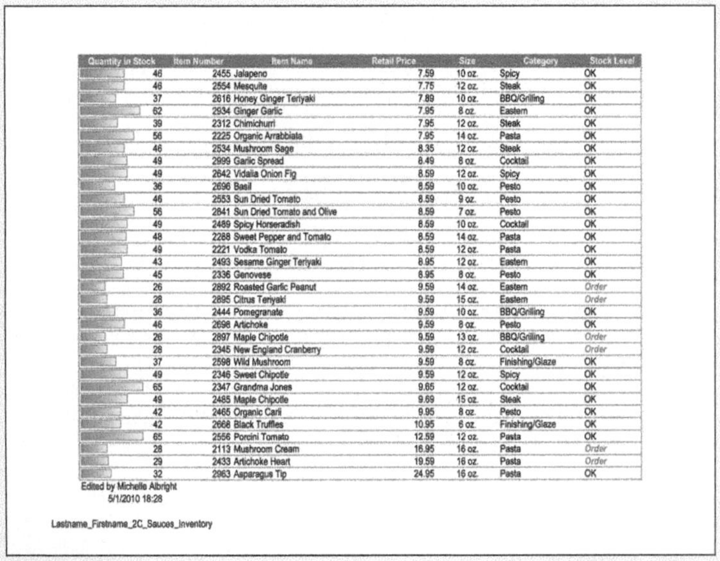

Quantity in Stock	Item Number	Item Name	Retail Price	Size	Category	Stock Level
46	2455	Jalapeno	7.59	10 oz.	Spicy	OK
46	2554	Mesquite	7.75	12 oz.	Steak	OK
37	2616	Honey Ginger Teriyaki	7.89	10 oz.	BBQ/Grilling	OK
62	2934	Ginger Garlic	7.95	8 oz.	Eastern	OK
39	2312	Chimichurri	7.95	12 oz.	Steak	OK
56	2225	Organic Arrabbiata	7.95	14 oz.	Pasta	OK
46	2534	Mushroom Sage	8.35	12 oz.	Steak	OK
49	2999	Garlic Spread	8.49	8 oz.	Cocktail	OK
49	2642	Vidalia Onion Fig	8.59	12 oz.	Spicy	OK
36	2696	Basil	8.59	10 oz.	Pesto	OK
46	2553	Sun Dried Tomato	8.59	9 oz.	Pesto	OK
56	2841	Sun Dried Tomato and Olive	8.59	7 oz.	Pesto	OK
49	2489	Spicy Horseradish	8.59	10 oz.	Cocktail	OK
48	2288	Sweet Pepper and Tomato	8.59	14 oz.	Pasta	OK
49	2221	Vodka Tomato	8.59	12 oz.	Pasta	OK
43	2493	Sesame Ginger Teriyaki	8.95	12 oz.	Eastern	OK
45	2336	Genovese	8.95	8 oz.	Pesto	OK
26	2892	Roasted Garlic Peanut	9.59	14 oz.	Eastern	Order
28	2895	Citrus Teriyaki	9.59	15 oz.	Eastern	Order
36	2444	Pomegranate	9.59	10 oz.	BBQ/Grilling	OK
46	2698	Artichoke	9.59	8 oz.	Pesto	OK
26	2897	Maple Chipotle	9.59	13 oz.	BBQ/Grilling	Order
28	2345	New England Cranberry	9.59	12 oz.	Cocktail	Order
37	2598	Wild Mushroom	9.59	8 oz.	Finishing/Glaze	OK
49	2346	Sweet Chipotle	9.59	12 oz.	Spicy	OK
65	2347	Grandma Jones	9.65	12 oz.	Cocktail	OK
49	2485	Maple Chipotle	9.69	15 oz.	Steak	OK
42	2465	Organic Carli	9.95	8 oz.	Pesto	OK
42	2668	Black Truffles	10.95	6 oz.	Finishing/Glaze	OK
65	2556	Porcini Tomato	12.59	12 oz.	Pasta	OK
28	2113	Mushroom Cream	16.95	16 oz.	Pasta	Order
29	2433	Artichoke Heart	19.59	16 oz.	Pasta	Order
32	2963	Asparagus Tip	24.95	16 oz.	Pasta	OK

Edited by Michelle Albright
5/1/2010 18:28

Lastname_Firstname_2C_Sauces_Inventory

Figure 2.53

(Project 2C Sauces Inventory continues on the next page)

Content-Based Assessments

Skills Review | Project 2C Sauces Inventory (continued)

1 **Start** Excel. From your student files, locate and open **e02C_Sauces_Inventory**. From **Backstage** view, display the **Save As** dialog box, navigate to your **Excel Chapter 2** folder, and then save the workbook as **Lastname_Firstname_2C_Sauces_Inventory**

- **a.** Click cell **B4**. Click the **Formulas tab**, and then in the **Function Library group**, click the **AutoSum** button. Select the range **A14:A68**, and then press Enter.
- **b.** With cell **B5** active, in the **Function Library group**, click the **More Functions** button. Point to **Statistical**, click **AVERAGE**, and then in the **Number1** box, type **d14:d68** Click **OK**.
- **c.** Click cell **B6**. In the **Function Library group**, click the **More Functions** button, point to **Statistical**, and then click **MEDIAN**. In the **Function Arguments** dialog box, to the right of the **Number1** box, click the **Collapse Dialog** button. Select the range **D14:D68**, click the **Expand Dialog** button, and then click **OK**.
- **d.** Click cell **B7**, and then by using a similar technique to insert a statistical function, insert the **MIN** function to determine the lowest **Retail Price**. Click cell **B8**, and then insert the **MAX** function to determine the highest **Retail Price**.

2 Right-click cell **B4**. On the Mini toolbar, click the **Comma Style** button, and then click the **Decrease Decimal** button two times. Select the range **B5:B8**, and apply the **Accounting Number Format**.

- **a.** Select the range **A4:B8**. Point to the right edge of the selected range to display the pointer. Drag the selected range to the right until the ScreenTip displays *D4:E8*, and then release the mouse button.
- **b.** With the range **D4:E8** selected, on the **Home tab**, in the **Styles group**, display the **Cell Styles** gallery, and then under **Themed Cell Styles**, click **20% - Accent1**.
- **c.** In cell **C6**, type **Sauce Statistics** Select the range **C4:C8**, right-click over the selection, and then click **Format Cells**. In the **Format Cells** dialog box, click the **Alignment tab**. Under **Text control**, select the **Merge cells** check box.
- **d.** In the upper right portion of the dialog box, under **Orientation**, point to the **red diamond**, and then drag the diamond upward until the **Degrees** box indicates *20*. Click **OK**.
- **e.** With the merged cell still selected, on the **Home tab**, in the **Font group**, change the **Font Size** to **18**, and then apply **Bold** and **Italic**. Click the **Font Color button arrow**, and then in the fourth column, click the first color—**Dark Blue, Text 2**.

3 Click cell **B10**. On the **Formulas tab**, in the **Function Library group**, click the **More Functions** button, and then display the list of **Statistical** functions. Click **COUNTIF**.

- **a.** At the right edge of the **Range** box, click the **Collapse Dialog** button, select the range **F14:F68**, and then press Enter. Click in the **Criteria** box, type **Pasta** and then click **OK** to calculate the number of *Pasta* types.
- **b.** Click cell **G14**. On the **Formulas tab**, in the **Function Library group**, click the **Logical** button, and then in the list, click **IF**. If necessary, drag the title bar of the **Function Arguments** dialog box up so that you can view **row 14** on your screen.
- **c.** With the insertion point in the **Logical_test** box, click cell **A14**, and then type **<30** Press Tab to move the insertion point to the **Value_if_true** box, and then type **Order** Press Tab to move the insertion point to the **Value_if_false** box, type **OK** and then click **OK**. Using the fill handle, copy the function in cell **G14** down through cell **G68**.

4 With the range **G14:G68** selected, on the **Home tab**, in the **Styles group**, click the **Conditional Formatting** button. In the list, point to **Highlight Cells Rules**, and then click **Text that Contains**.

- **a.** In the **Text That Contains** dialog box, with the insertion point blinking in the first box, type **Order** and then in the second box, click the **arrow**. In the list, click **Custom Format**.
- **b.** In the **Format Cells** dialog box, on the **Font tab**, under **Font style**, click **Bold Italic**. Click the **Color arrow**, and then under **Theme Colors**, in the sixth column, click the first color—**Red, Accent 2**. In the lower right corner of the **Format Cells** dialog box, click **OK**. In the **Text That Contains** dialog box, click **OK** to apply the font color, bold, and italic to the cells that contain the word *Order*.
- **c.** Select the range **A14:A68**. In the **Styles group**, click the **Conditional Formatting** button. In the list, point to **Data Bars**, and then under **Gradient Fill**, click **Orange Data Bar**. Click anywhere to cancel the selection.
- **d.** Select the range **F14:F68**. On the **Home tab**, in the **Editing group**, click the **Find & Select** button, and then click **Replace**. In the **Find and Replace** dialog box, in the **Find what** box, type **Hot** and then in the

(Project 2C Sauces Inventory continues on the next page)

Skills Review | Project 2C Sauces Inventory (continued)

Replace with box type **Spicy** Click the **Replace All** button and then click **OK**. In the lower right corner of the **Find and Replace** dialog box, click the **Close** button.

e. Scroll down as necessary, and then click cell **A70**. Type **Edited by Michelle Albright** and then press Enter. With cell **A71** as the active cell, on the **Formulas tab**, in the **Function Library group**, click the **Date & Time** button. In the list of functions, click **NOW**, and then click **OK** to enter the current date and time.

5 Select the range **A13:G68**. Click the **Insert tab**, and then in the **Tables group**, click the **Table** button. In the **Create Table** dialog box, if necessary, select the My table has headers check box, and then click **OK**. On the **Design tab**, in the **Table Styles group**, click the **More** button, and then under **Light**, locate and click **Table Style Light 9**.

a. In the header row of the table, click the **Retail Price arrow**, and then from the menu, click **Sort Smallest to Largest**. Click the **Category arrow**. On the menu, click the **(Select All)** check box to clear all the check boxes. Scroll as necessary and then click to select only the **Steak** check box. Click **OK**.

b. On the **Design tab**, in the **Table Style Options group**, select the **Total Row** check box. Click cell **A69**, click the **arrow** that displays to the right of cell **A69**, and then in the list, click **Sum**. In cell **B11**, type the result **6 (278 total items in stock)** and then press Enter.

c. In the header row of the table, click the **Category arrow** and then click **Clear Filter From "Category"** to redisplay all of the data. Click anywhere in the table. Click the **Design tab**, in the **Table Style Options group**, clear the **Total Row** check box, and then in the **Tools group**, click the **Convert to Range** button. Click **Yes**.

d. On the **Page Layout tab**, in the **Themes group**, click the **Themes** button, and then click **Horizon**.

6 On the **Page Layout tab**, click the **Margins** button, and then click **Custom Margins**. On the **Margins tab**, under **Center on page**, select the **Horizontally** check box. Click **OK**. On the **Page Layout tab**, in the **Scale to Fit group**, click the **Width button arrow**, and then click **1 page**.

a. In the **Page Setup group**, click the **Print Titles** button. Under **Print titles**, click in the **Rows to repeat at top** box, and then to the right, click the **Collapse Dialog** button. From the **row heading area**, select **row 13**, and then click the **Expand Dialog** button. Click **OK**.

b. On the **Insert tab**, in the **Text group**, click the **Header & Footer** button. Insert the **File Name** in the **left section** of the footer. Return to **Normal** view, make cell **A1** the active cell, and then delete the unused sheets.

c. Display the **Document Panel**, and then add your name, your course name and section, and the keywords **inventory, Portland Close** the **Document Information Panel**.

d. **Save** your workbook. Print or submit electronically as directed by your instructor. If required by your instructor, print or create an electronic version of your worksheets with formulas displayed by using the instructions in Activity 1.16, and then **Close** Excel without saving so that you do not save the changes you made to print formulas.

End **You have completed Project 2C**

Apply 2B skills from these Objectives:

- **7** Navigate a Workbook and Rename Worksheets
- **8** Enter Dates, Clear Contents, and Clear Formats
- **9** Copy and Paste by Using the Paste Options Gallery
- **10** Edit and Format Multiple Worksheets at the Same Time
- **11** Create a Summary Sheet with Column Sparklines
- **12** Format and Print Multiple Worksheets in a Workbook

Skills Review | Project 2D February Sales

In the following Skills Review, you will edit a workbook that summarizes in-store and online sales in the California and Oregon retail locations. Your completed workbook will look similar to Figure 2.54.

Project Files

For Project 2D, you will need the following file:

e02D_February_Sales

You will save your workbook as:

Lastname_Firstname_2D_February_Sales

Project Results

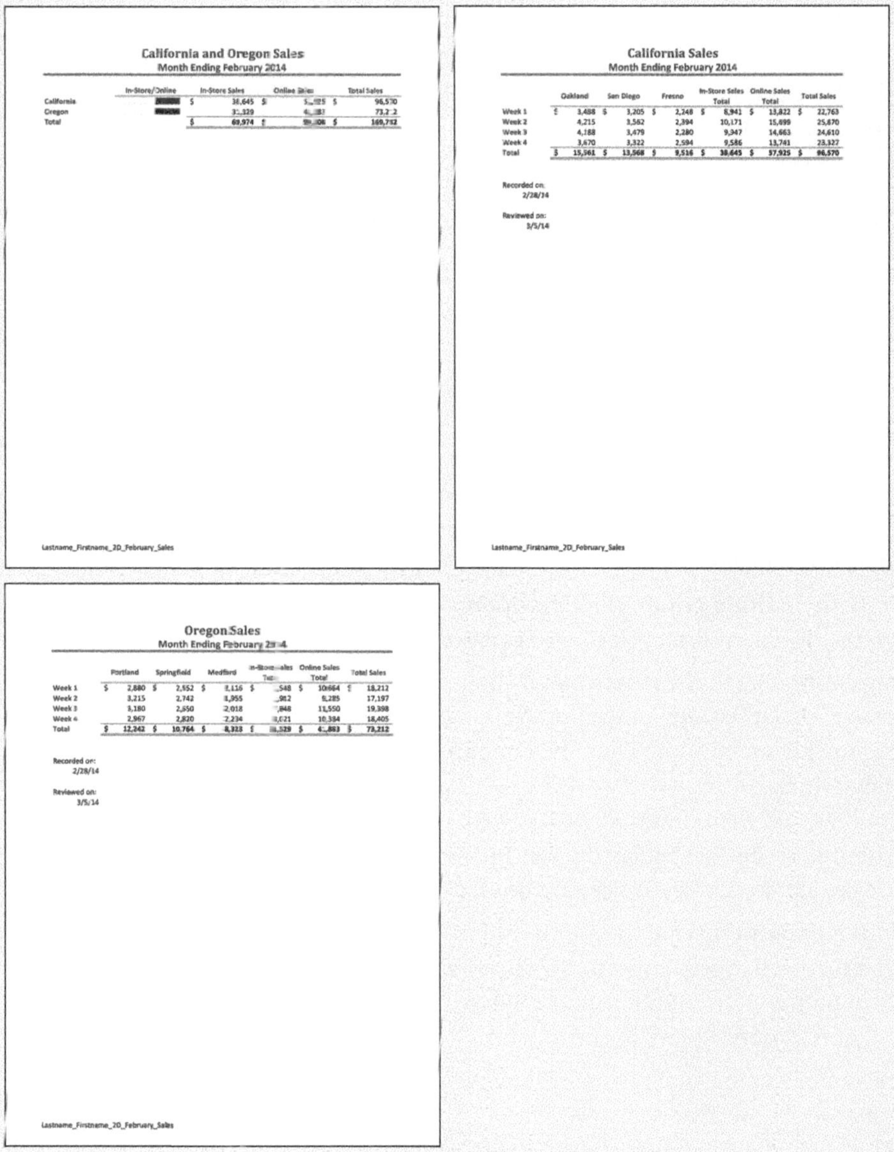

California and Oregon Sales
Month Ending February 2014

	In-Store/Online	In-Store Sales	Online Sales	Total Sales
California		$ 38,645	$ [illegible]	$ 96,570
Oregon		31,329	[illegible]	[illegible]
Total		$ 69,974	$ [illegible]	$ 169,782

Lastname_Firstname_2D_February_Sales

California Sales
Month Ending February 2014

	Oakland	San Diego	Fresno	In-Store Sales Total	Online Sales Total	Total Sales
Week 1	$ 3,488	$ 3,205	$ 2,248	$ 8,941	$ 13,822	$ 22,763
Week 2	4,215	3,562	2,394	10,171	15,699	25,870
Week 3	4,188	3,479	2,280	9,947	14,663	24,610
Week 4	3,670	3,322	2,594	9,586	13,741	23,327
Total	$ 15,561	$ 13,568	$ 9,516	$ 38,645	$ 57,925	$ 96,570

Recorded on:
2/28/14

Reviewed on:
3/5/14

Lastname_Firstname_2D_February_Sales

Oregon Sales
Month Ending February [illegible]

	Portland	Springfield	Medford	In-Store Sales Total	Online Sales Total	Total Sales
Week 1	$ 2,880	$ 2,552	$ [illegible]	$ [illegible]	$ [illegible]	$ 18,212
Week 2	3,215	2,742	[illegible]	[illegible]	[illegible]	17,197
Week 3	3,180	2,650	2,018	[illegible]	11,550	19,398
Week 4	2,967	2,820	2,234	[illegible]	10,384	18,405
Total	$ 12,242	$ 10,764	$ 8,323	$ [illegible]	$ [illegible]	$ 73,212

Recorded on:
2/28/14

Reviewed on:
3/5/14

Lastname_Firstname_2D_February_Sales

Figure 2.54

(Project 2D February Sales continues on the next page)

Skills Review | Project 2D February Sales (continued)

1 **Start** Excel. From your student files, locate and open **e02D_February_Sales**. Click the **File tab**, click **Save As**, navigate to your **Excel Chapter 2** folder, and then using your own name, save the file as **Lastname_Firstname_2D_February_Sales**

a. Point to the **Sheet1 tab**, and then double-click to select the sheet tab name. Type **California Sales** and then press Enter.

b. Point to the **Sheet2 tab**, right-click, and then from the shortcut menu, click **Rename**. Type **Oregon Sales** and press Enter.

c. Point to the **California Sales sheet tab** and right-click. On the shortcut menu, point to **Tab Color**, and then in the last column, click the first color—**Orange, Accent 6**.

d. Using the technique you just practiced, change the tab color of the **Oregon Sales sheet tab** to **Aqua, Accent 5**—in the next to last column, the first color.

e. Click the **California Sales sheet tab**, and then click cell **A13**. On the **Home tab**, in the **Number group**, click the **Number Format arrow**. From the bottom of the displayed menu, click **More Number Formats** to display the **Number tab** of the **Format Cells** dialog box. Click the **3/14/01** type, and then at the bottom of the dialog box, click **OK**.

f. Click cell **A16**, type **3/5/14** and then press Enter. Click cell **A13**, and then on the **Home tab**, in the **Clipboard group**, click the **Format Painter** button. Click cell **A16** to copy the date format from cell **A13** to cell **A16**.

g. Click cell **A1**. In the **Editing group**, click the **Clear** button. From the displayed list, click **Clear Formats**.

h. Select the range **A4:A16**. On the **Home tab**, in the **Clipboard group**, click the **Copy** button. At the bottom of the workbook window, click the **Oregon Sales sheet tab** to make it the active worksheet. Right-click cell **A4**, and then under **Paste Options**, click the first button—**Paste**. Display the **California Sales** sheet. Press Esc to cancel the moving border.

2 With the **California Sales** sheet active, press Ctrl + Home to make cell **A1** the active cell. Point to the sheet tab, right-click, and then on the shortcut menu, click **Select All Sheets**. Verify that *[Group]* displays in the title bar.

a. **Merge & Center** the text in cell A1 across the range **A1:G1**, and then apply the **Title** cell style. Select **columns A:G**, and then set their widths to **85 pixels**.

b. Click cell **A2**, type **Month Ending February 2014** and then on the **Formula Bar**, click the **Enter** button to keep cell **A2** as the active cell. **Merge & Center** the text across the range **A2:G2**, and then apply the **Heading 1** cell style.

c. Select the range **B4:G4**, and then apply the **Heading 3** cell style. In the **Alignment group**, click the **Center**, **Middle Align**, and **Wrap Text** buttons.

d. With the sheets still *grouped* and the **California Sales** sheet active, click cell **E5**. On the **Home tab**, in the **Editing group**, click the **Sum** button, and then press Enter. Click cell **E5**, and then drag the fill handle down to copy the formula through cell **E8**.

e. Click cell **G5**, type = click cell **E5**, type + click cell **F5**, and then press Enter. Copy the formula down through cell **G8**. In cell **A9**, type **Total** Select the range **B5:G9**, and then press Alt + = to enter the SUM function for all the columns. Select the range **A5:A9**, and then apply the **Heading 4** cell style.

f. Select the range **B5:G5**, hold down Ctrl, and then select the range **B9:G9**. Apply the **Accounting Number Format** and decrease the decimal places to zero. Select the range **B6:G8**, and then apply **Comma Style** with zero decimal places. Select the range **B9:G9** and apply the **Total** cell style.

3 Click the **Oregon Sales sheet tab** to cancel the grouping and display the second worksheet.

a. To the right of the **Oregon Sales** sheet tab, click the **Insert Worksheet** button. Rename the new worksheet tab **Summary** and then change the **Tab Color** to **Olive Green, Accent 3**—in the seventh column, the first color.

b. Widen **columns A:E** to **125** pixels. In cell **A1**, type **California and Oregon Sales** and then **Merge & Center** the title across the range **A1:E1**. Apply the **Title** cell style. In cell **A2**, type **Month Ending February 2014** and then **Merge & Center** the text across the range **A2:E2**. Apply the **Heading 1** cell style. In cell **A5**, type **California** and in cell **A6**, type **Oregon**

c. In cell **B4**, type **In-Store/Online** and press Tab. In cell **C4**, type **In-Store Sales** and press Tab. In cell **D4**, type **Online Sales** and press Tab. In cell **E4**, type **Total Sales** Select the range **B4:E4**, apply the **Heading 3** cell style, and then **Center** these column titles.

(Project 2D February Sales continues on the next page)

Skills Review | Project 2D February Sales (continued)

d. Click cell **C5**. Type = and then click the **California Sales sheet tab**. In the **California Sales** worksheet, click cell **E9**, and then press Enter. Click cell **D5**. Type = and then click the **California Sales sheet tab**. Click cell **F9**, and then press Enter.

e. By using the techniques you just practiced, in cells **C6** and **D6**, insert the total **In-Store Sales** and **Online Sales** data from the **Oregon Sales** worksheet.

f. Select the range **C5:E6**, and then click the **Sum** button to total the two rows. In cell **A7**, type **Total** and then select the range **C5:E7**. Click the **Sum** button to total the three columns. Select the nonadjacent ranges **C5:E5** and **C7:E7**, and then apply **Accounting Number Format** with zero decimal places. Select the range **C6:E6**, and then apply **Comma Style** with zero decimal places. Select the range **C7:E7**, and then apply the **Total** cell style. Select the range **A5:A7** and apply the **Heading 4** cell style.

g. Click cell **B5**. On the **Insert tab**, in the **Sparklines group**, click **Column**. In the **Create Sparklines** dialog box, with the insertion point blinking in the **Data Range** box, select the range **C5:D5** and then click **OK**.

h. Click cell **B6**, and then **Insert** a **Column Sparkline** for the range **C6:D6**. In the **Style group**, apply the second style in the second row—**Sparkline Style Accent 2, Darker 25%** to this sparkline.

4 Point to the **Summary sheet tab**, hold down the left mouse button to display a small black triangle, and drag to the left until the triangle and mouse pointer are to the left of the **California Sales sheet tab**, and then release the left mouse button.

a. Be sure the **Summary** worksheet is the active sheet, point to its sheet tab, right-click, and then click **Select All Sheets** to display *[Group]* in the title bar. On the **Insert tab**, in the **Text group**, click the **Header & Footer** button. Display the **Footer** area, and then in the **left section**, insert the **File Name**. Center the worksheets **Horizontally** on the page, return to **Normal** view, and make cell **A1** active.

b. Display the **Document Panel**, and then add your name, your course name and section, and the keywords **February sales Close** the **Document Information Panel**.

c. **Save** your workbook. To submit your workbook electronically, follow the instructions provided by your instructor. To print your workbook, continue to Step d.

d. Display **Backstage** view, verify that the worksheets in your workbook are still grouped—*[Group]* displays in the title bar—and then on the left click **Print**. Under **Settings**, verify that **Print Active Sheets** displays. At the top of the screen, verify that the **Number of Copies** is **1**. Click the **Print** button.

e. If required by your instructor, print or create an electronic version of your worksheets with formulas displayed by using the instructions in Activity 1.16, and then **Close** Excel without saving so that you do not save the changes you made to print formulas.

End You have completed Project 2D

Apply 2A skills from these Objectives:

1. Use the SUM, AVERAGE, MEDIAN, MIN, and MAX Functions
2. Move Data, Resolve Error Messages, and Rotate Text
3. Use COUNTIF and IF Functions and Apply Conditional Formatting
4. Use Date & Time Functions and Freeze Panes
5. Create, Sort, and Filter an Excel Table
6. Format and Print a Large Worksheet

Mastering Excel | Project 2E Desserts

In the following Mastery project, you will edit a worksheet for Laura Morales, President, detailing the current inventory of desserts produced at the San Diego facility. Your completed worksheet will look similar to Figure 2.55.

Project Files

For Project 2E, you will need the following file:

e02E_Desserts

You will save your workbook as:

Lastname_Firstname_2E_Desserts

Project Results

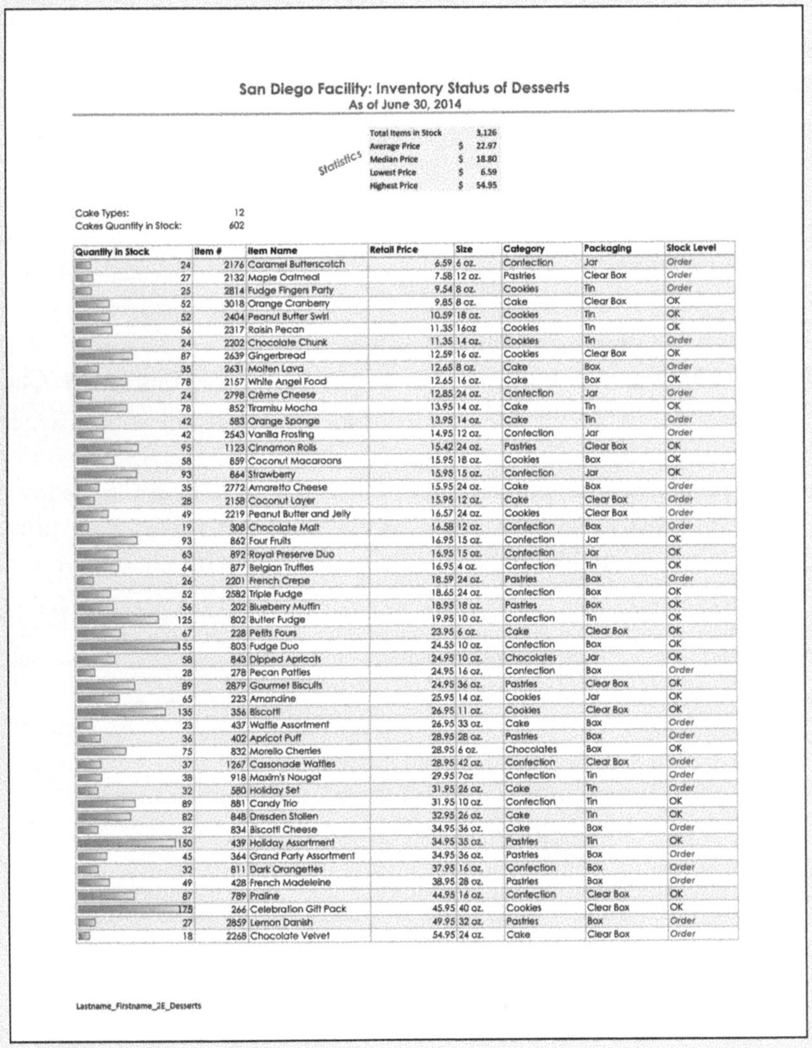

San Diego Facility: Inventory Status of Desserts
As of June 30, 2014

Statistics		
Total Items in Stock		3,126
Average Price	$	22.97
Median Price	$	18.80
Lowest Price	$	6.59
Highest Price	$	54.95

Cake Types: 12
Cakes Quantity in Stock: 602

Quantity in Stock	Item #	Item Name	Retail Price	Size	Category	Packaging	Stock Level
24	2176	Caramel Butterscotch	6.59	6 oz.	Confection	Jar	Order
27	2132	Maple Oatmeal	7.58	12 oz.	Pastries	Clear Box	Order
25	2814	Fudge Fingers Party	9.54	8 oz.	Cookies	Tin	Order
52	3018	Orange Cranberry	9.85	8 oz.	Cake	Clear Box	OK
52	2404	Peanut Butter Swirl	10.59	18 oz.	Cookies	Tin	OK
56	2317	Raisin Pecan	11.35	16oz	Cookies	Tin	OK
24	2202	Chocolate Chunk	11.35	14 oz.	Cookies	Tin	Order
87	2639	Gingerbread	12.59	16 oz.	Cookies	Clear Box	OK
35	2631	Molten Lava	12.65	8 oz.	Cake	Box	Order
78	2157	White Angel Food	12.65	16 oz.	Cake	Box	OK
24	2798	Crême Cheese	12.85	24 oz.	Confection	Jar	Order
78	852	Tiramisu Mocha	13.95	14 oz.	Cake	Tin	OK
42	583	Orange Sponge	13.95	14 oz.	Cake	Tin	Order
42	2543	Vanilla Frosting	14.95	12 oz.	Confection	Jar	Order
95	1123	Cinnamon Rolls	15.42	24 oz.	Pastries	Clear Box	OK
58	859	Coconut Macaroons	15.95	18 oz.	Cookies	Box	OK
93	864	Strawberry	15.95	15 oz.	Confection	Jar	OK
35	2772	Amaretto Cheese	15.95	24 oz.	Cake	Box	Order
28	2158	Coconut Layer	15.95	12 oz.	Cake	Clear Box	Order
49	2219	Peanut Butter and Jelly	16.57	24 oz.	Cookies	Clear Box	Order
19	308	Chocolate Malt	16.58	12 oz.	Confection	Box	Order
93	862	Four Fruits	16.95	15 oz.	Confection	Jar	OK
63	892	Royal Preserve Duo	16.95	15 oz.	Confection	Jar	OK
64	877	Belgian Truffles	16.95	4 oz.	Confection	Tin	OK
26	2201	French Crepe	18.59	24 oz.	Pastries	Box	Order
52	2582	Triple Fudge	18.65	24 oz.	Confection	Box	OK
56	202	Blueberry Muffin	18.95	18 oz.	Pastries	Box	OK
125	802	Butter Fudge	19.95	10 oz.	Confection	Tin	OK
67	228	Petits Fours	23.95	6 oz.	Cake	Clear Box	OK
155	803	Fudge Duo	24.55	10 oz.	Confection	Box	OK
58	843	Dipped Apricots	24.95	10 oz.	Chocolates	Jar	OK
28	278	Pecan Patties	24.95	16 oz.	Confection	Box	Order
89	2879	Gourmet Biscuits	24.95	36 oz.	Pastries	Clear Box	OK
65	223	Amandine	25.95	14 oz.	Cookies	Jar	OK
135	356	Biscotti	26.95	11 oz.	Cookies	Clear Box	OK
23	437	Waffle Assortment	26.95	33 oz.	Cake	Box	Order
36	402	Apricot Puff	28.95	28 oz.	Pastries	Box	Order
75	832	Morello Cherries	28.95	6 oz.	Chocolates	Box	OK
37	1267	Cassonade Waffles	28.95	42 oz.	Confection	Clear Box	Order
38	918	Maxim's Nougat	29.95	7oz	Confection	Tin	Order
32	580	Holiday Set	31.95	26 oz.	Cake	Tin	Order
89	881	Candy Trio	31.95	10 oz.	Confection	Tin	OK
82	848	Dresden Stollen	32.95	26 oz.	Cake	Tin	OK
32	834	Biscotti Cheese	34.95	36 oz.	Cake	Box	Order
150	439	Holiday Assortment	34.95	35 oz.	Pastries	Tin	OK
45	364	Grand Party Assortment	34.95	36 oz.	Pastries	Box	Order
32	811	Dark Orangettes	37.95	16 oz.	Confection	Box	Order
49	428	French Madeleine	38.95	28 oz.	Pastries	Box	Order
87	789	Praline	44.95	16 oz.	Confection	Clear Box	OK
175	266	Celebration Gift Pack	45.95	40 oz.	Cookies	Clear Box	OK
27	2859	Lemon Danish	49.95	32 oz.	Pastries	Box	Order
18	2268	Chocolate Velvet	54.95	24 oz.	Cake	Clear Box	Order

Lastname_Firstname_2E_Desserts

Figure 2.55

(Project 2E Desserts continues on the next page)

Mastering Excel | Project 2E Desserts (continued)

1 **Start** Excel, from your student files, locate and open **e02E_Desserts**, and then **Save** the file in your **Excel Chapter 2** folder as **Lastname_Firstname_2E_Desserts**

2 In cell **B4**, calculate the **Total Items in Stock** by summing the **Quantity in Stock** data, and then apply **Comma Style** with zero decimal places to the result. In each cell in the range **B5:B8**, insert formulas to calculate the Average, Median, Lowest, and Highest retail prices, and then apply the **Accounting Number Format** to each result.

3 Move the range **A4:B8** to the range **D4:E8**, and then apply the **20% - Accent1** cell style. Widen **column D** to **130 pixels**. In cell **C6**, type **Statistics** select the range **C4:C8**, and then from the **Format Cells** dialog box, merge the selected cells. Change the text **Orientation** to **25 Degrees**, and then apply **Bold** and **Italic**. Change the **Font Size** to **14** and the **Font Color** to **Pink, Accent 1, Darker 25%**. Apply **Middle Align** and **Align Text Right**.

4 In cell **B10**, use the **COUNTIF** function to count the number of **Cake** items. In the **Packaging** column, **Replace All** occurrences of **Cellophane** with **Clear Box**

5 In cell **H14**, enter an **IF** function to determine the items that must be ordered. If the **Quantity in Stock** is less than **50** the **Value_if_true** is **Order** Otherwise the **Value_if_false** is **OK** Fill the formula down through cell **H65**. Apply **Conditional Formatting** to the **Stock Level** column so that cells that contain the text *Order* are formatted with **Bold Italic** and with a **Color** of **Blue, Accent 5**. Apply conditional formatting to the **Quantity in Stock** column by applying a **Gradient Fill Orange Data Bar**.

6 Format the range **A13:H65** as a **Table** with headers, and apply the **Table Style Light 16** style. Sort the table from smallest to largest by **Retail Price**, and then filter on the **Category** column to display the **Cake** types. Display a **Total Row** in the table and then in cell **A66**, **Sum** the **Quantity in Stock** for the **Cake** items. Type the result in cell **B11**, and apply appropriate number formatting. Click in the table, and then on the **Design tab**, remove the total row from the table. Clear the **Category** filter and convert the table to a range.

7 Change the theme to **Composite**. Display the footer area, and insert the **File Name** in the **left section**. Center the worksheet **Horizontally**, and then use the **Scale to Fit** option to change the **Width** to **1 page**. Return to **Normal** view and make cell **A1** the active cell. In **Backstage** view, display the **Print Preview**, and then make any necessary corrections.

8 Add your name, your course name and section, and the keywords **desserts inventory, San Diego** to the Document Panel. **Save**, and then print or submit electronically as directed. If required by your instructor, print or create an electronic version of your worksheets with formulas displayed by using the instructions in Activity 1.16, and then **Close** Excel without saving so that you do not save the changes you made to print formulas.

End **You have completed Project 2E**

Content-Based Assessments

Apply 2B skills from these Objectives:

- 7 Navigate a Workbook and Rename Worksheets
- 8 Enter Dates, Clear Contents, and Clear Formats
- 9 Copy and Paste by Using the Paste Options Gallery
- 10 Edit and Format Multiple Worksheets at the Same Time
- 11 Create a Summary Sheet with Column Sparklines
- 12 Format and Print Multiple Worksheets in a Workbook

Mastering Excel | Project 2F Compensation

In the following Mastery project, you will edit a workbook that summarizes the Laurales Herb and Spices salesperson compensation for the month of November. Your completed worksheet will look similar to Figure 2.56.

Project Files

For Project 2F, you will need the following file:

e02F_Compensation

You will save your workbook as:

Lastname_Firstname_2F_Compensation

Project Results

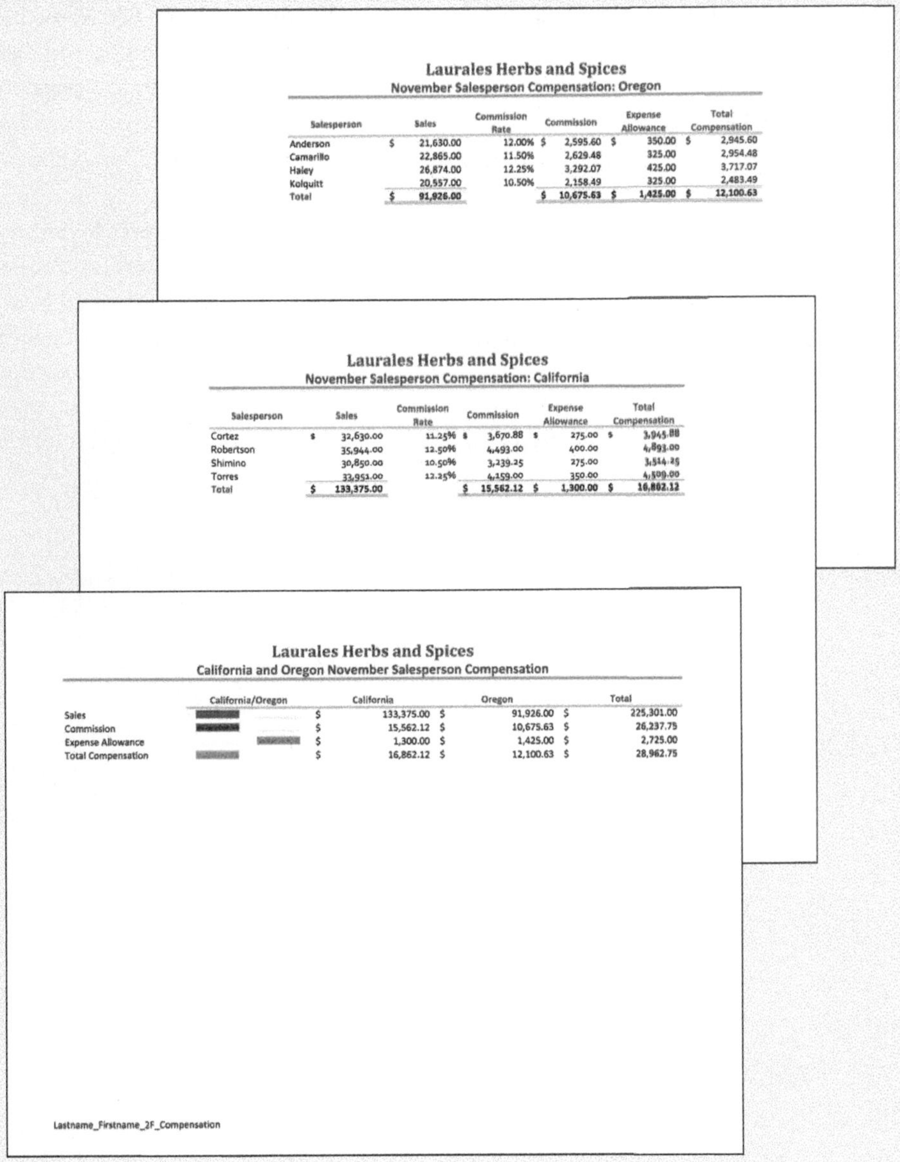

Laurales Herbs and Spices
November Salesperson Compensation: Oregon

Salesperson	Sales	Commission Rate	Commission	Expense Allowance	Total Compensation
Anderson	$ 21,630.00	12.00%	$ 2,595.60	$ 350.00	$ 2,945.60
Camarillo	22,865.00	11.50%	2,629.48	325.00	2,954.48
Haley	26,874.00	12.25%	3,292.07	425.00	3,717.07
Kolquitt	20,557.00	10.50%	2,158.49	325.00	2,483.49
Total	$ 91,926.00		$ 10,675.63	$ 1,425.00	$ 12,100.63

Laurales Herbs and Spices
November Salesperson Compensation: California

Salesperson	Sales	Commission Rate	Commission	Expense Allowance	Total Compensation
Cortez	$ 32,630.00	11.25%	$ 3,670.88	$ 275.00	$ 3,945.88
Robertson	35,944.00	12.50%	4,493.00	400.00	4,893.00
Shimino	30,850.00	10.50%	3,239.25	275.00	3,514.25
Torres	33,951.00	12.25%	4,159.00	350.00	4,509.00
Total	$ 133,375.00		$ 15,562.12	$ 1,300.00	$ 16,862.12

Laurales Herbs and Spices
California and Oregon November Salesperson Compensation

	California/Oregon	California	Oregon	Total
Sales		$ 133,375.00	$ 91,926.00	$ 225,301.00
Commission		$ 15,562.12	$ 10,675.63	$ 26,237.75
Expense Allowance		$ 1,300.00	$ 1,425.00	$ 2,725.00
Total Compensation		$ 16,862.12	$ 12,100.63	$ 28,962.75

Lastname_Firstname_2F_Compensation

Figure 2.56

(Project 2F Compensation continues on the next page)

Mastering Excel | Project 2F Compensation (continued)

1 **Start** Excel, from your student files, open **e02F_Compensation**, and then save the file in your **Excel Chapter 2** folder as **Lastname_Firstname_2F_Compensation**

2 Rename **Sheet1** as **California** and change the **Tab Color** to **Green, Accent 1**. Rename **Sheet2** as **Oregon** and change the **Tab Color** to **Gold, Accent 3**.

3 Click the **California sheet tab** to make it the active sheet, and then group the worksheets. In cell **A1**, type **Laurales Herbs and Spices** and then **Merge & Center** the text across the range **A1:F1**. Apply the **Title** cell style. **Merge & Center** the text in cell **A2** across the range **A2:F2**, and then apply the **Heading 1** cell style.

4 With the sheets still grouped, in cell **D5** calculate **Commission** for *Cortez* by multiplying the **Sales** by the **Commission Rate**. Copy the formula down through cell **D8**. In cell **F5**, calculate **Total Compensation** by summing the **Commission** and **Expense Allowance** for *Cortez*. Copy the formula down through the cell **F8**.

5 In **row 9**, sum the **Sales**, **Commission**, **Expense Allowance**, and **Total Compensation** columns. Apply the **Accounting Number Format** with two decimal places to the appropriate cells in **row 5** and **row 9** (do not include the percentages). Apply the **Comma Style** with two decimal places to the appropriate cells in **rows 6:8** (do not include the percentages). Apply the **Total** cell style to the appropriate cells in the Total row.

6 Insert a new worksheet. Change the sheet name to **Summary** and then change the **Tab Color** to **Periwinkle, Accent 5**. Widen **columns A:E** to **165** pixels, and then move the **Summary** sheet so that it is the first sheet in the workbook. In cell **A1**, type **Laurales Herbs and Spices** **Merge & Center** the title across the range **A1:E1**, and then apply the **Title** cell style. In cell **A2**, type **California and Oregon November Salesperson Compensation** and then **Merge & Center** the text across the range **A2:E2**. Apply the **Heading 1** cell style.

7 In the range **A5:A8**, type the following row titles and then apply the **Heading 4** cell style:

Sales
Commission
Expense Allowance
Total Compensation

8 In the range **B4:E4**, type the following column titles, and then **Center** and apply the **Heading 3** cell style.

California/Oregon
California
Oregon
Total

9 In cell **C5**, enter a formula that references cell **B9** in the **California** worksheet so that the total sales for California displays in **C5**. Create similar formulas to enter the total **Commission**, **Expense Allowance** and **Total Compensation** for California in the range **C6:C8**. Using the same technique, enter formulas in the range **D5:D8** so that the **Oregon** totals display.

10 Sum the **Sales**, **Commission**, **Expense Allowance**, and **Total Compensation** rows.

11 In cell **B5**, insert a **Column Sparkline** for the range **C5:D5**. In cells **B6**, **B7**, and **B8**, insert **Column** sparklines for the appropriate ranges to compare California totals with Oregon totals. To the sparkline in **B6**, apply the second style in the third row—**Sparkline Style Accent 2, (no dark or light)**. In **B7** apply the third style in the third row—**Sparkline Style Accent 3, (no dark or light)**. In **B8** apply the fourth style in the third row—**Sparkline Style Accent 4, (no dark or light)**.

12 **Group** the three worksheets, and then insert a footer in the left section with the **File Name**. Center the worksheets **Horizontally** on the page, and then change the **Orientation** to **Landscape**. Return the document to **Normal** view.

13 Display the **Document Panel**. Add your name, your course name and section, and the keywords **November sales** **Save** your workbook, and then print or submit electronically as directed. If required by your instructor, print or create an electronic version of your worksheets with formulas displayed by using the instructions in Activity 1.16, and then **Close** Excel without saving so that you do not save the changes you made to print formulas.

End **You have completed Project 2F**

Content-Based Assessments

Apply 2A and 2B skills from these Objectives:

1. Use the SUM, AVERAGE, MEDIAN, MIN, and MAX Functions
2. Move Data, Resolve Error Messages, and Rotate Text
3. Use COUNTIF and IF Functions and Apply Conditional Formatting
4. Use Date & Time Functions and Freeze Panes
5. Create, Sort, and Filter an Excel Table
6. Format and Print a Large Worksheet
7. Navigate a Workbook and Rename Worksheets
8. Enter Dates, Clear Contents, and Clear Formats
9. Copy and Paste by Using the Paste Options Gallery
10. Edit and Format Multiple Worksheets at the Same Time
11. Create a Summary Sheet with Column Sparklines
12. Format and Print Multiple Worksheets in a Workbook

Mastering Excel | Project 2G Inventory Summary

In the following Mastery project, you will edit a worksheet that summarizes the inventory status at the Petaluma production facility. Your completed workbook will look similar to Figure 2.57.

Project Files

For Project 2G, you will need the following file:

e02G_Inventory_Summary

You will save your workbook as:

Lastname_Firstname_2G_Inventory_Summary

Project Results

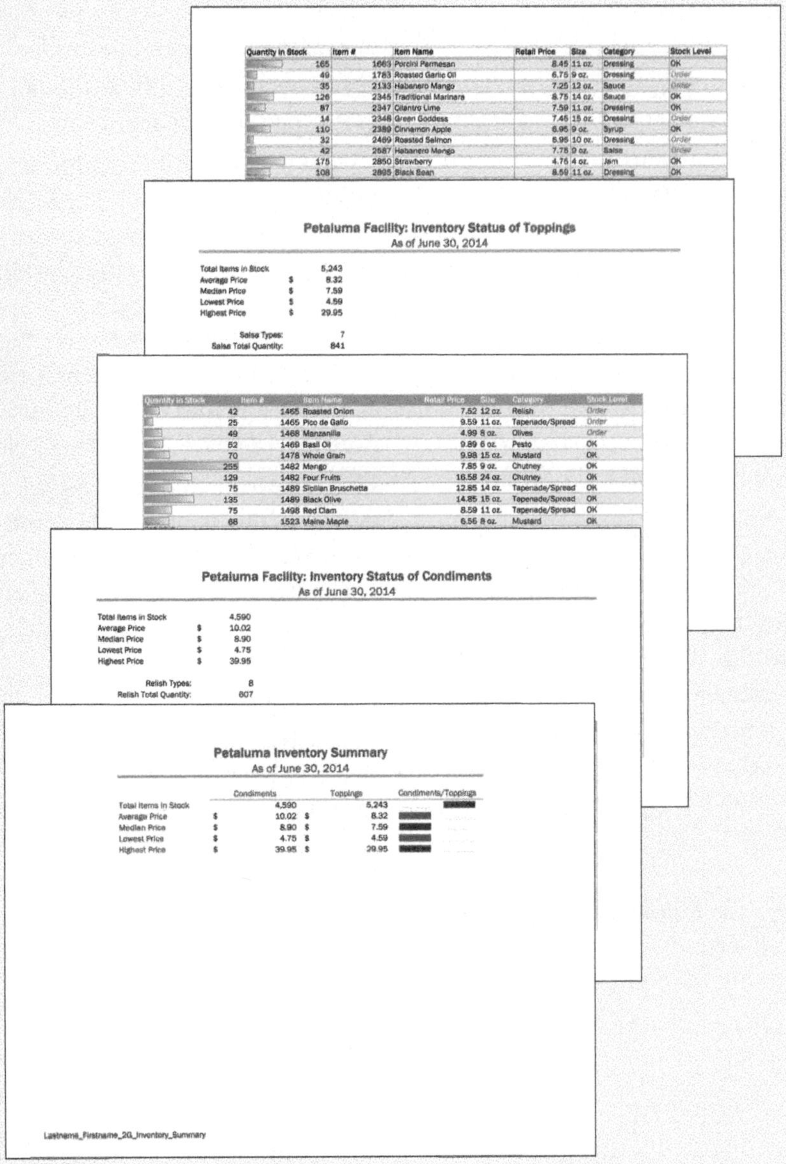

Figure 2.57

(Project 2G Inventory Summary continues on the next page)

Mastering Excel | Project 2G Inventory Summary (continued)

1 **Start** Excel. From your student files, open **e02G_Inventory_Summary**. Save the file in your **Excel Chapter 2** folder as **Lastname_Firstname_2G_Inventory_Summary**

2 Rename **Sheet1** as **Condiments** and **Sheet2** as **Toppings** Make the following calculations in each of the two worksheets *without* grouping the sheets:

- In cell **B4**, enter a formula to sum the **Quantity in Stock** data, and then apply **Comma Style** with zero decimal places to the result.
- In cells **B5:B8**, enter formulas to calculate the Average, Median, Lowest, and Highest retail prices, and then apply the **Accounting Number Format**.

3 In each of the two worksheets, make the following calculations *without* grouping the sheets:

- In cell **B10**, enter a COUNTIF function to determine how many different types of **Relish** products are in stock on the **Condiments** sheet and how many different types of **Salsa** products are in stock on the **Toppings** worksheet.
- In cell **G15**, enter an **IF** function to determine the items that must be ordered. If the **Quantity in Stock** is less than **50** the **Value_if_true** is **Order** Otherwise the **Value_if_false** is **OK** Fill the formula down through all the rows.
- Apply **Conditional Formatting** to the **Stock Level** column so that cells that contain the text *Order* are formatted with **Bold Italic** with a **Font Color** of **Gold, Accent 1, Darker 25%**. Apply **Gradient Fill Green Data Bars** to the **Quantity in Stock** column.

4 In the **Condiments** sheet, format the range **A14:G64** as a table with headers and apply **Table Style Medium 2**. Insert a **Total Row**, filter by **Category** for **Relish**, and then **Sum** the **Quantity in Stock** column. Record the result in cell **B11**.

5 Select the table, clear the filter, **Sort** the table on the **Item #** column from **Smallest to Largest**, remove the **Total Row**, and then convert the table to a range. On the **Page Layout tab**, set **Print Titles** so that **row 14** repeats at the top of each page.

6 In the **Toppings** sheet, format the range **A14:G61** as a table with headers and apply **Table Style Light 16**. Insert a **Total Row**, filter by **Category** for **Salsa**, and then **Sum** the **Quantity in Stock** column. Record the result in cell **B11**.

7 Select the table, clear the filter, **Sort** the table on the **Item #** column from **Smallest to Largest**, remove the **Total Row**, and then convert the table to a range.

8 On the **Page Layout tab**, set **Print Titles** so that **row 14** repeats at the top of each page, and then **Save** your workbook. **Group** the two worksheets. **Center** the worksheets **Horizontally**, and then use the **Scale to Fit** option to change the **Width** to **1 page**.

9 Insert a new worksheet. Change the sheet name to **Summary** and then widen **columns A:D** to **170** pixels. Move the **Summary** sheet so that it is the first sheet in the workbook. In cell **A1**, type **Petaluma Inventory Summary** **Merge & Center** the title across the range **A1:D1**, and then apply the **Title** cell style. In cell **A2**, type **As of June 30, 2014** and then **Merge & Center** the text across the range **A2:D2**. Apply the **Heading 1** cell style.

10 On the **Condiments sheet**, **Copy** the range **A4:A8**. Display the **Summary sheet** and **Paste** the selection to cell **A5**. Apply the **Heading 4** cell style to the selection. In the **Summary sheet**, in cell **B4**, type **Condiments** In cell **C4**, type **Toppings** and in cell **D4**, type **Condiments/Toppings** **Center** the column titles, and then apply the **Heading 3** cell style.

11 In cell **B5**, enter a formula that references cell **B4** in the **Condiments sheet** so that the **Condiments Total Items in Stock** displays in **B5**. Create similar formulas to enter the **Average Price**, **Median Price**, **Lowest Price**, and **Highest Price** from the **Condiments sheet** into the **Summary** sheet in the range **B6:B9**.

12 Enter formulas in the range **C5:C9** that reference the appropriate cells in the **Toppings** worksheet. To the range **B5:C5**, apply **Comma Style** with zero decimal places. In cells **D5**, **D6**, **D7**, **D8**, and **D9**, insert **Column** sparklines using the values in the *Condiments* and *Toppings* columns. Format each sparkline using the first five Sparkline styles in the first row.

13 Center the **Summary** worksheet **Horizontally** and change the **Orientation** to **Landscape**. **Group** the worksheets and insert a footer in the left section with the **File Name**. In **Normal** view, make cell **A1** the active cell. Display the **Document Panel**. Add your name, your course name and section, and the keywords **Petaluma inventory**

14 **Save** your workbook, and then print or submit electronically as directed. If required by your instructor, print or create an electronic version of your worksheets with formulas displayed by using the instructions in Activity 1.16, and then **Close** Excel without saving so that you do not save the changes you made to print formulas.

End **You have completed Project 2G**

Apply a combination of the 2A and 2B skills.

GO! Fix It | Project 2H Confections

Project Files

For Project 2H, you will need the following file:

e02H_Confections

You will save your workbook as:

Lastname_Firstname_2H_Confections

In this project, you will correct a worksheet that contains the confection inventory for the month of June at the Laurales Herb and Spices Petaluma production facility. From the student files that accompany this textbook, open the file e02H_Confections, and then save the file in your chapter folder as **Lastname_Firstname_2H_Confections**

To complete the project, you must find and correct errors in formulas and formatting. View each formula in cells B4:B8 and edit as necessary. In addition to errors that you find, you should know:

- The table should be sorted smallest to largest by Item #.
- New stock should be ordered when the Quantity in Stock is less than 50, and the word *Order* should be formatted with bold, italic, in font color Red, Accent 3.
- The table should be converted to a range.
- Gradient fill red data bars should be applied to the Quantity in Stock column.

Insert the file name in the left section of the footer, center the worksheet horizontally, and repeat the table column titles on each page. Edit the document properties with your name, course and section, and the keywords **Petaluma, confections** Save your file, and then print or submit your worksheet electronically as directed by your instructor. If required by your instructor, print or create an electronic version of your worksheets with formulas displayed by using the instructions in Activity 1.16, and then Close Excel without saving so that you do not save the changes you made to print formulas.

End You have completed Project 2H

Content-Based Assessments

Apply a combination of the 2A and 2B skills.

GO! Make It | Project 2I Salary Summary

Project Files

For Project 2I, you will need the following file:

e02I_Salary_Summary

You will save your workbook as:

Lastname_Firstname_2I_Salary_Summary

Open e02I_Salary_Summary and save the file in your Excel Chapter 2 folder as **Lastname_Firstname_2I_Salary_Summary** Edit the worksheet as shown in Figure 2.58. To calculate Commission for each salesperson, multiply the Sales by the Commission Rate, using absolute cell references as necessary. To determine the Bonus, construct an IF function where the Logical Test determines if Sales are greater than 21,500, the Value_if_true is 500, and the Value_if_false is 0. Calculate Total Compensation by adding the Commission and the Bonus for each salesperson. Determine the Sales and Compensation totals, averages, medians, and highest and lowest amounts. Insert a table, apply Table Medium Style 16, sort the table as shown in Figure 2.58, apply cell styles and number formatting as indicated, and convert the table to a range. Insert a footer with the file name in the left section, center the worksheet horizontally, and add your name, your course name and section, and the keywords **commission, sales** to the document properties. Print or submit electronically as directed by your instructor.

Project Results

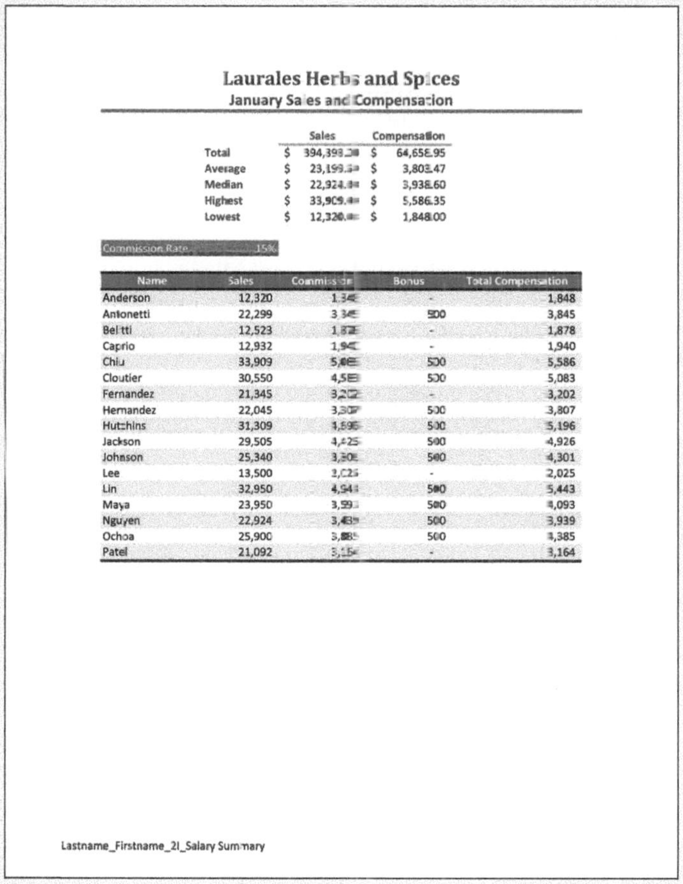

Laurales Herbs and Spices

January Sales and Compensation

	Sales	Compensation
Total	$ 394,398.[illegible]	$ 64,658.95
Average	$ 23,199.[illegible]	$ 3,803.47
Median	$ 22,924.[illegible]	$ 3,938.60
Highest	$ 33,909.[illegible]	$ 5,586.35
Lowest	$ 12,320.[illegible]	$ 1,848.00

Commission Rate 15%

Name	Sales	Commission	Bonus	Total Compensation
Anderson	12,320	1,34[illegible]	-	1,848
Antonetti	22,299	3,34[illegible]	500	3,845
Belitti	12,523	1,8[illegible]	-	1,878
Caprio	12,932	1,94[illegible]	-	1,940
Chiu	33,909	5,0[illegible]	500	5,586
Cloutier	30,550	4,5[illegible]	500	5,083
Fernandez	21,345	3,20[illegible]	-	3,202
Hernandez	22,045	3,30[illegible]	500	3,807
Hutchins	31,309	4,696	500	5,196
Jackson	29,505	4,425	500	4,926
Johnson	25,340	3,80[illegible]	500	4,301
Lee	13,500	2,025	-	2,025
Lin	32,950	4,943	500	5,443
Maya	23,950	3,593	500	4,093
Nguyen	22,924	3,439	500	3,939
Ochoa	25,900	3,885	500	4,385
Patel	21,092	3,164	-	3,164

Lastname_Firstname_2I_Salary Summary

Figure 2.58

End **You have completed Project 2I**

Apply a combination of the 2A and 2B skills.

GO! Solve It | Project 2J Toppings

Project Files

For Project 2J, you will need the following file:

e02J_Toppings

You will save your workbook as:

Lastname_Firstname_2J_Toppings

Open the file e02J_Toppings and save it as **Lastname_Firstname_2J_Toppings** Complete the worksheet by entering appropriate formulas in cells B5 and B6. In the Stock Level column, enter an IF function that determines whether the quantity in stock is greater than 65. If the Quantity in Stock is greater than 65, then the Stock Level should display the text **OK** Otherwise the Stock Level should display the text **Order** Insert a Table with a total row and apply an attractive table style. Sort the table by Item #, calculate the values for B7 and B8, and then clear all filters and remove the total row from the table. Convert the table to a range. Format the worksheet attractively, and apply appropriate Data Bars to the Quantity in Stock column and conditional formatting to the Stock Level column so that items that need to be ordered are easily identified. Include the file name in the footer, add appropriate properties, and submit as directed.

Performance Element	Performance Level: Exemplary: You consistently applied the relevant skills	Performance Level: Proficient: You sometimes, but not always, applied the relevant skills	Performance Level: Developing: You rarely or never applied the relevant skills
Create formulas	All formulas are correct and are efficiently constructed.	Formulas are correct but not always constructed in the most efficient manner.	One or more formulas are missing or incorrect; or only numbers were entered.
Insert and format a table	Table was created and formatted properly.	Table was created but incorrect data was selected or the table was not formatted.	No table was created.
Format worksheet data attractively and appropriately	Formatting is attractive and appropriate.	Adequately formatted but difficult to read or unattractive.	Inadequate or no formatting.

End **You have completed Project 2J**

Apply a combination of the 2A and 2B skills.

GO! Solve It | Project 2K First Quarter Summary

Project Files

For Project 2K, you will need the following file:

e02K_First_Quarter

You will save your workbook as:

Lastname_Firstname_2K_First_Quarter

Open the file e02K_First_Quarter and save it as **Lastname_Firstname_2K_First_Quarter** This workbook contains two worksheets; one that includes California sales data by product and one that includes Oregon sales data by product. Complete the two worksheets by calculating totals by product and by month. Then calculate the Percent of Total by dividing the Product Total by the Monthly Total, using absolute cell references as necessary. Format the worksheets attractively with a title and subtitle, and apply appropriate financial formatting. Insert a new worksheet that summarizes the monthly totals by state. Enter the months as the column titles and the states as the row titles. Include a Product Total column and a column for sparklines titled **Jan./Feb./March** Format the Summary worksheet attractively with a title and subtitle, insert column sparklines that compare the months, and apply appropriate financial formatting. Include the file name in the footer, add appropriate document properties, and submit as directed.

Performance Element	Performance Level: Exemplary: You consistently applied the relevant skills	Proficient: You sometimes, but not always, applied the relevant skills	Developing: You rarely or never applied the relevant skills
Create formulas	All formulas are correct and are efficiently constructed.	Formulas are correct but not always constructed in the most efficient manner.	One or more formulas are missing or incorrect; or only numbers were entered.
Create Summary worksheet	Summary worksheet created properly.	Summary worksheet was created but the data, sparklines, or formulas were incorrect.	No Summary worksheet was created.
Format attractively and appropriately	Formatting is attractive and appropriate.	Adequately formatted but difficult to read or unattractive.	Inadequate or no formatting.

End **You have completed Project 2K**

Outcomes-Based Assessments

Rubric

The following outcomes-based assessments are *open-ended assessments*. That is, there is no specific correct result; your result will depend on your approach to the information provided. Make *Professional Quality* your goal. Use the following scoring rubric to guide you in *how* to approach the problem, and then to evaluate *how well* your approach solves the problem.

The *criteria*—Software Mastery, Content, Format and Layout, and Process—represent the knowledge and skills you have gained that you can apply to solving the problem. The *levels of performance*—Professional Quality, Approaching Professional Quality, or Needs Quality Improvements—help you and your instructor evaluate your result.

	Your completed project is of Professional Quality if you:	Your completed project is Approaching Professional Quality if you:	Your completed project Needs Quality Improvements if you:
1-Software Mastery	Choose and apply the most appropriate skills, tools, and features and identify efficient methods to solve the problem.	Choose and apply some appropriate skills, tools, and features, but not in the most efficient manner.	Choose inappropriate skills, tools, or features, or are inefficient in solving the problem.
2-Content	Construct a solution that is clear and well organized, contains content that is accurate, appropriate to the audience and purpose, and is complete. Provide a solution that contains no errors in spelling, grammar, or style.	Construct a solution in which some components are unclear, poorly organized, inconsistent, or incomplete. Misjudge the needs of the audience. Have some errors in spelling, grammar, or style, but the errors do not detract from comprehension.	Construct a solution that is unclear, incomplete, or poorly organized; contains some inaccurate or inappropriate content; and contains many errors in spelling, grammar, or style. Do not solve the problem.
3-Format and Layout	Format and arrange all elements to communicate information and ideas, clarify function, illustrate relationships, and indicate relative importance.	Apply appropriate format and layout features to some elements, but not others. Overuse features, causing minor distraction.	Apply format and layout that does not communicate information or ideas clearly. Do not use format and layout features to clarify function, illustrate relationships, or indicate relative importance. Use available features excessively, causing distraction.
4-Process	Use an organized approach that integrates planning, development, self-assessment, revision, and reflection.	Demonstrate an organized approach in some areas, but not others; or, use an insufficient process of organization throughout.	Do not use an organized approach to solve the problem.

Outcomes-Based Assessments

Apply a combination of the 2A and 2B skills.

GO! Think | Project 2L Seasonings

Project Files

For Project 2L, you will need the following file:

e02L_Seasonings

You will save your workbook as:

Lastname_Firstname_2L_Seasonings

Laura Morales, President of Laurales Herbs and Spices, has requested a worksheet that summarizes the seasonings inventory data for the month of March. Laura would like the worksheet to include the total Quantity in Stock and Number of Items for each category of items and she would like the items to be sorted from lowest to highest retail price.

Edit the workbook to provide Laura with the information requested. Format the worksheet titles and data and include an appropriately formatted table so that the worksheet is professional and easy to read and understand. Insert a footer with the file name and add appropriate document properties. Save the file as **Lastname_Firstname_2L_Seasonings** and print or submit as directed by your instructor.

End You have completed Project 2L

Apply a combination of the 2A and 2B skills.

GO! Think | Project 2M Expense Summary

Project Files

For Project 2M, you will need the following file:

e02M_Expense_Summary

You will save your workbook as:

Lastname_Firstname_2M_Expense_Summary

Sara Lopez, Director of the San Diego production facility, has requested a summary analysis of the administrative expenses the facility incurred in the last fiscal year. Open e02M_Expense_Summary and then complete the calculation in the four worksheets containing the quarterly data. Summarize the information in a new worksheet that includes formulas referencing the totals for each expense category for each quarter. Sum the expenses to display the yearly expense by quarter and expense category. Format the worksheets in a manner that is professional and easy to read and understand. Insert a footer with the file name and add appropriate document properties. Save the file as **Lastname_Firstname_2M_Expense_Summary** and print or submit as directed by your instructor.

End You have completed Project 2M

Outcomes-Based Assessments

Apply a combination of the 2A and 2B skills.

You and GO! | Project 2N Annual Expenses

Project Files

For Project 2N, you will need the following file:

New blank Excel workbook

You will save your workbook as:

Lastname_Firstname_2N_Annual_Expenses

Develop a workbook that details the expenses you expect to incur during the current year. Create four worksheets, one for each quarter of the year and enter your expenses by month. For example, the Quarter 1 sheet will contain expense information for January, February, and March. Some of these expenses might include, but are not limited to, Mortgage, Rent, Utilities, Phone, Food, Entertainment, Tuition, Childcare, Clothing, and Insurance. Include monthly and quarterly totals for each category of expense. Insert a worksheet that summarizes the total expenses for each quarter. Format the worksheet by adjusting column width and wrapping text, and by applying appropriate financial number formatting and cell styles. Insert a footer with the file name and center the worksheet horizontally on the page. Save your file as **Lastname_Firstname_2N_Annual_Expenses** and submit as directed.

End **You have completed Project 2N**

Apply a combination of the 2A and 2B skills.

GO! CD-ROM

GO! Collaborate | Project 2O Bell Orchid Hotels Group Running Case

This project relates to the Bell Orchid Hotels. Your instructor may assign this group case project to your class. If your instructor assigns this project, he or she will provide you with information and instructions to work as part of a group. The group will apply the skills gained thus far to help the Bell Orchid Hotels achieve their business goals.

End **You have completed Project 2O**

Analyzing Data with Pie Charts, Line Charts, and What-If Analysis Tools

OUTCOMES

At the end of this chapter you will be able to:

OBJECTIVES

Mastering these objectives will enable you to:

PROJECT 3A
Present budget data in a pie chart.

1. Chart Data with a Pie Chart (p. 355)
2. Format a Pie Chart (p. 358)
3. Edit a Workbook and Update a Chart (p. 364)
4. Use Goal Seek to Perform What-If Analysis (p. 365)

PROJECT 3B
Make projections using what-if analysis and present projections in a line chart.

5. Design a Worksheet for What-If Analysis (p. 371)
6. Answer What-If Questions by Changing Values in a Worksheet (p. 378)
7. Chart Data with a Line Chart (p. 381)

Shutterstock

In This Chapter

In this chapter, you will work with two different types of commonly used charts that make it easy to visualize data. You will create a pie chart in a separate chart sheet to show how the parts of a budget contribute to a total budget. You will also practice using parentheses in a formula, calculate the percentage rate of an increase, answer what-if questions, and then chart data in a line chart to show the flow of data over time. In this chapter you will also practice formatting the axes in a line chart.

The projects in this chapter relate to **The City of Orange Blossom Beach**, a coastal city located between Fort Lauderdale and Miami. The city's access to major transportation provides both residents and businesses an opportunity to compete in the global marketplace. Each year the city welcomes a large number of tourists who enjoy the warm climate and beautiful beaches, and who embark on cruises from this major cruise port. The city encourages best environmental practices and partners with cities in other countries to promote sound government at the local level.

Project 3A Budget Pie Chart

Project Activities

In Activities 3.01 through 3.11, you will edit a worksheet for Lila Darius, City Manager, that projects expenses from the city's general fund for the next fiscal year, and then present the data in a pie chart. Your completed worksheet will look similar to Figure 3.1.

Project Files

For Project 3A, you will need the following file:

e03A_Fund_Expenses

You will save your workbook as:

Lastname_Firstname_3A_Fund_Expenses

Project Results

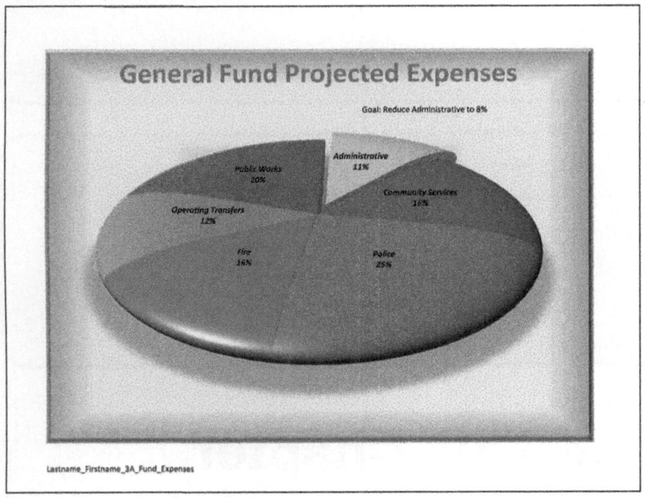

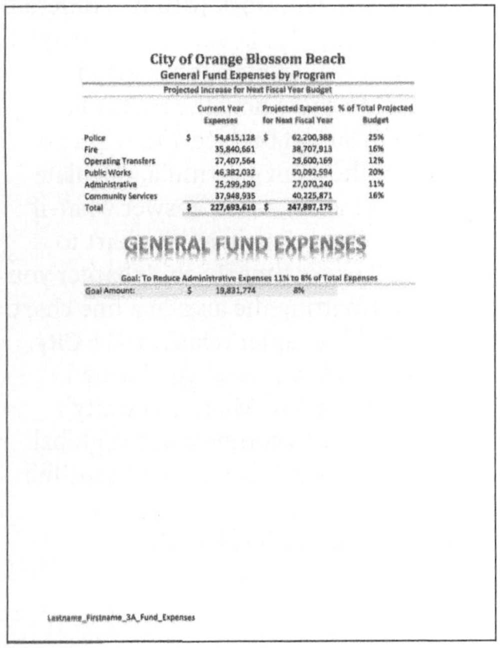

City of Orange Blossom Beach

General Fund Expenses by Program

Projected Increase for Next Fiscal Year Budget

	Current Year Expenses	Projected Expenses for Next Fiscal Year	% of Total Projected Budget
Police	$ 54,815,128	$ 62,200,388	25%
Fire	35,840,661	38,707,913	16%
Operating Transfers	27,407,564	29,600,169	12%
Public Works	46,382,032	50,092,594	20%
Administrative	25,299,290	27,070,240	11%
Community Services	37,948,935	40,225,871	16%
Total	$ 227,693,610	$ 247,897,175	

GENERAL FUND EXPENSES

Goal: To Reduce Administrative Expenses 11% to 8% of Total Expenses

Goal Amount: $ 19,831,774 8%

Lastname_Firstname_3A_Fund_Expenses

Figure 3.1
Project 3A Fund Expenses

Objective 1 | Chart Data with a Pie Chart

A ***pie chart*** shows the relationship of each part to a whole. The size of each pie slice is equal to its value compared to the total value of all the slices. The pie chart style charts data that is arranged in a single column or single row, and shows the size of items in a single data series proportional to the sum of the items. Whereas a column or bar chart can have two or more data series in the chart, a pie chart can have only one data series.

Consider using a pie chart when you have only one data series to plot, you do not have more than seven categories, and the categories represent parts of a total value.

Activity 3.01 | Creating a Pie Chart and a Chart Sheet

A ***fund*** is a sum of money set aside for a specific purpose. In a municipal government like the City of Orange Blossom Beach, the ***general fund*** is money set aside for the normal operating activities of the city, such as police, fire, and administering the everyday functions of the city.

1. **Start** Excel. From the student files that accompany this textbook, open **e03A_Fund_Expenses.** From **Backstage view**, display the **Save As** dialog box. Navigate to the location where you are storing projects for this chapter.

2. Create a new folder named **Excel Chapter 3** and open the new folder. In the **File name** box, type **Lastname_Firstname_3A_Fund_Expenses** Click **Save** or press Enter.

   The worksheet indicates the expenses for the current year and the projected expenses for the next fiscal year.

3. Click cell **D5**, and then type **=** to begin a formula.

4. Click cell **C5**, which is the first value that is part of the total Projected Expenses, to insert it into the formula. Type **/** to indicate division, and then click cell **C11**, which is the total Projected Expenses.

   Recall that to determine the percentage by which a value makes up a total, you must divide the value by the total. The result will be a percentage expressed as a decimal.

5. Press F4 to make the reference to the value in cell **C11** absolute, which will enable you to copy the formula. Compare your screen with Figure 3.2.

   Recall that an ***absolute cell reference*** refers to a cell by its fixed position in the worksheet. The reference to cell C5 is a ***relative cell reference***, because when you copy the formula, you want the reference to change *relative* to its row.

   Recall also that dollar signs display to indicate that a cell reference is absolute.

Excel | Chapter 3

Figure 3.2

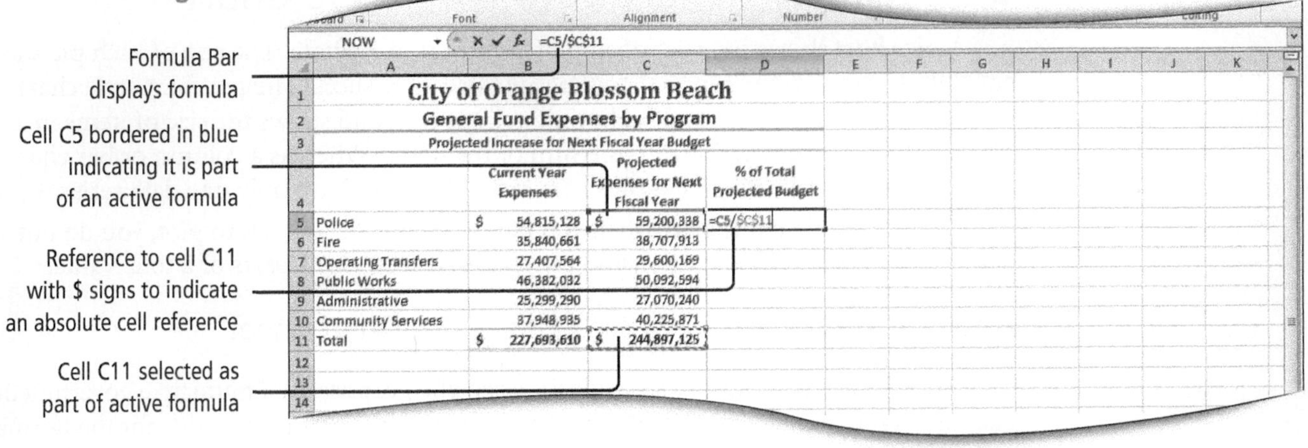

6 On the **Formula Bar**, click the **Enter** button to confirm the entry and to keep cell **D5** the active cell. Copy the formula down through cell **D10**, and then compare your screen with Figure 3.3.

Figure 3.3

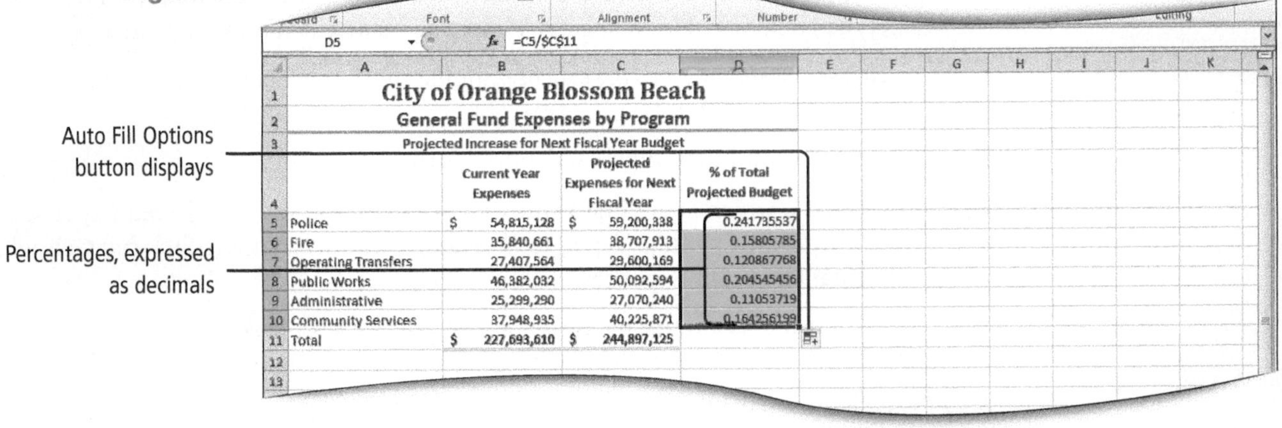

7 With the range **D5:D10** still selected, right-click over the selection, and then on the Mini toolbar, click the **Percent Style** button and the **Center** button. Click cell **A1** to cancel the selection, and then **Save** your workbook. Compare your screen with Figure 3.4.

Figure 3.4

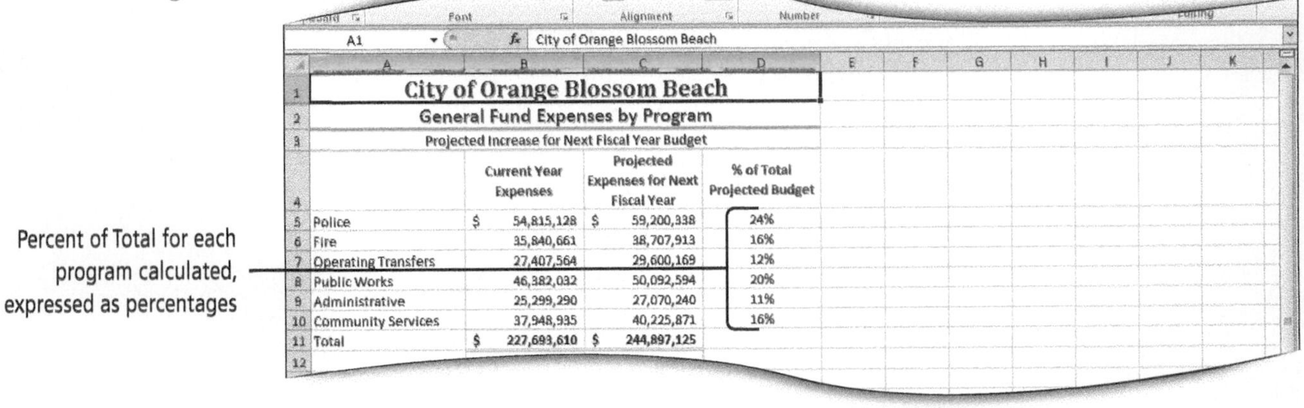

8 Select the range **A5:A10**, hold down Ctrl, and then select the range **C5:C10** to select the nonadjacent ranges with the program names and the projected expense for each program.

To create a pie chart, you must select two ranges. One range contains the labels for each slice of the pie chart, and the other range contains the values that add up to a total. The two ranges must have the same number of cells and the range with the values should *not* include the cell with the total.

The program names (Police, Fire, and so on) are the category names and will identify the slices of the pie chart. Each projected expense is a ***data point***—a value that originates in a worksheet cell and that is represented in a chart by a ***data marker***. In a pie chart, each pie slice is a data marker. Together, the data points form the ***data series***—related data points represented by data markers—and determine the size of each pie slice.

9 With the nonadjacent ranges selected, click the **Insert tab**, and then in the **Charts group**, click **Pie**. Under **3-D Pie**, click the first chart—**Pie in 3-D**—to create the chart on your worksheet.

10 On the **Design tab**, at the right end of the Ribbon in the **Location group**, click the **Move Chart** button. In the **Move Chart** dialog box, click the **New sheet** option button.

11 In the **New sheet** box, replace the highlighted text *Chart1* by typing **Projected Expenses Chart** and then click **OK** to display the chart on a separate worksheet in your workbook. Compare your screen with Figure 3.5.

The pie chart displays on a separate new sheet in your workbook, and a ***legend*** identifies the pie slices. Recall that a legend is a chart element that identifies the patterns or colors assigned to the categories in the chart.

A ***chart sheet*** is a workbook sheet that contains only a chart; it is useful when you want to view a chart separately from the worksheet data. The sheet tab indicates *Projected Expenses Chart.*

Figure 3.5

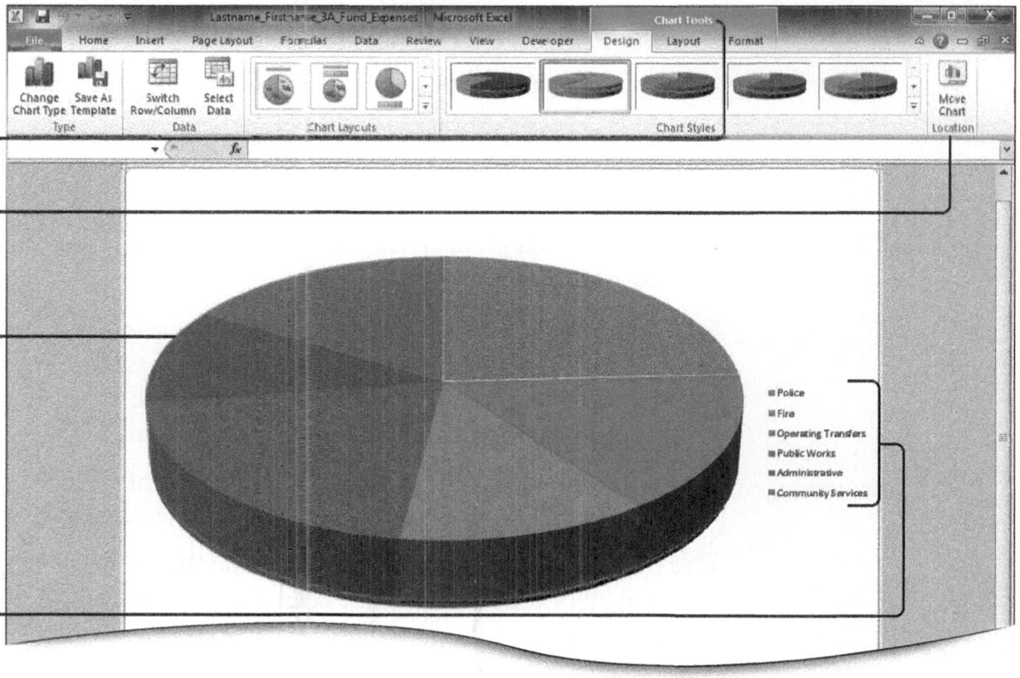

Chart Tools active

Move Chart button on Design tab

Chart displays on a separate new worksheet

Legend identifies pie slices

Objective 2 | Format a Pie Chart

Activity 3.02 | Applying Percentages to Labels in a Pie Chart

In your worksheet, for each expense, you calculated the percent of the total in column D. These percentages can also be calculated by the Chart feature and added to the pie slices as labels.

1 On the Ribbon under **Chart Tools**, click the **Layout tab**, and then in the **Labels group**, click the **Chart Title** button. On the displayed list, click **Above Chart**.

2 With the **Chart Title** box selected, watch the **Formula Bar** as you type **General Fund Projected Expenses** and then press Enter to create the new chart title in the box.

3 Point to the chart title text, right-click to display the Mini toolbar, and then change the **Font Size** to **36** and change the **Font Color** to **Olive Green, Accent 1, Darker 25%**—in the fifth column, the fifth color. Compare your screen with Figure 3.6.

Figure 3.6

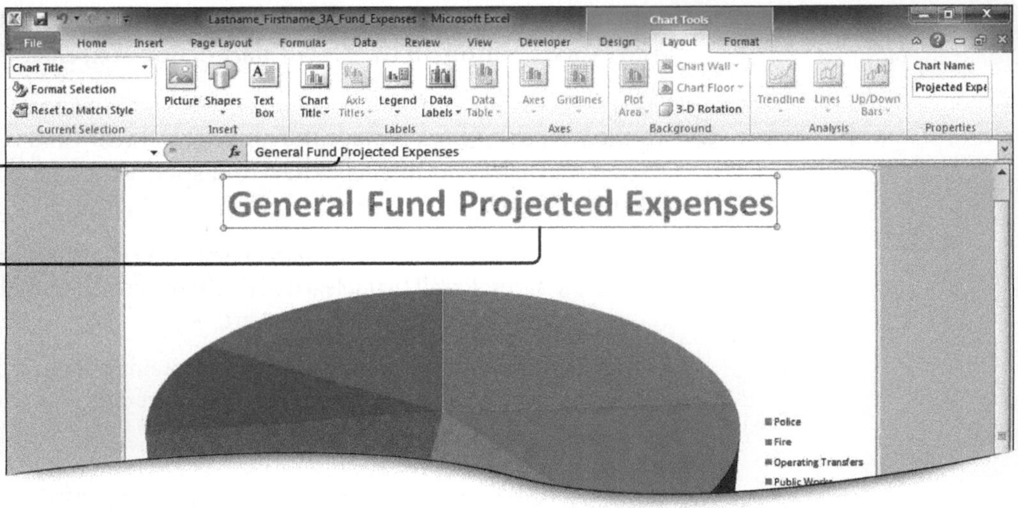

4 In the **Labels group**, click the **Legend** button, and then click **None**.

The chart expands to fill the new space. In a pie chart, it is usually more effective to place the labels within, or close to, each pie slice. Because you will place the program names (the categories) on the pie slices, a legend is unnecessary.

5 In the **Labels group**, click the **Data Labels** button, and then at the bottom, click **More Data Label Options**.

6 In the **Format Data Labels** dialog box, on the left, be sure **Label Options** is selected. On the right, under **Label Contains**, click as necessary to select the **Category Name** and **Percentage** check boxes. *Clear* any other check boxes in this group. Under **Label Position**, click the **Center** option button.

In the worksheet, you calculated the percent of the total in column D. Here, the percentage will be calculated by the Chart feature and added to the chart as a label.

7 In the lower right corner of the **Format Data Labels** dialog box, click **Close**, and notice that all of the data labels are selected and display both the category name and the percentage.

8. Point to any of the selected labels, right-click to display the Mini toolbar, and then change the **Font Size** to **11**, apply **Bold** [B], and apply **Italic** [I].

9. **Save** your workbook. Press Esc to deselect the labels, and then compare your screen with Figure 3.7.

Figure 3.7

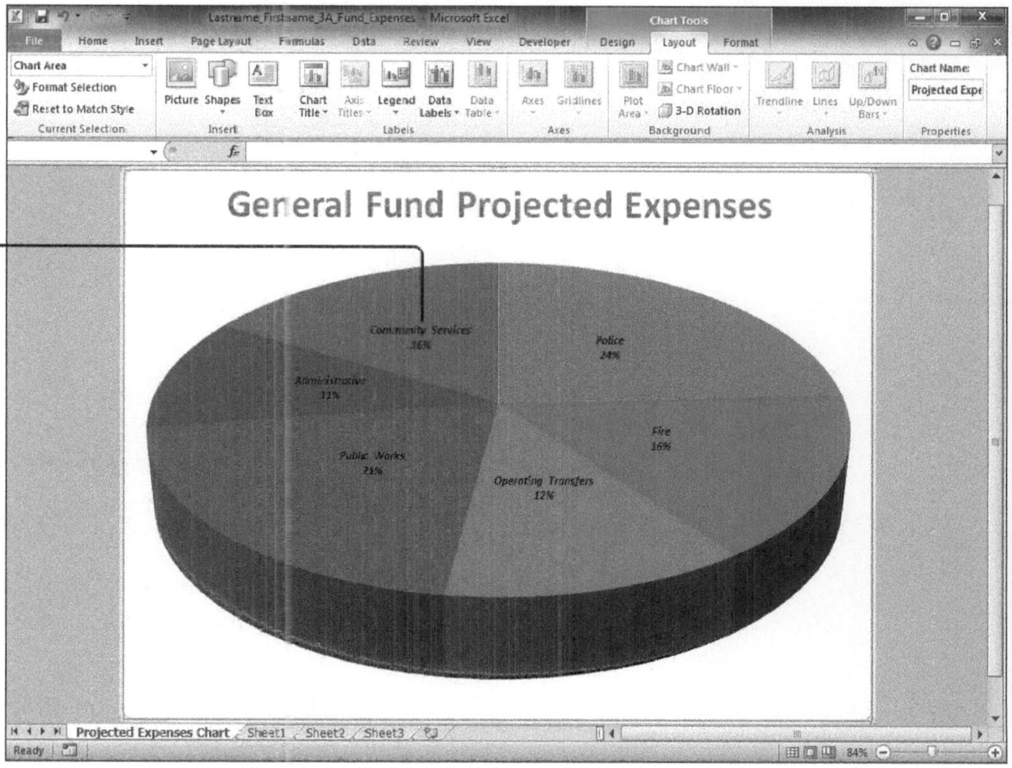

Data labels on pie slices replace legend; labels include category name and percentage; data labels centered in slice, 11 pt font, bold and italic

Activity 3.03 | Formatting a Pie Chart with 3-D

3-D, which is short for *three-dimensional*, refers to an image that appears to have all three spatial dimensions—length, width, and depth.

1. Click in any pie slice outside of the label to select the entire pie; notice that selection handles display on the outside corners of each slice.

2. Click the **Format tab**. In the **Shape Styles group**, click the **Shape Effects** button, point to **Bevel**, and then at the bottom of the gallery, click **3-D Options**.

3. In the **Format Data Series** dialog box, on the right, under **Bevel**, click the **Top** button. In the displayed gallery, under **Bevel**, point to the first button to display the ScreenTip *Circle*. Click the **Circle** button. Then click the **Bottom** button, and apply the **Circle** bevel.

   Bevel is a shape effect that uses shading and shadows to make the edges of a shape appear to be curved or angled.

4. In the four **Width** and **Height** spin boxes, type **512 pt** and then compare your screen with Figure 3.8.

Figure 3.8

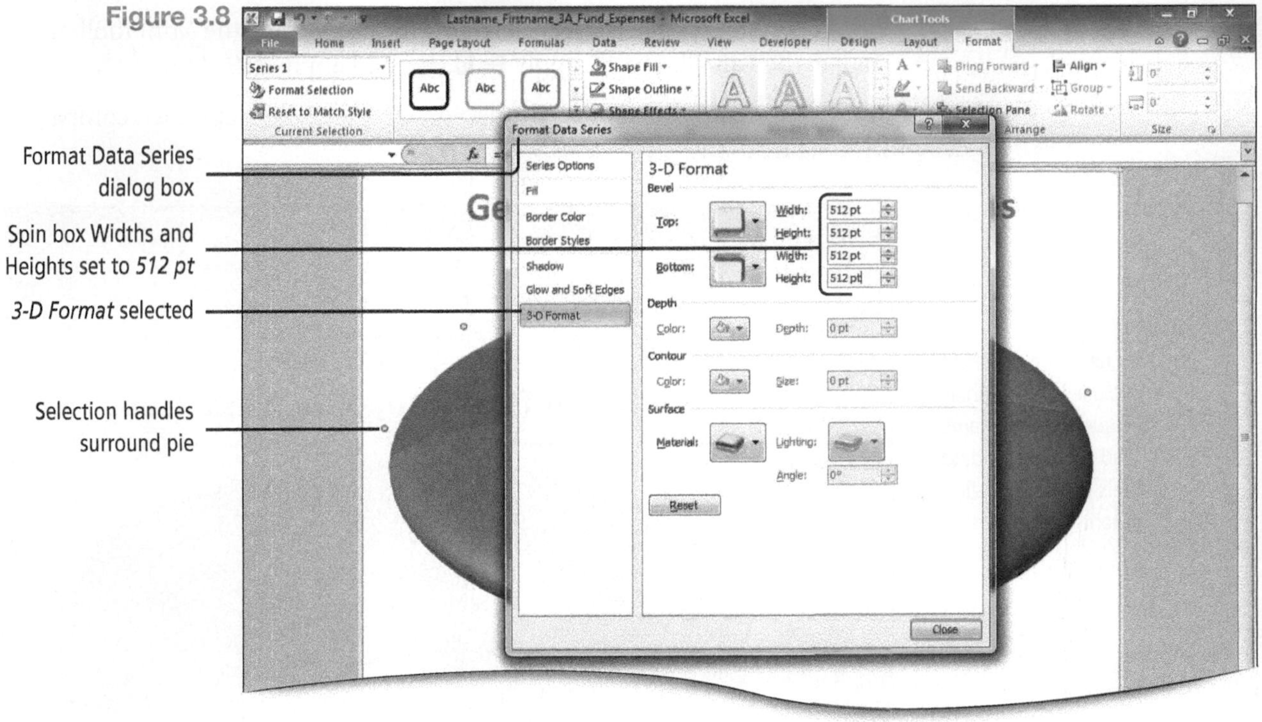

5 In the lower portion of the dialog box, under **Surface**, click the **Material** button. Under **Standard**, click the third button—**Plastic**. In the lower right corner, click **Close**.

6 With the pie still selected, on the **Format tab**, in the **Shape Styles group**, click **Shape Effects**, and then point to **Shadow**. At the bottom of the displayed gallery, scroll if necessary, and then under **Perspective**, click the third button, which displays the ScreenTip *Below* to display a shadow below the pie chart. Click **Save**.

Activity 3.04 | Rotating a Pie Chart

The order in which the data series in pie charts are plotted in Excel is determined by the order of the data on the worksheet. To gain a different view of the chart, you can rotate the chart within the 360 degrees of the circle of the pie shape to present a different visual perspective of the chart.

1 Notice the position of the **Fire** and **Police** slices in the chart. Then, with the pie chart still selected—sizing handles surround the pie—point anywhere in the pie and right-click. On the displayed shortcut menu, click **Format Data Series**.

> **Another Way**
> Drag the slider to 100.

2 In the **Format Data Series** dialog box, on the left, be sure **Series Options** is selected. On the right, under **Angle of first slice**, click in the box and type **100** to rotate the chart 100 degrees to the right.

3 Close the **Format Data Series** dialog box. Click **Save**, and then compare your screen with Figure 3.9.

Rotating the chart can provide a better perspective to the chart. Here, rotating the chart in this manner emphasizes that the Fire and Police programs represent a significant portion of the total expenses.

Figure 3.9

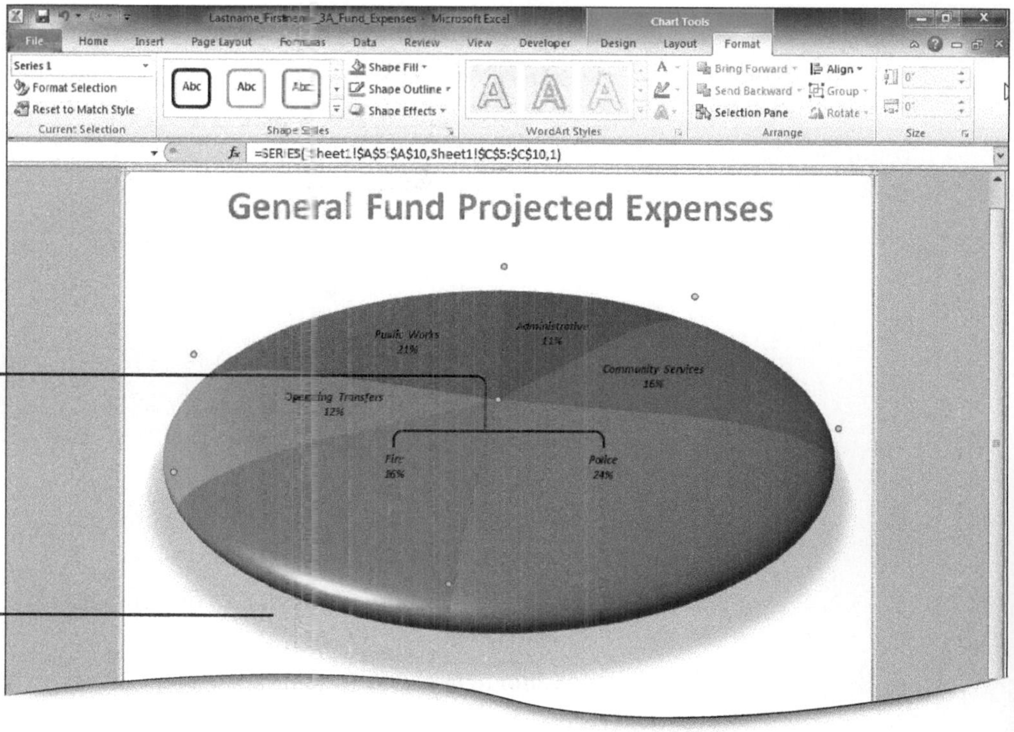

Fire and Police slices prominent

Shadow below chart

Activity 3.05 | Exploding and Coloring a Pie Slice

You can pull out—***explode***—one or more slices of a pie chart to emphasize a specific slice or slices. Additionally, there is a different chart type you can select if you want *all* the slices to explode and emphasize all the individual slices of a pie chart—the exploded pie or exploded pie in 3-D chart type. The exploded pie chart type displays the contribution of *each* value to the total, while at the same time emphasizing individual values.

1 Press Esc to deselect all chart elements. Click any slice to select the entire pie, and then click the **Administrative** slice to select only that slice. Compare your screen with Figure 3.10.

Figure 3.10

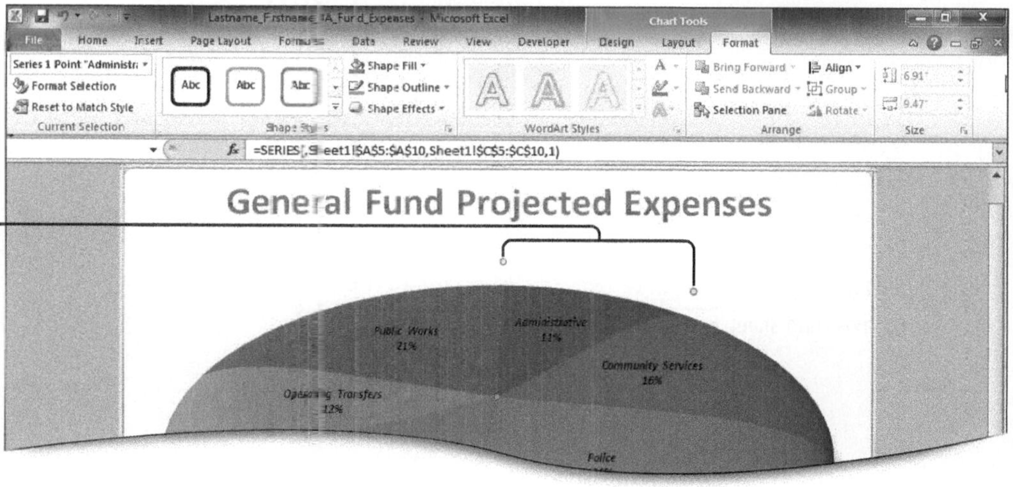

Only *Administrative* slice selected

2 Point to the **Administrative** slice to display the pointer, and then drag the slice slightly upward and away from the center of the pie, as shown in Figure 3.11, and then release the mouse button.

Figure 3.11

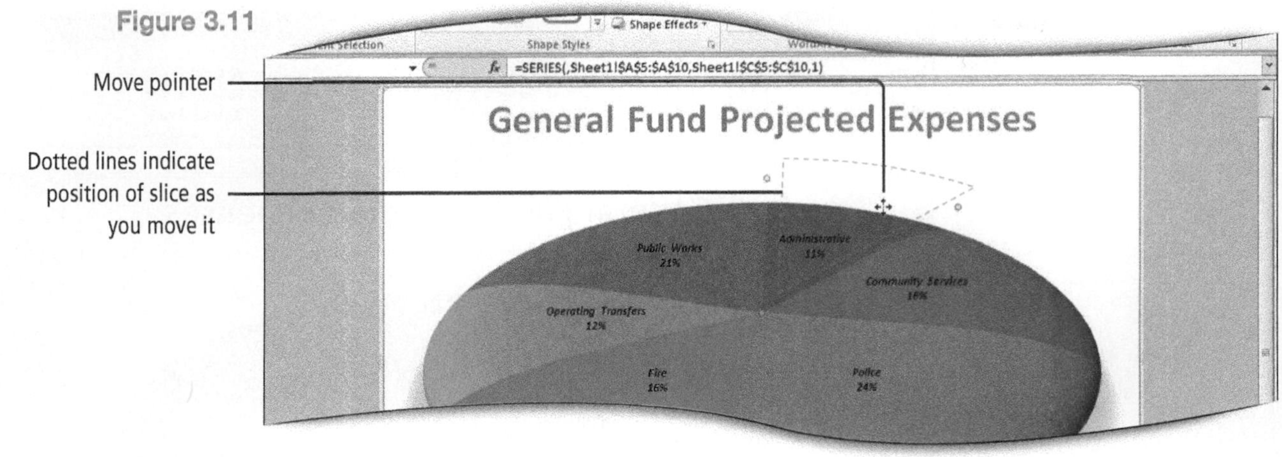

3. With the **Administrative** slice still selected, point to the slice and right-click, and then on the shortcut menu, click **Format Data Point**.
4. In the **Format Data Point** dialog box, on the left, click **Fill**. On the right, under **Fill**, click the **Solid fill** option button.
5. Click the **Color arrow**, and then under **Theme Colors**, in the seventh column, click the fourth color—**Gold, Accent 3, Lighter 40%**.
6. In the lower right corner of the **Format Data Point** dialog box, click the **Close** button.

Activity 3.06 | Formatting the Chart Area

The entire chart and all of its elements comprise the ***chart area***.

1. Point to the white area just inside the border of the chart to display the ScreenTip *Chart Area*. Click one time.
2. On the **Format tab**, in the **Shape Styles group**, click the **Shape Effects** button, point to **Bevel**, and then under **Bevel**, in the second row, click the third bevel—**Convex**.
3. Press Esc to deselect the chart element and view this effect—a convex beveled frame around your entire chart—and then compare your screen with Figure 3.12.

Figure 3.12

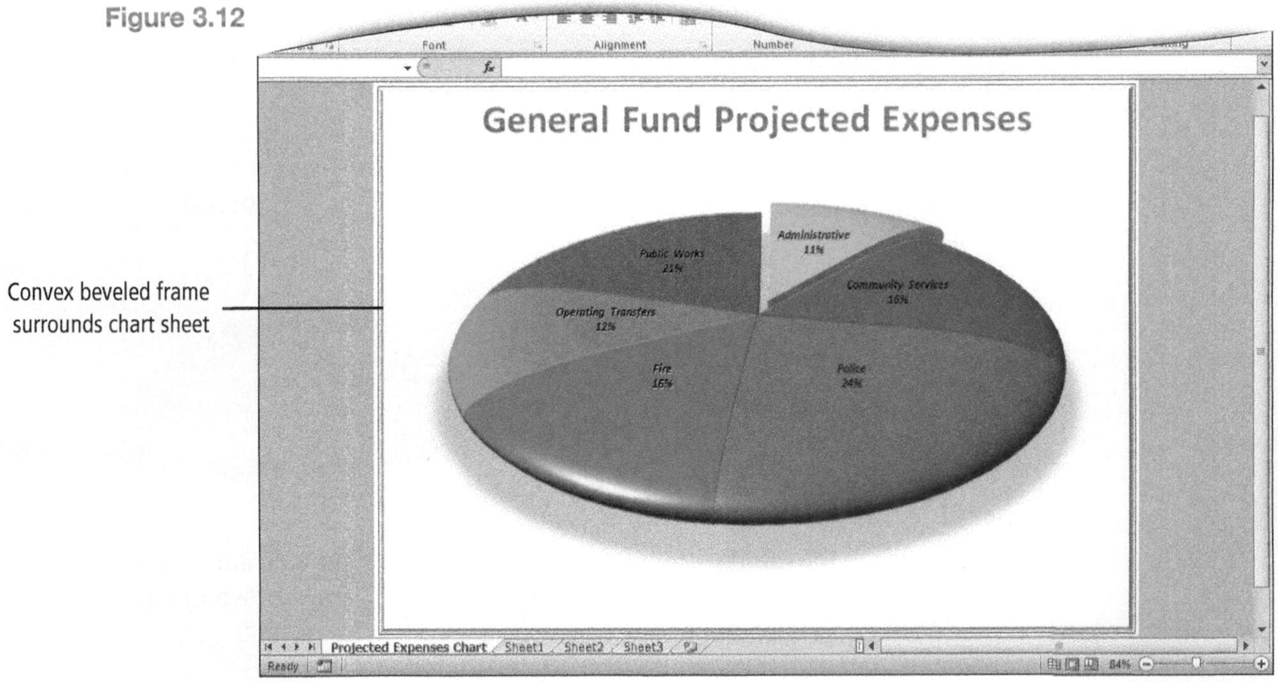

4. Point slightly inside the border of the chart to display the ScreenTip *Chart Area*, right-click, and then on the shortcut menu, click **Format Chart Area.**

5. In the **Format Chart Area** dialog box, on the left, be sure that **Fill** is selected. On the right, under **Fill**, click the **Gradient fill** option button.

6. Click the **Preset colors** arrow, and then in the second row, click the last preset, **Fog**. Click the **Type arrow**, and then click **Path**. Click the **Close** button.

7. Compare your screen with Figure 3.13, and then **Save** your workbook.

Figure 3.13

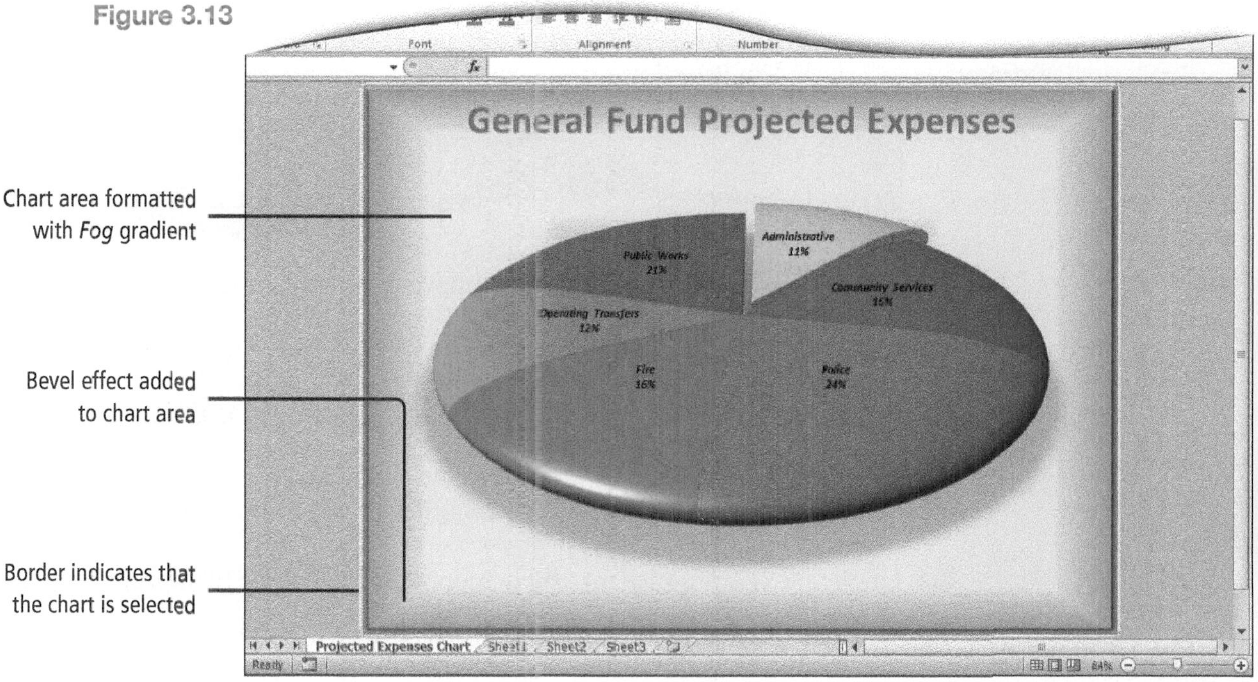

Activity 3.07 | Inserting a Text Box in a Chart

A ***text box*** is a movable, resizable container for text or graphics.

1. With the Chart Area still selected, click the **Layout tab**, and then in the **Insert group**, click the **Text Box** button, and then move the pointer into the chart area.

2. Position the displayed pointer under the *c* in *Projected* and about midway between the title and the pie—above the *Administrative* slice. Hold down the left mouse button, and then drag down and to the right approximately as shown in Figure 3.14; your text box need not be precise.

Figure 3.14

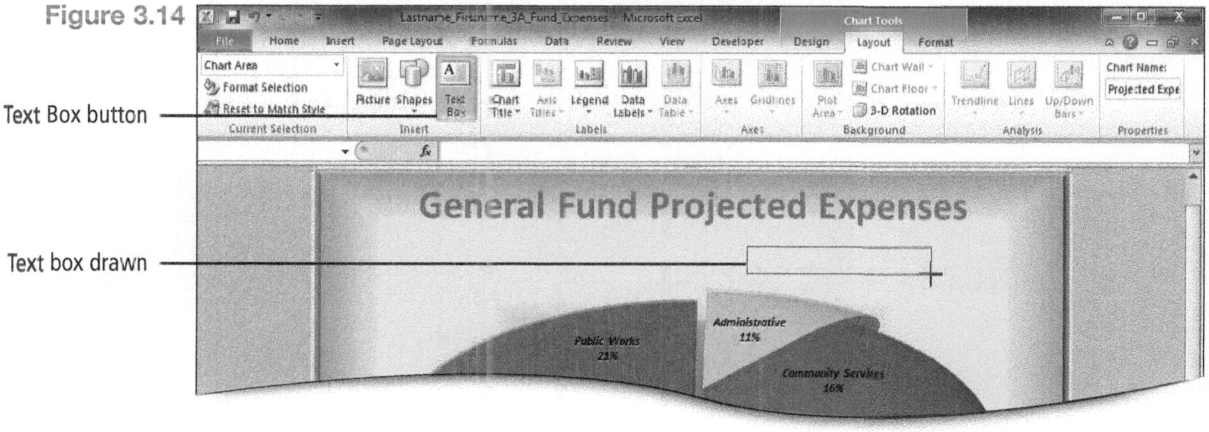

3 With the insertion point blinking inside the text box, type **Goal: Reduce Administrative to 8%** Press Esc or click outside the chart area to deselect the chart element, and then compare your screen with Figure 3.15.

Figure 3.15

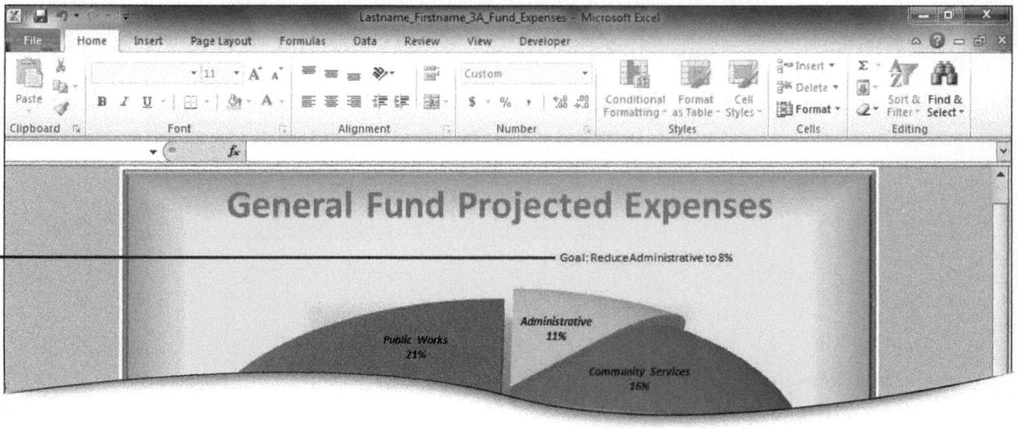

Text Box with inserted text

4 If necessary, select and then adjust or move your text box. **Save** your workbook.

Objective 3 | Edit a Workbook and Update a Chart

Activity 3.08 | Editing a Workbook and Updating a Chart

If you edit the data in your worksheet, the chart data markers—in this instance the pie slices—will adjust automatically to accurately represent the new values.

1 On the pie chart, notice that *Police* represents 24% of the total projected expenses.

2 In the sheet tab area at the bottom of the workbook, click the **Sheet1 tab** to redisplay the worksheet.

Another Way

Double-click the cell to position the insertion point in the cell and edit.

3 Click cell **C5**, and then in **Formula Bar**, change *59,200,338* to **62,200,388**

4 Press Enter, and notice that the total in cell **C11** recalculates to *$247,897,175* and the percentages in **column D** also recalculate.

5 Display the **Projected Expenses Chart** sheet. Notice that the pie slices adjust to show the recalculation—*Police* is now *25%* of the projected expenses. Click **Save**, and then compare your screen with Figure 3.16.

Figure 3.16

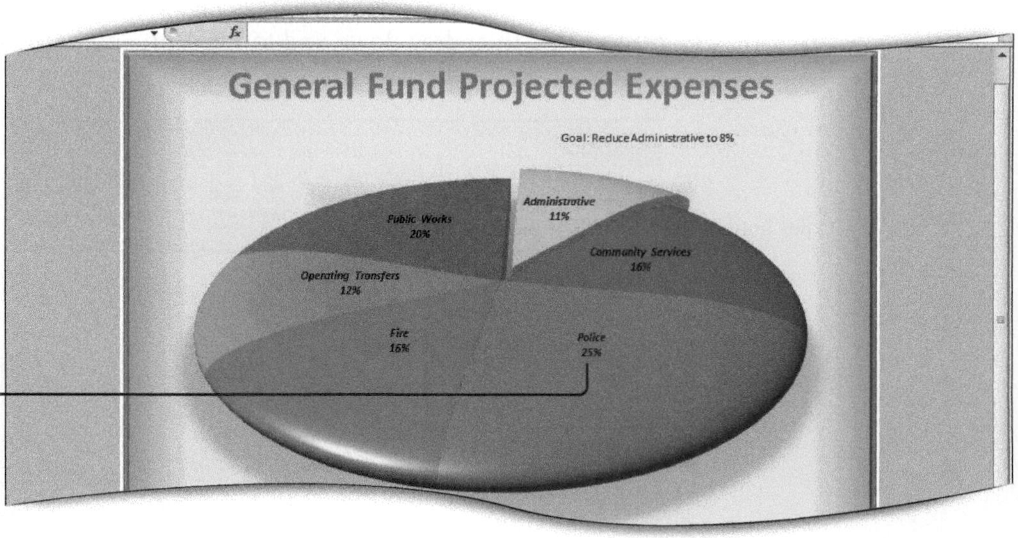

Police slice displays 25%

Activity 3.09 | Inserting WordArt in a Worksheet

WordArt is a gallery of text styles with which you can create decorative effects, such as shadowed or mirrored text. In an Excel worksheet, WordArt can be effective if you plan to display your worksheet in a PowerPoint presentation, or if readers will be viewing the worksheet data online.

1. In the sheet tab area at the bottom of the workbook, click the **Sheet1 tab** to redisplay the worksheet. Click the **Insert tab**, and then in the **Text group**, click the **WordArt** button.

2. In the WordArt gallery, in the last row, click the last style—**Fill – Olive Green, Accent 1, Metal Bevel, Reflection**.

   The WordArt indicating *YOUR TEXT HERE* displays in the worksheet.

3. With the WordArt selected, type **general fund expenses** and then point anywhere on the dashed border surrounding the WordArt object. Click the dashed border one time to change it to a solid border, indicating that all of the text is selected.

4. On the **Home tab**, in the **Font group**, change the **Font Size** to **28**.

5. Point to the WordArt border to display the pointer, and then drag to position the upper left corner of the WordArt approximately as shown in Figure 3.17. If necessary, hold down Ctrl and press any of the arrow keys on your keyboard to move the WordArt object into position in small increments. Click any cell to deselect the WordArt, and then click **Save**.

Figure 3.17

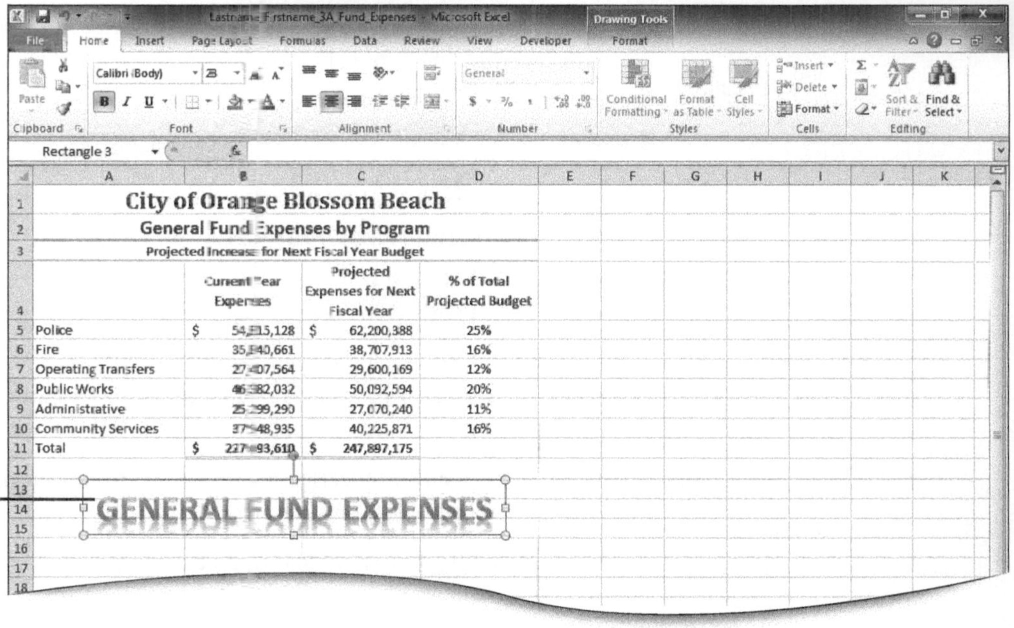

WordArt

Objective 4 | Use Goal Seek to Perform What-If Analysis

Activity 3.10 | Using Goal Seek to Perform What-If Analysis

The process of changing the values in cells to see how those changes affect the outcome of formulas in your worksheet is referred to as ***what-if analysis***. A what-if analysis tool that is included with Excel is ***Goal Seek***, which finds the input needed in one cell to arrive at the desired result in another cell.

1 In cell **A17**, type **Goal: To Reduce Administrative Expenses from 11% to 8% of Total Expenses** Merge and center the text across the range **A17:D17**, and then apply the **Heading 3** Cell Style.

2 In cell **A18**, type **Goal Amount:** and press Enter.

3 Select the range **C9:D9**, right-click over the selection, and then click **Copy**. Point to cell **B18**, right-click, and then under **Paste Options**, click the **Paste** button.

4 Press Esc to cancel the moving border, click cell **C18**, and then compare your screen with Figure 3.18.

Figure 3.18

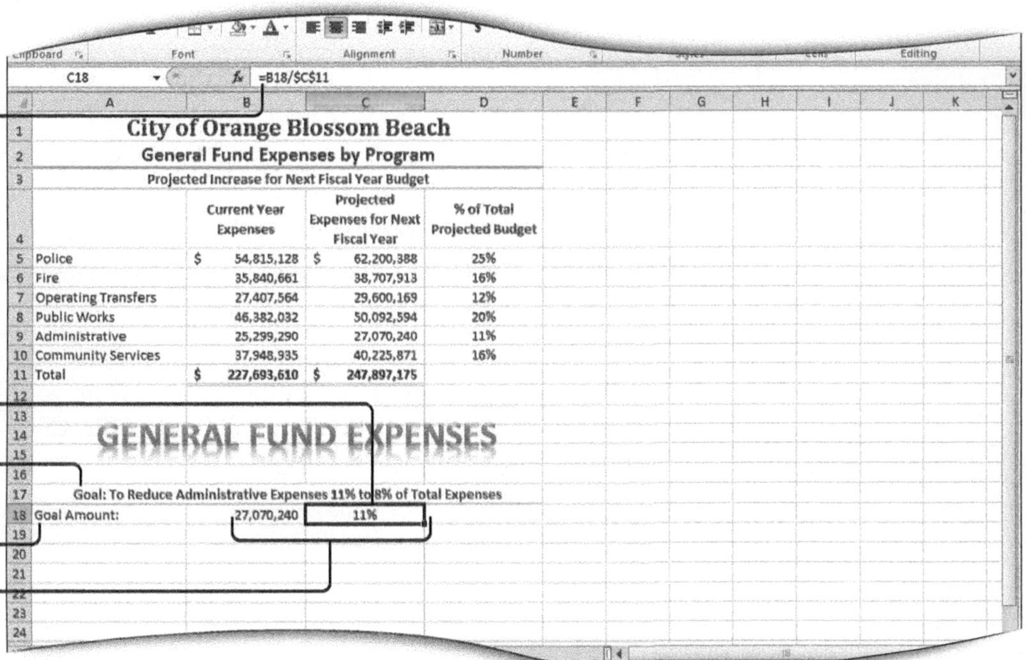

5 Be sure cell **C18** is the active cell. On the **Data tab**, in the **Data Tools group**, click the **What-If Analysis** button, and then click **Goal Seek**.

6 In the **Goal Seek** dialog box, notice that the active cell, **C18**, is indicated in the **Set cell** box. Press Tab to move to the **To value** box, and then type **8%**

C18 is the cell in which you want to set a specific value; 8% is the percentage of the total expenses that you want to budget for Administrative expenses. The Set cell box contains the formula that calculates the information you seek.

7 Press Tab to move the insertion point to the **By changing cell** box, and then click cell **B18**. Compare your screen with Figure 3.19.

Cell B18 contains the value that Excel changes to reach the goal. Excel formats this cell as an absolute cell reference.

Figure 3.19

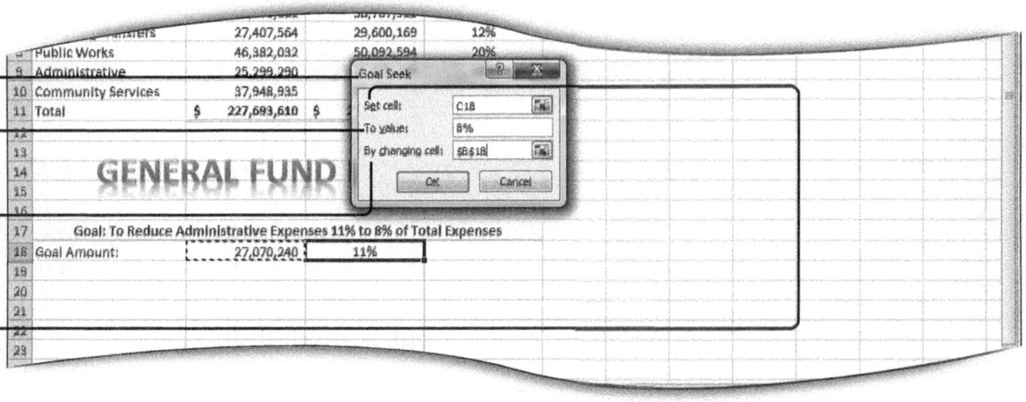

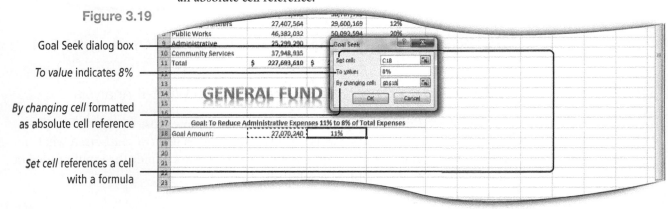

8 Click **OK**. In the displayed **Goal Seek Status** dialog box, click **OK**.

9 Select the range **A18:C18**. From the **Home tab**, display the **Cell Styles** gallery. Under **Themed Cell Styles**, apply **20% - Accent3**. Click cell **B18**, and then from the **Cell Styles** gallery, at the bottom of the gallery under **Number Format**, apply the **Currency [0]** cell style.

10 Press Ctrl + Home, click **Save**, and then compare your screen with Figure 3.20.

Excel calculates that the City must budget for *$19,831,774* in Administrative expenses in order for this item to become 8% of the total projected budget.

Figure 3.20

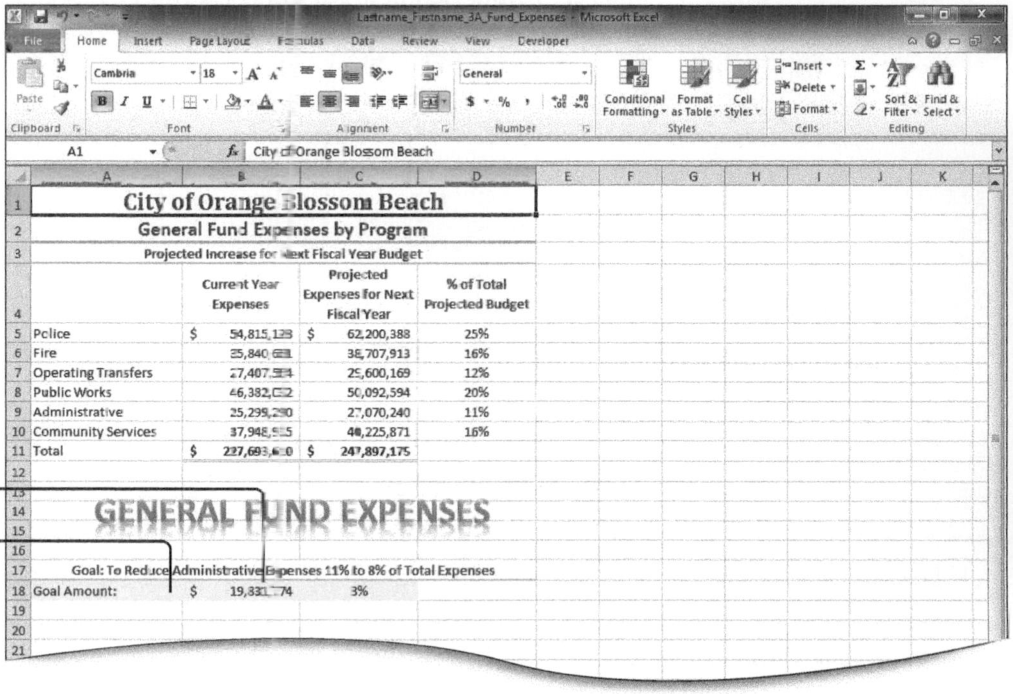

Activity 3.11 | Preparing and Printing a Workbook with a Chart Sheet

> **Another Way**
>
> Right-click the sheet tab, click Rename, type, and press Enter.

1 With your worksheet displayed, in the sheet tab area, double-click *Sheet1* to select the text, and then type **Projected Expenses Data** and press Enter.

2 Select **Sheet2** and **Sheet3**, right-click over the selected tabs, and then click **Delete** to delete the unused sheets.

3 On the **Insert tab**, click **Header & Footer**. In the **Navigation group**, click the **Go to Footer** button, click in the **left section** above the word *Footer*, and then in the **Header & Footer Elements group**, click the **File Name** button.

4 Click in a cell above the footer to deselect the **Footer area** and view your file name. On the **Page Layout tab**, in the **Page Setup group**, click the **Margins** button, and then at the bottom click **Custom Margins**.

5 In the displayed **Page Setup** dialog box, under **Center on page**, select the **Horizontally** check box. Click **OK**, and then on the status bar, click the **Normal** button to return to Normal view.

Recall that after displaying worksheets in Page Layout View, dotted lines display to indicate the page breaks when you return to Normal view.

6 Press Ctrl + Home to move to the top of the worksheet.

7 Click the **Projected Expenses Chart** sheet tab to display the chart sheet. On the **Insert tab**, in the **Text group**, click **Header & Footer** to display the **Header/Footer tab** of the **Page Setup** dialog box.

8 In the center of the **Page Setup** dialog box, click **Custom Footer**. With the insertion point blinking in the **Left section**, in the row of buttons in the middle of the dialog box, locate and click the **Insert File Name** button. Compare your screen with Figure 3.21.

Use the Page Setup dialog box in this manner to insert a footer on a chart sheet, which has no Page Layout view in which you can see the Header and Footer areas.

Figure 3.21

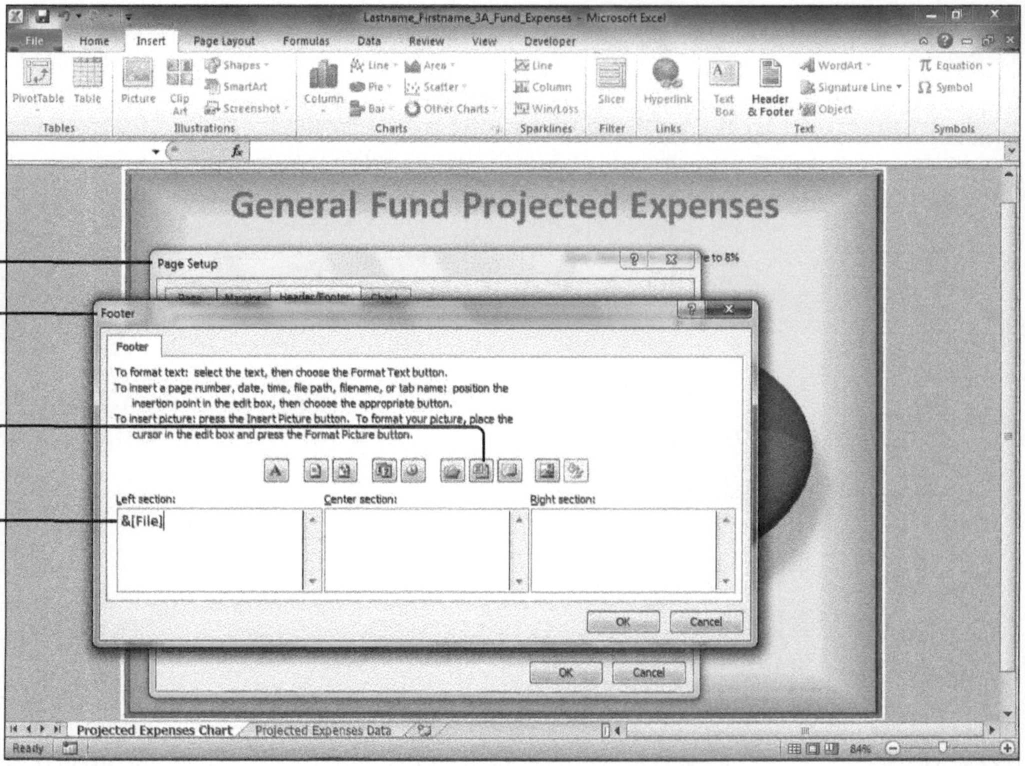

9 Click **OK** two times. Display **Backstage** view, on the right under the thumbnail, click **Properties**, and then click **Show Document Panel**. In the **Author** box, replace the existing text with your firstname and lastname. In the **Subject** box, type your course name and section number. In the **Keywords** box type **general fund, expenses, pie chart** and then **Close** the **Document Information Panel**.

10 Right-click either of the sheet tabs, and then click **Select All Sheets**. Verify that *[Group]* displays in the title bar.

Recall that by selecting all sheets, you can view all of the workbook pages in Print Preview.

11 Press Ctrl + F2 to display the **Print Preview**. Examine the first page, and then at the bottom of the **Print Preview**, click the **Next Page** button to view the second page of your workbook.

Note | Printing a Chart Sheet Uses More Toner

Printing a chart that displays on a chart sheet will use more toner or ink than a small chart that is part of a worksheet. If you are printing your work, check with your instructor to verify whether or not you should print the chart sheet.

12 Click **Save** to redisplay the workbook. Print or submit electronically as directed by your instructor.

13 If you are directed to submit printed formulas, refer to Activity 1.16 in Project 1A to do so.

14 If you printed your formulas, be sure to redisplay the worksheet by clicking the Show Formulas button to turn it off. **Close** the workbook. If you are prompted to save changes, click **No** so that you do not save the changes to the worksheet that you used for printing formulas. **Close** Excel.

More Knowledge | Setting the Default Number of Sheets in a New Workbook

By default, the number of new worksheets in a new workbook is three, but you can change this default number. From Backstage view, display the Excel Options dialog box, click the General tab, and then under When creating new workbooks, change the number in the Include this many sheets box.

End You have completed Project 3A

Project 3B Growth Projection with Line Chart

Project Activities

In Activities 3.12 through 3.19, you will assist Lila Darius, City Manager, in creating a worksheet to estimate future population growth based on three possible growth rates. You will also create a line chart to display past population growth. Your resulting worksheet and chart will look similar to Figure 3.22.

Project Files

For Project 3B, you will need the following files:

e03B_Population_Growth
e03B_Beach

You will save your workbook as:

Lastname_Firstname_3B_Population_Growth

Project Results

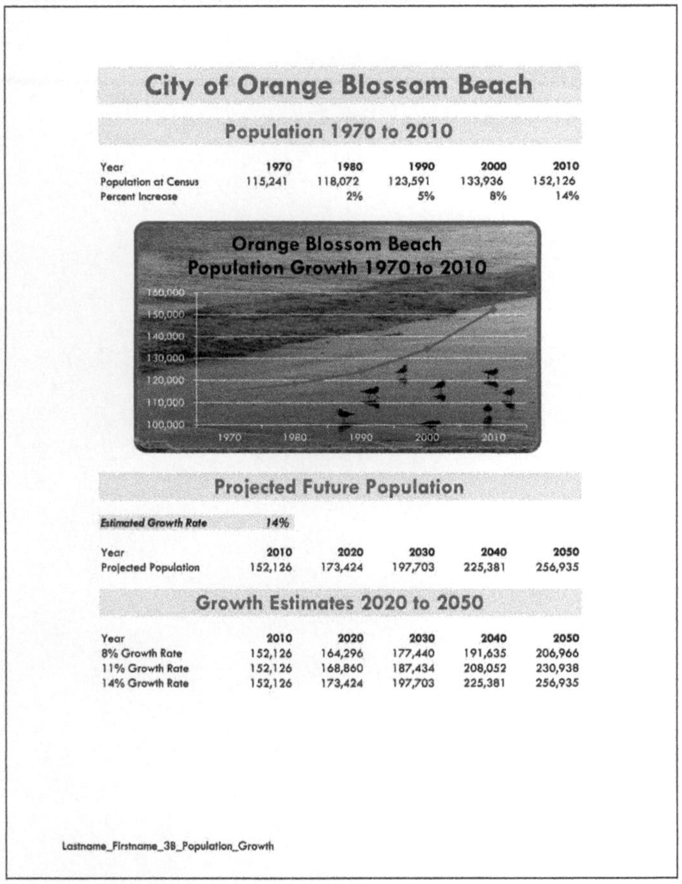

City of Orange Blossom Beach

Population 1970 to 2010

Year	1970	1980	1990	2000	2010
Population at Census	115,241	118,072	123,591	133,936	152,126
Percent Increase		2%	5%	8%	14%

Projected Future Population

Estimated Growth Rate	14%

Year	2010	2020	2030	2040	2050
Projected Population	152,126	173,424	197,703	225,381	256,935

Growth Estimates 2020 to 2050

Year	2010	2020	2030	2040	2050
8% Growth Rate	152,126	164,296	177,440	191,635	206,966
11% Growth Rate	152,126	168,860	187,434	208,052	230,938
14% Growth Rate	152,126	173,424	197,703	225,381	256,935

Lastname_Firstname_3B_Population_Growth

Figure 3.22
Project 3B Population Growth

Objective 5 | Design a Worksheet for What-If Analysis

Excel recalculates; if you change the value in a cell referenced in a formula, Excel automatically recalculates the result of the formula. Thus, you can change cell values to see *what* would happen *if* you tried different values. Recall that this process of changing the values in cells to see how those changes affect the outcome of formulas in your worksheet is referred to as what-if analysis.

Activity 3.12 | Using Parentheses in a Formula to Calculate a Percentage Rate of Increase

Ms. Darius has the city's population figures for the past five 10-year census periods. In each 10-year census period, the population has increased. In this activity, you will construct a formula to calculate the ***percentage rate of increase***—the percent by which one number increases over another number—for each 10-year census period since 1970. From this information future population growth can be estimated.

1 **Start** Excel. From your student files, open the file **e03B_Population_Growth**. From **Backstage** view, display the **Save As** dialog box. Navigate to your **Excel Chapter 3** folder, in the **File name** box, name the file **Lastname_Firstname_3B_Population_Growth** and then click **Save** or press Enter.

2 Leave **row 4** blank, and then click cell **A5**. Type **Year** and then press Tab. In cell **B5**, type **1970** and then press Tab.

3 In cell **C5**, type **1980** and then press Tab. Select the range **B5:C5**, and then drag the fill handle to the right through cell **F5** to extend the series to 2010.

By establishing a pattern of 10-year intervals with the first two cells, you can use the fill handle to continue the series. The AutoFill feature will do this for any pattern that you establish with two or more cells.

4 With the range **B5:F5** still selected, right-click over the selection, and then on the Mini toolbar, click **Bold** B. Compare your screen with Figure 3.23.

Figure 3.23

AutoFill used to fill 10-year periods to create column titles

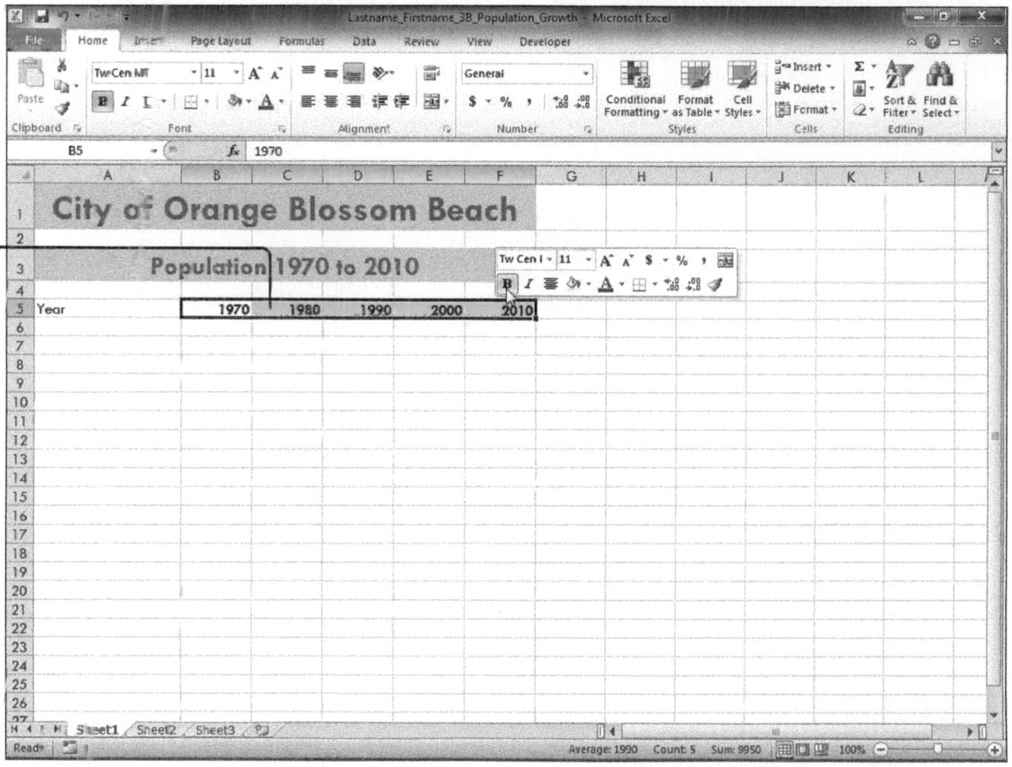

5 In cell **A6**, type **Population at Census** and press Enter. In cell **A7**, type **Percent Increase** and press Enter.

6 Click cell **B6**, and then beginning in cell **B6**, and pressing Tab to move across the row, enter the following values for the population in the years listed:

1970	1980	1990	2000	2010
115241	**118072**	**123591**	**133936**	**152126**

7 Select the range **B6:F6**, right-click, on the Mini toolbar, click **Comma Style**, and then click **Decrease Decimal** two times.

8 Click cell **C7**. Being sure to include the parentheses, type **=(c6-b6)/b6** and then on the **Formula Bar**, click the **Enter** button to keep cell **C7** active; your result is *0.02456591* (or *0.02*). Compare your screen with Figure 3.24.

Recall that as you type, a list of Excel functions that begin with the letter *C* and *B* may briefly display. This is ***Formula AutoComplete***, an Excel feature which, after typing an = (equal sign) and the beginning letter or letters of a function name, displays a list of function names that match the typed letter(s). In this instance, the letters represent cell references, *not* the beginning of a function name.

Figure 3.24

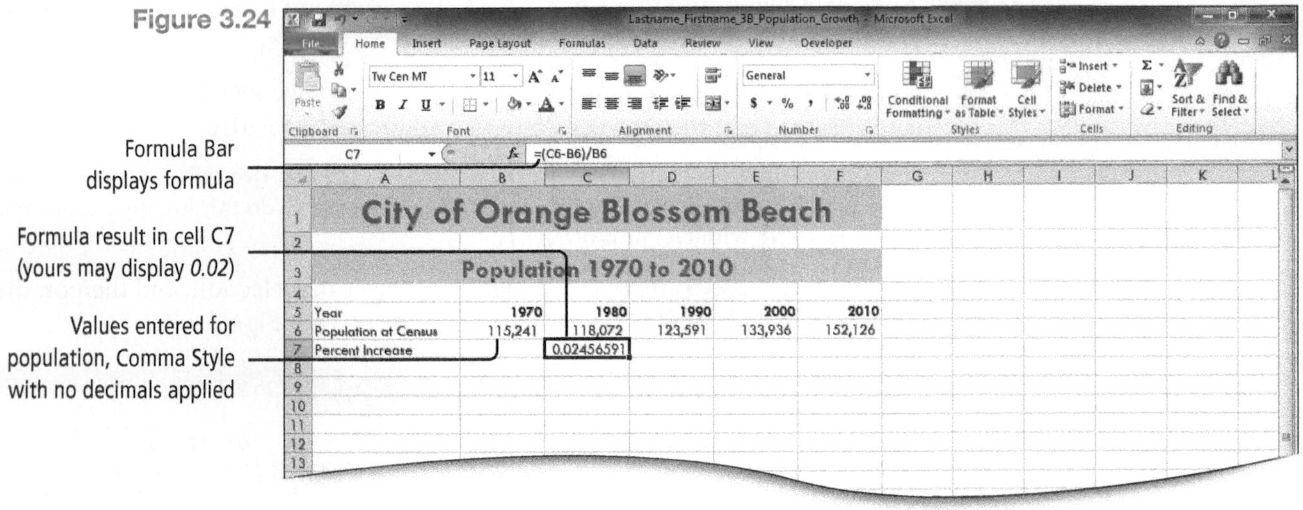

9 With cell **C7** active, on the **Home tab**, in the **Number group**, click the **Percent Style** button, and then examine the formula in the **Formula Bar**.

The mathematical formula ***rate*** = ***amount of increase/base*** is used to calculated the percentage rate of population increase from 1970 to 1980. The formula is applied as follows:

First, determine the *amount of increase* by subtracting the ***base***—the starting point represented by the 1970 population—from the 1980 population. Thus, the *amount of increase* = 118,072 – 115,241 or 2,831. Between 1970 and 1980, the population increased by 2,831 people. In the formula, this calculation is represented by *C6-B6*.

Second, calculate the *rate*—what the amount of increase (2,831) represents as a percentage of the base (1970's population of 115,241). Determine this by dividing the amount of increase (2,831) by the base (115,241). Thus, 2,831 divided by 115,241 is equal to 0.02456591 or, when formatted as a percent, 2%.

10 In the **Formula Bar**, locate the parentheses enclosing *C6-B6*.

Excel follows a set of mathematical rules called the ***order of operations***, which has four basic parts:

- Expressions within parentheses are processed first.
- Exponentiation, if present, is performed before multiplication and division.
- Multiplication and division are performed before addition and subtraction.
- Consecutive operators with the same level of precedence are calculated from left to right.

11 Click cell **D7**, type = and then by typing, or using a combination of typing and clicking cells to reference them, construct a formula similar to the one in cell **C7** to calculate the rate of increase in population from 1980 to 1990. Compare your screen with Figure 3.25.

Recall that the first step is to determine the *amount of increase*—1990 population minus 1980 population—and then to write the calculation so that Excel performs this operation first; that is, place it in parentheses.

The second step is to divide the result of the calculation in parentheses by the *base*—the population for 1980.

Figure 3.25

Formula to calculate percent increase from 1980 to 1990

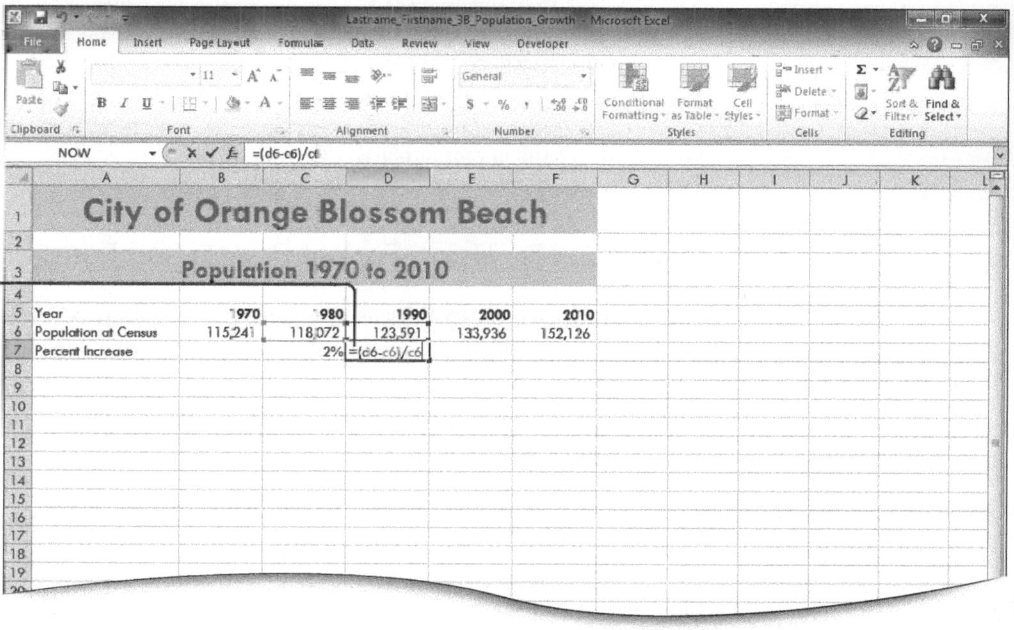

12 Press Enter; your result is *0.04674267* (or *0.05*). Format cell **D7** with the **Percent Style** %.

Your result is *5%*; Excel rounds up or down to format percentages.

13 With cell **D7** selected, drag the fill handle to the right through cell **F7**. Click any empty cell to cancel the selection, **Save** your workbook, and then compare your screen with Figure 3.26.

Because this formula uses relative cell references—that is, for each year, the formula is the same but the values used are relative to the formula's location—you can copy the formula in this manner. For example, the result for 1990 uses the 1980 population as the base, the result for 2000 uses the 1990 population as the base, and the result for 2010 uses the 2000 population as the base.

The formula results show the percent of increase for each 10-year period between 1970 and 2010. You can see that in each 10-year period, the population has grown as much as 14%—from 2000 to 2010—and as little as 2%—from 1970 to 1980.

Figure 3.26

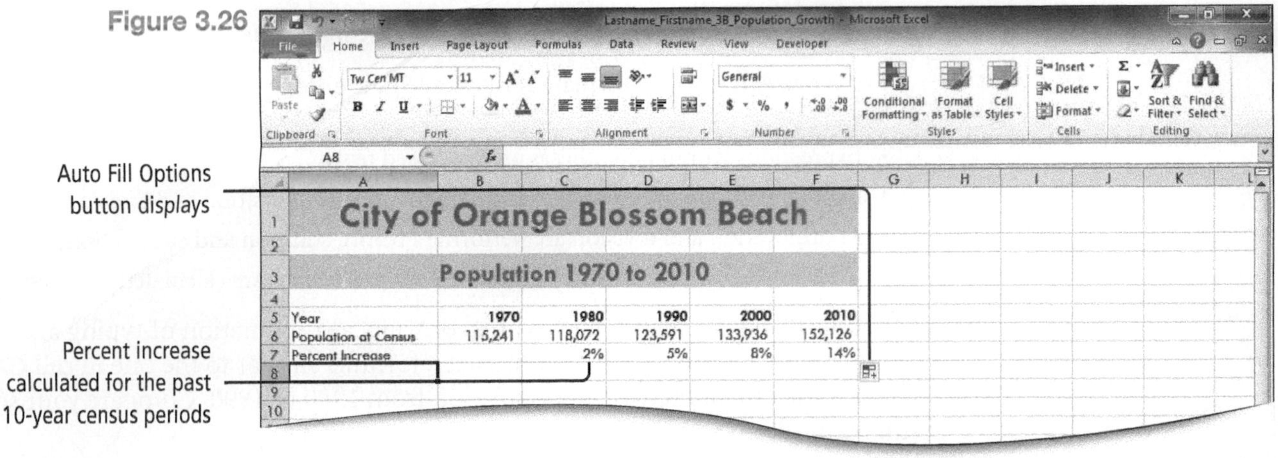

More Knowledge | **Use of Parentheses in a Formula**

When writing a formula in Excel, use parentheses to communicate the order in which the operations should occur. For example, to average three test scores of 100, 50, and 90 that you scored on three different tests, you would add the test scores and then divide by the number of test scores in the list. If you write this formula as =100+50+90/3, the result would be 180, because Excel would first divide 90 by 3 and then add 100+50+30. Excel would do so because the order of operations states that multiplication and division are calculated *before* addition and subtraction.

The correct way to write this formula is =(100+50+90)/3. Excel will add the three values, and then divide the result by 3, or 240/3 resulting in a correct average of 80. Parentheses play an important role in ensuring that you get the correct result in your formulas.

Activity 3.13 | Using Format Painter and Formatting as You Type

You can format numbers as you type them. When you type numbers in a format that Excel recognizes, Excel automatically applies that format to the cell. Recall that once applied, cell formats remain with the cell, even if the cell contents are deleted. In this activity, you will format cells by typing the numbers with percent signs and use Format Painter to copy text (non-numeric) formats.

1 Leave **row 8** blank, and then click cell **A9**. Type **Projected Future Population** and then press Enter.

Another Way

On the Home tab, in the Clipboard group, click the Format Painter button.

2 Point to cell **A3**, right-click, on the Mini toolbar click the **Format Painter** button, and then click cell **A9**.

The format of cell A3 is *painted*—applied to—cell A9, including the merging and centering of the text across the range A9:F9.

3 Leave **row 10** blank, and then click cell **A11**, type **Estimated Growth Rate** and then press Enter.

4 Leave **row 12** blank, and then click cell **A13**. Type **Year** and then in cell **A14**, type **Projected Population**

5 In cell **B13**, type **2010** and then press Tab. In cell **C13**, type **2020** and then press Tab.

6 Select the range **B13:C13**, and then drag the fill handle through cell **F13** to extend the pattern of years to *2050*. Apply **Bold** B to the selected range. Compare your screen with Figure 3.27.

Figure 3.27

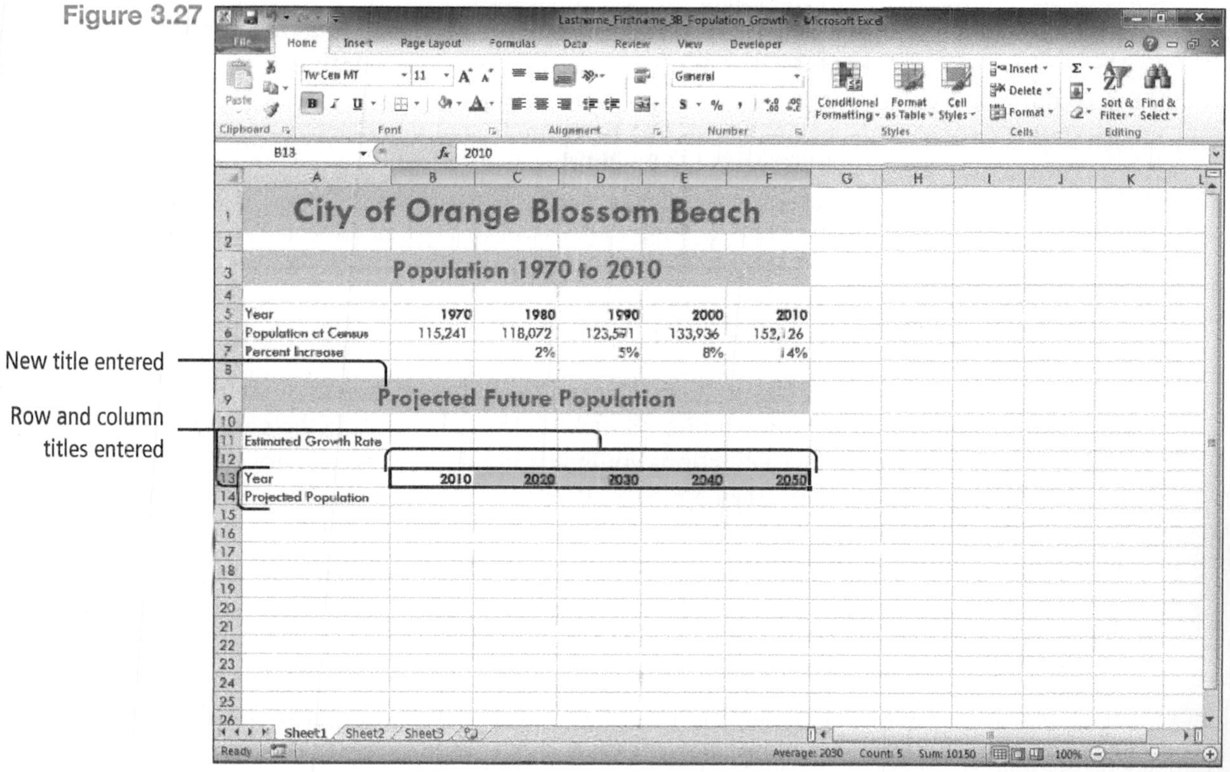

7 Click cell **B14**, and then on the **Home tab**, in the **Number group**, notice that the **Number Format** box indicates *General*. Then, being sure to type the comma, type **152,126**

8 On the **Formula Bar**, click the **Enter** button ✓ to keep the cell active, and then in the **Number group**, notice that the format changed to *Number*.

9 Press Del, and then in the **Number group**, notice that the *Number* format is still indicated.

Recall that deleting the contents of a cell does not delete the cell's formatting.

10 *Without* typing a comma, in cell **B14**, type **152126** and then press Enter.

The comma displays even though you did not type it. When you type a number and include a formatting symbol such as a comma or dollar sign, Excel applies the format to the cell. Thus, if you delete the contents of the cell and type in the cell again, the format you established remains applied to the cell. This is referred to as ***format as you type***.

11 Examine the format of the value in cell **B14**, and then compare it to the format in cell **B6** where you used the **Comma Style** button to format the cell. Notice that the number in cell **B14** is flush with the right edge of the cell, but the number in cell **B6** leaves a small amount of space on the right edge.

When you type commas as you enter numbers, Excel applies the *Number* format, which does *not* leave a space at the right of the number for a closing parenthesis in the event of a negative number. This is different from the format that is applied when you use the *Comma Style* button on the Ribbon or Mini toolbar, as you did for the numbers entered in row 6. Recall that the Comma Style format applied from either the Ribbon or the Mini toolbar leaves space on the right for a closing parenthesis in the event of a negative number.

12 In cell **B11**, type **8%** Select the range **A11:B11**, and then from the Mini toolbar, apply **Bold** [B] and **Italic** [I]. **Save** your workbook.

> **More Knowledge | Percentage Calculations**
>
> When you type a percentage into a cell—for example *8%*—the percentage format, without decimal points, displays in both the cell and the Formula Bar. Excel will, however, use the decimal value of *0.08* for actual calculations.

Activity 3.14 | Calculating a Value After an Increase

A growing population results in increased use of city services. Thus, city planners in Orange Blossom Beach must estimate how much the population will increase in the future. The calculations you made in the previous activity show that the population has increased at varying rates during each 10-year period from 1970 to 2010, ranging from a low of 2% to a high of 14% per 10-year census period.

Population data from the state and surrounding areas suggests that future growth will trend close to that of the recent past. To plan for the future, Ms. Darius wants to prepare three forecasts of the city's population based on the percentage increases in 2000, in 2010, and for a percentage increase halfway between the two; that is, for 8%, 11%, and 14%. In this activity, you will calculate the population that would result from an 8% increase.

1 Click cell **C14**. Type **=b14*(100%+b11)** and then on the **Formula Bar**, click the **Enter** [✓] button to display a result of *164296.08*. Compare your screen with Figure 3.28.

This formula calculates what the population will be in the year 2020 assuming an increase of 8% over 2010's population. Use the mathematical formula ***value after increase* = *base* × *percent for new value*** to calculate a value after an increase as follows:

First, establish the *percent for new value*. The ***percent for new value* = *base percent* + *percent of increase***. The *base percent* of 100% represents the base population and the *percent of increase* in this instance is 8%. Thus, the population will equal 100% of the base year plus 8% of the base year. This can be expressed as 108% or 1.08. In this formula, you will use 100% + the rate in cell B11, which is 8%, to equal 108%.

Second, enter a reference to the cell that contains the *base*—the population in 2010. The base value resides in cell B14—*152,126*.

Third, calculate the *value after increase*. Because in each future 10-year period the increase will be based on 8%—an absolute value located in cell B11—this cell reference can be formatted as absolute by typing dollar signs.

Figure 3.28

Formula includes absolute reference to cell B11

Formula result

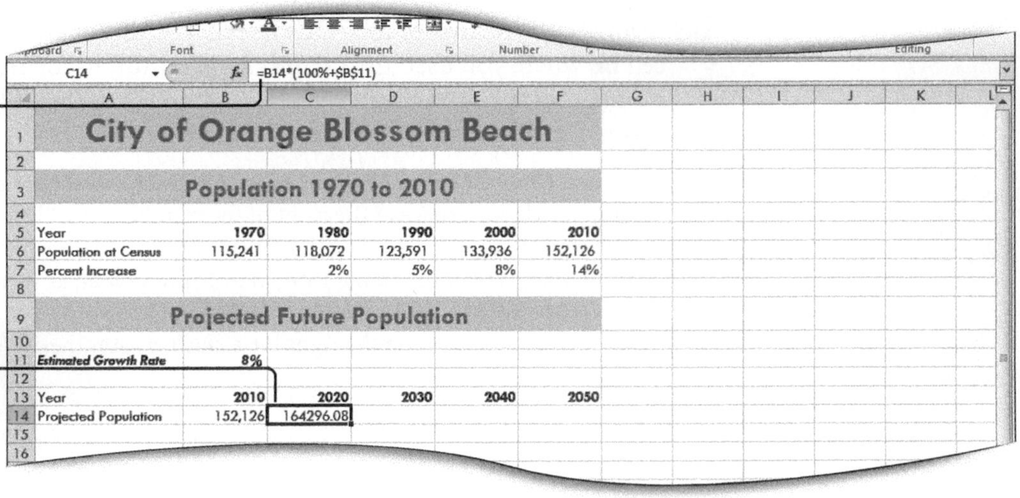

2 With cell **C14** as the active cell, drag the fill handle to copy the formula to the range **D14:F14.**

3 Point to cell **B14**, right-click, click the **Format Painter** button, and then select the range **C14:F14.** Click an empty cell to cancel the selection, click **Save** and then compare your screen with Figure 3.29.

This formula uses a relative cell address—B14—for the *base*; the population in the previous 10-year period is used in each of the formulas in cells D14:F14 as the *base* value. Because the reference to the *percent of increase* in cell B11 is an absolute reference, each *value after increase* is calculated with the value from cell B11.

The population projected for 2020—*164,296*—is an increase of 8% over the population in 2010. The projected population in 2030—*177,440*—is an increase of 8% over the population in 2020 and so on.

Figure 3.29

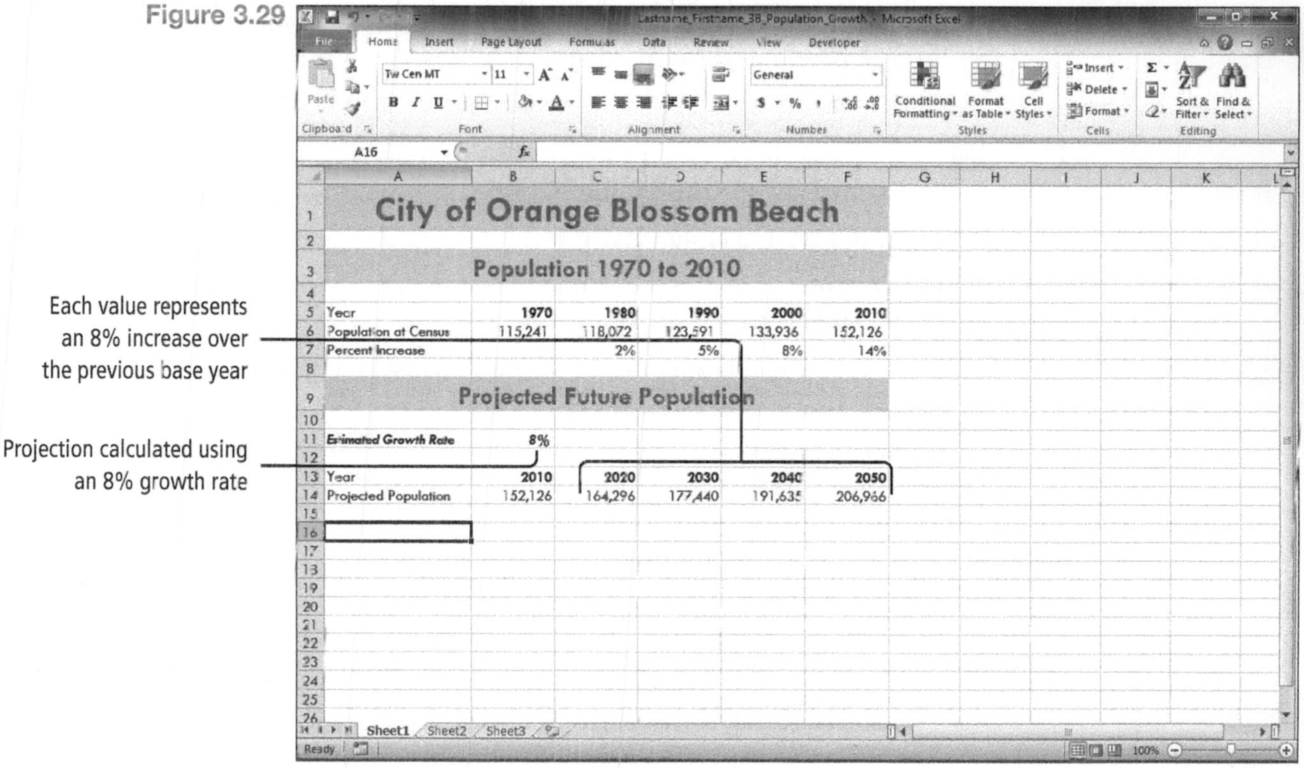

More Knowledge | Percent Increase or Decrease

The basic formula for calculating an increase or decrease can be done in two parts. First determine the percent by which the base value will be increased or decreased, and then add or subtract the results to the base. The formula can be simplified by using (1+amount of increase) or (1–amount of decrease), where 1, rather than 100%, represents the whole. Thus, the formula used in Step 1 of Activity 3.14 could also be written =b14*(1+b11), or =(b14*b11)+b14.

Objective 6 | Answer What-If Questions by Changing Values in a Worksheet

If a formula depends on the value in a cell, you can see what effect it will have if you change the value in that cell. Then, you can copy the value computed by the formula and paste it into another part of the worksheet where you can be compare it to other values.

Activity 3.15 | Answering What-If Questions and Using Paste Special

A growth rate of 8% in each 10-year period will result in a population of almost 207,000 people by 2050. The city planners will likely ask: *What if* the population grows at the highest rate (14%)? *What if* the population grows at a rate that is halfway between the 2000 and 2010 rates (11%)?

Because the formulas are constructed to use the growth rate displayed in cell B11, Ms. Darius can answer these questions quickly by entering different percentages into that cell. To keep the results of each set of calculations so they can be compared, you will paste the results of each what-if question into another area of the worksheet.

1 Leave **row 15** blank, and then click cell **A16**. Type **Growth Estimates 2020 to 2050** and then press Enter. Use **Format Painter** to copy the format from cell **A9** to cell **A16**.

2 Select the range **A11:B11**, right-click to display the Mini toolbar, click the **Fill Color button arrow**, and then under **Theme Colors**, in the first column, click the third color—**White, Background 1, Darker 15%.**

3 Leave **row 17** blank, and then in the range **A18:A21**, type the following row titles:

Year

8% Growth Rate

11% Growth Rate

14% Growth Rate

4 Select the range **B13:F13**, right-click over the selection, and then on the shortcut menu, click **Copy**.

Another Way

Press Ctrl + C; or, on the Home tab, in the Clipboard group, click the Copy button.

5 Point to cell **B18,** right-click, and then on the shortcut menu, under **Paste Options**, click the **Paste** button.

Recall that when pasting a group of copied cells to a target range, you need only point to or select the first cell of the range.

6 Select and **Copy** the range **B14:F14**, and then **Paste** it beginning in cell **B19**.

7 Click cell **C19**. On the **Formula Bar**, notice that the *formula* was pasted into the cell, as shown in Figure 3.30.

This is *not* the desired result. The actual *calculated values*—not the formulas—are needed in the range.

Figure 3.30

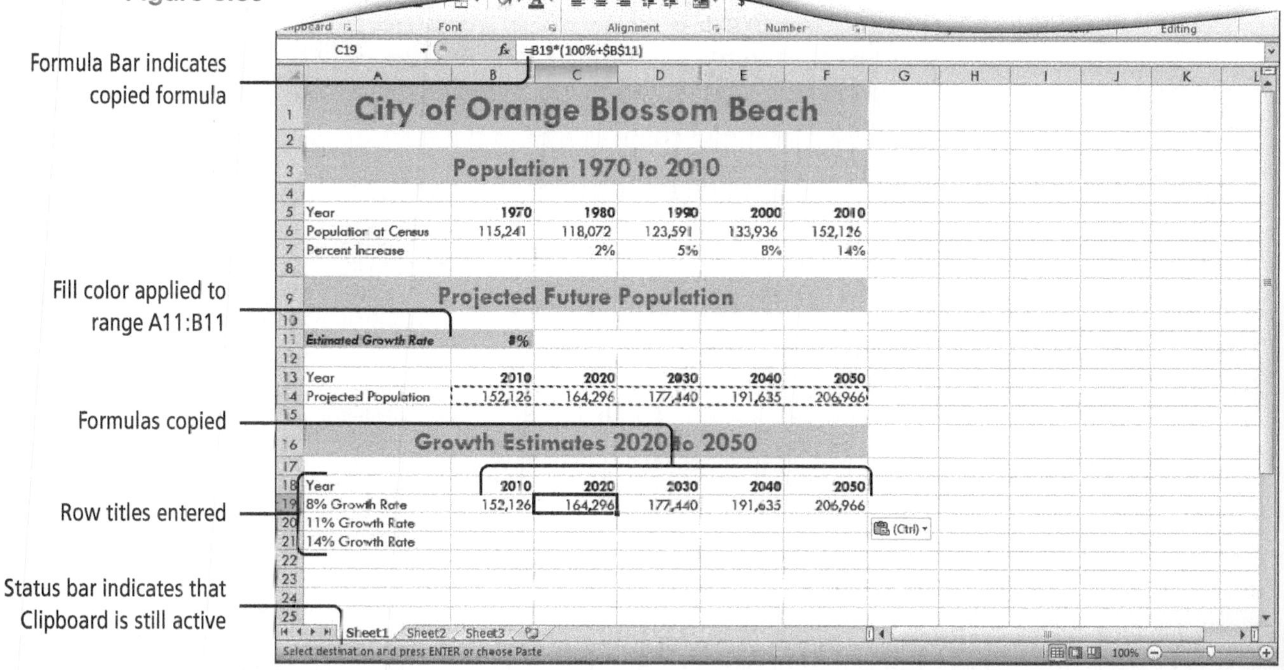

8 On the Quick Access Toolbar, click the **Undo** button. With the range **B14:F14** still copied to the Clipboard—as indicated by the message in the status bar and the moving border—point to cell **B19**, and then right-click to display the shortcut menu.

9 Under **Paste Options**, point to **Paste Special** to display another gallery, and then under **Paste Values**, point to the **Values & Number Formatting** button to display the ScreenTip as shown in Figure 3.31.

The ScreenTip *Values & Number Formatting (A)* indicates that you can paste the *calculated values* that result from the calculation of formulas along with the formatting applied to the copied cells. *(A)* is the keyboard shortcut for this command.

Figure 3.31

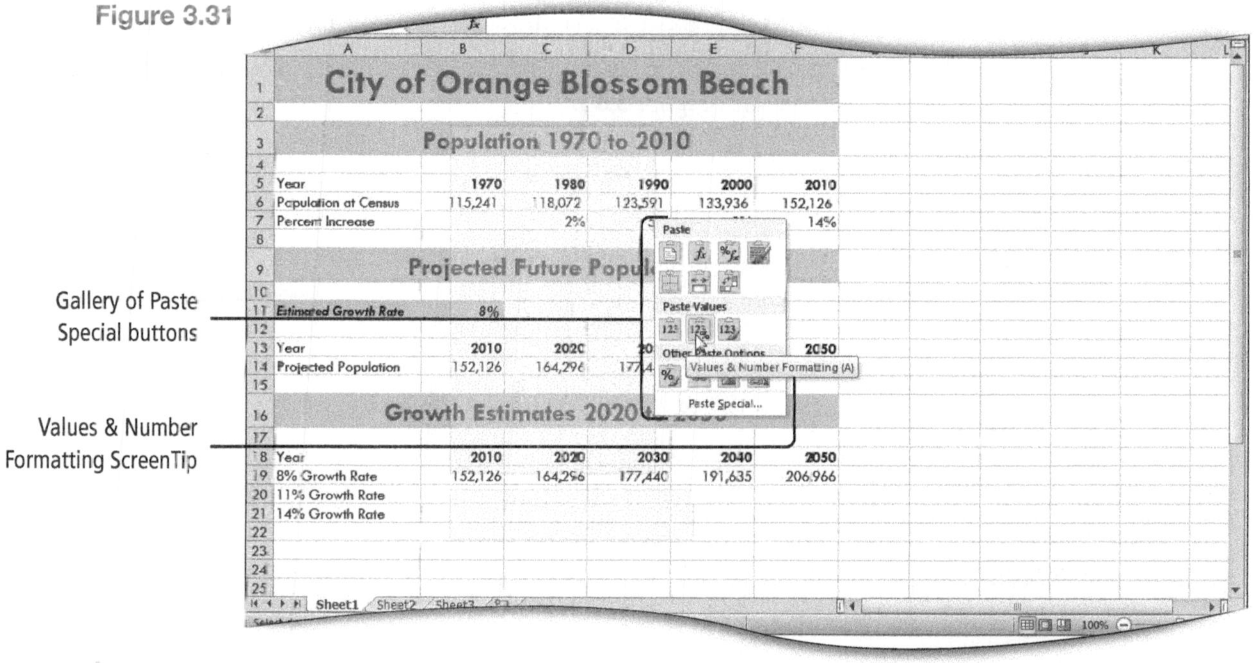

10 Click the **Values & Number Formatting** button, click cell **C19** and notice on the **Formula Bar** that the cell contains a *value*, not a formula. Press Esc to cancel the moving border. Compare your screen with Figure 3.32.

The calculated estimates based on an 8% growth rate are pasted along with their formatting.

Figure 3.32

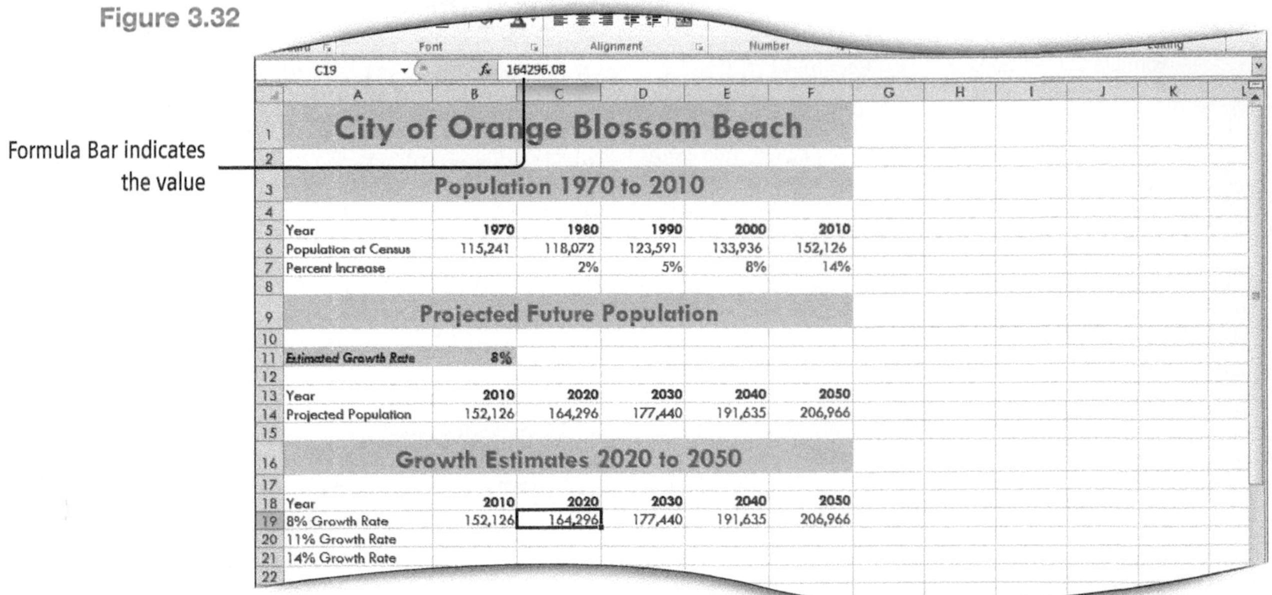

11 Click cell **B11**. Type **11** and then watch the values in **C14:F14** *recalculate* as, on the **Formula Bar**, you click the **Enter** button.

The value *11%* is halfway between 8% and 14%—the growth rates from the two most recent 10-year periods.

12 Select and **Copy** the new values in the range **B14:F14**. Point to cell **B20**, right-click, and then on the shortcut menu, point to **Paste Special**. Under **Paste Values**, click the **Values & Number Formatting** button.

13 In cell **B11**, change the percentage by typing **14** and then press Enter. Notice that the projected values in **C14:F14** recalculate.

14 Using the skills you just practiced, select and copy the recalculated values in the range **B14:F14**, and then paste the **Values & Number Formatting** to the range **B21:F21**.

15 Press Esc to cancel the moving border, click cell **A1**, click **Save**, and then compare your screen with Figure 3.33.

With this information, Ms. Darius can answer several what-if questions about the future population of the city and provide a range of population estimates based on the rates of growth over the past 10-year periods.

Figure 3.33

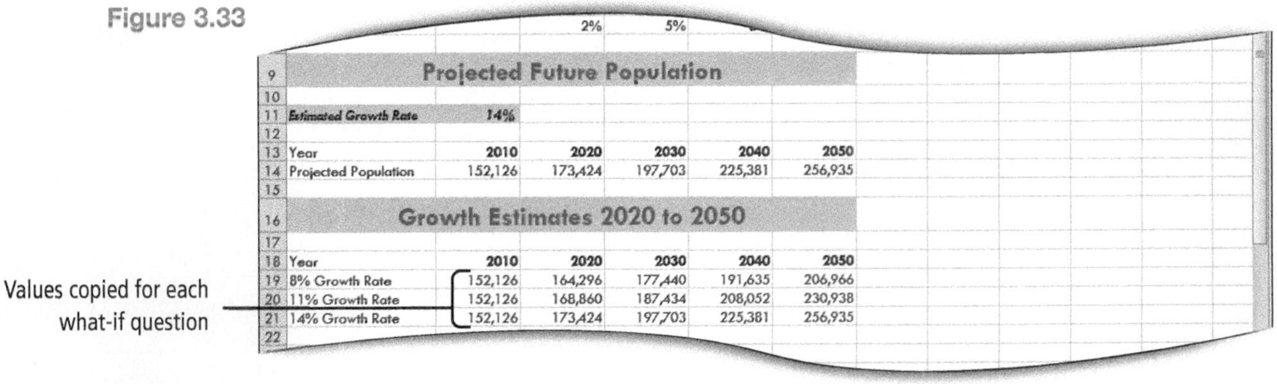

Objective 7 | Chart Data with a Line Chart

A ***line chart*** displays trends over time. Time is displayed along the bottom axis and the data point values connect with a line. The curve and direction of the line makes trends obvious to the reader.

Whereas the columns in a column chart and the pie slices in a pie chart emphasize the distinct values of each data point, the line in a line chart emphasizes the flow from one data point value to the next.

Activity 3.16 | Inserting Multiple Rows and Creating a Line Chart

So that city council members can see how the population has increased over the past five census periods, in this activity, you will chart the actual population figures from 1970 to 2010 in a line chart.

1 In the **row header area**, point to **row 8** to display the [→] pointer, and then drag down to select **rows 8:24**. Right-click over the selection, and then click **Insert** to insert the same number of blank rows as you selected. Compare your screen with Figure 3.34.

Use this technique to insert multiple rows quickly.

Figure 3.34

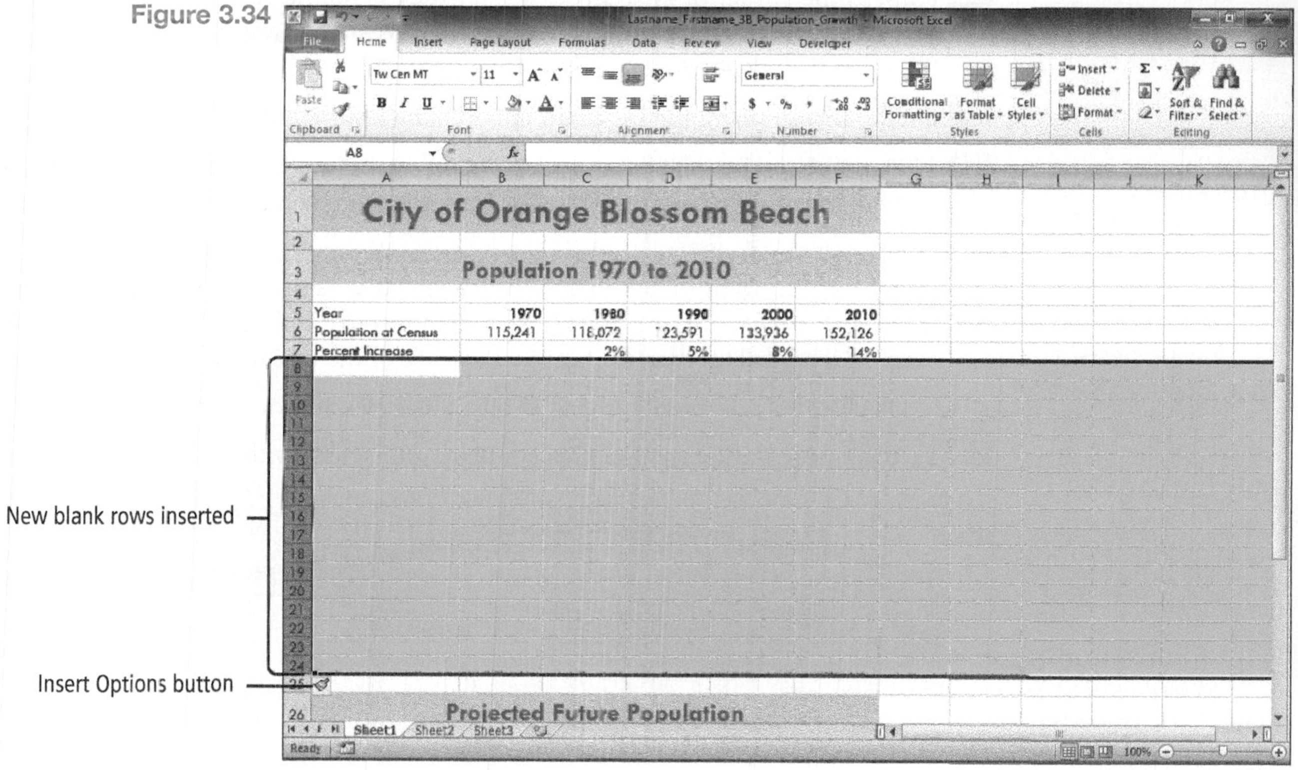

2 Near **row 25**, click the **Insert Options** button [icon], and then click the **Clear Formatting** option button to clear any formatting from these rows.

You will use this blank area in which to position your line chart.

3 Select the range **A6:F6**. On the **Insert tab**, in the **Charts group**, click the **Line** button.

4 In the displayed gallery of line charts, in the second row, point to the first chart type to display the ScreenTip *Line with Markers*. Compare your screen with Figure 3.35.

Figure 3.35

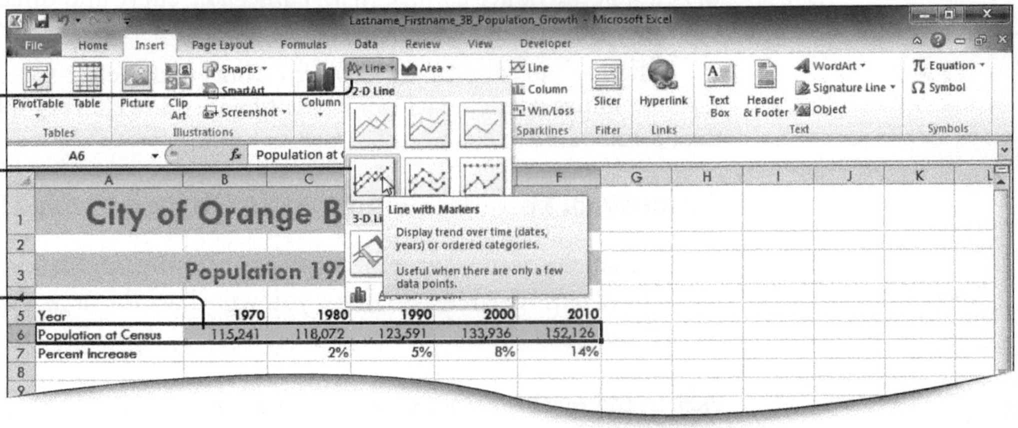

5 Click the **Line with Markers** chart type to create the chart as an embedded chart in the worksheet.

6 Point to the border of the chart to display the pointer, and then drag the chart so that its upper left corner is positioned in cell **A9**, aligned approximately under the *t* in the word *Percent* above.

7 On the **Layout tab**, in the **Labels group**, click the **Legend** button, and then click **None.**

8 Click the chart title one time to select it and display a solid border around the title. Watch the **Formula Bar** as you type **Orange Blossom Beach** and then press Enter.

9 In the chart title, click to position the insertion point following the *h* in *Beach*, and then press Enter to begin a new line. Type **Population Growth 1970 to 2010** Click the dashed border around the chart title to change it to a solid border, right-click, and then on the Mini toolbar, change the **Font Size** of the title to **20.**

Recall that a solid border around an object indicates that the entire object is selected.

10 **Save** your workbook, and then compare your screen with Figure 3.36.

Figure 3.36

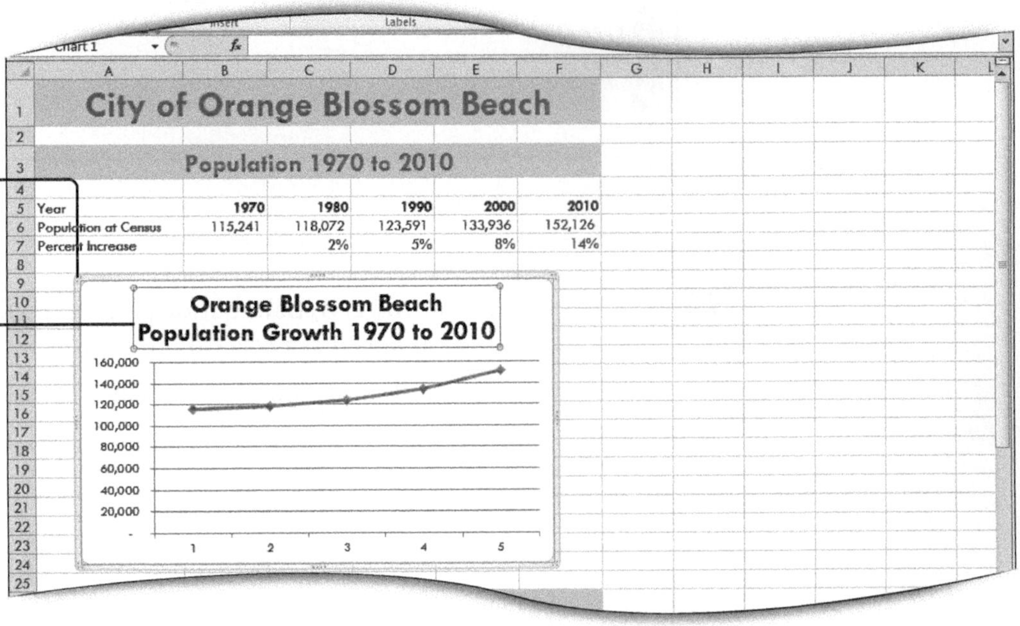

Activity 3.17 | Formatting Axes in a Line Chart

An ***axis*** is a line that serves as a frame of reference for measurement; it borders the chart ***plot area***. The plot area is the area bounded by the axes, including all the data series. Recall that the area along the bottom of a chart that identifies the categories of data is referred to as the ***category axis*** or the ***x-axis***. Recall also that the area along the left side of a chart that shows the range of numbers for the data points is referred to as the ***value axis*** or the ***y-axis***.

In this activity, you will change the category axis to include the names of the 10-year census periods and adjust the numeric scale of the value axis.

Another Way

At the bottom of the chart, point to any of the numbers 1 through 5 to display the ScreenTip *Horizontal (Category) Axis*. Right-click, and then from the shortcut menu, click Select Data.

1 Be sure the chart is still selected—a pale frame surrounds the chart area. Click the **Design tab**, and then in the **Data group**, click the **Select Data** button.

2 On the right side of the displayed **Select Data Source** dialog box, under **Horizontal (Category) Axis Labels**, locate the **Edit** button, as shown in Figure 3.37.

Figure 3.37

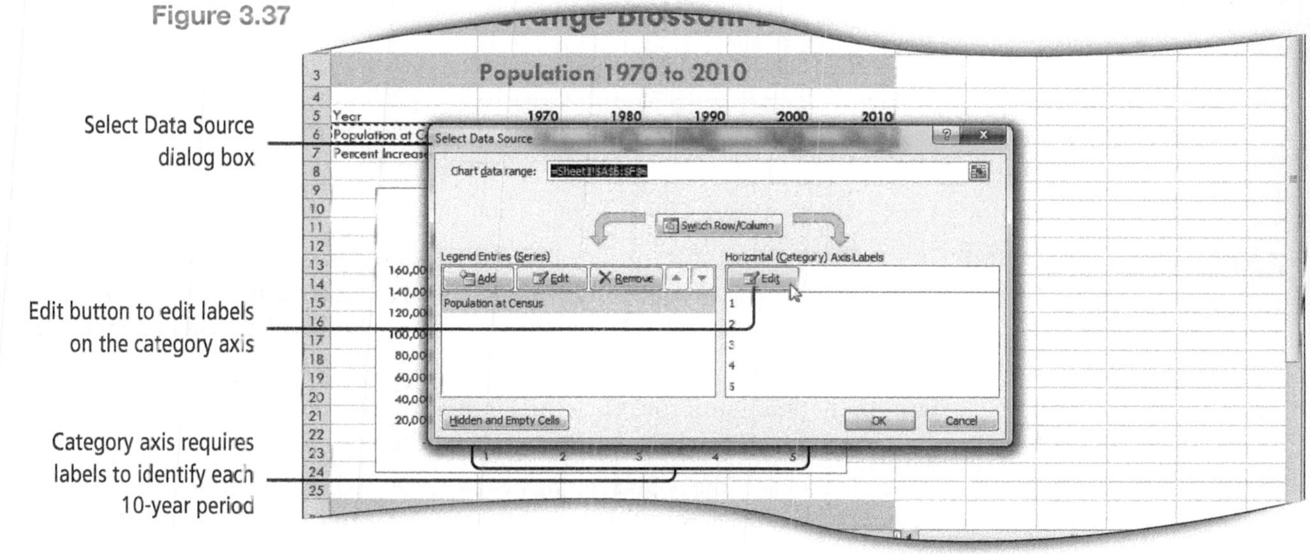

3 In the right column, click the **Edit** button. If necessary, drag the title bar of the **Axis Labels** dialog box to the right of the chart so that it is not blocking your view of the data, and then select the years in the range **B5:F5**. Compare your screen with Figure 3.38.

Figure 3.38

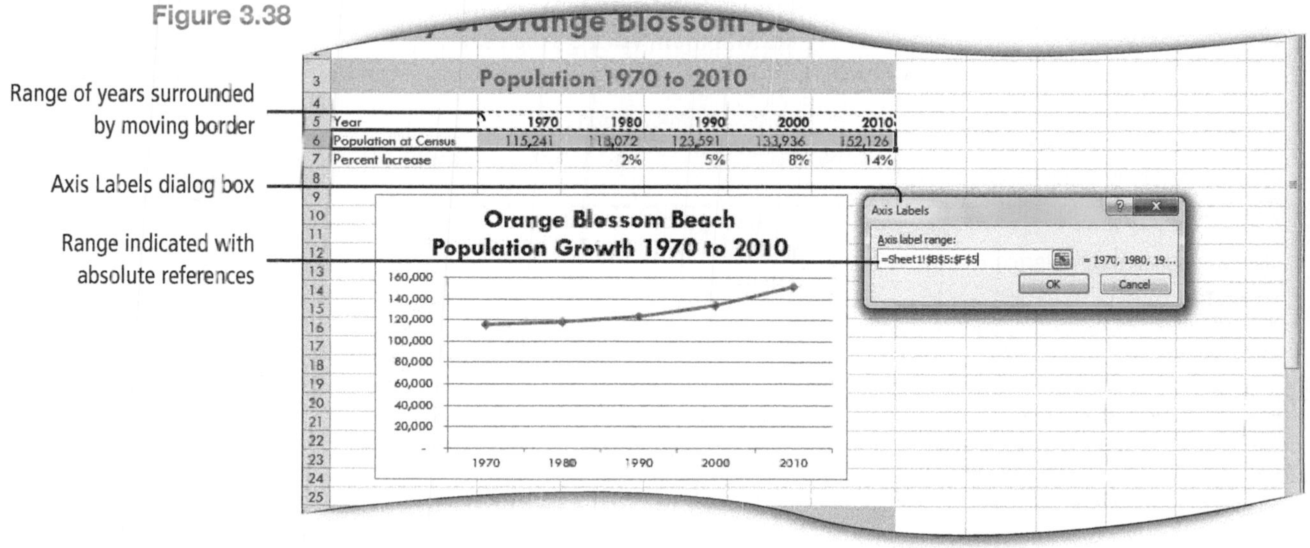

4 In the **Axis Labels** dialog box, click **OK**, and notice that in the right column of the **Select Data Source** dialog box, the years display as the category labels. Click **OK** to close the **Select Data Source** dialog box. Compare your screen with Figure 3.39.

Figure 3.39

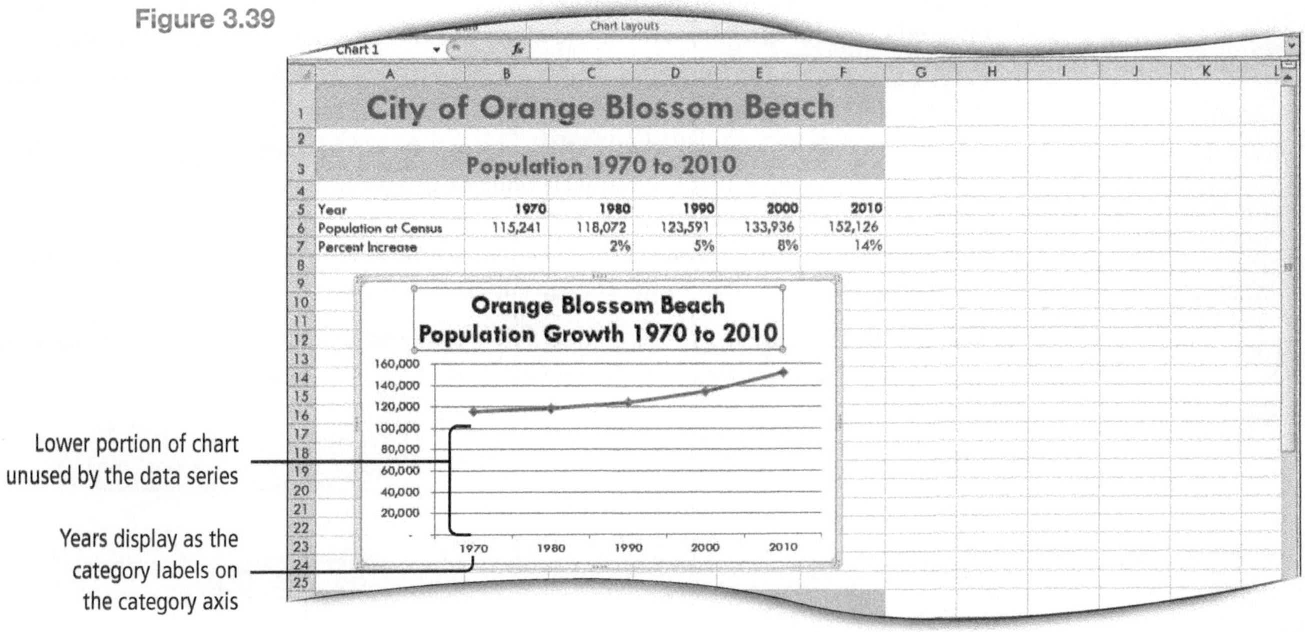

> **Another Way**
>
> On the left side of the chart, point to any of the numbers to display the ScreenTip *Vertical (Value) Axis*, and then right-click. From the shortcut menu, click Format Axis.

5 On the chart, notice that the blue line—the data series—does not display in the lower portion of the chart. Then, on the **Layout tab**, in the **Axes group**, click the **Axes** button. Point to **Primary Vertical Axis**, and then click **More Primary Vertical Axis Options**.

6 In the **Format Axis** dialog box, on the left, be sure **Axis Options** is selected. On the right, in the **Minimum** row, click the **Fixed** option button. In the box to the right, select the existing text *0.0*, and then type **100000**

Because none of the population figures are under 100,000, changing the Minimum number to 100,000 will enable the data series to occupy more of the plot area.

7 In the **Major unit** row, click the **Fixed** option button, select the text in the box to the right *20000.0*, and then type **10000** In the lower right corner, click **Close**. **Save** your workbook, and then compare your screen with Figure 3.40.

The ***Major unit*** value determines the spacing between ***tick marks*** and thus between the gridlines in the plot area. Tick marks are the short lines that display on an axis at regular intervals. By default, Excel started the values at zero and increased in increments of 20,000. By setting the Minimum value on the value axis to 100,000 and changing the Major unit from 20,000 to 10,000, the line chart shows a clearer trend in the population growth.

Figure 3.40

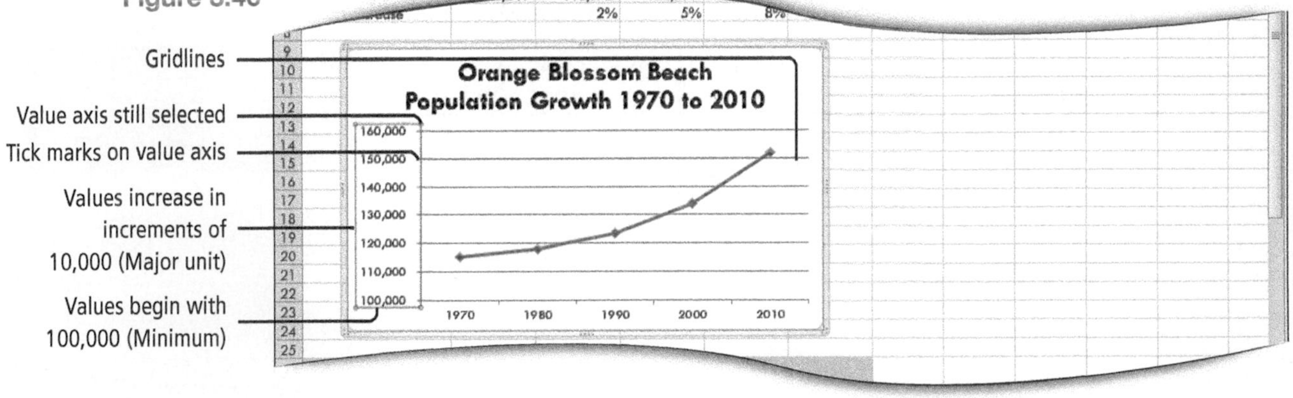

Activity 3.18 | Formatting the Chart and Plot Areas

An Excel chart has two background elements—the plot area and the chart area—which, by default display a single fill color. To add visual appeal to a chart, you can insert a graphic image as the background.

When formatting chart elements, there are several ways to display the dialog boxes that you need. You can right-click the area you want to format and choose a command on the shortcut menu. In this activity, you will use the Chart Elements box in the Current Selection group on the Format tab of the Ribbon, which is convenient if you are changing the format of a variety of chart elements.

1 Click the **Format tab**, and then in the **Current Selection group**, point to the small arrow to the right of the first item in the group to display the ScreenTip *Chart Elements*. Compare your screen with Figure 3.41.

From the ***Chart Elements box***, you can select a chart element so that you can format it.

Figure 3.41

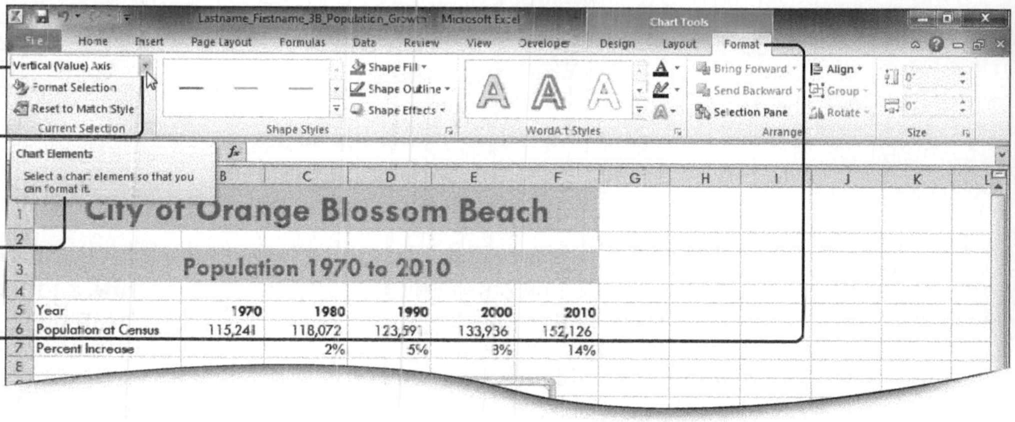

2 Click the **Chart Elements arrow**, and then from the displayed list, click **Chart Area**. Directly below the **Chart Elements** box, click the **Format Selection** button.

The Format Chart Area dialog box displays. Use this technique to select the chart element that you want to format, and then click the Format Selection button to display the appropriate dialog box.

3 In the **Format Chart Area** dialog box, on the left, be sure that **Fill** is selected.

4 On the right, under **Fill**, click the **Picture or texture fill** option button, and then under **Insert from**, click the **File** button. In the **Insert Picture** dialog box, navigate to your student files, and then insert the picture **e03B_Beach**. Leave the dialog box open, and then compare your screen with Figure 3.42.

Figure 3.42

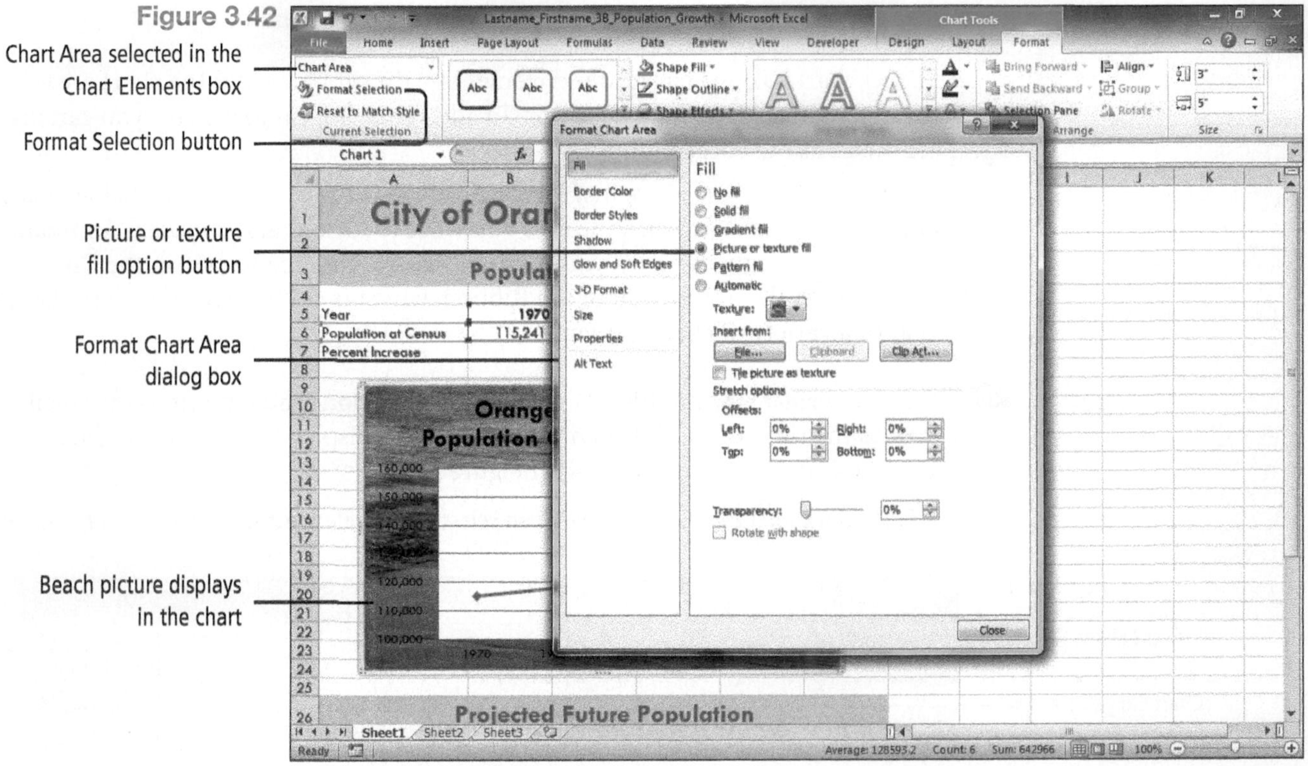

5 In the **Format Chart Area** dialog box, on the left, click **Border Color**, on the right click the **Solid line** option button, click the **Color arrow**, and then under **Theme Colors**, in the fourth column, click the first color—**Dark Teal, Text 2**.

6 On the left, click **Border Styles**. On the right, select the text in the **Width** box and type **4 pt** At the bottom select the **Rounded corners** check box, and then **Close** the dialog box.

A 4 pt teal border with rounded corners frames the chart.

7 In the **Current Selection group**, click the **Chart Elements arrow**, on the list click **Plot Area**, and then click the **Format Selection** button.

8 In the **Format Plot Area** dialog box, on the left, be sure that **Fill** is selected, and then on the right, click the **No fill** option button. **Close** the dialog box.

The fill is removed from the plot area so that the picture is visible as the background.

9 Click the **Chart Elements arrow**, on the list click **Vertical (Value) Axis**, and then click the **Format Selection** button.

10 In the **Format Axis** dialog box, on the left click **Line Color**, on the right click the **Solid line** option button, click the **Color arrow**, and then click the first color—**White, Background 1**. Compare your screen with Figure 3.43.

The vertical line with tick marks displays in white.

Figure 3.43

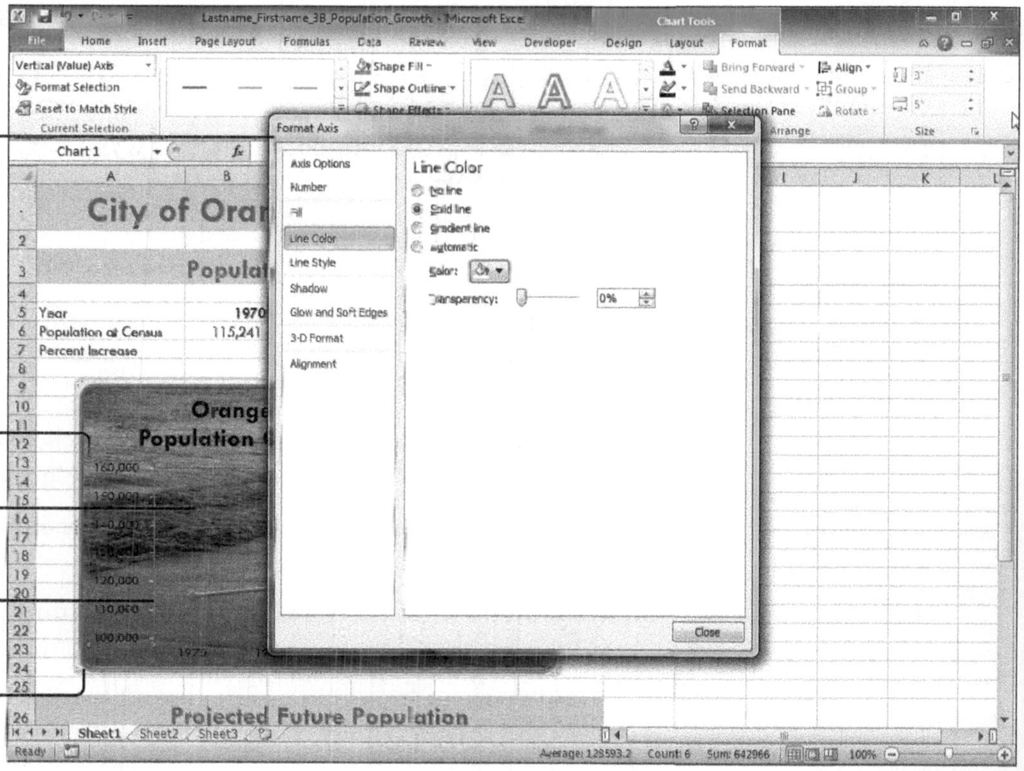

11 **Close** the dialog box. From the **Chart Elements** box, select the **Vertical (Value) Axis Major Gridlines**, and then click **Format Selection**. Change the **Line Color** to a **Solid line**, and then apply the **White, Background 1** color. **Close** the dialog box.

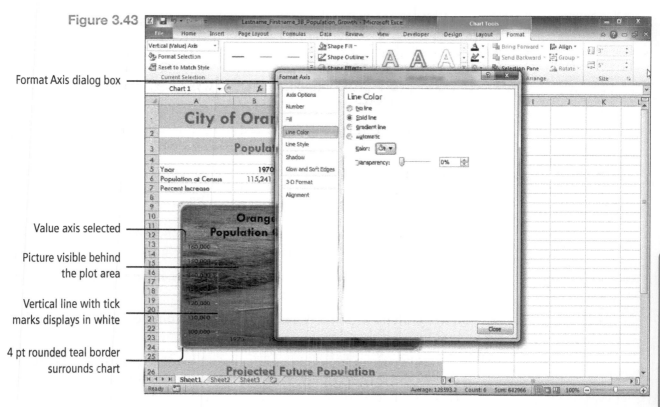

12 From the **Chart Elements** list, select the **Horizontal (Category) Axis**, and then click **Format Selection**. In the **Format Axis** dialog box, change the **Line Color** to a **Solid line**, and then apply the **White, Background 1** color. **Close** the dialog box.

13 Point to any of the numbers on the vertical value axis, right-click, and then on the Mini toolbar, change the **Font Color** [A] to **White, Background 1**. Point to any of the years on the horizontal category axis, right-click, and then change the **Font Color** [A] to **White, Background 1**.

For basic text-formatting changes—for example changing the size, font, style, or font color—you must leave the Chart Tools on the Ribbon and use commands from the Home tab or the Mini toolbar.

14 Click any cell to deselect the chart, press Ctrl + Home to move to the top of your worksheet, click **Save** [Save], and then compare your screen with Figure 3.44.

Figure 3.44

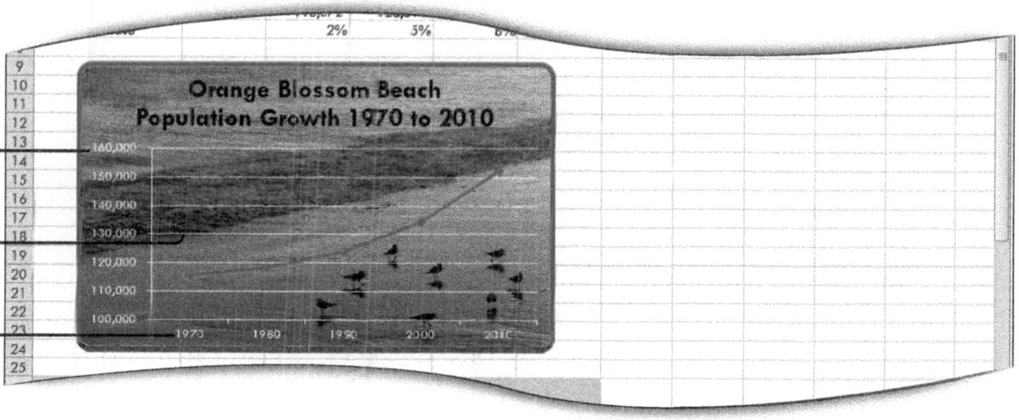

Activity 3.19 | Preparing and Printing Your Worksheet

1 From **Backstage** view, display the **Document Panel**. In the **Author** box, replace the existing text with your firstname and lastname. In the **Subject** box, type your course name and section number. In the **Keywords** box, type **population** and then **Close** [×] the **Document Information Panel**.

2 Click the **Insert tab**, and then in the **Text group**, click the **Header & Footer** button to switch to **Page Layout View** and open the **Header area**.

3 In the **Navigation group**, click the **Go to Footer** button, click just above the word *Footer*, and then in the **Header & Footer Elements group**, click the **File Name** button. Click in a cell just above the footer to exit the **Footer area** and view your file name.

4 Click the **Page Layout tab**. In the **Page Setup group**, click the **Margins** button, and then at the bottom of the **Margins** gallery, click **Custom Margins**.

5 In the displayed **Page Setup** dialog box, under **Center on page**, select the **Horizontally** check box. Click **OK** to close the dialog box.

6 On the status bar, click the **Normal** button [▦] to return to Normal view, and then press Ctrl + Home to move to the top of your worksheet.

7 At the lower edge of the window, click to select the **Sheet2 tab**, hold down Ctrl, and then click the **Sheet3 tab** to select the two unused sheets. Right-click over the selected sheet tabs, and then on the displayed shortcut menu, click **Delete**.

8 **Save** [💾] your workbook before printing or submitting. Press Ctrl + F2 to display the **Print Preview** to check your worksheet. Compare your screen with Figure 3.45.

Figure 3.45

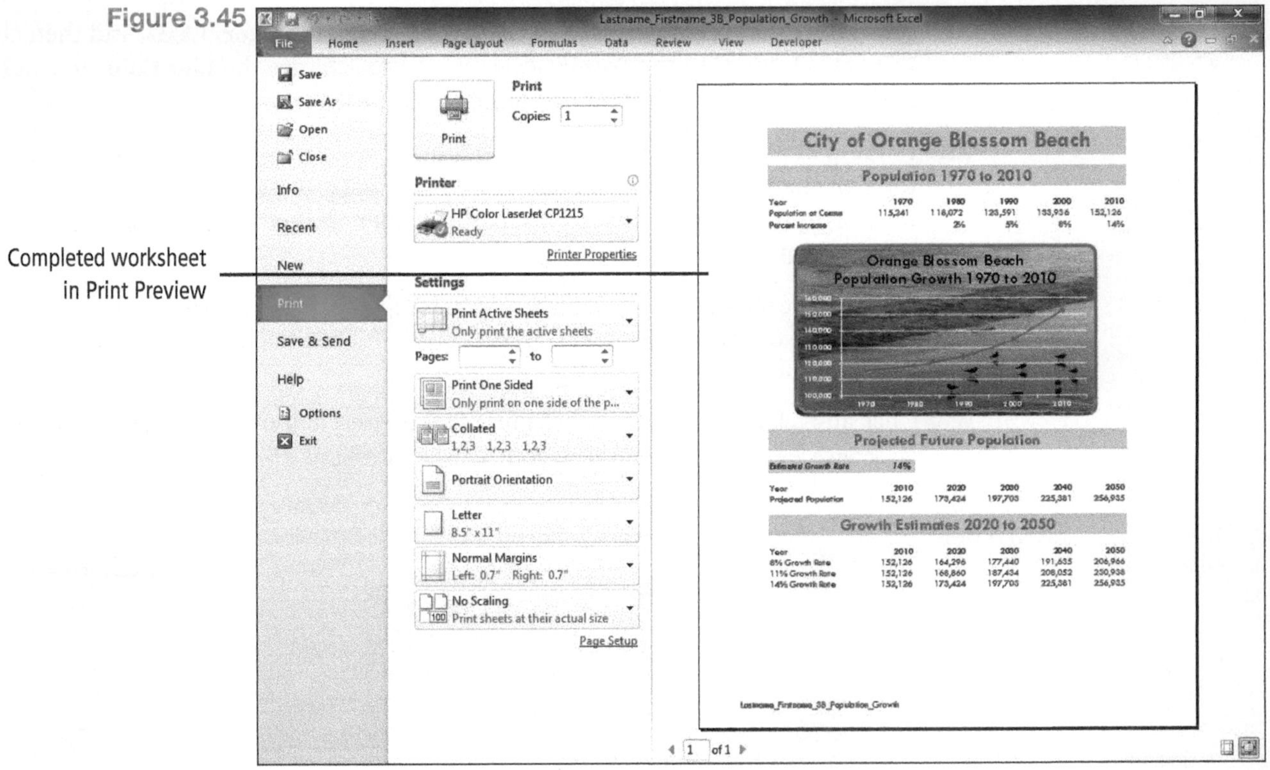

9 If necessary, return to the worksheet to make any necessary adjustments or corrections, and then **Save**.

10 Print or submit electronically as directed. If you are directed to submit printed formulas, refer to Activity 1.16 to do so.

11 If you printed your formulas, be sure to redisplay the worksheet by clicking the Show Formulas button to turn it off. From **Backstage** view, click **Close**. If the dialog box displays asking if you want to save changes, click **No** so that you do *not* save the changes you made for printing formulas. **Close** Excel.

End You have completed Project 3B

Content-Based Assessments

Summary

In this chapter, you created a pie chart to show how the parts of a budget contribute to a total budget. Then you formatted the pie chart attractively and used Goal Seek. You also practiced using parentheses in a formula, calculating the percentage rate of an increase, answering what-if questions, and charting data in a line chart to show the flow of data over time.

Key Terms

Matching

Match each term in the second column with its correct definition in the first column by writing the letter of the term on the blank line in front of the correct definition.

____ 1. A chart that shows the relationship of each part to a whole.

____ 2. The term used to describe money set aside for the normal operating activities of a government entity such as a city.

____ 3. In a formula, the address of a cell based on the relative position of the cell that contains the formula and the cell referred to.

____ 4. A column, bar, area, dot, pie slice, or other symbol in a chart that represents a single data point.

____ 5. A workbook sheet that contains only a chart.

____ 6. A shape effect that uses shading and shadows to make the edges of a shape appear to be curved or angled.

____ 7. The entire chart and all of its elements.

____ 8. The process of changing the values in cells to see how those changes affect the outcome of formulas in a worksheet.

____ 9. The mathematical formula to calculate a rate of increase.

A Axis
B Bevel
C Category axis
D Chart area
E Chart sheet
F Data marker
G Format as you type
H General Fund
I Order of operations
J Pie chart
K Rate=amount of increase/base
L Relative cell reference
M Tick marks
N Value axis
O What-if analysis

_____ 10. The mathematical rules for performing multiple calculations within a formula.

_____ 11. The Excel feature by which a cell takes on the formatting of the number typed into the cell.

_____ 12. A line that serves as a frame of reference for measurement and that borders the chart plot area.

_____ 13. The area along the bottom of a chart that identifies the categories of data; also referred to as the x-axis.

_____ 14. A numerical scale on the left side of a chart that shows the range of numbers for the data points; also referred to as the y-axis.

_____ 15. The short lines that display on an axis at regular intervals.

Multiple Choice

Circle the correct answer.

1. A sum of money set aside for a specific purpose is a:
   A. value axis B. fund C. rate
2. A cell reference that refers to a cell by its fixed position in a worksheet is referred to as being:
   A. absolute B. relative C. mixed
3. A value that originates in a worksheet cell and that is represented in a chart by a data marker is a data:
   A. point B. cell C. axis
4. Related data points represented by data markers are referred to as the data:
   A. slices B. set C. series
5. The action of pulling out a pie slice from a pie chart is called:
   A. extract B. explode C. plot
6. A gallery of text styles with which you can create decorative effects, such as shadowed or mirrored text is:
   A. WordArt B. shape effects C. text fill
7. The percent by which one number increases over another number is the percentage rate of:
   A. decrease B. change C. increase
8. A chart type that displays trends over time is a:
   A. pie chart B. line chart C. column chart
9. The area bounded by the axes of a chart, including all the data series, is the:
   A. chart area B. plot area C. axis area
10. The x-axis is also known as the:
    A. category axis B. value axis C. data axis

Apply 3A skills from these Objectives:

1. Chart Data with a Pie Chart
2. Format a Pie Chart
3. Edit a Workbook and Update a Chart
4. Use Goal Seek to Perform What-If Analysis

Skills Review | Project 3C Fund Revenue

In the following Skills Review, you will edit a worksheet for Jennifer Carson, City Finance Manager, which details the City general fund revenue. Your completed worksheets will look similar to Figure 3.46.

Project Files

For Project 3C, you will need the following file:

e03C_Fund_Revenue

You will save your workbook as:

Lastname_Firstname_3C_Fund_Revenue

Project Results

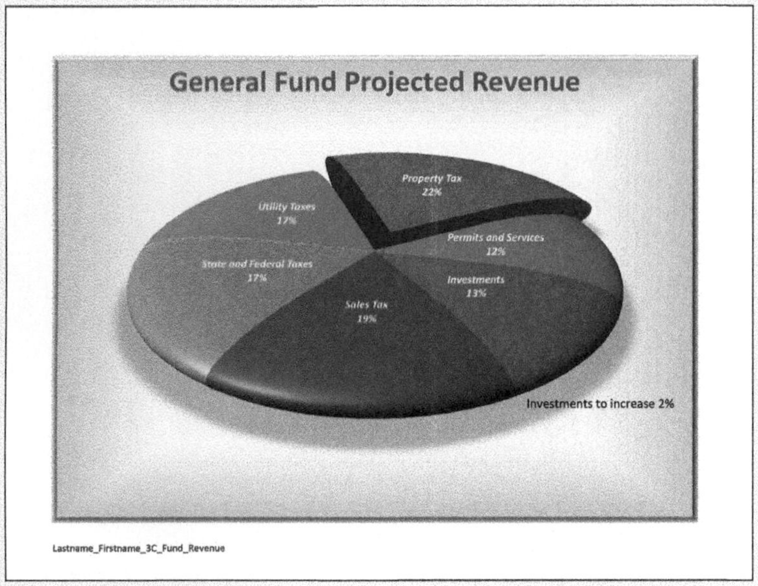

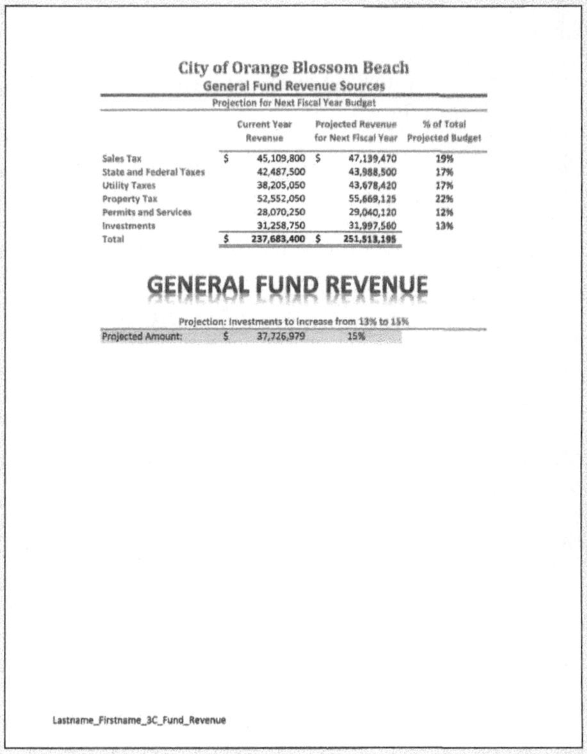

City of Orange Blossom Beach
General Fund Revenue Sources
Projection for Next Fiscal Year Budget

	Current Year Revenue	Projected Revenue for Next Fiscal Year	% of Total Projected Budget
Sales Tax	$ 45,109,800	$ 47,139,470	19%
State and Federal Taxes	42,487,500	43,988,500	17%
Utility Taxes	38,205,050	43,678,420	17%
Property Tax	52,552,050	55,669,125	22%
Permits and Services	28,070,250	29,040,120	12%
Investments	31,258,750	31,997,560	13%
Total	$ 237,683,400	$ 251,513,195	

GENERAL FUND REVENUE

Projection: Investments to increase from 13% to 15%

Projected Amount:	$ 37,726,979	15%

Lastname_Firstname_3C_Fund_Revenue

Figure 3.46

(Project 3C Fund Revenue continues on the next page)

Skills Review | Project 3C Fund Revenue (continued)

1 **Start** Excel. From your student files, open the file **e03C_Fund_Revenue. Save** the file in your **Excel Chapter 3** folder as **Lastname_Firstname_3C_Fund_Revenue**

a. Click cell **D5**, and then type = to begin a formula. Click cell **C5**, type / and then click cell **C11**. Press F4 to make the reference to the value in cell **C11** absolute. On the **Formula Bar**, click the **Enter** button, and then fill the formula down through cell **D10**.

b. With the range **D5:D10** selected, right-click over the selection, and then on Mini toolbar, click the **Percent Style** button and the **Center** button.

2 Select the nonadjacent ranges **A5:A10** and **C5:C10** to select the revenue names and the projected revenue. Click the **Insert tab**, and then in the **Charts group**, click **Pie**. Under **3-D Pie**, click the first chart—**Pie in 3-D**.

a. On the **Design tab**, in the **Location group**, click the **Move Chart** button. In the **Move Chart** dialog box, click the **New sheet** option button. In the **New sheet** box, replace the highlighted text *Chart1* by typing **Projected Revenue Chart** and then click **OK**.

b. On the **Layout tab**, in the **Labels group**, click the **Chart Title** button, and then click **Above Chart**. With the **Chart Title** box selected, type **General Fund Projected Revenue** and then press Enter to create the new chart title.

c. Point to the chart title text, and then right-click to display the Mini toolbar. Change the **Font Size** to **32** and change the **Font Color** to **Blue-Gray, Text 2**—in the fourth column, the first color.

d. Click in a white area of the chart to deselect the chart title. On the **Layout tab**, in the **Labels group**, click the **Legend** button, and then click **None**.

e. In the **Labels group**, click the **Data Labels** button, and then click **More Data Label Options**. In the **Format Data Labels** dialog box, on the left, be sure **Label Options** is selected. On the right, under **Label Contains**, click as necessary to select the **Category Name** and **Percentage** check boxes. *Clear* any other check boxes in this group. Under **Label Position**, click the **Center** option button. Click **Close**.

f. Point to any of the selected labels, right-click to display the Mini toolbar, and then change the **Font Size** to **12**, the **Font Color** to **White, Background 1, Darker 5%**, and then apply **Bold** and **Italic**.

3 3. Click in any pie slice outside of the label to select the entire pie. Click the **Format tab**, and then in the **Shape**

(Project 3C Fund Revenue continues on the next page)

Styles group, click the **Shape Effects** button. Point to **Bevel**, and then at the bottom of the gallery, click **3-D Options**.

a. In the **Format Data Series** dialog box, on the right, under **Bevel**, click the **Top** button. In the gallery, under **Bevel**, in the first row, click the first button—**Circle**. Then click the **Bottom** button, and apply the **Circle** bevel. In the four **Width** and **Height** spin boxes, type **512**

b. In the lower portion of the dialog box, under **Surface**, click the **Material** button. Under **Standard**, click the third button—**Plastic**. In the lower right corner, click the **Close** button.

c. On the **Format tab**, in the **Shape Styles group**, click **Shape Effects**, and then point to **Shadow**. Under **Perspective**, click the third button—**Below**.

d. With the pie chart still selected, point anywhere in the pie and right-click. On the displayed shortcut menu, click **Format Data Series**. In the **Format Data Series** dialog box, on the left, be sure **Series Options** is selected. On the right, click in the box under **Angle of first slice**, change *0* to type **150** to move the largest slice—*Property Tax*—to the top of the pie. Click **Close**.

e. Click in the area outside of the chart sheet to deselect all chart elements. Then, on the pie chart, click the outer edge of the **Property Tax** slice one time to select the pie chart, and then click the **Property Tax** slice again to select only that slice.

f. Point to the **Property Tax** slice, and then explode the slice by dragging it slightly away from the center of the pie.

g. With the **Property Tax** slice still selected, point to the slice and right-click. On the shortcut menu, click **Format Data Point**. In the displayed **Format Data Point** dialog box, on the left, click **Fill**. On the right, under **Fill**, click the **Solid fill** option button. Click the **Color arrow**, and then under **Theme Colors**, in the sixth column, click the fifth color—**Dark Yellow, Accent 2, Darker 25%**. Click **Close**.

4 Point to the white area just inside the border of the chart to display the ScreenTip **Chart Area**, and then click one time.

a. On the **Format tab**, in the **Shape Styles group**, click the **Shape Effects** button, point to **Bevel**, and then under **Bevel**, in the second row, click the third bevel—**Convex**.

b. With the chart area still selected, right-click in a white area at the outer edge of the chart, and then

Skills Review | Project 3C Fund Revenue (continued)

on the shortcut menu, click **Format Chart Area**. In the **Format Chart Area** dialog box, on the left, be sure that **Fill** is selected. On the right, under **Fill**, click the **Gradient fill** option button. Click the **Preset colors** arrow, and then in the third row, click the fourth preset, **Parchment**. Click the **Type arrow**, and then click **Path**. Click the **Close** button.

c. Click the **Layout tab**, and then in the **Insert group**, click the **Text Box** button. Position the pointer near the lower corner of the *Investments* slice. Hold down the left mouse button, and then drag down and to the right so that the text box extends to the end of the chart area and is approximately one-half inch high. With the insertion point blinking inside the text box, type **Investments to increase 2%** Select the text and then on the Mini toolbar, change the **Font Size** to **12**. If necessary, use the sizing handles to widen the text box so that the text displays on one line.

5 In the sheet tab area at the bottom of the workbook, click the **Sheet1 tab** to redisplay the worksheet.

a. Click the **Insert tab**, and then in the **Text group**, click the **WordArt** button.

b. In the **WordArt** gallery, in the last row, click the last style—**Fill – Red, Accent 1, Metal Bevel, Reflection**. Type **general fund revenue** and then point anywhere on the dashed border surrounding the WordArt object. Click the dashed border one time to change it to a solid border, indicating that all of the text is selected. Right-click the border to display the Mini toolbar, and then change the **Font Size** to **28**.

c. Drag to position the upper left corner of the WordArt in cell **A13**, centered below the worksheet.

6 In cell **A17**, type **Projection: Investments to Increase from 13% to 15%** and then **Merge & Center** the text across the range **A17:D17**. Apply the **Heading 3** cell style.

a. In cell **A18**, type **Projected Amount:** and press Enter. Select the range **C10:D10**, right-click over the selection, and then click **Copy**. Point to cell **B18**, right-click, and then under **Paste Options**, click the **Paste** button. Press Esc to cancel the moving border.

b. Click cell **C18**. On the **Data tab**, in the **Data Tools group**, click the **What-If Analysis** button, and then click **Goal Seek**. In the **Goal Seek** dialog box, press Tab to move to the **To value** box, and then type **15%**

c. Press Tab to move the insertion point to the **By changing cell** box, and then click cell **B18**. Click **OK**. In the displayed **Goal Seek Status** dialog box, click **OK**.

d. Select the range **A18:C18**. From the **Home tab**, display the **Cell Styles** gallery. Under **Themed Cell Styles**, apply **40% - Accent3**. Click cell **B18**, and then from the **Cell Styles** gallery, apply the **Currency [0]** cell style.

7 With your worksheet displayed, in the sheet tab area, double-click *Sheet1* to select the text, and then type **Projected Revenue Data** and press Enter.

a. On the **Insert tab**, in the **Text group**, click **Header & Footer**. In the **Navigation group**, click the **Go to Footer** button, click in the **left section** above the word *Footer*, and then in the **Header & Footer Elements group**, click the **File Name** button. Click in a cell above the footer to deselect the **Footer area** and view your file name.

b. On the **Page Layout tab**, in the **Page Setup group**, click the **Margins** button, and then at the bottom of the **Margins gallery**, click **Custom Margins**. In the **Page Setup** dialog box, under **Center on page**, select the **Horizontally** check box. Click **OK**, and then on the status bar, click the **Normal** button. Press Ctrl + Home to move to the top of your worksheet.

c. Click the **Projected Revenue Chart** sheet tab to display the chart sheet. On the **Insert tab**, click **Header & Footer**. In the center of the **Page Setup** dialog box, click **Custom Footer**. With the insertion point blinking in the **Left section**, in the row of buttons in the middle of the dialog box, locate and click the **Insert File Name** button. Click **OK** two times.

d. Right-click either of the sheet tabs, and then click **Select All Sheets**. From **Backstage** view, show the **Document Panel**. In the **Author** box, replace the existing text with your firstname and lastname. In the **Subject** box, type your course name and section number. In the **Keywords** box type **general fund, projected revenue** **Close** the **Document Information Panel**.

e. With the two sheets still grouped, press Ctrl + F2 to display the **Print Preview**, and then view the two pages of your workbook.

f. **Save** your workbook. Print or submit electronically as directed by your instructor. If required by your instructor, print or create an electronic version of your worksheets with formulas displayed by using the instructions in Activity 1.16, and then **Close** Excel without saving so that you do not save the changes you made to print formulas.

End **You have completed Project 3C**

Content-Based Assessments

Apply 3B skills from these Objectives:

- 5 Design a Worksheet for What-If Analysis
- 6 Answer What-If Questions by Changing Values in a Worksheet
- 7 Chart Data with a Line Chart

Skills Review | Project 3D Revenue Projection

In the following Skills Review, you will edit a worksheet for Jennifer Carson, City Finance Manager, which forecasts the permit revenue that the City of Orange Blossom Beach expects to collect in the next five years. Your completed worksheet will look similar to Figure 3.47.

Project Files

For Project 3D, you will need the following files:

e03D_Revenue_Projection
e03D_Shoreline

You will save your workbook as:

Lastname_Firstname_3D_Revenue_Projection

Project Results

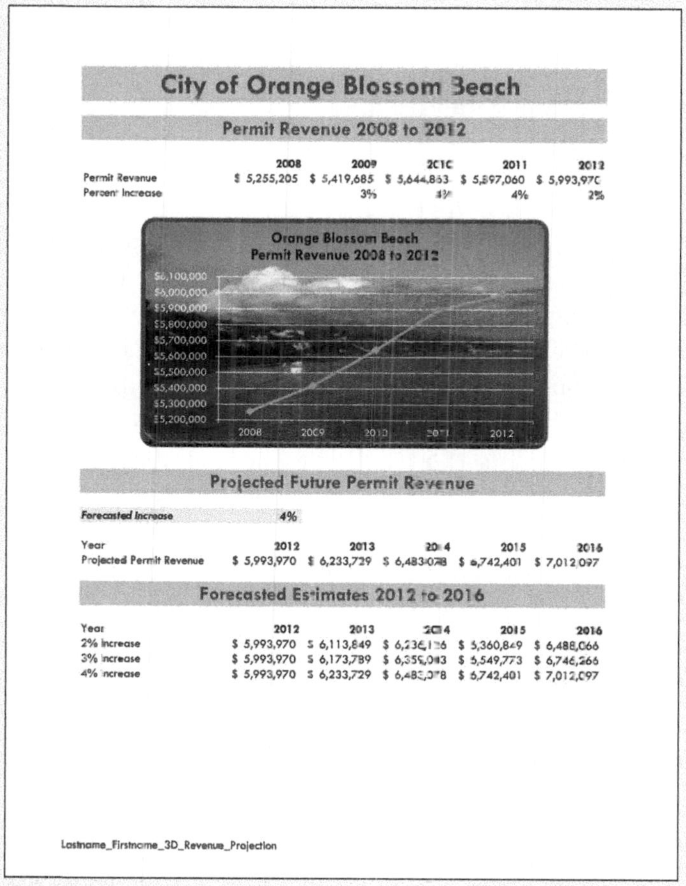

City of Orange Blossom Beach

Permit Revenue 2008 to 2012

	2008	2009	2010	2011	2012
Permit Revenue	$ 5,255,205	$ 5,419,685	$ 5,644,853	$ 5,897,060	$ 5,993,970
Percent Increase		3%	4%	4%	2%

Projected Future Permit Revenue

Forecasted Increase 4%

Year	2012	2013	2014	2015	2016
Projected Permit Revenue	$ 5,993,970	$ 6,233,729	$ 6,483,078	$ 6,742,401	$ 7,012,097

Forecasted Estimates 2012 to 2016

Year	2012	2013	2014	2015	2016
2% Increase	$ 5,993,970	$ 6,113,849	$ 6,236,136	$ 6,360,849	$ 6,488,066
3% Increase	$ 5,993,970	$ 6,173,789	$ 6,359,043	$ 6,549,773	$ 6,746,266
4% Increase	$ 5,993,970	$ 6,233,729	$ 6,483,078	$ 6,742,401	$ 7,012,097

Lastname_Firstname_3D_Revenue_Projection

Figure 3.47

(Project 3D Revenue Projection continues on the next page)

Skills Review | Project **3D** Revenue Projection (continued)

1 **Start** Excel. From your student files, open the file **e03D_Revenue_Projection. Save** the file in your **Excel Chapter 3** folder with the file name **Lastname_Firstname_3D_Revenue_Projection**

a. Click cell **C7**. Being sure to include the parentheses, type **=(c6-b6)/b6** and then on the **Formula Bar**, click the **Enter** button. In the **Number group**, click the **Percent Style** button.

b. Click cell **D7**, type **=** and then by typing, or using a combination of typing and clicking cells to reference them, construct a formula similar to the one in cell **C7** to calculate the rate of increase in population from 2009 to 2010. Format cell **D7** with the **Percent Style**. With cell **D7** selected, drag the fill handle to the right through cell **F7**.

c. In cell **A9**, type **Projected Future Permit Revenue** and then press Enter. Point to cell **A3**, and then right-click. On the Mini toolbar, click the **Format Painter** button, and then click cell **A9**. In cell **A11**, type **Forecasted Increase** and then in cell **A13**, type **Year**

d. In cell **A14**, type **Projected Permit Revenue** and then in cell **B13**, type **2012** and press Tab. In cell **C13**, type **2013** and then press Tab. Select the range **B13:C13**, and then drag the fill handle through cell **F13** to extend the pattern of years to *2016*. Apply **Bold** to the selection.

e. Click cell **B14**, type **5993970** and then from the **Cell Styles** gallery, apply the **Currency [0]** style.

f. In cell **B11**, type **2%** which is the percent of increase from 2011 to 2012, and then on the **Formula Bar**, click **Enter**. Select the range **A11:B11**, and then from the Mini toolbar, apply **Bold** and **Italic**.

2 Click cell **C14**. Type **=b14*(100%+b11)** and then on the **Formula Bar**, click the **Enter** button. With cell **C14** as the active cell, drag the fill handle to copy the formula to the range **D14:F14**.

a. Point to cell **B14**, right-click, click the **Format Painter** button, and then select the range **C14:F14**.

b. Click cell **A16**. Type **Forecasted Estimates 2012 to 2016** and then press Enter. Use **Format Painter** to copy the format from cell **A9** to cell **A16**.

c. Select the range **A11:B11**, right-click to display the Mini toolbar, click the **Fill Color button arrow**, and then under **Theme Colors**, in the first column, click the third color—**White, Background 1, Darker 15%**.

d. In the range **A18:A21**, type the following row titles:

Year

2% Increase

3% Increase

4% Increase

3 Select the range **B13:F13**, right-click over the selection, and then on the shortcut menu, click **Copy**. **Paste** the selection to the range **B18:F18**.

a. Select the range **B14:F14**, right-click over the selection, and then on the shortcut menu, click **Copy**. Point to **B19**, right-click, and then from the shortcut menu, point to **Paste Special**. Under **Paste Values**, click the second button—**Values & Number Formatting**. Press Esc to cancel the moving border,

b. Click cell **B11**. Type **3** and then press Enter. **Copy** the new values in the range **B14:F14**. Point to cell **B20** and right-click, and then point to **Paste Special**. Under **Paste Values**, click the **Values & Number Formatting** button.

c. In cell **B11**, type **4** and then press Enter. Select and copy the range **B14:F14**, and then paste the values and number formats to the range **B21:F21**. Press Esc to cancel the moving border.

4 In the **row header area**, point to **row 8** to display the pointer, and then drag down to select **rows 8:24**. Right-click over the selection, and then click **Insert** to insert the same number of blank rows as you selected. Under the selection area near cell **A25**, click the **Insert Options** button, and then click the **Clear Formatting** option button to clear any formatting from these rows.

a. Select the range **A6:F6**. On the **Insert tab**, in the **Charts group**, click the **Line** button. In the displayed gallery of line charts, in the second row, click the **Line with Markers** chart type to create the chart as an embedded chart in the worksheet.

b. Point to the border of the chart to display the pointer, and then drag the chart so that its upper left corner is positioned in cell **A9**, aligned approximately under the *r* in the word *Increase* above.

c. On the **Layout tab**, in the **Labels group**, click the **Legend** button, and then click **None**. Click the chart title one time to select it. Type **Orange Blossom Beach** and then press Enter.

(Project 3D Revenue Projection continues on the next page)

Skills Review | Project 3D Revenue Projection (continued)

d. In the chart title, click to position the insertion point following the *h* in *Beach*, and then press Enter to begin a new line. Type **Permit Revenue 2008 to 2012** Click the dashed border around the chart title to change it to a solid border, right-click the solid border, and then on the Mini toolbar, change the **Font Size** of the title to **14**.

5 With the chart selected, click the **Design tab**, and then in the **Data group**, click the **Select Data** button. On the right side of the **Select Data Source** dialog box, under **Horizontal (Category) Axis Labels**, in the right column, click the **Edit** button. If necessary, drag the title bar of the Axis Labels dialog box to the right of the chart so that it is not blocking your view of the data, and then select the years in the range **B5:F5**. Click **OK** two times to enter the years as the category labels.

a. On the **Layout tab**, in the **Axes group**, click the **Axes** button. Point to **Primary Vertical Axis**, and then click **More Primary Vertical Axis Options**. In the **Format Axis** dialog box, on the left, be sure **Axis Options** is selected. On the right, in the **Minimum** row, click the **Fixed** option button. In the box to the right, select the existing text, and then type **5200000**

b. In the **Major unit** row, click the **Fixed** option button, select the value *200000.0* in the box to the right, and then type **100000** In the lower right corner, click **Close**.

c. Click the **Format tab**, and then in the **Current Selection group**, click the **Chart Elements arrow**. From the displayed list, click **Chart Area**. Directly below the **Chart Elements** box, click the **Format Selection** button.

d. In the **Format Chart Area** dialog box, on the left, be sure that **Fill** is selected. On the right, under **Fill**, click the **Picture or texture fill** option button, and then under **Insert from**, click the **File** button. In the **Insert Picture** dialog box, navigate to your student files, and then insert the picture **e03D_Shoreline**. In the **Format Chart Area** dialog box, on the left, click **Border Color**. On the right click the **Solid line** option button, and then click the **Color arrow**. Under **Theme Colors**, in the fourth column, click the first color—**Brown, Text 2**.

e. On the left, click **Border Styles**. On the right, select the text in the **Width** box and type **4** Select the **Rounded corners** check box, and then **Close** the dialog box.

6 In the **Current Selection group**, click the **Chart Elements arrow**, on the list click **Plot Area**, and then click the **Format Selection** button. In the **Format Plot Area** dialog box, on the left, be sure that **Fill** is selected, and then on the right, click the **No fill** option button. **Close** the dialog box.

a. Click the **Chart Elements arrow**, on the list click **Vertical (Value) Axis**, and then click the **Format Selection** button. In the **Format Axis** dialog box, on the left, click **Line Color**. On the right, click the **Solid line** option button, click the **Color arrow**, and then click the first color—**White, Background 1**. **Close** the dialog box.

b. From the **Chart Elements** box, select the **Vertical (Value) Axis Major Gridlines**, and then click **Format Selection**. Change the **Line Color** to a **Solid line**, and then apply the **White, Background 1** color. **Close** the dialog box.

c. From the **Chart Elements** box, select the **Horizontal (Category) Axis**, and then click **Format Selection**. Change the **Line Color** to a **Solid line**, and then apply the **White, Background 1** color. **Close** the dialog box.

d. Point to any of the numbers on the **vertical value axis**, right-click, and then on the Mini toolbar, change the **Font Color** to **White, Background 1**. Point to any of the years on the **horizontal category axis**, right-click, and then change the **Font Color** to **White, Background 1**.

e. Click any cell to deselect the chart. Insert a **Header & Footer** with the **file name** in the **left section** of the footer, and then center the worksheet **Horizontally** on the page. Return to **Normal** view, and press Ctrl + Home. From **Backstage** view, show the **Document Panel**. In the **Author** box, replace the existing text with your firstname and lastname. In the **Subject** box, type your course name and section number. In the **Keywords** box type **permit revenue, forecast** **Close** the **Document Information Panel**.

f. **Save** your workbook. Print or submit electronically as directed by your instructor. If required by your instructor, print or create an electronic version of your worksheet with formulas displayed by using the instructions in Activity 1.16, and then **Close** Excel without saving so that you do not save the changes you made to print formulas.

End You have completed Project 3D

Apply 3A skills from these Objectives:

1. Chart Data with a Pie Chart
2. Format a Pie Chart
3. Edit a Workbook and Update a Chart
4. Use Goal Seek to Perform What-If Analysis

Mastering Excel | Project 3E Investments

In the following project, you will you will edit a worksheet for Jennifer Carson, City Finance Manager, that summarizes the investment portfolio of the City of Orange Blossom Beach. Your completed worksheets will look similar to Figure 3.48.

Project Files

For Project 3E, you will need the following file:

e03E_Investments

You will save your workbook as:

Lastname_Firstname_3E_Investments

Project Results

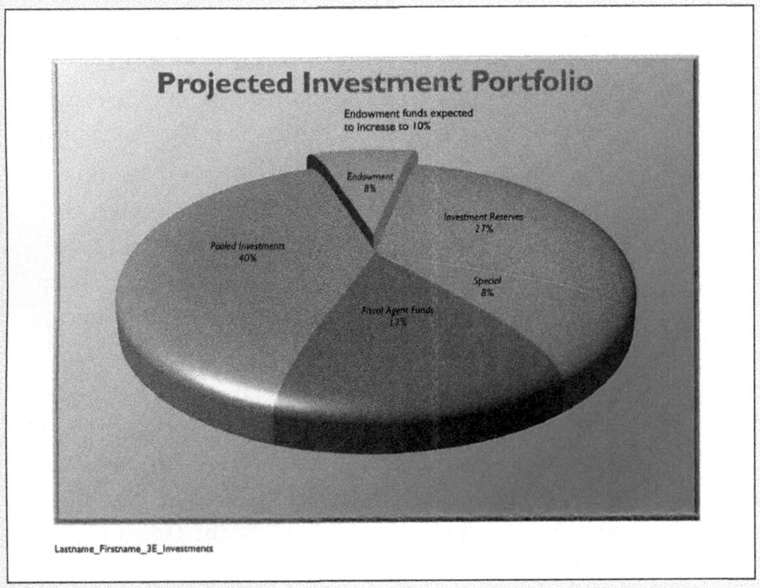

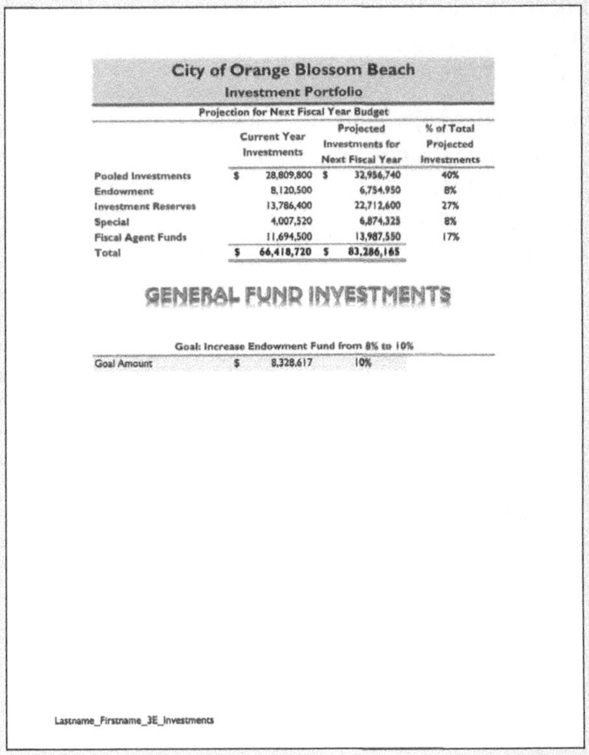

City of Orange Blossom Beach
Investment Portfolio
Projection for Next Fiscal Year Budget

	Current Year Investments	Projected Investments for Next Fiscal Year	% of Total Projected Investments
Pooled Investments	$ 28,809,800	$ 32,956,740	40%
Endowment	8,120,500	6,754,950	8%
Investment Reserves	13,786,400	22,712,600	27%
Special	4,007,520	6,874,325	8%
Fiscal Agent Funds	11,694,500	13,987,550	17%
Total	$ 66,418,720	$ 83,286,165	

GENERAL FUND INVESTMENTS

Goal: Increase Endowment Fund from 8% to 10%

Goal Amount	$ 8,328,617	10%

Lastname_Firstname_3E_Investments

Figure 3.48

(Project 3E Investments continues on the next page)

Mastering Excel | Project 3E Investments (continued)

1 **Start** Excel. From your student files, locate and open **e03E_Investments**. **Save** the file in your **Excel Chapter 3** folder as **Lastname_Firstname_3E_Investments**

2 In cells **B10** and **C10**, enter formulas to calculate totals for each column. Then, in cell **D5**, enter a formula to calculate the % of Total Projected Investments for Pooled Investments by dividing the **Projected Investments for Next Fiscal Year** for the **Pooled Investments** by the **Total Projected Investments for Next Fiscal Year**. Use absolute cell references as necessary, format the result in **Percent Style**, and **Center** the percentage. Fill the formula down through cell **D9**.

3 Select the nonadjacent ranges **A5:A9** and **C5:C9**, and then insert a **Pie in 3-D** chart. Move the chart to a **New sheet** named **Projected Investment Chart** Insert a **Chart Title** above the chart with the text **Projected Investment Portfolio** Change the chart title **Font Size** to **32** and change the **Font Color** to **Brown, Accent 6**—in the last column, the first color.

4 Remove the **Legend** from the chart, and then add **Data Labels** formatted so that only the **Category Name** and **Percentage** display positioned in the **Center**. Change the data labels **Font Size** to **11**, and then apply **Italic**.

5 Select the entire pie, display the **Shape Effects** gallery, point to **Bevel**, and then at the bottom of the gallery, click **3-D Options**. Change the **Top** and **Bottom** options to the last **Bevel** type—**Art Deco**. Set the **Top Width** and **Height** boxes to **256** and then set the **Bottom Width** and **Height** boxes to **0** Change the **Material** to the third **Standard** type—**Plastic**.

6 With the pie chart selected, display the shortcut menu, and then click **Format Data Series**. Change the **Angle of first slice** to **200** to move the *Endowment* slice to the top of the pie. Select the **Endowment** slice, and then explode the slice slightly.

7 Change the **Fill Color** of the **Pooled Investments** slice to **Gray-50%, Accent 1, Lighter 40%**. Format the **Chart Area** by applying a **Convex Bevel**. To the **Chart Area**, apply the **Moss, Preset Gradient fill**. In the **Angle** box, type **45** and then **Close** the **Format Chart Area** dialog box.

8 **Insert** a **Text Box** positioned approximately halfway between the *Endowment* pie slice and the *v* in the word *Investment* in the title. In the text box, type **Endowment funds expected to increase to 10%** Select the text and then on the Mini toolbar, change the **Font Size** to **12**. Size the text box as necessary so that the text displays on two lines as shown in Figure 3.48.

9 Display **Sheet1** and rename the sheet as **Projected Investment Data** Insert a **WordArt**—in the fifth row, insert the last WordArt style—**Fill – Gray-50%, Accent 1, Plastic Bevel, Reflection**. Type **General Fund Investments** and then change the **Font Size** to **20**. Drag to position the upper left corner of the WordArt in cell **A12**, centered below the worksheet.

10 In cell **A16**, type **Goal: Increase Endowment Fund from 8% to 10%** and then **Merge & Center** the text across the range **A16:D16**. Apply the **Heading 3** cell style. In cell **A17**, type **Goal Amount**

11 **Copy** the range **C6:D6** to cell **B17**. Click cell **C17**, and then use **Goal Seek** to determine the projected amount of endowment funds in cell **B17** if the value in **C17** is **10%**.

12 Select the range **A17:C17**, and then apply the **20% - Accent2** cell style. In **B17**, from the **Cell Styles** gallery, apply the **Currency [0]** cell style.

13 Insert a **Header & Footer** with the file name in the **left section** of the footer. In Page Layout view, check that the WordArt is centered under the worksheet data. Center the worksheet **Horizontally** on the page, and then return to **Normal** view. Display the **Projected Investment Chart** sheet and insert a **Custom Footer** with the file name in the **Left section**.

14 Group the sheets, and then display the **Document Panel**. Add your name, your course name and section, and the keywords **investment portfolio**

15 **Save** your workbook. Print or submit electronically as directed by your instructor. If required by your instructor, print or create an electronic version of your worksheets with formulas displayed by using the instructions in Activity 1.16, and then **Close** Excel without saving so that you do not save the changes you made to print formulas.

End **You have completed Project 3E**

Apply 3B skills from these Objectives:

- 5 Design a Worksheet for What-If Analysis
- 6 Answer What-If Questions by Changing Values in a Worksheet
- 7 Chart Data with a Line Chart

Mastering Excel | Project 3F Benefit Analysis

In the following project, you will edit a worksheet that Jeffrey Lovins, Human Resources Director, will use to prepare a five-year forecast of the annual cost of city employee benefits per employee. Your completed worksheet will look similar to Figure 3.49.

Project Files

For Project 3F, you will need the following file:

e03F_Benefit_Analysis

You will save your workbook as:

Lastname_Firstname_3F_Benefit_Analysis

Project Results

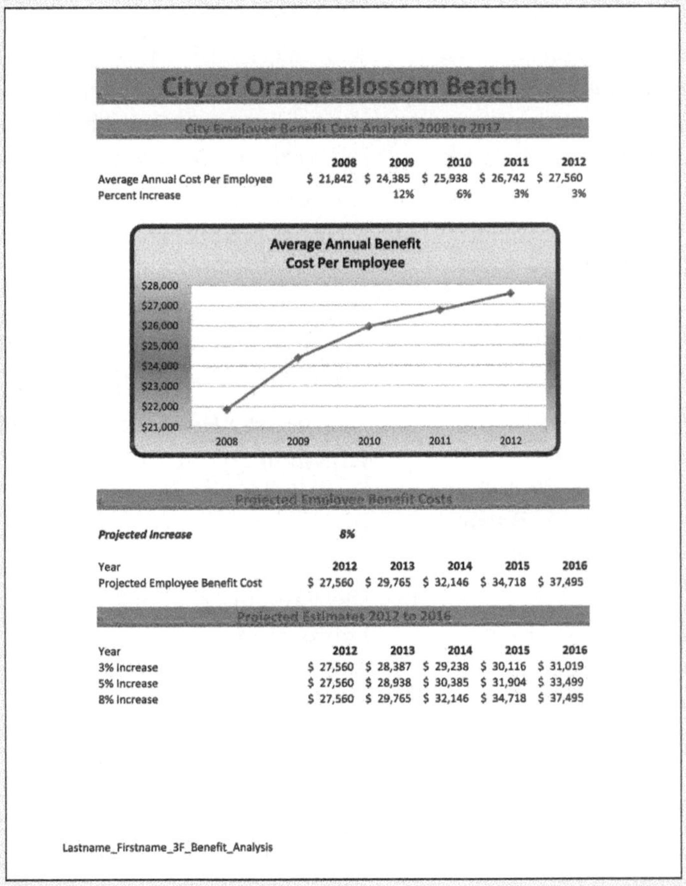

City of Orange Blossom Beach

City Employee Benefit Cost Analysis 2008 to 2012

	2008	2009	2010	2011	2012
Average Annual Cost Per Employee	$ 21,842	$ 24,385	$ 25,938	$ 26,742	$ 27,560
Percent Increase		12%	6%	3%	3%

Projected Employee Benefit Costs

Projected Increase 8%

Year	2012	2013	2014	2015	2016
Projected Employee Benefit Cost	$ 27,560	$ 29,765	$ 32,146	$ 34,718	$ 37,495

Projected Estimates 2012 to 2016

Year	2012	2013	2014	2015	2016
3% Increase	$ 27,560	$ 28,387	$ 29,238	$ 30,116	$ 31,019
5% Increase	$ 27,560	$ 28,938	$ 30,385	$ 31,904	$ 33,499
8% Increase	$ 27,560	$ 29,765	$ 32,146	$ 34,718	$ 37,495

Lastname_Firstname_3F_Benefit_Analysis

Figure 3.49

(Project 3F Benefit Analysis continues on the next page)

Mastering Excel | Project 3F Benefit Analysis (continued)

1 **Start** Excel. From your student files, open the file **e03F_Benefit_Analysis. Save** the file in your **Excel Chapter 3** folder as **Lastname_Firstname_3F_Benefit_Analysis**

2 In cell **C7**, construct a formula to calculate the percent of increase in employee annual benefit costs from 2008 to 2009. Format the result with the **Percent Style** and then fill the formula through cell **F7**.

3 In cell **A9**, type **Projected Employee Benefit Costs** and then use **Format Painter** to copy the formatting from cell **A3** to cell **A9**. In cell **A11**, type **Projected Increase** and then in cell **A13**, type **Year** In cell **A14**, type **Projected Employee Benefit Cost** and then in the range **B13:F13**, use the fill handle to enter the years 2012 through 2016. Apply **Bold** to the years. In cell **B14**, type **27560** and then from the **Cell Styles** gallery, apply the **Currency [0]** format. In cell **B11**, type **3%** which is the percent of increase from 2011 to 2012. To the range **A11:B11**, apply **Bold** and **Italic**.

4 In cell **C14**, construct a formula to calculate the annual cost of employee benefits for the year 2013 after the projected increase of 3% is applied. Fill the formula through cell **F14**, and then use **Format Painter** to copy the formatting from cell **B14** to the range **C14:F14**.

5 In cell **A16**, type **Projected Estimates 2012 to 2016** and then use **Format Painter** to copy the format from cell **A9** to cell **A16**. In cells **A18:A21**, type the following row titles:

Year
3% Increase
5% Increase
8% Increase

6 **Copy** the range **B13:F13**, and then **Paste** the selection to **B18:F18**. Copy the range **B14:F14** and then paste the **Values & Number Formatting** to the range **B19:F19**. Complete the Projected Estimates section of the worksheet by changing the *Projected Increase* in **B11** to **5%** and then to **8%** copying and pasting the **Values & Number Formatting** to the appropriate ranges in the worksheet.

7 Select **rows 8:24**, and then **Insert** the same number of blank rows as you selected. **Clear Formatting** from the inserted rows. By using the data in **A5:F6**, insert a **Line with Markers** chart in the worksheet. Move the chart so that its upper left corner is positioned in cell **A9** and centered under the data above. Remove the **Legend**, and then replace the existing chart title with the two-line title **Average Annual Benefit Cost Per Employee** The text *Cost per Employee* should display on the second line. Change the title **Font Size** to **14**.

8 Format the **Primary Vertical Axis** so that the **Minimum** is **21000** and the **Major unit** is **1000** Format the **Chart Area** with a **Gradient fill** by applying the third **Preset color** in the third row—**Wheat**. Change the **Border Color** by applying a **Solid line—Orange, Accent 1, Darker 50%**. Change the **Width** of the border to **4** and apply the **Rounded corners** option.

9 Deselect the chart, and then insert a **Header & Footer** with the file name in the **left section** of the footer; center the worksheet **Horizontally** on the page. In the **Document Panel**, add your name, your course name and section, and the keywords **employee benefits, forecast**

10 **Save** your workbook. Print or submit electronically as directed by your instructor. If required by your instructor, print or create an electronic version of your worksheets with formulas displayed by using the instructions in Activity 1.16, and then **Close** Excel without saving so that you do not save the changes you made to print formulas.

End **You have completed Project 3F**

Apply 3A and 3B skills from these Objectives:

1. Chart Data with a Pie Chart
2. Format a Pie Chart
3. Edit a Workbook and Update a Chart
4. Use Goal Seek to Perform What-If Analysis
5. Design a Worksheet for What-If Analysis
6. Answer What-If Questions by Changing Values in a Worksheet
7. Chart Data with a Line Chart

Mastering Excel | Project 3G Operations Analysis

In the following project, you will you will edit a workbook for Jennifer Carson, City Finance Manager, that summarizes the operations costs for the Public Works Department. Your completed worksheets will look similar to Figure 3.50.

Project Files

For Project 3G, you will need the following file:

e03G_Operations_Analysis

You will save your workbook as:

Lastname_Firstname_3G_Operations_Analysis

Project Results

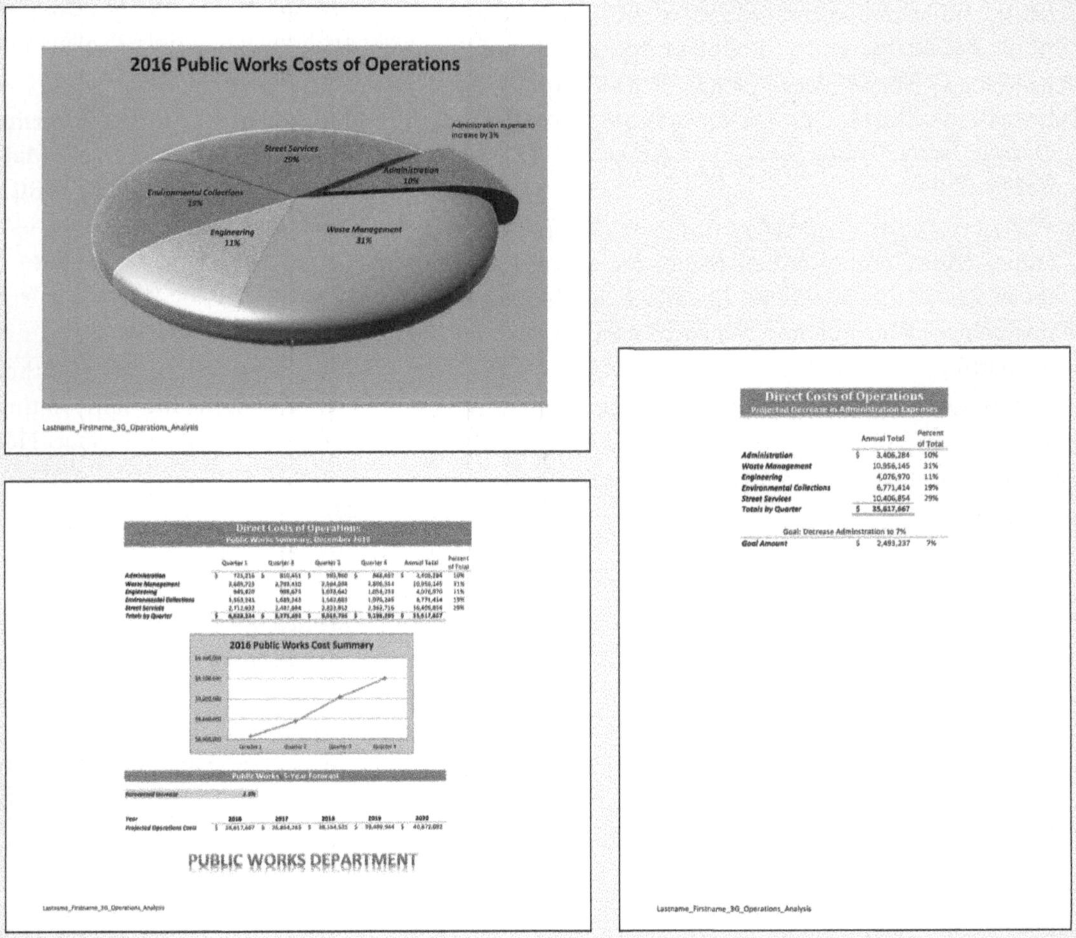

Figure 3.50

(Project 3G Operations Analysis continues on the next page)

Mastering Excel | Project 3G Operations Analysis (continued)

1 **Start** Excel. From your student files, open **e03G_Operations_Analysis. Save** the file as in your **Excel Chapter 3** folder as **Lastname_Firstname_3G_Operations_Analysis**

2 In the **Public Works** sheet, calculate totals in the ranges **F5:F9** and **B10:F10**. In cell **G5**, construct a formula to calculate the **Percent of Total** by dividing the **Annual Total** for **Administration** in cell **F5** by the **Annual Total** for all quarters in cell **F10**. Use absolute cell references as necessary, format the result in **Percent Style**, and then **Center**. Fill the formula down through cell **G9**.

3 Select the nonadjacent ranges **A5:A9** and **F5:F9**, and then insert a **Pie in 3-D** chart. Move the chart to a **New sheet** with the name **Public Works Summary Chart** Insert a **Chart Title** above the chart with the text **2016 Public Works Costs of Operations** and then change the **Font Size** to **28**.

4 Remove the **Legend** from the chart and then add **Data Labels** formatted so that only the **Category Name** and **Percentage** displays positioned in the **Center**. Change the data labels **Font Size** to **12**, and apply **Bold** and **Italic**.

5 Select the chart, and then modify the pie chart **Shape Effects** by changing the **Bevel, 3-D Options**. Change the **Top** and **Bottom** options to the first **Bevel** type—**Circle**. Set the **Top Width** and **Height** boxes to **256 pt** and then set the **Bottom Width** and **Height** boxes to **50 pt** Change the **Material** to the fourth **Standard Effect** type—**Metal**.

6 In the displayed **Format Data Series** dialog box, on the left, click **Series Options**, and then change the **Angle of first** slice to **50** Explode the **Administration** slice slightly away from the pie. Format the **Chart Area** with a **Solid fill**—**Aqua, Accent 2**—in the sixth column, the first color.

7 Insert a **Text Box** positioned outside the upper corner of the **Administration** pie slice extending to the edge of the chart area and that is about one-half inch in height. In the text box, type **Administration expense to increase by 3%** Change the **Font Size** to **10.5**. Size the text box so that the text displays on two lines. On this chart sheet, insert a **Custom Footer** with the file name in the **left section**.

8 In the **Public Works** sheet, using the data in the nonadjacent ranges **B4:E4** and **B10:E10**, insert a **Line with Markers** chart in the worksheet. Move the chart so that its upper left corner is positioned in cell **A12**, aligned approximately under the *t* in the word *Collections* above. Remove the **Legend** and then add a **Chart Title** above the chart with the text **2016 Public Works Cost Summary** Edit the **Primary Vertical Axis** so that the **Minimum** is **Fixed** at **8600000** and the **Major unit** is **Fixed** at **200000** Format the **Chart Area** with a **Solid fill** by applying **Aqua, Accent 2, Lighter 40%**—in the sixth column, the fourth color.

9 In cell **B35**, type **35617667** and then apply the **Currency [0]** cell style. In cell **C35**, construct a formula to calculate the **Projected Operations Costs** after the forecasted increase is applied. Fill the formula through cell **F35**, and then use **Format Painter** to copy the formatting from cell **B35** to the range **C35:F35**.

10 Insert a **WordArt** using the last style—**Fill - Brown, Accent 1, Metal Bevel, Reflection** Type **Public Works Department** and then change the **Font Size** to **32**. Drag to position the WordArt in cell **A38**, centered below the worksheet.

11 Change the **Orientation** to **Landscape**, and then use the **Scale to Fit** options to fit the **Height** to **1 page**. Insert a **Header & Footer** with the **file name** in the left area of the footer. In **Page Layout** view, check and adjust if necessary the visual centering of the chart and the WordArt. Center the worksheet **Horizontally** on the page, and then return to **Normal** view.

12 Display the **Projected Decrease sheet**. In cell **C5**, calculate the **Percent of Total** by dividing the *Administration Annual Total* by the *Totals by Quarter*, using absolute cell references as necessary. Apply **Percent Style** and then fill the formula from **C5:C9**.

13 **Copy** cell **B5**, and then use **Paste Special** to paste the **Values & Number Formatting** to cell **B13**. **Copy** and **Paste** cell **C5** to **C13**. With cell **C13** selected, use **Goal Seek** to determine the goal amount of administration expenses in cell **B13** if the value in **C13** is set to **7%**

14 On the **Projected Decrease** sheet, insert a **Header & Footer** with the file name in the **left section** of the footer, and then center the worksheet **Horizontally** on the page. Show the **Document Panel**. Add your name, your course name and section, and the keywords **public works**

15 **Save** your workbook. Print or submit electronically as directed by your instructor. If required by your instructor, print or create an electronic version of your worksheets with formulas displayed by using the instructions in Activity 1.16, and then **Close** Excel without saving so that you do not save the changes you made to print formulas.

End **You have completed Project 3G**

Apply a combination of the 3A and 3B skills.

GO! Fix It | Project 3H Recreation

Project Files

For Project 3H, you will need the following file:

e03H_Recreation

You will save your workbook as:

Lastname_Firstname_3H_Recreation

In this project, you will correct a worksheet that contains the annual enrollment of residents in city-sponsored recreation programs. From the student files that accompany this textbook, open the file e03H_Recreation, and then save the file in your chapter folder as **Lastname_Firstname_3H_Recreation**

To complete the project, you must find and correct errors in formulas and formatting. View each formula in the worksheet and edit as necessary. Review the format and title of the pie chart and make corrections and formatting changes as necessary. In addition to errors that you find, you should know:

- The pie chart data should include the Age Group and the Total columns.
- The Chart Area should include a blue solid fill background and the title font color should be white.
- The pie chart should be in a separate worksheet named **Enrollment Analysis Chart**

Add a footer to both sheets, and add your name, your course name and section, and the keywords **Parks and Recreation, enrollment** to the document properties. Save your file and then print or submit your worksheet electronically as directed by your instructor. If required by your instructor, print or create an electronic version of your worksheets with formulas displayed by using the instructions in Activity 1.16, and then close Excel without saving so that you do not save the changes you made to print formulas.

End **You have completed Project 3H**

Apply a combination of the 3A and 3B skills.

GO! Make It | Project 3I Tax Projection

Project Files

For Project 3I, you will need the following file:

New blank Excel workbook

You will save your workbook as:

Lastname_Firstname_3I_Tax_Projection

Start a new blank Excel workbook and create the worksheet shown in Figure 3.51. In the range C7:F7, calculate the rate of increase from the previous year. In the range C31:F31, calculate the projected property tax for each year based on the forecasted increase. Complete the worksheet by entering in the range B36:F38, the projected property tax revenue for each year based on 2%, 3%, and 4% increases. Insert the chart as shown, using the 2010 through 2014 Property Tax Revenue data. Fill the chart area with the Daybreak gradient fill and change the chart title font size to 14. Scale the width to fit to one page, and then add your name, your course name and section, and the keywords **property tax** to the document properties. Save the file in your Excel Chapter 3 folder as **Lastname_Firstname_3I_Tax_Projection** and then print or submit electronically as directed by your instructor.

Project Results

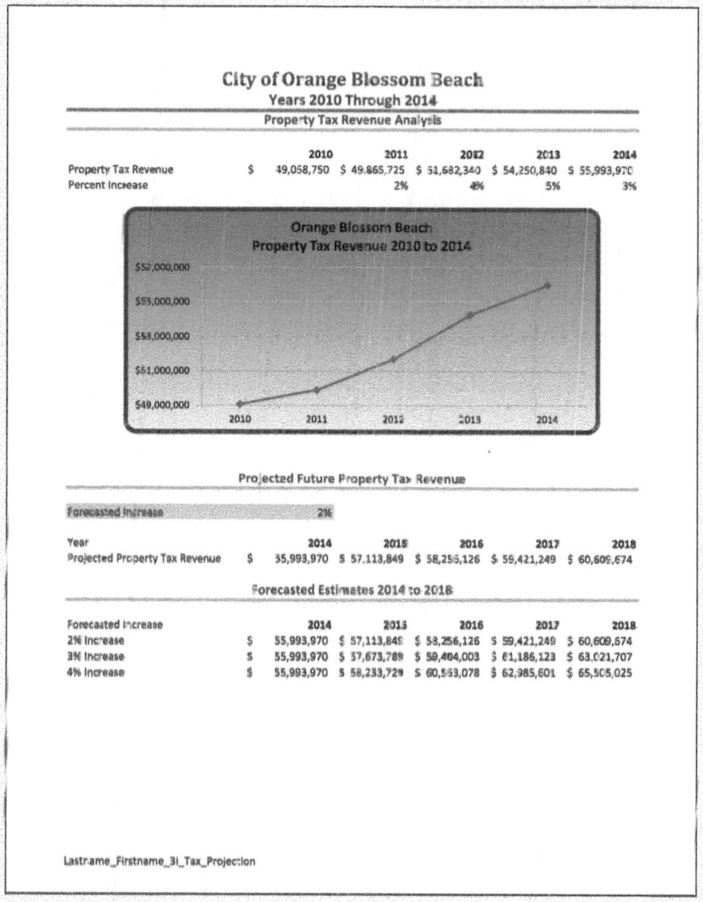

City of Orange Blossom Beach

Years 2010 Through 2014

Property Tax Revenue Analysis

		2010	2011	2012	2013	2014
Property Tax Revenue	$	49,058,750	$ 49,865,725	$ 51,682,340	$ 54,250,840	$ 55,993,970
Percent Increase			2%	4%	5%	3%

Projected Future Property Tax Revenue

Forecasted Increase		2%				
Year		2014	2015	2016	2017	2018
Projected Property Tax Revenue	$	55,993,970	$ 57,113,849	$ 58,256,126	$ 59,421,249	$ 60,609,674

Forecasted Estimates 2014 to 2018

Forecasted Increase		2014	2015	2016	2017	2018
2% Increase	$	55,993,970	$ 57,113,849	$ 58,256,126	$ 59,421,249	$ 60,609,674
3% Increase	$	55,993,970	$ 57,673,789	$ 59,404,003	$ 61,186,123	$ 63,021,707
4% Increase	$	55,993,970	$ 58,233,729	$ 60,563,078	$ 62,985,601	$ 65,505,025

Lastname_Firstname_3I_Tax_Projection

Figure 3.51

End You have completed Project 3I

Apply a combination of the 3A and 3B skills.

GO! Solve It | Project 3J Staffing

Project Files

For Project 3J, you will need the following file:

e03J_Staffing

You will save your workbook as:

Lastname_Firstname_3J_Staffing

Open the file e03J_Staffing and save it as **Lastname_Firstname_3J_Staffing** Complete the worksheet by calculating totals and the % of Total Employees. Format the worksheet attractively including appropriate number formatting. Insert a pie chart in a separate sheet that illustrates the Two-Year Projection staffing levels by department and use the techniques that you practiced in this chapter to format the chart so that it is attractive and easy to understand. Change the angle of the first slice so that the Public Safety slice displays below the title. Then, insert a text box that indicates that the increase in Public Safety staffing is contingent upon City Council approval. Include the file name in the footer, add appropriate properties, save and submit as directed.

Performance Criteria	Performance Level: Exemplary: You consistently applied the relevant skills	Proficient: You sometimes, but not always, applied the relevant skills	Developing: You rarely or never applied the relevant skills
Create formulas	All formulas are correct and are efficiently constructed.	Formulas are correct but not always constructed in the most efficient manner.	One or more formulas are missing or incorrect; or only numbers were entered.
Chart inserted and formatted	Chart was inserted and formatted properly.	Chart was inserted but incorrect data was selected or the chart was not formatted.	No chart was inserted.
Format attractively and appropriately	Formatting is attractive and appropriate.	Adequately formatted but difficult to read or unattractive.	Inadequate or no formatting.

End **You have completed Project 3J**

Apply a combination of the 3A and 3B skills.

GO! Solve It | Project 3K Water Usage

Project Files

For Project 3K, you will need the following file:

New blank Excel workbook
e03K_Beach

You will save your workbook as:

Lastname_Firstname_3K_Water_Usage

The City of Orange Blossom Beach is a growing community and the City Council has requested an analysis of future resource needs. In this project, you will create a worksheet for the Department of Water and Power that lists residential water usage over the past ten years and that forecasts the amount of water that city residents will use in the next ten years. Create a worksheet with the following data:

	2008	2010	2012	2014	2016
Water Use in Acre Feet	62500	68903	73905	76044	80342

Calculate the percent increase for the years 2010 to 2016. Below the Percent Increase, insert a line chart that illustrates the city's water usage from 2008 to 2016. Below the chart, add a section to the worksheet to calculate the projected water usage for the years 2016 to 2024 in two-year increments based on a 4% annual increase. The 2016 amount is 80,342. Format the chart and worksheet attractively with a title and subtitle, and apply appropriate formatting. If you choose to format the chart area with a picture, you can use e03K_Beach located with your student files. Include the file name in the footer and enter appropriate document properties. Save the workbook as **Lastname_Firstname_3K_Water_Usage** and submit it as directed.

Performance Criteria	Exemplary: You consistently applied the relevant skills	Proficient: You sometimes, but not always, applied the relevant skills	Developing: You rarely or never applied the relevant skills
Create formulas	All formulas are correct and are efficiently constructed.	Formulas are correct but not always constructed in the most efficient manner.	One or more formulas are missing or incorrect or only numbers were entered.
Insert and format line chart	Line chart created correctly and is attractively formatted.	Line chart was created but the data was incorrect or the chart was not appropriately formatted.	No line chart was created.
Format attractively and appropriately	Formatting is attractive and appropriate.	Adequately formatted but difficult to read or unattractive.	Inadequate or no formatting.

(Performance Level)

End You have completed Project 3K

Outcomes-Based Assessments

Rubric

The following outcomes-based assessments are *open-ended assessments*. That is, there is no specific correct result; your result will depend on your approach to the information provided. Make *Professional Quality* your goal. Use the following scoring rubric to guide you in *how* to approach the problem, and then to evaluate *how well* your approach solves the problem.

The *criteria*—Software Mastery, Content, Format and Layout, and Process—represent the knowledge and skills you have gained that you can apply to solving the problem. The *levels of performance*—Professional Quality, Approaching Professional Quality, or Needs Quality Improvements—help you and your instructor evaluate your result.

	Your completed project is of Professional Quality if you:	**Your completed project is Approaching Professional Quality if you:**	**Your completed project Needs Quality Improvements if you:**
1-Software Mastery	Choose and apply the most appropriate skills, tools, and features and identify efficient methods to solve the problem.	Choose and apply some appropriate skills, tools, and features, but not in the most efficient manner.	Choose inappropriate skills, tools, or features, or are inefficient in solving the problem.
2-Content	Construct a solution that is clear and well organized, contains content that is accurate, appropriate to the audience and purpose, and is complete. Provide a solution that contains no errors in spelling, grammar, or style.	Construct a solution in which some components are unclear, poorly organized, inconsistent, or incomplete. Misjudge the needs of the audience. Have some errors in spelling, grammar, or style, but the errors do not detract from comprehension.	Construct a solution that is unclear, incomplete, or poorly organized; contains some inaccurate or inappropriate content; and contains many errors in spelling, grammar, or style. Do not solve the problem.
3-Format and Layout	Format and arrange all elements to communicate information and ideas, clarify function, illustrate relationships, and indicate relative importance.	Apply appropriate format and layout features to some elements, but not others. Overuse features, causing minor distraction.	Apply format and layout that does not communicate information or ideas clearly. Do not use format and layout features to clarify function, illustrate relationships, or indicate relative importance. Use available features excessively, causing distraction.
4-Process	Use an organized approach that integrates planning, development, self-assessment, revision, and reflection.	Demonstrate an organized approach in some areas, but not others; or, use an insufficient process of organization throughout.	Do not use an organized approach to solve the problem.

Apply a combination of the 3A and 3B skills.

GO! Think | Project 3L School Enrollment

Project Files

For Project 3L, you will need the following file:

New blank Excel workbook

You will save your workbook as:

Lastname_Firstname_3L_School_Enrollment

Marcus Chavez, the Superintendent of Schools for the City of Orange Blossom Beach, has requested an enrollment analysis of students in the city public elementary schools in order to plan school boundary modifications resulting in more balanced enrollments. Enrollments in district elementary schools for the past two years are as follows:

School	2014 Enrollment	2015 Enrollment
Orange Blossom	795	824
Kittridge	832	952
Glenmeade	524	480
Hidden Trails	961	953
Beach Side	477	495
Sunnyvale	515	502

Create a workbook to provide Marcus with the enrollment information for each school and the total district enrollment. Insert a column to calculate the percent change from 2014 to 2015. Note that some of the results will be negative numbers. Format the percentages with two decimal places. Insert a pie chart in its own sheet that illustrates the 2015 enrollment figures for each school and format the chart attractively. Format the worksheet so that it is professional and easy to read and understand. Insert a footer with the file name and add appropriate document properties. Save the file as **Lastname_Firstname_3L_School_Enrollment** and print or submit as directed by your instructor.

End **You have completed Project 3L**

Outcomes-Based Assessments

Apply a combination of the 3A and 3B skills.

GO! Think | Project 3M Park Acreage

Project Files

For Project 3M, you will need the following files:

New blank Excel workbook
e03M_Park

You will save your workbook as:

Lastname_Firstname_3M_Park_Acreage

The City of Orange Blossom Beach wants to maintain a high ratio of parkland to residents and has established a goal of maintaining a minimum of 50 parkland acres per 1,000 residents. The following table contains the park acreage and the population, in thousands, since 1980. Start a new blank Excel workbook and then enter appropriate titles. Then, enter the following data in the worksheet and calculate the *Acres per 1,000 residents* by dividing the Park acreage by the Population in thousands.

	1980	1990	2000	2010
Population in thousands	118.4	123.9	133.5	152.6
Park acreage	5,800	6,340	8,490	9,200
Acres per 1,000 residents				

Create a line chart that displays the Park Acres Per 1,000 Residents for each year. Format the chart professionally and insert the picture e03M_Park from your student files in the chart fill area. Below the chart, create a new section titled **Park Acreage Analysis** and then copy and paste the Years and the Park acreage values to the new section. Calculate the *Percent increase* from the previous ten years for the 1990, 2000, and 2010 years. Below the Park Acreage Analysis section, create a new worksheet section titled **Park Acreage Forecast** and then enter the following values.

	2010	2020	2030	2040
Population in thousands	152.6	173.2	197.7	225.3
Park acreage necessary				
Percent increase				

Calculate the *Park acreage necessary* to reach the city's goal by multiplying the Population in thousands by 50. Then calculate the *Percent increase* from the previous ten years for the 2020, 2030, and 2040 years. Use techniques that you practiced in this chapter to format the worksheet professionally. Insert a footer with the file name and add appropriate document properties. Save the file as **Lastname_Firstname_3M_Park_Acreage** and print or submit as directed by your instructor.

End **You have completed Project 3M**

Outcomes-Based Assessments

Apply a combination of the 3A and 3B skills.

You and GO! | Project 3N Expense Analysis

Project Files

For Project 3N, you will need the following file:

New blank Excel workbook

You will save your workbook as:

Lastname_Firstname_3N_Expense_Analysis

Develop a worksheet that details the expenses you have incurred during the past two months and list the expenses for each month in separate columns. Calculate totals for each column and then add a column in which you can calculate the percent change from one month to the next. Insert and format a pie chart that illustrates the expenses that you incurred in the most recent month. After reviewing the pie chart, determine a category of expense in which you might be overspending, and then pull that slice out of the pie and insert a text box indicating how you might save money on that expense. Insert a footer with the file name and center the worksheet horizontally on the page. Save your file as **Lastname_Firstname_3N_Expense_Analysis** and submit as directed.

End You have completed Project 3N

Apply a combination of the 3A and 3B skills.

GO! Collaborate | Project 3O Bell Orchid Hotels Group Running Case

This project relates to the **Bell Orchid Hotels**. Your instructor may assign this group case project to your class. If your instructor assigns this project, he or she will provide you with information and instructions to work as part of a group. The group will apply the skills gained thus far to help the Bell Orchid Hotels achieve their business goals.

End You have completed Project 3O

Business Running Case

Razvan CHIRNOAGA/Shutterstock

This project relates to **Front Range Action Sports**, which is one of the country's largest retailers of sports gear and outdoor recreation merchandise. The company has large retail stores in Colorado, Washington, Oregon, California, and New Mexico, in addition to a growing online business. Major merchandise categories include fishing, camping, rock climbing, winter sports, action sports, water sports, team sports, racquet sports, fitness, golf, apparel, and footwear.

In this project, you will apply the skills you practiced from the Objectives in Excel Chapters 1 through 3. You will develop a workbook for Frank Osei, the Vice President of Finance, that contains year-end sales and inventory summary information. In the first two worksheets, you will summarize and chart net sales. In the next three worksheets, you will detail the ending inventory of the two largest company-owned production facilities in Seattle and Denver. Mr. Osei is particularly interested in data regarding the new line of ski equipment stocked at these two locations. In the last worksheet, you will summarize and chart annual expenses. Your completed worksheets will look similar to Figure 1.1.

Project Files

For Project BRC1, you will need the following files:

eBRC1_Annual_Report
eBRC1_Skiing

You will save your workbook as:

Lastname_Firstname_BRC1_Annual_Report

Project Results

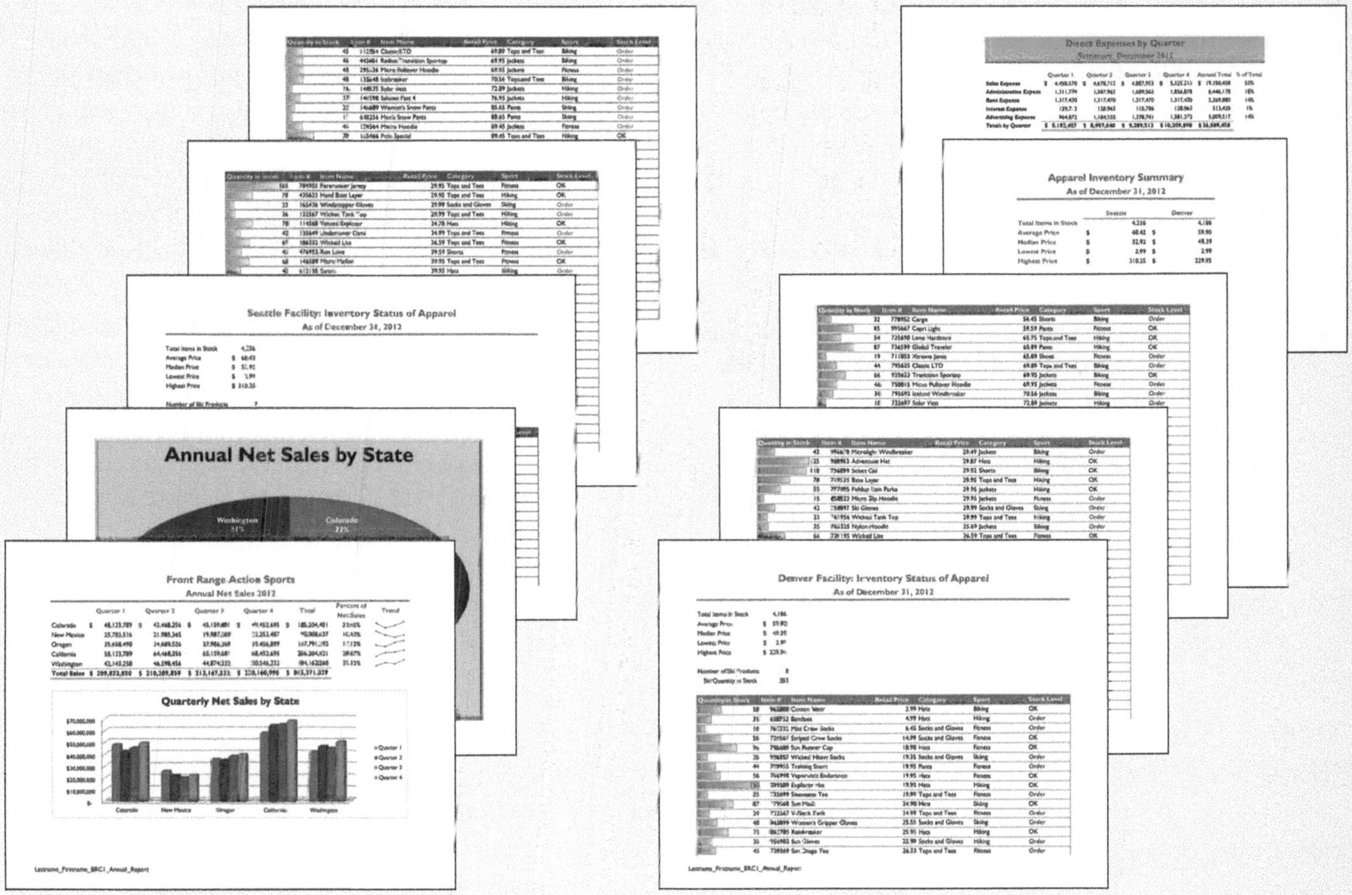

Figure 1.1

Business Running Case

Front Range Action Sports

1 **Start** Excel. From the student files that accompany this textbook, locate and open **eBRC1_Annual_Report**. In the location where you are storing your projects, create a new folder named **Front_Range_Action_Sports** or navigate to this folder if you have already created it. **Save** the new workbook as **Lastname_Firstname_BRC1_Annual_Report**

a. Familiarize yourself with the workbook by clicking each sheet tab, and then display the **Net Sales** worksheet. Click cell **B3**, and then use the fill handle to enter *Quarter 2*, *Quarter 3*, and *Quarter 4* in the range **C3:E3**. In the range **C4:E8**, enter the sales data for Quarter 2, Quarter 3, and Quarter 4 shown in **Table 1** at the bottom of the page.

b. Adjust the width of columns **B:F** to **125** pixels. Adjust the width of columns **G:H** to **100** pixels. In cell **F3**, type **Total** and then in the range **F4:F8**, calculate the annual total sales for each state. In the range **B9:F9**, calculate totals. In cell **G3**, type **Percent of Net Sales** and apply **Wrap Text** formatting to this cell. In cell **H3**, type **Trend** Using absolute cell references as necessary, in cell **G4**, construct a formula to calculate the percent that the *Colorado Total* is of the *Total Sales*. Fill the formula down through the range **G5:G8**. **Center** the results and then format the percentages with **Percent Style** and **two decimal places**.

c. Apply **Accounting Number Format** with **no decimal places** to the nonadjacent ranges **B4:F4** and **B9:F9**. Apply **Comma Style** with **no decimal** places to the range **B5:F8**. **Merge & Center** the two worksheet titles across columns **A:H**, and then to cell **A1**, apply the **Title** style and to cell **A2**, apply the **Heading 1** style. Apply the **Total** style to the range **B9:F9** and apply the **Heading 4** style to the range **B3:H3**. **Center** the column headings in **B3:H3** both horizontally and vertically.

d. In the range **H4:H8**, insert **Line** sparklines to represent the trend of each state across the four quarters. Add **Markers** and apply **Sparkline Style Accent 2 (no dark or light)**.

e. Select the range **A3:E8**, and then insert a **3-D Clustered Column** chart. Align the upper left corner of the chart inside the upper left corner of cell **A11**, and then size the chart so that its lower right corner is slightly inside cell **H24**. Apply chart **Style 26** and chart **Layout 1.** Replace the chart title text with **Quarterly Net Sales by State** Insert the file name in the **left section** of the footer, set the orientation to **Landscape**, and center the worksheet horizontally. Return to **Normal** view.

2 To show the percent that each state contributes to the total sales, select the nonadjacent ranges that represent the state names and state totals. Insert a **Pie in 3-D** chart and move the chart to a **New sheet.** Name the sheet **Net Sales by State** and then move the sheet so that it is the second sheet in the workbook.

a. Insert a **Chart Title** above the chart with the text **Annual Net Sales by State** Change the chart title **Font Size** to **36**. Remove the **Legend** from the chart, and then add **Data Labels** that display only the **Category Name** and **Percentage** positioned in the **Center**. Change the data labels **Font Size** to **14**, and then apply **Bold** and **Italic**. Change the **Font Color** to **White, Background 1**.

b. Select the entire pie, display the **Shape Effects** gallery, point to **Bevel**, and then at the bottom of the gallery, click **3-D Options**. Change the **Top** and **Bottom** options to the first **Bevel** type—**Circle**. Set all of the **Width** and **Height** boxes to **512** and then change the **Material** to the third **Standard** type—**Plastic**.

c. Format the **Chart Area** by applying a **Convex Bevel** and a **Solid fill—Dark Green, Accent 4, Lighter 60%**. Insert a **Custom Footer** with the **File Name** in the **left section**, and then **Save** the workbook.

Table 1

	Quarter 1	Quarter 2	Quarter 3	Quarter 4
Colorado	48123789	**42468256**	**45159681**	**49452695**
New Mexico	25783516	**21985365**	**19987269**	**22252487**
Oregon	35658498	**34689526**	**37986369**	**39456899**
California	58123789	**64468256**	**65159681**	**68452695**
Washington	42143258	**46598456**	**44874332**	**50546222**

---> (Return to Step 1-b)

(Business Running Case: Front Range Action Sports continues on the next page)

Front Range Action Sports (continued)

3 Display the **Seattle Inventory** worksheet, and then in cell **B4**, construct a formula to calculate the *Total Items in Stock* by summing the **Quantity in Stock** column. Format the result with **Comma Style** and **no decimal places**.

a. In cell **B5**, construct a formula to calculate the average of the **Retail Price** column. In the range **B6:B8**, construct similar formulas to calculate the median, lowest, and highest retail prices. Format the results in **B5:B8** with **Accounting Number Format**. In cell **B10**, use the **COUNTIF** function to count the number of **Skiing** items that the Seattle location stocks.

b. In cell **G14**, enter an **IF** function to determine the items that must be ordered. If the **Quantity in Stock** is less than **50** then **Value_if_true** is **Order** Otherwise the **Value_if_false** is **OK** Fill the formula down through cell **G87**. Apply **Conditional Formatting** to the **Stock Level** column so that cells that contain the text *Order* are formatted with **Bold Italic** and with a **Font Color** of **Orange, Accent 1**. Apply **Orange Gradient Fill Data Bars** to the **Quantity in Stock** column.

c. Insert a table with headers using the range **A13:G87**. Apply **Table Style Light 11**. **Sort** the table from smallest to largest on the **Retail Price** column, and then filter the table on the **Sport** column to display the **Skiing** types. Display a **Total Row** in the table, and then in cell **A88**, **Sum** the **Quantity in Stock** for the **Skiing** items. Type the result in cell **B11**. Remove the total row from the table, clear the **Sport** filter so that all of the data displays, and then convert the table to a range.

d. Change the **Print Titles** option so that **row 13** prints at the top of each page. Insert the file name in the **left section** of the footer, set the orientation to **Landscape**, and center the worksheet horizontally. Return to **Normal** view.

4 Display the **Denver Inventory** worksheet, and then in cell **B4**, construct a formula to calculate the *Total Items in Stock* by summing the **Quantity in Stock** column. Format the result with **Comma Style** and **no decimal places**.

a. In the range **B5:B8**, use the appropriate statistical functions to calculate the price data. Format the results with **Accounting Number Format**. In cell **B10**, use the **COUNTIF** function to count the number of **Skiing** items that the Denver location stocks.

b. In cell **G14**, enter an **IF** function to determine the items that must be ordered. If the **Quantity in Stock** is less than **50** **Value_if_true** is **Order** Otherwise the **Value_if_false** is **OK** Fill the formula down through cell **G87**. Apply **Conditional Formatting** to the **Stock Level** column so that cells that contain the text *Order* are formatted with **Bold Italic** and with a **Font Color** of **Dark Blue, Accent 3**. Apply **Light Blue Gradient Fill Data Bars** to the **Quantity in Stock** column.

c. Create a table with headers using the range **A13:G87**. Apply **Table Style Light 9**. **Sort** the table from smallest to largest on the **Retail Price** column, and then filter the table on the **Sport** column to display the **Skiing** types. Display a **Total Row** in the table and then in cell **A88**, **Sum** the **Quantity in Stock** for the **Skiing** items. Type the result in cell **B11**. Remove the total row from the table, clear the **Sport** filter so that all of the data displays, and then convert the table to a range.

d. Change the **Print Titles** option so that **row 13** prints at the top of each page. Insert the file name in the **left section** of the footer, set the orientation to **Landscape**, and center the worksheet horizontally. Return to **Normal** view.

e. Display the **Inventory Summary** sheet. In cell **B5**, enter a formula that references cell **B4** in the **Seattle Inventory** sheet so that the Seattle *Total Items in Stock* displays in **B5**. Create similar formulas to enter the **Average Price, Median Price, Lowest Price,** and **Highest Price** in the range **B6:B9**. Enter similar formulas in the range **C5:C9** so that the **Denver** totals display. Be sure the range **B6:C9** is formatted with **Accounting Number Format**. Insert the file name in the **left section** of the footer, set the orientation to **Portrait**, and center the worksheet horizontally. Return to **Normal** view. **Save** the workbook.

5 Display the **Annual Expenses** worksheet. Construct formulas to calculate the *Totals by Quarter* in the range **B10:E10** and the *Annual Totals* in the range **F5:F10**.

a. Using absolute cell references as necessary, in cell **G5**, construct a formula to calculate the *% of Total* by dividing the **Sales Expense Annual Total** by the **Annual Totals by Quarter**. Apply **Percent Style**, fill the formula down through the range **G6:G9**, and **Center** the percentages.

(Business Running Case: Front Range Action Sports continues on the next page)

Front Range Action Sports (continued)

b. Apply appropriate financial formatting to the data using no decimal places, and apply the **Total** cell style to the *Totals by Quarter*. **Center** the column headings and apply the **Heading 4** cell style.

c. **Merge & Center** the worksheet title and subtitle across columns **A:G**, and then to cell **A1**, apply the **Title** style and to cell **A2**, apply the **Heading 1** style. To the range **A1:A2**, apply a **Fill Color** using **Dark Blue, Accent 3, Lighter 60%**.

d. Using the data in the nonadjacent ranges **B4:E4** and **B10:E10**, insert a **Line with Markers** chart. Position the upper left corner of the chart slightly inside cell **B12** and resize the chart so that the lower right corner is inside cell **F25**. Remove the **Legend** and then add a **Chart Title** above the chart with the text **2012 Direct Expenses**

e. Apply chart **Style 13**, and then format the **Chart Area** with the picture **eBRC1_Skiing** from your student files. Format the **Plot Area** by changing the **Fill** option to **No fill**. Edit the **Vertical (Value) Axis** so that the **Minimum** is **8000000** and the **Major unit** is **1000000**

6 Use **Format Painter** to copy the formatting from cell **A2** to **A27**. In cell **B32**, enter a formula that references the value in cell **F10**.

a. Using absolute cell references as necessary, in cell **C32**, construct a formula to calculate the projected expenses for 2013 after the *Forecasted increase* in cell **B29** is applied. Fill the formula through cell **F32**. If necessary, use Format Painter to copy the format in cell B32 to the remaining cells in the row.

b. On the **Page Layout tab**, in the **Scale to Fit group**, set both the **Width** and **Height** to scale to **1 page**. Insert the file name in the **left section** of the footer, set the orientation to **Landscape**, and center the worksheet horizontally. Return to **Normal** view. Display the **Document Properties**. Add your name, your course name and section, and the keywords **annual report**

c. **Save** your workbook. Select all the sheets, and then display and check the Print Preview. There are a total of 10 pages. Print or submit electronically as directed. If required by your instructor, print or create an electronic version of your worksheets with formulas displayed by using the instructions in Activity 1.16, and then **Close** Excel without saving so that you do not save the changes you made to print formulas.

End **You have completed Business Running Case 1**

Getting Started with Microsoft Office PowerPoint

OUTCOMES

At the end of this chapter you will be able to:

OBJECTIVES

Mastering these objectives will enable you to:

PROJECT 1A
Create a new PowerPoint presentation.

1. Create a New Presentation (p. 623)
2. Edit a Presentation in Normal View (p. 627)
3. Add Pictures to a Presentation (p. 634)
4. Print and View a Presentation (p. 637)

PROJECT 1B
Edit and format a PowerPoint presentation.

5. Edit an Existing Presentation (p. 643)
6. Format a Presentation (p. 647)
7. Use Slide Sorter View (p. 650)
8. Apply Slide Transitions (p. 653)

In This Chapter

In this chapter you will study presentation skills, which are among the most important skills you will learn. Good presentation skills enhance your communications—written, electronic, and interpersonal. In this technology-enhanced world, communicating ideas clearly and concisely is a critical personal skill. Microsoft PowerPoint 2010 is presentation software with which you create electronic slide presentations. Use PowerPoint to present information to your audience effectively. You can start with a new, blank presentation and add content, pictures, and themes, or you can collaborate with colleagues by inserting slides that have been saved in other presentations.

The projects in this chapter relate to **Lehua Hawaiian Adventures**. Named for the small, crescent-shaped island that is noted for its snorkeling and scuba diving, Lehua Hawaiian Adventures offers exciting but affordable adventure tours. Hiking tours go off the beaten path to amazing remote places on the islands. If you prefer to ride into the heart of Hawaii, try the cycling tours. Lehua Hawaiian Adventures also offers Jeep tours. Whatever you prefer—mountain, sea, volcano—our tour guides are experts in the history, geography, culture, and flora and fauna of Hawaii.

Project 1A Company Overview

myitlab
Project 1A Training

Project Activities

In Activities 1.01 through 1.13, you will create the first four slides of a new presentation that Lehua Hawaiian Adventures tour manager Carl Kawaoka is developing to introduce the tour services that the company offers. Your completed presentation will look similar to Figure 1.1.

Project Files

For Project 1A, you will need the following files:

New blank PowerPoint presentation
p01A_Helicopter
p01A_Beach

You will save your presentation as:

Lastname_Firstname_1A_LHA_Overview

Project Results

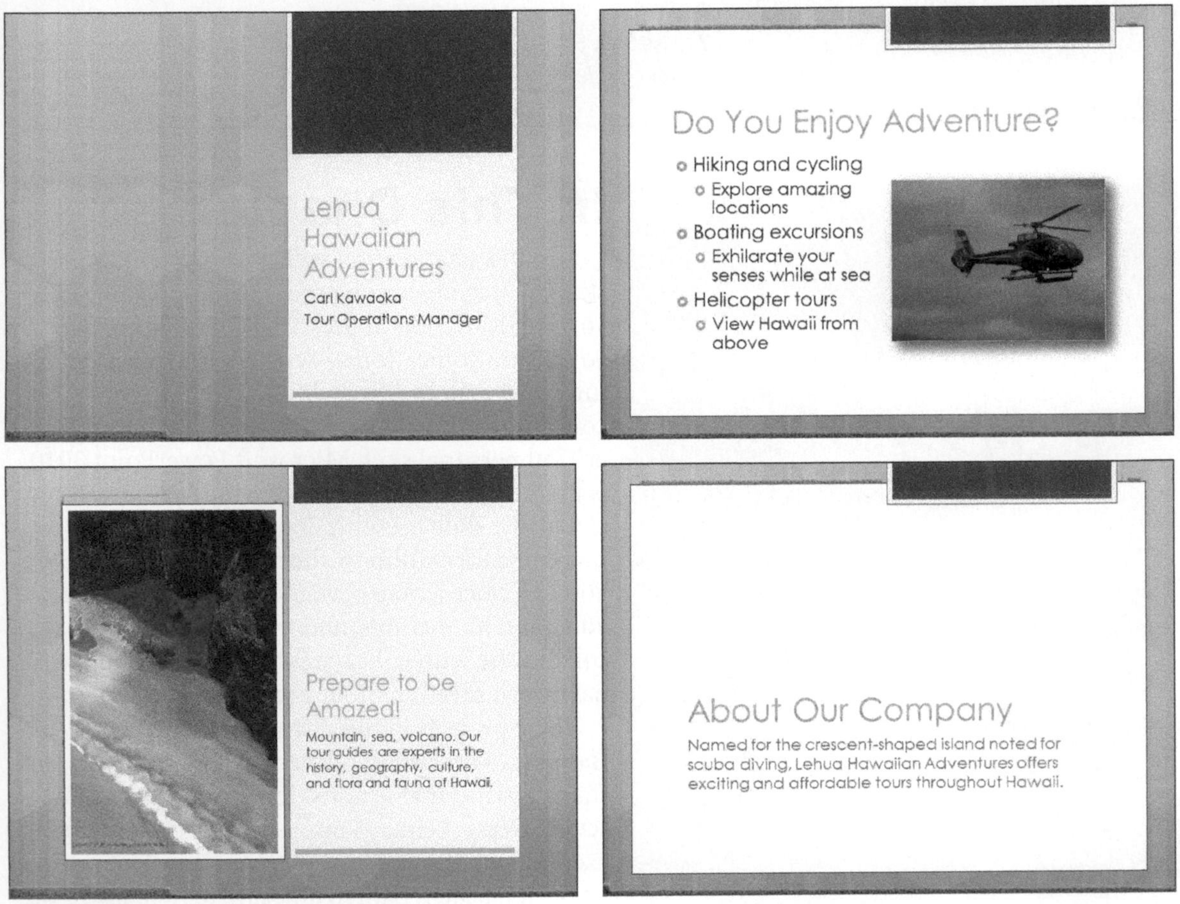

Figure 1.1
Project 1A LHA Overview

Objective 1 | Create a New Presentation

Microsoft PowerPoint 2010 is software with which you can present information to your audience effectively. You can edit and format a blank presentation by adding text, a presentation theme, and pictures.

Activity 1.01 | Identifying Parts of the PowerPoint Window

In this activity, you will start PowerPoint and identify the parts of the PowerPoint window.

1 **Start** PowerPoint to display a new blank presentation in Normal view, and then compare your screen with Figure 1.2.

Normal view is the primary editing view in PowerPoint where you write and design your presentations. Normal view includes the Notes pane, the Slide pane, and the Slides/ Outline pane.

Figure 1.2

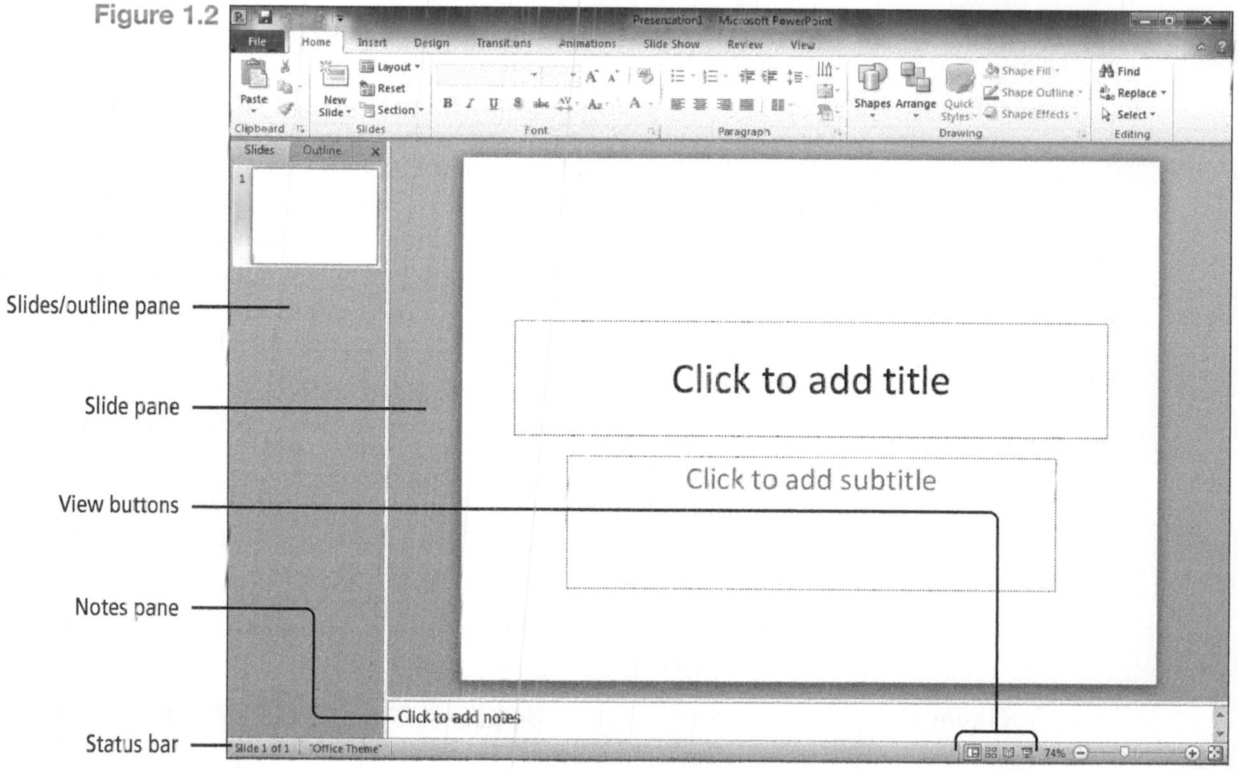

2 Take a moment to study the parts of the PowerPoint window described in the table in Figure 1.3.

Microsoft PowerPoint Screen Elements

Screen Element	Description
Notes pane	Displays below the Slide pane and provides space for you to type notes regarding the active slide.
Slide pane	Displays a large image of the active slide.
Slides/Outline pane	Displays either the presentation in the form of miniature images called ***thumbnails*** (Slides tab) or the presentation outline (Outline tab).
Status bar	Displays, in a horizontal bar at the bottom of the presentation window, the current slide number, number of slides in a presentation, theme, View buttons, Zoom slider, and Fit slide to current window button; you can customize this area to include additional helpful information.
View buttons	Control the look of the presentation window with a set of commands.

Figure 1.3

Activity 1.02 | Entering Presentation Text and Saving a Presentation

On startup, PowerPoint displays a new blank presentation with a single ***slide***—a ***title slide*** in Normal view. A presentation slide—similar to a page in a document—can contain text, pictures, tables, charts, and other multimedia or graphic objects. The title slide is the first slide in a presentation and provides an introduction to the presentation topic.

1. In the **Slide pane**, click in the text *Click to add title*, which is the title ***placeholder***.

   A placeholder is a box on a slide with dotted or dashed borders that holds title and body text or other content such as charts, tables, and pictures. This slide contains two placeholders, one for the title and one for the subtitle.

2. Type **Lehua Hawaiian Adventures** point to *Lehua*, and then right-click. On the shortcut menu, click **Ignore All** so *Lehua* is not flagged as a spelling error in this presentation. Compare your screen with Figure 1.4.

   Recall that a red wavy underline indicates that the underlined word is not in the Microsoft Office dictionary.

Figure 1.4

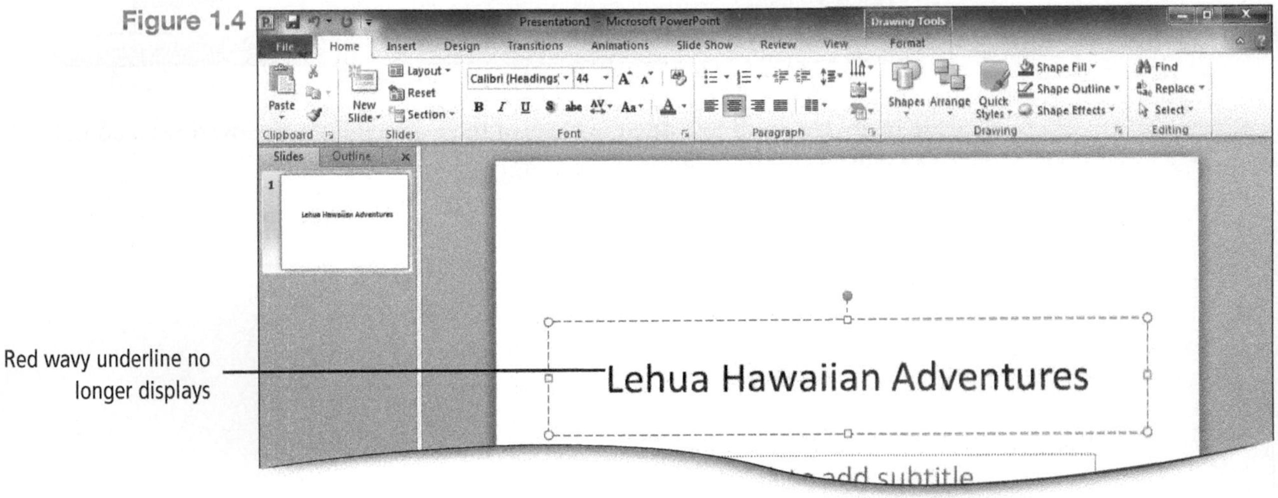

3 Click in the subtitle placeholder, and then type **Carl Kawaoka**

4 Press Enter to create a new line in the subtitle placeholder. Type **Tour Manager**

5 Right-click **Kawaoka**, and then on the shortcut menu, click **Ignore All**. Compare your screen with Figure 1.5.

Figure 1.5

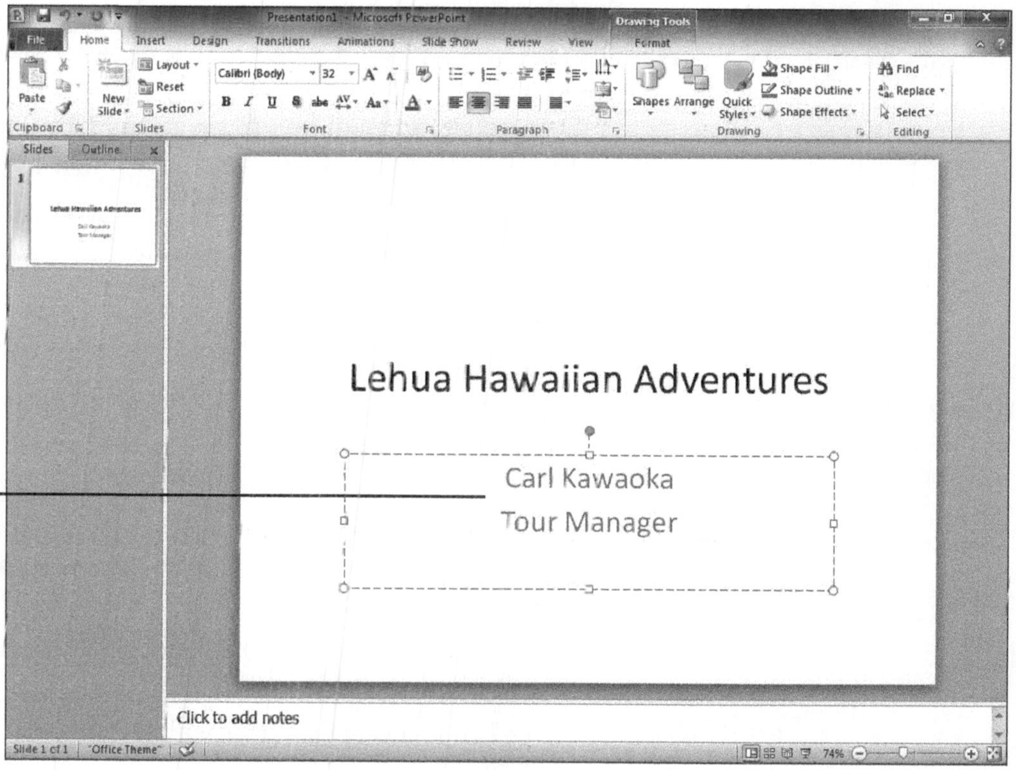

Text typed in subtitle placeholder

6 In the upper left corner of your screen, click the **File tab** to display **Backstage** view, click **Save As**, and then in the **Save As** dialog box, navigate to the location where you will store your files for this chapter. Create a new folder named **PowerPoint Chapter 1** In the **File name** box, replace the existing text with **Lastname_Firstname_1A_LHA_Overview** and then click **Save**.

Activity 1.03 | Applying a Presentation Theme

A ***theme*** is a set of unified design elements that provides a look for your presentation by applying colors, fonts, and effects.

1. On the Ribbon, click the **Design tab**. In the **Themes group**, click the **More** button [More button icon] to display the **Themes** gallery. Compare your screen with Figure 1.6.

Figure 1.6

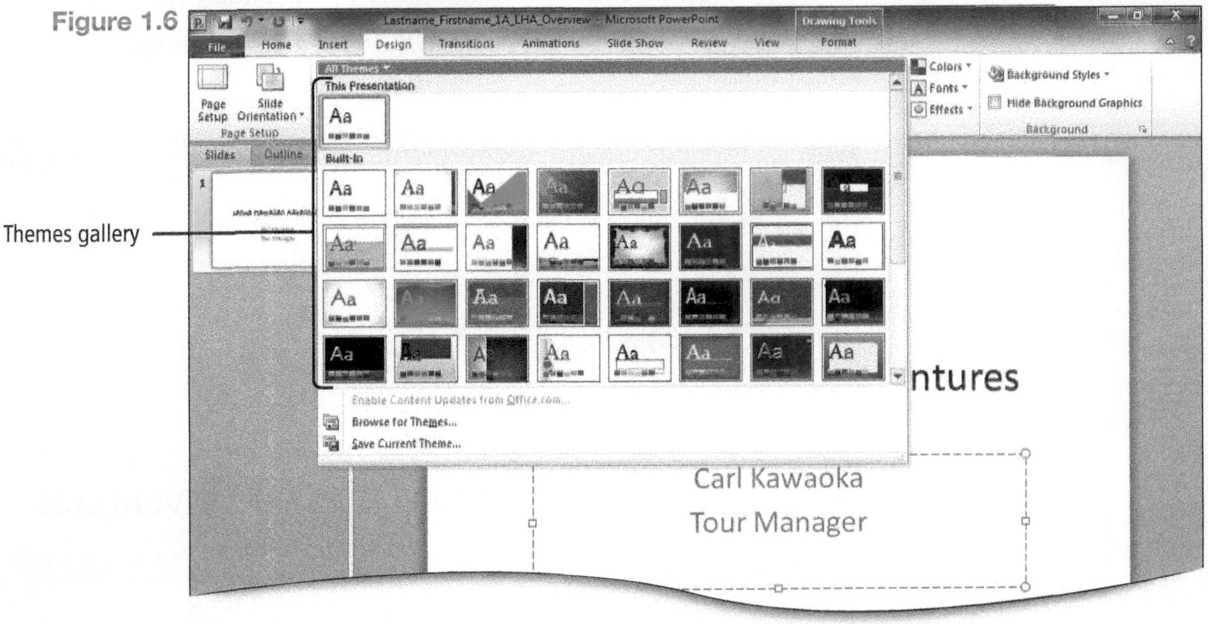

2. Under **Built-In**, point to several of the themes and notice that a ScreenTip displays the name of each theme and the Live Preview feature displays how each theme would look if applied to your presentation.

   The first theme that displays is the Office theme. Subsequent themes are arranged alphabetically.

3. Use the ScreenTips to locate the theme with the green background—**Austin**—as shown in Figure 1.7.

Figure 1.7

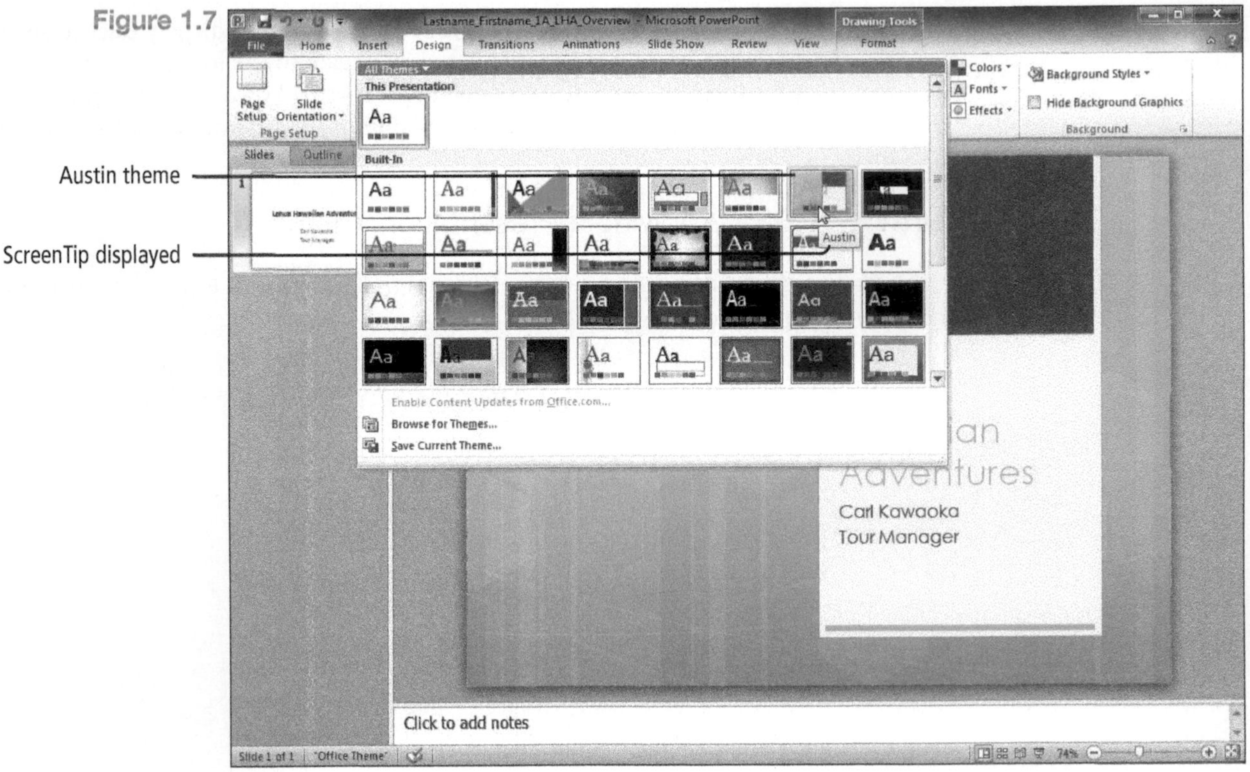

4. Click the **Austin** theme to change the presentation theme and then **Save** [Save icon] your presentation.

Objective 2 | Edit a Presentation in Normal View

Editing is the process of modifying a presentation by adding and deleting slides or by changing the contents of individual slides.

Activity 1.04 | Inserting a New Slide

To insert a new slide in a presentation, display the slide that will precede the slide that you want to insert.

1 On the **Home tab**, in the **Slides group**, point to the **New Slide** button. Compare your screen with Figure 1.8.

The New Slide button is a split button. Recall that clicking the main part of a split button performs a command and clicking the arrow opens a menu, list, or gallery. The upper, main part of the New Slide button, when clicked, inserts a slide without displaying any options. The lower part—the New Slide button arrow—when clicked, displays a gallery of slide ***layouts***. A layout is the arrangement of elements, such as title and subtitle text, lists, pictures, tables, charts, shapes, and movies, on a slide.

Figure 1.8

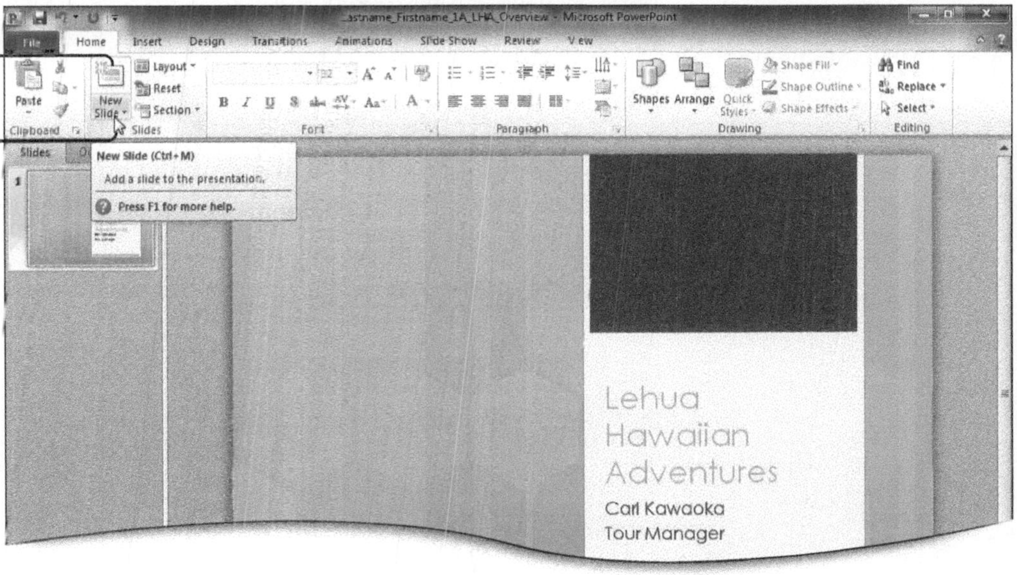

2 In the **Slides group**, click the lower portion of the New Slide button—the **New Slide button arrow**—to display the gallery, and then compare your screen with Figure 1.9.

PowerPoint | Chapter 1

Figure 1.9

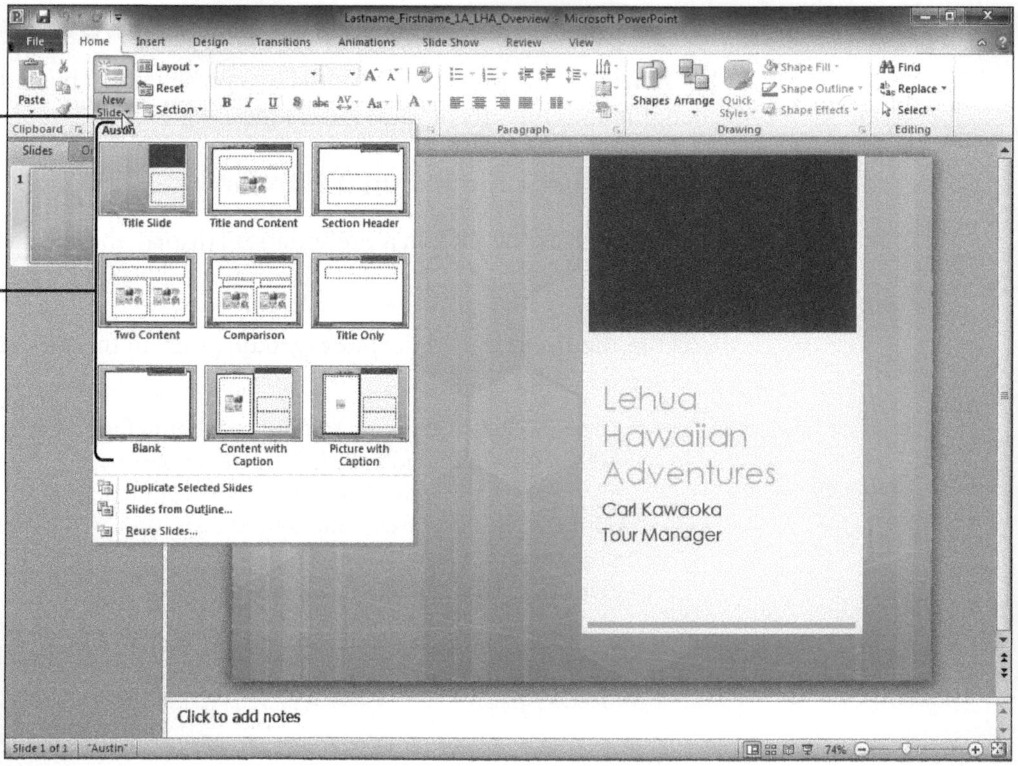

3 In the gallery, click the **Two Content** layout to insert a new slide. Notice that the new blank slide displays in the **Slide pane** and in the **Slides/Outline pane**. Compare your screen with Figure 1.10.

Figure 1.10

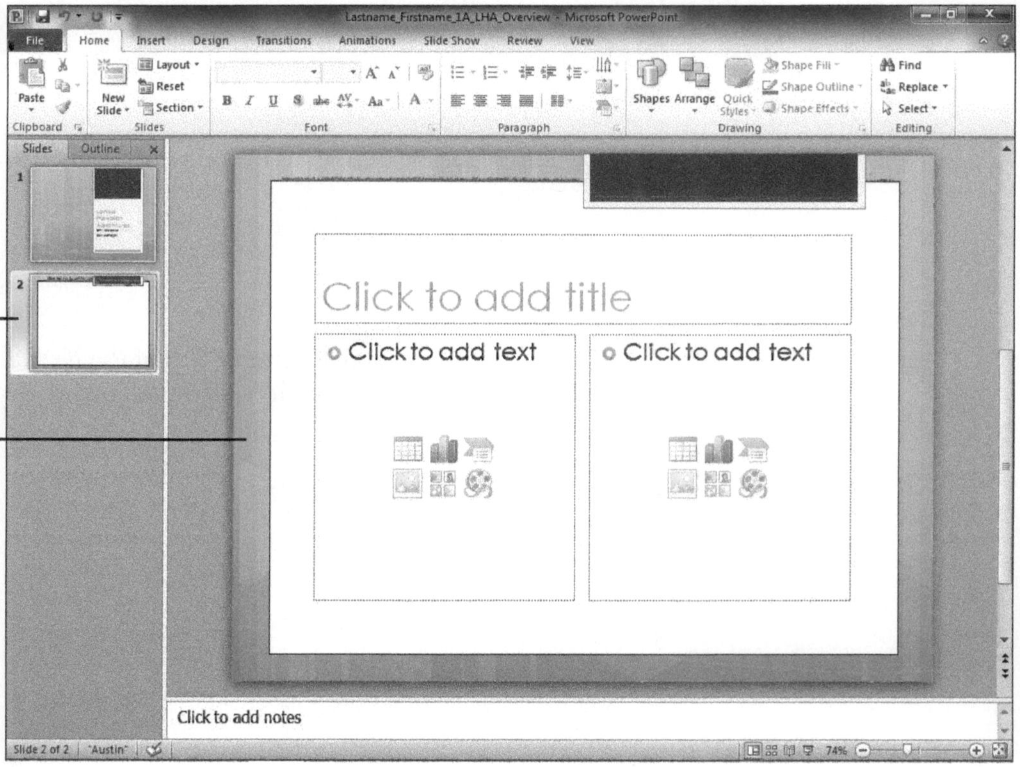

4 In the **Slide pane**, click the text *Click to add title*, and then type **Do You Enjoy Adventure?**

5 On the left side of the slide, click anywhere in the content placeholder. Type **Hiking and cycling** and then press Enter.

6 Type **Explore locations** and then compare your screen with Figure 1.11.

Figure 1.11

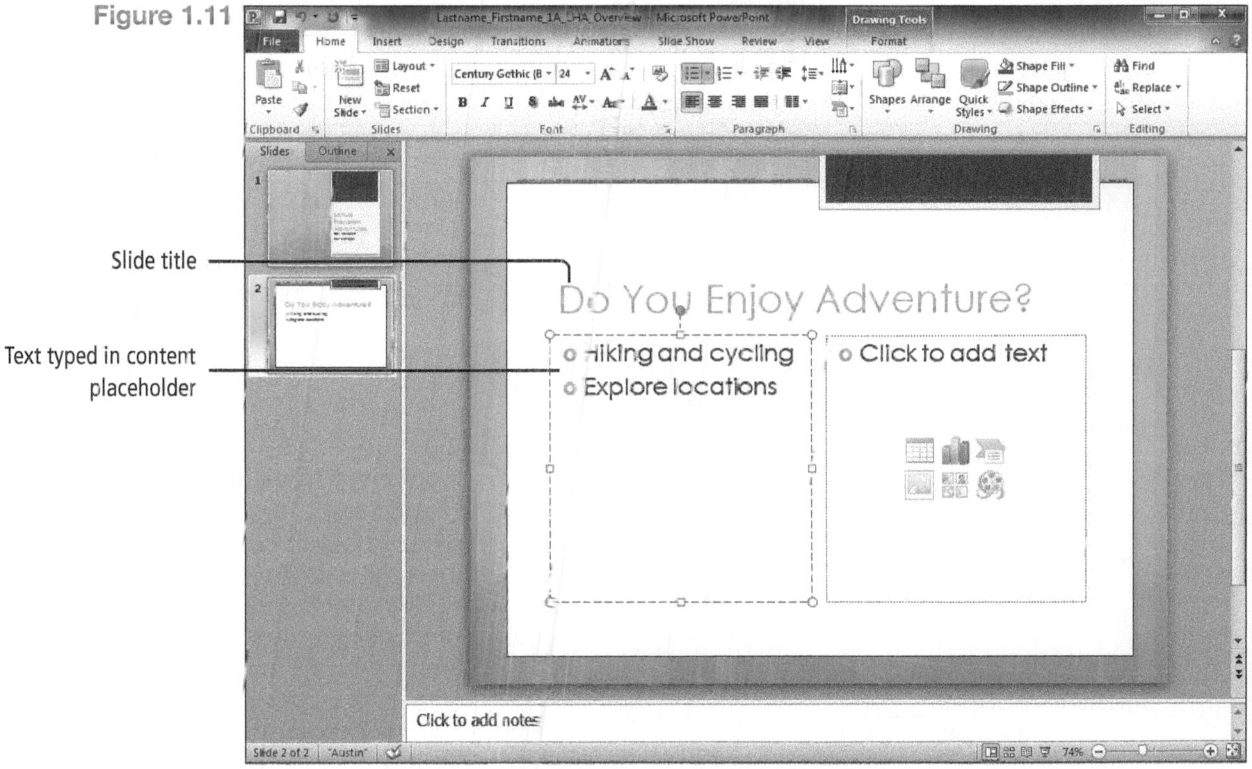

7 **Save** your presentation.

Activity 1.05 | Increasing and Decreasing List Levels

Text in a PowerPoint presentation is organized according to ***list levels***. List levels, each represented by a bullet symbol, are similar to outline levels. On a slide, list levels are identified by the bullet style, indentation, and the size of the text.

The first level on an individual slide is the title. Increasing the list level of a bullet point increases its indent and results in a smaller text size. Decreasing the list level of a bullet point decreases its indent and results in a larger text size.

1 On **Slide 2**, if necessary, click at the end of the last bullet point after the word *locations*, and then press Enter to insert a new bullet point.

2 Type **Boating excursions** and then press Enter.

3 Press Tab, and then notice that the green bullet is indented. Type **Exhilarate your senses while at sea**

By pressing Tab at the beginning of a bullet point, you can increase the list level and indent the bullet point.

PowerPoint | Chapter 1

4 Press Enter. Notice that a new bullet point displays at the same level as the previous bullet point. Then, on the **Home tab**, in the **Paragraph group**, click the **Decrease List Level** button. Type **Helicopter tours** and then compare your screen with Figure 1.12.

The Decrease List Level button promotes the bullet point. The text size increases and the text is no longer indented.

Figure 1.12

Decrease List Level button

List level of bullet point increased

List level of bullet point decreased

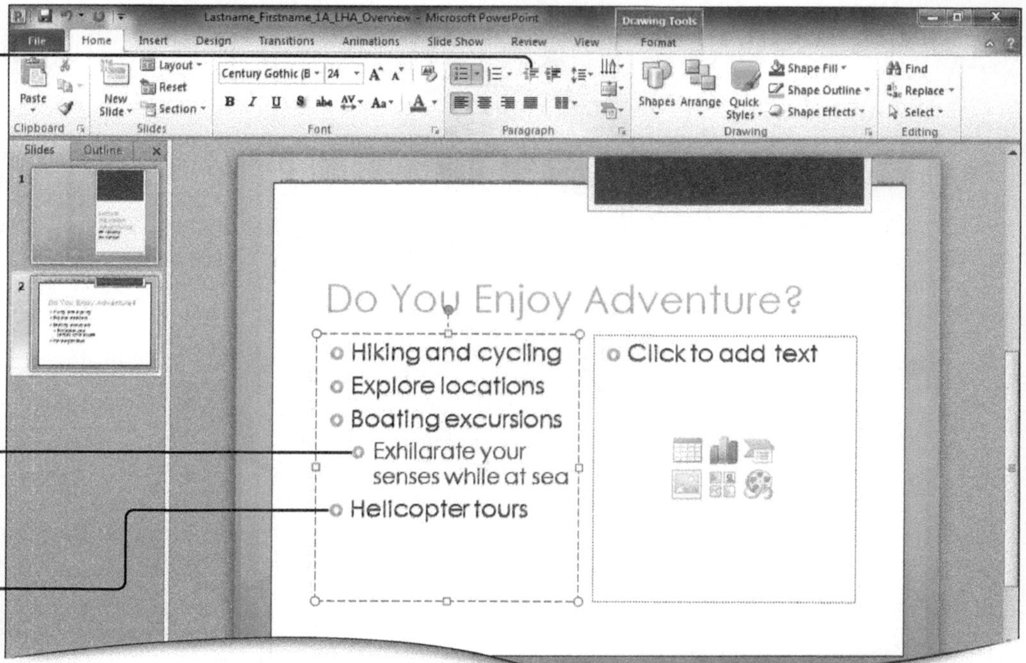

5 Press Enter, and then press Tab to increase the list level. Type **View Hawaii from above**

6 Click anywhere in the second bullet point—*Explore locations*. On the **Home tab**, in the **Paragraph group**, click the **Increase List Level** button. Compare your screen with Figure 1.13.

The bullet point is indented and the size of the text decreases.

Figure 1.13

Increase List Level button

List level of two bullet points increased

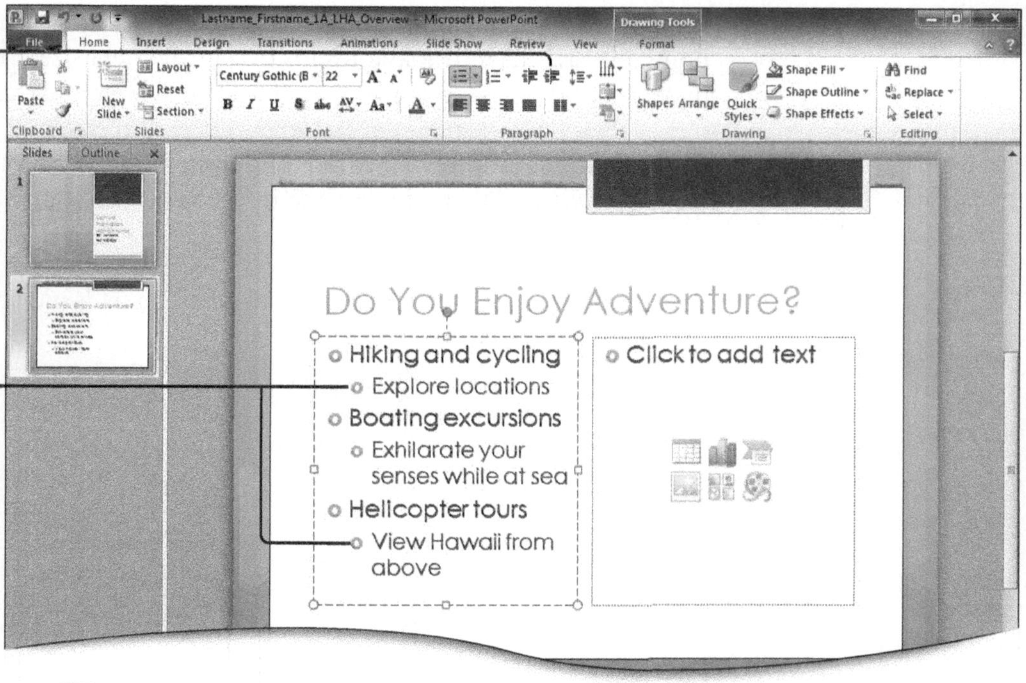

7 **Save** your presentation.

Activity 1.06 | Adding Speaker's Notes to a Presentation

Recall that when a presentation is displayed in Normal view, the Notes pane displays below the Slide pane. Use the Notes pane to type speaker's notes that you can print below a picture of each slide. Then, while making your presentation, you can refer to these printouts while making a presentation, thus reminding you of the important points that you want to discuss during the presentation.

1 With **Slide 2** displayed, on the **Home tab**, in the **Slides group**, click the **New Slide button arrow** to display the **Slide Layout** gallery, and then click **Section Header**.

The section header layout changes the look and flow of a presentation by providing text placeholders that do not contain bullet points.

2 Click in the title placeholder, and then type **About Our Company**

3 Click in the content placeholder below the title, and then type **Named for the crescent-shaped island noted for scuba diving, Lehua Hawaiian Adventures offers exciting and affordable tours throughout Hawaii.** Compare your screen with Figure 1.14.

Figure 1.14

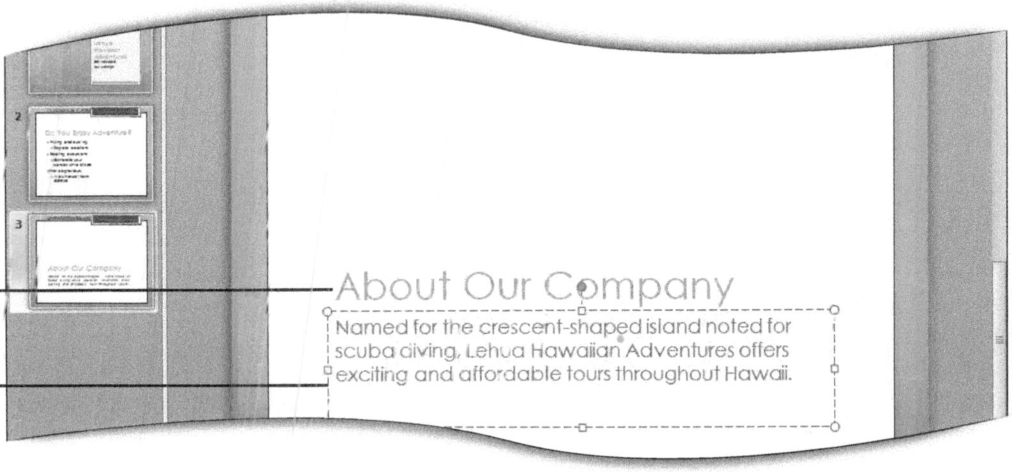

Slide title

Text typed in content placeholder

4 Below the slide, click in the **Notes pane**. Type **Lehua Hawaiian Adventures is based in Honolulu but has offices on each of the main Hawaiian islands.** Compare your screen with Figure 1.15, and then **Save** your presentation.

Figure 1.15

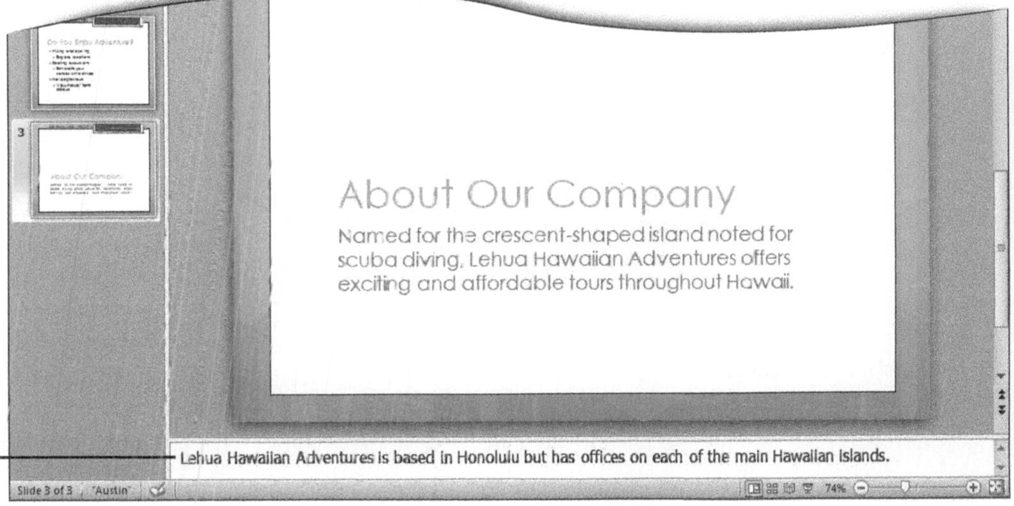

Text typed in the Notes pane

PowerPoint | Chapter 1

Activity 1.07 | Displaying and Editing Slides in the Slide Pane

To edit a presentation slide, display the slide in the Slide pane.

1. Look at the **Slides/Outline pane**, and then notice that the presentation contains three slides. At the right side of the PowerPoint window, in the vertical scroll bar, point to the scroll box, and then hold down the left mouse button to display a ScreenTip indicating the slide number and title.

2. Drag the scroll box up until the ScreenTip displays *Slide: 2 of 3 Do You Enjoy Adventure?* Compare your slide with Figure 1.16, and then release the mouse button to display **Slide 2**.

Figure 1.16

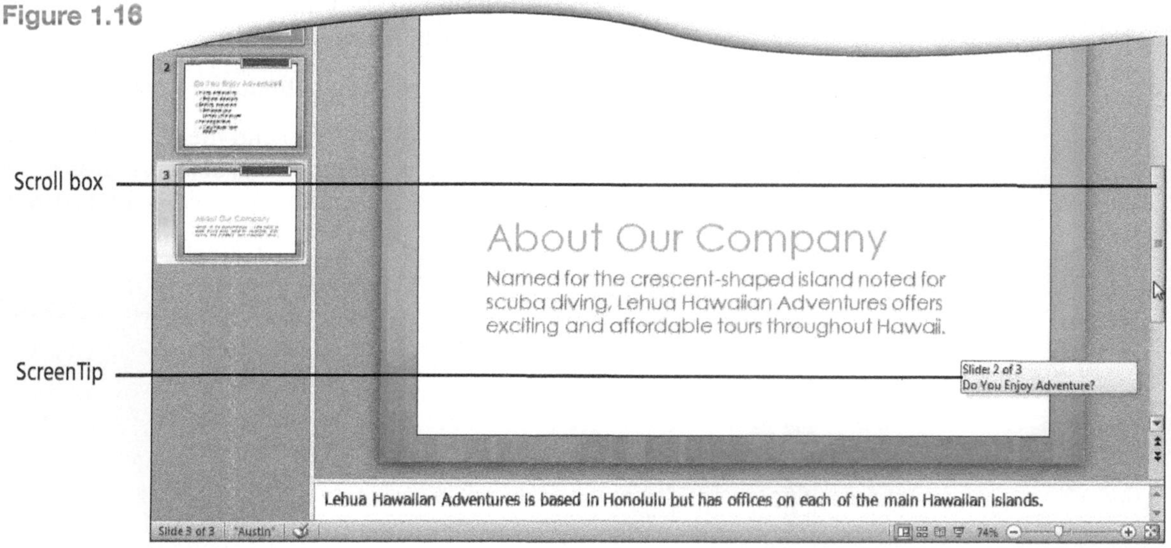

3. In the second bullet point, click at the end of the word *Explore*. Press Spacebar, and then type **amazing** Compare your screen with Figure 1.17.

   The placeholder text is resized to fit within the placeholder. The AutoFit Options button displays.

Figure 1.17

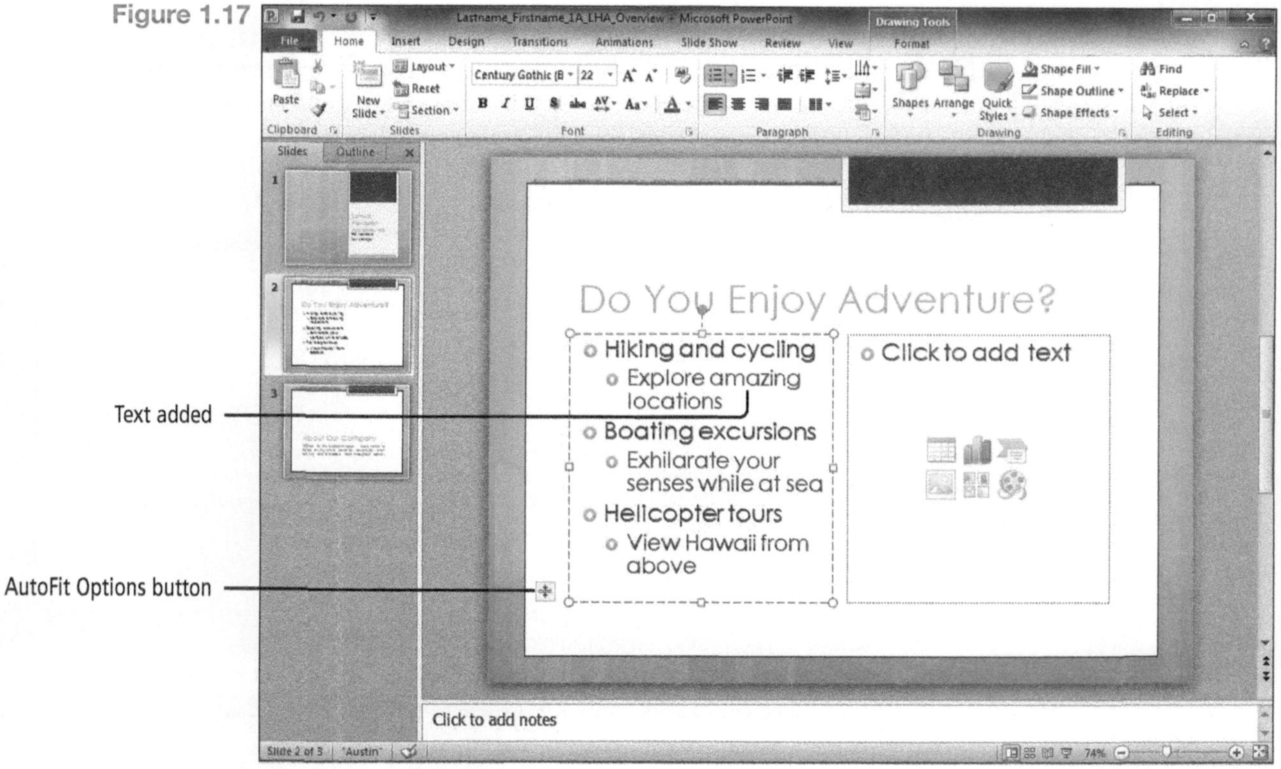

4 Click the **AutoFit Options** button, and then click **AutoFit Text to Placeholder**.

The *AutoFit Text to Placeholder* option keeps the text contained within the placeholder by reducing the size of the text. The *Stop Fitting Text to This Placeholder* option turns off the AutoFit option so that the text can flow beyond the placeholder border; the text size remains unchanged.

5 Below the vertical scroll bar, locate the **Previous Slide** and **Next Slide** buttons as shown in Figure 1.18.

Figure 1.18

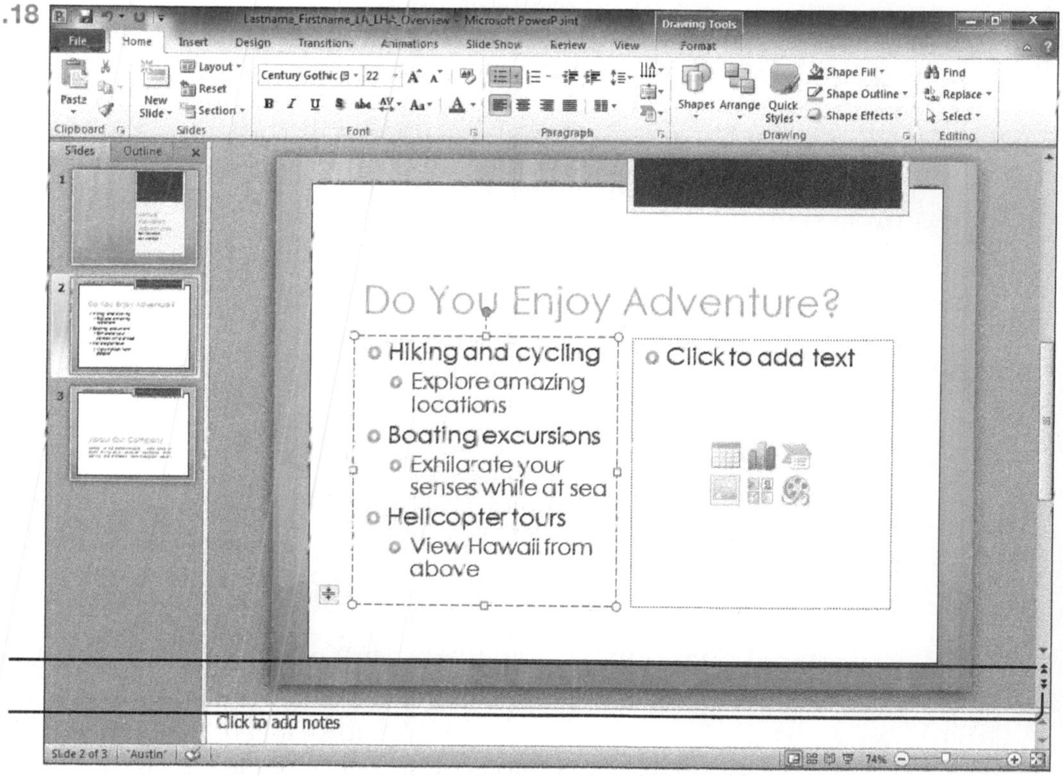

6 In the vertical scroll bar, click the **Previous Slide** button so that **Slide 1** displays. Then click the **Next Slide** button two times until **Slide 3** displays.

By clicking the Next Slide or the Previous Slide buttons, you can scroll through your presentation one slide at a time.

7 On the left side of the PowerPoint window, in the **Slides/Outline pane**, point to **Slide 1**, and then notice that a ScreenTip displays the slide title. Compare your screen with Figure 1.19.

In the Slides/Outline pane, the slide numbers display to the left of the slide thumbnails.

Figure 1.19

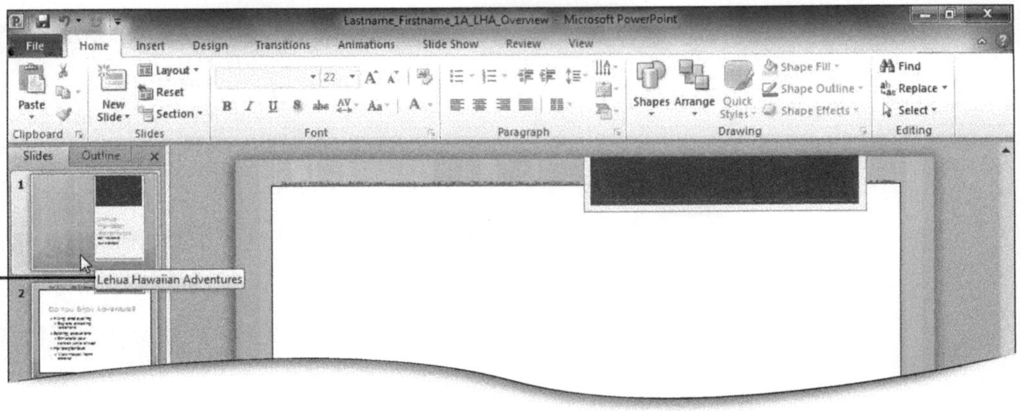

ScreenTip displays slide title

8 Click **Slide 1** to display it in the **Slide pane**, and then in the slide subtitle, click at the end of the word *Tour*. Press Spacebar, and then type **Operations**

Clicking a slide thumbnail is the most common method used to display a slide in the Slide pane.

9 **Save** your presentation.

Objective 3 | Add Pictures to a Presentation

Photographic images add impact to a presentation and help the audience visualize the message you are trying to convey.

Activity 1.08 | Inserting a Picture from a File

Many slide layouts in PowerPoint accommodate digital picture files so that you can easily add pictures you have stored on your system or on a portable storage device.

1 In the **Slides/Outline pane**, click **Slide 2** to display it in the **Slide pane**. On the **Home tab**, in the **Slides group**, click the **New Slide button arrow** to display the **Slide Layout** gallery. Click **Picture with Caption** to insert a new **Slide 3**. Compare your screen with Figure 1.20.

In the center of the large picture placeholder, the *Insert Picture from File* button displays.

Figure 1.20

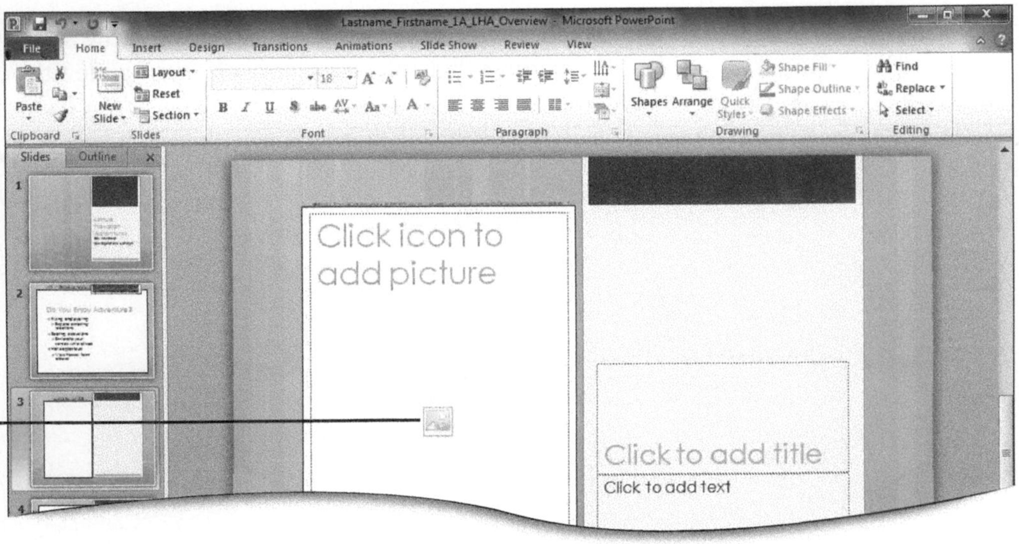

Insert Picture from File button

2 In the picture placeholder, click the **Insert Picture from File** button to open the **Insert Picture** dialog box. Navigate to the location in which your student files are stored, click **p01A_Beach**, then click **Insert** to insert the picture in the placeholder.

3 To the right of the picture, click in the title placeholder. Type **Prepare to be Amazed!**

4 Below the title, click in the caption placeholder, and then type **Mountain, sea, volcano. Our tour guides are experts in the history, geography, culture, and flora and fauna of Hawaii.** Compare your screen with Figure 1.21.

Figure 1.21

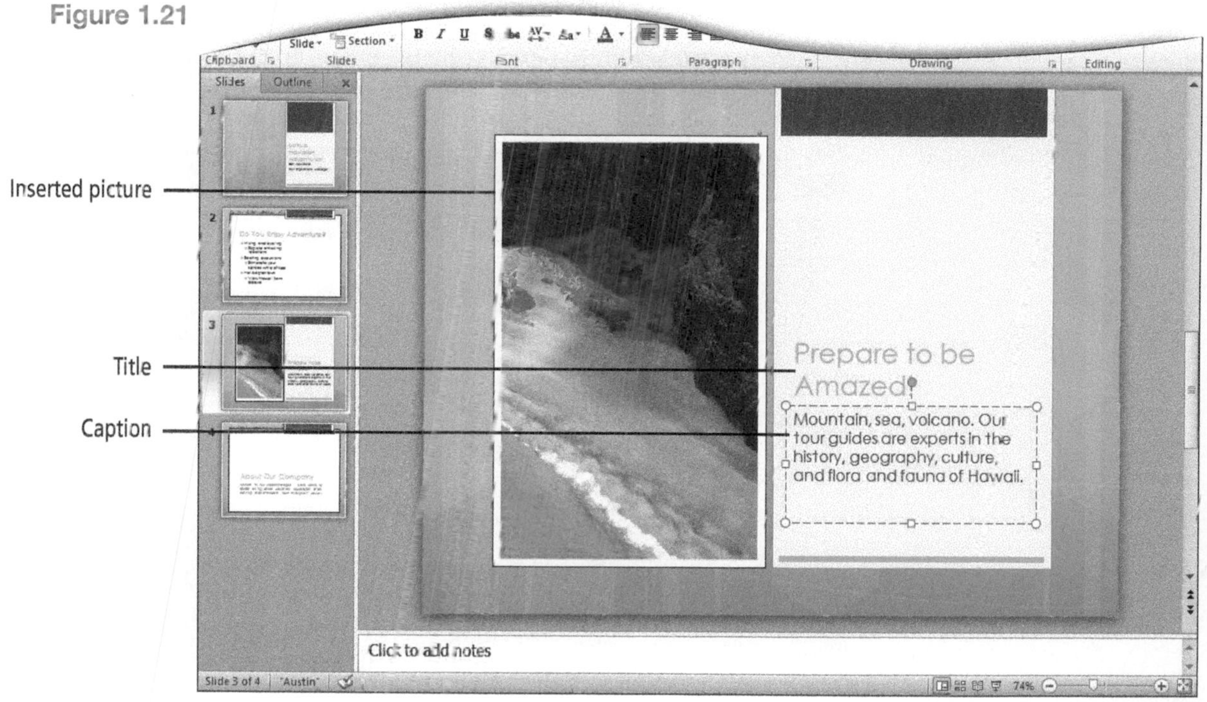

5 Display **Slide 2**. In the placeholder on the right side of the slide, click the **Insert Picture from File** button. Navigate to your student files, and then click **p01A_Helicopter**. Click **Insert**, and then compare your screen with Figure 1.22.

Small circles and squares—***sizing handles***—surround the inserted picture and indicate that the picture is selected and can be modified or formatted. The ***rotation handle***—a green circle above the picture—provides a way to rotate a selected image.

Figure 1.22

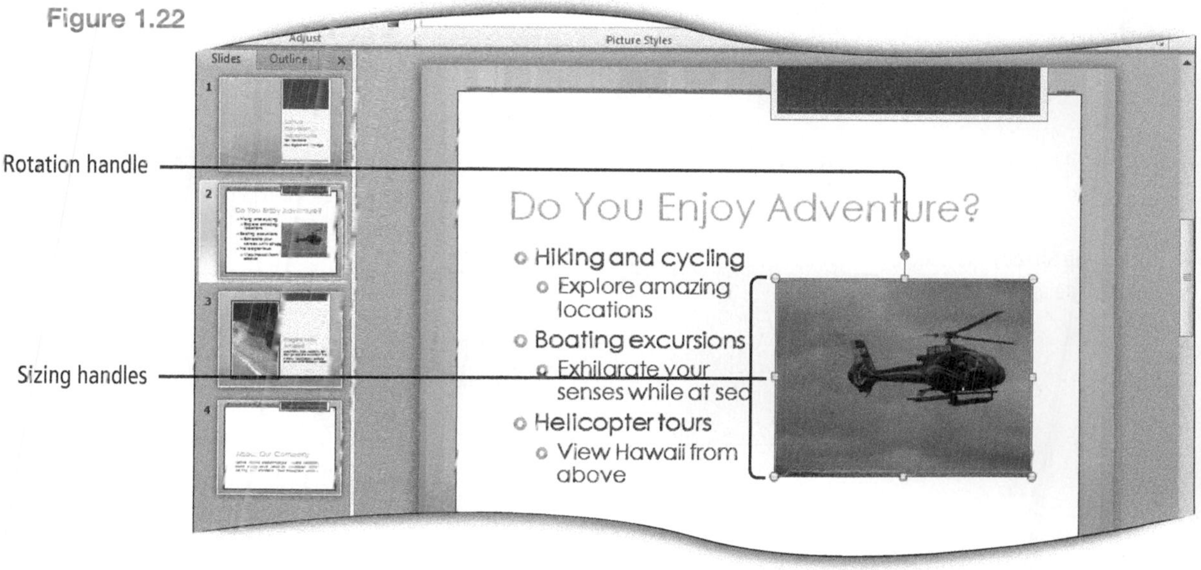

PowerPoint | Chapter 1

6 **Save** the presentation.

Activity 1.09 | Applying a Style to a Picture

The Picture Tools add the Format tab to the Ribbon, which provides numerous ***styles*** that you can apply to your pictures. A style is a collection of formatting options that you can apply to a picture, text, or an object.

1 With **Slide 2** displayed, if necessary, click the picture of the helicopter to select it. On the Ribbon, notice that the Picture Tools are active and the Format tab displays.

2 On the **Format tab**, in the **Picture Styles group**, click the **More** button to display the **Picture Styles** gallery, and then compare your screen with Figure 1.23.

Figure 1.23

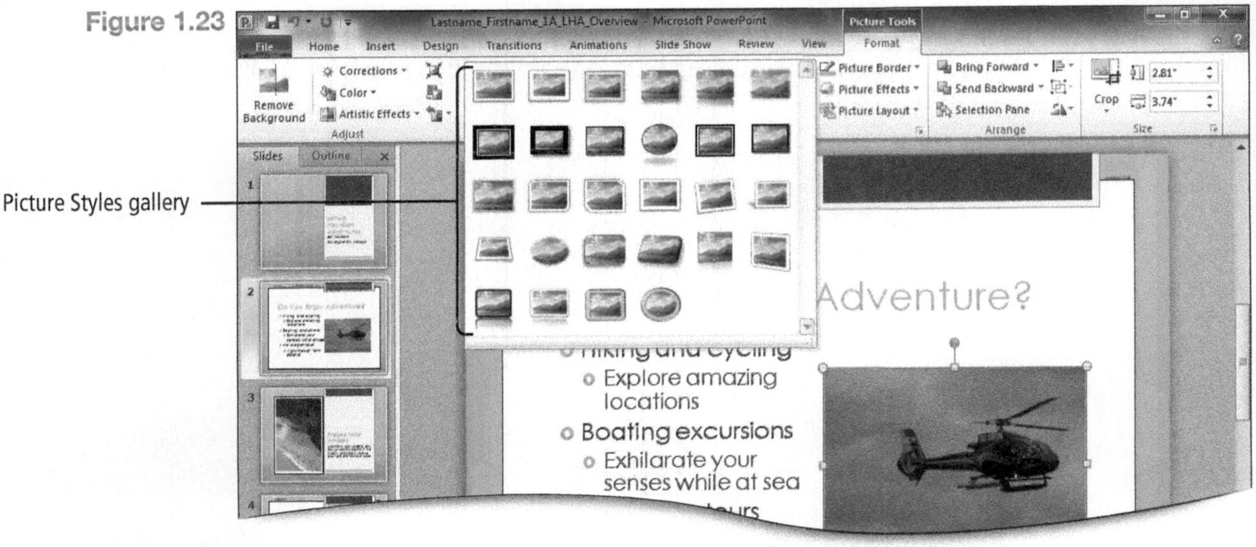

3 In the gallery, point to several of the picture styles to display the ScreenTips and to view the effect on your picture. In the first row, click **Drop Shadow Rectangle**.

4 Click in a blank area of the slide, and then compare your screen with Figure 1.24.

Figure 1.24

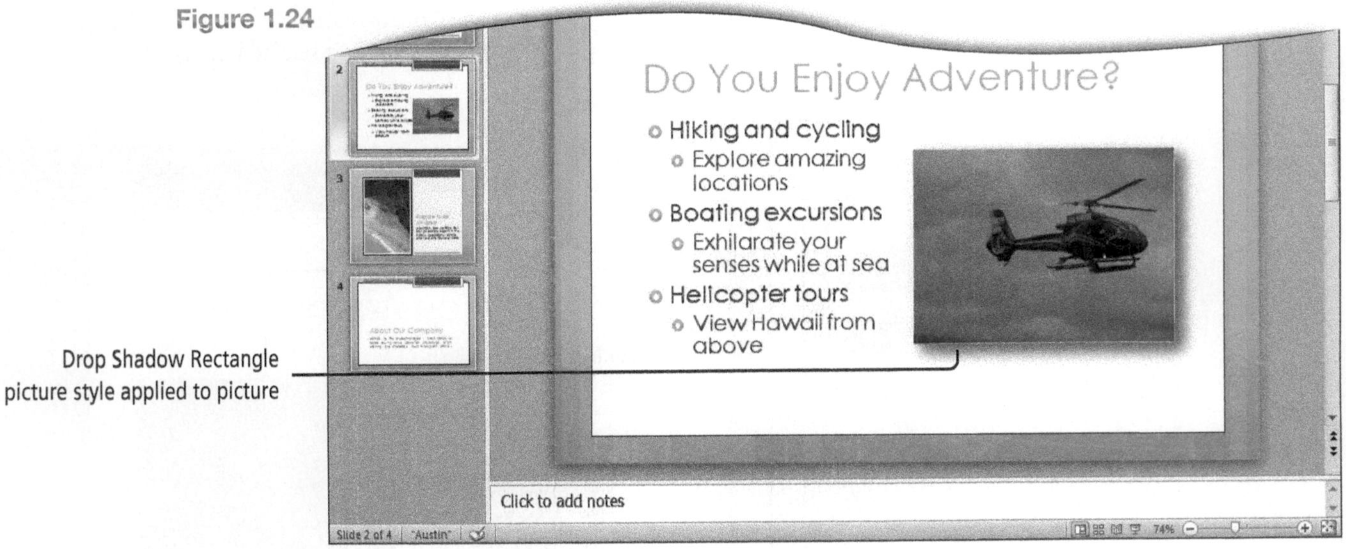

5 **Save** the presentation.

Activity 1.10 | Applying and Removing Picture Artistic Effects

Artistic effects are formats applied to images that make pictures resemble sketches or paintings.

1 With **Slide 2** displayed, select the picture of the helicopter.

2 Click the **Format tab**, and then in the **Adjust group**, click the **Artistic Effects** button to display the **Artistic Effects** gallery. Compare your screen with Figure 1.25.

Figure 1.25

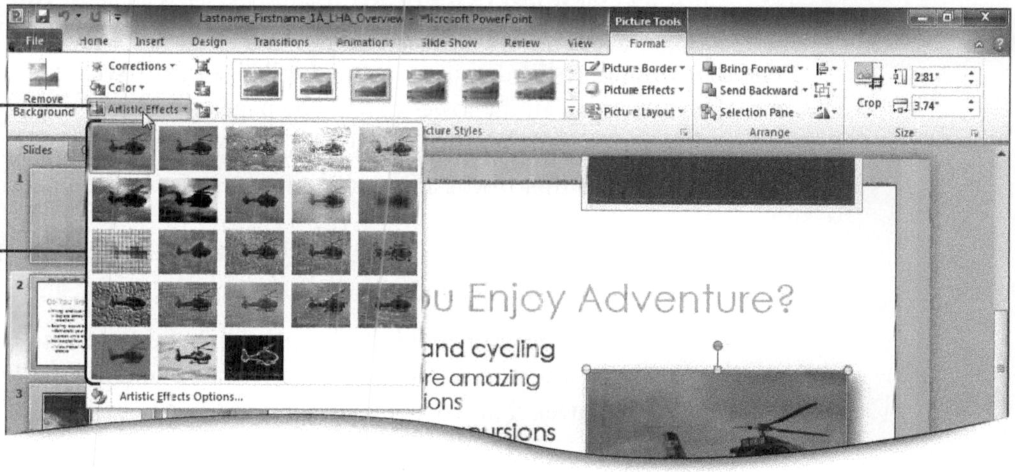

3 In the gallery, point to several of the artistic effects to display the ScreenTips and to have Live Preview display the effect on your picture. Then, in the second row, click the **Paint Strokes** effect.

4 With the picture still selected, on the **Format tab**, in the **Adjust group**, click the **Artistic Effects** button to display the gallery. In the first row, click the first effect—**None**—to remove the effect from the picture and restore the previous formatting.

5 **Save** the presentation.

Objective 4 | Print and View a Presentation

Activity 1.11 | Viewing a Slide Show

When you view a presentation as an electronic slide show, the entire slide fills the computer screen, and an audience can view your presentation if your computer is connected to a projection system.

> **Another Way**
>
> Press F5 to start the slide show from the beginning. Or, display the first slide you want to show and click the Slide Show button on the lower right side of the status bar; or press Shift + F5.

1 On the Ribbon, click the **Slide Show tab**. In the **Start Slide Show group**, click the **From Beginning** button.

The first slide fills the screen, displaying the presentation as the audience would see it if your computer was connected to a projection system.

2 Click the left mouse button or press Spacebar to advance to the second slide.

3 Continue to click or press Spacebar until the last slide displays, and then click or press Spacebar one more time to display a black slide.

After the last slide in a presentation, a ***black slide*** displays, indicating that the presentation is over.

4 With the black slide displayed, click the left mouse button or press Spacebar to exit the slide show and return to the presentation.

Activity 1.12 | Inserting Headers and Footers

A ***header*** is text that prints at the top of each sheet of ***slide handouts*** or ***notes pages***. Slide handouts are printed images of slides on a sheet of paper. Notes pages are printouts that contain the slide image on the top half of the page and notes that you have created on the Notes pane in the lower half of the page.

In addition to headers, you can insert ***footers***—text that displays at the bottom of every slide or that prints at the bottom of a sheet of slide handouts or notes pages.

1 Click the **Insert tab**, and then in the **Text group**, click the **Header & Footer** button to display the **Header and Footer** dialog box.

2 In the **Header and Footer** dialog box, click the **Notes and Handouts tab**. Under **Include on page**, select the **Date and time** check box, and as you do so, watch the Preview box in the lower right corner of the Header and Footer dialog box.

The Preview box indicates the placeholders on the printed Notes and Handouts pages. The two narrow rectangular boxes at the top of the Preview box indicate placeholders for the header text and date. When you select the Date and time check box, the placeholder in the upper right corner is outlined, indicating the location in which the date will display.

3 If necessary, click the Update automatically option button so that the current date prints on the notes and handouts each time the presentation is printed.

4 If necessary, *clear* the Header check box to omit this element. Notice that in the **Preview** box, the corresponding placeholder is not selected.

5 Select the **Page number** and **Footer** check boxes, and then notice that the insertion point displays in the **Footer** box. Using your own name, type **Lastname_Firstname_1A_LHA_Overview** so that the file name displays as a footer, and then compare your dialog box with Figure 1.26.

Figure 1.26

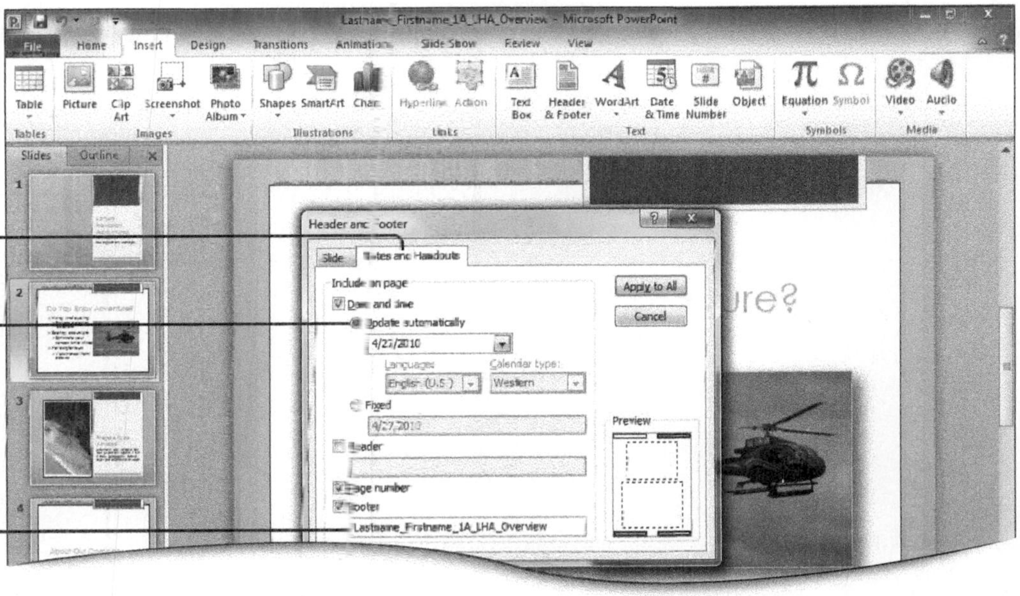

6 In the upper right corner of the dialog box, click **Apply to All**. **Save** your presentation.

> **More Knowledge | Adding Footers to Slides**
>
> You can also add footers to the actual slides, which will display during your presentation, by using the Slide tab in the Header and Footer dialog box. Headers cannot be added to individual slides.

Activity 1.13 | Printing a Presentation

Use Backstage view to preview the arrangement of slides on the handouts and notes pages.

1 Display **Slide 1**. Click the **File tab** to display **Backstage** view, and then click the **Print tab**.

The Print tab in Backstage view displays the tools you need to select your settings and also to view a preview of your presentation. On the right, Print Preview displays your presentation exactly as it will print.

2 In the **Settings group**, click **Full Page Slides**, and then compare your screen with Figure 1.27.

The gallery displays either the default print setting—Full Page Slides—or the most recently selected print setting. Thus, on your system, this button might indicate the presentation Notes Pages, Outline, or one of several arrangements of slide handouts—depending on the most recently used setting.

Figure 1.27

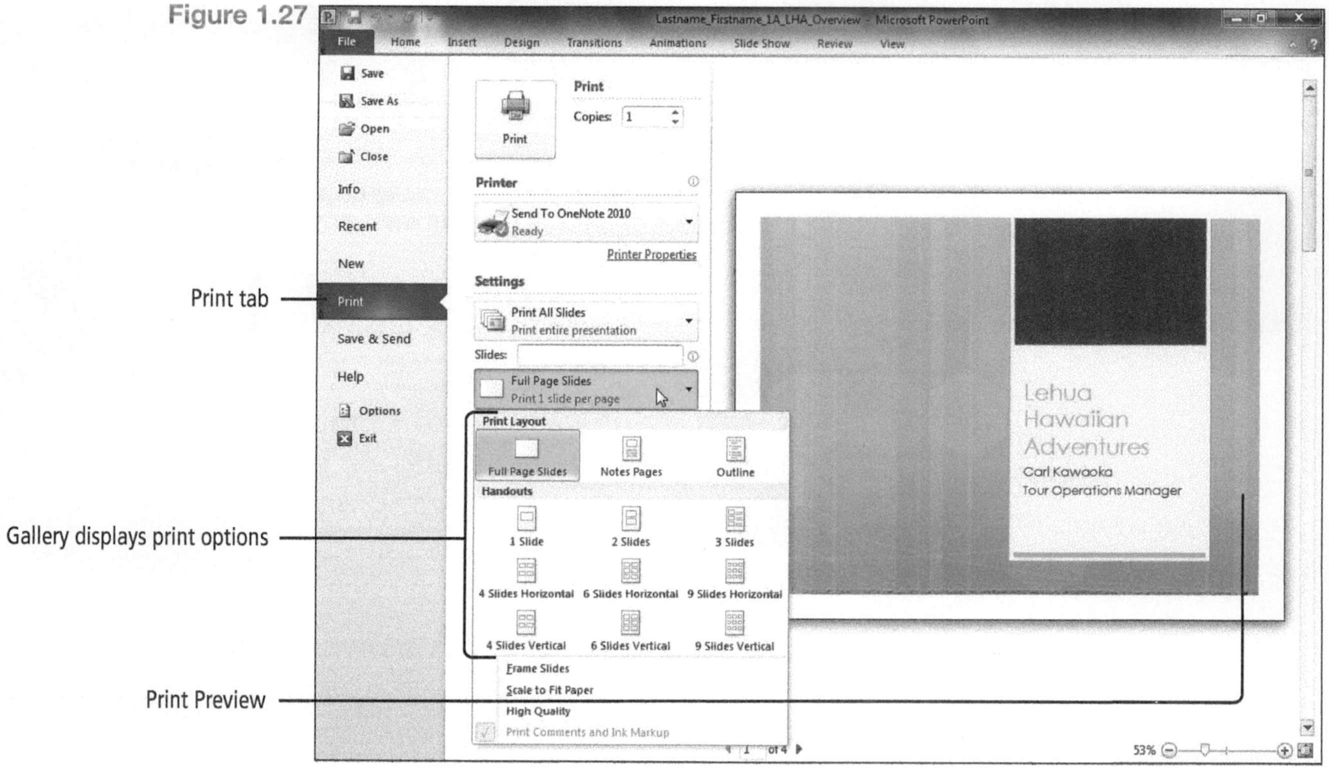

3 In the gallery, under **Handouts**, click **4 Slides Horizontal**. Notice that the **Print Preview** on the right displays the slide handout, and that the current date, file name, and page number display in the header and footer.

In the Settings group, the Portrait Orientation option displays so that you can change the print orientation from Portrait to Landscape. The Portrait Orientation option does not display when Full Page Slides is chosen.

4 To print your handout, be sure your system is connected to a printer, and then in the **Print group**, click the **Print** button.

The handout will print on your default printer—on a black and white printer, the colors will print in shades of gray. Backstage view closes and your file redisplays in the PowerPoint window.

5 Click the **File tab** to display **Backstage** view, and then click the **Print tab**. In the **Settings group**, click **4 Slides Horizontal**, and then under **Print Layout**, click **Notes Pages** to view the presentation notes for **Slide 1**; recall that you created notes for **Slide 4**.

Indicated below the Notes page are the current slide number and the number of pages that will print when Notes page is selected. You can use the Next Page and Previous Page arrows to display each Notes page in the presentation.

6 At the bottom of the **Print Preview**, click the **Next Page** button ▶ three times so that **Page 4** displays. Compare your screen with Figure 1.28.

The notes that you created for Slide 4 display below the image of the slide.

Figure 1.28

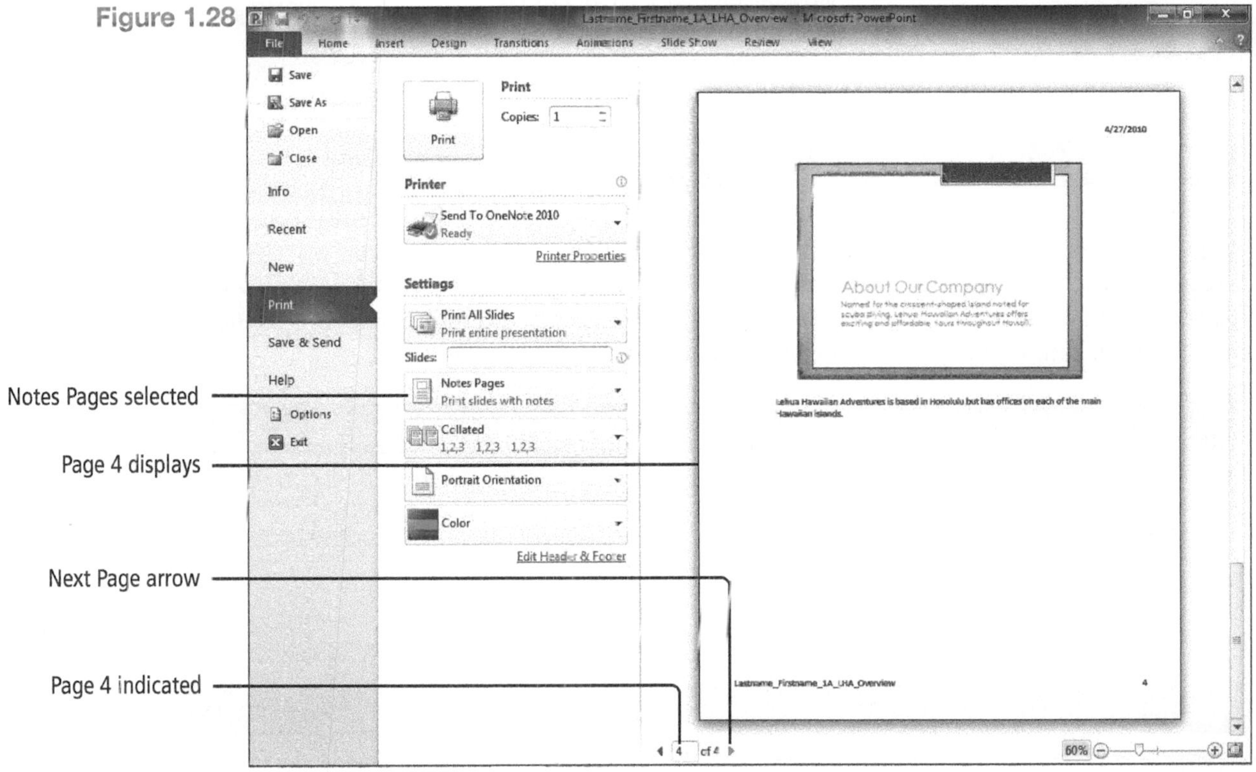

7 In the **Settings group**, click in the **Slides** box, and then type **4** so that only the Notes pages for **Slide 4** will print. In the **Settings group**, click **Notes Pages**, and then below the gallery, select **Frame Slides**. In the **Print group**, click the **Print** button to print the Notes page.

8 Click the **File tab** to redisplay **Backstage** view, be sure the **Info tab** is active, and then in the third panel, click **Properties**. Click **Show Document Panel**, and then in the **Author** box, delete any text and type your firstname and lastname.

9 In the **Subject** box, type your course name and section number. In the **Keywords** box, type **company overview** and then **Close** the Document Information Panel.

10 **Save** your presentation. On the right end of the title bar, click the **Close** button to close the presentation and close PowerPoint.

End **You have completed Project 1A**

Project 1B New Product Announcement

myitlab Project 1B Training

Project Activities

In Activities 1.14 through 1.23, you will combine two presentations that the marketing team at Lehua Adventure Travels developed describing their new Ecotours. You will combine the presentations by inserting slides from one presentation into another, and then you will rearrange and delete slides. You will also apply font formatting and slide transitions to the presentation. Your completed presentation will look similar to Figure 1.29.

Project Files

For Project 1B, you will need the following files:

p01B_Ecotours
p01B_Slides

You will save your presentation as:

Lastname_Firstname_1B_Ecotours

Project Results

Figure 1.29
Project 1B—Ecotours

Objective 5 | Edit an Existing Presentation

Recall that editing refers to the process of adding, deleting, and modifying presentation content. You can edit presentation content in either the Slide pane or the Slides/Outline pane.

Activity 1.14 | Displaying and Editing the Presentation Outline

You can display the presentation outline in the Slides/Outline pane and edit the presentation text. Changes that you make in the outline are immediately displayed in the Slide pane.

1 **Start** PowerPoint. From your student files, open **p01B_Ecotours**. On the **File tab**, click **Save As**, navigate to your **PowerPoint Chapter 1** folder, and then using your own name, save the file as **Lastname_Firstname_1B_Ecotours**

2 In the **Slides/Outline pane**, click the **Outline tab** to display the presentation outline. If necessary, below the Slides/Outline pane, drag the scroll box all the way to the left so that the slide numbers display. Compare your screen with Figure 1.30.

The outline tab is wider than the Slides tab so that you have additional space to type your text. Each slide in the outline displays the slide number, slide icon, and the slide title in bold.

Figure 1.30

Outline tab

Slide numbers and titles

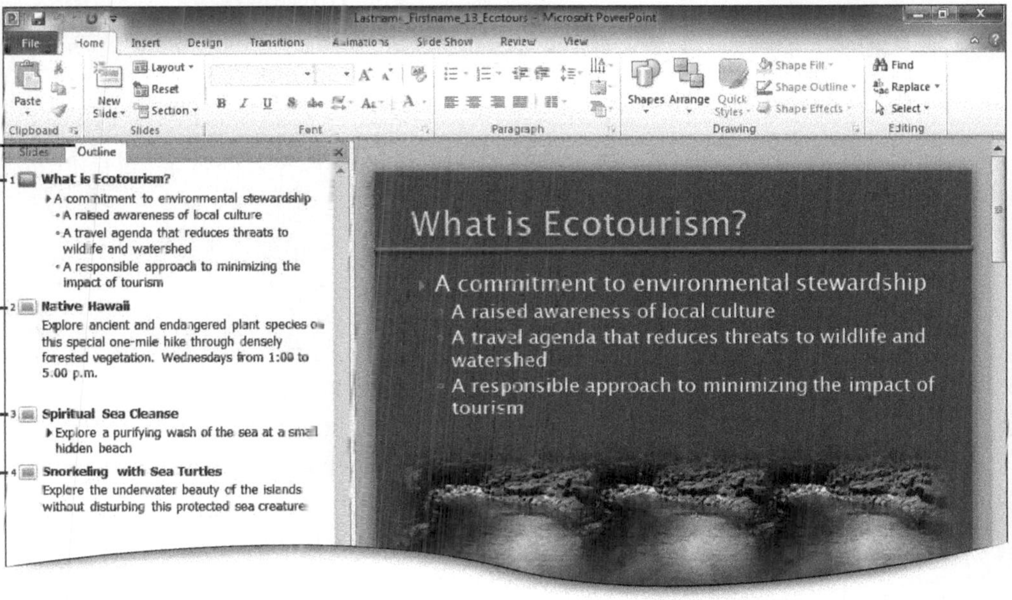

3 In the **Outline tab**, in **Slide 1**, select the last three bullet points, and then compare your screen with Figure 1.31.

Figure 1.31

Three bullet points selected

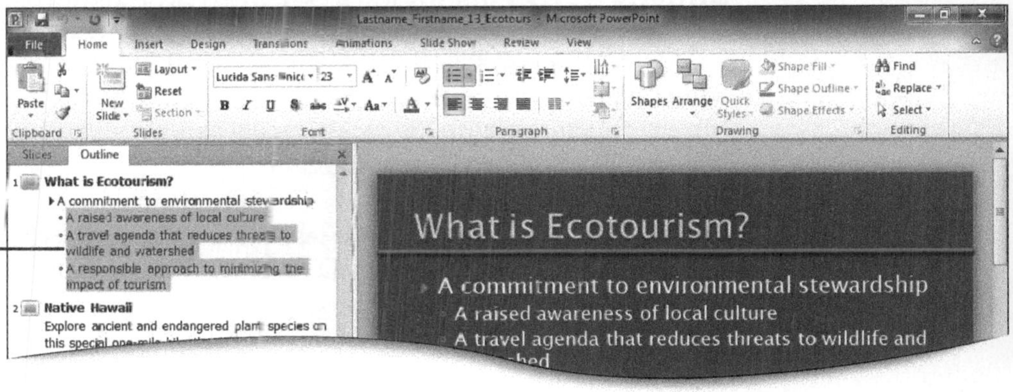

PowerPoint | Chapter 1

4 On the **Home tab**, in the **Paragraph group**, click the **Decrease List Level** button one time to decrease the list level of the selected bullet points.

When you type in the outline or change the list level, the changes also display in the Slide pane.

5 In the **Outline tab**, click anywhere in **Slide 3**, and then click at the end of the last bullet point after the word *beach*. Press Enter to create a new bullet point at the same list level as the previous bullet point. Type **Offered Tuesdays and Thursdays one hour before sunset, weather permitting**

6 Press Enter to create a new bullet point. Type **Fee: $30** and then compare your screen with Figure 1.32.

Figure 1.32

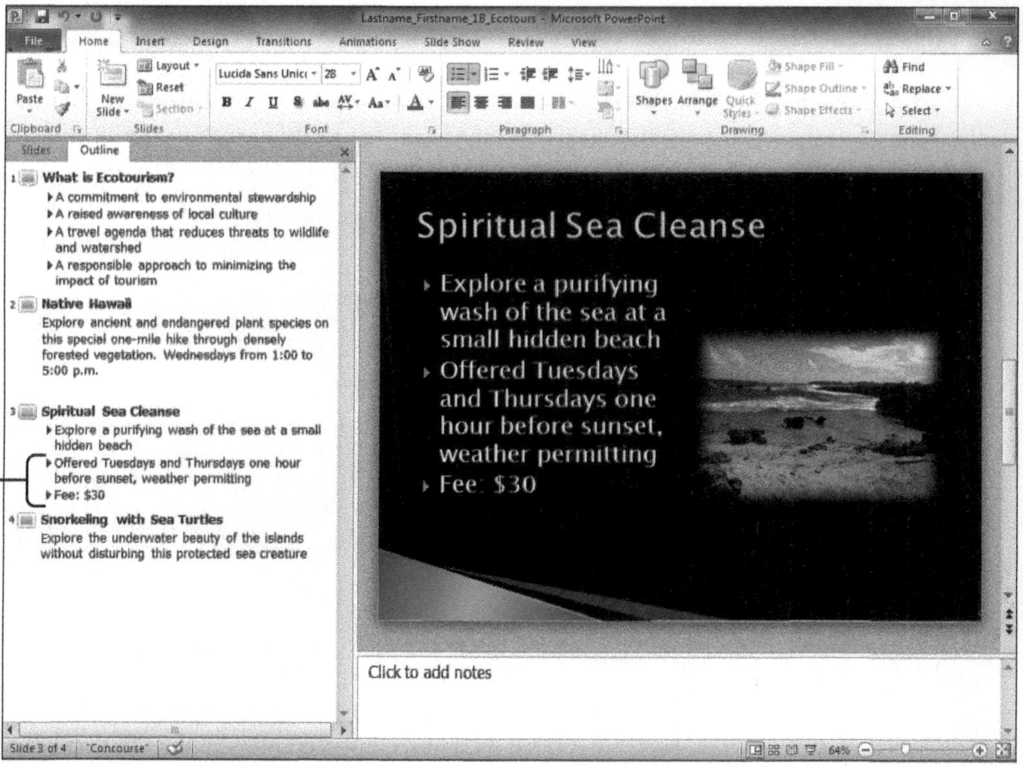

Two bullet points typed

7 In the **Slides/Outline pane**, click the **Slides tab** to display the slide thumbnails, and then **Save** the presentation.

You can type text in the Slide tab or in the Outline tab. Displaying the Outline tab enables you to view the entire flow of the presentation.

Activity 1.15 | Inserting Slides from an Existing Presentation

Presentation content is commonly shared among group members in an organization. Rather than re-creating slides, you can insert slides from an existing presentation into the current presentation. In this activity, you will insert slides from an existing presentation into your 1B_Ecotours presentation.

1 Display **Slide 1**. On the **Home tab**, in the **Slides group**, click the **New Slide button arrow** to display the **Slide Layout** gallery and additional commands for inserting slides. Compare your screen with Figure 1.33.

Figure 1.33

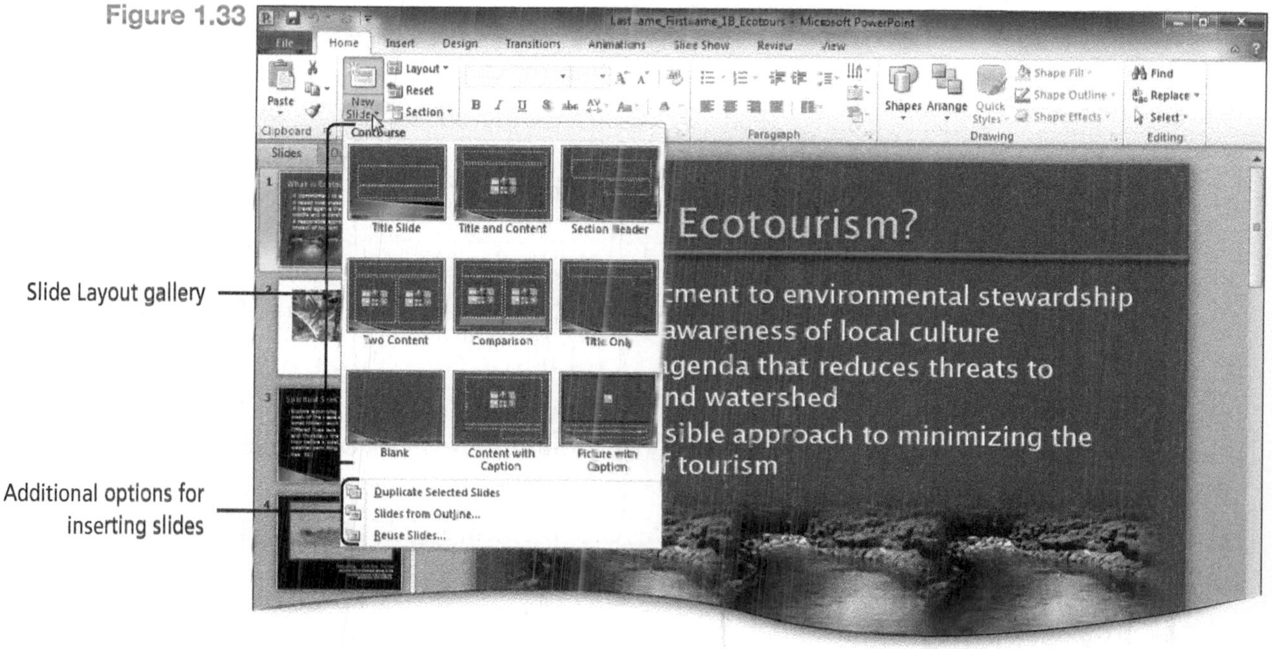

2. Below the gallery, click **Reuse Slides** to open the Reuse Slides pane on the right side of the PowerPoint window.

3. In the **Reuse Slides** pane, click the **Browse** button, and then click **Browse File**. In the **Browse** dialog box, navigate to the location where your student files are stored, and then double-click **p01B_Slides** to display the slides in the Reuse Slides pane.

4. At the bottom of the **Reuse Slides** pane, select the **Keep source formatting** check box, and then compare your screen with Figure 1.34.

By selecting the *Keep source formatting* check box, you retain the formatting applied to the slides when inserted into the existing presentation. When the *Keep source formatting* check box is cleared, the theme formatting of the presentation in which the slides are inserted is applied.

Figure 1.34

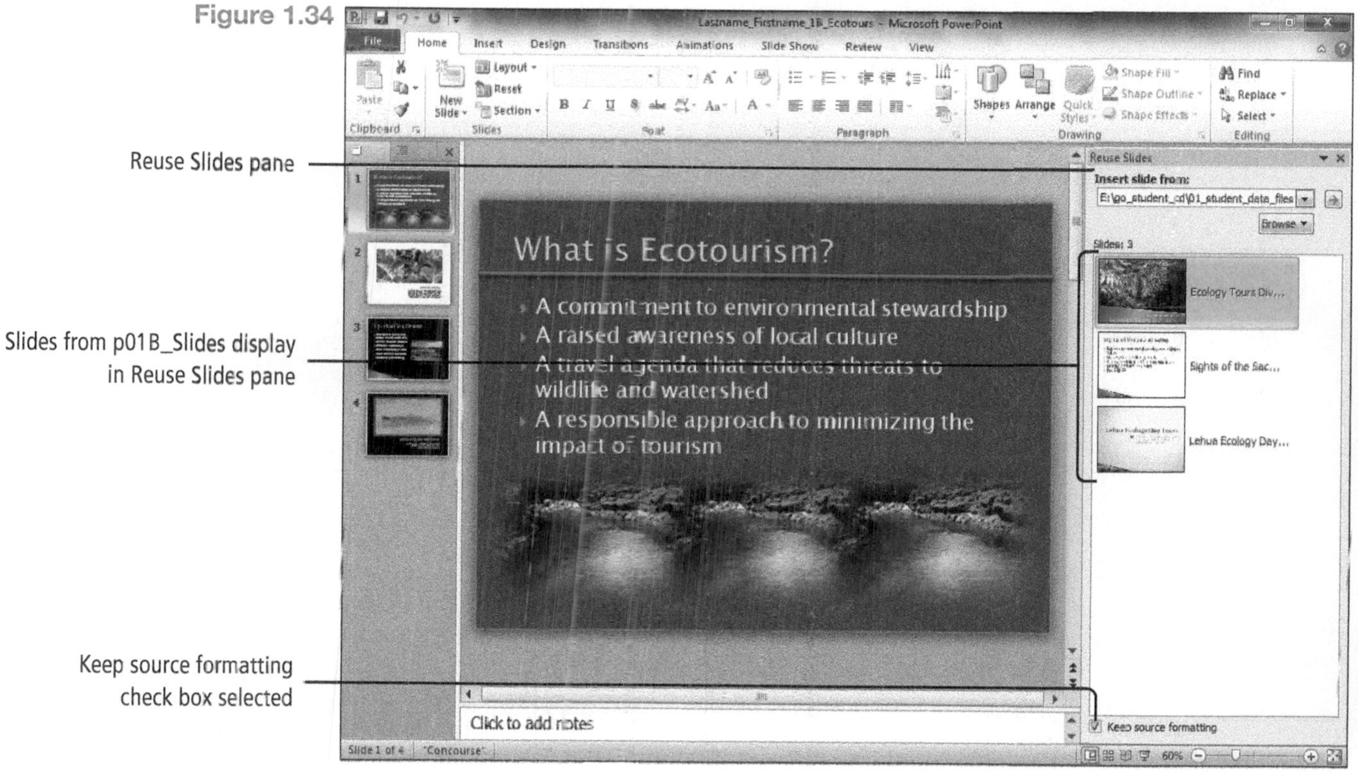

5 In the **Reuse Slides** pane, point to each slide to view a zoomed image of the slide and a ScreenTip displaying the file name and the slide title.

6 In the **Reuse Slides** pane, click the first slide—**Ecology Tours Division**—to insert the slide into the current presentation after Slide 1, and then notice that the original slide background formatting is retained.

> **Note | Inserting Slides**
>
> You can insert slides into your presentation in any order; remember to display the slide that will precede the slide that you want to insert.

7 In your **1B_Ecotours** presentation, in the **Slides/Outline pane**, click **Slide 5** to display it in the **Slide pane**.

8 In the **Reuse Slides** pane, click the second slide and then click the third slide to insert both slides after **Slide 5**.

Your presentation contains seven slides.

9 On **Slide 7**, point to *Lehua*, and then right-click to display the shortcut menu. Click **Ignore all**. Use the same technique to ignore the spelling of the word *Ecotour*. Compare your screen with Figure 1.35.

Figure 1.35

Inserted slide

Inserted slides

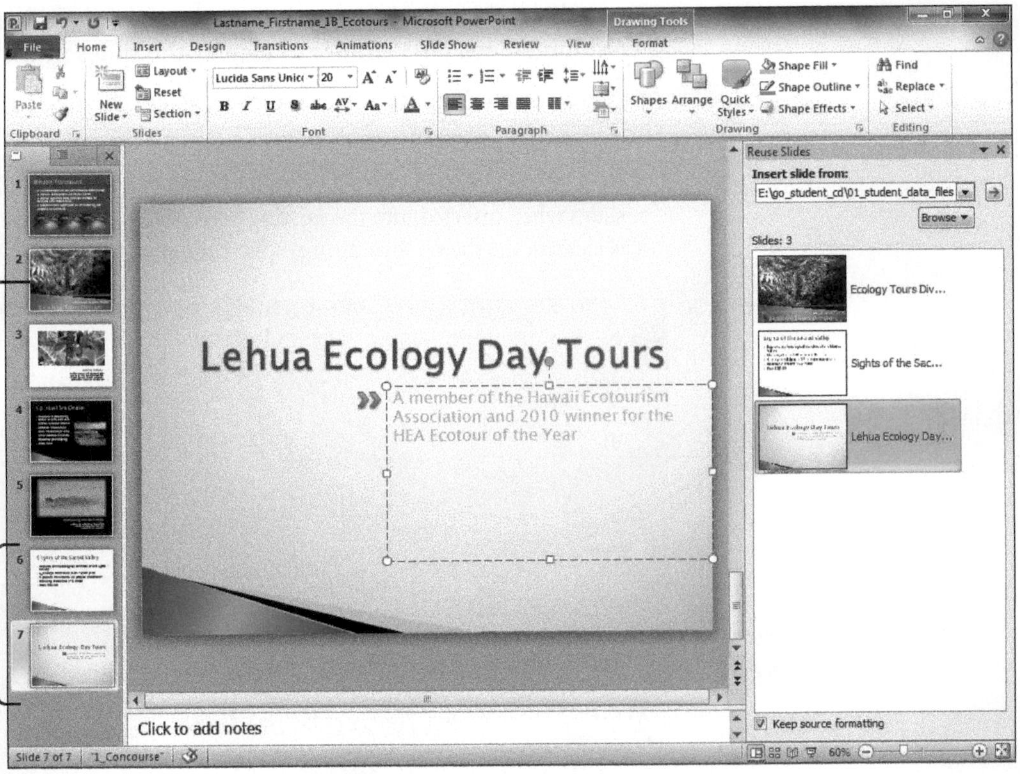

10 **Close** the **Reuse Slides** pane; click **Save**.

> **More Knowledge | Inserting All Slides**
>
> You can insert all of the slides from an existing presentation into the current presentation at one time. In the Reuse Slides pane, right-click one of the slides that you want to insert, and then click Insert All Slides.

Activity 1.16 | Finding and Replacing Text

The Replace command enables you to locate all occurrences of specified text and replace it with alternative text.

1 Display **Slide 1**. On the **Home tab**, in the **Editing group**, click the **Replace** button. In the **Replace** dialog box, in the **Find what** box, type **Ecology** and then in the **Replace with** box, type **Eco** Compare your screen with Figure 1.36.

Figure 1.36

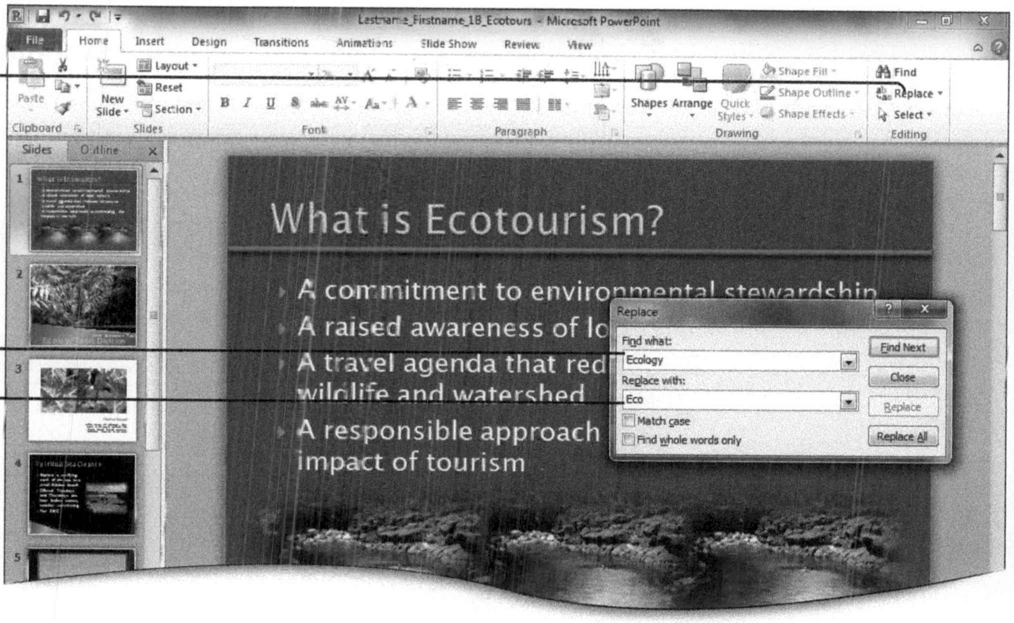

2 In the **Replace** dialog box, click the **Replace All** button.

A message box displays indicating the number of replacements that were made.

3 In the message box, click **OK**. **Close** the **Replace** dialog box, and then click **Save**.

Objective 6 | Format a Presentation

Formatting refers to changing the appearance of the text, layout, and design of a slide. You will find it easiest to do most of your formatting changes in PowerPoint in the Slide pane.

Activity 1.17 | Changing Fonts, Font Sizes, Font Styles, and Font Colors

Recall that a font is a set of characters with the same design and shape and that fonts are measured in points. Font styles include bold, italic, and underline, and you can apply any combination of these styles to presentation text. Font styles and font color are useful to provide emphasis and are a visual cue to draw the reader's eye to important text.

1 On the right side of the **Slides/Outline pane**, drag the scroll box down until **Slide 7** displays, and then click **Slide 7** to display it in the **Slides** pane.

When a presentation contains a large number of slides, a scroll box displays to the right of the slide thumbnails so that you can scroll and then select the thumbnails.

2 Select the title text—*Lehua Eco Day Tours*. Point to the Mini toolbar, and then click the **Font button arrow** to display the available fonts. Click **Arial Black**.

3 Select the light green text in the placeholder below the title, and then on the Mini toolbar, change the **Font** to **Arial Black** and the **Font Size** to **28**. Then, click the **Font Color button arrow** [A ▾], and compare your screen with Figure 1.37.

The colors in the top row of the color gallery are the colors associated with the presentation theme—*Concourse*. The colors in the rows below the first row are light and dark variations of the theme colors.

Figure 1.37

4 Point to several of the colors and notice that a ScreenTip displays the color name and Live Preview displays the selected text in the color to which you are pointing.

5 In the second column of colors, click the first color—**Black, Text 1**—to change the font color. Notice that on the Home tab and Mini toolbar, the lower part of the Font Color button displays the most recently applied font color—Black.

When you click the Font Color button instead of the Font Color button arrow, the color displayed in the lower part of the Font Color button is applied to selected text without displaying the color gallery.

6 Display **Slide 2**, and then select the title *Eco Tours Division*. On the Mini toolbar, click the **Font Color button** [A ▾] to apply the font color **Black, Text 1** to the selection. Select the subtitle—*Lehua Adventure Tours*—and then change the **Font Color** to **Black, Text 1**. Compare your screen with Figure 1.38.

Figure 1.38

7 Display **Slide 3**, and then select the title—*Native Hawaii*. From the Mini toolbar, apply **Bold** [B] and **Italic** [I], and then **Save** your presentation.

Activity 1.18 | Aligning Text and Changing Line Spacing

In PowerPoint, ***text alignment*** refers to the horizontal placement of text within a placeholder. You can align left, centered, right, or justified.

1 Display **Slide 2**. Click anywhere in the title—*Eco Tours Division*.

2 On the **Home tab**, in the **Paragraph group**, click the **Align Text Right** button to right align the text within the placeholder.

3 Display **Slide 7**. Click anywhere in the text below the title. In the **Paragraph group**, click the **Line Spacing** button. In the list, click **1.5** to change from single-spacing between lines to one-and-a-half spacing between lines. **Save** your presentation, and then compare your screen with Figure 1.39.

Figure 1.39

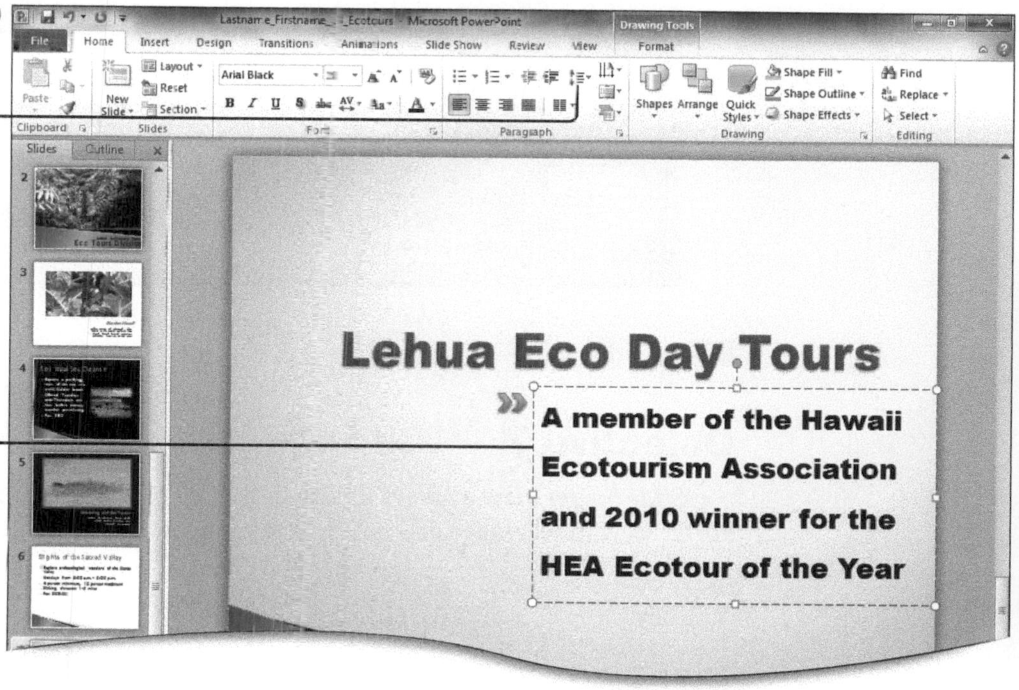

Activity 1.19 | Modifying Slide Layout

Recall that the slide layout defines the placement of the content placeholders on a slide. PowerPoint includes predefined layouts that you can apply to your slide for the purpose of arranging slide elements.

For example, a Title Slide contains two placeholder elements—the title and the subtitle. When you design your slides, consider the content that you want to include, and then choose a layout with the elements that will display the message you want to convey in the best way.

1 Display **Slide 3**. On the **Home tab**, in the **Slides group**, click the **Layout** button to display the **Slide Layout** gallery. Notice that *Content with Caption* is selected.

The selection indicates the layout of the current slide.

2 Click **Picture with Caption** to change the slide layout, and then compare your screen with Figure 1.40.

The Picture with Caption layout emphasizes the picture more effectively than the Content with Caption layout.

Figure 1.40

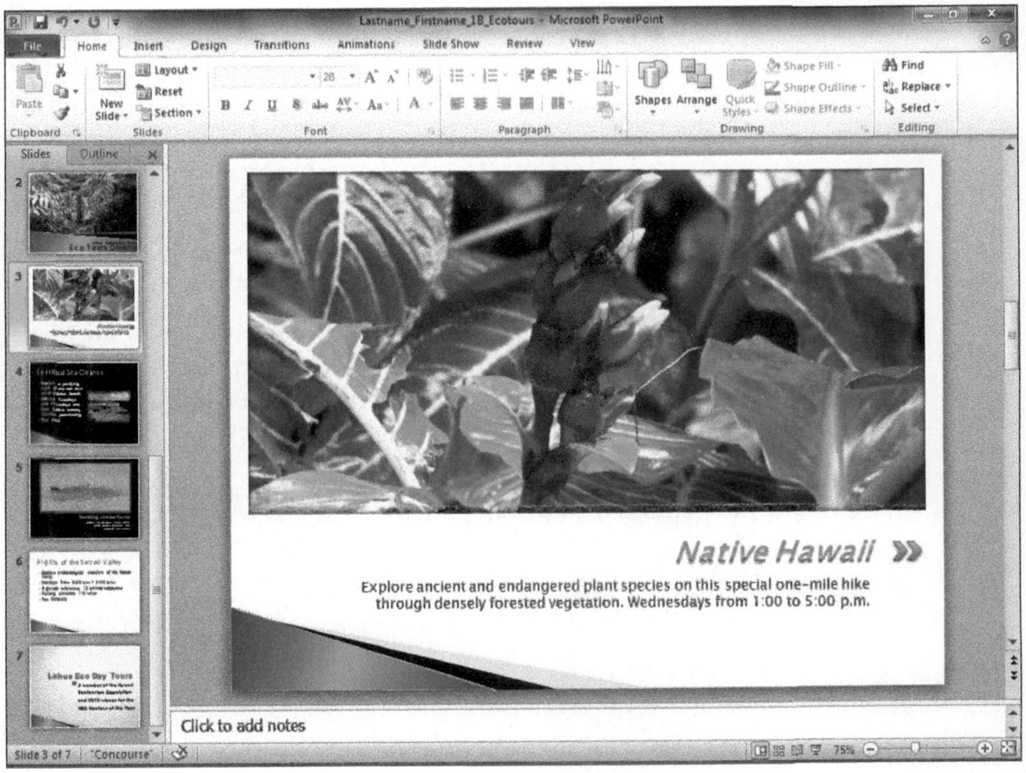

3 **Save** your presentation.

Objective 7 | Use Slide Sorter View

Slide Sorter view displays thumbnails of all of the slides in a presentation. Use Slide Sorter view to rearrange and delete slides and to apply formatting to multiple slides.

Activity 1.20 | Deleting Slides in Slide Sorter View

> **Another Way**
>
> On the Ribbon, click the View tab, and then in the Presentation Views group, click Slide Sorter.

1 In the lower right corner of the PowerPoint window, click the **Slide Sorter** button to display all of the slide thumbnails.

2 Compare your screen with Figure 1.41.

Your slides may display larger or smaller than those shown in Figure 1.41.

Figure 1.41

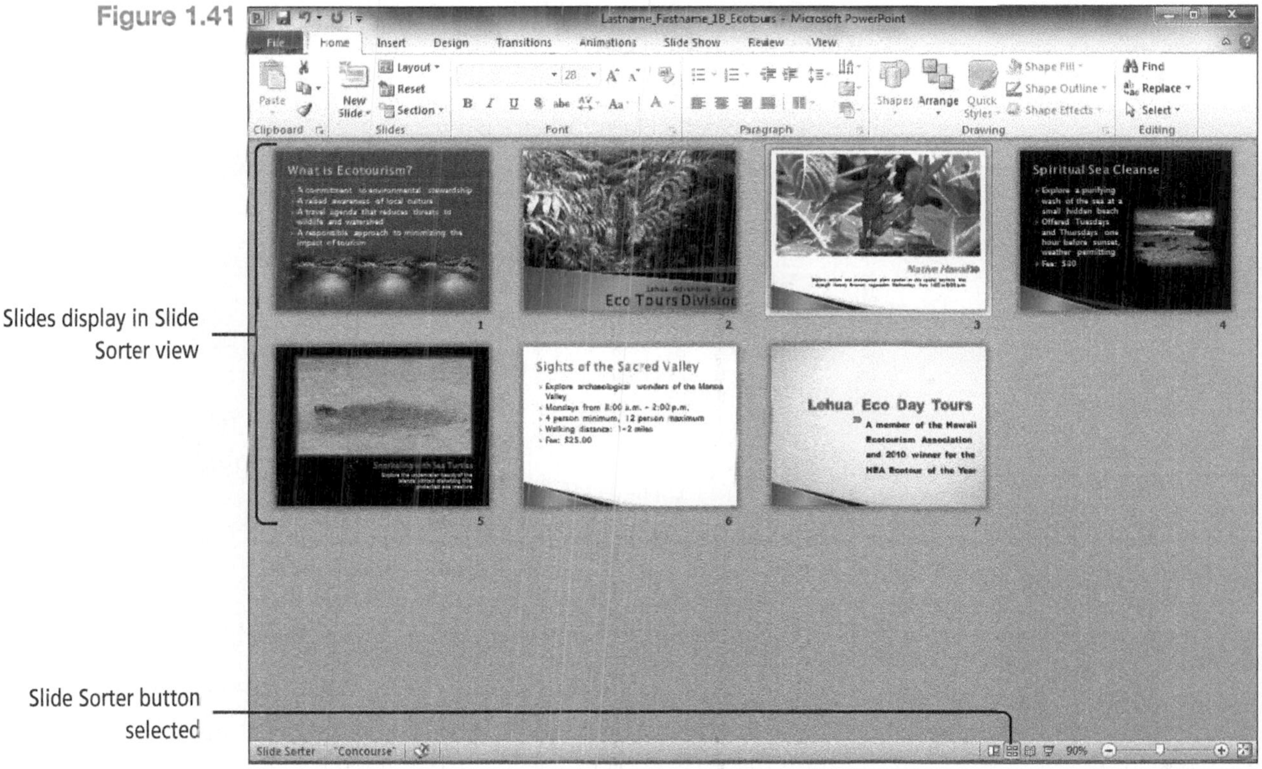

3 Click **Slide 6**, and notice that a thick outline surrounds the slide, indicating that it is selected. On your keyboard, press Del to delete the slide. Click **Save**.

Activity 1.21 | Moving Slides in Slide Sorter View

1 With the presentation displayed in Slide Sorter view, point to **Slide 2**. Hold down the left mouse button, and then drag the slide to the left until the vertical move bar and pointer indicating the position to which the slide will be moved is positioned to the left of **Slide 1**, as shown in Figure 1.42.

Figure 1.42

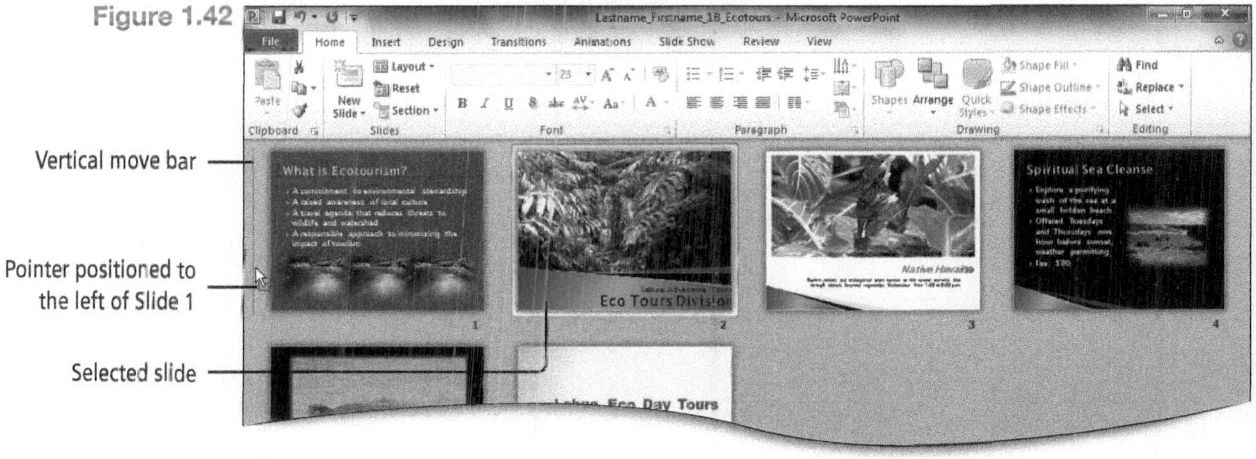

PowerPoint | Chapter 1

2 Release the mouse button to move the slide to the Slide 1 position in the presentation.

3 Click **Slide 4**, hold down Ctrl, and then click **Slide 5**. Compare your screen with Figure 1.43.

Both slides are outlined, indicating that both are selected. By holding down Ctrl, you can create a group of selected slides.

Figure 1.43

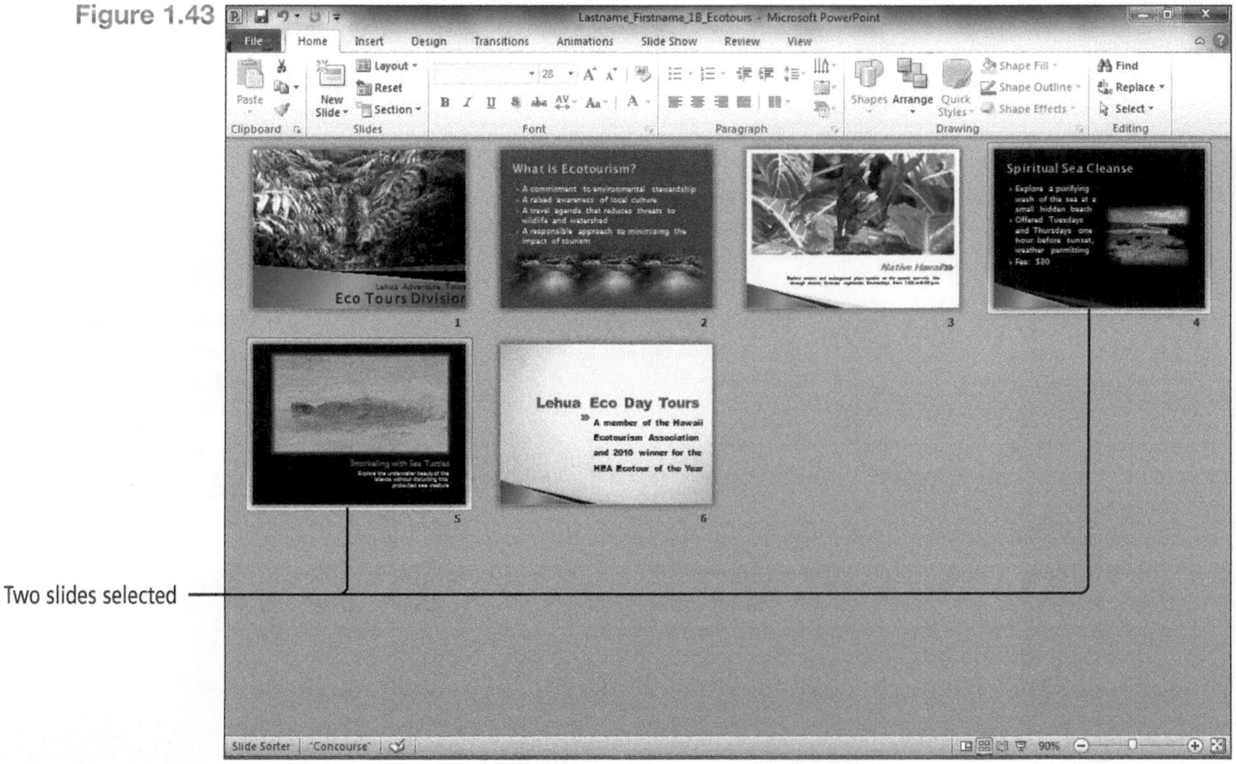

4 Point to either of the selected slides, hold down the left mouse button, and then drag to position the vertical move bar to the left of **Slide 3**. Release the mouse button to move the two slides, and then compare your screen with Figure 1.44.

Figure 1.44

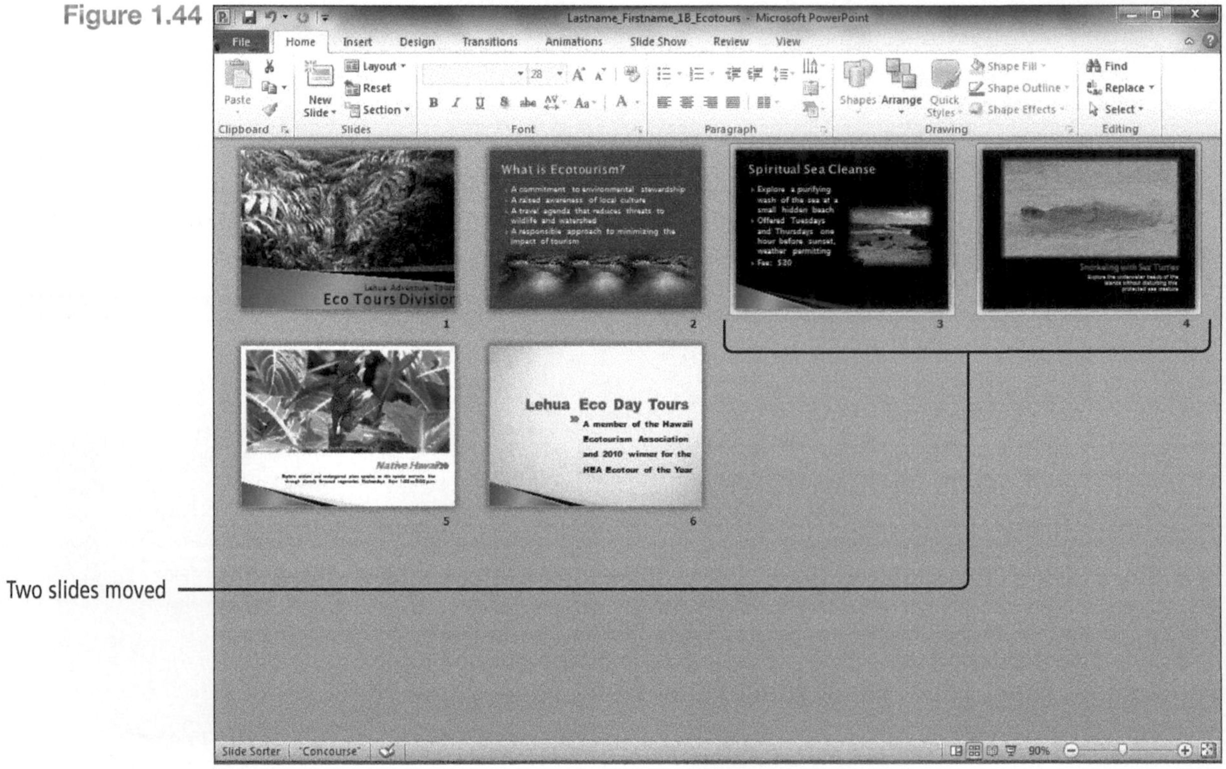

5 In the status bar, click the **Normal** button to return to Normal view. **Save** your presentation.

Objective 8 | Apply Slide Transitions

Slide transitions are the motion effects that occur in Slide Show view when you move from one slide to the next during a presentation. You can choose from a variety of transitions, and you can control the speed and method with which the slides advance.

Activity 1.22 | Applying Slide Transitions to a Presentation

1 Display **Slide 1**. On the **Transitions tab**, in the **Transition to This Slide group**, click the **More** button to display the **Transitions** gallery. Compare your screen with Figure 1.45.

Figure 1.45

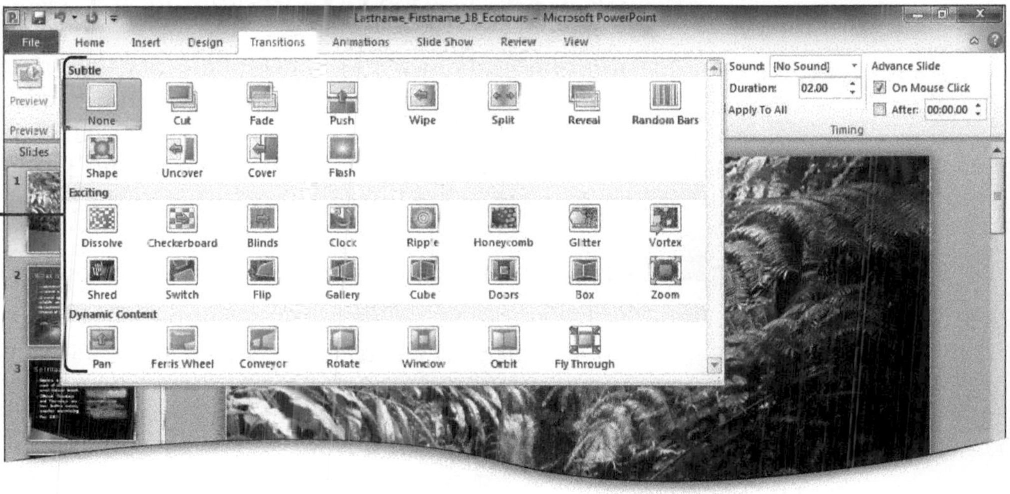

Transitions gallery

2 Under **Exciting**, click **Doors** to apply and view the transition. In the **Transition to This Slide group**, click the **Effect Options** button to display the directions from which the slide enters the screen. Click **Horizontal**.

The Effect Options vary depending upon the selected transition and include the direction from which the slide enters the screen or the shape in which the slide displays during the transition.

3 In the **Timing group**, notice that the **Duration** box displays *01.40*, indicating that the transition lasts 1.40 seconds. Click the **Duration** box **up spin arrow** two times so that *01.75* displays. Under **Advance Slide**, verify that the **On Mouse Click** check box is selected; select it if necessary. Compare your screen with Figure 1.46.

When the On Mouse Click option is selected, the presenter controls when the current slide advances to the next slide by clicking the mouse button or by pressing Spacebar.

Figure 1.46

On Mouse Click check box selected

Doors transition selected

Duration changed to *01.75*

4 In the **Timing group**, click the **Apply To All** button so that the Doors, Horizontal with a Duration of 1.75 seconds transition is applied to all of the slides in the presentation. Notice that in the Slides/Outline pane, a star displays below the slide number providing a visual cue that a transition has been applied to the slide.

5 Click the **Slide Show tab**. In the **Start Slide Show group**, click the **From Beginning** button, and then view your presentation, clicking the mouse button to advance through the slides. When the black slide displays, click the mouse button one more time to display the presentation in Normal view. **Save** your presentation.

> **More Knowledge | Applying Multiple Slide Transitions**
>
> You can apply more than one type of transition in your presentation by displaying the slides one at a time, and then clicking the transition that you want to apply instead of clicking the Apply To All button.

Activity 1.23 | Displaying a Presentation in Reading View

Organizations frequently conduct online meetings when participants are unable to meet in one location. The ***Reading view*** in PowerPoint displays a presentation in a manner similar to a slide show but the taskbar, title bar, and status bar remain available in the presentation window. Thus, a presenter can easily facilitate an online conference by switching to another window without closing the slide show.

> **Another Way**
>
> On the View tab, in the Presentation Views group, click Reading View.

1 In the lower right corner of the PowerPoint window, click the **Reading View** button. Compare your screen with Figure 1.47.

In Reading View, the status bar contains the Next and Previous buttons, which are used to navigate in the presentation, and the Menu button which is used to print, copy, and edit slides.

Figure 1.47

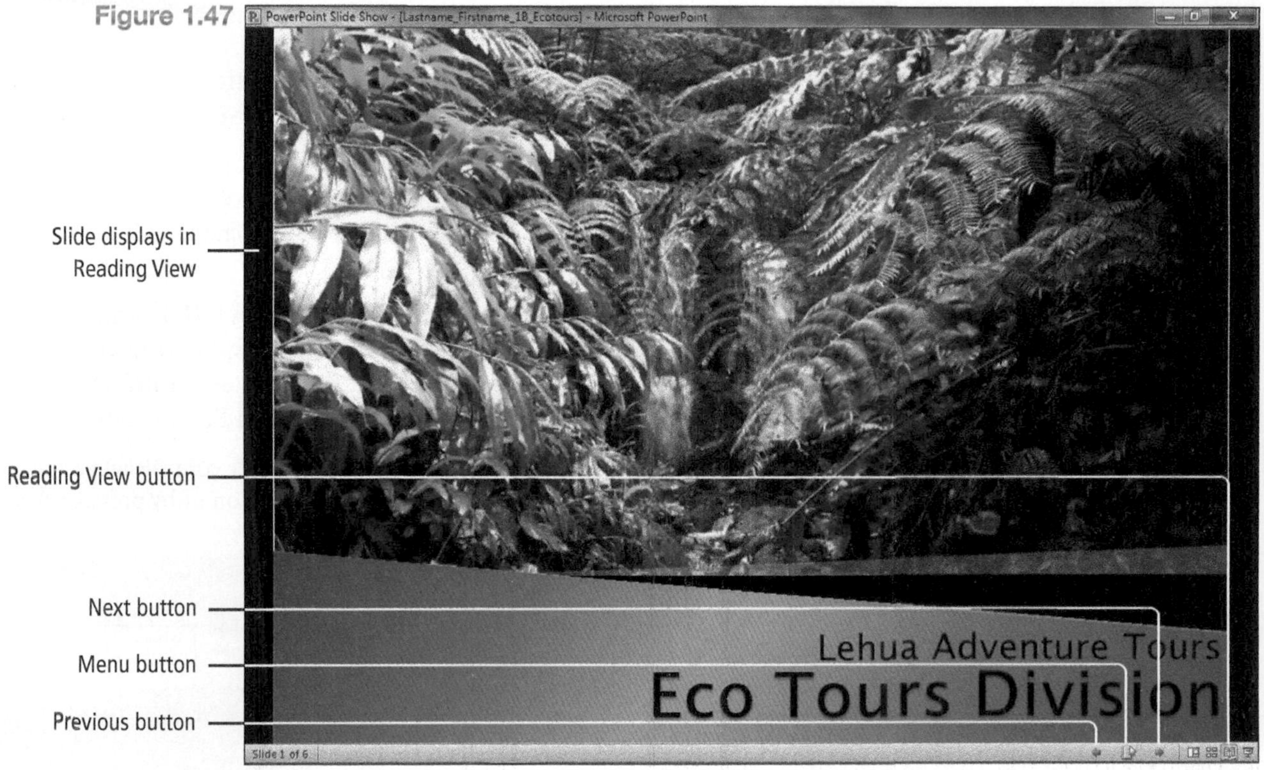

2 In the status bar, click the **Next** button to display **Slide 2**. Press [Spacebar] to display **Slide 3**. Click the left mouse button to display **Slide 4**. In the status bar, click the **Previous** button to display **Slide 3**.

> **Another Way**
> Press [Esc] to exit Reading view and return to Normal view.

3 In the status bar, click the **Menu** button to display the Reading view menu, and then click **End Show** to return to Normal view.

4 On the **Insert tab**, in the **Text group**, click the **Header & Footer** button, and then click the **Notes and Handouts tab**. Under **Include on page**, select the **Date and time** check box, and if necessary, select **Update automatically**. Clear the **Header** check box, and then select the **Page number** and **Footer** check boxes. In the **Footer** box, using your own name, type **Lastname_Firstname_1B_Ecotours** and then click **Apply to All**.

5 Display **Backstage** view, and then on the right, click **Properties**. Click **Show Document Panel**, and then in the **Author** box, delete any text and type your firstname and lastname. In the **Subject** box, type your course name and section number, and in the **Keywords** box, type **ecotours, ecotourism Close** [X] the Document Information Panel.

6 **Save** your presentation. Submit your presentation electronically or print **Handouts, 6 Slides Horizontal**, as directed by your instructor.

7 **Close** the presentation and **Exit** PowerPoint.

More Knowledge | Broadcasting a Slide Show

You can broadcast a slide show to remote viewers by using the PowerPoint Broadcast Service or another broadcast service. To broadcast a slide show, on the Slide Show tab, in the Start Slide Show group, click Broadcast Slide Show, and then follow the instructions in the Broadcast Slide Show dialog box to start the broadcast.

End You have completed Project 1B

Content-Based Assessments

Summary

In this chapter, you created a new PowerPoint presentation and edited an existing presentation by reusing slides from another presentation. You entered, edited, and formatted text in Normal view; worked with slides in Slide Sorter view; and viewed the presentation as a slide show. You also added emphasis to your presentations by inserting pictures, applying font formatting, and modifying layout, alignment, and line spacing.

Key Terms

Matching

Match each term in the second column with its correct definition in the first column by writing the letter of the term on the blank line in front of the correct definition.

____ 1. The PowerPoint view in which the window is divided into three panes—the Slide pane, the Slides/Outline pane, and the Notes pane.

____ 2. A presentation page that can contain text, pictures, tables, charts, and other multimedia or graphic objects.

____ 3. The first slide in a presentation, the purpose of which is to provide an introduction to the presentation topic.

____ 4. A box on a slide with dotted or dashed borders that holds title and body text or other content such as charts, tables, and pictures.

____ 5. A set of unified design elements that provides a look for your presentation by applying colors, fonts, and effects.

____ 6. An outline level in a presentation represented by a bullet symbol and identified in a slide by the indentation and the size of the text.

____ 7. Small circles and squares that indicate that a picture is selected.

____ 8. A green circle located above a selected picture with which you can rotate the selected image.

____ 9. A collection of formatting options that can be applied to a picture, text, or object.

____ 10. A slide that displays at the end of every slide show to indicate that the presentation is over.

____ 11. Printed images of slides on a sheet of paper.

A Black slide
B Formatting
C List level
D Normal view
E Notes page
F Placeholder
G Rotation handle
H Sizing handles
I Slide
J Slide handouts
K Slide transitions
L Style
M Text alignment
N Theme
O Title slide

_____ 12. A printout that contains the slide image on the top half of the page and notes that you have created in the Notes pane on the lower half of the page.

_____ 13. The process of changing the appearance of the text, layout, and design of a slide.

_____ 14. The term that refers to the horizontal placement of text within a placeholder.

_____ 15. Motion effects that occur in Slide Show view when you move from one slide to the next during a presentation.

Multiple Choice

Circle the correct answer.

1. In Normal view, the pane that displays a large image of the active slide is the:
A. Slide pane **B.** Slides/Outline pane **C.** Notes pane

2. In Normal view, the pane that displays below the Slide pane is the:
A. Slide Sorter pane **B.** Slides/Outline pane **C.** Notes pane

3. The buttons in the lower right corner that control the look of the presentation window are the:
A. Normal buttons **B.** View buttons **C.** Thumbnails buttons

4. The process of modifying a presentation by adding and deleting slides or by changing the contents of individual slides is referred to as:
A. Editing **B.** Formatting **C.** Aligning

5. The arrangement of elements, such as title and subtitle text, lists, pictures, tables, charts, shapes, and movies, on a PowerPoint slide is referred to as:
A. Theme modification **B.** Editing **C.** Layout

6. Text that prints at the top of a sheet of slide handouts or notes pages is a:
A. Header **B.** Footer **C.** Page number

7. Text that displays at the bottom of every slide or that prints at the bottom of a sheet of slide handouts or notes.
A. Header **B.** Footer **C.** Page number

8. The command that locates all occurrences of specific text and replaces it with alternative text is:
A. Replace **B.** Find **C.** Edit

9. The view in which all of the slides in your presentation display in miniature is:
A. Slide Sorter view **B.** Normal view **C.** Reading view

10. A view similar to Slide Show view but that also displays the title bar, status bar, and taskbar is:
A. Slide Sorter view **B.** Normal view **C.** Reading view

Apply 1A skills from these Objectives:

1. Create a New Presentation
2. Edit a Presentation in Normal View
3. Add Pictures to a Presentation
4. Print and View a Presentation

Skills Review | Project 1C Tour Hawaii

In the following Skills Review, you will create a new presentation by inserting content and pictures, adding notes and footers, and applying a presentation theme. Your completed presentation will look similar to Figure 1.48.

Project Files

For Project 1C, you will need the following files:

New blank PowerPoint presentation
p01C_Harbor
p01C_View

You will save your presentation as:

Lastname_Firstname_1C_Tour_Hawaii

Project Results

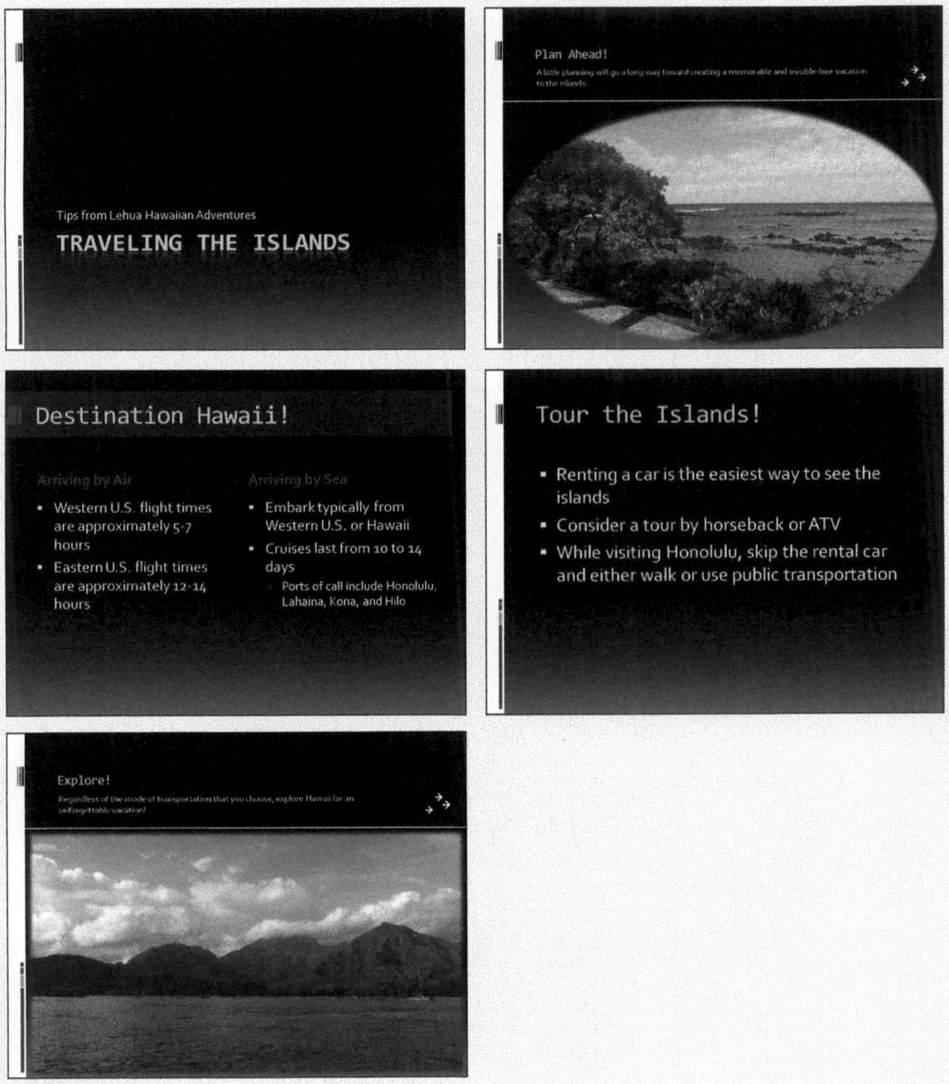

Figure 1.48

(Project 1C Tour Hawaii continues on the next page)

Skills Review | Project 1C Tour Hawaii (continued)

1 **Start** PowerPoint to display a new blank presentation in Normal view.

a. In the **Slide pane**, click in the title placeholder, which contains the text *Click to add title*. Type **Traveling the Islands**

b. Click in the subtitle placeholder, and then type **Tips from Lehua Hawaiian Adventures**

c. Right-click *Lehua*, and then on the shortcut menu, click **Ignore All**.

d. On the Ribbon, click the **Design tab**. In the **Themes group**, click the **More** button to display the **Themes gallery**. Recall that the themes display alphabetically. Using the ScreenTips, locate and then click **Metro** to apply the Metro theme to the presentation.

e. On the Quick Access Toolbar, click the **Save** button, navigate to your **PowerPoint Chapter 1** folder, and then **Save** the presentation as **Lastname_Firstname_1C_Tour_Hawaii**

2 On the **Home tab**, in the **Slides group**, click the **New Slide button arrow**. In the gallery, click the **Picture with Caption** layout to insert a new slide.

a. In the **Slide pane**, click the text *Click to add title*, and then type **Plan Ahead!**

b. Click in the text placeholder below the title, and then type **A little planning will go a long way toward creating a memorable and trouble-free vacation to the islands.**

c. In the picture placeholder, click the **Insert picture from File** button, and then navigate to your student data files. Click **p01C_View**, and then press Enter to insert the picture.

d. With the picture selected, on the **Format tab**, in the **Picture Styles group**, click the **More** button to display the **Picture Styles** gallery. Use the ScreenTips to locate, and then click the style **Soft Edge Oval**.

e. In the **Adjust group**, click the **Artistic Effects** button, and then in the fourth row, click the second effect—**Texturizer**.

3 On the **Home tab**, in the **Slides group**, click the **New Slide button arrow**. In the gallery, click the **Comparison** layout to insert a new slide. In the title placeholder, type **Destination Hawaii!**

a. Below the title, on the left side of the slide, click in the placeholder containing the pink words *Click to add text*. Type **Arriving by Air**

b. On the right side of the slide, click in the placeholder containing the pink words *Click to add text*. Type **Arriving by Sea**

c. On the left side of the slide, click in the content placeholder. Type **Western U.S. flight times are approximately 5–7 hours** and then press Enter. Type **Eastern U.S. flight times are approximately 12–14 hours**

d. On the right side of the slide, click in the content placeholder. Type **Embark typically from Western U.S. or Hawaii** and then press Enter. Type **Cruises last from 10 to 14 days**

e. Press Enter, and then on the **Home tab**, in the **Paragraph group**, click the **Increase List Level** button, and then type **Ports of call include Honolulu, Lahaina, Kona, and Hilo**

f. Right-click *Lahaina*, and then on the shortcut menu, click **Ignore All**. **Save** your presentation.

4 On the **Home tab**, in the **Slides group**, click the **New Slide button arrow**. In the gallery, click **Title and Content** to insert a new slide. In the title placeholder, type **Tour the Islands!**

a. In the content placeholder, type the following three bullet points:

Renting a car is the easiest way to see the islands

Consider a tour by horseback or ATV

While visiting Honolulu, skip the rental car and either walk or use public transportation

b. Below the slide, click in the **Notes pane**, and then type **Rental car company offices are located at each major airport.**

5 Insert a **New Slide** using the **Picture with Caption** layout.

a. In the title placeholder, type **Explore!** In the text placeholder, type **Regardless of the mode of transportation that you choose, explore Hawaii for an unforgettable vacation!**

b. In the center of the large picture placeholder, click the **Insert Picture from File** button. Navigate to your student files, and then insert **p01C_Harbor**.

c. With the picture selected, on the **Format tab**, in the **Picture Styles group**, click the **More** button to display the **Picture Styles** gallery. In the first row, click the sixth style—**Soft Edge Rectangle**.

(Project 1C Tour Hawaii continues on the next page)

Skills Review | Project 1C Tour Hawaii (continued)

6 On the Ribbon, click the **Slide Show tab**. In the **Start Slide Show group**, click the **From Beginning** button.

a. Click the left mouse button or press Spacebar to advance to the second slide. Continue to click or press Spacebar until the last slide displays, and then click or press Spacebar one more time to display a black slide.

b. With the black slide displayed, click the left mouse button or press Spacebar to exit the slide show and return to the presentation.

7 Click the **Insert tab**, and then in the **Text group**, click the **Header & Footer** button to display the **Header and Footer** dialog box.

a. In the **Header and Footer** dialog box, click the **Notes and Handouts tab**. Under **Include on page**, select the **Date and time** check box. If necessary, click the Update automatically option button so that the current date prints on the notes and handouts.

b. If necessary, clear the Header check box to omit this element. Select the **Page number** and **Footer** check boxes. In the **Footer** box, type **Lastname_Firstname_1C_Tour_Hawaii** and then click **Apply to All**.

c. Click the **File tab** to display **Backstage** view, and then on the right, click **Properties**. Click **Show Document Panel**, and then in the **Author** box, delete any text and type your firstname and lastname. In the **Subject** box, type your course name and section number, and in the **Keywords** box, type **travel tips, tour tips, trip planning Close** the Document Information Panel.

d. **Save** your presentation. Submit your presentation electronically or print **Handouts, 6 Slides Horizontal** as directed by your instructor. **Close** the presentation.

End You have completed Project 1C

Apply 1B skills from these Objectives:

5 Edit an Existing Presentation
6 Format a Presentation
7 Use Slide Sorter View
8 Apply Slide Transitions

Skills Review | Project 1D Luau Information

In the following Skills Review, you will edit an existing presentation by inserting slides from another presentation, applying font and slide formatting, and applying slide transitions. Your completed presentation will look similar to Figure 1.49.

Project Files

For Project 1D, you will need the following files:

p01D_Luau_Information
p01D_History_of_Luaus

You will save your presentation as:

Lastname_Firstname_1D_Luau_Information

Project Results

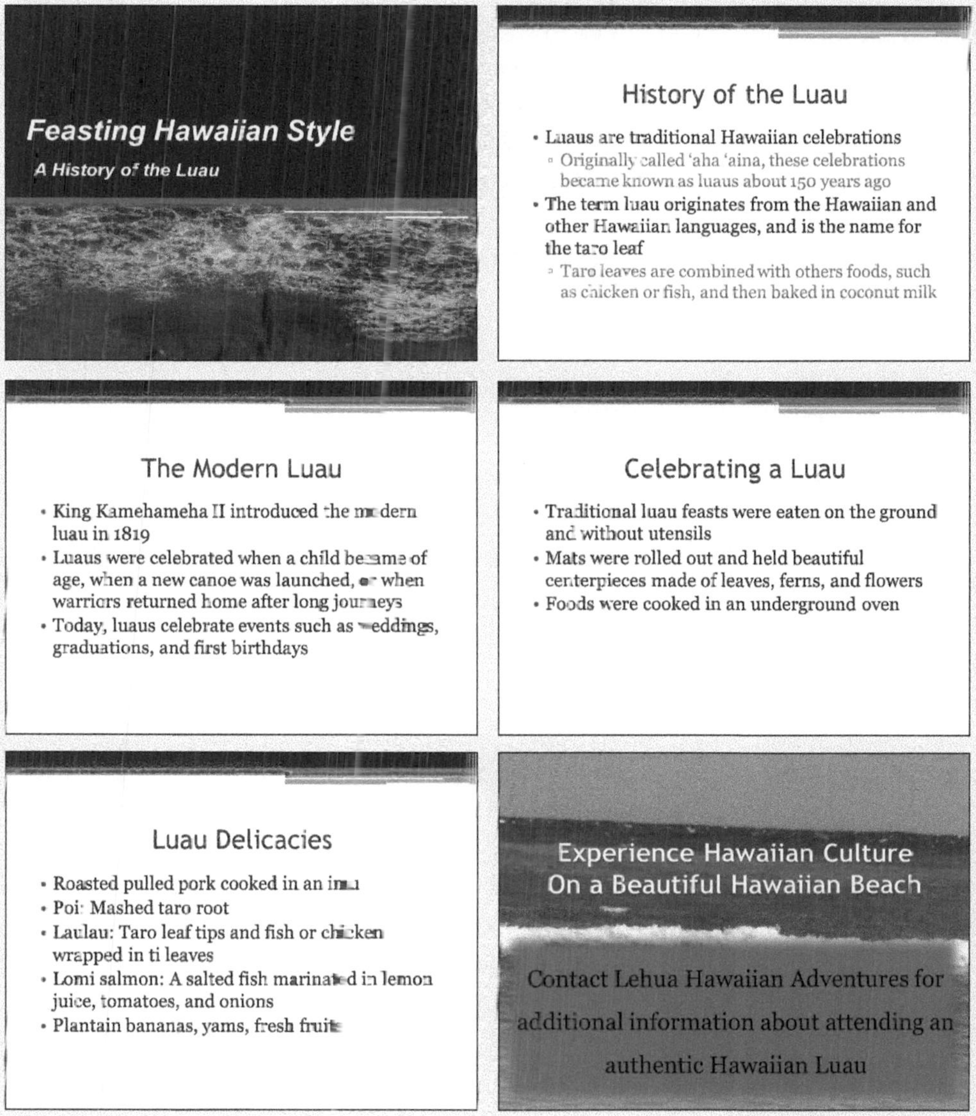

Figure 1.49

(Project 1D Luau Information continues on the next page)

Skills Review | Project 1D Luau Information (continued)

1 **Start** PowerPoint. From your student files, open **p01D_Luau_Information**. Click the **File tab** to display **Backstage** view, click **Save As**, navigate to your **PowerPoint Chapter 1** folder, and then using your own name, **Save** the file as **Lastname_Firstname_1D_Luau_Information** Take a moment to examine the content of the presentation.

a. In the **Slides/Outline pane**, click the **Outline tab** to display the presentation outline.

b. In the **Outline tab**, in **Slide 2**, click anywhere in the last bullet point, which begins with the text *Luaus were celebrated.*

c. On the **Home tab**, in the **Paragraph group**, click the **Decrease List Level** button one time.

d. In the **Outline tab**, click at the end of the second bullet after the word *journeys*. Press Enter to create a new bullet point at the same list level as the previous bullet point. Type **Today, luaus celebrate events such as weddings, graduations, and first birthdays**

e. In the **Slides/Outline pane**, click the **Slides tab** to display the slide thumbnails.

2 Display **Slide 1**. On the **Home tab**, in the **Slides group**, click the **New Slide button arrow** to display the **Slide Layout** gallery and additional options for inserting slides.

a. Below the gallery, click **Reuse Slides** to open the **Reuse Slides** pane on the right side of the PowerPoint window.

b. In the **Reuse Slides** pane, click the **Browse** button, and then click **Browse File**. In the **Browse** dialog box, navigate to your student files, and then double-click **p01D_History_of_Luaus**.

c. At the bottom of the **Reuse Slides** pane, select the **Keep source formatting** check box.

d. In the **Reuse Slides** pane, click the first slide—*Luau Information*—to insert the slide into the current presentation after **Slide 1**. In the **Reuse Slides** pane, click the second slide—**Celebrating a Luau** to insert it as the third slide in your presentation.

e. In your **1D_Luau_Information** presentation, in the **Slides/Outline pane**, click **Slide 5** to display it in the **Slide pane**.

f. In the **Reuse Slides** pane, click the third slide—*History of the Luau*—and then click the fourth slide—*Luau Delicacies*—to insert both slides after **Slide 5**. In the **Reuse Slides** pane, click the **Close** button.

3 Display **Slide 1**, and then select the title—*Feasting Polynesian Style.*

a. Point to the Mini toolbar, and then click the **Font arrow** to display the available fonts. Click **Arial**, and then click the **Font Size arrow**. Click **44** to change the font size. Use the Mini toolbar to apply **Bold** and **Italic** to the title.

b. Select the subtitle—*A History of the Luau*. Use the Mini toolbar to change the **Font** to **Arial** and the **Font Size** to **28**.

c. On the **Home tab**, in the **Editing group**, click the **Replace** button. In the **Replace** dialog box, click in the **Find what** box. Type **Polynesian** and then in the **Replace with** box, type **Hawaiian**

d. In the **Replace** dialog box, click the **Replace All** button to replace three occurrences of *Polynesian* with *Hawaiian*. Click **OK** to close the message box, and then in the **Replace** dialog box, click the **Close** button.

e. Display **Slide 6**, and then select the second bullet point, which begins *Originally*. On the Mini toolbar, click the **Font Color button arrow**. Under **Theme Colors**, in the sixth column, click the first color—**Teal, Accent 2**.

f. Select the last bullet point, which begins *Taro leaves*. On the Mini toolbar, click the **Font Color button** to apply **Teal, Accent 2** to the selection.

4 With **Slide 6** displayed, click anywhere in the title.

a. On the **Home tab**, in the **Paragraph group**, click the **Center** button to center the text within the placeholder.

b. Display **Slide 7**, and then **Center** the slide title.

c. Display **Slide 5**, and then click anywhere in the text in the lower portion of the slide. In the **Paragraph group**, click the **Line Spacing** button. In the list, click **1.5** to change from single-spacing between lines to one-and-a-half spacing between lines.

d. Display **Slide 3**. On the **Home tab**, in the **Slides group**, click the **Layout** button to display the **Slide Layout** gallery. Click **Title and Content** to change the slide layout.

5 In the lower right corner of the PowerPoint window, in the **View** buttons, click the **Slide Sorter** button to display the slide thumbnails in Slide Sorter view.

(Project 1D Luau Information continues on the next page)

Skills Review | Project 1D Luau Information (continued)

a. Click **Slide 2**, and then notice that a thick outline surrounds the slide, indicating that it is selected. Press Del to delete the slide.

b. Point to **Slide 5**, hold down the mouse button, and then drag to position the vertical move bar to the left of **Slide 2**. Release the mouse button to move the slide.

c. Point to **Slide 5**, hold down the mouse button, and then drag so that the vertical move bar displays to the right of **Slide 6**. Release the mouse button to move the slide so that it is the last slide in the presentation.

d. Point to **Slide 4**, hold down the mouse button, and then drag so that the vertical move bar displays to the left of **Slide 3**. Release the mouse button to move the slide.

e. In the **View** buttons, click the **Normal** button to return the presentation to Normal view.

6 Display **Slide 1**. On the **Transitions tab**, in the **Transition to This Slide group**, click the **Wipe** button to apply the Wipe transition to the slide.

a. In the **Transition to This Slide group**, click the **Effect Options** button, and then click **From Top**.

b. In the **Timing group**, click the **Duration** box **up spin arrow** twice to change the Duration to *01.50*.

c. In the **Timing group**, under **Advance Slide**, verify that the **On Mouse Click** check box is selected, and select it if necessary.

d. In the **Timing group**, click the **Apply To All** button so that the transition settings are applied to all of the slides in the presentation.

e. Click the **Slide Show tab**. In the **Start Slide Show group**, click the **From Beginning** button, and then view your presentation, clicking the mouse button to advance through the slides. When the black slide displays, click the mouse button one more time to display the presentation in Normal view.

f. On the **Insert tab**, in the **Text group**, click the **Header & Footer** button to display the **Header and Footer** dialog box. Click the **Notes and Handouts tab**. Under **Include on page**, select the **Date and time** check box, and then if necessary, select Update automatically.

g. Clear the **Header** check box if necessary, and then select the **Page number** and **Footer** check boxes. In the **Footer** box, using your own name, type **Lastname_Firstname_1D_Luau_Information** and then click **Apply to All**.

h. Click the **File tab**, and then on the right side of the window, click **Properties**. Click **Show Document Panel**, and then in the **Author** box, delete any text and type your firstname and lastname. In the **Subject** box, type your course name and section number, and in the **Keywords** box, type **luau, Hawaiian history, Hawaiian culture** **Close** the Document Information Panel.

i. **Save** your presentation. Submit your presentation electronically or print **Handouts, 6 Slides Horizontal** as directed by your instructor. **Close** the presentation.

End **You have completed Project 1D**

Apply 1A skills from these Objectives:

1. Create a New Presentation
2. Edit a Presentation in Normal View
3. Add Pictures to a Presentation
4. Print and View a Presentation

Mastering PowerPoint | Project 1E Boat Tours

In the following Mastering PowerPoint project, you will create a new presentation describing the types of boat tours offered by Lehua Hawaiian Adventures. Your completed presentation will look similar to Figure 1.50.

Project Files

For Project 1E, you will need the following files:

New blank PowerPoint presentation
p01E_Catamaran
p01E_Raft

You will save your presentation as:

Lastname_Firstname_1E_Boat_Tours

Project Results

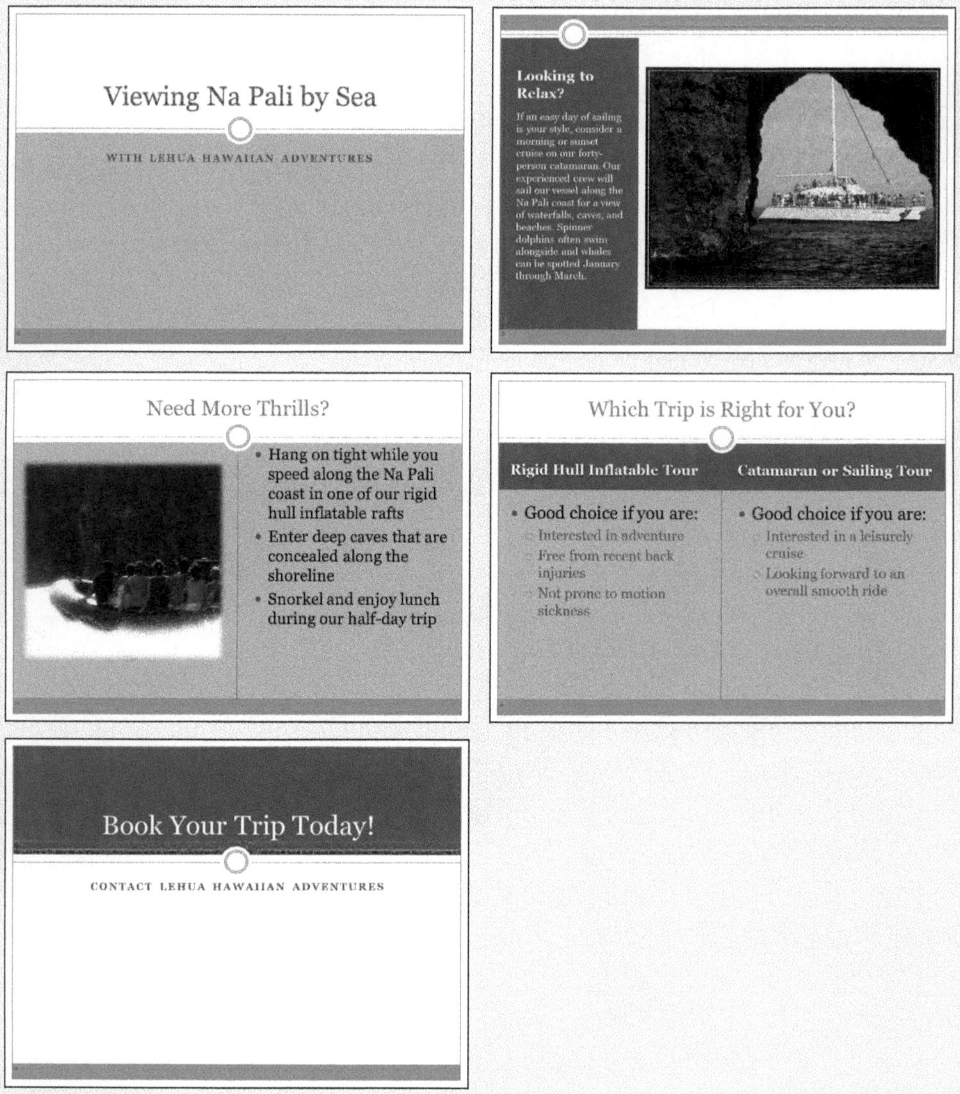

Figure 1.50

(Project 1E Boat Tours continues on the next page)

Mastering PowerPoint | Project 1E Boat Tours (continued)

1 **Start** PowerPoint to display a new blank presentation, and then change the **Design** by applying the **Civic** theme. As the title of this presentation type **Viewing Na Pali by Sea** and as the subtitle type **With Lehua Hawaiian Adventures**

2 Correct spelling errors on this slide by choosing the **Ignore All** option for the words *Pali* and *Lehua*. Save the presentation in your **PowerPoint Chapter 1** folder as **Lastname_Firstname_1E_Boat_Tours**

3 Insert a **New Slide** using the **Content with Caption** layout. In the title placeholder, type **Looking to Relax?** In the large content placeholder on the right side of the slide, from your student files, insert the picture **p01E_Catamaran.** Format the picture with the **Compound Frame, Black** picture style and the **Texturizer** artistic effect.

4 In the text placeholder, type **If an easy day of sailing is your style, consider a morning or sunset cruise on our forty-person catamaran. Our experienced crew will sail our vessel along the Na Pali coast for a view of waterfalls, caves, and beaches. Spinner dolphins often swim alongside and whales can be spotted January through March.**

5 Insert a **New Slide** using the **Two Content** layout. In the title placeholder, type **Need More Thrills?** In the content placeholder on the left side of the slide, from your student files, insert the picture **p01E_Raft**. Format the picture with the **Soft Edge Rectangle** picture style and the **Glow Diffused** artistic effect. In the content placeholder on the right side of the slide, type the following three bullet points:

Hang on tight while you speed along the Na Pali coast in one of our rigid hull inflatable rafts

Enter deep caves that are concealed along the shoreline

Snorkel and enjoy lunch during our half-day trip

6 Insert a **New Slide** using the **Comparison** layout. In the title placeholder, type **Which Trip is Right for You?** In the orange placeholder on the left side of the slide, type **Rigid Hull Inflatable Tour** and in the orange placeholder on the right side of the slide, type **Catamaran or Sailing Tour**

7 In the content placeholder on the left, type each of the following bullet points, increasing the list level for the last three bullet points as indicated:

Good choice if you are:

- **Interested in adventure**
- **Free from recent back injuries**
- **Not prone to motion sickness**

8 In the content placeholder on the right, type each of the following bullet points, increasing the list level for the last two bullet points as indicated:

Good choice if you are:

- **Interested in a leisurely cruise**
- **Looking forward to an overall smooth ride**

9 On **Slide 4**, type the following notes in the **Notes pane**: **If you need assistance deciding which boat tour is right for you, we'll be happy to help you decide.** Insert a **New Slide** using the **Section Header** layout. In the title placeholder, type **Book Your Trip Today!** In the text placeholder, type **Contact Lehua Hawaiian Adventures**

10 Insert a **Header & Footer** on the **Notes and Handouts**. Include the **Date and time** updated automatically, the **Page number**, and a **Footer**—using your own name—with the text **Lastname_Firstname_1E_Boat_Tours** and apply to all the slides.

11 Display the **Document Information Panel.** Replace the text in the **Author** box with your own firstname and lastname. In the **Subject** box, type your course name and section number, and in the **Keywords** box, type **Na Pali, boat tours, sailing Close** the Document Information Panel.

12 **Save** your presentation, and then view the slide show from the beginning. Submit your presentation electronically or print **Handouts, 6 Slides Horizontal** as directed by your instructor. **Close** the presentation.

End **You have completed Project 1E**

Apply 1B skills from these Objectives:

- 5 Edit an Existing Presentation
- 6 Format a Presentation
- 7 Use Slide Sorter View
- 8 Apply Slide Transitions

Mastering PowerPoint | Project 1F Helicopter Tour

In the following Mastering PowerPoint project, you will edit a presentation describing the helicopter tours offered by Lehua Hawaiian Adventures. Your completed presentation will look similar to Figure 1.51.

Project Files

For Project 1F, you will need the following files:

p01F_Helicopter_Tour
p01F_Aerial_Views

You will save your presentation as:

Lastname_Firstname_1F_Helicopter_Tour

Project Results

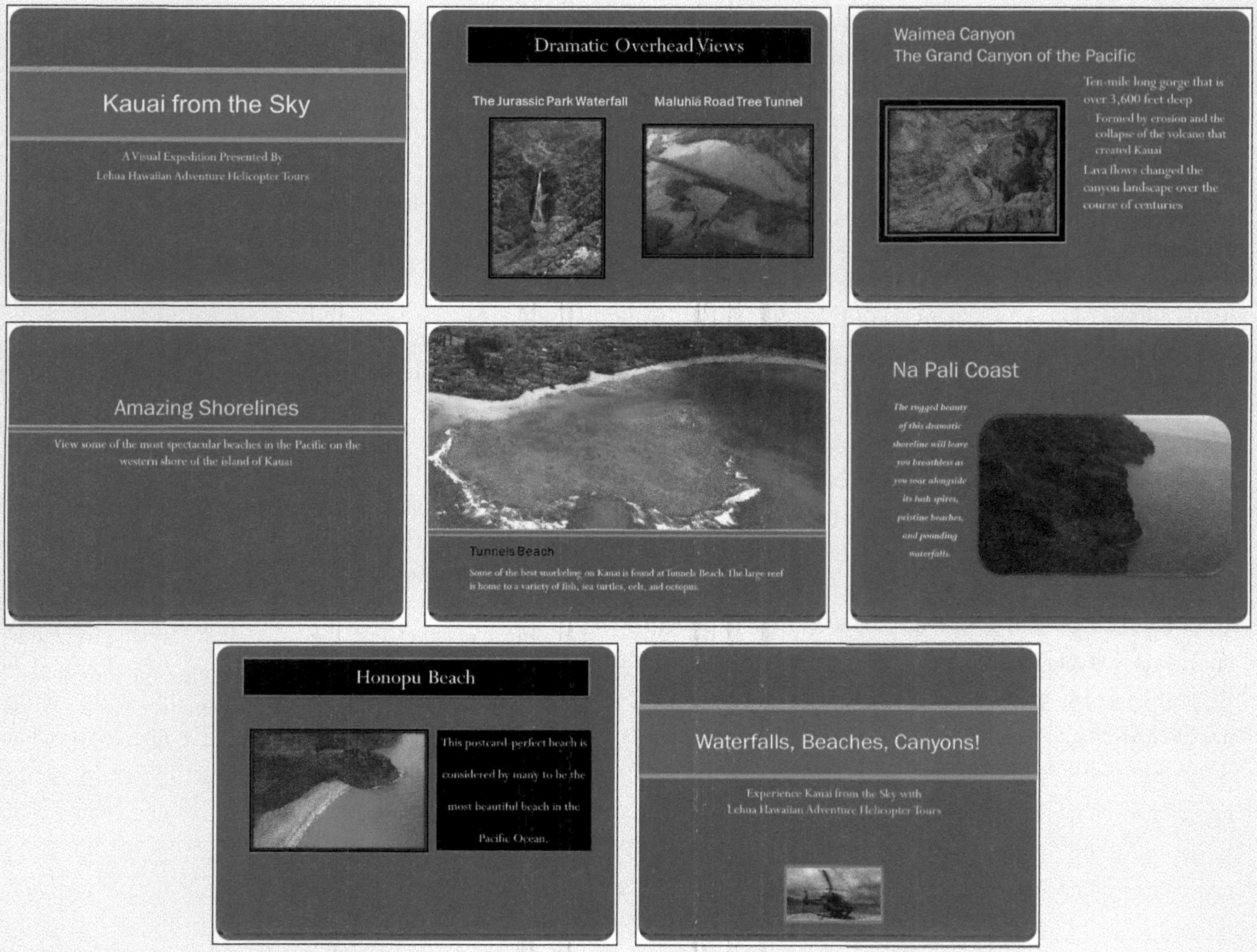

Figure 1.51

(Project 1F Helicopter Tour continues on the next page)

Mastering PowerPoint | Project 1F Helicopter Tour (continued)

1 **Start** PowerPoint, and then from your student data files, open the file **p01F_Helicopter_Tour.** In your **PowerPoint Chapter 1** folder, **Save** the file as **Lastname_Firstname_1F_Helicopter_Tour**

2 Display the presentation **Outline**. In the **Outline tab**, in **Slide 2**, increase the list level of the bullet point that begins *Formed by erosion*. In the **Outline tab**, click at the end of the second bullet point after the word *Kauai*. Press Enter, and then decrease the list level of the new bullet point. Type **Lava flows changed the canyon landscape over the course of centuries**

3 In the **Slides/Outline pane**, click the **Slides tab** to display the slide thumbnails, and then display **Slide 1**. Display the **Reuse Slides** pane, and then click the **Browse** button. Click **Browse File**, and then in the **Browse** dialog box, from your student files, open **p01F_Aerial_Views.** Select the **Keep source formatting** check box, and then from this group of slides, insert the first and second slides—*Aerial View of Kauai* and *Dramatic Overhead.*

4 In the **Slides/Outline pane**, click **Slide 4** to display it in the **Slide pane**, and then from the **Reuse Slides** pane, insert the third, fourth, fifth, and sixth slides—*Na Pali Coast, Honopu Beach, Amazing Shorelines, Tunnels Beach.* **Close** the **Reuse Slides** pane.

5 Display **Slide 1**, and then select the title—*Maui from the Sky*. Change the **Font** to **Arial**, and the **Font Size** to **44**. Change the **Font Color** to **White, Text 1**. Display the **Replace** dialog box. **Replace All** occurrences of the word **Maui** with **Kauai** and then **Close** the **Replace** dialog box.

6 Display **Slide 5**, and then select the paragraph in the content placeholder. Apply **Bold** and **Italic**, and then **Center** the text. Change the **Line Spacing** to **1.5**. Display **Slide 7**, and then change the **Slide Layout** to **Section Header**. **Center** the text in both placeholders.

7 In **Slide Sorter** view, delete **Slide 2**. Then select **Slides 6** and **7** and move both slides so that they are positioned after **Slide 3**. In **Normal** view, display **Slide 1**. Apply the **Split** transition and change the **Effect Options** to **Horizontal Out**. Apply the transition to all of the slides in the presentation. View the slide show from the beginning.

8 **Insert** a **Header & Footer** on the **Notes and Handouts**. Include the **Date and time** updated automatically, the **Page number**, and a **Footer** with the text **Lastname_Firstname_1F_Helicopter_Tour** Apply to all the slides.

9 Check spelling in the presentation. If necessary, select the Ignore All option if proper names are indicated as misspelled.

10 Display the **Document Information Panel**. Replace the text in the **Author** box with your own firstname and lastname. In the **Subject** box, type your course name and section number, and in the **Keywords** box, type **helicopter, Kauai** **Close** the Document Information Panel.

11 **Save** your presentation, and then submit your presentation electronically or print **Handouts, 4 Slides Horizontal** as directed by your instructor. **Close** the presentation.

End **You have completed Project 1F**

Content-Based Assessments

Apply 1A and 1B skills from these Objectives:

1. Create a New Presentation
2. Edit a Presentation in Normal View
3. Add Pictures to a Presentation
4. Print and View a Presentation
5. Edit an Existing Presentation
6. Format a Presentation
7. Use Slide Sorter View
8. Apply Slide Transitions

myitlab grader

Mastering PowerPoint | Project 1G Volcano Tour

In the following Mastering PowerPoint project, you will edit an existing presentation that describes the tour of Volcanoes National Park offered by Lehua Hawaiian Adventures. Your completed presentation will look similar to Figure 1.52.

Project Files

For Project 1G, you will need the following files:

p01G_Crater_Information
p01G_Lava
p01G_Volcano_Tour

You will save your presentation as:

Lastname_Firstname_1G_Volcano_Tour

Project Results

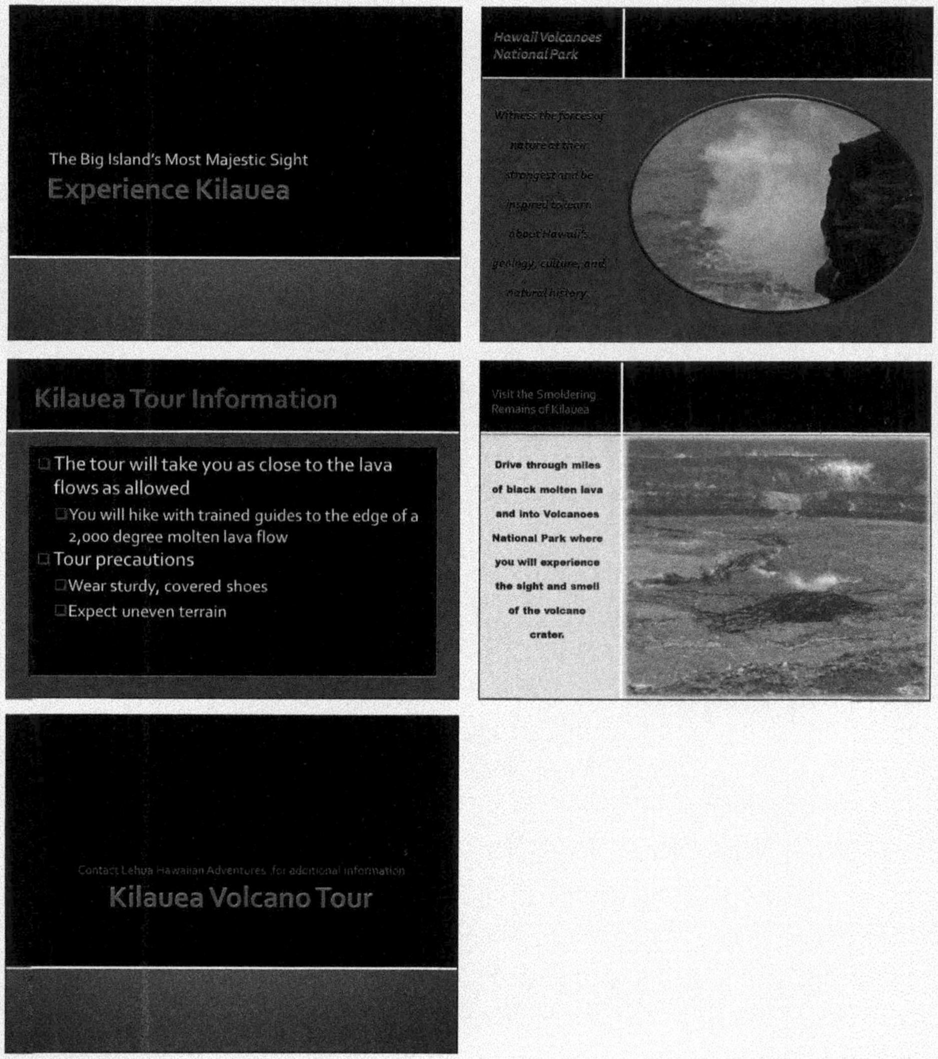

Figure 1.52

(Project 1G Volcano Tour continues on the next page)

Mastering PowerPoint | Project 1G Volcano Tour (continued)

1 **Start** PowerPoint, and then from your student files, open the file **p01G_Volcano_Tour**. In your **PowerPoint Chapter 1** folder, **Save** the file as **Lastname_Firstname_1G_Volcano_Tour**

2 Replace all occurrences of the text **Diamond Head** with **Kilauea** Display **Slide 3**, open the **Reuse Slides** pane, and then from your student files browse for and display the presentation **p01G_Crater_Information**. If necessary, clear the Keep source formatting check box, and then insert both slides from the **p01G_Crater_Information** file. **Close** the **Reuse Slides** pane.

3 Display the presentation outline, and then in **Slide 3**, increase the list level of the bullet point beginning *You will hike*. In either the **Slide pane** or the **Outline**, click at the end of the last bullet point after the word *flow*, and then insert a new bullet point. Decrease its list level. Type **Tour precautions** and then press Enter. Increase the list level, and then type the following two bullet points.

Wear sturdy, covered shoes

Expect uneven terrain

4 Display the slide thumbnails. In **Slide 1**, select the subtitle—*The Big Island's Most Majestic Sight*—and then change the **Font Color** to **White, Text 1** and the **Font Size** to **28**. On **Slide 2**, center the caption text located below the slide title and apply **Bold** and **Italic**. Change the **Line Spacing** to **2.0**. Click in the content placeholder on the right, and then from your student files, insert the picture **p01G_Lava**. Format the picture with the **Beveled Oval, Black** picture style and the **Paint Brush** artistic effect.

5 In **Slide Sorter** view, move **Slide 5** between **Slides 3** and **4**. In **Normal** view, on **Slide 5**, change the slide **Layout** to **Title Slide**, and then type the following notes in the **Notes pane**: **Recent volcanic activity at the national park site may result in changes to the tour itinerary.** Apply the **Uncover** transition and change the **Effect Options** to **From Top**. Change the **Timing** by increasing the **Duration** to **01.50**. Apply the transition effect to all of the slides. View the slide show from the beginning.

6 **Insert** a **Header & Footer** on the **Notes and Handouts**. Include the **Date and time** updated automatically, the **Page number**, and a **Footer**, using your own name, with the text **Lastname_Firstname_1G_Volcano_Tour**

7 Check spelling in the presentation. If necessary, select the Ignore All option if proper names are indicated as misspelled.

8 Display the **Document Information Panel**. Replace the text in the **Author** box with your own firstname and lastname. In the **Subject** box, type your course name and section number, and in the **Keywords** box, type **Kilauea, volcano** **Close** the Document Information Panel.

9 **Save** your presentation. Submit your presentation electronically or print **Handouts, 6 Slides Horizontal** as directed by your instructor. **Close** the presentation.

End **You have completed Project 1G**

Apply a combination of the 1A and 1B skills.

GO! Fix It | Project 1H Hawaii Guide

Project Files

For Project 1H, you will need the following files:

p01H_Hawaii_Guide
p01H_Islands

You will save your presentation as:

Lastname_Firstname_1H_Hawaii_Guide

In this project, you will edit a presentation prepared by Lehua Hawaiian Adventures that describes some of the activities on each of the Hawaiian Islands. From the student files that accompany this textbook, open the file p01H_Hawaii_Guide, and then save the file in your chapter folder as **Lastname_Firstname_1H_Hawaii_Guide**

To complete the project, you should know:

- All of the slides in the p01H_Islands presentation should be reused in this presentation and inserted after Slide 2. Correct two spelling errors and ignore all instances of proper names that are indicated as misspelled.
- The Opulent theme should be applied.
- Slides 3 through 8 should be arranged alphabetically according to the name of the island
- On the Maui and Molokai slides, the list level of the second bullet points should decreased.
- The Layout for Slide 2 should be Section Header, the slide should be moved to the end of the presentation, and the Flip transition using the Left effect option should be applied to all of the slides in the presentation.
- Document Properties should include your name, course name and section, and the keywords **guide, islands** A Header & Footer should be inserted on the Notes and Handouts that includes the Date and time updated automatically, the Page number, and a Footer with the text **Lastname_Firstname_1H_Hawaii_Guide**

Save your presentation and submit electronically or print Handouts, 4 Slides Horizontal as directed by your instructor. Close the presentation.

End You have completed Project 1H

Content-Based Assessments

Apply a combination of the 1A and 1B skills.

GO! Make It | Project 1I Dolphin Encounter

Project Files

For Project 1I, you will need the following files:

p01I_Dolphin_Encounters
p01I_Dolphin

You will save your presentation as:

Lastname_Firstname_1I_Dolphin_Encounters

From your student files, open p01I_Dolphin_Encounters, and then save it in your PowerPoint Chapter 1 folder as **Lastname_Firstname_1I_Dolphin_Encounters**

By using the skills you practiced in this chapter, create the slide shown in Figure 1.53 by inserting a new Slide 2 with the layout and text shown in the figure. The title font size is 36, and the font color is Black, Background 1. The caption text font is Arial, and the font size is 16 with bold and italic applied. To complete the slide, from your student files, insert the picture p01H_Dolphin. Insert the date and time updated automatically, the file name, and a page number in the Notes and Handouts footer. In the Document Information Panel, add your name and course information and the keyword **dolphin** Save your presentation, and then print or submit electronically as directed by your instructor.

Project Results

Dolphin Encounters!
Learn about dolphins during our 30-minute training program. Then join the trainers in our pool as you swim and play with our dolphin friends!

Figure 1.53

End You have completed Project 1I

PowerPoint | Chapter 1

Apply a combination of the 1A and 1B skills.

GO! Solve It | Project 1J Planning Tips

Project Files

For Project 1J, you will need the following file:

p01J_Planning_Tips

You will save your presentation as:

Lastname_Firstname_1J_Planning_Tips

Open the file p01J_Planning_Tips and save it as **Lastname_Firstname_1J_Planning_Tips** Complete the presentation by applying a theme and by correcting spelling errors. Format the presentation attractively by applying appropriate font formatting and by changing text alignment and line spacing. Change the layout of at least one slide to a layout that will accommodate a picture. Insert a picture that you have taken yourself, or use one of the pictures in your student data files that you inserted in other projects in this chapter. On the last slide, insert an appropriate picture, and then apply picture styles to both pictures. Apply slide transitions to all of the slides in the presentation, and then insert a header and footer that includes the date and time updated automatically, the file name in the footer, and the page number. Add your name, your course name and section number, and the keywords **planning, weather** to the Properties area. Save and print or submit as directed by your instructor.

Performance Elements	Performance Level: Exemplary: You consistently applied the relevant skills	Proficient: You sometimes, but not always, applied the relevant skills	Developing: You rarely or never applied the relevant skills
Apply a theme	An appropriate theme was applied to the presentation.	A theme was applied but was not appropriate for the presentation.	A theme was not applied.
Apply font and slide formatting	Font and slide formatting is attractive and appropriate.	Adequately formatted but difficult to read or unattractive.	Inadequate or no formatting.
Use appropriate pictures and apply styles attractively	Two appropriate pictures are inserted and styles are applied attractively.	Pictures are inserted but styles are not applied or are inappropriately applied.	Pictures are not inserted.

End **You have completed Project 1J**

Apply a combination of the 1A and 1B skills.

GO! Solve It | Project 1K Hikes

Project Files

For Project 1K, you will need the following file:

p01K_Hikes

You will save your presentation as:

Lastname_Firstname_1K_Hikes

Open the file p01K_Hikes and save it as **Lastname_Firstname_1K_Hikes** Complete the presentation by applying an appropriate theme. Move Slide 2 to the end of the presentation, and then change the layout to one appropriate for the end of the presentation. Format the presentation attractively by applying font formatting and by changing text alignment and line spacing. Review the information on Slide 3, and then increase list levels appropriately on this slide. Apply picture styles to the two pictures in the presentation and an artistic effect to at least one picture. Apply slide transitions to all of the slides. Insert a header and footer that includes the date and time updated automatically, the file name in the footer, and the page number. Add your name, your course name and section number, and the keywords **hiking Akaka Falls, Waimea Canyon** to the Properties area. Save and print or submit as directed by your instructor.

Performance Elements	Performance Level: Exemplary: You consistently applied the relevant skills	Proficient: You sometimes, but not always, applied the relevant skills	Developing: You rarely or never applied the relevant skills
Apply a theme	An appropriate theme was applied to the presentation.	A theme was applied but was not appropriate for the presentation.	A theme was not applied.
Apply appropriate formatting	Formatting is attractive and appropriate.	Adequately formatted but difficult to read or unattractive.	Inadequate or no formatting.
Apply appropriate list levels	List levels are applied appropriately.	Some, but not all, list levels are appropriately applied.	Changes to list levels were not made.

End You have completed Project 1K

Outcomes-Based Assessments

Rubric

The following outcomes-based assessments are *open-ended assessments*. That is, there is no specific correct result; your result will depend on your approach to the information provided. Make *Professional Quality* your goal. Use the following scoring rubric to guide you in *how* to approach the problem, and then to evaluate *how well* your approach solves the problem.

The *criteria*—Software Mastery, Content, Format and Layout, and Process—represent the knowledge and skills you have gained that you can apply to solving the problem. The *levels of performance*—Professional Quality, Approaching Professional Quality, or Needs Quality Improvements—help you and your instructor evaluate your result.

	Your completed project is of Professional Quality if you:	**Your completed project is Approaching Professional Quality if you:**	**Your completed project Needs Quality Improvements if you:**
1-Software Mastery	Choose and apply the most appropriate skills, tools, and features and identify efficient methods to solve the problem.	Choose and apply some appropriate skills, tools, and features, but not in the most efficient manner.	Choose inappropriate skills, tools, or features, or are inefficient in solving the problem.
2-Content	Construct a solution that is clear and well organized, contains content that is accurate, appropriate to the audience and purpose, and is complete. Provide a solution that contains no errors in spelling, grammar, or style.	Construct a solution in which some components are unclear, poorly organized, inconsistent, or incomplete. Misjudge the needs of the audience. Have some errors in spelling, grammar, or style, but the errors do not detract from comprehension.	Construct a solution that is unclear, incomplete, or poorly organized; contains some inaccurate or inappropriate content; and contains many errors in spelling, grammar, or style. Do not solve the problem.
3-Format and Layout	Format and arrange all elements to communicate information and ideas, clarify function, illustrate relationships, and indicate relative importance.	Apply appropriate format and layout features to some elements, but not others. Overuse features, causing minor distraction.	Apply format and layout that does not communicate information or ideas clearly. Do not use format and layout features to clarify function, illustrate relationships, or indicate relative importance. Use available features excessively, causing distraction.
4-Process	Use an organized approach that integrates planning, development, self-assessment, revision, and reflection.	Demonstrate an organized approach in some areas, but not others; or, use an insufficient process of organization throughout.	Do not use an organized approach to solve the problem.

Apply a combination of the 1A and 1B skills.

GO! Think | Project 1L Big Island

Project Files

For Project 1L, you will need the following files:

New blank PowerPoint presentation
p01L_Fishing
p01L_Monument

You will save your presentation as:

Lastname_Firstname_1L_Big_Island

Carl Kawaoka, Tour Operations Manager for Lehua Hawaiian Adventures, is developing a presentation describing sea tours on the Big Island of Hawaii to be shown at a travel fair on the mainland. In the presentation, Carl will be showcasing the company's two most popular sea excursions: The Captain Cook Monument Snorkeling Tour and the Kona Deep Sea Fishing Tour.

On the Captain Cook Monument Snorkeling Tour, guests meet at 8:00 a.m. at the Lehua Hawaiian Adventures Kona location and then board a 12-passenger rigid hull inflatable raft. Captained by a U.S. Coast Guard licensed crew, the raft is navigated along the Hawaii coastline, exploring sea caves, lava tubes, and waterfalls. Upon arrival at the Monument, guests snorkel in Hawaii's incredible undersea world of colorful fish, sea turtles, and stingrays. Lehua Hawaiian Adventures provides the lunch, snacks, drinks, and snorkeling equipment and asks that guests bring their own towels, sunscreen, swim suits, and sense of adventure. This tour lasts 5 hours and the fee is $85.

On the Kona Deep Sea Fishing Tour, guests meet at 7:00 a.m. at the Lehua Hawaiian Adventures Kona location and then board a 32-foot Blackfin fishing boat. The boat is captained by a U.S. Coast Guard licensed crew of three. A maximum of six guests are allowed on each trip, which sails, weather permitting, every Wednesday, Friday, and Saturday. For deep sea fishing, there is no better place than the Kona coast. On full-day adventures, it is common for guests to catch marlin, sailfish, ahi, ono, and mahi-mahi. This tour lasts 8 hours and the fee is $385.

Using the preceding information, create a presentation that Carl can show at the travel fair. The presentation should include four to six slides describing the two tours. Apply an appropriate theme and use slide layouts that will effectively present the content. From your student files, insert the pictures p01L_Fishing and p01L_Monument on appropriate slides and apply picture styles or artistic effects to enhance the pictures. Apply font formatting and slide transitions, and modify text alignment and line spacing as necessary. Save the file as **Lastname_Firstname_1L_Big_Island** and then insert a header and footer that include the date and time updated automatically, the file name in the footer, and the page number. Add your name, your course name and section number, and the keywords **sea tours, deep sea fishing, snorkeling tours** to the Properties area. Save and print or submit as directed by your instructor.

End You have completed Project 1L

Apply a combination of the 1A and 1B skills.

GO! Think | Project 1M Beaches

Project Files

For Project 1M, you will need the following files:

New blank PowerPoint presentation
p01M_Black_Sand
p01M_Kite_Surf
p01M_Lithified_Cliffs
p01M_Reef
p01M_Tide_Pools

You will save your presentation as:

Lastname_Firstname_1M_Beaches

Katherine Okubo, President of Lehua Hawaiian Adventures, is making a presentation to groups of tourists at a number of hotels on the Hawaiian Islands. She would like to begin the presentation with an introduction to the beaches of Hawaii before discussing the many ways in which her company can assist tourists with selecting the places they would like to visit. The following paragraphs contain some of the information about the shorelines and beaches that Katherine would like to include in the presentation.

The shorelines of Hawaii vary tremendously, from black sand beaches with pounding surf to beaches of pink and white sand with calm waters perfect for snorkeling. Many of the shorelines provide picturesque hiking, shallow tide pools for exploring, beautiful reef where fish and turtles delight snorkelers, and waves that the most adventurous kite and board surfers enjoy. The terrain and the water make it easy for visitors to find a favorite beach in Hawaii.

The northern shore of Oahu is famous for its surfing beaches, while the southern shores of Kauai provide hikers with amazing views of the lithified cliffs formed by the power of the ocean. Black sand beaches are common on Hawaii, formed by the lava flows that created the islands. The reef that buffers many beaches from the open ocean is home to a wide variety of sea life that can be enjoyed while scuba diving and snorkeling.

Using the preceding information, create the first four to six slides of a presentation that Katherine can show during her discussion. Apply an appropriate theme and use slide layouts that will effectively present the content. Several picture files listed at the beginning of this project have been provided that you can insert in your presentation. Apply font formatting, picture styles, and slide transitions, and modify text alignment and line spacing as necessary. Save the file as **Lastname_Firstname_1M_Beaches** and then insert a header and footer that include the date and time updated automatically, the file name in the footer, and the page number. Add your name, your course name and section number, and the keywords **beaches, Black Sands beach, tide pools, lithified cliffs, scuba, snorkeling** to the Properties area. Save and print or submit as directed by your instructor.

End You have completed Project 1M

Outcomes-Based Assessments

Apply a combination of the 1A and 1B skills.

You and GO! | Project 1N Travel

Project Files

For Project 1N, you will need the following files:

New blank PowerPoint presentation

You will save your presentation as:

Lastname_Firstname_1N_Travel

Choose a place to which you have traveled or would like to travel. Create a presentation with at least six slides that describes the location, the method of travel, the qualities of the location that make it interesting or fun, the places you can visit, and any cultural activities in which you might like to participate. Choose an appropriate theme, slide layouts, and pictures, and then format the presentation attractively. Save your presentation as **Lastname_Firstname_1N_Travel** and submit as directed.

End You have completed Project 1N

Apply a combination of the 1A and 1B skills.

GO! CD-ROM

GO! Collaborate | Project 1O Bell Orchid Hotels Group Running Case

This project relates to the **Bell Orchid Hotels**. Your instructor may assign this group case project to your class. If your instructor assigns this project, he or she will provide you with information and instructions to work as part of a group. The group will apply the skills gained thus far to help the Bell Orchid Hotels achieve their business goals.

End You have completed Project 1O

Formatting PowerPoint Presentations

OUTCOMES

At the end of this chapter you will be able to:

OBJECTIVES

Mastering these objectives will enable you to:

PROJECT 2A
Format a presentation to add visual interest and clarity.

1. Format Numbered and Bulleted Lists (p. 681)
2. Insert Clip Art (p. 685)
3. Insert Text Boxes and Shapes (p. 690)
4. Format Objects (p. 694)

PROJECT 2B
Enhance a presentation with WordArt and diagrams.

5. Remove Picture Backgrounds and Insert WordArt (p. 703)
6. Create and Format a SmartArt Graphic (p. 708)

Nikolay Okhitin\Shutterstock

In This Chapter

A PowerPoint presentation is a visual aid in which well-designed slides help the audience understand complex information while keeping them focused on the message. Color is an important element that enhances your slides and draws the audience's interest by creating focus. When designing the background and element colors for your presentation, be sure that the colors you use provide contrast so that the text is visible on the background

Fascination Entertainment Group operates 15 regional theme parks across the United States, Mexico, and Canada. Park types include traditional theme parks, water parks, and animal parks. This year the company will launch three of its new "Fascination Parks" where attractions combine fun and the discovery of math and science information, and where teens and adults enjoy the free Friday night concerts.

Project 2A Employee Training Presentation

myitlab Project 2A Training

Project Activities

In Activities 2.01 through 2.14, you will format a presentation for Yuki Hiroko, Director of Operations for Fascination Entertainment Group, that describes important safety guidelines for employees. Your completed presentation will look similar to Figure 2.1.

Project Files

For Project 2A, you will need the following file:

p02A_Safety

You will save your presentation as:

Lastname_Firstname_2A_Safety

Project Results

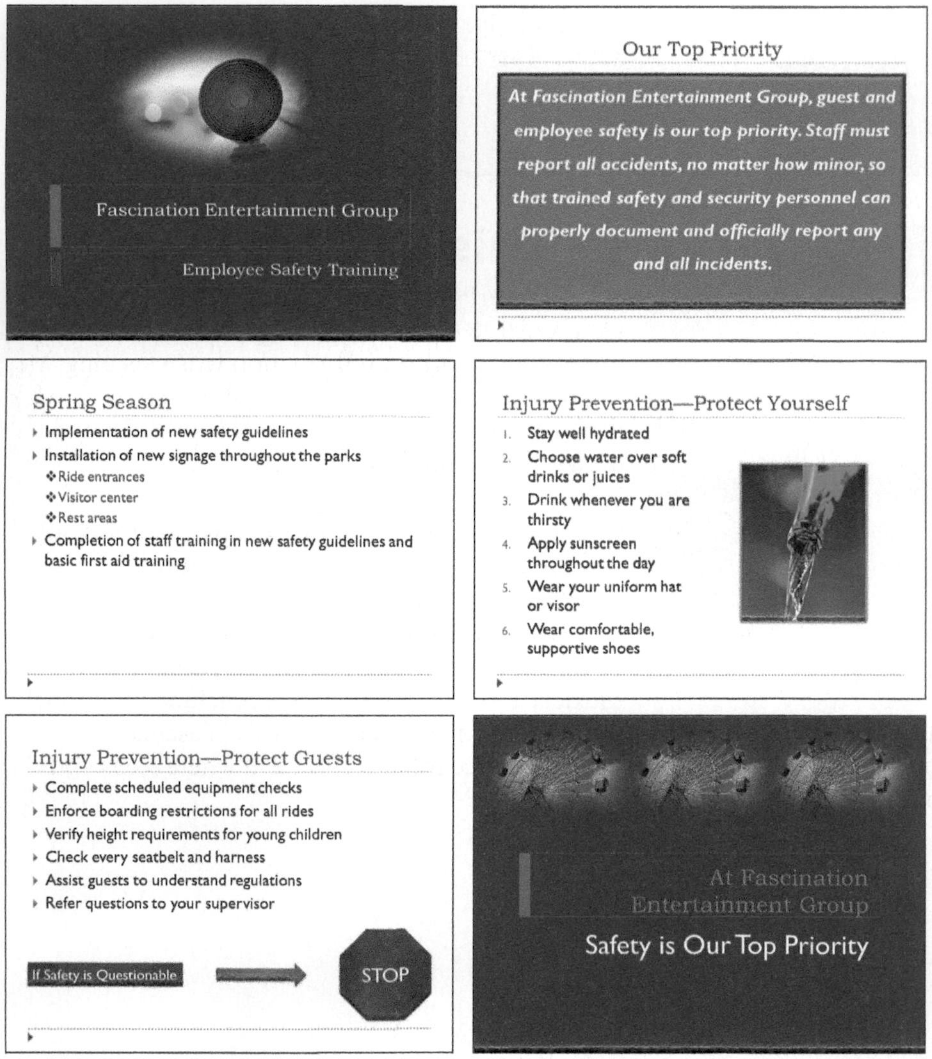

Figure 2.1
Project 2A Safety

Objective 1 | Format Numbered and Bulleted Lists

Recall that formatting is the process of changing the appearance of the text, layout, or design of a slide. You can format slide content by changing the bulleted and numbered list styles and colors.

Activity 2.01 | Selecting Placeholder Text

Recall that a placeholder is a box on a slide with dotted or dashed borders that holds title and body text or other content such as charts, tables, and pictures. You can format placeholder contents by selecting text or by selecting the entire placeholder.

1. **Start** PowerPoint. From the student files that accompany this textbook, locate and open **p02A_Safety**. On the **File tab**, click **Save As**, and then navigate to the location where you are storing your projects for this chapter. Create a new folder named **PowerPoint Chapter 2** and then in the **File name** box and using your own name, type **Lastname_Firstname_2A_Safety** Click **Save** or press Enter. Take a moment to view each slide and become familiar with the contents of this presentation.

2. Display **Slide 2**. Click anywhere in the content placeholder with the single bullet point, and then compare your screen with Figure 2.2.

   A dashed border displays, indicating that you can make editing changes to the placeholder text.

Figure 2.2

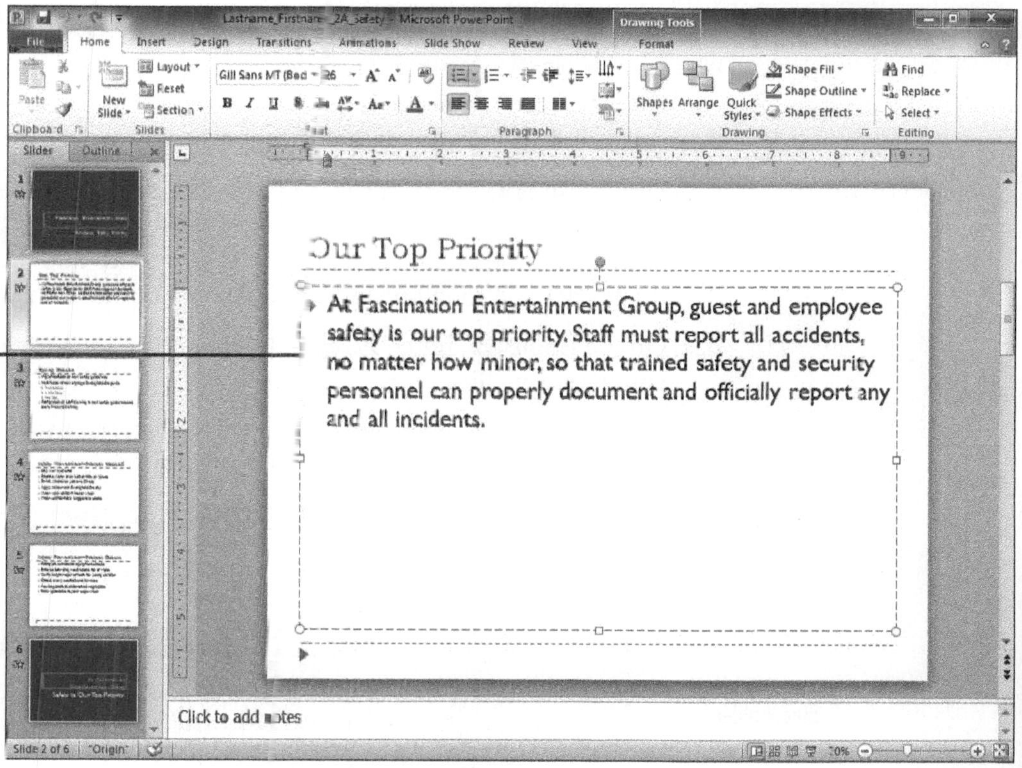

3 Point anywhere on the dashed border to display the [pointer icon] pointer, and then click one time to display the border as a solid line. Compare your screen with Figure 2.3.

When a placeholder's border displays as a solid line, all of the text in the placeholder is selected, and any formatting changes that you make will be applied to *all* of the text in the placeholder.

Figure 2.3

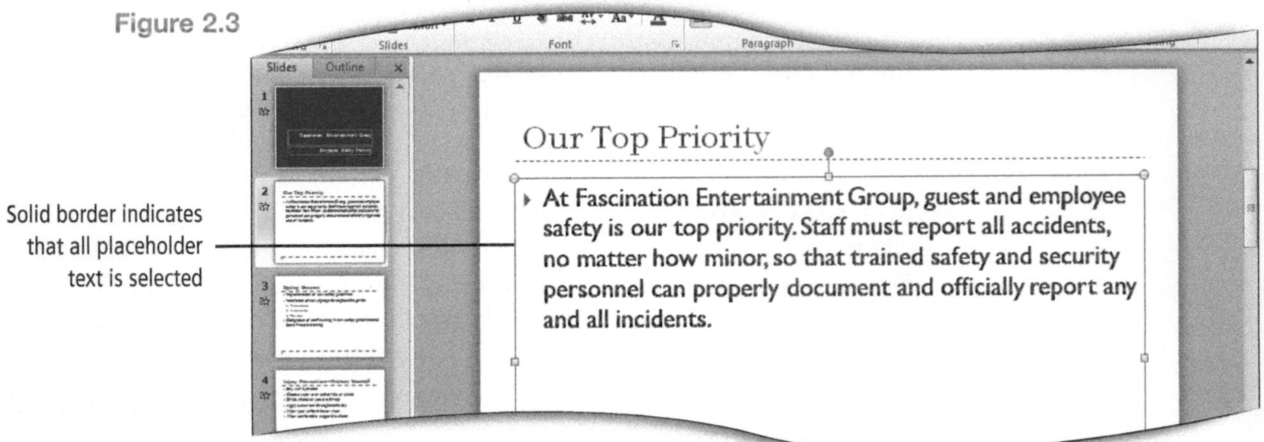

4 With the border of the placeholder displaying as a solid line, click in the **Font Size** box [44] to select the number, and then type **30** and press Enter. Notice that the font size of *all* of the placeholder text increases.

5 **Save** [save icon] your presentation.

Activity 2.02 | Changing a Bulleted List to a Numbered List

1 Display **Slide 4**, and then click anywhere in the bulleted list. Point to the blue dashed border (the red dashed lines at the top and bottom are part of the decorative elements of the theme) to display the [pointer icon] pointer, and then click one time to display the border as a solid line indicating that all of the text is selected.

2 On the **Home tab**, in the **Paragraph group**, click the **Numbering** button [numbering icon], and then compare your slide with Figure 2.4.

All of the bullet symbols are converted to numbers. The color of the numbers is determined by the presentation theme.

Figure 2.4

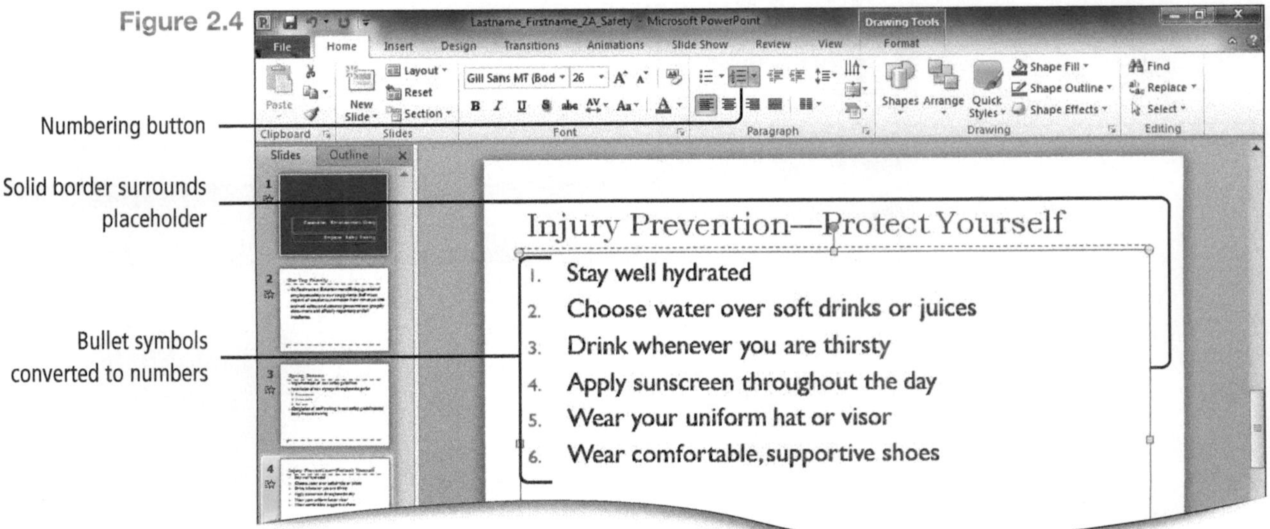

> **Alert! | Did You Display the Numbering Gallery?**
>
> If you clicked the Numbering button arrow instead of the Numbering button, the Numbering gallery displays. Click the Numbering button arrow again to close the gallery, and then click the Numbering button to convert the bullets to numbers.

3 **Save** your presentation.

Activity 2.03 | Modifying a Bulleted List Style

The presentation theme includes default styles for the bullet points in content placeholders. You can customize a bullet by changing its style, color, and size.

1 Display **Slide 3**, and then select the three second-level bullet points—*Ride entrances*, *Visitor center*, and *Rest areas*.

2 On the **Home tab**, in the **Paragraph group**, click the **Bullets button arrow** to display the **Bullets** gallery, and then compare your screen with Figure 2.5.

The Bullets gallery displays several bullet characters that you can apply to the selection.

Figure 2.5

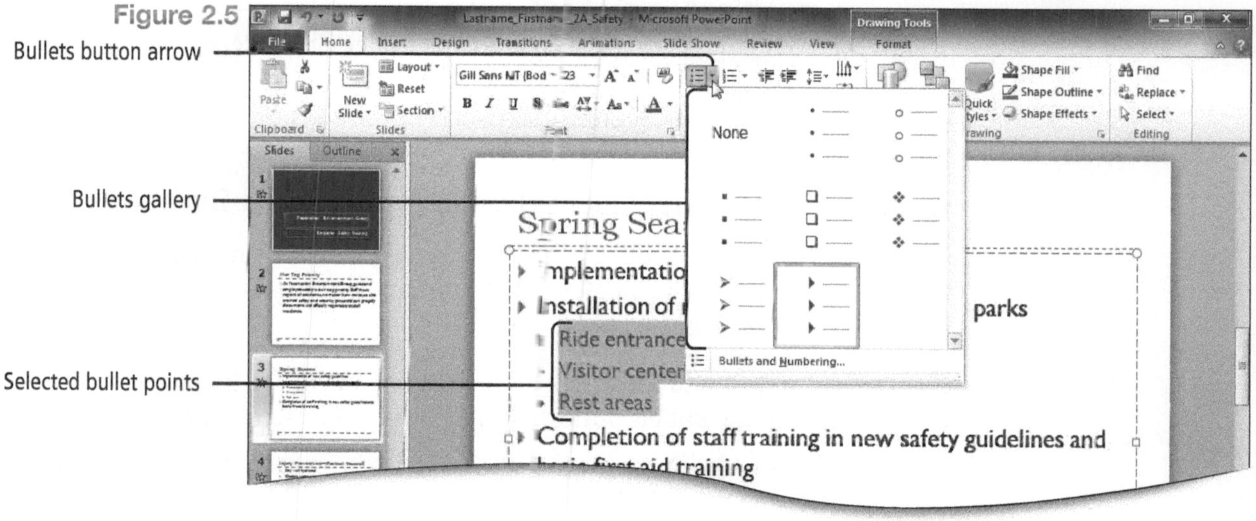

> **Alert! | Were the Bullets Removed?**
>
> If the bullets were removed, then you clicked the Bullets button instead of the Bullets button arrow. Click the Bullets button arrow, and then continue with Step 3.

3 At the bottom of the **Bullets** gallery, click **Bullets and Numbering**. In the **Bullets and Numbering** dialog box, point to each bullet style to display its ScreenTip. Then, in the second row, click **Star Bullets**. If the Star Bullets are not available, in the second row of bullets, click the second bullet style, and then click the Reset button.

4. Below the gallery, click the **Color** button. Under **Theme Colors**, in the sixth column, click the fifth color—**Red, Accent 2, Darker 25%**. In the **Size** box, select the existing number, type **100** and then compare your dialog box with Figure 2.6.

Figure 2.6

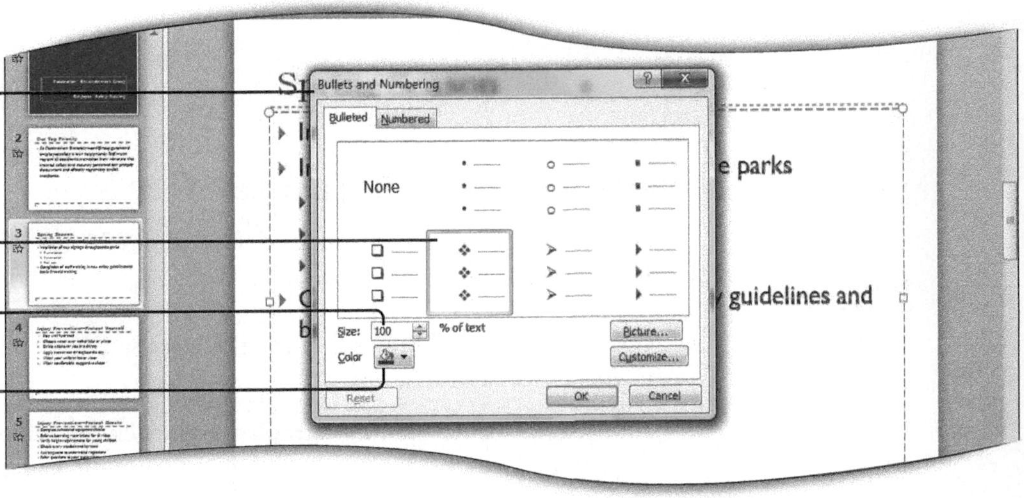

Bullets and Numbering dialog box

Star Bullets selected

Bullet size changed to 100% of text

Bullet color changed

5. Click **OK** to apply the bullet style, and then **Save** your presentation.

> **More Knowledge** | **Using Other Symbols as Bullet Characters**
>
> Many bullets styles are available to insert in your presentation. In the Bullets and Numbering dialog box, click the Customize button to view additional bullet styles.

Activity 2.04 | Removing a Bullet Symbol from a Bullet Point

The Bullet button is a toggle button, enabling you to turn the bullet symbol on and off. A slide that contains a single bullet point can be formatted as a single paragraph *without* a bullet symbol.

1. Display **Slide 2**, and then click in the paragraph. On the **Home tab**, in the **Paragraph group**, click the **Bullets** button. Compare your screen with Figure 2.7.

   The bullet symbol no longer displays, and the bullet button is no longer selected. Additionally, the indentation associated with the list level is removed.

2. **Center** the paragraph. On the **Home tab**, in the **Paragraph group**, click the **Line Spacing** button, and then click **1.5**.

Figure 2.7

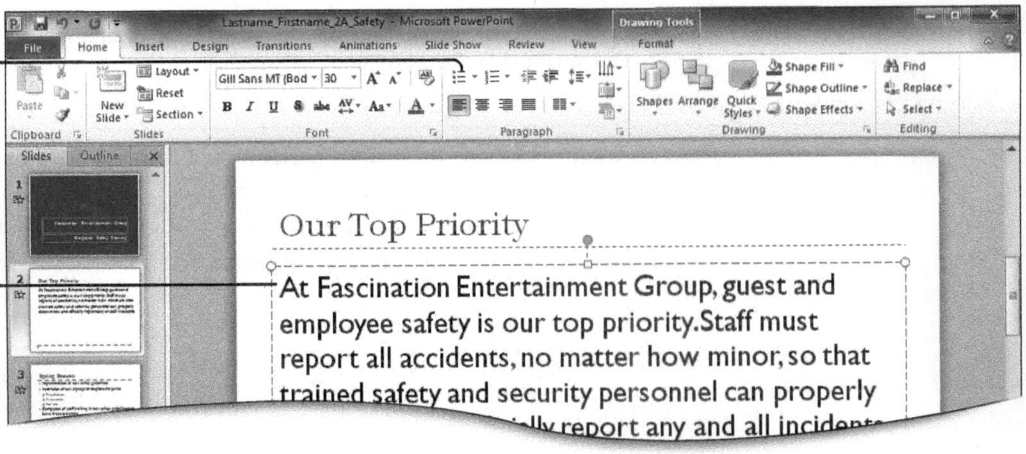

Bullets button

Bullet symbol and indentation removed from paragraph

3. Click the dashed border to display the solid border and to select all of the text in the paragraph, and then apply **Bold** and **Italic**. Click in the slide title, and then click the **Center** button. **Save** your presentation.

Objective 2 | Insert Clip Art

There are many sources from which you can insert images into a presentation. One type of image that you can insert is a ***clip***—a single media file such as art, sound, animation, or a movie.

Activity 2.05 | Inserting Clip Art

1. Display **Slide 4**, and then on the **Home tab**, in the **Slides group**, click the **Layout** button. Click **Two Content** to change the slide layout.

2. In the placeholder on the right side of the slide, click the **Clip Art** button to display the **Clip Art** pane, and then compare your screen with Figure 2.8.

Figure 2.8

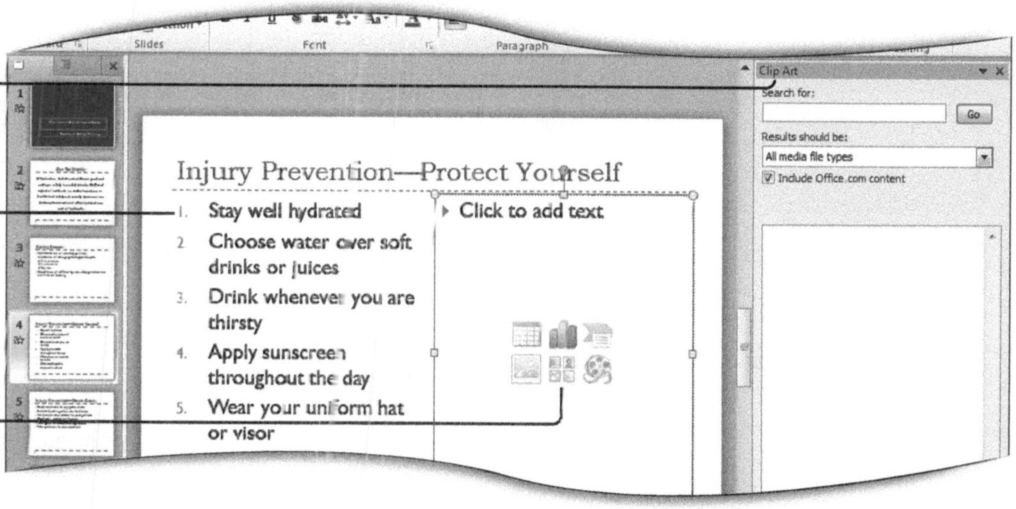

3. In the **Clip Art** pane, click in the **Search for** box, and then replace any existing text with **bottled water** so that PowerPoint can search for images that contain the keyword *bottled water*.

4. Click the **Results should be arrow**, and then click as necessary to *clear* the **Illustrations**, **Videos**, and **Audio** check boxes and to select only the **Photographs** check box. Compare your screen with Figure 2.9.

   With the Photographs check box selected, PowerPoint will search for images that were created with a digital camera or a scanner.

Figure 2.9

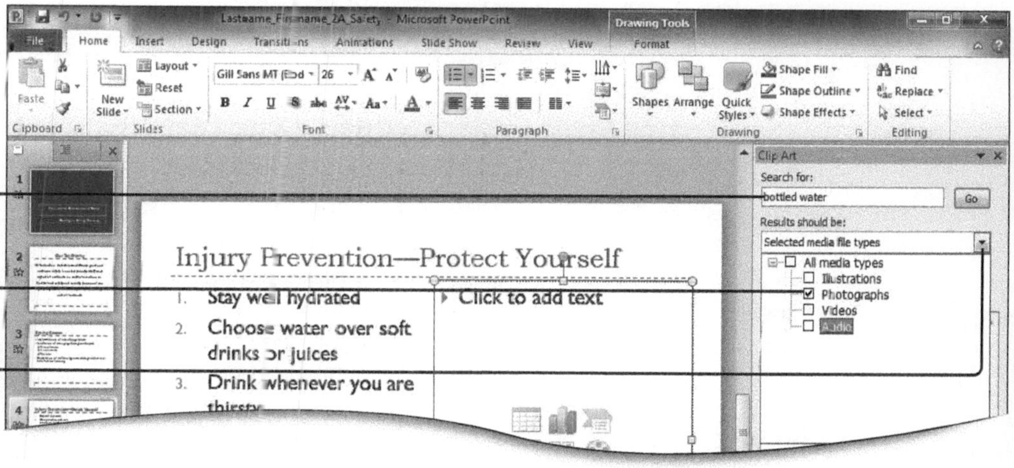

5 In the **Clip Art** pane, click the **Results should be arrow** to close the list. Then, if necessary, select the **Include Office.com content** check box so that images available on Office.com are included in the search.

6 In the **Clip Art** pane, click **Go** to display clips in the Clip Art pane. Scroll through the clips, and then locate and point to the image of the water pouring from a glass water bottle on a blue background. Compare your screen with Figure 2.10.

When you point to an image in the Clip Art pane, a ScreenTip displays the keywords and information about the size of the image.

Figure 2.10

Selected picture

ScreenTip

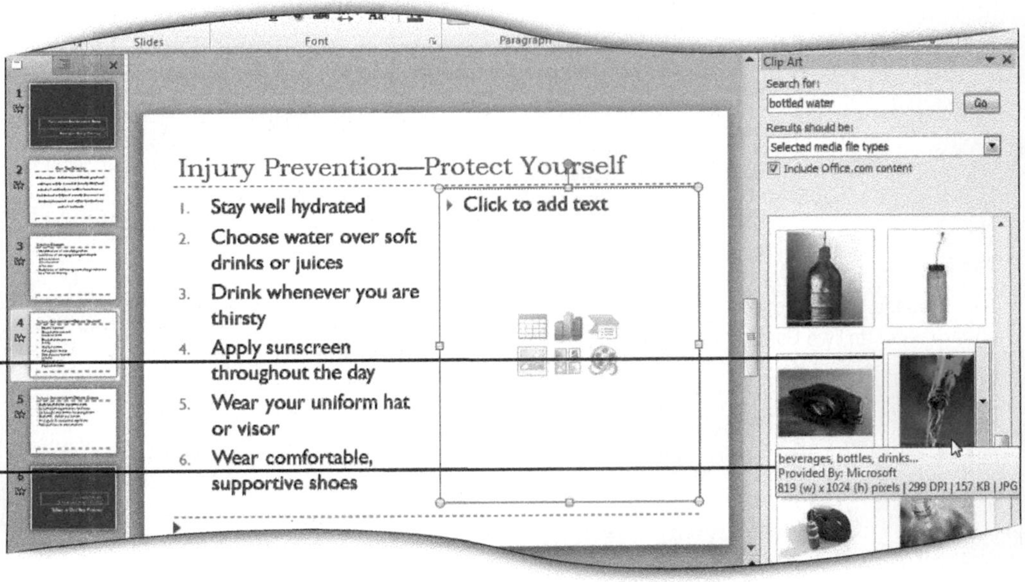

> **Alert! | Is the Water Bottle Picture Unavailable?**
>
> If you are unable to locate the suggested picture, choose another similar image.

7 Click the water bottle picture to insert it in the content placeholder on the right side of the slide. **Close** the **Clip Art** pane, and then compare your slide with Figure 2.11.

On the Ribbon, the Picture Tools display, and the water bottle image is surrounded by sizing handles, indicating that it is selected.

Figure 2.11

Picture Tools display

Picture inserted and selected

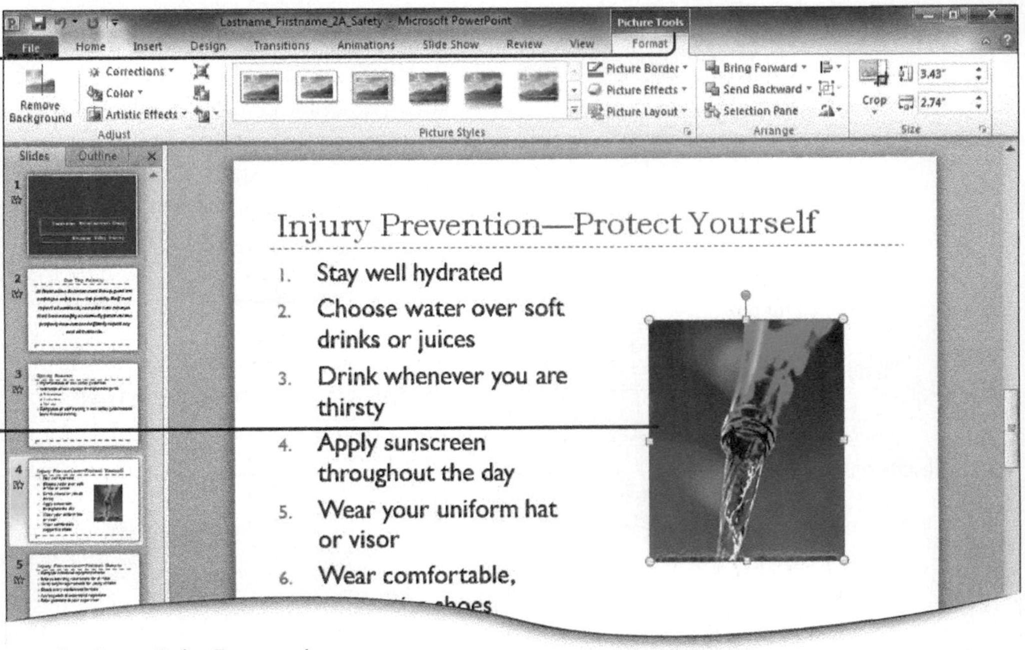

8 Display **Slide 1**. Click the **Insert tab**, and then in the **Images group**, click **Clip Art**.

9 In the **Clip Art** pane, in the **Search for** box, search for **red lights** and then click **Go**. Scroll as necessary to locate the picture of the single red warning light. Point to the picture, and then compare your screen with Figure 2.12.

If you cannot locate the picture, select another appropriate image.

Figure 2.12

red lights typed in Search for box

Selected picture

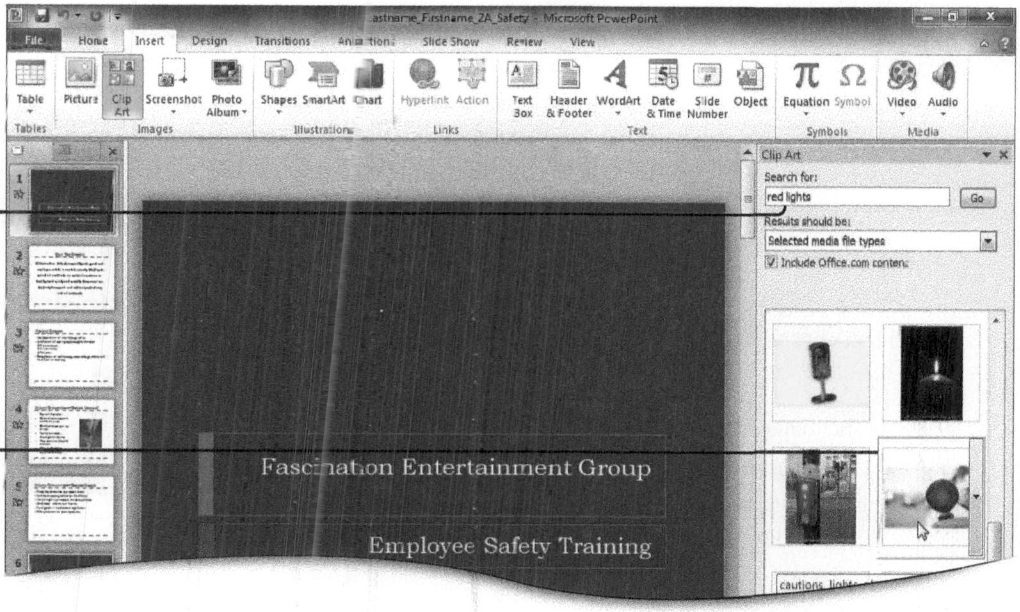

10 Click the **red light** picture to insert it in the center of the slide, and then **Close** the **Clip Art** pane. **Save** your presentation.

When you use the Clip Art command on the Ribbon instead of the Clip Art button in a content placeholder, PowerPoint inserts the image in the center of the slide.

Activity 2.06 | Moving and Sizing Images

Recall that when an image is selected, it is surrounded by sizing handles that you can drag to resize the image. You can also resize an image using the Shape Height and Shape Width boxes on the Format tab. When you point to the image, rather than pointing to a sizing handle, the move pointer—a four-headed arrow—displays, indicating that you can move the image.

> **Another Way**
> Alternatively, drag a corner sizing handle to resize an image proportionately.

1 If necessary, select the picture of the red light. On the **Format tab**, in the **Size group**, click in the **Shape Height** box, and then replace the selected number with **3.5**

2 Press Enter to resize the image. Notice that the picture is resized proportionately, and the **Width** box displays *5.26*. Compare your screen with Figure 2.13.

When a picture is resized in this manner, the width adjusts in proportion to the picture height.

Figure 2.13

3.5 typed in Shape Height box

PowerPoint | Chapter 2

3 Display the **View tab**. In the **Show group**, verify that the **Ruler** check box is selected and if necessary, select it. On the horizontal and vertical rulers, notice that *0* displays in the center.

Horizontally, the PowerPoint ruler indicates measurements from the center *out* to the left and to the right. Vertically, the PowerPoint ruler indicates measurements from the center up and down.

4 Point to the picture to display the pointer. Hold down Shift, and then drag the picture to the right until the left edge of the picture is aligned with the **left half of the horizontal ruler at 3 inches**. If necessary, hold down Ctrl and press an arrow key to move the picture in small increments in any direction for a more precise placement. Compare your screen with Figure 2.14.

Pressing Shift while dragging an object constrains object movement in a straight line either vertically or horizontally. Here, pressing Shift maintains the vertical placement of the picture.

Figure 2.14

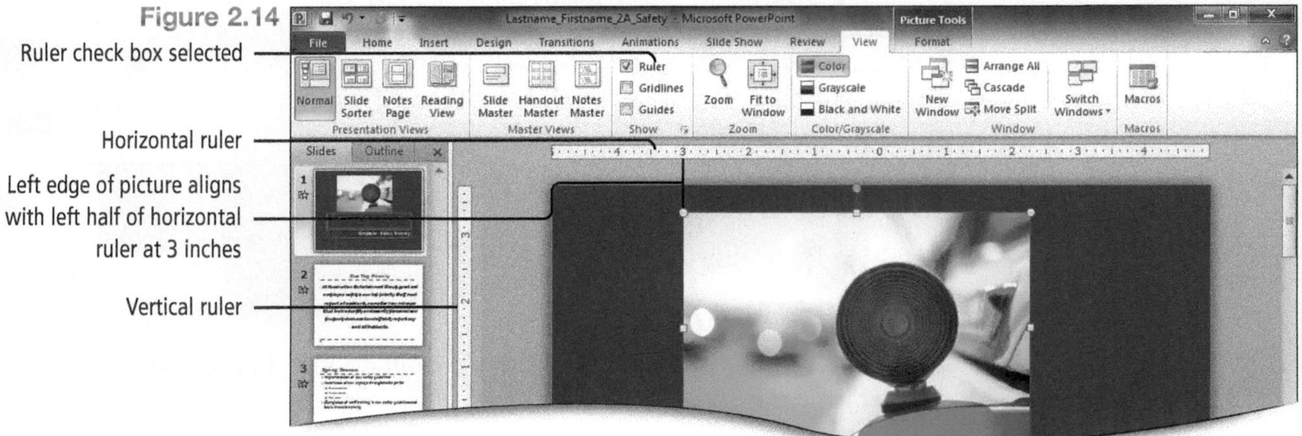

5 Display **Slide 6**. On the **Insert tab**, in the **Images group**, click the **Clip Art** button. In the **Clip Art** pane, search for **amusement park** and then click **Go**. Locate and click the picture of the Ferris wheel with the sky and clouds in the background, and then compare your slide with Figure 2.15.

Figure 2.15

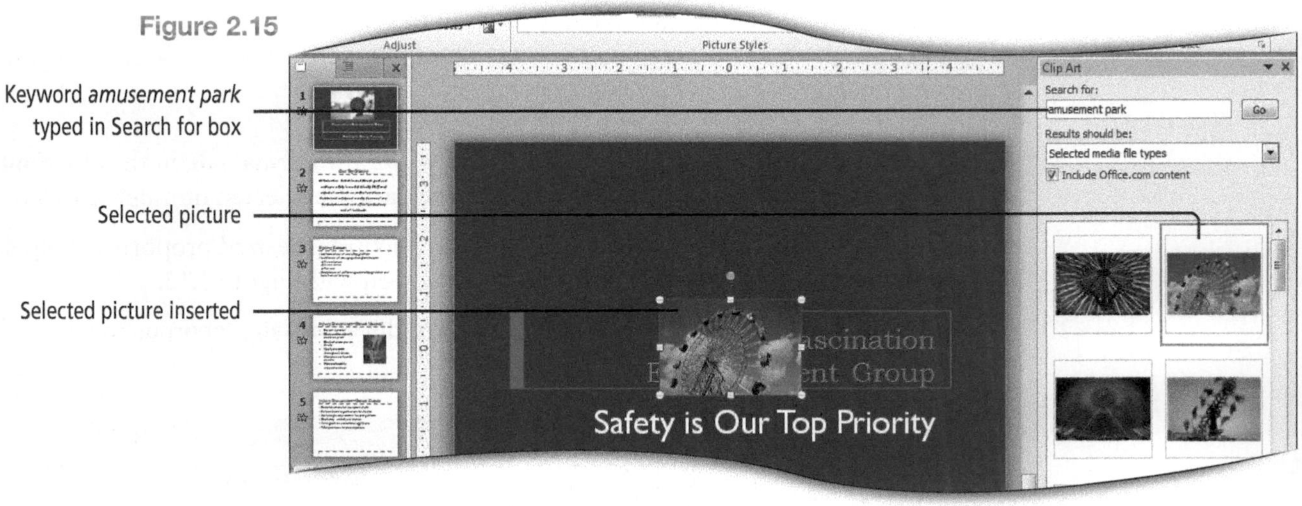

6 **Close** the **Clip Art** pane, and be sure that the picture is still selected. On the **Format tab**, in the **Size group**, click in the **Shape Height** box. Replace the displayed number with **2.5** and then press Enter to resize the picture. Compare your screen with Figure 2.16.

Figure 2.16

2.5 typed in Shape Height box

Picture resized

7 **Save** your presentation.

> **More Knowledge | Moving an Object by Using the Arrow Keys**
>
> You can use the directional arrow keys on your keyboard to move a picture, shape, or other object in small increments. Select the object so that its outside border displays as a solid line. Then, on your keyboard, hold down the Ctrl key and press the directional arrow keys to move the selected object in precise increments.

Activity 2.07 | Changing the Shape of a Picture

An inserted picture is rectangular in shape; however, you can modify a picture by changing its shape.

1 Display **Slide 1**, and then select the picture.

2 On the **Format tab**, in the **Size group**, *point* to the **Crop button arrow**, and then compare your screen with Figure 2.17.

The Crop button is a split button. The upper section—the Crop button—enables the ***crop*** feature, which reduces the size of a picture by removing vertical or horizontal edges. The lower section—the Crop arrow—displays cropping options, such as the option to crop a picture to a shape.

Figure 2.17

Crop button arrow

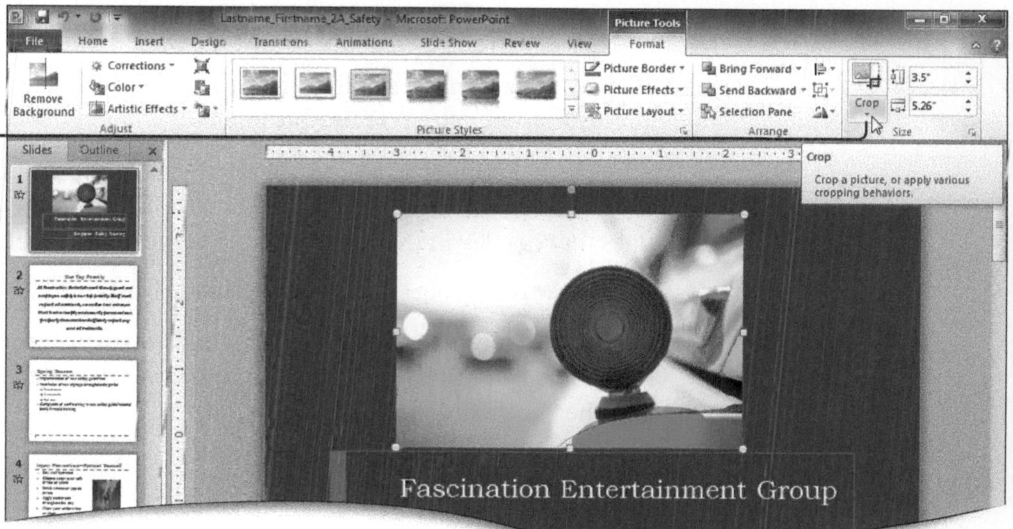

3. Click the **Crop button arrow**, and then point to **Crop to Shape** to display a gallery of shapes. Compare your screen with Figure 2.18.

Figure 2.18

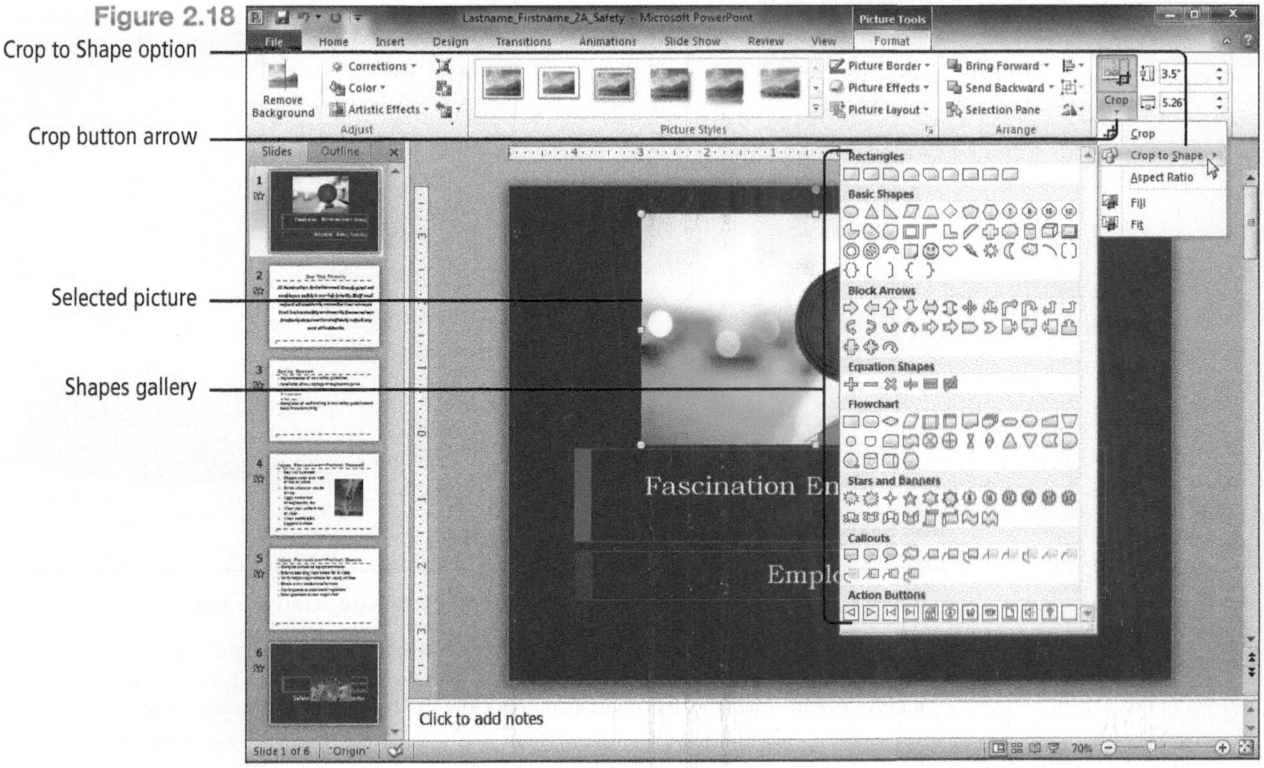

4. Under **Basic Shapes**, in the first row, click the first shape—**Oval**—to change the picture's shape to an oval. **Save** your presentation.

Objective 3 | Insert Text Boxes and Shapes

You can use objects, including text boxes and shapes, to draw attention to important information or to serve as containers for slide text. Many shapes, including lines, arrows, ovals, and rectangles, are available to insert and position anywhere on your slides.

Activity 2.08 | Inserting a Text Box

A ***text box*** is an object with which you can position text anywhere on a slide.

1. Display **Slide 5** and verify that the rulers display. Click the **Insert tab**, and then in the **Text group**, click the **Text Box** button.

2. Move the pointer to several different places on the slide, and as you do so, in the horizontal and vertical rulers, notice that ***ruler guides***—dotted vertical and horizontal lines that display in the rulers indicating the pointer's position—move also.

   Use the ruler guides to help you position objects on a slide.

3. Position the pointer so that the ruler guides are positioned on the **left half of the horizontal ruler at 4.5 inches** and on the **lower half of the vertical ruler at 1.5 inches**, and then compare your screen with Figure 2.19.

Figure 2.19

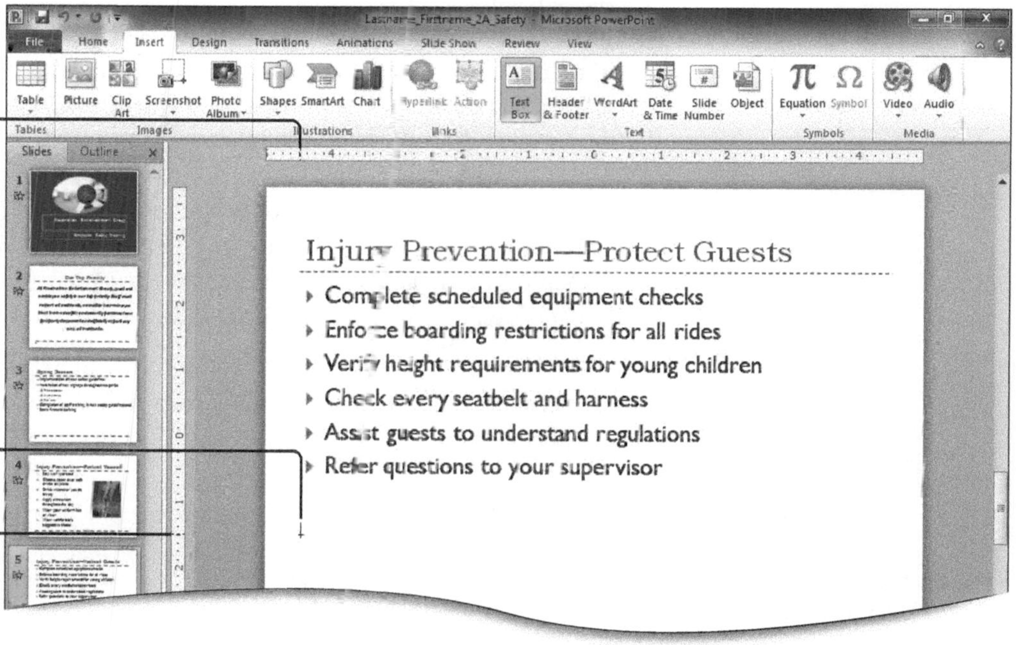

4 Click one time to create a narrow rectangular text box. With the insertion point blinking inside the text box, type **If Safety is Questionable** Notice that as you type, the width of the text box expands to accommodate the text. Compare your screen with Figure 2.20.

Do not be concerned if your text box is not positioned exactly as shown in Figure 2.20.

Figure 2.20

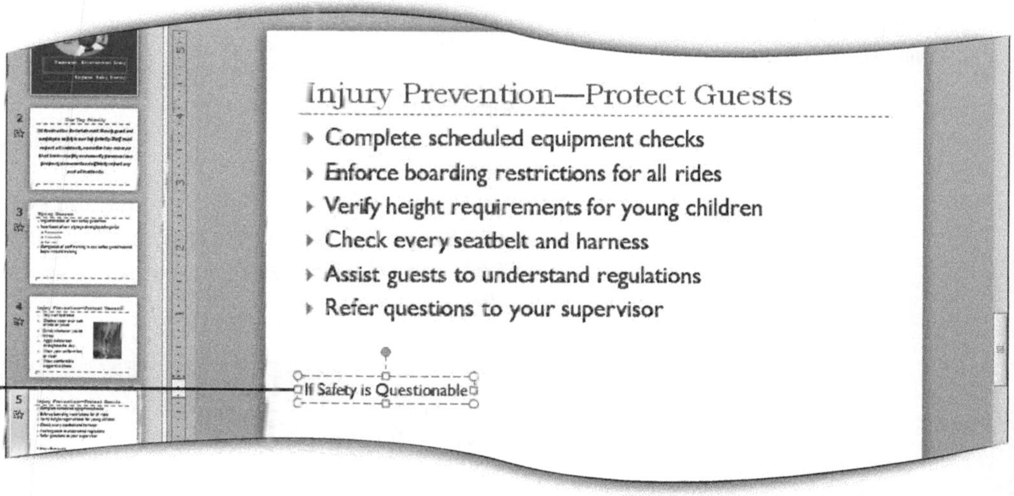

Alert! | Does the Text in the Text Box Display Vertically, One Character at a Time?

If you move the pointer when you click to create the text box, PowerPoint sets the width of the text box and does not widen to accommodate the text. If this happened to you, your text may display vertically instead of horizontally or it may display on two lines. Click Undo, and then repeat the steps again, being sure that you do not move the mouse when you click to insert the text box.

5 Select the text that you typed, change the **Font Size** to **24** and then **Save** your presentation.

You can format the text in a text box by using the same techniques that you use to format text in any other placeholder. For example, you can change the font, font style, font size, and font color.

Activity 2.09 | Inserting, Sizing, and Positioning Shapes

Shapes include lines, arrows, stars, banners, ovals, rectangles, and other basic shapes you can use to illustrate an idea, a process, or a workflow. Shapes can be sized and moved using the same techniques that you use to size and move clip art images.

1 With **Slide 5** displayed, click the **Insert tab**, and then in the **Illustrations group**, click the **Shapes** button to display the **Shapes** gallery. Under **Block Arrows**, click the first shape—**Right Arrow**. Move the pointer into the slide until the [+] pointer—called the ***crosshair pointer***—displays, indicating that you can draw a shape.

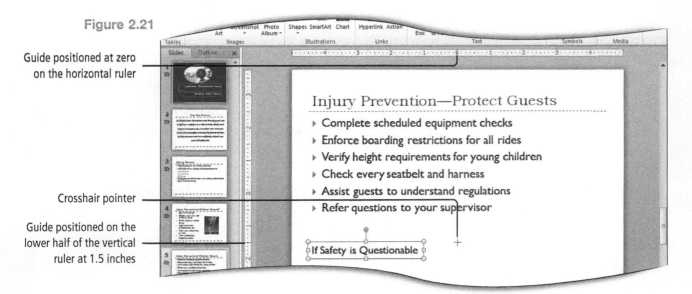

2 Move the [+] pointer to position the ruler guides at approximately **zero on the horizontal ruler** and on the **lower half of the vertical ruler at 1.5 inches**. Compare your screen with Figure 2.21.

Figure 2.21

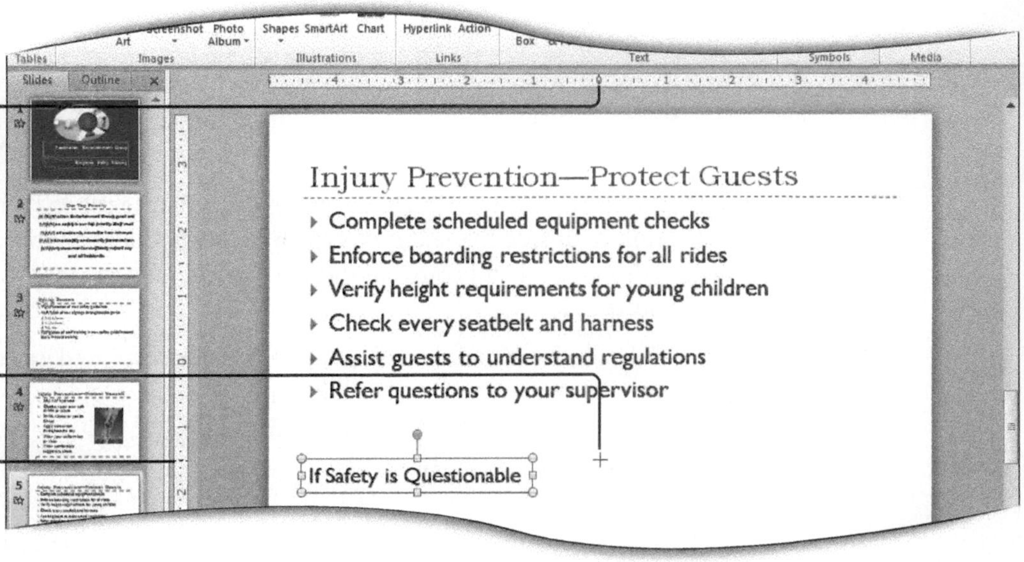

3 Click the mouse button to insert the arrow. Click the **Format tab**, and then in the **Size group**, click in the **Shape Height** box to select the number. Type **.5** and then click in the **Shape Width** box. Type **2** and then press Enter to resize the arrow. Compare your screen with Figure 2.22.

Figure 2.22

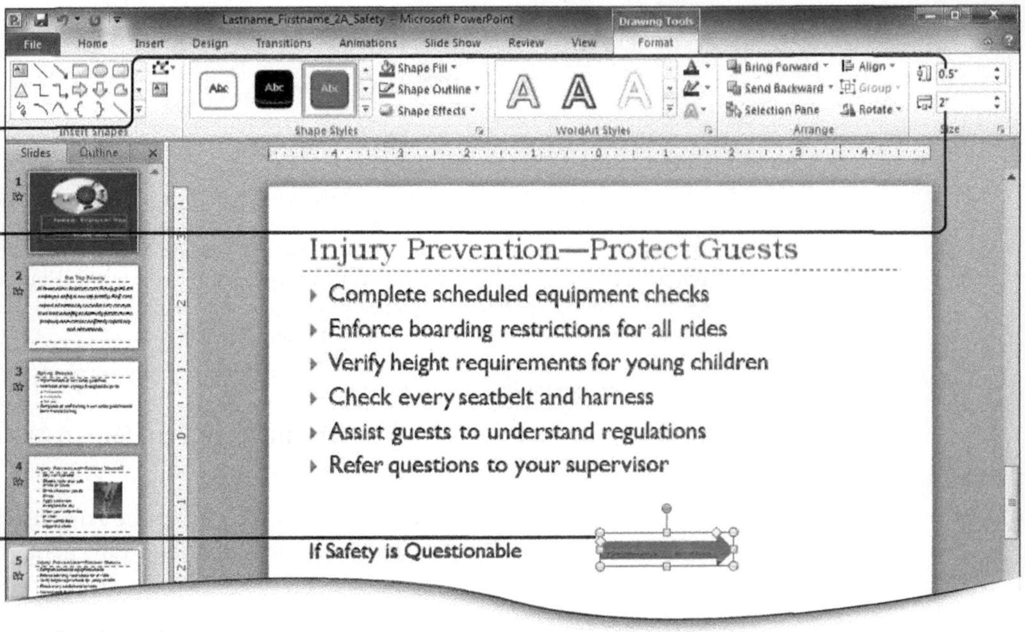

4. On the **Format tab**, in the **Insert Shapes group**, click the **More** button. In the gallery, under **Basic Shapes**, in the first row, click the second to last shape—**Octagon.**

5. Move the pointer to position the ruler guides on the **right half of the horizontal ruler at 2.5 inches** and on the **lower half of the vertical ruler at 1 inch**, and then click one time to insert an octagon.

6. On the **Format tab**, in the **Size group**, click in the **Shape Height** box to select the number. Type **2** and then click in the **Shape Width** box. Type **2** and then press Enter to resize the octagon. Compare your slide with Figure 2.23. Do not be concerned if your shapes are not positioned exactly as shown in the figure.

Figure 2.23

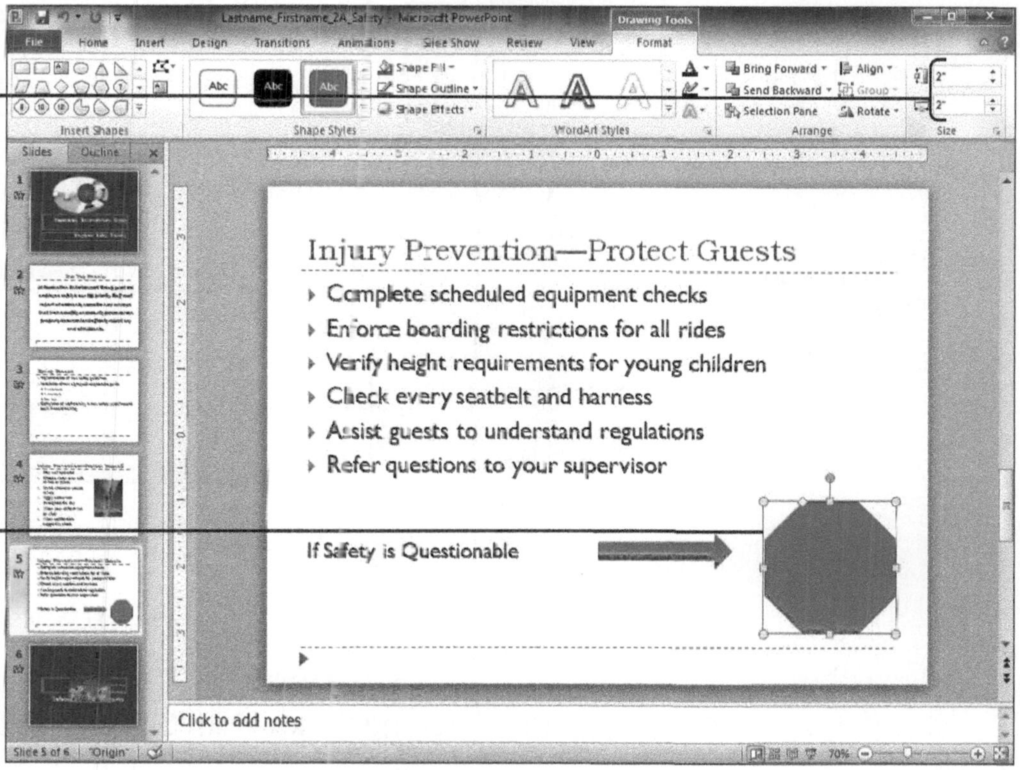

Shape Height and Width each changed to 2″

Octagon inserted and sized

7. **Save** your presentation.

Activity 2.10 | Adding Text to Shapes

Shapes can serve as a container for text. After you add text to a shape, you can change the font and font size, apply font styles, and change text alignment.

1. On **Slide 5**, if necessary, click the octagon so that it is selected. Type **STOP** and notice that the text is centered within the octagon.

2 Select the text *STOP*, and then on the Mini toolbar, change the **Font Size** to **32**. Compare your screen with Figure 2.24, and then **Save** your presentation.

Figure 2.24

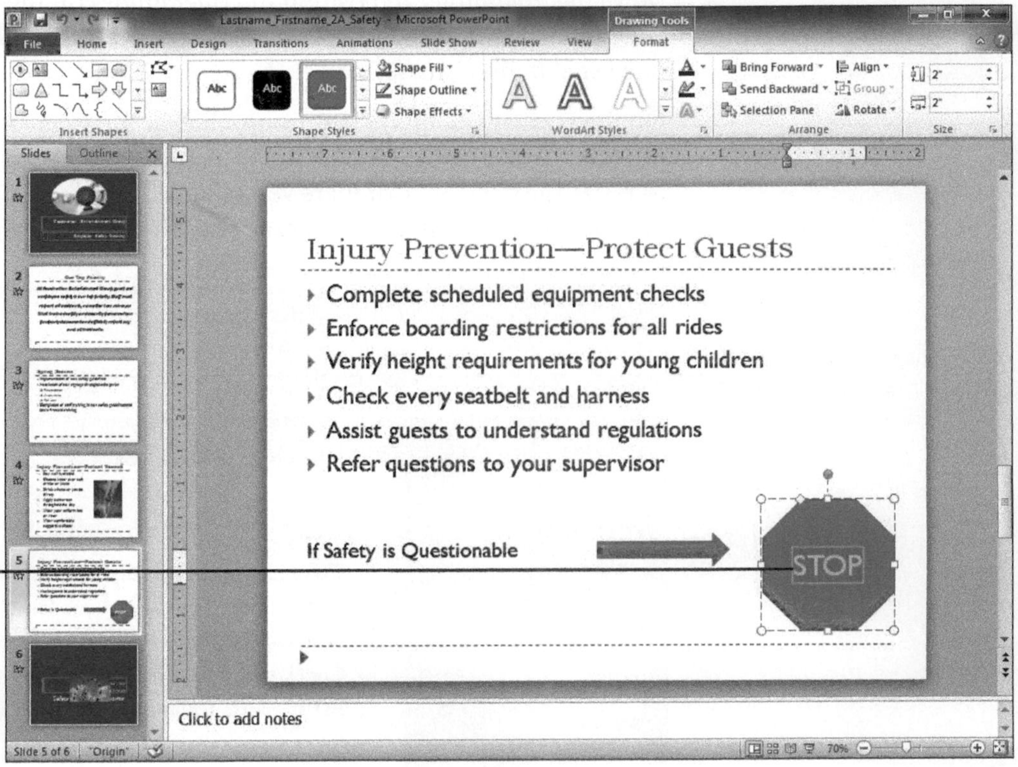

Text typed and font size changed to 32

Objective 4 | Format Objects

Apply styles and effects to clip art, shapes, and text boxes to complement slide backgrounds and colors.

Activity 2.11 | Applying Shape Fills, Outlines, and Styles

Changing the inside ***fill color*** and the outside line color is a distinctive way to format a shape. A fill color is the inside color of text or of an object. Use the Shape Styles gallery to apply predefined combinations of these fill and line colors and also to apply other effects.

1 On **Slide 5**, click anywhere in the text *If Safety is Questionable* to select the text box. On the **Format tab**, in the **Shape Styles group**, click the **More** button to display the **Shape Styles** gallery.

2 In the last row, click the third style—**Intense Effect - Red, Accent 2**. Select the **octagon** shape, and then apply the same style you applied to the text box—**Intense Effect - Red, Accent 2**.

3 Select the **arrow**, and then display the **Shape Styles** gallery. In the last row, click the second style—**Intense Effect - Blue, Accent 1**.

4 Click in a blank part of the slide so that no objects are selected, and then compare your screen with Figure 2.25.

Figure 2.25

Shape styles applied to three objects

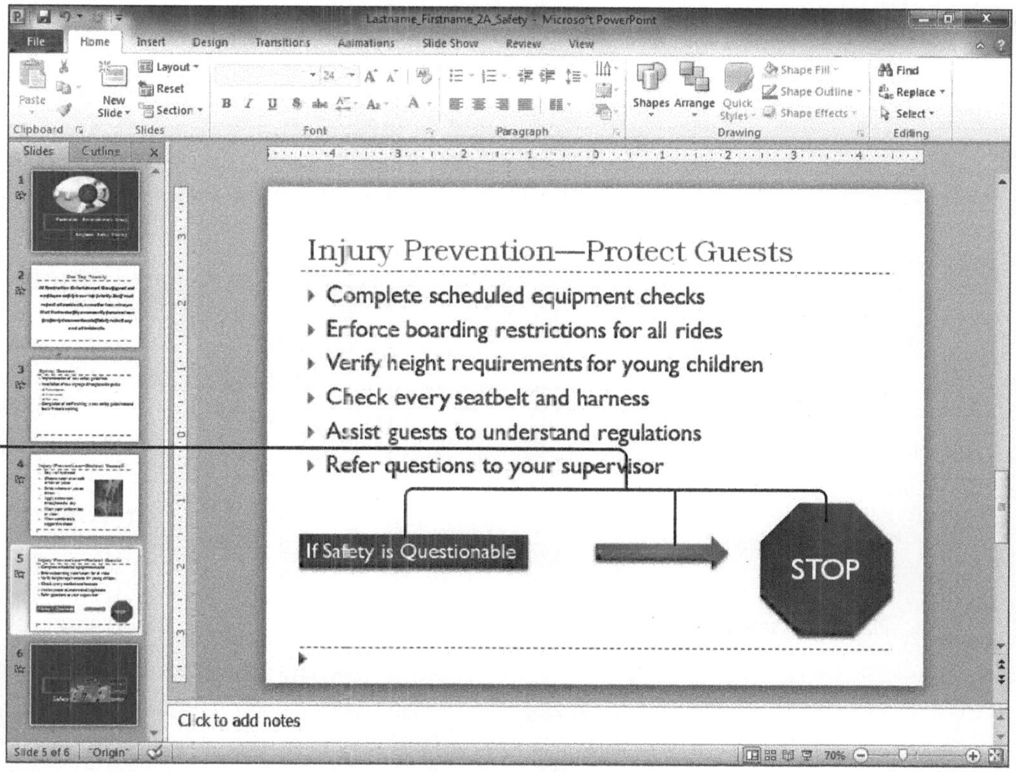

5 Display **Slide 2**, and then click anywhere in the paragraph of text to select the content placeholder.

6 On the **Format tab**, in the **Shape Styles group**, click the **Shape Fill** button, and then point to several of the theme colors and watch as Live Preview changes the inside color of the text box. In the fifth column, click the first color—**Blue, Accent 1**.

7 In the **Shape Styles group**, click the **Shape Outline** button. Point to **Weight**, click **3 pt**, and notice that a thick outline surrounds the text placeholder. Click in a blank area of the slide so that nothing is selected, and then compare your slide with Figure 2.26.

You can use combinations of shape fill, outline colors, and weights to format an object.

Figure 2.26

Shape fill and 3 pt outline applied to text placeholder

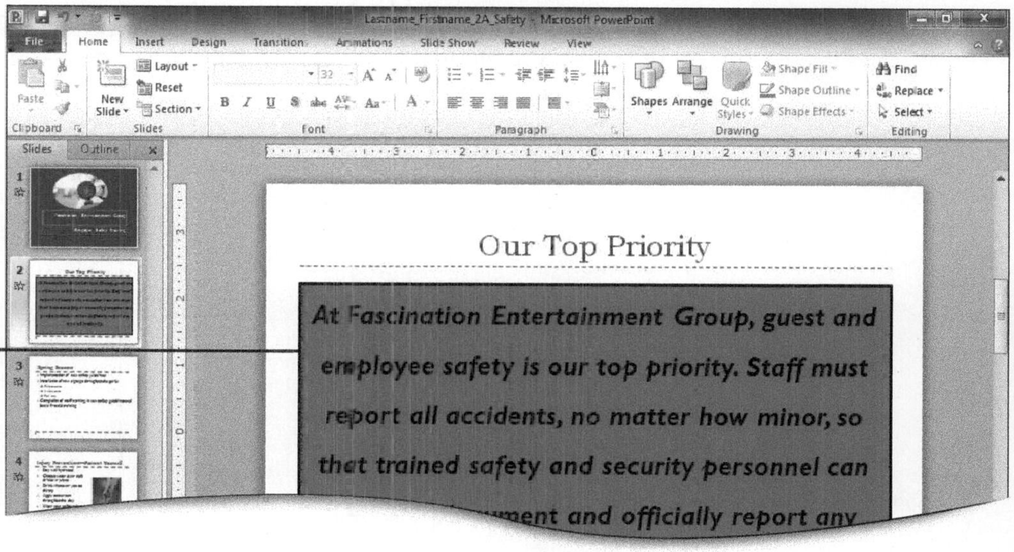

8 Click in the paragraph, and then press Ctrl + A to select all of the paragraph text, right-click in the selection to display the Mini toolbar, and then click the **Font Color button arrow** to display the **Theme Colors** gallery. Click the first color—**White, Background 1. Save** your presentation.

PowerPoint | Chapter 2

Activity 2.12 | Applying Shape and Picture Effects

1 On **Slide 2**, if necessary, select the blue content placeholder. On the **Format tab**, in the **Shape Styles group**, click the **Shape Effects** button, and then compare your screen with Figure 2.27.

A list of effects that you can apply to shapes displays. These effects can also be applied to pictures and text boxes.

Figure 2.27

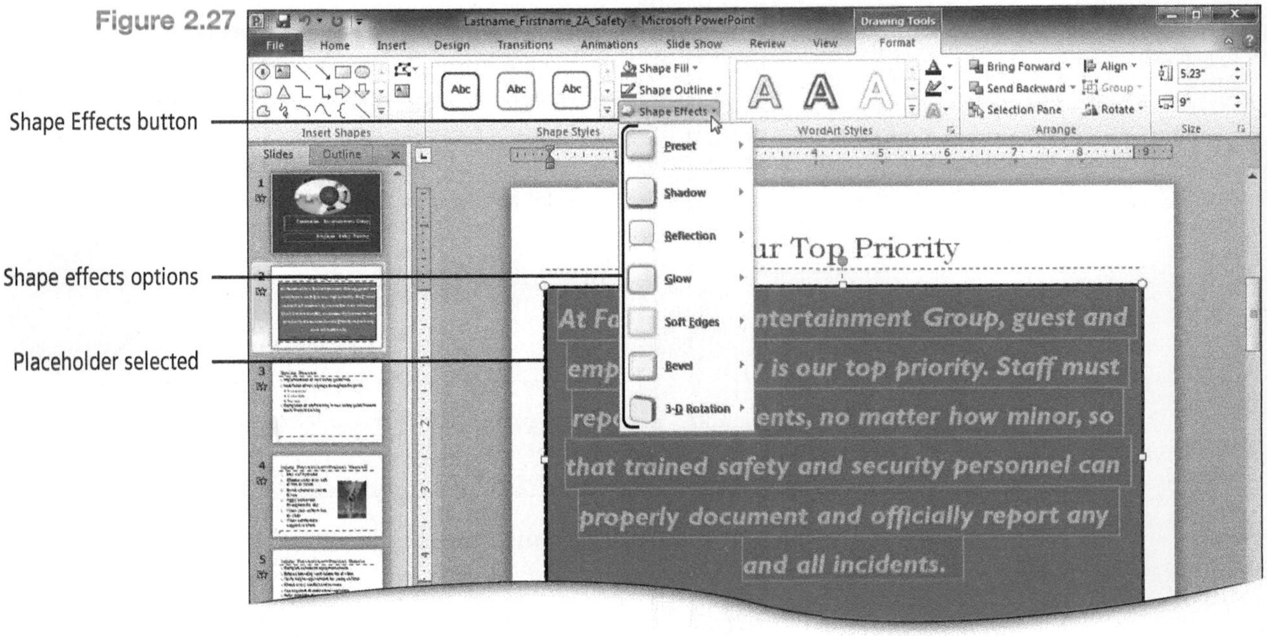

2 Point to **Bevel** to display the **Bevel** gallery. Point to each bevel to view its ScreenTip and to use Live Preview to examine the effect of each bevel on the content placeholder. In the last row, click the last bevel—**Art Deco**.

3 Display **Slide 1**, and then select the picture. On the **Format tab**, in the **Picture Styles group**, click the **Picture Effects** button.

4 Point to **Soft Edges**, and then in the **Soft Edges** gallery, point to each style to view its effect on the picture. Click the last **Soft Edges** effect—**50 Point**, and then compare your screen with Figure 2.28.

The soft edges effect softens and blurs the outer edge of the picture so that it blends into the slide background.

Figure 2.28

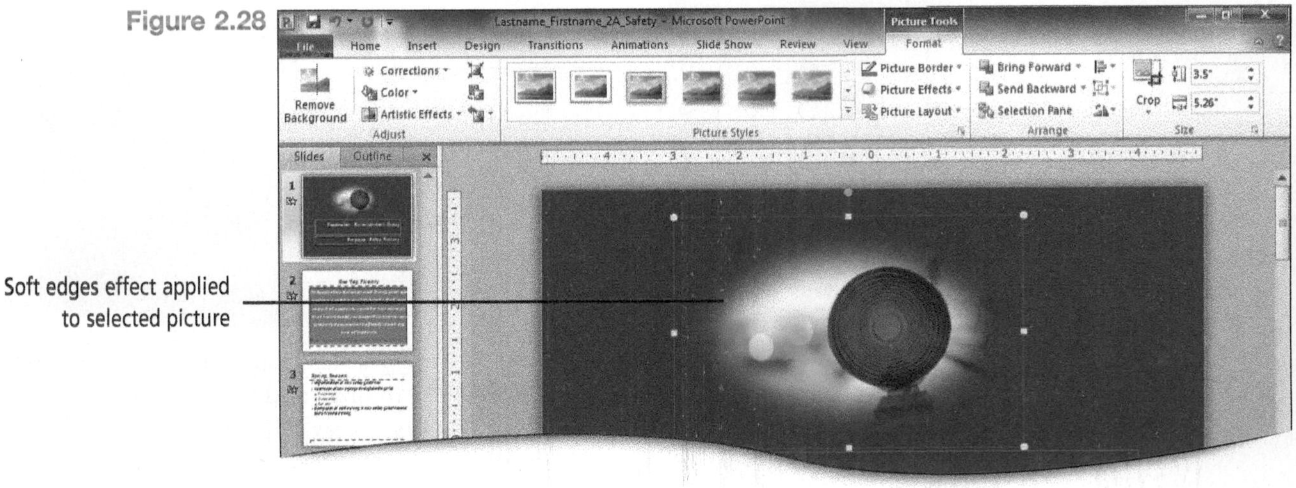

5 Display **Slide 4**, and then select the picture. On the **Format tab**, in the **Picture Styles group**, click the **Picture Effects** button, and then point to **Glow**.

6 Point to several of the effects to view the effect on the picture, and then under **Glow Variations**, in the second row, click the second glow effect—**Red, 8 pt glow, Accent color 2**. Click in a blank area of the slide to deselect the picture. Compare your slide with Figure 2.29, and then **Save** your presentation.

The glow effect applies a colored, softly blurred outline to the selected object.

Figure 2.29

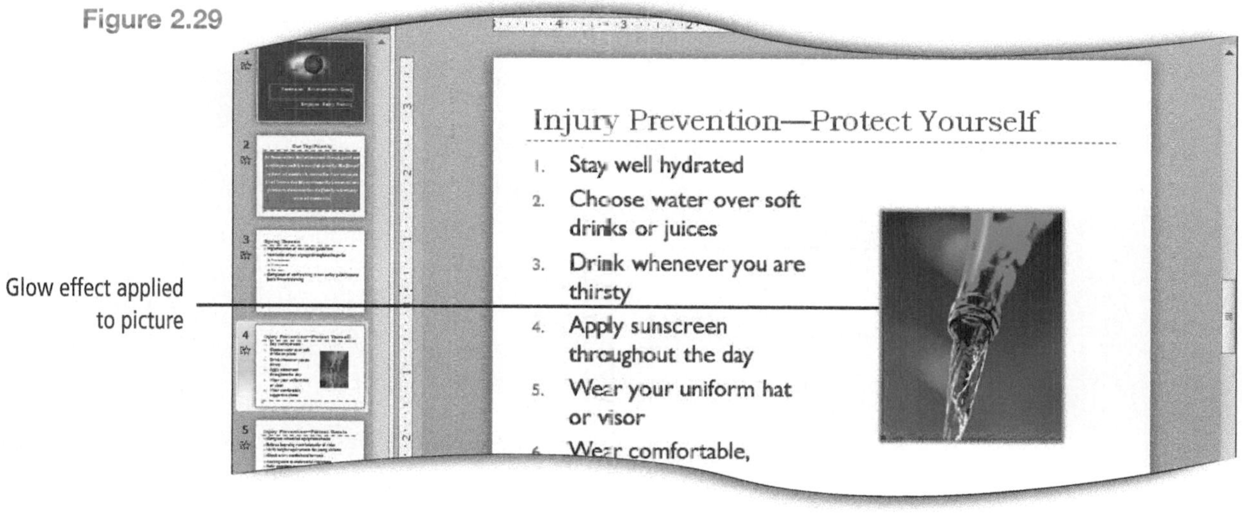

Activity 2.13 | Duplicating Objects

1 Display **Slide 6**, point to the picture to display the pointer, and then drag up and to the left so that the upper left corner of the picture aligns with the upper left corner of the slide.

2 Press and hold down Ctrl, and then press D one time. Release Ctrl.

A duplicate of the picture overlaps the original picture and the duplicated image is selected.

3 Point to the duplicated picture to display the pointer, and then drag down and to the right approximately 1 inch in both directions so that both pictures are visible. Compare your screen with Figure 2.30. Do not be concerned if your pictures are not positioned exactly as shown in the figure.

Figure 2.30

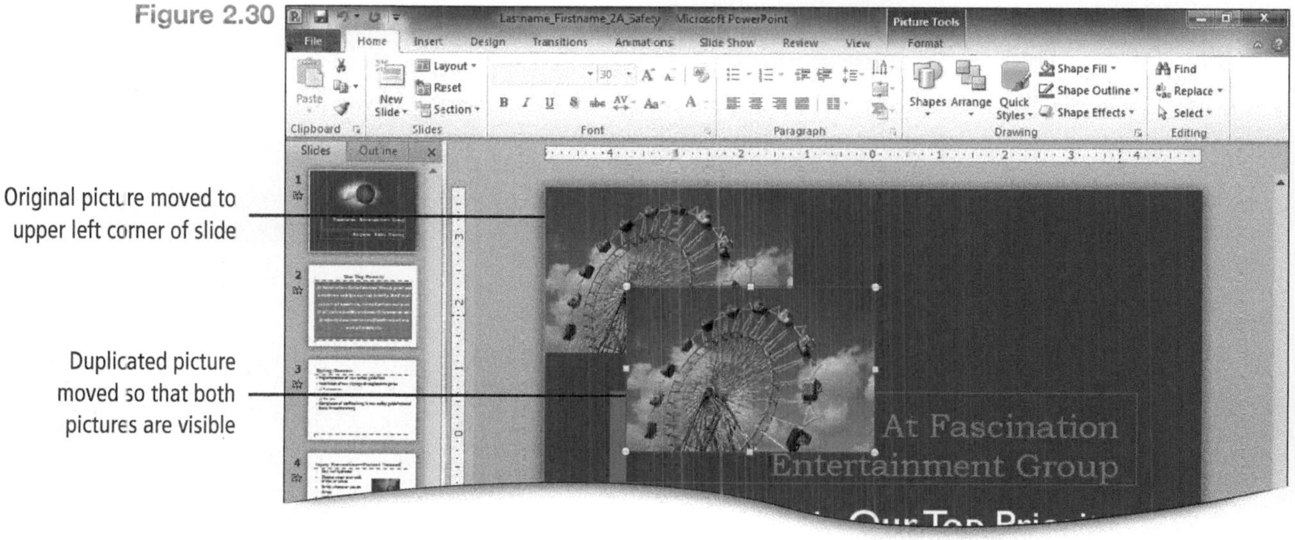

4 With the duplicated image selected, hold down Ctrl, and then press D to insert a third copy of the image.

5 Click anywhere on the slide so that none of the three pictures are selected. **Save** your presentation, and then compare your screen with Figure 2.31. Do not be concerned if your pictures are not positioned exactly as shown.

Figure 2.31

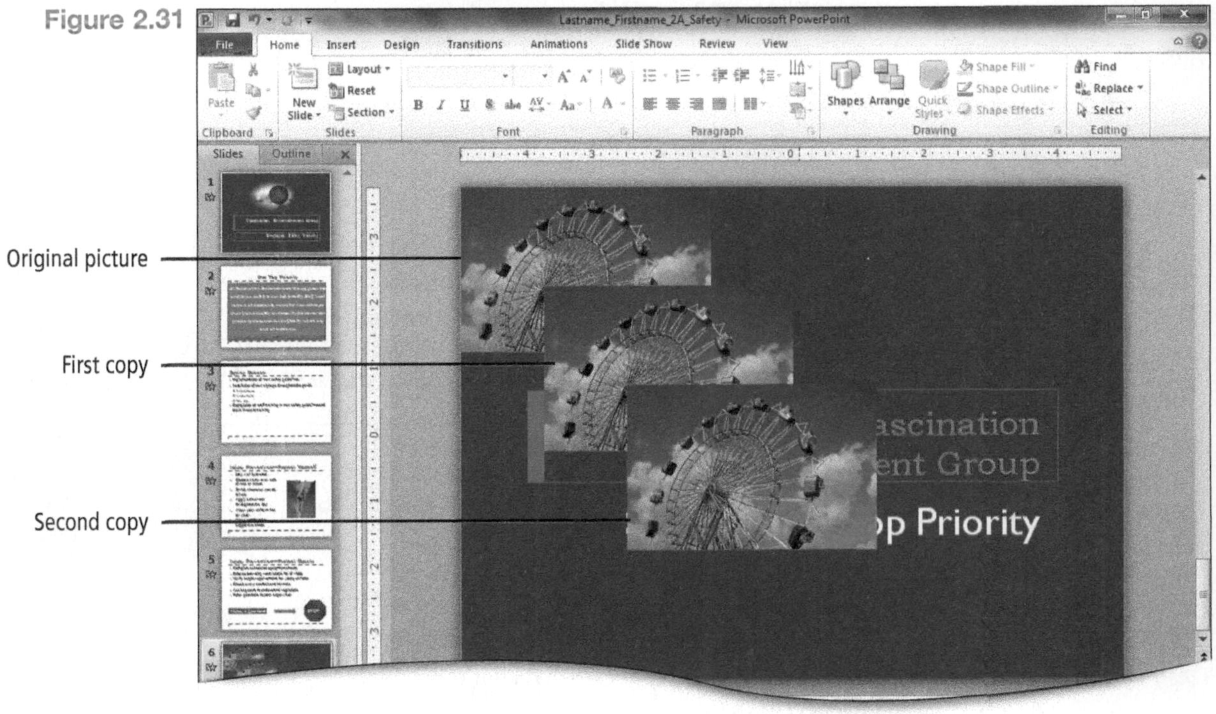

Activity 2.14 | Aligning and Distributing Objects

When you insert multiple objects on a slide, you can use commands on the Ribbon to align and distribute the objects precisely.

> **Another Way**
> Hold down Shift and click each object that you want to select.

1 With **Slide 6** displayed, position the pointer in the gray area of the Slide pane just outside the upper left corner of the slide to display the pointer. Drag down and to the right to draw a transparent blue rectangle that encloses the three pictures. Compare your slide with Figure 2.32.

Figure 2.32

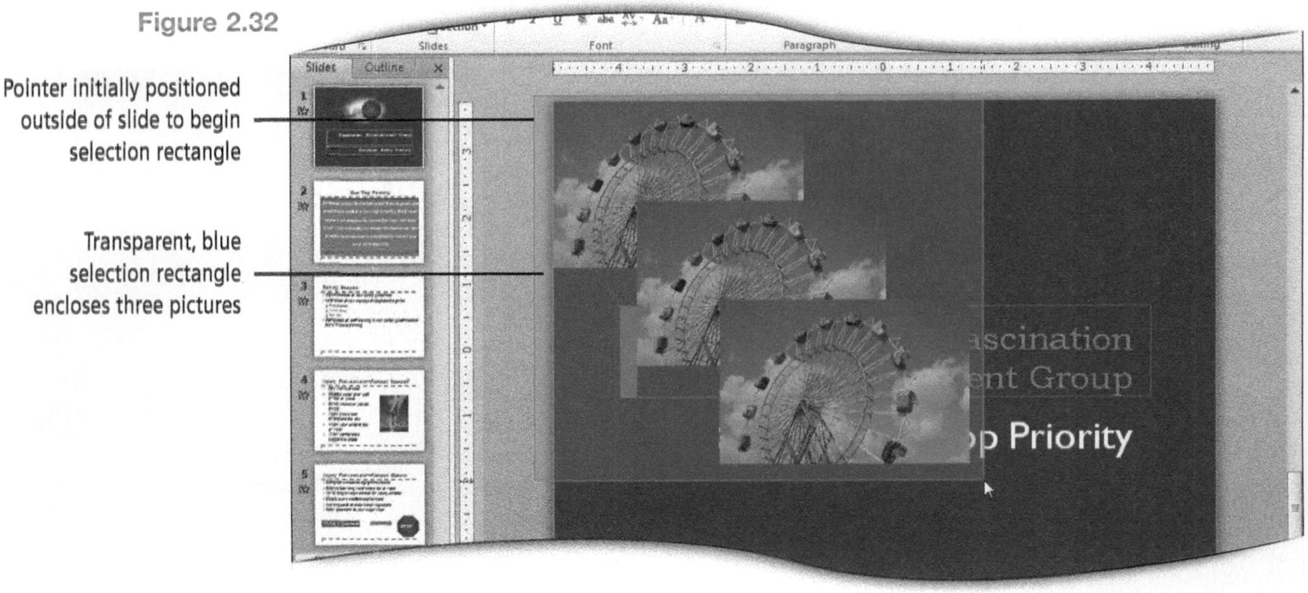

2 Release the mouse button to select the three objects, and then compare your screen with Figure 2.33.

Objects completely enclosed by a selection rectangle are selected when the mouse button is released.

Figure 2.33

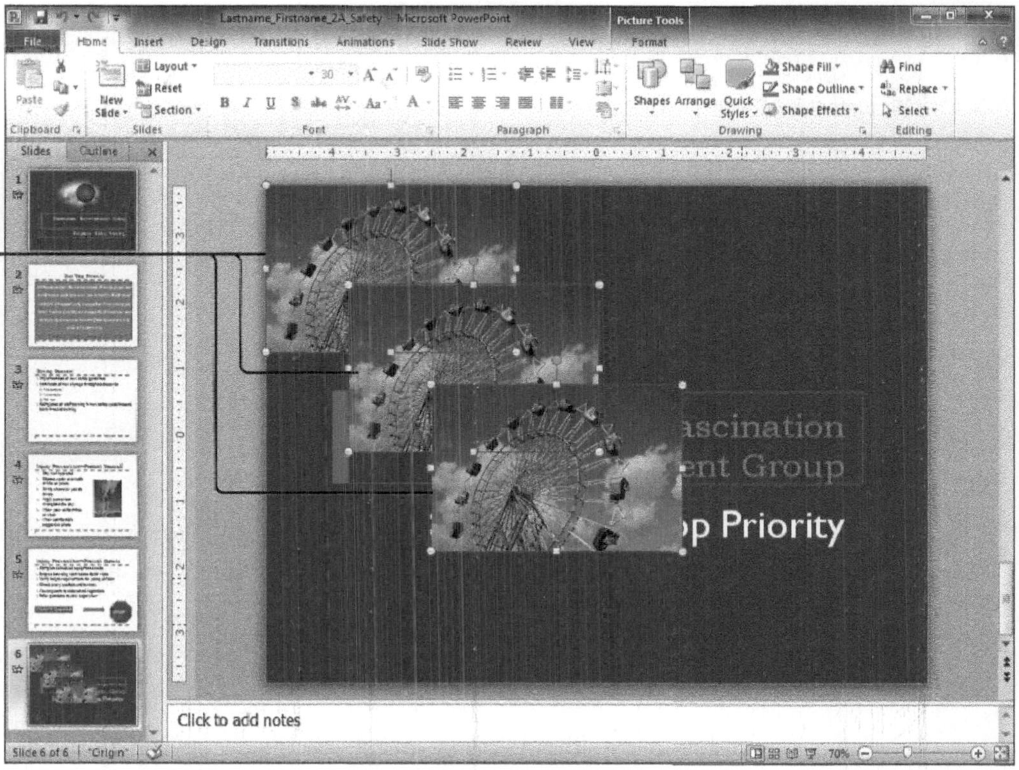

3 Click the **Format tab**, and then in the **Arrange group**, click the **Align** button. Toward the bottom of the menu, click **Align to Slide** to activate this setting.

When you select an alignment option, this setting will cause the objects to align with the edges of the slide.

4 On the **Format tab**, in the **Arrange group**, click the **Align** button again, and then click **Align Top**.

The top of each of the three pictures aligns with the top edge of the slide.

5 Click in a blank area of the slide so that nothing is selected. Then, click the third picture. Point to the picture so that the pointer displays, and then drag to the right so that its upper right corner aligns with the upper right corner of the slide.

6 Hold down Shift and click the remaining two pictures so that all three pictures are selected. On the **Format tab**, in the **Arrange group**, click the **Align** button. Click **Align Selected Objects** to activate this setting.

When you select an alignment option, this setting will cause the objects that you select to align relative to each other.

7 With the three pictures still selected, on the **Format tab**, in the **Arrange group**, click the **Align** button [Align icon] again, and then click **Distribute Horizontally**. Compare your screen with Figure 2.34.

The three pictures are spaced and distributed evenly across the top of the slide and aligned with the top edge of the slide.

Figure 2.34

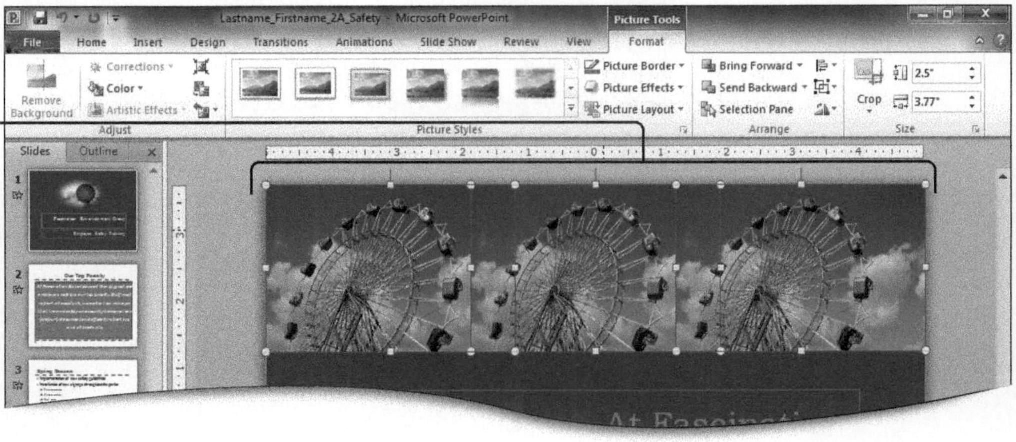

Pictures aligned with top edge of slide and distributed evenly across top edge of slide

8 With the three pictures selected, on the **Format tab**, in the **Picture Styles group**, click the **Picture Effects** button. Point to **Soft Edges**, and then click **50 Point** to apply the picture effect to all three images.

9 Display **Slide 5**, hold down Shift, and then at the bottom of the slide, click the **text box**, the **arrow**, and the **octagon** to select all three objects.

10 With the three objects selected, on the **Format tab**, in the **Arrange group**, click the **Align** button [Align icon]. Be sure that **Align Selected Objects** is still active—a check mark displays to its left. Then, click **Align Middle**. Click the **Align** button again, and then click **Distribute Horizontally**.

The midpoint of each object aligns and the three objects are distributed evenly.

11 Click anywhere on the slide so that none of the objects are selected, and then compare your screen with Figure 2.35.

Figure 2.35

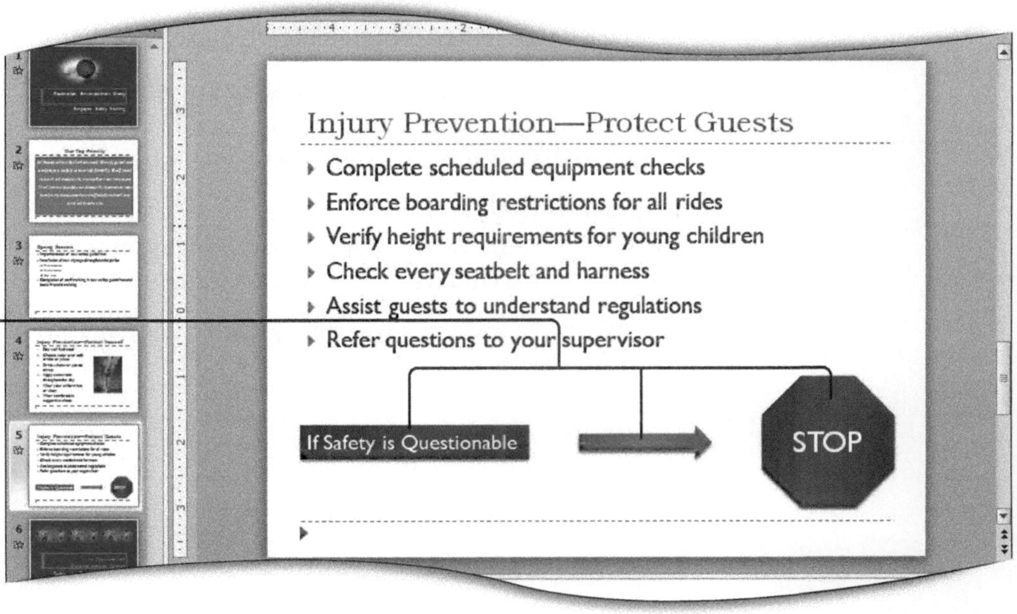

Text box, arrow, and shape are aligned and distributed

12 On the **Slide Show tab**, in the **Start Slide Show group**, click the **From Beginning** button, and then view the slide show. Press Esc when the black slide displays.

13 On the **Insert tab**, in the **Text group**, click the **Header & Footer** button to display the **Header and Footer** dialog box. Click the **Notes and Handouts tab**. Under **Include on page**, select the **Date and time** check box, and then select **Update automatically**. If necessary, clear the Header check box. Select the **Page number** and **Footer** check boxes. In the **Footer** box, using your own name, type **Lastname_Firstname_2A_Safety** and then click **Apply to All**.

14 Display the **Document Properties**. Replace the text in the **Author** box with your own firstname and lastname, in the **Subject** box, type your course name and section number, and in the **Keywords** box, type **safety, injury prevention** **Close** the **Document Information Panel**.

15 **Save** your presentation. Print **Handouts 6 Slides Horizontal**, or submit your presentation electronically as directed by your instructor.

16 **Close** the presentation and exit PowerPoint.

End **You have completed Project 2A**

PowerPoint | Chapter 2

Project 2B Event Announcement

Project Activities

In Activities 2.15 through 2.24, you will format slides in a presentation for the Fascination Entertainment Group Marketing Director that informs employees about upcoming events at the company's amusement parks. You will enhance the presentation using SmartArt and WordArt graphics. Your completed presentation will look similar to Figure 2.36.

Project Files

For Project 2B, you will need the following files:

p02B_Celebrations
p02B_Canada_Contact
p02B_Mexico_Contact
p02B_US_Contact

You will save your presentation as:

Lastname_Firstname_2B_Celebrations

Project Results

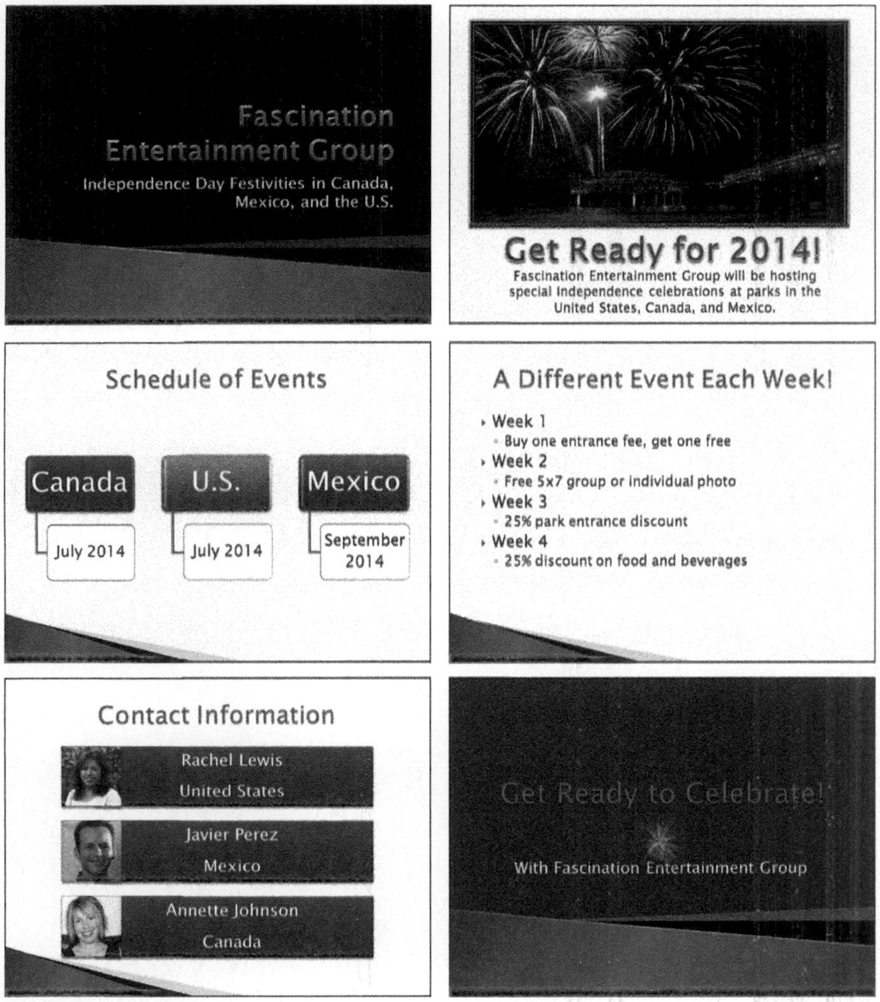

Figure 2.36
Project 2B Celebrations

Objective 5 | Remove Picture Backgrounds and Insert WordArt

To avoid the boxy look that results when you insert an image into a presentation, use ***Background Removal*** to flow a picture into the content of the presentation. Background Removal removes unwanted portions of a picture so that the picture does not appear as a self-contained rectangle.

WordArt is a gallery of text styles with which you can create decorative effects, such as shadowed or mirrored text. You can choose from the gallery of WordArt styles to insert a new WordArt object or you can customize existing text by applying WordArt formatting.

Activity 2.15 | Removing the Background from a Picture and Applying Soft Edge Options

1 **Start** PowerPoint. From your student files, open **p02B_Celebrations.** On the **View tab**, in the **Show group**, if necessary, select the Ruler check box. In your **PowerPoint Chapter 2** folder, save the file as **Lastname_Firstname_2B_Celebrations**

2 Display **Slide 6.** Notice how the picture is a self-contained rectangle and that it has a much darker black background than the presentation. Click the picture to select it, and then on the **Format tab**, in the **Adjust group**, click the **Remove Background** button. Compare your screen with Figure 2.37.

PowerPoint determines what portion of the picture is the foreground—the portion to keep—and which portion is the background—the portion to remove. The background is overlaid in magenta, leaving the remaining portion of the picture as it will look when the background removal is complete. A rectangular selection area displays that can be moved and sized to select additional areas of the picture. The Background Removal options display in the Refine group on the Ribbon.

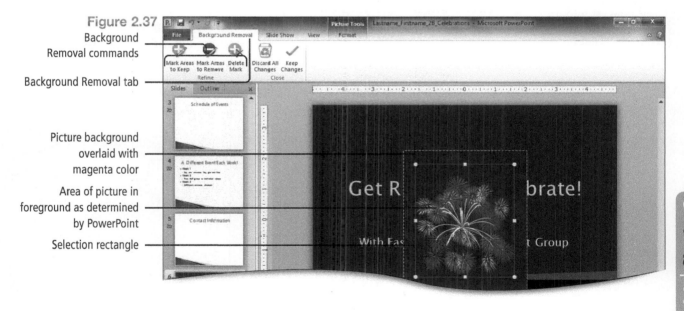

Figure 2.37

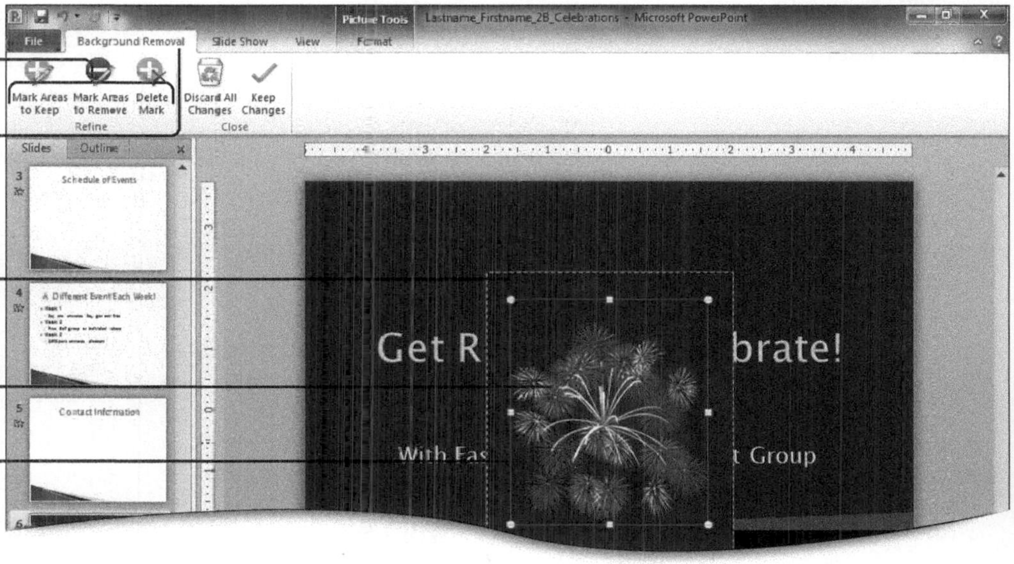

3 On the **selection rectangle**, point to the left center sizing handle to display the ↔ pointer, and then drag to the left so that the left edge of the selection area aligns with the dashed border surrounding the picture. Compare your screen with Figure 2.38.

When you move or size the selection area, the areas outside the selection are treated as background and are removed. Thus, you have control over which portions of the picture that you keep. Here, by resizing the selection area on the left, a larger area of each *flower* in the fireworks is included in the foreground of the picture. On the right side of the fireworks picture, some dark red shadowing is visible as part of the picture.

Figure 2.38

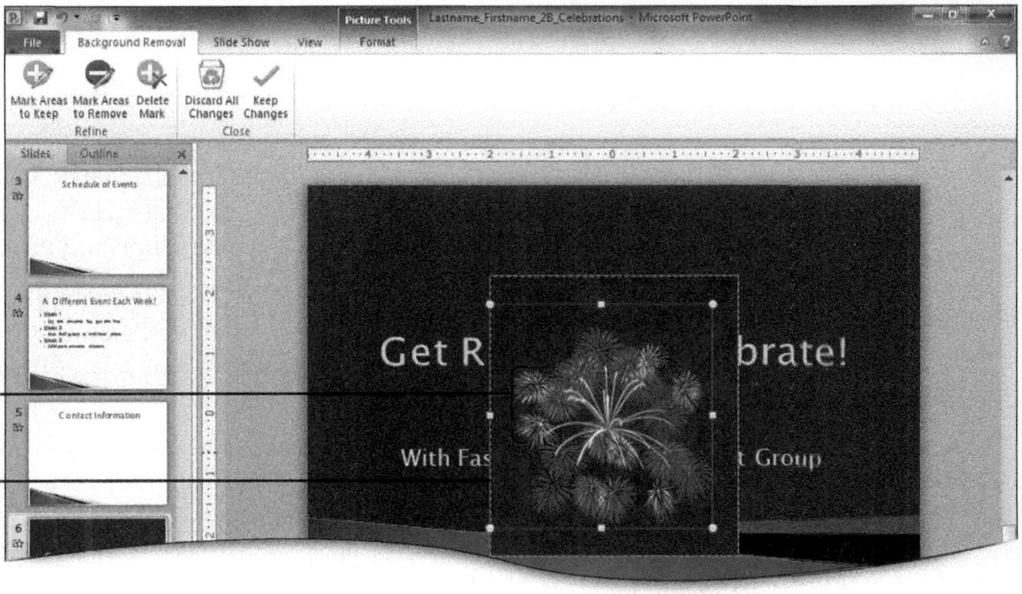

Additional portion of fireworks display as foreground

Selection rectangle aligns with dashed border

> **Another Way**
> In the status bar, use the Zoom Slider options to increase the Zoom to 100%.

4 On the **View tab**, in the **Zoom group**, click the **Zoom** button. In the **Zoom** dialog box, select **100%,** and then click **OK** to increase the size of the slide in the Slide pane. Notice on the right side of the fireworks picture the dark red shadowing in a triangular shape that is visible between some of the outer flowers of the fireworks display. Compare your slide with Figure 2.39.

Figure 2.39

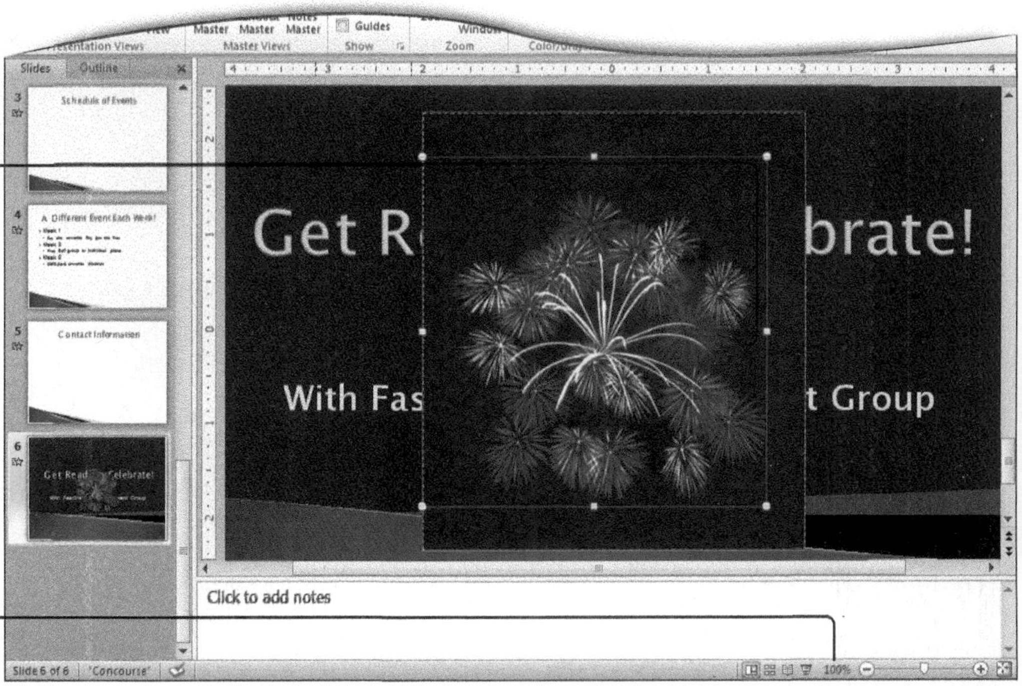

Dark red triangle-shaped shadowing between outer flowers

Zoom level set to 100%

5 On the **Background Removal tab**, in the **Refine group**, click the **Mark Areas to Remove** button, and then position the pencil pointer so that the ruler guides align on the **right half of the horizontal ruler at 1 inch** and on the **lower half of the vertical ruler at 0.5 inch**. Click one time to insert a deletion mark, and then compare your screen with Figure 2.40. If your mark is not positioned as shown in the figure, click Undo and begin again.

You can surround irregular-shaped areas that you want to remove with deletion marks. Here, you can begin to surround the dark red shadow by placing a deletion mark in one corner of the red triangular area.

Figure 2.40

6 With the pencil pointer still active, position the pointer to align the ruler guides on the **right half of the horizontal ruler at approximately 1.5 inches** and on the **lower half of the vertical ruler to 0.75 inch** so that the pointer is aligned on the right edge of the dark red triangle. Click one time to insert another mark. Compare your screen with Figure 2.41.

The two inserted marks provide PowerPoint sufficient information to remove the triangular-shaped red and black shadowed area. If the area is not removed as shown in the figure, insert additional deletion marks as necessary.

Figure 2.41

7 On the **Background Removal tab**, in the **Close group**, click the **Keep Changes** button to remove the background. On the far right edge of the status bar, click the **Fit slide to current window** button.

PowerPoint | Chapter 2

8 With the picture selected, on the **Format tab**, in the **Picture Styles group**, click the **Picture Effects** button, point to **Soft Edges**, and then click **50 Point**. In the **Adjust group**, click the **Artistic Effects** button, and then in the fourth row, click the third effect—**Crisscross Etching**.

9 In the **Size group**, click in the **Shape Height** box, replace the number with **3.5** and then press Enter. In the **Arrange group**, click the **Align** button, and then click **Align Center**. Click the **Align** button again, and then click **Align Middle**. Compare your slide with Figure 2.42, and then **Save** your presentation.

Figure 2.42

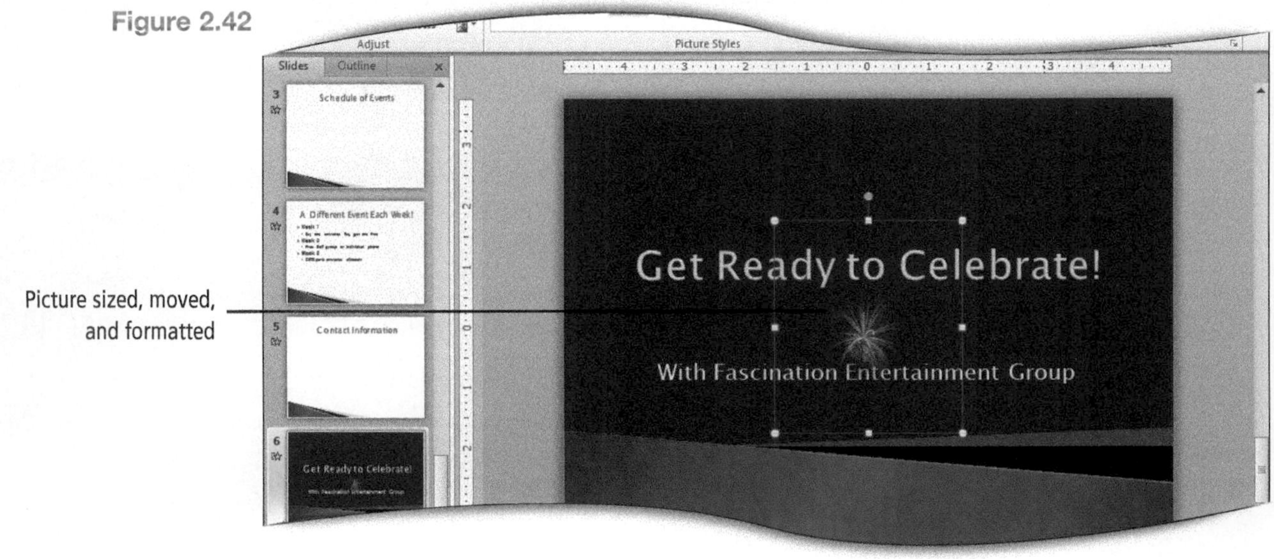

Activity 2.16 | Applying WordArt Styles to Existing Text

1 On **Slide 6**, click anywhere in the word *Get* to activate the title placeholder, and then select the title—*Get Ready to Celebrate*. Click the **Format tab**, and then in the **WordArt Styles group**, click the **More** button.

The WordArt Styles gallery displays in two sections. If you choose a WordArt style in the Applies to Selected Text section, you must first select all of the text to which you want to apply the WordArt. If you choose a WordArt style in the Applies to All Text in the Shape section, the WordArt style is applied to all of the text in the placeholder or shape.

2 Under **Applies to Selected Text**, in the first row, click the fourth style—**Fill – White, Outline – Accent 1**, and then compare your screen with Figure 2.43.

Figure 2.43

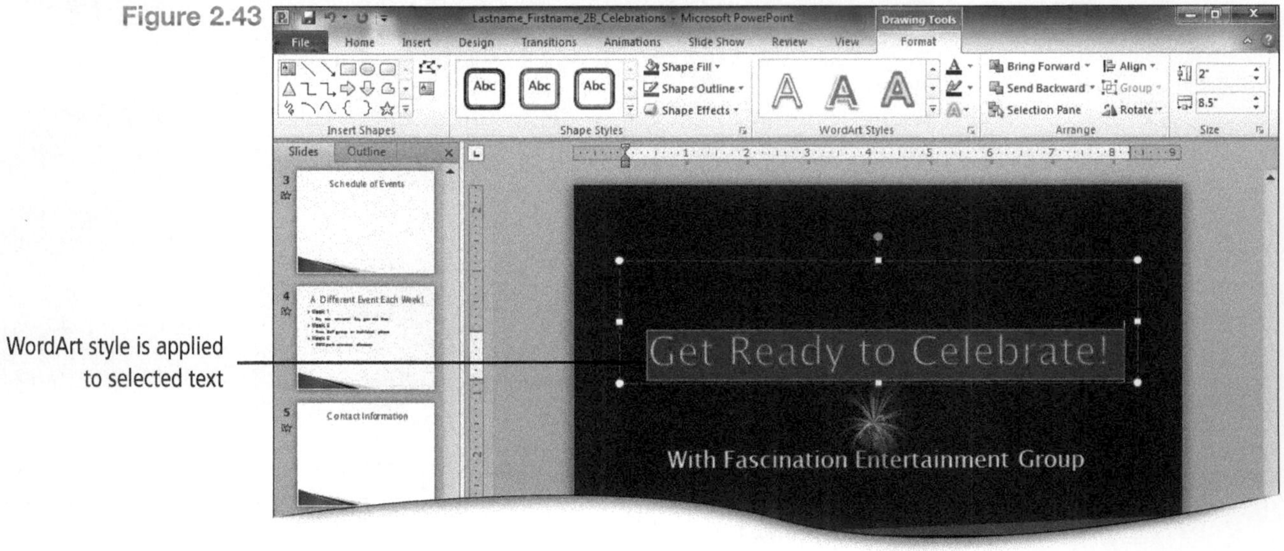

3 With the text still selected, in the **WordArt Styles group**, click the **Text Fill button arrow** [A]. Under **Theme Colors**, in the sixth column, click the fourth color—**Dark Red, Accent 2, Lighter 40%**, and then compare your screen with Figure 2.44.

Figure 2.44

Text Fill button reflects applied color

Text Fill color applied to WordArt

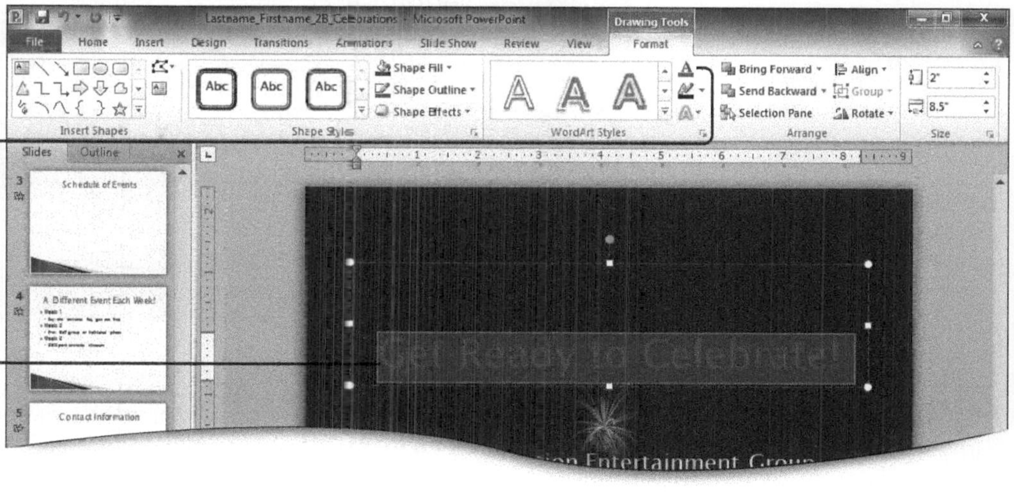

4 Display **Slide 1**, and then click anywhere in the title—*Fascination Entertainment Group.*

5 Click the **Format tab**, and then in the **WordArt Styles group**, click the **More** button [▾] to display the **WordArt Styles** gallery. Under **Applies to All Text in the Shape**, in the first row, click the third style—**Fill – Dark Red, Accent 2, Warm Matte Bevel**, and then compare your screen with Figure 2.45.

Figure 2.45

WordArt style applied to title

6 **Save** [💾] your presentation.

Activity 2.17 | Inserting a WordArt Object

In addition to formatting existing text using WordArt, you can insert a new WordArt object anywhere on a slide.

1 Display **Slide 2**. Click the **Insert tab**, and then in the **Text group**, click the **WordArt** button. In the gallery, in the last row, click the third WordArt style—**Fill – Dark Red, Accent 2, Matte Bevel.**

In the center of your slide, a WordArt placeholder displays *Your text here.* Text that you type will replace this text and the placeholder will expand to accommodate the text. The WordArt is surrounded by sizing handles with which you can adjust its size.

2 Type **Get Ready for 2014!** to replace the WordArt placeholder text. Compare your screen with Figure 2.46.

Figure 2.46

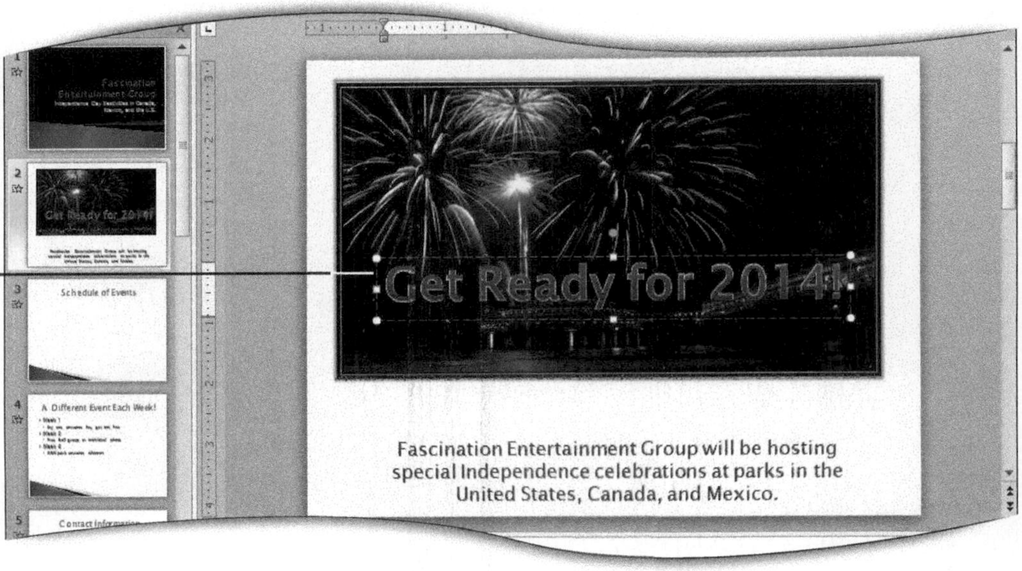

3 Point to the WordArt border to display the pointer. Hold down Shift, and then drag down to position the WordArt between the picture and the text at the bottom of the slide and centered between the left and right edge of the slide. Use Ctrl + any of the arrow keys to move the WordArt in small increments. Compare your slide with Figure 2.47 and move the WordArt again if necessary.

Recall that holding down Shift when dragging an object constrains the horizontal and vertical movement so that the object is moved in a straight line.

Figure 2.47

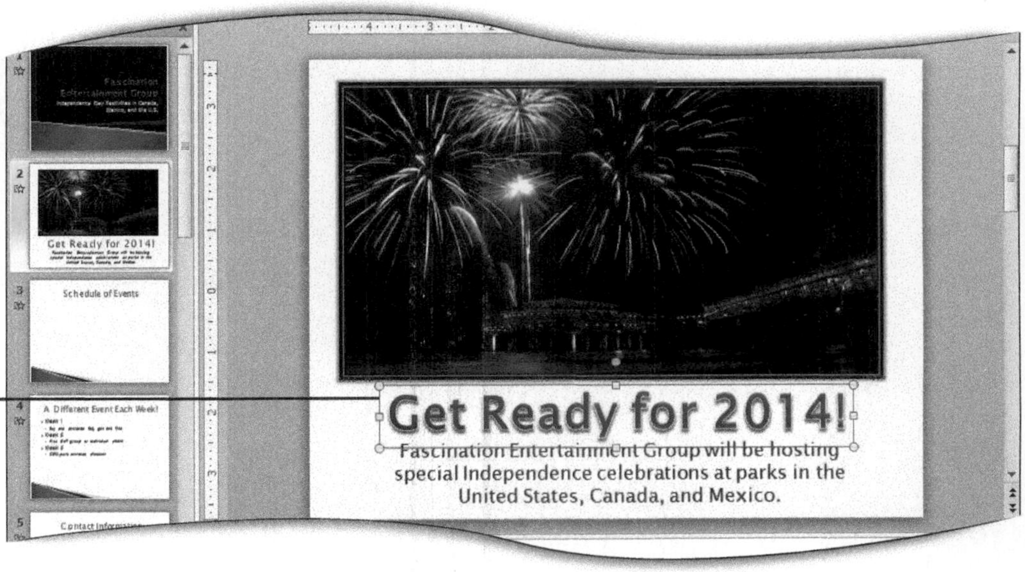

4 **Save** your presentation.

Objective 6 | Create and Format a SmartArt Graphic

A ***SmartArt graphic*** is a visual representation of information that you create by choosing from among various layouts to communicate your message or ideas effectively. SmartArt graphics can illustrate processes, hierarchies, cycles, lists, and relationships. You can include text and pictures in a SmartArt graphic, and you can apply colors, effects, and styles that coordinate with the presentation theme.

Activity 2.18 | Creating a SmartArt Graphic from Bulleted Points

You can convert an existing bulleted list into a SmartArt graphic. When you create a SmartArt graphic, consider the message that you are trying to convey, and then choose an appropriate layout. The table in Figure 2.48 describes types of SmartArt layouts and suggested purposes.

Microsoft PowerPoint SmartArt Graphic Types

Graphic Type	Purpose of Graphic
List	Shows non-sequential information
Process	Shows steps in a process or timeline
Cycle	Shows a continual process
Hierarchy	Shows a decision tree or displays an organization chart
Relationship	Illustrates connections
Matrix	Shows how parts relate to a whole
Pyramid	Shows proportional relationships with the largest component on the top or bottom
Picture	Includes pictures in the layout to communicate messages and ideas

Figure 2.48

> **Another Way**
> Right-click on a bulleted list to display the shortcut menu, and then click **Convert to SmartArt**.

1 Display **Slide 4**, and then click anywhere in the bulleted list placeholder. On the **Home tab**, in the **Paragraph group**, click the **Convert to SmartArt** button. Below the gallery, click **More SmartArt Graphics**.

Three sections comprise the Choose a SmartArt Graphic dialog box. The left section lists the SmartArt graphic types. The center section displays the SmartArt graphics according to type. The third section displays the selected SmartArt graphic, its name, and a description of its purpose.

2 On the left side of the **Choose a SmartArt Graphic** dialog box, click **List**. Use the ScreenTips to locate and then click **Vertical Bullet List**. Compare your screen with Figure 2.49.

Figure 2.49

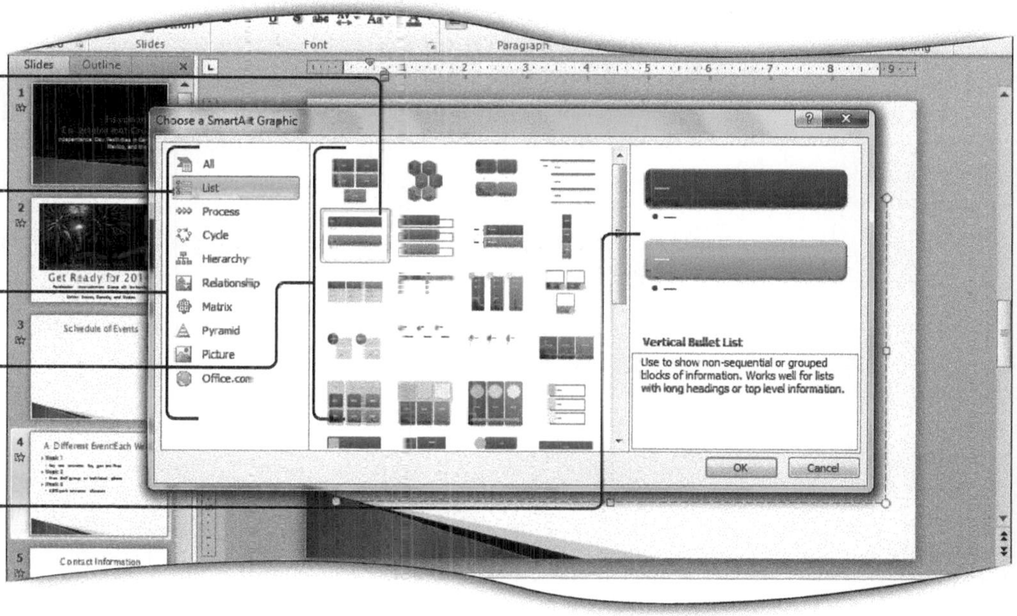

3 In the **Choose a SmartArt Graphic** dialog box, click **OK**. If the Text Pane displays to the right of the SmartArt graphic, click its Close button. Compare your screen with Figure 2.50, and then **Save** your presentation.

It is not necessary to select all of the text in the list. By clicking in the list, PowerPoint converts all of the bullet points to the selected SmartArt graphic. On the Ribbon, the SmartArt contextual tools display two tabs—Design and Format. The thick border surrounding the SmartArt graphic indicates that it is selected and displays the area that the object will cover on the slide.

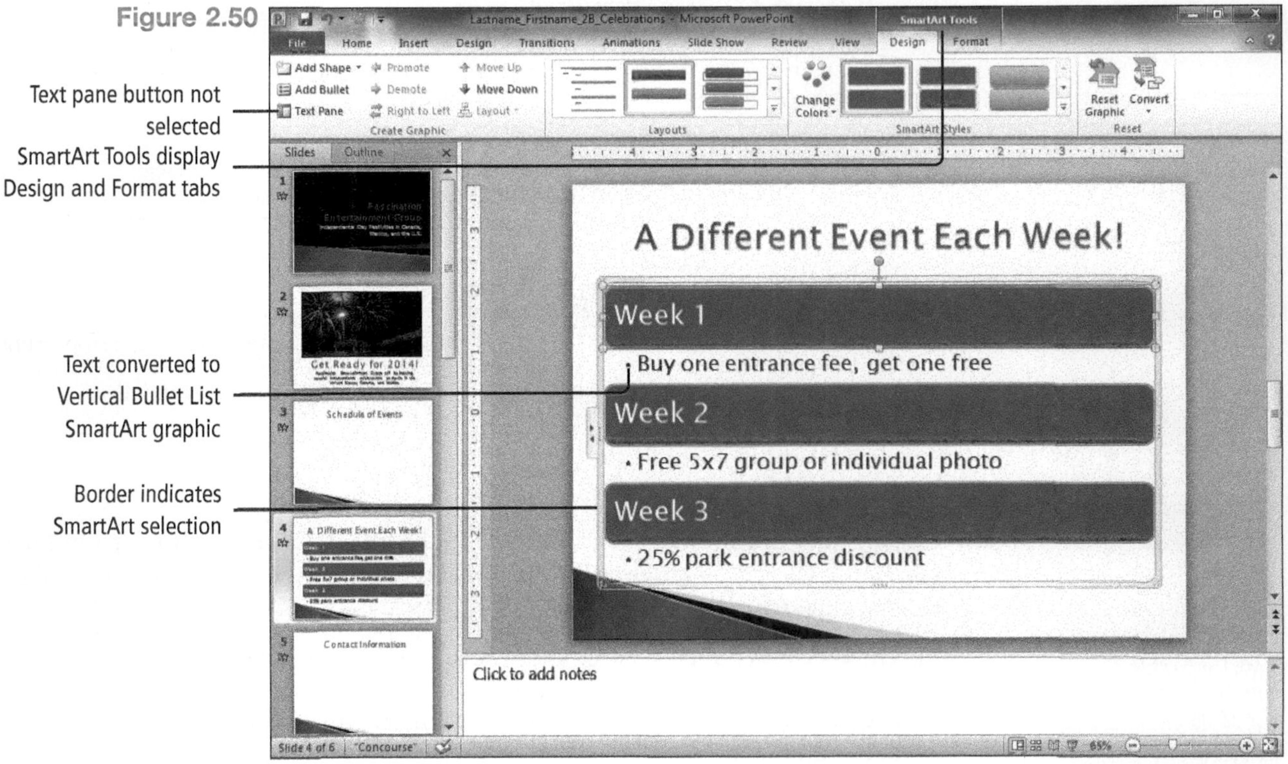

Figure 2.50

Activity 2.19 | Adding Shapes in a SmartArt Graphic

If a SmartArt graphic does not have enough shapes to illustrate a concept or display the relationships, you can add more shapes.

> **Another Way**
> Right-click the shape, point to **Add Shape**, and then click **Add Shape After**.

1 Click in the shape that contains the text *Week 3*. In the **SmartArt Tools**, click the **Design tab**. In the **Create Graphic group**, click the **Add Shape arrow**, and then click **Add Shape After** to insert a shape at the same level. Type **Week 4**

The text in each of the SmartArt shapes resizes to accommodate the added shape.

2 On the **Design tab**, in the **Create Graphic group**, click the **Add Bullet** button to add a bullet below the *Week 4* shape.

3 Type **25% discount on food and beverages** Compare your slide with Figure 2.51, and then **Save** your presentation.

Figure 2.51

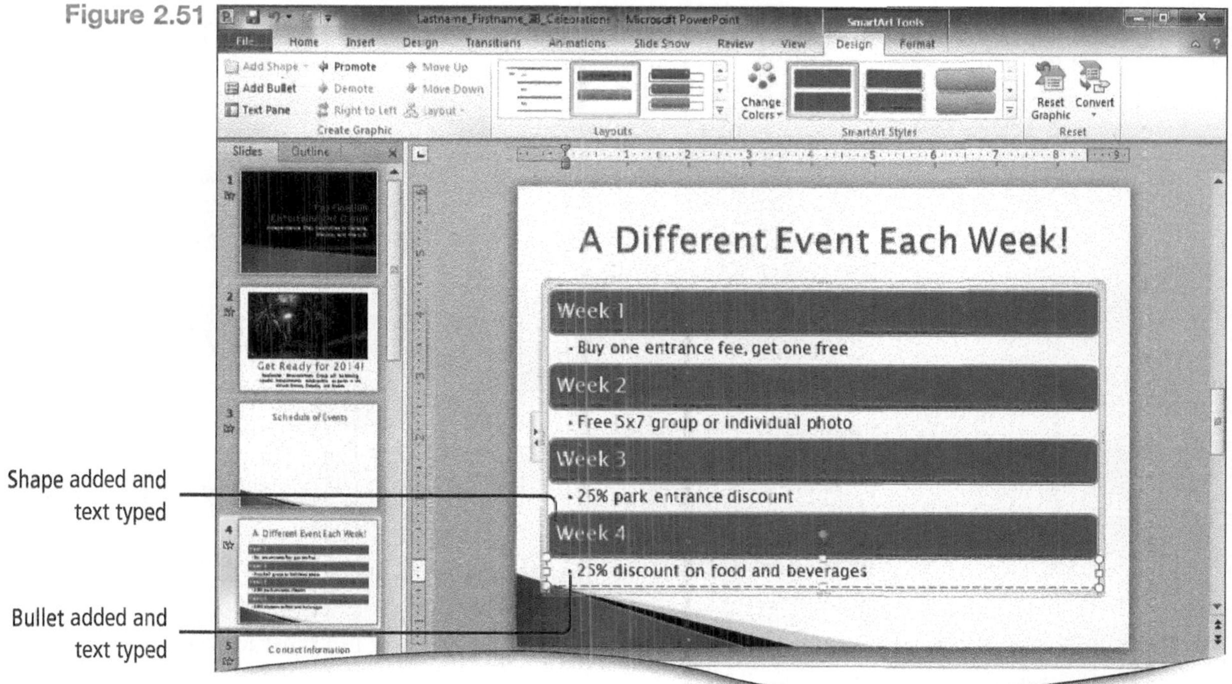

Activity 2.20 | Creating a SmartArt Graphic Using a Content Layout

1 Display **Slide 3**. In the center of the content placeholder, click the **Insert SmartArt Graphic** button to open the **Choose a SmartArt Graphic** dialog box.

2 On the left, click **Process**, and then scroll as necessary and use the ScreenTips to locate **Vertical Arrow List**. Click **Vertical Arrow List**. Compare your screen with Figure 2.52.

Figure 2.52

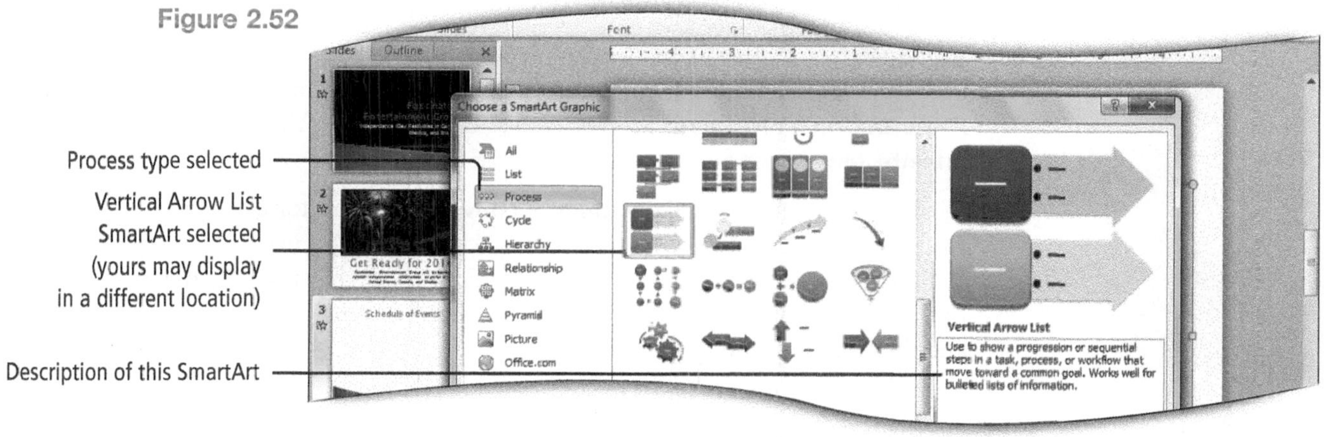

3 Click **OK** to insert the SmartArt graphic.

The SmartArt graphic displays with two rounded rectangle shapes and two arrow shapes. You can type text directly into the shapes or you can type text in the Text Pane, which may display to the left of your SmartArt graphic. You can display the Text Pane by clicking the Text Pane tab on the left side of the SmartArt graphic border, or by clicking the Text Pane button in the Create Graphic group. Depending on your software settings, the Text Pane may display.

4 In the SmartArt graphic, click in the first orange rectangle, and then type **Canada** In the arrow shape to the immediate right, click in the first bullet point. Type **July 2014** and then press Del to remove the second bullet point in the arrow shape.

5 Click in the second orange rectangle, and then type **U.S.** In the arrow shape to the immediate right, click in the first bullet point. Type **July 2014** and then press Del. Compare your slide with Figure 2.53.

Figure 2.53

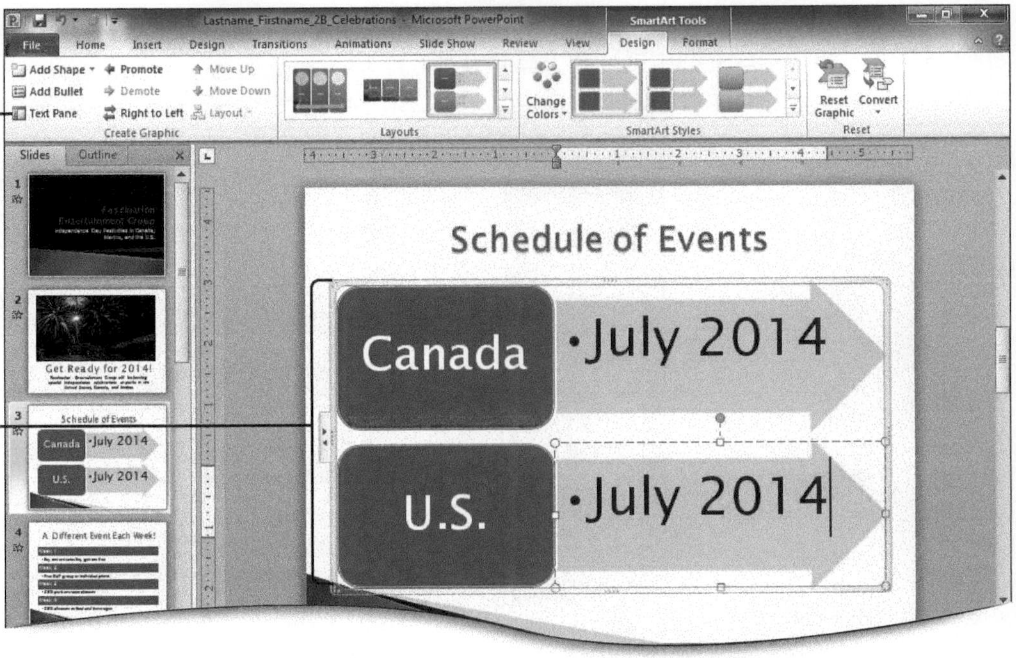

6 Click in the *U.S.* rectangle. On the **Design tab**, in the **Create Graphic group**, click the **Add Shape arrow**. Click **Add Shape After** to insert a new rectangle and arrow. Type **Mexico** and then in the arrow shape to the right, type **September 2014**

7 Display **Slide 5**. In the center of the content placeholder, click the **Insert SmartArt Graphic** button. In the **Choose a SmartArt Graphic** dialog box, click **Picture**, and then scroll as necessary to locate **Vertical Picture Accent List**. Click **Vertical Picture Accent List**, and then click **OK** to insert the graphic.

8 In the SmartArt graphic, in the top rectangle shape, type **Rachel Lewis** and then press Enter. Type **United States** and then click in the middle rectangle shape. Type **Javier Perez** and then press Enter. Type **Mexico** and then click in the last rectangle shape, type **Annette Johnson** and then press Enter. Type **Canada**

9 In the top circle shape, click the **Insert Picture from File** button. Navigate to your student files, click **p02B_US_Contact**, and then press Enter to insert the picture. Using the technique you just practiced, in the middle circle shape, insert **p02B_Mexico_Contact**. In the last circle shape, insert **p02B_Canada_Contact**. Compare your screen with Figure 2.54, and then **Save** your presentation.

Figure 2.54

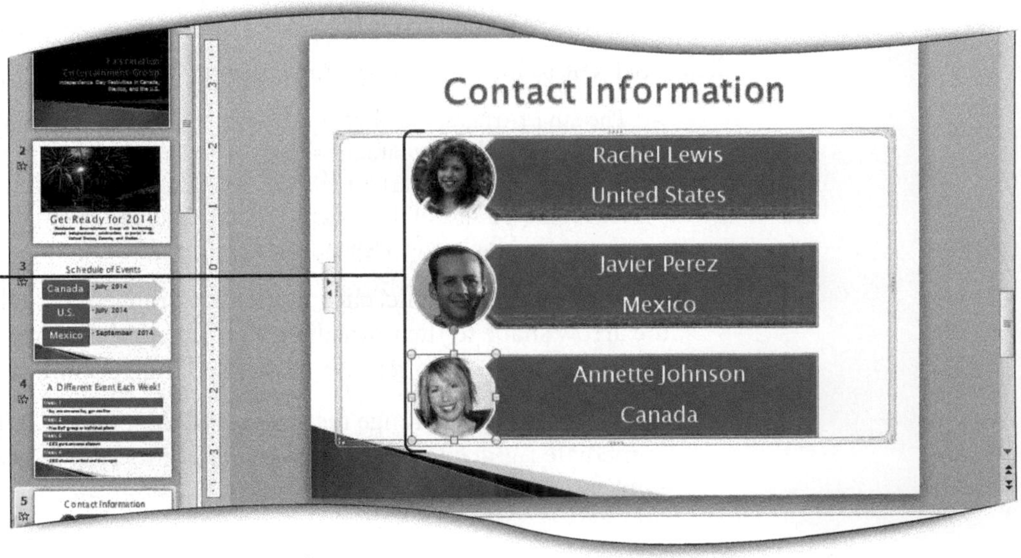

Activity 2.21 | Changing the SmartArt Layout

1 Display **Slide 3**, and then click anywhere in the SmartArt graphic. In the **SmartArt Tools**, click the **Design tab**. In the **Layouts group**, click the **More** button, and then click **More Layouts**. In the **Choose a SmartArt Graphic** dialog box, click **Hierarchy**. Locate and click **Hierarchy List**, and then click **OK**.

2 Compare your slide with Figure 2.55, and then **Save** the presentation.

Figure 2.55

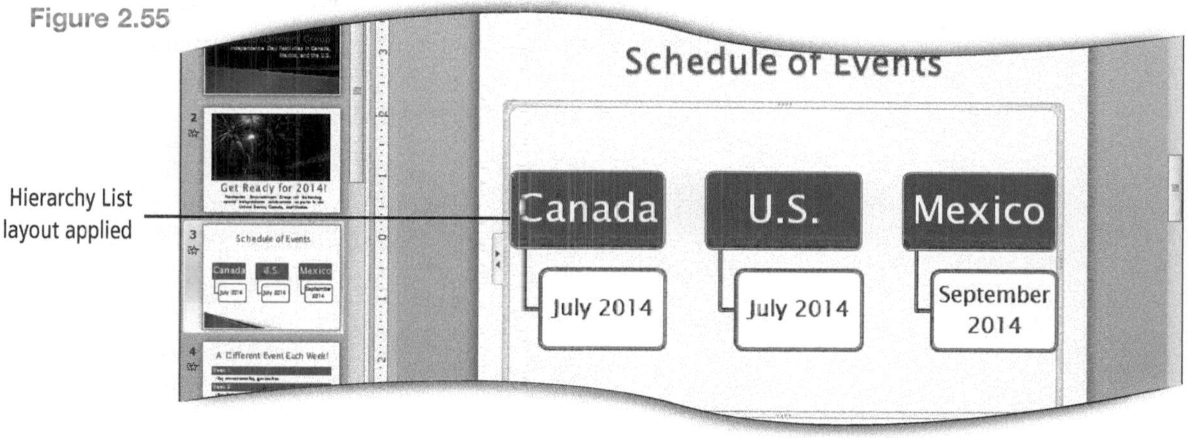

Activity 2.22 | Changing the Color and Style of a SmartArt Graphic

SmartArt Styles are combinations of formatting effects that you can apply to SmartArt graphics.

1 With **Slide 3** displayed and the SmartArt graphic selected, on the **Design tab**, in the **SmartArt Styles group**, click the **Change Colors** button. In the color gallery, under **Colorful**, click the first style—**Colorful - Accent Colors**—to change the color.

2 On the **Design tab**, in the **SmartArt Styles group**, click the **More** button to display the **SmartArt Styles gallery**. Under **3-D**, click the second style, **Inset**. Compare your slide with Figure 2.56.

Figure 2.56

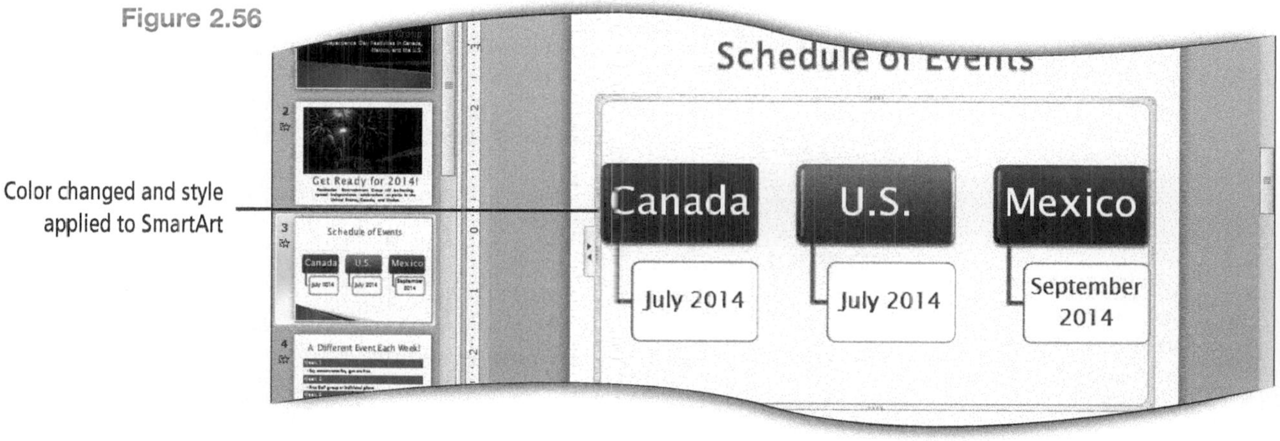

3 Display **Slide 5**, and select the SmartArt. On the **Design tab**, in the **SmartArt Styles group**, click the **Change Colors** button. Under **Accent 2**, click the second style—**Colored Fill - Accent 2**. On the **Design tab**, in the **SmartArt Styles group**, click the **More** button. Under **Best Match for Document**, click the last style, **Intense Effect**. **Save** the presentation.

Activity 2.23 | Customizing the Size and Shape of a SmartArt Graphic

You can select individual or groups of shapes in a SmartArt graphic and make them larger or smaller, and you can change selected shapes to another type of shape.

1 With **Slide 5** displayed, click in the upper red shape that contains the text *Rachel Lewis.* Hold down Shift, and then click in each of the two remaining red shapes containing the text *Javier Perez* and *Annette Johnson* so that all three text shapes are selected.

2 On the **Format tab**, in the **Shapes group**, click the **Larger** button two times to increase the size of the three selected shapes. Compare your screen with Figure 2.57.

Figure 2.57

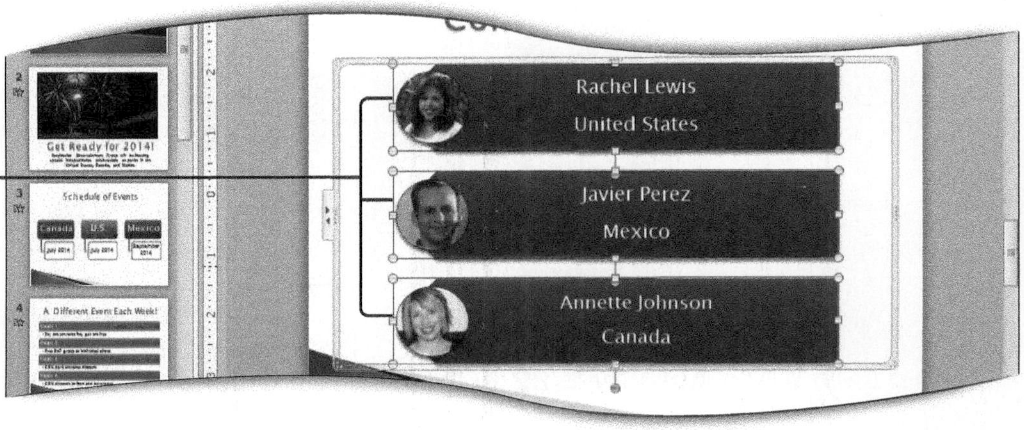

Three shapes selected and resized

3 With the three shapes selected, on the **Home tab**, in the **Font group**, increase the **Font Size** to **28**.

4 Select the first circle picture, and then hold down Shift and click the remaining two circles so that all three circles are selected. In the **SmartArt Tools**, on the **Format tab**, in the **Shapes group**, click the **Change Shape** button. Under **Rectangles**, click the first shape—**Rectangle**—to change the circles to rectangles. With the three shapes selected, in the **Shapes group**, click the **Larger** button two times. Compare your screen with Figure 2.58, and then **Save** the presentation.

Figure 2.58

Larger button

Change Shape button

Three shapes changed to rectangles and resized

Activity 2.24 | Converting a SmartArt to Text

1 Display **Slide 4**, and then click anywhere in the SmartArt graphic. On the **Design tab**, in the **Reset group**, click the **Convert** button, and then click **Convert to Text** to convert the SmartArt graphic to a bulleted list. Compare your screen with Figure 2.59.

Figure 2.59

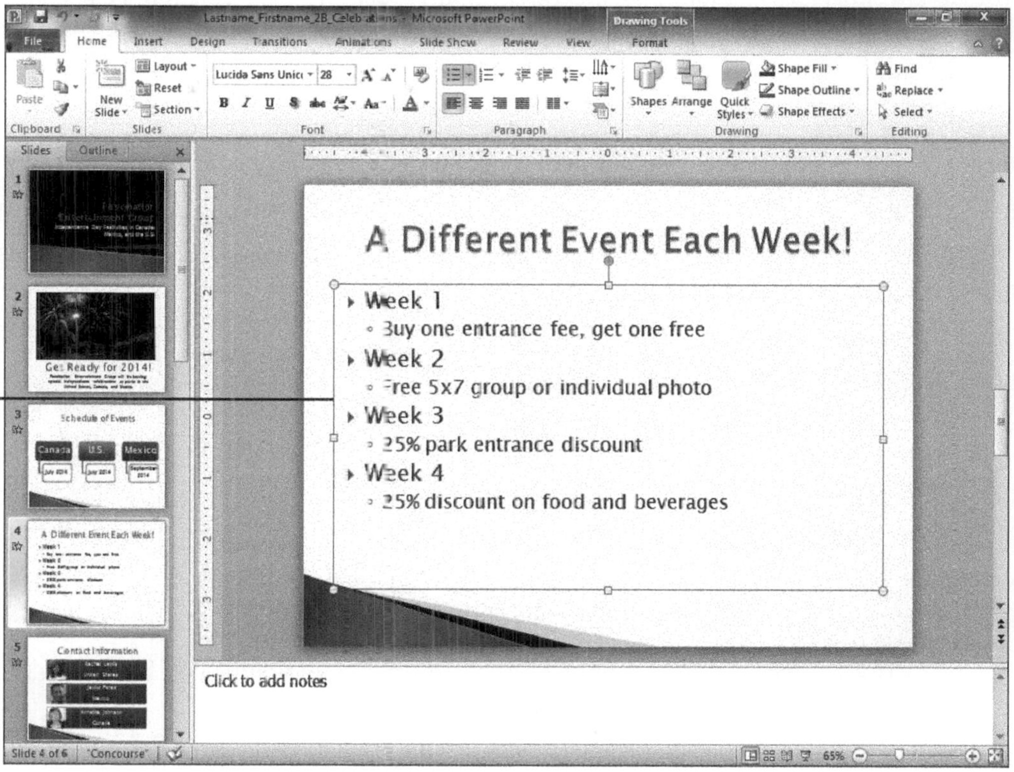

SmartArt graphic converted to text

2 Display the **Document Properties** Replace the text in the **Author** box with your own firstname and lastname, in the **Subject** box, type your course name and section number, and in the **Keywords** box, type **Independence day, celebrations** **Close** the **Document Information Panel**.

3 Insert a **Header & Footer** on the **Notes and Handouts**. Include the **Date and time updated automatically**, the **Page number**, and a **Footer** with the text **Lastname_Firstname_2B_Celebrations** Apply to all the slides. View the presentation from the beginning, and then make any necessary adjustments.

4 **Save** your presentation. Print **Handouts 6 Slides Horizontal**, or submit your presentation electronically as directed by your instructor.

5 **Close** the presentation.

End **You have completed Project 2B**

Content-Based Assessments

Summary

In this chapter, you formatted a presentation by changing the bullet style and by applying WordArt styles to text. You enhanced your presentations by inserting, sizing, and formatting shapes, pictures, and SmartArt graphics, resulting in a professional-looking presentation.

Key Terms

Background Removal..........703
Clip..........685
Crop..........689
Crosshair pointer..........692
Fill Color..........694
Ruler guides..........690
Shapes..........692
SmartArt graphic..........708
SmartArt Styles..........713
Text box..........690
WordArt..........703

Matching

Match each term in the second column with its correct definition in the first column by writing the letter of the term on the blank line in front of the correct definition.

____ 1. The line style in which a placeholder border displays, indicating that all of the text in the placeholder is selected.

____ 2. A common format for a slide that contains a single point without a bullet symbol.

____ 3. A single media file, for example art, sound, animation, or a movie.

____ 4. A four-headed arrow-shaped pointer that indicates that you can reposition an object or image.

____ 5. An object within which you can position text anywhere on the slide.

____ 6. Vertical and horizontal lines that display in the rulers to provide a visual indication of the pointer position so that you can draw a shape.

____ 7. Lines, arrows, stars, banners, ovals, or rectangles used to illustrate an idea, a process, or a workflow.

____ 8. The pointer that indicates that you can draw a shape.

____ 9. The inside color of text or an object.

____ 10. A style gallery displaying predefined combinations of shape fill and line colors.

____ 11. A setting used to align selected objects.

____ 12. The command that reduces the size of a picture by removing vertical or horizontal edges.

____ 13. A gallery of text styles from which you can create shadowed or mirrored text.

____ 14. A visual representation of information that you create by choosing from among layouts to communicate your message or ideas.

____ 15. Combinations of formatting effects that are applied to SmartArt graphics.

A Align to Slide
B Clip
C Crop
D Crosshair pointer
E Fill color
F Move pointer
G Paragraph
H Ruler guides
I Shapes
J Shape Styles
K SmartArt graphic
L SmartArt Styles
M Solid
N Text box
O WordArt

Content-Based Assessments

Multiple Choice

Circle the correct answer.

1. The color of the numbers or bullet symbols in a list is determined by the:
   A. Slide layout **B.** Presentation theme **C.** Gallery
2. When you point to an image in the Clip Art pane, the screen element that displays the keywords and information about the size of the image is the:
   A. ScreenTip **B.** Navigation bar **C.** Menu
3. To horizontally or vertically position selected objects on a slide relative to each other, use the:
   A. Align tools **B.** Distribute tools **C.** Crop tools
4. The command that removes unwanted portions of a picture so that the picture does not appear as a self-contained rectangle is:
   A. Shape height **B.** Picture adjust **C.** Background removal
5. The SmartArt type that shows steps in a process or timeline is:
   A. Radial **B.** Process **C.** List
6. The SmartArt type that shows a continual process is:
   A. Hierarchy **B.** Radial **C.** Cycle
7. The SmartArt type with which you can show a decision tree or create an organization chart is:
   A. Matrix **B.** Pyramid **C.** Hierarchy
8. The SmartArt type that illustrates connections is:
   A. Picture **B.** Radial **C.** Relationship
9. The SmartArt type that shows how parts relate to a whole is:
   A. Matrix **B.** Pyramid **C.** Radial
10. The SmartArt type that shows proportional relationships with the largest component on the top or bottom is:
    A. Matrix **B.** Pyramid **C.** Relationship

Apply 2A skills from these Objectives:

1. Format Numbered and Bulleted Lists
2. Insert Clip Art
3. Insert Text Boxes and Shapes
4. Format Objects

Skills Review | Project 2C Concerts

In the following Skills Review, you will format a presentation by inserting and formatting Clip Art, text boxes, and shapes, and by modifying bullets and numbering. Your completed presentation will look similar to Figure 2.60.

Project Files

For Project 2C, you will need the following file:

p02C_Concerts

You will save your presentation as:

Lastname_Firstname_2C_Concerts

Project Results

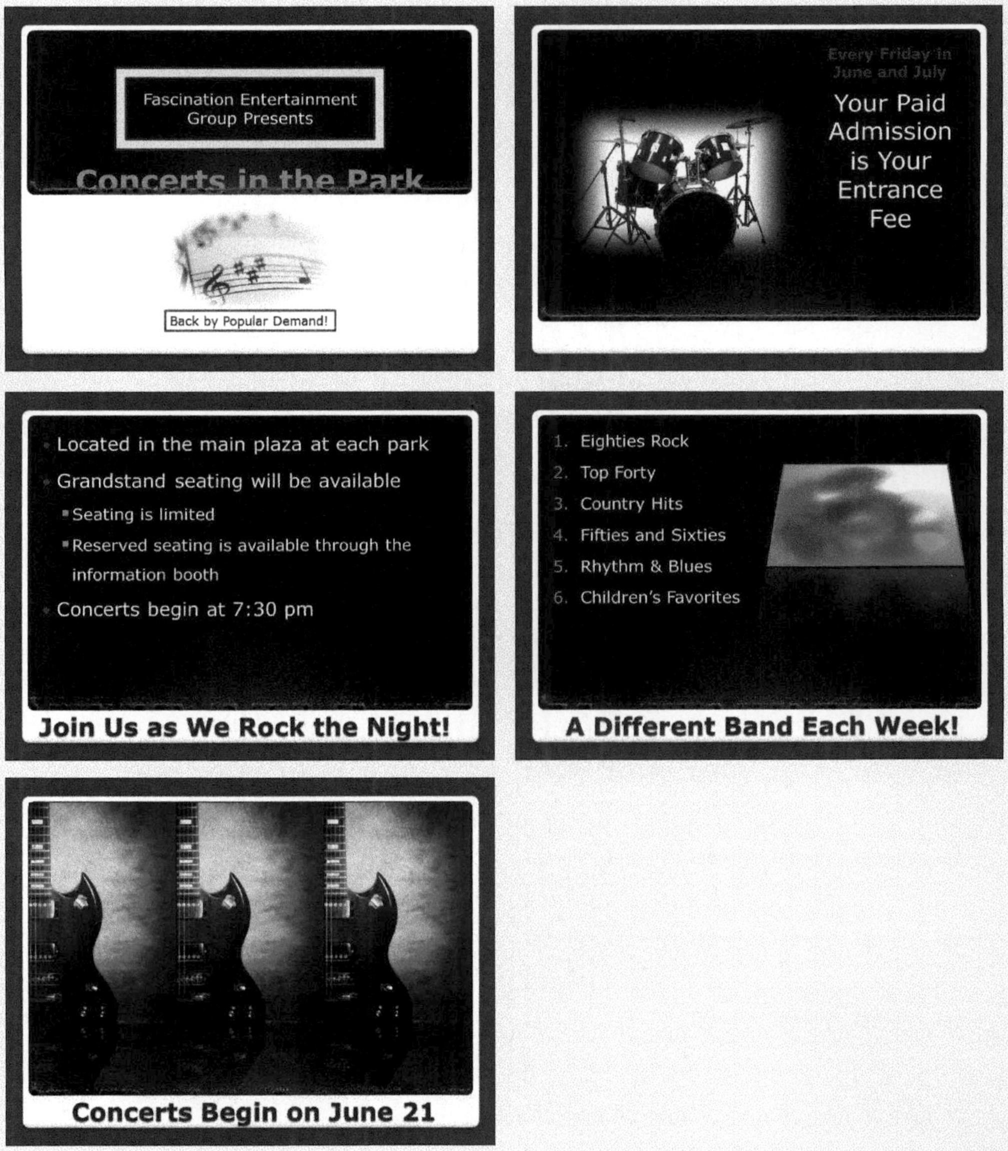

Figure 2.60

(Project 2C Concerts continues on the next page)

Skills Review | Project 2C Concerts (continued)

1 **Start** PowerPoint. From the student files that accompany this textbook, locate and open **p02C_Concerts. Save** the presentation in your **PowerPoint Chapter 2** folder as **Lastname_Firstname_2C_Concerts**

a. If necessary, display the Rulers. With **Slide 1** displayed, on the **Insert tab**, in the **Illustrations group**, click the **Shapes** button, and then under **Basic Shapes**, in the second row, click the fifth shape—**Frame**.

b. Move the pointer to align the ruler guides with the **left half of the horizontal ruler at 3 inches** and with the **upper half of the vertical ruler at 2.5 inches**, and then click to insert the Frame.

c. On the **Format tab**, in the **Size group**, click in the **Shape Height** box to select the number, and then type **1.7** Click in the **Shape Width** box. Replace the selected number with **5.5** and then press Enter to resize the shape.

d. With the frame selected, type **Fascination Entertainment Group Presents** and then change the **Font Size** to **24**. On the **Format tab**, in the **Shape Styles group**, click the **Shape Fill** button, and then under **Theme Colors**, in the fourth column, click the first color—**Lavender, Text 2**.

2 On the **Insert tab**, in the **Images group**, click the **Clip Art** button to display the **Clip Art** pane.

a. In the **Clip Art** pane, click in the **Search for** box and replace any existing text with **compositions musical notes** Click the **Results should be arrow**, and then click as necessary to so that only the **Photographs** check box is selected. Include Office.com content. Click **Go** to display the musical notes pictures.

b. Click the black and white picture of the two lines of music on a music sheet, and then **Close** the **Clip Art** pane. With the picture selected, on the **Format tab**, in the **Size group**, click in the **Shape Height** box. Replace the selected number with **2.5** and then press Enter to resize the image.

c. Point to the picture and then drag down and to the right so that it is centered just below the title—*Concerts in the Park*—and its top edge aligns with the lower edge of the black rounded rectangle.

d. With the picture selected, on the **Format tab**, in the **Size group**, click the **Crop arrow**, and then point to **Crop to Shape**. Under **Basic Shapes**, click the first shape—**Oval**. In the **Picture Styles group**, click the **Picture Effects** button, point to **Soft Edges**, and then click **25 Point**.

e. On the **Insert tab**, in the **Text group**, click the **Text Box** button. Move the pointer to position the ruler guides on the **horizontal ruler at 0 inches** and on the **lower half of the vertical ruler at 2.5 inches**, and then click to insert the text box.

f. On the **Format tab**, in the **Shape Styles group**, click the **More** button. In the first row, click the second style—**Colored Outline - Pink, Accent 1**. Type **Back by Popular Demand!**

g. With the text box selected, hold down Shift, and then click the frame shape, the title placeholder, and the picture so that all four objects are selected. Under **Drawing Tools**, on the **Format tab**, in the **Arrange group**, click the **Align** button, and then click **Align to Slide**. Click the **Align** button again, and then click **Align Center**. **Save** the presentation.

3 Display **Slide 2**, and then click in the title placeholder containing the text *Every Friday in June and July*.

a. On the **Home tab**, in the **Paragraph group**, click the **Bullets** button to remove the bullet symbol from the title.

b. On the left side of the slide, in the content placeholder, click the **Clip Art** button. In the **Clip Art** pane, in the **Search for** box, search for **cymbals** set the results to **Photographs**, include Office.com content, and then click **Go**. Insert the picture of the drum set on a white background.

c. On the **Format tab**, in the **Picture Styles group**, click the **Picture Effects** button, point to **Soft Edges**, and then click **50 Point**. **Close** the **Clip Art** pane.

4 Display **Slide 3**, and then select the third and fourth bullet points—the two, second-level bullet points.

a. On the **Home tab**, in the **Paragraph group**, click the **Bullets button arrow**, and then click **Bullets and Numbering**. In the first row of bullets, click the last style—**Filled Square Bullets**. Replace the number in the **Size** box with **125** and then click the **Color** button. In the eighth column, click the first color—**Gold, Accent 4**—and then click **OK** to change the bullet style.

b. Display **Slide 4**, and then click the bulleted list placeholder. Click the dashed border so that it displays as a solid line, and then on the **Home tab**, in the **Paragraph group**, click the **Numbering button** to change the bullets to numbers.

(Project 2C Concerts continues on the next page)

Skills Review | Project 2C Concerts (continued)

5 Display **Slide 5**. On the **Insert tab**, in the **Images group**, click the **Clip Art** button. In the **Clip Art** pane, in the **Search for** box, search for **electric guitar in monochrome** and then click **Go**. Insert the picture of the black electric guitar on the white, blue, and black background.

a. Change the picture **Height** to **4.5** and then drag the picture down and to the left so that its upper left corner aligns with the upper left corner of the black rectangle on the slide background. **Close** the **Clip Art** pane.

b. With the picture selected, on the **Format tab**, in the **Picture Styles group**, click **Picture Effects**, and then point to **Reflection**. Click the first reflection variation—**Tight Reflection, touching**.

c. With the picture selected, hold down Ctrl, and then press D to create a duplicate of the picture. Drag the duplicated picture to the right about 1 inch, and then hold down Ctrl and press D to create another duplicate.

d. Point to the third guitar picture that you inserted, and then drag to the right so that its upper right corner aligns with the upper right corner of the black rectangle on the slide background.

e. Hold down Shift, and then click the first two guitar pictures so that all three pictures are selected. On the **Format tab**, in the **Arrange group**, click the **Align** button, and then click **Align Selected Objects**. Click the **Align** button again, and then click **Align Top**. Click the **Align** button again, and then click **Distribute Horizontally**.

f. **Insert** a **Header & Footer** on the **Notes and Handouts**. Include the **Date and time updated automatically**, the **Page number**, and a **Footer** with the text **Lastname_Firstname_2C_Concerts** Click **Apply to All**.

g. Display the **Document Properties**. Replace the text in the **Author** box with your own firstname and lastname, in the **Subject** box, type your course name and section number, and in the **Keywords** box, type **concerts, summer events** **Close** the **Document Information Panel**.

h. View your slide show from the beginning, and then **Save** your presentation. Submit your presentation electronically or print **Handouts 6 Slides Horizontal** as directed by your instructor. **Close** the presentation and exit PowerPoint.

End **You have completed Project 2C**

Content-Based Assessments

Apply 2B skills from these Objectives:

- **5** Remove Picture Backgrounds and Insert WordArt
- **6** Create and Format a SmartArt Graphic

Skills Review | Project 2D Corporate Events

In the following Skills Review, you will format a presentation by inserting and formatting WordArt and SmartArt graphics. Your completed presentation will look similar to Figure 2.61.

Project Files

For Project 2D, you will need the following file:

p02D_Corporate_Events

You will save your presentation as:

Lastname_Firstname_2D_Corporate_Events

Project Results

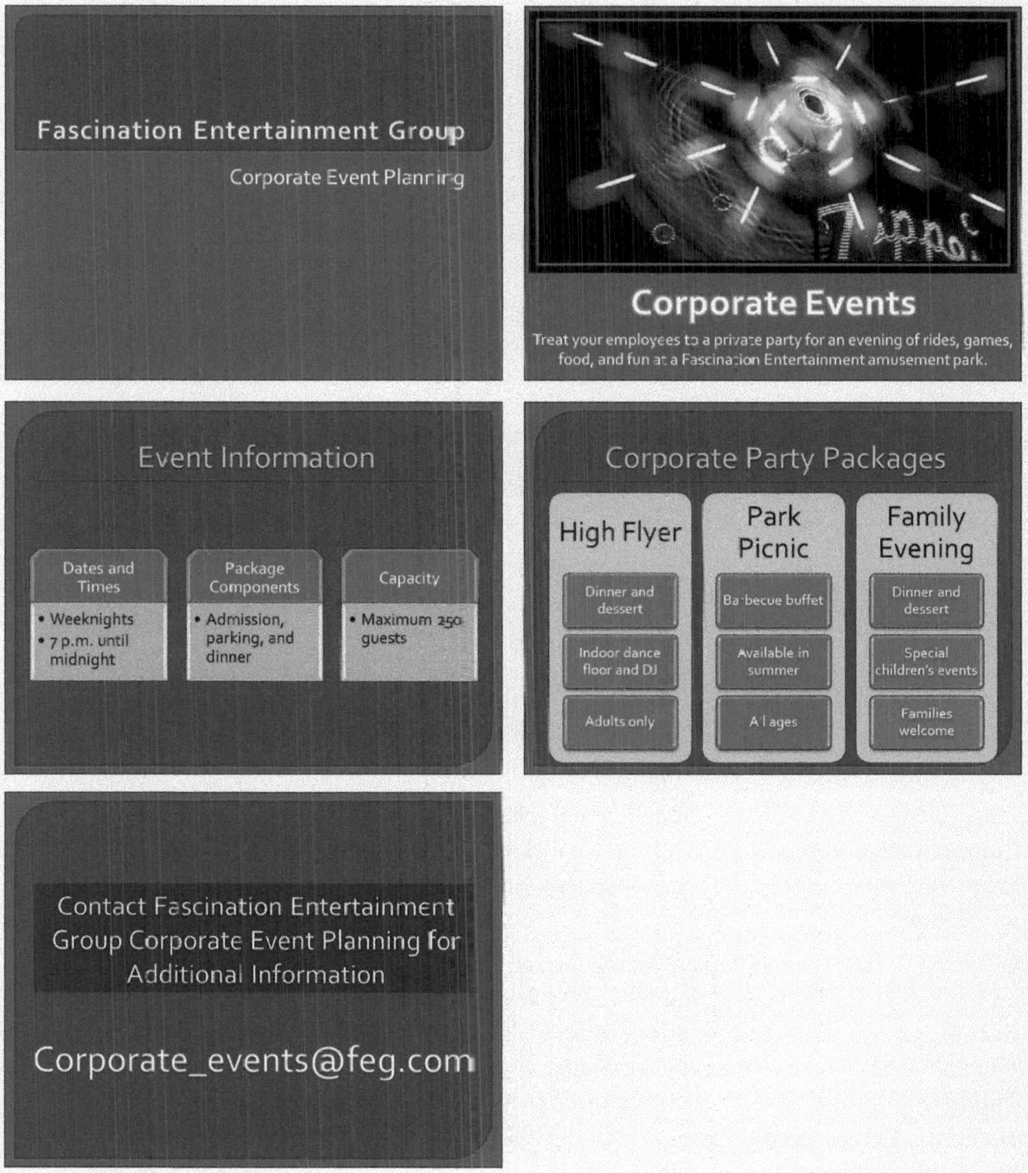

Figure 2.61

(Project 2D Corporate Events continues on the next page)

Skills Review | Project 2D Corporate Events (continued)

1 **Start** PowerPoint. From the student files that accompany this textbook, locate and open **p02D_Corporate_Events**. **Save** the presentation in your **PowerPoint Chapter 2** folder as **Lastname_Firstname_2D_Corporate_Events**

a. With **Slide 1** displayed, select the title—*Fascination Entertainment Group*. On the **Format tab**, in the **WordArt Styles group**, click the **More** button. Under **Applies to All Text in the Shape**, click the first style—**Fill - White, Warm Matte Bevel**. Change the **Font Size** to **40** so that all of the text displays on one line.

b. Display **Slide 2**. On the **Insert tab**, in the **Text group**, click the **WordArt** button. In the **WordArt** gallery, in the second row, click the second style—**Fill - Lime, Accent 6, Outline - Accent 6, Glow - Accent 6**. With the text *Your text here* selected, type **Corporate Events**

c. Point to the dashed, outer edge of the WordArt placeholder, hold down Shift, and drag straight down so that the WordArt is positioned between the picture and the text at the bottom of the slide.

d. With the WordArt selected, on the **Format tab**, in the **Arrange group**, click the **Align** button, and then click **Align Center** so that the WordArt is horizontally centered on the slide. **Save** the presentation.

2 Display **Slide 3**. In the center of the content placeholder, click the **Insert SmartArt Graphic** button to open the **Choose a SmartArt Graphic** dialog box. On the left, click **List**, and then use the ScreenTips to locate and then click **Vertical Bullet List**. Click **OK**.

a. In the SmartArt graphic, click *Text* in the first blue rectangle. Type **Dates and Times** and then click the bullet symbol below the first blue rectangle. Type **Weeknights** and then press Enter to insert a new bullet point. Type **7 p.m. until midnight**

b. Click in the second blue rectangle. Type **Package Components** and then click the bullet symbol below the second blue rectangle. Type **Admission, parking, and dinner**

c. Click in the *Package Components* rectangle, and then on the **SmartArt Tools Design tab**, in the **Create Graphic group**, click the **Add Shape arrow**. Click **Add Shape After** to insert a blue rectangle. Type **Capacity** and then on the **SmartArt Tools Design tab**, in the **Create Graphic group**, click the **Add Bullet** button. Type **Maximum 250 guests**

d. With the SmartArt selected, on the **SmartArt Tools Design tab**, in the **Layouts group**, click the **More** button, and then click **More Layouts**. On the left side of the dialog box, click **List**, and then in the center section of the dialog box, locate and click **Horizontal Bullet List**. Click **OK** to change the SmartArt layout.

e. On the **SmartArt Tools Design tab**, in the **SmartArt Styles group**, click the **More** button. Under **3-D**, in the first row, click the third style—**Cartoon**.

f. Hold down Shift, and then select the **Dates and Times**, **Package Components**, and **Capacity** rectangles. On the **Format tab**, in the **Shapes group**, click the **Change Shape** button, and then under **Rectangles**, click the fourth shape—**Snip Same Side Corner Rectangle**. **Save** the presentation.

3 Display **Slide 4**. In the content placeholder, right-click anywhere in the bulleted list. On the shortcut menu, point to **Convert to SmartArt**, and at the bottom of the gallery, click **More SmartArt Graphics**. On the left side of the **Choose a SmartArt Graphic** dialog box, click **Relationship**. Locate and click **Grouped List**, and then click **OK** to convert the list to a SmartArt graphic.

a. On the **SmartArt Tools Design tab**, in the **SmartArt Styles group**, click the **Change Colors** button. In the **Color** gallery, under **Accent 1**, click the last style—**Transparent Gradient Range - Accent 1**.

b. On the **Design tab**, in the **SmartArt Styles group**, click the **More** button to display the **SmartArt Styles gallery**. Under **3-D**, in the first row, click the third style—**Cartoon**. **Save** the presentation.

4 Display **Slide 5**, and if necessary, display the Rulers. On the **Insert tab**, in the **Text group**, click the **WordArt** button. In the **WordArt** gallery, in the first row, click the fourth style—**Fill - White, Outline - Accent 1**. With the text *Your text here* selected, type **Corporate_events@feg.com**

a. Point to the dashed, outer edge of the WordArt placeholder, and then drag down so that the top edge of the WordArt aligns with the **lower half of the vertical ruler at 1 inch**.

b. With the WordArt selected, on the **Format tab**, in the **Arrange group**, click the **Align** button, and then click **Align Center** so that the WordArt is horizontally centered on the slide.

(Project 2D Corporate Events continues on the next page)

Skills Review | Project 2D Corporate Events (continued)

c. **Insert** a **Header & Footer** on the **Notes and Handouts**. Include the **Date and time updated automatically**, the **Page number**, and a **Footer** with the text **Lastname_ Firstname_2D_Corporate_Events** and **Apply to All**.

d. Display the **Document Properties**. Replace the text in the **Author** box with your own firstname and lastname, in the **Subject** box, type your course name and section number, and in the **Keywords** box, type **corporate events, group packages Close** the **Document Information Panel**. View the presentation from the beginning.

e. **Save** your presentation. Submit your presentation electronically or print **Handouts 6 Slides Horizontal** as directed by your instructor. **Close** the presentation and exit PowerPoint.

End **You have completed Project 2D**

Apply **2A** skills from these Objectives:

1. Format Numbered and Bulleted Lists
2. Insert Clip Art
3. Insert Text Boxes and Shapes
4. Format Objects

Mastering PowerPoint | Project 2E Roller Coasters

In the following Mastering PowerPoint project, you will format a presentation describing new roller coaster attractions at the Fascination Entertainment Group theme parks. Your completed presentation will look similar to Figure 2.62.

Project Files

For Project 2E, you will need the following file:

p02E_Roller_Coasters

You will save your presentation as:

Lastname_Firstname_2E_Roller_Coasters

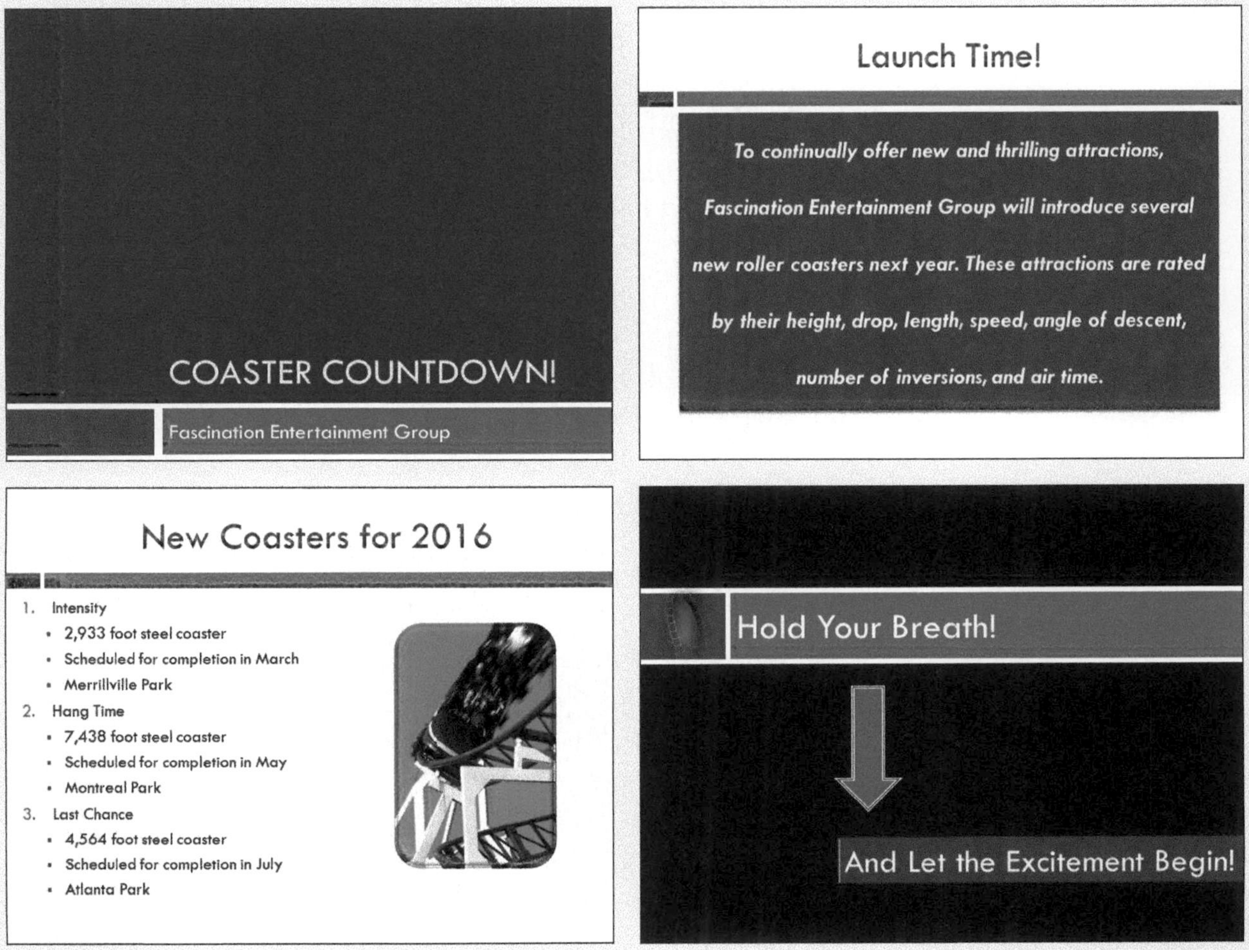

Figure 2.62

(Project 2E Roller Coasters continues on the next page)

Mastering PowerPoint | Project 2E Roller Coasters (continued)

1 **Start** PowerPoint. From the student files that accompany this textbook, locate and open **p02E_Roller_Coasters**. In your **PowerPoint Chapter 2** folder, **Save** the file as **Lastname_Firstname_2E_Roller_Coasters**

2 On **Slide 2**, remove the bullet symbol from the paragraph. **Center** the paragraph, apply **Bold** and **Italic** to the text, and then set the **Line Spacing** to **2.0**. With the content placeholder selected, display the **Shape Styles** gallery, and then in the fifth row, apply the third style—**Moderate Effect - Red, Accent 2**.

3 On **Slide 3**, apply **Numbering** to the first-level bullet points—*Intensity, Hang Time,* and *Last Chance*. Under each of the numbered items, change all of the hollow circle bullet symbols to **Filled Square Bullets**, and then change the bullet color to **Dark Blue, Text 2**—the first color in the fourth column.

4 In the content placeholder on the right side of the slide, insert a **Clip Art** photograph by searching for **roller coaster** Insert the close-up picture of the roller coaster with the red cars on the blue sky background, as shown in Figure 2.62 at the beginning of this project. Crop the picture shape to **Rounded Rectangle**, and then modify the **Picture Effect** by applying the last **Bevel** style—**Art Deco**.

5 On **Slide 4**, insert the picture of the white looped roller coaster on the lighter blue sky background. Change the picture **Height** to **1.5** and then apply a **25 Point Soft Edges** effect. Drag the picture up and to the left to position it in the center of the red rectangle to the left of the slide title. Deselect the picture.

6 From the **Shapes** gallery, under **Block Arrows**, insert a **Down Arrow** aligned with the **left half of the horizontal ruler at 1 inch** and the **upper half of the vertical ruler at 0.5 inches**. On the **Format tab**, from the **Shape Styles** gallery, in the third row, apply the second style—**Light 1 Outline, Colored Fill - Blue, Accent 1**. Change the **Shape Height** to **2** and the **Shape Width** to **1**

7 Insert a **Text Box** aligned with the **left half of the horizontal ruler at 1.5 inches** and with the **lower half of the vertical ruler at 2 inches**. On the **Format tab**, from the **Shape Styles** gallery, in the last row, apply the third style—**Intense Effect - Red, Accent 2**. In the inserted text box, type **And Let the Excitement Begin!** Change the **Font Size** to **40**, and then if necessary, drag the text box so that its right edge aligns with the right edge of the slide. Select the arrow and the text box, and then apply **Align Left** alignment using the **Align Selected Objects** option.

8 Select the title, the arrow, and the text box. Distribute the objects vertically using the **Align Selected Objects** option. Apply the **Box** transition to all of the slides in the presentation, and then view the slide show from the beginning.

9 **Insert** a **Header & Footer** on the **Notes and Handouts**. Include the **Date and time updated automatically**, the **Page number**, and a **Footer** with the text **Lastname_Firstname_2E_Roller_Coasters** Apply to all.

10 Display the **Document Properties**. Replace the text in the **Author** box with your own firstname and lastname, in the **Subject** box, type your course name and section number, and in the **Keywords** box, type **roller coasters, new attractions** **Close** the **Document Information Panel**.

11 **Save** your presentation. Submit your presentation electronically or print **Handouts 4 Slides Horizontal** as directed by your instructor. **Close** the presentation and exit PowerPoint.

End **You have completed Project 2E**

Apply **2B** skills from these Objectives:

- 5 Remove Picture Backgrounds and Insert WordArt
- 6 Create and Format a SmartArt Graphic

Mastering PowerPoint | Project 2F Coaster Club

In the following Mastering PowerPoint project, you will format a presentation describing an event sponsored by Fascination Entertainment Group for roller coaster club members. Your completed presentation will look similar to Figure 2.63.

Project Files

For Project 2F, you will need the following file:

p02F_Coaster_Club

You will save your presentation as:

Lastname_Firstname_2F_Coaster_Club

Project Results

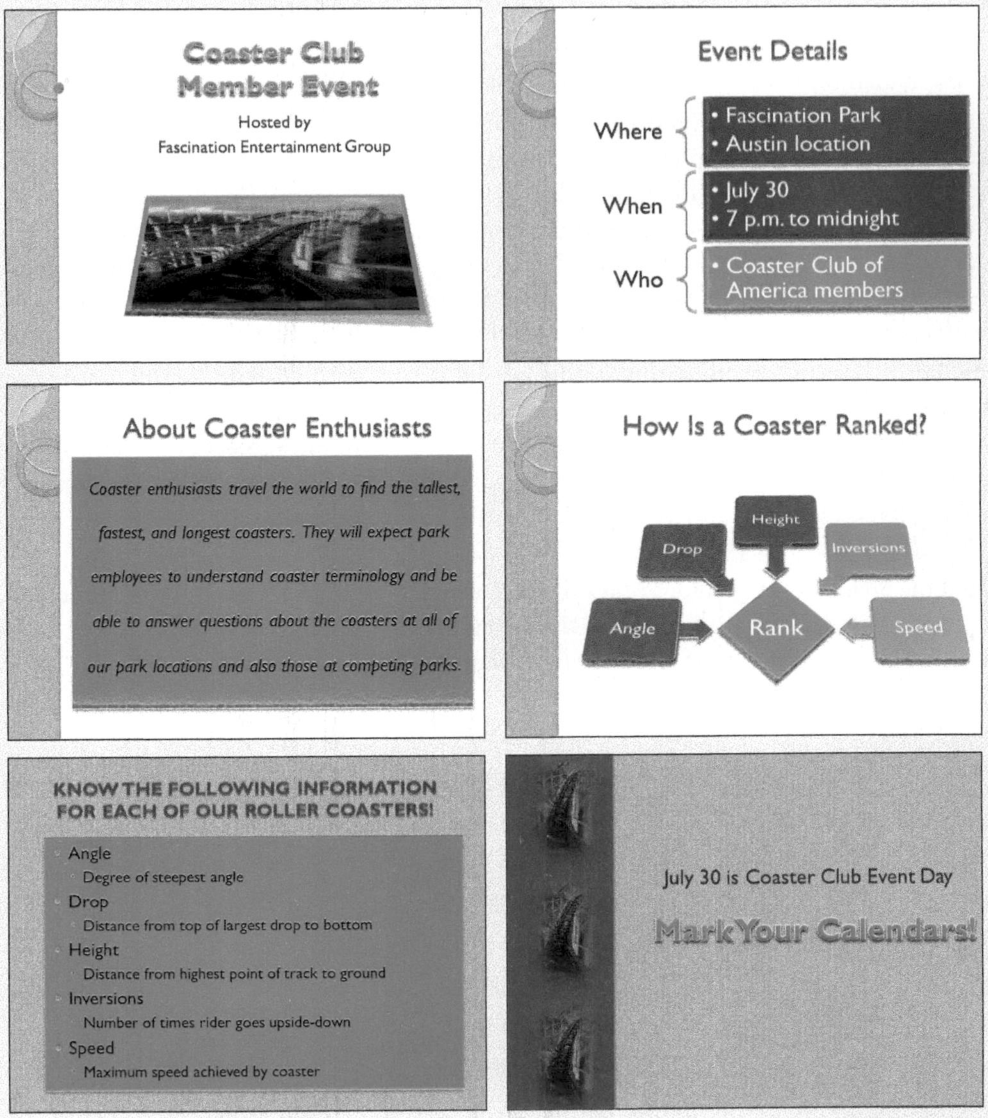

Figure 2.63

(Project 2F Coaster Club continues on the next page)

Mastering PowerPoint | Project 2F Coaster Club (continued)

1 **Start** PowerPoint. From the student files that accompany this textbook, open **p02F_Coaster_Club**, and then **Save** the file in your **PowerPoint Chapter 2** folder as **Lastname_Firstname_2F_Coaster_Club**

2 On **Slide 1**, select the title and display the **WordArt** gallery. In the last row, apply the third WordArt style—**Fill - Aqua, Accent 2, Matte Bevel**. On **Slide 2**, convert the bulleted list to a **SmartArt** graphic by applying the **Vertical Bracket List** graphic. Change the SmartArt color to **Colorful Range - Accent Colors 3 to 4**, and then apply the **Inset 3-D** style.

3 On **Slide 4**, in the content placeholder, insert a **Relationship** type **SmartArt** graphic—**Converging Radial**. In the circle shape, type **Rank** In the left rectangle, type **Angle** in the middle rectangle, type **Drop** and in the right rectangle type **Height** Add a shape after the *Height* rectangle, and then type **Inversions** Add a shape after the *Inversions* rectangle, and then type **Speed** so that your SmartArt contains five rectangular shapes pointing to the circle shape.

4 Change the SmartArt color to **Colorful Range - Accent Colors 3 to 4**, and then apply the **3-D Flat Scene** style. Change the circle shape to the **Diamond** basic shape. On the **Format tab**, in the **Shapes group**, click the **Larger** button two times to increase the size of the diamond.

5 On **Slide 5**, select the content placeholder, and then from the **Shape Styles** gallery, in the last row, apply the third style—**Intense Effect - Aqua, Accent 2**. Change the **Font Color** of all the text in the content placeholder to **Black, Text 1**.

6 On **Slide 6**, insert a **WordArt**—the third style in the last row—**Fill - Aqua, Accent 2, Matte Bevel**. Replace the WordArt text with **Mark Your Calendars!** Change the **Font Size** to **48**, and align the right edge of the WordArt placeholder with the right edge of the slide.

7 **Insert** a **Header & Footer** on the **Notes and Handouts**. Include the **Date and time updated automatically**, the **Page number**, and a **Footer** with the text **Lastname_Firstname_2F_Coaster_Club** Apply to all.

8 Display the **Document Properties**. Replace the text in the **Author** box with your own firstname and lastname, in the **Subject** box, type your course name and section number, and in the **Keywords** box, type **roller coasters, coaster club, events** **Close** the **Document Information Panel**.

9 **Save** your presentation, and then view the slide show from the beginning. Submit your presentation electronically or print **Handouts 6 Slides Horizontal** as directed by your instructor. **Close** the presentation and exit PowerPoint.

End **You have completed Project 2F**

Apply 2A and 2B skills from these Objectives:

1. Format Numbered and Bulleted Lists
2. Insert Clip Art
3. Insert Text Boxes and Shapes
4. Format Objects
5. Remove Picture Backgrounds and Insert WordArt
6. Create and Format a SmartArt Graphic

Mastering PowerPoint | Project 2G Orientation

In the following Mastering PowerPoint project, you will edit an existing presentation that is shown to Fascination Entertainment Group employees on their first day of a three-day orientation. Your completed presentation will look similar to Figure 2.64.

Project Files

For Project 2G, you will need the following files:

p02G_Orientation
p02G_Maya_Ruiz
p02G_David_Jensen
p02G_Ken_Lee

You will save your presentation as:

Lastname_Firstname_2G_Orientation

Project Results

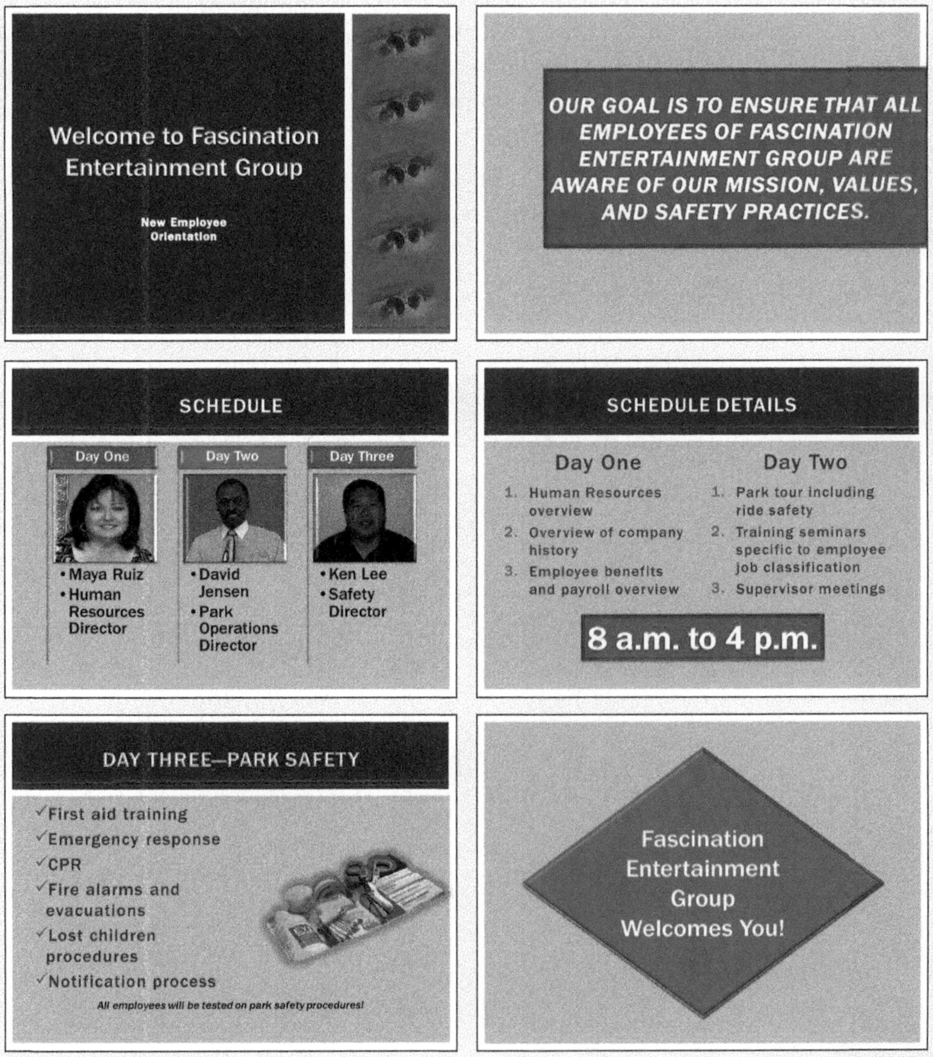

Figure 2.64

(Project 2G Orientation continues on the next page)

Mastering PowerPoint | Project 2G Orientation (continued)

1 **Start** PowerPoint, and then from your student data files, open the file **p02G_Orientation**. In your **PowerPoint Chapter 2** folder, **Save** the file as **Lastname_Firstname_2G_Orientation**

2 On **Slide 1**, format the title as a **WordArt** using the fourth style in the first row—**Fill - White, Outline - Accent 1**. Select the five pictures, and then using the **Align to Slide** option, align the pictures using the **Distribute Vertically** and **Align Right** commands. On **Slide 2**, change the **Shape Style** of the content placeholder to the second style in the last row—**Intense Effect - Tan, Accent 1**.

3 On **Slide 3**, convert the bulleted list to the **Picture** type **SmartArt** graphic—**Title Picture Lineup**. Change the color to **Colorful Range - Accent Colors 5 to 6**, and then apply the **3-D Inset** style. In the three picture placeholders, from your student files insert the following pictures: **p02G_Maya_Ruiz**, **p02G_David_Jensen**, and **p02G_Ken_Lee**.

4 On **Slide 4**, change the two bulleted lists to **Numbering**. Then, insert a **WordArt** using the **Fill - White, Drop Shadow** style with the text **8 a.m. to 4 p.m.** and position the WordArt centered below the two content placeholders. Apply a **Shape Style** to the WordArt using **Intense Effect - Tan, Accent 1**.

5 On **Slide 5**, change the bullet symbols to **Checkmark Bullets**, and then in the placeholder on the right, insert a **Clip Art** photograph by searching for **first aid kit** Insert the picture of the opened first aid box, and then remove the background from the picture so that only the items in the kit display. Mark areas to keep and remove as necessary. Change the **Shape Height** to **3.25** and then apply the **Brown, 18 pt glow, Accent color 4** picture effect.

6 On **Slide 5**, insert a **Text Box** aligned with the **left half of the horizontal ruler at 4 inches** and with the **lower half of the vertical ruler at 2.5 inches**. In the text box, type **All employees will be tested on park safety procedures!** Apply **Italic**, and then **Align Center** the text box using the **Align to Slide** option.

7 Insert a **New Slide** with the **Blank** layout. From the **Shapes** gallery, under **Basic Shapes**, insert a **Diamond** of any size anywhere on the slide. Then, resize the diamond so that its **Shape Height** is **6** and its **Shape Width** is **8** Using the **Align to Slide** option, apply the **Align Center**, and **Align Middle** alignment commands. Apply the **Moderate Effect - Tan, Accent 1** shape style to the diamond, and then in the diamond, type **Fascination Entertainment Group Welcomes You!** Change the **Font Size** to **40**, and then apply the **Art Deco Bevel** effect to the diamond shape.

8 **Insert** a **Header & Footer** on the **Notes and Handouts**. Include the **Date and time updated automatically**, the **Page number**, and a **Footer** with the text **Lastname_Firstname_2G_Orientation** Apply to all.

9 Display the **Document Properties**. Replace the text in the **Author** box with your own firstname and lastname, in the **Subject** box, type your course name and section number, and in the **Keywords** box, type **orientation, employee training** Close the **Document Information Panel**.

10 **Save** your presentation, and then view the slide show from the beginning. Submit your presentation electronically or print **Handouts 6 Slides Horizontal** as directed by your instructor. **Close** the presentation and exit PowerPoint.

End **You have completed Project 2G**

Apply a combination of the 2A and 2B skills.

GO! Fix It | Project 2H Summer Jobs

Project Files

For Project 2H, you will need the following file:

p02H_Summer_Jobs

You will save your presentation as:

Lastname_Firstname_2H_Summer_Jobs

In this project, you will edit several slides from a presentation prepared by the Human Resources Department at Fascination Entertainment Group regarding summer employment opportunities. From the student files that accompany this textbook, open the file p02H_Summer_Jobs, and then save the file in your chapter folder as **Lastname_Firstname_2H_Summer_Jobs**

To complete the project you should know:

- The Theme should be changed to Module and two spelling errors should be corrected.
- On Slide 1, the pictures should be aligned with the top of the slide and distributed horizontally.
- On Slide 2, the bulleted list should be converted to a Vertical Box List SmartArt and an attractive style should be applied. The colors should be changed to Colorful Range - Accent Colors 5 to 6.
- On Slide 3, the bulleted list should be formatted as a numbered list.
- On Slide 4, insert a Fill - White, Drop Shadow WordArt with the text **Apply Today!** and position the WordArt centered approximately 1 inch below the title placeholder.
- Document Properties should include your name, course name and section, and the keywords **summer jobs, recruitment** A Header & Footer should be inserted on the Notes and Handouts that includes the Date and time updated automatically, the Page number, and a Footer with the text **Lastname_Firstname_2H_Summer_Jobs**

Save and submit your presentation electronically or print Handouts 4 Slides Horizontal as directed by your instructor. Close the presentation.

End You have completed Project 2H

Content-Based Assessments

Apply a combination of the 2A and 2B skills.

GO! Make It | Project 2I Renovation Plans

Project Files

For Project 2I, you will need the following file:

New blank PowerPoint presentation

You will save your presentation as:

Lastname_Firstname_2I_Renovation_Plans

By using the skills you practiced in this chapter, create the first two slides of the presentation shown in Figure 2.65. Start PowerPoint to begin a new blank presentation, and apply the Urban theme and the Aspect color theme. Type the title and subtitle shown in Figure 2.65, and then change the background style to Style 12 and the title font size to 40. Apply the Fill - Black, Background 1, Metal Bevel WordArt style to the title. Save the file in your PowerPoint Chapter 2 folder as **Lastname_Firstname_2I_Renovation_Plans**

To locate the picture on Slide 1, search for a clip art photograph with the keyword **carnival rides** Resize the picture Height to **2** and then apply soft edges, duplicate, align, and distribute the images as shown in the figure.

Insert a new Slide 2 using the Content with Caption layout. Insert the Basic Matrix SmartArt layout shown in Figure 2.65 and change the color and style as shown. Type the title and caption text, changing the title Font Size to 28 and the caption text Font Size to 18. Modify line spacing and apply formatting to the caption text as shown in Figure 2.65. Insert the date, file name, and page number in the Notes and Handouts footer. In the Document Information Panel, add your name and course information and the Keywords **renovation, goals** Save, and then print or submit electronically as directed by your instructor.

Project Results

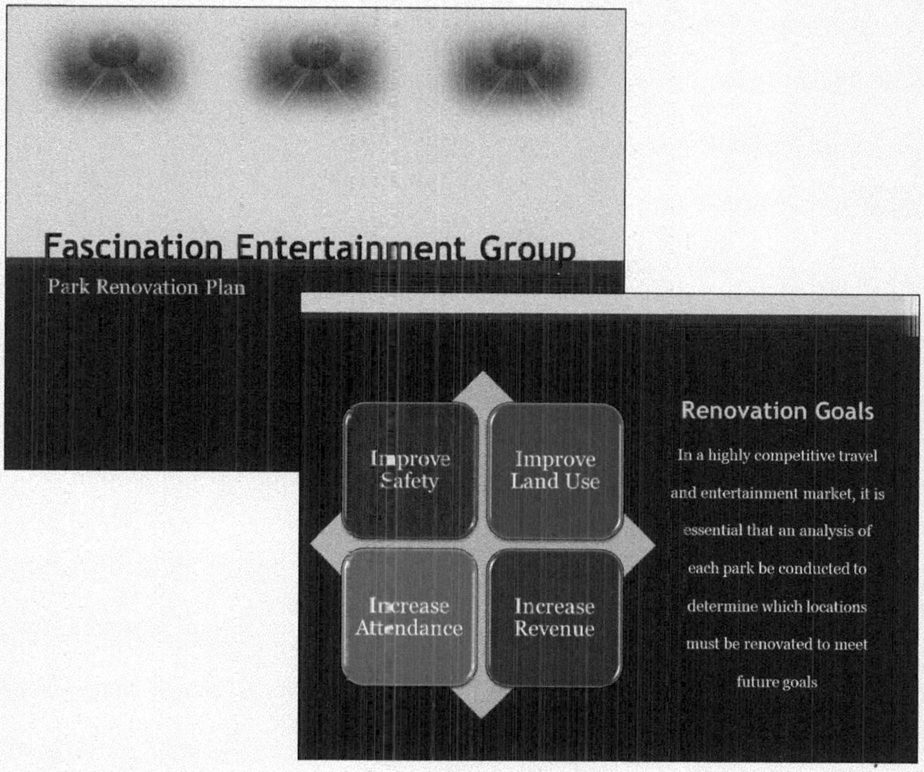

Figure 2.65

End You have completed Project 2I

PowerPoint | Chapter 2

Apply a combination of the 2A and 2B skills.

GO! Solve It | Project **2J** Business Summary

Project Files

For Project 2J, you will need the following file:

p02J_Business_Summary

You will save your presentation as:

Lastname_Firstname_2J_Business_Summary

Open the file p02J_Business_Summary and save it in your chapter folder as **Lastname_Firstname_2J_Business_Summary** Format the presentation attractively by applying appropriate font formatting and by changing text alignment and line spacing. Insert at least one clip art image and change the picture shape and effect. On Slide 2, align and format the text box and shape attractively and insert a clip art image that can be duplicated, aligned, and distributed across the bottom edge of the slide. On Slide 3, insert an appropriate photo on the right. On Slide 4, convert the bulleted list to an appropriate SmartArt graphic and format the graphic appropriately. Apply slide transitions to all of the slides in the presentation and insert a header and footer that includes the date and time updated automatically, the file name in the footer, and the page number. Add your name, your course name and section number, and the keywords **business summary, revenue** to the Properties area. Save, and then print or submit electronically as directed by your instructor.

Performance Elements	Performance Level		
	Exemplary: You consistently applied the relevant skills	**Proficient:** You sometimes, but not always, applied the relevant skills	**Developing:** You rarely or never applied the relevant skills
Insert and format appropriate clip art	Appropriate clip art was inserted and formatted in the presentation.	Clip art was inserted but was not appropriate for the presentation or was not formatted.	Clip art was not inserted.
Insert and format appropriate SmartArt graphic	Appropriate SmartArt graphic was inserted and formatted in the presentation.	SmartArt graphic was inserted but was not appropriate for the presentation or was not formatted.	SmartArt graphic was not inserted.
Format text boxes and shapes attractively	Text boxes and shapes were formatted attractively.	Text boxes and shapes were formatted but the formatting was inappropriately applied.	Inadequate or no formatting.
Insert transitions	Appropriate transitions were applied to all slides.	Transitions were applied to some, but not all slides.	Transitions were not applied.

End **You have completed Project 2J**

Apply a combination of the 2A and 2B skills.

GO! Solve It | Project 2K Hotel

Project Files

For Project 2K, you will need the following file:

p02K_Hotel

You will save your presentation as:

Lastname_Firstname_2K_Hotel

Open the file p02K_Hotel and save it as **Lastname_Firstname_2K_Hotel** Complete the presentation by inserting a clip art image on the first slide and applying appropriate picture effects. On Slide 2, format the bullet point as a single paragraph, and then on Slide 3, convert the bulleted list to an appropriate SmartArt graphic. Change the SmartArt color and apply a style. On Slide 4, insert and attractively position a WordArt with the text **Save the Date!** Apply slide transitions to all of the slides. Insert a header and footer that includes the date and time updated automatically, the file name in the footer, and the page number. Add your name, your course name and section number, and the keywords **hotel, accommodations** to the Properties area. Save your presentation. Print or submit as directed by your instructor.

Performance Elements	Performance Level		
	Exemplary: You consistently applied the relevant skills	**Proficient:** You sometimes, but not always, applied the relevant skills	**Developing:** You rarely or never applied the relevant skills
Insert and format appropriate clip art	Appropriate clip art was inserted and formatted in the presentation.	Clip art was inserted but was not appropriate for the presentation or was not formatted.	Clip art was not inserted.
Insert and format appropriate SmartArt graphic	Appropriate SmartArt graphic was inserted and formatted in the presentation.	SmartArt graphic was inserted but was not appropriate for the presentation or was not formatted.	SmartArt graphic was not inserted.
Insert and format appropriate WordArt	Appropriate WordArt was inserted and formatted in the presentation.	WordArt was inserted but was not appropriate for the presentation or was not formatted.	WordArt was not inserted.
Insert transitions	Appropriate transitions were applied to all slides.	Transitions were applied to some, but not all slides.	Transitions were not applied.

End **You have completed Project 2K**

Outcomes-Based Assessments

Rubric

The following outcomes-based assessments are *open-ended assessments*. That is, there is no specific correct result; your result will depend on your approach to the information provided. Make *Professional Quality* your goal. Use the following scoring rubric to guide you in *how* to approach the problem, and then to evaluate *how well* your approach solves the problem.

The *criteria*—Software Mastery, Content, Format and Layout, and Process—represent the knowledge and skills you have gained that you can apply to solving the problem. The *levels of performance*—Professional Quality, Approaching Professional Quality, or Needs Quality Improvements—help you and your instructor evaluate your result.

	Your completed project is of Professional Quality if you:	**Your completed project is Approaching Professional Quality if you:**	**Your completed project Needs Quality Improvements if you:**
1-Software Mastery	Choose and apply the most appropriate skills, tools, and features and identify efficient methods to solve the problem.	Choose and apply some appropriate skills, tools, and features, but not in the most efficient manner.	Choose inappropriate skills, tools, or features, or are inefficient in solving the problem.
2-Content	Construct a solution that is clear and well organized, contains content that is accurate, appropriate to the audience and purpose, and is complete. Provide a solution that contains no errors in spelling, grammar, or style.	Construct a solution in which some components are unclear, poorly organized, inconsistent, or incomplete. Misjudge the needs of the audience. Have some errors in spelling, grammar, or style, but the errors do not detract from comprehension.	Construct a solution that is unclear, incomplete, or poorly organized; contains some inaccurate or inappropriate content; and contains many errors in spelling, grammar, or style. Do not solve the problem.
3-Format and Layout	Format and arrange all elements to communicate information and ideas, clarify function, illustrate relationships, and indicate relative importance.	Apply appropriate format and layout features to some elements, but not others. Overuse features, causing minor distraction.	Apply format and layout that does not communicate information or ideas clearly. Do not use format and layout features to clarify function, illustrate relationships, or indicate relative importance. Use available features excessively, causing distraction.
4-Process	Use an organized approach that integrates planning, development, self-assessment, revision, and reflection.	Demonstrate an organized approach in some areas, but not others; or, use an insufficient process of organization throughout.	Do not use an organized approach to solve the problem.

Apply a combination of the 2A and 2B skills.

GO! Think | Project 2L Interactive Ride

Project Files

For Project 2L, you will need the following file:

New blank PowerPoint presentation

You will save your presentation as:

Lastname_Firstname_2L_Interactive_Ride

As part of its mission to combine fun with the discovery of math and science, Fascination Entertainment Group is opening a new, interactive roller coaster at its South Lake Tahoe location. FEG's newest coaster is designed for maximum thrill and minimum risk. In a special interactive exhibit located next to the coaster, riders can learn about the physics behind this powerful coaster and even try their hand at building a coaster.

Guests will begin by setting the height of the first hill, which determines the coaster's maximum potential energy to complete its journey. Next they will set the exit path, and build additional hills, loops, and corkscrews. When completed, riders can submit their coaster for a safety inspection to find out whether the ride passes or fails.

In either case, riders can also take a virtual tour of the ride they created to see the maximum speed achieved, the amount of negative G-forces applied, the length of the track, and the overall thrill factor. They can also see how their coaster compares with other coasters in the FEG family, and they can e-mail the coaster simulation to their friends.

Using the preceding information, create a presentation that Marketing Director, Annette Chosek, will present at a travel fair describing the new attraction. The presentation should include four to six slides with at least one SmartArt graphic and one clip art image. Apply an appropriate theme and use slide layouts that will effectively present the content, and use text boxes, shapes, and WordArt if appropriate. Apply font formatting and slide transitions, and modify text alignment and line spacing as necessary. Save the file as **Lastname_Firstname_2L_Interactive_Ride** and then insert a header and footer that includes the date and time updated automatically, the file name in the footer, and the page number. Add your name, your course name and section number, and the keywords **roller coaster, new rides** to the Properties area. Print or submit as directed by your instructor.

End You have completed Project 2L

Apply a combination of the 2A and 2B skills.

GO! Think | Project 2M Research

Project Files

For Project 2M, you will need the following file:

New blank PowerPoint presentation

You will save your presentation as:

Lastname_Firstname_2M_Research

As the number of theme park vacations continues to rise, Fascination Entertainment Group is developing plans to ensure that its top theme parks are a true vacation destination. Fascination Entertainment Group research has verified that visitors use several factors in determining their theme park destinations: top attractions, overall value, and nearby accommodations.

Visitors, regardless of age, look for thrills and entertainment at a good value. Fascination Entertainment Group owns four of North America's top 15 coasters and two of its top 10 water parks, thus making the parks prime attraction destinations. Typical costs for visitors include park entrance fees, food and beverages, souvenirs, transportation, and lodging. Beginning this year, FEG will offer vacation packages. Package pricing will vary depending on number of adults, number of children, length of stay, and number of parks attended (i.e., theme park, water park, and zoo). Each park will continue to offer annual passes at a discount.

Research shows that visitors who travel more than 100 miles one way will consider the need for nearby accommodations. For its top 10 theme parks, Fascination Entertainment Group will open hotels at any parks that do not currently have them within the next two years. Until then, the company will partner with area hotels to provide discounts to theme park visitors.

Using the preceding information, create the first four slides of a presentation that the Fascination Entertainment Group marketing director can show at an upcoming board of directors meeting. Apply an appropriate theme and use slide layouts that will effectively present the content. Include clip art and at least one SmartArt graphic. Apply font and WordArt formatting, picture styles, and slide transitions, and modify text alignment and line spacing as necessary. If appropriate, insert and format a text box or a shape. Save the file as **Lastname_Firstname_2M_Research** and then insert a header and footer that includes the date and time updated automatically, the file name in the footer, and the page number. Add your name, your course name and section number, and the keywords **visitor preferences, research findings** to the Properties area. Print or submit as directed by your instructor.

End You have completed Project 2M

Outcomes-Based Assessments

Apply a combination of the 2A and 2B skills.

You and GO! | Project 2N Theme Park

Project Files

For Project 2N, you will need the following file:

New blank PowerPoint presentation

You will save your presentation as:

Lastname_Firstname_2N_Theme_Park

Research your favorite theme park and create a presentation with at least six slides that describes the park, its top attractions, nearby accommodations, and the reasons why you enjoy the park. Choose an appropriate theme, slide layouts, and pictures, and format the presentation attractively, including at least one SmartArt graphic and one WordArt object or shape. Save your presentation as Lastname_Firstname_2N_Theme_Park and submit as directed.

End You have completed Project 2N

Apply a combination of the 2A and 2B skills.

GO! CD-ROM

GO! Collaborate | Project 2O Bell Orchid Hotels Group Running Case

This project relates to the **Bell Orchid Hotels**. Your instructor may assign this group case project to your class. If your instructor assigns this project, he or she will provide you with information and instructions to work as part of a group. The group will apply the skills gained thus far to help the Bell Orchid Hotels achieve their business goals.

End You have completed Project 2O

Enhancing a Presentation with Animation, Video, Tables, and Charts

OUTCOMES
At the end of this chapter you will be able to:

OBJECTIVES
Mastering these objectives will enable you to:

PROJECT 3A
Customize a presentation with animation and video.

PROJECT 3B
Create a presentation that includes data in tables and charts.

Travis Houston/Shutterstock

In This Chapter

Recall that a presentation theme applies a consistent look to a presentation. You can customize a presentation by modifying the theme and by applying animation to slide elements, and you can enhance your presentations by creating tables and charts that help your audience understand numeric data and trends just as pictures and diagrams help illustrate a concept. The data that you present should determine whether a table or a chart would most appropriately display your information. Styles applied to your tables and charts unify these slide elements by complementing your presentation theme.

The projects in this chapter relate to **Golden Grove**, a growing city located between Los Angeles and San Diego. Just 10 years ago the population was under 100,000; today it has grown to almost 300,000. Community leaders have always focused on quality and economic development in decisions on housing, open space, education, and infrastructure, making the city a model for other communities its size around the United States. The city provides many recreational and cultural opportunities with a large park system, thriving arts, and a friendly business atmosphere.

Project 3A Informational Presentation

myitlab Project 3A Training

Project Activities

In Activities 3.01 through 3.11, you will edit and format a presentation that Mindy Walker, Director of Golden Grove Parks and Recreation, has created to inform residents about the benefits of using the city's parks and trails. Your completed presentation will look similar to Figure 3.1.

Project Files

For Project 3A, you will need the following files:

p03A_Park
p03A_Pets
p03A_Trails
p03A_Walking_Trails
p03A_Trails_Video

You will save your presentation as:

Lastname_Firstname_3A_Walking_Trails

Project Results

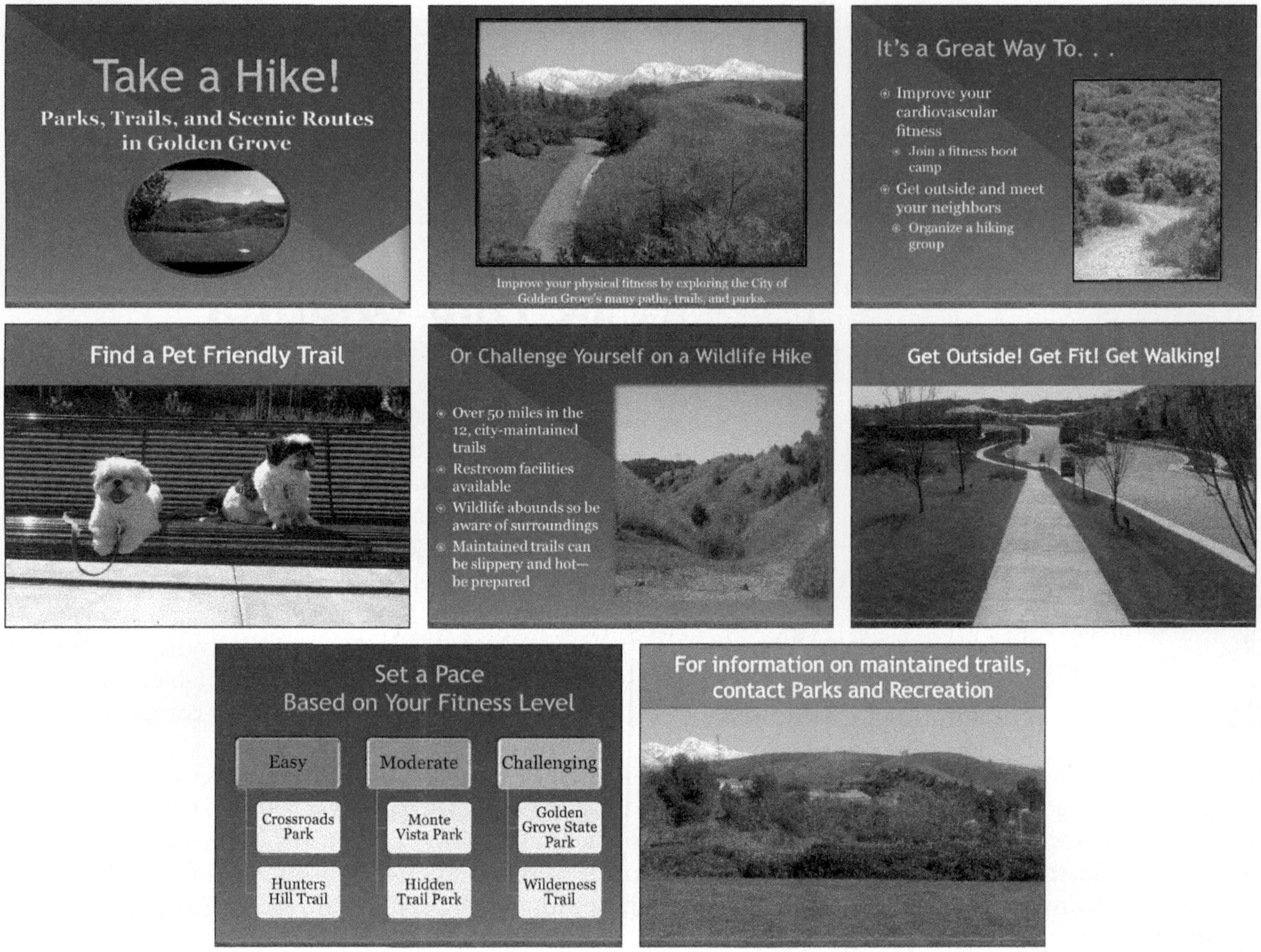

Figure 3.1
Project 3A Walking Trails

Objective 1 Customize Slide Backgrounds and Themes

You have practiced customizing presentations by applying themes with unified design elements, backgrounds, and colors that provide a consistent look in your presentation. Additional ways to customize a slide include changing theme fonts and colors, applying a background style, modifying the background color, or inserting a picture on the slide background.

Activity 3.01 | Changing the Theme Colors and Theme Fonts

Recall that the presentation theme is a coordinated, predefined set of colors, fonts, lines, and fill effects. In this activity, you will open a presentation in which the Verve theme is applied, and then you will change the ***theme colors***—a set of coordinating colors that are applied to the backgrounds, objects, and text in a presentation.

In addition to theme colors, every presentation theme includes ***theme fonts*** that determine the font to apply to two types of slide text—headings and body. The ***Headings font*** is applied to slide titles and the ***Body font*** is applied to all other text. When you apply a new theme font to the presentation, the text on every slide is updated with the new heading and body fonts.

1. From the student files that accompany this textbook, locate and open **p03A_Walking_Trails.** Display **Backstage** view, click **Save As,** and then navigate to the location where you are storing your projects for this chapter. Create a new folder named **PowerPoint Chapter 3** and then in the **File name** box and using your own name, type **Lastname_Firstname_3A_Walking_Trails** Click **Save** or press Enter.

2. Click the **Design tab**, and then in the **Themes group**, click the **Colors** button to display the list of theme colors. Point to several themes and notice the color changes on **Slide 1**. Scroll the **Theme Colors** list, and then click **Metro** to change the theme colors.

   Changing the theme colors does not change the overall design of the presentation. In this presentation, the *Verve* presentation theme is still applied to the presentation. By modifying the theme colors, you retain the design of the *Verve* theme. The colors of the *Metro* theme, which coordinate with the pictures in the presentation, are available as text, accent, and background colors.

3. With **Slide 1** displayed, click anywhere in the title placeholder. Click the **Home tab**, and then in the **Font group**, click the **Font button arrow**. Notice that at the top of the **Font** list, under **Theme Fonts**, Century Gothic (Headings) and Century Gothic (Body) display. Compare your screen with Figure 3.2.

Figure 3.2

Theme fonts

4. Click anywhere on the slide to close the Font list. Click the **Design tab**, and then in the **Themes group**, click the **Fonts** button.

   This list displays the name of each theme and the pair of fonts in the theme. The first and larger font in each pair is the Headings font and the second and smaller font in each pair is the Body font.

5. Point to several of the themes and watch as Live Preview changes the title and subtitle text. Then, scroll to the bottom of the **Theme Fonts** list and click **Urban**. Compare your screen with Figure 3.3, and then **Save** your presentation.

Figure 3.3

Activity 3.02 | Applying a Background Style

1. With **Slide 1** displayed, on the **Design tab**, in the **Background group**, click the **Background Styles** button. Compare your screen with Figure 3.4.

   A ***background style*** is a slide background fill variation that combines theme colors in different intensities or patterns.

Figure 3.4

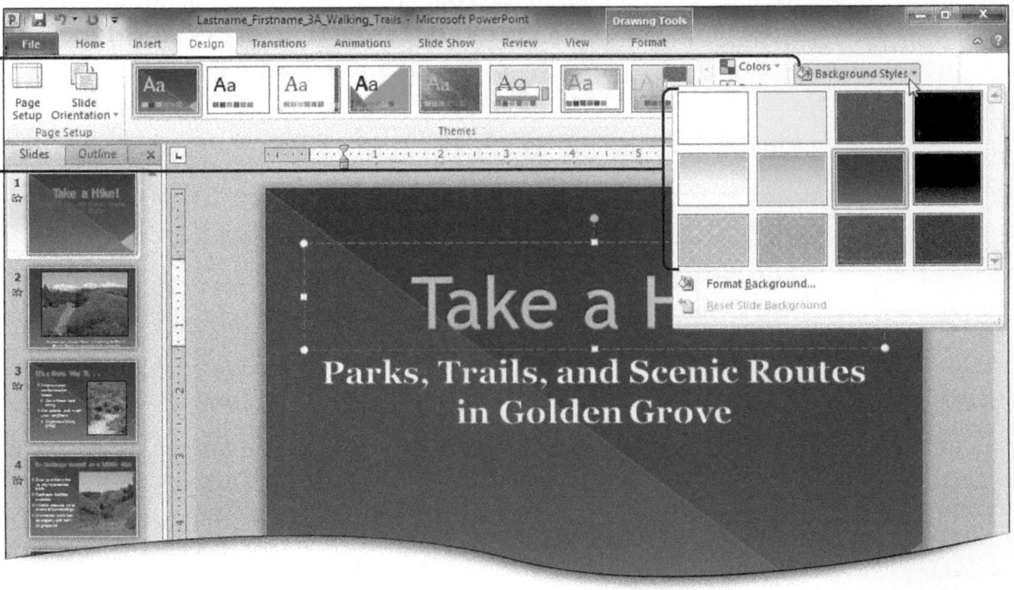

2. Point to each of the background styles to view the style on **Slide 1**. Then, in the first row, *right-click* **Style 2** to display the shortcut menu. Click **Apply to Selected Slides** and then compare your screen with Figure 3.5.

   The background style is applied only to Slide 1.

3. **Save** your presentation.

Figure 3.5

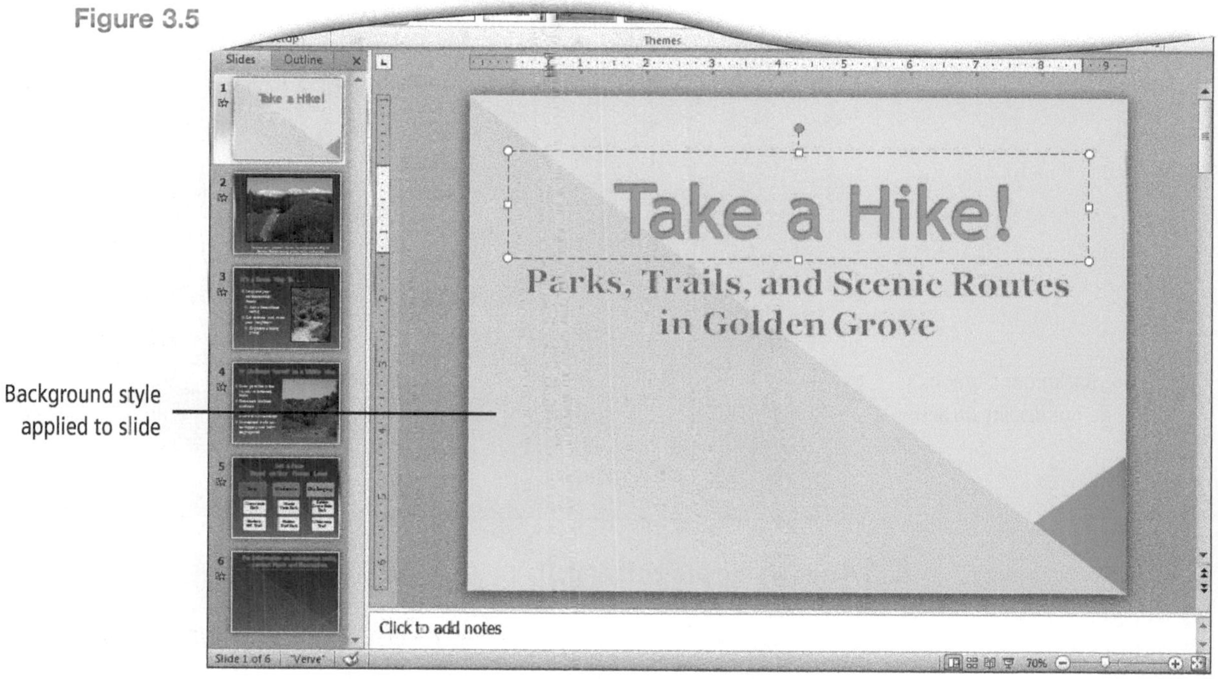

> **More Knowledge | Applying Background Styles to All Slides in a Presentation**
>
> To change the background style for all of the slides in the presentation, click the background style that you want to apply and the style will be applied to every slide.

Activity 3.03 | Hiding Background Graphics

Many of the PowerPoint 2010 themes contain graphic elements that display on the slide background. In the Verve theme applied to this presentation, the background includes a triangle and lines that intersect near the lower right corner of the slide. Sometimes the background graphics interfere with the slide content. When this happens, you can hide the background graphics.

1. Display **Slide 6**, and notice that on this slide, you can clearly see the triangle and lines on the slide background.

   You cannot delete these objects because they are a part of the slide background; however, you can hide them.

2. Display **Slide 5**, and notice that the background graphics distract from the connecting lines on the diagram. On the **Design tab**, in the **Background group**, select the **Hide Background Graphics** check box, and then compare your slide with Figure 3.6.

   The background objects no longer display behind the SmartArt diagram.

Figure 3.6

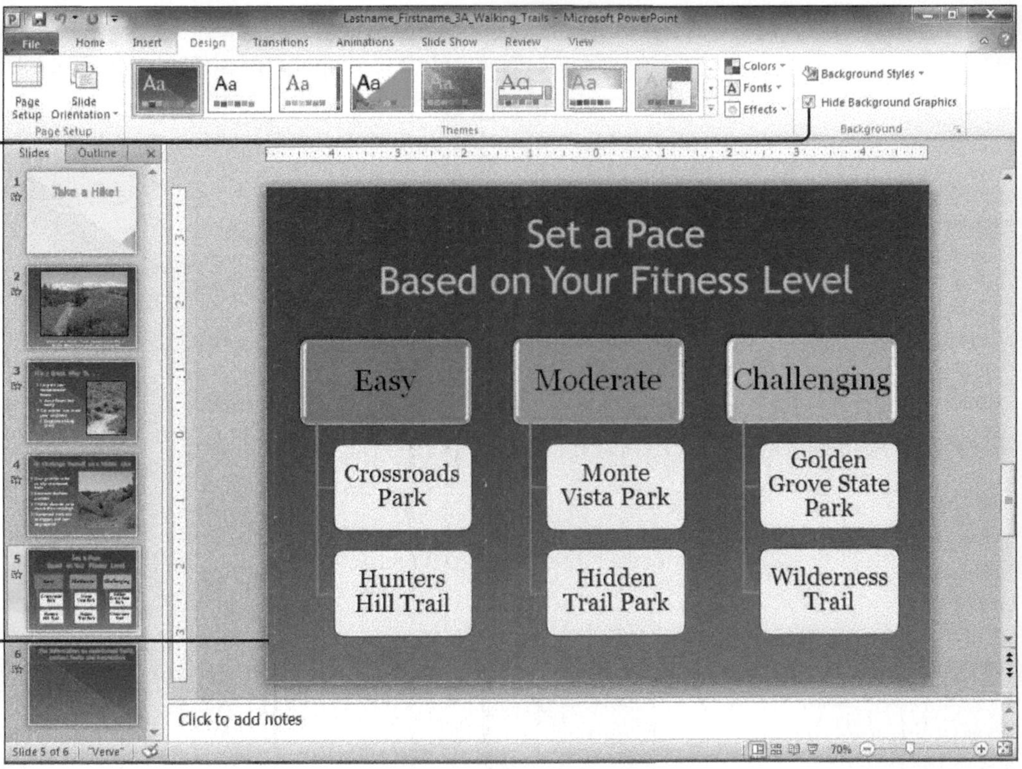

3 **Save** the presentation.

Activity 3.04 | Formatting a Slide Background with a Picture

You can insert a picture on a slide background so the image fills the entire slide.

1 Display **Slide 3**, and then click the **Home tab**. In the **Slides group**, click the **New Slide arrow**, and then click the **Title Only** layout to insert a new slide with the Title Only layout.

2 With the new **Slide 4** displayed, click the **Design tab**. In the **Background group**, select the **Hide Background Graphics** check box, and then click the **Background Styles** button. Below the displayed gallery, click **Format Background**.

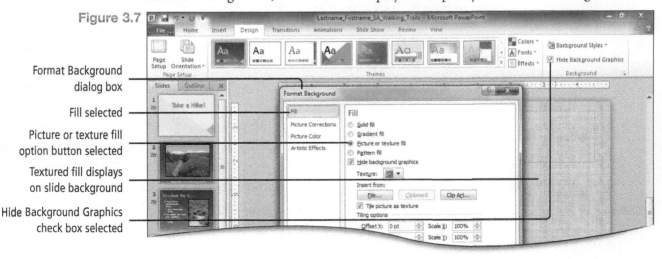

In the Format Background dialog box, you can customize a slide background by changing the formatting options.

3 If necessary, on the left side of the dialog box, click Fill. On the right side of the dialog box, under **Fill**, click the **Picture or texture fill** option button, and then notice that on the slide background, a textured fill displays. Compare your screen with Figure 3.7.

Figure 3.7

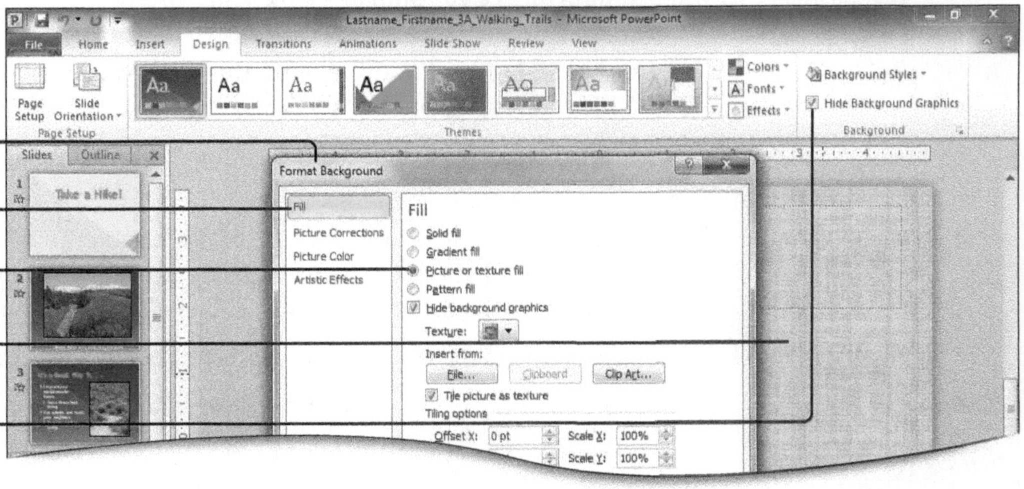

4 Under **Insert from**, click the **File** button to display the **Insert Picture** dialog box. Navigate to your student files, and then click **p03A_Pets**. Click **Insert**, and then at the bottom of the **Format Background** dialog box, click **Close**. Compare your slide with Figure 3.8 and notice that the picture displays as the background of Slide 4.

When a picture is applied to a slide background using the Format Background option, the picture is not treated as an object. The picture fills the background and you cannot move it or size it.

Figure 3.8

5 Click in the title placeholder, type **Find a Pet Friendly Trail** and then notice that the background picture does not provide sufficient contrast with the text to display the title effectively.

6 With your insertion point still in the title placeholder, click the **Format tab**. In the **Shape Styles group**, click the **Shape Fill button arrow**. In the fifth column, click the last color—**Green, Accent 1, Darker 50%**. Select the title text, and then on the **Format tab**, in the **WordArt Styles group**, in the first row, click the third style—**Fill - White, Drop Shadow**. **Center** the text.

The green fill color and the white WordArt style provide good contrast against the slide background so that the text is readable.

7 Point to the outer edge of the title placeholder to display the pointer, and then drag the placeholder up and to the left so that its upper left corner aligns with the upper left corner of the slide. Point to the center right sizing handle and drag to the right so that the placeholder extends to the right edge of the slide. Click outside of the placeholder, and then compare your slide with Figure 3.9.

Figure 3.9

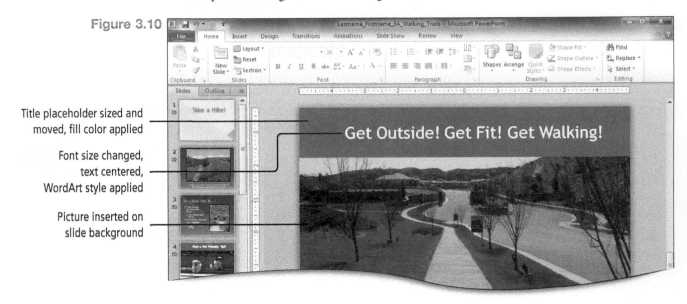

8 Display **Slide 5**, and then insert a **New Slide** with the **Title Only** layout. On the **Design tab**, in the **Background group**, select the **Hide Background Graphics** check box, and then click the **Background Styles** button. Click **Format Background**.

9 Under **Fill**, click the **Picture or texture fill** option button. Under **Insert from**, click **File**. Navigate to your student files, click **p03A_Trails**, click **Insert**, and then **Close** the dialog box. In the title placeholder, type **Get Outside! Get Fit! Get Walking!** and then **Center** the text.

10 Select the text, and then change the **Font Size** to **36**. Then, apply the same **Shape Fill** color and **WordArt** style to the title placeholder that you applied to the title on **Slide 4**. Size the placeholder so that it extends from the left edge of the slide to the right edge of the slide, and then drag the placeholder up so that its upper edge aligns with the upper edge of the slide. Click outside of the title so that it is not selected. Compare your slide with Figure 3.10.

The green fill color and white text provide good contrast with the slide background and complement the green color of the grass on the slide.

Figure 3.10

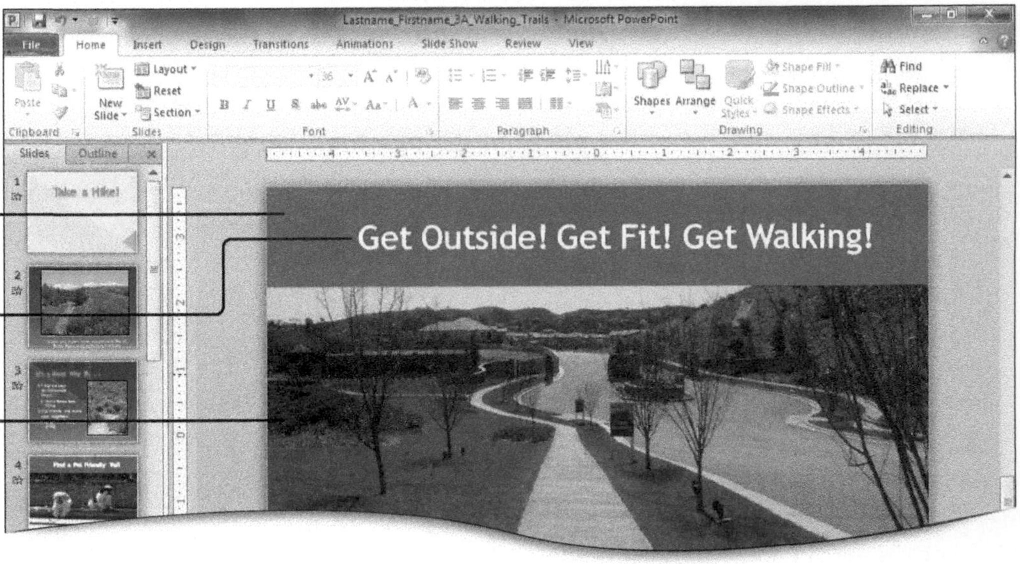

11 Display **Slide 8**, and then format the slide background with a picture from your student files—**p03A_Park**. On the **Design tab**, in the **Background group**, select the **Hide Background Graphics** check box.

12 Select the title placeholder. On the **Format tab**. In the **Shape Styles group**, click the **More** button. In the **Shape Styles** gallery, in the second row, click the sixth style—**Colored Fill – Periwinkle, Accent 5.**

13 Select the text, and then on the **Format tab**, in the **WordArt Styles group**, click the third style—**Fill - White, Drop Shadow**. Click outside of the placeholder, and then compare your slide with Figure 3.11. **Save** the presentation.

Figure 3.11

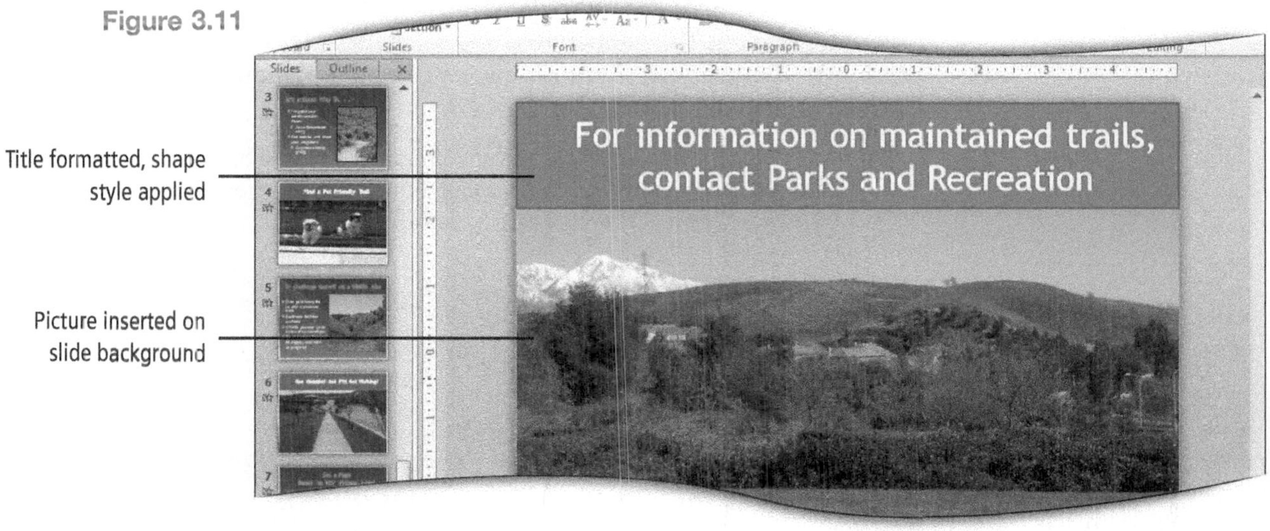

Activity 3.05 | Applying a Background Fill Color and Resetting a Slide Background

1 Display **Slide 1**, and then click the **Design tab.** In the **Background group**, click the **Background Styles** button, and then click **Format Background.**

2 In the **Format Background** dialog box, if necessary, click the Solid fill option button. Under **Fill Color**, click the **Color** button. Under **Theme Colors**, in the first column, click the last color—**White, Background 1, Darker 50%**. Click **Close.**

The solid fill color is applied to the slide background.

3 On the **Design tab**, in the **Background group**, click the **Background Styles** button. Below the gallery, click **Reset Slide Background**, and then **Save** the presentation.

After making many changes to a slide background, you may decide that the original theme formatting is the best choice for displaying the text and graphics on a slide. The Reset Slide Background feature restores the original theme and color theme formatting to a slide.

Objective 2 | Animate a Slide Show

Animation is a visual or sound effect added to an object or text on a slide. Animation can focus the audience's attention, providing the speaker with an opportunity to emphasize important points using the slide element as an effective visual aid.

Activity 3.06 | Applying Animation Entrance Effects and Effect Options

Entrance effects are animations that bring a slide element onto the screen. You can modify an entrance effect by using the animation Effect Options command.

1 Display **Slide 3**, and then click anywhere in the bulleted list placeholder. On the **Animations tab**, in the **Animation group**, click the **More** button. If necessary, scroll slightly so that the word *Entrance* displays at the top of the Animation gallery, and then compare your screen with Figure 3.12.

Recall that an entrance effect is animation that brings an object or text onto the screen. An ***emphasis effect*** is animation that emphasizes an object or text that is already displayed. An ***exit effect*** is animation that moves an object or text off the screen.

Figure 3.12

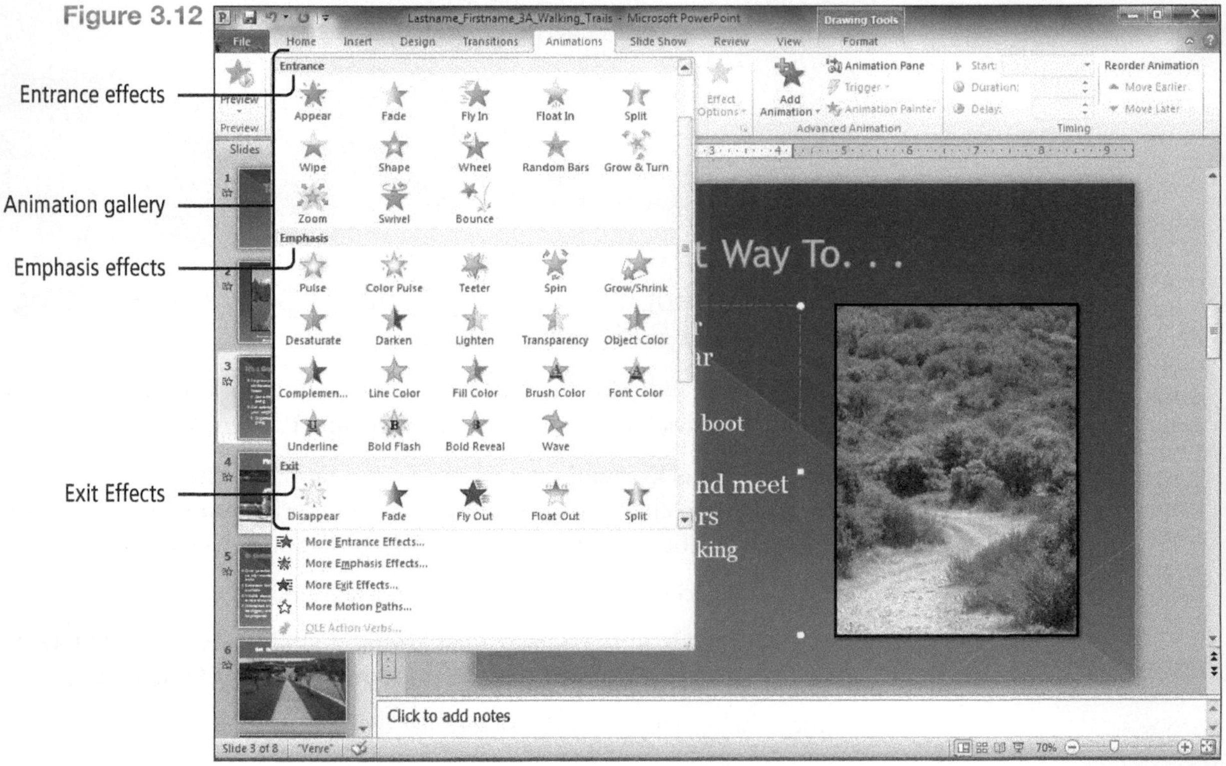

2 Under **Entrance**, click **Split**, and then notice the animation applied to the list. Compare your screen with Figure 3.13.

The numbers *1* and *2* display to the left of the bulleted list placeholder, indicating the order in which the bullet points will be animated during the slide show. For example, the first bullet point and its subordinate bullet are both numbered *1*. Thus, both will display at the same time.

Figure 3.13

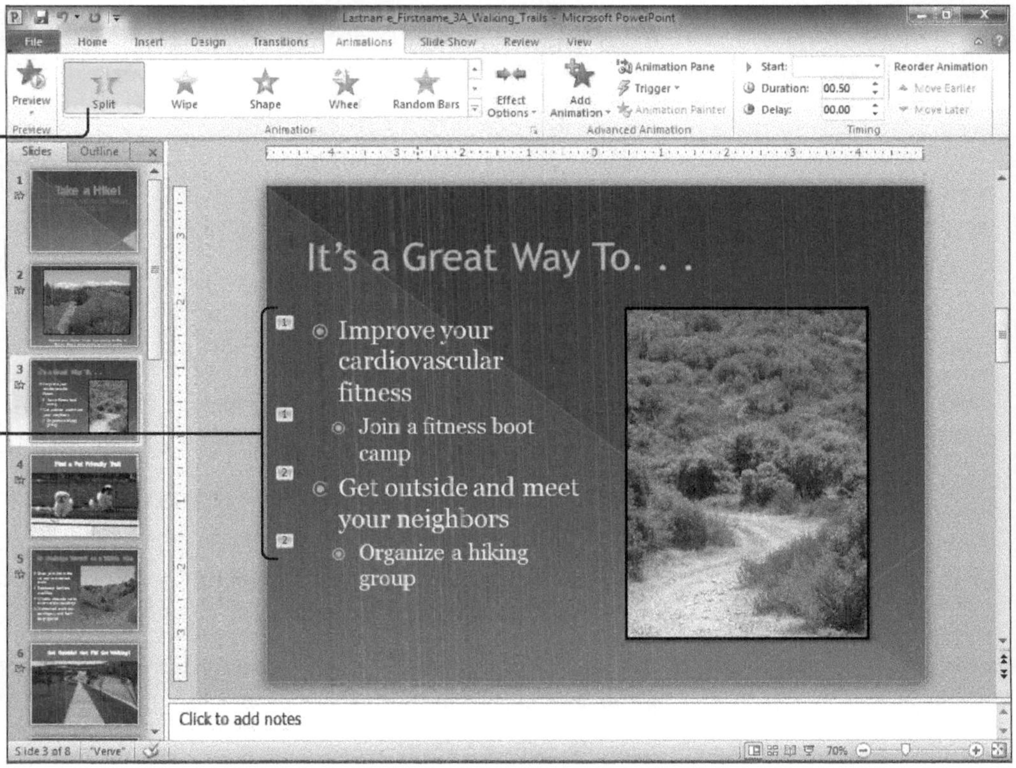

3 Select the bulleted text placeholder. In the **Animation group**, click the **Effect Options** button, and then compare your screen with Figure 3.14.

The Effect Options control the direction and sequence in which the animation displays. Additional options may be available with other entrance effects.

PowerPoint | Chapter 3

Figure 3.14

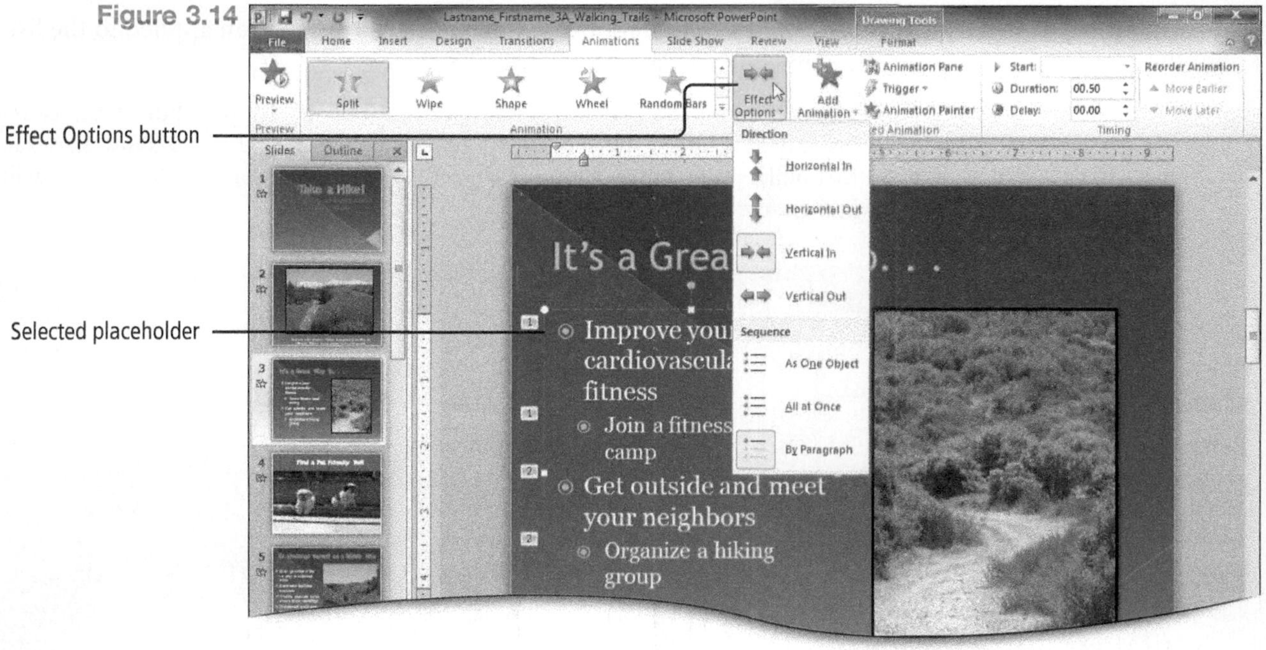

4. Click **Vertical Out** and notice the direction from which the animation is applied.

5. Select the picture. In the **Animation group**, click the **More** button, and then below the gallery, click **More Entrance Effects**. Compare your screen with Figure 3.15.

   The Change Entrance Effect dialog box displays additional entrance effects grouped in four categories: Basic, Subtle, Moderate, and Exciting.

Figure 3.15

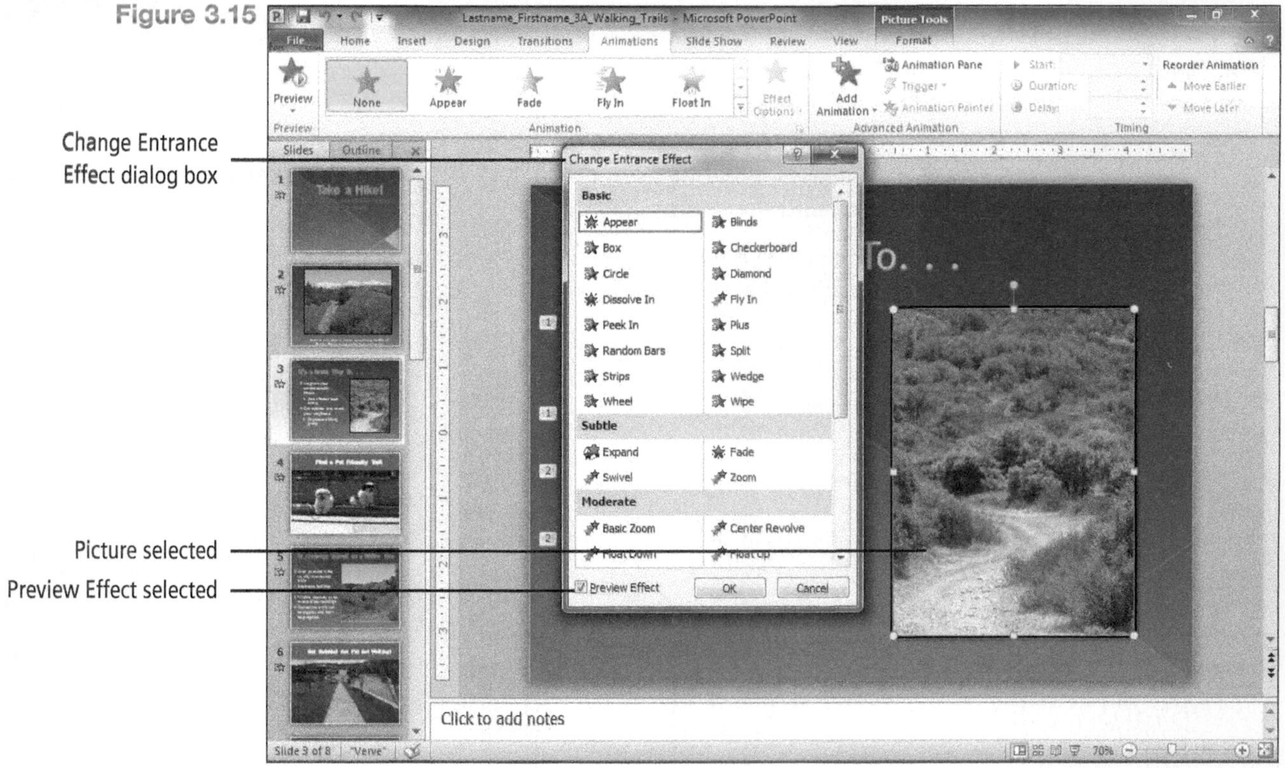

6 In the lower right corner of the **Change Entrance Effect** dialog box, verify that the **Preview Effect** check box is selected. Under **Basic**, click **Dissolve In**, and then watch as Live Preview displays the selected entrance effect. Click **OK**.

The number *3* displays next to the picture, indicating that it is third in the slide animation sequence.

7 Select the title. On the **Animations tab**, in the **Animation group**, click the **More** button, and then under **Entrance**, click **Split** to apply the animation to the title.

The number *4* displays next to the title, indicating that it is fourth in the slide animation sequence.

8 **Save** the presentation.

Activity 3.07 | Setting Animation Timing Options

Timing options control when animated items display in the animation sequence.

1 With **Slide 3** displayed, on the **Animations tab**, in the **Preview group**, click the **Preview** button.

The list displays first, followed by the picture, and then the title. The order in which animation is applied is the order in which objects display during the slide show.

2 Select the title. On the **Animations tab**, in the **Timing group**, under **Reorder Animation**, click the **Move Earlier** button two times, and then compare your screen with Figure 3.16.

To the left of the title placeholder, the number *1* displays. You can use the Reorder Animation buttons to change the order in which text and objects are animated during the slide show.

Figure 3.16

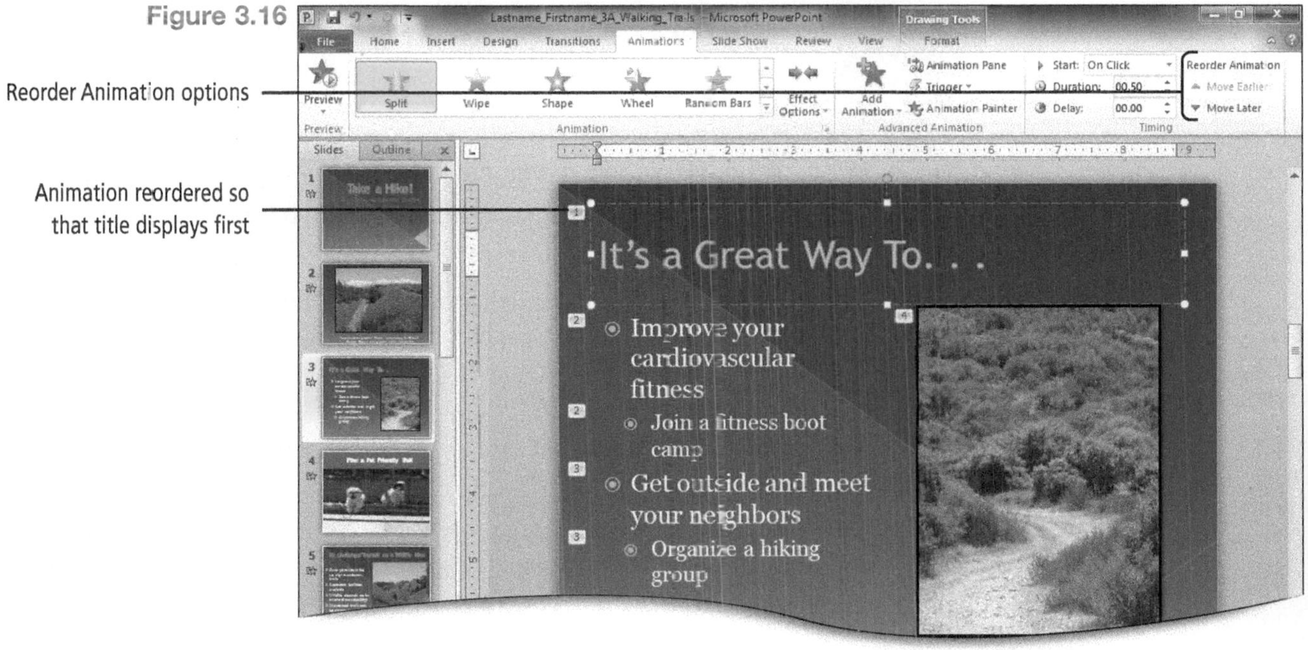

3 With the title selected, on the **Animations tab**, in the **Timing group**, click the **Start button arrow** to display three options—*On Click, With Previous*, and *After Previous*. Compare your screen with Figure 3.17.

The ***On Click*** option begins the animation sequence for the selected slide element when the mouse button is clicked or the Spacebar is pressed. The ***With Previous*** option begins the animation sequence at the same time as the previous animation or slide transition. The ***After Previous*** option begins the animation sequence for the selected slide element immediately after the completion of the previous animation or slide transition.

Figure 3.17

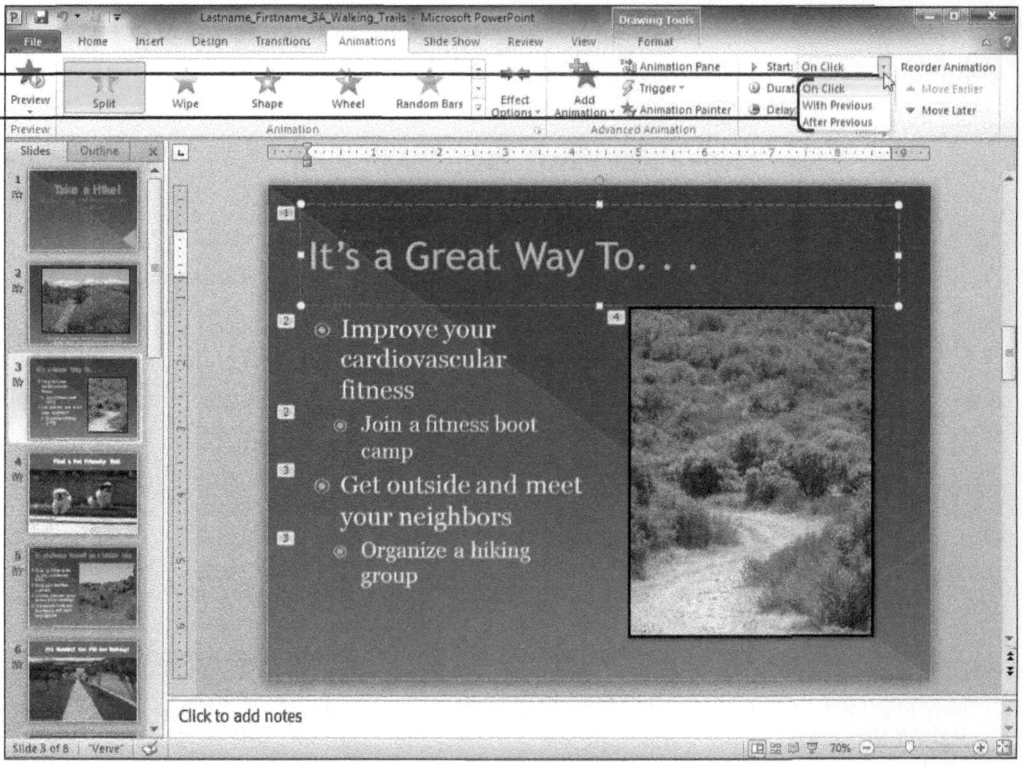

4 Click **After Previous**, and then notice that the number *1* is changed to *0*, indicating that the animation will begin immediately after the slide transition; the presenter does not need to click the mouse button or press Spacebar to display the title.

5 Select the picture, and then in the **Timing group**, click the **Start arrow**. Click **With Previous** and notice that the number is changed to *2*, indicating that the animation will begin at the same time as the second set of bullet points in the bulleted list.

6 On the **Animations tab**, in the **Preview group**, click the **Preview** button and notice that the title displays first, and that the picture displays at the same time as the second set of bullet points.

7 Display **Slide 1**, and then click in the title placeholder. On the **Animations tab**, in the **Animation group**, click the **Entrance** effect **Fly In**, and then click the **Effect Options** button. Click **From Top**. In the **Timing group**, click the **Start arrow**, and then click **After Previous.**

The number *0* displays to the left of the title indicating that the animation will begin immediately after the slide transition.

8 With the title selected, in the **Timing group**, click the **Duration** down arrow so that *00.25* displays in the **Duration** box. Compare your screen with Figure 3.18.

Duration controls the speed of the animation. You can set the duration of an animation by typing a value in the Duration box, or you can use the spin box arrows to increase and decrease the duration in 0.25-second increments. When you decrease the duration, the animation speed increases. When you increase the duration, the animation is slowed.

Figure 3.18

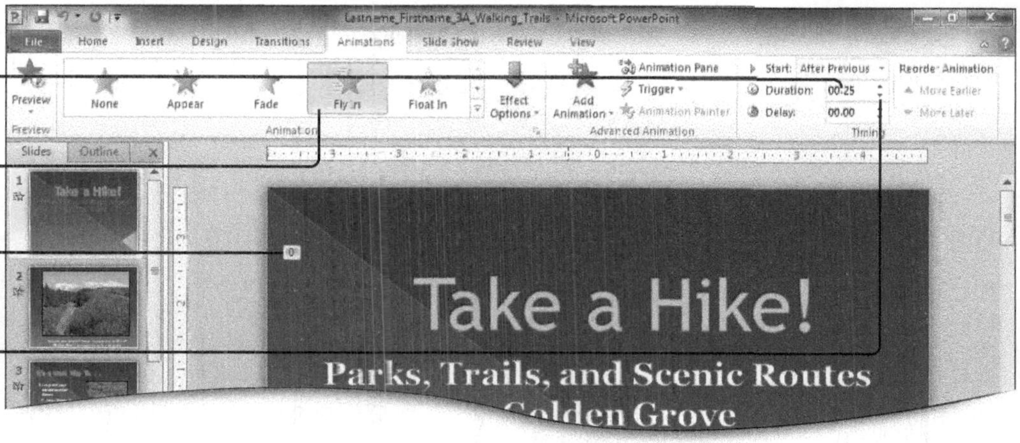

Duration set to *00.25*

Fly In animation applied to title

Zero displays to the left of title placeholder

Duration down arrow

9 Select the subtitle, and then in the **Animation group**, apply the **Fly In** entrance effect. In the **Timing group**, click the **Start arrow**, and then click **After Previous.** In the **Timing group**, select the value in the **Delay** box, type **00.50** and then press Enter. Compare your screen with Figure 3.19.

You can use Delay to begin a selected animation after a specified amount of time has elapsed. Here, the animation is delayed by one-half of a second after the completion of the previous animation—the title animation. You can type a value in the Delay or Duration boxes, or you can use the up and down arrows to change the timing.

Figure 3.19

Fly In animation applied to subtitle

Delay set to *00.50*

10 View the slide show from the beginning and notice the animation on Slides 1 and 3. When the black slide displays, press Esc to return to Normal view, and then **Save** the presentation.

Activity 3.08 | Using Animation Painter and Removing Animation

Animation Painter is a feature that copies animation settings from one object to another.

1. Display **Slide 3**, and then click anywhere in the bulleted list. On the **Animations tab**, in the **Advanced Animation group**, click the **Animation Painter** button. Display **Slide 5**, and then point anywhere in the bulleted list placeholder to display the Animation Painter pointer [pointer icon]. Compare your screen with Figure 3.20.

Figure 3.20

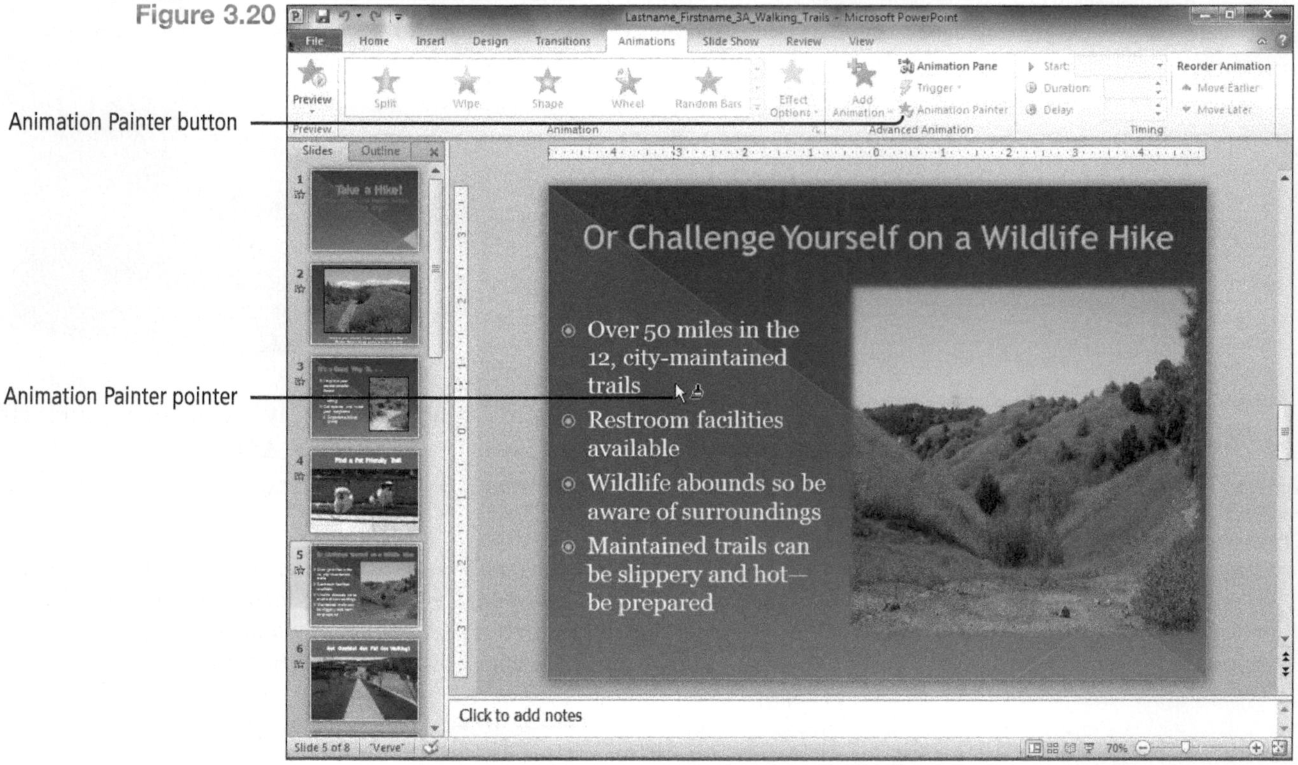

2. Click the bulleted list to copy the animation settings from the list on **Slide 3** to the list on **Slide 5**.

3. Display **Slide 3**, and then select the picture. Using the technique that you just practiced, use **Animation Painter** to copy the animation from the picture on **Slide 3** to the picture on **Slide 5**. With **Slide 5** displayed, compare your screen with Figure 3.21.

   The numbers displayed to the left of the bulleted list and the picture indicate that animation is applied to the objects.

Figure 3.21

Animation copied from Slide 3 to two placeholders

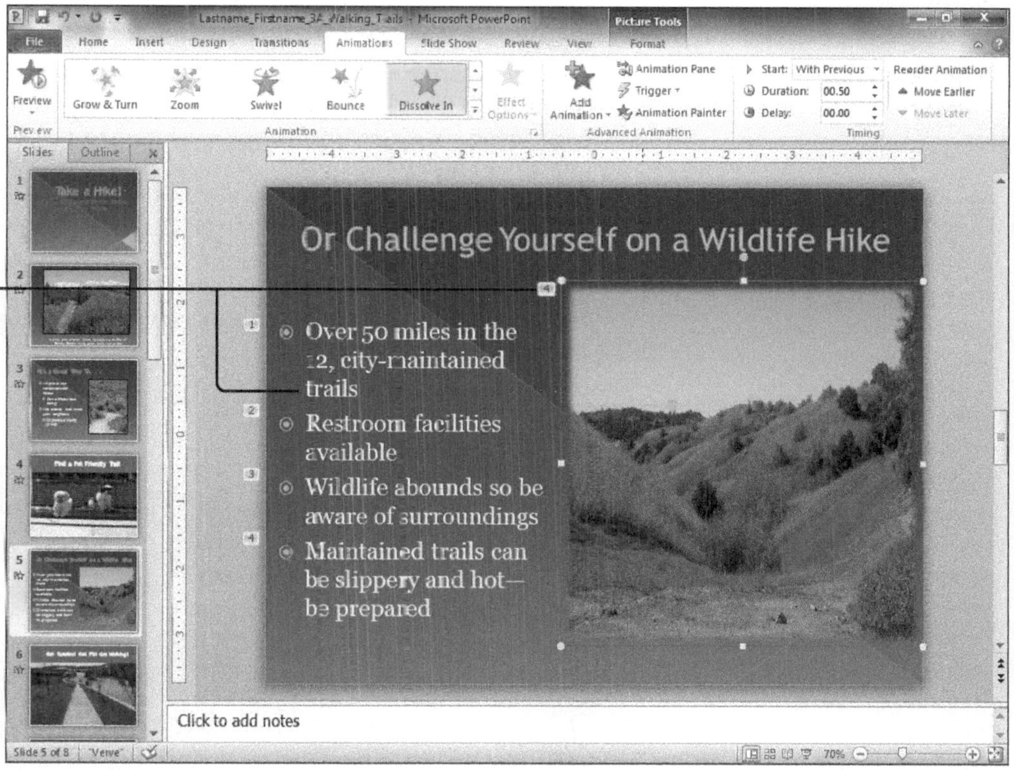

4 Display **Slide 3**, and then click in the title placeholder. On the **Animations tab**, in the **Animation group**, click the **More** button. At the top of the gallery, click **None** to remove the animation from the title placeholder. Compare your screen with Figure 3.22, and then **Save** the presentation.

Figure 3.22

Animation set to None

Animation removed from title

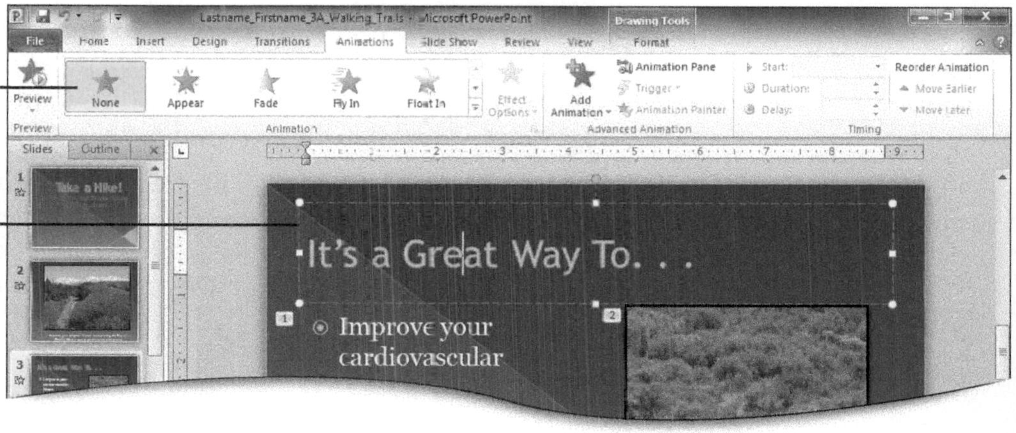

Objective 3 | Insert a Video

You can insert, size, and move videos in a PowerPoint presentation, and you can format videos by applying styles and effects. Video editing features in PowerPoint 2010 enable you to trim parts of a video and to fade the video in and out during a presentation.

Activity 3.09 | Inserting a Video

1 Display **Slide 1**. On the **Insert tab**, in the **Media group**, click the upper part of the **Video** button. In the **Insert Video** dialog box, navigate to your student files, and then click **p03A_Trails_Video**. Click **Insert**, and then compare your screen with Figure 3.23.

The video displays in the center of the slide, and playback and volume controls display in the control panel below the video. Video formatting and editing tools display on the Ribbon.

Figure 3.23

2 Below the video, on the control panel, click the **Play/Pause** button [▶] to view the video and notice that as the video plays, the control panel displays the time that has elapsed since the start of the video.

3 On the **Format tab**, in the **Size group**, click in the **Video Height** box. Type **3** and then press Enter. Notice that the video width adjusts proportionately.

4 Point to the video to display the pointer, and then drag the video down so that the top of the video is aligned at **zero on the vertical ruler**. On the **Format tab**, in the **Arrange group**, click the **Align** button, and then click **Align Center** to center the video horizontally on the slide. Compare your screen with Figure 3.24.

Figure 3.24

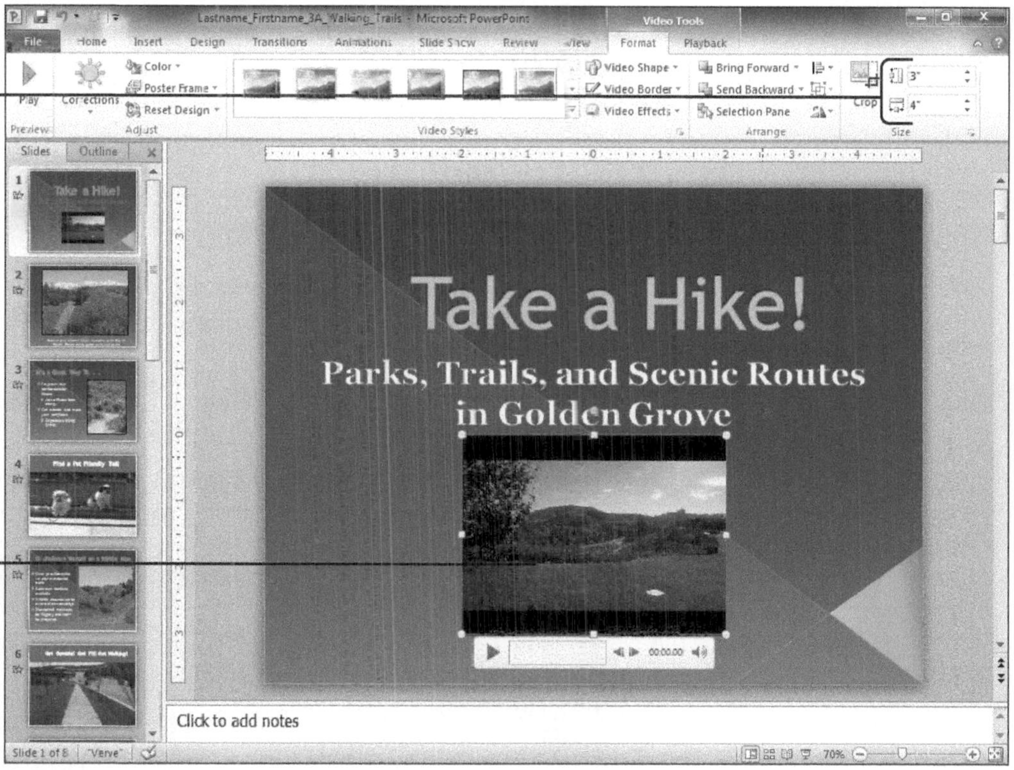

5 In the lower right corner of the PowerPoint window, in the **View** buttons, click the **Slide Show** button to display **Slide 1** in the slide show.

6 Point to the video to display the pointer, and then compare your screen with Figure 3.25.

When you point to the video during the slide show, the control panel displays.

Figure 3.25

PowerPoint | Chapter 3

7 With the pointer displayed, click the mouse button to view the video. Move the pointer away from the video and notice that the control panel no longer displays. When the video is finished, press Esc to exit the slide show.

8 **Save** the presentation.

Activity 3.10 | Formatting a Video

You can apply styles and effects to a video and change the video shape and border. You can also recolor a video so that it coordinates with the presentation theme.

1 With **Slide 1** displayed, select the video. On the **Format tab**, in the **Video Styles group**, click the **More** button to display the **Video Styles** gallery.

2 Using the ScreenTips to view the style name, under **Moderate**, click the first style—**Compound Frame, Black**. Compare your screen with Figure 3.26.

Figure 3.26

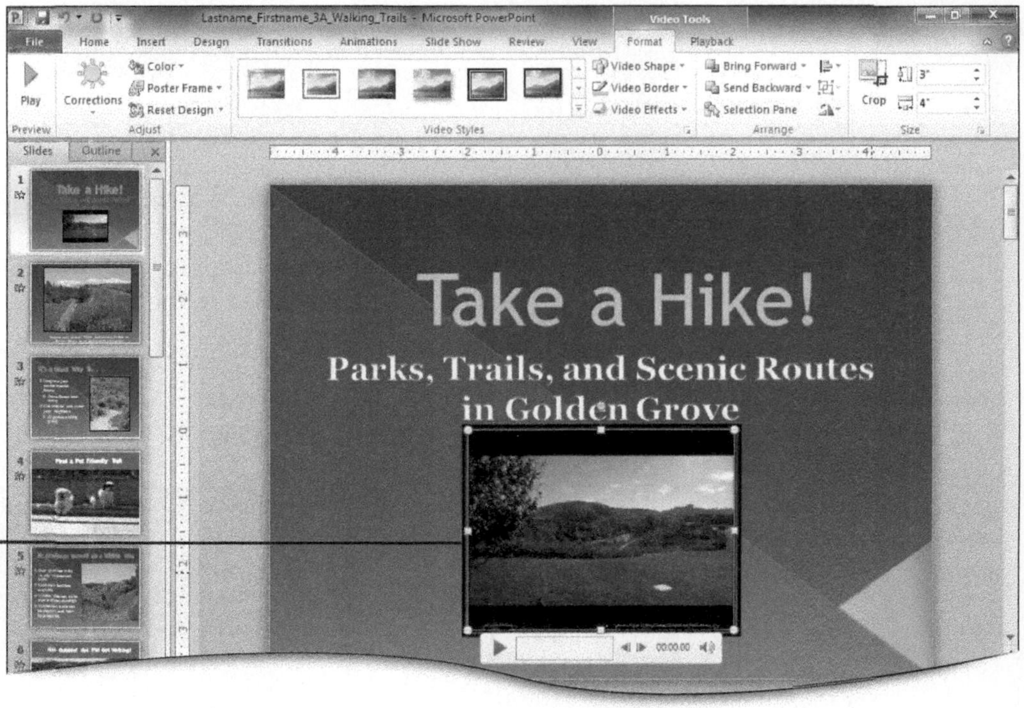

3 In the **Video Styles group**, click the **Video Shape** button, and then under **Basic Shapes**, click the first shape—**Oval**. In the **Video Styles group**, click the **Video Border** button, and then in the third column, click the fifth color—**Blue-Gray, Background 2, Darker 25%**. In the **Video Styles group**, click the **Video Effects** button, point to **Bevel**, and then click the last bevel—**Art Deco**. Compare your screen with Figure 3.27.

You can format a video with any combination of styles and effects.

Figure 3.27

Video shape changed, border and bevel applied

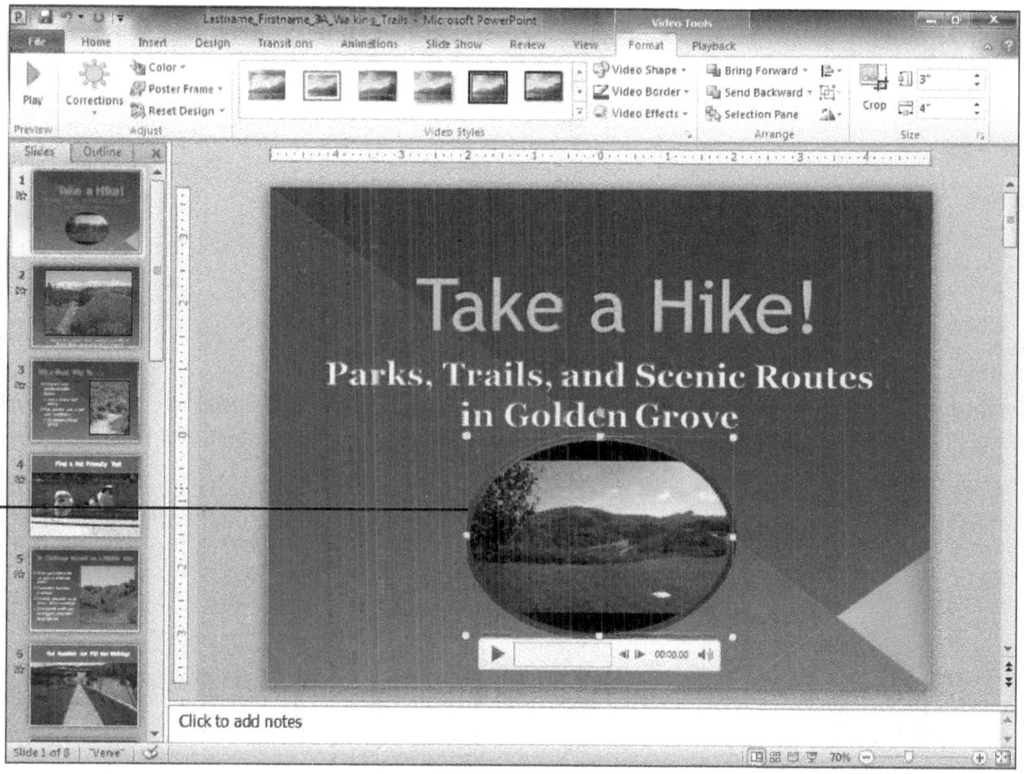

4 If necessary, select the video. On the **Format tab**, in the **Adjust group**, click the **Color** button to display the **Recolor** gallery.

The first row of the Recolor gallery displays options to recolor the video in grayscale, sepia, washout, or black and white variations. The remaining rows in the gallery display options to recolor the video in the theme colors.

5 In the **Recolor** gallery, in the second row, point to the first style—**Light Blue, Text color 2 Dark** and notice that Live Preview displays the video in the selected color. Compare your screen with Figure 3.28.

Figure 3.28

Color button

Recolor gallery

Selected color

Live Preview displays the video in the selected color

6 Click **Light Blue, Text color 2 Dark** to change the color of the video.

7 In the **Adjust group**, click the **Color** button to display the Recolor gallery. In the first row, click the first color—**No Recolor**, and then **Save** the presentation.

The No Recolor option restores the video to its original color.

Activity 3.11 | Editing and Compressing a Video

You can ***trim***—delete parts of a video to make it shorter—and you can compress a video file to reduce the file size of your PowerPoint presentation.

1 If necessary, select the video. On the **Playback tab**, in the **Editing group**, click the **Trim Video** button, and then compare your screen with Figure 3.29.

At the top of the displayed Trim Video dialog box, the file name and the video duration display. Below the video, a timeline displays with start and end markers indicating the video start and end time. Start Time and End Time boxes display the current start and end of the video. The Previous Frame and Next Frame buttons move the video forward and backward one frame at a time.

Figure 3.29

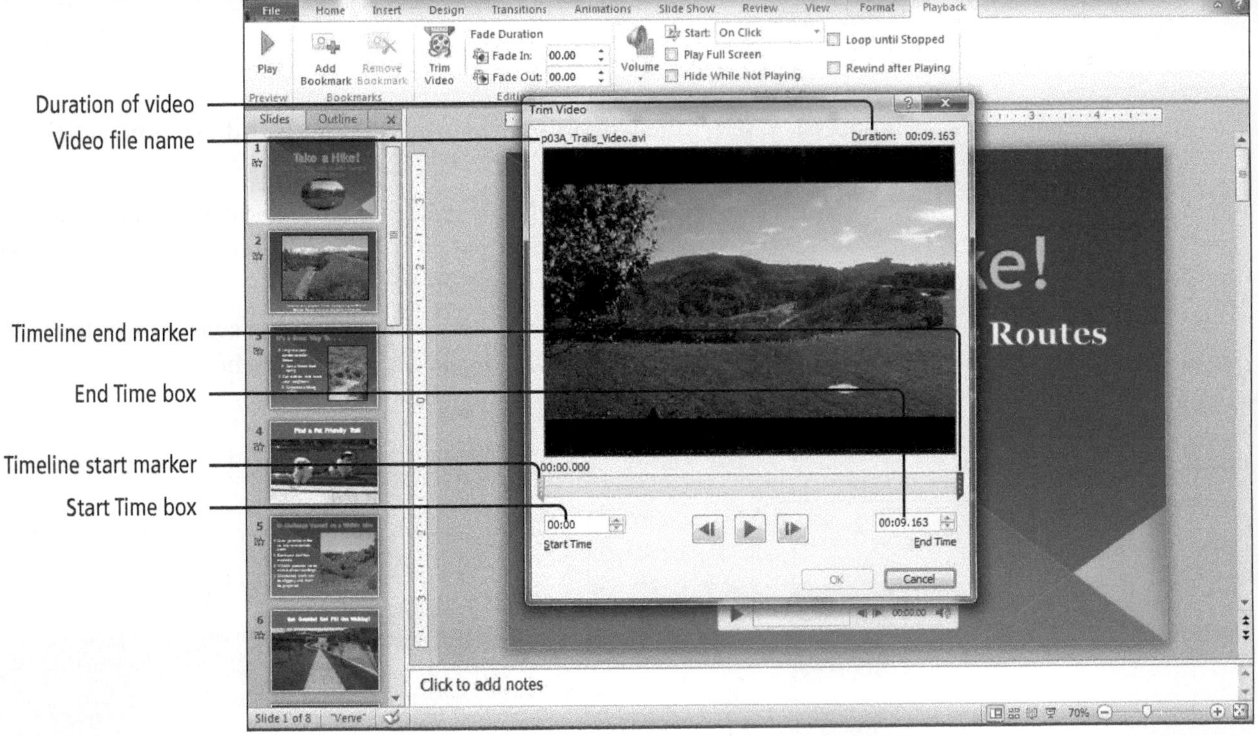

> **Another Way**
>
> Drag the red ending marking until its ScreenTip displays the ending time that you want; or type in the box.

2 Click in the **End Time** box, and then use the spin box arrows to set the End Time to **0:07.040**. Compare your screen with Figure 3.30.

The blue section of the timeline indicates the portion of the video that will play during the slide show. The gray section indicates the portion of the video that is trimmed.

Figure 3.30

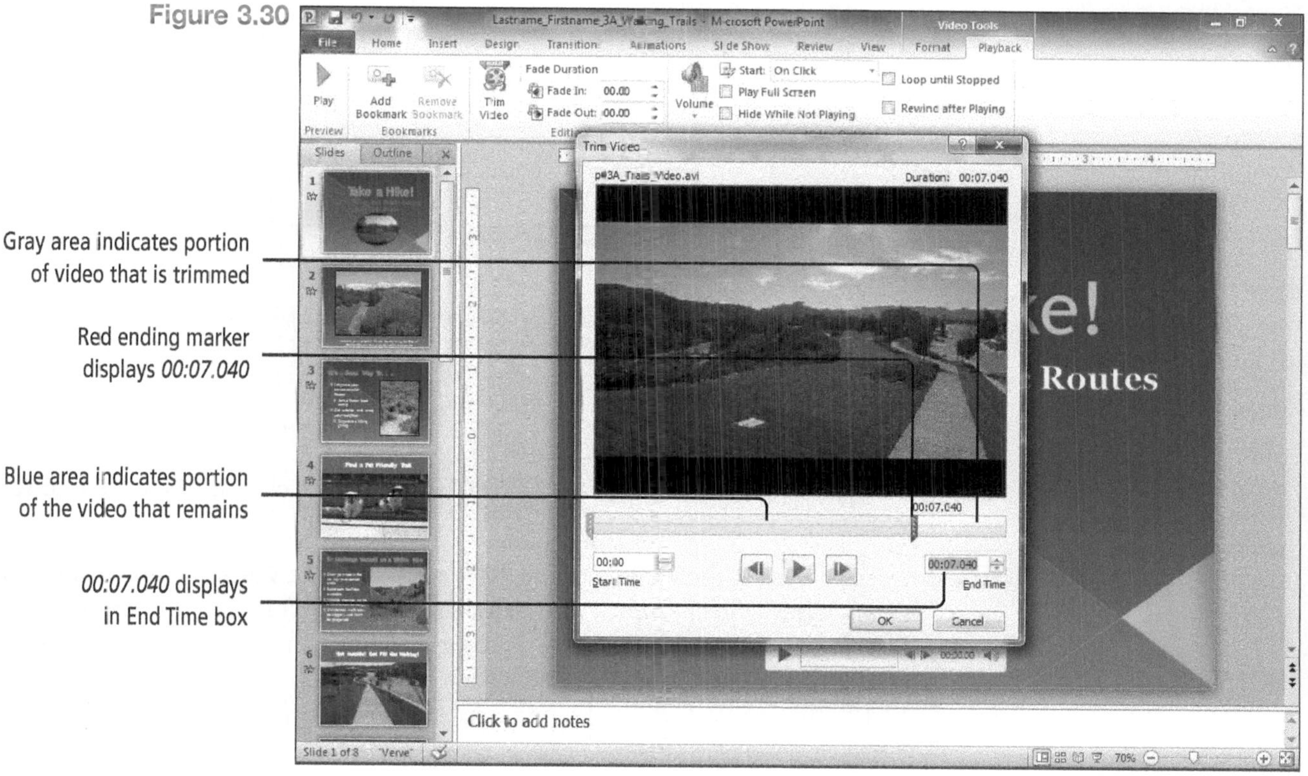

3 Click **OK** to apply the trim settings.

4 Display **Backstage** view, and then on the **Info tab**, click the **Compress Media** button. Read the description of each video quality option, and then click **Low Quality.** Compare your screen with Figure 3.31.

The Compress Media dialog box displays the slide number on which the selected video is inserted, the video file name, the original size of the video file, and when compression is complete, the amount that the file size was reduced.

Figure 3.31

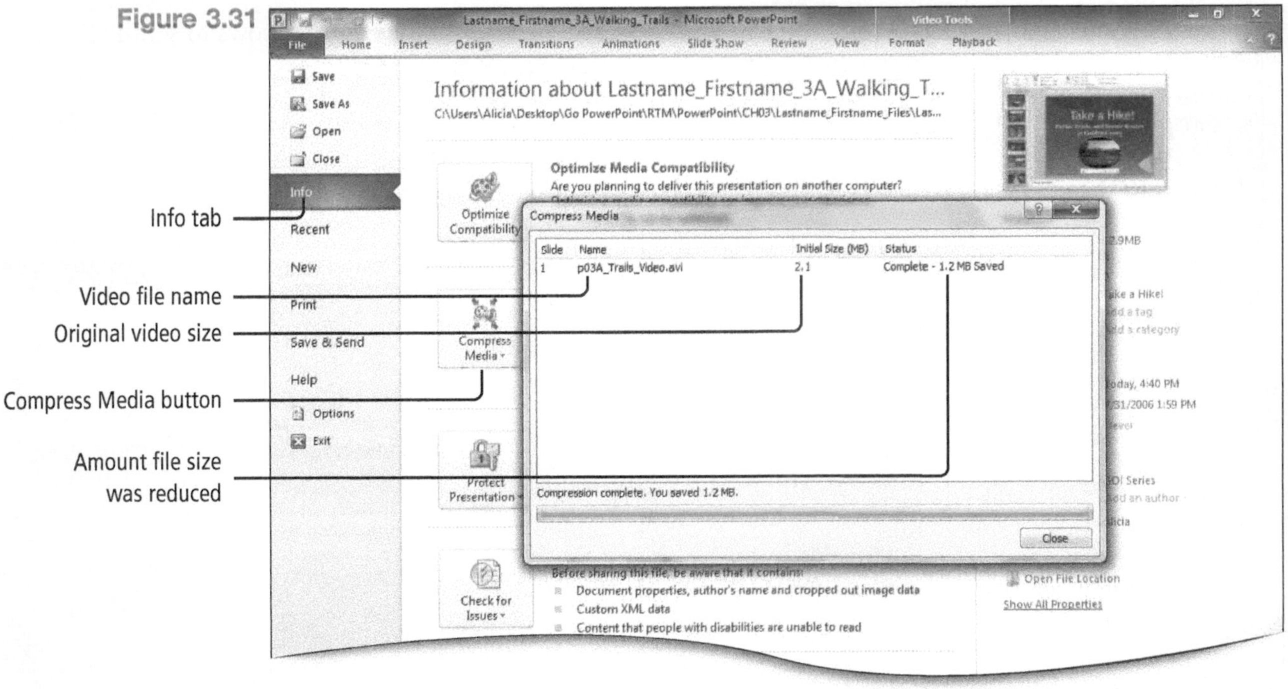

5 In the **Compress Media** dialog box, click **Close**, and then click the **Home tab** to return to **Slide 1**.

6 If necessary, select the video. On the **Playback tab**, in the **Video Options group**, click the **Start arrow**, and then click **Automatically** so that during the slide show, the video will begin automatically. Compare your screen with Figure 3.32.

Figure 3.32

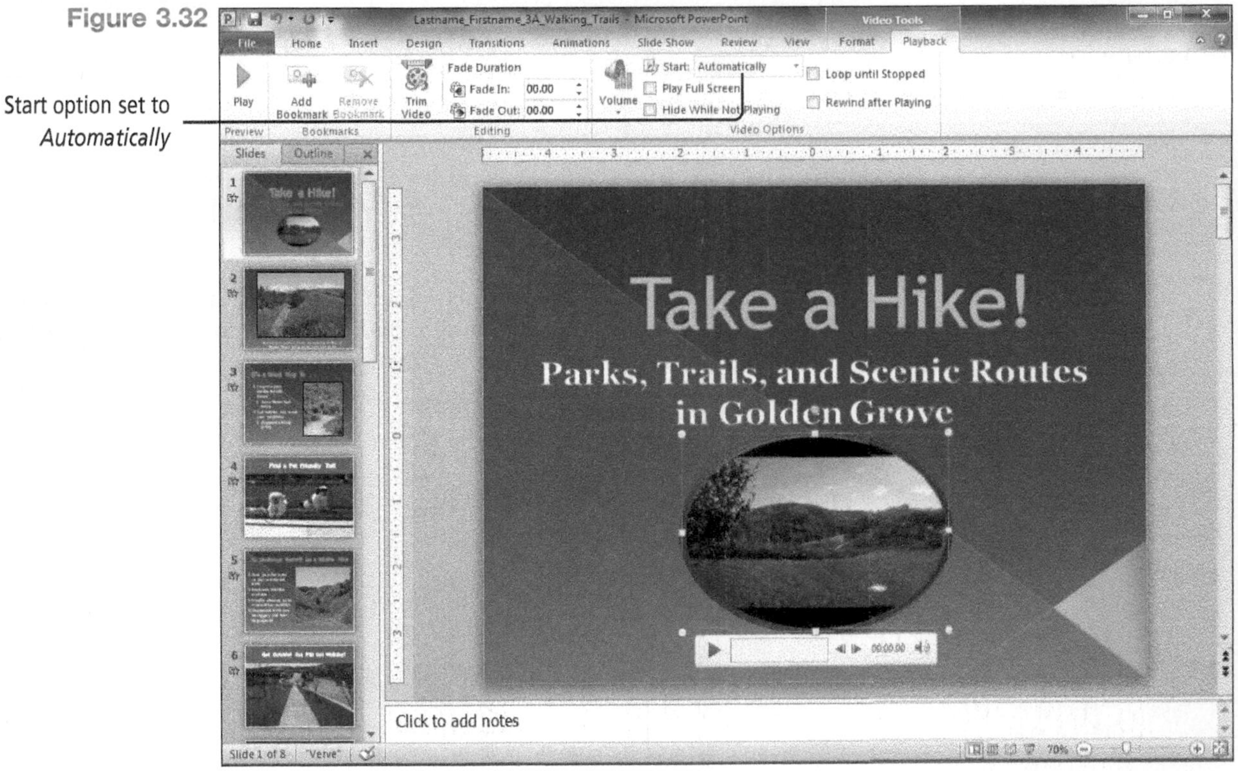

7 Click the **Slide Show tab**, in the **Start Slide Show group**, click the **From Beginning** button, and then view the slide show. Press Esc when the black slide displays.

> **Note | Your Video May Look Blurry**
>
> On playback, a compressed video may look slightly blurry. If you are certain that your presentation file will not be transmitted over the Internet, for example, in an e-mail message or in your learning management system, it is not necessary to compress the video.

8 On the **Insert tab**, in the **Text group**, click the **Header & Footer** button to display the **Header and Footer** dialog box. Click the **Notes and Handouts tab**. Under **Include on page**, select the **Date and time** check box, and then select **Update automatically**. If necessary, clear the **Header** check box, and then select the **Page number** and **Footer** check boxes. In the **Footer** box, using your own name, type **Lastname_Firstname_3A_Walking_Trails** and then click **Apply to All**.

9 Show the **Document Panel.** Replace the text in the **Author** box with your own firstname and lastname. In the **Subject** box, type your course name and section number, and in the **Keywords** box, type **trails, hiking Close** the **Document Information Panel.**

10 **Save** your presentation. Print **Handouts 4 Slides Horizontal**, or submit your presentation electronically as directed by your instructor.

11 **Close** the presentation and exit PowerPoint.

End You have completed Project 3A

PowerPoint | Chapter 3

Project 3B Summary and Analysis Presentation

Project Activities

In Activities 3.12 through 3.17, you will add a table and two charts to a presentation that Mindy Walker, Director of Parks and Recreation, is creating to inform the City Council about enrollment trends in Golden Grove recreation programs. Your completed presentation will look similar to Figure 3.33.

Project Files

For Project 3B, you will need the following file:

p03B_Recreation_Enrollment

You will save your presentation as:

Lastname_Firstname_3B_Recreation_Enrollment

Project Results

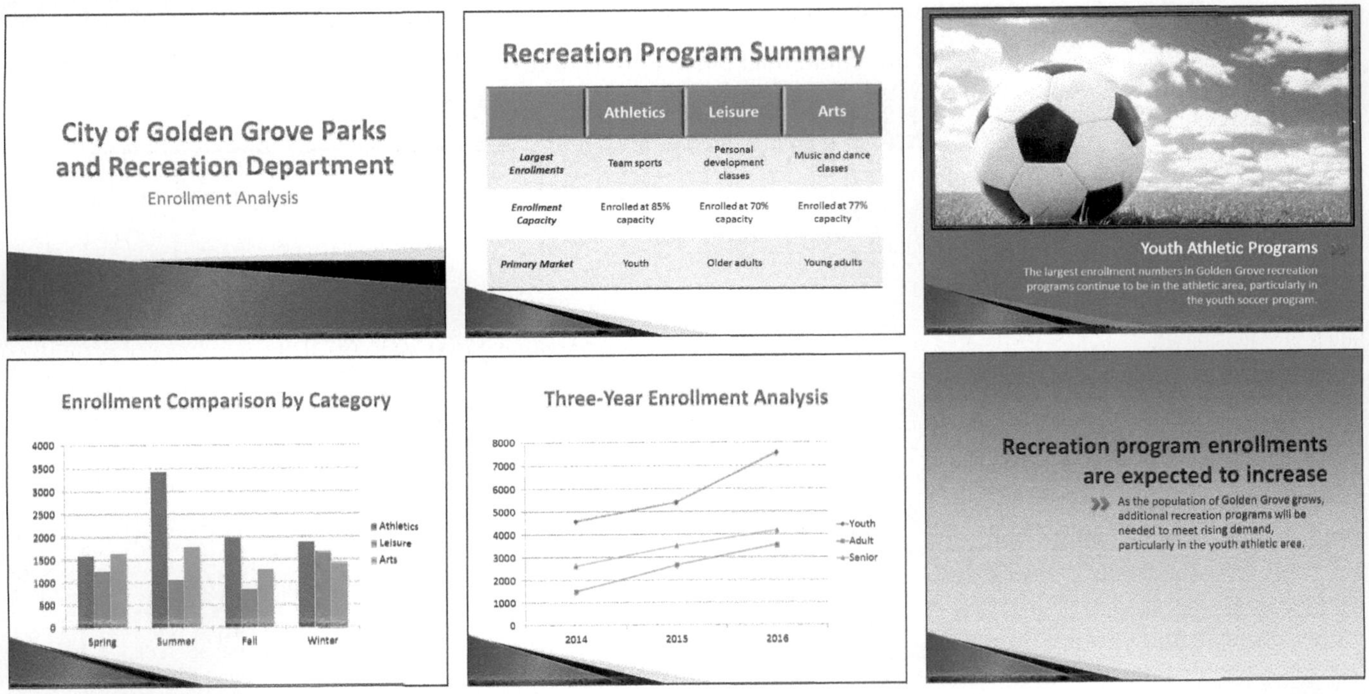

Figure 3.33
Project 3B Recreation Enrollment

Objective 4 | Create and Modify Tables

A ***table*** is a format for information that organizes and presents text and data in columns and rows. The intersection of a column and row is referred to as a ***cell*** and is the location in which you type text in a table.

Activity 3.12 | Creating a Table

There are several ways to insert a table in a PowerPoint slide. For example, you can use the Draw Table pointer, which is useful when the rows and columns contain cells of different sizes. Another way is to insert a slide with a Content Layout and then click the Insert Table button. Or, click the Insert tab and then click Table. In this activity, you will use a Content Layout to create a table.

1 **Start** PowerPoint. From your student files, open **p03B_Recreation_Enrollment**, and then **Save** the presentation in your **PowerPoint Chapter 3** folder as **Lastname_Firstname_3B_Recreation_Enrollment**

2 With **Slide 1** displayed, on the **Home tab**, in the **Slides group**, click the **New Slide** button to insert a slide with the **Title and Content** layout. In the title placeholder, type **Recreation Program Summary** and then **Center** the title.

3 In the content placeholder, click the **Insert Table** button to display the **Insert Table** dialog box. In the **Number of columns** box, type **3** and then press Tab. In the **Number of rows** box, type **2** and then compare your screen with Figure 3.34.

Here you enter the number of columns and rows that you want the table to contain.

Figure 3.34

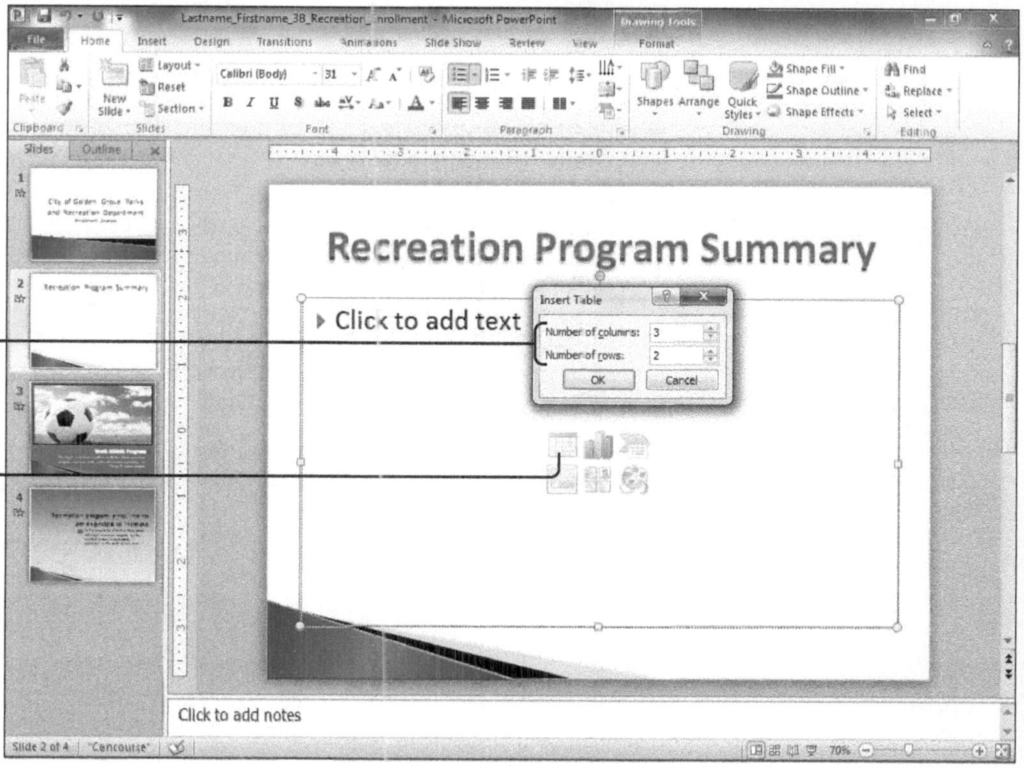

Table set for 3 columns and 2 rows

Insert Table button

4 Click **OK** to create a table with three columns and two rows. Notice that the insertion point is blinking in the upper left cell of the table.

The table extends from the left side of the content placeholder to the right side, and the three columns are equal in width. By default, a style is applied to the table.

5 With the insertion point positioned in the first cell of the table, type **Athletics** and then press [Tab].

Pressing [Tab] moves the insertion point to the next cell in the same row. If the insertion point is positioned in the last cell of a row, pressing [Tab] moves the insertion point to the first cell of the next row.

> **Alert! | Did You Press [Enter] Instead of [Tab]?**
>
> In a table, pressing [Enter] creates another line in the same cell. If you press [Enter] by mistake, you can remove the extra line by pressing [Backspace].

6 With the insertion point positioned in the second cell of the first row, type **Leisure** and then press [Tab]. Type **Arts** and then press [Tab] to move the insertion point to the first cell in the second row. Compare your table with Figure 3.35.

Figure 3.35

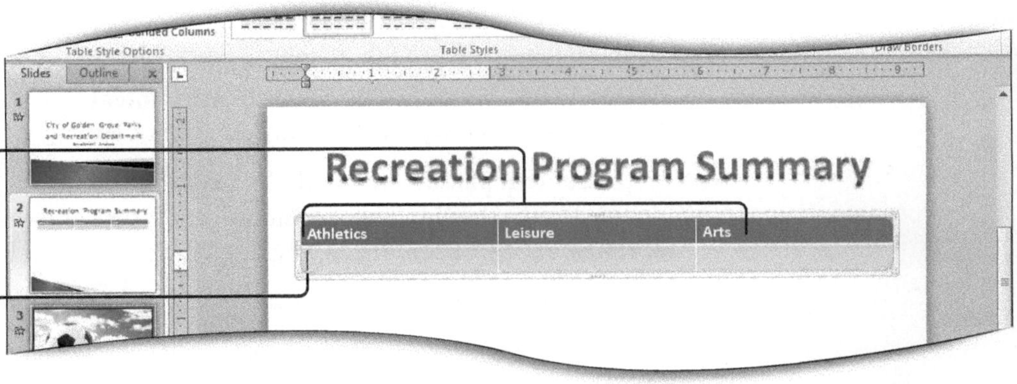

7 With the insertion point positioned in the first cell of the second row, type **Team sports** and then press [Tab]. Type **Personal development classes** and then press [Tab]. Type **Music and dance classes**

8 Press [Tab] to insert a new blank row.

When the insertion point is positioned in the last cell of a table, pressing [Tab] inserts a new blank row at the bottom of the table.

9 In the first cell of the third row, type **Youth** and then press [Tab]. Type **Older adults** and then press [Tab]. Type **Young adults** and then compare your table with Figure 3.36. **Save** your presentation.

Figure 3.36

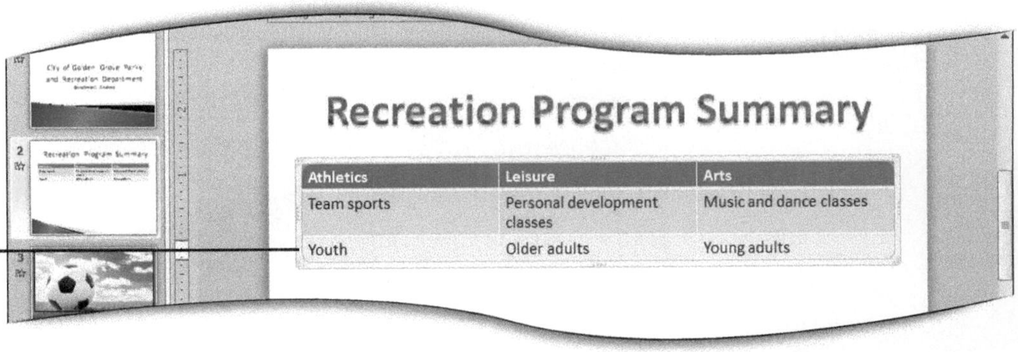

> **Alert! | Did You Add an Extra Row to the Table?**
>
> Recall that when the insertion point is positioned in the last cell of the table, pressing [Tab] inserts a new blank row. If you inadvertently inserted a blank row in the table, on the Quick Access Toolbar, click Undo.

Activity 3.13 | Modifying the Layout of a Table

You can modify the layout of a table by inserting or deleting rows and columns, changing the alignment of the text in a cell, adjusting the height and width of the entire table or selected rows and columns, and by merging multiple cells into one cell.

1 Click in any cell in the first column, and then click the **Layout tab**. In the **Rows & Columns group**, click the **Insert Left** button.

A new first column is inserted and the width of the columns is adjusted so that all four columns are the same width.

2 In the *second* row, click in the first cell, and then type **Largest Enrollments**

3 In the third row, click in the first cell, and then type **Primary Market** Compare your table with Figure 3.37.

Figure 3.37

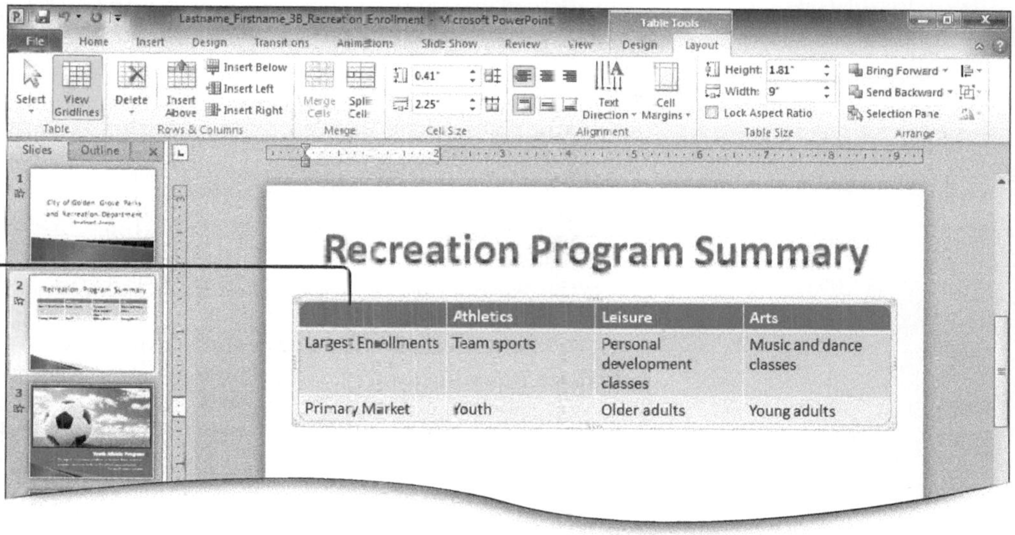

Column inserted and text typed

4 With the insertion point positioned in the third row, on the **Layout tab**, in the **Rows & Columns group**, click the **Insert Above** button to insert a new third row. In the first cell, type **Enrollment Capacity** and then press Tab. Type the remaining three entries, pressing Tab to move from cell to cell: **Enrolled at 85% capacity** and **Enrolled at 70% capacity** and **Enrolled at 77% capacity**

5 At the center of the lower border surrounding the table, point to the cluster of four dots—the sizing handle—to display the pointer. Compare your screen with Figure 3.38.

Figure 3.38

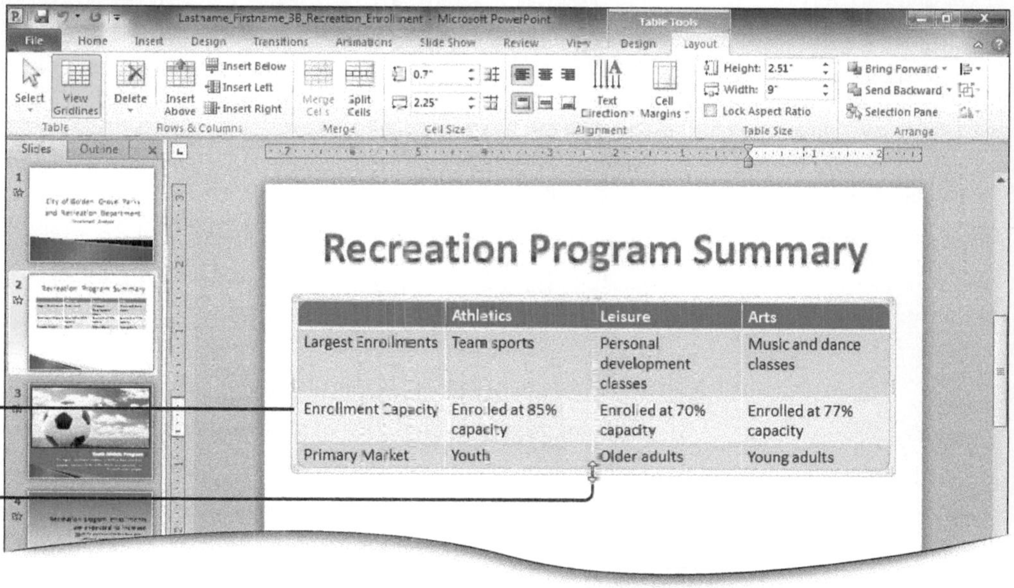

Row inserted and text typed

Vertical resize pointer positioned over sizing handle

6 Drag down to resize the table until the lower left corner of the table outline is just above the graphic in the lower left corner of the slide. Compare your screen with Figure 3.39.

Figure 3.39

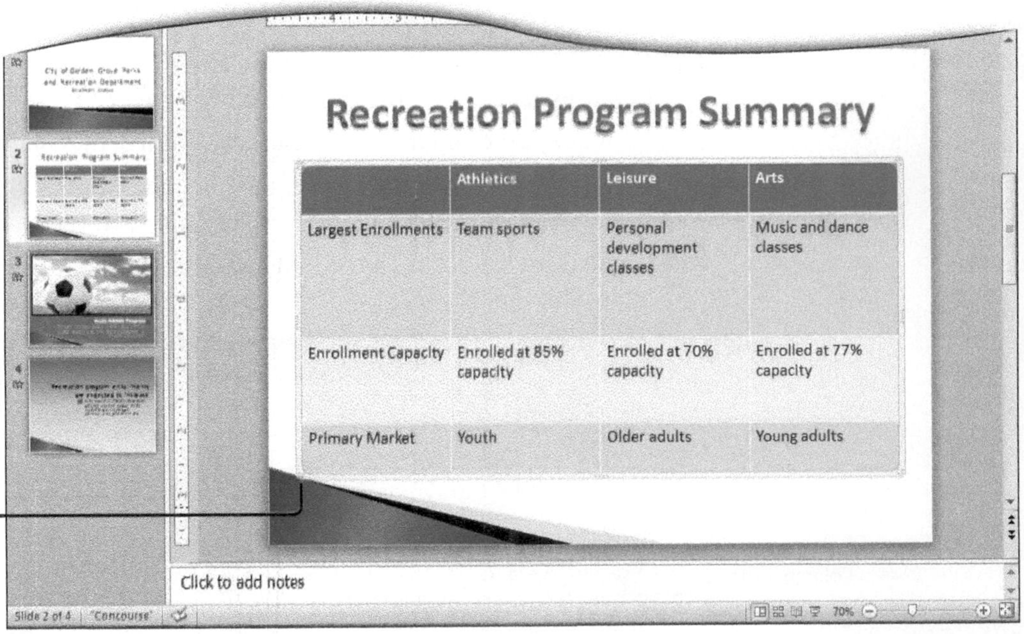

Table resized

7 Click in the first cell of the table. On the **Layout tab**, in the **Cell Size group**, click the **Distribute Rows** button. Compare your table with Figure 3.40.

The Distribute Rows command adjusts the height of the rows in the table so that they are equal.

Figure 3.40

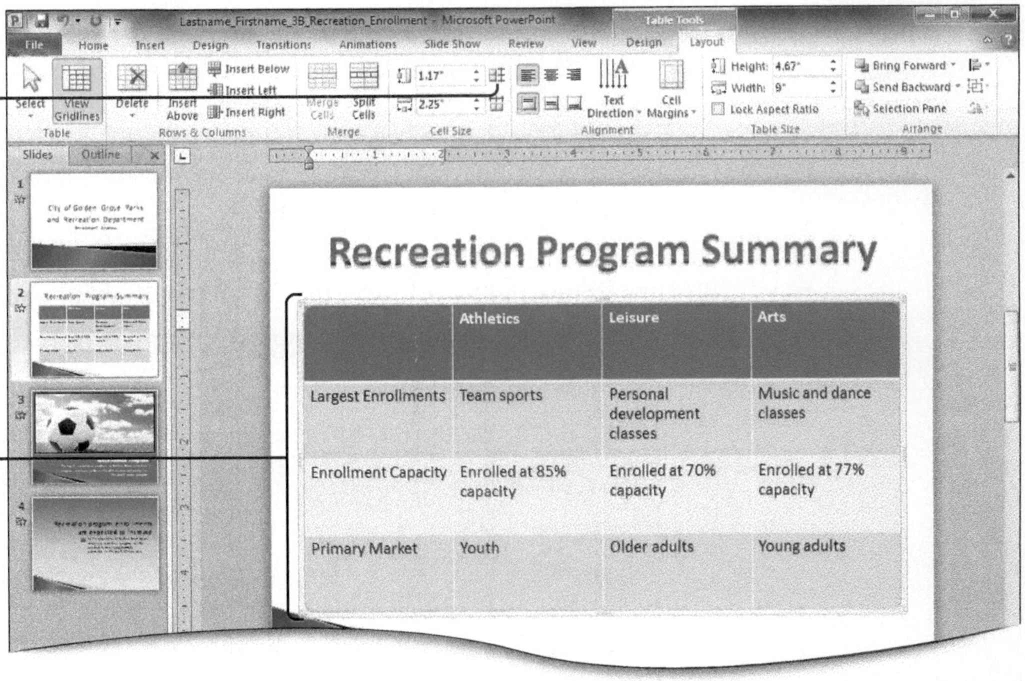

Distribute Rows button

Table rows equal in height

8 On the **Layout tab**, in the **Table group**, click **Select**, and then click **Select Table.** In the **Alignment group**, click the **Center** button, and then click the **Center Vertically** button.

All of the text in the table is centered horizontally and vertically within the cells.

9 **Save** your presentation.

> **More Knowledge | Deleting Rows and Columns**
>
> To delete a row or column from a table, click in the row or column that you want to delete. Click the Layout tab, and then in the Rows & Columns group, click Delete. In the displayed list, click Delete Columns or Delete Rows.

Activity 3.14 | Modifying a Table Design

You can modify the design of a table by applying a ***table style***. A table style formats the entire table so that it is consistent with the presentation theme. There are color categories within the table styles—Best Match for Document, Light, Medium, and Dark.

1. Click in any cell in the table. In the **Table Tools**, click the **Design tab**, and then in the **Table Styles group**, click the **More** button. In the displayed **Table Styles** gallery, point to several of the styles to view the Live Preview of the style.
2. Under **Medium**, scroll as necessary, and then in the third row, click the third button—**Medium Style 3 – Accent 2**—to apply the style to the table.
3. On the **Design tab**, in the **Table Style Options group**, clear the **Banded Rows** check box. Notice that each row except the header row displays in the same color.

   The check boxes in the Table Style Options group control where Table Style formatting is applied.
4. Select the **Banded Rows** check box.
5. Move the pointer outside of the table so that it is positioned to the left of the first row in the table to display the pointer, as shown in Figure 3.41.

Figure 3.41

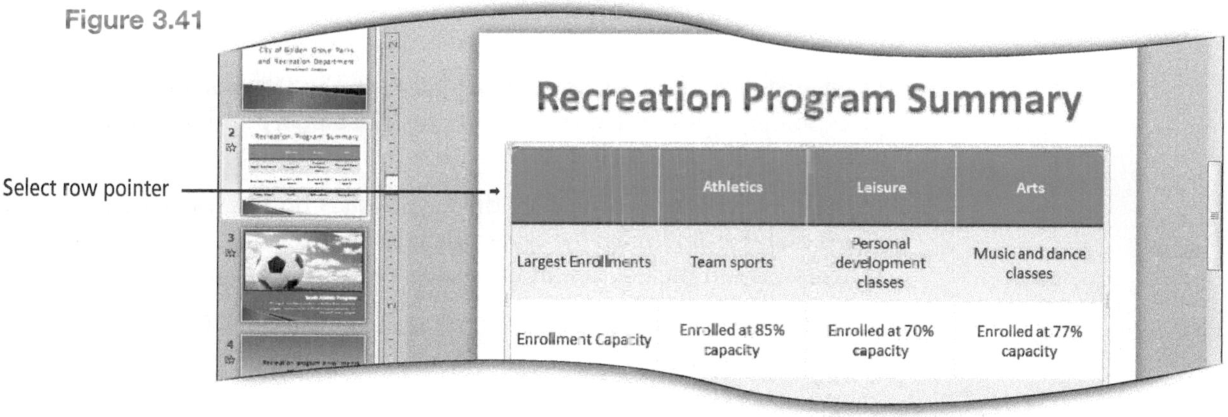

6. With the pointer pointing to the first row in the table, click the mouse button to select the entire row so that you can apply formatting to the selection. Move the pointer into the selected row, and then right-click to display the Mini toolbar and shortcut menu. On the Mini toolbar, change the **Font Size** to **28**.
7. With the first row still selected, in the **Table Tools**, on the **Design tab**, in the **Table Styles group**, click the **Effects** button. Point to **Cell Bevel**, and then under **Bevel**, click the first bevel—**Circle**.
8. Position the pointer above the first column to display the pointer, and then right-click to select the first column and display the shortcut menu. Click **Bold** and **Italic**.
9. Click in a blank area of the slide, and then compare your slide with Figure 3.42. **Save** the presentation.

Figure 3.42

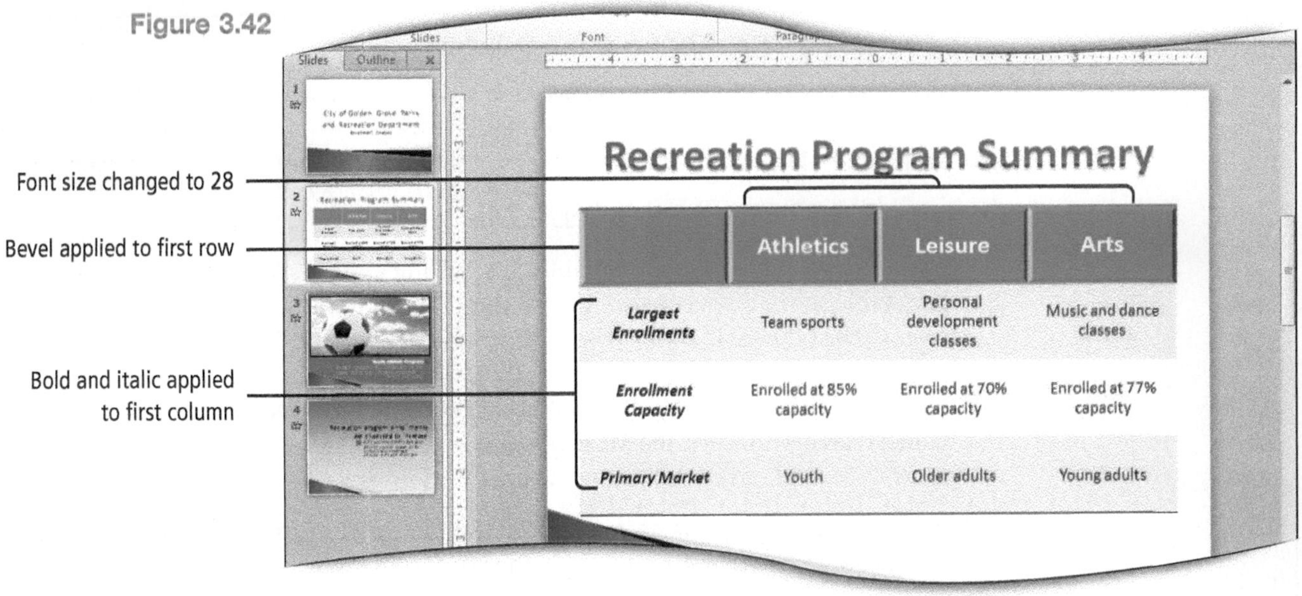

Objective 5 | Create and Modify Charts

A ***chart*** is a graphic representation of numeric data. Commonly used chart types include bar and column charts, pie charts, and line charts. A chart that you create in PowerPoint is stored in an Excel worksheet that is incorporated into the PowerPoint file.

Activity 3.15 | Creating a Column Chart and Applying a Chart Style

A ***column chart*** is useful for illustrating comparisons among related numbers. In this activity, you will create a column chart that compares enrollment in each category of recreation activities by season.

1. Display **Slide 3**, and then add a **New Slide** with the **Title and Content** layout. In the title placeholder, type **Enrollment Comparison by Category** and then **Center** the title and change the **Font Size** to **36**.
2. In the content placeholder, click the **Insert Chart** button to display the **Insert Chart** dialog box. Notice the types of charts that you can insert in your presentation. If necessary, on the left side of the dialog box, click Column.
3. Point to the first chart to display the ScreenTip *Clustered Column*. Compare your screen with Figure 3.43.

Figure 3.43

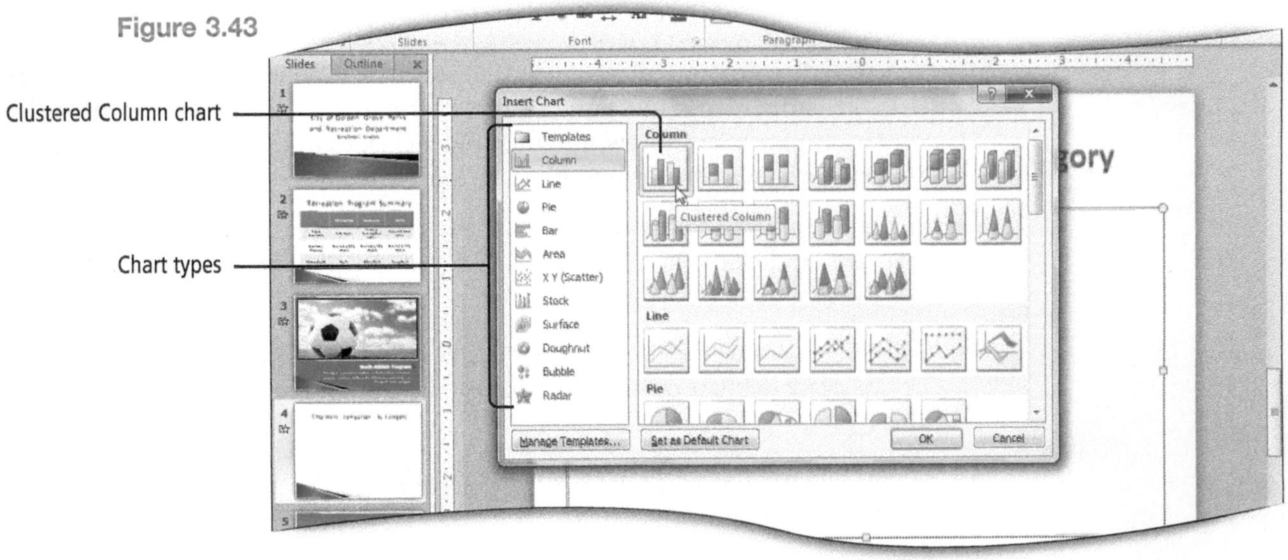

4 Click **Clustered Column**. Click **OK**, and then compare your screen with Figure 3.44.

The PowerPoint window displays a column chart on one side of your screen. On the other side of your screen, an Excel worksheet displays columns and rows. A cell is identified by the intersecting column letter and row number, forming the ***cell reference***.

The worksheet contains sample data in a data range outlined in blue, from which the chart in the PowerPoint window is generated. The column headings—*Series 1*, *Series 2*, and *Series 3* display in the chart ***legend*** and the row headings—*Category 1*, *Category 2*, *Category 3*, and *Category 4*—display as ***category labels***. The legend identifies the patterns or colors that are assigned to the data series in the chart. The category labels display along the bottom of the chart to identify the categories of data.

Figure 3.44

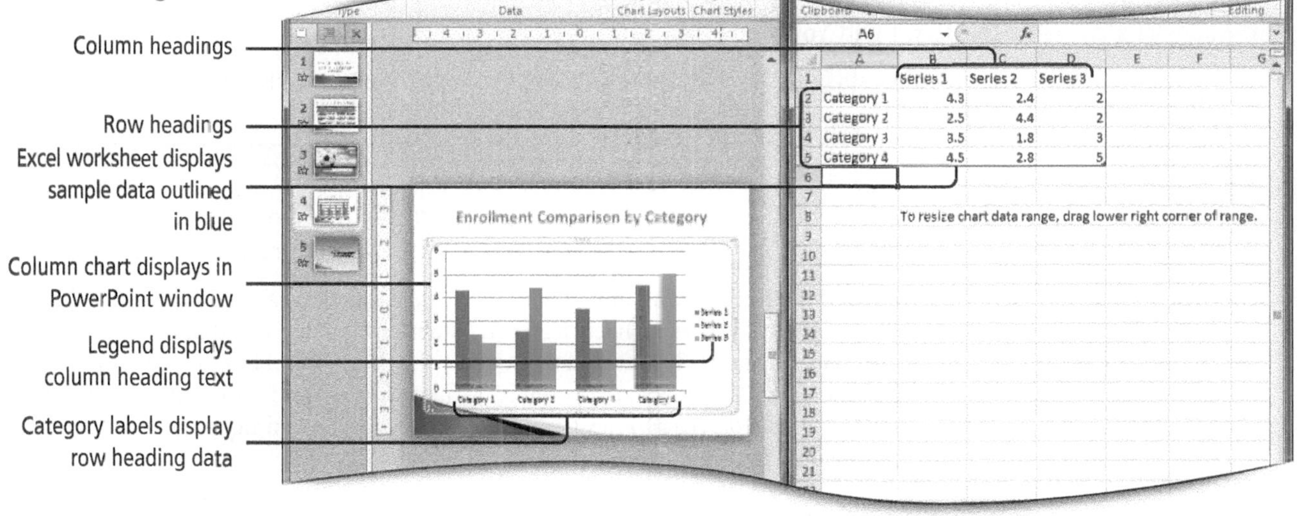

5 In the Excel window, click in cell **B1**, which contains the text *Series 1*. Type **Athletics** and then press Tab to move to cell **C1**.

The chart legend is updated to reflect the change in the Excel worksheet.

6 In cell **C1**, which contains the text *Series 2*, type **Leisure** and then press Tab to move to cell **D1**. Type **Arts** and then press Tab. Notice that cell **A2**, which contains the text *Category 1*, is selected. Compare your screen with Figure 3.45.

The blue box outlining the range of cells defines the area in which you are entering data. When you press Tab in the rightmost cell, the first cell in the next row becomes active.

Figure 3.45

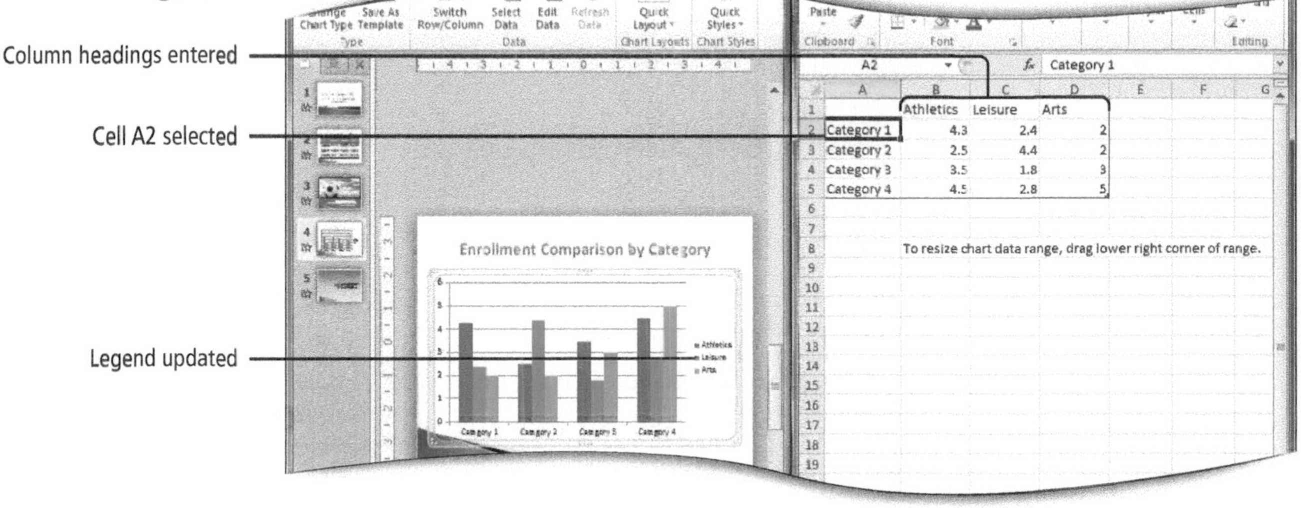

7 Beginning in cell **A2**, type the following data, pressing Tab to move from cell to cell.

	Athletics	Leisure	Arts
Spring	**1588**	**1263**	**1639**
Summer	**3422**	**1058**	**1782**
Fall	**1987**	**852**	**1293**
Winter	**1889**	**1674**	

8 In cell **D5**, which contains the value 5, type **1453** and then press Enter.

Pressing Enter in the last cell of the blue outlined area maintains the existing data range.

> **Alert! | Did You Press Tab After the Last Entry?**
>
> If you pressed Tab after entering the data in cell D5, you expanded the chart range. In the Excel window, click Undo.

9 Compare your worksheet and your chart with Figure 3.46. Correct any typing errors by clicking in the cell that you want to change, and then retype the data.

Each of the 12 cells containing the numeric data that you entered is a ***data point***—a value that originates in a worksheet cell. Each data point is represented in the chart by a ***data marker***—a column, bar, area, dot, pie slice, or other symbol in a chart that represents a single data point. Related data points form a ***data series***; for example, there is a data series for *Athletics*, *Leisure*, and *Arts*. Each data series has a unique color or pattern represented in the chart legend.

Figure 3.46

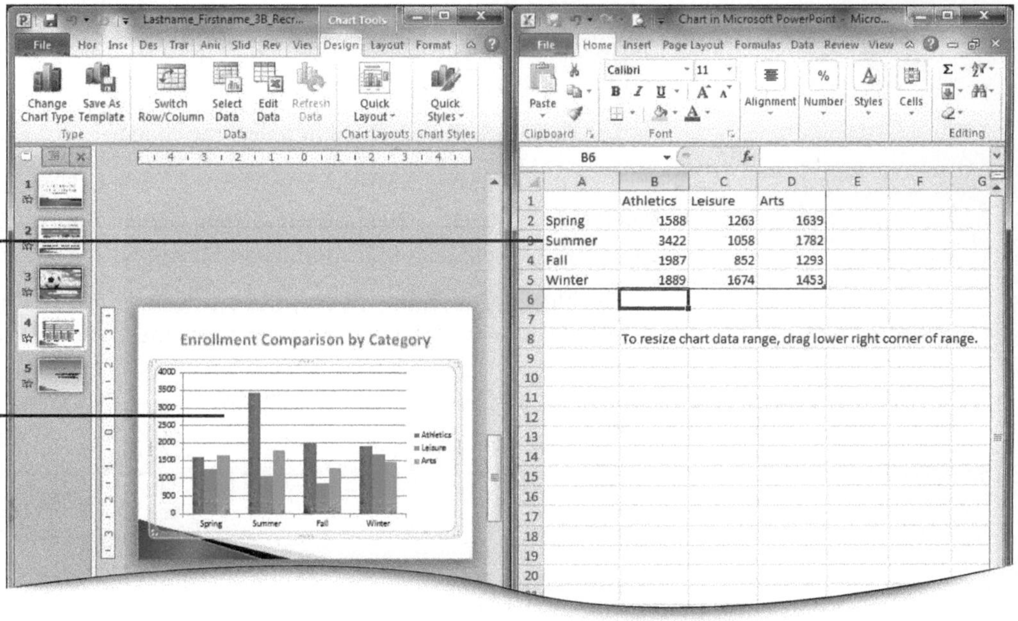

10 In the Excel window, click the **File tab**, and then click **Close**.

You are not prompted to save the Excel worksheet because the worksheet data is a part of the PowerPoint presentation. When you save the presentation, the Excel data is saved with it.

11 Be sure the chart is selected; click the outer edge of the chart if necessary to select it. In the **Chart Tools**, click the **Design tab**, and then in the **Chart Styles group**, click the **More** button.

12 In the **Chart Styles** gallery, the chart styles are numbered sequentially. Use ScreenTips to display the style numbers. Click **Style 10** to apply the style to the chart.

13 **Save** your presentation.

> **More Knowledge | Editing the Chart Data After Closing Excel**
>
> You can redisplay the Excel worksheet and make changes to the data after you have closed Excel. To do so, in PowerPoint, click the chart to select it, and then on the Design tab in the Data group, click Edit Data.

Activity 3.16 | Creating a Line Chart and Deleting Chart Data

To analyze and compare annual data over a three-year period, the presentation requires an additional chart. Recall that there are a number of different types of charts that you can insert in a PowerPoint presentation. In this activity, you will create a ***line chart***, which is commonly used to illustrate trends over time.

1 With **Slide 4** displayed, add a **New Slide** with the **Title and Content** layout. In the title placeholder, type **Three-Year Enrollment Analysis** and then **Center** the title and change the **Font Size** to **36**.

2 In the content placeholder, click the **Insert Chart** button. On the left side of the displayed **Insert Chart** dialog box, click **Line**, and then on the right, under **Line**, click the fourth chart—**Line with Markers**. Click **OK**.

3 In the Excel worksheet, click in cell **B1**, which contains the text *Series 1*. Type **Youth** and then press Tab. Type **Adult** and then press Tab. Type **Senior** and then press Tab.

4 Beginning in cell **A2**, type the following data, pressing Tab to move from cell to cell. If you make any typing errors, click in the cell that you want to change, and then retype the data.

	Youth	Adult	Senior
2014	**4586**	**1534**	**2661**
2015	**5422**	**2699**	**3542**
2016	**7565**	**3572**	**4183**

5 In the Excel window, position the pointer over **row heading 5** so that the pointer displays. Compare your screen with Figure 3.47.

Figure 3.47

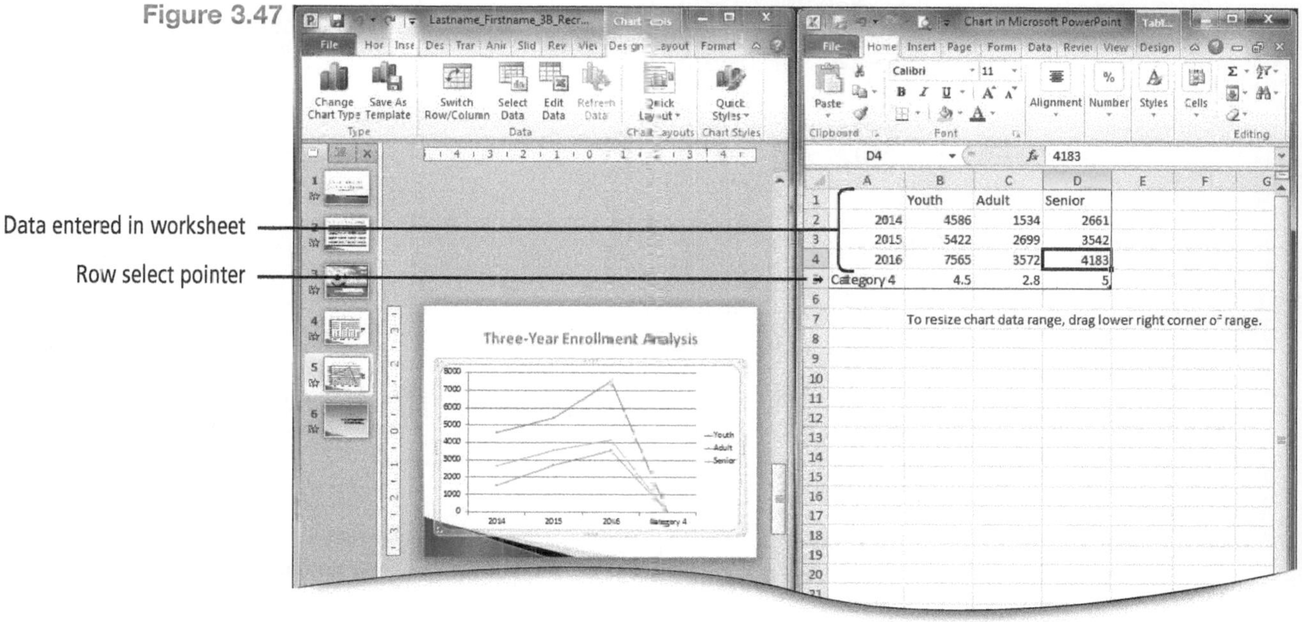

6 With the [→] pointer displayed, *right-click* to select the row and display the shortcut menu. On the shortcut menu, click **Delete** to delete the extra row from the worksheet, and then compare your screen with Figure 3.48.

The data in the worksheet contains four columns and four rows, and the blue outline defining the chart data range is resized. You must delete columns and rows that you do not want to include in the chart. You can add additional rows and columns by typing column and row headings and then entering additional data. When data is typed in cells adjacent to the chart range, the range is resized to include the new data.

Figure 3.48

Row with sample data deleted

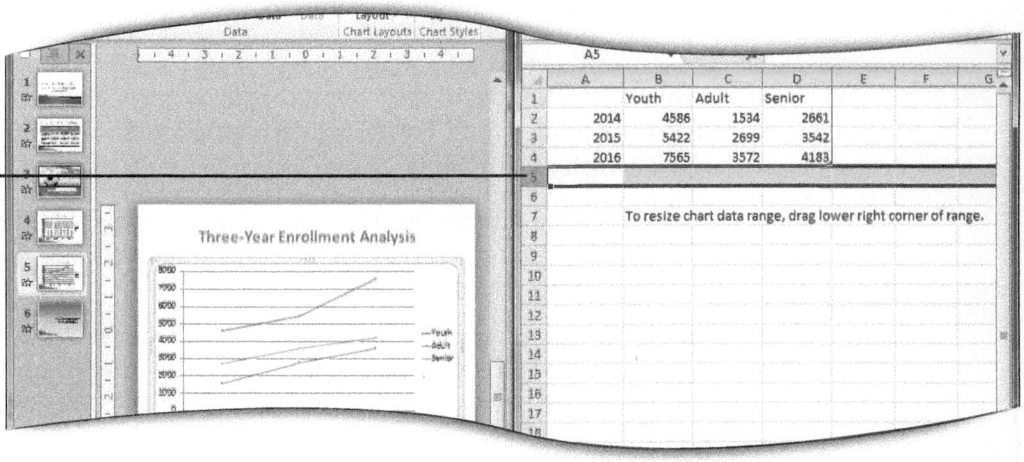

7 **Close** [X] the Excel window. In the **Chart Styles group**, click the **More** button [▾]. In the **Chart Styles** gallery, click **Style 26**, and then compare your slide with Figure 3.49. **Save** [💾] your presentation.

Figure 3.49

Chart Style 26 selected

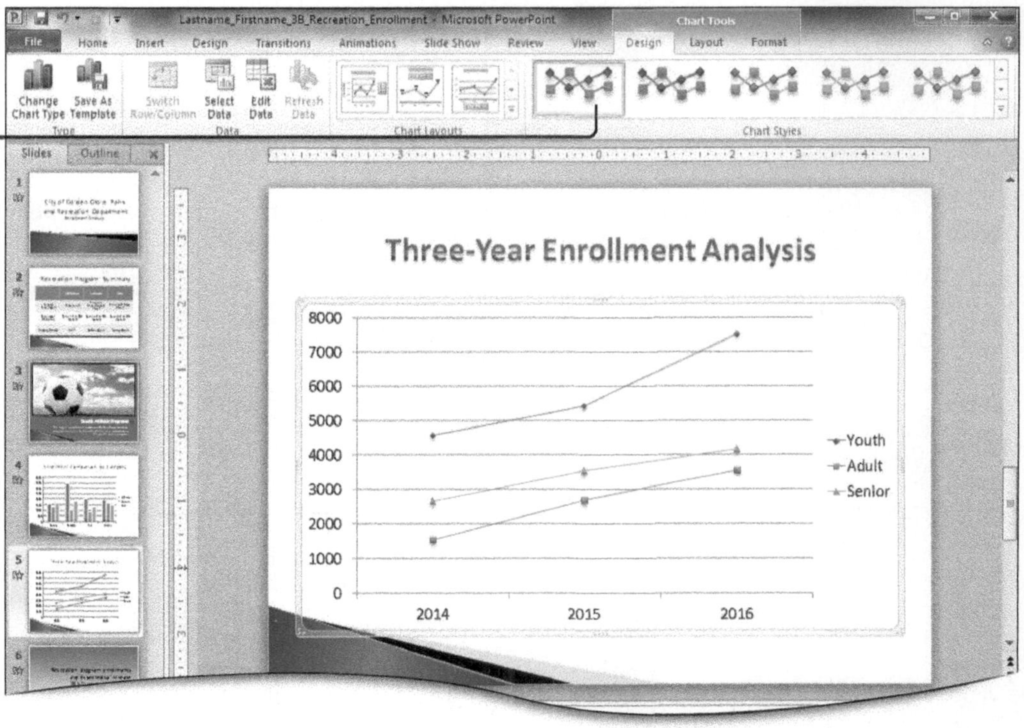

More Knowledge | Deleting Columns

To delete a worksheet column, position the pointer over the column letter that you want to select so that the [↓] pointer displays. Right-click to select the column and display the shortcut menu. Click Delete.

Activity 3.17 | Animating a Chart

1 Display **Slide 4**, and then click the column chart to select it. On the **Animations tab**, in the **Animation group**, click the **More** button, and then under **Entrance**, click **Split**.

2 In the **Animation group**, click the **Effect Options** button, and then under **Sequence**, click **By Series**. Compare your screen with Figure 3.50.

The By Series option displays the chart one data series at a time, and the numbers 1, 2, 3, and 4 to the left of the chart indicate the four parts of the chart animation sequence. The chart animation sequence includes the background, followed by the Athletics data series for each season, and then the Leisure series, and then the Arts series.

Figure 3.50

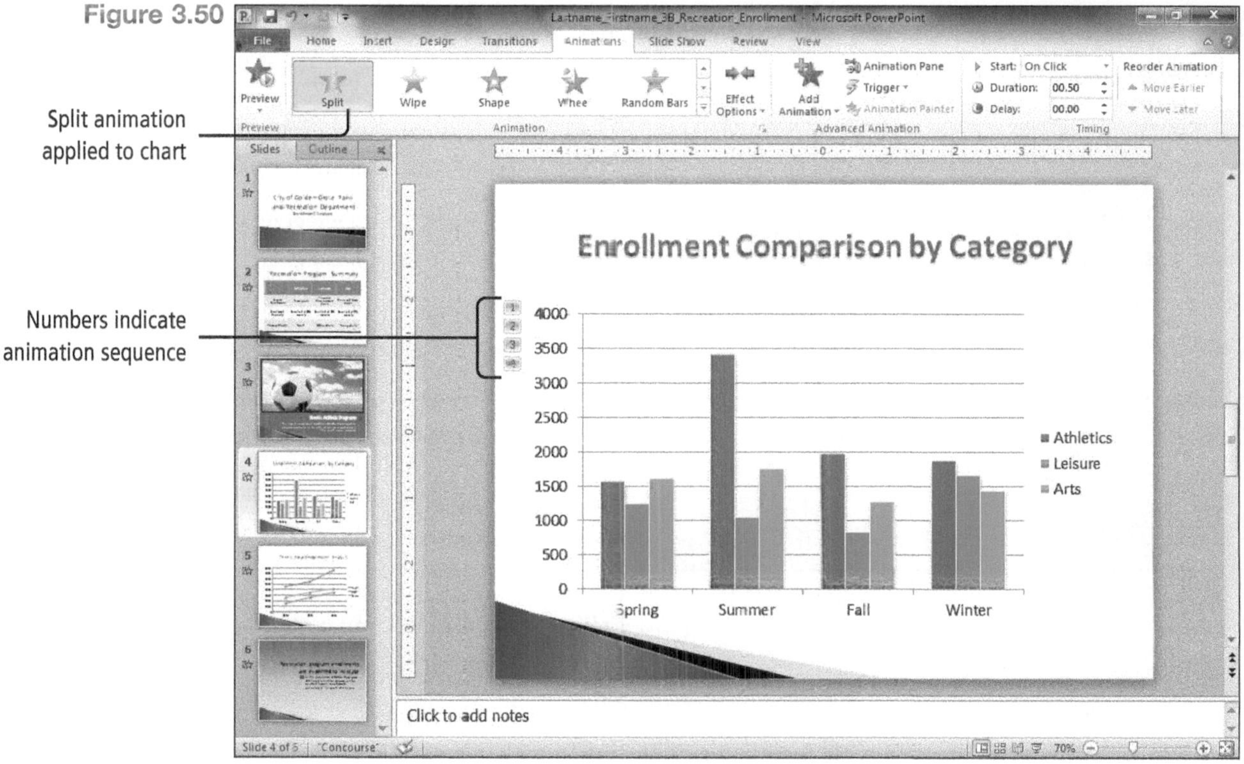

3 Click the **Slide Show tab**. In the **Start Slide Show group**, click **From Current Slide** to view the animation on **Slide 4**. Press Spacebar to display the legend and labels. Press Spacebar again to display the *Athletics* data.

4 Continue to press Spacebar to advance through the remaining animation effects. After the animations for Slide 4 are complete, press Esc to end the slide show and return to the presentation.

5 Insert a **Header & Footer** for the **Notes and Handouts**. Include the **Date and time updated automatically**, the **Page number**, and a **Footer** with the file name **Lastname_Firstname_3B_Recreation_Enrollment**

6 Show the **Document Panel**. Replace the text in the **Author** box with your own firstname and lastname. In the **Subject** box, type your course name and section number, and in the **Keywords** box, type **enrollment, recreation** **Close** the **Document Information Panel**.

7 **Save** your presentation. Print **Handouts 6 Slides Horizontal**, or submit your presentation electronically as directed by your instructor. **Close** the presentation and exit PowerPoint.

End **You have completed Project 3B**

Content-Based Assessments

Summary

In this chapter, you formatted a presentation by applying background styles, inserting pictures on slide backgrounds, and changing the theme fonts. You enhanced your presentation by inserting video, applying animation effects, and by changing effect and timing options. You practiced creating tables to present information in an organized manner, and you used charts to visually represent data.

Key Terms

Matching

Match each term in the second column with its correct definition in the first column by writing the letter of the term on the blank line in front of the correct definition.

____ 1. A slide background fill variation that combines theme colors in different intensities.

____ 2. A theme that determines the font applied to two types of slide text—headings and body.

____ 3. Of the two types of fonts in the theme font, the type that is applied to slide titles.

____ 4. Of the two types of fonts in the theme font, the type that is applied to all slide text except titles.

____ 5. A visual or sound effect added to an object or text on a slide.

____ 6. Animations that bring a slide element onto the screen.

____ 7. Animation that emphasizes an object or text that is already displayed.

____ 8. Animation that moves an object or text off the screen.

____ 9. A format for information that organizes and presents text and data in columns and rows.

____ 10. The intersection of a column and row.

____ 11. Formatting applied to an entire table so that it is consistent with the presentation theme.

____ 12. A graphic representation of numeric data.

____ 13. A type of chart used to compare data.

____ 14. A combination of the column letter and row number identifying a cell.

____ 15. A chart element that identifies the patterns or colors that are assigned to the each data series in the chart.

A Animation
B Background style
C Body font
D Cell
E Cell reference
F Chart
G Column chart
H Emphasis effect
I Entrance effect
J Exit effect
K Headings font
L Legend
M Table
N Table style
O Theme font

Content-Based Assessments

Multiple Choice

Circle the correct answer.

1. The set of coordinating colors applied to the backgrounds, objects, and text in a presentation is called:
   A. theme colors **B.** colors set **C.** coordinating colors
2. The command that is used to prevent background graphics from displaying on a slide is:
   A. Hide Background Styles **B.** Cover Background Graphics **C.** Hide Background Graphics
3. Animation options that control when animated items display in the animation sequence are called:
   A. timing options **B.** effect options **C.** sequence options
4. A feature that copies animation settings from one object to another is:
   A. copy **B.** format painter **C.** animation painter
5. The action of deleting parts of a video to make it shorter is referred to as:
   A. edit **B.** trim **C.** crop
6. A chart element that identifies categories of data is a:
   A. data marker **B.** category label **C.** category marker
7. A column, bar, area, dot, pie slice, or other symbol in a chart that represents a single data point is a:
   A. data marker **B.** data point **C.** data series
8. A chart value that originates in a worksheet cell is a:
   A. data marker **B.** data point **C.** data series
9. A group of related data points is called a:
   A. data marker **B.** data point **C.** data series
10. A type of chart that shows trends over time is a:
    A. pie chart **B.** column chart **C.** line chart

Content-Based Assessments

Apply 3A skills from these Objectives:

1. Customize Slide Backgrounds and Themes
2. Animate a Slide Show
3. Insert a Video

Skills Review | Project 3C Lake

In the following Skills Review, you will format a presentation by applying slide background styles, colors, pictures, and animation. Your completed presentation will look similar to Figure 3.51.

Project Files

For Project 3C, you will need the following files:

p03C_Lake
p03C_Scenery
p03C_Lake_Video

You will save your presentation as:

Lastname_Firstname_3C_Lake

Project Results

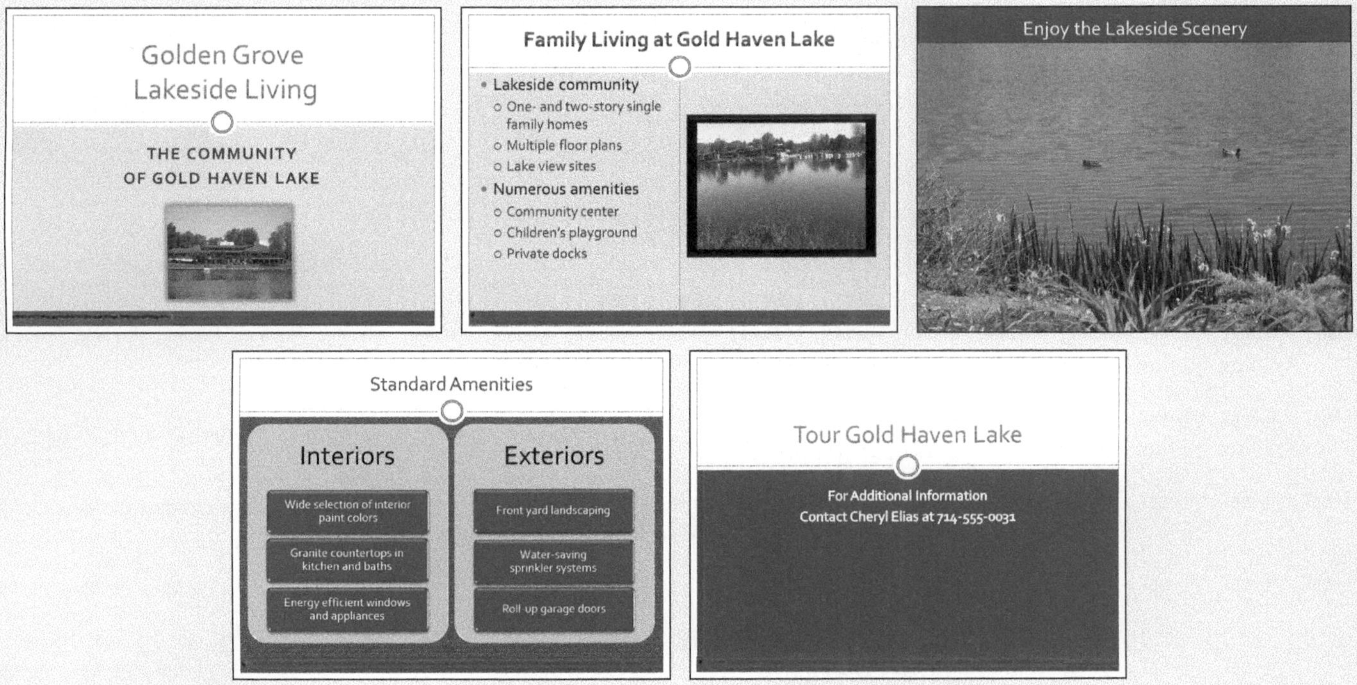

Figure 3.51

(Project 3C Lake continues on the next page)

Skills Review | Project 3C Lake (continued)

1 **Start** PowerPoint, from your student files open **p03C_Lake**, and then **Save** the presentation in your **PowerPoint Chapter 3** folder as **Lastname_Firstname_3C_Lake**

a. On the **Design tab**, in the **Themes group**, click the **Colors** button, and then click **Aspect** to change the theme colors. On the **Design tab**, in the **Themes group**, click the **Fonts** button, and then click **Module** to change the theme fonts.

b. Display **Slide 2**, and then on the **Home tab**, in the **Slides group**, click the **New Slide arrow**. Click **Title Only** to insert a new slide with the Title Only layout. On the **Design tab**, in the **Background group**, select the **Hide Background Graphics** check box. Click in the title placeholder, and then type **Enjoy the Lakeside Scenery**

c. On the **Design tab**, in the **Background group**, click the **Background Styles** button. Below the gallery, click **Format Background**, and then in the **Format Background** dialog box, verify that on the left side, **Fill** is selected. On the right side of the dialog box, under **Fill**, click the **Picture or texture fill** option button. Under **Insert from**, click the **File** button, and then navigate to your student data files. Click **p03C_Scenery**, and then click **Insert**. In the **Format Background** dialog box, click **Close** to format the slide background with the picture.

d. Click in the title placeholder. On the **Format tab**, in the **Shape Styles group**, click the **More** button, and then in the second row, click the fourth style—**Colored Fill - Dark Blue, Accent 3**.

e. Point to the outer edge of the title placeholder to display the [move] pointer, and then drag the placeholder up and to the left so that its top left corner aligns with the top left corner of the slide. Point to the center right sizing handle and drag to the right so that placeholder extends to the right edge of the slide.

2 Display **Slide 4**. On the **Design tab**, in the **Background group**, click the **Background Styles** button. In the second row, point to the third button—**Style 7**. *Right-click* to display the shortcut menu, and then click **Apply to Selected Slides** to apply the dark gray, patterned background to Slide 4.

a. Display **Slide 5**. On the **Design tab**, in the **Background group**, click the **Background Styles** button. Below the gallery, click **Format Background**.

b. In the **Format Background** dialog box, verify that on the left side, **Fill** is selected. On the right side, under **Fill**, click the **Solid Fill** option button, and then under **Fill Color**, click the **Color** button. In the seventh column, click the first color—**Dark Blue, Accent 3**, and then click **Close** to apply the background fill color to the slide.

3 Display **Slide 2**, and then on the **Insert tab**, in the **Media group**, click the **Video** button. Navigate to your student files, and then click **p03_Lake_Video**. Click **Insert** to insert the video.

a. With the video selected, on the **Format tab**, in the **Size group**, replace the value in the **Video Height** box with **3.25** and then press Enter.

b. Point to the video, and then hold down Shift and drag to the right so that its right edge aligns at **4.5 inches on the right side of the horizontal ruler**.

c. With the video selected, on the **Format tab**, in the **Video Styles group**, click the **Video Border** button, and then in the seventh column, click the first color—**Dark Blue, Accent 3**. Click the **Video Effects** button, point to **Bevel**, and then click the last style—**Art Deco**.

d. With the video selected, on the **Playback tab**, in the **Video Options group**, click the **Start arrow**, and then click **Automatically**. In the **Editing group**, click the **Trim Video** button. In the **Trim Video** dialog box, in the **End Time** box, use the spin box arrows to set the end time to **00:6.520** Click **OK**.

e. Display **Backstage** view. On the **Info page**, in the center panel, click the **Compress Media** button, and then click **Low Quality**. Recall that compressing in this manner facilitates sending your file over the Internet in an e-mail or in a learning management system, although it may make the video less clear when played. When the compression is complete, **Close** the **Compress Media** dialog box, and then click the **Home tab** to return to the presentation.

4 On **Slide 2**, click anywhere in the bulleted list placeholder. On the **Animations tab**, in the **Animation group**, click the **More** button, and then under **Entrance**, click **Split**.

a. In the **Animation group**, click the **Effect Options** button, and then click **Vertical Out**.

(Project 3C Lake continues on the next page)

Skills Review | Project 3C Lake (continued)

b. In the **Timing group**, click the **Start arrow**, and then click **With Previous** so that the list displays at the same time as the video begins to play.

c. In the **Timing group**, click the **Duration up arrow** two times so that *01.00* displays in the **Duration** box. Click the **Delay up arrow** one time so that *00.25* displays in the **Delay** box.

5 Display **Slide 5**, and then click in the title placeholder. On the **Animations tab**, in the **Animation group**, click the **More** button, and then under **Entrance**, click **Wipe**. In the **Timing group**, click the **Start arrow**, and then click **After Previous**.

a. Select the title, and then in the **Advanced Animation group**, click the **Animation Painter** button. Click the subtitle to apply the title animation effects to the subtitle.

b. Display **Slide 1**, and then select the title. On the **Animations tab**, in the **Animation group**, click the **More** button, and then click **None** to remove the animation from the title.

c. On the **Slide Show tab**, in the **Start Slide Show group**, click **From Beginning**, and then view your presentation, clicking the mouse button to advance through the slides.

d. Insert a **Header & Footer** for the **Notes and Handouts**. Include the **Date and time updated automatically**, the **Page number**, and a **Footer** with the file name **Lastname_Firstname_3C_Lake** Click **Apply to All**.

e. Show the **Document Panel**. Replace the text in the **Author** box with your own firstname and lastname. In the **Subject** box, type your course name and section number, and in the **Keywords** box, type **Gold Haven, lake** **Close** the **Document Information Panel**.

f. **Save** your presentation. Print **Handouts 6 Slides Horizontal**, or submit your presentation electronically as directed by your instructor. **Close** the presentation.

End **You have completed Project 3C**

Content-Based Assessments

Apply 3B skills from these Objectives:

4 Create and Modify Tables

5 Create and Modify Charts

Skills Review | Project 3D School Enrollment

In the following Skills Review, you will format a presentation by inserting and formatting a table, column chart, and line chart. Your completed presentation will look similar to Figure 3.52.

Project Files

For Project 3D, you will need the following file:

p03D_School_Enrollment

You will save your presentation as:

Lastname_Firstname_3D_School_Enrollment

Project Results

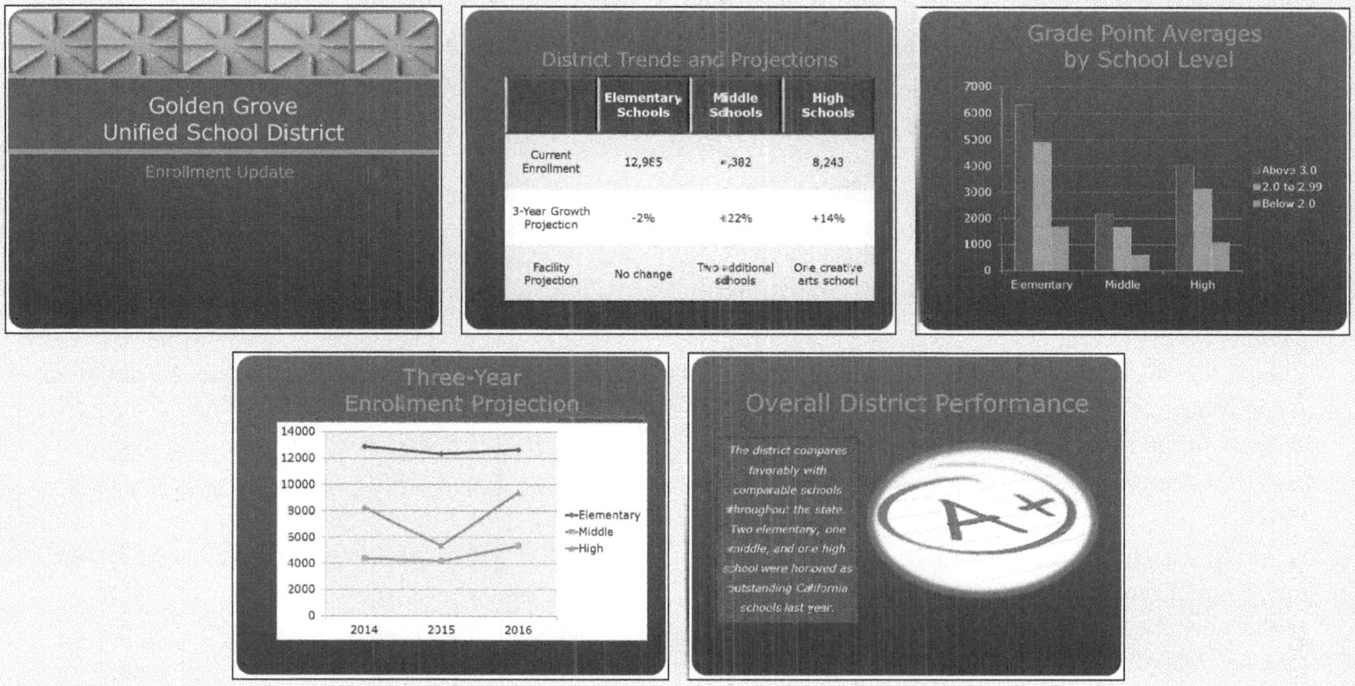

Figure 3.52

(Project 3D School Enrollment continues on the next page)

Skills Review | Project 3D School Enrollment (continued)

1 **Start** PowerPoint, from your student files open **p03D_School_Enrollment**, and then **Save** the presentation in your **PowerPoint Chapter 3** folder as **Lastname_Firstname_3D_School_Enrollment**

a. Display **Slide 2**. In the content placeholder, click the **Insert Table** button to display the **Insert Table** dialog box. In the **Number of columns** box, type **3** and then press Tab. In the **Number of rows** box, type **2** and then click **OK** to create the table.

b. In the first row of the table, click in the *second* cell. Type **Elementary Schools** and then press Tab. Type **High Schools** and then press Tab to move the insertion point to the first cell in the second row.

c. With the insertion point positioned in the first cell of the second row, type **Current Enrollment** and then press Tab. Type **12,985** and then press Tab. Type **8,243** and then press Tab to insert a new blank row. In the first cell of the third row, type **Facility Projection** and then press Tab. Type **No change** and then press Tab. Type **One creative arts school**

d. With the insertion point positioned in the last column, on the **Layout tab**, in the **Rows & Columns group**, click the **Insert Left** button. Click in the top cell of the inserted column, and then type **Middle Schools** In the second and third rows of the inserted column, type **4,382** and **Two additional schools**

e. With the insertion point positioned in the third row, on the **Layout tab**, in the **Rows & Columns group**, click the **Insert Above** button. Click in the first cell of the row you inserted, type **3-Year Growth Projection** and then press Tab. Type the remaining three entries in the row as follows: **-2%** and **+22%** and **+14%**

2 At the center of the lower border surrounding the table, point to the cluster of four dots—the sizing handle—and make the table larger by dragging down until the lower edge of the table aligns at **3 inches on the lower half of the vertical ruler**.

a. Click in the first cell of the table. On the **Layout tab**, in the **Cell Size group**, click the **Distribute Rows** button.

b. On the **Layout tab**, in the **Table group**, click **Select**, and then click **Select Table**. In the **Alignment group**, click the **Center** button, and then click the **Center Vertically** button.

c. Click in any cell in the table. In the **Table Tools**, click the **Design tab**, and then in the **Table Styles group**, click the **More** button. Under **Medium**, in the third row, click the second style—**Medium Style 3 – Accent 1**—to apply the style to the table.

d. Move the pointer outside of the table so that is positioned to the left of the first row in the table to display the ➡ pointer, click one time to select the entire row. Click the **Design tab**, and then in the **Table Styles group**, click the **Effects** button. Point to **Cell Bevel**, and then under **Bevel**, click the first bevel—**Circle**. Change the **Font Size** of the text in the first row to **20**.

3 Display **Slide 3**. In the content placeholder, click the **Insert Chart** button to display the **Insert Chart** dialog box. Click the first chart—*Clustered Column*—and then click **OK**.

a. In the Excel window, click in cell **B1**, which contains the text *Series 1*. Type **Above 3.0** and then press Tab to move to cell **C1**.

b. In cell **C1**, which contains the text *Series 2*, type **2.0 to 2.99** and then press Tab to move to cell **D1**, which contains the text *Series 3*. Type **Below 2.0** and then press Tab.

c. Beginning in cell **A2**, type the following data, pressing Tab to move from cell to cell.

	Above 3.0	2.0 to 2.99	Below 2.0
Elementary	**6318**	**4900**	**1676**
Middle	**2147**	**1665**	**596**
High	**4039**	**3132**	**1070**

d. In the Excel window, position the pointer over **row heading 5** so that the ➡ pointer displays. Then, *right-click* to select the row and display the shortcut menu. On the shortcut menu, click **Delete**. **Close** the Excel window.

e. If necessary, click the edge of the chart so that it is selected. In the **Chart Tools**, click the **Design tab**, and then in the **Chart Styles group**, click the **More** button. In the **Chart Styles** gallery, click **Style 10** to apply the style to the chart.

f. With the chart selected, click the **Animations tab**, and then in the **Animation group**, click the **More** button. Under **Entrance**, click **Split**. In the

(Project 3D School Enrollment continues on the next page)

Skills Review | Project 3D School Enrollment (continued)

Animation group, click the **Effect Options** button, and then under **Sequence**, click **By Series**.

4 Display **Slide 4**. In the content placeholder, click the **Insert Chart** button. On the left side of the displayed **Insert Chart** dialog box, click **Line**, and then under **Line**, click the fourth chart—**Line with Markers**. Click **OK**.

a. In the Excel worksheet, click in cell **B1**, which contains the text *Series 1*. Type **Elementary** and then press Tab. Type **Middle** and then press Tab. Type **High** and then press Tab.

b. Beginning in cell **A2**, type the following data, pressing Tab to move from cell to cell.

	Elementary	Middle	High
2014	12895	4382	8243
2015	12322	4156	5346
2016	12637	5346	9397

c. In the Excel window, position the pointer over **row heading 5** so that the ➡ pointer displays. Then, right-click to select the row and display the shortcut menu. On the shortcut menu, click **Delete**. **Close** the Excel window.

d. On the **Chart Tools Design tab**, in the **Chart Styles group**, click the **More** button. In the **Chart Styles** gallery, click **Style 34**.

e. Insert a **Header & Footer** for the **Notes and Handouts**. Include the **Date and time updated automatically**, the **Page number**, and a **Footer** with the file name **Lastname_Firstname_3D_School_Enrollment** Click **Apply to All**.

f. Show the **Document Panel**. Replace the text in the **Author** box with your own firstname and lastname. In the **Subject** box, type your course name and section number, and in the **Keywords** box, type **enrollment, schools Close** the **Document Information Panel**.

g. View the slide show from the beginning, and then **Save** your presentation. Print **Handouts 6 Slides Horizontal**, or submit your presentation electronically as directed by your instructor. **Close** the presentation and exit PowerPoint.

End You have completed Project 3D

Apply 3A skills from these Objectives:

1. Customize Slide Backgrounds and Themes
2. Animate a Slide Show
3. Insert a Video

Mastering PowerPoint | Project 3E Spotlight Neighborhood

In the following Mastering PowerPoint project, you will format a presentation created by the Golden Grove Public Relations department that announces the winner of the Spotlight Neighborhood award. Your completed presentation will look similar to Figure 3.53.

Project Files

For Project 3E, you will need the following files:

p03E_Spotlight_Neighborhood
p03E_Neighborhood
p03E_Neighborhood_Video

You will save your presentation as:

Lastname_Firstname_3E_Spotlight_Neighborhood

Project Results

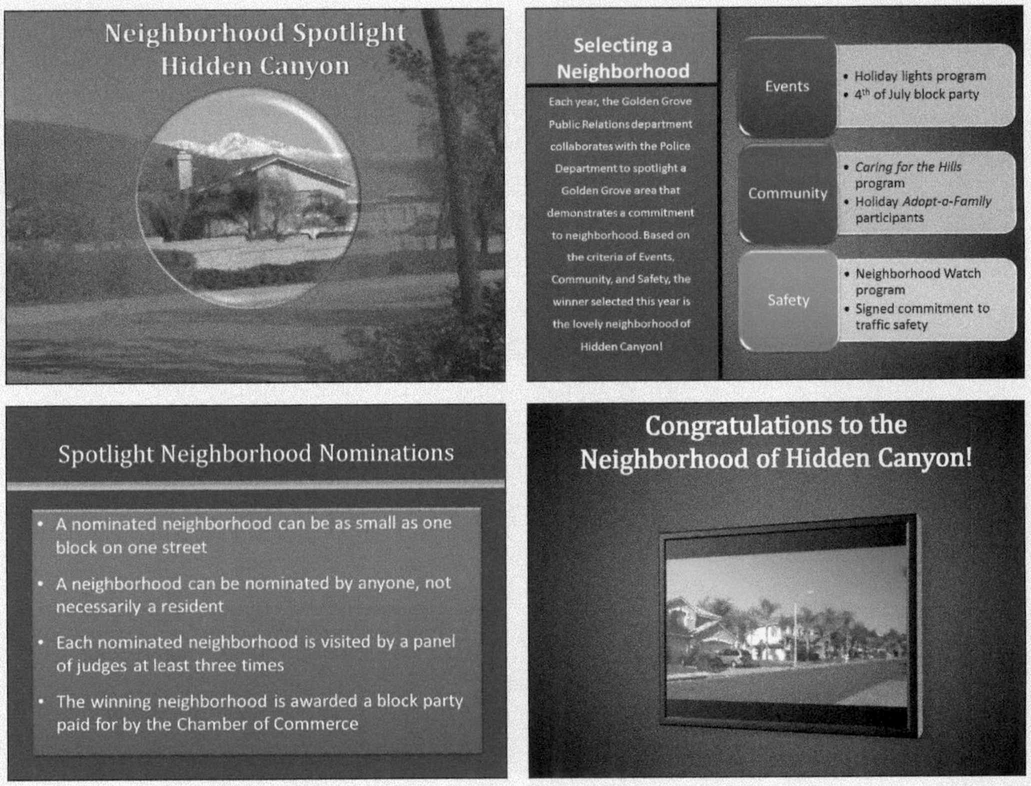

Figure 3.53

(Project 3E Spotlight Neighborhood continues on the next page)

Mastering PowerPoint | Project 3E Spotlight Neighborhood (continued)

1 **Start** PowerPoint. From the student files that accompany this textbook, locate and open **p03E_Spotlight_Neighborhood.** Change the **Theme Colors** for the presentation to **Office**, and the **Theme Fonts** to **Adjacency**. **Save** the presentation in your **PowerPoint Chapter 3** folder as **Lastname_Firstname_3E_Spotlight_Neighborhood**

2 On **Slide 1**, hide the background graphics, and then format the slide background by inserting a picture from your student files—**p03E_Neighborhood**. To the title, apply the first **WordArt** style—**Fill - Tan Text 2, Outline - Background 2**.

3 On **Slide 2**, display the **Background Styles** gallery, right-click **Background Style 12**, and then apply the style to this slide only. Select the paragraph on the left side of the slide, and then change the **Font Color** to **White, Text 1**. With the paragraph selected, apply the **Split** entrance effect, and then change the **Effect Options** to **Horizontal Out**. Change the **Start** setting to **After Previous**, and then change the **Duration** to **01.00**. Animate the **SmartArt** graphic by applying the **Fade** entrance effect and so that it starts **With Previous**.

4 On **Slide 3**, format the **Background Style** by applying a **Solid fill—Dark Blue, Text 2**. Change the **Font Color** of the title text to **White, Background 1**. Remove the entrance effect from the title.

5 On **Slide 4**, hide the background graphics, and then apply background **Style 12**. From your student files, insert the video **p03E_Neighborhood_Video**. Change the **Video Height** to **4** and **Align Center** the video. Format the video by applying, from the **Video Styles** gallery, an **Intense** style—**Monitor, Gray**. Change the **Start** setting to **Automatically**.

6 Display **Slide 2**, and then use **Animation Painter** to apply the animation from the paragraph on the left side of the slide to the bulleted list on **Slide 3**.

7 **Insert** a **Header & Footer** on the **Notes and Handouts**. Include the **Date and time updated automatically**, the **Page** number, and a **Footer** with the text **Lastname_Firstname_3E_Spotlight_Neighborhood**

8 Update the **Document Properties** with your name, course name and section number, and the **Keywords** **spotlight neighborhood** **Close** the **Document Information Panel**.

9 **Save** your presentation, and then view the slide show from the beginning. Submit your presentation electronically, or print **Handouts 4 Slides Horizontal** as directed by your instructor. **Close** the presentation.

End **You have completed Project 3E**

PowerPoint | Chapter 3

Apply 3B skills from these Objectives:

4 Create and Modify Tables

5 Create and Modify Charts

Mastering PowerPoint | Project 3F Water Conservation

In the following Mastering PowerPoint project, you will format a presentation that the Golden Grove Chief Water Engineer will present at a community forum. Your completed presentation will look similar to Figure 3.54.

Project Files

For Project 3F, you will need the following file:

p03F_Water_Conservation

You will save your presentation as:

Lastname_Firstname_3F_Water_Conservation

Project Results

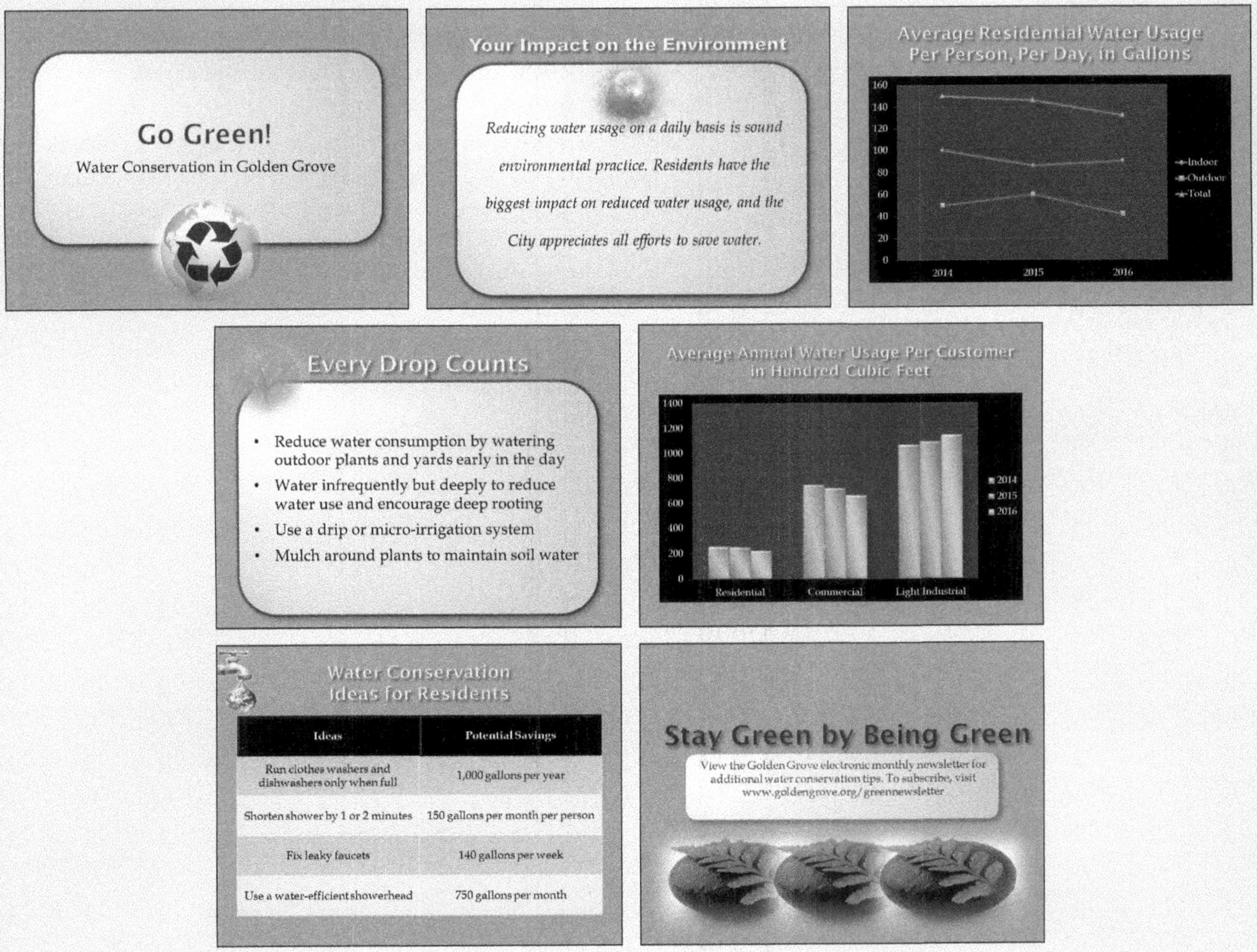

Figure 3.54

(Project 3F Water Conservation continues on the next page)

Mastering PowerPoint | Project 3F Water Conservation (continued)

1 **Start** PowerPoint. From your student files open **p03F_Water_Conservation**, and then **Save** the presentation in your **PowerPoint Chapter 3** folder as **Lastname_Firstname_3F_Water_Conservation**

2 On **Slide 3**, in the content placeholder, insert a **Line with Markers** chart. In the Excel worksheet, in cell **B1**, type **Indoor** and then enter the following data:

	Indoor	Outdoor	Total
2014	100	50	150
2015	86	60	146
2016	90	42	132

3 In the Excel window, delete **row 5**, and then **Close** the Excel window. Apply **Chart Style 42** to the chart, and then apply the **Wipe** entrance effect to the chart.

4 On **Slide 5**, in the content placeholder, insert a **Clustered Column** chart. In the Excel worksheet, in cell **B1**, type **2014** and then enter the following data:

	2014	2015	2016
Residential	256	249	225
Commercial	746	718	660
Light Industrial	1065	1092	1146

5 In the Excel window, delete **row 5**, and then **Close** the Excel window. Apply **Chart Style 42** to the chart, and then apply the **Wipe** entrance effect to the chart. Change the **Effect Options** so that the animation is applied **By Series**. Change the **Timing** so that the animation starts **After Previous**.

6 On **Slide 6**, in the content placeholder, insert a **Table** with **2 columns** and **5 rows**, and then type the text in **Table 1** at the bottom of the page.

7 Resize the table so that its lower edge extends to **3 inches on the lower half of the vertical ruler**, and then distribute the table rows. Align the table text so that it is centered horizontally and vertically within the cells. Apply table style **Medium Style 2**, and then apply a **Circle Bevel** to the first row. Change the table text **Font Size** to **20**.

8 Insert a **Header & Footer** for the **Notes and Handouts**. Include the **Date and time updated automatically**, the **Page number**, and a **Footer** with the file name **Lastname_Firstname_3F_Water_Conservation** Update the **Document Properties** with your name, course name and section number, and the **Keywords water conservation** **Close** the **Document Information Panel**.

9 View the slide show from the beginning, and then **Save** your presentation. Print **Handouts 4 Slides Horizontal**, or submit your presentation electronically as directed by your instructor. **Close** the presentation.

Table 1

Ideas	Potential Savings
Run clothes washers and dishwashers only when full	1,000 gallons per year
Shorten shower by 1 or 2 minutes	150 gallons per month per person
Fix leaky faucets	140 gallons per week
Use a water-efficient showerhead	750 gallons per month

---> (Return to Step 7)

End **You have completed Project 3F**

Apply 3A and 3B skills from these Objectives:

1. Customize Slide Backgrounds and Themes
2. Animate a Slide Show
3. Insert a Video
4. Create and Modify Tables
5. Create and Modify Charts

Mastering PowerPoint | Project 3G Restaurants

In the following Mastering PowerPoint project, you will format a presentation that the Golden Grove Public Relations Director will show at a meeting of the National Restaurant Owners Association to encourage new restaurant and catering business in the city. Your completed presentation will look similar to Figure 3.55.

Project Files

For Project 3G, you will need the following files:

p03G_Restaurants
p03G_Town_Center
p03G_Catering

You will save your presentation as:

Lastname_Firstname_3G_Restaurants

Project Results

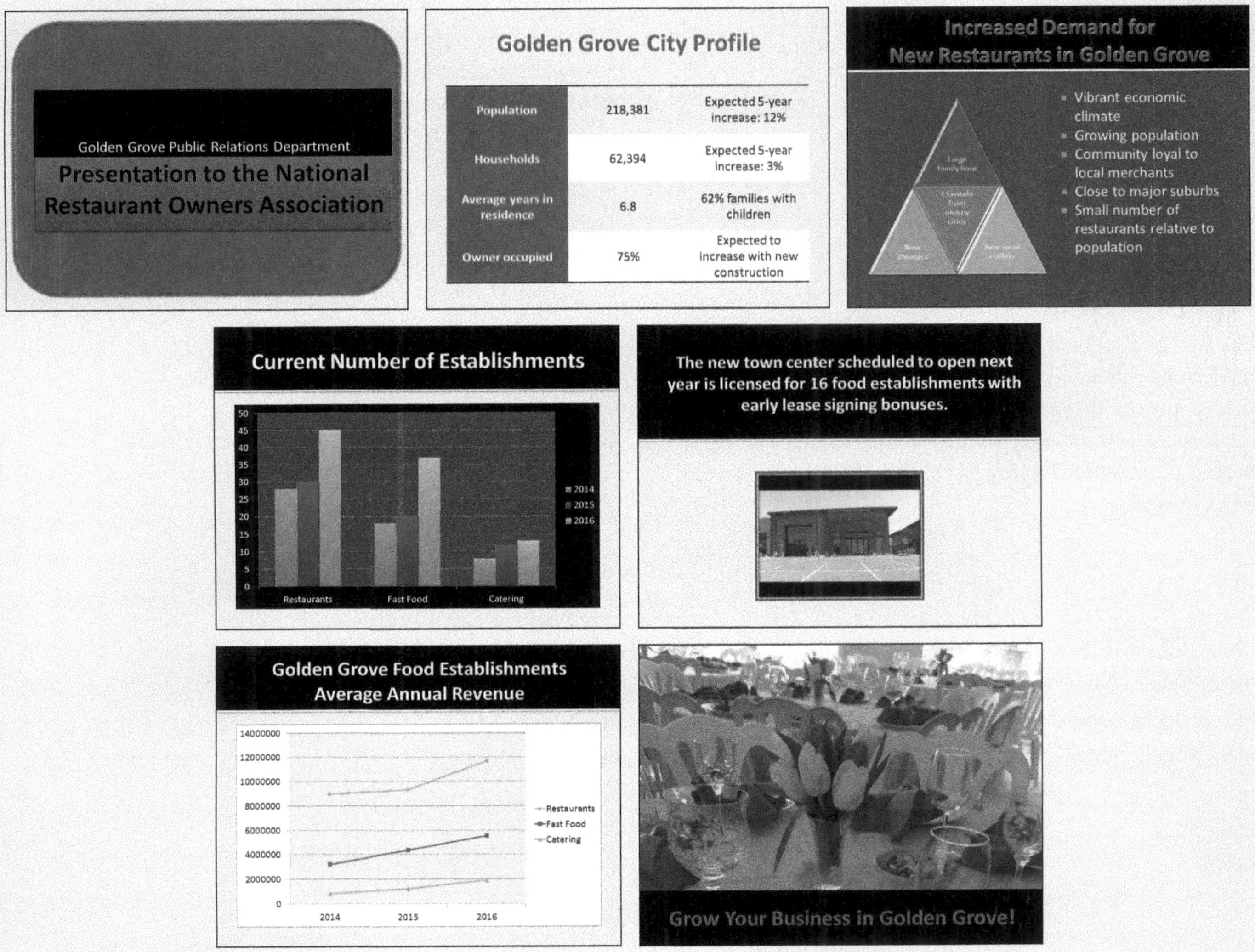

Figure 3.55

(Project 3G Restaurants continues on the next page)

Mastering PowerPoint | Project 3G Restaurants (continued)

1 **Start** PowerPoint. From the student files that accompany this textbook, locate and open **p03G_Restaurants**. Change the **Theme Colors** for the presentation to **Apothecary**, and the **Theme Fonts** to **Composite**. **Save** the presentation in your **PowerPoint Chapter 3** folder as **Lastname_Firstname_3G_Restaurants**

2 On **Slide 2**, insert a **Table** with **3 columns** and **4 rows**. Apply table style **Medium Style 3 - Accent 2**, and then type the information in **Table 1**, shown at the bottom of this page, into the inserted table.

3 On the **Design tab**, in the **Table Style Options group**, select *only* the **First Column** and **Banded Rows** check boxes. Resize the table so that its lower edge extends to **3 inches on the lower half of the vertical ruler**, and then distribute the table rows. Align the table text so that it is centered horizontally and vertically within the cells, and then change the **Font Size** of all of the table text to **24**.

4 On **Slide 3**, display the **Background Styles** gallery, right-click **Background Style 3**, and then apply the style to this slide only. Animate the **SmartArt** graphic using the **Wipe** entrance effect starting **After Previous**. Apply the **Split** entrance effect to the bulleted list placeholder, and then change the **Effect Options** to **Vertical Out**.

5 On **Slide 4**, insert a **Clustered Column** chart. In the Excel worksheet, in cell **B1** type **2014** and then enter the following data:

	2014	2015	2016
Restaurants	28	30	45
Fast Food	18	20	37
Catering	8	12	13

6 In the Excel window, delete **row 5**, and then **Close** the Excel window. Apply **Chart Style 42** to the chart, and then apply the **Wipe** entrance effect to the chart.

7 On **Slide 5**, from your student files, insert the video **p03G_Town_Center**. Change the **Video Height** to **3** and then drag the video down so that its top edge aligns at **zero on the vertical ruler**. Apply the **Align Center** alignment option, display the **Video Styles** gallery, and then apply the first **Moderate** style—**Compound Frame, Black**. Change the **Video Border** to **Gray-50%, Accent 1, Darker 50%**—in the fifth column, the last color.

8 On the **Playback tab**, change the **Video Options** to **Start** the video **Automatically**. **Trim** the video so that the **End Time** is **00:05.560**

9 On **Slide 6**, in the content placeholder, insert a **Line with Markers** chart. In the Excel worksheet, in cell **B1**, type **Restaurants** and then enter the following data:

	Restaurants	Fast Food	Catering
2014	8956231	3284680	856700
2015	9326852	4369571	1235640
2016	11689730	5526895	1894325

10 In the Excel window, delete **row 5**, and then **Close** the Excel window. Apply **Chart Style 34** to the chart, and then use **Animation Painter** to copy the animation from the column chart on **Slide 4** to the line chart on **Slide 6**.

11 On **Slide 7**, hide the background graphics. Format the slide background by inserting a picture from your student files—**p03G_Catering**. Change the title placeholder **Shape Fill** color to **Black, Text 1**, and then change the **Font Color** to **Red, Accent 2**. Size the placeholder so that it extends from the left edge of the slide to the right edge of the slide, and then position it so that its lower edge aligns with the lower edge of the slide. **Center** the text.

12 Insert a **Header & Footer** for the **Notes and Handouts**. Include the **Date and time updated automatically**, the **Page number**, and a **Footer** with the file name **Lastname_Firstname_3G_Restaurants** Update the **Properties** with your name, course name and section number, and the **Keywords catering, restaurants Close** the **Document Information Panel**.

13 View the slide show from the beginning, and then **Save** your presentation. Print **Handouts 4 Slides Horizontal**, or submit your presentation electronically as directed by your instructor. **Close** the presentation.

Table 1

Population	218,381	Expected 5-year increase: 12%
Households	62,394	Expected 5-year increase: 3%
Average years in residence	6.8	62% families with children
Owner occupied	75%	Expected to increase with new construction

---> (Return to Step 3)

End **You have completed Project 3G**

Apply a combination of the 3A and 3B skills.

GO! Fix It | Project 3H Housing Developments

Project Files

For Project 3H, you will need the following file:

p03H_Housing_Developments

You will save your presentation as:

Lastname_Firstname_3H_Housing_Developments

In this project, you will edit several slides from a presentation prepared by the Golden Grove Planning Department regarding real estate developments in the city. From the student files that accompany this textbook, open the file p03H_Housing_Developments, and then save the file in your chapter folder as **Lastname_Firstname_3H_Housing_Developments**

To complete the project, you should know:

- The Theme Colors should be changed to Module and the Theme Fonts should be changed to Apex.
- The titles on Slides 2 and 3 should be centered.
- On Slide 2, the table style Light Style 2 - Accent 2 should be applied and a column should be added to right of the last column in the table. In the inserted column, the following text should be entered in the three cells: **Bering** and **37%** and **August 2016**
- On Slides 3 and 4, the charts should be animated with the Wipe entrance effect.
- Document Properties should include your name, course name and section, and the keywords **property tax, housing** A Header & Footer should be inserted on the Notes and Handouts that includes the Date and time updated automatically, the Page number and a Footer with the text **Lastname_Firstname_3H_Housing_Developments**

Save and submit your presentation electronically or print Handouts 4 Slides Horizontal as directed by your instructor. Close the presentation.

End You have completed Project 3H

Apply a combination of the 3A and 3B skills.

GO! Make It | Project 3I Arboretum

Project Files

For Project 3I, you will need the following files:

New blank PowerPoint presentation
p03I_Flowers

You will save your presentation as:

Lastname_Firstname_3I_Arboretum

Start PowerPoint to begin a new blank presentation, and apply the Opulent theme. Save the file in your PowerPoint Chapter 3 folder as **Lastname_Firstname_3I_Arboretum**

By using the skills you practiced in this chapter, create the first two slides of the presentation shown in Figure 3.56. The layout for Slide 1 is Title Only, and the background is formatted with the picture from your student data file— p03I_Flowers. The title Shape Fill color is Purple, Accent 2, Darker 50%. On Slide 2, insert and format the table as shown. Change the Font Size of the text in the first row to 32. Insert the file name, date, and page number in the Notes and Handouts footer. In the Document Information Panel, add your name and course information and the Keywords **arboretum, events** Save, and then print or submit electronically as directed by your instructor.

Project Results

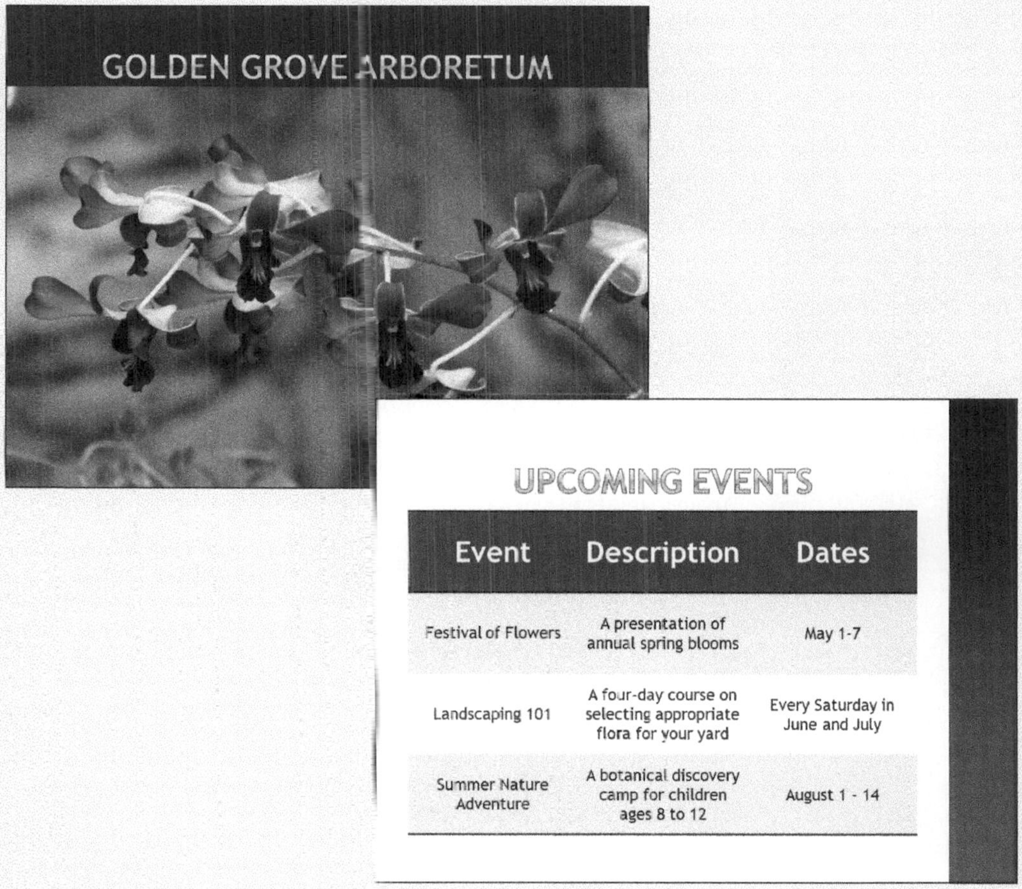

Figure 3.56

End **You have completed Project 3I**

Apply a combination of the 3A and 3B skills.

GO! Solve It | Project 3J Aquatic Center

Project Files

For Project 3J, you will need the following file:

p03J_Aquatic_Center

You will save your presentation as:

Lastname_Firstname_3J_Aquatic_Center

Open the file p03J_Aquatic_Center and save it as **Lastname_Firstname_3J_Aquatic_Center** Complete the presentation by changing the Theme Fonts and then formatting the slide background of at least one of the slides using a Background Style or Solid Fill color. On Slide 4, insert and format a table with the following information regarding the fee schedule for swim passes.

Membership	Monthly	Seasonal
Youth	$10	$25
Adult	$25	$50
Senior	$15	$30

Apply appropriate animation and slide transitions to the slides. Insert a header and footer that includes the date and time updated automatically, the file name in the footer, and the page number. Add your name, your course name and section number, and the keywords **aquatic center, swim program** to the Properties area. Save and then print, or submit it as directed by your instructor.

	Performance Level		
Performance Elements	**Exemplary:** You consistently applied the relevant skills	**Proficient:** You sometimes, but not always, applied the relevant skills	**Developing:** You rarely or never applied the relevant skills
Format slide with a background style	Slide background style was applied to at least one slide and text displayed with good contrast against the background.	Slide background was formatted but text did not display well against the chosen background.	Slide background was not formatted with a background style.
Insert and format appropriate table	Appropriate table was inserted and formatted.	A table was inserted but was not appropriately formatted.	Table was not inserted.
Apply appropriate animation	Appropriate animation was applied to the presentation.	Animation was applied but was not appropriate for the presentation.	Animation was not applied.

End **You have completed Project 3J**

Apply a combination of the 3A and 3B skills.

GO! Solve It | Project 3K Power

Project Files

For Project 3K, you will need the following files:

p03K_Power
p03K_Tower

You will save your presentation as:

Lastname_Firstname_3K_Power

Open the file p03K_Power and save it as **Lastname_Firstname_3K_Power** Complete the presentation by applying a theme and then formatting the slide background of one of the slides with the picture found in your student files—p03K_Tower. Adjust the size, position, fill color, and font color of the slide titles as necessary so that the title text displays attractively against the background picture. Format the background of at least one other slide using a Background Style or Solid Fill color. Insert a new Slide 3 that includes an appropriate title and a table with the following information regarding the power sources that the City uses.

Power Sources	Percent Used by City
Natural gas	32%
Hydroelectric	17%
Renewables	18%
Coal	23%
Nuclear	10%

On Slide 4, insert and format an appropriate chart to demonstrate the revenue collected from residential power sales over the past three years. Revenue in 2014 was 35.5 million dollars, in 2015 revenue was 42.6 million dollars, and in 2016 revenue was 48.2 million dollars. Apply appropriate animation and slide transitions to the slides. Insert a header and footer that includes the date and time updated automatically, the file name in the footer, and the page number. Add your name, your course name and section number, and the keywords **power sources, revenue** to the Properties area. Save and then print or submit the presentation as directed by your instructor.

Performance Elements	Performance Level: Exemplary: You consistently applied the relevant skills	Proficient: You sometimes, but not always, applied the relevant skills	Developing: You rarely or never applied the relevant skills
Format two slide backgrounds with pictures and styles	Two slide backgrounds were formatted attractively and text displayed with good contrast against backgrounds.	Slide backgrounds were formatted but text did not display well against the chosen background, or only one slide background was formatted.	Slide backgrounds were not formatted with pictures or styles.
Insert and format appropriate table and chart	Appropriate table and chart were inserted and formatted and the entered data was accurate.	A table and a chart were inserted but were not appropriate for the presentation or either a table or a chart was omitted.	Table and chart were not inserted.
Apply appropriate animation	Appropriate animation was applied to the presentation.	Animation was applied but was not appropriate for the presentation.	Animation was not applied.

End You have completed Project 3K

Rubric

The following outcomes-based assessments are *open-ended assessments*. That is, there is no specific correct result; your result will depend on your approach to the information provided. Make *Professional Quality* your goal. Use the following scoring rubric to guide you in *how* to approach the problem, and then to evaluate *how well* your approach solves the problem.

The *criteria*—Software Mastery, Content, Format and Layout, and Process—represent the knowledge and skills you have gained that you can apply to solving the problem. The *levels of performance*—Professional Quality, Approaching Professional Quality, or Needs Quality Improvements—help you and your instructor evaluate your result.

	Your completed project is of Professional Quality if you:	**Your completed project is Approaching Professional Quality if you:**	**Your completed project Needs Quality Improvements if you:**
1-Software Mastery	Choose and apply the most appropriate skills, tools, and features and identify efficient methods to solve the problem.	Choose and apply some appropriate skills, tools, and features, but not in the most efficient manner.	Choose inappropriate skills, tools, or features, or are inefficient in solving the problem.
2-Content	Construct a solution that is clear and well organized, contains content that is accurate, appropriate to the audience and purpose, and is complete. Provide a solution that contains no errors in spelling, grammar, or style.	Construct a solution in which some components are unclear, poorly organized, inconsistent, or incomplete. Misjudge the needs of the audience. Have some errors in spelling, grammar, or style, but the errors do not detract from comprehension.	Construct a solution that is unclear, incomplete, or poorly organized; contains some inaccurate or inappropriate content; and contains many errors in spelling, grammar, or style. Do not solve the problem.
3-Format and Layout	Format and arrange all elements to communicate information and ideas, clarify function, illustrate relationships, and indicate relative importance.	Apply appropriate format and layout features to some elements, but not others. Overuse features, causing minor distraction.	Apply format and layout that does not communicate information or ideas clearly. Do not use format and layout features to clarify function, illustrate relationships, or indicate relative importance. Use available features excessively, causing distraction.
4-Process	Use an organized approach that integrates planning, development, self-assessment, revision, and reflection.	Demonstrate an organized approach in some areas, but not others; or, use an insufficient process of organization throughout.	Do not use an organized approach to solve the problem.

Apply a combination of the 3A and 3B skills.

GO! Think | Project 3L Animal Sanctuary

Project Files

For Project 3L, you will need the following file:

New blank PowerPoint presentation

You will save your presentation as:

Lastname_Firstname_3L_Animal Sanctuary

The Golden Grove Animal Sanctuary, a non-profit organization, provides shelter and care for animals in need, including dogs, cats, hamsters, and guinea pigs. The Sanctuary, which celebrates its tenth anniversary in July, has cared for more than 12,000 animals since it opened and is a state-of-the-art facility. Funding for the Sanctuary comes in the form of business sponsorships, individual donations, and pet adoption fees. The following table indicates revenue generated by the Sanctuary during the past three years.

	Fees	Donations	Sponsorships
2014	125,085	215,380	175,684
2015	110,680	256,785	156,842
2016	132,455	314,682	212,648

In addition to shelter services, the Sanctuary offers community service and training programs, veterinarian services, and vaccine clinics. Examples of these services include Canine Obedience classes, microchipping ($25 fee), and the Healthy Pet Hotline (free). Canine Obedience classes are for puppies and adult dogs to improve obedience, socialization, and behavior. Classes last two, three, or four months and cost $150 to $250.

Using the preceding information, create the first five slides of a presentation that the director of the Golden Grove Animal Sanctuary will show at an upcoming pet fair. Apply an appropriate theme and use slide layouts that will effectively present the content. Include a line chart with the revenue data, a table with the community service programs information, and at least one slide formatted with a dog or cat on the slide background. Apply styles to the table and chart, and apply animation and slide transitions to the slides. Use the techniques that you practiced in this chapter so that your presentation is professional and attractive. Save the file as **Lastname_Firstname_3L_Animal_Sanctuary** and then insert a header and footer that includes the date and time updated automatically, the file name in the footer, and the page number. Add your name, your course name and section number, and the keywords **animals, pets** to the Properties area. Save and then print or submit the presentation as directed by your instructor.

End **You have completed Project 3L**

Outcomes-Based Assessments

Apply a combination of the 3A and 3B skills.

GO! Think | Project 3M Water Sources

Project Files

For Project 3M, you will need the following file:

New blank PowerPoint presentation

You will save your presentation as:

Lastname_Firstname_3M_Water_Sources

The Golden Grove Department of Water and Power operations are financed solely through sales of water and electric services. A portion of capital expenditures are funded through the sale of municipal bonds. The city's water supply is generated from a number of sources, with 35% from the Sierra Nevada aqueduct system, 42% from water districts, 18% from groundwater, and 5% from recycled sources. This supply provides water for the City's residents and commercial and industrial customers.

In the past three years, the Department has renovated several reservoirs and pump stations, resulting in better reserves and emergency preparedness capacity. The following table details the in-city reservoir capacities over the past three years. Water capacity is measured in acre feet, in which one acre foot is equal to approximately 325,000 gallons. Years in which zero or low capacity is specified indicates years in which the reservoir was undergoing renovation.

	2014	2015	2016
Elkhart Reservoir	350	1250	2243
Gold Lake Reservoir	3685	865	2865
Diamond Canyon Reservoir	2650	3850	4635

Using the preceding information, create a title slide and four additional slides of a presentation that the Golden Grove Chief Water Engineer can show at an upcoming City Council meeting. Apply an appropriate theme and use slide layouts that will effectively present the content. Include a table that details the water supply sources, and a column chart with the reservoir information. Apply animation and slide transitions and use the techniques that you practiced in this chapter so that your presentation is professional and attractive. Save the file as **Lastname_Firstname_3M_Water_Sources** and then insert a header and footer that includes the date and time updated automatically, the file name in the footer, and the page number. Add your name, your course name and section number, and the keywords **reservoirs, water capacity** to the Properties area. Save, and then print or submit the presentation as directed by your instructor.

End **You have completed Project 3M**

Outcomes-Based Assessments

Apply a combination of the 3A and 3B skills.

You and GO! | Project 3N Recreation Programs

Project Files

For Project 3N, you will need the following file:

New blank PowerPoint presentation

You will save your presentation as:

Lastname_Firstname_3N_Recreation_Programs

Research the recreation programs available in the city in which you live, and then create a presentation about the program. Include a table that describes some of the activities, the location in which they are held, and the fees. Choose an appropriate theme, slide layouts, and pictures, and format the presentation attractively, including at least one slide with a picture on the slide background. Save your presentation as **Lastname_Firstname_3N_Recreation_Programs** and submit as directed.

End **You have completed Project 3N**

Apply a combination of the 3A and 3B skills.

GO! Collaborate | Project 3O Bell Orchid Hotels Group Running Case

This project relates to the **Bell Orchid Hotels**. Your instructor may assign this group case project to your class. If your instructor assigns this project, he or she will provide you with information and instructions to work as part of a group. The group will apply the skills gained thus far to help the Bell Orchid Hotels achieve their business goals.

End **You have completed Project 3O**

Business Running Case

Razvan CHIRNOAGA/Shutterstock

This project relates to **Front Range Action Sports**, which is one of the country's largest retailers of sports gear and outdoor recreation merchandise. The company has large retail stores in Colorado, Washington, Oregon, California, and New Mexico, in addition to a growing online business. Major merchandise categories include fishing, camping, rock climbing, winter sports, action sports, water sports, team sports, racquet sports, fitness, golf, apparel, and footwear.

In this project, you will apply skills you practiced from the Objectives in PowerPoint Chapters 1 through 3. You will develop a presentation that Irene Shviktar, Vice President of Marketing, will show at a corporate marketing retreat that summarizes the company's plans to expand the winter sports product line. Your completed presentation will look similar to Figure 1.1.

Project Files

For Project BRC1, you will need the following files:

pBRC1_Company_Overview
pBRC1_Heights
pBRC1_Lake
pBRC1_Mountain
pBRC1_Skiing
pBRC1_Winter_Products

You will save your presentation as:
Lastname_Firstname_BRC1_Winter_Products

Project Results

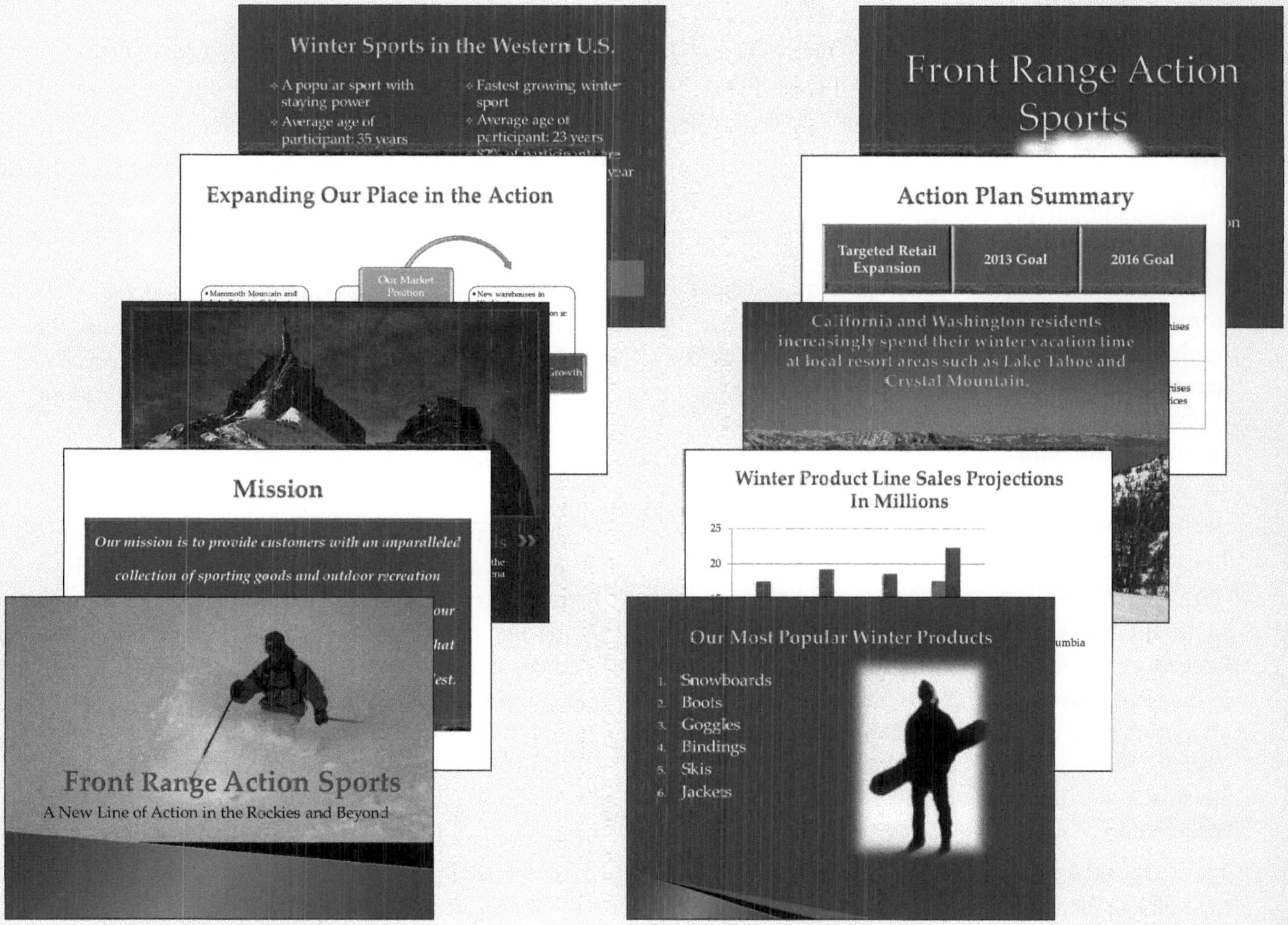

Figure 1.1

Front Range Action Sports (continued)

1 **Start** PowerPoint. From the student files that accompany this textbook, locate and open **pBRC1_Winter_Products**. In the location where you are storing your projects, create a new folder named **Front Range Action Sports** or navigate to this folder if you have already created it. **Save** the presentation as **Lastname_Firstname_BRC1_Winter_Products**

a. Display **Slide 1**. Change the presentation theme to **Concourse**, and then change the **Theme Colors** to **Office**. Change the **Theme Fonts** to **Elemental**. On **Slide 1**, format the background with a picture from your student files—**pBRC1_Skiing**.

b. Display the **Reuse Slides** pane. Browse your student files, and display in the **Reuse Slides** pane **pBRC1_Company_Overview**. Insert the second slide—**Mission**—as **Slide 2**, and then **Close** the **Reuse Slides** pane. Remove the bullet symbol from the paragraph, **Center** the text, and then apply **Bold** and **Italic**.

c. With **Slide 2** displayed, change the **Line Spacing** of the content placeholder text to **2.0**. Change the **Shape Fill** to the first color in the fourth column—**Dark Blue, Text 2**, and then change the **Font Color** to **White, Background 1**. Format the placeholder with the first **Bevel** shape effect—**Circle**—and then hide the background graphics on the slide.

d. Display **Slide 3**, and then in the picture placeholder, from your student files insert **pBRC1_Heights**. Apply the first **Glow** picture effect—**Blue, 5 pt glow, Accent color 1**. Format the slide background by applying **Style 12**, being sure to apply the background only to **Slide 3**.

2 Display **Slide 4**, and then in the content placeholder, insert the **Process** SmartArt graphic **Alternating Flow**. Change the color to **Colorful - Accent Colors**, and then apply **3-D Cartoon** style.

a. In the **red shape**, type **Washington and California Resorts** and then click in the first bullet point in the rounded rectangle above the red shape. Type **Mammoth Mountain and Lake Tahoe in California** Click in the second bullet point, and then type **Mission Ridge and Crystal Mountain in Washington**

b. In the **green shape**, type **Our Market Position** and then click in the first bullet point in the rounded rectangle below the green shape. Type **Trusted brand name in the sporting world** In the second bullet point, type **Winter sports product line not fully marketed in the Western United States**

c. In the **purple shape**, type **Poised for Growth** and then click in the first bullet point in the rounded rectangle above the purple shape. Type **New warehouses in Washington** In the second bullet point, type **Proposed retail division in Northern California**

d. Animate the SmartArt by applying the **Wipe** entrance effect. Change the **Start** option so that the SmartArt animation begins **After Previous**.

3 Display **Slide 5**, and then apply background **Style 3** to the slide. In both content placeholders, change the bullet symbol to **Star Bullets**, and then change the bullet **Color** to **Olive Green, Accent 3**. In the **blue shapes** at the bottom of the slide, change the **Font Color** to **White, Text 1**.

a. Insert a **Down Arrow** shape by clicking on the slide with the guides aligned with the **left half of the horizontal ruler at 3 inches** and with the **lower half of the vertical ruler at 1 inch.**

b. Change the arrow **Shape Height** to **1** and the **Shape Width** to **0.5** and then apply the fourth **Shape Style** in the first row—**Colored Outline - Olive Green, Accent 3**. Select the arrow, the content placeholder on the left, and the *Skiing* shape, and then on the **Format tab**, in the **Arrange group**, click the **Align** button. Click **Align Selected Objects**. Click the **Align** button again, and then click **Align Center.**

c. Duplicate the arrow shape, and then drag the duplicated arrow so that its left edge aligns with the **right half of the horizontal ruler at 2 inches** and its top edge aligns with the **lower half of the vertical ruler at 1 inch**. Select the arrow, the content placeholder on the right, and the *Snowboarding* shape, and then using the **Align Selected Objects** option apply **Align Center**. Select the two arrows, and then using the **Align Selected Objects** option, apply **Align Top** to the two arrow shapes.

4 With **Slide 5** displayed, insert a **New Slide** with the **Two Content** layout and then apply background **Style 3** to the inserted slide. Type the slide title **Our Most Popular Winter Products** Change the **Font Size** to **32** and then **Center** the title.

(Business Running Case: Front Range Action Sports continues on the next page)

Front Range Action Sports (continued)

a. In the content placeholder on the left, type the following six bullet points:

Snowboards
Boots
Goggles
Bindings
Skis
Jackets

b. Change the bulleted list to **Numbering**, and then change the number **Color** to **White, Text 1**.

c. In the placeholder on the right, insert a **Clip Art** by searching for a **Photograph** with the keyword **snowboard** Insert the black and white silhouette picture of the person holding a snowboard behind his back. If you cannot locate the picture, choose another image, and then **Close** the Clip Art pane.

d. Change the **Height** of the picture to **5** and then move the picture so that its upper left corner aligns with **zero on the horizontal ruler** and with the **upper half of the vertical ruler at 2.5 inches**. Apply a **Soft Edges** picture effect of **25 Point**.

e. Display **Slide 7**, and then in the content placeholder, insert a **Clustered Column** chart. In the **Excel** worksheet, enter the following data.

	Oregon	Colorado	British Columbia
2012	12.2	17.5	6.5
2013	14.5	19.2	8.7
2014	11.9	18.6	10.6
2015	17.6	22.4	11.3

f. **Close** the Excel worksheet. Apply **Chart Style 26**, and then animate the chart by applying the **Wipe** entrance effect.

5 Display **Slide 8**, and then hide the background graphics on the slide. Format the background with a picture from your student files—**pBRC1_Lake**.

a. Select the title placeholder, and then using the **Align to Slide** option, align the title using the **Align Top** and **Align Center** options.

b. Display **Slide 9**, and then in the content placeholder, insert a **Table** with **3** columns and **3** rows. Type the following text in the table.

Targeted Retail Expansion	2013 Goal	2016 Goal
Northern California	Three new franchises with rental services	Four new franchises
Central and Eastern Washington	Four new franchises with rental services and lessons	Eight new franchises with rental services

c. Apply the **Light Style 2 - Accent 1** table style, and then resize the table so that its lower left corner touches the graphic in the lower left corner of the slide. Distribute the table rows.

d. To the first row, apply the first **Cell Bevel** effect—**Circle**, and then change the **Font Size** to **24**. Center all of the text in the table horizontally and vertically, and then apply the **Wipe** entrance effect to the table.

6 Display **Slide 10**. Apply background **Style 3** to the slide, and then hide the background graphics. To the title, apply the fourth **WordArt** style in the first row **Fill - White, Outline -Accent 1**.

a. With **Slide 10** displayed, from your student files, insert the picture **pBRC1_Mountain**. Change the picture **Height** to **2.5** and then apply a **Soft Edges** picture effect of **25 Point**. Use the **Crop to Shape** option to change the picture shape to the tenth **Basic Shape** in the third row—**Cloud**. **Align Center** and **Align Middle** the picture using the **Align to Slide** option.

b. On **Slide 10**, insert a **WordArt** using the fourth **WordArt** style in the first row **Fill - White, Outline - Accent 1**. Type **Moving to the Top of the Winter Sports Action** and then change the **Font Size** to **28**. Drag the WordArt down so that its top edge aligns with the **lower half of the vertical ruler at 1 inch**. Select the title placeholder, picture, and WordArt, and then using the **Align to Slide** option, apply **Align Center**.

c. To all of the slides in the presentation, apply the **Box** transition, and then change the **Effect Options** to **From Top**. Display **Slide 6**, and then apply the **Split** entrance effect to the numbered list.

d. Display **Slide 3**. In the **Notes pane**, type **The key elements necessary to achieve our 2016 goals are the expansion of the winter sports product line, an aggressive marketing campaign, and new retail locations in California and Washington.**

(Business Running Case: Front Range Action Sports continues on the next page)

Front Range Action Sports (continued)

e. Insert a **Header & Footer** for the **Notes and Handouts**. Include the **Date and time** updated automatically, the **Page number**, and a **Footer** with the file name **Lastname_Firstname_BRC1_Winter_Products**

f. Display the **Document Properties**. Add your name, your course name and section, and the keywords **winter products, goals Close** the **Document Information Panel**.

g. View the slide show from the beginning, and then **Save** your presentation. Print **Handouts 6 Slides Horizontal**, or submit your presentation electronically as directed by your instructor. **Close** the presentation.

End **You have completed Business Running Case 1**

Integrating Word, Excel, Access, and PowerPoint

OUTCOMES
At the end of this chapter you will be able to:

OBJECTIVES
Mastering these objectives will enable you to:

PROJECT 1A
Create an Excel workbook that includes data exported from Access and data copied from Word.

1. Export Access Data to Excel (p. 805)
2. Create an Excel Worksheet from a Word Table (p. 808)
3. Copy and Paste an Excel Chart into Other Programs (p. 812)
4. Copy and Paste an Object from PowerPoint into Excel (p. 817)

PROJECT 1B
Link Excel data to a Word document and complete a mail merge in Word using Access data.

5. Link Excel Data to a Word Document (p. 821)
6. Modify Linked Data and Update Links (p. 823)
7. Create a Table in Word from Access Data (p. 824)
8. Use Access Data to Complete a Mail Merge in Word (p. 826)

Razvan CHIRNOAGA/Shutterstock

In This Chapter

One of the advantages of using the applications in a software suite is that all the applications work well with one another. By using the best application to complete the work with the data you have, you can create graphics or input data in one application and then export the data to another application without having to take the time to re-create or retype the graphic or data. You do need to identify the most appropriate software to produce solutions and to best utilize the functions of the various software.

In this chapter, you will copy and paste data and objects between software. You will practice linking the data in the destination file and then modify and update the link.

The projects in this chapter relate to **Front Range Action Sports**, one of the country's largest retailers of sports gear and outdoor recreation merchandise. The company has large retail stores in Colorado, Washington, Oregon, and New Mexico, in addition to a growing online business. Major merchandise categories include fishing, camping, rock climbing, winter sports, action sports, water sports, team sports, racquet sports, fitness, golf, apparel, and footwear.

Project 1A State Sales

Project Activities

In Activities 1.01 through 1.11, you will export Access data into an Excel workbook, and then you will copy and paste Word data into the Excel workbook. In Excel, you will create a chart based on the data, and then copy the chart into a PowerPoint presentation. Your completed documents will look similar to Figure 1.1.

Project Files

For Project 1A, you will need the following files:

New blank Excel workbook
i01A_Store_Locations.accdb
i01A_State_Sales.docx
i01A_Sales_Presentation.pptx

You will save your files as:

Lastname_Firstname_1A_Sales_Chart.xlsx
Lastname_Firstname_1A_Store_Locations.accdb
Lastname_Firstname_1A_State_Sales.docx
Lastname_Firstname_1A_Sales_Presentation.pptx

Project Results

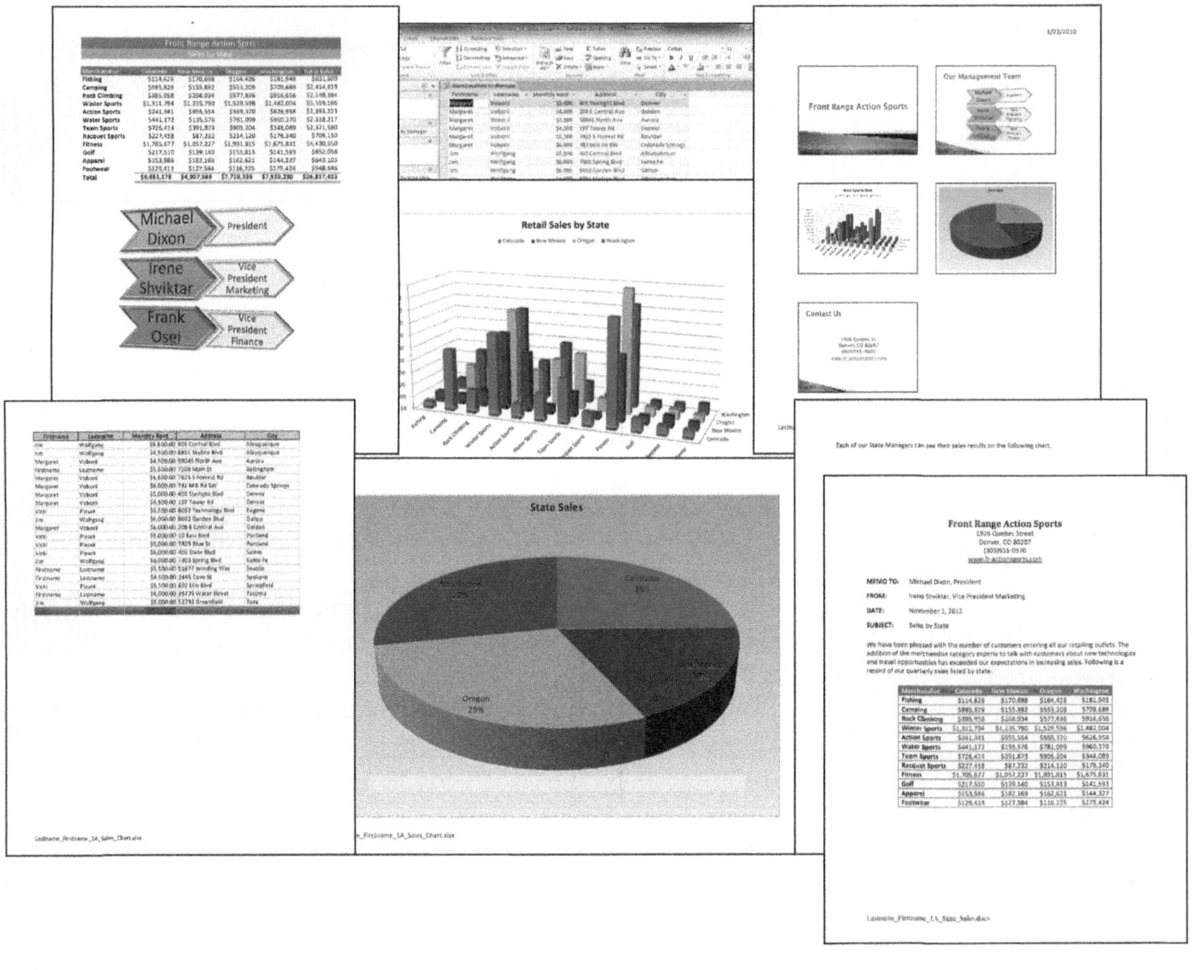

Figure 1.1
Project 1A State Sales

Objective 1 | Export Access Data to Excel

Access includes a tool to export data from an Access database into an Excel workbook. When you export Access data, you create a copy of the data in Excel.

Activity 1.01 | Exporting Access Data to Excel

In the following activity, you will export Access data into an Excel workbook.

1. Click **Start** . Click **Control Panel**, and then click **Appearance and Personalization.** Under **Folder Options**, click **Show hidden files and folders.** Under **Advanced settings**, clear the **Hide extensions for known file types** checkbox. Click **OK**, and then click **Close. Start** Access. Navigate to the student data files and then open the Access database **i01A_Store_Locations.** Click the **File tab** to display **Backstage** view, and then click **Save Database As.**

2. In the **Save As** dialog box, navigate to the location where you are saving your files. Click **New folder**, type **Integrated Projects** and then press Enter. In the **File name** box, name the file **Lastname_Firstname_1A_Store_Locations** and then press Enter. If the Security Warning message displays, click the Enable Content button.

3. In the **navigation pane**, double-click the **Managers** table. At the bottom of the table, replace *Firstname* with your **Firstname** and replace *Lastname* with your **Lastname** and then press Enter.

4. In the **navigation pane**, double-click the query **Store Locations by Manager**, and verify that your name displays. Compare your screen with Figure 1.2.

Figure 1.2

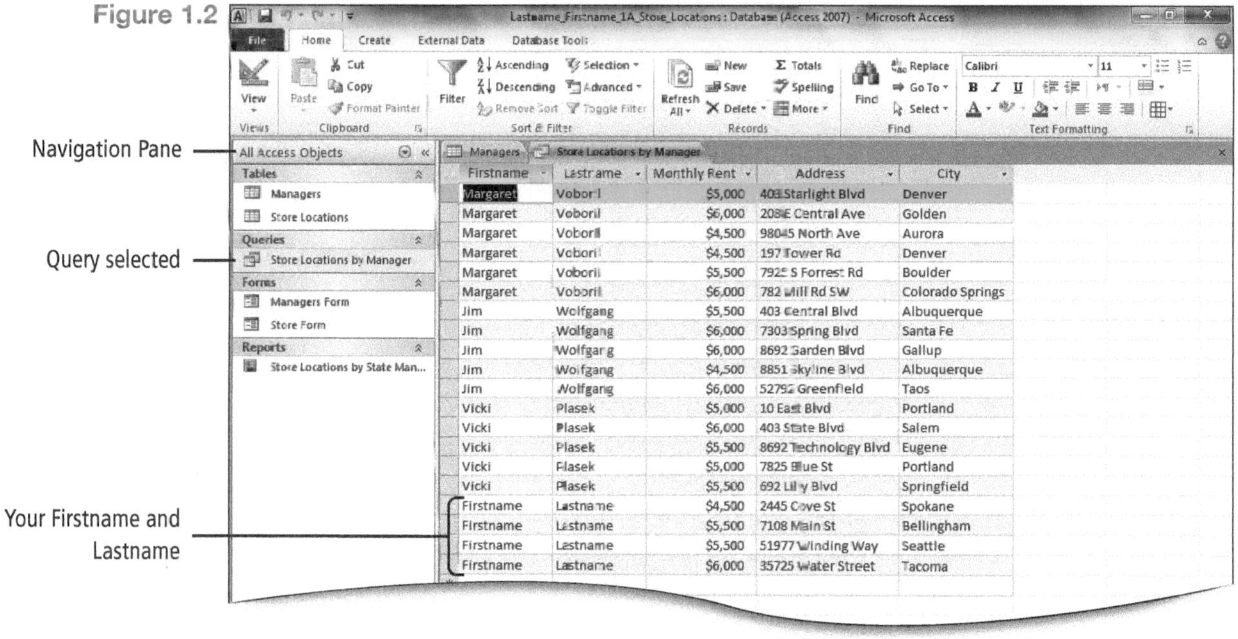

5. On the **External Data tab**, in the **Export group**, click the **Excel** button. In the **Export - Excel Spreadsheet** dialog box, click the **Browse** button. Navigate to your **Integrated Projects** folder, type the file name **Lastname_Firstname_1A_Sales_Chart** and then click **Save.**

6. In the **Export - Excel Spreadsheet** dialog box, verify that the **File format** is **Excel Workbook (*.xlsx)**. Select the **Export data with formatting and layout** check box, and then click **OK.** In the dialog box, verify that the **Save export steps** check box is not selected, and then click **Close.**

7 Click the **File tab** to display **Backstage** view, and then click **Exit.**

8 **Start** Excel. Navigate to your **Integrated Projects** folder, and then open the Excel workbook **Lastname_Firstname_1A_Sales_Chart.**

Notice the exported Access query name—*Store Locations by Manager*—becomes the Excel worksheet name.

Activity 1.02 | Creating and Sorting an Excel Table

To make managing and analyzing a group of related data easier, you can turn a range of cells into an Excel table. An Excel table typically contains data in a series of rows and columns, and the Excel table can be managed independently from the data in other rows and columns in the worksheet. In the following activity, you will change a range of data into an Excel table, and then sort the data.

1 Click cell **A1**. On the **Insert tab**, in the **Tables group**, click the **Table** button. In the **Create Table** dialog box, under **Where is the data for your table?**, verify that the range is **=$A$1:$E$21**, verify that the **My table has headers** check box is selected, and then compare your screen with Figure 1.3.

Figure 1.3

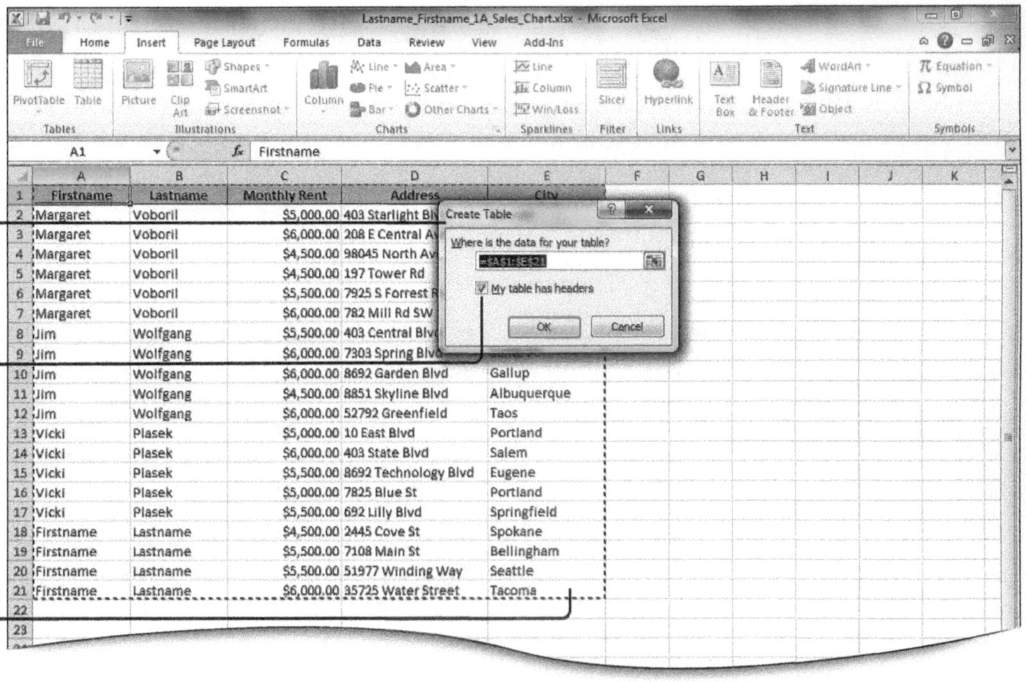

2 In the **Create Table** dialog box, click **OK**.

3 In cell **E1**, click the **Filter** button, and then click **Sort A to Z** to sort the entire table. Compare your screen with Figure 1.4.

The rows in column E—the City column—are sorted in ascending order.

After a column is sorted in ascending or descending order, a small arrow displays on the Filter button to indicate its sort order.

Figure 1.4

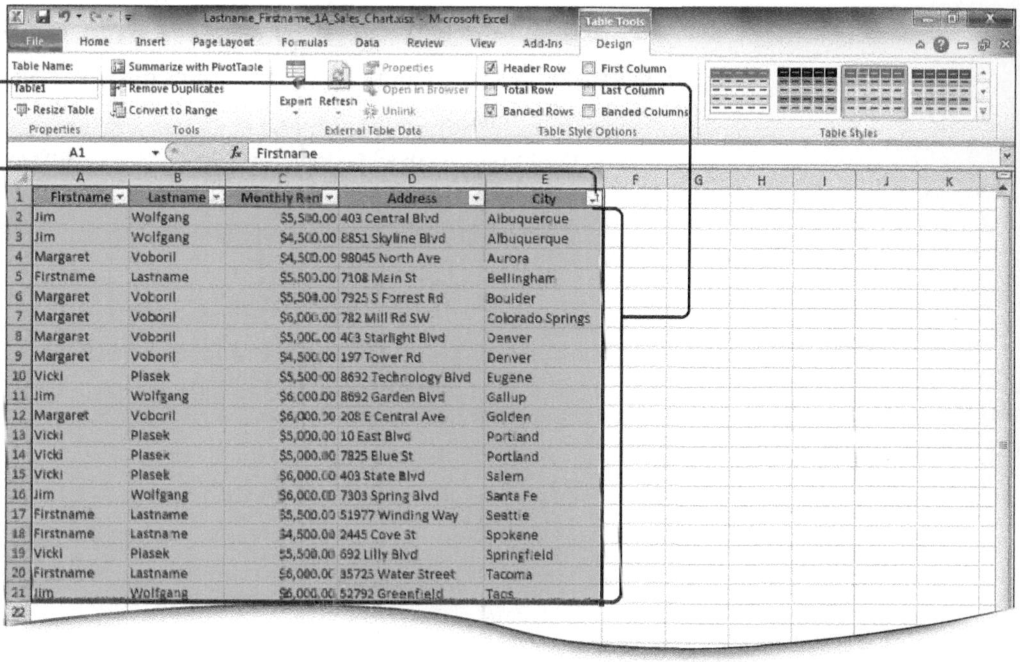

4 **Save** the Excel workbook.

Activity 1.03 | Inserting a Total Row in an Excel Table

An Excel table can help manage and analyze data. You can quickly total the data in an Excel table by displaying a Totals Row at the end of the table, and then by using the functions that are provided in drop-down lists for each totals row cell. In the following activity, you will insert a total row and sum a column using the total row.

1 On the **Design tab**, in the **Table Style Options group**, select the **Total Row** check box. Click cell **E22**, and then compare your screen with Figure 1.5.

Cell E22 displays the number 20. The Total Row counts the number of cells containing text in column E. The header row is not included in the Total Row calculations.

Figure 1.5

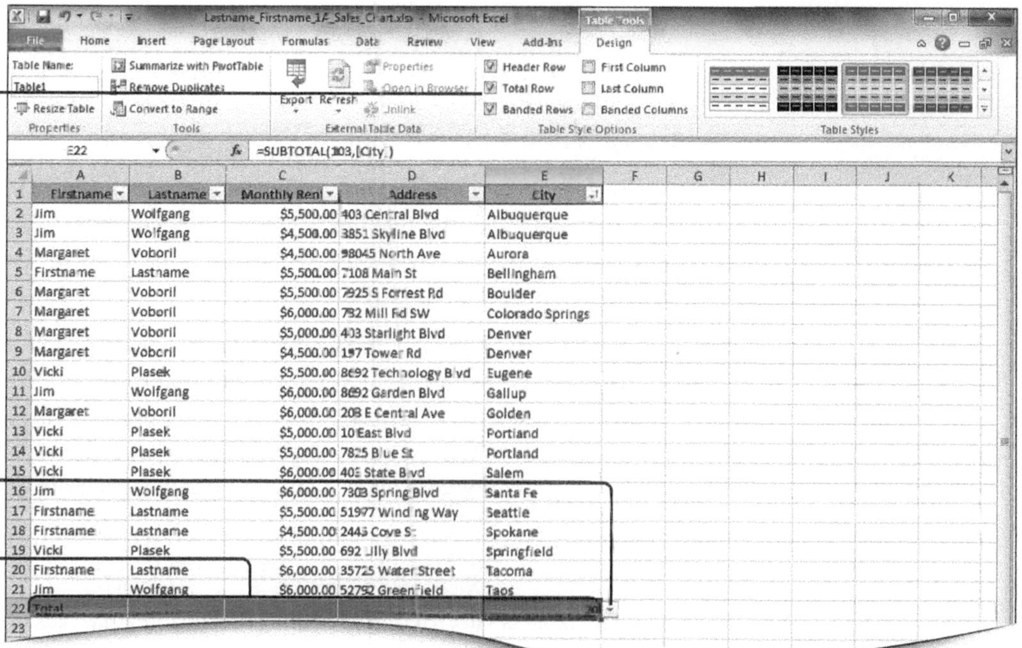

2 On the Total Row, in cell **E22**, click the **down arrow**, and then click **None**.

3 Click cell **C22**. Click the **down arrow** next to the active cell **C22**, and then click **Sum**. Compare your screen with Figure 1.6.

The Total Monthly Rent for all locations displays in cell C22.

Figure 1.6

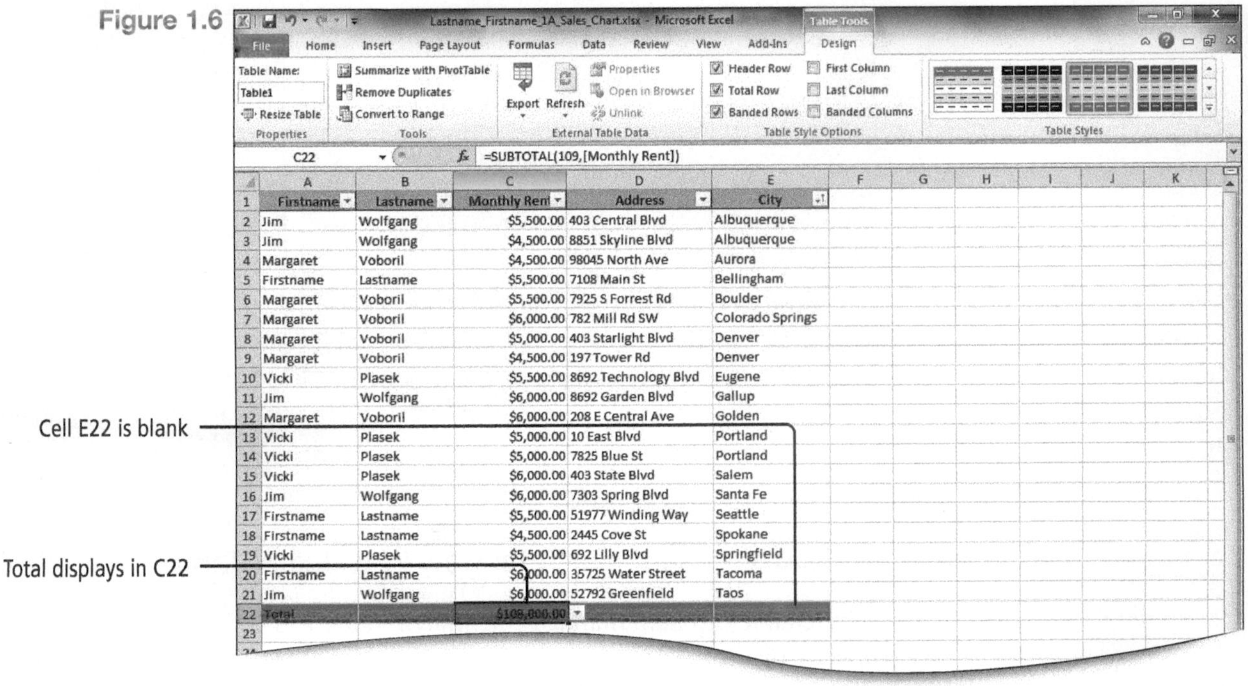

4 **Save** the Excel workbook.

Objective 2 | Create an Excel Worksheet from a Word Table

There are times when you might want to use some of the data from one file in a different program without having to retype the data. In the following activities, you will copy and paste data and objects from one program into another program.

Activity 1.04 | Formatting a Word Table

1 **Start** Word. Navigate to the student data files, and then open the document **i01A_State_Sales**. Click the **File tab** to display **Backstage** view, and then click **Save As**. Navigate to your **Integrated Projects** folder, and then **Save** the document as **Lastname_Firstname_1A_State_Sales**

2 Click the **Insert tab**. In the **Header & Footer group**, click the **Footer** button. At the bottom of the **Footer** gallery, click **Edit Footer**. On the **Design tab**, in the **Insert group**, click the **Quick Parts** button, and then click **Field**. In the **Field** dialog box, under **Field names**, scroll down to locate and click **FileName**, and then click **OK**. On the **Design tab**, in the **Close group**, click the **Close Header and Footer** button.

3 Scroll down to display the table. If necessary, display the formatting marks. Click the first cell in the table, and then compare your screen with Figure 1.7.

The table is selected and the Table Tools contextual tabs display.

Figure 1.7

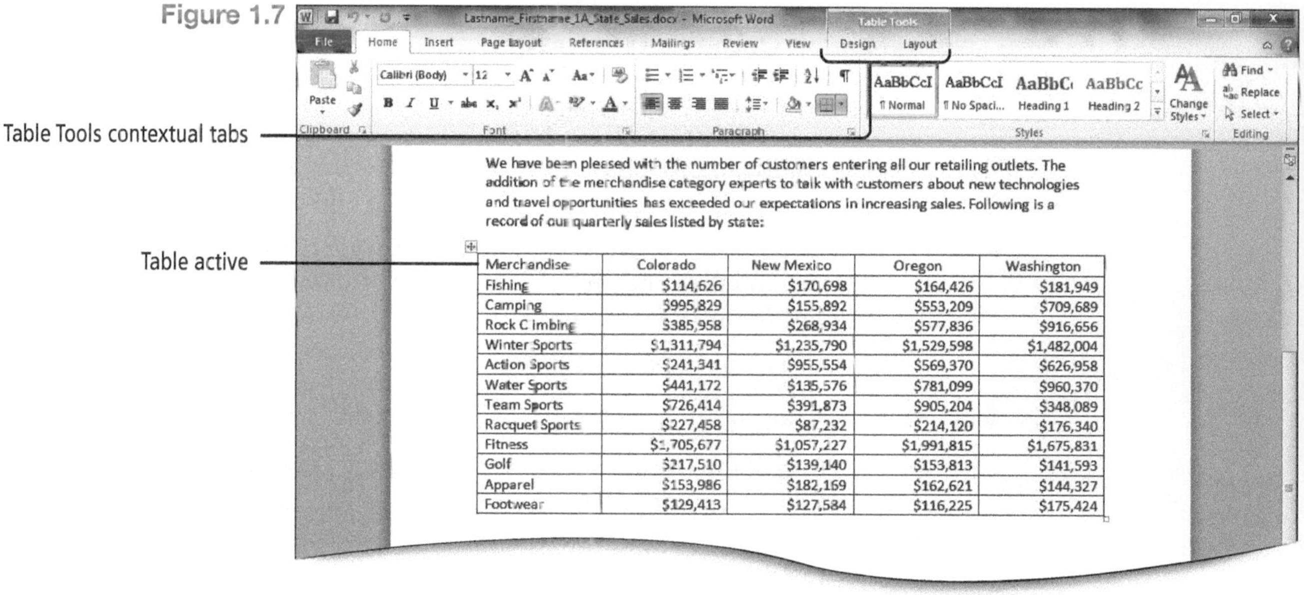

Table Tools contextual tabs
Table active
Lastname_Firstname_1A_State_Sales.docx - Microsoft Word
Table Tools
Design
Layout
We have been pleased with the number of customers entering all our retailing outlets. The addition of the merchandise category experts to talk with customers about new technologies and travel opportunities has exceeded our expectations in increasing sales. Following is a record of our quarterly sales listed by state:

4 Click the **Design tab**, and then in the **Table Styles group**, click the **More** button. In the **Table Styles** gallery, under **Built-In**, click the **Light List - Accent 1** button.

5 On the **Layout tab**, in the **Cell Size group**, click the **AutoFit** button, and then click **AutoFit Contents**. In the **Table group**, click the **Properties** button. In the **Table Properties** dialog box, under **Alignment**, click the **Center** button. Compare your screen with Figure 1.8.

Figure 1.8

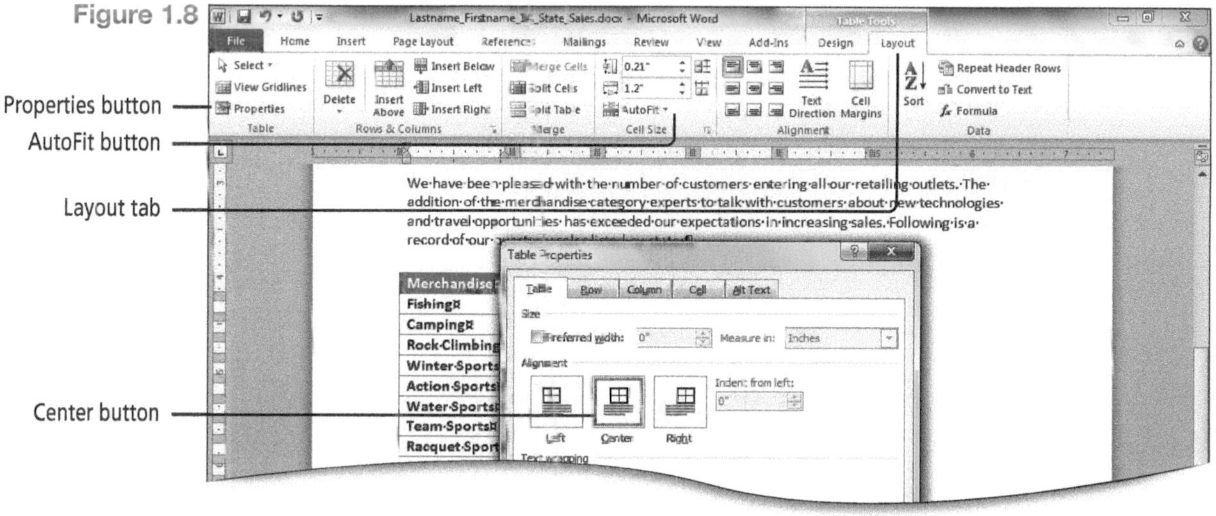

Properties button
AutoFit button
Layout tab
Center button
Table Properties
Left
Center
Right

6 In the **Table Properties** dialog box, click **OK** to center the table horizontally on the page.

7 **Save** the Word document.

Activity 1.05 | Copying and Pasting a Word Table into an Excel Workbook

After you have started a Word document, you may realize that you can manipulate the data better in another program, such as Excel. Instead of starting over and retyping all of the data, you can copy the data from Word and paste the data into Excel.

> **Note | Multiple Open Windows Notice**
>
> In this chapter, you will work with a number of different files and will have a number of different windows open. When you have completed the work in one file, save the file and minimize the window. When you need to use the file again, click the program icon on the taskbar to maximize that window.

1. Verify that Word is the active window. On the **Layout tab**, in the **Table group**, click the **Select** button, and then click **Select Table**. On the **Home tab** in the **Clipboard group**, click the **Copy** button.

   The entire table is selected and copied.

2. On the taskbar, click the **Excel** icon to make the Excel window active.

3. At the bottom of the worksheet, click the **Insert Worksheet** button to insert a new blank worksheet. Right-click the **Sheet1** worksheet tab, and then click **Rename**. Type **Sales** and then press Enter.

4. Click cell **A4** to make it the active cell. On the **Home tab**, in the **Clipboard group**, click the **Paste** button. Compare your screen with Figure 1.9.

   The Word data is pasted into the Excel worksheet, starting in cell A4—the active cell.

   The pound sign (#) will display if a column is not wide enough to display an entire number.

Figure 1.9

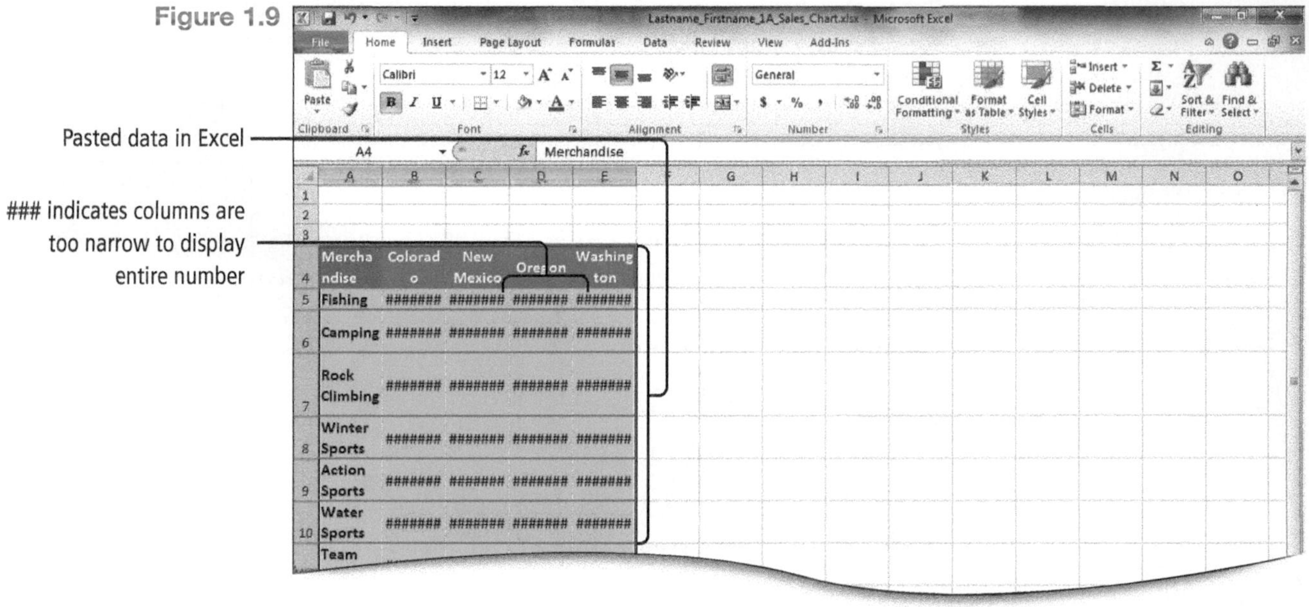

5. Select cell **A4**. On the **Home tab**, in the **Cells group**, click the **Format** button, and then click **Column Width**. In the **Column Width** dialog box, type **16** and then press **OK**.

6. Select the range **B4:E4**. In the **Cells group**, click the **Format** button, and then click **Column Width**. In the **Column Width** dialog box, type **12** and then click **OK**.

   All columns are wide enough to display all data.

7. Select the range **A4:A16**. In the **Cells group**, click the **Format** button, and then click **Row Height**. In the **Row Height** dialog box, type **17** and then click **OK**.

8 In cell **A1**, type **Front Range Action Sports** and then press Enter. In cell **A2**, type **Sales by State** and then press Enter. Select the range **A1:F1**, and then on the **Home tab**, in the **Alignment group**, click the **Merge & Center** button. In the **Styles group**, click the **Cell Styles** button, and then click **Accent1**. In the **Font group**, click the **Font Size** button, and then click **16**.

9 Select the range **A2:F2**. Using the same technique you just practiced, **Merge & Center** the range, apply the cell style **60% - Accent1**, and then change the **Font Size** to **14**. Compare your screen with Figure 1.10.

Figure 1.10

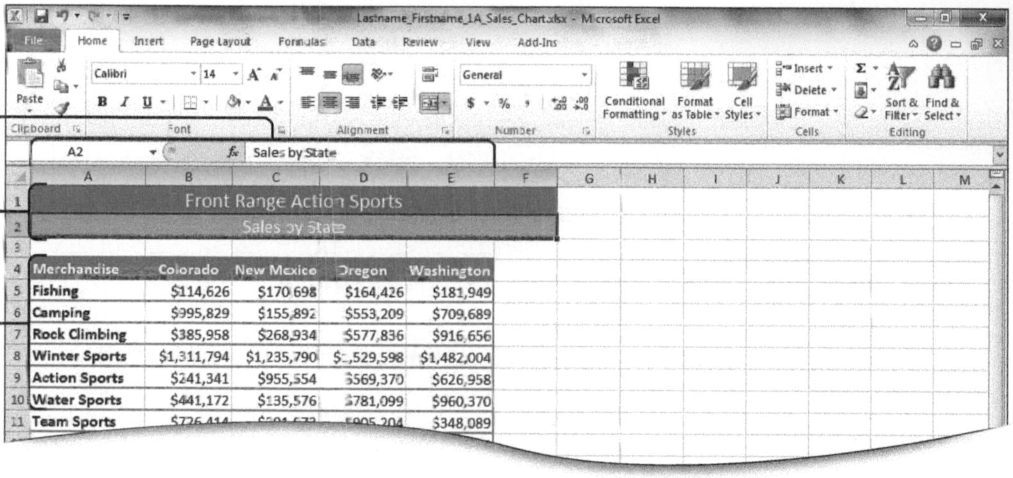

10 **Save** the Excel workbook.

Activity 1.06 | Using the SUM Function and Fill Handle in Excel

One of Excel's most powerful features is the capability to perform mathematical calculations. In the following activity, you will use the SUM function to add numbers.

1 Click cell **F4**, type **Total Sales** and then press Enter.

2 Verify that **F5** is the active cell. On the **Home tab**, in the **Editing group**, click the **Sum** button and then on the **Formula Bar**, click the **Enter** button to confirm the entry while keeping cell **F5** the active cell. Using the technique you previously practiced, widen column **F** to **13**

3 In cell **F5**, point to the fill handle to display the + pointer, hold down the left mouse button, and then drag down to cell **F16**. Release the mouse button. In the **Font group**, click the **Increase Font Size** button, and then compare your screen with Figure 1.11.

Figure 1.11

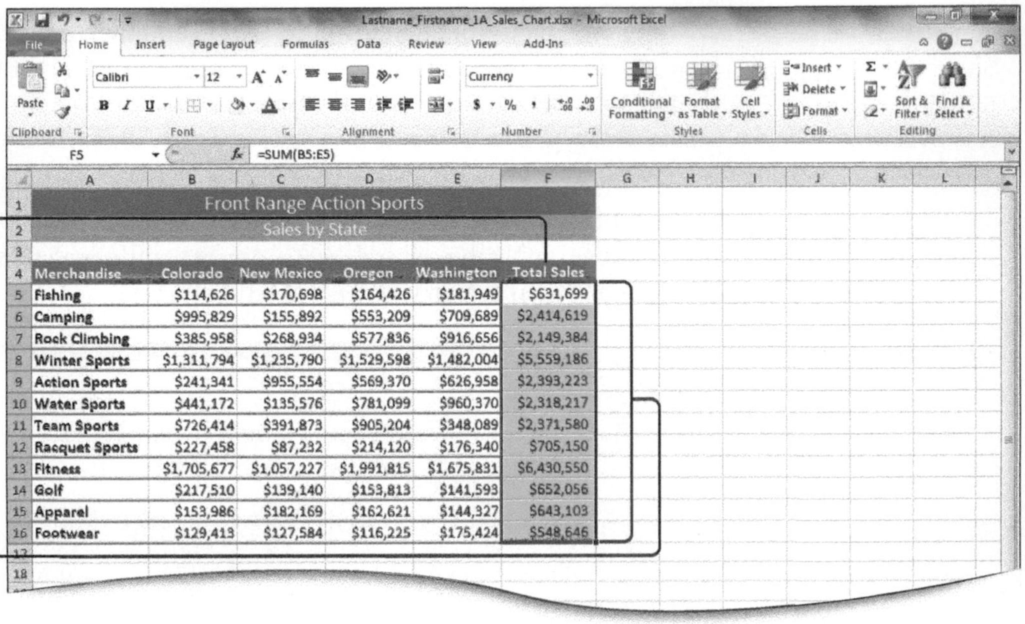

4 Click cell **A17**, type **Total** and then press Tab.

5 On the **Home tab**, in the **Editing group**, click the **Sum** button Σ and then on the **Formula Bar**, click the **Enter** button ✓. Using the technique you just practiced, use the fill handle to copy the formula to the right through cell **F17**.

6 Select the range **A5:E16**. In the **Font group**, click the **Border button arrow**, and then click **No Border**. Select the range **B17:F17**, in the **Styles group**, click the **Cell Styles** button, and then under **Titles and Headings**, click **Total**. In the **Font group**, click the **Increase Font Size** button A.

7 **Save** the Excel workbook.

Objective 3 | Copy and Paste an Excel Chart into Other Programs

When reviewing numbers in an Excel worksheet, sometimes it takes a minute to compare one number to another number. A chart is a visual way to illustrate the Excel data in an understandable manner. After a chart is created in Excel, it can be copied and pasted to other programs.

Activity 1.07 | Creating and Formatting Charts in Excel

In this activity you will create a column chart and a pie chart in Excel.

1 Select the range **A4:E16**. On the **Insert tab**, in the **Charts group**, click the **Column** button. Under **3-D Column**, click the fourth chart—**3-D Column**. On the **Design tab**, in the **Location group**, click the **Move Chart** button. In the **Move Chart** dialog box, click the **New sheet** option button, type **Merchandise Chart** and then click **OK**.

A 3-D column chart is created and moved to a new chart sheet named Merchandise Chart.

2 Click the **Layout tab**. In the **Labels group**, click the **Chart Title** button, and then click **Above Chart**. Type **Retail Sales by State** and then press Enter.

3 In the **Labels group**, click the **Legend** button, and then click **Show Legend at Top**. Compare your screen with Figure 1.12.

Figure 1.12

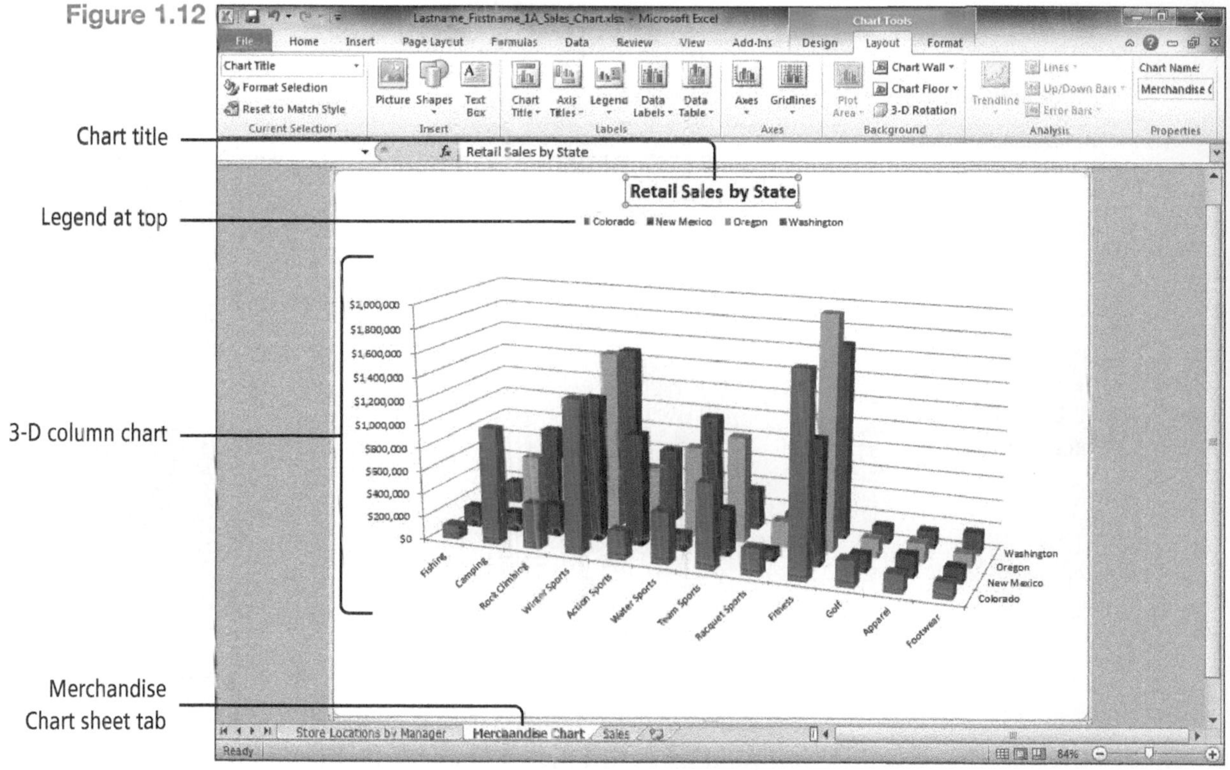

4 Click the **Sales** worksheet tab. Select the range **B4:E4**, hold down Ctrl, and then select the range **B17:E17**.

The range B4:E4 and the range B17:E17 are selected. Recall that holding down Ctrl enables you to select nonadjacent cells.

5 On the **Insert tab**, in the **Charts group**, click the **Pie** button, and then under **3-D Pie**, click **Pie in 3-D**. On the **Design tab**, in the **Location group**, click the **Move Chart** button. In the **Move Chart** dialog box, click the **New sheet** option button, type **State Sales Chart** and then click **OK**.

6 On the **Design tab**, in the **Chart Layouts group**, click the **More** button, and then click **Layout 5**. On the chart, click the **Chart Title**, type **State Sales** and then click outside of the title.

7 On the **Layout tab**, in the **Labels group**, click the **Data Labels** button, and then click **More Data Label Options**. In the **Format Data Labels** dialog box, under **Label Contains**, verify the **Category Name** check box is selected, select the **Percentage** check box, and clear any other check boxes. Under **Label Position**, verify that the **Best Fit** option button is selected and then click **Close**. With the data labels still selected, on the **Home tab**, in the **Font group**, click the **Font Size** button, and then click **14**.

8 On the **Layout tab**, in the **Current Selection group**, click the **Chart Elements arrow**, and then from the displayed list, click **Chart Area**. In the **Current Selection group**, click the **Format Selection** button. In the **Format Chart Area** dialog box, click the **Gradient fill** option button. Click **Close**, and then compare your screen with Figure 1.13.

Figure 1.13

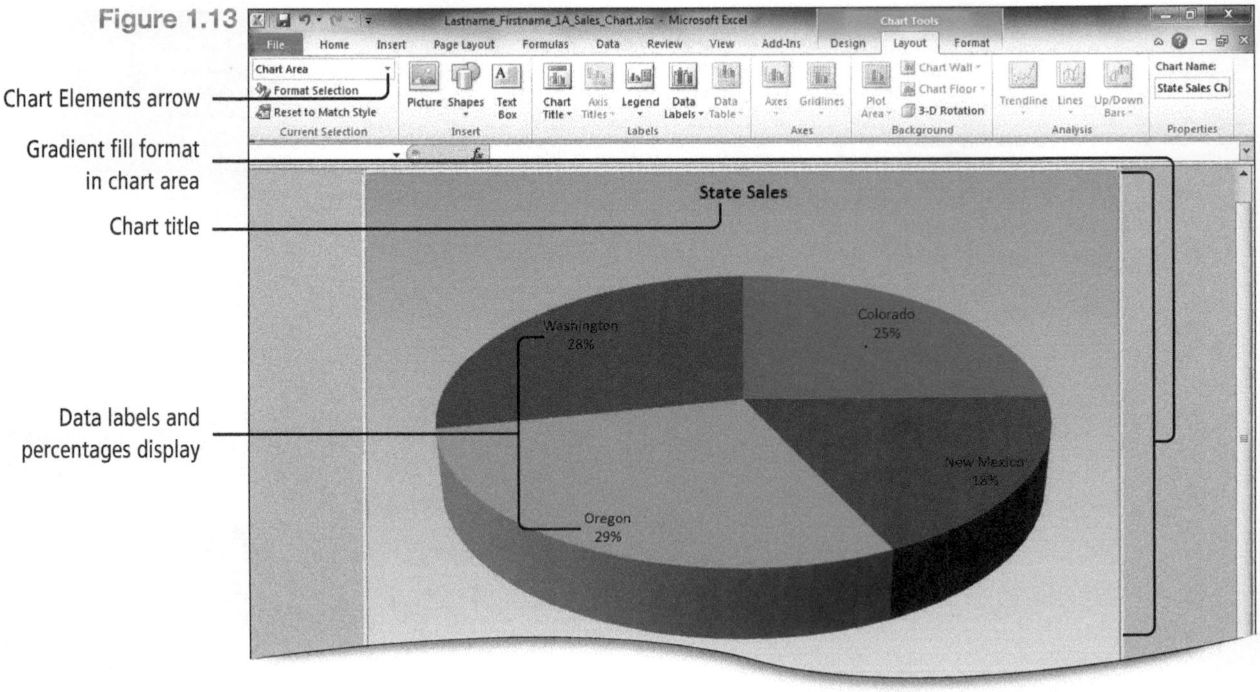

9 Press Ctrl, and then click the **Merchandise Chart** sheet tab.

With both chart sheets selected, the footer will be inserted on both sheets.

10 On the **Insert tab**, in the **Text group**, click the **Header & Footer** button. In the **Page Setup** dialog box, click the **Custom Footer** button. In the **Footer** dialog box, verify that the insertion point is in the *Left section*, and then click the **Insert File Name** button. In the **Footer** dialog box, click **OK**, and then in the **Page Setup** dialog box, click **OK**.

11 Click the **Sales** worksheet tab to make it the active worksheet and to deselect the chart sheets. Press Ctrl, and then click the **Store Locations by Manager** worksheet tab.

Footers are inserted differently in worksheets and in chart sheets.

Both worksheets are selected and the footer will be inserted on both worksheets.

12 On the **Insert tab**, in the **Text group**, click the **Header & Footer** button. On the **Design tab**, in the **Navigation group**, click the **Go to Footer** button. In the **Footer** area, click just above the word *Footer*, and then in the **Header & Footer Elements group**, click the **File Name** button. Click any cell in the workbook to exit the footer. On the status bar, click the **Normal** button to return to **Normal** view.

13 Press Ctrl + Home to display the top of the worksheet. Right-click a sheet tab, and then click Ungroup Sheets.

14 **Save** the Excel workbook.

Activity 1.08 | Copying and Pasting an Excel Chart into Word

1 On the **Home tab**, in the **Clipboard group**, click the **Dialog Box Launcher** to display the Clipboard. Click the **State Sales Chart** sheet tab, and then click the border of the pie chart to select the chart. On the **Home tab** in the **Clipboard group**, click the **Copy** button.

2 Click the **Merchandise Chart** sheet tab, and then click the border of the column chart to select the chart. In the **Clipboard group**, click the **Copy** button.

3 At the bottom of the screen, on the taskbar, click the **Word** icon. Press Ctrl + End to move the insertion point to the end of the document.

4 On the **Insert tab**, in the **Pages group**, click the **Page Break** button.

A new blank page 2 is inserted.

5 Type **Each of our State Managers can see their sales results on the following chart.** Press Enter two times.

6 On the **Home tab**, in the **Clipboard group**, click the **Dialog Box Launcher** to display the Clipboard task pane, as shown in Figure 1.14.

Figure 1.14

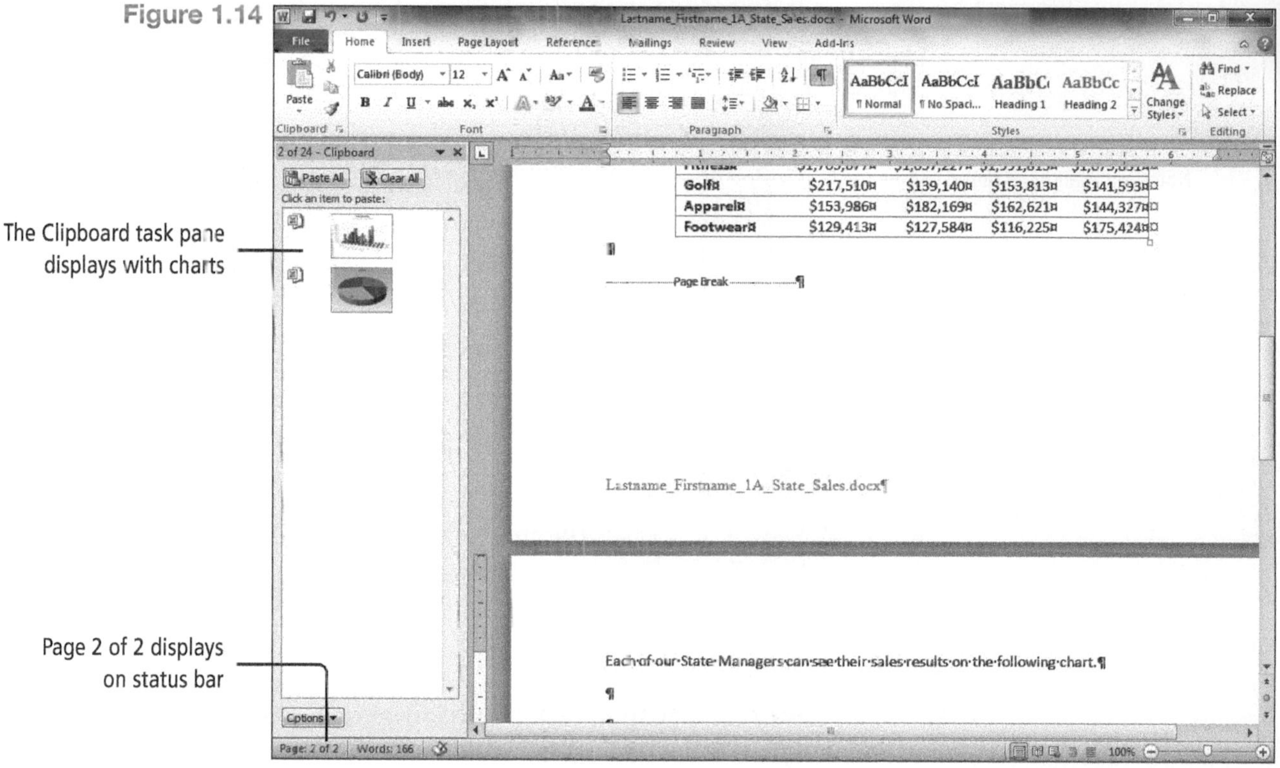

7 In the **Clipboard** task pane, click the **column chart.**

The column chart is pasted into the Word document.

8 **Close** the **Clipboard** task pane.

9 Click the chart and then click the **Layout tab**. In the **Background group**, click the **3-D Rotation** button. In the **Format Chart Area** dialog box, under **Chart Scale**, change the **Depth (% of base)** to **160** and then click **Close.**

All four state names display on the chart.

10 **Save** the Word document. **Print** or submit your file electronically as directed by your instructor.

11 **Close** the Word document, and then **Exit** Word.

Activity 1.09 | Pasting an Excel Chart in PowerPoint

1 **Start** PowerPoint. Navigate to the student data files and open the presentation **i01A_Sales_Presentation.** Click the **File tab** to display **Backstage** view, and then click **Save As.** Navigate to the **Integrated Projects** folder, and then **Save** the presentation as **Lastname_Firstname_1A_Sales_Presentation**

2 On the **Insert tab**, in the **Text group**, click the **Header & Footer** button. In the displayed **Header and Footer** dialog box, click the **Notes and Handouts** tab. Select the **Footer** check box, type **Lastname_Firstname_1A_Sales_Presentation** and then compare your screen with Figure 1.15.

Figure 1.15

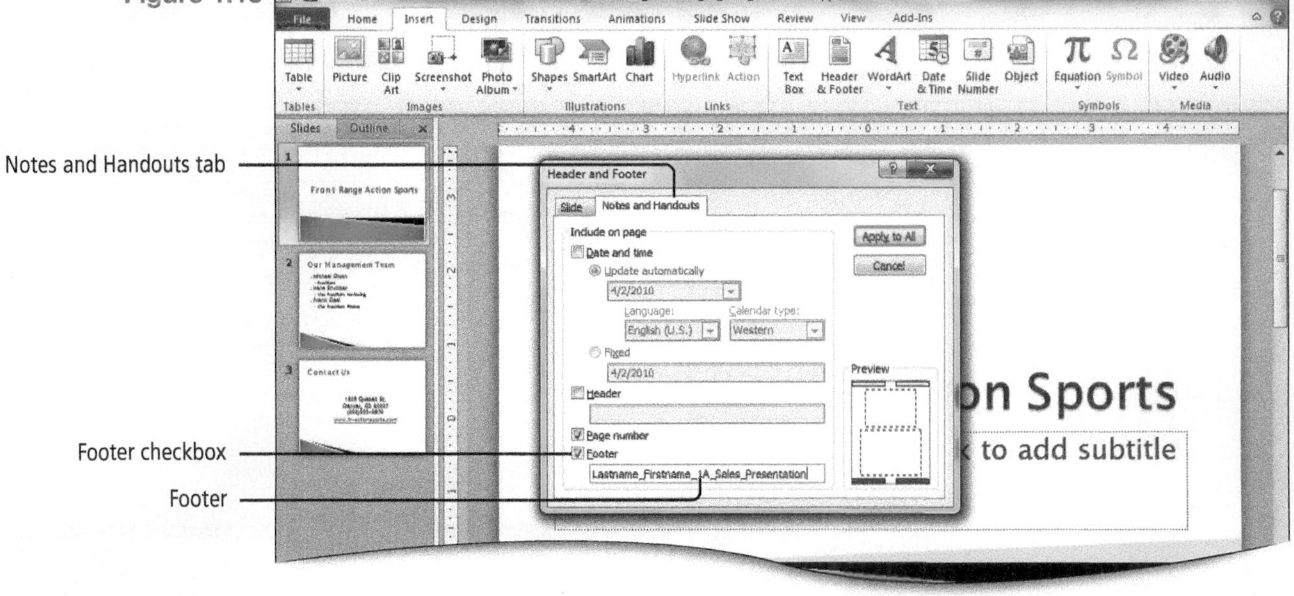

3 Click the **Apply to All** button.

4 Display **Slide 2**. On the **Home tab**, in the **Slides group**, click the **New Slide button arrow**, and then from the displayed gallery, click **Blank.** On the **Design tab**, in the **Background group**, select the **Hide Background Graphics** check box. Compare your screen with Figure 1.16.

A new blank Slide 3 is inserted into the presentation, and the background graphics do not display.

Figure 1.16

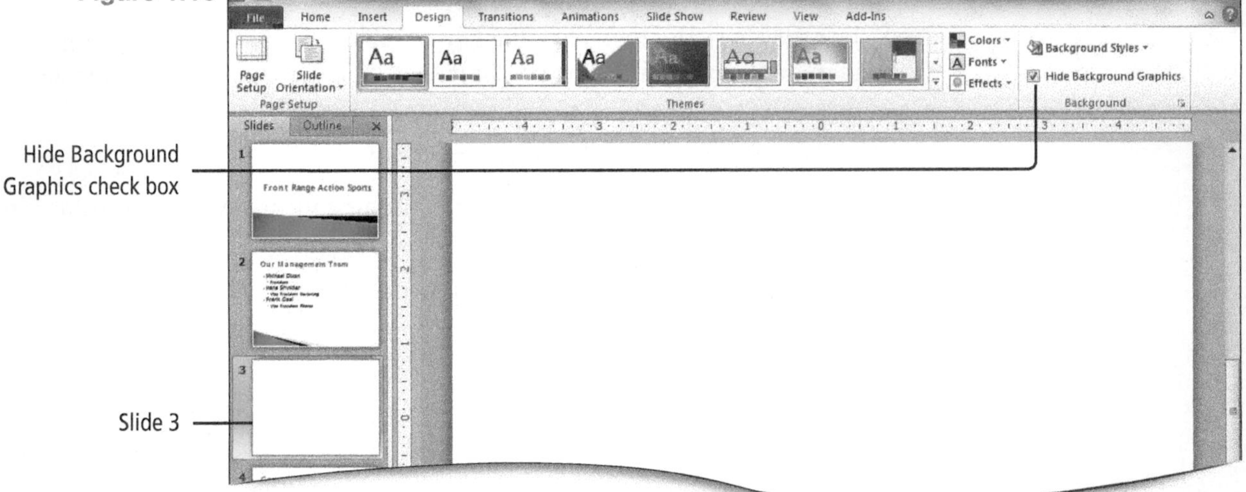

5 On the **Home tab**, in the **Clipboard group**, click the **Dialog Box Launcher** [icon]. In the **Clipboard** task pane, click the column chart.

The column chart is pasted into Slide 3 of the presentation.

6 Click the chart and then click the **Layout tab**. In the **Background group**, click the **3-D Rotation** button. In the **Format Chart Area** dialog box, under **Chart Scale**, change the **Depth (% of base)** to **160** and then click **Close**.

7 On the **Home tab**, in the **Slides group**, click the **New Slide button arrow**, and from the displayed gallery, click **Blank**. Using the technique you just practiced, select the **Hide Background Graphics** check box. In the **Clipboard** task pane, click the pie chart. Compare your screen with Figure 1.17.

Figure 1.17

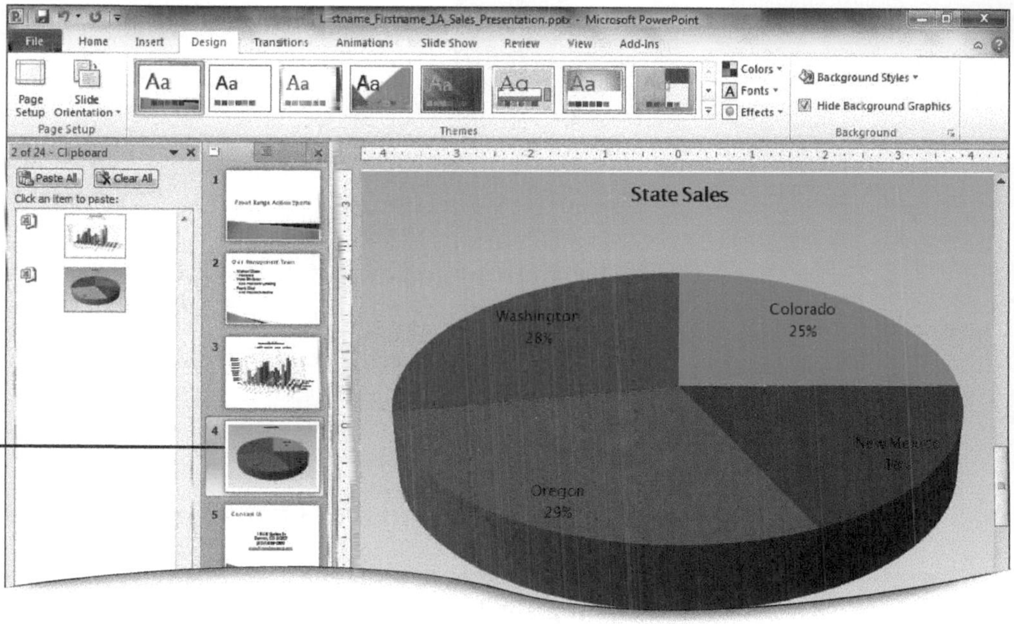

Pie chart in Slide 4

8 **Close** [icon] the **Clipboard** task pane, and then **Save** [icon] the presentation.

Objective 4 | Copy and Paste an Object from PowerPoint into Excel

In PowerPoint, bullet points can be converted into a SmartArt graphic to illustrate your message visually. After you have created a SmartArt graphic in PowerPoint, you can copy the graphic and paste it into another program. This saves you the time of recreating the graphic.

Activity 1.10 | Inserting a SmartArt Graphic

1 Make **Slide 2** the active slide. In **Slide 2**, click the placeholder containing the names of the managers. On the **Home tab**, in the **Paragraph group**, click the **Convert to SmartArt** button [icon]. In the displayed gallery, click **Chevron List**.

Notice on the Ribbon that there are now two Design tabs. The active tab is the Design tab to the right—the SmartArt Tools Design contextual tab is used to format the SmartArt graphic.

2 On the **Design tab**, in the **SmartArt Styles group**, click the **More** button [icon], and then under **3-D**, click **Metallic Scene**. Click on a blank area of the slide to deselect the SmartArt graphic, and then compare your screen with Figure 1.18.

Figure 1.18

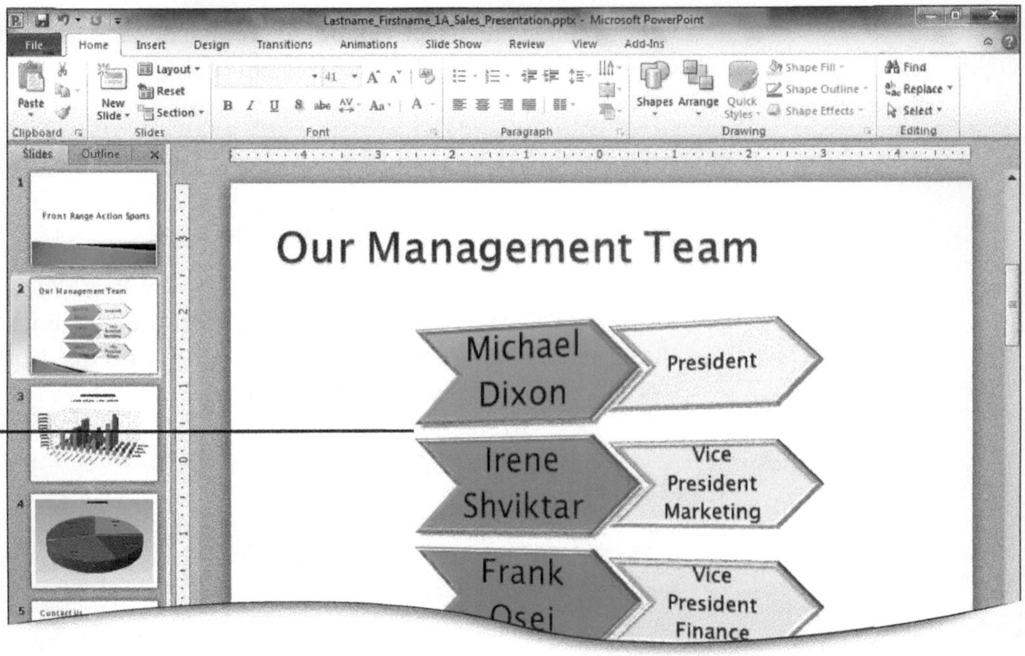

Bullet points converted to SmartArt graphic

3 Click the **SmartArt** graphic. On the **Animations tab**, in the **Animation group**, click the **More** button. From the displayed list, under **Entrance**, click **Float In**.

4 On the **Slide Show tab**, in the **Start Slide Show group**, click the **From Beginning** button to view the presentation. Press Enter to view each slide and to return to **Normal** view.

5 **Save** the presentation.

Activity 1.11 | Copying and Pasting a SmartArt Graphic

After you create an object in one program, you can copy and paste the object into a different program. In this activity, you will copy a SmartArt graphic in PowerPoint and paste it into an Excel workbook.

1 Click the border of the SmartArt graphic.

By clicking the border of an object, you select the entire object, not just a part of the object.

2 On the **Home tab**, in the **Clipboard group**, click the **Copy** button.

3 On the taskbar, click the Excel icon. Click the **Sales** worksheet tab, and then click cell **A20**. On the **Home tab**, in the **Clipboard group**, click the **Paste** button.

The SmartArt graphic is pasted into the Sales worksheet. The top left corner of the graphic is in cell A20.

4 Scroll down to view the graphic. On the **Format tab**, click the **Size** button. Click in the **Height** box, type **4** click in the **Width** box, type **5.5** and then press Enter. Compare your screen with Figure 1.19.

Figure 1.19

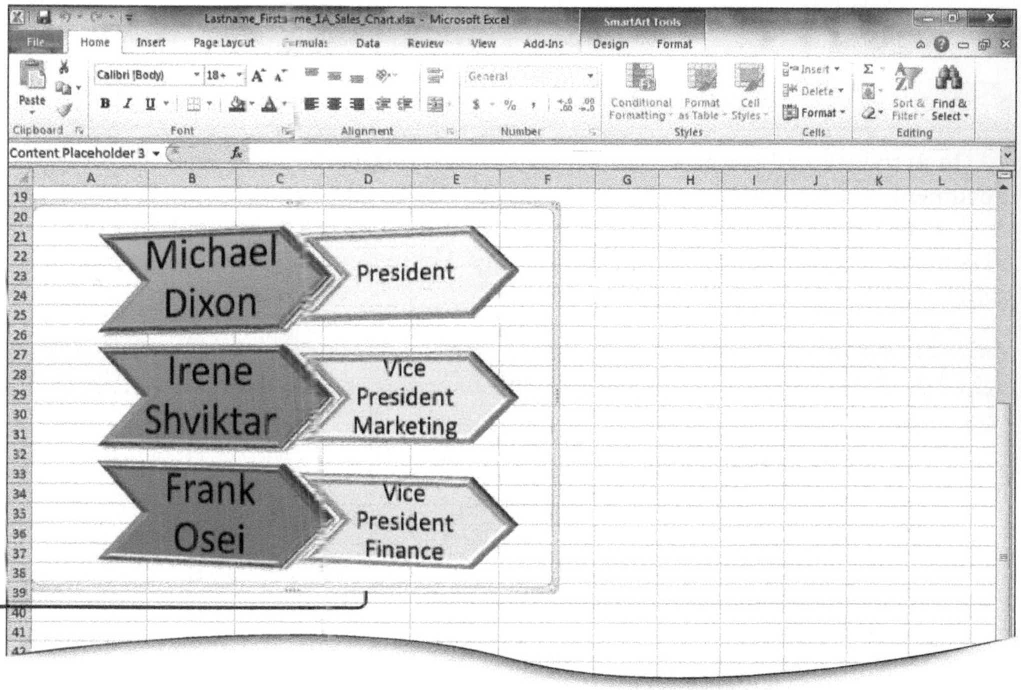

SmartArt graphic pasted in Sales worksheet

5 **Save** the Excel workbook.

6 Click the **File tab** to display **Backstage** view, and then click the **Print tab**. In the **Print** page, under **Settings**, click **Print Active Sheets**, and then click **Print Entire Workbook**. If you are directed by your instructor to print, click the **Print** button. To submit electronically, use the process provided by your instructor.

7 **Close** the Excel workbook, and then **Exit** Excel.

8 In PowerPoint, click the **File tab** to display **Backstage** view, and then click the **Print tab**. On the **Print** page, under **Settings**, click **Full Page Slides**. Under **Handouts** , click **6 Slides Vertical**. If you are directed by your instructor to print, click the **Print** button. To submit electronically, use the process provided by your instructor.

9 **Close** the PowerPoint presentation, and then **Exit** PowerPoint.

End You have completed Project 1A

Project 1B Taos Welcome

Project Activities

In Activities 1.12 through 1.18, you will link and update Excel data in a Word document. Microsoft Office programs can work together to quickly automate tasks such as creating letters from various data sources. You will use data from an Access database to complete memos in Word using Mail Merge. Your completed documents will look similar to Figure 1.20.

Project Files

For Project 1B, you will need the following files:

i01B_Welcome_Memo.docx
i01B_Taos_Inventory.xlsx
i01B_All_Associates.accdb

You will save your files as:

Lastname_Firstname_1B_Welcome_Memo.docx
Lastname_Firstname_1B_Taos_Memo.docx
Lastname_Firstname_1B_Taos_Inventory.xlsx
Lastname_Firstname_1B_All_Associates.accdb
Lastname_Firstname_1B_Store_Location.rtf

Project Results

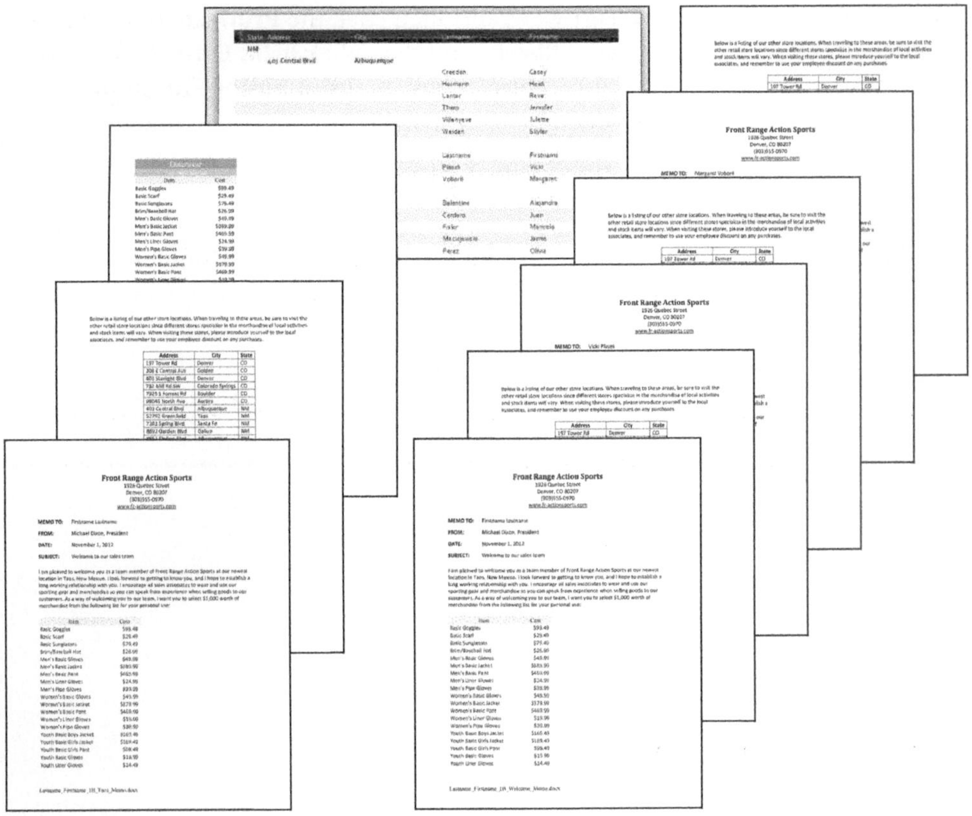

Figure 1.20
Project 1B Taos Welcome

Objective 5 | Link Excel Data to a Word Document

By using the linking tools in Office, you can refer to the contents of an Excel worksheet within a Word document. Changes you make in the Excel data will be updated in the linked Word document. If you link an Excel chart into a Word document, changes made in the Excel workbook will be shown in the chart in the Word document. Information about links is saved with the Word document. By default, when you open the Word document, Word checks the linked files and prompts you to apply any changes.

Activity 1.12 | Accessing Paste Special

In this activity, you will insert Excel data into a Word document. By selecting options in the Paste Special dialog box, you can link your Word document to the Excel data.

1. **Start** Word. Navigate to the student data files and then open the document **i01B_Welcome_Memo**. **Save** the document in your **Integrated Projects** folder as **Lastname_Firstname_1B_Welcome_Memo** If necessary, display the formatting marks.

2. Click the **Insert tab**, and then in the **Header & Footer group**, click the **Footer** button. At the bottom of the **Footer** gallery, click **Edit Footer**. On the **Design tab**, in the **Insert group**, click the **Quick Parts** button, and then click **Field**. In the **Field** dialog box, under **Field names**, locate and click **FileName**, and then click **OK**. In the **Close group**, click the **Close Header and Footer** button.

3. **Start** Excel. Navigate to the student data files, and then open the Excel workbook **i01B_Taos_Inventory**. **Save** the workbook in your **Integrated Projects** folder as **Lastname_Firstname_1B_Taos_Inventory**

4. On the **Insert tab**, in the **Text group**, click the **Header & Footer** button. On the **Design tab**, in the **Navigation group**, click the **Go to Footer** button. In the **Footer** area, click just above the word *Footer*, and then in the **Header & Footer Elements group**, click the **File Name** button. Click any cell in the workbook to exit the footer. On the status bar, click the **Normal** button.

5. Press Ctrl + Home to display the top of the worksheet, and then **Save** the Excel workbook.

6. Select the range **A3:B22**. On the **Home tab** in the **Clipboard group**, click the **Copy** button.

7. On the taskbar, click the **Word** icon. In the Word document, click the blank line below the paragraph that begins *I am pleased to welcome you.*

8. On the **Home tab**, in the **Clipboard group**, click the **Paste button arrow**, and then click **Paste Special**. In the **Paste Special** dialog box, click the **Paste link** option button, and under **As**, click **Microsoft Excel Worksheet Object**, as shown in Figure 1.21.

Figure 1.21

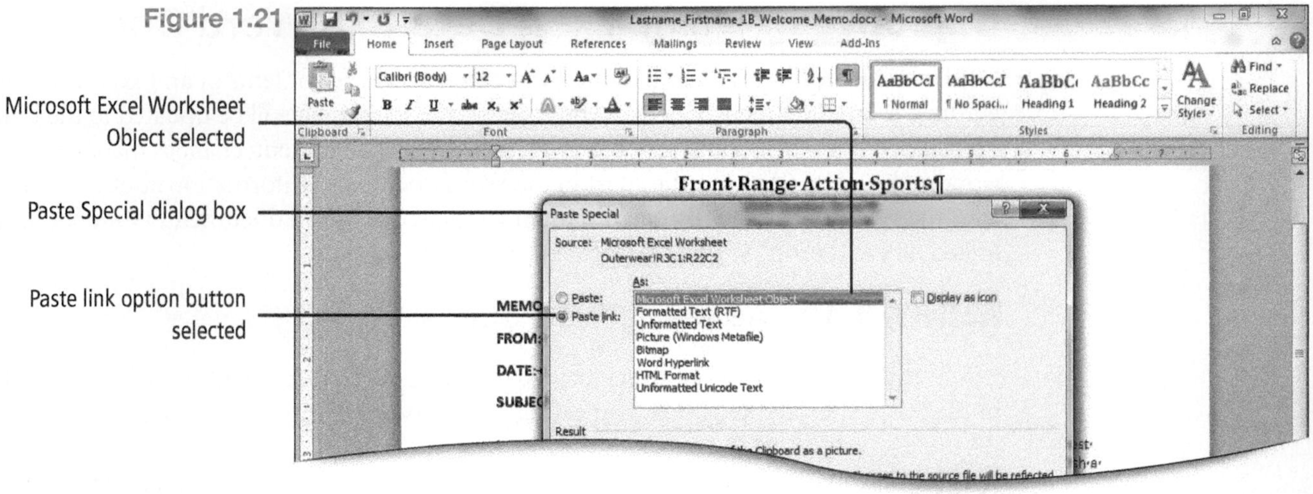

9 In the **Paste Special** dialog box, click **OK**.

The linked data from Excel is pasted into the Word document.

10 **Save**, and then **Close** the Word document.

Note | Security Notice

From this point forward, when you reopen a Word document that has a link to an external file, a Security Notice will automatically display. The notice will inform you that the file contains links and you have the option of updating the links or not updating them. If you trust the source of the file, you can update links. If you do not know where a file originated, you should cancel the update and investigate where the file came from before continuing.

11 In Word, navigate to your **Integrated Projects** folder, and then open the **Lastname_Firstname_1B_Welcome_Memo** document. A message box displays, as shown in Figure 1.22.

The message box informs you that the Word document is linked to another file, and it asks whether you want to update the data in the document.

Figure 1.22

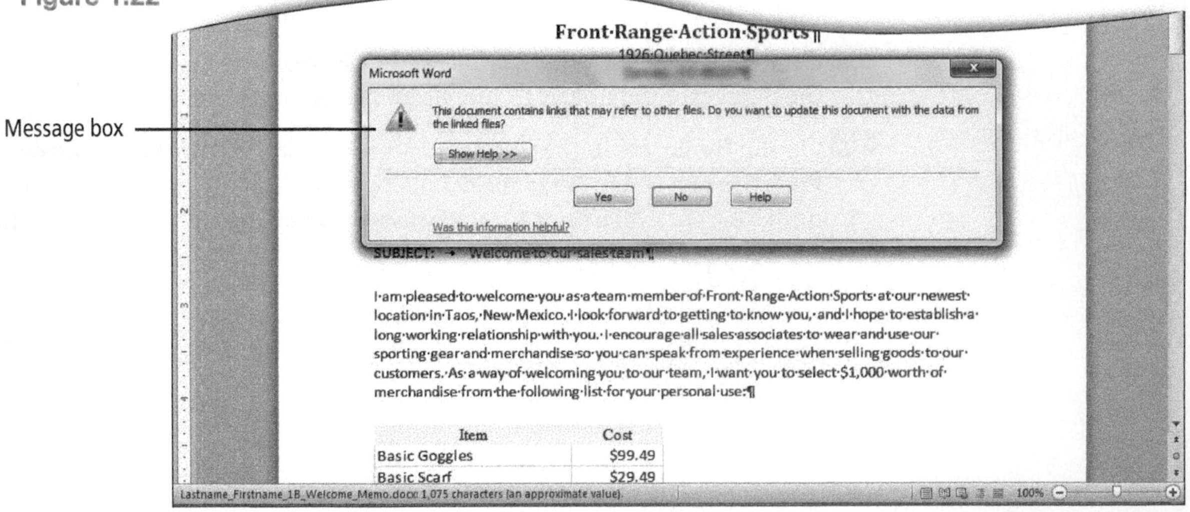

12 In the message box, click **Yes**.

The linked information has been updated.

Objective 6 | Modify Linked Data and Update Links

It is common to make changes to your data after you have completed your documents. You can modify the data in the source file and all linked data to that source file will be updated.

Activity 1.13 | Updating the Linked Data

In the following activity, you will update the Excel data, and then verify that the updated data displays in the Word document.

1 Double-click the pasted data in the Word document to access the Excel source file.

Excel becomes the active window.

2 If necessary, maximize the Excel worksheet, and then press Esc to cancel the copy. Click cell **B9**, type **389.99** and then press Enter. Click cell **B14**, type **379.99** and then press Enter.

3 **Save** the Excel workbook.

4 On the taskbar, click the **Word** icon. Notice the updates made to the Excel data are reflected in the linked Word document, as shown in Figure 1.23.

> **Alert! | What If the Data Is Not Updated?**
>
> If you do not see the new numbers in the Word document, click one time in the data to select it, and then press F9 to update the Excel data.

Figure 1.23

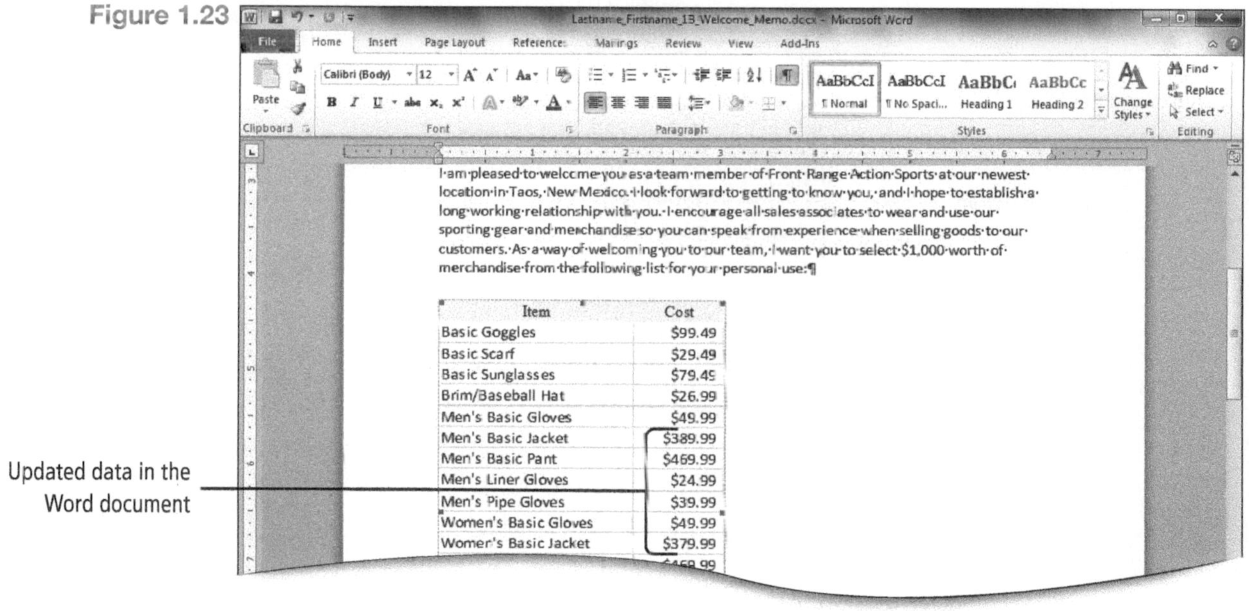
Lastname_Firstname_1B_Welcome_Memo.docx - Microsoft Word
I am pleased to welcome you as a team member of Front Range Action Sports at our newest location in Taos, New Mexico. I look forward to getting to know you, and I hope to establish a long working relationship with you. I encourage all sales associates to wear and use our sporting gear and merchandise so you can speak from experience when selling goods to our customers. As a way of welcoming you to our team, I want you to select $1,000 worth of merchandise from the following list for your personal use:
Item
Cost
Basic Goggles $99.49
Basic Scarf $29.49
Basic Sunglasses $79.49
Brim/Baseball Hat $26.99
Men's Basic Gloves $49.99
Men's Basic Jacket $389.99
Men's Basic Pant $469.99
Men's Liner Gloves $24.99
Men's Pipe Gloves $39.99
Women's Basic Gloves $49.99
Women's Basic Jacket $379.99
Updated data in the Word document

5 **Save** the Word document.

6 On the taskbar, click the **Excel** icon. **Print** or submit the workbook electronically as directed by your instructor.

7 **Close** the Excel workbook, and then **Exit** Excel.

Objective 7 | Create a Table in Word from Access Data

Exporting is a way to output Access data to another database, worksheet, or file format so another database or program can use the data. Exporting is similar to copying and pasting. You can export large amounts of data without having to select the data to copy it. If your data is up-to-date in an Access database, you can export an Access table to Word instead of retyping the information. Exporting saves you time and will reduce the number of errors.

Activity 1.14 | Exporting an Access Table to an RTF File

1. **Start** Access. Navigate to the student data files and then open the Access database **i01B_All_Associates.** Click the **File tab** to display **Backstage** view, and then click **Save Database As.**

2. In the **Save As** dialog box, navigate to your **Integrated Projects** folder, and then **Save** the database as **Lastname_Firstname_1B_All_Associates** If the Security Warning message displays, click the Enable Content button.

3. In the **navigation pane**, click the **Store Location** table to select the table. On the **External Data tab**, in the **Export group**, click the **More** button, and then click **Word.** Compare your screen with Figure 1.24.

   The Export - RTF File dialog box displays. You can click the Browse button to determine the location where the new file will be saved.

Figure 1.24

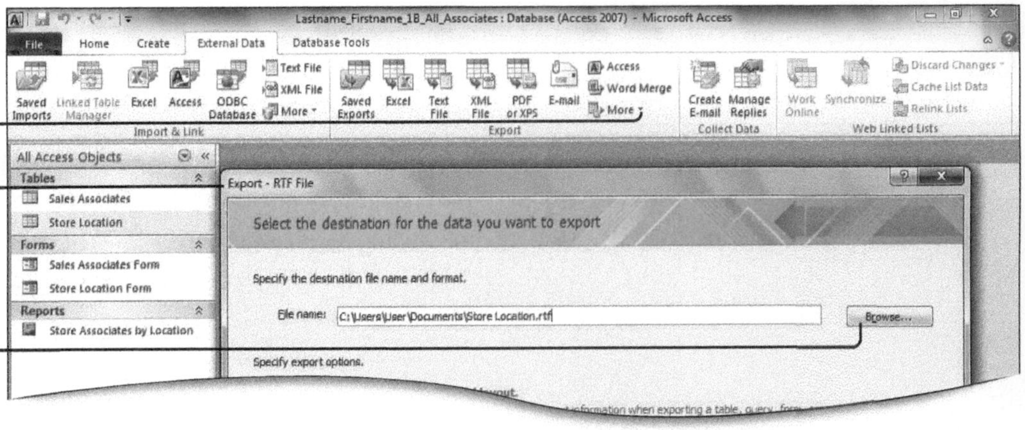

4. In the **Export – RTF File** dialog box, click the **Browse** button, and then navigate to your **Integrated Projects** folder. Save the file as **Lastname_Firstname_1B_Store_Location**

5. In the **Export – RTF File** dialog box, click the **OK** button. In the next dialog box, when asked, *Do you want to save these export steps?* the **Save export steps** check box should not be selected. Click the **Close** button.

   The Access table is saved as a rich text file.

Activity 1.15 | Inserting Access Data into a Word Document

1. On the taskbar, click the **Word** icon. Press Ctrl + End to move to the end of the document.

2. On the **Insert tab**, in the **Text group**, click the **Object button arrow**, and then click **Text from File.** In the **Insert File** dialog box, navigate to the **Integrated Projects** folder, click the file name **Lastname_Firstname_1B_Store_Location**, and then click **Insert.** Compare your screen with Figure 1.25.

Figure 1.25

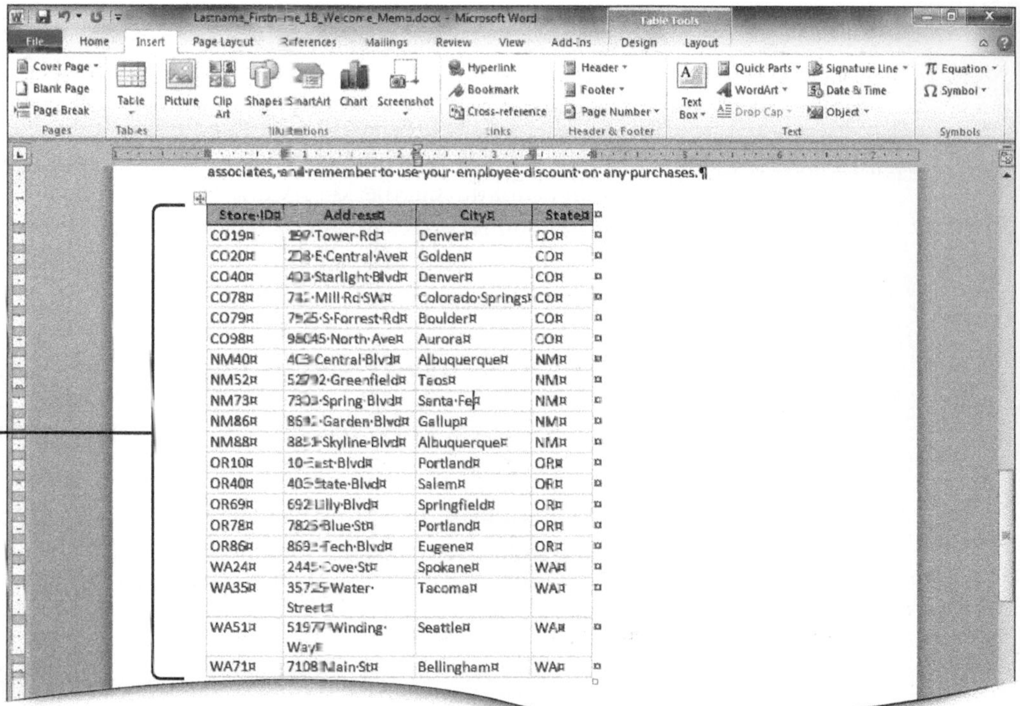

3 In the inserted table, click in the first cell, **Store ID,** to make the cell the active cell. On the **Design tab**, in the **Table Styles group**, click the **More** button, and then click **Light List - Accent 4.**

4 On the **Layout tab**, in the **Rows & Columns group**, click the **Delete** button, and then click **Delete Columns** to delete the Store ID column.

5 In the **Cell Size group**, click the **AutoFit** button, and then click **AutoFit Contents.**

The columns are automatically resized to fit the contents of the cells.

6 In the **Table group**, click the **Properties** button, and then click **Center.** Click **OK**, and then compare your screen with Figure 1.26.

The table is centered horizontally on the page.

Figure 1.26

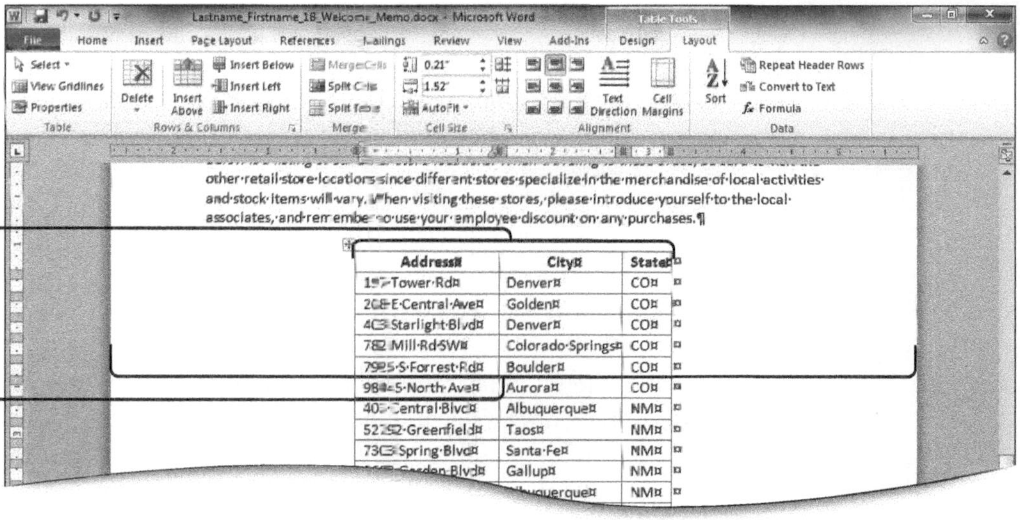

7 **Save** the Word document.

Objective 8 | Use Access Data to Complete a Mail Merge in Word

You can create a data source by entering names in the Mail Merge Wizard in Word, however, if you already have the names in an existing Access database, you do not need to enter them again during the Mail Merge process. You can filter data to quickly find a portion of the total records available. Filtered Access data displays only the records that meet the conditions you specify and hides the records that do not meet the conditions.

Activity 1.16 | Adding Records to an Access Table

1. On the taskbar, click the **Access** icon. In the **navigation pane**, double-click the **Sales Associates Form**.

2. In the navigation area at the bottom of the form, click the **New (blank) record** button. In the **ID** field, type **10-60531** and then press Tab. Type your **Firstname** press Tab, type your **Lastname** press Tab, type **Sales Associate** press Tab, type **NM52** and then compare your screen with Figure 1.27.

Figure 1.27

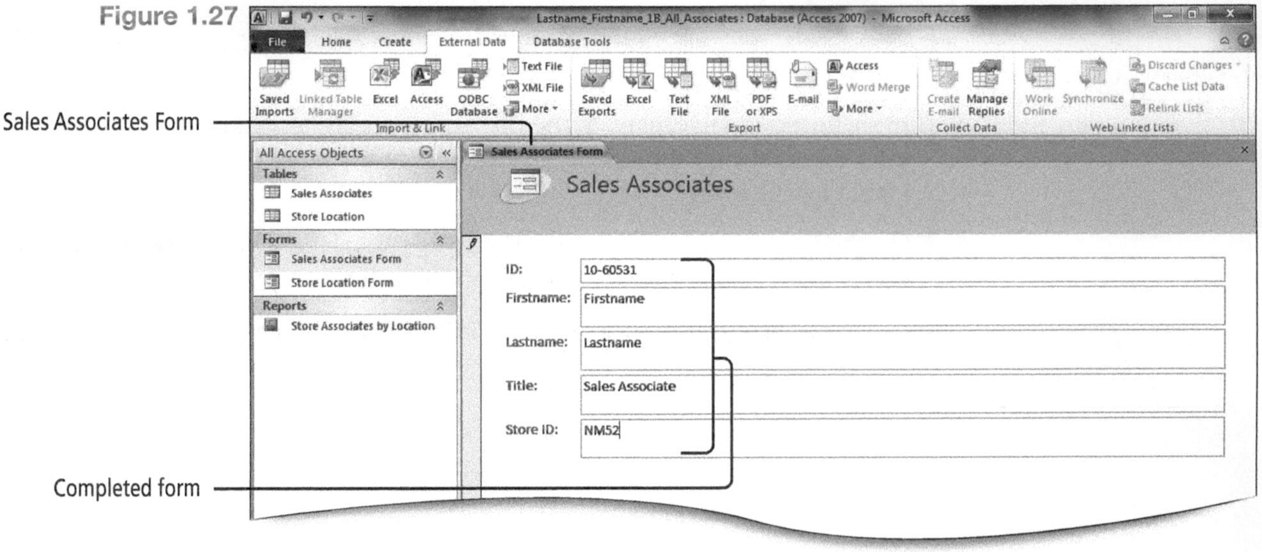

3. Press Tab to accept your record.

4. In the **navigation pane**, double-click the report **Store Associates by Location**. Scroll through the report and verify that your name displays under **NM** for the **Taos** location.

5. **Exit** Access.

Activity 1.17 | Starting Mail Merge in Word

Mail Merge can be used to add placeholders for inserting a data field into a document to make each document unique. In the following activity, you will start the mail merge process in Word and filter the Access records.

1 Make the **Word** document active.

2 On the **Mailings tab**, in the **Start Mail Merge group**, click the **Select Recipients** button, and then click **Use Existing List**.

3 In the **Select Data Source** dialog box, navigate to your **Integrated Projects** folder, select the **Lastname_Firstname_1B_All_Associates** database, and then click **Open** to display the **Select Table** dialog box. Compare your screen with Figure 1.28.

The Access database contains more than one table. You need to select which table will be used for the mail merge.

Figure 1.28

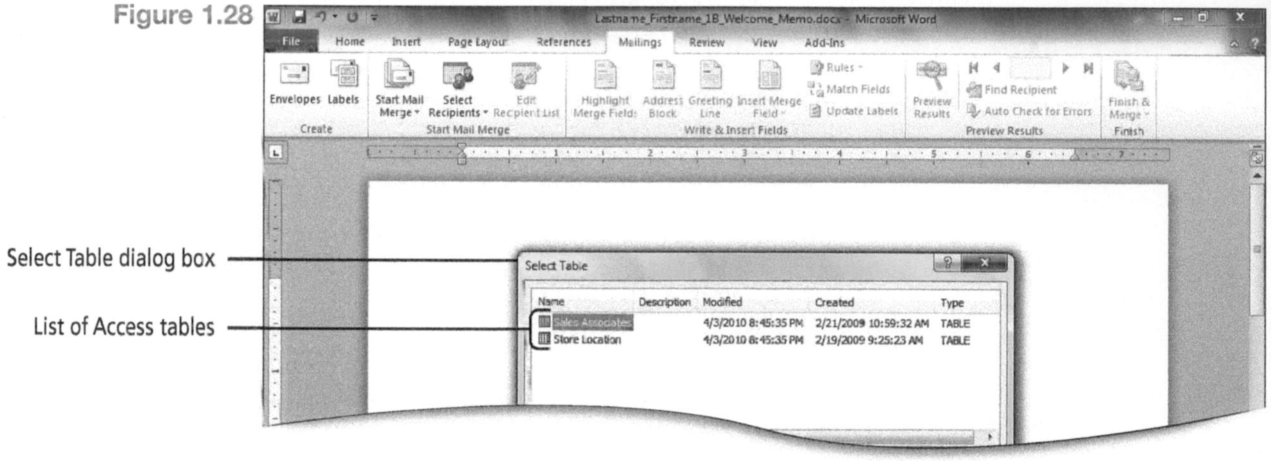

4 In the **Select Table** dialog box, verify that **Sales Associates** is selected, and then click **OK**.

5 In the **Start Mail Merge group**, click the **Edit Recipient List** button.

You can add or edit fields in the Mail Merge Recipients dialog box.

6 In the **Mail Merge Recipients** dialog box, under **Refine recipient list**, click **Filter**.

7 In the **Filter and Sort** dialog box, click the **Field arrow**, and then click **Store ID**. Under **Comparison**, verify that **Equal to** is selected. In the **Compare to** box, type **NM52** and then compare your screen with Figure 1.29.

You can filter on any of the fields.

Figure 1.29

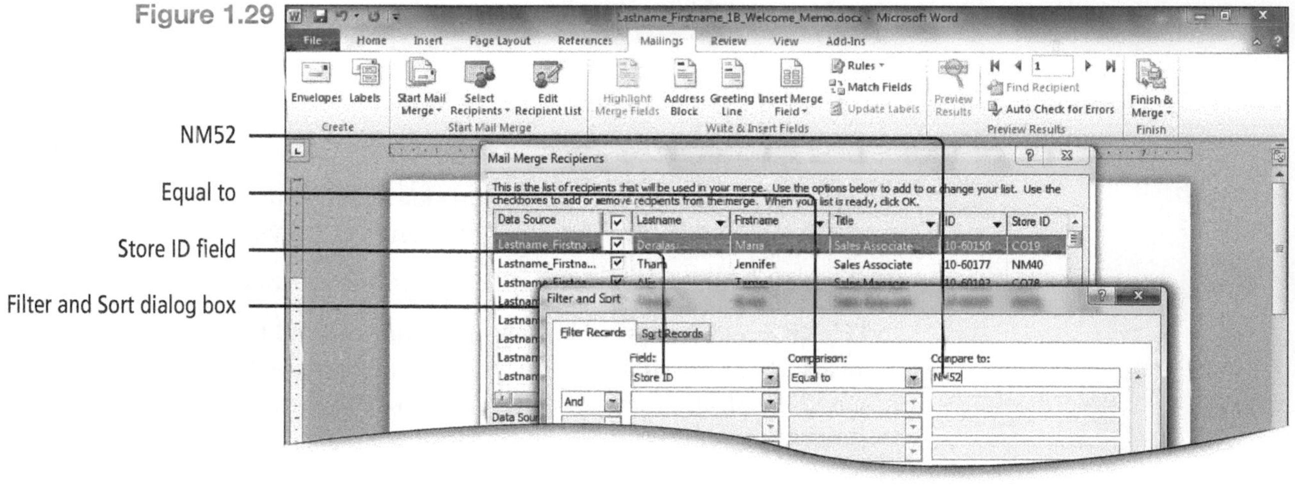

8 At the bottom of the **Filter and Sort** dialog box, click **OK**.

The three Taos records—including your record—display.

9 In the **Mail Merge Recipients** dialog box, click **OK**.

Activity 1.18 | Adding Merge Fields

You will add merge fields as placeholders in the Word document for the information that will be inserted from the Access database. The Mail Merge process includes the data source and the main document, and it will create a new Word document that contains the finished memos.

1 Scroll to the top of the Word document, and then click to place the insertion point after the heading *MEMO TO*.

This is the location in the memo where the sales associate names will be inserted.

2 On the **Mailings tab**, in the **Write & Insert Fields group**, click the **Insert Merge Field button arrow**, and then click **Firstname**. Compare your screen with Figure 1.30.

The Firstname field is inserted in the memo.

When you insert a mail merge field into the main document, the field name is always surrounded by chevrons (« »). These chevrons help distinguish the fields in the main document and will not display on the final document.

Figure 1.30

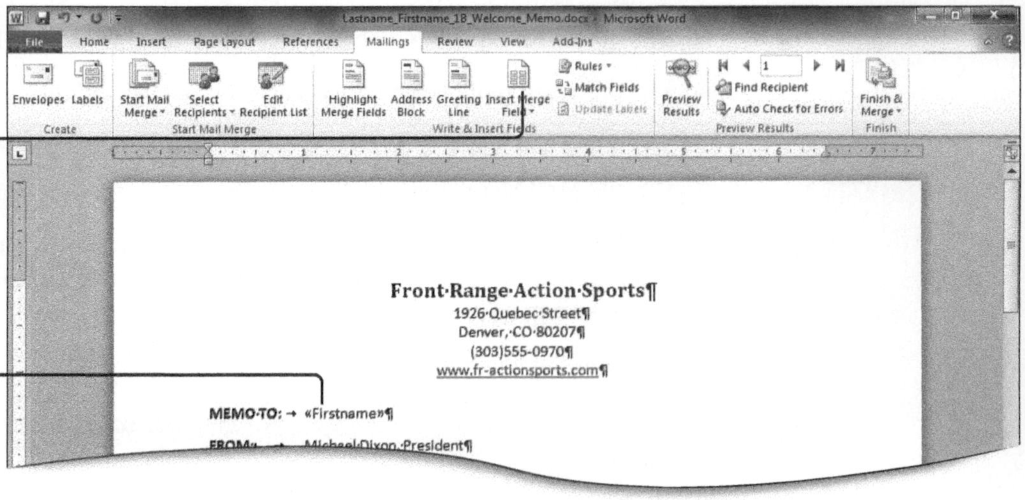

Insert Merge Field button

Firstname field displays in memo

3 Press Spacebar. Click the **Insert Merge Field button arrow**, and then click **Lastname**.

4 In the **Preview Results group**, click the **Preview Results** button. In the **Preview Results group**, click the **Next Record** button ▶ two times to preview the three memos.

The memos are the same except for the sales associate's name.

5 In the **Finish group**, click the **Finish & Merge** button, and then click **Edit Individual Documents.** In the **Merge to New Document** dialog box, verify that the **All** option button is selected, and then click **OK**. Compare your screen with Figure 1.31.

A new Word document with three memos has been created.

Figure 1.31

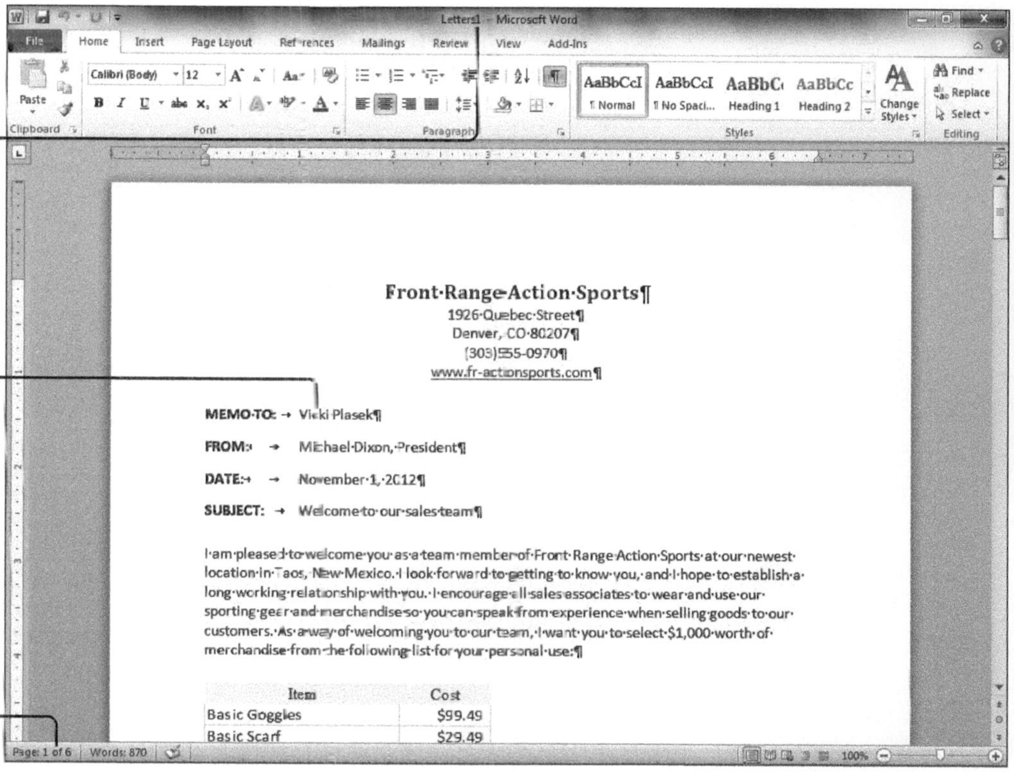
Letters1 - Microsoft Word
File
Home
Insert
Page Layout
References
Mailings
Review
View
Add-Ins
Paste
Clipboard
Calibri (Body)
12
Font
Paragraph
AaBbCcI
¶ Normal
¶ No Spaci...
Heading 1
Heading 2
Change Styles
Styles
Find
Replace
Select
Editing
Front·Range·Action·Sports¶
1926·Quebec·Street¶
Denver,·CO·80207¶
(303)555-0970¶
www.fr-actionsports.com¶
MEMO·TO: → Vicki·Plasek¶
FROM: → Michael·Dixon,·President¶
DATE: → November·1,·2012¶
SUBJECT: → Welcome·to·our·sales·team¶
I·am·pleased·to·welcome·you·as·a·team·member·of·Front·Range·Action·Sports·at·our·newest·location·in·Taos,·New·Mexico.·I·look·forward·to·getting·to·know·you,·and·I·hope·to·establish·a·long·working·relationship·with·you.·I·encourage·all·sales·associates·to·wear·and·use·our·sporting·gear·and·merchandise·so·you·can·speak·from·experience·when·selling·goods·to·our·customers.·As·a·way·of·welcoming·you·to·our·team,·I·want·you·to·select·$1,000·worth·of·merchandise·from·the·following·list·for·your·personal·use:¶
Item
Cost
Basic Goggles
$99.49
Basic Scarf
$29.49
Page: 1 of 6
Words: 870
100%

New document name

Merged name

6 pages

6 **Save** the new merged document in the **Integrated Projects** folder with the file name **Lastname_Firstname_1B_Taos_Memo**

7 Click the **Insert tab.** In the **Header & Footer group**, click the **Footer** button, and then click **Remove Footer**. Click the **Footer** button again, and then click **Edit Footer.** On the **Design tab**, in the **Insert group**, click the **Quick Parts** button, and then click **Field.** In the **Field** dialog box, under **Field names**, locate and click **FileName**, and then click **OK.** In the **Close group**, click the **Close Header and Footer** button.

8 **Save** the Word document.

9 **Print** or submit your Word documents electronically as directed by your instructor.

10 **Close** the Word documents, and then **Exit** Word.

End **You have completed Project 1B**

Glossary

3-D The shortened term for *three-dimensional*, which refers to an image that appears to have all three spatial dimensions—length, width, and depth.

Absolute cell reference A cell reference that refers to cells by their fixed position in a worksheet; an absolute cell reference remains the same when the formula is copied.

Accounting Number Format The Excel number format that applies a thousand comma separator where appropriate, inserts a fixed U.S Dollar sign aligned at the left edge of the cell, applies two decimal places, and leaves a small amount of space at the right edge of the cell to accommodate a parenthesis for negative numbers.

Active cell The cell, surrounded by a black border, ready to receive data or be affected by the next Excel command.

Address bar The bar at the top of a folder window with which you can navigate to a different folder or library, or go back to a previous one.

After Previous An animation command that begins the animation sequence for the selected PowerPoint slide element immediately after the completion of the previous animation or slide transition.

Aggregate functions Calculations such as MIN, MAX, AVG, and SUM that are performed on a group of records.

Alignment The placement of paragraph text relative to the left and right margins.

All Programs An area of the Start menu that displays all the available programs on your computer system.

American Psychological Association (APA) One of two commonly used style guides for formatting research papers.

Anchor The symbol that indicates to which paragraph an object is attached.

AND condition A condition in which only records where all of the values are present in the selected fields.

Animation A visual or sound effect added to an object or text on a slide.

Animation Painter A feature that copies animation settings from one object to another.

Append To add on to the end of an object; for example, to add records to the end of an existing table.

Application Another term for a program.

Arguments The values that an Excel function uses to perform calculations or operations.

Arithmetic operators The symbols +, –, *, /, %, and ^ used to denote addition, subtraction (or negation), multiplication, division, percentage, and exponentiation in an Excel formula.

Artistic effects Formats applied to images that make pictures resemble sketches or paintings.

Ascending order A sorting order that arranges text in alphabetical order (A to Z) or numbers from the lowest to highest number.

Auto Fill An Excel feature that generates and extends values into adjacent cells based on the values of selected cells.

AutoComplete (Excel) A feature that speeds your typing and lessens the likelihood of errors; if the first few characters you type in a cell match an existing entry in the column, Excel fills in the remaining characters for you.

AutoCorrect A feature that corrects common spelling errors as you type, for example, changing *teh* to *the*.

AutoFit An Excel feature that adjusts the width of a column to fit the cell content of the widest cell in the column.

AutoNumber data type A data type that describes a unique sequential or random number assigned by Access as each record is entered and that is useful for data that has no distinct field that can be considered unique.

AutoPlay A Windows feature that displays when you insert a CD, a DVD, or other removable device, and which lets you choose which program to use to start different kinds of media, such as music CDs, or CDs and DVDs containing photos.

AutoSum Another name for the *SUM* function.

AVERAGE function An Excel function that adds a group of values, and then divides the result by the number of values in the group.

Axis A line that serves as a frame of reference for measurement and which borders the chart plot area.

Back and Forward buttons Buttons at the top of a folder window that work in conjunction with the address bar to change folders by going backward or forward one folder at a time.

Background Removal A command that removes unwanted portions of a picture so that the picture does not appear as a self-contained rectangle.

Background style A slide background fill variation that combines theme colors in different intensities or patterns.

Backstage tabs The area along the left side of Backstage view with tabs to display various pages of commands.

Backstage view A centralized space for file management tasks; for example, opening, saving, printing, publishing, or sharing a file. A navigation pane displays along the left side with tabs that group file-related tasks together.

Bar tab stop A vertical bar that displays at a tab stop.

Base The starting point; used in calculating the rate of increase, which is the amount of increase divided by the base.

Best Fit An Access command that adjusts the width of a column to accommodate the column's longest entry.

Between ... And operator A comparison operator that looks for values within a range.

Bevel A shape effect that uses shading and shadows to make the edges of a shape appear to be curved or angled.

Bibliography A list of cited works in a report or research paper also referred to as *Works Cited*, *Sources*, or *References*, depending upon the report style.

Black slide A slide that displays at the end of an electronic slide show indicating that the presentation is over.

Blank database A database that has no data and has no database tools—you must create the data and the tools as you need them.

Blank Report tool An Access tool with which you can create a report from scratch by adding the fields you want in the order in which you want them to display.

Body font A font that is applied to all slide text except titles.

Body The text of a letter.

Bound control A control that retrieves its data from an underlying table or query; a text box control is an example of a bound control.

Bound The term used to describe objects and controls that are based on data that is stored in tables.

Bullets Text symbols such as small circles or check marks that precede each item in a bulleted list.

Bulleted list A list of items with each item introduced by a symbol such as a small circle or check mark, and which is useful when the items in the list can be displayed in any order.

Calculated control A control that contains an expression, often a formula, that uses one or more fields from the underlying table or query.

Calculated field A field that stores the value of a mathematical operation.

Caption A property setting that displays a name for a field in a table, query, form, or report other than that listed as the field name.

Category axis The area along the bottom of a chart that identifies the categories of data; also referred to as the *x-axis*.

Category label A chart element that identifies a category of data.

Category labels The labels that display along the bottom of a chart to identify the categories of data; Excel uses the row titles as the category names.

Cell The intersection of a column and a row.

Cell (Word) The box at the intersection of a row and column in a Word table.

Cell address Another name for a *cell reference.*

Cell content Anything typed into a cell.

Cell reference The identification of a specific cell by its intersecting column letter and row number.

Cell style A defined set of formatting characteristics, such as font, font size, font color, cell borders, and cell shading.

Center alignment An arrangement of text in which the text is centered between the left and right margins.

Center alignment The alignment of text or objects that is centered horizontally between the left and right margin.

Center tab stop A tab stop in which the text centers around the tab stop location.

Chart A graphic representation of numeric data.

Chart (Excel) The graphic representation of data in a worksheet; data presented as a chart is usually easier to understand than a table of numbers.

Chart area The entire chart and all of its elements.

Chart Elements box The box in the Chart Tools tabs from which you can select a chart element so that you can format it.

Chart layout The combination of chart elements that can be displayed in a chart such as a title, legend, labels for the columns, and the table of charted cells.

Chart Layouts gallery A group of predesigned chart layouts that you can apply to an Excel chart.

Chart sheet A workbook sheet that contains only a chart.

Chart style The overall visual look of a chart in terms of its graphic effects, colors, and backgrounds; for example, you can have flat or beveled columns, colors that solid or transparent, and backgrounds that are dark or light.

Chart Styles gallery A group of predesigned chart styles that you can apply to an Excel chart.

Chart types Various chart formats used in a way that is meaningful to the reader; common examples are column charts, pie charts, and line charts.

Citation A note inserted into the text of a research paper that refers the reader to a source in the bibliography.

Click The action of pressing the left button on your mouse pointing device one time.

Clip art Predefined graphics included with Microsoft Office or downloaded from the Web.

Clip A single media file, for example art, sound, animation, or a movie.

Column A vertical group of cells in a worksheet.

Column break indicator A single dotted line with the text *Column Break* that indicates where a manual column break was inserted.

Column chart A chart in which the data is arranged in columns and which is useful for showing data changes over a period of time or for illustrating comparisons among items.

Column chart A type of chart used to compare data.

Column heading The letter that displays at the top of a vertical group of cells in a worksheet; beginning with the first letter of the alphabet, a unique letter or combination of letters identifies each column.

Comma Style The Excel number format that inserts thousand comma separators where appropriate and applies two decimal places; Comma Style also leaves space at the right to accommodate a parenthesis when negative numbers are present.

Command An instruction to a computer program that causes an action to be carried out.

Common dialog boxes The set of dialog boxes that includes Open, Save, and Save As, which are provided by the Windows programming interface, and which display and operate in all of the Office programs in the same manner.

Common field A field in one or more tables that stores the same data.

Comparison operator Symbols that evaluate each value to determine if it is the same (=), greater than (>), less than (<), or in between a range of values as specified by the criteria.

Complimentary closing A parting farewell in a business letter.

Compound criteria Multiple conditions in a query or filter.

Compressed file A file that has been reduced in size and thus takes up less storage space and can be transferred to other computers quickly.

Conditional format A format that changes the appearance of a cell—for example, by adding cell shading or font color—based on a condition; if the condition is true, the cell is formatted based on that condition, and if the condition is false, the cell is *not* formatted.

Constant value Numbers, text, dates, or times of day that you type into a cell.

Content control In a template, an area indicated by placeholder text that can be used to add text, pictures, dates, or lists.

Context sensitive A command associated with activities in which you are engaged; often activated by right-clicking a screen item.

Context sensitive command A command associated with activities in which you are engaged.

Contextual tabs Tabs that are added to the Ribbon automatically when a specific object, such as a picture, is selected, and that contain commands relevant to the selected object.

Control An object on a form or report that displays data, performs actions, and lets you view and work with information.

Control layout The grouped arrangement of controls on a form or report.

Copy A command that duplicates a selection and places it on the Clipboard.

COUNTIF function A statistical function that counts the number of cells within a range that meet the given condition and that has two arguments—the range of cells to check and the criteria.

Criteria (Access) Conditions in a query that identify the specific records for which you are looking.

Criteria (Excel) Conditions that you specify in a logical function.

Crop A command that reduces the size of a picture by removing vertical or horizontal edges.

Crosshair pointer A pointer that indicates that you can draw a shape.

Crosstab query A query that uses an aggregate function for data that can be grouped by two types of information and displays the data in a compact, spreadsheet-like format.

Currency data type An Access data type that describes monetary values and numeric data that can be used in mathematical calculations involving data with one to four decimal places.

Cut A command that removes a selection and places it on the Clipboard.

Data Facts about people, events, things, or ideas.

Data (Excel) Text or numbers in a cell.

Data bar A cell format consisting of a shaded bar that provides a visual cue to the reader about the value of a cell relative to other cells; the length of the bar represents the value in the cell—a longer bar represents a higher value and a shorter bar represents a lower value.

Data entry The action of typing the record data into a database form or table.

Data marker A column, bar, area, dot, pie slice, or other symbol in a chart that represents a single data point; related data points form a data series.

Data point A value that originates in a worksheet cell and that is represented in a chart by a data marker.

Data series Related data points represented by data markers; each data series has a unique color or pattern represented in the chart legend.

Data source (Access) The table or tables from which a form, query, or report retrieves its data.

Data source (Word) A list of variable information, such as names and addresses, that is merged with a main document to create customized form letters or labels.

Data type The characteristic that defines the kind of data that can be entered into a field, such as numbers, text, or dates.

Database management system Database software that controls how related collections of data are stored, organized, retrieved, and secured; also known as a *DBMS*.

Database template A preformatted database designed for a specific purpose.

Database An organized collection of facts about people, events, things, or ideas related to a specific topic or purpose.

Datasheet view The Access view that displays data organized in columns and rows similar to an Excel worksheet.

Date control A control on a form or report that inserts the current date each time the form or report is opened.

Date line The first line in a business letter that contains the current date and that is positioned just below the letterhead if a letterhead is used.

DBMS An acronym for *database management system*.

Decimal tab stop A tab stop in which the text aligns with the decimal point at the tab stop location.

Default The term that refers to the current selection or setting that is automatically used by a computer program unless you specify otherwise.

Descending order A sorting order that arranges text in reverse alphabetical order (Z to A) or numbers from the highest to lowest number.

Deselect The action of canceling the selection of an object or block of text by clicking outside of the selection.

Design grid The lower area of the Query window that displays the design of the query.

Design view An Access view that displays the detailed structure of a query, form, or report; for forms and reports, may be the view in which some tasks must be performed, and only the controls, and not the data, display in this view.

Desktop In Windows, the opening screen that simulates your work area.

Destination table (Access) The table to which you import or append data.

Detail section The section of a form or report that displays the records from the underlying table or query.

Detail sheets The worksheets that contain the details of the information summarized on a summary sheet.

Details pane The area at the bottom of a folder window that displays the most common file properties.

Dialog Box Launcher A small icon that displays to the right of some group names on the Ribbon, and which opens a related dialog box or task pane providing additional options and commands related to that group.

Dialog box A small window that contains options for completing a task.

Displayed value The data that displays in a cell.

Document properties Details about a file that describe or identify it, including the title, author name, subject, and keywords that identify the document's topic or contents; also known as *metadata*.

Dot leader A series of dots preceding a tab that guides the eye across the line.

Double-click The action of clicking the left mouse button two times in rapid succession.

Drag The action of holding down the left mouse button while moving your mouse.

Drag and drop The action of moving a selection by dragging it to a new location.

Drawing objects Graphic objects, such as shapes, diagrams, lines, or circles.

Edit The actions of making changes to text or graphics in an Office file.

Editing The process of modifying a presentation by adding and deleting slides or by changing the contents of individual slides.

Ellipsis A set of three dots indicating incompleteness; when following a command name, indicates that a dialog box will display.

Emphasis effect Animation that emphasizes an object or text that is already displayed.

Enclosures Additional documents included with a business letter.

Endnote In a research paper, a note placed at the end of a document or chapter.

Enhanced ScreenTip A ScreenTip that displays more descriptive text than a normal ScreenTip.

Entrance effect Animation that brings a slide element onto the screen.

Excel table A series of rows and columns that contains related data that is managed independently from the data in other rows and columns in the worksheet.

Exit effect Animation that moves an object or text off the screen.

Expand Formula Bar button An Excel window element with which you can increase the height of the Formula Bar to display lengthy cell content.

Expand horizontal scroll bar button An Excel window element with which you can increase the width of the horizontal scroll bar.

Explode The action of pulling out one or more pie slices from a pie chart for emphasis.

Expression A formula.

Extract To decompress, or pull out, files from a compressed form.

Field A single piece of information that is stored in every record and formatted as a column in a database table.

Field (Word) A placeholder that displays preset content, such as the current date, the file name, a page number, or other stored information.

Field list A list of the field names in a table.

Field properties Characteristics of a field that control how the field displays and how data can be entered in the field.

Fields In a mail merge, the column headings in the data source.

File A collection of information stored on a computer under a single name, for example a Word document or a PowerPoint presentation.

File list In a folder window, the area on the right that displays the contents of the current folder or library.

Fill The inside color of an object.

Fill color The inside color of text or of an object.

Fill handle The small black square in the lower right corner of a selected cell.

Filter The process of displaying only a portion of the data based on matching a specific value to show only the data that meets the criteria that you specify.

Filter by Form An Access command that filters the records in a form based on one or more fields, or based on more than one value in the field.

Filter by Selection An Access command that retrieves only the records that contain the value in the selected field.

Filtering The process of displaying only a portion of the total records (a subset) based on matching a specific value.

Find and replace (Excel) A command that searches the cells in a worksheet—or in a selected range—for matches and then replaces each match with a replacement value of your choice.

First principle of good database design A principle of good database design stating that data is organized in tables so that there is no redundant data.

Flat database A simple database file that is not related or linked to any other collection of data.

Floating object A graphic that can be moved independently of the surrounding text characters.

Folder window In Windows, a window that displays the contents of the current folder, library, or device, and contains helpful parts so that you can navigate.

Folder A container in which you store files.

Font A set of characters with the same design and shape.

Font styles Formatting emphasis such as bold, italic, and underline.

Footer (PowerPoint) Text that displays at the bottom of every slide or that prints at the bottom of a sheet of slide handouts or notes pages.

Footer A reserved area for text or graphics that displays at the bottom of each page in a document.

Footnote In a research paper, a note placed at the bottom of the page.

Foreign key The field that is included in the related table so the field can be joined with the primary key in another table for the purpose of creating a relationship.

Form A database object used to enter data, edit data, or display data from a table or query.

Form (Access) An Access object you can use to enter new records into a table, edit or delete existing records in a table, or display existing records.

Form footer Information at the bottom of the screen in Form view that is printed after the last detail section on the last page.

Form header Information, such as a form's title, that displays at the top of the screen in Form view and is printed at the top of the first page when records are printed as forms.

Form tool The Access tool that creates a form with a single mouse click, which includes all of the fields from the underlying data source (table or query).

Form view The Access view in which you can view the records, but you cannot change the layout or design of the form.

Form Wizard The Access tool that creates a form by asking a series of questions.

Format (Excel) Changing the appearance of cells and worksheet elements to make a worksheet attractive and easy to read.

Format as you type The Excel feature by which a cell takes on the formatting of the number typed into the cell.

Format Painter An Office feature that copies formatting from one selection of text to another.

Formatting The process of establishing the overall appearance of text, graphics, and pages in an Office file—for example, in a Word document.

Formatting (PowerPoint) The process of changing the appearance of the text, layout, and design of a slide.

Formatting marks Characters that display on the screen, but do not print, indicating where the Enter key, the Spacebar, and the Tab key were pressed; also called *nonprinting characters.*

Formula AutoComplete An Excel feature which, after typing an = (equal sign) and the beginning letter or letters of a function name, displays a list of function names that match the typed letter(s).

Formula An equation that performs mathematical calculations on values in a worksheet.

Formula Bar An element in the Excel window that displays the value or formula contained in the active cell; here you can also enter or edit values or formulas.

Freeze Panes A command that enables you to select one or more rows or columns and freeze (lock) them into place; the locked rows and columns become separate panes.

Function A predefined formula—a formula that Excel has already built for you—that performs calculations by using specific values in a particular order or structure.

Fund A sum of money set aside for a specific purpose.

Gallery An Office feature that displays a list of potential results instead of just the command name.

General format The default format that Excel applies to numbers; this format has no specific characteristics—whatever you type in the cell will display, with the exception that trailing zeros to the right of a decimal point will not display.

General fund The term used to describe money set aside for the normal operating activities of a government entity such as a city.

Goal Seek A what-if analysis tool that finds the input needed in one cell to arrive at the desired result in another cell.

Graphics Pictures, clip art images, charts, or drawing objects.

Group footer Information printed at the end of each group of records; used to display summary information for the group.

Group header Information printed at the beginning of each new group of records, for example, the group name.

Group, Sort, and Total pane A pane that displays at the bottom of the screen in which you can control how information is sorted and grouped in a report; provides the most flexibility for adding or modifying groups, sort orders, or totals options on a report.

Groups On the Office Ribbon, the sets of related commands that you might need for a specific type of task.

Hanging indent An indent style in which the first line of a paragraph extends to the left of the remaining lines, and that is commonly used for bibliographic entries.

Header (PowerPoint) Text that prints at the top of each sheet of slide handouts or notes pages.

Header A reserved area for text or graphics that displays at the top of each page in a document.

Headings font The font that is applied to slide titles.

Horizontal window split box (Excel) An Excel window element with which you can split the worksheet into two horizontal views of the same worksheet.

HTML See Hypertext Markup Language (HTML).

Hypertext Markup Language (HTML) The language used to format documents that can be opened using any Web browser.

Icons Pictures that represent a program, a file, a folder, or some other object.

IF function A function that uses a logical test to check whether a condition is met, and then returns one value if true, and another value if false.

Import The process of copying data from another file, such as a Word table or an Excel workbook, into a separate file, such as an Access database.

Info tab The tab in Backstage view that displays information about the current file.

Information Data that is organized in a useful manner.

Inline object An object or graphic inserted in a document that acts like a character in a sentence.

Innermost sort field When sorting on multiple fields in Datasheet view, the field that will be used for the second level of sorting.

Insert Worksheet button Located on the row of sheet tabs, a sheet tab that, when clicked, inserts an additional worksheet into the workbook.

Insertion point A blinking vertical line that indicates where text or graphics will be inserted.

Inside address The name and address of the person receiving the letter; positioned below the date line.

Is Not Null A criteria that searches for fields that are not empty.

Is Null A criteria that searches for fields that are empty.

Join line In the Relationships window, the line joining two tables that visually indicates the related field and the type of relationship.

Justified alignment An arrangement of text in which the text aligns evenly on both the left and right margins.

Keyboard shortcut A combination of two or more keyboard keys, used to perform a task that would otherwise require a mouse.

KeyTips The letter that displays on a command in the Ribbon and that indicates the key you can press to activate the command when keyboard control of the Ribbon is activated.

Label control A control on a form or report that contains descriptive information, typically a field name.

Labels Another name for a text value, and which usually provides information about number values.

Landscape orientation A page orientation in which the paper is wider than it is tall.

Layout The arrangement of elements, such as title and subtitle text, lists, pictures, tables, charts, shapes, and movies, on a PowerPoint slide.

Layout selector A small symbol that displays in the upper left corner of a selected control layout in a form or report that is displayed in Layout view or Design view; used to move an entire group of controls.

Layout view The Access view in which you can make changes to a form or report while the object is running—the data from the underlying data source displays.

Leader characters Characters that form a solid, dotted, or dashed line that fills the space preceding a tab stop.

Left alignment An arrangement of text in which the text aligns at the left margin, leaving the right margin uneven.

Left alignment (Excel) The cell format in which characters align at the left edge of the cell; this is the default for text entries and is an example of formatting information stored in a cell.

Left tab stop A tab stop in which the text is left aligned at the tab stop and extends to the right.

Legend A chart element that identifies the patterns or colors that are assigned to the categories in the chart.

Lettered column headings The area along the top edge of a worksheet that identifies each column with a unique letter or combination of letters.

Letterhead The personal or company information that displays at the top of a letter.

Library In Windows, a collection of items, such as files and folders, assembled from various locations that might be on your computer, an external hard drive, removable media, or someone else's computer.

Line break indicator A small nonprinting bent arrow that displays where a manual line break was inserted.

Line chart A chart type that is useful to display trends over time; time displays along the bottom axis and the data point values are connected with a line.

Line spacing The distance between lines of text in a paragraph.

Link A connection to data in another file.

List level An outline level in a presentation represented by a bullet symbol and identified in a slide by the indentation and the size of the text.

Live Preview A technology that shows the result of applying an editing or formatting change as you point to possible results—*before* you actually apply it.

Location Any disk drive, folder, or other place in which you can store files and folders.

Logical functions A group of functions that test for specific conditions and that typically use conditional tests to determine whether specified conditions are true or false.

Logical operators Operators that combine criteria using AND and OR. With two criteria, AND requires that both conditions be met and OR requires that either condition be met.

Logical test Any value or expression that can be evaluated as being true or false.

Mail merge A Microsoft Word feature that joins a main document and a data source to create customized letters or labels.

Main document In a mail merge, the document that contains the text or formatting that remains constant.

Major unit The value in a chart's value axis that determines the spacing between tick marks and between the gridlines in the plot area.

Manual column break An artificial end to a column to balance columns or to provide space for the insertion of other objects.

Manual line break The action of ending a line, before the normal end of the line, without creating a new paragraph.

Manual page break The action of forcing a page to end and placing subsequent text at the top of the next page.

Margins The space between the text and the top, bottom, left, and right edges of the paper.

MAX function An Excel function that determines the largest value in a selected range of values.

MEDIAN function An Excel function that finds the middle value that has as many values above it in the group as are below it; it differs from AVERAGE in that the result is not affected as much by a single value that is greatly different from the others.

Merge & Center A command that joins selected cells in an Excel worksheet into one larger cell and centers the contents in the new cell.

Message Bar The area directly below the Ribbon that displays information such as security alerts when there is potentially unsafe, active content in an Office 2010 document that you open.

Metadata Details about a file that describe or identify it, including the title, author name, subject, and keywords that identify the document's topic or contents; also known as *document properties.*

Microsoft Access A database program, with which you can collect, track, and report data.

Microsoft Excel A spreadsheet program, with which you calculate and analyze numbers and create charts.

Microsoft InfoPath An Office program that enables you to create forms and gather data.

Microsoft Office 2010 A Microsoft suite of products that includes programs, servers, and services for individuals, small organizations, and large enterprises to perform specific tasks.

Microsoft OneNote An Office program with which you can manage notes that you make at meetings or in classes.

Microsoft Outlook An Office program with which you can manage e-mail and organizational activities.

Microsoft PowerPoint A presentation program, with which you can communicate information with high-impact graphics.

Microsoft Publisher An Office program with which you can create desktop publishing documents such as brochures.

Microsoft SharePoint Workspace An Office program that enables you to share information with others in a team environment.

Microsoft Word A word processing program, also referred to as an authoring program, with which you create and share documents by using its writing tools.

MIN function An Excel function that determines the smallest value in a selected range of values.

Mini toolbar A small toolbar containing frequently used formatting commands that displays as a result of selecting text or objects.

Modern Language Association (MLA) One of two commonly used style guides for formatting research papers.

Multiple Items form A form that enables you to display or enter multiple records in a table.

Name Box An element of the Excel window that displays the name of the selected cell, table, chart, or object.

Nameplate The banner on the front page of a newsletter that identifies the publication; also referred to as a *banner*, *flag*, or *masthead.*

Navigate The process of exploring within the organizing structure of Windows.

Navigate (Excel) The process of moving within a worksheet or workbook.

Navigation area An area at the bottom of the Access window that indicates the number of records in the table and contains controls (arrows) with which you can navigate among the records.

Navigation Pane (Access) An area of the Access window that displays and organizes the names of the objects in a database; from here, you open objects for use.

Navigation pane (Windows) In a folder window, the area on the left in which you can navigate to, open, and display favorites, libraries, folders, saved searches, and an expandable list of drives.

New from existing The Word command that opens an existing document as a new unnamed document, so that you can use it as a starting point for a new document.

No Spacing style The Word style that inserts *no* extra space following a paragraph and uses single spacing.

Nonprinting characters Characters that display on the screen, but do not print, indicating where the Enter key, the Spacebar, and the Tab key were pressed; also called *formatting marks.*

Normal template The template that serves as a basis for all new Word documents.

Normal view (Excel) A screen view that maximizes the number of cells visible on your screen and keeps the column letters and row numbers close to the columns and rows.

Normal view (PowerPoint) The primary editing view in PowerPoint in which you write and design your presentations; consists of the Notes pane, Slide pane, and the Slides/Outline pane.

Normalization The process of applying design rules and principles to ensure that your database performs as expected.

Note In a research paper, information that expands on the topic, but that does not fit well in the document text.

Notes page A printout that contains the slide image on the top half of the page and notes that you have created on the Notes pane in the lower half of the page.

Notes pane The PowerPoint screen element that displays below the Slide pane with space to type notes regarding the active slide.

NOW function An Excel function that retrieves the date and time from your computer's calendar and clock and inserts the information into the selected cell.

Nudge The action of moving an object on the page in small precise increments.

Number format A specific way in which Excel displays numbers in a cell.

Number values Constant values consisting of only numbers.

Numbered list A list of items in which each item is introduced by a consecutive number to indicate definite steps, a sequence of actions, or chronological order.

Numbered row headings The area along the left edge of a worksheet that identifies each row with a unique number.

Object window An area of the Access window that displays open objects, such as tables, forms, queries, or reports; by default, each object displays on its own tab.

Objects The basic parts of a database that you create to store your data and to work with your data; for example, tables, forms, queries, and reports.

Office Clipboard A temporary storage area that holds text or graphics that you select and then cut or copy.

On Click An animation command that begins the animation sequence for the selected PowerPoint slide element when the mouse button is clicked or the spacebar is pressed.

One-to-many relationship A relationship between two tables where one record in the first table corresponds to many records in the second table—the most common type of relationship in Access.

Open dialog box A dialog box from which you can navigate to, and then open on your screen, an existing file that was created in that same program.

Operators The symbols with which you can specify the type of calculation you want to perform in an Excel formula.

Option button A round button that allows you to make one choice among two or more options.

Options dialog box A dialog box within each Office application where you can select program settings and other options and preferences.

OR condition A condition in which records that match at least one of the specified values are displayed.

Order of operations The mathematical rules for performing multiple calculations within a formula.

Outermost sort field When sorting on multiple fields in Datasheet view, the field that will be used for the first level of sorting.

Page break indicator A dotted line with the text *Page Break* that indicates where a manual page break was inserted.

Page footer Information printed at the end of every page in a report; used to print page numbers or other information that you want to display at the bottom of every report page.

Page header (Access) Information printed at the top of every page of a report.

Page Layout view A screen view in which you can use the rulers to measure the width and height of data, set margins for printing, hide or display the numbered row headings and the lettered column headings, and change the page orientation; this view is useful for preparing your worksheet for printing.

Page number control A control on a form or report that inserts the page numbers when displayed in Print Preview or when printed.

Pane (Excel) A portion of a worksheet window bounded by and separated from other portions by vertical and horizontal bars.

Paragraph symbol The symbol ¶ that represents a paragraph.

Parenthetical citation In the MLA style, a citation that refers to items on the *Works Cited* page, and which is placed in parentheses; the citation includes the last name of the author or authors, and the page number in the referenced source.

Paste The action of placing text or objects that have been copied or moved from one location to another location.

Paste area The target destination for data that has been cut or copied using the Office Clipboard.

Paste Options Icons that provide a Live Preview of the various options for changing the format of a pasted item with a single click.

Paste Options gallery (Excel) A gallery of buttons that provides a Live Preview of all the Paste options available in the current context.

PDF (Portable Document Format) file A file format that creates an image that preserves the look of your file, but that cannot be easily changed; a popular format for sending documents electronically, because the document will display on most computers.

Percent for new value = base percent + percent of increase The formula for calculating a percentage by which a value increases by adding the base percentage—usually 100%—to the percent increase.

Percentage rate of increase The percent by which one number increases over another number.

Picture element A point of light measured in dots per square inch on a screen; 64 pixels equals 8.43 characters, which is the average number of digits that will fit in a cell in an Excel worksheet using the default font.

Picture styles Frames, shapes, shadows, borders, and other special effects that can be added to an image to create an overall visual style for the image.

Pie chart A chart that shows the relationship of each part to a whole.

Pixel The abbreviated name for a *picture element*.

Placeholder text Text in a content control that indicates the type of information to be entered in a specific location.

Placeholder A box on a slide with dotted or dashed borders that holds title and body text or other content such as charts, tables, and pictures.

Plot area The area bounded by the axes of a chart, including all the data series.

Point The action of moving your mouse pointer over something on your screen.

Point and click method The technique of constructing a formula by pointing to and then clicking cells; this method is convenient when the referenced cells are not adjacent to one another.

Pointer Any symbol that displays on your screen in response to moving your mouse.

Points A measurement of the size of a font; there are 72 points in an inch, with 10-12 points being the most commonly used font size.

Populate The action of filling a database table with records.

Portrait orientation A page orientation in which the paper is taller than it is wide.

Preview pane button In a folder window, the button on the toolbar with which you can display a preview of the contents of a file without opening it in a program.

Primary key The field that uniquely identifies a record in a table; for example, a Student ID number at a college.

Print Preview A view of a document as it will appear when you print it.

Print Titles An Excel command that enables you to specify rows and columns to repeat on each printed page.

Program A set of instructions that a computer uses to perform a specific task, such as word processing, accounting, or data management; also called an *application*.

Program-level control buttons In an Office program, the buttons on the right edge of the title bar that minimize, restore, or close the program.

Property Sheet A list of characteristics—properties—for fields or controls on a form or report in which you can make precise changes to each property associated with the field or control.

Protected view A security feature in Office 2010 that protects your computer from malicious files by opening them in a restricted environment until you enable them; you might encounter this feature if you open a file from an e-mail or download files from the Internet.

Pt. The abbreviation for *point*; for example when referring to a font size.

Query A database object that retrieves specific data from one or more database objects—either tables or other queries—and then, in a single datasheet, displays only the data you specify.

Quick Access Toolbar In an Office program, the small row of buttons in the upper left corner of the screen from which you can perform frequently used commands.

Quick Commands The commands Save, Save As, Open, and Close that display at the top of the navigation pane in Backstage view.

Range Two or more selected cells on a worksheet that are adjacent or nonadjacent; because the range is treated as a single unit, you can make the same changes or combination of changes to more than one cell at a time.

Range finder An Excel feature that outlines cells in color to indicate which cells are used in a formula; useful for verifying which cells are referenced in a formula.

Range finder An Excel feature that outlines cells in color to indicate which cells are used in a formula; useful for verifying which cells are referenced in a formula.

Rate = amount of increase/base The mathematical formula to calculate a rate of increase.

Read-Only A property assigned to a file that prevents the file from being modified or deleted; it indicates that you cannot save any changes to the displayed document unless you first save it with a new name.

Reading view A view in PowerPoint that displays a presentation in a manner similar to a slide show but in which the taskbar, title bar, and status bar remain available in the presentation window.

Record selector bar The bar at the left edge of a record when it is displayed in a form, and which is used to select an entire record.

Record All of the categories of data pertaining to one person, place, thing, event, or idea, and which is formatted as a row in a database table.

Record In a mail merge, a row of information that contains data for one person.

Record selector box The small box at the left of a record in Datasheet view that, when clicked, selects the entire record.

Record source The tables or queries that provide the underlying data for a form or report.

Redundant In a database, information that is repeated in a manner that indicates poor database design.

Referential integrity A set of rules that Access uses to ensure that the data between related tables is valid.

Relational database A sophisticated type of database that has multiple collections of data within the file that are related to one another.

Relationship An association that you establish between two tables based on common fields.

Relative cell reference In a formula, the address of a cell based on the relative position of the cell that contains the formula and the cell referred to.

Report A database object that summarizes the fields and records from a table or query in an easy-to-read format suitable for printing.

Report footer Information printed once at the end of a report; used to print report totals or other summary information for the entire report.

Report header Information printed once at the beginning of a report; used for logos, titles, and dates.

Report tool The Access tool that creates a report with one mouse click, which displays all of the fields and records from the record source that you select—a quick way to look at the underlying data.

Report Wizard An Access feature with which you can create a report by answering a series of questions; Access designs the report based on your answers.

Ribbon The user interface in Office 2010 that groups the commands for performing related tasks on tabs across the upper portion of the program window.

Ribbon tabs The tabs on the Office Ribbon that display the names of the task-oriented groups of commands.

Right alignment An arrangement of text in which the text aligns at the right margin, leaving the left margin uneven.

Right tab stop A tab stop in which the text is right aligned at the tab stop and extends to the left.

Right-click The action of clicking the right mouse button one time.

Rotation handle A green circle that provides a way to rotate a selected image.

Rounding A procedure in which you determine which digit at the right of the number will be the last digit displayed and then increase it by one if the next digit to its right is 5, 6, 7, 8, or 9.

Row A horizontal group of cells in a worksheet.

Row heading The numbers along the left side of an Excel worksheet that designate the row numbers.

Ruler guides Dotted vertical and horizontal lines that display in the rulers indicating the pointer's position.

Run The process in which Access searches the records in the table(s) included in the query design, finds the records that match the specified criteria, and then displays the records in a datasheet; only the fields that have been included in the query design display.

Salutation The greeting line of a business letter.

Sans serif A font design with no lines or extensions on the ends of characters.

Scale to Fit Excel commands that enable you to stretch or shrink the width, height, or both, of printed output to fit a maximum number of pages.

Scaling (Excel) The process of shrinking the width and/or height of printed output to fit a maximum number of pages.

Screenshot An image of an active window on your computer that you can paste into a document.

ScreenTip A small box that that displays useful information when you perform various mouse actions such as pointing to screen elements or dragging.

Scroll bar A vertical or horizontal bar in a window or a pane to assist in bringing an area into view, and which contains a scroll box and scroll arrows.

Scroll box The box in the vertical and horizontal scroll bars that can be dragged to reposition the contents of a window or pane on the screen.

Search box In a folder window, the box in which you can type a word or a phrase to look for an item in the current folder or library.

Second principle of good database design A principle stating that appropriate database techniques are used to ensure the accuracy of data entered into a table.

Section A portion of a document that can be formatted differently from the rest of the document.

Section bar A gray bar in a form or report that identifies and separates one section from another; used to select the section and to change the size of the adjacent section.

Section break A double dotted line that indicates the end of one section and the beginning of another section.

Select To highlight, by dragging with your mouse, areas of text or data or graphics, so that the selection can be edited, formatted, copied, or moved.

Select All box A box in the upper left corner of the worksheet grid that, when clicked, selects all the cells in a worksheet.

Select query A type of Access query that retrieves (selects) data from one or more tables or queries, displaying the selected data in a datasheet; also known as a *simple select query*.

Series A group of things that come one after another in succession; for example, January, February, March, and so on.

Serif font A font design that includes small line extensions on the ends of the letters to guide the eye in reading from left to right.

Shapes Lines, arrows, stars, banners, ovals, rectangles, and other basic shapes with which you can illustrate an idea, a process, or a workflow.

Sheet tab scrolling buttons Buttons to the left of the sheet tabs used to display Excel sheet tabs that are not in view; used when there are more sheet tabs than will display in the space provided.

Sheet tabs The labels along the lower border of the Excel window that identify each worksheet.

Shortcut menu A menu that displays commands and options relevant to the selected text or object.

Simple select query Another name for a select query.

Single File Web Page A document saved using HTML and that opens using a Web browser.

Single-record form A form that enables you to display or enter one record at a time in a table.

Sizing handles Small circles and squares that indicate that a picture is selected.

Slide A presentation page that can contain text, pictures, tables, charts, and other multimedia or graphic objects.

Slide handouts Printed images of slides on a sheet of paper.

Slide pane A PowerPoint screen element that displays a large image of the active slide.

Slide Sorter view A presentation view that displays thumbnails of all of the slides in a presentation.

Slide transitions The motion effects that occur in Slide Show view when you move from one slide to the next during a presentation.

Slides/Outline pane A PowerPoint screen element that displays the presentation either in the form of thumbnails (Slides tab) or in outline format (Outline tab).

Small caps A font effect, usually used in titles, that changes lowercase text into capital (uppercase) letters using a reduced font size.

SmartArt graphic A visual representation of information that you can create by choosing from among many different layouts to communicate your message or ideas effectively.

SmartArt Styles Combinations of formatting effects that you can apply to SmartArt graphics.

SmartArt A designer-quality visual representation of your information that you can create by choosing from among many different layouts to effectively communicate your message or ideas.

Sort The process of arranging data in a specific order based on the value in each field.

Source file When importing a file, refers to the file being imported.

Sparkline A tiny chart in the background of a cell that gives a visual trend summary alongside your data; makes a pattern more obvious.

Spin box A small box with an upward- and downward-pointing arrow that lets you move rapidly through a set of values by clicking.

Split button A button divided into two parts and in which clicking the main part of the button performs a command and clicking the arrow opens a menu with choices.

Spreadsheet Another name for a *worksheet.*

Stacked layout A control layout format that is similar to a paper form, with label controls placed to the left of each textbox control. The controls are grouped together for easy editing.

Start button The button on the Windows taskbar that displays the Start menu.

Start menu The Windows menu that provides a list of choices and is the main gateway to your computer's programs, folders, and settings.

Statistical functions Excel functions, including the AVERAGE, MEDIAN, MIN, and MAX functions, which are useful to analyze a group of measurements.

Status bar (Excel) The area along the lower edge of the Excel window that displays, on the left side, the current cell mode, page number, and worksheet information; on the right side, when numerical data is selected, common calculations such as Sum and Average display.

Status bar The area along the lower edge of an Office program window that displays file information on the left and buttons to control how the window looks on the right.

Structure In Access, the underlying design of a table, including field names, data types, descriptions, and field properties.

Style A group of formatting commands, such as font, font size, font color, paragraph alignment, and line spacing that can be applied to a paragraph with one command.

Style (PowerPoint) A collection of formatting options that can be applied to a picture, text, or an object.

Style guide A manual that contains standards for the design and writing of documents.

Subdatasheet A format for displaying related records when you click the plus sign (+) next to a record in a table on the *one* side of a relationship.

Subfolder A folder within a folder.

Subject line The optional line following the inside address in a business letter that states the purpose of the letter.

Subpoints Secondary-level information in a SmartArt graphic.

Subset A portion of the total records available.

SUM function A predefined formula that adds all the numbers in a selected range of cells.

Summary sheet A worksheet where totals from other worksheets are displayed and summarized.

Synonyms Words with the same or similar meaning.

Tab order The order in which the insertion point moves from one field to another in a form when you press the Tab key.

Tab stop Specific locations on a line of text, marked on the Word ruler, to which you can move the insertion point by pressing the Tab key, and which is used to align and indent text.

Table A format for information that organizes and presents text and data in columns and rows.

Table (Access) The database object that stores data organized in an arrangement of columns and rows, and which is the foundation of an Access database.

Table (Word) An arrangement of information organized into rows and columns.

Table area The upper area of the Query window that displays field lists for the tables that are used in the query.

Table style Formatting applied to an entire table so that it is consistent with the presentation theme.

Tables and Related Views An arrangement in the Navigation Pane that groups objects by the table to which they are related.

Tabs On the Office Ribbon, the name of each activity area in the Office Ribbon.

Tags Custom file properties that you create to help find and organize your own files.

Task pane A window within a Microsoft Office application in which you can enter options for completing a command.

Template An existing document that you use as a starting point for a new document; it opens a copy of itself, unnamed, and then you use the structure—and possibly some content, such as headings—as the starting point for the new document.

Text alignment (PowerPoint) The horizontal placement of text within a placeholder.

Text box A movable resizable container for text or graphics.

Text box (PowerPoint) An object within which you can position text anywhere on a slide.

Text box control The graphical object on a form or report that displays the data from the underlying table or query; a text box control is known as a bound control.

Text control A content control that accepts only a text entry.

Text data type An Access data type that describes text, a combination of text and numbers, or numbers that are not used in calculations, such as a number that is an identifier like a Student ID.

Text effects Decorative formats, such as shadowed or mirrored text, text glow, 3-D effects, and colors that make text stand out.

Text string A sequence of characters.

Text values Constant values consisting of only text, and which usually provides information about number values; also referred to as *labels*.

Text wrapping The manner in which text displays around an object.

Theme A predefined format that can be applied to the entire database or to individual objects in the database.

Theme A predesigned set of colors, fonts, lines, and fill effects that look good together and that can be applied to your entire document or to specific items.

Theme (PowerPoint) A set of unified design elements that provides a look for your presentation by applying colors, fonts, and effects.

Theme colors A set of coordinating colors that are applied to the backgrounds, objects, and text in a presentation.

Theme font A theme that determines the font applied to two types of slide text—headings and body.

Thesaurus A research tool that provides a list of synonyms.

Thumbnails (PowerPoint) Miniature images of presentation slides.

Tick marks The short lines that display on an axis at regular intervals.

Timing options Animation options that control when animated items display in the animation sequence.

Title bar The bar at the top edge of the program window that indicates the name of the current file and the program name.

Title slide The first slide in a presentation the purpose of which is to provide an introduction to the presentation topic.

Toggle button A button that can be turned on by clicking it once, and then turned off by clicking it again.

Toolbar In a folder window, a row of buttons with which you can perform common tasks, such as changing the view of your files and folders or burning files to a CD.

Top-level points The main text points in a SmartArt graphic.

Trim The action of deleting parts of a video to make it shorter.

Triple-click The action of clicking the left mouse button three times in rapid succession.

Truncated Refers to data that is cut off or shortened.

Trust Center An area of the Access program where you can view the security and privacy settings for your Access installation.

Trusted Documents A security feature in Office 2010 that remembers which files you have already enabled; you might encounter this feature if you open a file from an e-mail or download files from the Internet.

Unbound control A control that does not have a source of data, such as a title in a form or report.

Underlying formula The formula entered in a cell and visible only on the Formula Bar.

Underlying value The data that displays in the Formula Bar.

USB flash drive A small data storage device that plugs into a computer USB port.

Value Another name for a *constant value*.

Value after increase = base x percent for new value The formula for calculating the value after an increase by multiplying the original value—the base—by the percent for new value (see the *Percent for new value* formula).

Value axis A numerical scale on the left side of a chart that shows the range of numbers for the data points; also referred to as the *y-axis*.

Vertical window split box (Excel) A small box on the vertical scroll bar with which you can split the window into two vertical views of the same worksheet.

Views button In a folder window, a toolbar button with which you can choose how to view the contents of the current location.

Volatile A term used to describe an Excel function that is subject to change each time the workbook is reopened; for example the NOW function updates itself to the current date and time each time the workbook is opened.

What-if analysis The process of changing the values in cells to see how those changes affect the outcome of formulas in a worksheet.

Wildcard character In a query, a character that serves as a placeholder for one or more unknown characters in your criteria; an asterisk (*) represents one or more unknown characters, and a question mark (?) represents a single unknown character.

Window A rectangular area on a computer screen in which programs and content appear, and which can be moved, resized, minimized, or closed.

Windows Explorer The program that displays the files and folders on your computer, and which is at work anytime you are viewing the contents of files and folders in a window.

Windows taskbar The area along the lower edge of the Windows desktop that contains the Start button and an area to display buttons for open programs.

With Previous An animation command that begins the animation sequence on a PowerPoint slide at the same time as the previous animation or slide transition.

Wizard A feature in Microsoft Office that walks you step by step through a process.

WordArt A gallery of text styles with which you can create decorative effects, such as shadowed or mirrored text.

Wordwrap The feature that moves text from the right edge of a paragraph to the beginning of the next line as necessary to fit within the margins.

Workbook An Excel file that contains one or more worksheets.

Workbook-level buttons Buttons at the far right of the Ribbon tabs that minimize or restore a displayed workbook.

Workbook-level buttons Buttons at the far right of the Ribbon tabs that minimize or restore a displayed workbook.

Works Cited In the MLA style, a list of cited works placed at the end of a research paper or report.

Worksheet The primary document that you use in Excel to work with and store data, and which is formatted as a pattern of uniformly spaced horizontal and vertical lines.

Writer's identification The name and title of the author of a letter, placed near the bottom of the letter under the complimentary closing—also referred to as the *writer's signature block*.

Writer's signature block The name and title of the author of a letter, placed near the bottom of the letter, under the complimentary closing—also referred to as the *writer's identification*.

x-axis Another name for the *category axis*.

x-axis Another name for the horizontal *(category) axis*.

y-axis Another name for the *value axis*.

y-axis Another name for the vertical *(value) axis*.

Zoom The action of increasing or decreasing the viewing area on the screen.

Index

Symbols and Numbers

A

B

C

D

E

F

G

H

I

J

K

L

N

O

P

Q

R

T

U

V

X–Z

SINGLE PC LICENSE AGREEMENT AND LIMITED WARRANTY

READ THIS LICENSE CAREFULLY BEFORE OPENING THIS PACKAGE. BY OPENING THIS PACKAGE, YOU ARE AGREEING TO THE TERMS AND CONDITIONS OF THIS LICENSE. IF YOU DO NOT AGREE, DO NOT OPEN THE PACKAGE. PROMPTLY RETURN THE UNOPENED PACKAGE AND ALL ACCOMPANYING ITEMS TO THE PLACE YOU OBTAINED THEM. *THESE TERMS APPLY TO ALL LICENSED SOFTWARE ON THE DISK EXCEPT THAT THE TERMS FOR USE OF ANY SHAREWARE OR FREEWARE ON THE DISKETTES ARE AS SET FORTH IN THE ELECTRONIC LICENSE LOCATED ON THE DISK:*

1. GRANT OF LICENSE and OWNERSHIP: The enclosed computer programs ("Software") are licensed, not sold, to you by Prentice-Hall, Inc. ("We" or the "Company") and in consideration of your purchase or adoption of the accompanying Company textbooks and/or other materials, and your agreement to these terms. We reserve any rights not granted to you. You own only the disk(s) but we and/or our licensors own the Software itself. This license allows you to use and display your copy of the Software on a single computer (i.e., with a single CPU) at a single location for academic use only, so long as you comply with the terms of this Agreement. You may make one copy for back up, or transfer your copy to another CPU, provided that the Software is usable on only one computer.

2. RESTRICTIONS: You may not transfer or distribute the Software or documentation to anyone else. Except for backup, you may not copy the documentation or the Software. You may not network the Software or otherwise use it on more than one computer or computer terminal at the same time. You may not reverse engineer, disassemble, decompile, modify, adapt, translate, or create derivative works based on the Software or the Documentation. You may be held legally responsible for any copying or copyright infringement which is caused by your failure to abide by the terms of these restrictions.

3. TERMINATION: This license is effective until terminated. This license will terminate automatically without notice from the Company if you fail to comply with any provisions or limitations of this license. Upon termination, you shall destroy the Documentation and all copies of the Software. All provisions of this Agreement as to limitation and disclaimer of warranties, limitation of liability, remedies or damages, and our ownership rights shall survive termination.

4.DISCLAIMER OF WARRANTY: THE COMPANY AND ITS LICENSORS MAKE NO WARRANTIES ABOUT THE SOFTWARE, WHICH IS PROVIDED "AS-IS." IF THE DISK IS DEFECTIVE IN MATERIALS OR WORKMANSHIP, YOUR ONLY REMEDY IS TO RETURN IT TO THE COMPANY WITHIN 30 DAYS FOR REPLACEMENT UNLESS THE COMPANY DETERMINES IN GOOD FAITH THAT THE DISK HAS BEEN MISUSED OR IMPROPERLY INSTALLED, REPAIRED, ALTERED OR DAMAGED. THE COMPANY DISCLAIMS ALL WARRANTIES, EXPRESS OR IMPLIED, INCLUDING WITHOUT LIMITATION, THE IMPLIED WARRANTIES OF MERCHANTABILITY AND FITNESS FOR A PARTICULAR PURPOSE. THE COMPANY DOES NOT WARRANT, GUARANTEE OR MAKE ANY REPRESENTATION REGARDING THE ACCURACY, RELIABILITY, CURRENTNESS, USE, OR RESULTS OF USE, OF THE SOFTWARE.

5. LIMITATION OF REMEDIES AND DAMAGES: IN NO EVENT, SHALL THE COMPANY OR ITS EMPLOYEES, AGENTS, LICENSORS OR CONTRACTORS BE LIABLE FOR ANY INCIDENTAL, INDIRECT, SPECIAL OR CONSEQUENTIAL DAMAGES ARISING OUT OF OR IN CONNECTION WITH THIS LICENSE OR THE SOFTWARE, INCLUDING, WITHOUT LIMITATION, LOSS OF USE, LOSS OF DATA, LOSS OF INCOME OR PROFIT, OR OTHER LOSSES SUSTAINED AS A RESULT OF INJURY TO ANY PERSON, OR LOSS OF OR DAMAGE TO PROPERTY, OR CLAIMS OF THIRD PARTIES, EVEN IF THE COMPANY OR AN AUTHORIZED REPRESENTATIVE OF THE COMPANY HAS BEEN ADVISED OF THE POSSIBILITY OF SUCH DAMAGES. SOME JURISDICTIONS DO NOT ALLOW THE LIMITATION OF DAMAGES IN CERTAIN CIRCUMSTANCES, SO THE ABOVE LIMITATIONS MAY NOT ALWAYS APPLY.

6. GENERAL: THIS AGREEMENT SHALL BE CONSTRUED IN ACCORDANCE WITH THE LAWS OF THE UNITED STATES OF AMERICA AND THE STATE OF NEW YORK, APPLICABLE TO CONTRACTS MADE IN NEW YORK, AND SHALL BENEFIT THE COMPANY, ITS AFFILIATES AND ASSIGNEES. This Agreement is the complete and exclusive statement of the agreement between you and the Company and supersedes all proposals, prior agreements, oral or written, and any other communications between you and the company or any of its representatives relating to the subject matter. If you are a U.S. Government user, this Software is licensed with "restricted rights" as set forth in subparagraphs (a)-(d) of the Commercial Computer-Restricted Rights clause at FAR 52.227-19 or in subparagraphs (c)(1)(ii) of the Rights in Technical Data and Computer Software clause at DFARS 252.227-7013, and similar clauses, as applicable.

Should you have any questions concerning this agreement or if you wish to contact the Company for any reason, please contact in writing:

Multimedia Production,
Higher Education Division,
Prentice-Hall, Inc.,
1 Lake Street,
Upper Saddle River NJ 07458.